LIFE INSURANCE

LIFE
INSURANCE

Eighth Edition

S. S. Huebner

Late Emeritus Professor of Insurance
Wharton School of Finance
University of Pennsylvania

Kenneth Black, Jr.

Regents' Professor of Insurance
School of Business Administration
Georgia State University

PRENTICE-HALL, INC., Englewood Cliffs, New Jersey

ISBN: 0-13-535765-9

Library of Congress Catalog Card Number: 72-181734

10 9 8 7 6 5 4 3 2 1

Introduction reprinted, with permission, from the *Journal* of the American Society of Chartered Life Underwriters, Volume XXIII, No. 3 (July, 1969). Copyright 1969 by the American Society of Chartered Life Underwriters, 270 Bryn Mawr Avenue, Bryn Mawr, Pa. 19010.

PRENTICE-HALL INTERNATIONAL, INC., *London*
PRENTICE-HALL OF AUSTRALIA, PTY. LTD., *Sydney*
PRENTICE-HALL OF CANADA, LTD., *Toronto*
PRENTICE-HALL OF INDIA PRIVATE LIMITED, *New Delhi*
PRENTICE-HALL OF JAPAN, INC., *Tokyo*

TO
THE MEMORY OF

Frederick A. Huebner
and
Wilhelmina Dicke Huebner

TO
Kenneth Black
and
Margaret Virginia Black

Preface

THIS TEXTBOOK IS A thorough revision of its predecessor, published in 1969. Earlier editions were published in 1915, 1923, 1935, 1950, 1958, and 1964. Recent years have seen tremendous changes in the life insurance business. For example, the group insurance method of providing life, health, and pension benefits has grown with astonishing rapidity. During this period the life insurance industry has also entered the individual health insurance field actively and aggressively. In fact, life insurance companies are now the leading writers of health insurance benefits in this country. In order to recognize these dynamic changes within the business, this volume attempts to provide an integrated treatment of life and health insurance throughout. Both life and health insurance have an economic justification in the earning power of the human life (the so-called human life value) and play an essential role for the creative, concerned individual in a free, civilized society. It is hoped that this text on life *and* health insurance will meet the needs of the student, the underwriter, and the layman.

A special effort has been made to produce a text which is logically developed and easily assimilated. It aims to bring together in compact, classified form those facts, principles, and practices which will enable the student, underwriter, and layman to have a comprehensive understanding of life and health insurance and the legitimate ways they may and should be employed in the interest of personal, family, and business welfare. Special effort has been taken to make the presentation simple and compact.

The book is divided into nine distinct parts, dealing respectively with The Nature and Uses of Life and Health Insurance; The Life Insurance Product: Types of Contracts; The Life Insurance Product: Analysis of the Contract; The Health Insurance Product; The Mathematics of Life Insurance; The Mathematics of Health Insurance; Selection, Classification, and Treatment of Life and Health Insurance Risks; Special Forms of Life and Health Insurance; and Organization, Management, and Regulation of Life and Health Insurance Companies.

In the preceding editions, Dr. Bruce D. Mudgett and Bryan L. Daly received special acknowledgment. Insofar as this volume remains the same as its predecessor, this acknowledgment is again extended. Likewise, in the earlier editions, special acknowledgment was given to Dr. George L. Amrhein and Dr. Chester A. Kline. Again, insofar as this volume remains the same as its predecessor, this acknowledgment is again extended. Dr. Black would like to express his appreciation to a number of individuals within the life and health insurance business who reviewed chapters and/or sections of the volume. These included: Mr. Neils H. Fischer, Aetna Life Insurance Co.; Mr. Henry F. Scheig, Aid Association for Lutherans; Dr. Barnie E. Abelle, American College of Life Underwriters; Carl Bakal, Anna Rosenberg Associates; Mr. William H. Walpole, Associated Hospital Services of New York; Mr. Charles E. Farr, Bankers Life Company; Nancy Lee, Research, Blue Cross Association; Mr. Samuel Turner, Bowles and Tillinghast, Inc.; Mr. Charles L. Van House, Coastal States Life Insurance Company; Mr. Edwin L. Goldberg, The Commonwealth of Massachusetts; Mr. Edmond V. Villani, The Commonwealth of Massachusetts, Division of Savings Bank Life Insurance; Mr. Thomas E. Martin, Jr., Eastman Dillon Union Securities & Co.; Dr. W. Rogers Hammond, Dr. Albert W. Clark, Dr. W. Ray Bagwell, and Dr. Eli A. Zubay, Georgia State University; Mr. Gerald S. Parker, Guardian Life Insurance Co. of America; Mr. James R. Williams, Health Insurance Institute; Mr. William E. Kingsley, Institute of Life Insurance; Mr. John P. Nietmann, Life Insurance Association of America; Mr. Jason B. Gilliland, Mrs. Linda B. Emory, Life Insurance Company of Georgia; Mr. Charles N. Walker, Lincoln National Life Insurance Company; Mr. James W. Krause, Lutheran Brotherhood; Mr. Frank J. Gadient, Modern Woodmen of America; Tom K. Mura, National Association of Blue Shield Plans; Mr. Walter M. Robinson, Jr., National Life & Accident Insurance Company; Mr. Walter B. Prager, Mr. Charles M. Sternhell, and Mr. Edward H. Sweetser, New York Life Insurance Company; Mr. Christopher J. Cox, North American Reassurance Company; Mr. Gerald Farlow, Pensurdata, Inc.; Mr. Jack T. Kvernland, Mr. John K. Kittredge, Mr. Malcolm D. MacKinnon, Mr. Meyer Melnikoff, Mr. Paul E. Sarnoff, and Mr. James J. Olsen, Prudential Insurance Company of America; Mr. Theodore Fuller, Savings Bank Life Insurance Fund; Mr. Walter E. Rapp, Savings Bank Life Insurance Company; Mr. Joseph W. Satterthwaite, Towers, Perrin, Forster & Crosby, Inc.; Mrs. Marice C. Hart, Social Security Administration; Dr. Jack C. Keir, Temple University; Mr. F. J. Petraitis, Veterans Administration.

Special acknowledgment is due to Mr. B. Franklin Blair of the Provident Mutual Life Insurance Company for his help with the chapters on financial statements. Much of the material in these chapters is based upon Mr. Blair's paper, *Interpreting Life Insurance Company Annual Reports.*

The author is also indebted to Professor Robert W. Batten, Dr. Walter F. Berdal, Professor John E. Brown, Dr. John W. Hall, Professor Maurice

E. McDonald, Dr. Robert A. Marshall, Dr. Stuart Schwarzschild, and Professor Steven N. Weisbart, all members of the Department of Insurance, School of Business Administration, Georgia State University, who read individual chapters and in some cases entire sections, and gave generously of their criticism and judgment.

Finally, the author should like to record his appreciation to Mrs. Virginia Van Buren, Mrs. Polly Young, and Miss Sue Lambert for their efforts and personal interest in typing and editing this manuscript.

None of those who read the manuscript, it hardly need be said, bear any responsibility for the deficiencies that may remain in the completed work.

K.B., Jr.

Contents

I THE NATURE AND USE OF LIFE AND HEALTH INSURANCE

Insurance Defined, 3; Loss Sharing, 3; Principle of large numbers, 4; Nature of the perils, 4; Need for scientific accumulation of a fund, 5; *Methods of Providing Life and Health Insurance Protection, 7;* Yearly renewable term insurance, 7; The level-premium plan, 9; *Life and Health Insurance Are the Opposite of Gambling, 11.*

Economic Basis of Life and Health Insurance, 14; The concept of human capital, 14; The human life value concept, 15; *Management of Life Values, 20;* Capitalization and idemnification of a human life value, 21; Accounting principles, 22; Life insurance as a life will, 23; *The Amount of Life and Health Insurance to Acquire, 23;* Human life value approach, 24; Needs approach, 25; Human life value vs. needs ap-

II THE LIFE INSURANCE PRODUCT: TYPES OF CONTRACTS

III THE LIFE INSURANCE PRODUCT: ANALYSIS OF THE CONTRACT

IV THE HEALTH INSURANCE PRODUCT

V THE MATHEMATICS OF LIFE INSURANCE

VI THE MATHEMATICS OF HEALTH INSURANCE

serves, 494; Group reserves, 495; Other reserves, 495; *Surplus Distribution, 496;* Individual policies, 496; Group policies, 497.

VII SELECTION, CLASSIFICATION, AND TREATMENT OF LIFE AND HEALTH INSURANCE RISKS

Purpose of Selection, 501; Selection Philosophy, 503; The standard groups, 503; The substandard groups, 503; Balance within each risk or rate classification, 504; Emphasis on the unique impairment, 504; Equity among policyholders, 505; Recognition of underlying mortality assumptions, 505; *Factors Affecting the Life Risk, 506;* Age, 506; Build, 507; Physical conditions, 507; Personal history, 508; Family history, 508; Occupation, 509; Habits, 509; Moral hazard, 510; Sex, 511; Aviation, 511; Military service, 511; Other factors, 512; *Sources of Information Concerning Life Risks, 513;* The application, 513; The medical examination, 514; The agent's report, 514; Attending physicians, 515; The inspection report, 515; Intercompany data, 516; *Methods of Classification, 517;* The judgment method of rating, 517; The numerical rating system, 517; *Scale of Ratings, 519.*

Treatment of Substandard Life Insurance Risks, 521; Incidence of extra risk, 521; Methods of rating, 522; Improvement in the risk, 527; *Special Procedures and Problems, 528;* Nonmedical life insurance, 528; Guaranteed insurability option, 529; Insurance at extremes of age, 530; *Reinsurance, 531;* Concept of retention, 531; Reinsurance arrangements, 533; Source of funds, 535.

Factors Affecting the Health Risk, 537; Age, 537; Sex, 538; Occupation, 538; Physical condition, 539; Personal history,

VIII   SPECIAL FORMS OF LIFE AND HEALTH INSURANCE

34.   Group Insurance   551

35.   Insured Pension Plans   584

IX ORGANIZATION, MANAGEMENT, AND REGULATION OF LIFE INSURANCE COMPANIES

Trade publications, 730; Annual reports to the policyholders, 731; *Annual Reports, 732;* Nature of the balance sheet, 732; Interpreting the balance sheet, 736; Summary of operations (Income and Disbursements), 745; Surplus account, 752; Other statistical information, 753.

APPENDICES

Tables, Graphs, and Exhibits

TABLES

GRAPHS

EXHIBIT

Introduction

MAN'S QUEST for security is eternal. While security means different things to different people, there appears to be one common frame of reference, i.e., all views of security relate to man's needs.

THE INDIVIDUAL AND SECURITY

It is generally accepted that personal insecurity relates to the lack of confidence or the uncertainty of individuals regarding one or more of their needs. Social scientists agree that man's needs are unlimited and changing over time. As soon as he satisfies one of his needs, another appears. Social scientists generally agree, however, that broadly a *priority* of need levels exists that is applicable to most individuals.[1]

As the more basic needs are encountered, they claim priority, and efforts to satisfy the higher needs must be postponed. A. H. Maslow, a pioneer researcher in this area, developed a need priority of five levels:[2]

1. Basic physiological needs
2. Safety from external danger
3. Love, affection, and social activity
4. Esteem and self-respect
5. Self-realization and accomplishment

The significant point for the purpose of this discussion is that need levels have *a definite sequence of domination.* In the typical situation in the United States today, basic physiological needs are reasonably well satisfied. In parts of the world, however, where there is very low productivity or famine, or disaster, the priority of survival needs is clear. When man's

[1] Keith Davis, *Human Relations in Business* (New York: McGraw-Hill Book Company, Inc., 1957), pp. 24–49.

[2] A. H. Maslow, "A Theory of Human Motivation," *Psychological Review,* Vol. L (1943), pp. 370–396; and A. H. Maslow, *Motivation and Personality* (New York: Harper and Brothers, 1954).

physiological needs are satisfied reasonably, the safety and security needs tend to dominate. Physiological needs are essentially finite. Man can get too much food, warmth, and so forth. In fact, for both physiological needs and safety and security needs man can have too much—he can feel so safe that he can become careless or defenseless.

While physiological needs are essentially finite, needs at the third, fourth, and fifth levels are substantially infinite. Accordingly, these higher-order needs are likely to be the dominant ones in advanced civilizations. Man's lower-order needs are satisfied primarily through economic behavior. He needs money income to purchase satisfactions for physiological needs and security. Man's higher-order needs, on the other hand, are satisfied primarily through symbolic behavior of psychic and social content. He senses meaning in his experiences and derives satisfactions therefrom, a behavior of a totally different order from economic behavior. Thus, individuals strive to satisfy their needs, *as they perceive them,* each from a frame of reference which has been built over a lifetime of individual, family, and other environmental influences, and each is dominated by a need level which is reflective of his economic circumstances.

How Much Security

How much security is good? How much is bad? How does risk, qualitatively and quantitatively, relate to the family's life cycle or the human life cycle? There is considerable evidence that the response to risk varies widely, depending on personal criteria, such as education, sex, and age. Accepting and coping with risks up to a certain magnitude builds character; beyond this, the burden can be destructive.

Consider, for example, the attitudes and actions of individuals regarding the inevitability of death. A strong religious conviction tends to provide security and a sense of safety despite the eventuality of death and the other exigencies of life. The intimate relationship between religious commitment and security indicates that we are not dealing with a logical problem alone, but also with a psychological one. Attitudes and perception change. We live in a society today where some feel that "God is dead." Medical science has minimized the pain and suffering of illness, including that prior to the eventuality of death. For many, on the other hand, the major concern over death is for the economic and psychological welfare of dependents rather than for themselves. The psychological impact of risk and the feeling of uncertainty surrounding death and other aspects of human behavior are significant areas for investigation.[3]

[3] John W. Riley, Jr., "Old Age in American Society: Notes on Health, Retirement, and the Anticipation of Death," *Journal of the American Society of Chartered Life Underwriters,* Vol. XXII, No. 1 (January, 1968), p. 27.

Can one be too secure? For example, there is considerable evidence that creativity is stimulated by adversity. In fact, some researchers[4] have suggested that security is not the most important goal which motivates man. Ardrey suggests that the most significant force for a productive life is the drive for *identity*. Following this in significance is the drive for *stimulation* and then *security*.[5]

We shun anonymity, dread boredom and seek to dispel anxiety. The extent of a given need will vary from species to species, population to population, individual to individual. . . . But there is not the variation we might expect. There are few exceptions to the rule that the need for identity is the most powerful. The need for stimulation is not far behind. And security, normally, will be sacrificed for either of the other two.

Ardrey believes that the danger of security is boredom. While we may all agree that our societies should provide greater security for the individual, if all we produce is a social structure providing increased anonymity and boredom, we should not be surprised if ingenious man turns to such stimulating amusements as drugs, vandalism, riots, and strange haircuts.

Individual Value Systems

There is general agreement that man is most human at the point of choice or when he is engaged in decision-making. It is this ability to make conscious choices based on understanding of past events and prediction of future consequences which distinguishes man most markedly from other animals. Man is vastly superior to other animals in his capacity to visualize the long-range consequences of alternative courses of action.[6] It is the ability and the right and the freedom to make decisions and choices and to influence outcomes that permit a man to maintain his individual identity, to develop a self-image based upon a matrix of values—an individual value system—all his own. His individual reaction to varying degrees of uncertainty which influence his choice and decisions again provides him individualistic identity.

It is only with reasonable economic security (need levels 1 and 2 reasonably satisfied) that man can afford to be motivated by and make his decisions based upon the higher order of needs, such as self-determination

---

[4] See, for example, Robert Ardrey, *The Territorial Imperative* (New York: Atheneum, 1966).

[5] Robert Ardrey, "Man is a Territorial Animal," *Life*, September 2, 1966, p. 58. For a summary of management philosophies relating to motivation theory, see Saul W. Gellerman, *The Management of Human Relations* (New York: Holt, Rinehart and Winston, 1966), pp. 42–58.

[6] All animals are choice-making organisms. They all learn and make appropriate choices based on learning.

and understanding. Therefore, a reasonable level of economic security will provide the individual with the opportunity to be more human, to find greater meaning in life, and to ponder his interrelationships with other human beings. Man has a drive to belong, to relate without being subservient; this becomes a conscious matter under conditions of reasonable economic security.

AMERICAN SECURITY INSTITUTIONS

In the United States economic security, i.e., sufficient money as a medium of exchange to purchase satisfactions for physiological needs and security, is provided through an intricate blending of private and government enterprise. The primary basis of economic security that has resulted from individual, group (or corporate), and social (or government) effort is reflected in large measure in the growth and development of individual, group, and social insurance.

Individual insurance represents the oldest of the economic security systems. Its growth and development have come essentially from *voluntary decisions of individuals* based upon an awareness of security needs and an ability to pay premiums. Group insurance[7] has been developed through business, union, or other group action on behalf of well-defined groups, usually employees. Social insurance has evolved through government action to meet the economic security needs of broad segments of the population.

Gregg suggests[8] that our economic security system can be likened to a platform resting upon a tripod. At the turn of the century, only one leg, individual insurance, was of significance in the United States. The second leg, added early in the century, developed in the form of private pensions and group insurance. The third leg, social insurance, received a major thrust with the substantive entry of the Federal Government in the field of economic security through the passage of the Social Security Act of 1935.

All three legs of this tripod of security have grown remarkably, but the rate of growth has been in inverse relationship to the order in which they were introduced. In 1969 the individual leg of the security tripod represented 21% of the security dollar; group represented 33%; and social 46%. Over the past thirty years these percentages have changed from individual representing 68 per cent; group 20 per cent; and social 12 per cent.

---

[7] Defined to include insured and uninsured pensions, group life and health insurance, and other elements of employee benefit plans.

[8] Davis W. Gregg, "Security and Insurance: Some Issues and Unanswered Questions," *The Journal of the American Society of Chartered Life Underwriters,* Vol. XXI, No. 1 (January, 1967). See also Davis W. Gregg, "Freedom and Security," *1970 CLU Forum Report—Perceptions on Economic Security* (Bryn Mawr, Pa.: American Society of Chartered Life Underwriters, 1971), pp. 26–30.

Assuming that a significant measure of maturity is the willingness to choose to postpone present pleasure, then the rapid growth of our total security complex should please us because it implies individual and social maturity. It also reflects success in achieving satisfaction for a higher order of needs and wants for the individual and his family. On the other hand, the "institutionalization" of security through the great growth of the social and group mechanisms (from 32 per cent to 79 per cent of the security dollar), as well as the increasing role of government as reflected in the increase of its share of the security dollar from 12 per cent to 46 per cent, may or may not bode well for individual identity. The optimal balance of ways of achieving an optimal amount of economic security is a subject worthy of study.[9]

INDIVIDUALIZED ECONOMIC SECURITY PROGRAM

The freedom to make a decision based upon individual values is the final and finest criterion of self-determination. Freedom of choice is likewise the essence of personal identity in a situation in which individual value systems are pressured and molded by the interactions of a human being with his environment, his family, his friends, and others. In this area, the opportunity for creative response is a function of reasonable economic security. Social insurance and group insurance provide a foundation upon which a responsible individual can design an *individualized security program* providing an environment for creative life and living. Individual life and health insurance represent the opportunity to bring an appropriate level of economic security to the individual and his family that will permit him and his dependents to have the freedom to decide where to live, where to work, where to retire, when to marry, and so forth. Regardless of death or disability, life and health insurance can permit a family to continue to live in *their house;* to continue to enjoy a standard of living comparable to *their present life;* to continue to enjoy *their friends.* In short, economic need will note force them out of their own world. The decisions involved in setting up an individualized security program are made as a result of analyzing individual goals and needs, and guaranteeing attainment of these goals regardless of the risks of death, disability, or old age. The confidence which arises from the conscious, individualized decisions involved in build-

---

[9] See *ibid.* The *Future Outlook Study* conducted by the Institute of Life Insurance is a first effort to evaluate public attitudes toward the life and health insurance product, the companies that provide it, and the men who sell it. See statement by Florence Skelly of Daniel Yankelovich, Inc., to General Agents and Managers Conference. New York State Life Underwriters Association, *The National Underwriter,* life ed., November 9, 1968. p. 1.

ing a security program contributes materially to the creative risk-taking essential to individual fulfillment.

If there is truth to the view that human growth involves intelligent decision-making and that individual identity is critically important to human growth and fulfillment, then careful attention should be given to maintaining an environment wherein the individual retains a sense of personal responsibility for his own welfare and that of his family.[10] The opportunity to identify one's own goals and needs, to develop an individual matrix of values, and to implement these through individual decisions regarding one's tailor-made security program are critically important elements in maintaining a virile, creative society. American contemporary capitalism is a political, economic, and social system under which the individual and individual responsibility are paramount. It *assumes* that financial compensation is geared generally to contribution. It further assumes that free men with *reasonable* economic security can control their own destiny as individuals through risk-taking while protecting their loved ones by consciously arranging a tailor-made security program consistent with their individual goals and objectives.[11] Individual life and health insurance can play an essential role for the creative, concerned individual. This volume attempts to provide an understanding of the specific uses to which insurance can be put as well as an analysis of the life and health insurance institutions. It is submitted that a thorough understanding of life and health insurance is important to the individual in a free, civilized society.

---

[10] See Davis W. Gregg, "Family Life Cycle: A Conceptual Legacy," *Journal of the American Society of Chartered Life Underwriters,* Vol. XIV (Fall, 1960), p. 308.

[11] See Michael H. Mescon, "Management, Capitalism and the Individual," *Journal of the American Society of Chartered Life Underwriters,* Vol. XXII, No. 3 (July, 1968), pp. 21–26.

I The Nature and Uses of Life and Health Insurance

Nature of Life and Health Insurance 1
and the Underlying Basic Principles

INSURANCE DEFINED

Loss Sharing

MANKIND IS EXPOSED to many serious perils such as property losses from fire and windstorm and personal losses from disability and premature death. While it is impossible for the individual to foretell or completely prevent their occurrence, it is possible and highly important that he provide against their financial effects, the loss of property and/or earnings. It is the function of insurance in its various forms to safeguard against such misfortunes by having the losses of the unfortunate few paid by the contribution of the many who are exposed to the same risk. This is the essence of insurance—the sharing of losses and the substitution of certainty for uncertainty. If the peril under consideration be that of premature death, the financial loss suffered is indemnified through life insurance. If the peril under consideration be disability, the financial loss is indemnified through health insurance. From the community standpoint life or health insurance may be defined as that social device for making accumulations to meet uncertain losses resulting from premature death or disability which is carried out by the transfer of the risks of many individuals to one person or a group of persons.[1] From the standpoint of the individual, however, life or health insurance may be defined as consisting of a contract, whereby for a stipulated consideration, called the premium, one party (the insurer) agrees to pay to the other (the insured), or his beneficiary, a defined amount upon the occurrence of death, disability, or some other specified event.

Every insurance organization is a mechanism for distributing losses. This is true whether a group mutually insures each member of the group (mutual life insurance company) or an independent contractor for a consideration, called the premium, assumes the risk and pays the resulting losses (stock life insurance company).

[1] Allen H. Willett, *The Economic Theory of Risk and Insurance* (Philadelphia: University of Pennsylvania Press, 1951), p. 72.

Principle of Large Numbers

In order to eliminate the speculative element and reduce violent fluctuations in the losses shared from year to year, it is necessary to apply the principle of the law of large numbers to the insurance operation. This basic principle is that the larger the number of separate risks of a like nature combined into one group, the less uncertainty there will be as to the amount of loss that will be incurred within a given period.

To insure a single life against death for $1,000 during a given year is clearly a gamble. If the number of persons insured be increased to one hundred, the element of uncertainty will still be present to a large extent although the possibility of at least one death is much greater. If 500,000 lives of similar physical condition be combined into the same group, or if more than that number of lives are insured in each of a considerable number of companies, the fluctuation in the rate of death from year to year will likely vary by only a fraction of 1 per cent. The company will thus be able to determine in advance the approximate amount of its death claims and place its business on a nonspeculative basis. In fact, if the number of lives insured by a company were so large as virtually to make the application of the law of averages perfect, practically all uncertainty as to the amount of loss during a given period would be removed. As has been well said:

> When the insurance is furnished by a company with capital or surplus which answers as a given guarantee of stability, it becomes a business instead of a speculation, the distinction being that while an individual who assumes a single risk either loses or gains thereby the whole amount involved, the company which takes many, by means of the aggregate business reduces the possible variations to narrow limits and really makes of insurance a business attended with less peril than almost any other. . . . During a given year an individual either dies or he survives the year; the result is a 100 per cent loss or a 100 per cent gain, if one wagers upon the one life. But make one hundred thousand of these bets upon persons of the same age and like physical condition and the variation in the result will not be 2 per cent usually, instead of 200 per cent. There is nothing more uncertain than life and nothing more certain than life insurance.[2]

Nature of the Perils

While all forms of insurance are alike in that they require for their successful operation a combination of many risks into a group, they are vitally

[2] Miles M. Dawson, *The Business of Life Insurance* (New York: A. S. Barnes & Co., 1911), p. 4.

different as regards the nature of the perils covered. In this respect, the chief difference between life and other forms of insurance is that in the latter the contingency insured against may or may not happen, and in the great majority of cases, does not happen. In life insurance the event against which protection is granted, namely death, is an uncertainty for one year, but each year the probability of loss increases until it becomes a certainty, because death eventually comes to everyone. It is necessary, therefore, if a life insurance policy is to protect the insured during the whole of life, not only to provide against the risk of death each year, but also to accumulate an adequate fund for the purpose of meeting an absolutely certain claim that will eventually occur. Mr. Dawson said:

It was failure to see the necessity for providing for an increasing hazard, converging into certainty, which has caused many serious errors in the fundamental plans of some institutions formed to furnish life insurance, and the thing which separates plans of insurance into sound and unsound is precisely whether intelligent regard for this principle has guided the company in determining its rates of premium and the managements and disposition of its funds.[3]

In the case of health insurance not everyone does become disabled and the risk of disablement does not follow as consistent a pattern as in the case of the risk of dying. Where long-term level premium health insurance contracts are issued, however, and the risk insured against is an increasing one over time, it is necessary to accumulate an adequate fund to meet the high rate of claims which will inevitably develop as the policyholders in the group grow older.

Need for Scientific Accumulation of a Fund

In accumulating the fund referred to in the preceding section, it is important for insurance companies to take into account several other characteristics which differentiate life insurance from other forms of insurance. In the first place, the persons combining for life insurance are not of the same age. On the average those insuring at the younger ages will live much longer before claim is made on their policies than those who insure at the older ages. Equity, therefore, requires that the premium payments be graded upwards as the age at which the policy is issued increases. This is also true in health insurance to the extent that the risk of disablement increases with increasing age. Many types of policies are on the market, some insuring against death or disability for a limited number of years only, while others cover the whole of life; some provide for the payment of premiums for a stated number of years only and others for the entire duration of the con-

[3] *Ibid.,* p. 7.

tract. Some promise the payment of the face of the policy in one lump sum, others provide for the payment of that sum in a fixed number of installments, and so forth. Here again equity demands that the rates for each type of policy be determined not only with reference to the age of the insured at entry, but also according to the nature of the benefits promised.

These complex conditions cannot be treated justly by the companies unless they follow scientific principles in the computation of their rates. Life insurance policies promise defined amount in the event of death, and in some instances, in the event of survival at a stated time. Health insurance policies promise a definite benefit in the event of disability but also provide benefits which are a function of medical expenses incurred because of a particular disability. It is, therefore, essential that there be an accurate determination of the liability involved and that an adequate premium be charged which is equitable as between ages and types of policies. This is especially important because unlike most other types of insurance, life insurance contracts and some health insurance contracts extend throughout life or for a long period of time and cannot be cancelled by the company. Later chapters will outline the principles underlying the computation of rates; therefore, the matter will not be discussed in detail at this time. The reasons just mentioned make it essential for the companies to compute their premiums on the basis of tables of mortality and morbidity based on experience which will indicate the probability of death or disability at any age.

In addition to the foregoing, life insurance presents a further problem as regards the accumulation of the fund necessary to pay policy claims. Experience has shown the desirability of a level annual premium. Mathematically, it is possible to consider a life insurance policy as composed of a series of one-year renewable term insurances and to make each year's premium just cover the cost of current protection. Under this plan, however, since the rate of death increases with increasing age, the premium will gradually become more and more burdensome and at last prohibitive, with the result that the healthy members of the group will withdraw rather than continue to pay the greatly increased rates. From a practical standpoint, therefore, it is desirable, in the great majority of cases, to charge a uniform or level annual premium as contrasted with an increasing one. Mathematically, the two plans are the same, since they are computed on the basis of the same interest, mortality, and expense assumptions, but the level annual premium has the great advantage of being moderate in amount and the same from year to year, with the result that policyholders remain satisfied and soon become accustomed to its payment. This same situation exists in health insurance under long term contracts.

Keeping the premium the same from year to year, instead of increasing it in accordance with increasing age, involves the collection during the earlier years of a sum over and above that required to pay the current cost of insurance. This overcharge accumulates and will be drawn upon during the later years when the same level annual premium becomes insufficient to meet the current mortality cost. It does not belong to the company but is held in trust for the policyholder at an assumed rate of interest. This overcharge, or unearned premium, is called the policy reserve.[4] When combined with the reserves on a large number of policies, it represents that sum which, together with the future premiums to be paid by that group of policyholders, will just enable the company to meet its claims on all lives insured in the group, assuming deaths or disabilities occur according to the mortality or morbidity table in use. This method of accumulating a reserve fund is fundamental to any sound plan of permanent life or health insurance.

METHODS OF PROVIDING LIFE AND HEALTH INSURANCE PROTECTION

Yearly Renewable Term Insurance

The simplest form of life insurance protection is the "natural premium" plan or, as it is more commonly known, the yearly renewable term insurance plan. A brief explanation of this plan and the level-premium plan, which is discussed hereafter, will serve to illustrate the preceding discussion of basic principles.

Yearly renewable term insurance provides insurance for a period of one year only, but permits the insured policyholder to renew the policy without evidence of insurability.[5] In the event the insured dies while the policy is in force, the face amount will be paid to his designated beneficiary. If he does not die while the policy is in force, he will be entitled to no return of premium since the premium charged contemplated the fact that not all of those insured would die during the policy period. Every one insured has an equal chance of dying and thus receives the same "benefit"; the total contributions [6] of those insured were pooled to pay the losses of those who did actually die during the period of protection. Since each premium purchases only one year of insurance protection, the premium charged for yearly renewable term insurance is based on the death rate for the attained age of each insured individual. It is necessary to classify policyholders into groups by age in order that each will pay a fair share of total losses expected since the death rate increases with age.

The increasing probability of death may be seen in the following table

---

[4] Since the manner in which the fund is to be accumulated and invested is regulated by law, the policy reserve is frequently referred to as the legal reserve. It is a liability representing the assets accumulated fom the excess portions of the premiums paid.

[5] See pp. 188–189.

[6] Actually, part of the premiums contributed constitute a provision for the expense of operating the insurance plan as well as a margin for safety.

which shows the annual death rates per 1,000 at various ages according to the *Commissioners 1958 Standard Ordinary Table of Mortality* which is currently used by many American life insurance companies for valuation of policy liabilities.[7]

**TABLE 1-1.   Rates of Mortality
1958 CSO Table***

Male Age	Rate of Mortality per 1,000
20	1.79
30	2.13
40	3.53
50	8.32
60	20.34
70	49.79
80	109.98
90	228.14
99	1,000.00

* This table is required for minimum reserve and nonforfeiture value purposes in connection with ordinary business issued after January 1, 1966.

It will be seen from Table 1–1 that the rate of dying increases with age at an increasing rate, rising ultimately to a certainty. It is obvious, therefore, that it is necessary to classify people by age if each is to contribute his fair share to the pool for losses.

The death rate at male age 30, according to the *1958 CSO Table,* is 2.13 per 1,000. If 100,000 persons age 30 are insured for $1,000, a company would expect to receive 213 death claims aggregating $213,000. Since 100,000 persons are insured, the company would have to collect $2.13 from each one in order to accumulate a fund sufficient to meet the 213 death claims. It should be noted that the premium charged is exactly the same as the death rate,[8] and it is this fact which has led to calling yearly renewable term insurance the natural premium plan.

Since the death rate increases at an increasing rate, rising ultimately to a certainty, the premium which must be paid each year increases at exactly the same rate. As surviving members of a group of insured policyholders continue to renew their insurance year after year, the increasing premium causes them to question the advisability of continuing the insurance. As the increases become more burdensome, there is a tendency for

[7] See Chapter 24.
[8] This statement refers to the "insurance" charge only and ignores the provision for expenses and contingencies.

those in good health to drop their policies, while those in poor health naturally would make every effort to continue to renew their policies regardless of cost. This tendency is known as *adverse selection* and results in a continuing group of policyholders whose mortality experience exceeds the normal or expected death rates. In addition, the premiums would ultimately become prohibitive even for those in poor health. In view of the adverse selection producing abnormally high mortality rates and the ultimate prohibitive nature of the premium, the insurance process breaks down, and, consequently, those insurance companies which offer yearly renewable term insurance invariably place a limit on the period during which the insurance can be renewed. Since the majority of individuals need life insurance protection on a permanent basis regardless of the age at which they die, it was natural that the insurance industry developed the level-premium plan of insurance.

The Level-Premium Plan

The practical difficulties which arise out of the fact that the mortality rate increases with age have been solved through the use of the *level-premium* plan. The fundamental idea of the level-premium plan is that the company can agree to accept the same premium each year (a level premium), provided the level premiums collected are the mathematical equivalent of the increasing yearly renewable term premiums for the same period of time. As a result, the level premiums paid in the early years of the contract will be more than sufficient to pay current death claims but will be less than adequate to meet death claims that occur in later years.

This results in the creation of a fund from the annual level premiums paid in the early policy years when mortality rates are low. When interest on the fund is added and future premiums are collected, this fund is exactly sufficient to pay all death claims as they occur during the period of the policy.

The effect of substituting a level premium for a series of increasing premiums is illustrated in Graph 1-1. The graph shows that a level premium of $10.40 annually will develop a reserve fund during the early policy years which, *with interest,* will exactly make up the deficit in premiums during the later years of the contract.

The principle of the level-premium plan may be applied to the whole of life and thus provide the policyholder with permanent insurance protection for a level annual premium.

In any policy providing protection for the whole of life, the excess of the level premium over the actual death cost will have to be enough with compound interest to make up the deficits in later years and, at the same time, accumulate a fund which is equal to the face value of the policy at the end

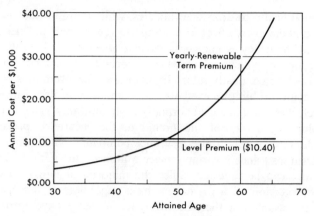

GRAPH 1-1.   Comparison of yearly renewable term premium with level premium for term to 65 issued at age 30.

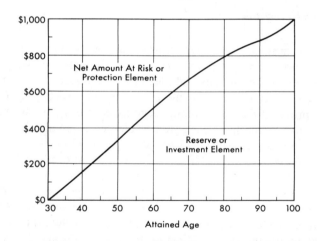

GRAPH 1-2.   Proportion of protection and investment elements in ordinary life contract issued at male age 30, 1958 CSO Table and 2½ per cent interest.

of the policy period. The *1958 CSO Table* assumes that all males who survive to age 99 will die during the year, and therefore, it is necessary to accumulate for each policy on those at attained age 99 a sum equal to the face of the policy by the end of the policy year. This is necessary since all will die (or are assumed to die) during this year and there are no survivors with whom to share the losses. Under the yearly renewable term plan, if it were issued at this age, each person would have to contribute the face amount of his policy as a premium,[9] since everyone is assumed to die and a pro rata share of the total losses will be exactly equal to the face of his own policy.

Under a level-premium type of contract the accumulated fund becomes a part of the face amount payable upon the death of a policyholder and, as a result, the insurance company has less than the face amount at risk. Therefore, at any point, the actual amount of pure life insurance protection is the difference between the fund accumulated at that point and the face amount of the contract. This difference is called the *net amount at risk*. It declines as the fund accumulation increases and, consequently, the rate per unit of protection at that age is applied to a smaller amount, thus reducing the cost for *pure insurance protection*.

As is apparent from the above comments, under the level-premium plan a $1,000 policy does not provide $1,000 of pure insurance. Rather it provides a decreasing amount of insurance and an increasing investment element which when combined are always just equal to the face of the policy. This combination of protection and investment is found in all level-premium plans. Fundamentally, the only difference in the several contracts is the relative proportions of the investment and protection elements.

Graph 1–2 shows a life insurance policy of $1,000 which is payable on the death of the insured and may be purchased by a level premium of $14.80 payable annually until death. The increasing investment element and the declining amount of pure protection are apparent.

Health insurance protection is also provided under the "yearly renewable term" and "level-premium" plans. The apparent differences in application reflect the difference in incidence of the peril insured against and the multiplicity of benefit forms found in health insurance policies.

LIFE AND HEALTH INSURANCE ARE THE OPPOSITE OF GAMBLING

Although life and health insurance serve indirectly to increase the productivity of the community by eliminating worry and increasing initiative, their direct economic function is to change uncertainty into certainty and thus enable the insured to transfer the peril of premature death or disability to the insurer at the lowest possible cost. The larger the number of separate risks combined into a group the less fluctuation in loss rate and, therefore, the greater the certainty that the premiums collected will exactly meet the claims and set up the required reserves. Unless certainty of loss is present, an insurance organization must charge a contingency margin or gamble its

[9] Technically, this premium would be less than the face to the extent of the interest to be earned during the year.

existence against the fact that its claim rate will not fluctuate to its detriment. Therefore, the larger the numbers insured the less the company needs to collect annually from the insured.

This function of insurance is perhaps most readily understood in connection with fire insurance. Let us assume that each of 5,000 persons owns a house valued at $10,000, that all the houses are alike, and that the annual loss by fire as regards the entire number, although varying slightly from year to year, averages one half of 1 per cent of the value, or $50. In the absence of any system of insurance making possible the application of the law of averages, it is clear that none of these owners can effect any arrangement which will place them in a position of absolute security. At best they can only anticipate their uncertain losses by practicing self-insurance, that is, by increasing their rentals by an amount considerably in excess of the average annual loss of $50. But even assuming that they can increase their rentals by 4 or 5 times the amount actually necessary under a system of insurance, they will still remain subject to a large gamble. At the end of the year the great majority of these owners, since they suffered no loss, will have the entire extra sum collected from tenants as a clear gain, while to those unfortunate few who suffered a total loss the extra sum collected will prove woefully inadequate to indemnify the value destroyed. But let us now assume that these 5,000 house owners can combine their risks into a group. By doing this they can substitute for the great *uncertainty* of loss which confronted them as individuals a *certain* definitely known annual loss, amounting on the average to $50 per house and $250,000 for the group. This sum, plus a proper addition for expenses, contingencies, and reasonable profit, is all that the company needs to charge in order to secure absolutely these owners against the risk of loss by fire. "The risk that an insurance company carries is far less than the sum of the risks of the insured, and as the size of the company increases, the disproportion becomes greater." [10]

Now, just as each house owner was enabled to use fire insurance to substitute certainty for uncertainty at the lowest possible cost, so is it also possible to hedge against the uncertainty of life through life insurance by providing for the payment of a definite sum of money at death, whenever that may occur, to replace the economic value of the deceased individual. From a family and business standpoint, nearly all lives possess an economic value which may at any time be snuffed out by death or lost temporarily or permanently through disability. It is as reasonable to insure against the loss of this value as it is to protect oneself against the loss of property. In the absence of insurance we saw that property owners could at best practice only some form of self-insurance, and that it was impossible for them to

[10] Willett, *op. cit.,* p. 108.

effect any arrangement which would give absolute certainty. Similarly, in the absence of a system of life and health insurance which makes possible the application of the law of averages, no arrangement can be found which will render certain the indemnification of the economic value of a human life lost through death or disability. The practice of saving such a sum in anticipation of probable death or disability by no means takes the place of insurance as an agency in substituting certainty for uncertainty, because saving requires time and because death or disability may occur before the savings fund has reached an appreciable size. Unlike the practice of saving, a life or health insurance policy means certainty because it guarantees a definite benefit from the moment the first premium is paid. Moreover, it furnishes this element of certainty to the public at the lowest possible cost since the companies are enabled through the combination of many risks to determine quite accurately the average cost of the protection for the entire group. From the company's point of view we have seen that life and health insurance are essentially nonspeculative; in fact, probably no other business operates with greater certainty.

From the insured's point of view life and health insurance are the antithesis of gambling. Nothing is more uncertain than life, and life and health insurance offer the only sure method of changing that uncertainty into certainty. Failure of the head of a family to insure his life against the sudden loss of his economic value through death or disability amounts to gambling with the greatest of life's values; and the gamble is a particularly mean one since, in case of loss, the dependent family and not the gambler must suffer the consequences.

Family and Personal Uses | 2
of Life and Health Insurance |

ECONOMIC BASIS OF LIFE AND
HEALTH INSURANCE

The Concept of Human Capital

WHILE ECONOMISTS HAVE long known that people are an important element of a nation's wealth, they have not stressed the simple truth that people invest in themselves and that these investments are substantial. Although economists are seldom timid in entering on abstract analysis, they have proceeded gingerly in coming to grips with this form of investment.[1] Free men are, after all, first and foremost the end to be served by economic endeavor; they are not property or marketable assets. Nevertheless, individuals have become capitalists from the acquisition of knowledge and skills that have economic value. Knowledge and skill are in great part the product of investment, and, combined with other human investment, predominantly account for the productive superiority of the technically advanced countries.[2]

Clearly, the most distinctive feature of our economic system is the growth in human capital.[3] The increased productivity arising from our investments in human capital is so significant that human resources management has come to the fore as a major management responsibility in every type of institution in our society. It would be useful, therefore, if we could establish a conceptual framework for estimating the value of assets in the form of human capital. Both the estimation of current human capital values and the

---

[1] Theodore W. Schultz, "Investment in Human Capital," *The American Economic Review,* Vol. LI, No. 1 (March, 1961), p. 2.

[2] *Ibid.,* p. 3.

[3] The significance of this point has led one author to label the United States as a "knowledge society." See Peter F. Drucker, *The Age of Discontinuity* (New York: Harper and Row, Publishers, 1969), Part IV.

estimation of how these values could be altered by various programs (such as in health and education) are matters worthy of attention.[4]

The Human Life Value Concept

The human life value concept is one segment of the general theory of human capital. While this general area of inquiry has been under discussion for over four centuries, only in recent times has the interrelationship between human capital and life insurance been acknowledged.[5] Some semblance of the idea existed in the old Anglo-Saxon law, where it was used to determine the compensation to be allowed to the relatives of an individual who was killed by a third party. In recent years the valuation of a human life in connection with legal actions seeking recovery for wrongful death has gained considerable prominence. A considerable body of literature has developed in this area, contributing to a more scientific approach to the calculation of damages (including human life values) in wrongful death cases.[6]

Apparently, the concept was first applied to life insurance in the 1880's through the efforts of Jacob L. Green, then president of the Connecticut Mutual Life Insurance Company. It was not, however, until the 1920's that the human life value became established as the economic foundation of life insurance.

Significance of the Human Life Value Concept.   In 1924, the late Dr. S. S. Huebner proposed the human life value concept as a philosophical framework for the analysis of basic economic risks faced by individuals. This concept has been widely accepted by those associated with the institution of life insurance and tends to change materially the

---

[4] Burton A. Weisbrod, "The Valuation of Human Capital," *The American Economic Review*, Vol. LXIX, No. 5 (October, 1961), pp. 425–426. See Gary S. Becher, *Human Capital* (New York: Columbia University Press, 1964) and also Mark Blaug, *Economics of Education, A Selected Annotated Bibliography*, 2nd ed. (New York: Pergamon Press, 1970).

[5] Sir William Petty (1623–1687) was the first economist to be credited with using the concept of the economic value of a man. Fifty years passed before another economist, Philip Cantillon (1680–1734), made another contribution to the concept of human capital. Then followed Adam Smith (1723–1798), Johann H. Von Thunen (1783–1850), John Stuart Mill (1806–1873), and others. In 1853, Sir William Farr, an economist and statistician, derived the first set of equations used to describe the human life value. In so doing he laid the basic foundation of the theory as we know it today. See Alred E. Hofflander, "The Human Life Value: An Historical Perspective," *The Journal of Risk and Insurance*, Vol. XXXIII, No. 3 (September, 1966), pp. 381–391.

[6] See, for example, Stuart M. Speiser, *Recovery for Wrongful Death—Economic Handbook* (Rochester, N.Y.: The Lawyers Co-operative Publishing Company, 1970).

widely held view that life insurance is essentially a physical death proposition, with no profit to the premium payor, and that life insurance selling does not require professional counseling. In Dr. Huebner's view, the concept means more than just a statement that a human life has an economic value. Rather, it involves the five important concepts:

1. The human life value, expressed with a dollar valuation, should be carefully appraised and capitalized. The human life value is based on the fact that every man who earns more than is necessary for his own self-maintenance has a monetary value to those who are dependent upon him. Thus, it may be defined as the capitalized value of that part of the earnings of the individual devoted to the support of family dependents, business associates, and others who benefit from his economic earning capacity.

The primary purpose of life and health insurance is the protection of the family. Every family is dependent for subsistence upon an income which necessarily varies in amount with the particular circumstances surrounding its case. In some instances this income is obtained from the return on invested funds which have been accumulated or inherited, but in the overwhelming majority of cases the subsistence of the family depends upon the *current earnings* of the family head. He is the breadwinner who has assumed responsibility for the support of those dependent upon him, and his wife and children have a right to look to him for adequate maintenance. His life has an economic value (and the same is also often true of the mother or son) to the dependent members of the family, and it is this value of one life in relation to another that justifies the existence of life and health insurance. Such a relationship may exist also with business associates whenever they pool their capital and skills in an enterprise. In fact, whenever continuance of a life is financially valuable to others, an economic basis for life and health insurance exists.

Obviously, many refinements could enter into a careful appraisal of an individual's human life value, but the logic of appraising and capitalizing the values inherent in a human life for life and health insurance purposes should be clear.

2. The human life value should be recognized as the creator of substantially all property values. The human life value is the key to the *turning of property into a productive force.*[7] In other words, the human life value is the cause, and property values are the effect.

3. The family is an economic unit, organized around the human life values of its members. The family should be regarded as man's first and

[7] Further, estimates now show that the income of the United States has been increasing at a much higher rate than the combined amount of land, man-hours worked, and the stock of reproducible capital used to produce the income. This would appear to represent a return to the investment we have been making in human capital. This is additional evidence of the critical role of the human capital in our total economic system.

most important enterprise. It needs to be organized originally, managed, and its economic values finally liquidated in the same manner that other enterprises are organized, operated, and liquidated.

4. *The human life value and its protection should be regarded as constituting the principal economic link between the present and succeeding generations.* The realization of the potential net earnings of the breadwinner constitutes the economic foundation for the proper education and development of the children in the event of the family head's premature death or disability, and the protection of the children against the burden of parental financial support.

5. *In view of the significance of human life values relative to property values, the scientific principles of business management utilized in connection with property values should be applied to life values.* Principles such as appraisal, conservation, indemnity and depreciation should be applied to the organization, management, and liquidation of human life values. These principles have been applied to property values for decades.

Qualitative Characteristics of the Individual Human Life Value. Man possesses two estates, an "acquired estate" and a "potential estate." The former refers to what he has acquired—his property estate. The latter refers to his monetary worth as an economic force, "existing in possibility," i.e., his capability of earning for others beyond the limits of his own self-maintenance and, if given time, his ability to accumulate surplus earnings into an acquired estate. The insurable value of an individual's economic possibilities may be defined as the monetary worth of the economic forces which incorporated within his being, namely, (1) good character; (2) good health; (3) industry, or the willingness to work; (4) willingness to make a proper investment in the mind by way of education, training, and experience; (5) creative ability and judgment; and (6) the patience and ambition to translate the economic dreams of the mind into tangible realities for the benefit of self, family, and mankind in general.

Nearly everybody will agree that good character is the main pedestal upon which all else in our economic career is essentially dependent. No one wants a lazy person in any line of economic endeavor. Good health is absolutely vital, and increasingly executives are recognizing the value of life conservation work, just as they have been accustomed to conserving their property assets against loss through loss-prevention activities. The investment in the mind by way of education and training is also vital, and was extolled by Benjamin Franklin about 175 years ago as the "investment above the ears," sure and dependable. As our economic system has become more complex and technically advanced, growth in knowledge and skill has become the *sine qua non* of earning capacity.[8] Creative ability

8 See Peter Drucker, *op. cit.*

and judgment are important to high earnings, since sound decision-making is the essence of the manager's function. The sixth and last factor—patience and ambition—is also important to the attainment of a high order of economic success. These qualitative characteristics underlie an individual's earning capacity. They are the basis of economic life itself.

The Quantitative Characteristics of the Human Life Value.
The human life value may be defined, quantitatively, as the capitalized value of the net earnings of an individual. The same economic and statistical principles are applicable whether one is concerned with the appraisal of the value of property or of the earning capacity of human beings. The general elements of appraising potential earnings for an individual require a projection over the expected work life of the individual, such items as *basic earnings, incentive earnings,* and *fringe benefits.* These elements may generally be expected to vary with such criteria as occupation and industry, age, sex, race, residence, education, mobility, marital status, and number of dependents. The process is still further complicated by the necessity to project change in each of these considerations. For purposes of this discussion, a simplified model will be utilized, but it should be noted that the considerable research and development presently under way is likely to lead to increasingly sophisticated approaches to the appraisal of human life values.[9]

Human Life Value Subject to Loss.   The human life value is subject to loss through a number of serious risks including: (1) premature death, (2) temporary disability, (3) total and permanent disability, (4) retirement, and (5) unemployment. While it should be clear that any event which affects an individual's earning capacity has a corresponding impact on his human life value (potential estate), it might be worthwhile to consider briefly the probability of losing one's potential estate by death or disability.

Even where the logic of the situation as it relates to religious, civic, and economic duty might not appear, it would seem that contemplation of the very extent of the probability of losing the potential estate should suffice to initiate action. According to the *Commissioners 1958 Standard Ordinary (CSO) Mortality Table,* beginning with male age 30, over 28 per cent die before they reach the retirement age of 65. At five-year intervals, during this most effective period of the working life, the *Table* indicates that 1.1 per cent of the total number starting at age 30 are expected to die during

[9] U.S. Bureau of the Census, "Present Value of Estimated Lifetime Earnings," Technical Paper No. 16 (Washington: U.S. Government Printing Office, 1967). See also John E. Brown, "A Study of the Economic Variables Affecting the Valuation of a Human Life in Legal Decisions" (unpublished Ph.D. thesis, Faculty of Political Science, Department of Economics, North Carolina State University, 1971).

the first five years, 2.5 per cent during the first ten years, 7.6 per cent during the first fifteen years, 12.1 per cent, or more than one out of every ten, during the first twenty years, and 18.8 per cent, or nearly one out of every five, during the first twenty-five years. Although the death record indicated by the *Table* is conservative, it is fairly correct to say that about one out of every three who start the working period of life fails to survive to the normal retirement age of 65. In other words, as is indicated by the above figures, nearly all, or a substantial part of, the potential estates are lost to about a third of the working population. No one should be willing to assume such a fearful ratio of loss when the cost of term insurance is so small and the future consequences of an uninsured loss to one's own family are so serious.

The potential estate also is subject to reduction through the loss of personal earning power due to disability. Experience has shown that extended total disability is clearly a major peril.

Recent studies show that in a year, four out of every five persons are disabled for at least one day from disease and one in every eighteen from accidental injury. The probability of long-term disability for insured persons ranges from about 7½ times the probability of death at age 22 to two times at age 62.[10]

The probability of loss from death and disability is significantly greater than the other commonly insured perils. Only about one building in every one hundred ever experiences a worthwhile fire loss throughout its entire history, whereas one out of every three working lives passes before age 65, and all remaining must pass thereafter. Moreover, the average fire loss in well-protected cities does not exceed 10 to 15 per cent of the property involved, that is, it is a partial loss. With respect to such cities it is said that only about one out of every thirty fires results in a substantially total loss. The death peril, on the contrary, always strikes a 100 per cent blow, and the loss to the potential estate is total. The same is probably also true in many total disability claims. It does seem, reasoning from this standpoint, that the death peril to the potential estate is at least one hundred times as serious as is the fire peril to acquired property. Similarly, disability is a much more serious peril to the potential estate than the fire peril is to acquired property. And yet, fire insurance is almost universally taken as a matter of course, even by the ignorant, while death and disability insurance protection is generally avoided and must be persistently emphasized and sold in order to bring about even the limited percentage of coverage of human life values prevailing today. One would think that solemn funerals and speeding ambulances ought to be as effective a spur to insurance action as are the sirens and all the other noises of fire-fighting equipment.

---

[10] See O. D. Dickerson, *Health Insurance,* 3rd ed. (Homewood, Ill.: Richard D. Irwin, Inc., 1968), pp. 15–16.

Even where a substantial amount of property exists in the family estate, it is undesirable to permit that fact to justify minimizing insurance needs. Material property, as we have pointed out, is very elusive in character when contrasted with the greater permanence of the human life value. There must be an allowance of a substantial factor of safety when a property estate is owned by a prospect. During the last depression, any number of people must have concluded that it would have been better to have ignored their business estate and other investments altogether in evaluating the adequacy of their life insurance program. Moreover, it is hard to see why insurance of the potential estate should be confused with the possession of a material estate. The two are entirely separate and each is a distinct possession. The material estate needs to be insured against shrinkage and other loss. But the potential estate also needs to be insured against loss. Why lose it any more than the material estate? It is certainly poor economics to protect the material possessions against loss, and then to feel that just because one has a material estate the potential estate can be lost with impunity. Both estates are valuable and both need to be insured. Even assuming that one is to be excluded, it should certainly not be the potential estate. That estate, as we have seen, is much the more significant of the two from every possible standpoint. It is, moreover, much more like "the good earth" than any other species of investment upon which a man and his family can place dependence.

MANAGEMENT OF LIFE VALUES

In view of the fact that the human life value is the predominant element in our national economic worth, we should apply to human life values (human capital) the same fundamental business principles or practices which we have applied as a matter of course to our property values. Despite the fact that there are obvious differences between persons and, say, machines, the principles of their economic valuation are the same. The work-life expectancy of a man or a woman is equivalent to the productive life of a physical asset. The projected earnings of a person are equivalent to the future returns expected from employment of a physical asset. The projected personal expenditures of an individual are equivalent to the projected depreciation and maintenance costs of a physical asset. When costs and revenues have been appropriately discounted, a comparison of value can be made between a person and a machine.

Capitalization and Indemnification of a Human Life Value

Acknowledging the economic value of a human life from either a family or a business standpoint, life and health insurance make possible the capitalization of that value. By guaranteeing this capitalized value in the event of death or disability, life and health insurance may be said to perpetuate the earning capacity of the life for the benefit of those dependent upon it. Through experience and effort, the value of a human life normally increases over time, the dependent family in the meantime becoming more and more accustomed to a higher standard of living; suddenly this entire value may be swept away by death or disability. Unless some substitute, some sort of hedge, can be found, there will be nothing to take the place of the economic value of the deceased. Life and health insurance constitute such a hedge, and men who have assumed family obligations should take out such an amount of insurance—to capitalize their potential earnings to such an extent—that the proceeds and benefits will yield an income equivalent to at least from one-third to one-half of their earning capacity during the remainder of their working lifetimes.

For years we have developed a science, "corporation finance," which deals with the capitalization and management of the value of land, buildings, equipment, and good will. But it is only in recent years that the same ideas have been applied to human life values. Life and health insurance, as already indicated, furnish the only known method of capitalizing the economic value of a human life and indemnifying for its loss in the event of premature death or disability.

Every business which owns a valuable machine appraises its value, charges depreciation against earnings as the machine wears out, accumulates a depreciation fund to provide for its ultimate replacement, and obtains protection against its damage or destruction. These same principles can be applied through life and health insurance by an individual in the financial management of his personal and family affairs.

By determining the value of the potential estate and capitalizing this value by the purchase of life and health insurance, a mechanism is available for depreciating the life value asset, accumulating a sinking fund to replace the asset when economic death occurs, and indemnifying for the lost potential estate in the event of disability or premature death. The analogy between life and health insurance and corporation finance is appropriate. Life and health insurance is corporation finance applied to human values.

Accounting Principles

Once a human life value has been appraised, it can be capitalized and managed through the initiation of a permanent life insurance contract. The level premium method of financing life insurance contracts provides in the early policy years for a premium in excess of the estimated death costs. Thus, to the extent that the (net) level premium, which is payable either for the life of the contract or for the premium payment period, is greater than the amount estimated as adequate to pay current death claims in the early policy years, there is established an increasing savings fund to the credit of the policyowner. The concept of an increasing investment can be illustrated best with an endowment at age 65 policy, the face amount of which is approximately equal to the insured's human life value, although it applies to any permanent life insurance policy as well. This "investment" element of the contract, which builds up over the life of the policy until finally reaching the face at maturity (age 65), has been likened to a sinking fund. Just as a business sinking fund builds up over time through periodic payments so that at the maturity of an outstanding debt a sufficient fund will be available to retire the debt, so does the cash value in an endowment policy accumulate to create a fund at retirement to provide for the insured's self-maintenance during his retirement years.

The fundamental business principle of charging depreciation against the annual earnings of a business also may be applied to our human life values. A person's human life value also normally declines with the passing of time. As a person approaches retirement age, the number of remaining productive years in his working lifetime will decline. Therefore, like depreciable business property, the economic worth of a person's life is subject to a gradual reduction in its value over the person's working lifetime. As the business firm does with respect to depreciable business property, an individual should allow for his declining human life value by making provision for this out of his current income. The portion of the annual premium for a permanent life insurance policy, which goes to increase the cash value of the policy, represents, in an economic sense, an annual charge against the insured's earnings for the depreciation of his human life value. In this way, the insured makes provision for the declining economic value of his life, and provides a fund for meeting his future obligations including his own self-maintenance—through the use of the annuity principle either directly in the form of a retirement income or through the use of income settlement options following his death.

Life Insurance as a Life Will

In most cases, the individual life value constitutes something like 90 per cent of all he owns, while his material possessions (property values) comprise only 10 per cent. Increasingly, men are recognizing that they should have two wills, a *life* will and a *property* will. The traditional "last will and testament" with which the insured policyowner bequeaths his property estate should be coupled with a life will under the terms of which he bequeaths the monetary value of his life, his potential life value. Where there is a named beneficiary other than the insured's estate, the insured is the testator, the named beneficiaries are the heirs, and the so-called beneficiary clause is the heart of the arrangement. An appropriate selection of settlement options and/or trust arrangements coupled with the careful naming of beneficiaries assures the insured policyowner that his life will will function effectively in distributing his life value following his death with the life insurance company serving as executor. This life will, as contrasted to a property will, however, has many advantages. The life value distributed through a life will is not subject to probate, there are no costs of administration, no delay in settlement, and no publicity with respect to the inheritance. Litigation between heirs is eliminated and the numerous annoying details usually connected with the settlement of an estate under a will are avoided. Moreover, there is a very favorable tax treatment under our Federal and state income, estate, and inheritance taxes.[11]

THE AMOUNT OF LIFE AND HEALTH INSURANCE TO ACQUIRE

In determining how much life and health insurance should be carried, there are two basic approaches: (1) the human life value approach and (2) the needs approach.

[11] For an excellent summary of the tax treatment of life insurance, see Stuart A. McCarthy, "Tax Treatment of Life Insurance," Chapter in Dan M. McGill, *Life Insurance,* rev. ed. (Homewood, Illinois: Richard D. Irwin, Inc., 1967); see also *The R & R Tax Handbook* which is published annually and provides questions and answers on the taxation of insurance, annuity, endowment contracts and other related areas (The Research and Review Service of America, Inc., Indianapolis).

Human Life Value Approach

This approach involves the capitalization of that part of the individual's earning capacity which is devoted to the maintenance of his dependents through the medium of life insurance. Logically, the amount of life and health insurance to be taken follows from the extent to which the individual wishes to capitalize his life value and protect his potential earning power.

From the standpoint of indemnifying for the lost earning power which would benefit dependents, consideration should be given to the amount of income produced through personal efforts which will be lost to the family in the event personal earnings are terminated by death or disability.

The technically accurate method of computing the monetary value of a man is considered too complex for general use.[12] The concept itself is not, however. It simply involves the present value of future net incomes with allowance for trends in earnings, certain deductions (for self-maintenance, life insurance premiums, and personal income taxes) and discounting for interest.

A relatively simple but reasonably accurate method of estimating the economic value of a man to his family and, consequently, the extent to which he should capitalize his earnings for life and health insurance purposes is as follows:

1. Determine the *amount of earned income devoted to the family.*
   - Estimate the individual's *average* annual earnings from future personal efforts.
   - Deduct Federal and state income taxes, personal life and health insurance premiums, and the cost of self-maintenance.
2. Determine the *working expectancy* of the individual, i.e., his probable productive working period.
   - Determine the number of years between the present age and the *contemplated* age of retirement.
3. Determine *economic value* of individual life.
   - Select a reasonable rate of interest at which future earnings should be discounted. The rate assumed should be in line with the rate generally payable on proceeds left with the insurance company.[13]

[12] See Louis J. Dublin and Alfred J. Lotka, *The Money Value of a Man,* rev. ed. (New York: Ronald Press Company, 1946) for a comprehensive discussion of the subject; see also Speiser, *op. cit.,* and Juan B. Aponte and Herbert S. Denenberg, "A New Concept of the Economics of Life Value and Human Life Value," *The Journal of Risk and Insurance,* Vol. XXXV, No. 3 (September, 1968), pp. 337–356.

[13] For a discussion of the factors involved in selecting an interest rate for human life valuation purposes, see Speiser, *op. cit.,* pp. 23–35.

■ Multiply the "amount of earned income devoted to the family" by the present value of $1 payable annually for the "working expectancy," utilizing the rate of interest selected above.

Thus, if an individual had an "amount of income devoted to the family" of $10,000 and a "working expectancy" of 30 years, he would be worth $173,000 to his family today, assuming a discount rate of interest of 4 per cent.[14] To the extent possible this income flow should be capitalized in the form of a life insurance policy on the producer of the income.

In establishing the appropriate amount of health insurance needed to indemnify for lost earnings, it is not necessary to capitalize the "amount of income devoted to the family." In this case, a disability income policy with an income benefit equal to $10,000 plus the cost of self-maintenance with the benefit payable for the "working expectancy" will be adequate. Thus, with appropriate amounts of life and health insurance the insured can be certain that the income flow to his family will continue uninterrupted whether he lives, dies, or is disabled.

Needs Approach

A second approach to the problem of determining how much life and health insurance a person should carry is to analyze the various needs that would be experienced by the family in the event that the breadwinner should die or become disabled. This technique is termed the "needs approach," and from a purely sales standpoint has been considered more practical than the "human life value" approach.

In order to determine the amount of life and health insurance the head of a family should own through the use of the "needs approach," it is first necessary to determine the financial objectives of the family in the event of the death or disability of the head of the family.

Naturally, the "needs" or financial objectives will differ from family to family and within a family group over a period of time. Nevertheless, certain general categories of needs can be established which generally will be applicable to the average family. Among the needs of the family normally would be included: (1) the cleanup fund (last illness and burial expenses, outstanding notes and loans, estate and inheritance taxes, probate costs, and so forth); (2) the readjustment income (an income sufficient to permit any required adjustment in the standard of living to be made gradually); (3) income for the family until children are self-supporting; (4) life income for the widow after the children are self-supporting; (5) special

---

[14] This computation can be made by consulting a compound discount table. In the instant case the $173,000 was determined by multiplying 17.30 × 10,000.

needs (mortgage redemption, emergency fund, educational fund, and other specific needs, depending upon the individual family); and (6) retirement needs.

The *income* needs arising out of disability are essentially the same as those arising out of death since the loss in each case is *income*. Therefore, all of the above needs (except the cleanup fund) are the same for both life and health insurance purposes since the only question is which condition, death or disability, causes the disruption in the flow of income to the family. In either case, the breadwinner has ceased to be an economic asset, and in fact, in the case of disability, he becomes an economic liability because of the need to provide for his maintenance as well as the extra cost of medical expenses incurred in attempting to repair and rehabilitate him. For these reasons the amount of income required for any specific need tends to be greater for disability than in the case of death. After burial and the closing of the estate, the breadwinner does not constitute any economic responsibility to the family in any way.

Although income needs are vitally important, health insurance also provides medical expense reimbursement coverage for all the members of the family including the breadwinner. Therefore, it is necessary to consider the family's need for medical expense insurance separately. In this case, the health insurance contracts are written with the needs as an integral part of the contract. For example, assuming that a hospitalization policy includes surgical coverage, only the insured member of the family who has surgery performed has a benefit available. The need produces the benefit subject to the limitations in the contract. If no one has surgery, no benefit is payable. In contrast, a life or health insurance contract, bought for the purpose of mortgage redemption, pays in the event of death or disability even if the mortgage has been paid off prior to death or disability.

In considering medical expense coverage, the primary considerations are establishing (1) the types of benefits for which coverage is desired; (2) acceptable limitations (including exclusions) in the various types of benefits; and (3) appropriate deductible and/or percentage participation (coinsurance) provisions in relation to the family's income.[15]

In connection with establishing income needs for life and health insurance purposes and appropriate medical expense coverage, all decisions as to financial objectives and needs are made *by the family* with the *advice* of a life underwriter. It is also necessary for the family to determine the order of priority of the various needs since the ability to pay premiums may prevent the attainment, currently, of the desired life and health insurance program.

---

[15] Chapters 16, 17, and 18 are devoted to a careful consideration of the multiplicity of available health insurance policies and their provisions.

Having determined the financial objectives and needs of the individual family and their order of priority, it is necessary next to determine what income or other benefits are available from other sources to meet these needs. Thus, consideration should be given to the benefits available to the family from Social Security, investment income, Veterans Administration, present life and health insurance, anticipated inheritances, and other sources.

The difference between the funds needed to meet the financial objectives of the family and those available from other sources represents the amount of life and health insurance needed.[16] In all cases, however, the ability to pay the premiums required must be considered, and it may be that only part of the needed life and health insurance program will be purchased immediately with the supposition that the remainder will be purchased as soon as it becomes practicable.

Naturally, an individual family's needs will change because of additional children being born, changes in sources of income, or otherwise, and it is essential that the life and health insurance program be reviewed periodically to take these changes into account.

Human Life Value vs. Needs Approach

Ideally, the productive head of each family unit should be insured for an amount equal to his full economic value to that family unit. As a practical matter this ideal is difficult to attain. The basic obstacle is that when the economic value of an individual is greatest (at the younger ages), income (and consequently the funds available for premium payments) tends to be lowest.

The needs approach, to a large extent in practice, is used to approach the one pressing need of the time. The human life value approach includes the entire group of needs for all of life. It includes the capitalization concept so that in the event of disability or premature death the entire group of family needs will be met. In addition, it includes in advance the need for protection against the economic or so-called "retirement death," now as great a problem in many respects as that of premature death. Upon economic death or retirement the insured life value—the potential estate—has become an acquired estate through the economic endeavors of the insured during his working lifetime. The depreciated life value is now represented by the savings element in the life insurance program and is available for scientific liquidation through annuities, thus protecting the insured life

---

[16] It is, of course, necessary to convert the income needed through new life insurance to a principal amount, since life insurance is usually purchased by paying a given rate per $1,000 face amount. This is not necessary for health insurance purposes.

against the retirement death and also benefiting the children by relieving them of the burden of parental support.

Various rule-of-thumb formulae have been devised in an effort to establish a proper relationship between income and the amount of insurance to be maintained. Probably the most popular is that 10 to 15 per cent of income should be placed in life and health insurance premiums, but as with any rule of thumb, this ratio is not reasonable at all income levels. This approach is probably not realistic, in terms of attainment, at income levels below $5,000 or above $15,000. The average American family in 1971 owned enough life insurance of all types to replace approximately twenty-four months of its disposable income after Federal income taxes.

The Duty to Insure

From the family standpoint, life and health insurance is a necessary business proposition which may be expected of every person with dependents as a matter of course, just like any other necessary business obligation which ordinary decency requires him to meet. The care of his family is man's first and most important business. The family should be established and run on a sound business basis. It should be protected against needless bankruptcy. The death or disability of the head of this business should not involve its impairment or dissolution any more than the death of the head of a bank, railroad, or store should affect their respective businesses. Every corporation and firm represents capitalized earning capacity and good will. Why, then, when men and women are about to organize the business called a family should there not be protection, in the form of life and health insurance policies, of the only real value and good will behind that business? Why is it not fully as reasonable to have life and health insurance policies accompany a marriage certificate as it is to have a marine insurance certificate invariably attached to a foreign bill of exchange. The voyage in the first instance is, on the average, much longer, subject to much greater risk, and in case of wreck the loss is of infinitely greater consequence.

The growth of life and health insurance implies an increasing development of the sense of responsibility. The idea of providing only for the present must give way to recognition of the fact that a person's responsibility to his family is not limited to the years of survival. Emphasis should be laid on the "crime of not insuring," and the finger of scorn should be pointed at any man who, although he has provided well while he was alive, has not seen fit to discount the uncertain future for the benefit of a dependent household. As already explained, life and health insurance is a sure means of changing uncertainty into certainty and is the opposite of gambling. He who does not insure gambles with the greatest of all values, and, if he loses, makes those dearest to him pay the forfeit. That the gamble is a risky one is easily demonstrated by any mortality or morbidity table, and even if life be granted until age 60 or 65, let it not be overlooked that less than one in ten of our population succeeds in accumulating a reasonable competency, and that through reverses a great majority of this limited number lose it by the time that age is reached. A mother's *right* as well as her *duty* in the matter of life and health insurance should also be emphasized. She should be taught that not only is it her husband's duty to protect the family adequately, if it is at all possible, but that it is also *her duty,* if necessary, to use her persuasive powers to get him to act, and if that does not avail, to insist on action as her *right.* Not only has she a right to personal protection, but her rights as regards life and health insurance are further increased by her interest in the children under her care.

ADVANTAGES TO THE INSURED POLICYHOLDER[17]

Aside from the advantage of capitalization of potential income and its direct protection for the family, life and health insurance also benefit the policyholder in a number of important ways. The policyholder, in other words, is a "beneficiary" under his life and health insurance, and that expression should not attach only to the insured's dependents. There are a number of advantages which deserve special mention in this respect, and all benefit the policyholder's family by qualifying him to meet its obligations and to protect its comfort and happiness.

Eliminates Worry and Increases Initiative

Writers have frequently asserted that life and health insurance are not to be regarded as producers of wealth and that their function is merely to distribute funds from the fortunate to the unfortunate. In reality, however, life and health insurance will be found to be powerful forces in the production of wealth in that they relieve the policyholder of worry and increase his efficiency. Constant worry is one of the greatest curses that can fall to the lot of man, and life and health insurance, if universally used, would lift that curse from innumerable shoulders. The knowledge of an assured estate from the moment the premium is paid will enable the insured to feel freer to take initiative. Let us assume that the head of a family is the possessor of $10,000 and is afforded an excellent opportunity for the invest-

[17] Huebner, *op. cit.,* pp. 143–240.

ment of this capital in a business pursuit. If it were not for life and health insurance, the owner of this capital could not safely afford to invest this sum and assume the speculative hazard connected with most business enterprises because of the fear that this capital might be lost, and that in case of disability or premature death no provision would exist for those dependent upon him. Life and health insurance, however, furnish a hedge against such a contingency and assure the prospective investor, in this instance, that, in case of the loss of his investment through his disability or death, the insurance company will reimburse his dependents at least to the extent of $10,000. The same advantage must also be apparent in the case of those who are without substantial capital, and whose economic effort is often largely stifled by fear. By removing a load of care from the mind, life and health insurance promote efficiency and make life happier. For this reason, life and health insurance should be regarded by the average man as among his most treasured possessions, and premium payments should not be looked upon merely as an expense to be borne grudgingly. It may safely be stated that the possession of an adequate amount of life and health insurance causes the average policyholder to eat better, sleep better, feel better, and as a result of these, to work better.

Makes Saving Possible

One constantly meets with those whose argument against life and health insurance is that they prefer to save. The habit of saving should be encouraged by all means, but it should be borne in mind that the saving of a competency involves the necessary time to save, and that life and health insurance are the only certain methods to use as a hedge against the possibility of the saving period being cut short by death or interrupted by disability. A policy of saving can yield only a small amount at the start, whereas a policy of insurance guarantees the full face value or income benefit from its beginning and thus guards the policyholder against failure through early death or disability to have sufficient working time to save adequately through other channels. Thus, if one is able to save $500 annually, it will take nearly fifteen years to accumulate a fund of $10,000, assuming that the accumulations are safely invested annually at 4 per cent compound interest. Yet a family head's resolution to protect the home with such a savings fund is contingent upon his survival for the full period and may be defeated by death or disability before the savings have reached any appreciable sum. To depend entirely on saving as a means of providing for the future of the family is a highly uncertain policy to pursue. The first requisite in providing for the future support of dependents is *certainty,* and this can be secured only by using life and health insurance as a hedge against the possible failure to continue the annual accumulations to the savings fund because of early death or disability. Through life and health insurance, the suggested fund of $10,000 can be assured in any case. Upon death the insurance company pays the face of the policy, while, in case of survival, the insured is given the necessary time to accumulate a competency. In the event that part of the time is lost through disability, health insurance will guarantee that the competency will continue to be accumulated.

Moreover, the roseate views which so many hold concerning their resolution and ability to accumulate and keep should be tempered by a frank statement of the facts. Eighty-five per cent of this country's adults leave no estate worthy of mention, and 90 per cent lack the comforts of life. The habit of saving, as already stated, should be encouraged, but the foregoing facts clearly indicate that it is unwise to practice saving to the exclusion of life and health insurance. Both should be practiced, and, if only one is possible because of limited means, insurance should be selected because of its much greater certainty in leaving a stipulated fund for the support of the family whenever the breadwinner's income-producing capacity is cut short by death or interrupted by disability.

For the great mass of people with dependents, life and health insurance should be the first type of security to be purchased. Where a dependent family is at stake, it is the height of folly to urge investment in other directions, and it is quite beside the point to offer laborious explanations of the relative merits of various classes of bonds, stocks, and other types of investment. The greatest purpose of life and health insurance is to protect. As already indicated, it takes time to save, and where dependents must be protected, life and health insurance alone guarantee the creation of a competency against the contingency of premature death cutting short the saving period or disability interrupting it. The great mass of people live only within the life and health insurance stage and are removed by thousands of dollars from the point where they can judiciously become direct investors along other lines. Even when contemplating the ownership of a home, no man with a family on his hands has a right to say, "I shall first buy and pay for a home, and then shall buy life and health insurance." The potential estate is the vital thing when a dependent family is at stake. Life and health insurance must come first. No man has a right to put money into any other type of investment until he has first made decent provision for a potential estate through life and health insurance, that being the only way in which to accomplish such a result.

Furnishes a Safe and Profitable Investment

In addition to guaranteeing an estate at once, life insurance contains an accumulating investment feature which is absolutely safe and which reaches large proportions in the later years of the policy. With the exception of a few types of policies only, life insurance, as an accumulation of savings, is admirably adapted to put small sums of money to prompt and profitable use, and in this respect has been aptly defined as "compound interest in harness." As will be explained later, nearly all types of life insurance policies gradually accumulate a so-called surrender value (savings element) which may be withdrawn by the insured if he decides to discontinue the policy, and which is paid to the designated party in the event of the insured's survival. This value, as will be shown later, represents an accumulation of a portion of the premiums paid by the policyholder which the company promptly invests. In participating companies, the interest earnings in excess of the interest rate assumed in calculating premiums are returned to the policyholder in the dividends paid. Because of this fact, participating companies usually assume a lower interest rate than non-participating companies in computing premium rates.[18] In other words, this value of the policy represents savings left with the company for investment.

The investment service of life insurance is so important to the policyholder and his family as to justify a separate treatment and a more detailed explanation.[19] Suffice it to say at this time that life insurance not only furnishes a profitable and safe investment, but modern policies also make it possible for the insured to arrange for the safeguarding of the proceeds of the policy for the benefit of his beneficiaries upon his death. Too frequently the competency which a husband or father has provided through saving or insurance is quickly lost by the heir or beneficiary through speculation, unwise investments, or excessive expenditures for unnecessary comforts. Such a contingency should always be contemplated by the insured and may be prevented in various ways. Modern income arrangements, especially, furnish a guarantee against such a contingency by providing that the beneficiary shall, following the death of the insured, receive during the whole of her life, or for a designated number of years, as the case may be, an annual, quarterly, or monthly income of a stipulated sum. Or, instead of having the proceeds of the policy paid in one lump sum upon death, the insured may arrange to have the company retain the sum upon the maturity of the policy and pay the same in a designated number of installments. Again, the proceeds of the policy may be left with the company at interest during the life-

---

[18] See Chapter 20.
[19] See Chapter 4.

time of the beneficiary or for a designated number of years.[20]

Forces and Encourages Thrift

Not only does life insurance render safe the insured's effort to accumulate a fund through saving by hedging him against early death, and furnish a profitable and safe investment, but for the great majority of people, it constitutes an excellent means of encouraging and even forcing thrift. There are few institutions, if any, which have given such excellent schooling along this line. Savings banks, of course, do their share in developing the saving instinct among the people and savings and loan associations have also assumed a prominent position in this respect. But, usually, institutions of this character have the shortcoming of permitting the depositor to withdraw all or nearly all of the funds after giving notice, with the result that a resolution to save over a long period may be broken when the depositor for one reason or another sees fit to withdraw the amount deposited.

In life insurance, nearly all the types of contracts sold contain a savings feature, and this is especially true of the so-called whole-life and endowment policies which, as will be explained more fully later, promise the payment of a stipulated sum not only upon the death of the insured during a given term of years but also upon his survival at the end of that term. Of course, in order to receive, say $10,000, at the end of the specified term the insured is obliged to pay to the company a sufficient amount in annual, semiannual, quarterly, or monthly premiums to enable the company, after improving these payments at compound interest, to accumulate a fund by the end of the period which will equal the sum stipulated in the contract. Furthermore, the regular payment of the premium from year to year will soon be looked upon by the insured in much the same manner as he regards interest on a mortgage. Consequently, to secure the necessary funds to pay the premium his industry will be considerably enhanced, or his efforts to save the required premiums out of income will be increased. In fact, it is the common assertion of innumerable individuals who were the holders of endowment policies that at the end of fifteen, twenty, or twenty-five years, they became the possessors of a considerable sum of money which, under other circumstances they would never have accumulated, or which, if they had succeeded in accumulating, would have been lost or dissipated. Life insurance, in other words, tends to bring about compulsory saving and represents the accumulation of small sums (which in all probability would not have been accumulated) over a long period of years into a substantial total. In brief, life insurance generally bears the relationship to thrift that

[20] See Chapter 15.

the modern utilization of byproducts (largely wasted in former years) bears to many of our leading manufacturing enterprises of today.

Affords Protection Against Claims of the Insured's Creditors

The desire for such protection is perfectly natural and also important in view of the great hazard of bankruptcy. It is a matter with which the insured public should be made familiar because of the variations in state exemption laws as well as court decisions rendered in different jurisdictions. The motto "Welcome" may be in every home, but it should not be for creditors in the event of the home owner's bankruptcy. Most states have enacted exemption laws protecting life insurance taken out after the passage of the act in favor of the wife, children, or other dependent relatives. Most frequently, the amount of such insurance thus declared exempt from creditors' claims is limited to some reasonable amount. But in some states the exemption act relates to all such policies, without respect to amount, and without regard to the fact that "the right to change the beneficiary named has been reserved by the insured or is permitted by the insurer."[21]

Furnishes an Assured Income in the Form of Annuities

Life insurance also proves valuable to a very considerable number of people, who, as the result of a life's work, have succeeded in saving only a limited amount of capital, and who have no one to whom they particularly care to transfer this sum in case of death. Thus, let us assume that a person aged 60 has accumulated $25,000, and that this represents the entire estate available for the maintenance of the owner during his later years. Owing to the limited size of the estate, the owner will be obliged to invest the same in the most careful manner, and the current rate of return for such investments would probably not exceed 4 to 5 per cent. Consequently, this individual's income will be limited to between $1,000 and $1,250 per year, an amount insufficient for proper maintenance during old age. Nor can he afford to take a portion of his principal for living expenses, because this would reduce his annual income. The danger confronting him is just the opposite of that facing the man who wants insurance against death. The latter wants insurance because he does not know how long he will live, while the former is confronted with the danger of living too long, that is, of outliving his income.

Just as the man who felt that death or disability might intervene too soon could hedge himself against that risk, so can our owner of the $25,000

[21] See Chapter 14.

fund, who feels that his income is too limited or that he might outlive this income, hedge against those risks by buying an "annuity." A life annuity is a contract under which an insurance company promises to pay the holder thereof a certain stipulated income every year as long as he lives, the payment ceasing upon death or, under refund annuities, at the end of a specified period following the death of the annuitant. Thus, for illustrative purposes, let us apply an annuity to a man aged 60 who has saved $25,000, which sum, as stated, will yield only $1,250 income a year if invested at 5 per cent. To quote the rates for annuities of a certain company, this man may deposit $1,330.83 and receive therefor a promise of an income of $100 a year throughout life. For his $25,000 he can purchase an annual income of $1,878.52 per year. This sum, it will be observed, represents a higher yield of 7.5 per cent, significantly higher than the assumed current rate of 5 per cent.[22] The older the annuitant is when the annuity is purchased, the larger is the annual return the company can afford to give. If, therefore, the holder of a limited estate does not particularly care to transfer his property to some individual or institution, life insurance makes it possible for him to pay the same to an insurance company in return for a promise of a certain definite income per year, thus relieving himself from all further worry as to the continuation of his future income. The companies can afford to give these larger returns at the later years of life because the death rate at age 60 and thereafter is high and because of the understanding that the annuity payments will cease just as soon as the annuitant dies,[23] in which case the remaining balance of the money deposited with the company redounds to the benefit of the other surviving annuitants.

Relation of the Foregoing Advantages to Society at Large

The many advantages discussed in the preceding pages, it is apparent, will benefit greatly the community as a whole if life and health insurance is widely used. Mr. Holcombe writes:

It is clear that any agency which improves the mental or moral attributes, or the material circumstances of any one of its citizens, raises the condition of the community of which he is a member, and thus benefits the state. Savings banks encourage thrift and produce accumulations which would in many cases be otherwise wasted, and thus they constitute a distinct and tangible benefit to the state. Life insurance promotes a sense of responsibility, strengthens family ties, and thus elevates the general character of the nation. It lessens those family discords which end in divorce, it checks intemperance, and often by its requirements brings a realization of the benefits of right living. . . .

[22] The "higher yield," of course, is due to the fact that principal is being liquidated under the annuity.

[23] Subject to certain minimum benefits, depending on the contract. See pp. 121–122.

There can be no doubt, furthermore, that life insurance curtails the expense to the public treasury, of almshouses and police, of criminal courts and prisons, and of the various other necessary branches of the public service which have to do with the prevention and punishment of crime, and the relief of the suffering and unfortunate. . . . It is certain that in many cases the proceeds of a life insurance policy are practically all that remain at the death of the one responsible for the support of helpless dependents, and in a vast number of these cases, were it not for this aid, many persons would be forced to accept public charity.[24]

The value of life and health insurance as an agency for increasing the individual's sense of responsibility, and for relieving the community of much needless expense in supporting members of destitute families, has been recognized for years by the governments of all civilized countries. But three additional general benefits of life and health insurance should be referred to briefly as vitally affecting the entire community. They are:

1. Through their investments, now exceeding $207,254 billion, life insurance companies have exerted a powerful influence in the upbuilding of the industrial life of the nation. Millions of policyholders have accumulated a huge total of savings, through installment thrift, and the life insurance business has served as the agency through which a vast aggregation of small sums has become available for the furtherance of the nation's leading business interests, as well as in the erection of homes and the development of farms. The life insurance business also pledged $2 billion in loans under its Urban Investment Program to improve housing, to create jobs and to promote community services in the core areas of the nation's cities. Total commitments as of year-end 1970 were almost $1.6 billion since the program was started in 1967.[25] In 1970, life insurance companies supplied about 9 per cent of the financial capital flowing from all investment sources in the United States.[26]

2. By carefully restricting the admission to membership and by requiring answers to numerous questions relating to intemperate habits, the life insurance companies forcefully direct the applicant's attention to the close relationship between temperate living and longevity. Physical ailments are also frequently discovered for the first time as a result of the physical examinations which the companies require applicants to undergo. The knowledge thus obtained leads to the application of remedies, and results in the conservation of the value of many lives for the benefit of the community.

3. There has also been a growing emphasis upon the conservation of health, that is, of the "potential life value estate." In this, many of the life

[24] *Yale Insurance Lectures,* I, 39–41.
[25] *Life Insurance Fact Book,* 1971, p. 9.
[26] *Ibid.,* p. 67.

and health insurance companies have taken an important part. All of the previous discussion of the potential estate would have little significance if it did not indicate the reasonableness of conserving this estate through prevention-of-loss efforts in the same sense that such efforts are applied to the conservation of material productive property. A family head, be he a wage or salary earner or a business man, simply cannot afford to be ill and therefore inefficient, or to die prematurely. In other forms of insurance, like fire, marine, title, steam-boiler, compensation, and fidelity insurance, the assumption of such prevention-of-loss work has long been recognized and is regarded as both a business and a social service. As a matter of fact, prevention of loss in the first instance is the greatest insurance of all. A maintained potential value is better than a premature payment of cash to indemnify its loss.

In 1970 a task force representing the life insurance business developed a sweeping set of recommendations for action in overcoming the critical shortcomings of our nation's health care system. These proposals, known as the Program for Health Care in the 1970's,[27] include innovations and greater involvement in the health care delivery system than ever before.

<hr />

[27] See pp. 650–651.

Business Uses of | 3
Life and Health Insurance

FAMILY vs. BUSINESS LIFE AND HEALTH INSURANCE

Distinction

THE DISTINCTION BETWEEN "family life and health insurance" and "business life and health insurance" is essentially one of convenience. All life and health insurance is really business life and health insurance, but by custom we have chosen the expression "family life and health insurance" when the insurance relates more directly to the family, and "business life and health insurance" when the insurance is apparently concerned more directly with the protection of the insured's business or vocation. For the overwhelming majority of the middle class, the family and the family head's business or vocation are inseparably interrelated. In the final analysis, protection of business assets is the object of business life and health insurance. Such protection of the "business assets" has, however, as we shall see, a most vital bearing upon the welfare of the insured's family.

So-called business life and health insurance has assumed large proportions only within the past thirty-five years. While the primary purpose of life and health insurance is to protect the family against the loss of the income-producing capacity of the breadwinner, it is clear that business enterprises likewise have need of protection against the loss of the valuable lives that give them vitality and success. In recent years the business world has become increasingly aware of this fact, and as a result, an enormous amount of insurance has been written on the lives of business men who have had in mind chiefly the stabilization of their businesses through the establishment of better credit relations, the procurement of protection against the loss through death or disability of those most valuable to its success, and the arrangement of a practical purchase plan for the retirement of their insured interests in the event of permanent disability or death. So large is the volume of business insurance becoming and so rapid is its increase that there is good reason to believe that the time is approaching when the life

38

insurance or health insurance policy will be almost as integral a part of the corporate and copartnership structure as are the charter, the bond, the stock certificate, and the partnership agreement. The business uses of life and health insurance afford a boundless field for study and thought because there are few men indeed who do not at some time face a business situation, the solution of which would be made simpler and less hazardous through the medium of life or health insurance. In any business situation where death or disability would produce a need for cash funds, life and health insurance represent the ideal solution. Here the contingency which produces the need for funds automatically produces those funds. There is no other financing medium available which can guarantee such a result.

Close Relationship Between the Home and Business

Business life and health insurance should particularly appeal to a business man when it is shown that in nearly all instances there is a very close relationship between his home and the business in which he is engaged. So close is this relation that a policy taken for the special conservation of the business may often prove even more valuable than a policy taken out for the direct protection of the family. The latter policy can seldom do more than alleviate in a measure the financial injury caused by the death or disability of the income producer, while the former may be the means of successfully continuing in operation the business of the deceased. Had not the former policy been taken out, the business might have failed or declined. The family policy usually assures the continuance of a portion only of the insured's income after his death or disability, while the business policy, since it conserves the efficiency of the insured's business, may be instrumental in bringing about the continuation of a much larger income, namely, the income from a successful business.

Moreover, the owner of a business, generally speaking, conducts the same primarily for the purpose of supporting a home, thus, again showing that the welfare of the home and the welfare of the business are so intimately related as to be inseparable. On the one hand, the advantages of family insurance, as discussed in the preceding chapter, such as freedom from worry, increase in initiative, and so forth, will produce a very wholesome effect upon the welfare of the insured's business. Business success means, as a rule, family happiness and contentment. On the other hand, business adversity practically always means family adversity, and, therefore, business insurance which protects the business against disaster is in reality also family insurance, since it preserves the family's interest in the income derived from that business.

Although life and health insurance serves the business world in a wide variety of ways, most of its important services are provided in connection with (1) the insurance of key men, (2) the enhancement of credit, (3) business continuation arrangements, and (4) employee welfare plans.

KEY MAN INDEMNIFICATION

The purpose of key man insurance is to *indemnify* a business firm for the loss of earnings brought about by the death or disability of a key officer or other employee. Many business firms have been built around some one man whose capital, energy, technical knowledge, experience, or power to plan and execute make him a most valuable asset of the organization and a necessity to its successful operation. Numerous examples may be pointed to as illustrating the dependence of a successful business upon the personal equation. Thus, a corporation or firm may be vitally interested in one of its officers whose financial worth as an endorser, or ability as an executive, may be the basis of its general credit rating. A manufacturing or mining enterprise may be dependent upon someone who alone possesses the chemical or engineering knowledge necessary to the concern. A publishing house may have engaged someone who alone can be the author of a proposed work and may be obliged to incur considerable outlay before it is written. The sales manager of a large business establishment may have made himself indispensable through his ability to organize an efficient body of salesmen, to employ the most effective methods of selling, and to develop profitable markets. Again, some officer of the concern, although not actively engaged in its daily operations, may prove indispensable because he is its principal owner and because his experience and business connections make him its chief adviser.

These are only a few illustrations of the many that might be given to show the importance of a human life as an asset to the successful operation of a business. Now why not insure the business against the loss of that life —that asset—through death or disability? Surely, the extinction or disabling of such valuable lives will in many instances prove a more serious loss than that by fire or any of the other sources of loss in business against which insurance is invariably procured. The loss of the officer whose endorsement or executive ability is the basis for the firm's credit might result in a refusal on the part of lenders to renew old and make new loans, thus possibly jeopardizing the business because of lack of capital. If insured, however, for the benefit of the business, the firm would, immediately upon his death, receive the face value of the policy or, in the event of his disability, receive income benefits in accordance with the policy. Not only would the insurance proceeds or benefits help the company meet any obligations falling due during the period of adjustment, but the mere knowledge that the business was the recipient of a large amount of cash or a steady flow of income would be a powerful factor in allaying doubt and in restoring confidence on the part of creditors. Similarly, the death or disability of the person who alone possessed the chemical and engineering knowledge required by his employer might result in the lowering of the quality or the volume of the output of the commodity in question, thus causing more inconvenience and possible loss of business, while the death or disability of the sales manager might involve the disintegration of the selling force and the consequent loss of profitable markets. Furthermore, in many instances an untimely death or disability may leave a special piece of work unfinished and subject the employer to a loss of the advances made, since no one else can be found to bring the unfinished project to completion. Here the amount of life and health insurance protection may be made to equal approximately the outlay incurred, and if the work is known to require only a few years for its completion, the term of the policy may be made to cover this limited period. Such short-term policies also often prove desirable for the protection of a new business against the death or disability of its owner or manager during the first five or ten years required for the business to become firmly established.

All losses of a character like those enumerated may be guarded against by making the business the beneficiary of appropriate policies on the lives of the officers or other employees under consideration. In the event of death or disability, the business will be indemnified promptly for the loss of the services of the deceased or disabled employee, and the proceeds received will enable it to bridge over the period necessary to secure the services of a worthy successor or substitute. As one author has expressed it:

> In the conservation of business, many other kinds of insurance, highly useful because deeply needed, are employed—fire, casualty, surety, employers' liability, title, plate glass, etc.,—but none of these, except casualty (and that only in case of accident), defends against loss or destruction caused by the death of a man who is the blood, brains, gold, and very life of the business. Curious omission, dangerous neglect, is it not?—fire? insurance; embezzlement? insurance; accident to a workman? insurance; title? insurance; broken pane of glass? insurance!—but against the staggering loss or the supreme disaster of total ruin following the snuffing out of a man upon whom the whole fabric of the business rests—*no insurance!* and that snuffing out occurs in innumerable cases as quickly and as suddenly as the smashing of a plate glass front. Business has greater need of life insurance than of any other kind, because it is the only form that completely encircles with impregnable protection against utter destruction through death.[1]

[1] Stewart Anderson, "Commercial Life Insurance," in H. P. Dunham, *The Business of Insurance* (New York: Ronald Press Co., 1912), I, p. 387.

In any specific case, it is difficult to determine accurately the economic loss that would be suffered by the business concern in the event of the key man's death or disability.

The problem of estimating the loss may be approached in terms of lost earnings, or measured by the additional compensation which is necessary to secure an experienced replacement. In either case, consideration should be given to the question of whether the loss is a temporary or a permanent one. The degree of accuracy with which the value of the economic loss produced by the death or disability of a key man can be determined varies according to the type of business, particular function of the key man, and other circumstances. In any case, it is not difficult to establish the possibility of loss. The extent to which the value of a key man should be capitalized is properly a management decision.

Procedurally, the insurance is taken out on the life of the key man, paid for by the business, and made payable to the business as beneficiary. In most cases some form of low premium permanent life insurance is taken out, and the accumulating cash value (savings element) is reflected as an asset in the balance sheet of the corporation. Naturally, if the need is a temporary one (such as a specific research project to be completed within five years), a temporary form of life insurance (term insurance) would be appropriate. Disability income coverage may be written jointly with the life insurance, or this hazard to the life value of a key man may be insured separately.

ENHANCEMENT OF CREDIT

General Credit Rating

Anything that stabilizes the financial position of a firm improves its general credit rating. Consequently, life and health insurance can serve to enhance the credit of a business organization by indemnifying for the loss of a key man and/or assuring the continuation of the firm as a "going concern" in the event of the death or disability of the owner(s). Insuring the lives of key men assures banks and other lending institutions as well as suppliers that the business will have a financial cushion in the event of the death or disability of one or more key personnel. In addition, if a permanent form of life insurance is used, the liquidity of the firm is improved through the accumulation of cash values (savings elements) which are available at all times. The cash values are properly shown on the firm's balance sheet as assets. Similarly, if prospective lenders or other creditors are assured of the continuation of the firm as a going concern in the event of the death or disability of the owner(s), the firm will not only be able to obtain a larger line of credit, but will usually be able to obtain it on better terms.

Life Insurance as Specific Collateral

In addition to the general improvement of a firm's credit rating, a life or health insurance contract may be pledged as collateral. The cash value (savings element) of a permanent form of life insurance may be pledged as collateral for a loan by assigning the policy to the lender. Under such an arrangement, the basic security for the loan lies in the savings or investment element of the contract, and the amount of the loan is always covered by the cash value of the policy. If the borrower dies before the loan is repaid, the lender simply deducts the borrower's obligation from the proceeds, the excess being paid to the insured's estate or designated beneficiary. In the event the borrower is unwilling or unable to repay the loan at maturity, the lender can recover his funds either by surrendering the policy for cash or by exercising the policy loan privilege. In the normal course of events the loan is repaid at maturity and the policy reassigned to the borrower. As will be pointed out later, the insured frequently borrows directly from the insurance company by utilizing the policy loan privilege. The concept of the loan is the same, however, with the policy being assigned to the insurance company instead of a bank or other lender.

A policy may also be pledged as collateral with a different purpose in mind. Its purpose may be to protect the lender only against loss arising out of the death or disability of a key man or the borrower. Thus, life and health insurance may be used advantageously in that large number of instances where a business man, already established in business, may need more credit for its proper development, but where the banker feels that the business, standing by itself, does not warrant the making of further loans. To the banker, the man at the head of the business is a very important asset, and he may feel that while the business itself does not warrant another loan, the business, plus the man who manages it, would justify the extension of further credit. Here, however, the contingency of early death or disability must be provided for, since in either event the last loan is apt to be unsecured. In other words, a life and/or health insurance policy in favor of the creditor is a hedge against the contingency of the loss of the value of the life upon which the repayment of the loan is primarily dependent.

In this case, it should be noted that the loan is not made against the cash value of the life policy itself. In fact, it is new life insurance taken for credit purposes and, therefore, does not as yet have a loan value. The real security behind the loan is the demonstrated business ability of the borrower. The situation is comparable to a fire insurance policy used as the basis of credit. Fire insurance policies possess no cash value for borrowing purposes. It is the real estate that serves as collateral, but only when insured against fire for the benefit of the creditor. So here, also, it is the demonstrated ability of the business man which serves as collateral, but only when insured against death or disability for the benefit of the creditor.

In addition to short term credit situations, life insurance may be used as collateral in connection with bond issues as well. Thus, let us assume that a firm raises $50,000 on bonds which mature in twenty years, and that the nature and organization of the business are such as to make it chiefly dependent for its credit and successful operation upon the life of one man. Under such circumstances, the unexpected death of this individual might impair the concern to such an extent that the liquidation of its assets might not prove sufficient for the full redemption of the bonds. Unless some means can be found which will assure the creditors that the bonds will be redeemed upon maturity, the loan will, in all probability, either not be effected at all or only under severe restrictions and at a very high rate of interest.

Proper security to the creditors may be furnished conveniently in this instance through the medium of endowment insurance. In other words, the head of the business may insure his life for $50,000 under a twenty-year endowment policy. In case of survival, the business is likely to prosper with the result that the security back of the bonds will greatly increase. In that case, the endowment policy will serve the purpose of creating a sinking fund which increases year after year until, at the end of twenty years, it will amount to $50,000, or just the sum needed to redeem the bond issue then falling due. On the other hand, should the insured die before the expiration of the twenty-year period, and this is the real contingency against which the creditors desire to be protected, the business at once receives the full value of the policy. The firm would thus have on hand sufficient funds to pay off the bonds at once if that were possible and desirable. But if it is found, instead, that the business can be continued advantageously, such a portion of the $50,000 of insurance money may be set aside in a sinking fund as will, at the current rate of interest, amount to $50,000, or the face of the bond issue, at the end of the twenty-year period. The balance of the insurance money not needed for the sinking fund may be used for the improvement of the business, thus, in turn, enhancing still more the security back of the bond issue. In order to hedge against the possibility of the business head's disability, a waiver of premium benefit can be added to the endowment policy which will assure the availability of the funds at the end of the twenty-year period even if the business head has not died and remains disabled.

Life Insurance as an Emergency Fund

As was mentioned above, the cash or loan value of a policy is a real asset which enhances the credit of the business man because it is available on demand, or on comparatively short notice, irrespective of the financial conditions which may prevail, and usually at the fixed rate of 5 or 6 per cent interest.

Bankers and other creditors always regard the cash value of a business man's policies as additional assets justifying larger extensions of credit on his firm's paper. But suppose the borrower must have additional credit at a time when the condition of the money market is such as to make it highly inconvenient or impossible for the banks to meet his requirements. It is at such times that the loan privilege contained in insurance contracts affords a convenient and most excellent means of relief, as has been amply testified to by many of the nation's leading business men. During periods of panic such stringency often prevails in the credit market as to make impossible the floating of loans even on the best collateral. At such times millions of dollars have been borrowed on life insurance policies and numerous business men, firms, and corporations have used their life insurance contracts as a means of securing funds to make up their payrolls or to meet other pressing obligations.

It is not intended here to encourage the altogether too common habit of borrowing the loan value of policies, because in many instances the privilege is exercised unnecessarily simply because some luxury is desired or because the security market seems low, or because some other apparent opportunity to make money quickly seems to present itself. And even where these considerations are not the motive, the insured frequently uses this asset because it is so easily obtained, never considering at the time the relation of that asset to his beneficiary and often overlooking some other available asset which should have been used in preference to the cash value of his policy.

This service of life insurance to the business community and the spirit in which it should be used is well exemplified by the experience of one of the nation's leading business men in the early years of this century. He wrote:

Never, except as a last resource, should a man use his insurance policies as the basis for borrowing. It should be a source of joy and satisfaction that this sacred investment is kept clear of encumbrance. Whatever advantageous financial operations might offer with reference to other investments, sums set aside for insurance should be regarded as of a different class, to be maintained unimpaired. It is a satisfaction to know that the gradually increasing cash value offers, however, a resource always available and unquestionable. It is a stout anchor to windward holding firm against any storm of family or business misfortune that may arise. In the autumn of 1907, there was a panic, during which there was a practical suspension both of currency payments and of credits. Rates of interest advanced to prohibitory figures, but notwithstanding the enhanced rates, loans were practically impossible to obtain. Three or four years before, one of my partners and I had taken out life insurance policies for considerable amounts. These gave the right to borrow from the insurance company at the fixed rate of 5 per cent. We were, therefore, enabled to place this credit at the disposal of the partnership of which we were members, and about $120,000 of cash was instantly available in a time of great need. Of course, these loans were repaid to the insurance company immediately upon the restoration of normal conditions. Such a privilege must in many cases mean the avoidance of actual disaster.[2]

BUSINESS CONTINUATION

In the case of the sole proprietorship, the partnership, and the close corporation [3] the problems of business stability and continuation following the death or disability of the owners are critically important to both the family of the deceased owner and the surviving owners and employees. It will be necessary to review briefly the effects which the death or disability of an owner can have on the stability and continuation of a business in order to understand the vital role which life and health insurance play in this regard.

Partnership

The partnership form of business organization has a number of advantages, but it is subject to the general rule of law that any change in the membership of the partnership causes its *dissolution*. The law provides that upon the death of a general partner the partnership is dissolved and the surviving partners become liquidating trustees, charged with the responsibility of immediately winding up the business and paying over to the estate of the deceased his fair share of the liquidated value of the business. Liquidation of a business, which involves the "forced sale" of assets, almost invariably results in severe shrinkages among the assets. Under such conditions accounts receivable will bring only a fraction of their normal value, inventory and plant must be disposed of at sacrifice prices, and good will is lost completely. From the viewpoint of the survivors, liquidation not only produces losses to them by shrinkage in asset values but, more important, destroys their very means of earning a living. The seriousness of the consequences often leads survivors to attempt to continue the business by buying out the interest of the deceased partner and reorganizing the partnership. This procedure is not practicable, however, for two reasons. In most cases

---

[2] Alba B. Johnson, "A Business Man's Views Upon Life Insurance." An address delivered before the Philadelphia Association of Life Underwriters, December 4, 1913.

[3] A close corporation may be defined as a corporation where a small group of business men own the company as stockholders, control it as directors, and run its affairs as officers.

it would not be possible to raise the necessary cash. But even if the surviving partners could raise the cash to purchase the interest of the deceased, they would have to prove that the price paid for the interest was fair. Their fiduciary status makes this impracticable; in fact, in some states they would not be permitted to purchase the interest since it in effect involves a trustee purchasing trust property. In the usual case it is also impracticable for the widow or other heir to become a member of the reorganized partnership or to purchase the interests of the surviving partners. The record of litigation clearly indicates that, in the absence of *advance* agreement among the partners, any attempt to continue the business is fraught with legal and practical complications.[4]

In order to avoid the consequences of inaction prior to death, it is increasingly common for the members of a partnership to enter into a so-called buy-and-sell agreement which binds the surviving partners to purchase the partnership interest of the first partner to die at a prearranged price set forth in the agreement and obligates the estate of the deceased partner to sell his interest to the surviving partners. The value of the various partnership interests is determined at the time the agreement is entered into and periodically revalued, or a formula for value determination is included in the agreement. Each partner is insured for the amount of his interest, the policies being owned by the other partners or the partnership itself. Upon the first death among the partners the operation of the plan is simple. The life insurance proceeds are used by the partnership or surviving partners, as the case may be, to purchase the interest of the deceased from his estate. The partnership is reorganized by the surviving partners and continued in operation, and the heirs of the deceased receive in cash the "going concern" value of his partnership interest. All parties benefit by the arrangement and the problems of liquidation are obviated. The surviving partners can enter into a new buy-and-sell agreement or amend the original agreement to account for changes in the value of their respective interests.

The *personal service partnership* (for example, lawyers, doctors, and the like) often uses an income-continuation agreement instead of a regular buy-and-sell arrangement. Here it is provided that for a specified number of years after the death of a partner the firm will share a percentage of its profits with the heirs of the deceased or pay a fixed sum for the period. In some cases there will be two agreements, one a regular buy-and-sell agreement covering the tangible assets, and the other an income-continuation agreement covering the deceased's share in future earnings. Life insurance is the ideal funding medium for both types of agreement.

When one of the partners is totally disabled, his special talents, knowl-

---

[4] For an excellent and thorough treatment of the problems of business continuation and the use of life and health insurance in solving the problems, see Edwin H. White, *Business Insurance,* 3rd ed. (Englewood Cliffs, N. J.: Prentice-Hall, Inc., 1963).

edge, and ability are no longer available to the partnership. Instead, the disabled partner becomes a drain on the business financially, and his partner(s) must assume his responsibilities and duties without adequate compensation. The nondisabled partners are faced with the problem of earning sufficient money to provide for their usual shares of the partnership profits as well as that of the disabled partner. If they hire a capable replacement for the disabled partner, it is even more difficult to maintain the disabled partner's salary. On the other hand, if a replacement is not hired, the burden on the nondisabled partners may become unbearable, particularly if the disability lasts for any length of time.

As in the case of death, the alternative of taking in family members is fraught with dangers and problems. Likewise liquidation is not a proper solution. Over and above the possible losses brought about by the forced sale of the business, the nondisabled partners must start all over again in building their careers. Here again, as in the case of the death of a partner, the ideal solution is a properly drawn buy-and-sell agreement which binds the nondisabled partners to purchase the partnership interest of the disabled partner at a prearranged price set forth in the agreement and obligates the disabled partner to sell his interest to the nondisabled partners. The agreement can be funded by disability income health insurance policies.

Although the principle of the arrangement is identical with that in the case of the death of a partner, there are some special problems. First, a proper definition for disability must be agreed upon that will not be subjective. Also, there must be agreement regarding the length of time during which the disabled partner should receive a predetermined income before the buy-out becomes mandatory. Finally, provision should be made for funds to provide income before the buy-out provisions take effect and afterwards. Health insurance policies in appropriate amounts should be used to fund the agreement.

Close Corporation

Although the death of a stockholder does not legally dissolve the corporation, the nature of a *close* corporation leads to practical problems making retirement of the deceased's interest a necessity. The practical difficulties encountered in attempting to continue the business in operation following the death of a stockholder stem from the facts that (1) the stockholders of a close corporation are also its officers, (2) earnings are distributed primarily in the form of salaries, and (3) there is no ready market for the stock. Close corporations are so similar to partnerships in basic operation that they have been described as "incorporated partnerships." Consequently, a prearranged plan to retire a stockholder's interest following his death is vital for the stockholders in a close corporation.

Upon the death of the principal stockholder in a close corporation the surviving stockholders have four alternatives: (1) to accept the widow or other adult heir of the deceased into the actual management of the firm; (2) to pay dividends, approximately equivalent to the salary of the deceased stockholder, to the widow or other heir without any participation in management on their part; (3) to admit into active management of the firm outside interests to whom the stock of the deceased may have been sold; or (4) to purchase the stock from the estate of the deceased.

All of these may prove undesirable or impracticable. In the first case a widow or other adult heir would normally be able to contribute little to the management of the business and might well be a constant source of disruption in its operation. The second alternative would be inherently unpalatable to the survivors since they would be bearing all of the burdens of management but would be sharing the fruits of their labor equally with another contributing nothing but capital to the firm. If the survivors chose to pay less in dividends than the approximate salary of their former associate, this would lead to dissatisfaction on the part of the widow and other complications. The entrance of outsiders into the management of the firm could well be very unsatisfactory. Associates in a close corporation, as in a partnership, join forces because they work well together and all have a certain contribution which, taken together, produces a vigorous, profitable combination. In many cases the outsiders may well not be acceptable and lead to a disruption of the business or, in extreme cases, even to liquidation of the firm. More important, if the outsiders' stock constitutes a majority interest, the survivors would be at the mercy of the new owners, who would control such matters as salary scales and dividend policy. The final alternative may not be practicable because the survivors may not be able to raise the cash, agreement may not be possible as to a fair price, or the heirs may simply refuse to sell.

From the widow's viewpoint, she faces the possibility of having to dispose of the stock at a sacrifice price either to the surviving stockholders or to outsiders, neither of whom would normally be inclined to offer a reasonable price. Alternatively, she faces the threat of receiving no dividends if she decides to retain the stock.

These and other difficulties can be avoided by a properly drawn buy-and-sell agreement financed by life insurance. The agreement binds the surviving stockholders or corporation, as the case may be, to purchase the stock of the deceased stockholder at a prearranged price set forth in the agreement and obligates the estate of the deceased stockholder to sell his stock to the surviving stockholders or the corporation. As in the case of the partnership agreement, each stockholder's interest is valued at the time the agreement is drawn up and periodically revalued.

Each stockholder is insured for the amount of his stock interest, the insurance being owned by either the corporation or the other stockholders.

Upon the first death among the stockholders the life insurance proceeds are used by the corporation or surviving stockholders, as the case may be, to purchase or retire the stock of the deceased from his estate. Thus, the business future of the survivors is assured and the widow receives cash for a speculative interest.

The stockholders of a close corporation, who are active in the business, are in a position similar to that of partners in a partnership. Consequently, the possibility of such a working owner becoming disabled over a long period is a serious risk for the business. The basic problems and available solutions follow the pattern discussed previously in connection with the partnership. The best available solution lies in funding a properly drawn buy-and-sell agreement with appropriate amounts of health insurance.[5]

Similar agreements can be worked out between a sole proprietor and one or more key employees to continue the business and at the same time protect the "going concern" value of the sole proprietorship for his heirs.

Life and Health Insurance the Best Means of Financing a Business Continuation Agreement

As already indicated, any business continuation agreement is necessarily dependent upon the accumulation of a cash sinking fund. Excepting life and health insurance, analysis will show that all other available financing arrangements are likely to be unreliable, inadequate, and inconvenient. To be reliable, the plan must produce the prearranged amount of cash at the time death or disability calls for the funds. But how can that be accomplished through an accumulating sinking fund which mathematically requires time, at an assumed rate of interest, to reach a stated amount? If death of the stockholder or partner occurs early, a mere pittance may have been accumulated. Again, the sinking fund requires investment management and is constantly faced with the danger of loss of principal or income. The life insurance plan, by way of contrast, furnishes the exact agreed amount *at any time,* even though death occurs within a week. In other words, life insurance guarantees the completion of the fund by protecting it with decreasing term insurance, which decreases at exactly the rate at which the cash sinking fund increases in the course of time. Insurance company management also means absolute solvency of the fund at all times, assures a reasonably large and fairly constant rate of return on the accumulated funds, and relieves all parties to the arrangement from all troubles of

---

[5] For a thorough discussion of the problems arising out of the disability of key men, sole proprietors, partners, and working owners of close corporations and the available alternative solutions, see William Harmelin and Robert W. Osler, *Business Uses of Health Insurance,* rev. ed. (Bryn Mawr, Pa.: American College of Life Underwriters, 1967).

investment managerial care. Likewise, health insurance can be used to fund a disability business continuation agreement.

Being mathematically sound, absolutely effective in the prompt fulfillment of promises, efficient in management, free from all investment cares and fears, and as reasonable in cost as any plan which can be proposed, the life and health insurance methods of financing a business continuation agreement stand without a competitor. If it be decided to have such an agreement, then it is difficult to see why the life or health insurance method should not be used. It creates a definite market for the deceased's interest, irrespective of time and conditions. It frees his heirs or dependents from the speculative hazard associated with a business interest and furnishes to them the agreed amount of cash promptly, fully, and in usable form. It protects the deceased's heirs against the acts of his surviving associates and the surviving associates against the acts of his heirs. It maintains the business intact and enhances the confidence of valuable employees as well as of those outside the business. It also helps to settle the estate of the deceased partner or stockholder by providing funds to meet the cash needs of the estate.

The uncertainties growing out of death or disability, as they relate to partnerships and close corporations, are many and, as we have seen, of such a serious nature as to be to the interested parties a constant gamble and a constant source of worry. By one stroke, through a business continuation agreement financed by life and health insurance, all of these uncertainties are converted into certainty. Surely there can be no argument against the contention that the problem of business continuation should be anticipated and provided against while the harmoniously working stockholders or partners are all still alive. Each stockholder or partner should realize, in the interest of his family's future welfare, that he cannot foretell what may happen to his interest in the business upon his death or disability, still less what the destiny of the business may be a few years or a decade thereafter. Clearly, the stockholders or partners should agree upon some plan which in the event of death or disability will assure to each a liquidation of his business interest on a basis compatible with the welfare of the surviving associates and sufficient to give promptly to his family the cash value of his interest.

EMPLOYEE WELFARE PLANS

Employee welfare plans include three broad forms of coverage provided by life insurance companies: (1) life insurance, (2) health insurance, and (3) pensions. These coverages, when used as part of an employee welfare plan, are usually provided through group contracts, although individual contracts may be used in connection with these benefits. Because of the increasing importance of pension programs and group insurance as a merchandising medium for life and health insurance benefits, later chapters will consider them in more detail.

OTHER USES

For tax and other reasons, various types of compensation and benefit arrangements have developed for top management employees which may be funded through life and health insurance. For example, deferred compensation agreements have become very popular, whereby a key employee is promised a fixed income (for example, $5,000) for a specified period following retirement (for example, ten years). The advantage to the employee of receiving the income after retirement is that normally he will be in a much lower tax bracket than if he received the benefit currently. Some arrangements provide for these payments to be made to the employee in the event of disability or to the employee's wife (or other beneficiary) if he should die prior to retirement. Life and health insurance, of course, are the ideal mediums through which to fund these liabilities assumed by the corporation. The corporation finds this arrangement attractive in that it helps hold the key employee, since the deferred compensation arrangement is normally contingent on continued employment.

In any case where a sum of money or an income is payable to an employee (or beneficiary) on disability or retirement, life and health insurance may be used to advantage, and where it is payable on death, life insurance has no peer as a funding medium.

Other Uses of Life and Health Insurance | 4

LIFE INSURANCE AS AN INVESTMENT

Investment Concept in Life Insurance

IN HIS DESIRE to accumulate a decent investment estate through thrift on the installment plan, extending over the working period of life, man is subject to five great perils, namely: (1) the danger of not living long enough to complete his savings and investment fund; (2) the danger of becoming disabled and not being able to pay the deposits necessary to the upbuilding of the savings fund; (3) the possible lack of industry and initiative to earn the wherewithal to pay the deposits; (4) the possible lack of will power to continue the arrangement for a long period of time; and (5) the inability, through faulty investment, to keep that which he may have saved. The preceding chapter has explained life and health insurance as a means of protection against these mentioned perils. But the last of the enumerated perils, namely, the inability, through faulty investment, to keep one's savings intact, deserves further consideration. Common observation shows the importance of this peril. Comparatively few succeed in keeping their thrift fund intact, owing to investment loss, and this is particularly true when we contemplate the investment slaughter occasioned by our numerous and more or less constantly recurring business recessions. During the last serious depression, about one estate in every five of America's millions of estates was substantially wiped out, and at least half of all of the remaining estates were cut to half of their former dollar valuation. Clearly, man needs to be protected in the maintenance of his savings through a sound investment plan, quite as much as he needs to be protected against the contingencies of disability and death. And this is an important function of legal reserve life insurance. The basic function of life insurance is to guarantee an estate of a stated amount, live or die. But both the death and the life sides of the account, it is important to note, constitute real protection. Assuming a $10,000 policy, the insured is protected to this extent in the event of premature death. But, likewise, he should also be protected to the same extent, should he live to the end of the policy period. The funds may be just as vital at that time as they are at the time of death.

Fortunately, there is a rapidly growing and much better understanding on the part of the public of the dual nature of a life insurance policy, namely, a combination of decreasing insurance with an accumulating investment element, the former decreasing at exactly the same rate as the latter increases until, when the contract matures, the decreasing insurance element (protecting the potential life value) is reduced to zero while the investment element has risen to 100 per cent of the face of the contract. The investment or savings element in permanent life insurance policies is the basis for the "living values" of such contracts. People are increasingly looking to their life insurance contracts for savings and investments.

Basic Characteristics

The life insurance business has an investment portfolio of over $207.3 billion owned by millions of policyholders. In evaluating life insurance as a fixed-dollar investment there are a number of standards which could be used, but by all of them life insurance is an ideal investment.

Security. Of the various attributes of an ideal investment, safety of principal is clearly the most important. It is the keystone in the investment arch; more people learned that lesson during the last depression than probably ever before. But life insurance, despite the thousands upon thousands of bankruptcies of depository institutions during this depression, has not given the American public anything to worry about. Dr. McCahan's detailed investigation,[1] covering the twenty-three-year period to 1932 (the time of the investigation) shows that "the average annual loss to policyholders during the past twenty-three years did not exceed 29 cents for every $1,000 of net reserve." Even with respect to companies suspending during the depression years of 1930–32, he concludes:

If the depression period (1930–32) be taken by itself, the average annual losses from companies failing during these three years will not exceed 91 cents for every $1,000 of average net reserve held by all life insurance companies in this country. Thus, it may truthfully be said that the institution was 99.9 per cent safe throughout a period of extraordinary financial strain.[2]

The reasons for such a high standard of solvency for so large a portfolio

[1] S. S. Huebner and David McCahan, *Life Insurance as an Investment* (New York: D. Appleton-Century Co., Inc., 1933), Chapter VII, "The Solvency Record of Life Insurance."

[2] *Ibid.*

need to be explained at least briefly. The main source of strength is found in the application of the principle of diversification or averages along seven distinctly different lines. Whereas the normal individual is unable to apply even one of these averages to his limited portfolio, and whereas other investment institutions can apply but two or three at best, medium-sized and large life insurance companies can easily apply all seven. The seven applications may be described briefly as follows:

1. *Distribution of the portfolio over the different economic enterprises of the country.* At the end of 1970 the $207,300,000,000 life insurance portfolio was distributed as follows over different economic interests: 35.9 per cent in mortgages, 32.9 per cent in U.S. corporate bonds, 2.2 per cent in foreign corporate bonds, 2.2 per cent in United States Government bonds, 1.7 per cent in state, county, and municipal bonds, 1.6 per cent in foreign government bonds, 5.7 per cent in common stocks, 1.7 per cent in preferred stocks, 3.0 per cent in real estate, 7.8 per cent in policy loans, 5.3 per cent in cash and other admitted assets. Life insurance investment managements avoid placing all of the investment risk in one basket. They have pursued a policy of spreading the risk over all of America's economic endeavors and have thus secured a stability practically synonymous with the nation's economic stability.

2. *Territorial distribution.* Distribution by industries, if confined to one or a few states, might nevertheless leave the portfolio endangered. The distribution of life insurance investments by territory may be illustrated by distribution of mortgage holdings of United States life insurance companies. Thus, in a recent year, 13.0 per cent were in the Northeast, 25.1 per cent in the North Central, 36.6 per cent in the South, 22.5 per cent in the West, and 2.8 per cent were located outside of the United States.

3. *Diversification by number.* Here, life insurance exceeds all other depository institutions. Many companies have from 5,000 to 10,000 different units of investment. It is easily conceivable that a policyholder may have $20,000 of life insurance cash values with a number of companies holding probably 100,000 to 200,000 different units of investment. This would mean an investment of about 10 or 20 cents in each of that large number of investments. Such distribution is clearly beyond the reach of the individual. Yet life insurance gives that service to the policyholder, and at a very small cost for the managerial service. It is not merely the number of investments that is important; the number should also be spread with respect to the types of industries and geographic location.

4. *Diversification by maturities.* As a bulwark against financial stringency, it is important to assure the regularity and volume of current maturities. With respect to life insurance companies this factor exists to a surprising degree. During the last depression most companies were in posi-

tion to meet about 80 per cent of all financial pressure by way of loans and surrenders with the cash flowing in from maturing mortgages and corporation bonds. In addition, they had the cash income from premiums and investments. Comparatively few companies were obliged to sell any securities to meet the current cash demands occasioned by surrenders and policy loans.

5. *Diversification as to the time of purchase.* A life insurance company's portfolio is built up over a long period of time, the purchases being made year by year. The average purchase price of the entire portfolio represents an average of time, including bad years as well as good. All of the investments acquired in the course of time are carried over from year to year, and the financial results may not, therefore, be measured by the decline of a single year or the decline from a given price level prevailing at a particular date.

6. *Diversification of clientele.* Banks, savings and loan associations, and most other depository institutions are essentially local in character with respect to their depositors. They are therefore apt to be subject to "runs" during periods of financial distress. Financial runs are seldom national or state in character, and life insurance companies have the advantage of a depositor clientele widely diffused throughout either the nation or a substantial part thereof. Should pressure by way of surrenders or policy loans assert itself, the procedure is gradual and can be substantially discounted; it can be met easily through cash from maturities and the income from premiums and investment income.

7. *Selective average.* If all securities be poor in quality, spread of risk along all of the aforementioned six lines will prove of little value. Life insurance investment managements recognize this, and give careful scrutiny to all of their investments, irrespective of number, in order to furnish a good average quality of investment. They pursue the trust viewpoint in all investment decisions and operate on a very conservative basis. They observe the first-lien principle with respect to both real estate loans and corporation bonds. Shares of common stock held by United States life insurance companies comprise only a small portion of the entire portfolio.[3] The investment managements also have relatively limited foreign investments (except Canadian government bonds), and have pursued a program emphasizing stability of income, with relatively limited attention to appreciation.

In addition to being able to apply these principles, probably no business is the subject of such strict governmental supervision as the life insurance business. The life insurance companies of America are subject to a degree of supervision by the insurance departments which makes it exceedingly difficult for the management of such companies to imperil the policy-

[3] At the end of 1970, common stocks comprised 5.7 per cent of total assets. See *Life Insurance Fact Book,* 1971, p. 77.

holder's funds by indulging in unsound investment practices or fraudulent methods of administration.[4]

In regard to the availability of information concerning a company's operations (investment and otherwise), life insurance meets the highest standards known to the investment world. Nearly all the states issue annual reports for the benefit of the public, and in the meantime various specialized services as well as the insurance press render the same service. Irrespective of where the policyholder may live, he has the benefit of the public reports of the strictest state in which his company transacts business.

Yield.   As already explained, the life insurance portfolio represents an accumulation of purchases over a long period of time, thus containing many long-running bonds of high yield, acquired at a favorable time, which will tend to maintain the average return on the entire portfolio. For the twenty years from 1912 to 1932, the average interest earned on the mean assets of American companies amounted to 5.22 per cent. Even during the severe depression years of 1932–33, the average annual yield was 4.91 per cent (5.08 per cent during 1932 and 4.75 during 1933). Even should interest rates decline for a long period, the life insurance portfolio would be slower to feel the decline than most other portfolios. For one thing, the insurance company may brace its average investment yield by turning to the territorial regions which offer the highest yield. Again, a large part of the portfolio consists of bonds, bought advantageously over a long period and having a long time to run before maturity. Thus, using a typical medium-sized company with a bond portfolio of approximately $150,000,-000, it appeared that in a given year, 77 per cent of that total portfolio was protected in its maturity for eleven years or more, with an average yield of 4.92 per cent on the purchase price; 63 per cent for sixteen years or more, with an average yield of 5.25 per cent; 44 per cent for twenty-one years or more, with an average yield of 5.09 per cent; and 27 per cent for twenty-six years or more, with an average yield of 4.96 per cent. A portfolio like the foregoing will certainly be able to resist better the effects of a long declining interest period.

It is important to note that in considering the yield on the investment element of a life insurance policy, it is necessary to take account of the fact that a part of each premium is used to pay for the current insurance protection—the decreasing amount at risk. If this is not done, and the cash value or maturity value of the policy is compared with the *total* premiums paid, the apparent yield will be much lower than the true rate of return.

Actually, it is not necessary to make any special calculations in order to determine the *approximate* rate of interest realized on the investment ele-

[4] See Chapter 44.

ment of any particular policy.[5] Since the investment portfolio is unsegregated as far as individual policies are concerned, the net rate of return earned on the portfolio is reasonably representative of the yield ultimately credited to individual policies.

In view of the high degree of security of life insurance investments, the rates of interest earned by the companies are high. Thus, at the present time, the life insurance companies are earning more than 5 per cent, which is as high as, or higher than, any other investment medium of *comparable safety*.

Another fact of considerable significance is that the rate of return earned by a life insurance company is exceptionally stable and changes very slowly. This is due to the facts that the life insurance business is long term in nature and that the current income of the companies has always exceeded its outgo. Because of this, the companies can invest in long-term securities which bring a higher yield and necessitate reinvestment less frequently than most investment media.

Liquidity.   1. *Nonfluctuation in value.* Investors usually wish to know whether an investment remains fairly stable in its market price and whether the money invested may be obtained at any time by sale. We have only to compare life insurance with other leading types of investment to show that it is entitled in this respect to the best rating. The life insurance investment, as shown in the cash value table of the insurance contract, experiences no fluctuation at all, and the policyholder need not concern himself with newspaper files to ascertain the value of his investment. Life insurance is a depository institution based upon the law of averages as it relates to investment, and as a consequence, the investment accumulation remains constant to the policyholder.

2. *Marketability at par.* Whenever desired, the policyholder may surrender (sell) to the insurance company his cross section of the company's investment portfolio at the price stipulated in the contractual cash value (quotation) table. As already indicated, the cash values set forth in the contract are free from fluctuation.[6]

3. *Suitability for quick borrowing.* As was explained in Chapter 2, the investment accumulation in life insurance policies may nearly always be borrowed without delay or publicity at a fair guaranteed rate of interest (usually 5 or 6 per cent) and for the full amount (after initial period during which expense charges apply) minus one year's interest. The loan is really made against the policyholder's ownership of a cross section of the company's investment portfolio.

[5] But see Stuart Schwarzschild, "A Model for Determining the Rate of Return on Investment in Life Insurance Policies," *Journal of Risk and Insurance,* September, 1967, pp. 435–444; see also Joseph M. Belth, "The Rate of Return on the Savings Element in Cash-Value Life Insurance," *Journal of Risk and Insurance,* Vol. XXXV, No. 4 (December, 1968), pp. 569–581.

[6] See Chapter 26.

Convenience of Plan

Avoidance of Managerial Care.   While safety of principal and reasonable rate of current income are easily the first considerations in a good investment, avoidance of managerial care is probably the next important factor. Efficient management is the heart of investment success. Life insurance company management of deposits entrusted to its care is certainly efficient, and at the same time the policyholder is freed from all managerial trouble and worry. The company gives the policyholder the benefit of its experience and skill with respect to inquiry, analysis and appraisal, its judgment of trends, its understanding and application of fundamental principles of investment, and its willingness to assume all routine cares. The policyholder need not even clip a coupon. He is left entirely free to tend to his own business, to earn the wherewithal to meet the necessary deposits (premiums). Thereafter, his troubles are over, all further managerial care being assumed by the company to which the deposit was paid.

Favorable Denomination.   Most nonspeculative investments, such as bonds and mortgages, are available only in the form of $1,000 denominations. The life insurance investment again meets the convenience of all. Practically all companies will issue policies for a face value of $1,000 or more in multiples of $500. The annual, semiannual, quarterly, or monthly premium under small-sized policies is exceedingly modest and within the reach of practically every person.

Acceptable Duration.   The policy term may be made short or long in accordance with the insured's desire. Usually, investors prefer to have the investment extend over considerable periods of time. Here life insurance affords a splendid opportunity. Endowment policies may be taken for any desired period such as ten, twenty, thirty, or forty years. The investment period may be made to coincide with the anticipated working period. A still longer period, if desired, need only be requested. The investment period may be made to run to any one of numerous maturity dates up to age 100. In the meantime, the cash value is readily obtainable for the promised amount, thus enabling the insured to terminate the investment prior to the maturity date of the contract.

Installment Method of Purchase.   Although the life insurance plan of investment may not be regarded strictly as an installment plan, it nevertheless furnishes all the conveniences associated with the installment method. A definite financial resolution is attained over a series of years through a distinct number of separate steps. A forty-year annual premium endowment policy for $20,000 is matured through forty separate steps.

Full Title to a Part.   Under other installment plans of investment, the purchaser does not obtain undisputed possession of the entire unit until the same has been fully paid for. But this is not the case in life insurance. Each payment buys an entity to which the insured has full title. Strictly speaking, life insurance is, therefore, not an installment plan of investment. It really consists of a series of separate parts, each being purchased separately with each premium.

Other Aspects

Favorable Tax Treatment.   Life insurance companies are subjected by the states to unfair special taxes, but from the policyholder's standpoint this disadvantage is clearly overbalanced by advantages extended to life and health insurance in the fields of income and inheritance taxation. Briefly stated, these tax advantages are four in number:

1. Exemption, in general, from income taxation of life insurance proceeds paid upon the happening of death, even though the proceeds received may greatly exceed the cost of the insurance.
2. Exemption (wholly or in part) from state inheritance taxation of life insurance proceeds payable to named beneficiaries.
3. Exemption from income taxation of all payments received by the policyholder himself (such as return premiums, dividends, cash value, or a matured endowment) to an amount equal to the premium cost of the contract.
4. Imposition of a moderate Federal income tax immediately upon the return from annuities, involving a favorable rule taxing the interest earnings on the principal sum being liquidated.[7]

Protection Against Creditors.   In the great majority of states, life insurance policies payable to wife, children, or other dependent relatives are protected under exemption laws against the claims of creditors of the insured arising from obligations incurred after the passage of the act. Often the amount of such insurance thus declared exempt from creditors claims is limited to some reasonable amount. Various states, however, have made their exemption acts relate to all such policies without respect to

---

[7] See *The R & R Tax Handbook—1971* (Indianapolis: The Research & Review Service of America, Inc.).

amount and without regard to the fact that "the right to change the beneficiary named has been reserved by the insured or is permitted by the insurer." [8]

Effectiveness in Meeting Essential Investment Objectives

Accumulation of an investment estate should certainly be motivated by appealing objectives, that is, future wants and obligations. Otherwise there would be no purpose in the sacrifice and trouble. For the overwhelming mass of people, the objectives of an investment program seem to be:

1. To provide against financial contingencies resulting from premature death.
2. To provide against financial contingencies resulting from disability during the working period of life.
3. To meet old age retirement needs or supplement Social Security benefits.
4. To meet unemployment and other serious business or family reverses.
5. To meet basic financial obligations, with a definite future due date, requiring solution through the accumulation of a scientifically managed sinking fund.

Life and health insurance certainly offer a complete program, designed to meet all of the aforementioned five factors.

A true emergency fund must have five vital attributes, namely: (1) dependable solvency of the fund, (2) reasonably rapid growth through compound interest at the highest rate consistent with absolute solvency, (3) freedom from all managerial care on the part of the individual accumulating the fund, (4) absolute stability as to the dollar valuation of the fund irrespective of business fluctuations, and (5) prompt availability whenever the acid test of an emergency may arise. The previous discussion clearly indicates that the life insurance investment, viewed as an emergency fund, possesses all of these attributes to an almost perfect degree.

LIFE INSURANCE AND EQUITY INVESTMENTS

As the previous discussion has shown, the savings element in permanent life insurance contracts has been considered a prime fixed-dollar investment. The security of principal and relatively high yield, reflecting the

---

[8] See *The R & R Advanced Underwriting and Estate Planning Service* (Indianapolis: The Research and Review Service of America, Inc., Current), Sec. 10.

basic characteristics of life insurance, have made life insurance an outstanding savings vehicle for the American public over the last decade. However, the proportion of total savings flowing into the life insurance business has been declining. This has been a result of aggressive competition from commercial banks, savings and loan associations, trusteed pension plans, and mutual funds, the success of which has been fostered by changing economic conditions.

The general inflationary trend in the United States has increased the public's interest in equities as an investment medium both as a hedge against inflation and to permit participation in the steady economic growth the country has experienced. A recent study by Lionel D. Edie and Company traced the long-run growth of the American economy, analyzed the forces behind the growth and pondered the implications of future economic trends for personal saving and investing and, in particular, for life insurance.[9]

The projections called for a very strong expansion of gross private domestic investment which implies a high rate of personal and business saving in the next ten to fifteen years if we are to escape very serious inflationary pressures. This, coupled with the fact that there is little prospect of a downward trend in interest rates in the same period, bodes well for fixed-dollar investments such as those standing behind the savings element of permanent life insurance.

In this same report, however, it was clear that the appeal of equity investments with the general public would undoubtedly strengthen in the next ten to fifteen years. Beyond the projected rise in corporate earnings, the study indicated that the rise of the price level will force investors to turn increasingly to equities as a hedge against inflation. Whether equities are a good hedge against inflation is open to question, but the report concluded that the public will see no other alternative.

What are the implications of this conclusion to life insurance? During the past decade, the life insurance business has been continually studying its products from the standpoint of their attractiveness to the public in the light of economic trends and prospects. Out of this process of self-examination have come changes in product design to adapt life insurance to our modern economy. The most notable, of course, are those designed to appeal to the increasing public attractiveness of equities. There are many critics who believe that the reaction of the life insurance business to changing economic trends has been too little and too late. In an industry so bound by statute and public regulation, and so conscious and conscientious about its public trust, it was inevitable that change in product design and in marketing concepts would be evolutionary rather than revolutionary. But there is now evidence that the life insurance business is moving swiftly and strongly to adapt

[9] See James J. O'Leary, "Economic Forces Influencing Personal Investing in the Future," *1967 Forum Report* (Bryn Mawr, Pa.: American Society of Chartered Life Underwriters, 1967), pp. 3–17.

its products to the emerging trends in our economy. The life insurance business seems ready to meet this challenge in the group pension field with the development of separate account funding and variable annuities on a group basis. It would appear, however, that much remains to be done in the field of ordinary cash value life insurance to design new products or to redesign old products in an imaginative way to make a greater appeal to the equity-conscious public. This means that more and more life companies will be establishing mutual funds. It probably means a major push into the marketing of variable annuities and variable life insurance to individuals in spite of regulatory and marketing problems.

As the regulatory and marketing problems are solved, it would appear that the life insurance contract may well become even more attractive as a savings and investment medium. The availability of adequate electronic data equipment coupled with a market demand for equity investments would appear to portend the movement to develop a so-called "life cycle" policy which would include in one master account a base contract and a multitude of options providing adequate flexibility to meet all of the personal investment and protection needs of an individual and his family.[10]

LIFE AND HEALTH INSURANCE AS PROTECTION FOR PROPERTY ESTATE

Expedites the Settlement of Insured's Property Estate

The majority of estates either are encumbered with claims of one kind or another or present serious problems of administration. To hedge against such a contingency, life and health insurance may again be used to great advantage. Reference has already been made to the way in which life insurance serves to liquidate mortgages in the event of the mortgagor's premature death. But the same principle is also applicable to a host of other obligations or difficulties of settlement that the deceased leaves to his heirs. Thus, the proceeds of life and health insurance will often serve to effect a *prompt* settlement of the estate through payment of loans on securities or other property, all bills outstanding at the time of death or incident thereto, such as administration costs, inheritance, income, or other post mortem taxes, and last illness expenses and funeral costs. In addition, life insurance payable directly to the heirs will provide for the upkeep of the family during the period of administration. This permits the executor or administrator

---

[10] See Institute of Life Insurance, *Highlights of the Future Outlook Study* (New York, 1967), pp. 14–15.

to handle the settlement of the estate in the most efficient and desirable manner without the problem of providing funds to maintain the family during the period of administration.

Where the business is so organized as to make its division into units undesirable, life insurance may be used to make proper provision in cash for various members of the family, thus avoiding the undesirable division of ownership of the business. And even where such an arrangement has not been effected, and it is found advantageous to sell the business of the deceased, particularly to certain of the beneficiaries under the will, life insurance proceeds may serve as a basis for a fair settlement among all the heirs.

Protection Against Forced Liquidation of Property

Not only does life insurance facilitate the prompt settlement of estates, but it also serves as a safeguard against depletion of the estate. Among those claims against the estate mentioned above, the tax items usually constitute the most serious, particularly in larger estates. Thus, in addition to last illness, funeral, and administration costs, an estate may stand in need of ready cash to pay (1) Federal and state estate and inheritance taxes, (2) property or other local taxes that have accrued since the last assessment, and (3) Federal or state income taxes for the current year up to the time of death. In addition, the estate is also responsible for the payment of any property or income taxes past due and unpaid.

Not only are estates subject to the Federal tax, but nearly every state has also seen fit to adopt this plan of taxation in one form or another. Space limits forbid a detailed discussion of the various laws since they differ greatly in many essentials, such as rates of taxation, classification of heirs, exemptions allowed, and the location of taxable property. Suffice it to say that the combined effect of both Federal and state taxes is often such as to cause a serious depletion of the estate, especially where it is large, and to constitute a serious burden in its settlement.

Life insurance serves as the ideal medium through which to provide liquidity in the estate, since the event which produces the need for cash, death, automatically produces the funds. Utilizing life insurance to provide cash for the prompt payment of taxes and other post mortem expenses avoids the necessity of selling a portion of the estate, probably at a most inopportune time. Taxes for which the deceased's estate is responsible must be paid in cash, irrespective of economic conditions that may prevail at the time the taxes fall due. Hence, it may be necessary, in the absence of adequate life insurance proceeds, to raise the necessary cash through the sale of very desirable items of real estate, possibly at a time when it is difficult to obtain a buyer except at great sacrifice. The estate may consist of stocks and bonds, with the tax falling due in the midst of a business depression, when such securities are selling at greatly depreciated prices. These are merely illustrations of how a forced sale at bottom prices in order to raise cash for tax-paying purposes may deplete an estate to an extraordinary degree. Such a situation, however, may be avoided through the carrying of adequate life insurance, the full face value of which becomes immediately available upon death for the payment of taxes, thus enabling other investments of the estate to remain undisturbed. Only one other plan suggests itself, namely, the maintenance at all times of a cash balance so large as to meet the contingency under consideration. Such a plan is clearly impossible for the great majority, and most unbusinesslike for the limited number who could afford to adopt it. Immediate availability of life insurance proceeds for the payment of post mortem taxes, it may be stated, also gives the added advantage of obtaining the discount of 5 per cent frequently allowed for the payment of inheritance taxes before the due date. In providing liquidity for an estate, life insurance has no peer.

Hedging Good Will and Intangible Assets

In many instances the appraised value of the estate consists in large part of good will dependent upon the continued life of the owner. With his death or disability, the money value of his good will soon disappears in large part or entirely. This is particularly true of the professions and semiprofessions. It is also true in innumerable other cases. The only possible method of protecting the money value of such good will against loss through death or disability is through life and health insurance. In the event of death or disability, the life or health insurance proceeds will reimburse the loss of the money value of the good will and will thus keep the estate intact.

Similarly, many are obliged to make intangible investments by way of advertising, the training of personnel, and so forth. The investment is ever so real, but it is intangible and unmarketable. A tree must be planted and must be allowed to grow before it can bear fruit in worthwhile fashion. So these intangible investments represent a planting and a growing. They will bear fruit in due course as the tree continues to survive. The death of the owner of the little business during its formative years usually means a loss of such intangible investments. Why not hedge such investments with life insurance? If the owner lives, the investment will likely become fruitful. But if the owner dies and the investment thus fails, the life insurance proceeds will reimburse the estate as far as the appraised money value of such expenditures is concerned. Probably one third of all business enterprises require life insurance for this particular purpose.

Hedging Serious Losses Already Sustained

Even during normal times, but particularly during periods of business depression, many business estates suffer serious shrinkage in their dollar valuation. The comment of the victim of such shrinkage is usually as follows: "My business estate has certainly received a bad blow; I have lost heavily and my business is flat. If I live, I confidently believe I can retrieve the loss and be wiser the next time; but if I die, my estate will certainly be in difficulty. I feel I need life insurance now to supplement my remaining estate in the event of death at just this time."

The one thing this man needs is time. Life and health insurance will give him that time. By insuring his life he can hedge against the possibility that premature death or disability will prevent him from recouping his losses. There is no other vehicle through which he can obtain such "time insurance."

MISCELLANEOUS

Life Insurance as a Means of Endowing Educational and Philanthropic Institutions

Philanthropic activity along its many lines constitutes one of the greatest of all of our financial efforts. Any number of institutions—educational, religious, medical, scientific, charitable, and so forth—are dependent in the main upon lives (donors) who need to be insured against loss to the recipients of the benefactions. The surface in bequest insurance has hardly been scratched, and a wonderful future lies ahead.

Also, in the past, philanthropic bequests have been derived largely from the wealthy few who could afford to give readily from their large accumulated capital. But we are more and more faced with the warning that there will soon be few rich men—owing to heavy surtaxes, estate and inheritance taxes—and that philanthropic institutions of all kinds will more and more have to rely upon the benefactions of the many. Now these many donors are not in a position to deplete their existing capital, and it is here that bequest life insurance fulfills an outstanding service otherwise unobtainable. Life insurance bequests are created out of current income in the sense that the insured sets aside periodically out of current income from 1 to 5 per cent for charity or other community purposes that he may have in mind. Creation of the bequest does not mean depletion of the insured's existing capital. Instead, the benefaction is created out of earnings and thrift following the taking of the insurance. In the absence of such insurance, the bequest would probably never have been started at all, and, in any case, it would have remained much smaller, viewing the problem in its relation to the wealth actually owned by the donor.

Life Insurance as a Means of Making Contingent Interests Marketable

One of the minor functions of life insurance is its use in making contingent interests marketable. Reference is made especially to the use of socalled contingent or survivorship policies which expressly provide that the face of the policy will be paid upon the death of the insured only if some other designated person is still living at the time, that is, the policy is said to insure one life against another. The function of such contracts becomes apparent when we reflect that frequently the owners of estates bequeath the entire income to the widow throughout her life, the property itself to be distributed upon her death to certain heirs who may then be living. Such heirs, it is clear, possess a valuable right under the will, but it is a contingent one and may be lost in case of death during the lifetime of the widow. Manifestly, it will be difficult for any such heirs to give this contingent interest a market value for the purpose of a sale or a loan unless some means can be found to protect the purchaser or lender against the loss of the interest through the death of the heir before the death of the widow. Such protection is furnished most cheaply through a so-called contingent or survivorship policy. Thus let us assume that A is entitled to property contingent upon surviving B, who is the life tenant of an estate. Save as a speculation, depending largely upon the condition of B's health, the contingent reversion has no realizable value. But this contingent interest may be converted into a marketable proposition through a life insurance policy payable only upon A's death during the lifetime of B. Such policies may be secured by the payment of a single premium in advance, or if preferred may be paid for by annual premiums continuing during the joint duration of the two lives.

Life Insurance as a Gift to Children

A life insurance policy on the life of a child makes an ideal gift. In many cases there are tax advantages, but, in addition, a policy on the life of a child represents a gift which (1) requires no supervision or investment management, (2) protects the child's insurability, and (3) can be purchased today at a price which the child could never match in the future. Procedurally, the donor would simply purchase life insurance on the child's life, with the initial premium plus all future premium payments being made directly to the life insurance company. The premium payments, as made, constitute the gifts to the child.

BIBLIOGRAPHY

The Nature and Uses of Life and Health Insurance

Advanced Underwriting and Estate Planning Service, Vol. 2 (Indianapolis: The Research and Review Service of America, Inc., 1971).

Becker, Gary S. *Human Capital* (New York: Columbia University Press, 1964).

Belth, Joseph M. "The Rate of Return on the Savings Element in Cash-Value Life Insurance," *The Journal of Risk and Insurance,* Vol. XXXV, No. 4 (December, 1968).

Blaug, Mark. *Economics of Education, A Selected Annotated Bibliography,* 2nd ed. (New York: Pergamon Press, 1970).

Brown, Robert A., Jr., and O'Neill, Jack. "Appraising the Human Asset for Business Life Insurance Requirements," *Journal of the American Society of Chartered Life Underwriters,* Vol. XI, No. 4 (Fall, 1957), pp. 340–352.

Drewry, James S. "Life Insurance is Good Property," *Journal of the American Society of Chartered Life Underwriters,* Vol. II, No. 2 (March, 1948), pp. 128-137.

————— *Why Life Insurance?* (Cincinnati: National Underwriter Company, 1952.)

Drucker, Peter F. *The Age of Discontinuity* (New York: Harper and Row, Publishers, 1969).

Ferrari, J. Robert. "Investment Life Insurance Versus Term Insurance and Separate Investment," *Journal of Risk and Insurance,* Vol. XXXV, No. 2 (June, 1968), pp. 181-198.

Gardiner, Harold W. "Programming Life Insurance," *Life and Health Insurance Handbook,* 2nd ed. (Homewood, Ill.: Richard D. Irwin, Inc., 1964), Chapter 61.

Gregg, Davis W. "Freedom and Security," *1970 CLU Forum Report—Perceptions on Economic Security* (Bryn Mawr, Pa.: American Society of Chartered Life Underwriters, 1971).

Harmelin, W., and Osler, R. W. *Business Uses of Health Insurance,* rev. ed. (Bryn Mawr, Pa.: American College of Life Underwriters, 1967).

Hofflander, Alfred E. "The Human Life Value: An Historical Perspective," *The Journal of Risk and Insurance,* Vol. XXIII, No. 3 (September, 1966).

Huebner, S. S. *Economics of Life Insurance,* 3rd ed. (New York: Appleton-Century-Crofts, Inc., 1959).

Institute of Life Insurance. *Highlights of the Future Outlook Study* (New York: 1967).

Linton, M. Albert. *Life Insurance Speaks for Itself* (New York: Harper and Brothers, 1962).

Osler, Robert W. "Programming Health Insurance," *Life and Health Insurance Handbook,* 2nd ed. (Homewood, Ill.: Richard D. Irwin, Inc., 1964), Chapter 62.

Schultz, Theodore W. "Investment in Human Capital," *The American Economic Review,* Vol. LI, No. 1 (March, 1961).

Schwarzschild, Stuart. "A Model for Determining the Rate of Return on Investment in Life Insurance Policies," *Journal of Risk and Insurance,* Vol. XXXIV, No. 3 (September, 1967), pp. 435-444.

Smith, J. Carlton. *Key Man Uses of Life Insurance,* rev. ed. (Bryn Mawr, Pa.: American College of Life Underwriters, 1964).

Speiser, Stuart M. *Recovery for Wrongful Death—Economic Handbook* (Rochester, N.Y.: The Lawyers Co-operative Publishing Company, 1970).

U. S. Bureau of the Census. "Present Value of Estimated Lifetime Earnings," Technical Paper No. 16 (Washington, D. C.: U. S. Government Printing Office, 1967).

Weisbrod, Burton A. "The Valuation of Human Capital," *The American Economic Review,* Vol. LXIX, No. 5 (October, 1961).

White, Edwin H. *Business Insurance,* 3rd ed. (Englewood Cliffs, N. J.: Prentice-Hall, Inc., 1963).

II The Life Insurance Product: Types of Contracts

Term Insurance | 5

THERE ARE FOUR basic classes of life insurance contracts issued by life insurance companies: (1) term, (2) whole-life, (3) endowment, and (4) annuities. Other classifications based on method of premium payment, period of coverage, method of distribution of proceeds, and combinations of these basic contracts are possible, but the above classification seems sufficient as a background for understanding the various life insurance contracts available today. Two other comments are worthy of mention at this point, however. First, while life insurance policies differ widely in form, it is important to note that the premiums charged for all policies, as will be shown later, are computed on the basis of actuarial assumptions which ensure that the cost of any policy is the amount actually required to provide the benefits guaranteed by that policy. Thus, it follows that, basically, all the policies issued by a given company are approximately equivalent to each other, from the standpoint of dollars and cents, insofar as their inherent worth is concerned.

Second, in a discussion of the various types of life insurance policies, it is vital that we bear in mind that the important function of all such policies is the creation of a stipulated fund, through either the operation of the term insurance or the operation of the accumulating investment account. In other words, all forms of life insurance policies have for their primary purpose the *upbuilding* of an investment fund. Annuities, on the contrary, have as their basic function the *liquidation,* that is, the *using up,* of a fund which may have been built up through life insurance or by methods other than insurance. This chapter is concerned with *term insurance* as the expression is used in the business today.

NATURE OF TERM INSURANCE

A term policy in life insurance may be defined as a contract which furnishes life insurance protection for a limited number of years, the face value of the policy being payable only if death occurs during the stipulated term, and nothing being paid in case of survival.

Such policies may be issued for a period as short as one year [1] or may

---

[1] So-called "preliminary" or "initial" term insurance is available for periods as

73

provide protection up to age 65 or 70. Customarily, term insurance policies are written for periods of five, ten, fifteen, or twenty years. Such policies may insure for the agreed term of years only, or may be renewed for successive term periods at the option of the insured and without evidence of insurability. Term insurance applications are carefully underwritten, and various restrictions are imposed by many companies on the issuance of term contracts, such as those limiting the size of the policy to a certain amount or the age beyond which it can be renewed.

Term insurance may, therefore, be regarded as temporary insurance, and, in principle, more nearly compares with property and casualty insurance contracts than any of the other life insurance contracts in use. If a building valued at $10,000 is insured for that amount under a five-year term policy, the company will pay this insurance in case of the destruction of the building during the term, but if at the end of the specified five-year period the owner neglects to insure the building again by renewing the policy and a fire thereafter ensues, the company is absolved from all liability in view of the expiration of the contract. Similarly, if a person insures his life for $10,000 under a five-year term policy, keeping the policy in force either by paying a single premium in advance or by paying, as is nearly always the case, annual premiums from year to year, the company will pay $10,000 in case of his death at any time before the expiration of the five years; nothing, however, is paid if death occurs after the expiration of the contract period since the term life policy, like the fire policy, has expired at that time. At the end of the policy term all premiums paid are fully earned whether or not a loss has occurred and the policy has no further value.

The premium for term insurance protection is relatively low despite the facts that expenses are a larger proportion of the outlay and the rate is increased to allow for adverse selection. This is due to the fact that term insurance protection is *temporary* and no charge is necessary to cover the high death rates at the older ages. Term insurance insures against a contingency only, whereas whole life contracts insure against a certainty.

SPECIAL FEATURES IN TERM POLICIES

Renewable Feature

Many five- and ten-year term policies contain an option to renew for a limited number of additional periods of protection. This option permits the insured, at the expiration of the first term period or at the end of any subse-

---

short as a month. This insurance is usually restricted to situations in which it is desired to have protection start immediately, with the policy having a formal effective date one or more months in the future.

quent term period, to renew the policy without a medical examination and irrespective of the insured's health at the time of renewal. The renewal of the policy, in other words, can be effected by the insured by paying the premium for the age then attained without furnishing any evidence of insurability. Usually, however, the companies limit the age (generally 60 or, at the latest, 65 years) at which such renewable term policies may be issued, and, in some instances, the number of renewals permitted is limited.

Where the term policy contains no renewal privilege, the insured may be placed at the disadvantage, at the end of the term, of being without insurance and of not being in a position, because of poor physical condition, hazardous occupation, or otherwise, to secure a renewal of the contract or to obtain any other form of life insurance protection. In many instances, also, the particular contingency which the term policy was designed to cover, may still exist at the expiration of the term, thus making highly desirable the privilege of renewing the contract for one or more terms at the will of the insured and without the possibility of denial on the part of the company. Most term policies have a convertible feature, hereinafter described more fully, which permits the insured to take other insurance near the end of the term period if the future need for the coverage is apparent at that time.

It should be noted that the premium, while level for a given period, increases with each renewal and is based on the attained age of the insured at the time of renewal. Thus, although the *scale* of rates in the contract is guaranteed, the rate increases with each renewal because of the higher attained age of the insured.

Renewable term insurance fills a valid need by protecting the insurability of the policyholder. The price on a net cost basis is high, however. As the premium rate increases with each renewal, adverse selection against the company develops at an increasing rate. Naturally, resistance to the higher premiums will cause many policyholders in good health to fail to renew while the great majority of those in poor health will renew even in face of the higher premium. As a result, the mortality experience among surviving insured policyholders will become increasingly unfavorable. The companies recognize this problem and the cost of this adverse selection is passed on to the policyholders through either a "loaded" premium or decreased dividends. The limitation of coverage to age 55, 60, or 65 and the limited number of renewals permitted are additional recognition of the increasing adverse selection evidenced in the face of the rising premium outlay necessary to continue such protection with increasing age. In fact, term insurance written on any basis is satisfactory for temporary protection only.

Convertible Feature

Most term insurance policies also include a convertible feature, that is, the privilege on the part of the insured to convert the policy into a permanent type of contract upon a proper adjustment in the premium charge, *without evidence of insurability*. Some companies extend this conversion privilege throughout the term period of five- and ten-year policies, but the great majority grant the right only for a limited number of years, such as the first four or seven years of the term or, on long-period term policies, to a date several years before expiration of the term period, in order to minimize adverse selection. Conversion into regular whole-life or endowment insurance is usually allowed. The exchange is usually allowed at any time during the period when conversion is permitted, and may be effected as of the "attained age" or as of the "original age."

The *attained age method* of conversion involves the issuance of a permanent policy of the form currently being issued at the date of conversion, and the premium rate for the new policy is that required at the attained age of the insured.[2]

The original age method involves a retroactive conversion with the permanent policy bearing the date and premium rate which would have been paid had the permanent policy been taken out originally, and taking the *form* of the permanent contract which was being issued at the original date. It should be apparent that this form of contract may be more or less liberal than the form being issued at the date of conversion and that the premium rate will be lower due to the younger effective age. Most companies require that retroactive conversions take place within five years of the date of issue of the term contract.

In the case of an original age conversion, most companies require the insured to pay the difference between the premiums which would have been paid on the new policy if it had been issued at the same time as the original policy, and the premiums paid thereunder for the same amount of insurance, with interest on such difference at a certain stipulated annual rate (5 or 6 per cent, currently). Some companies, after five or more years, require only that the insured pay the difference in reserves (in some companies the cash surrender values) under the two policies with or without interest plus a small service charge to pay premium taxes, commissions, and other costs. In any case, the purpose of the adjustment is to place the insurance company in the same financial position it would have held had the permanent policy been issued in the first place.

In making a choice between the two bases of conversion, the insured may be motivated by the lower premium rate payable under an original age conversion, or the availability of a more liberal contract at the original date, but other factors will affect such a decision. For example, if the insured is in ill health, he would be foolish to convert retroactively and pay a substantial sum of money to the insurance company. Such an action

---

[2] Most term policies have only a small reserve (investment element), but in case of conversions, companies usually allow a so-called conversion value based on this reserve against the premium.

would in effect reduce the protection element (net amount at risk), since the money paid becomes part of the reserve of the policy, immediately reducing the effective amount of insurance protection. It goes without saying that the availability of the sum required for retroactive conversion is a significant factor in such a decision. It can also be argued that, in lieu of a retroactive conversion, the insured should take any surplus funds and purchase additional insurance or prepay premiums on existing insurance, including the newly converted policy. Subject to certain limitations, many companies will permit the insured to prepay premiums, either in the form of "premium deposits" or by "discounting premiums." [3] These premiums are credited with interest at a guaranteed rate currently running about 5 to 5¼ per cent. Limitations as to withdrawal differ from company to company, but in the event of the insured's death, the balance of any such deposits is paid to the appropriate beneficiary in addition to the face of the policy.

The advisability of the purchase of additional insurance depends on the insured's needs and present insurance program. In the final analysis, the decision, as with most aspects of an insurance program, rests with the importance of the investment and protection elements of the contract to the insured.

Some companies issue term policies which provide for automatic conversion to a specific permanent plan, but the continuation of the insurance is still optional with the insured. There may be some sales and administrative advantages involved, but it is doubtful that such a provision is very effective in reducing adverse selection.

The advantages of the conversion privilege become apparent if we consider the disadvantages usually attaching to term insurance. At the time of taking out the policy the insured may not have definitely selected the type of policy best adapted for his needs. Following the issuance of the term policy, his circumstances may soon become such as to enable him to take out adequate permanent insurance. Or he may desire to utilize insurance as a means of accumulating an estate rather than to use it entirely for protection against death. As soon, therefore, as he concludes that term insurance does not meet his present and future needs, he may carry out his conclusions by exchanging his term contract for one on the whole-life or endowment plan in either of the two ways already suggested. Moreover, another great value of the conversion privilege also becomes apparent (where the policy does not contain a renewable privilege) when it is remembered that during even the first five or seven years following the issuance of the contract, a considerable percentage of the insured lives become physically impaired to such an extent as to make impossible the securing of any other plan of

---

[3] These two procedures are similar, differing in that under the discount method, credit is taken in advance for the interest to be earned on the funds deposited.

life insurance in a reliable company at standard rates. Under such circumstances a nonrenewable term policy may, because of its expiration before death, fail utterly to protect the insured. If, however, the policy contains the conversion privilege, and if the time limit for making an exchange of the policy has not yet expired, it will be to the insured's advantage to take this privilege and thus protect himself against the possibility of his insurance expiring before death occurs.

LONG TERM CONTRACTS

Most term contracts provide protection for a relatively short period of time, but term contracts are available which are written to cover the usual working lifetime of an individual. There are two types of contracts providing essentially the same protection: (1) life expectancy and (2) term to 60 or 65.

The term to expectancy provides protection for the life expectancy of the insured with the premium being level throughout this period. The exact number of years which the contract will run depends upon the age of the insured at date of application and the mortality assumption used. For example, the *1958 CSO Table* [4] shows a life expectancy of 47 years at age 24, while at age 55 it would be 20 years.[5] Although this contract is strictly a protection contract, the leveling of the premium over a long period of years produces a cash value (savings element) which increases to a point and then declines to zero at the termination of the policy. This is demonstrated in Graph 5–1.

The contract contains a conventional conversion feature which may be exercised prior to the expiration date of the contract. In addition, provision is made for automatic conversion of the contract into a form of whole-life at the end of the period of coverage. The insured usually has the option of taking a reduced amount of permanent insurance at no increase in premium or of continuing the original amount of insurance with an increase in premium.[6]

The term to 60 or 65 contract usually provides protection for a some-

---

[4] See pp. 325–326.

[5] In a technical sense, the term "life expectancy" is completely without meaning in relation to any one person. It has significance only to large numbers of individuals of a given age. In other words mortality tables do not show the life expectancy of any particular individual. See pp. 328–329.

[6] Some companies issue a contract known as the "term expectancy" which is virtually identical to the life expectancy contract but contains *no* conversion privileges. Naturally, the premiums are somewhat lower because of the elimination of the conversion privilege.

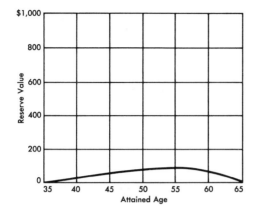

GRAPH 5-1.   Extent of reserve element in term to 65 contract issued at male age 35, 1958 CSO Table and 2½ per cent interest.

what shorter period than the life expectancy policy and consequently has a slightly lower premium. The rationale of the policy is that it provides protection during the period of the individual's productive effort, since 65 is usually regarded as the normal retirement age, or until his children are grown and the need decreases. As in the case of the life expectancy contract, there is a cash value during the term of the policy. The contract also usually provides for a conventional conversion privilege, but it must be exercised at some point before the expiration of the policy.

DECREASING AND INCREASING TERM INSURANCE

Another form of term insurance, decreasing in face amount, is widely used as a rider for permanent contracts and as a separate policy to provide so-called mortgage protection. The policy or rider, from a given initial amount of insurance, year by year declines in face amount, becoming zero at the end of the term of the contract. The premium is very low because of the facts that (1) the amount of insurance protection decreases and (2) the face amount decreases as the rate per unit of insurance increases. Most companies offer this coverage (not always as a separate contract) on a ten-, fifteen-, or twenty-year basis, and a conversion privilege is usually included. Level premiums are sometimes limited to a somewhat shorter period than the term of the policy to discourage policyholders from dropping the protection during the last few years when the amount of protection is quite low.

Increasing term insurance is virtually never sold as a separate contract.

Its primary use is in connection with combination or package policies where it will be included, as part of a contract, to provide a benefit which increases with time and is payable on death.[7]

EVALUATION OF TERM LIFE INSURANCE

Term life insurance has long been the subject of controversy. There are those who advocate the use of term insurance to the virtual exclusion of permanent life insurance. Some so-called "insurance consultants" will go so far as to advise an individual to surrender existing permanent insurance for cash and to replace it with term insurance. Life insurance companies themselves tend to discourage the indiscriminate use of term insurance. The fact is that there are both appropriate and inappropriate uses to which term insurance may be applied. The following sections attempt to illustrate the proper use of term insurance and to point out the disadvantages of its improper application in planning the financial affairs of an individual. Finally, some of the *fallacious* arguments advanced in favor of term insurance are analyzed briefly.

Uses of Term Insurance

Term policies are especially designed to afford protection against contingencies which either require only the taking out of temporary insurance or call for the largest amount of insurance protection for the time being at the lowest possible outlay of funds. Their purpose is to serve in the same way that property insurance contracts do, namely, to protect by way of indemnification against the loss of an asset of pecuniary value. In life insurance, such term insurance is designed to indemnify the loss of the capitalized earning value of the insured life. Briefly enumerated, pure term insurance seems justified under the following eight sets of circumstances:

1. For persons with small income for the present, with family obligations on their hands, but with good prospects for the development of a career. Emphasis, it will be noted, is placed upon the development of a career. The average worker, as a rule, has little prospect or inclination for a career. His accumulation of an investment fund must be secured as best he can during his working years. For him, ordinary life insurance or some limited-payment form of contract, to be explained later, will likely prove more efficacious than term insurance. But those who have a career to estab-

---

[7] The return of premium provision found in some contracts is an example of the use of increasing term insurance. See pp. 146–147.

lish and have a limited income temporarily should use all of their resources to establish a following and reputation. They should not overlook the importance of investing surplus within themselves during the early years for their own education and upbuilding for the specialized work which they are to do rather than placing such surplus funds into the investment portion of life insurance. Investment in the person for self-improvement during the early years will prove the greatest investment by far. It will yield rich dividends in money and satisfaction, and will constitute an asset that cannot be taken away by shrinkage in price quotations. One may wonder whether such persons have any right to turn to tangible material investments until they have first made a reasonable effort at investment for their own personal self-improvement. Yet it is essential that, while this investment in the person is being pursued, proper provision should be made, where a family is at stake, for a decent *potential estate* as a safeguard against the occurrence of an early death. Term insurance guarantees such a potential estate.

2. For persons who have placed substantially all their resources in the material assets of a new business which is still in its formative stages, and where premature death of the human factor in that business would spell serious loss, if not destruction, to the invested capital. New enterprises are particularly speculative and become more settled only as time elapses. Term insurance serves a very useful purpose, because of its low absolute dollar outlay, in the initial stages of such undertakings. It serves as a hedge against the possible loss of the business asset in the event of the early removal by death of the person behind the enterprise.

3. To protect one's insurability. Many young men recognize the need for additional life insurance. As their incomes and families grow, their need for life insurance becomes greater, but at the time the need is greatest it may be impossible to secure additional insurance because of an impairment in health. Term insurance, through its conversion feature, can serve as a hedge against this possibility. This was particularly important prior to the development of "guaranteed insurability coverage." [8]

4. As a supplement to investment insurance, for persons of ordinary means, during the child-raising period. The so-called Family Income Rider,[9] which is nothing more than pure term insurance, on the income plan, added to ordinary life insurance for a period equal to the difference between the age of the youngest child and the age of self-sufficiency of that child, has been widely adopted, and clearly indicates a wholehearted recognition of the value of term insurance as the solution of a pressing problem.

5. As a hedge against loss in the estate already sustained, where the owner of the estate is without current means, where a little time is required to repair the damage, and where there is hope that an economic revival will

[8] See pp. 529–530.
[9] See pp. 132–135.

again lift the dollar valuation of the depreciated assets. Such owners lack the funds to buy high premium insurance. They are, therefore, certainly served by pure term insurance. They are likely to appreciate the value of life insurance in the future, and to sense the wisdom of converting the term insurance into at least ordinary life insurance when happier financial days arrive.

6. As additional protection for loans. Here again, term insurance has been a boon during depression years to many who stood in need of loans and whose current income was pitifully small. Many creditors, after having satisfied themselves about the character and potential ability of the borrower, are willing to accept ten-year term insurance as the additional collateral. It is also important to note the supreme importance of a few dollars in a period of business depression, and consequently the importance of the smaller absolute expenditure for term insurance as compared with other types of contracts. Many students borrow funds for their education, particularly in the medical field, where costs are high and the returns are great. Term insurance becomes an essential coverage in such cases to protect the lender, because the student can and will pay his debts if he lives.

7. As a means of protecting mortgage obligations. One of the most common uses of term insurance is to provide proceeds from which a mortgage may be cancelled, redeemed, or retired upon the death of the breadwinner.

8. As a means of hedging definitely known contingencies. Innumerable instances of that nature will readily occur to us. Protection of a limited waiting period before a pension plan goes into operation for the individual, protection of contractual relations of a few years' standing only, and protection of a vested interest in payments extending over a fixed number of years only are illustrations.

Disadvantages of Term Insurance

While the foregoing illustrations serve to indicate the useful purposes that may often be derived from term insurance, it is important to note that this type of contract presents various dangers which are frequently overlooked and which should always be borne in mind by the person contemplating taking out such a policy. Although the absolute outlay for term contracts is very low in the younger years, the sole purpose of such policies is to furnish temporary protection. The entire premium represents payment for this protection and nothing is paid to the insured in case of survival at the expiration of the policy. It is a common assertion that the chief objection to this form of insurance is that the insured is apt to feel dissatisfied at the expiration of the contract, and that it is most difficult to make the average holder of such a policy, after he has paid ten or twenty premiums, appreciate the fact that he has already received full value in the form of protection for the premiums paid and is therefore not entitled to any refund.

While the insured may feel that he will be in a financial position later to make the carrying of insurance unnecessary, or to replace his term insurance with policies at a higher premium but which afford permanent protection, there is nearly always the danger that he may have miscalculated the future or may neglect to carry out his original ideas. Hence, if the usual term policy is not supplemented with other forms of insurance, such as whole-life or very long term insurance, there may come a day when the policyholder, upon the expiration of the term contract, will be without insurance at the very time when he may need it most. Assuming that he will be able to obtain other insurance at the time by passing the required medical examination, his advanced age will have greatly increased the premium, and possibly at that time, his early expectation of a larger income not having been realized, such increased cost may prove exceedingly burdensome. Moreover, other types of policies generally commend themselves in preference to term contracts in that they inculcate in the policyholder to a much greater extent a compulsory spirit of thrift and thus cause the great majority to have to their credit a substantial sum, accumulated from small payments promptly invested, which otherwise they would not have accumulated or would have lost or wasted. Term insurance, as already stated, represents cost for protection against death only, and the smallness of the premium should prove an attraction only where large protection is absolutely needed and where the available fund for premium payments makes a more permanent form of protection impossible.

Finally, it should be noted that, "per unit of protection," term insurance is the most expensive form of life insurance available, i.e., the rate per dollar of term protection in a term policy is higher than the rate per dollar of term protection in a whole-life or endowment plan. The reason is that the mortality experience on term insurance is clearly greater than on the other plans, due primarily to adverse selection. A person who knows that he is in relatively poor health, although still insurable, will usually select a plan of insurance which carries the lowest premium outlay. Also, persons in poor health will be more inclined to convert to permanent insurance rather than let their term insurance contracts expire, since it is available to them at "bargain" rates.

Term insurance is also expensive because of the relation between the loading and the low average premium rate. The loading for the *fixed, overhead type of expenses* is a greater proportion of the lower premium rate; this means that the insurance is more expensive than in the case of permanent contracts, where the average premium rate is higher. Thus, while term policies involve the *lowest premium outlay,* they are *the most expensive* form of life insurance protection.

Fallacious Arguments in Favor of Term Insurance

Most of the fallacious arguments advanced against term life insurance inherently flow out of unfounded criticism of the level-premium system of providing life insurance protection. One author [10] summarizes these arguments into two allegations:

(1) level-premium life insurance overcharges the policyholder and

(2) the investment and protection elements in permanent insurance should be separated.

The first allegation is, of course, simply not true. Where needs for life insurance protection are long-term or permanent, there is no way to provide that permanent protection without leveling the premium. The level premium, in face of the increasing probability of dying, admittedly results in charges greater than pure term insurance in the early years, but this "overcharge" offsets the inadequate level premiums in later years, when the pure term premiums would become prohibitive and lead to a breakdown in the insurance process. If long-term or permanent protection is desired, a level-premium plan is mandatory. Obviously, if one knew when one was going to die, one could select against the system and would know to buy either term or permanent life insurance. Experience has shown that relatively few are able to predict the date of their death.

The argument that an amount equal to the reserve belongs to the policyholder and should be paid in addition to the face of the policy is patently invalid. It fails to acknowledge the nature of the permanent level-premium plan, which results in a steadily decreasing amount of pure insurance protection as the reserve increases. It is this very reduction in the protection element that enables the level-premium plan to work.

The second allegation—that the protection and investment elements of the contract should be separated—is based upon the premise that an individual can invest his funds more wisely and with a greater return than can the life insurance company. Colloquially, this recommendation is stated as "buy term and invest the difference," the difference being the difference between the term premium and the premium which would be paid for level-premium permanent insurance. This argument is, of course, a matter for individual judgment. Chapter 4 clearly shows the remarkable record of the life insurance business in terms of safety, yield, liquidity, and other criteria of a sound investment program. The industry's present movement into equities makes the argument even less appropriate from the standpoint of the individual buyer of life insurance.

[10] See Dan M. McGill, *Life Insurance*, rev. ed. (Homewood, Ill.: Richard D. Irwin, Inc., 1967), pp. 54–57.

The above comments should not be considered a criticism of other forms of investments. All have a place in a financial program of an individual. Level-premium life insurance, however, should be the foundation of all financial planning.

Whole-Life Insurance | 6

IN CONTRAST WITH term insurance, which pays benefits only if death takes place during a specified number of years, whole-life insurance provides for the payment of the face value upon the death of the insured, regardless of when it may occur. Whole-life protection may be purchased under either of two principal types of contracts, the chief difference between the two being the method of payment therefor. One is known as an *ordinary or straight life policy;* the other as a *limited-payment life policy.*

PRINCIPAL TYPES OF WHOLE-LIFE INSURANCE

Ordinary Life Policy

The ordinary life insurance policy is based on the assumption that premiums will be paid throughout the lifetime of the insured. In many cases, however, the insured purchases the policy with no intention of paying premiums as long as he lives. His intention may be to use dividend refunds (if participating) to pay up the whole-life policy in a shorter period, to surrender the policy for a paid-up whole-life policy of smaller face amount, or to surrender the policy at retirement for an annuity. The point is that the ordinary life insurance policy is a very flexible contract, and it is important to recognize that the insured is not irrevocably committed to paying premiums as long as he lives. During the earlier years of the insured's life, this type of insurance affords *permanent protection* for wife and children or other dependents at the lowest possible premium outlay. In the later years of life, when it may be felt that such a program can and should be changed because of the children's being grown and other changing needs and circumstances, this type of policy provides the *greatest possible degree of flexibility* to meet such situations. This policy should be the foundation of every life insurance program, and is the most popular contract offered by

86

commercial life insurance companies. Due to its importance, a somewhat more detailed discussion follows.

Furnishes Permanent Protection. The ordinary life policy furnishes permanent protection in the sense that it never has to be renewed or converted. It gives the insured this *permanent* protection at moderate cost, and this is highly important for the average man of moderate salary or daily wage who requires considerable family protection and whose limited income does not enable him both to pay premiums and to accumulate a large savings fund. Term insurance is essentially designed to afford protection against a *temporary* family or business peril, and can be recommended safely only when it is definitely known that the peril under consideration is temporary in character. But such contracts, as we have noted, contain elements of danger which are inseparable from temporary insurance. The chief danger connected with such insurance is that the insured may have miscalculated the duration of the peril confronting him and his future need for protection, or may neglect to carry out his original purpose to convert his temporary insurance into, or replace it with, policies which afford protection for the whole of life. Under ordinary life insurance all danger as to miscalculations relative to future need or the failure to carry out original purposes is obviated. Such insurance is certain in its results as it provides protection that is *permanent,* payable in the event of death whether it occurs early or late, and purchasable at a moderate premium which remains uniform throughout life.

Furnishes Permanent Protection at the Smallest Initial Outlay. The ordinary life policy gives the maximum of permanent protection at a minimum annual charge. This may be seen in Table 6–1, which compares

TABLE 6-1. Nonparticipating Annual Premium Rates per $1,000 for a $10,000 Policy for Representative Contracts

Age	Ordinary Life	Paid-up at 65	20-Pay Life	Endowment at 65	20-Year Endowment
25	$13.45	$14.89	$22.29	$ 18.25	$43.81
30	15.83	17.99	25.12	22.13	44.04
35	18.99	22.40	28.61	27.79	44.66
40	22.97	28.35	32.65	35.64	45.76
45	27.94	37.47	37.47	47.47	47.47
50	34.06	51.99	42.88	65.08	49.90
55	41.93	80.92	49.46	101.60	53.67
60	52.83	—	58.46	—	60.09
65	67.46	—	70.79	—	—

the nonparticipating [1] gross premiums charged by a company for ordinary life with those required under the limited-payment and endowment plans. Thus, assuming a $10,000 policy size,[2] the annual premium at age 35 charged per $1,000 of ordinary life insurance is $18.99; on twenty-payment life, $28.61; and on an endowment policy, maturing in twenty years, the premium is $44.66. It is therefore seen that the ordinary life policy furnishes permanent protection at the smallest initial outlay, although, as will be shown later, the limited-payment and endowment policies will, if the insured continues to live, ultimately yield a larger savings fund, thus compensating for the higher premium. In case of early death, however, the insured would realize the same amount under each of the aforementioned policies, yet his outlay would have been considerably greater under the limited-payment and endowment plans than under the ordinary life policy.

Owing to its moderate annual cost, an ordinary life policy tends to bring adequate protection within the reach of nearly all. It is particularly well adapted to those whose income is small and who find desirable a considerable amount of permanent protection. To the successful business man, on the other hand, the policy affords ample protection and enables him to use any surplus money for business purposes. The policy is also well adapted to persons who, although having passed middle life, may still desire the largest amount of permanent protection at the lowest cost. Even at ages 45 and 50 the annual premiums charged by the aforementioned company are, respectively, only $27.94 and $34.06 per $1,000 of insurance, while a twenty-payment life policy costs annually $37.47 and $42.88 and an endowment policy, maturing in twenty years, $47.47 and $49.90.

Combines Savings with Insurance.   Besides its moderate cost and the permanent character of the protection afforded, the ordinary life policy furnishes the further advantage of combining saving with insurance. In term insurance, as already explained, practically all of the premium represents payment for the current protection so that there is no savings element. Moreover, under term insurance nothing is paid to the insured in case of survival at the expiration of the term, and it is this fact which constitutes one of the chief psychological objections to this type of insurance, it being most difficult, as previously stated, to make the average holder of such a policy, after he has paid ten or twenty premiums, appreciate the fact that he has already received full value in the form of protection for the premiums paid, and that he is therefore not entitled to receive any refund.

[1] Participating companies doing the larger share of the national life insurance business charge a somewhat higher gross premium but make a dividend refund to the policyholder at the end of the year. See Chapter 27.

[2] This is necessary because of the fact that the premiums are graded by size. See pp. 420–421.

As contrasted with this psychological shortcoming, the ordinary life policy presents an entirely different situation. In the early years of such a policy the annual level premium is much in excess of the amount required to pay the current cost of the insurance protection, the balance being retained by the company as a reserve (called the legal reserve) and improved at compound interest at an agreed rate for the purpose of making good the deficiency in the later years of life, when the annual level premium is no longer sufficient to pay for the actual cost of the insurance. The overcharges in the early premiums are conducive to thrift on the part of the insured, and, in the great majority of instances, represent a saving—an accumulation of small amounts promptly invested by the company—which would otherwise not have been earned or, if earned, would have been lost or needlessly wasted. The fund thus accumulated out of the overcharges in the early premiums is held in trust for the policyholder.

This is the savings or investment element in the policy. Thus, the ordinary life insurance policy, as in the case of all permanent plans of insurance, is a combination of protection and saving. Since the premiums are lowest, the savings element at all durations is lower than that of the other forms of permanent insurance. The emphasis in this contract is on the protection element, but the leveling of the premium produces a savings element which is significant, and can be used in a variety of ways. The "cash value" of the policy represents this saving element. Table 6–2 illustrates the cash values which will accumulate under a $10,000 ordinary life insurance contract issued at age 35. Cash values are not usually available during the first year (sometimes two and even three years depending on age at issue) because of the acquisition expenses incurred when the contract is initially written.[3]

Table 6–2 shows that the cash value of the $10,000 policy has accumulated to $4,280 during the first twenty-five years, and this accumulation continues until it reaches $10,000, the face value of the policy, by age 100, the last year in the mortality table used for current life insurance policies. Since a whole-life policy matures for its face value at age 100, it follows that such a contract, if entered into at age 35, may be truly regarded as a sixty-five-year term policy, that is, for a term equal to the whole of life, or as a sixty-five-year endowment policy, maturing for its face value at age 100. All are mathematical equivalents.

Flexibility.   As mentioned above, the ordinary life contract provides a high degree of flexibility. Certain policy provisions provide this flexibility both before and after maturity of the policy. After maturity, the contract provides for various alternative ways in which the proceeds may be paid to the designated beneficiaries. These "settlement" options

[3] See Chapters 25 and 26 for an explanation of the interdependence between expenses and cash values.

TABLE 6-2. Surrender Values for $10,000 Ordinary Life Issued at Male Age 35

(1958 CSO Table and 2½ Per Cent Interest)

Number of Years Policy Has Been in Force	Cash or Loan Value	Paid-up Insurance	Extended Term Insurance (CET Table)	
			Years	Days
1	—	—	0	0
2	—	$ 10	0	25
3	$ 170	380	4	38
4	340	740	6	363
5	510	1,100	9	47
6	690	1,440	10	268
7	870	1,780	11	354
8	1,040	2,100	12	338
9	1,230	2,420	13	245
10	1,410	2,720	14	91
11	1,600	3,020	14	252
12	1,780	3,310	15	8
13	1,970	3,590	15	93
14	2,160	3,860	15	150
15	2,350	4,120	15	183
16	2,540	4,380	15	194
17	2,740	4,620	15	186
18	2,930	4,860	15	162
19	3,120	5,090	15	124
20	3,320	5,310	15	72
Age 60	4,280	6,300	14	60
Age 65	5,210	7,130	12	310

will be discussed in Chapter 15. Before maturity a number of contract provisions permit adjustment to meet changing circumstances. For example, the nonforfeiture options permit the insured to surrender the policy for its then cash value or stop premium payments and accept the equivalent in the form of a paid-up whole-life policy for a reduced amount or term insurance for the full face amount for a limited period of time. Participating policies provide for dividend options which give the insured the option of taking dividends in cash, applying them to reduce premiums, applying them to purchase paid-up units of whole-life insurance, or accumulating them at interest. Again, most policies permit the insured, subject to certain conditions, to exchange the ordinary life policy for another form of life insurance. Provision is also made for the insured to assign his policy to the company as collateral and borrow up to the amount of the cash value, if he so desires. Surrender values can also be used to purchase an annuity or retirement income. Current contracts of many companies specifically give the insured the right to take the cash value in the form of a life income purchased at net rates. Other companies will grant the privilege upon request. Many people purchase ordinary life insurance to protect their families during the child-rearing period, with the specific objective of using the cash values for their own retirements. These and many other contract provisions make this contract sufficiently flexible to enable the insured to meet changing needs and circumstances.

Disadvantage of Premium Payments for Life. The chief objection usually advanced against ordinary life insurance is the continued payment of the premium throughout life. In view of the flexibility of the ordinary life contract, however, this objection is more apparent than real. Thus, where dividend refunds are granted, this objection may, at the option of the insured, be obviated by allowing the annual dividends to accumulate with the company with a view to either shortening the premium-payment period or hastening the maturity of the contract. Under the first option the contract becomes a paid-up policy for the full amount after a period of years—thus requiring no further premium payments—the insurance, however, being still payable at death only.

The cash surrender value and other options allowed under an ordinary life policy may also, under certain circumstances, make desirable a discontinuance of premium payments. Changing circumstances may cause the insured to desire the taking of any one of three important options customarily allowed by the companies. If the policy has served its protective purpose and the insured is satisfied that the change in his circumstances is such as no longer to require insurance protection and does not wish the full face value of the policy for legacies or bequests, he may surrender the policy to the company for its cash value. Or, instead of taking the cash value, the insured may choose the option of stopping premium payments and taking a paid-up policy for a reduced amount, payable upon death to his estate or designated beneficiary. The amount of paid-up insurance which the companies grant after the policy has been in force a specified number of years is indicated in the third column of Table 6–2, and represents the amount of insurance that can be purchased at the then-attained age with a net single premium equal to the surrender value. The amounts, it will be observed, are very considerable in the later years, the face value of the paid-up insurance granted on the $10,000 policy, after it has been in force twenty-five years, being $6,300.

Lastly, it may happen that the policyholder contracts some fatal disease or meets with some accident which incapacitates him for the earning of future premiums. Under such circumstances the necessity for insurance is greater than ever, and the policyholder is allowed to avail himself of the option of "extended term insurance," which means that he can, without further premium payments, enjoy the full benefit of his original policy for a designated number of years and days. This option may also be chosen, even though the ability to pay premiums continues, when the insured is satisfied that his physical condition is such as to prove fatal before the expiration of the term during which extended term insurance is granted.[4] The duration of the term of extended term insurance as allowed by the companies will again depend upon the cash value of the policy, which is used as a single premium to purchase term insurance at the then-attained age. The respective periods of time on the $10,000 policy, used for purposes of illustration, are shown in the fourth and fifth columns of Table 6–2. Thus, it will be observed, for example, that after this policy has been in force nineteen years it may be extended for its full face value, without further premium payments, for a term of fifteen years and one hundred and twenty-four days.

Limited-Payment Policies

Under the terms of limited-payment policies the face of the policy is not payable until death, but premiums are charged for a limited number of years only, after which the policy becomes paid up for its full amount. The limitation may be expressed in terms of the *number* of annual premiums or the *age* to which annual premiums must be paid.

Thus, instead of continuing until death, premium payments may be fixed at almost any number of years, that is, from one to thirty, or even more. Customarily the payments cease after ten, fifteen, or twenty years, but life policies providing for twenty-five or thirty premiums are not uncommon. The greater the number of premium payments, the more closely the contract approaches the ordinary life form. If premiums are limited to twenty years, for example, the policy is known as a twenty-payment life policy. Companies also make available contracts which limit premiums on the basis of a terminal age, such as 60, 65, 70, or even higher. The objective is to appeal to the buyer with the idea of paying up the policy during his working lifetime. Thus, a policy which requires premiums to age 65 would be known as a life paid up at 65 policy. It should be noted that a thirty-payment life and a life paid up at 65 policy both issued at age 35 would have the same premium, since actually both whole-life contracts have payments limited to thirty years.

Since limited-payment policies require the payment of premiums during a term which is less than the term of the contract, it follows that the annual level premium under this plan must be larger than that necessary when premium payments continue throughout the life of the policy. The purpose

---

[4] It should be noted that the disability waiver of premium benefit may make this option inappropriate under some circumstances. See pp. 196–197.

of the plan is to have the policyholder pay an extra amount annually during the fixed premium-paying period so that after the termination of this period the policy may remain in force and be carried to successful completion without further financial obligation on the part of the insured. Thus, in the case of a limited-payment policy, the ten, fifteen, or twenty premiums called for by the contract represent a sum which is sufficiently larger than the aggregate amount required during the same period for an ordinary life plan to enable the company, together with compound interest earnings at an assumed rate, to carry the policy to its maturity without further charges upon the insured. Although the mathematics underlying the computation of net premiums on the limited-payment plan is referred to in Chapter 23, the manner of applying the principle in practice may be illustrated by the following nonparticipating rates[5] taken from the rate book of the company already used for purposes of illustration in the two preceding chapters. The rates presented are those charged by the company at various selected ages for a whole-life policy on the ten-, fifteen-, and twenty-payment plans. The rates for the plan with premiums payable for life (ordinary life) are also given, in the second column, so that a comparison may be made.

TABLE 6-3. Nonparticipating Annual Premium Rates
per $1,000 Whole-Life Policies for a $10,000 Policy
with Varying Periods of Premium Payments

Age	Whole-Life	20 Years	Life Paid-up at 65
25	$13.45	$22.29	$14.89
30	15.83	25.12	17.99
35	18.99	28.61	22.40
40	22.97	32.65	28.35
45	27.94	37.47	37.47
50	34.06	42.88	51.99
55	41.93	49.46	80.92
60	52.83	58.46	—
65	67.46	70.79	—

An examination of Table 6–3 shows that the fewer the number of premium payments, the larger each payment will be. Thus at age 25 a whole-life policy with premiums payable until the policy becomes a claim will cost $13.45 in this company. If, however, the insured prefers to pay for the policy in installments to age 65, each premium will amount to $14.89; if

[5] These rates are used merely for illustrative purposes. It should be noted that the gross premiums charged by different companies vary somewhat. Moreover, in participating companies the gross premiums are considerably higher and are reduced at the end of the year through the distribution of dividend refunds.

paid in twenty installments, the premium will be $22.29. If the premiums were spread over ten and fifteen years, the annual premiums would be still higher.

Owing to th˜ higher premiums, the limited-payment plan is not well adapted to those whose income is small and whose need for insurance protection is so great as to require emphasis on the amount of protection rather than the accumulation of a fund with the company, especially when there is reason to believe that the income out of which premiums may conveniently be paid will be much greater in the future than it is at present. Furthermore, many policyholders, amply able to pay premiums, may feel that a policy requiring payments for life will fit their needs better than a limited-payment contract, since it enables them to use the difference in the premiums to better advantage than if they were allowed to accumulate with an insurance company.

On the other hand, the disadvantage of higher premiums is offset by the availability of a larger savings or investment element. The higher premiums produce greater cash values which are available for use in an emergency and at retirement. There is no presumptive financial advantage of one form over the other. All limited-payment policies contain the same nonforfeiture options, dividends options, settlement options, and other features of the ordinary life insurance policy which provide flexibility for the insured. It is important to remember that all permanent forms of life insurance are made up of protection and savings, and the major distinction between the many plans is the relative importance of these two elements.

The one-pay or single-premium whole-life policy is an extreme form of limited-payment life insurance. Naturally, under this form the savings element is the predominating feature and the protection element is substantially less than the face of the policy. Consequently, such contracts are purchased primarily for investment purposes. The other extreme is represented by the ordinary life insurance policy where premiums are payable until the maturity of the contract. The normal limited-payment contracts vary between these extremes. The five- and ten-pay life policies are closely allied to the single-premium policies, whereas a policy paid up at age 85 is, for all practical purposes, the equivalent of an ordinary life policy. As the number of premium payments increases, the annual premium and, consequently, the cash value or savings element becomes correspondingly smaller. The choice depends upon circumstances and personal preference.

Graph 6–1 shows the terminal reserve values when whole-life insurance, sold at male age 35, is paid for by means of a single premium, annual premiums covering ten years, annual premiums covering twenty years, and annual premiums payable for the whole of life. When a company sells a whole-life policy at male age 35, to be paid for according to one of these premium plans, the law requires that the proper reserve values be maintained. Such values represent the excess of premium payments over the cost of protection and, hence, may be viewed properly as representing sav-

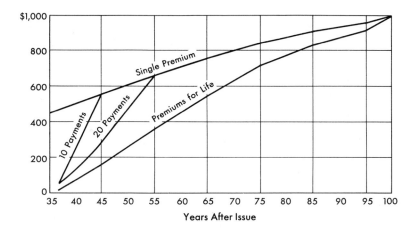

GRAPH 6-1.   Terminal reserve values per $1,000, male age 35, whole-life insurance, 1958 CSO Table and 2½ per cent interest.

ings belonging to the insured. The graph also illustrates what has already been explained, that is, the size of the savings fund represented by the reserve value varies inversely with the length of the premium-paying period. Thus, the ordinary life plan with payments for life has the smallest savings fund, and the single-premium plan, which involves only one payment, has the largest of all. It should be noted, however, that after the premium payments cease under the two limited-payment plans, the savings in each instance equal those under the single-premium plan. This must be the case, since after any limited-payment period expires, the company will not receive any more funds from the insured to help it carry the policy until death matures it as a claim.

OTHER FORMS OF WHOLE-LIFE

Modified Life Policies

A *modified life* policy is an ordinary life contract under which premiums are redistributed so that they are lower than normal during the first three or five years and higher than normal thereafter. Thus, one company under a "Modified Five" may set the premium during the first five years so that it will double thereafter. Other redistributions are also used. During the preliminary period, the premium is always something more than the level term premium for such a period, but less than the ordinary life premium at date of issue. Logically, after the preliminary period, the premium is always something larger than the ordinary life premium at the date of issue but less than the ordinary life premium at the insured's attained age at the end of the preliminary period. Regardless of the redistribution arrangement utilized, the company receives the actuarial equivalent of the regular ordinary life premiums.

A variation of the modified life is the *graded premium* ordinary life. In such a contract the premium advances *each year* during the preliminary period (usually five years) and then remains level. This is, of course, simply another premium redistribution which is the actuarial equivalent of the regular ordinary life premiums.

Modified life insurance policies are designed to overcome resistance of life insurance prospects to the premium outlay necessary to purchase permanent life insurance.[6] It is appropriate for the young family man or those completing their education whose need for protection is great but whose income is insufficient to afford regular ordinary life. The policy avoids some of the disadvantages of pure level term insurance, and enables a young man to embark on a program of permanent life insurance with some recognition of the fact that his income and, consequently, his ability to pay will normally increase each year.

It should be noted at this point that level term insurance with an automatic conversion feature may be considered an extreme case of premium redistribution. Under this arrangement no part of the premium goes toward savings and, consequently, at the end of the preliminary period the premium would simply be the ordinary life premium at the insured's attained age. This premium would, of course, be higher than the premium under the usual modified life plan after the preliminary period.

Under all modified life plans the cash values are smaller in the earlier years than they would be normally and are not payable at as early a date, but in all other respects the contract is usually identical with the ordinary life policy.

Joint-Life Insurance

Although the great majority of life insurance is written on the life of one person (single-life insurance), it is theoretically possible to write life insurance on any number of lives. Where a contract is written on two or more lives, it is known as a joint-life policy. The term *joint-life* policy promises to pay the face amount in the event of the *first* death among the two or more lives covered under the contract. If the face is payable upon the death

---

[6] Actually, one of the first modified life policies, the "Modified 3," introduced in 1928 by the Prudential, was intended to meet the competition of nonparticipating contracts which had lower initial premiums than the participating ordinary life policy. See E. C. May and W. C. Oursler, *The Prudential* (New York: Doubleday & Co., Inc., 1950), pp. 191–192.

of the *last* of two or more lives, it is known as a *last-survivor* policy. Neither of these policies are written in any volume, but the joint-life policy has been utilized to some extent.

The joint-life policy may be written on any whole-life or endowment plan, but it is virtually never written on a term basis. The premium for a given face amount of insurance would be smaller than the total of the separate premiums involved with individual policies each for the same face amount. But it must be remembered that following the death of one of the lives insured, the contract ceases, and the survivors would have no further protection.

PREFERRED RISK AND "SPECIAL" WHOLE-LIFE POLICIES

For many years some companies have issued so-called preferred risk policies with reduced premiums under selection standards which were intended to produce a better-than-normal mortality experience. In recent years there has been greatly increased activity in this area, and, in addition, other factors are now considered in determining the amount of reduction in the premium. Due to the fact that more is now involved than simply selecting superior risks, it has become the practice to refer to such policies as "specials."

Usually on the ordinary life plan, specials today are offered only (1) in a minimum amount (usually $5,000 to $25,000), (2) to preferred risks, or (3) both. These factors provide the main justification for the reduction in premium which in some cases is substantial.

The purpose of the minimum amount is to reduce the expense rate per $1,000 of insurance. Many items of expense do not vary directly with the premium, such as some administration expenses, medical examination fee, inspection report fee, servicing of a policy, premium collection processes, and so forth. Therefore, if the average size policy can be increased, the expense rate per $1,000 will be lower, and consequently, at least part of this savings will be passed on to the buyer who is willing to buy a larger policy.

Even those expenses which do vary directly with the premium, such as premium taxes and commissions, produce an additional savings when applied to a lower gross premium.

Other factors which affect the expense savings in specials of some companies include (1) an actual reduction in the agent's commission rate for such policies, (2) the *requirement* of an annual premium to reduce collection costs, (3) inclusion of less favorable settlement options in the contract, and (4) the possibility of a lower lapse ratio.

The "preferred risk" theory for lower rates on large contracts was widely used several years ago but is disappearing with the advent of specials based almost solely on size. The savings developed through superior selection standards depend upon the nature of the standard imposed. A large policy will always be medically examined whereas the smaller contract may not; therefore, the large contracts usually result in better mortality in the first few years. The potential savings involved may be substantial, but the only true test is the *actual* mortality experience. Anticipated mortality savings may or may not develop depending on a number of factors. Some quarters feel that the extreme competitive situation will not permit companies to hold the line from an underwriting standpoint. It is difficult to convince an agent, after he has sold a large case on the basis of a "special" to a man who would be standard for another plan, that the preferred risk contract cannot be issued because of a few extra mortality points assessed from an underwriting standpoint.

Those favoring the issuance of specials argue that it is only equitable to give a benefit in the form of reduced premiums to a policyholder who takes out a policy of such size that its expense rate is lower than average.

On the other hand, there is no magic in a minimum face amount of $5,000, $10,000, or $25,000, and logically, it can be argued that all life insurance premiums should be graded by size of risk (per $1,000) above a certain minimum. If there is an expense savings for policies averaging $5,000, why doesn't a $10,000 or $50,000 policy deserve an even greater discount? If the principle of granting rate reductions due to expense savings or mortality savings is valid, it should be extended to all kinds of policies.

As a result, an increasing number of companies are adopting the principle of grading premiums by size of policy as one of the features of their special, and a number of companies have applied the principle across the board to all plans and all ages.

The economics of the situation, because of increased complication in the operation of the business, naturally limits the extent to which equity can be attained. Unless the principle is extended to all forms of policies and graded by size of risk above an established minimum, the result is simply to substitute one form of discrimination for another.

Regardless of the soundness of the reasons advanced pro and con, the extremely competitive situation existing currently has resulted in a tremendous increase in the number of companies offering specials. In addition, it is anticipated that an increasing number of companies will accept the principle of gradation of premium by size of policy and apply it across the board to all contracts and all ages.

It should be remembered that total incurred expenses are the same, assuming the same volume of business and average size policy, and what is involved here is *allocating* expenses between various classes of policyholders. As expenses are reallocated to theoretically refined classifications, the cost of smaller policies must go up if the cost of larger policies goes down. The total expenses are the same. It should be noted, however, that if such reallocation leads to a higher average size policy or significantly greater volume of business, unit costs related to fixed expenses could decline for all policies.

VARIABLE LIFE INSURANCE

Inflation in our economy has become so accepted a fact of life in the minds of most people that it seems to be becoming the controlling influence in how individuals organize their financial affairs. In response to this perceived need, the life insurance business is developing an insurance product that has a guaranteed minimum death benefit and the potential of increased insurance benefits without necessarily requiring the spending of more premium dollars. In choosing such a variable benefit policy, in lieu of the traditional fixed-benefit policy, the policyholder will obtain a contract right to have the net investment return in excess of the assumed rate of return applied to increase his policy benefits. On the other hand, he will give up the guarantee of cash values and the elements of a fixed-benefit policy that depend on guaranteed cash values, specifically, the minimum nonforfeiture benefits and the traditional policy loan. The advent of variable life insurance has potential of working far-reaching changes in the life insurance business.

Product Design

Variable life insurance includes both an *index-linked* and an *equity-linked* product. The index-linked product is a contract under which the face varies according to some published index, such as the consumer price index. Under equity-linked contracts, the face value fluctuates with the investment performance of the reserve, which consists principally of common stocks. Equity based variable life insurance products may also be classified as *variable premium* or *fixed premium*. A variable premium plan has been on the market in Holland for fifteen years. Fixed premium equity-linked plans appeared in Great Britain about five years ago, and more recently in Canada. Interest in equity based insurance for the U.S. was sparked by the publication in November, 1969, of a paper by three New York Life actuaries.[7]

[7] Robert A. Beck, "Variable Life Insurance: A Perspective on Issues and Current Developments," *Proceedings of the National Conference on Variable Life Insurance* (Philadelphia, Pa.: Insurance Department, University of Pennsylvania, March, 1971), p. 3.

This paper considered variable life insurance under which (1) premiums were fixed at issue, (2) the assets backing up the policy were invested in common stocks, and (3) the benefits varied according to the investment results of the stock portfolio.

Review of Dutch Design.[8]   Under this design, the entire reserve for the variable life insurance policy is held in a separate account whose assets would be invested primarily in equities. The face amount varies at specific intervals (e.g., daily, monthly, or yearly). The face amount for any particular period is equal to the face amount for the prior period multiplied by an investment adjustment factor. The investment adjustment factor reflects the relationship between (a) the actual net investment experience of the separate account (adjusted where appropriate for taxes and other charges made by the insurance company) and (b) the interest rate assumed for the calculation of net premiums and reserves.

In order to maintain actuarial balance under this design, it is necessary to have variable premiums as well as variable benefits. The actual amounts of premium are determined by using the same investment adjustment factors that are used to determine face amounts. In other words, face amounts and premiums vary in exactly the same proportion; if the face amount has become twice the initial face amount due to favorable investment experience then the premium currently payable is twice the initial premium, and so on. The basic actuarial theory for the variable premium Dutch design, under which all premiums and benefits are expressed in terms of units instead of dollars is, of course, exactly the same as the basic actuarial theory for corresponding fixed dollar life insurance policies.

Despite the appealing basic simplicity of the variable premium Dutch design, there is a widespread feeling among actuaries and other insurance executives in the United States that the variable premium feature may prove to be a critical disadvantage from a marketing standpoint. Accordingly, most of the variable life insurance designs that have recently been discussed in the United States involve fixed rather than variable premiums.

New York Life Fixed Premium Design.[9]   The New York Life fixed premium benefit design was originally proposed in a paper written by John C. Fraser, Walter N. Miller, and Charles M. Sternhell and presented at the annual meeting of the Society of Actuaries in November, 1969. A basic feature that is common to both the New York Life design and the Dutch design is the fact that the entire reserve is held in a separate account whose assets would be invested primarily in equities.

[8] Charles M. Sternhell, "The New York Life Benefit Design and Its Practical Implementation," *Proceedings of the National Conference on Variable Life Insurance* (Philadelphia, Pa.: Insurance Department, University of Pennsylvania, March, 1971), pp. 70–74.

[9] *Ibid.*

A basic difference between the New York Life design and the Dutch design is the fact that, under the New York Life design, the face amount for any particular period is equal to the face amount for the prior period multiplied by two factors instead of by only one factor as under the Dutch design. The two factors involved in the New York Life design are: (1) an investment adjustment factor which is the same as that used under the Dutch design, and (2) a premium adjustment factor which reflects the fact that fixed, level premiums are payable instead of variable premiums.

Under the New York Life benefit design, reserves per $1,000 of actual face amount for a variable life insurance policy are exactly the same as reserves per $1,000 of face amount for a corresponding fixed-benefit policy. This important feature is also present in the variable premium Dutch design but is not present in any fixed premium design other than the New York Life design. This feature is significant because it helps to make the variable life insurance policy resemble as closely as possible the traditional fixed-benefit policy that agents are used to selling.

Illustrative Results Under Dutch and New York Life Designs. Table 6–4 shows illustrative face amounts and net premiums for a variable whole life policy with an initial face amount of $1,000 issued to a male age 55. Illustrative figures are shown for four different levels of assumed net annual investment experience of the separate account (after adjustment for any charges made by the company against separate account assets); namely, 0 per cent, 3 per cent, 6 per cent, and 9 per cent. Net premiums and reserves for each type of policy are calculated on the basis of the *1958 CSO Mortality Table* and an assumed interest rate of 3 per cent.

The first four columns of Table 6–4 show illustrative results for a policy of the Dutch design. The second column shows that the face amounts and net premiums will remain level if the actual net investment experience of the separate account is always equal to the 3 per cent assumed interest rate. The first column illustrates how the face amounts and premiums would go down if the actual net investment experience were 0 per cent, and the third and fourth columns show how the face amounts and premiums would go up if the actual net investment experience were 6 per cent or 9 per cent.

Under any fixed premium design, there must obviously be a dampening effect on the amounts of insurance that can be provided as compared with those provided under the variable premium Dutch design. The last four columns of Table 6–4 indicate that in all cases the face amounts for the New York Life fixed premium design are closer to the initial face amount than is the case for the variable premium Dutch design. If the net investment experience is less favorable than the assumed interest rate of 3 per cent, the New York Life design produces higher face amounts than the Dutch design. Conversely, if the net investment experience is more favor-

TABLE 6-4. Illustrative Face Amounts for Variable Benefit Whole-Life
Policy with an Initial Face Amount of $1,000 Issued to a Male
Age 55 Where Net Annual Investment Performance of
Separate Account is 0%, 3%, 6%, or 9%
*(Net level premiums and reserves based on 1958 CSO Table,
3% interest and traditional functions)*

End of Policy Year	Variable Premium (Dutch design) Per cent				Fixed Premium (New York Life design) Per cent			
	0	3	6	9	0	3	6	9
1	$971	$1,000	$1,029	$1,058	$971	$1,000	$1,029	$1,058
2	943	1,000	1,059	1,120	959	1,000	1,041	1,084
3	915	1,000	1,090	1,185	948	1,000	1,054	1,110
4	888	1,000	1,122	1,254	937	1,000	1,067	1,137
5	863	1,000	1,154	1,327	926	1,000	1,080	1,165
6	837	1,000	1,188	1,405	915	1,000	1,093	1,194
7	813	1,000	1,223	1,486	904	1,000	1,106	1,224
8	789	1,000	1,258	1,573	893	1,000	1,120	1,255
9	766	1,000	1,295	1,665	883	1,000	1,134	1,287
10	744	1,000	1,333	1,762	873	1,000	1,148	1,320
11	722	1,000	1,371	1,864	863	1,000	1,162	1,355
12	701	1,000	1,411	1,973	853	1,000	1,177	1,391
13	681	1,000	1,452	2,088	843	1,000	1,192	1,428
14	661	1,000	1,495	2,209	834	1,000	1,207	1,466
15	642	1,000	1,538	2,338	825	1,000	1,222	1,505
16	623	1,000	1,583	2,474	816	1,000	1,237	1,545
17	605	1,000	1,629	2,618	807	1,000	1,252	1,586
18	587	1,000	1,677	2,771	799	1,000	1,268	1,628
19	570	1,000	1,725	2,932	791	1,000	1,284	1,672
20	554	1,000	1,776	3,103	783	1,000	1,300	1,717
21	538	1,000	1,827	3,284	775	1,000	1,316	1,763
22	522	1,000	1,881	3,475	767	1,000	1,332	1,811
23	507	1,000	1,935	3,678	760	1,000	1,348	1,860
24	492	1,000	1,992	3,892	753	1,000	1,364	1,911
25	478	1,000	2,050	4,118	746	1,000	1,381	1,963
26	464	1,000	2,110	4,358	739	1,000	1,398	2,016
27	450	1,000	2,171	4,612	732	1,000	1,415	2,071
28	437	1,000	2,234	4,881	725	1,000	1,432	2,128
29	424	1,000	2,299	5,165	719	1,000	1,449	2,186
30	412	1,000	2,366	5,466	713	1,000	1,466	2,245

TABLE 6-4. (cont'd.)

End of Policy Year	Variable Premium (Dutch design) Per cent				Fixed Premium (New York Life design) Per cent			
	0	3	6	9	0	3	6	9
31	400	1,000	2,435	5,785	707	1,000	1,483	2,306
32	388	1,000	2,506	6,121	701	1,000	1,500	2,369
33	377	1,000	2,579	6,478	695	1,000	1,517	2,433
34	366	1,000	2,654	6,855	690	1,000	1,535	2,499
35	355	1,000	2,732	7,255	685	1,000	1,553	2,567
36	345	1,000	2,811	7,677	680	1,000	1,571	2,637
37	335	1,000	2,893	8,125	675	1,000	1,589	2,709
38	325	1,000	2,977	8,598	670	1,000	1,607	2,783
39	316	1,000	3,064	9,099	665	1,000	1,625	2,859
40	307	1,000	3,153	9,629	660	1,000	1,643	2,937
41	298	1,000	3,245	10,190	655	1,000	1,662	3,018
42	289	1,000	3,340	10,783	650	1,000	1,681	3,102
43	281	1,000	3,437	11,411	645	1,000	1,700	3,189
44	272	1,000	3,537	12,076	640	1,000	1,720	3,279
45	264	1,000	3,640	12,780	635	1,000	1,740	3,373

Net Premiums for Selected Policy Years

	0	3	6	9	0	3	6	9
1	$39.09	$39.09	$39.09	$39.09	$39.09	$39.09	$39.09	$39.09
5	34.71	39.09	43.86	49.02	39.09	39.09	39.09	39.09
10	29.94	39.09	50.62	65.08	39.09	39.09	39.09	39.09
15	25.84	39.09	58.44	86.35	39.09	39.09	39.09	39.09
20	22.28	39.09	67.43	114.61	39.09	39.09	39.09	39.09
25	19.23	39.09	77.87	152.14	39.09	39.09	39.09	39.09
30	16.57	39.09	89.87	201.90	39.09	39.09	39.09	39.09
35	14.31	39.09	103.74	267.96	39.09	39.09	39.09	39.09
40	12.35	39.09	119.77	355.68	39.09	39.09	39.09	39.09
45	10.63	39.09	138.26	472.05	39.09	39.09	39.09	39.09

able than the assumed interest rate of 3 per cent, the New York Life design produces lower face amounts than the Dutch design.

There are, of course, other fixed premium design possibilities. The New York Life actuaries believe that variable life insurance will be sold primarily as an insurance product rather than as an investment vehicle, and therefore believe that their design has favorable characteristics in that it places relatively more emphasis on the death benefit aspect of the policy than other fixed premium designs.

Practical Implementation

There are many specific decisions involved in implementing a particular approach to variable life insurance. For example, questions relating to the frequency of adjustments in face amount, cash surrender values, nonforfeiture benefits, policy loan provision, grace period, reinstatement provision, dividend options, settlement options, compensation to agents, and pricing policies are complex questions.

One of the basic questions upon which the rate of development of this life insurance product depends is whether this product will be considered a "security" for regulatory purposes or an "insurance product." Variable annuities legally have been considered "securities." In the case of variable life insurance, the industry's approach[10] to the SEC has been to define a class of policies over which the Commission was asked not to assert jurisdiction under the Federal security laws. This class was proposed to have the following four basic characteristics designed to assure that their insurance function and purpose is predominant and that they meet the needs of persons who are interested in protection:

(1) *The contract must provide lifetime insurance coverage.* This means only policies that provide "whole-life" coverage. This characteristic excludes all endowment policies but does not exclude limited payment life policies. Whole-life policies are believed to be purchased primarily for protection against the death of the insured for the benefit of his beneficiaries. Endowment policies may well be purchased by persons with both investment and insurance objectives.

(2) *The contract must be issued for an initial stated amount of death benefit and must guarantee payment of a death benefit at least equal to such amount.* Several companies have made extensive analyses which have persuaded them that they can incorporate in a variable life insurance contract a guarantee that, whatever the investment performance, the death benefit will not be less than the death benefit payable at the outset of the policy. Thus, an investment risk that is neither illusory nor trivial but is of real significance to the purchaser will be assumed by the insurance company. The purchaser is thereby assured that no matter how adverse the investment experience of the separate account, his beneficiaries will nonetheless receive not less than the initial coverage he purchased.

(3) *The amount payable upon the death of the insured in any year must be no less than a minimum multiple of the gross premium payable in that year by a person who meets standard underwriting requirements.* Under

---

[10] Ralph L. Gustin, Jr., "Federal Regulatory Aspects of Variable Life Insurance," *Proceedings of the National Conference on Variable Life Insurance* (Philadelphia, Pa.: Insurance Department, University of Pennsylvania, March, 1971), pp. 21–24.

this characteristic the multiple would vary with the issue age and sex of the insured. For example, the premium for a 60-year-old man is much higher than it is for a 20-year-old man for the same amount of insurance. The higher the multiple, the greater the restriction upon the kind of policy that can be sold. Without this requirement the investment element could be greatly increased either by charging premiums which are much higher than is customary and allowing the excess amounts, plus the investment results, to emerge in the form of increased benefits or by providing that the premiums under a lifetime policy are to be paid over a comparatively short period, such as a five- or ten-year payment whole-life policy. In effect this characteristic limits the amount of premium that may be charged for a given amount of death benefit.

The Committee offered to submit a fully developed set of multiples whenever the Commission deems appropriate.

(4) *The entire contract must be a life insurance contract subject to regulation under the state insurance laws, including required approvals by state insurance commissioners.* State regulation will assure that the benefits under the policy will be actuarially supported by adequate reserves and underlying assets and that the issuing company is subject to supervision as a life insurance company.

The industry hopes that variable life insurance policies that have these prior characteristics will necessarily retain their character as contracts of insurance and should be regulated as insurance contracts. Company interest and capacity to move ahead in making variable life insurance available in the United States depend to a considerable extent upon the SEC decision in this regard.

Endowment Insurance | 7

NATURE OF ENDOWMENT INSURANCE

THE TERM AND whole-life policies discussed in the preceding chapters provide for the payment of the full amount of the policy only in the event of death. Endowment policies, on the contrary, provide for not only the payment of the face of the policy upon the death of the insured during a fixed term of years, but also the payment of the full face amount at the end of said term *if the insured be living*. Whereas policies payable only in the event of death are taken out chiefly for the benefit of others, endowment policies, although affording protection to others against the death of the insured during the fixed term, usually revert to the insured if he survives the endowment period. Such policies have therefore become popular in recent years as a convenient means of accumulating a fund which will afterwards become available for the use of the policyholders.

There are two ways of looking at endowment insurance, that is, (1) the so-called mathematical concept, and (2) the economic concept.

Mathematical Concept

There are two promises made by the company under endowment insurance: (1) to pay the face amount in the event the insured dies during the endowment period, and (2) to pay the face amount in the event the insured survives to the end of the endowment period. The first promise is obviously identical with that made under a level term policy for an equivalent amount and period. The second introduces a new concept, the "pure endowment." Just as a company may actuarially estimate how many will die, it can also estimate the number who will live to attain a certain age. Thus, a *pure endowment* is defined as a contract which promises to pay the face amount *only* if the insured be living at the end of a specified period, nothing being paid in case of prior death. This contract is rarely sold separately since few people are willing to risk the loss of all premiums paid

106

in the event of death before the end of the endowment period. In order to provide a death benefit during the endowment period, only term insurance for the same period need be added. It can be seen that these two elements, (1) level term insurance and (2) a pure endowment, will together meet the two promises made under endowment insurance.

Economic Concept

Although the above analysis is correct and convenient for purposes of mathematical computation, there is another and perhaps more logical and meaningful analysis of endowment insurance, the *economic analysis*. This analysis of endowment insurance divides endowment insurance into two parts, namely, *decreasing term insurance* and *increasing investment*. The investment part of the contract is not considered, and in fact is not, a pure endowment, all of which is lost in case of death before the end of the term. Rather it is a savings accumulation which is available to the insured at any time after the first year or two, through surrender of or loan upon the policy. This investment feature is supplemented by term insurance, which is not, however, level term insurance for $1,000 throughout the term of the contract, but insurance for a constantly decreasing amount, which, when added to the investment accumulation at the date of death, will make the amount payable under the policy equal to its face, or $1,000. The insurance portion of the contract, therefore, is for a decreasing amount, being almost $1,000 in the early years of the contract and gradually decreasing throughout the term. Thus, if at a particular time a $1,000 endowment policy has an investment accumulation of $150, the insured will be protected against death by $850 of decreasing term insurance, but when the accumulation reaches $900 there will remain decreasing term insurance for only the difference between $1,000 and $900, or $100.

Finally, when the investment portion of the contract reaches 100 per cent of the face of the policy at the time of its maturity, the decreasing term insurance will have declined to zero. At any particular time, the accumulated savings fund on the one side and the decreasing term insurance on the other will always equal the face of the contract. In other words, there is no apparent forfeiture in the event of death. Upon death, the company pays to the policyholder's estate or to his heirs the face amount of the policy, which is made up of (1) the investment standing to his credit, and (2) decreasing term insurance equal to the difference between the investment accumulation and the face of the contract. The purpose of the decreasing term insurance is always to equal that portion of the policy which the policyholder intended to save if he had lived, but which he failed to save because of premature death. The premium paid for the policy may, in view of this explanation, be divided into three parts—one for the investment accumulation, another in payment for the cost of the decreasing term insurance, and still another (a comparatively small part) to meet the cost of managing the installment plan of the investment and other expenses incident to the insurance business.

The decreasing term insurance and increasing investment analysis may be understood better after a study of Graph 7–1, which shows the reserve values which the law requires under a thirty-year endowment policy issued at male age 35 and paid for by four different premium plans. The shorter the period over which premiums are to be paid for this type of policy, the larger the investment element represented by the reserve values at any particular time. As the investment increases, the protection decreases and, at the end of the endowment period, the investment element equals the face of the policy.

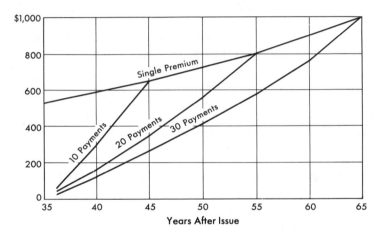

GRAPH 7-1.   Terminal reserve values per $1,000, male age 35, 30-year endowment insurance, 1958 CSO Table and 2½ per cent interest.

For each policy the amount above the graph or line equals the amount of term insurance at any given age, the amount below the graph or line equals the amount of reserve (or "investment") at the same age, and the sum of the two always equals $1,000 or face amount of the policy. Table 7–1 shows the increasing reserve or investment element and the decreasing term insurance or protection element on a thirty-year endowment insurance contract.

The above analysis, it should be noted, is equally applicable to whole-life policies with premiums payable for life, as well as to such policies under the various limited-payment plans. These contracts are also endowment insurance arrangements, although they are not customarily viewed in that manner. They are all investment policies to a stated extent. It is all a matter

TABLE 7-1. $1,000 Twenty-Year Endowment
Insurance, Male Age 35

(1958 CSO Table and 2½ Per Cent Interest)

End of Policy Year	Reserve Value	Net Amount at Risk
1	$ 13.57	$986.43
2	54.62	945.38
3	96.66	903.34
4	139.70	860.30
5	183.75	816.25
10	420.28	579.72
15	688.70	311.30
20	1,000.00	—

of the degree to which the installment investment plan is emphasized. As the reserve value—the investment side—of the contract increases, the death protection—the decreasing term insurance side—correspondingly decreases. On a whole-life policy the decreasing term insurance is reduced to zero at male age 100, when the investment side reaches 100 per cent of the face of the contract.

It might be worthwhile to note that permanent life insurance contracts have not always emphasized the increasing investment, decreasing term insurance concept. In the early days of the business there were no nonforfeiture values under life insurance contracts. If an individual were forced, because of inability to pay or otherwise, to cease premium payments under his contract, no return of any sort was available to him as a matter of contract. The contract promised to pay in the event of the occurrence of death or survival to a certain age, but if the contract were dropped prior to the occurrence of these contingencies, all premiums were considered fully earned, and the reserve or savings element was forfeited.[1] Actuaries, in calculating reserve values, also base their calculations on the mathematical concept because it is easier to work with pure endowment and term insurance mortality factors on a $1,000 basis than in a constantly changing amount. It was perfectly natural then to consider the mathematical interpretation the only valid explanation.

With the increasing emphasis on the living values of life insurance and because the economic approach is easier for the layman to understand and

---

[1] Some companies did allow a cash value, but even here the policy usually contained no provision for them so that the policyholder had no *right* to any surrender value. The values when allowed were small and generally were granted only if application was made within a short period after lapse. There was no *legal requirement* as to the allowance of a surrender value in any form until 1861, and no *legal requirement* for a *cash* surrender privilege until 1906.

produces identically the same results, the legal interpretation of the contract has been modified accordingly; similarly, the economic concept of all permanent forms of life insurance has become accepted as the more meaningful explanation. Both the mathematical and the economic concepts are sound, as one is the actuarial equivalent of the other. They are simply two different ways of looking at and of analyzing the same thing.

ENDOWMENT INSURANCE POLICIES

Types

An examination of the contracts issued by different companies shows many variations in the use of the endowment insurance principle. Such policies may be made payable in ten, fifteen, twenty, twenty-five, thirty, or more years, or the length of the term may be so arranged as to cause the policy to mature at certain ages, such as 60, 65, 70, and so forth. When the policy is written for a short term, its purpose is usually to combine immediate protection with heavy savings, whereas if written for a long term, or to mature at an advanced age, its object is usually to combine protection with old-age provision. Usually, the contracts are paid for by premiums (payable annually, semiannually, quarterly, or monthly) continuing throughout the term, but, if desired, the premiums may be paid on the limited-payment plan as, for example, a thirty-year endowment policy paid up in twenty years or an endowment at age 65 paid up in twenty years.

Besides the standard contracts, other applications of the endowment principle are sometimes made as, for example, in the case of the "retirement income" or "semi-endowments." In the case of the retirement income policy, it provides that the amount payable upon survival is greater than the face amount, and the amount payable at death is the face amount or cash value, whichever is greater.[2] The semi-endowment pays upon survival only half the sum payable in the event of death during the endowment period. Various kinds of "juvenile endowment policies" are also issued by certain companies. These include endowments maturing at specified ages for educational purposes. A return of premium benefit is offered which provides for the return of the premiums paid in the event of the child's death before reaching the endowment age. An extra benefit frequently added to juvenile endowments is a payor rider which, upon the death or disability of the premium payor, usually the father, provides that premium payments shall cease, the policy becoming fully paid in the event of death or the premiums waived during the parent's disability.

[2] See pp. 136–138.

Premiums Charged for Endowment Policies

Since the company's liability under an endowment policy involves not only payment of its face upon death but also payment of the full amount of the policy upon survival of the term, it follows that the annual premium on such policies is necessarily much higher, except for the very long endowment periods where the rate is only slightly higher than that charged on an ordinary life policy. An examination of Table 7–2 of nonparticipating rates

TABLE 7-2. Nonparticipating Annual Premium Rates per $1,000 Endowment Insurance Policies for $10,000 Policy with Varying Endowment Periods

Age	20 Years	Endowment at Age 65	Ordinary Life
25	$43.81	$ 18.25	$13.45
30	44.04	22.13	15.83
35	44.66	27.79	18.99
40	45.76	35.64	22.97
45	47.47	47.47	27.94
50	49.90	65.08	34.06
55	53.67	101.60	41.93
60	60.09	—	52.83
65	—	—	67.46

(charged by the same company whose rates were used for purposes of illustration in the preceding chapters) shows this to be especially true when the endowment period is a short one (e.g., endowment at 60 issued at age 50). The significant difference indicated here is due chiefly to the necessity for accumulating more rapidly the investment portion of the endowment policy in order to have it equal the full face value at the end of the term. In previous chapters we saw that the cash value of the $10,000 ordinary life policy at male age 35, used for illustrative purposes, was $3,320 after the policy had been in force twenty years whereas, for the same policy on the twenty-payment plan, the corresponding cash value is $6,250. The $10,000 twenty-year endowment policy, however, must, according to its definition, have a value of $10,000 at the end of the twenty-year period, and the difference between this value and the values noted for the other two policies must be obtained by the company through a higher premium.

In participating insurance the gross premiums will be somewhat higher, to be reduced annually by dividend distributions.

USES OF ENDOWMENT INSURANCE

The endowment insurance contract serves as an effective vehicle to accumulate a specific sum of money over a period of time with the savings program protected by insurance against the contingency of premature death. As with all permanent life insurance contracts, the endowment insurance policy provides excellent investment management of the funds being accumulated, and the semi-compulsory nature of the premium serves as an incentive to saving.

The real function of endowment insurance is not to yield an investment return larger than is obtainable from other gilt-edged investment plans, but rather to furnish a fairly remunerative means of inculcating the savings instinct and to afford a sure method of providing against old age or some other specific contingency by accumulating a definite sum of money within a definite time.

Reference has been made several times to the fact that the saving of a competence involves the time necessary to save and that life insurance affords the only known method of protecting a person against the possibility, owing to untimely death, of not being able to accumulate the desired amount. Were it not for the uncertainty of life and the inability of most people to carry out their resolution to adhere to a definite plan of saving, the accumulation of an estate could readily be accomplished by the deposit of certain sums at regular intervals. But, as we have seen, the effort to save a fixed amount is confronted by two dangers: (1) death or disability before there has been time to save the desired amount, and (2) failure of the individual to continue his plan of savings or to keep intact that which may already have been accumulated.

Endowment insurance, with waiver of premium for disability, like other kinds of investment insurance, is designed to protect the individual from both dangers. Let us assume that it is the purpose of a person aged 25 to accumulate $20,000 during the next forty years. The accomplishment of this purpose might be attempted by a twofold program: (1) the saving of a certain amount periodically for investment in business, securities, and so forth, and (2) the securing of insurance protection against the possibility of the saving period's being cut short by death, through the purchase of a term or whole-life policy. But it is also clear that the result can definitely be accomplished by the purchase of a $20,000 forty-year endowment policy, with waiver of premium, maturing at age 65. On the one hand, this policy, by requiring the payment of the premium at regular intervals, tends to enforce thrift on the part of the insured and places accumulations beyond the danger of loss to which private investments are usually subject. On the other hand, it hedges the insured's effort at thrift against disability or premature death. In explaining the nature of an endowment policy we saw that it can be regarded as a combination of saving (and investment) and decreasing term insurance. Thus, in the first year of the contract, when the investment portion of the contract is small, the term insurance amounts to nearly $20,000; but, if at a particular time the investment accumulation under this policy is $3,000, the insurance protection amounts to $17,000. When the investment portion equals $19,000, the insurance portion is only $1,000; likewise, when the accumulation of the $20,000 fund is completed and paid at age 65, the insurance portion is reduced to zero. It is thus seen that this policy assures an estate of $20,000, and protects the insured from the chief danger—death before the fund reaches the desired amount—attaching to any plan of saving which is not hedged with a life insurance policy. In the event the insured is disabled, the premiums are waived and the savings program is continued uninterrupted.

Briefly stated, endowment insurance may be useful in four main ways, namely:

1. *As an Incentive to Save.* Endowment insurance is advanced as a method of systematic saving in that it provides for the laying away of a moderate sum each year with a view to having all the accumulations available at the end of a fixed period. This era is recognized as a particularly extravagant one, and vast numbers of people, because of extravagant habits, never save a dollar although receiving good incomes. For such persons an endowment policy generally turns out to be a means of forcing thrift, since it compels them to do that which, if left entirely to their own option, would remain undone. By requiring the payment of specific sums at regular intervals during a period of years, endowment insurance enables many to save a worthwhile sum without being conscious of the sacrifice, whereas haphazard methods of saving seldom achieve this result. "Such a policy," it has been said, "gives a person a definite aim—he must save just so much every year, and experience soon teaches that he can do it easily." It should also be emphasized that in many instances the difference between the premium for an endowment policy and for a life insurance contract requiring a smaller payment is saved only because of the voluntarily assumed sacrifice of paying the higher rate. Endowment insurance, therefore, as it concerns those who find it difficult to save, represents a means of using the by-product of their earnings—the small sums otherwise wasted in needless expenditures—for the accumulation of a competence. Endowment insurance also furnishes the advantage of an absolutely safe plan of investment. Even assuming that these small sums are not wasted, it would still be true that in probably the majority of instances, they would be invested injudiciously

and would be subject to the hazard of business or, even if carefully invested, would be withdrawn later under the temptations of speculation or extravagant living.

It is also contended by many that endowment policies maturing in, say, twenty years afford to many young men, especially if they labor under the difficulty of not being able to save or to keep their savings, the advantage of yielding a cash capital "at the prime of life, when, ripened by years of experience, they can use it to the best advantage." Strange as it may seem, many of the nation's most prominent business men who we think could currently use all spare funds to the best advantage in their business, have publicly emphasized this feature of endowment insurance. One of the leading merchants of this country has related how he had been induced to take one endowment policy after another until he carried a huge amount of this type of insurance. He explained its advantages as a means of compulsory thrift, of accumulating sums little by little until a large fund existed, and expressed his belief that if it had not been for the sum realized upon the maturity of his endowments he might never have erected his splendid store.

2. *As a Means of Providing for Old Age.* Endowment insurance, if the term is so selected as to make the policy mature at an age like 60, 65, or 70, may serve as an excellent method of accumulating a fund for support in old age. Many who oppose endowments maturing at earlier periods because of their greater cost are ardent supporters of long-term endowments maturing at an age when a man's earning capacity usually ceases and when he naturally expects to retire from actual work. Relatively few individuals succeed in laying up a decent competence by the time this age is reached. Most people are therefore confronted with two contingencies: (1) an untimely death may leave their families unprotected, and (2) in case of survival until old age they may lack the means of proper support. Both of these contingencies may be conveniently provided for by a long-term endowment. If death should occur at any time during the term, the insurance proceeds revert to the family, but should the insured survive to old age, when the needs for insurance for family protection in the usual sense has largely or altogether passed,[3] he will himself receive the proceeds of the fund which his prudence and foresight enabled him to accumulate, to be used for his own support and comfort, either through the ordinary channels of investment or the exercise of the available options in the policy.

In this connection it should be remembered that a whole-life policy is an endowment at male age 100, since this age, according to the mortality table, is considered the extreme limit of life. At age 25 a whole-life policy is, therefore, an endowment policy for the term of seventy-five years. Now

---

[3] Actually, the availability of an annuity to protect against the "retirement death" is also "family protection" since it protects the children against assumption of parental care.

those upholding long-term endowments take the position that it is most illogical to choose age 100 as the age when the insured will have completed his savings fund under the policy, and that it accords much more with the real needs of the average man to move the maturity of the contract from the ridiculous age of 100 to the more reasonable age of 60 or 65, when the need of insurance protection is usually small while the need of a fund for comfortable maintenance in old age is usually pressing. Especially, it is argued, this change to an earlier date of maturity should be provided when the difference between the premium on an ordinary life policy taken at an early age and that on an endowment maturing at, say, 65 is so small that its payment does not involve any appreciable sacrifice and would in all probability not have been saved except for the voluntary determination to pay the slightly higher premium. Thus, at age 20, using the rates of a given company, the premium on a $1,000 endowment, maturing at age 65, is $15.33 as compared with a premium of $11.65 for an ordinary life policy, or a difference of only $3.68. In other words, the payment of this slight extra sum each year during the forty-five-year period insures the payment of the full amount of the policy in case of survival at age 65. This extra charge over 45 years makes a total additional investment of $165.60, for which the insured, at age 65, will have $412.00 more cash than he would have had with the ordinary life plan.

3. *As a Means of Hedging Against the Possibility of the Saving Period's Being Cut Short by Death.* Quite often we plan and actually start a savings program for a specific purpose to be completed by a specific date. It might be a plan to provide money for a college education for our children or an amount which we wish to donate to a worthwhile charity at a definite future date. We may divide the amount by the number of years and set aside a sum each year (considering interest) and put our plan into operation. If death occurred before the completion of the period, we would perhaps fall short of our goal. But putting the annual savings into an endowment policy to run for the definite period we would be assured that, live or die, our goal would be fully attained.

4. *As a Means of Accumulating a Fund for Specific Purposes.* Endowment insurance may serve admirably in accumulating a fund for specific purposes. Thus, endowment insurance lends itself to the accumulation of a fund for the benefit of such institutions as colleges, churches, hospitals, and so forth. Again, endowment insurance may be used to accumulate a retirement fund for the policyholder. It also may serve some special family purpose, especially as regards the making of proper and certain provision for starting children in life. It is to accomplish this purpose in the most convenient manner for parents or guardians that companies issue the various forms of "educational" and "children's" endowments already enumerated. By means of such policies, small savings, which would otherwise probably

be wasted, may be accumulated into a fund to be used for any specific purpose with assurance that the objective will be obtained despite the premature death or disability of the policyholder.

MISUSE OF ENDOWMENT INSURANCE

Endowment insurance, while serving useful purposes, can be misused. It is essentially a savings plan with insurance to protect the savings program against premature death. It should *not* be used where the need for protection is predominant. Due to the heavy savings element, the premiums are the largest of all life insurance plans but *provide the smallest amount of actual insurance protection for each dollar of premium paid*. In view of the fact that most families have limited funds available and need a program emphasizing life insurance *protection,* frequently the use of endowment insurance is a mistake since it soaks up available premiums without providing the actual protection needed. As in all uses of insurance, it is important to relate the product to the need. The only basis on which any contract, endowment or otherwise, should be criticized as far as its use goes, is that it fails to provide the optimum combination of savings and protection in the situation for which it has been recommended.

The lower premium forms of permanent insurance have the greatest flexibility to permit adjustments to meet changing circumstances. Therefore, younger individuals, who may have need for large amounts of protection, should consider using ordinary life or some other form of low-premium permanent life insurance. On the other hand, if the financial objective is specific and adequate funds are available, the endowment insurance contract is an appropriate vehicle for the accumulation of the savings fund.

Annuities | 8

NATURE OF ANNUITIES

BROADLY, AN ANNUITY may be defined as a periodic payment made during a fixed period or for the duration of a designated life or lives. If the payments are made with reference to life contingencies, the contract is known as a *life* annuity. Life annuities may be either *temporary* (payable for a fixed period or until the death of the annuitant, whichever is earlier) or *whole*. The term "life" in the title of an annuity simply indicates that payments are contingent upon the continued existence of one or more lives. In the following discussion reference to life annuities will mean *whole-life* annuities unless specifically indicated otherwise.

Liquidation, the Basic Mission of Annuities

Life insurance has as its principal mission the *creation* of an estate on both its decreasing term insurance and its investment sides. The annuity, on the contrary, has as its basic function the systematic liquidation of that which has been created either along life insurance or non-life insurance lines, such as savings bank accounts, stock or bond investments, or real estate.

In one sense the life annuity may be described as the opposite of insurance protection against death. In its pure form (that is, when not used in connection with some insurance arrangement) a life annuity may be defined as a contract whereby for a cash consideration one party (the insurer) agrees to pay the other (the annuitant) a stipulated sum (the annuity) periodically throughout life, the understanding being that the principal sum standing to the credit of the annuitant shall be considered liquidated immediately upon the death of the recipient of the annuity payments. The purpose of the annuity, it is seen, is to protect against a risk—the outliving of one's income—which is just the opposite of that confronting a person who desires life insurance as protection against the loss of income through premature death.

117

Each payment under an annuity is composed partly of principal and partly of the income earned on the unliquidated principal. If a person exactly lived out his life expectancy, he would have neither gained nor lost through utilizing the annuity contract. If he outlived his life expectancy under the contract, the additional payments would be derived from the funds contributed by those who failed to survive their expectancy. On the other hand if he died in advance of his life expectancy, he would not have recovered his entire contributions, the excess going to provide income for those who outlived their expectancy. Since no one knows into which category he will fall, it is an equitable arrangement, and can succeed from the company's point of view only through the operation of the law of large numbers. There is no other arrangement under which a given sum can be scientifically liquidated in equal installments over the duration of a human life.

Despite the difference in function, sight should not be lost of the fact that annuities are simply another important means of insurance and are based on the same fundamental principles. Technically, the two types of contracts are closely related, since both employ the pooling technique, and premiums in each case are computed on the basis of probabilities of death and survival as reflected by a mortality table.

Insurance is a pooling arrangement whereby a group of individuals make contributions so that the dependents of the unfortunate few who die each year may be indemnified for loss of the breadwinner's income, whereas the annuity is a pooling arrangement whereby those who die prematurely and do not need further income make a contribution so that those who live beyond their expectancy may receive more income than their contributions alone would provide. From an economic standpoint life insurance and annuities have been regarded as vastly different from one another. Although different in their application (since "creation" constitutes the insurance in the one case and "liquidation" in the other), in essence they are both *insurance* in the true sense of the term. Life insurance protects against the absence of income in the event of premature death or disability, whereas the annuity protects (insures) against the absence of income on the part of those "afflicted" with undue longevity. Both mean dependable protection to two unfortunate groups, the one dying too soon and the other living too long. They are both insurance arrangements, the one pertaining to the years of ascendancy, and the other to the years of decline. When coupled together, the two forms of insurance complete the economic program from start to finish on a basis of financial dependability.

Classification of Annuities

Annuities may be classified in a number of ways, but the following descriptive groups are generally used in describing an annuity's function. Understanding them will be helpful in understanding the life annuity contract. They are (1) number of lives, (2) method of premium payment, (3) time when income commences, (4) presence or absence of a refund feature, and (5) units in which benefits expressed.

Number of Lives.   This classification involves simply the question of whether annuity payments are made with reference to a single life or more than one life. If the contract covers two or more lives it is known generally as a *joint*-life annuity. The two most important types of joint-life contracts, the joint-life annuity and the joint and survivor annuity, will be discussed later in this chapter.

Method of Premium Payment.   Both single-life and joint-life annuities may be purchased with either *single premiums* or *level periodic premiums*. Thus, a single-life annuity could be purchased with a lump sum accumulated through savings, inheritance, or other media, or an individual may choose to spread the cost over a specified period by paying periodic (usually annual) premiums.

Time When Income Payments Commence.   In terms of this classification there are two categories: *immediate* and *deferred*. An immediate annuity is one under which the first benefit payment is due one payment interval (monthly, annually, or other) from the date of purchase. This type of life annuity must always be purchased with a single premium. It is basic to life annuity underwriting that no benefit payments are ever made until the entire purchase price of the annuity is in the hands of the insurance company.

The deferred annuity, on the other hand, may be purchased with either a single premium or a periodic level premium. Under a deferred life annuity, there must be a period longer than one benefit payment interval before benefit payments begin. The longer the deferred period, the more flexibility may be permitted in premium payments, with the basic underwriting rule mentioned above still being met. Normally, a number of years elapse before benefit payments commence. The majority of individual deferred-annuity contracts are sold on a level-premium basis with premiums continuing until the stated date for commencement of benefit payments or until prior death of the annuitant. In the case of deferred life annuities purchased under a group annuity pension contract the single-premium method of purchase is utilized almost exclusively.

Presence of Refund Feature.   Under this basis of classification the presence or absence of a refund feature is considered as well as the various forms which the refund benefit may take. This subject is discussed in the following section under the nature of the insurer's obligation before and after the commencement of income payments.

Units in Which Benefits Expressed.   Traditionally, annuity benefits have been expressed in fixed dollars. With the advent of the variable annuity (see below), the units in which payout benefits are expressed forms another basis of classification.

Nature of Insurance Companies' Obligation

This discussion classification is based on the benefits payable in the event of death prior to or following the commencement of income payments under the contract, that is, during the accumulation period or the liquidation period.

Accumulation Period.   As was indicated above, the immediate annuity is always purchased with a single premium and the income commences at the end of the first benefit interval following the purchase of the contract. Obviously, there is no obligation on the company before it receives the purchase price. Under a deferred annuity, however, there may be an obligation to pay some benefit before the income begins, that is, during the *accumulation period*. A deferred annuity may be written on a pure or refund basis in this connection. Under the pure deferred annuity the premiums are discounted for mortality during the accumulation period, and in event of death prior to the commencement of income payments there would be no refund of premiums paid, since they would be fully earned. Where a refund feature is applicable during the accumulation period, premiums with or without interest would be refunded if death occurred before annuity income begins. Naturally, a deferred annuity with such a refund feature would cost more than the pure deferred annuity mentioned above.

Liquidation Period.   Regardless of the manner in which funds are accumulated, the amount of money necessary to provide a given amount and form of income starting at a stated age is the same. Consequently, the following discussion of the nature of the company's obligation during the liquidation period is applicable to both immediate and deferred annuities. In fact, the discussion in principle is equally applicable to life income settlement options (to be discussed below). The discussion is simply a description of the various arrangements under which a given sum can be liquidated on the basis of life contingencies.

Broadly, there are two arrangements: (1) pure and (2) refund. The pure life annuity, frequently referred to as a straight life annuity, provides periodic income payments that continue as long as the annuitant lives, but *terminate upon his death*. The annuity premium is considered fully earned upon the death of the annuitant, no matter how soon that may occur after the commencement of income, and *no refund is payable* to the annuitant's estate or any beneficiary. Under this form of income the entire purchase price is applied to provide income to the annuitant, no part of it going to pay for any refund benefit following the annuitant's death. Thus, the pure life annuity provides the *maximum income per dollar of outlay,* and is appropriate where only a limited amount of capital is available. It should be pointed out, however, that at the younger ages, because of the high probability of survival, the difference in income between a pure life annuity and one with a refund feature is too small to take a chance on an early death (see below).

Regardless of the questions of equity and technical soundness, most people are opposed to placing a substantial sum of money into a contract which promises little or no return if they should die shortly after income payments commence. Therefore, most companies have added a refund feature to life annuities in order to make them more salable. In contrast to the pure life annuity, not all of the purchase price goes to provide income payments to the annuitant. Part of the purchase price is applied to meet the cost of *guaranteeing a minimum amount of benefits,* whether or not the annuitant lives to receive them himself. Thus, for a given premium outlay a smaller periodic income payment will be available under a refund life annuity than would be available under the pure life annuity form. The minimum benefit guarantee or refund feature may be stated either in terms of a guaranteed number of annuity payments whether the annuitant lives or dies, or in terms of a refund of the purchase price (or some portion thereof) in the event of the annuitant's early death.

The first form of life annuity with a refund feature mentioned above is named, variously, "life annuity certain and continuous," "life annuity with installments certain," and "life annuity with minimum guaranteed return." This arrangement calls for a guaranteed number of monthly (or annual) payments to be made whether the annuitant lives or dies, with payments to continue for the whole of the annuitant's life if he should live beyond the guaranteed period. Contracts are usually written with payments guaranteed for five, ten, fifteen, or twenty years. The size of the income payments available from a given principal is less for the longer guarantee period.

There are two important forms of annuity income which promise to return all or a portion of the purchase price. They are the installment refund annuity and the cash refund annuity. The *installment refund* annuity promises that in the event the annuitant dies before receiving income installments equal to the purchase price, the payments will be continued to a beneficiary until the full cost has been paid. The *cash refund* annuity, on the other hand, promises to pay in a *lump sum* to the annuitant's estate or a contingent beneficiary, the difference, if any, between the purchase price of the annuity and the sum of the installment payments made prior to the death of the annuitant. The only difference between the cash refund and the installment refund annuity is that under the former the unrecovered portion of the purchase price is refunded in a lump sum at the annuitant's death, whereas in the latter the installments are continued until the purchase price has been completely recovered.[1] The cash refund will provide somewhat less in absolute amount since the insurance company loses the interest which it would have earned had the balance been liquidated in installments. In either case the payments to the annuitant continue as long as he lives even after the guaranteed minimum benefits have been recovered.

It might be well at this point to compare the income which can be provided under some of the important forms of annuities for a given amount of principal sum. The figures in Table 8–1 are all based on the same rate basis, and variations are intended to show the impact which the form of annuity income, the age of the annuitant at the date of commencement of income, and the sex of the annuitant have on the yield (in this case monthly) available from $1,000 of the principal sum.

TABLE 8-1. Immediate Life Annuity Monthly Incomes per $1,000 Nonparticipating Premiums

Age Last Birthday	Pure Life Annuity		10 Years Certain Annuity		Cash	
	M	F	M	F	M	F
50	$ 5.00	$ 4.54	$4.91	$4.51	$4.68	$4.40
55	5.54	4.97	5.37	4.90	5.09	4.75
60	6.26	5.54	5.95	5.41	5.58	5.18
65	7.22	6.34	6.64	6.06	6.19	5.73
70	8.57	7.46	7.40	6.83	6.93	6.42
75	10.47	9.06	8.15	7.68	7.85	7.28
80	13.05	11.35	8.77	8.46	8.96	8.37

It should be apparent from Table 8–1 that the cost of the refund feature is inconsequential at the younger ages, but becomes quite expensive at the higher ages. Since the death rate is quite low at the younger ages, and most of the annuitants would survive anyway, the difference in income available under the various annuities is too small to take a chance on an early death. For example, at male age 50 an annuity with ten years' installments guaranteed will provide only nine cents difference in monthly income, since so few will actually die during that ten-year period. It is not until about age 60 or 65 that any appreciable difference in income is given up to add a refund feature. Consequently, it would appear to be economically unsound

---

1 It should be noted that the insurance company *can* afford to refund the full purchase price in the annuity contract whether the annuitant lives or dies and still continue the benefit payments to those annuitants who have recovered their full premium outlay, because the interest earnings on the funds while they are in the hands of the insurance company will serve as a premium to provide the life income to begin after the purchase price has been refunded.

to purchase a pure life annuity below age 60. It should also be remembered that the benefits under each of these income forms are actuarial equivalents of those under the others, and the choice should be the appropriate one, considering the annuitant's individual circumstances.

INDIVIDUAL ANNUITY CONTRACTS

Retirement Annuity Contract

The most significant individual annuity contract sold today is the *retirement annuity contract* which is offered by the great majority of companies. The retirement annuity contract is a deferred annuity with a wide range of options which make the contract very flexible. Prior to maturity the contract is simply a pure investment contract for the accumulation of a principal sum to be applied to provide an income for the annuitant at retirement. As will be brought out below, it is possible for the annuitant to adjust the contract to changes of circumstances not anticipated when the contract was issued.

Level premiums are "deposited" with the insurance company during the deferred period and accumulated at a rate of compound interest specified in the contract. In the event of the *death* of the annuitant prior to age 65 or other selected maturity date of the contract, the contract provides for the return of the accumulated gross premiums (without interest) or the cash value, *whichever is larger*. Because of the expenses incurred in the early years, the cash value does not exceed the accumulated gross premiums (without interest) until after a number of years. During this initial period, when the death benefit exceeds the cash value, there is a minor insurance element in this annuity contract equal to the excess of the premiums over the cash value.

During the deferred period the annuitant may withdraw the cash value at any time and terminate the contract. On the other hand, most contracts provide that if the contract lapses, the cash value is automatically applied (after thirty-one days) to produce a paid-up deferred annuity in a reduced amount. The annuitant may, however, surrender the paid-up annuity at any time thereafter.

Premiums for this contract are usually quoted on the basis that the accumulated sum *at maturity* will be applied under a life annuity with 120 or 240 monthly installments guaranteed. At maturity, however, the annuitant may, optionally, elect any form of life annuity, the actual monthly income being appropriately adjusted. In addition, the annuitant usually has the further option of taking the accumulated sum in cash instead of in the form of an annuity. This so-called *cash option* exposes the company to serious adverse selection both from a financial and a mortality standpoint. Persons who are in poor health tend to elect the cash option while those in excellent health usually choose to take an annuity income. In addition, since the basis for application of the accumulated sum at maturity is specified in the contract at issue, this retirement annuity is, in effect, a contract to sell, at the buyer's option at a future date, an annuity on terms now guaranteed. The purchaser may exercise the option at maturity date either to buy the annuity or to take a cash settlement as he sees fit. The rates in the contract, relative to the open market rates, may be favorable or unfavorable and the holder of a retirement annuity again has the possibility of selecting against the company.

It should be noted that the amount of income purchased under a retirement annuity contract is usually much less than could have been obtained for the same premium outlay under a pure deferred life annuity where there are no death or withdrawal benefits during the deferred period.

The usual form of retirement annuity permits the annuitant to have the income commence at an earlier or later date than the one originally specified in the contract with an appropriate adjustment in the amount of income. Under this arrangement, the accumulated cash value is applied at the selected age as a single premium to purchase an immediate life annuity with the amount of annuity income depending upon the amount of the cash value, the age selected, and the form of life annuity chosen. The option to postpone the commencement of income payments may be particularly attractive if the increasing longevity produces an increasingly greater working expectancy.

Retirement annuities written by mutual companies are virtually always participating during the accumulation period and may be participating during the liquidation phase, particularly during any period of guaranteed installments.

Joint-Life Annuities

Joint Annuity.   A joint-life annuity is a contract which provides a specified amount of income for two or more persons named in the contract, with the income ceasing upon the *first* death among the covered lives. Although the cost of such a contract is relatively inexpensive, this contract has a very limited market.

Joint and Last-Survivor Annuity.   In contrast to the straight joint-life annuity, the joint and last-survivor annuity is increasingly finding acceptance, primarily as an alternative income settlement form under individual life insurance and endowment contracts, and in private pension plans. It is more appealing since it provides that the income payments continue as long as *either* of two or more persons lives. Its most obvious use is for a husband and wife or other family relationships.

Since the annuity provides for payment until the *last* death among the covered lives, it will pay to a later date on the average and therefore is naturally more expensive than other annuity forms. Saying it in another way, a given principal sum will provide less income under a joint and last-survivor form than would a normal single-life annuity form at either of the two ages.

The joint and survivorship form is usually offered on either a pure life basis or with a certain number of installments guaranteed. In its normal form the joint and last-survivor annuity continues the *same* income until the death of the *last survivor*. Most companies, however, offer a modified form which provides (assuming two covered lives) that the income will be reduced following the death of the first annuitant to two thirds (or one half, depending upon the contract) of the original income. This contract (or option) is known as a *joint and two-thirds annuity* (or *joint and one-half*). Naturally, for a given amount of principal sum, the modified form will provide more income initially because of the later reduction.[2]

The Variable Annuity

In times of deflation the value of such a fixed and guaranteed annuity income increases because of a falling price structure, that is, the purchasing power of a fixed dollar income tends to go up in periods of falling prices. On the other hand, when inflation produces a rising price level the purchasing power of the same fixed dollar income tends to fall off. Consequently, in times of deflation the fixed dollar annuity finds much popularity, whereas in periods of inflation annuity incomes providing a decreasing amount of purchasing power tend to cause wide criticism. The impact of inflation since 1941 has led to a search for a way of providing a guaranteed life annuity with a reasonably stable purchasing power. The variable life annuity based on the equity type of investments has been advanced as a possible answer to this problem.

Nature of the Variable Annuity.[3]   As in the case of conventional deferred annuity, during the accumulation period, a level annual premium is paid to the insurance company, and, along with other variable

[2] The joint and last-survivor form found in private pension plans commonly provides that the income is reduced *only* when the *employee* dies first.

[3] See Edward J. Day and Meyer Melnikoff, "The Variable Annuity as a Life Insurance Company Product," *Journal of the American Society of Chartered Life Underwriters*, Vol. X, No. 1 (December, 1955), pp. 45–56.

annuity premiums, placed in a special "Variable Annuity Account." The funds in this account are invested separately from the company's other assets, mostly in common stocks. Each year the level premiums, after deduction of a portion of each premium for expenses, are applied to purchase units of credit in the special account, the number of units depending upon the current valuation of a unit in dollars. Thus, if each unit, based on current investment results, is valued at $10, a level premium of $100 after expenses will purchase ten units the following year. If the value of a unit is changed (depending upon investment results), however, the level premium of $100 would purchase more or less than ten units. This procedure would continue until the maturity of the contract. At that time the accumulated total number of units credited would be applied according to actuarial principles and based on the current valuation of a unit, to convert credited units to a retirement income of so many units to be valued annually for the lifetime of the annuitant.

Instead of providing for the payment each month of a *fixed number of dollars,* the variable annuity provides for the payment each month or year of the current value of a *fixed number of annuity units.* Thus, the dollar amount of each payment would depend on the dollar value of an annuity unit when the payment is made. The valuation assigned to a unit would depend upon the investment results of the special account which would be invested mostly in common stocks. For example, if an annuitant were entitled to a payment of ten annuity units each month and the dollar value of an annuity unit for three consecutive months were $10.20, $9.90, and $10.10, the annuitant would receive an income for these months of $102.00, $99.00, and $101.00. In order to minimize the temptation to "play the market," a participant in a variable annuity would not normally be permitted routinely to surrender his accumulation units for cash. When the variable annuity is used as part of a pension plan, surrender values generally are not made available at all. Where the variable annuity is sold as an individual contract, surrender privileges are made available but on a much more restricted basis than in connection with ordinary annuities. Under all plans, the current value of the accumulation units is payable, usually as a continuing income, upon the death of the participant during the accumulation period.

Investment Risk Assumed by Annuitant.   Under a conventional annuity the insurance company assumes the mortality, expense, and investment risks. The company invests the assets behind conventional annuities mostly in stable fixed-dollar investments. This is necessary to implement their *guarantee* of fixed-dollar incomes. Under a variable annuity, the insurance company assumes only the risk of fluctuations due to mortality and expenses. The assets behind variable annuities are invested in equity type investments, and dollar income is permitted to fluctuate accordingly on the theory that the dollar income, while varying, will provide a more stable amount of purchasing power. The annuitant, then, is assuming the investment risk, but it is important to remember that the insurance company is still absorbing expense fluctuations and guaranteeing that the annuitant will not *outlive* his income. Equity type investments, it is asserted by the proponents of the plan, yield more under normal business conditions, and the annuitant has a more than reasonable chance of receiving a higher income than he would receive under a guaranteed annuity. On the other hand, in times of depressed business conditions, the variable annuitant will receive somewhat less in dollars of income than in the case of a conventional fixed-dollar annuity.

Marketing Developments.[4]   Since the pioneering adaptation of the variable annuity concept by the Teachers Insurance and Annuity Association in 1952, a number of companies have been organized to sell variable annuities, on either an individual or a group basis, to members of the general public. In view of the unique characteristics of the variable annuity contract, it was necessary to modify the law in most jurisdictions (or obtain liberal administrative interpretations) in order to permit the sale of variable annuities. The majority of states now permit the writing of variable annuities on a group basis, i.e., in connection with a pension plan, and a growing number have approved their sale on an individual basis.

In the VALIC decision,[5] the United States Supreme Court held that an individual variable annuity contract is a security within the meaning of the Securities Act of 1933 and that any organization which offers such a contract is an investment company and subject to the Investment Company Act of 1940. Thus, any company which offers individual variable annuity contracts is subject to *dual supervision* by the Securities and Exchange Commission and the various state insurance departments. Group variable annuity contracts are currently exempt from supervision by the Securities and Exchange Commission, provided that certain restrictions are observed.

SETTLEMENT OPTIONS

Virtually all life insurance contracts contain a series of options with regard to the disposition of life insurance proceeds. These so-called settlement options fall into three categories: (1) retention of the proceeds at interest, (2) systematic liquidation of the proceeds *without* reference to a

---

[4] See Arthur L. Blakesly, III, "The Variable Annuity Today," *Journal of the American Society of Chartered Life Underwriters,* Vol. XXII, No. 2 (April, 1968), pp. 9–17.

[5] *Securities and Exchange Commission v. Valic,* 359 U.S. 65 (1959).

life contingency, and (3) systematic liquidation of the proceeds *with* reference to a life contingency.

The basic concept of the so-called interest option is that the beneficiary is to receive the interest earnings, the principal being held until some future date or the occurrence of some specific event. The second and third categories involve options known as installment options and are in reality forms of annuities. The so-called installment amount and installment period options provide for periodic payments either over a predetermined period (installment period) or until the entire principal sum with interest earnings thereon is exhausted (installment amount). Since neither of these periodic payments are contingent upon survival, they are simply temporary annuities and come within the second category of options. The other category of installment options involving the scientific liquidation of a principal sum with reference to life contingencies are forms of life annuities, and are referred to in the policy as *life income options.* Most companies make available by contract or, as a matter of practice, a pure or straight life income, a cash refund life income, an installment refund life income, a life income with installments guaranteed, and a joint and last-survivor life income option. It is important to remember that these installment options are simply immediate annuities, in effect, purchased by applying the proceeds of the policy as a single premium. Settlement options, as such, and their uses will be discussed in greater detail in a later chapter, but it seems appropriate to take cognizance of their relationship to annuities at this point.

The insurance and annuity ideas need to be coupled together during the working period of life to create an assured financial program for old age support. As the public becomes educated to the liquidation function of annuities, and to the helpfulness of insurance in the creation of that which is later to be liquidated through the means of some annuity plan, we may confidently look forward to an enormous growth in both the insurance and the annuity fields. Many believe that the growth of the annuity business will be the outstanding feature in the life insurance business during the next quarter of a century. While this may be true, there is more reason to believe that life insurance for ultimate annuity purposes will be much the more popular item.

SERVICES RENDERED BY ANNUITIES

Briefly described, the benefits derived from annuities are the following:

1. *The Service of Investment Management.* The high quality of the investment management offered to holders of insurance policies has already been explained in Chapter 4. All that was said there is also equally applica-

ble to the annuitant. The old are particularly anxious to be freed of investment cares, and as stated elsewhere: "Dread of loss of income is a constant harassment to the old. Aged people should not be bothered, and as a matter of fact do not wish to be, with financial cares. For them the time has come to receive and use income and not to make income. Investment management is one of the strongest arguments for the sale of annuities."

2. *The Dependable Solvency of the Investment.* The extraordinary certainty of the solvency of life insurance companies was also explained in Chapter 4, and all that was said there is equally applicable to the annuitant. Instead of living in hope as younger people usually do, old folks nearly always live in a state of financial fear. Old age is certainly not the time to lose one's investment principal. For reasons already explained, there is little or no risk of such a loss when the principal is entrusted to life insurance companies. This is certainly true if the fund is split up among two or three companies. And even if a company should suspend operations (a very rare occurrence), the loss is confined usually to only a small fraction of the total principal.

3. *A Large and Certain Annual Income Guaranteed.* Along with freedom from fear, owing to the dependable solvency of the investment, the annuitant will enjoy monthly an income equal (at the retirement age) significantly higher than that obtainable through the customary channels of conservative investment, if he is willing to have his principal liquidated. Each year the company will give him the current income on his investment plus a portion of the investment itself. The large income is certain, and the annuitant may spend it without fear. It will last as long as life lasts. The annuity is the only available arrangement whereby people of ordinary means may enjoy the principal sum of their labor and thrift, and do so without fear. In the absence of an annuity, old folks scarcely ever use any part of the principal of their savings. They live on the income alone—a regular boarding house variety of life—and finally are obliged to leave it all to others at the time of their death. In the absence of an annuity, there is always the danger of spending too much or too little. But with the annuity the scale of spending is not only greatly increased but is definite as to amount.

4. *Hedging Shrunken Estates.* Mention has already been made of the extent to which the last depression cut into the dollar value of American estates. Any number of old folks, formerly in comfortable circumstances, were left with a greatly reduced income. Under such circumstances the annuity can come to the rescue of innumerable people as a means of equalizing in income the shrinkage which has occurred in principal. Thus the owner of a $50,000 estate in 1929 thought fondly in terms of $2,500 of income. But when the estate shrank, let us say, to $25,000, the income also declined to $1,250. Lack of comfort took the place of contentment. But by investing the $25,000 in an annuity at ages 60 to 65, a certain yield is ob-

tainable for life significantly higher than the ordinary investment yield. In other words, the $25,000 as regards income for life, is about equivalent to the $50,000 estate, that is, before the shrinkage occurred.

5. *Releases Funds to Philanthropic Institutions*. Educational, religious, medical, and other philanthropic institutions are turning as never before to insurance and annuities as a means of creating endowments for the future. Often donations are accepted from aged donors on the basis of a guaranteed life income to the benefactor. It may be questioned, however, whether any such institutions have a right to assume such a risk. In addition, the benefaction lies idle, waiting for the donor to die, at which time the fund is released to the institution. How much better to release a portion of the donation at once, by securing the stipulated income (equal to the investment return) for the donor through an annuity. Where the age of the donor is around 65, a portion of the donation (about half) can be invested in an annuity to yield to the donor an income equivalent to a 4 per cent return on the entire benefaction. The other half of the donation is thus released for immediate use if the terms of the grant permit.

6. *A Parent May Finance a Child*. Much the same reasoning as that explained in the preceding section may be followed by a father desirous of aiding his son financially at a time when such aid is apt to do the greatest good. The father may own an estate of $20,000, yielding about $600 of income annually. In the absence of an annuity he is obliged to hang tenaciously to the estate. He tells his son that he would like to help him, but that is impossible. However, the $20,000 will go to the son upon the father's death. How much better, if the father is about age 65, to split the $20,000 into two equal parts, investing $10,000 in an annuity, yielding about as much as the whole $20,000 can at 3 per cent. The father thus has the income for life which he previously had from the entire estate. The other $10,000 he may give to the son at once, and not keep him waiting until death makes an income unnecessary. In ever so many instances the son might reach the age of retirement himself before receiving the money. In many instances such a plan would also save a great deal in taxes.

7. *Distribution of Estates to Children by Wealthy Parents Is Made Possible*. Annuities make such a distribution possible, because such parents are enabled to live comfortably on the balance retained for investment in an annuity.

8. *The Making of Wills Is Facilitated*. Frequently, testators leave lump-sum cash bequests to their immediate heirs, their friends, or their servants. But such lump-sum payments are extremely uncertain and certainly not so advantageous as definite income settlements. The very purpose of the bequest is to provide an income and not a principal sum to again be left to the heirs or others under the terms of the beneficiary's will. How much better to provide in the will that the cash bequest should be invested for the heir in an annuity. This has the double advantage of insuring the bequest

against loss and of greatly enlarging the income. Through the use of annuities the testator is enabled to accomplish greater results with a given sum of money either by way of a greater income to his heirs or by way of bequests to a larger number of heirs.

9. *The Life of Annuitants Is Prolonged.* It is a common saying that annuitants are long livers. Freedom from financial worry and fear, and contentment with an adequate income are conducive to longevity. If it be true that half of human ailments are probably attributable at least in part to fear and worry, then the effectiveness of annuities towards health and happiness must be apparent. Annuities serve in old age much the same economic purpose that periodic medical examinations do during the working years of life—life conservation.

Special Life and 9
Annuity Contracts

IN ADDITION TO the regular life insurance and annuity contracts already discussed, life insurance companies issue a wide variety of special policies or policy combinations. These special forms contain no basic principles different from those already discussed. They differ only in the sense that they present a combination, such as whole-life with term insurance, designed to serve a particular group of buyers. Most of these contracts were developed for merchandising purposes, and while a few have met a real need and have found wide acceptance, it is important to remember that they do not offer the same flexibility as do the regular forms of contracts. Taken as a whole, the amount of insurance protection sold under these contracts is small in proportion to that sold each year in the United States under the ordinary forms of insurance.

COMBINATION CONTRACTS

Family Income Policy or Rider

This type of policy was designed to appeal to young men with family responsibilities. The purpose of the combination is to provide an income during the child-raising period in the event of the father's premature death, and also to provide the foundation for a permanent life insurance program.

This type of policy provides for monthly income payments to the beneficiary beginning at death of the insured and running to the end of the policy period, which usually is ten, fifteen, or twenty years from date of issue. The monthly income is usually in the amount of 1 per cent of the face of the policy ($10 for each $1,000 of insurance), although a few companies are now using 2 per cent and even 4 per cent family income benefits. In addition, the policy provides for a face amount which becomes payable at the end of the income period if the insured dies before the expiration of the ten, fifteen, or twenty years from date of issue. If the insured lives beyond the specified period, only the face amount is payable upon his death. In the latter event the contract is the same as a regular whole-life policy. The specified income period chosen ideally should be long enough to protect the family until the youngest child is self-supporting.

Some contracts also provide for a lump sum, payable at death, to be used to meet the last illness and funeral expenses.

To illustrate the principles underlying this type of contract, assume a young man buys a $10,000 twenty-year family income policy. In the event he dies five years later, the company will pay his beneficiary $100 a month for the remaining fifteen years of the income period selected and $10,000 at the end of fifteen years. If he dies eighteen years after the policy is issued, $100 a month will be payable for two years and $10,000 at the end of two years. If he dies any time after the expiration of the twenty-year period (even twenty years and one day), only the face amount will be payable and it will be payable immediately. In all cases, the $10,000 face amount will be payable either in one lump sum or under any one of the settlement options found in the usual life insurance contract.

The family income policy is a combination of *whole-life insurance* and *decreasing term insurance*. The whole-life insurance provides for the payment of the face amount whenever the insured dies, before or after the expiration of the income period selected. Decreasing term insurance is added to the whole-life contract in an amount sufficient, with the interest on the proceeds from the whole-life policy (which it should be remembered matures immediately upon the death of the insured), to provide the monthly payments during the specified period selected. The *maximum* number of *income payments* which would have to be made under a twenty-year period would be 240, in the event the insured died immediately. The *minimum* number of *income payments* would be none, in the event the insured died at the end of or after the expiration of the twenty-year period. As is indicated in Graph 9–1, the amount of the term insurance necessary to provide for the income payments decreases from an initial maximum to zero at the end of the specified period. It is important to remember, however, that the actual amount of term insurance needed is reduced by the amount of income provided by the interest on the whole-life proceeds which are held by the company until the end of the period. A few contracts provide for the payment of the face of the policy immediately rather than at the end of the income period. This arrangement necessitates a larger amount of term insurance to offset the loss of interest on the whole-life proceeds.

The benefits provided by the family income *policy* may also be provided by a family income *rider* attached to any form of permanent insurance. In such cases, the basic amount of insurance is payable at death instead of at the end of the family income period, as in the case of the family income policy. The rider provides the appropriate amount of decreasing term insurance. The rider may be written for any period desired, and can be writ-

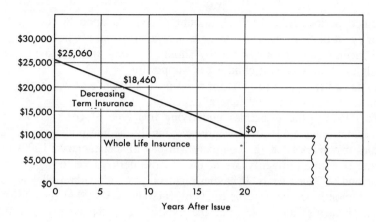

GRAPH 9-1.   Relative proportions of whole-life and decreasing term insurance in a $10,000 family income policy, 1958 CSO Table and 2½ per cent interest.

ten either with new policies or added to existing permanent insurance, provided that evidence of insurability is furnished. The family income rider attached to a permanent policy provides the same benefits as the family income policy, with greater flexibility. In fact, some companies will issue a "family income to 65" rider which goes far beyond the original purpose of the family income policy. It is not surprising to note that the rider arrangement has almost completely supplanted the special policy form.

The premium for a family income policy or rider is level throughout the specified income period but drops down at the expiration of the period to that payable for the permanent insurance as of the issue date of the contract. Some companies provide for the cost of the term portion by means of a level premium payable over a period shorter than the specified income period because of the very small amount of term insurance actually in force in the last few years of the income period. Disability and double indemnity benefits, when written in connection with a family income policy, relate only to the permanent part of the policy.

The underlying purpose of the family income policy or rider is more adequate family protection in the event of the insured's death before his children have reached maturity. The policy was designed chiefly for the young married man who is unable to afford a sufficient amount of insurance under one of the regular forms of protection. The advantages of the policy, therefore, are those connected with the sale of ordinary life protection plus term insurance to this class of individuals. It is one of the most popular forms of combination contracts.

One of the chief handicaps in the sale of this policy is that often the insured does not understand its provisions regarding the income period. The income is payable only if the insured dies during the income period, and then only until the end of the income period, which may be ten, fifteen, or twenty years from date of issue. The policy does *not* provide for income benefits for ten, fifteen, or twenty years from date of death. The longer the insured lives, the shorter will be the income period; but this does not prevent the income period from covering the time of maximum need of the insured's family.

Because of the disadvantages connected with the term insurance element in this policy, many companies provide that while it is in full force, and without evidence of insurability, the family income policy may be exchanged for any of the regular forms of whole-life or endowment policies.

Another criticism of the policy is that it is inelastic. Changing circumstances may take away some of its value. For instance, it makes no allowance for future family additions, and the convertibility and other features of the policy may not help the insured in such changed circumstances. The regular forms of life and endowment policies offer advantages to those individuals who can afford the more adequate protection.

In order that it will be used in such a manner as to fulfill its fundamental purpose, this type of policy usually has certain limitations imposed upon it by the company. The twenty-year income plan is sometimes limited to applicants whose ages range from 20 to 45. Within this age range will be found, generally, the young married man who, in case of death, wants to provide his family with an income until the youngest child is grown to self-sufficiency. The fifteen-year income plan is often limited to applicants whose ages range from 20 to 50, while the ten-year income plan is sold to applicants up to 55 years of age. The ten- and fifteen-year plans are recommended for those whose children are older and who have no probability of requiring the income payments for longer than these short periods. So, also, there are certain limits on the amount of insurance sold. For example, an amount less than $2,500 is not accepted by most companies. Maximum limits set by one company vary somewhat by age, reaching $50,000 for men ages 25 to 50 and $25,000 for women ages 30 to 55.

These limits are usually less than the regular life or endowment limits, so that if the insured can afford to take amounts of insurance above those specified, it is logical to advise that at least the excess be issued on the regular plans of insurance.

Family Maintenance Policy or Rider

The family maintenance policy is very similar to the family income policy. The distinguishing feature of the family maintenance policy is that if the individual dies during the specified period elected (for example, twenty years), the income payments will be payable for a full twenty years regardless of the point within the specified period at which the insured dies. In other respects the family maintenance policy provides the same benefits as the family income policy. Just as in the family income policy if the insured dies after the specified period has expired, only the face of the policy is payable. (See Graph 9–2.)

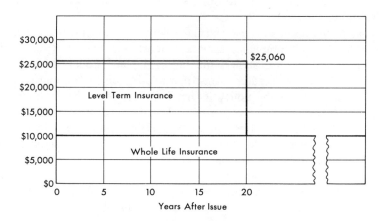

GRAPH 9-2.   Relative proportions of whole-life and level term insurance in a $10,000 20-year family maintenance policy, 1958 CSO Table and 2½ per cent interest.

The family maintenance policy is a combination of permanent insurance and term insurance. The term insurance portion in this case, however, is *level* and not decreasing in nature. Since the same benefits are promised even if the insured dies the last day of the specified period, it follows that a level amount of term insurance will be needed to provide the income payments promised. Interest on the proceeds of the permanent insurance serves to reduce the amount of term insurance necessary. The benefits are most frequently provided by a rider arrangement in connection with existing or new permanent policies.

Today, the family maintenance policy as such is sold by relatively few companies. It has been virtually supplanted by the family income rider and the use of level term riders. The analysis of this special policy form is included here, however, because it demonstrates clearly the principles involved in designing special policy forms utilizing the basic forms of insurance protection.

Retirement Income Contract

The retirement income contract is very popular. Not only is it the most significant contract for providing retirement income to the individual policyholder, but it is also the standard form used in insured pension plans utilizing individual contracts. The contract goes under other names including "income endowment," "retirement endowment," "endowment annuity," and "insurance with annuity."

This contract is practically identical with the retirement annuity contract discussed earlier. The main distinction involves the death benefit prior to maturity, which is greater under the retirement income contract. In contrast to the retirement annuity, which promises only to return the premiums or the cash value, whichever is larger, the retirement income contract promises $1,000 for each $10 [1] unit of monthly life income or the cash value, whichever is larger.

The additional death benefits are provided by decreasing term insurance. The amount of term insurance is exactly sufficient at each age, when supplemented with the reserve value, to pay the face of the policy. After the point at which the cash value exceeds the face of the policy, the reserve and cash value are the same and also become the death benefit.

Most retirement income policies are written to mature at age 55, 60, or 65. Because of the additional insurance element, they do not provide as much flexibility as the retirement annuity with respect to optional maturity dates.

The retirement income contract is thus a combination of a savings fund arrangement (as explained above in connection with the retirement annuity) and term insurance, with the amount of term insurance decreasing each year so that it is always just enough to make up the difference between the savings fund and the face amount payable in the event of the annuitant's death during the deferred period. Graph 9–3, based upon the figures of a 2½ per cent company, illustrates these two elements of the contract. In this case the policyholder wishes to have $10,000 protection for his beneficiary and $100 per month income for himself, with payments guaranteed for 120 months, should he live to the retirement age of 65. In order to provide this income, the company must have on hand at age 65, not $10,000 but $16,640. Hence, during the later years of the deferred period, the savings fund will exceed the $10,000 of initial protection. In the policy discussed above, the fund will exceed the $10,000 initial protection after the twentieth year. If the policyholder dies after this date and before the retirement age, the beneficiary will receive the larger fund then on hand.

Multiple Protection Policies

A number of companies have introduced combination policies which may appropriately be characterized as "multiple protection" policies. These

[1] Other contracts are available providing up to $2,000 of insurance for each $10 unit of monthly income.

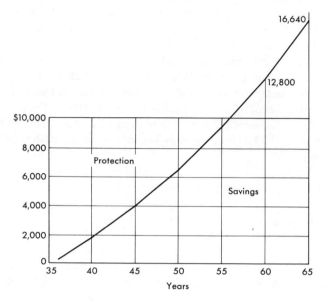

GRAPH 9-3. **Terminal reserves per $10,000 insurance and $100 monthly income retirement income policy, 1958 CSO Table, male age 35 and 2½ per cent interest.**

contracts promise to pay a multiple of the face amount if the insured should die within a specified period and only the face if he should die after the expiration of the period. The period of multiple protection may run ten, fifteen, or twenty years or to a specified age, such as 60 or 65. The death benefits during the specified period are usually double or triple the face of the policy.

If, for example, double protection is provided to age 60, with the face of the policy payable thereafter, the combination represents the simple combination of level term insurance and modified whole-life insurance in equal amounts. The total premium is applied to the modified life after the term insurance expires. In the event triple protection is promised, the amount of term insurance involved will be exactly twice as much as the underlying whole-life policy. As in the case of the other combination forms involving term insurance, the coverage may be provided by a special policy or by attachment of a term rider to a permanent policy. Also, the term insurance portion is usually convertible into permanent insurance without evidence of insurability.

It should be noted that a twenty-year double protection policy is similar in construction to the twenty-year family maintenance policy, the term insurance being for a level amount in both cases.

Family Policy

A number of companies are now issuing policies insuring an entire family in one contract, commonly called the Family Policy. Most family *policies* provide whole-life or other permanent forms on the father, designated as the insured, with a premium based on his age. Term insurance is provided on the wife and children. The wife's coverage may be a stated amount or vary in amount with her age and is usually term insurance to the husband's age 65, but whole-life may also be used. Insurance on the children is term for a fixed amount. All children living under the family roof are covered, even if adopted or born *after* the policy is issued. Coverage is effective for children over a few days old (for example, fifteen days) and under a stated age, usually 18. The children's term insurance coverage expires at a stated age, such as 18, 21, or 25, and is usually convertible to any permanent plan of insurance without evidence of insurability. Most plans permit conversion for children up to $5,000 per unit of coverage.

A unit of coverage may consist of $5,000 whole-life on the insured and $1,000 or $1,250 whole-life or term on the wife and $1,000 term on each child. In the event the insured dies prior to age 65, some companies provide that all term coverage is paid up. Others provide conversion privileges. The paid-up feature is provided by a survivorship annuity feature (see below) in the amount of the premium for the beneficiary's insurance, since the beneficiary must survive the insured for the benefit to be payable.

The premium does not change in the event of either the wife's death [2] or the inclusion of additional children. The premium for the children's coverage is based on an average number of children, but in the event of the wife's death prior to the insured's, her insurance is paid to her beneficiary and at the same time the husband's insurance is increased by the same amount for the period of the insurance that was on her life.

There are many features of the family policies currently being issued which vary widely, but the basic provisions follow a pattern similar to that outlined above. It should be noted that some companies are providing the benefits of a family *policy* by attaching a *rider* to a permanent form of life insurance. The significance of the family policy lies in the fact that it has been enthusiastically received by the public. It satisfies the need for coverage on every member of the family during the period when the husband is liable for all expenses in the event of the death of any member of his family, and it provides protection at low cost. It is unique in that it departs from the tradition of a single policy on each individual. Although more than one life has previously been covered in joint-life policies, the idea of including an

[2] Some companies do provide for a reduction in premium in the event of the wife's death.

undetermined number of individuals whose ages may not be known to the insurance company, as in the case of future children unborn at the time of issue, has not been previously attempted. It also represents another example of the combination of the basic forms of life insurance to provide a given set of benefits. Under most policies, the premium rate for the entire package of protection depends entirely upon the age of the insured. The premium is computed on the assumption that the wife is the same age as the husband, and that the number and ages of the children conform to a particular pattern. If the wife is not the same age as the husband, the predetermined premium will be used to purchase whatever amount of insurance can be obtained at her actual age. Deviations from the assumed number and ages of children are ignored for premium and dividend purposes.

SURVIVORSHIP ANNUITY CONTRACTS

Survivorship Annuity

Nature.   This type of contract is unique in that it furnishes an income benefit under a policy which does not provide for a lump-sum settlement. Actually, the survivorship or reversionary annuity, as it is sometimes called, is a life insurance policy combined with an annuity agreement. The contract provides that if the beneficiary should outlive the insured, the beneficiary will receive a *predetermined* income for life regardless of her age at the insured's death. In the event the beneficiary predeceases the insured, however, the contract terminates and no further premiums or benefits are payable.

Although the survivorship annuity provides for the payment of a life annuity to a beneficiary commencing upon the death of the insured, it is life insurance because the proceeds from which the life annuity is to be paid must be on hand at the insured's death. The amount of money which the company needs at the death of the insured is the present value of the predetermined payments promised the beneficiary. Since the present value of an immediate life annuity declines with each increase in age of the beneficiary, the effective amount of insurance under a survivorship annuity is at the maximum at time of issue and decreases steadily thereafter. Since there is no way to know the age of the beneficiary at the insured's future death, the beneficiary's life expectancy must also be considered in determining the proper rate for a survivorship annuity. For this same reason, the contract does not permit a *change* of beneficiary. It must be remembered that if the beneficiary predeceases the insured, the contract is terminated and the premium is considered fully earned. Although the insured must furnish evidence of insurability, the beneficiary does not, since an early death would be favorable to the insurance company. Insurance companies never require evidence of insurability of annuitants.

Uses of the Survivorship Annuity. This contract provides income payments which, regardless of the beneficiary's age at the insured's death, are definite as to amount, and which continue for the life of the beneficiary. It thus provides protection of a kind which cannot be obtained under any of the settlement options discussed in the previous chapter. It will be remembered that a life annuity may be obtained under one of the settlement options but the size of the annuity depends upon the age of the beneficiary at the death of the insured, and cannot be known beforehand. The survivorship annuity also provides income protection for the beneficiary at relatively low cost if the policy is taken out when the insured is young and the beneficiary is old. For this reason, the policy is attractive when a child desires to protect an aged parent or other aged relative. It may be paid for either by a single premium or by annual premiums.

There are a number of features connected with the survivorship annuity which many people consider disadvantages. The beneficiary cannot be changed. This point is of considerable importance since history shows that it frequently happens that the original beneficiary under a life insurance contract is not the one who finally receives its proceeds. It is obvious, however, that such a right cannot be allowed, since a substitution of a younger or more healthy beneficiary would increase the risk which the company is assuming in granting the protection. If the beneficiary dies before the insured, the contract is ended. It is impossible to enter into a new contract protecting a new beneficiary without having the insured submit himself again for a medical examination. When the ages are nearly equal, or when the beneficiary is younger than the insured, the survivorship annuity is seldom used because of its relatively high cost. The survivorship annuity fails to make provision for those who may become dependent upon the insured after the contract is written, and consequently, are not included in it. If a man should protect his wife by purchasing a survivorship annuity and upon his death be survived by children and his widow, the children would receive the benefits of the annuity only during the lifetime of the mother. Finally, there is no old-age protection. If a man names his wife as beneficiary, both may live a long time. Payments will not be made under the policy while both insured and beneficiary are living, and yet income may be greatly needed in old age.

Life Income Policy

The life income policy is a modified form of survivorship annuity. It differs from the pure survivorship annuity *only* in that a minimum number of payments are guaranteed following the insured's death, *whether or not the beneficiary is alive to receive them.*

If the beneficiary survives the guaranteed period (usually twenty years), she will receive a predetermined income as long as she lives. If she does not live to receive any or lives to receive only part of the guaranteed installments, the remainder of the guaranteed payments are paid to contingent beneficiaries. It can be seen that this arrangement overcomes most of the objections to the reversionary annuity. The income's being certain to the estate for twenty years, regardless of whether the beneficiary lives or not, ensures that children will be protected until they are self-supporting. For the guaranteed benefits, the beneficiary may be changed or a cash surrender value may be demanded in case it is necessary or desirable to discontinue the contract. In case the original beneficiary dies prior to the insured, the premiums are reduced. A new beneficiary normally cannot be substituted for the pure annuity benefits.

An analysis of the life income policy reveals, as in the case of the pure survivorship annuity, that the amount of insurance (risk) involved is that sum which, at the death of the insured, will be sufficient to give the beneficiary the promised annuity for the rest of life, with a number of payments guaranteed. The amount of money thus required will be less from year to year, since the risk decreases as the beneficiary grows older. It is apparent, however, that the amount of insurance cannot fall below the sum necessary to meet the guaranteed payments, since these must be paid regardless of the age or death of the beneficiary. The life income policy, therefore, consists of, first, an amount of insurance which is determined not by the age of the beneficiary, but by the present value of the guaranteed payments and, second, an amount of insurance (which decreases each year the insured lives) sufficient to provide a fixed amount of annuity to the beneficiary starting after the guaranteed payment period and continuing for the rest of life. The premium charge for this annuity depends upon the age of the beneficiary as well as the age of the insured when the policy is taken out. The discounted value of the guaranteed payments is often called the commuted value, and the technical term for the annuity is a *deferred survivorship annuity.* If the beneficiary dies before the insured, the company is no longer under obligation to pay the deferred survivorship annuity and hence the premium for this part of the contract is thereafter discontinued. The "reduced premium" is paid until the death of the insured when the guaranteed payments will be made, or, if the policy so provides, a lump-sum payment equal to their "commuted value" will be made.

The insured may change the beneficiary if he desires, and has reserved this right. If such change is made, the premium is reduced, because the insurance for the deferred survivorship annuity is discontinued. The reason for this is obvious when it is recalled that the original premium for this part of the contract was based upon the age of the beneficiary as well as that of the insured. To allow the free substitution of beneficiaries might increase the risk of the company. If the new beneficiary is younger or in better health than the original, the risk is greatly increased. Some companies, subject to approval, will permit the insured to purchase a new deferred survivorship annuity in favor of the new beneficiary in order to provide the same protection as existed for the old beneficiary.

Income and Principal Policy

The income and principal policy is a special contract which provides that upon the death of the insured, a life income of a specified amount is paid to the primary beneficiary, with the face of the policy being payable to a secondary beneficiary upon the death of the first. If the primary beneficiary predeceases the insured, the face of the policy is paid directly to the secondary beneficiary upon the death of the insured.

The specific purpose served by this policy is to provide for the lifetime needs of one beneficiary and to have the face of the policy ultimately distributed to a secondary beneficiary. This could be accomplished, of course, by leaving the proceeds of life insurance with the company under the interest option with no right of withdrawal. The problem with this solution is that it would take a very large amount of life insurance for the interest income alone to be adequate for the needs of the primary beneficiary.

The income and principal policy guarantees a higher rate of interest on the proceeds held at interest than the rate at which such proceeds are usually held, thus reducing the amount of insurance required to provide the larger income needed. The policy is in reality a combination of *whole-life insurance* and a *survivorship annuity*. The whole-life insurance proceeds furnish the funds that will eventually be paid to the secondary beneficiary upon the death of the primary beneficiary. The survivorship annuity provides the additional amount needed to increase the income from the use of the interest option on the whole-life policy to the amount of insurance promised for the primary beneficiary under the income and principal policy. The added protection will *increase the premium* by an amount that will depend upon the age of the insured and the primary beneficiary.

In the event the primary beneficiary dies before the insured, the survivorship annuity ceases, with a reduction in the premiums corresponding to that in effect for the whole-life portion of the policy. Upon the death of the insured, in these circumstances, the proceeds of the whole-life policy are payable to the secondary beneficiary.

Here, as in the case of all contracts, the insured pays for what he gets, but there is a practical objection to this contract in that the insured may be misled into believing that he is getting a higher return than normal for his beneficiary when, in reality, he is paying an extra premium for the additional income promised.

JUVENILE INSURANCE

Nature

Juvenile insurance is insurance written on the lives of children from age 1 day to 14 or 15 years of age issued *on the application of a parent* or other person responsible for the support of the child. In the past most companies have attempted to limit the amount of juvenile policies, because of the limited insurable value of a child. This skepticism was shared by several states which enacted statutes for the purpose of establishing strict limits on the amount of insurance which could be written on the lives of young children. It was feared that indiscriminate insuring of children might lead to speculation in the lives of young children. The companies have gradually relaxed their limitations, however, and unless restricted by statute, will write substantial amounts on juvenile lives.

In those states where statutory limitations exist, the pattern is to specify the maximum amount of insurance that can be in force on the life of a child at each age during the early years. In most cases the statutory limitations usually apply only up to age 5, but they may extend to age 10 or 15. Consequently, in those states with statutory limitations, juvenile policies are issued on a graded death benefit basis, in accordance with state law. Table 9–1 shows a typical graded death benefit plan.

TABLE 9-1. Graded Death Benefits per $1,000 of Ultimate Face Amount

Age at Issue Nearest Birthday	1st Year	2nd Year	3rd Year	4th Year	5th Year
0	$ 100	$ 200	$ 400	$ 600	$ 800
1	200	400	600	800	1,000
2	400	600	800	1,000	
3	600	800	1,000		
4	800	1,000			
5	1,000				

It can be seen from Table 9–1 that a $5,000 policy (ultimate face amount) issued at age 2 would pay a death benefit in the first policy year of $2,000 ($400 × 5), in the second year $3,000 ($600 × 5), and so on.

Some companies prefer to issue policies in states which impose restrictions on juvenile policies that promise, in event of death before a specified age, such as 15 or 18, only to return all premiums paid with interest. Since such contracts provide no *insurance* prior to the specified age, there is no possibility of contravening any state law regardless of the face amounts of such policies.

In those states which do not impose restrictions on juvenile insurance, it is now possible to obtain full coverage from age 0 and there is a trend in this direction. Some companies will insure a child from 1 day, but many require that the child be at least 1 month old. Because the insured under a juvenile policy is a minor, control of the policy is usually vested in the applicant (usually a parent) until the child attains age 21 or the prior death of the applicant. Many companies will issue regular policies to minors on their *own application,* provided they are above the juvenile age limit set by the particular state involved.[3] Technically, this is not juvenile insurance since the insured individual is the applicant.

Plans Available

Juvenile insurance is usually available in the following forms: (1) life paid up at 65; (2) twenty-payment life; (3) thirty-payment life; (4) endowment at eighty-five; (5) twenty-payment endowment at eighty-five; and (6) endowments maturing at ages 16 to 21.

Estate Builder.   A special juvenile policy known variously as a jumping juvenile, junior estate builder, and similar names, has been introduced in recent years with some success. It is usually issued at ages 1 to 15 in units of $1,000 with the face amount automatically increasing to $5,000 (five times the original face) at age 21 with no increase in premium. The basic policy is usually endowment at 65, life paid-up at 65, or ordinary life. This arrangement of coverage has proved very attractive, and many companies have been quite successful in merchandising this form.

Payor Benefits.   Provision can be made in all forms of juvenile insurance for continuance of the insurance in the event of the death or total disability of the person responsible for the payment of the premiums (usually the parent). A so-called payor clause is added to the juvenile policy which provides that premiums will be waived until the insured (the child) attains a specified age, usually 25, or the maturity date of the contract, whichever is earlier, in the event the premium payor dies or becomes disabled. Naturally, evidence of insurability must be furnished by the premium payor, or nominator, as he is sometimes referred to, before the payor clause can be attached to a contract.

---

[3] This is done in spite of the risk of disaffirmation of the contract by the minor-applicant when he attains his majority. See pp. 155. Some states, including New York, have by statute conferred legal capacity on minors above a certain age, usually 14, to enter life insurance transactions.

Uses of Juvenile Insurance

Juvenile insurance can serve to provide funds (1) for last illness and funeral expenses, (2) for college education, (3) to start a permanent insurance program for a child at a low premium rate, and (4) to assure a child will have some life insurance even if he later becomes uninsurable. Probably the last two purposes served by juvenile insurance are the most significant. It is important to remember, however, that juvenile insurance should not be considered until an adequate program of life insurance is carried by the breadwinner. Too often people have insured their children to develop a "college fund" or for similar purposes, and ignored the major risk, the loss of the earning capacity of the breadwinner.

OTHER SPECIAL CONTRACTS

Miscellaneous

Mortgage Redemption.   Many companies issue a special policy form which is intended solely to cancel or redeem a mortgage in the event of the death of the head of the family. Such policies, known variously as mortgage redemption, mortgage protection, home protector, or by other descriptive titles, are really nothing but pure decreasing term insurance for the period of the mortgage. They are so arranged that the amount of term insurance follows the amortization of the mortgage. Due to its temporary nature and declining face amount, this policy is quite low in cost. This type of policy has the same limitations as other temporary (term) insurance, and the importance of redeeming the mortgage must be considered in light of the family's other needs.

There is nothing unique about a mortgage redemption policy; it is simply term life insurance. The proceeds of a whole-life or any policy may be used to retire a mortgage upon the death of the breadwinner.

This policy is sometimes written in conjunction with a base plan of permanent insurance. It should be apparent that such arrangements are similar in nature to the family-income policy discussed above.

Return-of-Premium Contracts.   Such policies differ from the usual forms of life insurance in that they promise upon death to pay not only the face of the policy, but in addition thereto a sum equal to all or to a portion of the premiums paid. The premiums returned may comprise the entire amount paid during the existence of the contract, but usually such return is limited to the premiums paid during a limited period, such as ten, fifteen, or twenty years, or to a stated age, such as 60. A promise of this kind should cause no surprise since the policy merely represents *increasing term life insurance* under a level-premium plan. In other words, the face value of the policy increases as the number of premium payments increases, but the increasing amount of term insurance must be paid for by an extra charge, that is, the premium on a policy allowing a return of all or a portion of the premiums is higher than the premium for the same kind of policy when not containing a return-of-premium privilege. Thus, for an additional premium, an increasing term rider could be added to any policy and grant a return-of-premium privilege.

A similar contract is available where the term "rider" is used to provide a return of an amount equal to the cash value. Such contracts are essentially the same as return-of-premium contracts except that the amount of the increasing term insurance is slightly different.

Guaranteed Dividend Policy.   Some nonparticipating companies add a guaranteed dividend benefit to their contracts. This annual "dividend" is a specified amount and usually is attached in the form of a sheet of coupons, resembling the coupons attached to bonds. In life insurance, the term "dividend" refers to a policy's share in the divisible surplus earnings of the company, and the size of such dividends varies, depending on the future earnings of the company. Guaranteed dividends, then, are not normal life insurance dividends; rather they are an extra benefit for which an extra premium must be charged. The benefit is, in reality, a series of *one-year pure endowments,* each maturing annually in the amount of the dividend coupon.

Adjusting Benefit Policy.   Recently, a number of companies [4] have introduced policies or options which use dividends to provide some form of level constant additional coverage. The details, including the name given the plan, vary from company to company, but the purpose is basically the same. Under one plan the face amount of a special straight life policy is reduced after a few years. The dividends then are used to purchase paid-up additions and one-year term insurance in varying combinations sufficient to replace the reduction in face amount (based on current dividend scales). In the plans of most companies a time might come where more dividends would be available than needed to purchase the requisite amount of additional coverage. The excess dividends are handled in a variety of ways, but most companies issuing this type of policy use the excess to purchase paid-up additions. If the occasion arises when the divi-

[4] The impetus for the development of this policy came from a plan started by a Canadian company in 1962. See LIAMA, *Products and Services,* Bulletin No. 62, July 10, 1967.

dends are insufficient to purchase the scheduled amount of term and paid-up additions, the majority of plans with such schedules require that one-year term be purchased to stretch dividends as far as possible. The plan has been used primarily in competition as a substitute for term insurance or as an alternative to nonparticipating policies.

Cost-of-Living Policy.   A steadily growing number of life insurance companies are offering a cost-of-living rider which automatically increases coverage in accordance with increases in the consumer price index (CPI). The rider provides for term insurance as an addition to the face of the base permanent policy, the amount varying in accordance with changes in the CPI. Assuming the CPI advances 5 per cent during a year, $5,000 of 1-year term insurance automatically is written for the following year and the insured is billed for the additional coverage in his premium notice. No evidence of insurability is required for the additional term insurance. If the CPI declines, the amount of insurance is never decreased below the face amount of the base permanent plan.

Individual life insurance companies are offering other index-linked products.[5] They may be broadly grouped into two categories depending upon whether the policyholder or the company assumes the inflation risk. In the first case, the inflation risk is borne in the main by the policyholder. The company merely undertakes to provide additional insurance, at the expense of the policyholder, in event of an increase in the index. This additional insurance is normally made available on a favorable cost basis (avoiding high first-year charges) and without evidence of insurability. The additional cost is sometimes prefunded by one means or another, but not in a manner which places the company on the inflation risk.

In the second group of products, the inflation risk is borne by the life insurance company. A provision for this risk-bearing is included in the overall premium paid by the policyholder.

Other.   There is no end to the possible combinations of the basic forms of life insurance which can be made to produce a particular life insurance product. All such combinations, however, are subject to the type of analysis illustrated with the contracts discussed in this chapter.

Selecting the Proper Policy

Any policy which apparently gives something for nothing will inevitably upon further analysis prove to be simply a combination of the basic forms

---

[5] John M. Bragg, "Life Insurance with Guaranteed Purchasing Power," *Proceedings of the National Conference on Variable Life Insurance* (Philadelphia, Pa.: Insurance Department, University of Pennsylvania, March, 1971), pp. 47–60.

of insurance for which the proper actuarial premium has been charged. Although policies differ greatly in form, it is important to note that the premiums charged for all policies, as will be shown later, are computed on the basis of actuarial assumptions which ensure that the cost of any policy is the amount actually required to provide the benefits guaranteed by that policy. As mentioned earlier, all the policies issued by a given company are approximately equivalent to each other from the standpoint of dollars and cents insofar as their inherent worth is concerned.

Although the policies issued by a given company are usually on a basis of equivalency as regards net cost, it is highly important to remember that one form of policy may be much better suited to the needs of the policyholder than another.

All permanent forms of life insurance represent different combinations of protection and investment. The "mixture" or relative proportion of these two elements desired will determine the appropriate contract. If the greater weight is to be given protection with some investment, then some low premium form of whole-life insurance should be used. If greater investment is desired, but with strong protection need, a high premium form of whole-life insurance is indicated. If great weight is to be given savings and investment with less emphasis on protection, endowment insurance is appropriate. At the extremes, if pure protection with no investment is desired, term insurance should be used; if all investment with no protection is desired, a deferred annuity is suitable. Much has been written concerning "programming" and the "fitting of the policy to the client," by which is meant that the various kinds of policies have certain advantages or disadvantages, depending upon the circumstances surrounding the applicant and the particular purpose that he wishes to realize by the taking of life insurance. It is therefore highly important for the life underwriter, after ascertaining the prospective applicant's financial ability to pay premiums and the object which he desires to accomplish through insurance, to recommend impartially that contract which will serve his client best. The matter may be illustrated by the following example: A merchant may display a large variety of suits of clothes, all priced correctly from the standpoint of their inherent value. But, despite their common value, these suits may differ in color, style, and material. One suit may be totally unfit for the use of a prospective buyer, although inherently worth just as much as another suit which may be selected by him as meeting his requirements. In life insurance, likewise, the many policies on the market may, from a mathematical standpoint, be valued correctly from the standpoint of cost. But in selecting a contract the prospective buyer should be careful to see, and in such selection it is the professional duty of the agent to render impartial advice, that the character of the policy is such as to give him what the family or business circumstances surrounding his life require.

BIBLIOGRAPHY

The Life Insurance Product: Types of Contracts

Couch, George James. *Couch Cyclopedia of Insurance Law,* 2nd ed. by Ronald A. Anderson (Rochester, N. Y.: Lawyers Cooperative Publishing Co., 1959–1968).

Day, J. Edward, and Melnikoff, Meyer. "The Variable Annuity as a Life Insurance Company Product," *Journal of the American Society of Chartered Life Underwriters,* Vol. X, No. 1 (December, 1955).

Eilers, Robert D. *Regulation of Blue Cross and Blue Shield Plans* (Homewood, Ill.: Richard D. Irwin, Inc., 1963).

Elliott, C. B. *A Treatise on the Law of Insurance* (Indianapolis, Ind.: The Bobbs-Merrill Co., 1907).

Greider, Janice E., and Beadles, William T. *Law and the Life Insurance Contract,* rev. ed. (Homewood, Ill.: Richard D. Irwin, Inc., 1968).

Herrick, Kenneth W. *Total Disability Provisions in Life Insurance Contracts.* S. S. Huebner Foundation Studies (Homewood, Ill.: Richard D. Irwin, Inc., 1958).

Johnson, George E. "The Variable Annuity," *Journal of the American Society of Chartered Life Underwriters,* Vol. VII, No. 1 (December, 1952).

Krueger, Harry, and Waggoner, Leland T., eds. *The Life Insurance Policy Contract* (Boston: Little, Brown and Company, 1953).

McGill, Dan M., ed. *The Beneficiary in Life Insurance.* S. S. Huebner Foundation Lectures (Homewood, Ill.: Richard D. Irwin, Inc., 1956).

Mehr, Robert I., and Osler, Robert W. *Modern Life Insurance,* 3rd ed. (New York: The Macmillan Company, 1961).

National Underwriter Company. *Who Writes What?* (Cincinnati, 1968).

Patterson, E. W. *Essentials of Insurance Law* (New York: McGraw-Hill Book Company, Inc., 1957).

Proceedings of the National Conference on Variable Life Insurance (Philadelphia, Pa.: Insurance Department, University of Pennsylvania, March, 1971).

Redecker, Harry S., and Reid, Charles K., II. *Life Insurance Settlement Options,* rev. ed. (Homewood, Ill.: Richard D. Irwin, Inc., 1964).

Richards, George. *The Law of Insurance,* 5th ed. (posthumous), by Warren Freedman (New York: Baker Voorhis & Company, Inc., 1952).

Schwarzschild, Stuart. *Rights of Creditors in Life Insurance Policies.* S. S. Huebner Foundation Studies (Homewood, Ill.: Richard D. Irwin, Inc., 1963).

Vance, W. R., and Anderson, B. M. *Handbook of the Law of Insurance,* 3rd ed. (St. Paul: West Publishing Company, 1951).

III The Life Insurance Product: Analysis of the Contract

Fundamental Legal 10
Concepts: I

IN THIS AND the succeeding chapter, consideration will be given to the fundamental legal concepts applicable to the making of the life insurance contract. The basic purpose of the discussion is to lay the foundation for an analysis and interpretation of the contractual relationship which provides the legal vehicle for the life insurance process. This will include the general rules of contract and agency law as they apply to the life insurance business. It should be remembered that the rules of law may be established either by constitutional provisions, by statutory enactments, by proper administrative regulations or rulings, or by precedent through court decisions.

THE LIFE INSURANCE CONTRACT

In order for any contract to be valid there are four requirements which must be met: (1) There must be an agreement based on an *offer* made by one of the parties to the contract, and an *acceptance* of that offer by the other party *in the same terms.* (2) The parties to the contract must be *legally capable* of making a contract. (3) There must be a *valid consideration.* (4) The *purpose* of the agreement must be lawful.[1] A life insurance policy is a contract and must, therefore, conform to these requirements. Before examining these basic rules as they apply to the life insurance contract, however, attention will be directed to the distinguishing characteristics of the insurance contract. This is important, since these characteristics underlie the distinctive judicial interpretation and court application of contract law to the life insurance contract.

Distinguishing Characteristics

In the first place, the insurance contract is one of *utmost good faith*— that is, each party is entitled to rely upon the representations of the other without attempt to deceive or withhold material information. The rule of

---

[1] Some types of contracts have to be in a particular *form* in order to be legal. From a practical standpoint, this aspect of the formation of a contract refers to whether or not the contract has to be in writing or can be in oral form. In the absence of specific legislation requiring a life insurance contract to be in writing, such a contract can be oral in nature. New York, Georgia and several other states have statutes requiring life insurance contracts to be in writing. Practically, oral contracts are completely unsuitable for a transaction involving life insurance.

caveat emptor[2] does not generally apply. It is not surprising to find that this is so if it is remembered that the company must depend to a great extent on the statements of prospective policyholders in assessing their acceptability for insurance purposes, and that the insurance contract is an extremely intricate and highly technical contract which forces the buyer to rely upon the good faith of the insurer. The fact that the contract is highly specialized and technical in nature also prevents it from being a bargaining contract. Its terms and provisions are fixed by the insurer and must be accepted or rejected by the prospective buyer. The contract is thus referred to as one of *adhesion*. The implications of these characteristics will be brought out later in the discussion of the construction and interpretation of the contract.

The contract of life insurance is not a contract of indemnity, as is the case of most other insurance contracts. Under a contract of indemnity the insured is never entitled to profit by reason of the insurance. Under such contracts the insurer simply puts the insured in the same financial position he would have been in had a loss not occurred. On the other hand, under a life insurance contract the insured promises to pay a definite sum of money which does not purport to measure the loss; it is a *valued* policy. The rules relating to insurable interest discussed below reflect this characteristic.

The contract is *conditional* in that the obligation of the insurer to pay a claim depends upon the performance of certain acts by the insured, such as the payment of premiums and the furnishing of proofs of death by the beneficiary.

In addition, the life insurance contract is *unilateral* in nature in that it involves an enforceable promise of one party only, the insurer. The owner of the contract makes no promise to pay the premiums. On the other hand, if he does choose to pay them, the insurer is bound to accept them and meet its obligations under the contract.

Finally, the life insurance contract may be classified as an *aleatory* contract as opposed to a *commutative* contract. In a commutative contract there is an exchange of approximately equivalent values, whereas in an aleatory contract the element of chance enters, and one party may receive much more in value than he gives under the contract. This important distinction is discussed further below.

Elements of the Life Insurance Contract

Capacity of the Parties.   In order to have a valid contract the parties must have the legal capacity to contract. If the insurance company is licensed to transact business in the state under consideration, and otherwise complies with the state insurance code, its capacity to contract is clear.

---

[2] "Let the buyer beware."

Where the insurer is incompetent by reason of noncompliance or incomplete compliance with the requirements of the state in which the contract is executed, the questions of the validity of the contract and the respective rights of the parties are not uniformly decided. The contract may be void in its inception; it may be voidable, that is, enforceable for the benefit of the innocent party; or, and by far the majority rule, the execution of the contract is penalized rather than being prohibited, that is, the contract remains binding upon both parties.[3] The insured can also sue the nonadmitted insurer in the state courts where the insured resides under the so-called Long Arm Statute.[4]

In connection with the legal capacity of the insured to contract, no problem arises unless the insured is (1) a minor, (2) intoxicated, (3) insane, or (4) an enemy alien.

In the absence of contrary state law, contracts made by minors are voidable except for the reasonable value of necessaries. Legal majority is 21 in most states, although a few states permit minors to enter into contracts at 18 or upon marriage or a combination of age and marriage. A number of states also have special statutes giving minors 14 or over the capacity to make a binding life insurance contract. These laws recognize that although *life insurance is not a necessity* it has important values to the insured and his family. In the absence of special statutes, when an insurance company enters into a contract with a minor, that contract is voidable at the option of the minor. The insurer is bound by the contract unless the minor *chooses* to repudiate the contract during minority or within a reasonable time thereafter. If the minor does repudiate his contract, the company must usually refund *all* premiums paid. Much insurance is written on the application of minors despite the danger of repudiation. There is, of course, no problem in the case of juvenile insurance where the application for insurance on the life of a minor is made by a competent adult.

A person who is under the influence of intoxicating liquor, to the extent that he is unable to understand the nature of the transaction in which he is engaged, lacks legal capacity. The effect is to make his contracts *voidable,* and he may thus repudiate the contract within a reasonable length of time after he becomes sober, or he may ratify the contract.

In the case of mental incompetency, if no guardian has been appointed, the contracts made by an insane person are *voidable* and are treated in the same manner as are the contracts made by minors. On the other hand, if a person has been declared legally insane and a guardian appointed, all contracts made by the ward are *void.* As in the case of minors, an insane person may be held liable for the reasonable value of necessaries.

Trading with an enemy in time of war is illegal, and no valid contract could be entered into during such a period. On the other hand, contracts may already be in force between domestic citizens and enemy aliens. Such

[3] Janice E. Greider and William T. Beadles, *Law and the Life Insurance Contract,* rev. ed. (Homewood, Ill.: Richard D. Irwin, Inc., 1968), pp. 44–48.

[4] *McGee vs. International Life Insurance Company* (1957), 355 U. S. 220, 78 S. C. + 199, 2 L. Ed 2nd 223 (AAAN).

contracts are either suspended or terminated by a declaration of war. Court decisions in regard to life insurance contracts under such conditions are not at all uniform.[5]

Mutual Assent.   As in the case of other simple contracts, there must be an offer and an acceptance before the life insurance contract is created. The offer may be made by either the insurance company or the applicant, depending upon the circumstances. There are three ways in which the life insurance contract can be created: (1) the applicant may pay the premium at the time the application is submitted and receive a conditional receipt; (2) the application may be submitted but no premium paid; or (3) the applicant may pay the premium with the application but receive no conditional receipt.

Conditional Receipt.   Where the usual conditional receipt is utilized, the insurer is considered as having made an offer conditional upon the applicant's insurability, and the applicant as having accepted the conditional offer by payment of the premium. The insurance becomes effective as of the time of the medical examination (or date of conditional receipt if later) provided that the applicant is found insurable, and delivery of the policy itself is not essential. Under this arrangement, a claim would be paid even if death occurred before the papers reached the company's home office, provided that the applicant *would* have been insurable according to the company's normal standards. The purpose of this type of transaction is, of course, to provide protection, assuming the applicant is insurable, between the time of the medical examination and the time of delivery of the policy.[6]

Application Without Premium.   In case the applicant does not pay the premium when the application is submitted, if the company approves the application, the issuance of the policy and its delivery to the applicant while in good health constitutes the offer. By paying the first premium when the policy is delivered, the applicant accepts the company's offer and the contract becomes effective at that point.

Premium Paid Without Conditional Receipt.   Less frequently, the premium is paid with the application but no conditional receipt is issued. In such cases there is no contract in force until the policy is issued *and* delivered. Here the applicant is considered to have made an offer which he may withdraw at any time before acceptance by the company. Since the final act which makes the contract effective is the delivery of the policy, just what constitutes delivery, legally, becomes important.

[5] Greider and Beadles, *op. cit.,* pp. 313–315.

[6] *Ibid.,* pp. 98–106. The conditional receipt described here is widely used. There are other forms in use. A fair number of companies use a conditional receipt which makes the insurance effective the date the application is approved at the home office. This is, of course, not as favorable as the more widely used form.

Delivery need not necessarily involve an actual physical transfer of the policy into the possession of the insured. Constructive delivery may be effected if the company has intentionally and unconditionally given up control over the policy and placed it in control of someone acting for the policyholder, including the company's own agent. For example, if the company mails the policy, addressed to the insured, this constitutes constructive delivery even if he never receives it—the post office in this case is regarded as the insured's agent. Again, mailing the policy to the company's agent for unconditional delivery makes the delivery effective even if the agent never actually places the policy in the insured's hands. But, if an agent is instructed not to deliver the policy unless the applicant is in good health (the usual case), there is no constructive delivery. It should be noted, however, that undue delay by the agent in delivering the policy to the insured has been construed as constructive delivery.

Mere possession of a policy does not establish delivery if all conditions have not been met. For instance, it is not uncommon to leave the policy with the applicant for inspection, but his possession of it does not establish legal delivery if it can be established that the premium has not been paid. In this connection it is usual to obtain an inspection receipt from the applicant setting forth his acknowledgment of the circumstances under which he is granted possession of the policy. Such a receipt is not legally necessary, but it is a practical precaution,[7] and will prevent misunderstanding with the beneficiary in the event something happens to the applicant before he pays the premium.

In a majority of cases the date written on the policy is not the same as the effective date of the policy. Commonly, the contract is dated as of the date of the application. In some cases it is given the date on which the policy is actually written. Again, the policy may be antedated to give the policyholder the benefit of a date nearest his earlier birthday to gain the advantage of lower rates. This does not alter the effective date of the protection, but it does raise two important questions: (1) when does the next premium come due and (2) from what date do the incontestable and suicide periods run?[8] The courts, in general, have held that except in conditional receipt cases, the date written on the policy determines the date on which premiums are due even though this means less than one full year's protection is granted. With regard to the suicide and incontestable clauses, the general rule is that when the policy bears a date earlier than the date when actual protection began, the date of the policy establishes the point of departure. On the other hand, when the policy bears a date later than the actual date of issue, the clauses are held to run from the date when protection began. Where the

---

[7] Possession of a life insurance policy at the death of the insured, in the absence of fraud, creates a presumption that the initial premium was paid. See *ibid.*, pp. 289–291.

[8]*Ibid.*, p. 291. See also *Lentin vs. Continental Assurance Co.* (1952) 412 Ill. 158, 105 N.E. 2d 735, 44 A.L.R. 2d 463.

clauses themselves specify a certain date as the date of issue for the purposes of these clauses, this date is usually recognized.

Consideration.   In the life insurance contract the consideration given by the applicant for the promises of the company are the statements in the application and the payment of the first annual premium or, in the event premiums are paid less frequently than annually, the first installment thereof. Premiums subsequent to the first premium or installment are not part of the "legal consideration," but are simply conditions which must be performed to keep the contract in existence.[9]

Payment of the premium is usually required in cash. The insurer may, however, agree to accept a check, note, or, in the absence of a prohibitive statute, services. Although a check is customarily considered cash, payment by check is usually accepted only as *conditional* payment. This means that if a check is not paid when presented, there has been no payment, and the insurer's promise is no longer binding, regardless of the good faith of the insured. The insurer may, of course, agree to accept a check as absolute payment, in which case the check would constitute valid consideration whether it were paid on presentment or not.

In the case of a promissory note, if the agent has authority from his company to deal in premium notes, a note is adequate consideration. Thus, unless the note has a provision to the effect that the policy will be repudiated if the note is not honored at maturity, the premium is considered paid and constitutes adequate consideration for the contract. In such cases the note is a separate transaction and the company's action is limited to its rights on the note if it is not honored at maturity.[10]

Legal Purpose.   To be valid a contract must be for a legal purpose and not contrary to public policy. For example, in most states gambling transactions have been declared illegal by statute. Such agreements are, therefore, unenforceable at law. Both a gambling transaction and a life insurance contract are in the same class, in that they are aleatory in character as contrasted to commutative.

In a commutative agreement an approximate exchange of equal values is intended. For example, in an agreement to sell real estate, the seller undertakes to obtain in money at least approximately what the property is worth to him, and the buyer expects to pay in money the approximate worth of the property which he undertakes to buy. Opposed to the commutative agreement is the *aleatory* agreement. In such an agreement the element of chance plays a significant role. Each party to such an agreement

---

[9] *Ibid.*

[10] There are conflicting decisions as to the effect of a forfeiture provision when it is included in only the policy or the note. Where the forfeiture provision is contained in both the policy and note, the provisions have uniformly been held valid and enforceable. See *ibid.*, p. 298.

recognizes that one of them may obtain far more in equivalent worth under the contract than the other, but each also recognizes that which one will gain and which will lose is governed by the operations of chance. The typical aleatory agreement is the wager or gambling agreement, which is, in general, illegal. The insurance contract is also aleatory, yet it is entirely legal and universally recognized as conducive to the public good. The distinction between the contract of insurance and the illegal wagering contract is vitally important. Insofar as the applicant is concerned, the distinction is fundamental. One's purpose in entering a wager is to gain at the expense of others through the operation of the inequalities of chance. One's purpose in entering an insurance contract is the precise converse—it is to avoid the inequalities of chance and transform uncertainty into certainty. The requirement of an *insurable interest* in insurance takes the agreement out of the gambling category. This subject of *insurable interest* is so vital that it will be discussed in detail in a separate section below.

From the insurer's standpoint the insurance agreement is removed from the category of gambling by the *elimination of chance* through the operation of the law of large numbers.

In addition to the fact that a life insurance contract will fail if there is no insurable interest on the part of the applicant in the insured, a contract may be illegal and against public policy for other reasons. As was mentioned earlier, a contract with an enemy alien is held to be against public policy and void. Again, a contract is illegal and void where it is negotiated with intent to murder.

Insurable Interest

Nature of Insurable Interest.　　A contract of life insurance must, according to law, be supported by an interest in the continuance of the life of the insured. Such an *insurable interest* may assume many forms and may have its origin, as we shall see, in a great variety of relationships. An exact definition of the term in a few words is therefore difficult, if not impossible. Mr. Justice Field briefly summarized the nature of the interest in the following words:[11]

It is not easy to define with precision what will in all cases constitute an insurable interest so as to take the contract out of the class of wager policies. It may be stated generally, however, to be such an interest, arising from the relations of the party obtaining the insurance, either as creditor of or surety for the assured, or from the ties of blood or marriage to him, as will justify a reasonable expectation of advantage or benefit from the continuance of his life. It is not necessary that the expectation of advantage or benefit should be always capable of pecuniary estimation, for a parent has an insurable interest in the life of his child, and a child in the life of his parent, a husband in the life of his wife, and

[11] *Warnock vs. Davis* (1881) 104 U.S. 775, 779; (1938) 94 Fed. 2d. 409.

a wife in the life of her husband. The natural affection in cases of this kind is considered more powerful—as operating more efficaciously—to protect the life of the insured than any other consideration. But in all cases there must be a reasonable ground, founded upon the relations of the parties to each other, either pecuniary or of blood or affinity, to expect some benefit or advantage from the continuance of the life of the assured. Otherwise, the contract is a mere wager, by which the party taking the policy is directly interested in the early death of the assured. Such policies have a tendency to create a desire for the event. They are, therefore, independently of any statute on the subject, condemned as being against public policy.

As indicated in the above decision, life insurance policies in the absence of insurable interest are unenforceable at law, first, because they are wagers and void as against public policy or contrary to statutes prohibiting gaming and, second, because they are an incentive to crime in that they encourage the taking of human life. This doctrine has been developed out of regard for public welfare rather than for the protection of insurance companies. Although a policy of insurance involves risk or speculation, it is not ordinarily a wagering transaction. It differs from the latter in that it is the purpose of the contract to eliminate a risk that already exists, whereas, in a purely wagering contract, the risk is created by the contract itself. It is the presence of insurable interest that transforms the insurance policy from an instrument of wager into one of insurance. In discussing insurable interest in life insurance it is helpful to analyze the question from the standpoint of whether the policy is taken out by the insured upon his own life or whether the policy is taken out upon the life of some other person.

Insurable Interest of the Insured in His Own Life.   It is a fundamental principle of law that every man possesses an insurable interest to an unlimited extent in his own life, and that he may make his insurance payable to any person he chooses to name as beneficiary.[12] In this respect life insurance affords a striking contrast to fire and other forms of property insurance. Fire insurance policies, for example, are contracts of indemnity and the company's liability is limited to the value of the property at the time of the fire, that is, the face of the policy, owing to depreciation of the property or other causes, is not necessarily the sum that will be paid when a total loss of the property occurs. Life insurance contracts, however, are not regarded purely as contracts of indemnity, and in cases where the insurance is taken out by the person whose life is insured, the courts have refused to establish any degree of relationship between the amount of insurance and the value of the life on which it is taken. When the contract is taken without collusion and without intent to violate the laws prohibiting wagers, the natural love of life is held to constitute a sufficient insurable in-

---

[12] 29 Am. Jur. Sec. 355.

terest to support a policy for any amount. It should be stated, however, that although *legally* there is no limit to the amount of insurance that may be taken out by an individual on his own life, nevertheless, in practice the companies are concerned with this problem, and in order to avoid over-insurance and consequent moral hazard, they usually limit the amount that they will write on one life to a sum that is not unreasonably large relative to the insured's financial status and earning capacity.

Insurable Interest of Another in the Life of the Insured. Turning now to a consideration of the subject from the standpoint of insurance taken out by persons on the lives of other persons, we unfortunately meet with a great variety of court decisions. This lack of harmony in the court law presents itself in nearly all relationships that may arise out of commercial dealings or out of the ties of affection or kinship. As a general rule a person taking out insurance on the life of another must have insurable interest. It has been held, however, that if the beneficiary has such an interest the person taking out the insurance need have none. But even where the interest exists, a policy obtained without the knowledge and consent of the insured is contrary to public policy and void.[13] Insurable interest may arise out of one or more of the following three classes of relationships:

1. *Insurable interest arising out of ties of affection, blood, or marriage.* The courts have generally held that certain ties of near relationship create an insurable interest, even though the element of dependence is not present. Thus, the relationship of husband and wife is conclusively presumed to establish an insurable interest on behalf of either party in the other's life. Some courts have added the relationship of parent and child and of brother and sister, but have refused to extend it further. As regards other relationships, the courts have generally taken the position that the interest must be based upon a reasonable expectation of deriving pecuniary benefit from the continuance of the insured's life. In this theory, for example, American courts have repeatedly held that a woman has an insurable interest in the life of her fiancé, since that relationship gives to her a reasonable right to expect pecuniary benefit. An excellent review of the numerous decisions referring to insurable interest arising out of ties of blood or affection is furnished by the Circuit Court of Appeals.[14] Following a review of the decisions bearing on the subject the court held:

The sum of the decisions and of textbook discussion upon the subject of insurable interest may, we think, be fairly stated thus: No person has an insurable interest in the life of another unless he would in reasonable probability suffer a pecuniary loss, or fail to make a pecuniary gain, by the other's death;

---

[13] Some states (for example, Louisiana) permit either a husband or wife to take insurance on the life of the other without consent of the one insured.

[14] *Life Insurance Clearing Company vs. O'Neill* (1901; C.C.A.) 106 Fed. 800, 201.

or (in some jurisdictions) unless, in the discharge of some undertaking, he has spent money, or is about to spend money, for the other's support or advantage. The extent of the insurable interest—the amount for which a policy may be taken out, or for which recovery may be had—is not now under consideration. What is often called "relationship insurance" must be governed by this rule. It must rest upon the foundation of a pecuniary interest, although the interest may be contingent, and need not be capable of exact estimation in dollars and cents. Sentiment or affection is not sufficient of itself, although it may often be influential in persuading a court or jury to reach the conclusion that a beneficiary had a reasonable expectation of pecuniary advantage from the continued life of the insured. In one relation only—the relation of husband and wife—is the actual existence of such a pecuniary interest unimportant; the reason being that a real pecuniary interest is found in so great a majority of cases that the courts conclusively presume it to exist in every case, whatever the fact may be, and therefore will not inquire into the true state of a few exceptional instances. This, we think, is essentially what is meant by the declaration of courts and textbook writers that the mere relationship of husband and wife is sufficient to give an insurable interest. . . .

In all other relationships there is no presumption of interest, and no insurable interest exists, unless the reasonable likelihood of pecuniary loss or gain is present in actual fact. No doubt, judicial language is to be found supporting the view that the mere relationship of parent and child is sufficient to give an insurable interest.

2. *Insurable interest growing out of the creditor–debtor relationship.* The rule is well settled that a creditor has an insurable interest in the life of his debtor. In this respect the important question is the amount of insurance, as compared with the amount of the debt, which the creditor shall be allowed to take on the life of the debtor. Manifestly, the creditor's insurable interest should not be limited to the face of the indebtedness, because under such circumstances the creditor, upon the death of the debtor, would be enabled to indemnify himself only to the extent of his debt, and would be unsecured as regards the premiums paid together with interest thereon. The courts are not uniform in establishing a rule concerning the validity of a policy where the amount of insurance exceeds the debt. Where there is a substantial interest, however, mere overvaluation is not conclusive evidence that the policy is a wager contract.

The rule adopted by the United States Supreme Court places an indefinite restriction upon the insurable interest of the creditor by providing that the relationship between the amount of insurance and the amount of the debt must not be so disproportionate as to make the policy take on the appearance of a wagering contract as distinguished from its legitimate purpose, namely, security for the indebtedness. In *Cammack vs. Lewis*,[15] for example, the court declared a policy of $3,000 taken out by a creditor to

[15] (1872) 15 Wall. (U.S.) 643.

secure a debt of $70 to be "a sheer wagering policy, without any claim to be considered as one meant to secure the debt." Mr. Justice Miller stated in his opinion that "to procure a policy for $3,000 to cover a debt of $70 is of itself a mere wager. The disproportion between the real interest of the creditor and the amount to be received by him deprives it of all pretense to be a bona fide effort to secure the debt, and the strength of this proposition is not diminished by the fact that Cammack was only to get $2,000 out of the $3,000; nor is it weakened by the fact that the policy was taken out in the name of Lewis and assigned by him to Cammack."[16] But while making the relationship between the amount of insurance and the amount of the debt an important factor to be considered on the merits of each case, the Supreme Court has never undertaken to define this relationship precisely.

Although it is perhaps better to decide each case in the light of its own circumstances, some states have attempted definitely to limit the amount of insurance that may be taken out by the creditor. Thus, Pennsylvania has adopted a rule to the effect that the policy is limited to the amount of the debt with interest and the amount of premiums with interest thereon during the expectancy of the life insured according to the Carlisle tables.[17] Such attempts to define precisely the creditor's interest, however, have not met with the favorable opinion of legal critics but, instead, have been opposed on the grounds that:

First, the validity of the contract should be determined according to the motives of the parties and the contract as viewed at its date, rather than after the death of the insured; and secondly, the total amount of premium, as thus computed with interest thereon, will generally exceed the face amount of the policy, no matter how large or how small the amount of insurance, leaving to the creditor nothing at all to apply upon the debt.[18]

Opposed to the foregoing rules are those decisions which, while limiting the creditor in his right of recovery on a policy, permit him to secure as much insurance on the debtor's life as he may choose to take out. His right to recover, however, is limited to the amount of the debt and the premiums plus interest thereon, the balance, if any, passing to the debtor. This rule, sometimes referred to as the Texas rule, is well exemplified by the case of *Cheeves vs. Anders*.[19] Here the court declared that:

The limit of interest of a creditor in a policy upon the life of his debtor is the amount of such debt and interest plus the amount expended to preserve the policy with interest thereon. The remainder of the proceeds of the policy, the court

---

[16] *Ibid.*, p. 647.

[17] *Wheeland vs. Atwood* (1899) 192 Pa. 237.

[18] *Richards on the Law of Insurance*, 5th ed. (New York: Baker, Voorhis & Co., Inc., 1952), p. 397.

[19] (1894) 87 Tex. 287.

held, should go to the estate of the insured on the ground that "if the person named as beneficiary, or the assignee of such policy, has no insurable interest in the life of the insured, he will hold the proceeds as the trustee for the benefit of those entitled by law to receive it."

3. *Insurable interest growing out of other business relations.* Numerous business relations, other than that of creditor and debtor, justify the taking of insurance by one person on the life of another. Thus, an employer may insure the life of an employee and the employee the life of the employer, a partner the life of a copartner, and the partnership the life of each partner, and the corporation the life of an officer. Similarly, a surety on a bond, though no default on the bond has occurred, has an insurable interest in the life of the principal. Again, the holder of a property interest contingent upon another person's reaching a certain age may protect himself against the loss of his contingent right through the death of that person before attaining the prescribed age. The courts have even refused to hold that those furnishing funds for corporate enterprises have no insurable interest in the lives of the managers and promoters of said corporations; and it is stated that certain stockholders in the United States have taken out insurance on the lives of prominent financiers who were instrumental in financing and promoting the corporations whose stock they held.[20]

Insurable Interest of the Assignees.   The assignment of a policy and the appointment of a beneficiary, it should be noted, have been held by the courts to be subject to contract and statutory restrictions. The important question for consideration under this heading, however, is: Can a policy taken out by a person on his own life, and valid at its inception, be subsequently assigned to one who has no insurable interest in the life of the insured? In answering this question the courts are by no means a unit, but a review of the decisions indicates an increasingly liberal attitude. Some of the earlier decisions of the United States Supreme Court would indicate its disapproval of such a practice.[21] Where, however, the assignment is made in good faith, and it is not a device to conceal wagering, speculation in insurance, or evasion of the law, an assignee of an existing life policy that was valid when effected, is entitled to demand and require payment of the whole sum insured. This rule has been adopted by the majority of the juris-

---

[20] Richards, *op. cit.*, pp. 398–401.

[21] In *Warnock vs. Davis* (1881) 104 U.S. 775, 782, the court states: "But if there be any sound reason for holding a policy invalid when taken out by a party who has no interest in the life of the assured, it is difficult to see why that reason is not as cogent and operative against a party taking an assignment of a policy upon the life of a person in which he has no interest. The same ground which invalidates the one should invalidate the other—so far, at least, as to restrict the right of the assignee to the sums actually advanced by him. In the conflict of decisions on this subject we are free to follow those which seem more fully in accord with the general policy of the law against speculative contracts upor human life." See also (1938) 94 Fed. 2d., 409.

dictions, and the reason for its adoption may be obtained from the decision in the case of *Gordon vs. Ware National Bank*.[22] In commenting on the ruling of the Supreme Court of Indiana to the effect that an assignment of a policy to one having no insurable interest was void, and that certain other states had adopted it, the court stated:[23]

The rule adopted by these states greatly detracts from the value of life insurance policies, and restricts their commercial value; for, if their possible purchasers are limited to those who have insurable interests in the lives they insure, it is obvious that buyers will be few, and their commercial value and the traffic in them must be much less than if all men may become their lawful purchasers. In view of this fact the Supreme Court of the United States and the courts of the great commercial communities of this country—of New York, Ohio, Massachusetts, Illinois, Michigan, New Jersey, California, Minnesota, Connecticut, Louisiana, Rhode Island, Wisconsin, Nebraska, Tennessee, South Carolina, Mississippi, and Maryland—have repudiated the old declaration of the Supreme Court of Indiana, and have adopted the more modern and national rule that "any person has a right to procure an insurance on his own life, and to assign it to another, provided it is not done by way of cover for a wager policy." . . . This is a great commercial nation. The policy of the nation, the business habits and acts of its citizens, and the tendency of the decisions of its courts are to depart more and more from the old rule that choses in action are not assignable, to make them more and more subject of traffic and commerce, and to sustain their transfers in the ordinary course of business.

It may be added that many of the cases declaring an assignment without interest to be illegal involve a consideration of facts which indicate strongly that the transaction under consideration constituted an attempt to secure speculative insurance. Generally speaking, assignments of policies are not regarded by the courts as creating new contracts, but merely as continuing the old ones. The modern tendency in business is to make the transfer of life insurance policies as free as possible, and if the transfer is effected with the consent of the parties, the courts are more and more inclined to regard objections on the ground of public policy as of little consequence. Thus, Mr. Justice Holmes decided that "the danger that might arise from a general license to all to insure whom they like does not exist [in assignment]. Obviously, it is a very different thing from granting such a general license, to allow the holder of a valid insurance upon his own life to transfer it to one whom he, the party most concerned, is not afraid to trust."[24]

The Time and Continuity of Insurable Interest.   Recent cases affecting insurance on property exhibit a strong tendency to apply the rule that an insurable interest existing at some time during the risk and at the time of the loss is sufficient to validate the policy, and that it is unnecessary to have the interest exist at the time of the issuance of the contract. As

[22] (1904; C.C.A.) 132 Fed. 444.
[23] *Ibid.*, pp. 447, 448.
[24] *Grigsby vs. Russell* (1911) 222 U.S. 149, 155; (1940) 116 Fed. 2d. 261.

regards life insurance, the weight of authority is to the opposite effect, that is, the interest must exist at the time the contract is made, and a policy, valid at its inception, will not thereafter be voided if it should happen that the interest ceases before the maturity of the contract, unless the provisions of the policy are such as to bring about that result. The fact that insurable interest need exist only at the inception of the contract is a corollary of the views of present-day courts that life insurance policies are not contracts of indemnity. In former times this was not true. Although the principle of indemnity has never been applied to insurance taken out by an individual on his own life, it was adopted as the correct view when the question involving the insurance of the life of a debtor by his creditor was first presented. Thus, if a *creditor* obtained a policy upon the life of his debtor and paid premiums thereon, and the debtor subsequently repaid the debt, and then died, the courts held that no recovery could be had upon the life insurance policy, since it was one of indemnity. The debt having been paid to the creditor, he suffered no loss by the death of the insured and therefore could not collect upon his policy. This ruling to the effect that life insurance policies, like fire and marine policies, were contracts of indemnity, found little favor with the life insurance companies at the time. In practice it was disregarded, and finally the courts of England changed their attitude. In overturning the former rule in the case of *Dalby vs. India*,[25] the presiding judge stated that a life insurance policy is a mere contract to pay a certain sum of money on the death of the person stipulated. In the decision it was emphasized that the view hitherto prevailing, whereby the right to recover was limited to the amount of the interest, if any, at the time of the death, was contrary to practice and fair dealing and common honesty. The later English doctrine was adopted by the American courts, and with a very few exceptions is the present rule.[26] The result may be, therefore, that the creditor will be twice paid for his debt, once by his debtor and again by recovery on the policy. So, too, the courts generally have decided that a policy naming a married woman as beneficiary remains in force even though she obtains a divorce before the insured's death. Some states' divorce laws specifically mention insurance policies and cut off the divorced wife's interest.[27]

Where, however, the *debtor* takes out the policy, the creditor is not entitled to double payment. As stated by the United States Supreme Court,[28] "if a policy of insurance be taken out by a debtor on his own life, naming a creditor as beneficiary, or with a subsequent assignment to a creditor, the general doctrine is that on payment of the debt the creditor loses all interest therein, and the policy becomes one for the benefit of the insured, and collectible by his executors or administrators."

[25] *Dalby vs. The India and London Life-Insurance Co.* (1845) 15 C.B. (Eng.) 365.
[26] At one time Texas and Virginia were exceptions, but both now follow the general rule.
[27] *McCain vs. Yost* (1955) 155 Tex. 174, 284 S.W. 2d 898; and Texas Insurance Code 3.49–1.
[28] *Crotty vs. Union Mut. Life Ins. Co.* (1892) 144 U.S. 621, 624.

Fundamental Legal Concepts: II | 11

CONSTRUCTION AND INTERPRETATION OF THE POLICY AND APPLICATION

As WAS POINTED out in the preceding chapter, the validity of a policy of insurance depends upon the same common law principles that apply to every other legal contract. The agreement between competent parties, resulting from an offer and acceptance, must comply with legal requirements as to form and have for its purpose a legal object. There must be a valuable consideration, an insurable interest, and the contract must be made with full knowledge of material facts and be free from fraud, mistake, or misunderstanding. The relationship established is that of conditional debtor and creditor, and not that of trustee and *cestui que trust*.

General Rules Underlying Court Decisions Affecting Life Insurance

Policy forms are necessarily general in character, and are drawn to meet a general situation and not with reference to particular cases. Yet, it is apparent that innumerable instances arise which require a special interpretation of the general terms of the contract in order to realize the essential purpose of the contract, namely, to protect against loss. There is scarcely a provision in the policy today which has not been the subject of interpretation by the courts, and chiefly because of ambiguity in the wording, varying circumstances surrounding the loss, or statutory requirements, there are few provisions concerning which there are not conflicting opinions. Frequently also, the interests of the insured seem at variance with the interests of the insurer, with the result that the attitude of state legislatures has often been one of hostility. Under these conditions, it is to be expected that disputes will frequently occur as to the interpretation which shall be given to the general provisions of the policy when unexpected circumstances surround the particular loss. However great the conflict of authority has become, there are certain legal principles underlying the interpretation of the appli-

167

cation, as well as of policy provisions, that are kept in mind by the courts as guiding principles in their efforts to interpret the contract. Briefly summarized, these principles are discussed below.

Not Contracts of Indemnity.   Unlike fire insurance contracts, life insurance policies, although the indemnification of the value of human life in case of premature death should be their essential objective, cannot be regarded by the courts as purely contracts of indemnity. In fire insurance, for example, no matter what the stated value of the property may be in the policy, as a general rule the insured can collect no more than the actual value of the property at the time of the fire. Life insurance contracts, however, are held to be contracts to pay a certain sum of money in the event of death. This general ruling has an important bearing upon the subject of insurable interest in life insurance. The chief difficulty that the courts have encountered in disposing of this legal phase of the subject seems to have presented itself in those cases where creditors (or persons similarly situated) take out policies on the lives of their debtors with a view to securing the indebtedness.

Contract of Adhesion.   Whenever the wording of any provision in the contract permits of more than one construction, the courts will give the benefit of the doubt to the insured on the ground that the contract is not a bargaining contract but rather one of "adhesion"; that is, that the insured is obliged to take the form of policy offered by the company and which was framed by it in its own interest. Few persons understand the subject of insurance or the rules of law governing the negotiations, and they have no voice in fixing the provisions of the contract. Forfeitures are not favored by the courts, and conflicting provisions or ambiguous language will, therefore, be so construed as to give effect to the contract. As the United States Supreme Court has ruled: [1]

> Where a policy of insurance is so framed as to leave room for two constructions, the words used should be interpreted most strongly against the insurer. This exception rests upon the ground that the company's attorneys, officers, or agents prepared the policy, and it is its language that must be interpreted.

Admitting that this is a reasonable rule where the company is free to frame the policy, the question arises as to whether this same ruling should be applied where the policy forms, or portions thereof, are prescribed and made compulsory by law.[2] Where the policy is in a form required by

[1] *Liverpool, etc., Insurance Company vs. Kearney* (1901) 180 U.S. 132, 136; (1939) 102 Fed. 2d. 561.

[2] Although Massachusetts adopted a standard fire policy as early as 1873, it was not until 1906 that such action was taken by any of the states for the purpose of prescribing the form of the life insurance contract. New York passed a law, effective

statute, the above rule is not universally enforced, but probably the weight of authority, especially as it pertains to the insurance, is to the effect that the insured should be favored. The principle has been stated as follows: [3]

> Although a standard form of policy is prescribed by statute, nevertheless upon its acceptance by the parties it becomes a voluntary contract between them which derives its force and efficacy from their consent. It constitutes their contract, and it must be construed by the same rules as similar contracts voluntarily entered into. And the fact that the legislature has prescribed a standard form of policy affords no reason for giving to a clause any different construction from that theretofore given by the courts to all similar contracts made without legislative sanction. So where the terms employed in a standard policy have been in previous use in insurance contracts and have had a judicial construction, it will be assumed that said terms were used in the standard forms in the sense in which they were previously used and defined.

Endorsements Take Precedence Over Policy Form.   Since policy forms are necessarily general in character and cannot meet all particular contingencies, although this is not so generally true in life insurance as in fire and other forms of property insurance, it follows that special or written agreements must often be endorsed on the contract with a view to modifying the original terms of the policy form. Where this is done, it is a universally recognized principle that whenever there is a difference in meaning between any endorsement and the policy form itself, the superimposed parts of the contract, whether written, stamped, or printed, control the regular provisions of the policy. This principle is based on the theory that endorsements on the policy must be considered as later in date than the policy itself, thus representing the latest agreement between the parties. If ambiguity exists in the wording of any such endorsements, the insured must again be given the benefit of the doubt. Similarly, if the written portion of the regular policy is inconsistent with the printed portion, the former will be upheld, since it refers to this particular contract as distinguished from the general form which the parties frequently do not bother to revise in conformity with the written portion.

January 1, 1907, in which the wording of various types of contracts was established, but this method was not regarded as satisfactory and the law was repealed several years later. In its place the legislature substituted a statute requiring that all policies must contain certain clauses with established minimum standards of liberality, although companies may issue policies which are more favorable to the insured. Statutes of this nature are typical of those passed in many states, although some, in addition, prohibit absolutely the inclusion of certain clauses. In addition, some few states at the present time have made provision for complete standard forms, but these are *optional.*

[3] *Gratz vs. Ins. Co. of N.A., Appellant* (1925) 282 Pa. 224, 230, quoting *Joseph A. Joyce on Insurance,* 2nd ed. (Rochester, N. Y.: Lawyers Co-operative Publishing Co., 1917), pp. 546–547.

Contract Enforced as It Stands.   In the absence of conflicting provisions or ambiguity in language, however, no discretion can be exercised by the court to modify the contract in such a way as to bring about an adjustment which it may regard as more just than the strict enforcement of the contract as it stands. The reason for the rule has been set forth as follows: [4]

Parties competent to contract may enter into such agreements with each other as they see fit, and it is the purpose of the law and function of the court to enforce their contract if not in violation of law or opposed to public policy. Courts do not make contracts for parties who are fully capable of making their own agreements, and if there is no ambiguity about a contract the courts cannot permit a construction contrary to its terms.

Again, stated more succinctly: [5]

Courts have no more right by strained construction to make a policy more beneficial by extending the coverage contracted for than they would have to increase the amount of insurance.

Governing Law.   Generally speaking, the construction of the contract as to its *validity* will be governed by the law and usages of the place where the contract is made. This is held to be where the last and essential acts necessary to formation of a contract took place.[6] Assignments and other matters relating to the *performance* of the contract, however, are governed by the law of the place of performance, regardless of the place where the original contract was made.

[4] *Hancock vs. Knights of Security* (1922) 303 Ill. 66, 73.

[5] *Davis vs. Jefferson Life Ins. Co.* 73 Fed. 2d. 330.

[6] In discussing this rule and exceptions thereto, Richards makes the following comments:

"This rule is peculiarly appropriate to this branch of the law because in insurance there may be several places where the contract is operative—one place for the payment of premiums, another for the payment of loss, and a third for the location of the subject of insurance. But if the policy provides that the premiums and loss are to be payable at the home office, the latter place would seem to be the place of performance, and there would in that case be cogent reason for holding, in analogy to the general rule, that its law is to prevail in the construction of the policy.

"It is often important to determine by what law the validity and effect of the policy are to be governed, because the statutory provisions, as well as usages and decisions, relating to the insurance contract vary greatly in different states, and such statutes generally have no extraterritorial effect. If the policy provides that it will not be binding until countersigned at a certain agency, the agency is ordinarily the place of contract. So, if the policy is sent to the agent for delivery on receipt of the premium; but if the application is accepted at the home office, and the policy mailed from there to the applicant in another state, the home office will be the place of contract. As a general thing, the contract is considered made where the last act necessary to complete it is done." *Richards on the Law of Insurance,* 5th ed. (New York: Baker, Voorhis & Co., 1952), pp. 1319–1320.

The Application and Its Interpretation

An application for life insurance may be defined as the insured's proposal to the insurer for protection, and may be considered as the beginning of the policy contract. In this document the applicant is required to give true answers to a large number of questions, relating principally to his personal and family history, habits, total insurance already taken out, and other applications for insurance which are either pending or have been postponed or refused. The policy usually stipulates that insurance is granted in consideration of the application for the policy, which is declared to be a part thereof, and most generally contains an additional clause to the effect that the policy and the application therefor (a copy of which is attached to the policy when issued) "constitute the entire contract between the parties."

Until about 1870 it was not customary to attach to the policy a copy of the application. In the following years many companies, realizing that it was desirable for the insured to know from his policy just what his contract provided, made it a practice to attach a copy of the application. At the present time many states have laws requiring the annexation of applications to policies, on penalty of the company's being estopped from denying the correctness or truth of such application. Other states have adopted statutes requiring every policy to contain the entire contract between the parties and forbidding the incorporation therein, by reference, of any rules, application, or other writings unless the same are endorsed upon or attached to the policy when issued. This applies to statements made to the medical examiner if signed by the insured.

Full Knowledge and Disclosure.   In deciding whether to assume a given risk, the insurer relies in part on information furnished by the applicant. Consequently, the company is entitled to have all information which would have an influence on its decision to assume or not assume a given risk. This is particularly true in connection with a highly aleatory contract such as the life insurance contract. As a result, the applicant must act in good faith, and if the information given is *false* or *incomplete* the insurer may be in a position to rescind or cancel the contract. Thus, either the failure of the applicant to disclose fully all pertinent information (doctrine of concealment) or the falsity of positive statements made by the applicant may be grounds for rescinding the contract (doctrines of warranties and representations).

Concealment.   As stated above, the courts have repeatedly stated that insurance policies are contracts involving the utmost good faith. In the early cases it was held that they were based upon chance and that the withholding of any essential facts by either party rendered the risk actually insured different from that intended to be run. The validity of the policy therefore depended upon the full disclosure of all material information. The test of the materiality of a fact concealed is whether its knowledge by the company would have influenced it in accepting or rejecting the risk, or if it would have been a fair reason for increasing the premium. In other words, was the concealment so materially important as to have induced the company, had the information been known, to have declined the risk or to have altered the rate? Whether a fact is material and should have been revealed is generally a question for the jury.

The doctrine of concealment which was developed in connection with marine insurance was primarily for the protection of the underwriter and at one time was applied to all branches of insurance, but, as the business developed, the courts recognized that some distinction should be made between marine insurance and fire or life insurance. It should be remembered that, as contrasted to marine insurance, where the property to be insured may be thousands of miles away, the life insurer is in a position to examine the applicant in person, ask questions on important points, and have the advice of a physician who examines the applicant. It is only natural that the duty to disclose should be relaxed somewhat in life insurance. The question was very thoroughly reviewed in the case of *Penn Mutual Life Insurance vs. Mechanics' Savings Bank and Trust Company*,[7] and at the present time the rule relative to life policies is well settled that "no failure to disclose a fact material to the risk, not inquired about, will void the policy, unless such nondisclosure was with intent to conceal from the insurer a fact believed to be material; that is, unless the nondisclosure was fraudulent." [8]

Representations.   In general, a representation is a statement made to the insurer for the purpose of giving information or inducing him to accept the risk. It may be designated as a misrepresentation when the information is incorrect. "Affirmative representations" are those dealing with facts existing at the time the contract is made. "Promissory representations" pertain to statements made by the insured concerning what is to happen during the term of insurance. Since the courts permitted the insurer to escape liability where there was a nondisclosure of *material* facts, it may be presumed what their attitude would be when the insured, instead of merely remaining silent, actually made a statement that was false and material. To render the policy invalid, however, the insurer must prove the falsity of the statement relied upon as a defense, and its materiality is a question for the jury.

Construction of Misstatements Made by Applicant.   As a general rule, representations are construed liberally in favor of the insured

---

[7] (1896; C.C.A.) 72 Fed. 413; *Blair vs. National Security Insurance Co.* (1942) 126 Fed. 2d. 955.
[8] *Ibid.*, 434, 441.

and need be only substantially correct. The tendency of court decisions has been in the direction of protecting the insured by giving him the benefit of the doubt wherever possible and by placing favorable constructions upon the materiality of inquiries contained in the application. Whereas it was formerly the rule that a material false representation rendered the policy voidable at the option of the company even though there was no fraudulent intent on the part of the insured, this rule has been modified in certain states either by court decision or by statute. Thus, one court has stated that "a forfeiture does not follow where there has been no deliberate intent to deceive, and the known falsity of the answer is not affirmatively shown." [9] Statutes on this question are quite common among the states. Some provide that the policy will not be invalidated unless the misrepresentation is made with intent to deceive; others, that the misrepresentation must be either material or fraudulent; and still others, that the misrepresentation must have contributed to the loss. In all cases the general purpose of such laws is to prevent a forfeiture of the policy unless the company has been deceived to its detriment.

Due to the importance of the answers to the questions contained in the application, it may be worthwhile to consider a little further the attitude of the courts in construing disputes that grow out of misstatements made by the applicant.

1. *Statements as to health, freedom from disease, habits, and medical attendance.* An unusually large number of decisions have been rendered in connection with such statements, owing principally to the varied phraseology used by the companies in formulating the questions. While much depends upon the exact phraseology used, in determining whether or not the contract has been violated, the courts have generally taken the view that the expression "good health," or words to that effect, does not preclude indispositions but means freedom from such diseases or ailments as tend to undermine the general healthfulness of the system.[10] If such words as "to the best of my knowledge or belief" are used to qualify the applicant's answers, the insurer in order to void the policy must show that the insured acted in bad faith and had actual knowledge of the facts. But as Richards points out: "Without such qualifying words, where the answer of the applicant is made in good faith and relates to an unknown and obscure disease, or to a long list of diseases, some of them obscure, the courts are disposed to construe the answers as relating to matter of opinion of the applicant rather than to matter of fact." [11]

Answers relating to habits, while regarded by the courts as matters of fact rather than opinion, have in many instances been construed leniently, as may, for example, be judged from the expression of opinion of the

---

[9] *Kuhns vs. N. Y. Life Ins. Co., Appellant* (1929) 297 Pa. 418, 423.
[10] *Plumbs vs. Penn Mutual Life Ins. Co.* (1895) 108 Mich. 94.
[11] Richards, *op. cit.,* p. 1145.

United States Supreme Court that one occurrence of delirium tremens does not necessarily violate a warranty covering temperate habits.[12] Similarly, the courts, while holding that untrue answers to questions relating to medical attendance or consultation with physicians invalidate the policy, will whenever possible, especially if the questions are in the least ambiguous, interpret the language favorably to the insured.

2. *Statements relating to family relationships and family history.* Untrue answers of the applicant to questions relating to his family *relationships* have, in nearly all instances, been held to invalidate the policy. With respect to family *history,* however, the courts have shown reluctance to nullify a policy where the insured's incorrect answers were not made in bad faith. In other words the courts have manifested a strong tendency to construe statements of this class, if made in good faith, as mere matters of opinion on the ground that such questions are in the nature of collateral inquiries and that the applicant can hardly be expected to keep himself thoroughly posted on the ages at death, the condition of health during life, and the causes of death of his relatives and ancestors.

3. *Statements relating to the age of the applicant.* It must be apparent that the insurer is entitled to a correct statement of the insured's age, since the rate of premium is based on that age. In the absence, therefore, of any policy provision relating to the matter, the courts have consistently held that an understatement of age increases the risk as a matter of law and will void the policy. Such a harsh consequence is avoided today by a clause, required in most states by statute, which provides for an adjustment by stipulating that "if the age of the insured has been misstated, and the error shall not have been adjusted during his lifetime, the amount payable hereunder shall be such as the premium paid would have purchased at the correct age."

4. *Statements relating to other insurance and to rejected or postponed applications.* The importance of inquiries along these lines as a means of preventing overinsurance and uncovering or preventing attempts at fraud is obvious, and false answers to such inquiries have consistently been held to invalidate the policy. The only question of importance in this respect, concerning which court decisions do not agree, is whether the term "other insurance," when used in the application of a regular insurance company, includes certificates issued by and applications made to fraternal and mutual benefit societies. Most of the decisions rendered take the position that only policies or applications in regular companies are included in the inquiry, although some of the courts regard fraternal orders and other benefit societies as insurance concerns and, therefore, consider membership therein as other insurance. The doubt occasioned by this conflict of legal authority, however, can easily be overcome by making the inquiry in the application specifically cover benefit certificates as well as other insurance in companies.

[12] *Insurance Co. vs. Foley* (1881) 105 U.S. 350; (1887) 7 S.C. 1221.

Warranties. Closely associated with the common law doctrines of concealment and representation was that of warranty. Although severely criticized by many writers, it should be recalled that at the time of its introduction the underwriter was quite often entirely dependent upon the insured's statements for his knowledge of the risk. Since it was often difficult for the insurer to prove the materiality of a misstatement, there was frequently incorporated in the policy a warranty clause in which the applicant warranted the truth of his statements. Thus, some life policies called attention, not merely once but several times, and usually in special print, to the fact that answers in the application were made a part of the contract and would have the effect of warranties. By this practice the companies gave added force to the information furnished in the application with a view to protecting themselves as fully as possible against fraud and against the difficulty of proving the materiality of inquiries to the satisfaction of a jury. Such references were also common in the policies of many other types of insurance. The standard fire policy formerly provided that "if an application, survey, plan, or description of property be referred to in this policy it shall be a part of this contract and a warranty by the insured." The marine insurance contract also usually furnishes a striking illustration of numerous provisions and endorsements which are declared in the contract to be warranties.

The distinguishing characteristic of a warranty is that it must be absolutely and literally true, and a forfeiture will result if merely the falsehood of the statement can be shown, irrespective of its materiality. Where statements are construed as warranties, in order to escape liability the company need prove only that the statement is incorrect. The courts assume that the materiality of the thing warranted has been established and that all inquiry on the subject is precluded. As stated by the United States Supreme Court: [13] "It is only necessary to reiterate that all the statements contained in the proposal must be true; that the materiality of such statements is removed from the consideration of a court or jury by the agreement of the parties that such statements are absolutely true, and that, if untrue in any respect, the policy shall be void."

Because of the hardship and injustice which the technical enforcement of the common law rule pertaining to warranties might sometimes cause, and also largely because there was a time when certain insurance companies took undue advantage of warranties in their policies as a means of bringing about a technical forfeiture of the contract, the vast majority of states have passed statutes which protect the insured against technical avoidance of the contract because of statements which he may have made, unless they relate to a matter material to the risk or were made with fraudulent intent. These statutes differ widely in their wording, but are similar to the New York statute which provides in effect that all statements

[13] *Aetna Life Ins. Co. vs. France* (1875) 91 U.S. 510, 512.

purporting to be made by the insured shall be deemed representations and not warranties.[14] As previously stated in discussing representations, some of the statutes go much further.

Statutory provisions relating to concealment, misrepresentation, and warranty are quite within the police power of the legislature, and their constitutionality has been upheld by both the United States Supreme Court [15] and various state supreme courts. Furthermore, the operation of the statute may not be set aside by specific agreement in the policy itself. Such laws, therefore, control all policies to which they apply, issued subsequently to their enactment. While some of them have been criticized as being too liberal to the insured, they are supported by many writers on the ground that most policyholders are ignorant of the true significance of warranties, and that many may thus incur a technical forfeiture of the contract through inadvertent misstatements in their applications.

The Incontestable Clause.   The severity of warranties is also greatly alleviated by the existence in present-day policies of the incontestable clause. By this provision of the contract, the company agrees not to set up as a defense any error, concealment, misstatement, or even fraud, on the part of the insured after the policy has been in effect a certain length of time. The incontestable clause is unique in that contrary to the general law that fraud vitiates all contracts, it permits the legal enforcement of a contract that has been procured by fraud. Such clauses represent a clear illustration of the modern tendency on the part of the companies to liberalize their contracts, and much can be said in their favor. From the standpoint of the insured and the beneficiary such clauses remove the fear of lawsuits especially at a time—namely, after the death of the insured—when it may be difficult for the beneficiary successfully to combat with competent testimony the company's charge of a violation of the contract. From the standpoint of the company the existence of the clause increases business by making the policy attractive to the public. Again, from the standpoint of public policy it is undesirable to have widows, children, or other dependents protected by a contract throughout the lifetime of the insured which may be subject to forfeiture for violations that might remain unknown until the death of the insured, and thus leave the dependents without the protection which it is the essential purpose of life insurance to give. Moreover, if policies can be contested at the time of the insured's death, the issue must be determined in the courts, thus involving long delay in the settlement of the claim at the very time when the need for speedy payment is greatest. Considerations like these have no doubt been responsible for the requirement of incontestable clauses in life insurance policies by the statutes of a considerable number of states.

Whether or not a life insurance policy obtained by fraud would be en-

---

[14] New York Insurance Law, Sec. 142 (3).
[15] *Hancock Mutual Life Insurance Company vs. Warren* (1901) 181 U.S. 73.

forced by the courts after the period of contestability had expired was a question frequently raised in the various jurisdictions. It was contended by some of the companies that a clause condoning fraud would be contrary to public policy. The economic justification of the clause was very clearly analyzed in the case of *Kansas Mutual Life Insurance Company vs. Whitehead,*[16] in which the court gave its reason for enforcing the contract, even though it had been fraudulently obtained. To quote:

This view does not exclude the consideration of fraud, but allows the parties to fix by stipulation the length of time which the fraud of the insured can operate to deceive the insurer. It recognizes the right of the insurer, predicated upon a vast experience and profound knowledge in such matters, to agree that in a stipulated time, fixed by himself, he can unearth and drag to light any fraud committed by the insured, and protect himself from the consequences. This clause is of vast importance and benefit, both to the insured and to the insurer. It enables the latter to increase his business by giving an assurance to persons doubtful of the utility of insurance, that neither they nor their families, after the lapse of a given time, shall be harassed with lawsuits when the evidence of the original transaction shall have become dim, or difficult of retention, or when, perhaps, the lips of him who best knew the facts are sealed by death. That this consideration is a powerful inducement, especially to the poor and obscure, to take out insurance, cannot be doubted; and after the lapse of this reasonable time, it must, of necessity, be of great consolation to the insured to feel that the insurance money, to secure which he has, perhaps, so often endured privation, will be paid over to his family undiminished by court costs or lawyers' fees. To permit an insurance company to induce persons to insure their lives under the pleasing expectation of an incontestable clause and then, when the insured is dead, to undertake, as against his family, to contest the policy on the ground of fraud, would be to permit the perpetration of as great fraud as the insured could possibly have committed in the obtention of the policy. There is no more public policy against the fraud of the insured than against the fraud of the insurer. The incontestable clause is upheld in law, not for the purpose of upholding fraud, but for the purpose of shutting off harassing defenses based upon alleged fraud; and, in so doing, the law merely adopts the certificate of the insurer that within a given time he can expose and render innocuous any fraud in the preliminary statement of the insured. . . . We are acquainted with no rule which forbids one party from relying upon his own acumen in protecting his interest in a proposed contract, and refusing to rely upon the statements or warranties of the opposing party.

THE LAW PERTAINING TO THE AGENT

Since life insurance is written almost exclusively by corporations, in most instances transacting business in many states, the agent is a necessary factor in the successful prosecution of the business. It is also apparent that if the

[16] (1906) 123 Ky. 21, 26.

agent is to perform properly the duties connected with the solicitation of business on behalf of his employer, he must be given a certain amount of authority. To govern his relations with the company and the public, there was, to begin with, the general law of agency. But there has since developed a large body of statute and court law dealing with insurance agents in particular, and it is from this law that we are able to comprehend the status of the life insurance agent.

In General

It is a general rule of law that the position of the agent carries with it authority to do and say those things and use those means which are appropriate to the proper fulfillment of the services which he is employed to render. Almost invariably the company gives its agents a written commission defining their authority. But the absence of such written authority does not relieve the company of responsibility for the conduct of those who are in reality its agents, because to hold otherwise would enable the insurer at any time to avoid all responsibility for the misconduct or errors of its agents by simply sending them into the field without written authority. Agency is a fact depending on circumstances independent of any provisions that may exist in the policy or application, and in cases where the question has come up for decision the courts have outlined the evidence that may be considered as proof establishing the fact and character of the agency. This evidence may consist of an express contract between the company and agent, as already stated, or a recognition by the company that a certain person is its agent. Again, the fact and character of the agency may be shown by the possession of certain papers or by other evidence from which agency may legally be inferred. It is important, however, to note that the insured must not presume the existence of the agency relationship, but must satisfy himself of it and the extent of its character by some tangible evidence. Naturally, the problem of presumption of agency is not likely to arise in view of the state laws requiring agents to be licensed and because of the care exercised by most companies in appointing agents and in supervising their activities.

Powers of the Agent

A general agent's powers are coextensive with those of his principal within the limit of the particular business or territory in which such general agent operates, whereas a special agent's powers extend to all acts necessary to the accomplishment of the particular transaction which he is engaged to perform. If they are acting within the apparent scope of their powers, agents make the company liable for their wrongful or fraudulent acts, omissions, and misrepresentations. Provided that the policy or application contains no restrictions on the agent's authority to waive forfeitures—and even here we have noted disagreement in the court decisions—the acts and knowledge of the agent in relation to anything pertaining to the application or policy are generally held by the courts to be the acts and knowledge of the company, thus estopping it from taking advantage of any forfeiture occasioned by the agent's errors or fraudulent acts.

While there is not unanimity in the decisions, the weight of authority is to the effect that, in the absence of restrictions, the company is liable not only for the acts of its agents, but also for the acts and knowledge of the subagents and employees to whom the agent has delegated authority. In insurance it is a common practice, and is frequently found necessary, for agents to employ others to assist them in their work, and having delegated authority to them, the courts have regarded it as "just and reasonable that insurance companies should be held responsible not only for acts of their agents, but also for the acts of the subagents employed within the scope of their agents' authority." Although it may be argued that the company has not authorized its agents to delegate their authority to others, and that it would therefore be an unreasonable extension of the company's liability, it must be remembered that agents are employed by the companies in accordance with the usages and necessities of the business.

Policy Limitations

As a general rule, life insurance companies insert a provision in their policies or application forms prohibiting their agents from in any way altering the contract. Although the wording of such clauses is not uniform, the following may be regarded as representative of the usual provision:

No agent or other person except the President, Vice-President, a Second Vice-President, or a Secretary of the Company has power on behalf of the Company to bind the Company by making any promises respecting benefits or accepting any representations or information not contained in the written application for this Policy, or to make or modify this contract, or to extend the time for payment of a premium, or to waive any lapse or forfeiture or any of the Company's rights or requirements.

The reasonableness of stipulations like the above must be conceded when one takes into account the fact that most life insurance companies are represented by hundreds and sometimes thousands of agents and that in the desire to obtain business many are often tempted to make promises not covered by the policy, or to overlook or conceal representations or information which, had the same been known to the company, would have caused it to refuse to issue the policy. It therefore seems reasonable that the companies should seek to protect themselves against such contingencies by stating expressly in the contract itself that the agent is not authorized to modify or alter the policy in any particular. It may be added that a clause is found in fire and various other kinds of insurance policies providing, among other things, that a waiver of any provision or condition of the policy, permitted to be waived, must be in writing added thereto.

Despite the apparent reasonableness of such policy provisions, however, the various court decisions dealing with the matter are by no means in harmony as to the legal force of the same, and as a result various rules have been formulated.[17] One such rule is to the effect that policy limitations upon an agent's authority operate as notice to the insured of the limited extent of the agent's powers, and thus protect the company.[18] In another group of cases the courts have adopted an attitude more favorable to the insured by holding that such policy restrictions upon an agent's authority are not conclusive as to those matters involved before the contract is completed, but relate only "to the exercise of the agent's authority in matters concerning the policy after its delivery and acceptance, the theory in the main being that no presumption can reasonably attach that the insured was cognizant of such provisions, or could anticipate that they would be incorporated into the policy." [19] Still another rule holds, in effect, that restrictions in the policy relate only to acts before a loss has occurred.[20]

Perhaps the rule at present having the support of the weight of authority is one prohibiting the company from forfeiting the insurance in case of policy violation (1) where the company or any agent clothed with actual or apparent authority has waived, either orally or in writing, any provision of the policy, or (2) where the company because of some knowledge or act on its part, or on the part of its agent, is estopped from setting up as a defense the violation of the terms of the contract.[21] Whether the courts rely upon the doctrine of parol waiver or upon the doctrine of estoppel,[22] the ultimate result is that in most of the cases, as stated above under the majority rule, the company is held bound even though some provision of the contract has been violated and the policy contains a provision limiting the agent's power to make policy changes. Various reasons have been offered by the courts for taking this view. One court regards the doctrine "as peculiar to the law of insurance and as founded on the laudable design of preventing the perpetration of a fraud through obtaining a premium by the insurance company of a policy known to be void *ab initio*." [23] Other

---

[17] *Couch on Insurance* 2d, § 26:82.

[18] *Ibid.,* § 26:83.

[19] *Ibid.,* § 26:86.

[20] *Ibid.,* § 26:88.

[21] *Ibid.,* § 26:90.

[22] For a discussion of this point see W. R. Vance and B. M. Anderson, *Handbook of the Law of Insurance,* 3rd ed. (St. Paul, Minn.: West Publishing Co., 1951), Chapters VIII and IX.

[23] *Chismore vs. Anchor Fire Ins. Co.* (1906) 131 Iowa 180, 182.

courts refuse to uphold the provision in the interest of fair dealing [24] or on the ground that since the principal has an inherent power to waive either orally or in writing, so has the agent.[25] But it should be noted that in the famous *Northern Assurance Company* case,[26] the United States Supreme Court refused to uphold the aforementioned doctrine of oral waiver and repudiated it as fundamentally unsound. Despite this decision, however, many state courts have continued to render opinions to the opposite effect. Moreover, as previously stated, some states seek to neutralize policy provisions like those discussed under this heading by enacting laws which make notice to the agent notice to the company as regards the insured's health, habits, and occupation.

In the course of their daily business, agents are frequently asked to express opinions on the meaning of policy provisions, and it is of the utmost importance that definite relations should exist between the company and its agents as regards the expression of such opinions. What, then, is the legal effect of the agent's opinion? The general rule is that no legal effect can be given to such opinions. This view is based on the theory that an agent's opinion as to the meaning of any section of the contract does not create new or change old obligations. It is followed particularly where the authority of the insurer's agent is limited, where the terms of the contract are clear and unambiguous, and where the opinion of the agent is in contravention thereof. However, in certain jurisdictions the company is bound by the opinions of its agents, especially where such opinion is not inconsistent with the language of an ambiguous clause in the policy, and is relied upon by the insured.[27]

Agent's Liability to His Principal for Injury Occasioned by Misconduct

The relation of the agent to his employer is such that he must never further his own personal interests by disobeying or exceeding his instructions. Any misconduct of the agent makes him personally liable to his principal for the damage occasioned. This responsibility is based on the basic law of agency which states that wherever an agent violates his duties or obligations to his principal, whether it be by exceeding his authority or by positive misconduct, or by mere negligence or omission in the proper functions of his agency, or in any other manner, and any loss or damage thereby falls on his principal, he is responsible, and must indemnify the principal. In practice, however, most cases involving serious violation of agency agreements are resolved by the agent being discharged with a revocation of license.

[24] *Lewis vs. Guardian Fire & Life Assur. Co.* (1905) 181 N.Y. 392.
[25] *Thompson vs. Traders' Ins. Co.* (1902) Mo. 12.
[26] *Northern Assurance Company vs. Grand View Building Association* (1902) 183 U.S. 308.
[27] *Couch on Insurance* 2d, § 26:92.

OTHER BASIC CONCEPTS

Presumptions

There are three areas of law where "presumptions" have an important application to the life insurance business: (1) the question of survival in common disaster cases; (2) the presumption of death after a specified period following the disappearance of an individual; and (3) the presumption against suicide. All of these presumptions set up in the law are "rebuttable," that is, they merely shift the burden of proof to the party against whom they operate. Once evidence is presented rebutting the presumption it disappears, having served simply to justify a legal inference without evidence until overcome by rebutting evidence.

Common Disaster.   The right of a beneficiary to receive the proceeds of a life insurance policy is usually conditioned on his *surviving* the insured. Usually, there is no problem of showing adequate evidence of survivorship, but where the insured and the beneficiary die in the same accident and there is no evidence to show who died first, the question arises as to whose estate the proceeds are payable. There is no common law presumption based on age or sex as to which died first.[28] Although there has been much diversity of decisions, most courts have awarded the proceeds to the insured's estate, particularly where the insured has reserved the right to change the beneficiary. In order to meet this problem the Uniform Simultaneous Death Act has been enacted in most states. This act, which is not confined to insurance, provides in a section on insurance that "Where the insured and the beneficiary in a policy of life or accident insurance have died and there is no sufficient evidence that they have died otherwise than simultaneously, the proceeds of the policy shall be distributed as if the insured had survived the beneficiary." This, of course, resolves the question of survival in those states where the act is effective, but it does not solve the main problems which face the insurance companies. Specifically, if the proceeds are payable in a lump sum, in the absence of proper planning, no matter who is determined to have survived, the proceeds will go into the estate of the insured or the beneficiary. This will subject the proceeds to depletion through unnecessary probate costs, additional taxes, and the claims of creditors.

Related to this situation are the much more frequent "short-term survivorship" situations where the beneficiary survives the insured by a very short period of time. Here there is no question of survivorship, but all of the above problems remain plus the possibility of shrinkage in the proceeds

[28] Vance, *op. cit.,* p. 724.

because of prior election of a life income settlement option, under which the entire proceeds are considered fully earned even though the beneficiary lived to receive only one or a few installments.[29]

In approaching this problem, many companies use a so-called survivorship clause which simply provides that the beneficiary must survive the insured by a fixed period after the insured's death in order to be entitled to the proceeds. This clause in conjunction with the naming of contingent beneficiaries will prevent the proceeds from falling into the estate of either the insured or the original beneficiary. Another provision utilized is a direction that the proceeds be payable to the beneficiary only if he is alive at the time of payment. This latter provision, with the proper use of the income settlement options, will also avoid most of the problems mentioned above.

Presumption of Survival—Suicide.

As is pointed out in a later chapter, usually there is a provision in the life insurance contract[30] excepting coverage when death occurs as a result of suicide within one (or two) years after the date of issue of the contract. Accidental self-destruction is, of course, not suicide, and it is necessary to delineate between such cases and actual suicides. In the case of doubt as to whether the death occurred through suicide or accident, the *presumption is always against suicide* because of the instinct of self-preservation and the natural love of life. The significance of this presumption will be considered further in the discussion of the suicide provision itself.

Disappearance—Presumption of Death.

It is a well-settled rule of law that when a person leaves his usual place of residence and is neither heard of nor known to be living for a term of seven years, the presumption of his life ceases and that of his death arises. Therefore, if the insured disappears for a period of seven years and his absence is unexplained, he is presumed to be dead, and the insurance company is required to pay the claim. The only presumption, however, is that of death; there is none as to the time of death. But if it appears in evidence "that the absent person, within the seven years, encountered some specific peril, or within that period came within the range of some impending or immediate danger, which might reasonably be expected to destroy life, the court or jury may infer that life ceased before the expiration of the seven years."[31] In such cases, the insurer must pay the face of the policy plus interest thereon from the date of *proof* of death. It should be noted that the insured is presumed to exist until the end of the seven-year period. Therefore, if premiums are not paid, the beneficiary is not entitled to the insurance, unless she

---

[29] If there is a guarantee feature, installments equal to the guarantee would, of course, be paid.

[30] Missouri has a statute prohibiting the use of such a provision. See pp. 193–194.

[31] *Davis vs. Briggs* (1878) 97 U.S. 628; (1937) 93 Fed. 2d. 1; *Tobin vs. United States,* 286 Fed. 2d. 480 (1961).

can prove that death occurred before the due date of the next premium, or unless the policy has remained in force because of the operation of one of its nonforfeiture provisions.

Murderer–Beneficiary

It is clear that when a beneficiary murders the insured, public policy prohibits the payment of the proceeds to such a beneficiary. The rule of public policy is invoked to prevent the murderer from profiting and not, however, to relieve the insurer from liability on its policy. Under such circumstances the proceeds are paid to an innocent contingent beneficiary, if one exists, or to the estate of the insured.[32]

If, however, a beneficiary procures insurance *himself* with the intent to murder the insured and thus defraud the company, the insurance company is absolved from any liability and need only refund the premiums.

In manslaughter cases the courts have been somewhat less than uniform, but most hold that the beneficiary may collect the life insurance proceeds if he commits involuntary manslaughter.[33]

Execution of Insured for a Crime

In general, life insurance contracts are not defeated where the insured meets death by execution for a crime. Actually, there is no reason to penalize the innocent parties involved (the beneficiaries) for the crime of another. There is no selection against the company involved, and it would appear to be sound public policy to pay the proceeds in accordance with the policy provisions. There are many jurisdictions, however, where a contrary result has been reached.

---

[32] Statutes in some states provide that if a beneficiary feloniously kills the insured the proceeds are payable to heirs under descent and distribution laws. See Greider and Beadles *op. cit.,* pp. 410–413.

[33] See E. W. Patterson, *Essentials of Insurance Law* (New York: McGraw-Hill Book Co., Inc., 1957), p. 160.

Policy Provisions I: 12
General Provisions

INTRODUCTION

THE LIFE INSURANCE contract is a very flexible document which can be easily adjusted to meet changing circumstances and needs. Much of the flexibility arises out of the dual nature of the modern life insurance contract.

Dual Nature of the Modern Contract

Repeatedly, this volume has stressed the importance of the fact that all permanent life contracts are made up of an increasing savings or investment element and a decreasing amount of pure life insurance. This, of course, arises out of the level-premium approach to the risk of death which increases at an increasing rate, rising ultimately to a certainty. The so-called savings element in a life insurance contract under the level-premium system was not caused by a desire to set aside savings as in a savings bank, but was rather a means of saving the insured from a loss of protection which would result if annual premiums reached impossibly high figures in the late years of his life. Notwithstanding the original intent, the presence of this savings element naturally led to increasing emphasis on the lifetime features of an unmatured life insurance policy. The values built up *have* actually been "saved" by the policyholder as he goes along. With the introduction of the nonforfeiture provisions, the dual nature of the modern life insurance contract emerged, and the so-called prematurity rights have continued to be enlarged.

The contract provisions relating to nonforfeiture, assignment, and policy loans arise essentially out of the savings side of the contract. In addition, the savings element may be applied under the settlement options to provide retirement income *to the insured* and/or other beneficiaries. Again, the savings element side permits individuals to *save* through their policy and utilize the investment services of the life insurance company. The point here is that although the basic purpose of the life insurance contract is to *provide a fund of fixed dollar value* at maturity, the prematurity rights in the modern life insurance policy are of increasing significance and importance. The dual nature of the modern life insurance contract is important in understanding its structure and design.

Statutory Control

Although there is no statutory standard policy, the provisions of the life insurance contract are subject to considerable state control and regulation. The system of state control of the policy contract involves the requirements (1) that no policy form may be used until approved by the state insurance department and (2) that policies must contain certain *standard provisions,* specified in the insurance law. Although both requirements are intended to ensure fair and equitable treatment of policyholders, the latter was also intended to promote a degree of uniformity in important areas. The statutes do not, in general, prescribe the exact wording to be used in the "standard provisions." Provisions must provide *in substance* the same effect, and it is important to note that provisions *more favorable* than those required by the statutes may be used. Consequently, policies of different companies are not necessarily identical in regard to these provisions.

The standard provisions generally required by the various states include those relative to (1) the grace period, (2) the entire contract provision, (3) misstatement of age, (4) reinstatement, (5) incontestability, (6) annual dividends, (7) policy loans, (8) nonforfeiture values, and (9) settlement options. Each of these standard provisions will be discussed in this and the succeeding chapters.

Individual states may have other regulations which relate to the policy contract or its terms. New York, for example, expressly prohibits any exclusion from liability for death except for those set forth in the law.[1] Again, many states require that each form be coded and that a brief description of the policy be placed at the bottom of the *first* page (for example, twenty-payment life).

Due to the expense of maintaining different forms of policies for use in different states, each company attempts to produce a contract which meets the requirements of all or substantially all of the states in which they do business. Thus, in practice, a New York requirement will have an effect on policies issued in other states by New York-licensed companies. Occasionally, conflicting state requirements or company preference will cause the use of special policy forms or modification of the regular forms in particular states.

---

[1] Permissive exclusions: (1) war clause; (2) suicide clause, limited to two years; (3) aviation exclusion clause, unlimited; and (4) an occupational or residence exclusion, limited to two years. New York Law, Sec. 155 (2).

STANDARD PROVISIONS

The Entire Contract Clause

The *entire contract* clause provides that the policy itself and the application, if a copy is attached to the policy, constitutes, legally, the entire contract between the parties. The reasons for and practical effect of such a provision were set forth in connection with the earlier discussion of the application and its interpretation.

Incontestable Clause

The incontestable clause was introduced by life insurance companies on a voluntary basis to provide greater assurance on the part of the public that they would not have relatively unimportant misstatements used to deny liability under the doctrine of warranties.[2]

A typical policy provision consistent with the standard provision requirements of the New York Insurance Law would read as follows:

After this policy has been in force during the lifetime of the Insured for a period of two years from the date of issue it shall be incontestable except for nonpayment of premiums, and except as to provisions and conditions relating to benefits in the event of total and permanent disability, and those granting additional insurance specifically against death by accidental means, contained in any supplemental agreement attached to, and made a part of, this policy.

This clause has been given a very broad application—far beyond the intention of the companies when it was originally introduced. The question is settled today that this clause prevents a life insurance company from voiding a life insurance contract even on grounds of *material misrepresentation* or *fraud* in the application for the contract. The reasoning behind this broad application was discussed earlier.

The incontestable clause may be considered similar to a short statute of limitations. By inserting this policy provision the company undertakes to make all necessary investigations concerning the good faith and all other circumstances surrounding the insured's application within the time limit stipulated in the clause. The company also definitely agrees not to resist the payment of the claim if no violation of the contract has come to light during the stipulated time limit following the issuance of the policy and if during

---

[2] See pp. 175–176.

the time the company has taken no action to rescind the contract. It is understood, however, that the clause does not waive any of the remedies and the provisions which the contract provides must be compiled with by the claimant following the death of the insured.

Grace Period

The usual provision for days of grace in payment of premiums after the first, permits payments up to thirty or thirty-one days after the due dates without any charge for interest. During this period, the policy remains in full force and effect. In the event death occurs during the grace period the company is permitted to deduct the overdue premium plus interest from the settlement with the beneficiary. The purpose of this provision is to protect the policyholder against "unintentional lapse." If it were not for this provision, and the insured's payment were even one day late, technically he would have to furnish evidence of insurability in order to reinstate the policy.

Since premiums are calculated on the assumption that they will be received and invested on their due dates, the company suffers a loss in interest to the extent of payment past the due date. Although the company is permitted under the law to charge interest, practically the interest charge is waived, due to the small amounts involved and the expense of collection.

It should also be noted that all those who allow their policies to lapse are insured for an extra month. Since the company collects a premium *only* in the event of death within the grace period, most of those who lapse pay no share of the cost of insurance for that period.

Reinstatement

Another so-called standard provision is that relating to *reinstatement.* The term refers to the situation where an individual has failed to pay a premium within the grace period following the due date, his policy has lapsed, and he desires to reinstate the policy. The provision usually gives the insured the right to reinstate it within a period of three years of any default in payment of premiums, subject to certain conditions and limitations.

In the first place the insured must *furnish evidence of insurability satisfactory to the company*. This is essential, since otherwise an undue proportion of reinstatements would involve those in bad health; that is, there would be "selection against the company," for experience shows that the impaired are more apt to ask for reinstatement than are the unimpaired.

Most lapses are unintentional and are followed within a short period of time (two–four weeks) by an application for reinstatement. The insurer should take a liberal view in such cases (and usually does), since the chance of antiselection is slight. Up to within, say, two months of lapse the only evidence required for reinstatement is a statement from the *insured* that he is in good health and that there has been no material change in health since lapse. The longer the period since lapse, the more nearly the requirements coincide with those imposed in the case of new applications. Naturally, company practice varies somewhat, but companies have the contractual right to require a medical examination and other evidence of insurability.

The term "evidence of insurability" has a much broader scope than "good health." Insurability connotes standards with regard to such subjects as occupation, travel, other insurance, and financial conditions as well as the physical characteristics or health status of the applicant. The classic example of the distinction between "good health" and "insurability" is the case of a criminal condemned to death—he may be in perfect health but he's hardly insurable.[3]

The term "satisfactory to the company" generally has been held to allow the insurer to require evidence which would be satisfactory to a reasonable insurer.[4] It should be remembered that an insurer is in business to insure, not to decline applications, and if the applicant is insurable, the presumption must be that he will be accepted.

A second condition which must be met for reinstatement is the payment of premiums in arrears with interest thereon. The usual terms are payment of overdue premiums, less any dividends which would have been payable, with interest at 5 per cent.

Finally, any outstanding policy loan must be either repaid or reinstated.

The reinstatement provision was originally included voluntarily by the companies in order to safeguard the insured against certain hardships which were possible, since there were no nonforfeiture provisions in the older policies. Under such contracts, if the insured failed to pay a premium when due, the policy not only lapsed, but the insured also forfeited the values which had accumulated on account of his policy.[5] Although the presence of nonforfeiture provisions in modern contracts has made the reinstatement clause less vital, it still serves a useful function in today's contracts.

Although company practice is liberal, due to the high cost, reinstatement is seldom requested more than five years after lapse, the insured preferring to take a new policy. The most important reasons why reinstatement might be preferred to taking a new policy include: (1) the new policy will usu-

[3] *Kallman vs. Equitable Life Assurance Society,* 248 App. Div. 146, 288 N.Y. Supp. 1032 (1st Dept. 1936); affirmed, 272 N.Y. 648, 5 N.E. 2d 375 (1936).

[4] 18 Cal. 2d 635, 117 P. 2d at 7 (1941).

[5] Harold M. Horne and D. Bruce Mansfield, *The Life Insurance Contract,* 2nd ed. (New York: Life Office Management Association, 1948), p. 198.

ally involve paying a higher premium; (2) the incontestable and suicide clauses (see below) of the old policy may have run out; [6] (3) the new contract will not show a cash value for one or two years; (4) many old contracts contain provisions (for example, settlement options based on a more favorable rate base than found in new contracts) and/or benefits on a more liberal basis and at lower rates than in current contracts.

It should be noted that the standard provision for reinstatement does not require that reinstatement be permitted if the policy either has been surrendered for its cash value or has been continued as extended term insurance and the full period has expired. Many companies include this restriction in their contract.

Nonforfeiture Provision

The nature and uses of the "nonforfeiture options," that is, (1) cash surrender value; (2) reduced paid-up insurance; and (3) extended term insurance, are explained later. At this point consideration is given only to the policy provisions relating to these options. The policy provisions required under the Standard Nonforfeiture Law [7] include the following:

1. A *cash* value is *required* only after premiums have been paid for three years. The *minimum* amount of cash value which may be granted is calculated by the so-called adjusted-premium method, which will be discussed later. It should be remembered that the minimum value developed by the adjusted-premium method must be provided in the form of reduced paid-up insurance or extended term insurance (see below), even if the policy has been in force less than three years.

2. The policy must contain a provision specifying *optional* nonforfeiture benefits available in lieu of a *cash* value and stating that one of the optional nonforfeiture benefits (that is, reduced paid-up insurance or extended term insurance) will take effect *automatically* if no specific request is made by the insured. In this regard, the law requires that the insured be permitted to claim the full *cash* within sixty days of default, *even* though insurance protection has been provided from date of lapse to the date the insured claims the *cash* value. The law further requires that the insured must at all times have the right to take the net cash value for either reduced paid-up insurance or extended term insurance, provided that either of these optional benefits took effect after premiums had been paid for at least three years.

---

[6] The law is not entirely clear, but the general rule is that the incontestable clause is reinstated, making the policy contestable again. See cases cited in Harry Krueger and Leland T. Waggoner, *The Life Insurance Policy Contract* (Boston: Little, Brown & Co., 1953), p. 78, footnote 3. In contrast the courts have been virtually unanimous in holding that the suicide clause does not run again. *Ibid.*, p. 214.

[7] Effective in most states about January 1, 1948.

3. The policy must contain a statement of the *mortality table* and *rate of interest* as well as a description of the *method* used in calculating the nonforfeiture values. In addition, a *table* is required showing the cash and other nonforfeiture options for each of the first twenty years.

The policy must contain a provision giving the company the *right* to defer payment of any *cash* value for six months after request is made for it. This provision is usually referred to as the *delay* clause and is intended to protect the company against "runs," where investments might have to be liquidated under adverse circumstances. Although this clause serves a vital function, it has never been evoked by any life insurance company to date.

Policy Loans

In most states the standard provisions required in all policies include a provision for policy loans in connection with the permanent forms of insurance. Thus, the policy usually provides in effect (1) that the company will lend, on the security of the policy, an amount which, with interest thereon to the next policy anniversary, will not exceed the guaranteed cash value of the policy on that anniversary; (2) that interest is payable annually at a rate specified in the policy; (3) that interest which is not paid when due shall be added to the loan and shall bear interest at the same rate; (4) that if the *total* indebtedness equals or exceeds the cash value, the policy shall terminate, subject to thirty-one days' notice to the insured or other owner of the policy; and (5) that the policyholder *may* repay the loan either in whole or in part at any time.

As with other *cash* prematurity rights, the policy also provides that the company *may* defer the granting of a cash loan but not a loan for the purpose of paying premiums. The *amount* of loan available usually includes the cash value of any paid-up additions. A policy loan is not actually due and repayable until either the policy itself matures or the total indebtedness, including unpaid interest, equals the cash value. The automatic continuation of the loan, as long as the cash value provides security, is one of the unique features of policy loans.

The interest rate required to be specified in the policy is of significance. Currently, the rate of interest specified in the policy *for policy loans* is usually 5 per cent. The recent high market rates of interest and the significant increase in policy loans have led some companies to increase their contract loan rate above 5 per cent. This rate should be fairly high, since it is a long-term guarantee extending over the entire future duration of the policy. In addition, the great majority of policy loans are small, and the expense of handling such loans is relatively high. It should be noted that at least one company includes in its contract an *interest schedule* graded by the size of the loan.

The policies of many companies now include a provision for *automatic premium loans* (not a standard provision), that is, a provision that if a premium is unpaid at the end of the grace period, and if the policy has a sufficient cash value, the amount of the premium will be advanced automatically as a loan against the policy.[8] Under some policy forms, as required by some states, the policy owner must specifically elect to make the provision operative. The major purpose of the automatic premium loan provision is protection against *unintentional* lapse, as where the payment of premium is overlooked because of illness. If the policy were allowed to lapse, the nonforfeiture options would be effective, but if the policyholder wanted to reinstate his policy, the insured would have to furnish evidence of insurability satisfactory to the company.

In the case of the automatic premium loan, the policyholder need only pay back the loan, and the policy continues in full force and effect. The major disadvantage of the automatic premium loan is that it may tend to encourage laxity in payment of premiums.

Annual Dividends

As will be brought out in the discussion of surplus and its distribution,[9] most states require annual apportionment of divisible surplus. Thus, the New York Law requires "that the insurer shall annually ascertain and apportion *any* divisible surplus accruing on the policy." Naturally, nonparticipating policies do not have this provision.

Misstatement of Age

The laws of most states require that all policies include a provision that in the event the age of the insured is found to have been misstated, the amount of insurance shall be such as could have been purchased by the premiums actually paid at the correct age of the insured. For example, consider an ordinary life policy for $10,000 issued at age 35 at an annual premium of $300. If, when a death claim is filed, it is found that the true age at issue was 36, which would have required a premium of, say, $320, the amount payable by the company would be 300/320 of $10,000, or $9,375. Similarly, the amount payable would increase if the age had been overstated.

In the event the error in age is discovered while the policy is still in force, the procedure followed depends upon whether the age has been under- or overstated. In the case where age has been understated, the insured is

---

[8] Rhode Island, for example, requires that all new policies issued in that state shall contain an automatic premium loan. This is not a statutory requirement in other states.

[9] See Chapter 27.

usually given the option of paying the difference in premiums with interest or of having the policy reissued for the reduced amount. In the case of over-statement of age, a refund is usually made by paying the difference in reserves.

SPECIAL PROVISIONS

After it has complied with the different statutory requirements, each company will include some policy provisions which are not required, such as assignment, change of plan, and automatic premium loan privileges. In addition, subject to statutory restrictions, certain risks may be excluded, such as aviation, war, and suicide risks.

Suicide Clause

A typical suicide clause reads as follows:

If within two years following the date of issue of this policy and while it is in force, the insured, whether sane or insane, shall die by his own hand or act, the Company will be liable only for the amount of the premiums paid here-under, which shall be paid in one sum to the beneficiary herein.

At one time, life insurance contracts excluded the risk of suicide entirely. This was unfortunate, since in a given case the whole purpose of the policy —usually to protect dependents—could be defeated. In addition, it was not necessary to protect the company. Suicide is, of course, one of the causes of death which make up the total mortality rate, and such deaths can be in-cluded in the mortality tables upon which premiums are based. Conse-quently, it is not necessary to exclude suicide completely. It is necessary, however, for the company to protect itself against cases where insurance is purchased in contemplation of suicide. Adequate protection against this "selection against the company" can be obtained by excluding the risk of suicide for one or two years after the date of issue of the policy.

It is important to remember that the clause is intended to protect against adverse selection, not to exclude the risk of suicide as such. Most state laws permit a two-year exclusion, and this is the usual practice. A number of companies, however, use a one-year exclusion. In view of this, it might appear that suicide by one *insane* should be an insurable risk, even from the first day of coverage. The act is involuntary and cannot in the nature of things involve adverse selection. In theory this is correct, but in practice it is too difficult to distinguish between "sane" and "insane" suicides.

It was pointed out earlier [10] that there is a legal presumption that a person will not take his own life. This fact plus the tendency on the part of the courts to lean over backwards to hold for dependents makes it difficult to prove suicide even where the facts clearly point to it. The courts have gone to extraordinary lengths at times in holding that suicide had not been proved and in deciding that the company was liable.

Where suicide, proved or agreed to, has been the cause of death within the restricted period, the company will refund the premiums paid, with or without interest, depending on the contract.

Aviation Exclusion

Restriction of coverage in case of death from aviation, except as regards the insured as passenger, is virtually universal in double indemnity provisions. At one time it was also quite common to exclude death caused by aviation from the basic life insurance coverage. The rapid advancement of the aviation industry, its excellent safety record, and the increasing acceptance and utilization of aviation facilities by the public have led to liberal coverage of the aviation risk by most companies. All companies cover fare-paying passengers on regularly scheduled airlines. Increasingly, similar flight on unscheduled airlines will not result in any policy restriction or increased rate. Even private pilots and the pilot and crews of commercial airlines are being written standard or with much reduced extra rates. Perhaps the major area where the aviation restrictions are still strictly applied is in the case of military aircraft. It is important to note that virtually all restrictions as to coverage can be eliminated if the insured is willing to pay an extra premium.

At one time there was some question as to the effect of the incontestable clause on an aviation exclusion. It is clearly settled today that a company has the right to exclude a given risk from coverage despite the presence of an incontestable clause. The courts have held that just as in the case of the suicide exclusion, denial of a claim for an excluded aviation risk is not a contest of the policy but rather enforcement of a policy provision.[11]

War Exclusion

Companies usually insert so-called war clauses in their contracts during periods of impending war and of wartime. This is particularly true of poli-

[10] See pp. 183–184.
[11] The leading case on this point was the famous Conway Decision, which developed out of the refusal of the Superintendent of Insurance of the State of New York to approve for issue a policy containing an aviation exclusion rider, on the grounds that it conflicted with the prescribed incontestable clause. *Met. Life Ins. Co. vs. Conway* (1930) 252 N. Y. 449, 169 N.E. 642.

cies issued to young men of draft age. The clauses normally provide for a return of premium with interest or a refund equal to the reserve element of the policy in event death occurs under conditions excluded in the policy. War clauses are usually cancelled at the end of the war period.

The major purpose of war clauses is to control adverse selection on the part of buyers of insurance. It is clear not only that those going into military service would be a larger proportion than normal of individuals buying insurance but also that they would be inclined to buy larger policies than they would have in peacetime. The experience of many companies after both World Wars I and II showed that they could have covered the war risk without extra premium. Without such clauses, however, the potential adverse selection involved could undoubtedly lead to serious disturbance of the overall mortality experience.

In general, there are two types of war clauses: (1) the "status" type and (2) the "results" type. Under the status type of clause, the policy will not pay for the death of the insured *while* he is in the military service, regardless of the *cause* of death. Some companies liberalize this clause by only excluding death outside the "home area," as defined in the clause. Usually, this home area is defined as the United States, District of Columbia, and Canada, but other definitions are not infrequent. Under the results type of clause there is no coverage *if* the death is a *result* of war. The basic distinction between the clauses is the significance of the cause of death: under the status clause it is immaterial; under the results clause it is vital.

The validity of war clauses has not been the subject of much litigation, but the interpretation of the clauses has given rise to a large volume of cases. Much litigation has evolved around the question of whether a particular clause is a status clause or a results clause.

Since the results type of clause is more liberal, unless the wording is very clear that the clause is a status clause, the courts tend to bend over backward to interpret it as a results clause. Other litigation has related to the nature of death and over the existence of the war itself.[12]

Change of Plan

Many policies contain a provision granting the insured the right to change the policy to one of another form. Most companies limit the contract provision to changes to plans of insurance involving a *higher* premium rate. In connection with such an exchange the insured must usually pay the difference between the then reserve (savings element) on the new form and the then reserve under the original policy with interest. In addition, changes

[12] See *Beley vs. Pennsylvania Mutual Life Insurance Company,* 373 Pa. 231, 95A. (2d) 202 (Pa., 1953). *Stucker vs. College Life Insurance Co. of America,* 208 N.E. (2d) 731 (Ind., 1965).

to plans with a higher premium rate do not necessitate evidence of insurability. A few companies permit changes to plans of insurance involving a *lower* premium by contract right. In such cases, evidence of insurability is required to protect the company against adverse selection. Most of the companies that do not grant changes to lower premium plans as a matter of contract right will do so as a matter of practice.

THE DISABILITY CLAUSE

The basic ordinary life insurance contract does not include any disability benefits.[13] It is quite common, however, to attach riders to a life insurance contract which provide certain benefits in the event of total and permanent disability. The two most common disability benefits so provided are (1) waiver of premium or (2) waiver of premium *and* disability income. The definition of disability is usually the same for both waiver of premium and disability income benefits.

Definition of Disability

As mentioned, under the disability clauses in life insurance policies, the risk covered pertains to *total and permanent* disability. Although there is a lack of uniformity in the phraseology employed, the customary wording of the clause declares the insured to be entitled to the benefits promised when he "has become wholly and permanently disabled so that he is and will be permanently, continuously, and wholly prevented thereby from performing any work or engaging in any occupation for compensation or profit." Sometimes the clause also contains the thought that the disability must be the "result of disease or of bodily injury." Moreover, there is a further stipulation in most instances that "the entire and irrecoverable loss of the sight of both eyes, or the use of both hands or both feet, or one hand and one foot will be considered total disability."

The words "total" and "permanent" have proved difficult to interpret legally, and this has been one of the outstanding problems to life insurance companies. Strictly interpreted, the wording of the clause would seem to deny benefits to all except the absolutely helpless. Yet the courts, as well as the companies, have, in the main, been disposed to grant a liberal interpretation, so that disability as viewed under the clause contemplates all cases where the insured is unable to pursue his own occupation or any other calling for which he is fitted by ability or training. In some states, however,

---

[13] Industrial life insurance policies do include certain disability benefits with no separate premium charge. See pp. 616–617.

the courts have refused to follow this particular interpretation, holding either that "any occupation" means the insured's "own occupation" or (in a few instances) that the wording of the clause must be given a literal meaning.[14]

Similarly, there has been doubt as to the meaning of the word "permanency." There is hesitancy, with respect to the great majority of cases of total disability, to declare the case a permanent one. So many cases, apparently permanent, are nevertheless subject to possible cure. To delay payment of benefits until the question of permanency is definitely settled would often mean postponement until death itself settled the matter. The problem, however, is usually settled by the companies themselves, in that the clause specifies that total disability, continuous for a stated period (usually for six months), shall be presumed to be permanent until recovery.[15]

Waiver of Premium

The waiver of premium provision may be, and quite frequently is, added to the life insurance contract for a small extra premium. It provides that in the event the insured becomes totally and permanently disabled before age 60 (in some cases 65), premiums on the contract will be waived during the continuance of disability beyond a specified period, usually six months. The operation of the contract continues just as if the insured himself were paying the premiums. Thus, dividends are continued on a participating policy,[16] the cash value continues to increase, a loan may be secured, and so forth.

It should be noted that all premiums are waived during disability, not just those falling due after the expiration of the elimination period. This is different from the disability income provision and from most waivers of premium provisions in individual health insurance policies. Almost all companies require six months of disability in order for the waiver of premium benefit to take effect. As long as disability commences during the period of coverage, *all* premiums are waived while it continues, even those falling due after age 60. The maximum age limit for women is often five years lower than for men, and the rate is often much higher. Married women usually are not eligible for this coverage, since it primarily is for the benefit of a person whose earned income is cut off.

[14] For a discussion of various definitions of disability found in individual health insurance contracts, see pp. 270–273.

[15] A disability income contract which occupies a place midway between noncancellable individual health insurance and life insurance riders is issued by the Mutual Benefit Life Insurance Company of Newark, New Jersey. See O. D. Dickerson, *Health Insurance*, 3rd ed. (Homewood, Ill.: Richard D. Irwin, Inc., 1968), pp. 458–460.

[16] The dividend formula of most companies recognizes the presence or absence of disability coverage, however.

Disability Income

Until recently the customary monthly disability income benefit provided by riders on life insurance policies was ½ of 1 per cent of the face of the policy ($5 per month per $1,000). In face of favorable underwriting experience and strong competitive conditions, an increasing number of companies using the disability income clause pay monthly, 1 per cent of the face of the policy ($10 per month per $1,000).[17] Many companies limit the maximum monthly income they will issue to some stated figure, like $500, with a further limit on the amount the company will participate in in all companies. This latter limit may range up to $1,000, with an additional limit based on a percentage of net earned income frequently imposed. The great majority consider six months' total disability as permanent, and commence payments at the end of the sixth month. Since the first check is usually payable at the end of the sixth month, this is really the equivalent of a six-month elimination period with a one-month retroactive payment. Some companies impose a four- or six-month elimination period, but the above is by far the most common. Most companies also make payments retroactive for only six months, or for one year when claim is made some period after disability develops.

Dividends which would have become payable during the period of disability are allowed, and in other respects the basic life contract continues as though no disability had occurred. Should the insured recover, income payments will cease, and premiums becoming due thereafter must be paid. Moreover, provision is usually made in the case of endowment policies that income is to cease at the maturity date of the endowment.

Until about 1931, the clause usually covered disability occurring prior to age 60. After 1930–31, many companies reduced the age to 55; in recent years there has been a trend back to a limit of age 60. Any disability which develops after age 55 (or 60) is thus not covered. In the event of disability prior to age 55 (or 60), however, payments continue to be made for life or to age 65, depending on the contract. Those companies terminating income at 65 usually mature the contract as an endowment and pay the face at that time.

Many companies refuse to issue the disability clause in conjunction with term policies. It is also the general practice not to extend disability income insurance to married women and women not gainfully employed, except at greatly increased rates; some companies exclude women without exception.

---

[17] At least two companies issue a $20 benefit, one of which reduces to $10 after age 60.

With respect to substandard risks, the disability coverage is also either entirely refused or restricted. Although the clause is often written without restrictions, it is the more general practice for companies to apply certain restrictions (as regards cause of disability) to all purchasers of the disability clause, such as disability resulting from self-inflicted injuries, from military and naval service in time of war, and (a much more infrequent restriction) from aerial or submarine activities or violation of law. The misstatement of age clause in the basic life insurance policy applies, but other prorating clauses are usually not included in disability riders, nor would they be applicable to waiver of premium benefits.

It is important to recognize that these disability clauses are one form of health insurance. Many of the companies offering disability riders in connection with their life insurance contracts also provide separate health insurance contracts which provide temporary and partial as well as total and permanent disability benefits. Health insurance will be discussed in some detail in later chapters.

DOUBLE INDEMNITY

A *double indemnity* clause or rider may also be added to a life insurance contract. It provides that double the face amount of insurance is payable if the death of the insured is caused by accidental means.

From an economic standpoint there is no reason why double indemnity should be paid in the event of death from accident, as compared with death from disease. The loss to the family is equally great under either cause of death. In fact, the risk of death from disease is, with respect to most persons, many times greater than the risk of death from accident. The clause has value, of course, and its cost is comparatively small, owing to the relatively small risk when viewed in relation to all causes of death. This small cost is probably the main reason for its appeal to many people as well as for its inclusion in the life insurance contract as a means of effecting sales.

Definition of Accidental Death

A typical clause includes the following definition of accidental death: "Death resulting from bodily injury effected solely through external, violent, and accidental means independently and exclusively of all other causes and within ninety days after such injury."

The expression "accidental means" insists that both the *cause* and the *result* of what happened must be accidental. For example, if death occurs as a result of the insured's jumping from a moving vehicle, the results may be accidental but the means are not accidental. The intention of such a definition is to limit the coverage to deaths which are purely and entirely accidental.

The requirement that death must be caused solely by "external, violent, and accidental means" is intended primarily to eliminate "accidental" deaths where disease was the real or a contributing cause. Thus, where the insured has a heart attack while driving his car and is killed in an ensuing automobile accident, the real cause of death was disease, and double indemnity is not intended to cover. The courts, however, have tended to disregard the distinction and companies have frequently been required to pay death claims which were clearly not a result of "accidental means."[18]

Exclusions

Certain causes of death (even where the means and result are accidental) are excluded by the double indemnity provision. These exclusions fall into five classes: (1) deaths resulting from certain illegal activities; (2) deaths where an accident was involved but where illness, disease, or mental infirmity was also involved; (3) deaths from certain specified causes where there may be considerable doubt about the accidental character of the death; (4) deaths resulting from war; and (5) deaths resulting from aviation, except passenger travel on scheduled airlines. The rather numerous exclusions in the double indemnity clause indicate the practical difficulties inherent in this form of coverage.

Time and Age Limits

To be covered, a death must occur within ninety days of an accident. The purpose of this restriction is to assure, reasonably, that the accident was the sole cause of death. Double indemnity coverage usually is limited to age 60, 65, or, in a few cases, 70. The majority of companies grade their premium charges by age and a number of companies now offer multiple indemnity (two, three, or more times the face amount) coverage.

[18] See pp. 268–269.

OTHER PROVISIONS

In addition to the general provisions discussed above, there are a number of discretionary provisions found in a life insurance contract which provide its flexibility and adaptability to changing needs and circumstances. For example, dividend options, nonforfeiture options, and policy loans, which were discussed earlier, provide such flexibility. In the following chapter attention will be directed to the provisions relating to the designation of beneficiaries and their rights, assignment of the rights under the policy, and the relation of creditor's rights and life insurance. The succeeding chapter considers the provisions of the contract relating to settlement options.

IT IS THE purpose of this and the following chapter to review (1) the respective interests of the insured and the beneficiary in the life insurance contract, (2) creditor's rights in life insurance, and (3) the assignment of rights in connection with the life insurance contract.

THE BENEFICIARY CLAUSE

It is a fundamental rule of law that a person has an insurable interest in his own life. A man may be expected to prefer to remain alive regardless of the amount of insurance which would be paid to someone if he died. Accordingly, a man may insure his own life for the benefit of anyone he wishes regardless of whether or not the beneficiary has an insurable interest in his life.[1]

Nature of Designation

Vested Rights of the Beneficiary. The rights of the insured and designated beneficiaries depend to a considerable extent on the form of the beneficiary designation, that is, whether it is revocable or irrevocable. Where the policy does not reserve to the insured the power to change the beneficiary, that is, an irrevocable designation, such beneficiary is held to have acquired a vested right in the policy immediately upon its issuance. This vested right is so complete that neither the insured nor his creditors

---

[1] Prior to 1953 the public policy of Texas required such an interest on the part of *all* beneficiaries. This was changed in 1953 by Article 3.49–1 of the Texas statutes. Until recently Virginia also did not follow the general rule. But in the case of *Smith vs. Coleman* (325.E. (2) 704; 355.E. (2) 107), the Virginia Supreme Court held definitely that in a policy procured by the insured the beneficiary named by the insured was not required to have an insurable interest in his life to be entitled to the death benefit.

can impair the same without the beneficiary's consent. This general principle of law is well stated in *Condon vs. New York Life:* [2]

> It is held by the great weight of authority that the interest of a designated beneficiary in an ordinary life policy vests upon the execution and delivery thereof, and, unless the same contains a provision authorizing a change of beneficiary without the consent thereof, the insured cannot make such change. And this applies to a policy to which there are attached the incidents of a loan value, cash surrender value, and automatic extension by premiums paid.

Thus, in the case of an irrevocable beneficiary designation, unless there is some specific provision in the policy authorizing the insured to make policy loans, surrender the policy, or exercise other specific prematurity rights or privileges, he may not take any action which will in any way diminish or affect the irrevocable right of the beneficiary to receive the full amount of insurance at the death of the insured. In the usual case it is as if the beneficiary and the insured were joint owners of the policy. The insured cannot act without the consent of the irrevocable beneficiary.

Although not usual, a contract may be written where, in connection with an irrevocable beneficiary designation, specific rights, such as policy loans or the right to receive the cash value, may be reserved to the insured. Such a contract has been upheld [3] on the grounds that the terms and conditions of the policy are what control the rights of the insured and determine the interest of the beneficiary. In contracts where certain rights are reserved, even though the insured may be able to diminish the value of the beneficiary's interest by a policy loan or destroy it absolutely by surrender, he may not revoke that beneficiary's interest, such as it may be, without the beneficiary's consent. It should be noted that in the majority of policies issued, there are no specific conditions that would permit the insured to impair or destroy the interest of an irrevocably designated beneficiary.

Reserving the Right to Change the Beneficiary.   As the prematurity rights under life insurance contracts became more important, insureds became more desirous of maintaining control over their life insurance contracts. To enable the insured to bring this about, some companies inserted a provision in the contract giving to the insured the right of disposing of his insurance as he saw fit. At the present time all companies grant this right, if desired, and virtually all policies now contain a provision reserving to the insured full power to change the beneficiary or beneficiaries at will while the policy is in force and subject to any previous assignment. When this right is reserved, the policy remains the property of the insured and the original beneficiary obtains no vested rights in the policy or its

[2] 183 Iowa 658; 166 N.W. 452.
[3] *Nielsen vs. General American Life Co.,* 89 Fed. 2d 90.

proceeds but possesses only a "mere expectancy until after the maturity of the contract." Thus, where the insured reserves the right to change the beneficiary, he is regarded as the complete owner of the policy.[4]

Various methods may be used in arranging such revocable beneficiary designations. Some companies provide in their policies words to the effect that:

when the right of revocation has been reserved, or in case of the death of any beneficiary under either a revocable or irrevocable designation, the insured, if there be no existing assignment of the policy made as herein provided, may, while the policy is in force, designate a new beneficiary, with or without reserving the right of revocation, by filing written notice thereof at the home office of the company accompanied by the policy for suitable endorsement thereon. Such change shall take effect when endorsed on the policy by the company and not before.

Other policies state that the insured may at any time change the beneficiary or beneficiaries under the policy, and where this is done it is frequently stipulated that the insured may, however, declare the designation of any beneficiary to be irrevocable. In other instances the change of beneficiary clause may contain stipulations to the effect that if any beneficiary shall die before the insured, the interest of such beneficiary shall vest in the insured, or that the insured reserves the right, without the beneficiary's consent, to surrender the policy for its cash value or to borrow thereon.

In contrast to the foregoing provisions, a few companies purposely omit a change of beneficiary clause in their contracts, and ask the insured to state specifically in his application his position in regard to this privilege. These companies, while admitting that the right of revocation may in occasional instances prove of great practical use, call attention to the fact that "a policy containing the unconditional reservation of the right to change the beneficiary may produce an instrument identical with the one in which the estate is made the beneficiary." They, therefore, hold that the danger connected with such an unconditional reservation, regarded by them as a questionable privilege, should always be called to the attention of the applicant by the agent. Then, if the applicant still insists on having the privilege, the company will gladly grant it; but under these circumstances it is felt that the insured asked for the privilege with a full understanding of what he was doing and what his request might mean to himself and family in the future. On the other hand, the advocates of a special beneficiary

---

[4] Possibly only three states, Colorado, Massachusetts, and New Jersey, still maintain the view that a revocable beneficiary has an interest in a life insurance policy that is more than a mere expectancy. In these states, such a beneficiary is considered as having a qualified vested interest that is subject to divestment if a change of beneficiary is effected in accordance with policy provisions. See James S. Burke, "Designation of the Beneficiary," *The Beneficiary in Life Insurance* (Homewood, Ill.: S. S. Huebner Foundation for Insurance Education, Richard D. Irwin, Inc., 1956), p. 9.

clause for every contract consider the practice to be supported by reasons of expediency and equity and contend that the insured should, as a matter of right, have the privilege of doing as he wishes with his own.

Whatever the practice in designating the insured's right of revocation, it is highly important, relative to the question of creditors' rights, that the legal significance of the privilege to change the beneficiary at will should be clearly comprehended by the policyholder. The possibilities of future bankruptcy do not seriously occupy the thoughts of the average person, yet statistics reveal a surprisingly large number of business failures.

Before leaving this subject, brief reference should be made to the beneficiary's interest under a fraternal or mutual benefit certificate. Here the right of revocation is usually reserved to the insured by the constitution or by-laws governing the members, and under such circumstances the interest of the beneficiary is not a vested one. But should the rules or certificates of the order or society, or any statute, contain restrictions as to the classes of beneficiaries that may be named, the holder of the certificate is obliged to observe them. It has been held that under such conditions the properly named beneficiary can contest an appointment illegally made at a future time. In the absence, however, of any right of revocation by statute or by the rules of the association, or in case of a definite agreement with the beneficiary originally named, the insured is precluded from substituting another appointment.

In industrial policies, it should be stated, it is frequently the practice to include a provision known as the facility-of-payment clause, permitting the company to choose the beneficiary under certain circumstances. Usually, the clause is given some such wording as the following:

> The company may pay the amount due under this policy to either the beneficiary named below, or to the executor or administrator, husband or wife, or any relative by blood or connection by marriage of the insured, or to any other person appearing to said company to be equitably entitled to the same by reason of having incurred expenses on behalf of the insured, or for his or her burial; and the production of a receipt signed by either of said persons shall be conclusive evidence that all claims under this policy have been satisfied.

Such provisions have been repeatedly upheld by the courts as reasonable in this form of insurance.

Designating the Beneficiary

Need for Clarity.   Judging from the unusually large number of court decisions which relate to this subject, it is apparent that the beneficiary often is designated carelessly in a life insurance policy, and that because of such carelessness the real intention of the insured upon his death might be difficult to determine and possibly be defeated. It is the general rule of the courts, if at all possible, so to construe the language used in designating the beneficiary as to enforce the intentions of the parties thereto. But in doing this the courts cannot set aside the language expressly used if the same is not ambiguous.

Numerous illustrations may be cited as indicating the necessity of care in describing the beneficiary. Thus, where the policy is payable to the "insured's children" the term includes those by a former wife but not his wife's children by a former husband. A policy payable "to the wife and upon her death before the insured to 'their children' " does not give an interest to a child by a marriage contracted by the insured after his first wife's death. Adopted children are included in the term "children," and the term "dependents" is limited strictly to those actually dependent for support upon the insured. Again, the term "relatives" has been held to "include those by marriage as well as by blood, but not an illegitimate child"; the term "heirs" refers to "those who take under the statute of descent and distribution."[5]

In addition to naming a "primary" beneficiary carefully, it is important that the insured should provide definite instructions relative to the payment of the proceeds in such cases where the primary beneficiary *predeceases* the insured. This is usually handled by naming "contingent" beneficiaries at the time the policy is issued and the primary beneficiary is designated. The use of contingent beneficiaries is particularly important under conditions which bring about the death of the insured and of the primary beneficiary at the same time or within a few hours of each other. As mentioned earlier, many companies also include a so-called survivorship clause which provides that the beneficiary must survive the insured by a specified period of time after the insured's death in order to be entitled to the proceeds.[6] Provision can be made to fit exceptional cases by appropriate wording of the beneficiary designation. As explained in more detail below, such proper wording may be important also in protecting the life insurance fund from attachments by the beneficiary's creditors.

Nonindividual Designations.   The insured may designate as beneficiary a partnership, association, corporation, or trustee as well as an individual. In most cases life insurance policies for the benefit of business firms or corporations are procured by such firms or corporations and owned by them, or are assigned outright to them by the insured. From time to time, however, there are cases where the insured merely designates a partnership, association, or corporation as beneficiary. In those cases the interest of such beneficiaries is essentially no different from that of an individual beneficiary, the rights of the insured and beneficiary being de-

[5] C. B. Elliott, *Treatise of the Law of Insurance* (Indianapolis, Ind.: The Bobbs-Merrill Company, 1907), pp. 383–387. Here is presented a detailed list of the numerous interpretations which American courts have given to the various terms that are commonly used in designating beneficiaries in life insurance policies.

[6] See pp. 182–183.

pendent on whether the designation is made revocably or irrevocably. It is important, of course, to anticipate complications brought about by mergers, reorganizations, and so forth.

A Minor as a Beneficiary. The designation of a minor as beneficiary presents unique problems. For example, if a minor beneficiary is named irrevocably, the insured is prevented in the future from exercising any rights under the policy, since the minor must consent and he lacks the capacity to do so.[7] It would be necessary to have a guardian appointed, and even then the guardian, in protecting the minor's rights, might not acquiesce in the action the insured desired to take.

Minor beneficiaries also raise the question of how payment is to be accomplished in the event the policy matures and becomes payable to such beneficiary before he has reached his majority. A minor is not legally competent to receive payment and cannot give a binding receipt for it. In order to avoid the possibility of having to pay a second time, the insurer generally will not make payment of any substantial amount directly to minor beneficiaries, but will insist upon the appointment of a general guardian. This process is expensive. In a number of states, statutes have been passed authorizing waiver of guardianship and permitting payments due a minor to be made to another for the benefit of the minor, usually a parent or person taking care of the minor. The amounts authorized, however, are nominal, being less than $500 as a rule, although a few states permit payments up to $1,000 without a guardian's being appointed.

Some states [8] have statutes providing that a minor who has attained the age of 16 or 18 years shall be competent to receive and give a valid receipt for an amount not exceeding $2,000 or $3,000 in any one year as benefits payable upon the death of the insured, provided that the contract specifically provides for payments directly to the minor.

Change of Beneficiary. In applying for a life insurance policy, the insured will state whether he wants to reserve the right to change the beneficiary, and the policy will be written accordingly. As long as the right to change is reserved, the insured may successively change the beneficiary at will. The policy provides the method by which such changes may be accomplished. Conformance with the required procedure is usually insisted upon, and in the great majority of cases the change of beneficiary is a routine matter.

The procedure for change provided for in the policy is simple. The company, of course, must be notified of the insured's desire to change the beneficiary. Some policies merely provide for written notice to the com-

---

[7] Although not generally the case, the designation could be made subject to a policy provision specifically permitting the insured to exercise certain prematurity rights without the consent of the beneficiary.

[8] Arizona, Georgia, Kentucky, Louisiana, Maryland, Michigan, New York, Oklahoma, Utah and Washington.

pany. Others require written notice to the company, accompanied by the policy for endorsement. The latter procedure is the general rule.

There may be times when the insured is unable to present the policy for endorsement because it has been lost or for other reasons. The courts have universally held that the requirements for changing the beneficiary are for the protection of the insurance company and that the company may waive them in a proper case. In general the courts have held that where the insured has complied substantially with the requirements for changing the beneficiary, or where the insured has done all that he could but for reasons beyond his control, a change of beneficiary will be deemed to have been accomplished notwithstanding the failure to comply fully with the policy requirements.

Other Aspects

Transmissibility of the Beneficiary's Interest.   Where the beneficiary has been named absolutely and without any qualifying restrictions, the important question arises: Are the rights of the beneficiary in the policy such as to pass to his or her representatives in case of death before the insured dies? This question may be discussed conveniently from two standpoints: (1) when all the designated beneficiaries die before the insured, and (2) when some of them die before the insured and others outlive him. Assuming that the sole beneficiary designated in the policy dies before the insured, is the latter at liberty to make a new appointment? Today, virtually all policies overcome this difficulty by including a so-called *reverter clause* in the contract. It usually provides to the effect that "if any beneficiary shall die before the insured, the interest of such beneficiary shall vest in the insured." The majority of decisions permit him to make a new appointment, and this ruling is regarded as the better one by legal writers on the subject. It is contended that since the insured's original intention as to the disposition of the proceeds of the policy has failed, the power to indicate a new beneficiary should revert to him. His original intention to protect his wife and children, it is argued, cannot be construed as implying that he meant to waive all control over his own policy in case he should happen to become the sole survivor. To hold otherwise would seem inequitable and would likely prove ineffective, since the insured could at any time lapse his policy.

Now assuming in the second case, that the policy simply names the "wife and children" or the "children" as beneficiaries, and that it contains no conditions governing the matter, how shall the proceeds of the policy be shared when some of the designated beneficiaries die before the insured dies while others survive him? In other words, are those beneficiaries who outlived the insured entitled to the entire proceeds of the policy, or is the interest of the surviving beneficiaries still limited to the share which they originally held under the policy, while the respective interests of those beneficiaries whose deaths preceded the insured's pass to their representatives or assigns? Here again the courts are not in accord. Where the policy is payable to "the wife of the insured, if living, otherwise to their children," it is clear that the interest of the children is a contingent one, depending upon the life of the wife. But suppose that the husband survives the wife, shall the proceeds of the policy pass only to those children who survive the mother, or shall all the children living at the time of the issuance of the contract participate in the distribution? Some courts hold (sometimes called the New York rule) that only the children surviving the mother come into possession of the entire policy. Other courts, however, follow the rule (sometimes called the Connecticut rule) that all the children alive when the policy was issued acquire a vested right therein, and that the interest of those dying before their mother dies passes to their representatives.

Effect of Cessation of the Beneficiary's Insurable Interest in the Life of the Insured Prior to Maturity of the Contract.   Earlier it was stated as a general rule that a person has an insurable interest in his own life and may accordingly insure that life to any amount and name anyone as beneficiary under the policy, even though such beneficiary may not have an insurable interest at the time. The only general exception to this rule, we saw, consists of those instances where the policy is a mere cover for fraud or speculative insurance and thus constitutes an evasion of the law against wagering. Since in a policy taken out by the insured on his own life it is not necessary that the beneficiary have an insurable interest, it follows that if such an interest did exist at the time the policy was issued, its loss before the maturity of the contract would not prevent the beneficiary from collecting the proceeds. But assuming that the policy is taken out legally by one person on the life of another, will a subsequent loss of that interest adversely affect the vested rights of such beneficiary? Here the prevailing rule holds that a policy valid at its inception because supported by an insurable interest will not, unless its provisions clearly stipulate to the contrary, be affected thereafter by a loss of that interest on the part of the beneficiary. A married woman, for example, who has taken a policy on her husband's life has generally been held to have the right to maintain the existence of the policy following a divorce and to be entitled to the proceeds upon his death. Certificates or the rules of some fraternal and mutual benefit societies, however, provide that the relation of husband and wife, or other family relationship under consideration, must exist at the time of the insured's death.

Death of the Insured at the Hands of the Beneficiary.   As a matter of public policy, where the beneficiary or the assignee has feloniously taken the life of the insured, he is not entitled to the insurance proceeds. The New York Court of Appeals has stated that:

all laws as well as all contracts may be controlled in their operation and effect by general, fundamental maxims of the common law. No one shall be permitted to profit by his own fraud, or to take advantage of his own wrong, or to found any claim upon his own iniquity, or to acquire property by his own crime. These maxims are dictated by public policy, have their foundation in universal law administered in all civilized countries, and have nowhere been superseded by statutes.[9]

Although the beneficiary and anyone claiming through him are not allowed to profit by his act, nevertheless the insurance company is not excused from payment. In the event there are no contingent beneficiaries, the policy stands as without a beneficiary, and the proceeds become the property of the insured's estate.

[9] *Riggs vs. Palmer* (1889) 115 N.Y. 506, 511.

Policy Provisions III: Creditor Rights and Assignment

14

CREDITOR RIGHTS IN LIFE INSURANCE [1]

Rights of Creditors of the Insured

The National Bankruptcy Act. The foregoing considerations assume importance when the change of beneficiary clause is viewed from the standpoint of claims of creditors. The statutes and court decisions governing the extent to which cash values and the proceeds of life insurance policies are available to creditors of the insured in case of insolvency are of great importance. As previously indicated, it is generally accepted by the legislatures and the courts that a moderate amount of insurance may be taken for family protection without its being subject to attachment by creditors. The following paragraph will indicate the attitude of the United States Supreme Court on this question: [2]

This argument in the interest of creditors concedes that the debtor may rightfully preserve his family from suffering and want. It seems to us that the same public policy which justifies this, and recognizes the support of wife and children as a positive obligation in law as well as morals, should be extended to protect them from destitution after the debtor's death, by permitting him, not to accumulate a fund as a permanent provision, but to devote a moderate portion of his earnings to keep on foot a security for support already, or which could thereby be, lawfully obtained, at least to the extent of requiring that, under such circumstances, the fraudulent intent of both parties to the transaction should be made out.

The rights of creditors in claiming life insurance funds are determined by (1) the nature of the beneficiary designation, (2) the National Bankruptcy Act, and (3) the exemption statutes of the various states. As

[1] For a thorough study of this entire field, see Stuart Schwarzschild, *Rights of Creditors in Life Insurance Policies* (Homewood, Ill.: Richard D. Irwin, Inc., 1963).
[2] *Central National Bank of Washington vs. Hume* (1888) 128 U.S. 195, 211; (1941) 117 Fed. 2d 582; *U.S. vs. Bess*, 243 Fed. 2d 675 (1957).

211

stated below, the latter are of vital importance in modifying the effect of the National Bankruptcy Act. However, it is desirable first to have a clear understanding of the provisions of the Bankruptcy Act, and then to note the significance of the state statutes. In either case the manner in which the beneficiary is named is of great importance.

Where the insured has named a beneficiary other than himself, his estate, or legal representatives and has not reserved to himself the right to change such beneficiary, the latter has a vested interest in the policy, and the creditors of the insured have no interest in the proceeds of the insurance, and cannot deprive the beneficiary of its benefits.[3] But where the policy is made payable to the insured, his estate, or legal representatives, such policy is subject to the claims of creditors in case of bankruptcy. So too if the insured names a beneficiary not in the above classes, but reserves the unqualified right to change the beneficiary, the policy, if it has a cash surrender value and to the extent of such value, will pass to the trustee in bankruptcy as provided under Section 70-a of the Federal Bankruptcy Law. To quote from the decision of the United States Supreme Court: [4]

The declaration of subdivision 3 is that "powers which he might have exercised for his own benefit" "shall in turn be vested" in the trustee, and there is vested in him as well all property that the bankrupt could transfer or which by judicial process could be subjected to his debts, and especially as to insurance policies which have a cash surrender value payable to himself, his estate or personal representative. It is true the policies in question here are not so payable, but they can be or could have been so payable at his own will and by simple declaration. Under such conditions to hold that there was nothing of property to vest in a trustee would be to make an insurance policy a shelter for valuable assets, and, it might be, a refuge for fraud. And our conclusions would be the same if we regarded the proviso alone.

If, as seems probable, the courts will generally interpret a revocable beneficiary designation as giving the trustee in bankruptcy the power to distribute the cash value of a policy among creditors, it follows that a policy taken out for family protection, if containing such a clause, will have connected with it a risk that the insured, in view of the future possibility of bankruptcy, should bear in mind and carefully consider. Numerous statutes, as we have seen, have purposely made it possible for men to make suitable provision for their families in case of premature death by creating an insurance fund that is immune from seizure by creditors. Yet the introduction of a clause giving the insured a free hand to change the beneficiary, or to surrender the policy, or use it for borrowing purposes, introduces an element of uncertainty in a contract that in most instances should be made

---

[3] *Central Bank of Washington vs. Hume* (1888) 128 U.S. 195; (1938) 100 Fed. 2d. 593.

[4] *Cohen vs. Samuels* (1917) 145 U.S. 50, 53; (1928) 28 Fed. 2d. 438.

absolutely secure for the benefit of those for whose protection it was expressly taken out and who have the right to expect that the insured fund, which is their sole provision against want after the death of the breadwinner, shall not have constantly hanging over it an element of uncertainty. Not to protect a policy against creditors may often result as has been well said, "in accumulating trouble for a time when misfortune would be amply abundant."

There are certain provisions and rules, however, that afford some measure of protection against creditors, even when the beneficiary is not irrevocably named. Thus, the National Bankruptcy Act expressly permits a bankrupt, having a policy with a cash surrender value payable to himself, his estate, or his legal representatives, to keep the policy free from the claims of creditors by paying such surrender value to the trustee within thirty days after the ascertainment of the amount.[5] So, too, if the policy has no surrender value, the courts have held that the trustee has no interest therein. In *Morris vs. Dobb, trustee,* where a husband took out a policy payable to his legal representatives and subsequently transferred the same to his wife four months prior to the filing of a petition in bankruptcy, the court held:[6] "A policy of insurance on the life of a bankrupt, which has no cash surrender value, and no value for any purpose except the contingency of its being valuable at the death of the bankrupt if the premiums are kept paid, does not vest in the trustee as assets of the estate."

Cases often arise where shortly following the filing of the petition in bankruptcy a policy, payable to the insured or his representatives, matures through the death of the bankrupt. In that event, are the creditors entitled to the proceeds of the policy? The question was decided by the Supreme Court of the United States in *Burlingham vs. Crouse,*[7] *Everett vs. Judson,*[8] and *Andrews vs. Partridge.*[9] According to the facts of the first case, the bankrupt carried $200,000 of insurance which, owing to loans on the policies protected with an assignment to the insurance company as well as to an additional third party, had a negligible cash surrender value at the time of the filing of the petition in bankruptcy. Shortly after becoming

---

[5] The U. S. Bankruptcy Act, Sec. 70-a, provides that: "Property which prior to the filing of the petition he could by any means have transferred, or which might have been levied upon and sold under judicial process against him, provided that when any bankrupt shall have any insurance policy which has a cash surrender value, payable to himself, his estate or personal representatives, he may, within thirty days after the cash surrender value has been ascertained and stated to the trustee by the company issuing the same, pay or secure to the trustee the sums so ascertained and stated and continue to hold, own and carry such policy free from the claims of the creditors participating in the distribution of his estate under the bankruptcy proceedings; otherwise the policy shall pass to the trustee as assets."

[6] (1900) 110 Ga. 606, quoting *In re Buelow,* 98 Fed. 86. *Burlingham vs. Crouse,* 228 U.S. 459 (1913).

[7] (1913) 228 U.S. 459.

[8] (1913) 228 U.S. 474.

[9] (1913) 228 U.S. 479.

bankrupt the insured died, thus maturing the contracts. The trustees undertook to set aside the assignment as preferential and contended that the proceeds of the policy belonged to the bankrupt's estate. As opposed to this view, the assignee contended that the creditors were entitled only to the available cash surrender value at the time of the filing of the petition in bankruptcy, and this, as previously noted, was negligible. The court upheld this view and ruled: [10] "We think it was the purpose of Congress to pass to the trustee that sum which was available to the bankrupt at the time of bankruptcy as a cash asset, otherwise to leave to the insured the benefit of his life insurance." This is the general rule even where there are no loans outstanding and the cash values are substantial.

State Exemption Statutes.　　From earliest times it has been the policy of Congress to give effect to state exemption statutes, and the National Bankruptcy Act of 1898 has a provision to this effect.[11] In *Holden vs. Stratton* [12] the United States Supreme Court definitely decided that according to Section 6, a life insurance policy that is exempt from the claims of creditors under any state statute is also exempt in bankruptcy proceedings. The exemptions governing are those prescribed by the state laws in force at the time of filing the petition in the state of the bankrupt's domicile.

State statutes relative to the rights of creditors may be divided into two broad groups, the first exempting proceeds of life insurance policies payable at the time of the death of the insured, and the second exempting not only the proceeds payable at death, but the cash values as well. The statutes first enacted were of the type of the first group, and since, as previously stated, they were passed at a time when cash values were relatively unimportant and when the beneficiary ordinarily had a vested interest in the policy, they were as a general rule adequate. The first law of this nature was passed by New York in 1840. This was followed by similar laws in other states so that by 1875 such laws were general. For illustrative purposes, the law of Pennsylvania may be cited. It read as follows: [13]

All policies of life insurance or annuities upon the life of any person which may hereafter mature, and which have been or shall be taken out for the benefit of, or *bona fide* assigned to the wife or children or any relative dependent upon such person, shall be vested in such wife or children or other relative, full and clear from all claims of the creditors of such person.

[10] (1913) 228 U.S. 459, 473.
[11] Act of July 1, 1898, c.541, § 6. "Section 6. This Act shall not affect the allowance to bankrupts of the exemptions which are prescribed by the State laws in force at the time of the filing of the petition in the State where they (the bankrupts) have had their domicile for the six months or greater portion thereof immediately preceding the filing of the petition."
[12] (1905) 198 U.S. 202; *Meyer vs. U.S.,* 375 U.S. 233, 239 (1963).
[13] Act of April 15, 1868 (P.L. 103).

Acts of this nature were so construed by the courts that where a policy had a cash value and where the insured had reserved the right to change the beneficiary, the creditors were able to claim such cash value. Additional legislation was therefore necessary to protect such policies, and statutes of the second group above described became increasingly common. Without attempting to trace in detail the development of such laws in Pennsylvania, it may be stated that at the present time life insurance policies, in which certain beneficiaries are named, are free from the claims of creditors even when the insured has reserved the right to change the beneficiary. To quote the law now in force: [14]

That the net amount payable under any policy of life insurance or under any annuity contract upon the life of any person, heretofore or hereafter made for the benefit of or assigned to the wife or children or dependent relative of such person, shall be exempt from all claims of the creditors of such person arising out of or based upon any obligation created after the passage of this Act, whether or not the right to change the named beneficiary is reserved by or permitted to such person.

Section 55-A of the New York Insurance Law, effective March 31, 1927, is intended to provide similar protection.[15] This act as interpreted protects the *proceeds and avails* from attachment by the creditors of the insured; and in the term "proceeds and avails" are included cash surrender values and dividends left to accumulate. Any payments, however, that have been made to the insured, such as cash surrender values, or dividends that have been deposited to his account, or disability payments that are made to the insured directly are not exempt, since the act states that in a policy of insurance the

---

[14] Act of June 28, 1923 (P.L. 884). The law as passed in 1919 omitted the phrase "arising out of or based upon any obligation created after the passage of this act." This provision was inserted, since a law exempting policies from claims of creditors arising before it was passed would be contrary to the Federal Constitution in that it impaired the obligation of existing contracts.

[15] It provides as follows: "If a policy of insurance, whether heretofore or hereafter issued, is effected by any person on his own life or on another life, in favor of a person other than himself, or, except in cases of transfer with intent to defraud creditors, if a policy of life insurance is assigned or in any way made payable to any such person, the lawful beneficiary or assignee thereof, other than the insured or the person so effecting such insurance, or his executors or administrators, shall be entitled to its proceeds and avails against the creditors and representatives of the insured and of the person effecting the same, whether or not the right to change the beneficiary is reserved or permitted, and whether or not the policy is made payable to the person whose life is insured if the beneficiary or assignee shall predecease such person; provided, that, subject to the statute of limitations, the amount of any premium for said insurance paid with intent to defraud creditors, with interest thereon, shall enure to their benefit from the proceeds of the policy; but the company issuing the policy shall be discharged of all liability thereon by payment of its proceed in accordance with its terms, unless before such payment the company shall have written notice, by or in behalf of a creditor, of a claim to recover for transfer made or premiums paid with intent to defraud creditors, with specification of the amount claimed."

lawful beneficiary or assignee *other than the insured* shall be entitled to its proceeds and avails against the creditors and representatives of the insured.

According to Howard C. Spencer, Section 55-a of the New York Law "has been held to cover endowments as have the California, Ohio, Washington, and Wisconsin statutes. But, on the other hand, the contrary has been held of the Nebraska and New Hampshire statutes." [16] With respect to annuities, Mr. Spencer summarizes the situation as follows: "The cash value of the deferred annuity is not protected by the ordinary insurance exemption statute, unless annuities are expressly included. The protection of payments made under the annuity presents a far more serious problem. Impressive arguments can be presented for the need of some minimum protection. But equally weighty reasons can be advanced for the need of limiting this protection." [17]

Although the above laws might be considered somewhat typical, it should be noted that the exemption statutes relating to life insurance are distinguished by their lack of uniformity. Because so much depends upon the language and scope of the particular statute involved, only a generalized discussion is possible.

Some of the laws are applicable only where the named beneficiary is of a certain class, such as the insured's wife or children, or a dependent relative. Others are broader in scope. Some enactments limit the amount of the annual premiums payable for exempt insurance. Under other statutes the limitation is based on the total amount of insurance proceeds, instead of on the amount of annual premiums paid. Proceeds in excess of the stipulated figure are available to creditors.

Rights of Beneficiary's Creditors

Prior to Maturity.   In the absence of a statute exempting the avails or cash values of life insurance from the claims of creditors of the beneficiary, the question of whether such creditors can reach the cash values depends upon whether or not the beneficiary possesses a property right in the policy. If the beneficiary does not possess such a right in the policy, his creditors cannot reach the cash values. It was pointed out earlier that a revocable beneficiary has a mere expectancy, and, consequently, no property right exists to be attached. Even in the case of an irrevocably named beneficiary, creditors of such a beneficiary cannot reach the cash

---

[16] Howard C. Spencer, "Rights of Creditors in Life Insurance," *The Beneficiary in Life Insurance* (Homewood, Ill.: S. S. Huebner Foundation for Insurance Education, Richard D. Irwin, Inc., 1956), pp. 101–102.

[17] *Ibid.,* p. 102. In 1939, in the revision of the Insurance Law of New York, Section 55-a was repealed and Section 166 was enacted. This Section is not new law but the old law with a few changes plus a consolidation of a number of special statutes.

value of the policy, since the beneficiary does not possess the right to obtain the cash value without the consent of the insured.

At Maturity.   The rights of a beneficiary, whether designated revocably or irrevocably, vest absolutely upon the *death* of the insured. In the case of maturity of a policy as an endowment, the rights of beneficiaries may or may not vest immediately, depending upon the contract. For example, an endowment policy which provides that the proceeds are to be paid in installments upon maturity as an endowment may perhaps be held to remain in force as long as payments are being made in accordance with the policy terms. It appears that the insured should have the right to change a revocable beneficiary during such time, in spite of the fact that the policy has matured as an endowment.[18]

In the absence of statutory provision, the creditors of the beneficiary are entitled to the proceeds of the insurance as soon as a right thereto vests in the beneficiary.[19] The New York Court of Appeals has stated that "Just as any money or property which is left by a decedent may be taken for the debts or liabilities of those to whom it is given after it has been paid to them, so the proceeds of an insurance policy or certificate may be compulsorily devoted to the same purpose when the beneficiary comes into possession thereof." [20]

Most of the state laws exempting life insurance proceeds and avails from claims of creditors expressly refer only to creditors of the insured. Such statutes have been held generally not to provide any protection against the claims of creditors of the beneficiaries. It should be noted, however, that a few states have very broad statutes which exempt the proceeds of life insurance against the creditors of both the insured and the beneficiary.

Spendthrift Trust Clauses.   In addition to the few broad statutes which exempt life insurance proceeds from the claims of the creditors of both the insured and the beneficiary, a majority of states have laws permitting the insured, if he so desires, to include in the policy installment settlement provisions, a so-called spendthrift trust clause which will protect the proceeds from claims of the beneficiary's creditors. The clause provides that the benefits payable to any beneficiary after the death of the insured are not assignable nor transferable nor subject to commutation or encumbrance, nor to any legal process, execution, garnishment, or attach-

---

[18] "Beneficiary Clauses," in Harry Krueger and Leland T. Waggoner (eds.), *The Life Insurance Policy Contract* (Boston: Little, Brown & Company, 1953), p. 91.

[19] *Murray vs. Wells* (1880) 53 Iowa 256. In the case of *Holmes, appellant, vs. Marshall* (1905) 145 Cal. 777, the court held that under certain conditions the exemption extends "not only against the debts of the person whose life was insured, and who paid the premiums, but also to the debts of the beneficiary to whom it is payable after the death of the insured." See also S. Dak. L. (1930) Ch. 170.

[20] *Bull vs. Case* (1901) 165 N.Y. 578, 581.

ment proceeding. In a majority of such states the provisions extend only to beneficiaries other than the insured.

The outstanding characteristic of these spendthrift statutes is the permissive nature of the exemption. The company and someone else must agree on the exemption for it to be operative. Practically, this means that the *insured* must provide for the clause in the installment settlement provisions of the policy. The protection would not be effective if a beneficiary requested the inclusion of such a clause following the death of the insured. The spendthrift trust clause protects only the money being held by the company. As soon as the beneficiary receives the money, it may be available to his creditors.

More than half the states have statutes recognizing spendthrift trusts. In the majority of those states where no statute exists, the courts have upheld the use of spendthrift trust clauses. Actually, there are only a few states where such clauses are not valid and even in these a discretionary trust may be used to accomplish the same thing.[21]

Misappropriation of Funds.   Although the rights of beneficiaries in life insurance policies have been greatly enlarged by legislation of the type described above, nevertheless, it is contrary to public policy to permit life insurance to act as a shelter for assets that equitably belong to some third party. Thus, where premiums are paid out of misappropriated funds, the right to follow the embezzled funds is not lost merely because such money was used to buy life insurance. As stated by a Wisconsin court: [22] "The statutes guarding the rights of married women in insurance policies and homesteads are beneficent statutes, which are liberally construed in their behalf. But they are not designed to encourage fraud or to make such property a safe depository for stolen funds." Where premiums are paid with wrongfully acquired funds, the rights of the aggrieved party vary according to jurisdiction. In some cases he is able to reclaim the entire proceeds of the policies purchased by his money. In other cases he can get from the proceeds only the money taken from him. In the third group of states he is awarded merely the amount of money traceable to premium payments. So too, when it is clearly evident that it is the insured's intention to defraud his creditors by taking out insurance or by assigning it, the beneficiary is not protected against creditors' claims. In some such cases the premiums paid by the insured following his insolvency are obtainable by his creditors, and in others the creditors obtain the insurance money in the proportion that the premiums paid subsequent to the insolvency bear to the sum total of the premiums paid on the policy.

[21] For a comprehensive review of creditors' rights in life insurance as well as a digest of state insurance exemption laws, see *Advanced Underwriting Service* (Indianapolis: The Research and Review Service of America, Inc.), Sec. 10.

[22] *Truelsch vs. Miller* (1925) 186 Wis. 239, 252.

THE ASSIGNMENT CLAUSE

Distinctions Between Assignment of Life Insurance and Other Policies

There are few types of contracts which are so frequently assigned as insurance policies, and any discussion of the subject must distinguish clearly the underlying difference between the assignment of life policies and the assignment of policies in fire and most other lines of property insurance. The fire insurance policy, being strictly a personal contract, that is, insuring the particular owner of the property rather than the property itself, can be assigned only with the consent of the company. The standard fire policy now in general use provides that "Assignment of this policy shall not be valid except with the written consent of this Company." Therefore, in case of the transfer of insured property, the company may refuse its consent to the transfer of the policy to the new owner, and if such transfer of the policy has been undertaken without the company's knowledge or consent, it will be relieved of all further liability.

A life insurance policy, however, being in the nature of a chose in action, has been held by the courts to be freely assignable for a valuable consideration in the absence of (1) restrictive provisions in the policy, or (2) attempts at concealment of fraud or more speculative insurance.[23] To hold otherwise might often diminish the value of a life policy to its owner as a means of securing credit or other benefits. Unlike a fire policy, the life insurance contract in most instances provides for payment upon death, an event that is certain to occur sooner or later. For this reason the courts have held the life policy to resemble an ordinary chose in action, and have generally inclined to the view that sufficient reasons against its assignability cannot be given so long as there is no infringement of the vested rights of

[23] "It is desirable that the insured should have the opportunity of making free commercial use of his life insurance as available property, for it may often be convenient to secure money, by loan or otherwise, upon it. Unlike the case of a fire policy, a life policy was considered assignable at common law; and, by the better opinion, a policy of life insurance may be assigned or made payable to one who has no insurable interest, if the transaction is not a mere cover for a wager. The demands of business quite outweigh the remote possibility that some unscrupulous assignee may succumb to the temptation of murdering or shortening the life of the insured for the sake of hastening payment of the insurance money. Moreover, there would seem to be room for the operation of any such sinister designs regardless of whether the assignee has an insurable interest. A creditor, for example, may be quite as strongly tempted, as the donee of a gift, to realize a prompt payment of the insurance upon the life of the assignor." *Richards on the Law of Insurance,* 5th ed. (New York: Baker, Voorhis & Co., 1952), pp. 539–540.

the beneficiary. But, as already stated, if the assignment is based upon an immoral or illegal consideration, the courts will refuse to uphold it; and cases are on record where even executors or administrators of the insured have been permitted to oppose the legality of an assignment on such grounds. After death has occurred, it may be added, the interest in the policy is held to be purely a chose in action subject to assignment by the beneficiary without regard to the "notice of assignment" or any other provisions of the policy.

Distinction Between Assignment and Change of Beneficiary

The assignment of a life insurance policy and a change of beneficiary under such a policy are not the same thing. The Circuit Court of Appeals has stated: [24] "An assignment is the transfer by one of his right or interest in property to another. It rests upon contract, and, generally speaking, the delivery of the thing assigned is necessary to its validity. The power to change the beneficiary is the power to appoint. The power of appointment must be exercised in the manner agreed upon in the contract of insurance."

Unless the insured has reserved the right to change the beneficiary, he cannot assign a policy payable to a third person as beneficiary without the beneficiary's consent. But where the right to change the beneficiary has been reserved, the courts are not in agreement upon the effect of an assignment of a policy upon the interest of the beneficiary. The majority of courts hold that the assignee's rights are superior to those of the beneficiary. However, in some jurisdictions, the beneficiary is held to have a vested interest which can be divested only by following exactly the procedure set forth in the policy for a change of beneficiary.[25]

Assignments Classified

Assignments are of several kinds, and in determining the effect of the assignment the courts as a general rule look to the intention of the parties. When a policy is conditionally assigned to secure creditors, they are entitled only to the amount of premiums, debt, and interest thereon, any balance going to the insured or to his estate. In an absolute assignment, voluntarily made, in good faith, and not in fraud of creditors, the assignee gets the entire amount of the insurance. The same rule applies, generally, where the policy has been transferred absolutely to a purchaser for value. As a general

---

[24] *The Mutual Benefit Life Insurance Co. vs. Swett, et al.* (1915; C.C.A.) 222 Fed. 200, 205.

[25] Janice E. Greider and William T. Beadles, *Law and the Life Insurance Contract,* rev. ed. (Homewood, Ill.: Richard D. Irwin, Inc., 1968), pp. 361–365.

rule, however, if the assignment is merely a cloak for a wager, it is unenforceable.[26]

Frequently, an absolute assignment is made to secure a debt. Attention should therefore be called to the prevailing doctrine that such an assignment does not give to the assignee the entire proceeds of the policy. The courts will look to the intent of the parties. This rule has been stated as follows: [27] "Although the assignment was absolute in form, it was a fair deduction, from the evidence, that it was intended merely as security for an indebtedness due by the insured to the assignee, and thus that all right in the policy in excess of such debt was the equitable property of the insured and descended to his administratrix at his death."

Policy Restrictions Relating to the Assignment of Policies

Although policies are assignable in the absence of restrictive policy provisions, it is the universal practice today of life insurance companies to include an assignment clause of some kind in them. Although much variation exists in the wording adopted by the companies, the provision usually reads that "no assignment of this policy shall be binding upon the company unless in writing and until filed at its home office. The company assumes no responsibility as to the validity of any assignment." In many policies, however, the provision is more elaborate, some companies stipulating that in addition to the filing of the assignment, or a duplicate thereof, the assignment must be approved in writing by certain officers of the company; that the original assignment and due proof of interest must be produced when the policy is presented for payment; and that all assignments shall be subject to any indebtedness to the company at its home office.

Where an assignment has thus been brought to the attention of the company and has been consented to, it is held to constitute a new contract between the company and the assignee. The latter, however, simply obtains the rights of the original insured—that is, takes the position of the assignor —and is protected only to the extent that the assignor was protected under the policy. In other words, the assignee takes only what the assignor can assign; if the policy is void at the time of assignment because of acts of violation on the part of the assignor, the assignee is not in a position to recover.

The assignee's position in this respect has been greatly improved through the general use of the incontestable clause, which, as we have seen, protects the policy against the acts of the insured after the lapse of a stipulated period. The principle, however, is worthy of emphasis in that it applies before the incontestable feature goes into operation, and in that it has a most important bearing upon other forms of insurance. In fire insurance, ordi-

[26] W. R. Vance and B. M. Anderson, *Handbook on the Law of Insurance,* 3rd ed. (St. Paul: West Publishing Co., 1951), pp. 768–769.
[27] *Saville vs. Lee* (1931) 43 Ga. App. 263, 264.

nary assignments of policies are considered so dangerous, because of the possible invalidity of the contract at the time of assignment, that it is almost the universal practice for mortgagees either to insure their own interest as mortgagee or to require the mortgagor to have a so-called mortgagee clause endorsed on the policy protecting the premises offered as security for the loan, which provides that "this insurance, as to the interest of the mortgagee (or trustee) only therein, shall not be invalidated by any act or neglect of the mortgagor or owner of the within described property, nor by any foreclosure or other proceedings or notice of sale relating to the property, nor by any change in the title of ownership of the property, nor by the occupation of the premises for purposes more hazardous than are permitted by this policy, etc." In some jurisdictions the courts have even held that the endorsement of such a clause does not revive a policy already void at the time the endorsement is made, and for this reason it is the practice of certain large lending institutions—a number of life insurance companies resort to the practice—to require fire insurance companies to consent by special agreement to protect them, as mortgagees, against all acts and neglect of the mortgagor whether occurring prior or subsequent to the issuance of the mortgagee clause.

It should also be observed that the assignment provisions of life insurance policies to which reference was made do not prohibit an assignment without consent, but simply provide that the company need not recognize the assignment until it has received written notice of the same, and that it assumes no responsibility as to its validity. As is well stated in one case [28] where the court had under consideration an assignment similar to those mentioned above:

The consent of the company to an assignment is not necessary. All that is required is that the assignment be in writing on the policy, and a copy of it furnished to the company, within thirty days. This provision is not, one which is intended to guard against increased risks, and does not go to, or infuse itself into, the essence of the contract. Its sole purpose is to protect the company against the danger of having to pay the policy twice, by requiring written evidence of any change of beneficiaries to be put in reliable form and promptly furnished to the company.

All that could, at the very most, be claimed as the effect of noncompliance with this stipulation, is that the company might disregard an attempted assignment, and pay the money to the original beneficiary; in other words, such attempted assignment would be merely voidable at the option of the company.

Elliott, in reviewing the cases affecting notice of assignment to the insurer, concludes: [29] "At the most, a failure to give the required notice invalidates an attempted assignment, but does not void the policy. A notice

---

[28] *Hogue vs. Minnesota Packing and Provision Company* (1894) 59 Minn. 39, 44.
[29] C. B. Elliott, *A Treatise on the Law of Insurance* (Indianapolis, Ind.: The Bobbs-Merrill Company, 1902), p. 406.

given within a reasonable time after an assignment is sufficient, although the insured may have died in the meantime."

When the writing of the assignment is required, it is unnecessary to use any particular wording, and the content of the assignment may assume any form that the parties thereto may agree upon, such for example as a special agreement between debtor and creditor as to the final disposition of any balance of the proceeds of the policy after full payment of the actual indebtedness. Where nothing to the contrary is stipulated in the agreement of assignment, the assignee of a policy held as collateral security for a debt of the assignor cannot dispose of the same by sale or surrender to the company for its cash value, without first giving the insured proper notice and a reasonable time for redemption. Moreover, actual delivery of the policy to the assignee is not necessary to make an assignment binding; in fact, the courts have held that the assignee's rights may be fully supported even in cases where neither the policy nor the assignment has been delivered to him.

American Bankers Association Collateral Assignment Form

Most assignments of life insurance policies are made to facilitate the insured's personal or business credit or to provide collateral security for bank loans. The banking world has therefore been deeply interested in bringing about a uniformity of assignment practice under proper conditions, a desire attributable partly to the varying procedures followed by insurance companies, partly because life insurance contracts contain a third party (the beneficiary) with varying degrees of interest, and partly because the law of the various states, both common and statute, differs considerably with respect to the rights of all of the parties involved in an assignment of a life insurance contract. In the course of time many different assignment forms came into being, some designed by the banks and others by insurance companies which they either required or recommended.

After detailed investigation, the Bank Management Commission of the American Bankers Association, in collaboration with representatives of the Association of Life Insurance Counsel, approved a form of Assignment of Life Insurance Policy as Collateral.

The ABA form attempts to provide adequate protection to the lender, but at the same time permit the insured to retain certain rights under the policy. Thus, the *assignee* gets the right to (1) collect the proceeds at maturity, (2) surrender the policy pursuant to its terms, (3) obtain policy loans, and (4) receive dividends and exercise and receive benefit of nonforfeiture rights.[30] On the other hand the *insured* retains the right to (1)

---

[30] The form perhaps should but *does not* permit the assignee to reach prepaid premiums.

collect any disability benefits, (2) change the beneficiary (subject to the assignment), and (3) elect optional modes of settlement (subject to the assignment). Under the form the assignee also agrees (1) to pay over to the beneficiary any proceeds or avails in excess of the insured's debt to him, (2) not to surrender or obtain a loan from the insurance company (except for paying premiums) unless there is default on the debt or premium payments and then not until twenty days after notification to the insured, and (3) to forward the policy to the company for endorsement of any change of beneficiary or election of settlement option. As explained by Robert Dechert,[31] "The ABA form operates as a satisfactory middle ground between the completely absolute type of form which theretofore was often demanded by bank lenders and the old type of collateral assignment form used by some life insurance companies, under which lenders often found themselves in difficulties because insurance companies would not permit any action to be taken without specific approval by the insured."

State Statutes Affecting Assignments by Beneficiaries

In the absence of restraining statutes, beneficiaries may assign their contingent interest in a life policy, although there are legal cases affirming the position that the holder of a certificate in a fraternal or mutual benefit society may not assign the same, unless the restriction is waived by the society, to persons who do not come within the group of permitted beneficiaries. Unless prohibited by statute, even the wife has been held to have the right to assign her interest in a policy in order to secure a debt of her husband. But, as noted in the preceding section, many states have adopted laws which have for their purpose the protection of the interest of the wife and children of the insured by providing that the proceeds of his life insurance made payable to them shall not be liable to seizure or appropriation for the satisfaction of the claims of creditors. In New York and Wisconsin the courts have construed such statutes as meaning that the wife is prohibited altogether from assigning her interests, while in other states similar statutes were construed as not precluding such an assignment. By subsequent enactment, however, the New York law now provides that "a policy of insurance on the life of any person for the benefit of a married woman, is also assignable and may be surrendered to the company issuing the same, by her, or her legal representative, with the written consent of the assured." [32]

---

[31] Dan M. McGill (ed.), *The Beneficiary in Life Insurance* (Homewood, Ill.: S. S. Huebner Foundation for Insurance Education, Richard D. Irwin, Inc., 1956), p. 38. For a complete copy of the ABA form see Appendix A.

[32] N. Y. Dom. Rel. Law, 52.

Assignment of the Policy by the Assignee—A Policy of Life Insurance Is Not a Negotiable Instrument

Although an assignee cannot, in the absence of an agreement to the contrary, sell or surrender the policy without giving the insured a reasonable opportunity to redeem it, he may, under proper circumstances, reassign the policy to another. Thus, in *Corcoran vs. Mutual Life Insurance Company* [33] it was held that where a policy was given as collateral security for the payment of a note, the holder has the right to assign the same to the endorsee of the note, who will then be entitled to hold the policy as security for the note.

But a life insurance policy is not to be regarded as a negotiable instrument, as is exemplified by the case of *Brown vs. Equitable Life Assurance Society.*[34] Here the insured assigned a policy as security for a debt, and the assignee subsequently assigned the same to a bank as security for another loan. The court held that despite the absoluteness of the form of assignment, "the bank took the policy subject to the equities existing in favor of the insured, unless the conduct of the latter was such as to create an estoppel." According to the facts of the case, the insured had neglected to pay premiums for eleven years, and during that period had made no effort to recover the policy. These circumstances, together with the fact that the bank kept the policy from lapsing by paying the premiums itself, caused the court to hold that the insured was prevented from claiming any rights under the policy as against either the first assignee or the bank.

[33] (1898) 183 Pa. 443.
[34] (1899) 75 Minn. 412.

Policy Provisions IV: | 15
Settlement Options

ONE OF THE most important things which the insured should consider at the time he purchases a life insurance policy is the manner in which the proceeds will be paid when it matures or becomes a claim. Failure on the insured's part to arrange for the proper payment of proceeds may defeat the purpose for which the insurance was taken out, even though apparently a sufficient amount of protection is carried. It is the purpose of the following discussion to consider the policy provisions relating to the settlement of life insurance proceeds as well as company practices which impinge on the planning of settlement arrangements.

NATURE OF THE OPTIONS

Settlement options are usually designated in the contract either by number or letter, and the order in which they appear varies with the company. Most ordinary contracts today provide for settlement under several of the options discussed below. The other options are often provided or may be secured upon request.

Cash or Lump Sum

In a strict sense, a "lump-sum" settlement is not an "option," because life insurance contracts usually provide for lump-sum settlement in the *absence* of some other direction by the policyowner. But practically, it can be considered an option selected by *default* when the insured fails to make some more appropriate arrangement. There are life insurance contracts which provide for an income settlement in the absence of other direction by the insured, and if a cash payment is desired, it must be selected specifically.

Most companies, where proceeds are payable in cash, will permit a named beneficiary to place them under one of the settlement options provided in the contract. Notwithstanding this, there are a number of disadvantages to a lump-sum settlement. A major drawback is that there is no protection against the so-called common disaster or the much more common short-term-survivorship situation which was discussed earlier. The beneficiary may never live to take advantage of her "right to place the proceeds under one of the settlement options." Even with a delayed payment or common disaster clause, full protection is not available, and the proceeds may be subject to shrinkage due to probate costs and creditors and may also have undesirable estate tax consequences.

A second disadvantage of such a settlement is that it usually affords no protection against the creditors of the beneficiary. As was pointed out in the preceding chapter, such protection can usually be arranged in connection with the income options, if elected before the insured's death.

Company practice will not usually permit a beneficiary who elects an income option in lieu of a cash settlement to designate contingent beneficiaries. This is an additional disadvantage in that in many such cases any proceeds remaining in the company's hands at the primary beneficiary's death must go to the primary beneficiary's estate.

Although most companies permit many arrangements not specifically granted by contract, virtually all companies are more *liberal* respecting income settlement plans adopted by the insured before death than for those requested by a beneficiary entitled to a lump-sum payment. A further disadvantage in this regard is the possibility of future changes in company practices before the beneficiary requests a specific settlement arrangement. Finally, most policies do not provide for interest to be paid from the date of death unless a settlement option has been elected while the insured was living.

Although there are circumstances where a lump-sum settlement may be indicated, in connection with *personal* life insurance, a planned settlement utilizing one or more of the income options discussed below is usually recommended for the average policyholder. It should be noted, however, that in the case where significant amounts are involved and where the insured is not in financial difficulties, use of trust arrangements with a bank may well be preferable to the use of the regular settlement options.

Interest Option

Under the interest option the proceeds remain with the company and only the interest earned thereon is paid to the beneficiary. In most companies the interest cannot be left to accumulate and compound, but must be paid out monthly, quarterly, semiannually, or annually, commencing at the end of the first such period. Interest earned above the guaranteed rate (the only source of surplus considered) is usually paid with the guaranteed payments. There are legal limits to the length of time the principal may be kept intact [1]

---

[1] See pp. 243–244.

and company practice frequently limits this to the lifetime of the primary beneficiary or thirty years, whichever is the longer. The rate of interest guaranteed under this option varies slightly between companies, and, in addition, some companies guarantee a lower rate where withdrawal privileges are granted to the beneficiary. Current policies generally guarantee a lower rate than older contracts in the same company.

Table 15–1 shows the yields per $1,000 of proceeds placed under the interest option at various guaranteed rates.

TABLE 15-1.   Interest Option

Rate	Annual Payment	Monthly Payment
2.0%	$20	$1.65
2.5	25	2.06
3.0	30	2.47
3.5	35	2.87

It should be noticed that the monthly yield is less than one twelfth of the corresponding annual amount, due to an adjustment made for loss of interest.

The interest option is the most *flexible* of all options and therefore is one of the most widely used. Basically, the main advantage of the interest option is that it assures the beneficiary freedom from investment worries while guaranteeing both principal and a minimum rate of return. In addition, however, depending upon individual company rules and state laws, the beneficiary *may* be given:

1. The right to name who is to receive any balance at the primary beneficiary's death, or the right to change the contingent beneficiaries previously designated by the insured or other policyowner.

2. The right to make withdrawals of all or part of the principal, subject to the limitations included in the settlement agreement. Most companies will permit any reasonable combination of limiting factors (so much per year, at certain ages, and so forth), or the proceeds may be held without any withdrawal privileges.

3. The right to elect to change to another settlement option at a later time, when circumstances may have changed. Thus, for example, the proceeds may be left under the interest option with the right in the primary beneficiary to change to any other option, including the life income option (see below), at a later date. This privilege of electing to change "at any time" subjects the company to adverse selection (obviously a beneficiary in bad health at age 65 would not elect to change to a life income option). In

view of this, many companies provide that if election to change options is not made within a reasonable but limited time following the death of the insured, income rates being included in current contracts will apply instead of those included in the original contract.

Provision may be made for an automatic or mandatory change to another option at some specified later date or age, or upon the happening of an event such as entry into college.

4. Protection from most creditors, under a spendthrift clause included in the policy.

The right of withdrawal and the right to change to another option are the sources of flexibility in the interest option, and it usually is the foundation upon which most comprehensive settlement agreements are formulated.

Fixed Period Option

This is one of the two options based on the concept of scientifically liquidating principal and interest over a period of years, *without* reference to a life contingency. The other is the fixed amount option which is discussed below. The fixed period option, as its name indicates, provides for the payment of the proceeds in equal installments over a definite period of months or years, usually not longer than twenty-five or thirty years. The amount of proceeds, the period of time, the guaranteed rate of interest, and the frequency of payments determine the amount of each installment. Surplus interest is usually credited at the end of each year. Table 15–2 shows the

TABLE 15-2. Guaranteed Installments per
$1,000 of Proceeds

(2½ Per Cent Interest)

Number of Years Payable	Annually	Monthly
5	$210.00	$17.70
10	111.47	9.39
15	78.80	6.64
20	62.58	5.27

payments which would be provided by $1,000 of proceeds payable over specified periods.

The fixed period option is valuable where the most important consideration is to provide income for a definite period, as in the case of a readjustment period following the insured's death, while the children are in school, or others. Most companies will permit the insured to give the beneficiary the right to commute, or discount, all remaining installments and receive a lump sum, and some companies will permit the beneficiary to select the date when payments are to begin; but aside from these, the fixed period option is very inflexible.

Since the basic characteristic of this option is the period of time selected, a policy loan which is outstanding at the insured's death will reduce the *amount* of each installment but will *not* affect the number of installments. For the same reason, any dividend accumulations or paid-up additions payable with the proceeds will operate to increase the beneficiary's income, the number of installments remaining the same.

Fixed Amount Option

Under the fixed amount option the amount of income is the primary consideration, rather than the period of time over which the proceeds and interest are to be liquidated. Here a specified rate of income is designated, such as $100 per month, $75 per month, or any other rate, and payments are continued until the principal and interest thereon are exhausted.

In most situations the fixed amount option is more advantageous than the fixed period option because it is much more flexible. Most companies permit the insured to specify varying amounts of income at different times, and the beneficiary may be given the right of withdrawal in whole or in part at any time and from time to time, or the right to withdraw up to a certain sum in any one year on a cumulative or noncumulative basis. In the case of both the fixed period and fixed amount options, the commencement of these installments can be deferred to a particular time by holding the proceeds under the interest option until that time. As in the case of the interest option, most companies will permit a beneficiary to direct that any unpaid balance be placed under some other option (usually the life income option).

Since the *amount* of each installment is the controlling factor under this option, dividend accumulations or additions payable with the proceeds, together with any excess interest earned while installments are being paid, increase the number of installments but do not affect the amount of each installment. Conversely, loans outstanding at the insured's death or withdrawals of principal by the beneficiary serve to decrease the number of installments.

There is usually a special rule governing minimum installments under the fixed amount option. Usually, at least $50 per year is required to be paid out for each $1,000 of proceeds. Sometimes the minimum is set at $10 per month. The rule is in keeping with the purpose of the option; that is, to exhaust the principal and interest within some reasonable length of time.

It should be noted that basically the fixed amount and fixed period options represent the same idea expressed in different ways. Both scientifically liquidate principal and interest over a period of years, without reference to a life contingency. For this reason, the guaranteed interest factor is usually the same for both options in a given contract.

Life Income Options

The several forms of life income options represent the other broad class of settlement options—those scientifically liquidating principal and interest *with* reference to life contingencies. These options are unique to life insurance companies; no other financial institution can make such an arrangement with its clients. As was pointed out earlier,[2] life income options are in reality forms of life annuities and thus serve the same economic functions.

The amount of each installment depends on the type of life income (annuity) selected, the amount of the proceeds, the rate of interest assumed, the age of the beneficiary when the income commences, and the sex of the beneficiary. The most common forms of life income options are (1) the life income option, (2) the refund life income option, and (3) the life income option with "period certain" or "installments guaranteed." In recent years, a number of companies have begun to include a joint and survivorship life income option in their contracts. Although all of these are not included in every contract, most companies will, on request, add those not shown in the contract. Virtually all contracts contain the third type in some form.

Life Income Option.   Installments are payable only so long as the primary beneficiary lives, with no return of principal guaranteed. Since no principal return is guaranteed, the pure life income option provides the largest life income per $1,000 of proceeds for a given beneficiary. As was pointed out in the chapter on annuities, most people hesitate to take the risk of forfeiting a large part of the principal in the event of an early death. This is particularly true where there are relatives to whom they wish to leave funds they do not need for themselves. Thus, for example, this form would obviously be inappropriate for a widow with young children, as it affords no protection to the children in the case of the early death of their mother.

Refund Life Income Option.   The refund life income options may take the form of a "cash refund annuity" or an "installment refund annuity." It will be remembered that both annuities guarantee the

[2] See pp. 127–128.

return of an amount no less than the principal sum, the difference in the two forms being that under the "cash refund" option a lump-sum settlement is made following the death of the primary beneficiary instead of continuing the installment payments.

Life Income with Period Certain.   Under this, the most widely used life income option, installments are payable as long as the primary beneficiary lives, but should this beneficiary die before a predetermined number of "years (or months) certain," the company will continue the installments to a second beneficiary until the end of the certain period. Usually, the certain period runs for five, ten, fifteen, or twenty years (or equivalent months). The usual contract contains two or three alternative periods, the most popular being ten and twenty years, but again, others may be obtained on request. This option is frequently used where a widow and minor children are concerned, since it assumes the desired income for life while still guaranteeing that the income will last until the children are grown regardless of the date of death of their mother.

Joint and Survivorship Life Income Option.   The joint and survivorship life income option is not always included in the original contract or available in all companies. Under this option, if at the death of the first beneficiary the second beneficiary is still living, installments are continued during the latter's lifetime. As in the case of joint and survivorship annuities, this option may continue the same income to the surviving beneficiary or reduce the installments to two thirds ("joint and two thirds"), three fourths ("joint and three fourths") or one half ("joint and one half") of the original amount and continue this reduced amount for the lifetime of the surviving beneficiary. A few companies will grant joint and survivorship options with a certain period of ten or twenty years.

The joint and survivorship option is most useful in providing for the retirement income of the insured and his wife. In such cases the proceeds of a matured endowment or retirement income policy or the cash value of any permanent form of insurance may be applied under this option.

Other Settlement Arrangements

Although virtually any desired pattern of income may be obtained by using the various options described above, either singly or in a combination, some companies provide options which are designed to meet a specific need or serve a particular purpose. Actually, these special options are usually a combination of the basic options to fit a particular situation, with an attractive sales title applied thereto. For example, a so-called educational plan option provides a fixed-dollar income during nine or ten months of each college year, with a modest "graduation present" in cash after the final installment. This is really a combination of the amount and interest options with appropriate limitations placed thereon to produce the desired result.

Notwithstanding the wide variety of settlement plans offered by the various options or combinations of options, situations do arise where the standard options do not seem to fit. Upon proper submission of the facts the company will usually be willing to work out a special settlement plan within reasonable limits.

In those cases where an individual desires greater flexibility than the insurance company will permit, consideration should be given to the services of a trust company. This is particularly true if discretionary powers are indicated. An insurance company normally will not accept any arrangement whereby it must exercise discretion in carrying out the terms of the agreement. This is a proper function of the trust department of a bank. In such cases the proceeds are paid over to a corporate trustee to be administered as a trust by that trustee for individual beneficiaries.

A relatively small percentage of the total proceeds which become payable under life insurance contracts are paid over to a trustee for administration. The reasons are several. In the first place the trust operates on the segregated fund principle, and each fund must stand on its own. This means that it is difficult to obtain adequate diversification unless the amount of proceeds is quite substantial.[3] Besides providing greater diversification and, hence, security of principal and income, the insurance company *guarantees* the principal and a minimum rate of income. A trust company cannot provide any guarantees. In addition, the insurance company can guarantee a life income which the trust company cannot. Also, the relative cost of a trust arrangement is greater on smaller trusts. Consequently, a trust arrangement is not usually considered except in conjunction with larger estates, and in those cases where unusual flexibility is indicated.

USES OF SETTLEMENT OPTIONS

In General

An examination of the above options shows that the life insurance companies offer the insured (or beneficiary) a great amount of flexibility in the distribution of the proceeds. The insured may elect in writing, filed with the

[3] It should be noted that in some states today, banks and trust companies are permitted to set up a so-called common trust fund wherein small trust accounts may be merged for investment purposes only. Obviously, if the fund is large enough, diversification similar to that of a life insurance company portfolio could be obtained.

company, to have the proceeds of his policy paid according to any one or more of these methods. He may reserve the right to revoke his selection of a particular installment method of settlement and elect any other method. This renders the contract flexible and permits the insured to choose a more desirable form of settlement if changed circumstances warrant. If the insured does not make such selection, any beneficiary entitled to receive such proceeds may, when the policy becomes payable, exercise such right of election. The proper use of these options permits the insured to leave the proceeds with the company and thus "insure his insurance." The beneficiary does not obtain a lump-sum settlement and, therefore, cannot squander or lose the money through bad investments. In this connection it should be remembered, also, that the insurance company is strictly accountable for the funds left in its possession. Other fiduciary institutions cannot be held responsible for the loss of a segregated trust, if due care and diligence have been exercised. Under these options, however, there is no segregation of the fund, and the insurance company as a whole guarantees the payments. Also, many life insurance companies operate on the participating plan, and beneficiaries, therefore, receive a share of whatever extra interest the company may make on its investments. Finally, the selection of one of these options eliminates the details and heavy expenses usually connected with the administration of an estate. The charge made by the company for administering the funds is generally small as compared with other methods. The beneficiary has no expense of reinvestment and no need to exercise judgment in placing investments. There are no legal expenses or contests between heirs, and no fluctuations in the value of the estate or in the income derived therefrom.

In spite of the apparent attractiveness of these options, however, there are certain circumstances under which particular options should not be used. The objection most frequently connected with the fixed amount and fixed period options is that the beneficiary may outlive the installment period and be without the steady income to which he or she has been accustomed. This situation is particularly serious when the age and physical condition of the beneficiary, at the time the installments cease, are such as to prevent the earning of a livelihood. If the insured (or beneficiary) selects the fixed amount option, he or she gets the advantage of an installment which is satisfactory as to size, but, as stated, the proceeds plus interest may be exhausted at a time when it is greatly needed. If, on the other hand, the fixed period option is used, and an attempt is made to gauge the period over which the payments should be spread, the size of each installment may be unsatisfactory unless the amount of insurance is sufficiently large. It is difficult in many cases to determine just how long the beneficiary will need the installments, and where the duration of life is involved, this becomes impossible.

It should be noted that regardless of the option selected, the insured takes out his insurance in multiples of $1,000 and pays his premiums accordingly. The premiums for the insurance are exactly the same as though the policy were payable in a lump sum. They are based upon the age of the insured alone at the time the policy is issued.

The shortcomings of the fixed amount and fixed period options are remedied by the life income option, which provides a life income with or without stipulated payments. Here the insurance company, in effect, keeps the face of the matured policy and sells the beneficiary an annuity payable for life with or without a certain number of guaranteed payments, the amount of which is determined by the age and sex of the beneficiary at the time the proceeds of the policy become payable. It is thus impossible for the beneficiary to be left at any time without an income, such as was the case under the fixed amount and fixed period options. It should not be forgotten, however, that the size of each installment cannot be determined beforehand, since neither the insured nor anyone else can know what the age of the beneficiary will be at the death of the insured. This disadvantage may be illustrated by an assumption that the insured will die while the beneficiary is young and a comparison of the installment received then with the installment which would be obtained should the insured die when the beneficiary is older. For example, according to Table 15–3, showing several forms of

TABLE 15-3. Life Income Options: Installments per $1,000 Proceeds

Age of Beneficiary	Pure Life Income		With 10 Years Period Certain		With 20 Years Period Certain	
	Male	Female	Male	Female	Male	Female
20	$ 2.91	$2.79	$2.90	$2.78	$2.88	$2.77
30	3.23	3.05	3.22	3.04	3.18	3.02
40	3.73	3.45	3.70	3.43	3.59	3.37
50	4.51	4.08	4.42	4.02	4.12	3.84
60	5.80	5.07	5.48	4.90	4.70	4.41
70	8.02	6.75	6.91	6.16	4.94	4.94
80	12.06	9.72	8.39	7.69	4.94	4.94

the life income option, if the insured dies when the beneficiary is 30, she will receive for each $1,000 of insurance proceeds $3.05 monthly with no payments guaranteed, $3.04 per month with payments guaranteed for at least ten years, or $3.02 per month with payments guaranteed for at least twenty years; however, if the insured dies when the beneficiary is 60 years of age, she will receive $5.07 with no payments guaranteed, $4.90 per month with payments guaranteed for at least ten years, or $4.41 per month with payments guaranteed for at least twenty years. Thus, as the beneficiary grows older (assuming the insured does not die) the amount of insurance in force is sufficient, automatically, to provide for larger payments to the beneficiary beginning at the insured's death and continuing thereafter.

The life income option often is attractive to an insured who has an endowment policy. In addition to providing for his beneficiary by having the proceeds payable under any suitable optional settlement plan in the event of his death during the policy term, he can also provide an income for himself for the remainder of his own lifetime, should he survive the endowment period. In other words, if the policy matures as a death claim, the beneficiary receives the proceeds under the settlement option elected by the insured, whereas, if it matures as an endowment, the insured receives the proceeds in the form of an annuity for the rest of his life. In the latter case the amount of each installment depends upon the age of the insured when the endowment matures, the sex of the insured, and also upon the number of payments which are guaranteed, if any.

The interest option has some of the advantages and some of the disadvantages of the lump-sum method of settlement. It may be used to advantage in cases where the insured desires to have interest go to a beneficiary and, after a certain period, or after a death, or upon the happening of a certain event, the principal paid to a third party or institution. Its main advantage arises out of its flexibility through proper use of the withdrawal privilege and the right to change to another option. Thus, for example, it is not usually advisable to elect a life income option until the beneficiary attains age 55, 60, or over 65. Where the insured dies early, the proceeds can be left under the interest option until the beneficiary attains, say, age 65, at which time he may or may not elect the life income option, depending upon the circumstances.

Concurrent and Successive Uses of Settlement Options

It has already been indicated that the insured may have the proceeds of his insurance paid under more than one of the settlement options. In many instances the insured may find that he can better provide for his beneficiaries by selecting, not one, but a combination of settlement options. Furthermore, he may have the selected options operate concurrently, successively, or both. For example, the options may be used concurrently by dividing the amount of insurance into two or more parts for the purpose of having each part paid separately under one of the options. Thus, provision may be made for a lump-sum settlement to pay for last illness, burial, estate, and other readjustment expenses, and for the retention of the remainder by the company. Part of the balance so retained may be administered under the interest option, with one or more primary beneficiaries being designated to receive the interest payments. If the insured desires, he may name one or more secondary beneficiaries to receive the interest payments in the event of the death of a primary beneficiary before a certain number of years have elapsed. Provision should be made for the eventual disposal of the principal sum.[4] The remainder of the proceeds may be paid by the company to a given beneficiary in the form of a life income with or without a certain number of payments guaranteed. Should a certain number of payments be specified, one or more secondary beneficiaries should be named to receive any unpaid installments which may be due at the death of the primary beneficiary.

The insured may elect to use the options in a successive rather than in the concurrent manner just explained. Thus, he may desire his beneficiary to receive a life income, starting at a given age, such as 60. He may specify that if at his death the beneficiary has not reached the designated age, the funds are to be retained by the company under the interest option, the interest being paid as directed to one or more beneficiaries. In either event, when the beneficiary reaches the stipulated age, the funds on hand are to be used to purchase a life income, with or without guaranteed payments.

The options may be used both concurrently and successively. A good example of this combination would be the above illustration of the concurrent use of options, with a slight addition thereto. In this example it was assumed that part of the proceeds were to be left at interest for a designated period, but nothing was said regarding the method of disposing of the principal sum. At the end of the stated interest period the insured may have this principal paid in the form of equal installments over a stated number of years (fixed period option), in the form of installments of a given size as long as the funds together with interest earnings will provide such payments (fixed amount option), or in any other manner permitted by the insurance company.

Basic Rules of Practice

It will be remembered that the settlement provisions of many contracts merely grant the insured, or the beneficiary of a lump-sum settlement after his death, the right to elect just one of the income settlement options in lieu of cash, with payments to commence immediately. In practice, the companies have recognized that the needs of many policyholders could not be met by strict adherence to the letter of the settlement option provisions in their policies. In attempting to render a complete service to their policyholders, companies generally have permitted arrangements extending far beyond the restricted provisions included in the contract. In view of the fact that judgment, philosophy, and experience are the basis of rules of practice,

[4] The common law "rule against perpetuities" prohibits the tying up of funds for a period longer than the lives of those in existence at the date of settlement and for twenty-one years thereafter. Some states have statutes which are more strict. See pp. 243–244.

however, it is only natural that there will be marked variations in the extra-contractual services of different companies in connection with settlement agreements.

There are detailed services,[5] revised annually, that provide a summary of the practices of individual companies, but the most logical and reliable source of such information is the companies themselves. Here only certain of the basic rules will be discussed briefly in order to provide a working understanding of the problems involved.

Who May Elect Options.   Normally, the insured possesses the right to specify that proceeds be payable under one of the income settlement options. Also, a beneficiary usually may elect an income settlement option in lieu of a lump-sum settlement, or be granted the privilege of electing an option under the terms of a prearranged agreement.

Most policies are issued on the application of the person to be insured who becomes the policyowner. There are, however, many policies issued under which someone other than the insured applies for the insurance and owns all of the "incidents of ownership" (absolute ownership). In such cases the third-party owner usually pays the premium. For example, such contracts are often found in corporate insurance cases and in family situations where a wife may insure her husband or a child his parents, or vice versa. The question of ownership is important in applying the general rule that a policyowner may select settlement options. In practice, whether a settlement plan can be worked out for a given case may depend upon whether the policyowner is a natural person or business entity, as well as the nature of the beneficiary. For example, many companies provide that the beneficiary (under an income settlement plan) must be a natural person in his or her own right. Again, some companies will not permit an assignee to elect a settlement option. Normally, the policyowner may elect to use the settlement options for payments to himself either in utilizing the proceeds of a matured endowment, retirement income contracts, or by placing the cash value of a policy under the settlement options. It is important to note that many contracts do not grant, *by contract,* the right to place the *cash value* under the settlement options. Usually, however, the company will be willing to add this privilege by amendment upon specific request.

There are usually no restrictions on the election of settlement options by a corporate owner for individual, natural beneficiaries. In addition, where a corporation (other than a trustee) requests the use of options for *its own benefit* in connection with a legitimate business purpose, most companies will go along. For example, a corporation may wish to pay a retirement income to the insured or to continue his salary to his dependents for some period after his death.

---

[5] *Diamond Life Bulletins; Flitcraft Compend, Settlement Options* by Flitcraft; *Handy Guide; Little Gem; The Insurance Research and Review, Inc., Advanced Underwriting Service.*

As a general rule, most companies will not permit trustees to use settlement options but will usually permit trustees as owners or named beneficiaries of life insurance policies to elect settlement options for the benefit of specific trust beneficiaries.

Minimum Amount Requirements.   In general, most contracts provide that not less than $1,000 will be retained under an option. Recently, some companies have raised the minimum amount to $2,000. In addition, installment payments must be not less than $10 per month (in some companies not less than $20 or $25 per month). These minimum amount requirements apply to *each share* held for a separate beneficiary and to *each fund* if the proceeds of a policy are split into two or more funds for use with *different options.*

In connection with the fixed amount option there is usually an additional requirement that payments under this option shall not be less than 5 per cent of the original principal in any one year. The purpose of this latter rule is to assure that the principal and interest will be paid out within a reasonable period.

Duration of Planned Settlement.   The duration of a settlement plan is related to the types of beneficiaries and types of options involved. The great majority of companies will provide deferred settlement service to meet the needs of the primary and secondary beneficiary. This means, normally, that the plan may be continued during the lifetime of the widow of the policyowner and at least until his children are of mature age. In the usual case, settlement with the secondary beneficiary is in a lump sum, but when parents of the owner are named as secondary beneficiaries, many companies will permit the plan to be extended to provide income for them. The basic concept is to extend the deferred settlement service to meet the needs of the immediate family of the policyowner.

The choice of settlement option may further limit the duration of a settlement plan. For example, the interest option generally cannot be elected for several successive classes of beneficiaries, thereby extending the guaranteed interest income far into the future. Company practice in this regard, however, varies considerably. Most companies are willing to retain proceeds at interest for the lifetime of the primary beneficiary or thirty years, whichever is longer. Some companies will extend this period for the lifetime of the secondary beneficiary. There are still other variations, but in general, most companies will not continue interest income to a third beneficiary.

Under the life income options guaranteed periods are usually limited to periods of twenty years or less except in the case of a refund life income option elected at a very young age. In the case of the fixed period and fixed amount options thirty years is usually the maximum period permitted.

Withdrawal Privilege.   The right of withdrawal is vital to provide flexibility in any settlement plan. The maximum limitations placed on the right of withdrawal are usually determined by the person electing the settlement option. In general, the companies' main concern is usually to avoid unduly long and complex agreements. Most companies do, however, have rules as to the *frequency* of permitted withdrawals and the *minimum amount* of each withdrawal. Thus, agreements usually provide that withdrawals may be made only on any interest or installment date (sometimes limited to three, four, or six per year), and the minimum which may be withdrawn at any one time will run about $100, although the minimum may range from no minimum to as high as $500.

In this regard, companies usually reserve the right to delay cash withdrawals under the settlement options for a period of up to six months. This corresponds to the standard policy provision which permits deferment of payment up to 180 days in connection with loan and cash surrender values.

The withdrawal privilege is available if the fund is retained under the *interest or fixed amount* options, but generally is not available under the fixed period or life income options. The essential nature of these options would be upset if a withdrawal privilege was granted. Some companies will, however, permit a provision for withdrawal of the *entire* commuted value of the period certain payments under these latter options.

Right to Change from One Option to Another.   In order to introduce flexibility into settlement plans the beneficiary is often given the right to change from one option to another. The interest option and fixed amount options afford the most flexibility in this regard, but some companies will permit such a privilege in connection with the fixed period or life income options. In the latter options the privilege is usually available with respect to settling the commuted value of the remaining installments to secondary beneficiaries.

Right to Increase Payments.   Another privilege which can be incorporated within a settlement plan is the right to increase the amount of income, usually under the fixed amount option. The need for this power, which is of comparatively recent origin, arose because of the need to coordinate benefits with those provided by the Social Security Act. In addition, this power has been emphasized as a means whereby income can be increased to meet the higher living costs or to overcome loss of income from other property. The policyowner may establish upper limits of income, such as "not to exceed five hundred dollars per month." This power to increase income may be limited to the period after a specified date, within a fixed period, or the agreement may permit the exercise of the power at any time. Some companies also limit the *number* of times this power can be exercised.

Primary and Secondary Beneficiaries.   Almost any reasonable combination of options is available to meet the needs of a primary beneficiary. In connection with secondary beneficiaries, the restrictions deal not only with the special powers discussed above but also with option combinations. The term "secondary beneficiary" is used here to mean the situation in which the primary beneficiary survives the insured, dies before receiving all the fund, and the balance of the fund or of the installments becomes payable to a *secondary* beneficiary. The liberality of company rules in this situation varies, depending upon the type of option operative at the date of the primary beneficiary's death.

If the primary beneficiary dies while the interest option is operative, virtually all companies will permit settlement with the secondary beneficiary under any one of the installment options, or even under the interest option for at least a limited period of time. In connection with the fixed amount, fixed period, and life income options, company practice has varied, but the trend is to permit commutation of the guaranteed installments and settlement of this commuted value under the interest option or under one of the other installment options. It should be noted that automatic arrangements should be avoided in those situations where the balance of the fund, upon the death of the primary beneficiary, is apt to be relatively small.

Practically all companies will permit a settlement agreement to provide that following the death of the primary beneficiary, the installments then being paid will be continued to the secondary beneficiary. In fact, most companies encourage such arrangements, particularly where the insurance estate is small.

As pointed out earlier, the right of a primary beneficiary, entitled to a lump-sum settlement, to elect an option is usually granted by contract. In the event the primary (original) beneficiary predeceases the insured, the first contingent beneficiary may elect settlement under an option. On the other hand, where a primary beneficiary survives the insured, and dies, it is a general practice not to grant a *lump-sum secondary beneficiary* the right to elect a settlement option. In addition, some companies will not permit a *primary beneficiary* the right to designate a secondary beneficiary to receive any remaining unpaid installments which otherwise would be paid to the primary beneficiary's estate in a lump sum.

LEGAL ASPECTS RELATING TO SETTLEMENT OPTIONS

The preceding material has discussed many of the legal aspects of settlement options. There are several important concepts, however, which have not been considered directly. They are important in that their understanding will facilitate an appreciation of the reasons which motivate companies in establishing limitations and restrictions in the use of settlement options.

It should be remembered that each state has the right to pass statutes affecting the interpretation of life insurance contracts in that state. Also, where no statute is applicable, reference must be made to the "common law" of that particular state. In addition, Federal law may also enter the picture, as in the case of bankruptcy and in connection with the enforcement of various Federal tax liens. It should be noted, however, where states provide specific exemptions from liens, the Federal laws observe the state regulations.

Fundamental Legal Nature

It is well settled today that if two parties make a life insurance contract for the benefit of a third party, it may be enforced by the *third party beneficiary*.

The beneficiary provision and related settlement agreements of a life insurance contract represent a typical example of such a contract. Thus, the beneficiary may, in his or her own name, bring an action for payment of the proceeds after the contract conditions have been complied with in regard to proof of death.

Following the insured's death a contractual relationship exists between the insurance company and the beneficiary—a debtor–creditor relationship —whether the proceeds are payable in a lump sum or under the interest or income options. If the policyowner, during the insured's lifetime, sets up the settlement arrangement, performance of that agreement after the insured's death is regarded merely as a continuation of the third party beneficiary arrangement. If, on the other hand, a primary beneficiary entitled to a lump-sum settlement elects to receive the proceeds under one of the settlement options, some courts have held that a *new direct* contractual relationship exists between the company and the beneficiary. In either case, however, as a party to a direct contractual relationship or as a third party beneficiary, the beneficiary may enforce his or her rights under the life insurance contract or subsequent settlement agreement.

Settlement Agreement Distinguished from Trust

It is well settled that a settlement agreement as currently handled does not constitute a trust.[6] The relationship created by the insurance company and the beneficiary is that of debtor and creditor. The insurance company obligates itself to pay, and this is a general obligation supported by *all the assets* of the company, not an obligation to preserve a segregated fund. The

[6] George G. Bogert, *Law of Trust and Trustees* (Kansas City, Mo.: Vernon Law Book Co., 1951).

insurance company's obligation is absolute no matter how much or how little income it earns on its assets. The provision in the settlement agreement providing that the company may mingle the proceeds with its general corporate assets is fundamentally contrary to the trust concept.

It should be noticed, however, that a life insurance company could (where charter powers permit) retain proceeds as a trustee. In practice, however, insurance companies have very rarely chosen to exercise such powers. Today, the companies almost universally follow the practice of holding the policy proceeds under a debtor–creditor relationship. It is this practice and the consequent merging of assets which enables a well-managed life insurance company to offer safety and stability which few investments can equal.

Settlement Agreements as a Disposition of Property

The term "testamentary disposition" connotes the transfer of property by the owner at the time of his death. The law requires that such disposition may be made only by a will that complies with the required formalities of the particular state statute of wills. The provisions of life insurance policies for payment of proceeds at death have been upheld even though such policies are not wills, are not generally given away during lifetime, and even though the policyowner reserves the right to change the beneficiary until the insured dies.[7] The provisions for payment, where the proceeds are payable in a lump sum or in installments, are upheld as a firmly established exception to the testamentary disposition rule.[8]

Rule Against Perpetuities

It is in the public interest to see that property stays in circulation. To this end there are rules that limit the length of time during which property owners can reserve to themselves enjoyment of property. The common law "rule against perpetuities" provides that the vesting of the ownership of property cannot be deferred for longer than a life or lives in being and twenty-one years (plus the period of gestation) thereafter. Simply, this time limit is twenty-one years after the death of persons living and identified with a given transaction, measured from the date the property is transferred or the interest in the property is created.

[7] See Harry S. Redecker and Charles Reid, *Life Insurance Settlement Options,* rev. ed. (Boston: Little, Brown & Co., 1964), pp. 133–135.

[8] The question has been raised in two cases involving the election of a settlement option by a *beneficiary* where she was entitled to a lump-sum settlement. See *Mutual Benefit Life Insurance Co. vs. Ellis,* 125 Fed. 2d 127 (2d Cir. 1942) and *Hall vs. Mutual Life Ins. Co. of N. Y.,* 109 NYS 2d 646, affirmed, 122 NYS 2d 239 (1953).

The common law rule has been modified by statute in a few states. Thus, in New York the law provides [9] that absolute ownership of personal property shall not be suspended by any limitation or condition that could extend beyond two individual lives in being at the date of the instrument creating the limitation or condition.

Although there has been little litigation on this point,[10] it is generally felt today that the rule against perpetuities is not applicable to settlement agreements because such agreements merely create a debtor–creditor relationship. Companies, however, usually avoid any possible application of the rule against perpetuities by prohibiting agreements that would violate such rules. Practically, family needs usually can be met within such limits.

Rule Against Accumulations

The rule against accumulations prohibits the accumulation of *income* for any unreasonable period. In this connection all state laws permit such accumulations during the minority of a beneficiary entitled to the income, but many prohibit such accumulations for an adult. The law of a few states will permit the accumulation of income during some specified period, such as ten years, even though the beneficiary is an adult.

In general, laws restricting the accumulation of income are felt to apply to life insurance settlement options. Life insurance companies will usually permit accumulations of interest under settlement options *only* during the minority of beneficiaries, regardless of whether or not the law in a given state specifically refers to settlement options. In fact, some companies will not permit any accumulations.

[9] Section 11, New York Personal Property Law.
[10] In *Holmes vs. John Hancock Mutual Life Insurance Company,* 228 N.Y. 106, 41 N.E. 2d 909 (1942), the court held that the New York statute regarding perpetuities did not apply to a settlement agreement.

BIBLIOGRAPHY

The Life Insurance Product: Analysis of the Contract

Couch, George James. *Couch Cyclopedia of Insurance Law,* 2nd ed. by Ronald A. Anderson (Rochester, N. Y.: Lawyers Cooperative Publishing Co., 1959–1968).

Day, J. Edward, and Melnikoff, Meyer. "The Variable Annuity as a Life

Insurance Company Product," *Journal of the American Society of Chartered Life Underwriters,* Vol. X, No. 1 (December, 1955).

Elliott, C.B. *A Treatise on the Law of Insurance* (Indianapolis, Ind.: The Bobbs-Merrill Co., 1907).

Greider, Janice E., and Beadles, William T. *Law and the Life Insurance Contract,* rev. ed. (Homewood, Ill.: Richard D. Irwin, Inc., 1968).

Herrick, Kenneth W. *Total Disability Provisions in Life Insurance Contracts.* S. S. Huebner Foundation Studies (Homewood, Ill.: Richard D. Irwin, Inc., 1958).

Johnson, George E. "The Variable Annuity," *Journal of the American Society of Chartered Life Underwriters,* Vol. VII, No. 1 (December, 1952).

Krueger, Harry, and Waggoner, Leland T., eds. *The Life Insurance Policy Contract* (Boston: Little, Brown and Company, 1953).

McGill, Dan M., ed. *The Beneficiary in Life Insurance.* S. S. Huebner Foundation Lectures (Homewood, Ill.: Richard D. Irwin, Inc., 1956).

Mehr, Robert I., and Osler, Robert W. *Modern Life Insurance,* 3rd ed. (New York: The Macmillan Company, 1961).

National Underwriter Company. *Who Writes What?* (Cincinnati, 1963).

Patterson, E. W. *Essentials of Insurance Law* (New York: McGraw-Hill Book Company, Inc., 1957).

Redecker, Harry S., and Reid, Charles K., II. *Life Insurance Settlement Options,* rev. ed. (Homewood, Ill.: Richard D. Irwin, Inc., 1964).

Richards, George. *The Law of Insurance,* 5th ed. (posthumous), by Warren Freedman (New York: Baker Voorhis & Company, Inc., 1952).

Schwarzschild, Stuart. *Rights of Creditors in Life Insurance Policies.* S. S. Huebner Foundation Studies (Homewood, Ill.: Richard D. Irwin, Inc., 1963).

Vance, W. R., and Anderson, B. M. *Handbook of the Law of Insurance,* 3rd ed. (St. Paul: West Publishing Company, 1951).

IV   The Health Insurance Product

Plans Meeting Health Costs[1] | 16

THE MOST COMPLETE coverage against the financial consequences of disability is offered by *commercial health insurance*.[2] In addition to "ordinary" individual health insurance, a considerable amount of commercial health insurance protection is provided by (1) life insurance disability riders, (2) industrial contracts, and (3) group policies.

Other plans meeting health costs include (1) private noncommercial and (2) social insurance plans. The former includes *hospitalization* (Blue Cross), *medical service* (Blue Shield), and *independent plans* (labor unions, fraternal benefit societies, medical societies, private group plans, and others). Social insurance is represented by two significant types of *state plans* (workmen's compensation and compulsory cash sickness plans) and various *Federal insurance programs* (OASDI, Medicare and Medicaid, government life insurance, disability benefits, veterans' benefits, Railroad Retirement System, and others).

This present chapter reviews briefly the basic structure of the most important of these plans established to meet health costs. The following chapters analyze the provisions of the individual health insurance contract and the methods of arranging coverage in use today through private insurance companies. Table 16-1 shows the number of persons with health insurance protection by type of coverage through commercial insurance companies and other nongovernmental organizations.

---

[1] As used here, the term "plan" includes any instrument or mechanism, public or private, which facilitates the financing of the costs of health care.

[2] As used in this volume, "commercial health insurance" refers to protection provided by private insurance companies (life and health, health, and casualty). Disability income and medical expense benefits, payable in dollars to the insured, are available. Traditionally, the term "commercial health insurance" has been reserved for an individual, cancellable disability income contract.

TABLE 16-1. Number of Persons with Health Insurance
Protection by Type of Coverage in the United States
(000 omitted)

End of year	Hospital expense	Surgical expense	Regular medical expense	Major medical expense	Disability income Short- term	Long- term
1965	153,133	140,462	111,696	51,946	46,347	4,457
1966	158,022	144,715	116,462	56,742	49,372	5,002
1967	162,853	150,396	122,570	62,226	51,230	6,682
1968	169,497	155,725	129,105	66,861	54,955	7,718
1969	175,221	162,144	134,930	72,292	57,004	9,076
1970	181,511	168,961	145,294	78,217	57,595	10,740

Source: *Sourcebook of Health Insurance Data,* 1971, p. 16

COMMERCIAL HEALTH INSURANCE PLANS

One of the most significant characteristics of commercial health insurance plans is the wide variety of contracts available. The relatively great
number of contracts currently offered by a single company is compounded
by the intercompany variations, and by the fact that there are many older
policies in force with still different provisions. Since it would be impossible to describe in detail the multiplicity of available policies, this discussion is general.

Individual Health Insurance[3]

Individual health insurance coverages can be classified into two major
categories—disability income insurance and medical expense insurance.
    Disability income insurance provides periodic payments when the in-
sured is unable to work as a result of illness, disease, or injury. The basic
benefit provided is a form of substitute income to replace a *portion* of
the insured's *earned* income should this earned income terminate because
of disability caused by sickness or injury.

[3] In this volume, unless specifically noted to the contrary, individual health insurance relates to health insurance issued to individuals other than industrial health
insurance contracts.

In general, disability income policies may be subdivided into two major classes: those which cover only disability caused by accidental injury and those covering the risk of both sickness and injury. These two classes of policies are similar in most basic respects except as to the extent of the risk to be covered. Since sickness is a far more common cause of disability than accident, an "accident only" policy should be recognized as a policy providing only limited coverage.

The total amount of benefits payable under a particular disability income policy is, in a large measure, defined and controlled in accordance with three policy specifications: (1) the monthly (or weekly) indemnity, (2) the elimination periods, and (3) the maximum benefit periods. In each area the insured usually has a wide variety of choices in structuring the overall coverage best suited to his own needs.

Medical expense insurance provides benefits for *medical care*. The term "medical care" includes not only medical and surgical services of a physician but hospital, nursing, and related health services, supplies and equipment as well. Medical expense insurance, therefore, is a *reimbursement* type of coverage which provides broad benefits that can cover virtually all of the expenses connected with medical care and related services. Since every individual is subject to the hazards of sickness or injury and thus to substantial medical expenses, this type of insurance is designed to cover all members of a family unit instead of just the wage earner as in the case of disability income insurance.

The total field of medical care covers a wide range of services and supplies, the expenses for which can be grouped into the following broad subdivisions: hospital expenses, surgical expenses, medical expenses (used in the limited sense of nonsurgical services of a physician), and nursing expenses. Coverage against these different expenses is available in varying degrees through the many different health insurance policy forms offered by insurance companies. Some policies cover only one major category. The following chapters will consider individual health insurance in detail including the typical coverage arrangements available to individuals and families.

Industrial Health Insurance

Individual health insurance policies may also be obtained on an industrial basis with premiums collected weekly or monthly at the home of the insured. Industrial health insurance, as with industrial life insurance, is sold in small amounts, with the amount of insurance being determined primarily by the insured's ability to pay rather than his economic need. Because of the small premium involved, it is necessary to streamline all procedures pertaining to the issuance of policies. For this same reason, it is not possible to make an extensive investigation prior to issuance, and a copy of the application is not attached to the policy. A simple benefit schedule is used to indicate the benefits and the premiums therefor. There are no riders or endorsements, nor are premiums rated for occupation. Claim settlement procedures are simplified to the extent that nearly all claims are handled through the same local district office which collects and accounts for premiums. Although procedures vary, the agent often assists in completing claim forms and delivers the amounts to be paid. It is also usual to substitute more restricted definitions of the perils insured and less liberal benefit provisions for the more complex underwriting and claim procedures common to other individual health insurance.

Industrial policies are offered to those who, for underwriting reasons or cost, cannot buy other individual health insurance. They are sold to individuals to whom a weekly or monthly collection service is important in order to maintain their insurance in force. They are purchased by or for housewives, children, and workers in all occupational classifications. Most newly issued industrial health insurance is now sold in the southern states to the lower income groups.

It is common to require that a minimum amount of industrial life insurance be purchased with the health insurance policy. The minimum life insurance premium may vary from 10 cents to 25 cents a week.

Group Health Insurance

Another major source of health insurance protection is available through group plans. Health insurance benefits of varying types are provided for groups of individuals under a single master contract. The master contract is issued to the employer, association, or union securing protection for its employees or members without selection of individual risks.[4] Each member of the insured group is provided a certificate of insurance as evidence of participation. The employer, association, or union may pay the entire premium under the group contract, but in most group plans the individuals covered contribute to the payment of the premium by payroll deductions or by additional dues. The basic concepts and principles of group insurance, including group health insurance, are discussed in Chapter 34.

---

[4] In some states, where there is no group insurance law, much so-called Association group business is written on a master policy and certificate basis, subject to full evidence of good health.

Blanket Insurance[5]

Blanket insurance is like group insurance in that a group of individuals is insured through one policy issued to a company or other organization. It has some distinctive characteristics, however. The nature of the risk insured against is more limited or temporary than that ordinarily covered by group insurance. For example, a blanket policy issued to a volunteer fire department providing coverage only while they are engaged in fighting fires or undergoing a fire drill. Again, the individuals covered may be constantly changing as in the case of a blanket policy issued to a common carrier to cover its passengers. Consequently, the individuals covered under a blanket policy are not specifically identified as they would be under a group health plan.

The types of benefits normally available under a blanket policy include: (1) medical expense, (2) accidental death and dismemberment, and (3) disability income. Of these, medical expense is the most predominant, probably because it is the customary benefit on the many blanket policies issued to school and camp groups. Accidental death and dismemberment is the next most important by volume. This is the most common benefit provided by blanket policies covering travel hazards.

Blanket insurance is a rapidly growing phase of the health insurance business. The factors leading to this growth include: the significant increase in the number of athletic teams which travel, the increasing concern of organizations to protect their key people who travel, and the increasing interest of school districts in protection for children traveling to and from school.

Franchise Insurance

Individual policies are sold to various types of groups under the general term of franchise insurance. This term is applied often to insurance sold to small employer-employee groups usually involving less than 25 employees. Such insurance is similar to "wholesale" or "employee" life insurance. A second type of franchise insurance is the professional group franchise under which individual policies are sold to members of professional societies such as county medical societies. Group underwriting procedures are customarily used under both of these forms of "franchise in-

[5] HIAA, *Principles of Individual Health Insurance* I (New York, 1968), pp. 57–58.

surance" if some minimum of the eligible members, such as 50 per cent, apply for the insurance. Also, under these circumstances, some insurers waive the exclusion of losses due to sickness or injury predating the policy, a customary exclusion in individually issued policies. The term "franchise insurance" is applied also to policies sold through individual solicitation under a payroll deduction or salary allotment plan similar to that commonly employed in connection with life insurance. Such policies are generally subject to the usual underwriting procedures of individual insurance, including substandard ratings and the use of exclusion riders. Under all forms of franchise insurance, the insurer usually agrees to waive its right to discontinue or modify any individual policy, unless it simultaneously discontinues or modifies all other policies in the same group. This general concept forms the basis of a distinct class of policies referred to in the Annual Statement as "collectively renewable" forms.

Life Insurance Disability Riders

As pointed out earlier,[6] life insurance companies provide total and permanent disability insurance through riders attached to ordinary life insurance policies. The two disability benefits provided are (1) waiver of premium and (2) disability income. The definition of disability is usually the same for both benefits, but is usually more restrictive than the definitions of disability normally found in individual health insurance contracts.[7]

Disability Income.   These clauses insure against total and permanent disability only, thus differing in the scope of their protection from other health insurance coverage. Specifications of what constitutes total and permanent disability vary, but a typical clause provides:

> If the insured, after the payment of the premiums for the first year, while the policy is in full force and before attaining the age of 60 years, shall furnish due proof that he has become wholly and permanently disabled so that he is and will be permanently, continuously, and wholly prevented thereby from performing any work, or engaging in any occupation for compensation or profit, and that the disability has existed continuously for a period of six months, the company will waive future premiums and pay the benefits stipulated herein.

A major advantage of having the disability clause incorporated in the life contract is the saving in acquisition cost. The coverage is easy to sell in connection with life insurance, and the underwriting is facilitated be-

---

[6] See pp. 196–199.
[7] See pp. 270–272.

cause of the medical examination required for the life contract. There is no basic conflict between the disability provisions of a life insurance contract rider and those of individual health insurance contracts which provide broad coverage. The life insurance policy disability rider offers only partial protection against the perils of accident and sickness. It does not purport to cover partial or temporary total disabilities, persons over 60 or 65 years of age, substandard risks, or female risks in general. It offers no hospital, medical, or surgical benefits, such as provided by the usual individual health contracts.

Although many life insurance companies abandoned this line following the disastrous experience of the thirties, many companies have re-entered the market, but with a chastened attitude toward limits and amounts of issue, and a recognition of the need to underwrite the risk from a morbidity as well as a mortality standpoint.

Disability income is now quite generally available to standard male risks under age 60. The monthly income paid is $5 or $10 per $1,000 of life insurance face amount if the insured becomes totally and permanently disabled before age 60. Most companies limit the amount of monthly income that they will issue to $500 with further limits on the entire line of indemnity (including individual health insurance) in which they will participate. A much smaller number of companies offers disability income to standard female risks but generally restrict the amount to $100 per month.

Waiver-of-Premium.   Waiver-of-premium disability insurance is widely written, covering standard males for total and permanent disability incurred before age 60 or 65 and standard females so disabled before age 55. The rate charged females for this benefit is often 200 per cent of the male rate. As with additional death benefits for accidental death, life insurance companies set a limit on the amount of waiver-of-premium benefit that they will issue on a single life. These limits vary with the size and underwriting attitude of the company from $25,000 to $250,000.

Accidental Death.   In addition to the disability income and waiver-of-premium clauses, a life insurance policy may have added to it, by means of a rider or supplementary agreement, a provision which stipulates that an additional sum—equal to the face of the policy—shall be payable in the event that the insured's death should be caused by accidental means. For a small added premium, a life insurance policy will pay double (or in some cases more) the contract proceeds in the event that the insured dies through accidental bodily injury. Accidental death for double indemnity purposes is typically defined as "death resulting from bodily injury effected solely through external, violent, and accidental means independently and exclusively of all other causes within ninety days after such injury." As pointed out in the next chapter,[8] the use of the expression "accidental means" is intended to eliminate liability in those cases where the *result* of what happened could be considered accidental but where the *cause* of that result was not accidental.

Some companies issue accidental death benefits from age 0 to age 60, but the more usual limits are ages 10 or 15 to age 55, with coverage continuing to age 65, when it terminates in most companies. Amounts of issue for most companies have been restricted to $100,000, with a few going as high as $200,000. Recently, a number of companies have made multiple indemnities available and the limits have been increased accordingly.

PRIVATE NONCOMMERCIAL PLANS[9]

There are numerous health insurance plans set up on a nonprofit basis to provide hospital, surgical, or other benefits for a privately organized group. Such plans are set up by employers, unions, hospitals, medical societies, and others. Normally, they are organized under laws exempting them from certain taxes imposed on commercial insurance companies. In general, such plans may be divided into two groups: (1) Blue Cross and Blue Shield and (2) other independent plans.

Blue Cross and Blue Shield Plans

In 1970, there were 80 Blue Cross and 72 Blue Shield plans operating in the United States and Puerto Rico with affiliated plans in Canada and Jamaica.[10] All operate in a restricted geographic area, some being statewide and others being limited to a region within a state or to a single community.[11] These associations are by all odds the most important nongovernmental competitors of the commercial insurance companies in providing medical expense benefits. Their basic approach is somewhat different from that of the commercial companies providing health insurance.

---

[8] See pp. 268–269 for a more detailed analysis of the accidental means insuring clause.

[9] For an excellent summary of such plans see E. J. Faulkner, *Health Insurance* (New York: The McGraw-Hill Book Co., 1960), Chapter 2. See also John G. Turnbull, C. Arthur Williams, Jr., and Earl F. Cheit, *Economics and Social Security*, 3rd ed. (New York: The Ronald Press Co., 1967), and O. D. Dickerson, *Health Insurance*, 3rd ed. (Homewood, Ill.: Richard D. Irwin, Inc., 1968).

[10] *Blue Cross and Blue Shield Fact Book* (Chicago: Blue Cross Association and National Association of Blue Shield Plans, 1971), pp. 3, 14.

[11] J. F. Follman, Jr., *Medical Care and Health Insurance* (Homewood, Ill.: Richard D. Irwin, Inc., 1963), pp. 121–122.

Blue Cross. Blue Cross plans are nonprofit hospital expense prepayment plans designed primarily to provide benefits for hospitalization coverage, with certain restrictions on the type of accommodation to be used. Usually, only semiprivate accommodations are considered. These plans have representatives on the Committee on Blue Cross of the American Hospital Association.[12] There is a large number of locally autonomous Blue Cross plans in the United States. Most plans were organized by hospitals in the area served by the plan. Member hospitals usually elect the board of directors, although the board will normally include a significant number of members of the public and medical profession as well as hospital administrators. The Committee on Blue Cross has little direct authority over the independent local plans except to establish minimum standards for membership.

Under many Blue Cross plans subscribers are provided "service-type" benefits. Policies issued by commercial health insurance companies provide for payment directly to the insured of a specific number of dollars in reimbursement for various types of expenses incurred. The customary Blue Cross approach, however, is to guarantee the availability of certain types and amounts of hospital services. Under this arrangement there is no direct payment by Blue Cross to the insured. Instead the insured is billed only for those services not covered by the Blue Cross certificate and the Blue Cross organization through a separate contract with the member hospitals reimburses the hospital for the covered services which the hospital renders to the insured.

Initially, Blue Cross contracts were sold only to members of eligible groups, although today individual enrollments are permitted. In virtually all Blue Cross plans, if an individual leaves the group, he is permitted to purchase an individual contract without providing evidence of insurability, but usually at a somewhat higher premium.

Each Blue Cross plan enters into a contract with its subscribers and its member hospitals. All plans do not use the same contract; in fact, many offer more than one contract to their subscribers.

There is an increasing trend to provide dollar limitations to the services provided, in view of the rapidly rising cost of medical services.[13] For example, a given Blue Cross contract may provide for a semiprivate room up to $30 a day. Any charge for a semiprivate room in excess of $30

[12] Under the American Hospital Association Approval Program, a nonprofit hospital service plan may call itself a Blue Cross Plan and use the Blue Cross symbol if the plan meets the standards set forth.

[13] Initially, the Blue Cross plans operated on a pure "service" basis as contrasted to the "cash indemnity" approach utilized by the commercial carriers. Gradually dollar limitations and coinsurance features have been introduced into Blue Cross plans for a variety of reasons, and there is considerably less difference between the commercial and Blue Cross approaches today than was formerly the case.

under such a plan would be charged to the member personally. The usual practice is to permit the application of a specified dollar allowance toward a private room notwithstanding the fact that the contract basically calls for semiprivate accommodations.

Today, most Blue Cross plans also cover some outpatient services (usually for accidental injury and/or minor surgery) in their basic certificates. In addition, most Blue Cross plans offer supplementary or extended benefits beyond the basic certificate. This supplementary or extended care may include nursing home care, care in the home after hospitalization, dental treatment, prescription drugs, and catastrophic illness coverage. Members of one Blue Cross plan moving into the area of another plan are entitled to transfer membership to the new home area. The majority of Blue Cross plans are coordinated with Blue Shield plans, which offer medical and surgical care protection.

On those Blue Cross plans that cover some surgical or physician's expenses, cash indemnity payments are made to the subscriber. This violates the unique concept of service and care which underlies the hospitalization benefits, but represents additional evidence that there is less difference between the commercial and Blue Cross approaches today than was formerly the case.

In order to provide service to national or multistate accounts, the Blue Cross Association was brought into existence in 1948, and its responsibilities were enlarged in 1956. Some such organization was necessary because the Blue Cross plans are separate corporations in separate jurisdictions, each plan having its own contracts and its own schedule of rates and hospital benefits. The Association also represents Blue Cross to provide care for the dependents of servicemen under the Federal Medicare program.

In addition to the Association, Blue Cross plans also operate a stock casualty insurance company, Health Service, Inc., which was organized in 1948 to help meet the needs of national organizations for uniform contracts. Health Service, Inc., will underwrite benefits needed by members of a national group which are not available under a particular Blue Cross plan.

Blue Cross subscribers normally go to a hospital cooperating with the plan. In the event a member or subscriber is hospitalized in a nonplan hospital, usually a special per diem benefit is allowed, often less liberal than that normally provided. If a subscriber is hospitalized outside the area of the plan to which he belongs, the Inter-Plan Service Benefit Bank enables him to be treated temporarily as a member of the Blue Cross plan of the area where he is hospitalized, receiving the benefits of that plan. Thus, with such a clearing house, benefit coverage is continuous.

Implementing Medicare for millions of the elderly has been a major undertaking of the Blue Cross system. In 1966, the Blue Cross Association entered into a contract with the U.S. Government to operate a nation-wide administrative service for Medicare. As Medicare and Medicaid intermediary for a large majority of the nation's hospitals, extended care facilities, and home health agencies, Blue Cross performs a wide range of services necessary for the operation of the program, including claims payment for the health care these institutions provide to Medicare and Medicaid beneficaries. During 1970, Blue Cross served an additional 20,500,000 persons through its administrative role in government programs.

Blue Shield.   Blue Shield Plans are voluntary nonprofit organizations offering prepayment plans covering medical and surgical expenses and are members of the National Association of Blue Shield Plans. These plans, which are usually closely coordinated with the local Blue Cross plan, were originally initiated and controlled by a local medical society. Most plans are now controlled by a Board of Directors representing both the consumer and the medical profession with contractual agreements with physicians to provide the care promised under the plan.

Blue Shield plans fall into three broad categories based on the nature of the benefits provided:[14]

1. The full service contracts entitle the subscriber to complete payment of expenses incurred for the benefits listed in the contract, payment being made direct to the physician. (In many plans coverage is available on a "usual, customary, and reasonable paid in full" basis.)

2. Straight indemnity plans are cash-benefit plans paying specific predetermined cash benefits to the subscriber for a listed schedule of procedures.

3. The third and most prevalent type of contract is that which offers a combination of the foregoing types of plans. The subscriber is accorded the full service type of coverage in this plan if his income is below a fixed amount. Although this income level ceiling varies widely among the many combination type contracts, a representative ceiling would be $6,000 for individuals and $7,500 for families. If an individual's or family's income is above this fixed amount, he is subject to the same benefits used in the indemnity contract.

As in the case of Blue Cross, there are some variations from plan to plan, each of which is operated essentially autonomously. For national accounts (groups whose membership spans a number of Plan areas) the National Association of Blue Shield Plans has developed a set of comprehensive contract definitions. This assures common definition and administration of Blue Shield benefits from Plan to Plan for members of large groups. In general, surgical expense is usually covered under these plans regardless of where the surgery is performed. The majority of people, how-

---

[14] Follman, *op. cit.*, p. 123.

ever, limit their purchases of medical coverage to those services performed by a physician during a period of hospital confinement, although most plans provide home and office coverage to groups. Thus, the typical Blue Shield plan provides benefits similar in nature to those provided under the surgical and in-hospital physicians' benefits provisions of hospital-surgical policies issued by insurance companies.

In order to service national accounts, to provide nonstandard benefits, and to complement the local plan's underwriting ability, the National Association of Blue Shield Plans, along with the Blue Cross Association, organized two insurance companies, Health Service, Inc., and the Medical Indemnity of America, Inc.

Blue Shield members who require medical care while traveling outside the area covered by their Blue Shield contract are taken care of by the plan dealing directly with the physician and the patient. It should be noted, however, that a new system is to be initiated in 1972 which will provide universal coverage for Blue Shield subscribers.

Blue Cross–Blue Shield Major Medical Coverage.   Recently, a number of Blue Cross–Blue Shield plans have introduced major medical plans even though certain key major medical features such as large deductibles and coinsurance (percentage participation) are contradictory to fundamental Blue Cross philosophy.

The major medical coverage provided by these plans is in most respects very similar to the major medical benefits offered by insurance companies. One Blue Cross major medical expense certificate, for example, provides that after the subscriber has exhausted his benefits under his basic Blue Cross–Blue Shield certificates, his continuing covered expenses are subject to a $100 deductible after which the major medical contract pays 80 per cent of covered medical expenses up to an aggregate maximum of $10,000. Covered medical expenses would include not only hospital and surgical expenses but any customary charges for necessary treatment received in a hospital, at home, in a doctor's office or elsewhere. To date Blue Cross–Blue Shield major medical coverage has been limited almost entirely to group subscribers and has not yet been offered extensively on an individual or family policy basis.[15]

Distinctive Characteristics of Blue Cross and Blue Shield.[16] Although there are many similarities between Blue Cross–Blue Shield coverages and practices, and corresponding insurance company operations, there are several significant characteristics which distinguish Blue Cross–Blue Shield from commercial health insurance.

---

[15] HIAA, *Principles of Individual Health Insurance I* (New York, 1968), p. 65. As of September 15, 1971, fifteen plans offered major medical coverage direct to individual subscribers.

[16] *Ibid.*, pp. 65–68.

(1) Service Approach. As mentioned earlier, one of the more important distinguishing characteristics of Blue Cross–Blue Shield is the *service approach* followed in regard to benefits. The insurance company *indemnity type contract* provides for cash payments up to specified maximums which may be less than the actual total charge, and these cash benefits are payable directly to the insured. Under the pure service approach, however, the agreement between Blue Cross–Blue Shield and their subscribers does not involve cash reimbursement for covered expenses but rather a guarantee that certain contractural services will be provided without charge to the subscribers.

(2) Contractual Relationship with Hospitals and Doctors. Flowing out of the service concept, another unique feature of Blue Cross–Blue Shield plans is the contractual arrangements made between Blue Cross–Blue Shield and the hospitals and physicians who provide the covered services. The heart of the typical contract between a Blue Cross organization and the member hospitals is the hospital reimbursement schedule. This schedule sets forth the amounts and the basis on which the Blue Cross plan agrees to reimburse the member hospitals for the services which they provide "without charge" to Blue Cross subscribers. A comparatively simple such schedule is the so-called per diem reimbursement type. Under this arrangement, Blue Cross agrees to pay member hospitals a stated number of dollars for each day of hospital care provided a subscriber.

Corresponding to the hospital reimbursement schedules are the fee schedules which form the heart of the contracts between Blue Shield organizations and participating physicians. These fee schedules determine the rate of reimbursement by Blue Shield to the physician for the covered surgical and medical services which he renders to subscribers.

These contractual relationships between Blue Cross–Blue Shield and the providers of hospital and medical care represent a privilege which insurance companies do not enjoy and as such can provide Blue Cross–Blue Shield with a competitive advantage. This advantage stems from the fact that the level of payments required by the reimbursement and fee schedules frequently is such that Blue Cross–Blue Shield receives a discount on the true costs of the care provided. These "discounts" have long been a source of discontent on the part of the insurance industry since insurance company policyholders are in turn required to pay not only full hospital costs but also, in effect, to make up for certain hospital financing deficits which may be partly, at least, attributable to the discounts afforded Blue Cross–Blue Shield. Blue Cross representatives question the validity of this position and point out that they do have a real advantage in working with hospitals to control costs.

(3) Rating Procedures. Blue Cross–Blue Shield has traditionally used what is known as a *community rating system.* In connection with group

coverage, this involves simply a "pooling" of the overall experience of *all* covered groups and the setting of an average rate sufficient to support this experience. This rate then would be applicable to all groups insured under the plan. Thus, under the community rating system, groups with the higher claim rates would pay basically the same premiums as the groups with better experience.

Insurance companies on the other hand generally have followed the experience rating principle in connection with their group plans. Experience rating involves a recognition of the different levels of losses experienced by the various covered groups and the charging of different premiums based on the claim experience. In recent years Blue Cross–Blue Shield has, of necessity, begun to deviate from their community rating philosophy to avoid losing some of their larger and more desirable clients. The competition from insurance companies has forced Blue Cross–Blue Shield to adopt an experience rating system whereby the more favorable experience of such groups is reflected in producing lower premiums for them.

Blue Cross–Blue Shield has also used the community rating system for nongroup coverages as well. In general, they establish three broad classifications: single subscribers, subscribers with one dependent, and subscribers with two or more dependents. Then three different rate levels are developed, one for each classification group. Thus, all single subscribers would pay the same premium regardless of the age at which the subscriber became a member of the plan. Similarly, a family made up of husband, wife, and one child is charged the same as a family with 6 or 8 covered children.

The insurance company approach in connection with individual and family hospital-surgical coverage is to charge premiums more in line with the anticipated total claim experience. This is accomplished through a premium structure with rates graded by age at issue which includes an additional premium charge for each covered person.

Regardless of the rating philosophy, however, it is worthwhile to note that there is a significant difference between the rates of retention of Blue Cross–Blue Shield and commercial insurers. In 1969, the retentions (amounts retained by insuring organizations for operating expenses, additional reserves, and profits) of Blue Cross–Blue Shield insurers equaled 4.1 per cent of subscription income whereas 16.7 per cent of premium income was retained by commercial insurers. It should be noted, however, that the retention on the group business of commercial insurers was only 5.9 per cent.[17]

(4) Nonprofit Status and Favorable Tax Treatment. The Blue Cross and Blue Shield Plans operate on a nonprofit basis which practically means that any net gain realized from operations will eventually be returned to

[17] See *Social Security Bulletin* (February, 1971), p. 17.

the plan's subscribers through either reduced premiums or more comprehensive coverage. This nonprofit philosophy is a feature shared by the mutual insurance companies whose net earnings are also distributed to policyowners in the form of yearly dividends.

Another advantage enjoyed by Blue Cross–Blue Shield is the favorable tax treatment afforded these organizations by Federal, state, and local taxing authorities. Insurance companies have long been subjected to Federal income taxes, a variety of state taxes, including a significant tax on premiums received, and even certain local taxes. Blue Cross–Blue Shield, on the other hand, has always been virtually immune to the more significant of these taxes. They pay no Federal income tax and many states, as well, exempt them from all taxes. Even in those states which do assess Blue Cross–Blue Shield, many of these taxes are minor compared to the levies on insurance companies with similar operations.

The reasoning behind this general immunity from taxes still enjoyed by Blue Cross–Blue Shield goes back to the beginning days of their development. Originally, these organizations performed a unique community service by providing much needed hospital and medical coverage to many persons who could not otherwise have obtained such insurance. The prepayment mechanism pioneered by Blue Cross–Blue Shield contributed greatly to the financial stability of the hospitals and thus to a large degree relieved the states of the burden of hospital support. Thus, the Blue Cross and Blue Shield organizations were considered to be civic and social welfare institutions and this was the primary reason for their favored tax treatment.

The conditions on which this original tax exempt status was based have changed considerably over the years. For example, insurance companies now also serve wide areas of the population with even a wider variety of health insurance coverages than offered by Blue Cross–Blue Shield. Then, too, Blue Cross–Blue Shield has abandoned, to a degree at least, certain of their practices such as community rating that originally marked them as unique social organizations. The favorable tax status afforded Blue Cross–Blue Shield has been a major point of dissatisfaction among insurance companies who point to the distinct competitive advantage accruing to Blue Cross–Blue Shield as the result of their relatively favorable tax treatment.

Independent Plans

The so-called independent plans include formal sick leave plans provided by employers, *supplementary* workmen's compensation plans under which a firm seeks to supplement workmen's compensation benefits in the event of occupational injury or disease, and a heterogeneous group of medical expense plans.[18]

The independent medical expense plans may be classified broadly as industrial and nonindustrial. An example of the former is the Welfare and Retirement Fund of the United Mine Workers of America. The nonindustrial group includes plans sponsored by fraternal benefit societies, medical societies (other than Blue Shield), communities, or private group clinics. An example of the nonindustrial community plan is the Health Insurance Plan of Greater New York.

SOCIAL INSURANCE PLANS

Health insurance benefits are provided, often in restricted form, through state and Federal social insurance plans. Prior to the advent of Medicare, the most important of these included workmen's compensation and nonoccupational disability plans established by state law.

All states have passed Workmen's Compensation laws, based on the principle that industrial accidents and disease should be a part of the cost of production and should be compensated regardless of fault. These laws establish a schedule of benefits, for death and for each type of injury, which are payable by the employer.[19] Except in a few states where a monopolistic state fund has been created, most states permit the employer to insure his liability with commercial companies. The benefits provided are not too liberal and vary widely from jurisdiction to jurisdiction.

California, New York, New Jersey, and Rhode Island have passed laws requiring employers to provide *nonoccupational* disability benefits for employees on a contributory basis.[20] Except in Rhode Island, where coverage must be placed with a monopolistic state fund, employers may insure with either commercial companies or the state carrier set up in each state. Bills to establish similar plans in other states are constantly being introduced, but to date no other state has passed such a law.[21]

---

[18] HIAA, *Principles of Individual Health Insurance I* (New York, 1968).

[19] Workmen's compensation is "elective" in many jurisdictions, but the consequences of electing out from under the law are such that, for practical purposes, all the laws are compulsory.

[20] For a detailed discussion of these plans see Paul A. Brinker, *Economic Insecurity and Social Security* (New York: Appleton-Century-Crofts, 1968), pp. 241–247. See also, Grant M. Osborne, *Compulsory Temporary Disability Insurance in the United States* (Homewood, Ill.: Richard D. Irwin, Inc., 1958).

[21] Puerto Rico passed such a law in 1968. A law was also passed in Washington in 1949, but it was defeated in a referendum in 1950. See Dickerson, *op. cit.*, p. 183. There are, of course, other state and social insurance programs providing, among othe benefits, certain health insurance benefits. See futher the sources cited in this chapter.

The rapid growth of the number of older persons in our economy in recent decades has focused attention upon their need for health insurance, particularly medical expense coverage. The Social Security Amendments of 1965 included three separate elements of significance to those concerned with plans meeting health costs. The first[22] is "Title XVIII" of the Amendments, popularly known as "Medicare." The Medicare program placed the Federal Government, for the first time, squarely in the business of health insurance, with a comprehensive program of medical benefits covering essentially all persons over the age of 65.

The second significant element in the Amendments is "Title XIX," popularly referred to as "Medicaid." Medicaid significantly expanded the role of the Federal Government in assistance to the states in the provision of medical care for the needy, the program operating as an expansion and extension of the Kerr-Mills Law.

The third area of significance was a liberalization of the disability provisions of the Social Security Act, through the 1965 and 1967 amendments to the act. The changes involved did not introduce major new concepts into the Social Security legislation as was the case with Medicare and Medicaid, but the liberalization was sufficient to cause many insurers to make adjustments in their underwriting of disability income benefits.

Medicare is, in general, a two-part program of Federal health insurance. Under "Part A," the Hospital Insurance Plan, essentially all persons age 65 or over are covered for extensive hospitalization benefits. "Part B," which is optional, provides a supplementary program of surgical, doctors' care, and certain other benefits for persons over age 65 who enroll. This program is discussed later, in Chapter 37.

[22] See Robert J. Myers, *Medicare* (Homewood, Ill.: Richard D. Irwin, Inc., 1969).

Individual Health Insurance Contracts: I | 17

THIS AND THE following chapter are devoted to an analysis of the individual health insurance contract, including an examination of the most important coverage combinations provided under schedule or package policy forms.

All individual health insurance policies, whether they provide disability income and principal sum benefits, or medical expense benefits, or a combination of both, will contain (1) an insuring clause; (2) benefit provisions; (3) a consideration clause (which cites the application, if made a part of the contract, and the premium as the insured's consideration); (4) a statement of the conditions and terms of cancellation and renewal; (5) the exclusions, exceptions, and reductions; and (6) the general provisions or conditions.

The insurance contract is a conditional promise to pay, i.e., the insured must meet the terms of the contract before the company is obligated to pay the sums stipulated. In order to collect the benefits provided by a health insurance policy, the insured must (1) have a policy validly issued and in force, (2) have suffered a physical-economic loss as defined in the policy which was caused by the perils insured, and (3) comply with the various contract conditions.

INSURING CLAUSE

Except for the exclusions and limitations, the covered perils or *causes* of eligible loss are stated in the insuring clause. While many medical expense policies are written on an "all risks" basis, nearly every policy which includes disability income benefits is a "specified peril" contract, i.e., the perils insured are accident and/or sickness usually with separate benefit provisions, benefit amounts, and other provisions for each peril.

As a general rule, companies offer broad or unlimited accident policies providing nearly every form of benefit customarily written. However, with the exception of limited-sickness medical expense policies, sickness as a peril is generally insured in conjunction with accident coverage.

The great variety of insuring clauses traditionally utilized in health insurance policies has resulted in varying and sometimes conflicting court interpretations. As a result of these court decisions, and because of outside pressures, there has been a tendency to use somewhat simplified wording in the newly issued individual health policies. The following insuring clause is typical of the traditional form widely used as late as 1954 in policies granting disability income benefits. It is found in many outstanding individual health policies and is still utilized in newly issued *industrial* business.

The Company hereby insures (1) against loss resulting directly and independently of all other causes from bodily injury sustained during the term of this policy and effected solely through accidental means and (2) against loss resulting directly and independently of all other causes from disease contracted during the policy term, as herein limited and provided.

Most of the confusion arising from the use of this clause is directly attributable to the desire of the companies (1) to write the single peril of accident in one policy; (2) to provide additional and more liberal benefits for loss caused by accidental injury than for sickness in combination policies; and (3) to provide benefits for accidental injury or illness incurred only within the policy period.[1] A typical example of a liberal insuring clause which is being utilized increasingly in newly issued individual health insurance policies (for disability income and/or medical expense benefits) follows:

The Company hereby insures against the loss, as specified in this policy that results from accidental bodily injuries sustained, or sickness contracted, while this policy is in force.

Two phrases are important to an understanding of the difference between the traditional and the more modern insuring clause. These are (1) "loss resulting *directly and independently* of all other causes," and (2) "bodily injuries . . . effected solely through *accidental means.*"

Directly and Independently

The phrase "loss resulting directly and independently of all other causes" is designed to exclude disease or bodily infirmity as a factor which causes or contributes to loss (both loss frequency and/or severity). It is the insurance company's intention that accident benefits will be paid only if accidental injury is the *proximate cause of the loss* (i.e., the injury must be

---

[1] It is significant that the trend toward the simplification of the insuring clause was first evident in the early 1950's in medical expense policies providing benefits for "accidental injury or disease." Since similar benefits were granted for medical expense caused by either peril, these insuring clauses expressed the scope of the contract in very simple terms.

the *sole* as well as the *original* cause of an unbroken chain of events causing the loss). If disease or abnormality was the contributing factor to the injury, or the amount of the loss resulting from the injury, then the loss did not result "directly and independently of all other causes." Similarly, with regard to sickness, if any abnormality or pre-existing condition [2] was a contributing factor to the cause of the illness, or its duration, then the loss did not result "directly and independently of all other causes." Of course, even a literal interpretation of this phrase would permit the recovery of accident benefits for a disease which followed an accident, providing that it can be shown that the injury was the predominant, efficient, controlling, or producing cause of the loss (doctrine of proximate cause). Death or disability caused by pneumonia resulting from confinement following an accident may be covered under the accident benefit provisions. Only pre-existing diseases or conditions that increase the loss frequency or severity are meant to be eliminated as covered causes of loss.

Although it is omitted from the modern, more liberal insuring clause mentioned above, the phrase "directly and independently of all other causes," remains in many of the individual health insurance policies and in nearly all of the limited and industrial contracts issued today.

Literally interpreted, this clause can work a hardship upon the insured. On the other hand, the courts have not always interpreted it literally or in fact upheld the intent. Since the court decisions tend to set the companies' claim policies, the court history has to be recognized. The courts of most jurisdictions will hold for the insured where an accident, which would have caused injuries in the absence of any impairments, triggers or aggravates an existing impairment which has been neither under treatment nor disabling immediately before the accident, and death or disability ensues. On the other hand, if the underlying infirmity or disease had been under treatment and causing some problems, the courts of many jurisdictions would uphold the company. In the case where the impairment actually is a contributing cause of the accident itself, from which the injuries flow, then in almost all jurisdictions the recovery would be denied.

Accidental Means

Perhaps the greatest confusion surrounding the traditional insuring clause is centered in the *accidental means* provisions. Rather than stating that the policy provides benefits for "bodily injury effected solely through accidental means" the newer insuring clause refers simply to "accidental bodily injury." A distinction between the two phrases is important since not all accidental bodily injuries result from accidental means.

[2] The term "pre-existing" is used by the industry to refer to conditions and diseases existing prior to the policy issue date.

Under the accidental means clause, a bodily injury must meet two tests in order to be covered; both (1) the *cause* of the injury and (2) the *result* (the injury itself) must have been unexpected or unforeseen. Mere unintentional injury to the body is not covered. For example, the traditional definition would not provide the more liberal accident benefits for sunstroke as a result of sunbathing since the "means" or *cause* of the sunstroke was intentional. Since the result was accidental, however, such a claim would be considered under the "accidental bodily injury" provision. Similarly, when a man breaks his leg by jumping from a wall, the *result* was unexpected but his voluntary leap was not. However, if the man's leg has been broken from an unintentional fall from the wall, both the *cause* (or "means") and *result* would be accidental, and the accident benefits would be payable.

In order to clarify further their intention as regards accidental injury, many insurers added the words "external and violent" to the accidental means clause. Thus, the clause would read "bodily injuries . . . effected solely through external, violent and accidental means."

Since most courts have interpreted the accidental means clause to mean accidental bodily injury, insurance companies are increasingly adopting the language of the more modern insuring agreement. However, the clause, often modified by the words "external" and "violent," is still found in industrial and in some individual policies today.

TYPES OF BENEFITS

After determining that a peril insured is the cause of the loss, the insured must look to the benefit provision in order to determine (1) his eligibility for payment (i.e., has the covered *cause* of loss had the required *effect*—disability or medical expense?) and (2) the nature of the benefit payment. Broadly, the various types of benefits available may be classified as (1) *disability income benefits;* (2) *collateral benefits for accidental injury,* and (3) *incurred medical expense benefits.* With the exception of the major medical expense benefit, which is usually written separately, coverage arrangements may be purchased to include one or all of the above types of benefits.

Disability Income Benefits

Disability income benefits provide monthly or weekly payments during a period of disability as defined and limited by the policy. Four major factors should be considered in evaluating the benefit: (1) the definition of disability, (2) the benefit amount, (3) the duration of benefit payment, and (4) other provisions limiting the company's liability.

Definition of Disability.   As policies are presently drafted, payment of disability income benefit, together with the amount and duration of benefit, depends upon the insured's ability to qualify as a disabled person and the status of his disability. A person who is disabled as defined in the policy is *presumed* to have suffered a reduction in his income. He may be totally disabled by reasons of accident or sickness, or he may be partially disabled. The definition of disability may be located in the same clause which states the amount and duration of benefits payable. There is a tendency to define disability in a separate provision.

(1) Total Disability.   The traditional definition, and the one still utilized in the less liberal individual policies, defines total disability as the inability to engage in *any* occupation for wage or profit. Company practice and most court decisions, however, have imparted to this definition a broader meaning than the words convey. As a result most companies have adopted the most liberal of the court interpretations of "any occupation" by incorporating the "any occupation for which he is reasonably suited by education, training, or experience" definition into their contracts.

Perhaps because it has found the greatest favor among the courts, the definition most often used in currently issued individual policies imposes a double standard, i.e., the insured must be unable to perform the duties of *his* occupation for a specified period of time; thereafter the standard is raised to the duties of any occupation.

This latter definition, which distinguishes the time period between occupational (one's own occupation) and general (any occupation) disability, and thus states clearly the insurer's intentions, is the only one that has strict policy terminology which has influenced the courts. This specific initial period (one's occupation) has come to be, most commonly, two years, although there is considerable variation among insurers. Some insurers will provide for as long as five years of the insured's occupation for the least hazardous occupational classes, especially the professional classifications, while providing the usual two years with respect to other occupational classes. Again, some insurers after the initial period, revert to the "reasonably fitted" definition instead of the "any occupation" language mentioned above.

Regardless of the definition of disability used, a few companies follow the sound practice of adding a statement to the effect that no total disability income benefit will be paid during any period in which the insured is gainfully employed. The purpose of this provision is to clarify the insurer's intent to provide benefits only when the insured is totally disabled.

It is still the practice of some insurers to distinguish between total disability and total confining disability. Sickness policies may require that, in addition to meeting the requirements of the basic definition of total disability, the insured must be "necessarily confined within doors" in order to collect benefits. Some industrial policies may require bed or hospital confinement. Because of the great moral hazard surrounding sickness disability, especially long-term sickness disability, a few companies have felt the peril uninsurable at a reasonable cost unless the confinement provision is included.

Again, because of the harshness and ambiguity of the confinement provision, the courts have construed it liberally in favor of the insured. Thus, the insured may leave the house or hospital for treatment or therapeutic reasons without loss of benefit. Most disability income policies, particularly where the maximum benefit duration for sickness does not exceed one or two years, no longer incorporate the confinement provision. Individual health policies currently incorporating this provision provide that the benefit will be payable for up to six or twelve months of total disability resulting from sickness, regardless of whether or not it results in house confinement, with *lifetime* benefits payable thereafter if the disability confines the insured to his home.

Some contracts, in order to encourage participation in formal rehabilitation programs, expand the normal definition of total disability to include limited periods, such as six to twelve months, during which the individual drawing benefits is earning income while participating in an "organized" rehabilitation program. This is usually defined as an "employer- or government-sponsored" program.

(2) Partial Disability. Most accident policies provide a reduced payment for partial disability, which is often defined as "the inability of the Insured to perform one or more of the important daily duties of his occupation." A similar benefit is sometimes provided for partial disability due to sickness as a convalescent benefit for partial disability which *follows* compensable total disability. Otherwise, sickness benefits are not available.

In theory, partial disability benefits were designed to reduce the frequency and duration of total disability payments in those circumstances where the insured is capable of some work. In practice, however, partial disability benefits are payable often after the insured has returned to full-time employment at full earnings. Under such circumstances, the benefit ceases to be an income replacement benefit and is not related to an economic loss except as it may fortuitously suffice to pay for the medical expenses involved. For this reason and the fact that total disability is more liberally defined, policies are now being offered which do not include any partial disability benefit.

Waiver of premium during continued total disability is almost universally provided in guaranteed renewable noncancellable policies. Some insurers also include this benefit in optionally renewable policies. Premiums are usually waived after total disability has continued beyond the specific elimination period (see below), usually three to six months. Usually, only premiums falling due *after* the waiver of premium elimination period has expired are waived.

An increasingly common feature of disability income benefits is some form of "guaranteed insurability" provision. In some cases the guarantee is "absolute," the provision being that on a specified anniversary, such as the third or fifth, the insured may purchase a specified additional amount of monthly income, with no evidence of insurability required, even as to earnings. Others provide a "conditional" guarantee, requiring evidence that the insured's *earnings,* as of each option date, are sufficient to qualify the increased monthly amount under the insurer's underwriting rules.

Amount and Duration of Benefits.   The amount and duration of the disability income benefit varies with the degree of the insured's disability (total or partial) and the peril involved (accident or sickness).

The total disability benefit is usually written on a *valued basis.* Subject to the company's underwriting rules, the benefit amount is selected by the applicant. With the exception of the noncancellable or guaranteed renewable policies (where the "Average Earnings Clause" may be used [3]), the amount of the benefit is not adjusted to the insured's level of earnings at the time of the loss.

This utilization of the valued concept, together with the potential fluctuations in the insured's earnings potential (because of age, changes in motivation and skills, and general economic fluctuations) and the obvious moral hazard, has forced insurance companies to establish definite underwriting rules as regards maximum benefits.

While issue limits vary by company, most often 50 per cent to 60 per cent of gross earned income is the maximum amount companies are willing to insure. This limit is reasonable in most cases due to the tax-free nature of disability income benefits where policies are purchased personally, and because most disabled persons find expenditures decrease during disability. This is particularly true where major medical and basic medical coverage is also a part of the policyholder's program.

Most companies also limit the dollar amount they will issue to monthly amounts between $500 and $1,000 although it is now possible to buy noncancellable disability income policies paying up to $2,500 per month with benefits to age 65 or beyond. "All company" participation limits further limit the amount an insured may purchase in all companies combined. These limits vary by company and are usually in the range of $1,000 to $2,500 per month, depending on the duration of benefit.

It is the common practice for companies to pay accidental total disability income benefits for the lifetime of the insured, provided that he can qualify under the definition of total disability. A few companies will pay lifetime benefits for *confining* sickness disability. Nonconfining sickness benefits are sometimes limited to a maximum of two or five years, although benefits to age 65 are now generally available.

Accidental partial disability benefits are customarily a reduced amount,

[3] See p. 276.

usually 50 per cent of the total disability benefit. Although the duration of the partial disability benefit is usually twenty-six weeks, benefits may be payable for as long as one year.

The amount and duration of the disability income benefits payable under industrial policies is considerably less than for individual health insurance.

A special form of disability benefit that has become somewhat more prevalent in recent years is the "Business Expense Disability" or "Business Overhead" benefit. This coverage provides payment, during total disability of the insured, for certain *eligible expenses* required for the maintenance of his business staff and facilities. Any salary to the insured is normally excluded from "eligible expenses" since the coverage is not intended to provide disability income, but only to maintain business or professional staff and facilities during a temporary period of inability to produce the gross income necessary to support these. Benefits are limited to some specified monthly amount, subject to a fourteen- or thirty-day elimination period and up to a twelve-month maximum benefit period. The coverage is usually available only to sole proprietors and partners.

Provisions Limiting the Insurer's Obligation to Pay.   In addition to the definitions of disability and the provisions relating to the amount and duration of benefits, certain other provisions further clarify the company's obligation to pay. These provisions may be found either in the benefit provision itself, in the exclusions, or in the general policy conditions.

(1) Limitations Customarily Found in the Benefit Provisions.   The benefit provisions of an individual disability income policy may contain one or more of five limitations which condition the company's obligation to pay.

The first is the *elimination period,* or that period of time beginning with the first day of disability during which no benefits are paid. In the case of total disability caused by sickness, the elimination period may run from the date of first treatment by a licensed physician after the commencement of disability. The duration of the elimination period may vary from 7 to 365 days, or longer.

It is common for accident benefits to be payable from the first day of disability. A few companies offer benefits starting with the first day of sickness disability.

There can be no question about the propriety of the elimination period. It is a waiting period—a form of deductible—and is designed to eliminate entirely the many short disabilities for which benefits would otherwise be payable, and which do not ordinarily cause the insured severe economic hardship. In addition, disability income protection is rarely needed during the first few days of any disability because of private salary continuation plans. Of course, with an elimination period, the cost of insurance is greatly reduced, since the small, highly frequent, budgetable loss has been eliminated. The longer the elimination period, the lower the premium.

The second benefit phrase limiting the company's obligation to pay requires that the insured be *regularly attended by a legally qualified physician* as a condition precedent to recovery. This requirement is universally included in individual health insurance policies.

The third provision refers to *total and partial disability which does not immediately follow an accident.* Because of the difficulty in establishing a direct relationship between disability and accidental bodily injury, companies at one time required that the insured be continuously disabled from the date of injury. However, since legitimate cases do arise where disability may not immediately follow the injury, disability income contracts now usually provide that the disability must commence within a limited period following injury—usually thirty to ninety days. Some companies have no time limit within which the disability must begin. Partial disability immediately following a period of total disability may also be eligible for benefit.

The necessity for this provision arises out of the differences between accident and sickness insurance as regards the nature of the benefits, benefit amounts, and benefit duration. Disabilities which cannot be traced to an accidental injury are (and should be) payable as though caused by sickness.

The *probationary period* provision, which states that no benefits shall be paid for sickness contracted or commencing during the first fifteen (or thirty) days of the policy period, is designed to clarify further the company's intention not to provide benefits for sickness which commenced prior to the policy period (pre-existing disease). It is designed to minimize the number of borderline cases where it is difficult to establish the origin of the disease, and to serve as a deterrent to adverse selection. This clause may be found occasionally in the exclusions, but when it is used, it is ordinarily a part of the insuring clause.

Finally, when a period of temporary recovery separates two periods of disability, a serious question may arise as to whether the later disability is an entirely new event or merely a continuation of a previous disability. This is especially important since the maximum duration for sickness disability is usually expressed as a limit per disability, and benefits could be extended indefinitely simply by effecting a temporary recovery and then claiming a new illness. The problem is compounded when the policy is noncancellable or guaranteed renewable.

In order that there can be no misunderstanding, nearly all noncancellable or guaranteed renewable policies and many of the newer "optionally renewable" policies contain *a definition of a recurrent disability.* Such a definition usually specifies that before the later disability can be considered caused by a new illness, the insured must have returned to full-time work for a continuous period of at least six months. There is both an advantage and a disadvantage in this provision which is sometimes overlooked. If the recurrence is within the six-month period, then only the unused portion of the monthly indemnity limit is available, but the elimination period is not re-applied. If the recurrence is after more than six months of work resumption, then the elimination period is re-applied, but a complete new duration of benefit limit is available.

(2) Limitations Customarily Found in the Exclusions. Although most modern individual health insurance policies provide broad coverage, they are not designed to provide protection for all accidents or sicknesses. As regards both perils, most policies exclude loss contributed to or caused by (1) pre-existing injury or conditions; (2) war, whether declared or undeclared, or any act of war; (3) any injuries sustained or sickness contracted while the insured is serving in the armed forces of a country or international authority such as the United Nations; (4) any injury sustained in an aircraft other than when the insured is a passenger on a regularly scheduled airline; (5) intentional self-destruction sane or insane; and (6) pregnancy.

Since both the insuring clause and the benefit provisions usually state that the cause of the disability must have occurred while the policy is in force, the pre-existing condition exclusion is intended merely to clarify the intent of the insurer. It is interesting to note however, that a few companies are following the usual court interpretation of this provision and are stating that pre-existing illnesses or conditions will be excluded as causes of loss only when they have manifested themselves prior to the effective date of the policy. It should also be noted that pre-existing conditions are subject to the time limit on a company's defenses in virtually all jurisdictions.[4]

Increasingly, companies are liberalizing the aircraft exclusion so that the policy includes flight as a passenger on any aircraft, and a few have no aviation exclusion at all.

Certain exclusions, which are applicable specifically to the peril of accident, include (1) disease or mental infirmity; (2) any infection, whether sustained accidentally or otherwise, except septic infection of and through a visible wound accidentally sustained, and (3) hernia. All of these exclusions reflect a clarification of the company's attempt to distinguish between the perils of accident and sickness.

Occupational injury or disease is sometimes excluded as a cause of loss from policies intended for wage earners and others who are protected against occupational accidents and diseases through workmen's compensation programs. In this manner, the price of the protection is considerably reduced, and the danger of overinsurance from this source is alleviated.

(3) Limitations Found in the General Conditions. Broadly, the provisions found in the general conditions pertain to matters that are of an administrative nature. However, two provisions, at times found in disability

---

[4] Uniform provisions provide for three years; for variations, see Edwin L. Bartleson *et al., Health Insurance,* 2nd ed. (Chicago: The Society of Actuaries, 1968), p. 232.

income policies, operate to limit the amount of the benefits recoverable from a single insurance company. Still others may be included which result in a limitation on the benefit payable. These so-called prorating provisions,[5] dealing with change of occupation and misstatement of age, merely are intended to adjust the benefit level to conform to the proper rating classification. The others, relating to other insurance and earned income, are designed to limit moral hazard.

The other insurance provisions (optional uniform provisions 4 and 5), often labeled *"Insurance With Other Insurers,"* permit the pro rata reduction of benefit payments if additional insurance is *discovered* at the time of claim. The reduction allowed is determined by a comparison of the benefits provided under the policy of one company together with all benefits under policies of other companies *of which the first company had no notice,* with all similar benefit amounts payable under all valid policies. Thus, if the insured had a policy providing $400 per month income benefit and failed to notify the company of another policy of the same amount, the application of this clause would reduce the payments to 400/800 of $400, or $200 per month. The formula would be:

$$\frac{\text{Benefits in this policy}}{\text{Total benefits in all policies}} \times \frac{\text{Amount this policy would pay if it were the only one in force}} = \frac{\text{Amount paid by this policy}}$$

When benefits are reduced by this clause, a pro rata portion of the premium must be returned to the insured.

Another provision, entitled *"Relation of Earnings to Insurance"* (optional uniform provision 6) may be found in noncancellable or guaranteed renewable disability income benefit policies. Broadly, this clause provides that when the total income amount exceeds the insured's prior monthly income, the benefit of the policy shall be reduced its proportionate share of the amount of the prior income. For example, if the insured has two policies providing $200 and $400 per month, respectively, but his earnings are only $500 per month, only 500/600 of the stated benefit amount would be paid by a policy with such a clause. In terms of a formula:

$$\frac{\text{Average earnings}}{\text{Total benefits in all policies}} \times \frac{\text{Benefit in this policy}} = \frac{\text{Amount paid by this policy}}$$

[5] These provisions are among the "optional standard" provisions provided for under the Uniform Individual Policy Provisions Law. See pp. 295–296.

This clause further provides that it is not applicable if the sum of all monthly benefits is less than $200, or to the extent that it would operate to reduce the benefit payable to less than $200 per month. Again, the pro rata premium proportionate to the reduction in benefits must be returned to the insured.

Obviously, the purpose of these prorating clauses is to discourage the purchase of unduly large amounts of income benefits and also to provide some protection to the company against the hazard of overinsurance, whether it is due to deflation and economic recession or the insured's purchase of new insurance in the future.[6] The "other insurance" clause usually is used in cancellable or nonrenewable policies where the insurance company has a chance to get off the risk when notified of other insurance. It is little protection for the company under a noncancellable or guaranteed renewable policy. As mentioned earlier, the "relation of earnings to insurance clause" is common in the latter types of contracts, especially where the maximum benefit period is long.

Since disability income contracts are generally based upon an occupational classification, the *"Change of Occupation"* provision (optional uniform provision 1) provides that if an insured suffers a disability after having changed to a more hazardous occupation than that which he followed at the time of applying for the policy, his benefits will be reduced to that proportion of the stated benefits which the premium rate for the original occupation bears to the premium rate for the new and more hazardous occupation.

The *"Misstatement of Age"* clause (optional uniform provision 2) provides in effect that the benefit paid will be equal to what the premium the insured is paying would have purchased if the age had been correctly stated. The benefit is adjusted (either up or down) in the proportion that the premium the insured actually paid bears to the premium he should have paid, had the age been correctly stated.

Finally, the *"Other Insurance With The Same Insurer"* clause (optional uniform provision 3) relates to the situation where more than one contract is in force concurrently in the same company. This provision makes the portion of the aggregate benefit for a specified coverage or coverages in excess of a specified benefit limit void.

It should be noted that many policies do not contain any of these prorating provisions and probably no policy contains all of them.

---

[6] The definition of total disability was liberalized in Section 303 of the Title III Amendments to the Social Security Act in 1965. This liberalization increases the hazard of overinsurance under voluntary disability benefits and has led many insurers to tighten up their issue and participation rules for disability income in relation to earnings. It is possible to include Social Security disability benefits as "other valid coverage" under the "Relation of Earnings to Insurance" provision, provided an appropriate definition of "other valid coverage" is employed.

Collateral Benefits

The disability income benefit (whether it be payable for loss resulting from accident or from sickness) is often supplemented by other benefits payable only as a result of accidental injury as defined. Alternatively, combinations of these supplemental benefits may be written separately or as a package.

Accidental Death Benefit.   Companies have traditionally offered the accidental death benefit as a part of the disability income policy. The amount of this benefit is the *Principal Sum* of the contract. Although the Principal Sum varies from a few hundred dollars to several thousand dollars, companies have endeavored to write the benefit on a *level basis,* i.e., in such a way that the ratio of the Principal Sum to the weekly income benefit does not exceed 200 to 1. Experience has shown that a greater ratio contributes to adverse underwriting results. However, with the development of the new *schedule policies,* where the insured may select the amount of the Principal Sum and/or income benefits, there is developing a tendency to reduce the amount of the Principal Sum benefit and to give greater attention to adequate amounts of disability income insurance.

Accidental Dismemberment and Loss of Sight Benefits.   A benefit is often paid for certain disabilities which, because of their severity, are *presumed to be total and permanent.* When the Principal Sum or a portion of it is paid for dismemberment or loss of sight, it is called a Capital Sum payment.[7] A typical schedule of Capital Sum dismemberment and loss of sight benefits follows:

LOSS	CAPITAL SUM BENEFIT
Both hands or both feet or sight of both eyes	The Principal Sum
One hand and one foot	The Principal Sum
Sight of one eye and either one hand or one foot	The Principal Sum
One hand or one foot or sight of one eye	One half of the Principal Sum

[7] In contracts providing weekly or monthly income benefits, the Capital Sum benefits may be expressed in relation to the income benefits (e.g., two hundred weeks of benefits).

For purposes of this provision loss of hand or foot means complete severance at or above the wrist or ankle joints respectively. Loss of sight must be entire and irrecoverable.

These benefits are payable under a variety of arrangements. The most liberal would make them *payable in addition* to all other income benefits due under the policy. Most policies tie the payment of these benefits with the income benefit in some manner as follows:

1. The least liberal provision makes the benefits payable automatically in lieu of all other policy benefits. (This provision is now prohibited in some jurisdictions.)

2. The insured may elect, usually within a certain number of days following injury, to receive income indemnity for the rest of life, or some other specified period of time, in lieu of the lump-sum indemnity. (This provision is now prohibited in some jurisdictions.)

3. The insured may elect, usually within a certain number of days following injury, to receive the lump-sum indemnity in lieu of the income benefit.

4. The Capital Sum benefits will be the minimum amount which the insured receives because of the specified dismemberment or loss of sight. Any amounts remaining unpaid on the insured's death are made payable to his estate or beneficiary. Thus, if the income benefits paid prior to death were less than the Capital Sum benefit, the difference would be payable to the insured's estate or beneficiary.

As regards the second and third of the above four provisions, many policies provide that income benefits will be payable from the beginning of total disability to the date of the loss of life, limb, or sight, in addition to the Capital Sum benefit.

Double Indemnity Benefits. Many disability contracts contain a double indemnity provision which provides that all collateral benefits, other than those for medical expense, will be doubled, provided that the injury was sustained under certain conditions. Usually, benefits are doubled when the injury results from an accident (1) while the insured is a passenger on a common carrier or passenger elevator or (2) caused by boiler explosion, hurricane, tornado, lightning, collapse of building walls, or fire. In some cases triple or quadruple indemnity may be payable. Because of the remoteness of these events, it appears that this benefit is designed to appeal to the speculative instinct of the insured and, at best, to induce him to buy the other coverages that are more important to his personal security.

Accumulations. Occasionally, policies provide that the Principal Sum benefits shall be increased by a stipulated percentage per year if the policy is continued in force, until the *accumulations* reach a stated limit (usually 50 per cent of the Principal Sum benefit). The purpose of this provision is to encourage the insured to renew his policy periodically in the same company. It is a reflection of the competitive aspects inherent in this type of insurance.

Elective Indemnity Benefit.   Many policies give the insured the option of taking a specified sum for certain minor or partial disabilities, (fractures, dislocations, amputations) in lieu of the disabilty benefit, or in lieu of all other benefits payable under the policy for such injury. The specified amounts are listed in a schedule, usually in terms of multiples of the total disability benefit. In more liberal policies, these elective indemnity benefits are stated as the minimum benefit which the insured shall receive under the disability income provision.

Nondisabling Injury Benefit.   Many disability income policies include a blanket medical expense benefit which provides for the payment of the actual cost of medical treatment for nondisabling injuries up to an amount equal to one fourth of the monthly income benefit. This benefit payment is usually in lieu of all other benefit payments.

Medical Expense Benefits

Although blanket benefits are available, most of the existing individual health insurance covering the expense of medical care is provided on a specified benefit basis, i.e., there are separate benefit provisions and amount limits for hospital, surgical, and other medical expense. These benefits may be combined with the disability income benefit in a single policy. Alternatively, hospital expense benefits may be written separately in a single contract, to which the other medical expense benefits may be added to form a medical expense policy. Other medical expense benefits which may be included in the disability income or medical expense policy include the nurses' care benefit and the maternity benefit. Unless specific mention is made to the contrary, the insured perils or causes of loss are both accidental bodily injury and sickness.

The insured is primarily responsible for the medical expense costs, and he is paid by his insurer for expense incurred. However, the general acceptance of the Hospital Admissions Plan, as proposed by the Health Insurance Council, now makes it possible for the insured to assign his policy benefits to the hospital. He is then billed for the difference between the hospital charges and the amount of the benefits paid by his contract. These benefits are usually written on a so-called indemnity basis. The company pays the actual costs of the service up to a specified maximum amount. However, benefits may follow the traditional *valued* approach. The *valued* or *fixed hospital benefit* provides for the payment of a specified amount for each day of confinement, regardless of the actual cost of the facilities used.

Medical expense benefits are customarily extended to cover the dependents of the named insured. When these benefits form a part of the disability income policy, a *dependents' rider* is attached. A *family group* provision is usually included as a part of the medical expense policy. The usual policy defines family dependents as the insured's spouse and children dependent upon the insured not over the age of eighteen. Newborn children are often extended automatic protection, although a specified period of days following the date of birth may be required before the protection becomes effective. Premiums are adjusted on the renewal date for changes in the number of dependents.

Hospital Expense Benefits. Two types of hospital expense benefits are customarily written: (1) the daily hospital benefit and (2) the miscellaneous expense or hospital services benefit.

The *daily hospital benefit* is designed to provide payment for the hospital charges for room, board, floor nursing, and other routine services which are subject to a per diem charge. As previously mentioned, this benefit may be on an "indemnity" or a "valued" basis, with the amount of the benefit ranging from a nominal amount of $5 to as much as $50 per day. The benefit period, or the duration of benefits, ranges from thirty days to as long as one year, with a period of seventy to ninety days being common.

The *miscellaneous expense* or *hospital services benefit,* which is nearly always on an indemnity basis, provides payment for hospital charges not covered under the daily hospital benefit. Specifically, it provides payment toward the cost of anesthetics, including the administration thereof; ambulance service to and from the hospital; and operating room, x-ray and fluoroscope, medicines, drugs, surgical dressings, oxygen, and any other medical equipment or supplies for which a charge is made by the hospital. Usually, the maximum amount of the benefit payment is expressed in terms of a multiple of the amount paid under the daily hospital benefit, i.e., ten, fifteen, or twenty times the daily hospital benefit. Some companies offer a choice of dollar limits, so that with any given daily room maximum the purchaser can select any desired amount of hospital services coverage, from as little as $50 up to $1,000, $2,500, or more. There are other variations including the use of an 80 per cent percentage participation (coinsurance) provision with high dollar benefit amounts and a flat deductible such as $25 or $50 applicable to the combined room and services benefit.[8]

Most policies specifically define a hospital. Typically, the word "hospital" "means only an institution operated pursuant to the law for the care and treatment of sick and injured persons, with organized facilities for major surgery and 24-hour nursing service." The purpose of the hospital definition

[8] The use of a deductible and/or a coinsurance or percentage participation clause helps keep premiums down. See pp. 285–287.

is to eliminate benefits for confinement in institutions primarily providing board and room care, i.e., rest and nursing homes.

Hospital expense benefits are payable only to a person who qualifies as an in-patient, i.e., a person who is confined to a bed in a hospital and who is billed for at least one day's room and board. Some policies may establish a benefit for out-patient hospital care for injuries which require emergency treatment in the hospital, or if surgery is performed. The amount of this benefit, always written on an indemnity basis, is often expressed as being equal to the miscellaneous hospital expense benefit.[9]

Surgical Expense Benefits. The surgical expense benefit provides for the payment of the charges made by a physician for surgical operations, subject to the schedule of limits for each listed procedure. The schedule, which may contain as many as one hundred procedures, is designed to establish relative costs as between the most expensive and the least expensive operations, and is based upon a careful intercompany study of the relative costs for the various procedures.

Since the schedule is designed to reflect the relative costs of the various procedures, the amount of the surgical benefit is expressed in terms of the maximum benefit payable. Amounts range from $100 to a maximum as high as $600 or more for people who live in high-cost areas or who enjoy higher incomes. The premium for the surgical benefit varies with the amount of the maximum benefit selected.

Since it is impossible to name all of the surgical procedures that may be performed, the list contained in the policy refers only to those operations which occur most frequently. Nonlisted operations are usually covered, however, with the amount of benefit payable varying according to the relative cost of the procedure when compared with the procedures which are specifically listed.

Following are listed some operations taken from a $100 schedule. Benefits payable under a $200 schedule would be twice as large; a $300 schedule three times as large, etc.

Title of Operation	Amount
Appendectomy	$ 50.00
Gall bladder removal	75.00
Removal of lung	100.00
Tonsillectomy	15.00
Treatment of simple fracture—	
thigh	37.00
forearm	12.50
Hysterectomy	75.00

[9] Some companies will write "out-patient diagnostic" coverage for accident or sickness, usually subject to a low maximum limit.

Herniotomy—	
single	50.00
double	62.50
Delivery of child	25.00
Caesarean section	50.00
Hemorrhoidectomy—	
external	12.50
internal	25.00

It is customary that where two or more surgical procedures are performed through the same incision, or because of the same or related conditions, the maximum payment applicable will be the larger of the benefits applicable to all such procedures. In recognition of the fact that unusually complex sickness or injuries may require multiple surgery, some companies provide "elastic" schedules, under which it is provided that an amount exceeding the listed limit may be payable in cases of abnormal complications. In addition, there is usually a definition of surgical procedure. A typical definition reads as follows:

"Operations" means only the following surgical procedures performed by a legally qualified physician: cutting, suturing, treatment of fracture, reduction of dislocation, electrocauterization, tapping, administration of artificial pneumothorax or pneumoperitoneum, removal of stone or foreign body by endoscopic means, or the injection treatment of hernia, hemorrhoids or varicose veins.

Recently, so-called "Relative Value Schedules" have been developed, in which values assigned to each listed procedure are "units" or point values. The actual dollar benefit limit is then determined by assigning a dollar "unit value" to the schedule, such as $3.00, $5.00 or even $10.00. The advantage of this approach is that it provides greater flexibility in determining the dollar value of any one policy schedule, thus permitting it to be adapted, conveniently, to the locality or income level of the purchaser.[10]

Doctors' Expense Benefit.   Another medical expense benefit, relatively rare in individual health insurance forms, is designed to reimburse the insured for the cost of the doctor's services for other than surgical operations or post-operative care. Benefits are usually on a valued basis and are considerably less than the customary charge for the services rendered.

There are two broad limits of recovery. The *limit per call* varies with the doctor's charges. Limits for office and hospital calls are usually $3; home visit $5. The *overall maximum limit* may be expressed either as a

[10] These relative value schedules have been widely adopted by state medical societies in an effort to bring the relative weighting of procedure values more under control of the medical profession. The oldest and most widely used relative value schedule is the California Relative Value Study, originally published in 1954. See Bartleson *et al., op. cit.*, p. 31.

maximum number of calls and/or a maximum dollar limit for each sickness or injury. Many policies limit this benefit to visits by the doctor in the hospital.

The unusually high moral hazard, the danger of adverse selection, and the relatively high frequency of these comparatively small payments have generally operated to make this type of benefit uninsurable in individual policies (where the experience of the individual risk cannot be considered). It should be noted, however, that these benefits are included in the major medical expense policy discussed below.

Nurses' Expense Benefit.   Occasionally, the policies are written to include a benefit for nursing care. Benefits are similar to the hospital expense benefit in that there is a maximum limit per day and an overall time limit. A nurse is defined as "a private duty, registered, professional nurse." Although benefits are usually payable only while the insured is in the hospital, the policy may be extended to include the home.

Maternity Benefits.   Although pregnancy and childbirth do not meet the usual standards for an insurable peril, individual insurance policies often provide limited benefits. A probationary period of at least nine months (often ten months) usually applies in order to eliminate the possibility of adverse selection. A few more-liberal policies provide benefits if the pregnancy commences after the policy date or after a short probationary period, making it possible to pay benefits for miscarriage when a full-term birth would have been compensated.

The most common maternity benefit provides payment for hospital expense, usually limited to a specified multiple of the daily hospital benefits. No miscellaneous hospital benefit is available. The obstetrical benefit sometimes pays for the cost of surgery necessary in connection with pregnancy.

Usually, the maternity benefits are made available only in family policies where both the husband and wife are insured.

Dental Care.   A few insurers have offered dental care policies or riders on an individual basis, usually employing a dental services schedule similar to the surgical schedule. The difficulties of underwriting this benefit, however, combined with the high frequency of very small claims, have limited the availability of this coverage in individual policies.[11]

Major Medical Expense Benefits.[12]   Although the medical expense benefits described above are designed to pay a substantial portion

---

[11] *Ibid.,* p. 33.

[12] See HIAA, *Principles of Individual Health Insurance I* (New York, 1968), pp. 109–114.

of the costs of relatively minor injuries and illnesses, they fail to provide adequate insurance for the substantial cost of the serious injury or illness. Since the purpose of insurance is to alleviate the economic effects of serious injury or illness, and since the insurance mechanism functions efficiently only where loss frequency is relatively low, it is only natural that the concept of major medical expense insurance would be devised.

The earlier major medical expense benefits were developed to pay only for expense incurred as the result of accidental injury. The *blanket accident expense benefit,* found only in disability income or accidental death and dismemberment policies, provides indemnification for the expense of medical care necessitated by accidental injury. The amount of the benefit may be as high as $5,000 for any one accident, and covers all expenses (hospital, medical, nurses') on a blanket basis, sometimes with the use of a deductible provision.

The great failing of this accident benefit is that it does not pay for the major sickness. To meet this need the *major medical expense benefit* was devised. Major medical expense insurance is designed to complement basic hospital and surgical expense insurance and provides benefits in cases where substantial expenses are incurred within a reasonably short period of time, constituting a potential financial catastrophe to the individual or family unit. Major medical insurance can be provided in the form of a rider attached to a basic hospital and surgical expense policy or issued as a separate policy.

If a major medical insurance rider is attached to a basic hospital and surgical expense policy, it will, in effect, after the deductible is satisfied, cover losses after the hospital and surgical limits of the basic policy are exhausted or substantially exceeded. There is no underwriting requirement that an individual or family unit have basic hospital and sickness coverage. The insured may elect to be self-insured up to the deductible amount.

Major medical expense insurance is written on an *expense incurred basis* and anticipates that *eligible medical expenses,* in excess of an expressed deductible amount, shall be incurred within a limited period of time which is called the *accumulation period.* In the event eligible medical expenses exceed the deductible amount, the insurer will pay a certain portion of such expenses with the insured coinsuring a portion of such expenses usually to a limit of 20 to 25 per cent. This percentage participation gives the insured a vested financial interest in expenses incurred and should tend to guide him away from unnecessary or unduly expensive medical care.

The general provisions relating to such things as insuring clause, renewability, termination of coverage, definitions, and similar matters resemble substantially such provisions in a basic hospital and surgical expense policy.

The definition of sickness, however, will usually be quite different from that included in the basic hospitalization policy form. Such definition can be drafted so that the benefits of the policy apply on an *each sickness basis*. In the event of two or more separate sicknesses occurring during a single benefit period, this would require that the deductible be applied separately to the expenses incurred in connection with each such sickness. Sickness may also be defined as each sickness or disease *due to the same or related causes* including all recurrences. It also may be defined as including *all sicknesses or diseases suffered concurrently* whether or not there is any relationship between the sicknesses or diseases. The significance of this latter definition is that all medical expenses incurred on behalf of an insured person, whether from one or more causes, would be eligible for benefit payments during the benefit period upon satisfaction of the initial deductible amount.

As in the case of other health insurance policies covering medical care expenses, both the definitions of injury and sickness will exclude any injury or sickness for which the insured person would be entitled to benefits under any workmen's compensation, occupational disease, employer's liability or similar law.

(1) Eligible Expenses. The major medical expense policy includes a provision defining the kinds of medical care expenditures that will be considered an eligible expense. Only eligible expenses are considered in (1) satisfying the deductible amount, and (2) determining the benefits payable under the policy. It is important to note that major medical expense policies vary considerably in the kinds of expenses they consider eligible and the manner in which they are treated.

Expenditures for *hospital room and board*, including general nursing care, may or may not be limited to a specific dollar amount for eligible-expense purposes. For example, two approaches to room and board benefits might be as follows: (1) Hospital room and board, including general nursing care, but not to exceed the hospital room and board limit per day specified in the policy schedule. (2) Charges made by a hospital for: room and board and services customarily included in the hospital room and board charge up to the lesser of either the hospital's regular daily rate for semiprivate room accommodations plus $6.00 per day of hospital confinement or $30 per day of hospital confinement.

Miscellaneous expense items such as medical services or supplies, other than board and room and general nursing care services, provided by the hospital may be considered an eligible expense on an unallocated basis or it may be expressed as containing certain limitations such as a dollar limit on the cost of the operating room, a dollar limit for X-ray examination or X-ray therapy, and similar items.

Eligible expenses for *surgical procedures* may be expressed as follows: (1) it may be unlimited, i.e., the customary charge for such procedure without other limitations; (2) it may be limited to an express dollar limitation; or (3) it may be limited pursuant to a schedule of operations with values listed for various surgical procedures.

Charges for *other services* customarily qualifying as eligible expenses would include dental care of fractures or dislocations of the jaw or injury to natural teeth, services of a graduate registered nurse or professional anesthetist, X-ray examination or laboratory tests, prescription drugs and medicines as well as various devices such as artificial limbs or eyes, and other special medical care expenditures.

Any charge which is subjected to a limitation per unit of charge or a maximum for certain kinds of charges is described as an "inner limit."

(2) Deductible Amount. The deductible amount may be expressed as (1) a specific dollar amount, (2) a dollar amount determined by reference to a table which is based on the net income of the husband and wife, or (3) the greater of either benefits afforded under other insurance coverages or a stated dollar amount. The most commonly used approach is the first, based on a fixed dollar deductible amount.

(3) Benefit Period. A *benefit period*, usually a period of two or three years, will be established if eligible expenses in excess of the deductible amount by reason of a covered sickness or injury shall be accumulated within the specified *accumulation period* of 90 or 180 days. Once the benefit period has been established the insurance company will pay benefits in accordance with the provision of the policy usually captioned "Major Medical Benefit."

(4) Major Medical Benefit. The major medical benefit expresses the promise of the insurer to pay a specified percentage, usually 75 or 80 per cent, of the eligible expenses incurred which is in excess of the deductible amount. This promise is, of course, subject to any inner limit controls which may apply to specific kinds of eligible expenses and is subject to the maximum limit of the policy which may be any amount ranging from $5,000 to $25,000 or more.

(5) Common Accident. The major medical expense policy usually provides that, if two or more insured members of a family sustain injuries as the result of a common accident, only one deductible need be satisfied. The maximum benefit limit, however, still applies severally to each insured person.

(6) Exclusions. The exclusions of the major medical expense policy generally relate to war, full-time active military duty, elective cosmetic surgery, eye refraction or the fitting of eyeglasses, dental care or treatment except that specifically provided for with respect to injury to natural teeth, sickness or injury for which benefits are payable under workmen's compensation, occupational disease, employer's liability or similar law, care extended to ex-members of the armed forces by any governmental hospital or hospital providing services to such person at the direction of the government.

Major medical policies also usually contain limitations with respect to pregnancy, childbirth, or miscarriage except for occurrences that may come within a definition of what constitutes a "complication of pregnancy" for which benefits may be payable. Certain limitations may be expressed as applicable to expenses incurred in the care and treatment of mental illness. This may take many forms, including outright exclusion, limitation to expenses incurred while confined in a general hospital, or a fixed dollar limitation which may be expressed as a limit for each period of sickness or as a lifetime limit.

In face of rapidly increasing costs, severely adverse experience, and repeated rate increases under such "uncontrolled" plans, many insurers have turned toward reliance on various types of "inside limit" devices mentioned above to put some control on their losses in relation to medical cost inflation. The most common inside limit is a daily hospital room maximum. Many contracts now also use a surgical schedule or else place some aggregate limit on surgeons' fees, and provide aggregate inside limits on private duty nursing and doctors' visits. Inside limits, of course, break with the original philosophy of major medical insurance, and their use continues to be a subject of controversy within the health insurance industry.[13]

Provisions Limiting the Insurer's Obligation to Pay.   Most of the appropriate provisions limiting the insurer's obligation to pay which were previously described as being applicable to disability income benefits are also applicable to medical expense benefits. In addition there are a few provisions which are peculiar to the expense policies.

(1) Limitations Customarily Found in the Benefit Provisions. Medical expense policies may include a *deductible*, applicable to hospital and/or surgical expense benefits. Unlike the major medical benefit, the amount of the deductible is relatively small, i.e., $25 to $50.

Some medical expense policies contain a *probationary* period applicable to the policy as a whole. The length of this period may range from seven to thirty days. An additional probationary period may be required for elective surgery such as (1) repair of an abdominal hernia; (2) removal or treatment of hemorrhoids; (3) removal of tonsils or adenoids, or both; (4) removal of appendix; or (5) treatment caused by, or contributed to, any condition of the female generative organs. As with the probationary period applying to the entire policy, the purpose of this additional six-month period is to eliminate the possibility of adverse selection. Although the probationary period is usually described in the benefit provisions, it may be found in the exclusions.

[13] Bartleson *et al., op. cit., pp.* 37-38.

As previously mentioned, noncancellable or guaranteed renewable disability income policies customarily include a provision for *recurrent disabilities*. Medical expense policies, regardless of the renewability and cancellation provisions, often include provisions defining the company's intent as regards *recurrent hospitalization* and/or *successive operations*. The recurrent hospitalization provision states that successive periods of hospitalization shall be considered as one confinement unless (1) the cause of the subsequent confinement is entirely unrelated to the causes and conditions for which treatment was furnished during the prior confinement, or (2) the successive periods of confinement are separated by an interval during which the insured resumes full normal activities for a continuous period of at least six months. The *successive operations* provision is worded in a similar manner. As previously mentioned, these definitions of recurrent hospitalization and successive operations are necessary because the policy usually specifies a maximum period of hospital confinement, or a maximum amount for a surgical operation due to one injury or illness. Without these provisions it would be possible for the insured to collect multiple limits for the same condition simply by effecting a temporary recovery.

(2) Limitations Found in the Exclusions.   In addition to the exclusions customarily found in the disability income policy, the medical expense policy usually excludes the expense of dental service and eye refractions; expense associated with a rest cure; expense due to injury or sickness for which benefits are payable under any workmen's compensation or occupational disease law; and expenses which are incurred while the insured is confined to any hospital owned, or contracted for, or operated by a national, state, or provincial government, or any political subdivision thereof, or on account of the treatment of members or ex-members of the armed forces; and sometimes mental disease. It should be noted that dental surgery is frequently covered when it is caused by accidental injury. Coverage of mental disease and benefits for confinement to government or veterans' hospitals is excluded primarily since care in these institutions is provided as a matter of right without an effective "means" test. Additional exclusions may be included in policies.

(3) Limitations Found in the General Conditions.   Some companies are including in optionally renewable medical expense policies, the "Insurance With Other Insurers" provision. This condition states, in essence, that where the insured has duplicate coverage with other companies, on an expense incurred or provision of service basis, of which he has not given written notice to this company, benefits will be paid under this policy in the proportion that this company's indemnities, together with those of all other companies of which this company has had notice, bears to the total benefits guaranteed by all policies. Premiums for that proportion of the benefits not paid are refunded.

Recently, there has been some confusion and difficulty with several states over the subject of governmental hospitals. The problem arises because many states charge for treatment in state-supported institutions if the patient has means. They do not charge the indigent. The position the states are taking is that the existence of hospital insurance is prima facie evidence of means. On this basis, they want the companies to pay the bills to the extent of the insurance, or the charges which would have been made in the absence of insurance to persons who had the means to pay. There is a division among the companies as to how far they should go in meeting this request. It would appear that the request is reasonable.

Federal Medicare[14]

The passage of Title XVIII of the 1965 Amendments to the Social Security Act created immediate problems for private health insurance, because the threat of massive overinsurance through widespread duplication of benefits became a reality.

The majority of insurers undertook immediate revision of their individual portfolios so as to discontinue the further sale of lifetime guaranteed renewable policies and similar programs involving substantial duplication with Medicare. They also initiated efforts toward discontinuance or conversion of existing in force business involving similar duplicate coverage.[15]

The insurance industry has developed three different approaches to providing appropriate coverage supplemental to Medicare:

(1) Benefits of broad scope containing a general *exclusion* of any expenses *eligible* for reimbursement under Medicare, or, in some contracts, *actually* reimbursed under Medicare. This latter distinction is significant in relation to "Part B" of Title XVIII which provides coverage for doctors' and surgeons' fees on an *optional basis*.

(2) Benefits designed to cover, specifically, various expenses not covered by Medicare.

(3) Benefits which, in effect, duplicate to some extent the benefits included in Medicare, but which are issued on a limited basis so that actual overinsurance is not anticipated.

Most insurers are using one of two basic methods to avoid eventual duplication of Medicare under medical expense policies sold originally to cover

[14] This summary based on *ibid.*, pp. 49–55.

[15] The NIAC, through its Subcommittee to Study the Effect of Medicare on Health Insurance, promulgated a series of permissive recommendations to enable insurers to take such steps as they desired in adjusting to Medicare. See O. D. Dickerson, "The Impact of Medicare on Private Medical Expense Insurance," *Annals of the Society of C.P.C.U.*, Vol. 19, No. 3 (Fall, 1966).

persons below the age of Medicare eligibility:

(1) Automatic termination of persons attaining age of Medicare eligibility (selected, usually, by those insurers not wishing to become involved in any program of supplementation of Medicare);

(2) Automatic change in benefits as of Medicare eligibility, to supplemental coverage, including the use of a general Medicare exclusion (selected by those insurers desiring to continue lifetime benefits in supplementation of Medicare).

Each of these approaches has advantages and disadvantages, and each must contemplate future liberalizations in Medicare benefits.

In addition to the Medicare adjustments, private health insurance is faced with potentially enormous duplication problems arising from Title XIX of the Social Security Act. This Title, popularly known as Medicaid, deals with grants to states for medical assistance programs. The problem here will be more difficult to deal with since it does not create a clearcut plan of benefits taking effect at a specified age, as does Medicare.[16]

[16] See Robert J. Myers, "Medicaid Legislative Provisions," *Medicare* (Homewood: Ill.: Richard D. Irwin, Inc., 1969).

Individual Health Insurance | 18
Contracts: II

CONTINUANCE PROVISIONS

INDIVIDUAL HEALTH INSURANCE policies may be classified according to their cancellation and renewal provisions[1] into (1) Noncancellable, (2) Guaranteed Renewable, (3) Conditionally Renewable, (4) Collectively Renewable, (5) Renewable at Insurer's Option, (6) Cancellable, and (7) Term.

Noncancellable contracts are those which the insured has the right to continue in force by the timely payment of premiums set forth in the contract, for a substantial period of time during which the insurer has no right to make unilaterally any change in any provision of the contract while the contract is in force. These contracts are not cancellable and the right of renewal or continuance until an advanced age, for example age 60, is guaranteed. The premium may be level from date of issue, or increase in accordance with a schedule contained in the contract at issue. The insurance company may not modify the premium or the coverage while the contract is in force.

Guaranteed renewable contracts give the insured the right to continue his contract in force by the timely payment of premiums for a substantial period of time, during which the insurance company has no right to make unilaterally any change in any provision of the contract while the contract is in force, other than a change in the premium rate for classes of insureds. The classes of insureds may be based on contract form, territory, age, period of issue, or other objective bases and may or may not be established at issue of the contract.

Conditionally renewable contracts provide that the insured may renew the contract from period to period, until a stated date or an attained age, subject to the right of the insurer to decline renewal only at anniversary or premium dates, and then only for defined causes such as retirement but

[1] This classification is based on O. D. Dickerson, *Contract Analysis in Health Insurance* (Bryn Mawr, Pa.: American College of Life Underwriters, 1970), pp. 9–10.

other than deterioration of the insured's health; *or* they provide that the insurer relinquishes the right of termination for certain causes including deterioration of the insured's health.

Collectively renewable health insurance contracts give the insured the right to continue his contract in force by timely payment of premiums unless the insurance company terminates coverage of all policies of a given class or in a given state (or of a class in a state). The term also is used for association franchise plans where individual policies are used which may not be terminated by the insurance company except when it terminates all policies of the association.

Contracts renewable at insurer's option are those in which the insurance company reserves the right to terminate coverage at any anniversary or premium due date but does not have the right to terminate coverage between such dates.

Cancellable contracts are those which may be terminated by the insurance company (and/or insured) at any time (subject to requirements as to notice, etc.).

Term contracts make no provision for renewal or termination other than by expiration of the policy term. These usually are very short-term contracts.

While noncancellable contracts are best from the insured's point of view, they are more expensive than the others, and not every individual will want to or can pay the higher premium involved. Guaranteed renewable contracts provide the same security as noncancellable contracts except that the premium is subject to change. They are somewhat less expensive than noncancellable contracts. Medical expense contracts are seldom noncancellable since the right to change premiums is felt to be necessary to protect the insurance company against future increases in medical expense costs. Most individual medical expense policies are guaranteed renewable or collectively renewable. The term "commercial" has been commonly applied to contracts which are conditionally renewable, renewable at the insurer's option, or cancellable. These contracts are lower in cost than noncancellable or guaranteed renewable contracts and, because of the less strict underwriting standards, they are available to wider markets.

EXCLUSIONS AND SUSPENSION OF COVERAGE

As indicated in the preceding chapter, there are certain exclusions and suspensions of coverage in the usual individual health insurance contract. They may be classified broadly as: (1) certain types of losses; (2) situations involving excessive risk; and (3) situations involving duplication of benefits.

Some types of losses, such as the exclusion of pre-existing conditions or of pregnancy or of a certain disease for a period of time, are intended primarily as "underwriting through the policy" to relieve the company of responsibility for conditions the knowledge of which might have led the insured to purchase the insurance. Some, such as aviation activities or military service, exclude a risk that the companies consider too great to cover. In the latter case, there is no need for insurance since government provisions cover both incurred costs and income loss for service-connected disabilities. Insurance cannot soundly cover deliberate acts of the insured, so suicide and self-inflicted injuries are excluded. For the same reasons, benefits for pregnancy and childbirth are usually quite limited or may be excluded entirely. Finally, in order to prevent duplication of coverage and benefit payment, policies often exclude coverage where Workmen's Compensation benefits, Medicare, or other government benefits are applicable. The Workmen's Compensation exclusion is used in medical expense policies primarily to avoid duplication of benefits, because the majority of Workmen's Compensation and occupational disease laws provide rather complete medical care. This same reasoning applies to Medicare benefits for those eligible for such benefits. It is used in disability income policies primarily as a means of reducing the premium, and secondarily as a means of avoiding duplicate benefits.

The exclusion relating to war or military service may be of a different nature. This may provide that loss occurring *while* the insured is in military service, as defined, will not be covered. This type of provision suspends the coverage for a period of time, but provides for a return premium for such period. The distinction between a "status" and a "results" type of war clause must also be considered. The first suspends coverage while a specified "status" exists, while the latter excludes loss resulting from a specified peril. A careful reading of the contract is necessary to distinguish one from the other.

House confinement is sometimes required as a prerequisite to benefit collection under disability income policies covering disability arising out of sickness. Sometimes benefits are paid only for house-confining illness; sometimes a reduced benefit is paid for nonconfining sickness, or a shorter duration is covered for nonconfining than for confining disability. At one time the use of house-confining clauses was the rule in regard to sickness income benefits. Today the clause is rather rare, and it is diminishing in importance.

Other clauses that look like exclusions are merely intended as controls on moral hazard and to define more specifically the event insured against. Such clauses include the requirement that the insured be under the care of a legally qualified physician other than himself. This is common to almost all health insurance contracts. Policies that cover hospital expense will require admission to a "hospital," perhaps as a "registered bed patient."

Similar definitions are used in regard to reimbursement for nurse expense and related benefits. All these operate to exclude losses not permitted by the definition but are intended primarily as claim controls.

GENERAL PROVISIONS

The preceding discussion has brought out a number of the so-called general provisions of an individual health insurance contract. Many of the general provisions are standard provisions required by law. All states regulate the policy forms for individual health insurance. The Uniform Individual Accident and Sickness Policy Provisions Law recommended by the National Association of Insurance Commissioners in 1950, or a reasonable approximation thereof, has been enacted in all jurisdictions where the laws otherwise could have been in conflict. The Uniform Law [2] sets forth twelve mandatory and eleven optional provisions. As with the life insurance standard provisions, if they are included, the required or optional provisions must be in the language of the statute or in language at least as favorable to the insured.

In addition to prescribing the uniform provisions, the law contains certain other requirements relating to typography, to the application, to who may be covered, and to the general administration of the law. The twelve *Required Provisions,* in substance, state:

1. *Entire Contract.* Specifies that the endorsements and attached papers constitute the entire contract of insurance.
2. *Time Limit on Certain Defenses or Incontestible.* Provides that after the policy has been in force for more than three years (two years in most states), the company cannot deny claims because of pre-existing conditions or misstatements on application.
3. *Grace Period.* Requires a stipulated grace period (7 days for weekly premium contracts, 10 days for monthly premium contracts and 31 days for all other contracts) be granted for payment of each premium falling due after the first premium, during which grace period the contract shall continue in force.
4. *Reinstatement.* Outlines requirements for reinstatement after lapse.
5. *Notice of Claim.* Specifies how the policyholder gives notice of claim.
6. *Claim Forms.* Specifies when the company shall furnish claim forms.
7. *Proofs of Loss.* Specifies the time limit within which the insured shall give proof of loss to the company.

[2] See Appendix B.

8. *Time of Payment of Claims.* Specifies the time after proof of loss within which payment must be made.

9. *Payment of Claims.* Specifies the person to whom claim payments are made.

10. *Physical Examination and Autopsy.* Gives the company the right to examine the person of the insured during a claim or to perform an autopsy, where not prohibited by law.

11. *Legal Actions.* Gives the time limits within which the insured may bring legal actions against the company.

12. *Change of Beneficiary.* Gives the insured the right to change the beneficiary.

An outline of the *Optional Policy Provisions* is as follows:

1. *Change of Occupation.* Permits a pro rata benefit reduction in event of change of occupation to a more hazardous occupation and reduction of premium in event of change to a less hazardous occupation. (See p. 277.)

2. *Misstatement of Age.* Provides for an adjustment of benefits in event of misstatement of age. (See p. 277.)

3. *Other Insurance in this Insurer.* Provides for a pro rata benefit reduction in event of other insurance in this insurer. (See p. 277.)

4. *Insurance with Other Insurers.* Provides for a pro rata reduction of *expense incurred benefits* in event of insurance with other insurers without written notice to the company. (See p. 276.)

5. *Insurance with Other Insurers.* Provides for a pro rata reduction of *indemnity benefits* in event of insurance with other insurers without written notice to the company. (See p. 276.)

6. *Relation of Earnings to Insurance.* Provides for a pro rata reduction of disability income benefits (in noncancellable and guaranteed renewable policies) where all benefits payable for loss-of-time exceed the insured's average earnings for the 2-year period prior to claim. (See pp. 276–277.)

7. *Unpaid Premium.* Permits any unpaid premium due at time of claim to be deducted from the claim.

8. *Cancellation.* Permits cancellation of the policy at any time by the company or insured.

9. *Conformity with State Statutes.* Amends any policy provision to effect conformity with state law.

10. *Illegal Occupation.* Excludes benefits for loss resulting from the insured engaging in an illegal occupation.

11. *Intoxicants and Narcotics.* Excludes benefits for loss resulting from the insured's use of intoxicants and narcotics.

COVERAGE ARRANGEMENTS

Traditionally, individual health insurance policies have been written on a package basis, with the insurance company combining benefits of various types and liberality on a predetermined basis and offering the result under a particularly alluring name. Accident policies were written to include disability income; death, dismemberment, and loss of sight; and blanket medical expense benefits. Alternatively, an accident policy might be written to include just the accidental death, dismemberment, and loss of sight benefits together with the blanket medical expense benefit. Accident and sickness policies might combine the disability income and principal sum benefits with the hospital and surgical expense benefits. Again, medical expense policies might combine hospital and surgical benefits in one policy.

Two departures from previous practice are becoming evident. First, there seems to be a trend to separate disability income and medical expense benefits into separate policies. Second, there is a tendency to write all benefits on a scheduled basis, i.e., the company devises a form which includes several benefits in such a way that the insured may elect the benefit and the benefit amounts which he desires. Examples of this schedule technique which are already familiar to most insureds would include property and liability insurance contracts such as the family automobile policy and the owners', landlords', and tenants' liability policy.

Many advantages accrue to this approach. The insured is given an opportunity to see the various types of benefits and to select those benefits which are important to him. He has a greater understanding of the policy. The company may be in a better position to re-underwrite on renewal. Finally, it facilitates the collection of statistical experience by policy benefit rather than by a policy package.

In order to bring into focus the preceding discussion of the multiplicity of variations in health insurance benefits, it might be helpful to review briefly a summary, including premium rates, of three basic individual health insurance coverage arrangements offered by particular insurance companies. Also, a summary of a basic Blue Cross–Blue Shield plan is included for comparison.

Hospital and Surgical Expense Plan

Insurance Company Plan.   Table 18–1 presents a summary of a hospital and surgical expense plan. The benefits are relatively liberal and typical. It may be renewed to age 65 with the right to change

TABLE 18-1. Illustrative Hospital and Surgical Expense Plan

Brief Description of Plan

I. Hospital Expense Benefits
   A. Hospital, room, board, and routine services: Up to $40 per day for as long as 120 days of resident in-patient hospital confinement, or confinement due to any one sickness or accident
   B. Additional hospital expenses: Up to $600 for hospital confinement or confinements as a resident inpatient due to any one sickness or accident, including charges incurred for operating room, anesthetics, surgical dressings, laboratory, medicines and drugs, X-ray and fluoroscope, oxygen, ambulance service, and other medical services
   C. Hospital calls by a physician: Up to $6 per day of hospital confinement but not to exceed $300 for all calls during all confinements due to any one sickness or accident (The four weeks following an operation are included in this coverage only if elected in lieu of the surgical benefit for the operation.)

II. Surgical and Radiotherapy Expense Benefits
   A. Surgical operations: Up to $900 according to a schedule and depending on the nature of the operation(s), due to any one sickness or accident
   B. Radiotherapy: Up to $600 according to a schedule and depending on the nature of the radiotherapy due to any one sickness or accident

III. Convalescent Nursing Home Expense Benefit
   A. Convalescent nursing home room, board, and routine services: Up to $20 per day for as long as 60 days of convalescent nursing home confinement(s) due to any one sickness or accident (Such a confinement must start within seven days after a continuous hospital stay of at least five days.)

IV. Expenses Not Covered
   A. Sickness or injury covered by any workmen's compensation act or occupational disease law
   B. Sickness or injury arising out of war, declared or undeclared
   C. Hospital confinement, convalescent nursing home confinement, services or supplies in U. S. Government facilities
   D. Hospital confinement, convalescent nursing home confinement, services or supplies during the first six months of coverage due to the following: repair of injuinal, femoral, or umbilical hernia; removal of tonsils and adenoids; hemorrhoids; disorders of the female generative organs; appendectomy concurrent with an operation on the female generative organs
   E. Hospital confinement, convalescent nursing home confinement, services or supplies provided under any national or state government program or law that is not restricted to employees of such government
   F. Physicians' services in connection with specified mouth and foot conditions
   G. Pregnancy, except certain unusual complications
   H. With respect to full-time active duty in the armed forces (other than active duty for training purposes only for two months or less),
      (1) any loss incurred while on such duty,
      (2) any loss resulting from injury sustained or sickness contracted while on such duty
      The company will refund premiums paid for the person in military service for any such period for which no coverage is provided

V. Other Features
   A. Guaranteed renewable and full coverage continues on each adult to age 65, and on each child until his 23rd birthday unless he marries or ceases to be a dependent prior to that age. Coverage of incapacitated children may be continued beyond age 23 (A "conversion privilege" is available for children).

B. Premium rate cannot be changed unless company changes the table of premium rates for all policies in class. Benefits cannot be reduced even at 65 – nor can re-strictive rider be placed on the policy after issue

Illustrative Participating Gross Premium Rates

Benefit Pattern	Plan #1	Plan #2
Hospital confinement benefits		
maximum daily hospital benefit	$ 30	$ 40
maximum duration (days)	120	120
Maximum additional hospital expense benefit	$300	$600
Physician's in-hospital calls benefits		
maximum daily benefit	$ 4	$ 6
maximum benefit	$200	$300
Convalescent nursing home expense benefits		
maximum daily benefit	$ 15	$ 20
maximum duration (days)	60	60
Maximum surgical benefit	$600	$900
Maximum radiotherapy benefit	$600	$600

Issue Age	Plan #1 $30 DHB			Plan #2 $40 DHB		
		Women			Women	
	Men	With Husband	All Other	Men	With Husband	All Other
25	$ 99.60	$129.15	$137.15	$135.13	$179.67	$187.67
30	101.52	131.11	139.11	137.69	182.31	190.31
35	112.41	140.74	148.74	152.23	195.20	203.20
40	125.55	149.94	157.94	169.72	207.51	215.51
45	140.48	158.67	166.67	189.70	219.08	227.08
50	156.92	167.56	175.56	211.72	230.73	238.73
55	174.03	177.04	185.04	234.63	243.30	251.30
59	189.12	182.81	190.81	256.61	251.25	259.25

Issue Limits and Eligibility Requirements

Hospital Expense coverage may not be written in addition to any other basic hospital, comprehensive, or extended type hospital and medical expense coverage. It may be written in addition to Major Medical Expense subject to the following limits on the amount of DHB under the Hospital Expense Policy:

Major Medical deductible amount	Maximum DHB available
less than $500	Hospital Expense not available
$500 but less than $750	$20
$750 but less than $1,000	$30
$1,000 or over	$40

Premium for Children (0–17)

Plan #1: Each Child $49.82
Plan #2: Each Child $67.90

On applications covering more than one person, all eligible family members must be included.

premiums by class reserved to the company. Coverage on children is provided until age 23 unless they marry or cease to be dependents prior to that age. Coverage of incapacitated children may be continued beyond age 23 for an additional premium. A conversion privilege is available to children within thirty-one days after their coverage terminates.

The policy is issued in most occupational classifications and is available to the following:

1. Unmarried men and women, ages 18–59.
2. Heads of families to cover themselves and all eligible family members. Eligible family members are husband and wife, up to age 59, and dependent children age 15 days to less than 18 years. Application for coverage must be made on all eligible family members except:

(a) Family members in military service are excluded.

(b) Where husband or wife alone is covered under a group hospital or Blue Cross plan, the policy can be issued excluding him or her from coverage.

In Table 18–1 the specific benefit amounts have been indicated for two plans. The premium for Plan #1, if the contract were issued to a husband aged 35, including his wife aged 30 and one child aged 6, would be a total annual premium of $293.34. The comparable premium for Plan #2 would be $462.44. Other benefit combinations are available.

It is important to note that this policy is liberal in terms of benefits and provides guaranteed renewable coverage to age 65 with the right to adjust the premium rates by class reserved to the company.

Blue Cross–Blue Shield Plan. As pointed out earlier, basic Blue Cross benefits for hospital care and Blue Shield benefits for physician care have moved from the full service approach toward the insurance company approach of utilizing dollar limitations on services provided. As is frequently the case, competition and similar environmental constraints have caused both Blue Cross–Blue Shield and insurers to adopt certain practices and procedures originally unique to one or the other.

Table 18–2[3] presents a summary of a Blue Cross–Blue Shield basic medical expense plan. This plan's 365 coverage on hospital expense is relatively liberal. As in the case of insurance company plans, for certain kinds of expenses there are dollar limitations on benefits provided. In general, except for possible differences in acquisition costs, tax treatment, and savings in loss costs due to any discounts allowed Blue Cross by associated hospitals, unit benefit costs should be similar to insurance company plans.

[3] See pp. 302–303.

Major Medical Expense Plan

Insurance Company Plan. Table 18-3[4] presents a summary of an individual major medical expense plan with a deductible amount of $500, $1,000, or $1,500 depending upon the plan selected, and subject correspondingly to a maximum benefit of $10,000, $20,000, or $30,000. The coverage follows the usual major medical pattern, although it does not utilize a percentage participation (coinsurance) provision on all expenses and provides for a maximum benefit period of three years in connection with any particular injury or illness.

The plan provides "internal limits" on the daily room and board charge, surgical procedures, and all other eligible medical expenses. Virtually all companies have found it advisable and necessary to have such internal limits because of their experience with unlimited benefits.

As in the case of the hospital-surgical plan described above, this policy is a variable-premium guaranteed renewable policy. It may be renewed until the covered individuals reach age 65, at which time Medicare is available. The policy provides, however, the privilege of purchasing, without evidence of insurability, any policy offered by the company to persons age 65. A conversion privilege is also available to children covered under the policy. The policy is guaranteed renewable with the right to change premiums by class reserved to the company.

This policy is issued in most occupational classifications (medical examinations required for men ages 51 through 60) and is available to the following:

1. Unmarried men and women ages 18 to 60.

2. Heads of families to cover themselves and all eligible family members. Eligible family members are husband and wife, up to age 60, and dependent children age 15 days to 23 years. Application for coverage must be on all eligible family members. However, family members in military service are not eligible for coverage.

A person is not eligible for coverage under this policy if he or she is covered by any other major medical expense policy. The annual premium for the plan presented in Table 18-2 for a man aged 35, with a wife *or* with a wife and one or more children, would be $297.55. The fact that a family has children does not alter the premium under this particular policy; it is written on a family basis. Newborn children are automatically covered.

---

[4] See pp. 304–307.

TABLE 18-2. Illustrative Blue Cross–Blue Shield Basic Medical Expense Plan

Brief Description of Plan

I. Hospital Expense Benefits (Blue Cross)
    A. Hospital, room, board, and routine services: Covered in full in a semi-private room (average charge credited toward cost of private room) for up to 365 days of hospital care per calendar year for each "separate" hospital confinement. For certain disorders benefit is limited
    B. Additional hospital expenses: Virtually all expenses covered in full including use of operating room, anesthetics, surgical dressings, laboratory, medicine, and drugs, x-ray and fluoroscope, oxygen, therapy and other medical services
    C. Hospital calls by a physician: Covered up to per diem limits for 365 days per hospital admission ($15.00 the first day; $10.00 the second day; $4.00 each day the third through the tenth day; $3.00 each day thereafter.) For certain disorders, benefit is limited to 30 days (when concurrent with either surgical or obstetrical care, benefits limited to one or the other)
    D. Out-patient care: Full coverage for emergency treatment within 72 hours of accidental injury, or when minor surgery is required
    E. Maternity benefits: Full benefits provided for up to 10 days of care per period of pregnancy. Includes delivery room and ordinary nursery care during the mother's hospital stay

II. Surgical Expense Benefits (Blue Shield)
    A. Surgical care: Up to $300 allowed toward surgeon's fees according to a schedule and depending on the nature of the operation(s)
    B. Out-of-hospital diagnostic x-ray and laboratory services: Allowances provided in accordance with schedule subject to maximum of $50 for diagnostic x-rays and $50 for laboratory services during any period of twelve consecutive months.
    C. In-hospital visits by a surgeon: (See Blue Cross hospital calls above)

III. Services Not Covered
    A. By Blue Cross: Services of persons not employed by the hospital; hospitalization primarily for diagnostic studies or physical therapy; services not consistent with diagnosis; for the following conditions, after a clear diagnosis as such: chronic alcoholism, drug addiction
    B. By Blue Shield: Care furnished by other than a Doctor of Medicine or Doctor of Dental Surgery. Any fee charged by a physician for consultation, or screening examinations; cosmetic surgery; for removal or care of teeth
    C. By Blue Cross or Blue Shield: Ambulance service; blood or blood plasma; procurement or use of special braces, appliances or equipment; convalescent, custodial or sanitaria care; rest cures; on-the-job injuries or when coverage is provided in full or in part at the expense of any Federal, state or local government; service rendered in connection with injuries sustained as a result of war, declared or undeclared, or any act of war. Expenses covered under Medicare

TABLE 18-2. (cont'd.)

IV. Other Features (Blue Cross–Blue Shield)
   A. Renewable to age 65 for husband and wife, and also covers each unmarried child from birth to 19 years of age who is living with family in a parent-child relationship. (A "conversion privilege" is available for children)
   B. Special coverage is available at age 65 to *supplement* Medicare benefits
   C. Premium rate may be adjusted periodically by Blue Cross–Blue Shield
   D. Membership may be transferred to another Blue Cross and Blue Shield Plan in the case of a permanent move.

The premium for the major medical coverage reflects the fact that the deductible in the case of the major medical plans is substantial, and the elimination of many small frequent losses materially reduces the premium which would otherwise have to be charged. This demonstrates also that basic hospital-surgical expense plans are really prepayment plans covering frequent, small, and in many cases budgetable expenses. Major medical expense insurance, on the other hand, provides true insurance where the catastrophic risk of the individual is transferred to an insurance company to be pooled with the risks of others, thus permitting major health care costs to become a budgetable expense for the individual. While prepayment plans serve a valid purpose and what constitutes a financial problem varies with individuals, it is clear that the major medical insurance provides the medical expense insurance protection needed by most families.

Blue Cross–Blue Shield.   Since the mid 1960's major medical coverage has been written by Blue Cross–Blue Shield *group* plans, particularly on large national accounts. In addition, fifteen Blue Cross–Blue Shield plans have made major medical coverage available on a nongroup basis. Some organizations still have a basic Blue Cross–Blue Shield plan in conjunction with a group major medical plan provided by an insurance company. Since this is a relatively inefficient system, it is declining in acceptance. Blue Cross–Blue Shield major medical coverage has followed the typical insurance company pattern utilizing a deductible amount, 75 or 80 per cent coinsurance (percentage participation) and a dollar maximum benefit.

TABLE 18-3. Illustrative Individual Major Medical Expense Insurance Plan

Brief Description of Plan

I. Eligible Medical Expenses
   A. Hospital: Charges by a hospital for room, board, and general nursing care not to exceed a daily charge of $_____; charges by a hospital for room, board, and nursing care in an Intensive Care Unit, up to a daily charge of $_____
   B. Surgery: Charges by a licensed physician or surgeon for the performance of surgery, including any postoperative care during the period of two weeks immediately following such surgery, up to the maximum amount determined in accordance with the policy's surgical schedule; charges by licensed physicians or surgeons assisting in the performance of surgery up to a maximum of 15 per cent of surgical schedule amount
   C. Physician's fees: Charges by a licensed physician for medical care, other than the performance of surgery or administration of anesthetics; separate limits for specialists and for initial versus follow-up visits
   D. Nursing services: 80 per cent of the charges for the private duty nursing services of a licensed nurse incurred while hospital confined other than in an Intensive Care Unit; 50 per cent of such charges incurred while not hospital confined
   E. Convalescent home: Charges by a convalescent home for room, board, and general nursing care for as long as 30 days for each confinement, up to a total of 100 days in any Benefit Period, not to exceed a daily charge of $_____. Confinement must be preceded by at least 5 days' confinement in a hospital for the same condition and begin within 14 days after discharge from such hospital confinement
   F. Medical services and supplies: 80 per cent of most other medical services and supplies
   G. Transportation: 80 per cent of the charges for transportation by a professional ambulance
   H. Dental work: Charges for dental work required (i) as a result of injury to sound natural teeth or (ii) in connection with treatment on account of a malignant tumor; 80 per cent of any other charges which are for dental work by a licensed dentist or for dental prosthetics
   I. Cosmetic surgery: Charges incurred for cosmetic surgery (i) to correct a condition resulting from injury, or (ii) to correct a congenital anomaly of a child born while coverage is in effect on both husband and wife
   J. Mental illness: Eligible medical expenses incurred for the treatment of mental illness or nervous disorders will be those incurred only while confined in a hospital, up to a Maximum Benefit of $_____

II. Policy Does Not Cover
   A. Expenses arising from: Injury occurring or sickness contracted or commencing before coverage is in effect under the policy; normal pregnancy, childbirth, or miscarriage; attempted suicide; war or while in Armed Forces; injuries or sickness covered by workmen's compensation, occupational disease, or similar law; medical care or services fur-

TABLE 18-3. (cont'd.)

nished or performed by the Insured or the Insured's spouse or their children, parents, brothers, or sisters

B. Confinement in rest homes, homes for the aged, places for custodial care or which are primarily for the treatment of alcoholism or drug addiction, or in a hospital owned or operated by an agency of a national government for the treatment of members or ex-members of the Armed Forces

C. No coverage is provided for medical care, services, or supplies which are paid for, or covered under, any plan (including "Medicare") established by a national, state, or local government, or any agency thereof; however, charges for such care, services, or supplies which would otherwise qualify as eligible medical expenses may be used to satisfy the *Deductible Amount,* in determining any benefits payable under the policy

III. Benefit Period: Three years from beginning of a 120 day period during which *Eligible Medical Expenses* exceed the *Deductible Amount*

IV. Deductible Amount: $500, $1,000, or $1,500 depending upon plan selected and "Total Family Income"

V. Maximum Benefit: The policy pays 100 per cent of all Eligible Medical Expenses in excess of the Deductible Amount up to the plan limit selected until three years after the first charge is incurred

VI. Other Features
   A. Waiver of premium: All premiums falling due after 120 days of continuous total disability, which begins before age 60, will be waived for as long as such total disability continues. When both husband and wife are covered this benefit will be for the husband's total disability, otherwise it will be for the one adult covered under the policy
   B. Guaranteed renewable: To age 65, coverage will continue on each adult to the first policy anniversary occurring on or after such person's 65th birthday, and on each unmarried dependent child until age 23
   C. Privilege of policy purchase at age 65: Any person covered at age 65, whose coverage then automatically terminates, can purchase within 31 days after such termination, a policy providing benefits then being issued by the Company to persons age 65. *No evidence of insurability will be required* and the premium for such policy will be based on the person's attained age and the insurance plan
   D. Conversion privilege for children
   E. Automatic coverage for new-born children

Illustrative Gross Participating Premium Rates

Plan A:	$ 500 Deductible Amount—$10,000 Maximum Benefit
Plan B:	$1,000 Deductible Amount—$20,000 Maximum Benefit
Plan C:	$1,500 Deductible Amount—$30,000 Maximum Benefit
	(Premiums are the same for Plans A, B, or C)

TABLE 18-3. (cont'd.)

Age at Issue	Men* A	Men* Q	Women* A	Women* Q	Family† A	Family† Q
18–25	$ 89.96	$23.39	$110.30	$28.68	$213.59	$ 55.53
30	111.53	29.00	132.94	34.56	256.14	66.60
35	134.09	34.86	153.45	39.90	297.55	77.36
40	173.39	45.08	179.55	46.68	354.60	92.20
45	218.93	56.92	207.68	54.00	419.94	109.18
50	270.13	70.23	237.61	61.78	487.74	126.81
55	326.24	84.82	269.05	69.95	561.95	146.11

*Separate policies will not be issued to a husband and wife.

†The rate is the same whether the policy is to cover only the husband and wife, or is to cover husband, wife, and one or more children. Include all eligible family members on the application. Premiums for the policy and the Optional Increased Daily Hospital Room and Board Amount, issued on a family basis, depend only on the issue age of the husband.

Coverage on one parent and child or children (where permitted by issue rules below):
Add to the appropriate policy premium rate shown above under Men or Women the following charge (which is the same for one or more children): Annual—$40; Quarterly—$10.40.

Medical Examination:
Men—Age 50 and under . . . Nonmedically; Ages 51–50 . . . Medically
Women—Nonmedically

Summary of Plan Limits and Availability

Total Income Limit*	$15,000 or less	$15,001 to $50,000	$50,001 to $100,000
Plan(s) Available	A, B, or C	B or C	C

	Plan A	Plan B	Plan C
Deductible amount	$ 500	$ 1,000	$ 1,500
Maximum benefit	$10,000	$20,000	$30,000
Maximum benefit for mental illness	$ 2,500	$ 5,000	$ 7,500
Hospital room and board Daily charges			
Regular confinement	$ 30†	$ 40†	$ 50†
Intensive care confinement	$ 60	$ 80	$ 100
Surgical expenses from:	$6–$1,200	$8–$1,600	$10–$2,000
Illustrative operations:			
Stomach ulcer or tumor	$ 360	$ 480	$ 600
Compound hip fracture, open repair	$ 480	$ 640	$ 800
Removal of disc in spine with spinal fusion	$ 720	$ 960	$ 1,200
Brain tumor	$ 900	$ 1,200	$ 1,500
Heart valve repair	$ 1,200	$ 1,600	$ 2,500

*"Total family income" means total annual income of the family from all sources, including investment income. Applicants with such income over $100,000 are not eligible.

†If Optional Increased Daily Hospital Room and Board Amount is added to the policy, increase this amount by the appropriate amount ($10 or $20).

TABLE 18-3. (cont'd.)

	Spe-cial-ist	Other	Spe-cial-ist	Other	Spe-cial-ist	Other
Medical care by physician:						
Initial visit	$30	$18	$40	$24	$50	$30
Follow-up visit (Dr.'s office, hospital)	$12	$ 6	$16	$ 8	$20	$10
Other follow-up visits	$18	$12	$24	$16	$30	$20
Post-hospital convalescent home care	$ 15		$ 20		$ 25	

Disability Income Plan

Table 18–4 presents a summary of a long-term disability income plan. In general, the coverage arrangement follows the usual pattern. It provides lifetime accident total disability benefits and sickness coverage extending to age 65. The disability income benefits begin after 30 days of total disability although other combinations of waiting periods are available.

The definition of disability is liberal, being defined in terms of the insured's own occupation for the first five years of disability with the increasingly standard definition "any reasonably gainful occupation for which he is or may become reasonably fitted by education, training or experience" applying thereafter.

The policy is noncancellable and guaranteed renewable to age 65. From age 65 it is conditionally renewable to age 70 at an attained age premium so long as the insured works full time. From age of issue to age 65 no right is reserved to the company to change premiums, even by class, as the policy is noncancellable. This is long-term health insurance protection and a medical examination is required of most applicants.

For the husband in a family who wishes to protect the income flow to himself and his family in the event he becomes disabled, this plan meets that need. He has lifetime benefits if disabled before age 50, and benefits to age 65 if he is disabled after age 50 but before age 65. After age 65 his need for coverage is dubious, under the assumption that this is the age of economic retirement. If he does remain employed, however, he can keep this policy on a year to year basis at an attained age premium—subject to a two-year maximum duration of benefit.

Assuming a husband aged 35, the annual premium for a $100 monthly income benefit (thirtieth-day accident and sickness) would be $64.25. It is worth noting that accepting a deductible of 365 days on accident and sickness benefits would save $27.76 over seventh-day accident and sickness coverage. This is a 29.1 per cent reduction in cost, and demonstrates the savings in cost which is available through the elimination of the smaller, more frequent loss from coverage.

TABLE 18-4. Illustrative Long-Term Disability Income Plan

Brief Description of Plan

I. Disability Income Benefits

    A. Total disability—sickness or accident

    Disability income benefit: $500 monthly while disabled, beginning with the thirty-first day of disability. Benefits may continue for life if disability begins before age 50; to age 65 if disability begins after 50 but before age 63; for a maximum of two years if disability begins after age 63

    Definition of disability: The benefits for total disability outlined above are payable for the first five years if the individual is unable to work at his own occupation or profession and thereafter if he is unable to work at any reasonably gainful occupation for which he is or may become fitted by education, training, or experience, having due regard for the nature of his previous occupation and for his prior average earnings.

    The entire and irrecoverable loss of the sight of both eyes, or of the power of speech, or of the use of any two extremities (arms or legs) because of sickness or accident will be considered total disability as long as such loss continues

    B. Partial disability—sickness or accident

    Disability income benefit: $250 monthly for as long as six months following a period of total disability for which benefits have been paid

    Definition of partial disability: Inability to perform one or more, but not all the important daily duties of own occupation or inability to perform the usual daily duties of own occupation at least 50 per cent of the time

II. Other Benefits

    A. Waiver of premium: If totally disabled for at least three months, premiums waived during continued total disability to age 65, retroactive to beginning of total disability

    B. Capital sum benefit: A sum equal to the total disability indemnity for one year ($6,000) in the event of the loss of the sight of an eye, the power of speech, or a hand or a foot by severance (up to twice this amount for a double loss)

    C. Rehabilitation benefit: Participation in a government-sponsored or other professionally planned rehabilitation program, approved by the company in advance, will not alone be deemed a recovery from total disability

    D. Benefits increased by 5 per cent or 10 per cent respectively if premiums are paid semiannually or annually

III. Limitations

    A. Policy does not pay benefits for:

        (1) injuries sustained or illness beginning before the policy is issued;

        (2) injury or illness resulting from war or sustained while in military service;

        (3) intentionally self-inflicted injuries

TABLE 18-4. (cont'd.)

B. Monthly indemnity not payable unless under care of a physician except that such care is not required if total disability shall have resulted from loss of eyesight or of any two extremities by severance

IV. Other Features
A. Guarantees the right of renewal until the policy anniversary following 65th birthday. The premium rate is guaranteed until age 65; it is conditionally renewable thereafter until age 70 at the premium rate then in effect for the covered individual's attained age, as long as he continues to be employed full-time
B. Policy is participating. Dividends (not guaranteed) may reduce premium outlay
C. Does not require house confinement
D. Elimination period not applied to any period of total disability that commences while policy is in force and within five years after termination of a prior period of total disability (1) for which monthly indemnity shall have been payable and (2) which shall have lasted more than six months

Illustrative Participating Gross Premium Rates

Men Only, Occupational Class 5
Premiums per $100 Monthly Income Benefit

Issue Age	*Elimination Periods (Sickness and Accident)*						
	7 days	14 days	30 days	2 months	3 months	6 months	1 year
25	$ 69.10	$ 61.77	$ 51.45	$ 46.53	$ 44.42	$42.25	$41.34
30	75.99	68.91	58.79	53.83	51.63	49.27	48.24
35	80.84	74.09	64.25	59.20	56.86	54.28	53.08
40	95.85	88.88	78.22	72.57	69.86	66.74	65.19
45	113.84	105.85	93.50	86.99	83.76	79.84	77.76
50	128.90	119.71	105.33	97.93	94.13	89.30	86.54
55	146.13	134.27	116.36	108.00	103.57	97.64	93.93

Add for Other Classes

Class							
4	$ 3.20	$ 2.60	$ 2.00	$ 1.60	$ 1.20	$ 0.80	$ 0.00
3	8.00	6.50	5.00	4.00	3.00	2.00	0.00

Add for Accident and Sickness Partial

Accident	Sickness	5	4	3
none	30 days or less	$11.00	$11.68	$12.70
30 days or less	30 days or less	9.00	9.52	10.30
over 30 days	over 30 days	7.00	7.52	8.30

TABLE 18-4. (cont'd.)

Add for Lifetime Accident (Applicant Age 50 or Older)	*$3.00*

Maximum Issue and Participation Limits

Benefit Period	Monthly Issue and Participation Limits
Two years or less	$1,800
All other benefit periods	1,500

Subject to the company's issue and participation limits, it will insure 60 per cent of a man's income less the following charge for Social Security benefits:

— less $100 per month, if insurance age is not over 35 and occupational Class 5, 4, or 3;
— less $200 per month for all others.

Social Security charge does not apply to one-year plans or to doctors of medicine

For semiannual premiums, divide by 2. For quarterly premiums, divide by 4

BIBLIOGRAPHY

The Health Insurance Product

American College of Life Underwriters. *Readings for Health Insurance—I* (Bryn Mawr, Pa.: 1968).

Angell, Frank J. *Health Insurance* (New York: The Ronald Press Company, 1963).

Bartelson, Edwin L., *et al. Health Insurance,* 2nd ed. (Chicago: The Society of Actuaries, 1968).

Bassford, Horace R. "Premium Rates, Reserves, and Nonforfeiture Values for Participating Policies," *Transactions of the Actuarial Society of America,* XLIII, 328–364.

Blue Cross Association and National Association of Blue Shield Plans. *The Blue Cross and Blue Shield Fact Book* (Chicago: 1971).

Brinker, Paul A. *Economic Insecurity and Social Security* (New York: Appleton-Century-Crofts, 1968).

Dickerson, O. D. *Health Insurance,* 3rd ed. (Homewood, Ill.: Richard D. Irwin, Inc., 1968).

Faulkner, E. J. *Health Insurance* (New York: McGraw-Hill Book Company, Inc., 1960).

Follman, J. F., Jr. *Medical Care and Health Insurance* (Homewood, Ill.: Richard D. Irwin, Inc., 1963).

Health Insurance Association of America. *Principles of Individual Health Insurance I* (New York: 1968).

Herrick, Kenneth W. *Total Disability Provisions in Life Insurance Contracts.* S. S. Huebner Foundation Studies (Homewood, Ill.: Richard D. Irwin, Inc., 1958).

Myers, Robert J. *Medicare* (Homewood. Ill.: Richard D. Irwin, Inc., 1969).

Osborne, Grant M. *Compulsory Temporary Disability Insurance in the United States.* S. S. Huebner Foundation Studies (Homewood, Ill.: Richard D. Irwin, Inc., 1958).

Pickerell, Jesse F. *Group Health Insurance,* rev. ed. S. S. Huebner Foundation Studies (Homewood, Ill.: Richard D. Irwin, Inc., 1961).

Turnbull, John G., Williams, C. Arthur, and Cheit, Earl F. *Economics and Social Security,* 3rd ed. (New York: The Ronald Press Company, 1968).

V The Mathematics
of Life Insurance

The Measurement of Risk | 19
in Life Insurance

INSURANCE HAS BEEN defined as an institution which eliminates risk or which substitutes certainty for uncertainty. The occurrence of events insured against cannot be wholly prevented, but the uncertainty of financial loss through such occurrences can be eliminated by distributing the loss over a group. Thus, a man cannot be sure whether or not his house will burn even if he uses all the preventive measures known. If the house burns, the property is lost and gone forever; that much material value has been actually destroyed. But it is not necessary that the owner should stand the entire loss. Before the fire occurred it was not known whether his house would burn or someone else's, and he could agree with other owners of houses that they would all contribute to a common fund from which any unfortunate owner who lost his house by fire should be reimbursed. Thus, instead of the loss falling on one it can be divided equally among all. This is the essence of insurance and it illustrates the meaning of the statement that insurance is the elimination of uncertainty or the replacement of uncertainty by certainty. The common contribution to the fund referred to above constitutes the certain loss and is measured by the premium; the uncertain loss refers to the uncertainty that a particular house will burn. The same situation exists with respect to life insurance. It is not death itself that can be distributed, that is, parceled out among a number of insurance companies, but the financial consequences of death. Man has an earning power during a certain period of his life which is lost to his business or his family by premature death, but it is not known in advance upon whom death will fall prematurely. Hence, all men can reasonably contribute to a fund which will be used to help satisfy the business and family needs of those who die early.

These two illustrations suggest the possibilities that exist for the application of the insurance principle. In whatever field risk is found to exist, the insurance principle has a possibility of application. The working out of a scientific insurance plan necessitates some method of measuring the risk involved in order to determine the amount of each individual's contribution to the common fund. The correct measurement of risk, therefore, lies at the foundation of any system of insurance. The measurement of risk is possible through the application to statistical data covering the phenomenon in question of mathematical laws known collectively as the theory of probability. These laws are discussed briefly before proceeding to a consideration of their application in the calculation of life insurance premium rates.

THE LAWS OF PROBABILITY

The laws of probability furnish three principles of which practical use is made in life and health insurance: (1) the law of certainty, (2) the law of simple probability, and (3) the law of compound probability. The use of these principles facilitates the description of risk in terms of mathematical values. The three laws may be stated as follows:

(1) certainty may be expressed by unity, or 1;

(2) simple probability, or the probability or chance that an event will happen or that it will not happen may be expressed by a fraction which may take a value of from 0 to 1; and

(3) compound probability, or the chance that two mutually independent events will happen [1] is the product of the separate probabilities that the events, taken separately, will happen.

An illustration should help to clarify these statements. If a box contains twenty marbles and it is known that five of the marbles are black and the remainder white, what is the probability that a marble, drawn at random from the box, will be black? If any marble has an equal chance with any other of being drawn, then there are twenty different draws that might be made. Since if five of the marbles are black, there are five chances out of twenty of drawing a black marble, the probability is in the ratio of five to twenty, or 5/20. Similarly, it might be desired to know the chance that the marble will not be black, and by similar reasoning it is found that this probability equals 15/20. From these facts it is possible to formulate a general statement of the method of determining *simple probabilities* as follows: The *denominator* will equal the total number of possible trials or chances that an event may happen or may not happen or the total number of instances dealt with—in the example above, total number of marbles. The *numerator* will be composed of only those instances which satisfy the conditions imposed—in the first example, the number of black marbles.

In the illustration used here there are marbles of two kinds only, black and white, and any marble withdrawn from the box must be one or the other color. The total existing probabilities are therefore two, the probability of drawing a black marble and the probability of drawing a white one. If

---

[1] There are laws of compound probability, for instance, where the separate events are dependent, but they do not enter into the present discussion.

certainty is represented by unity, then unity, or the value "1" will represent the fact of drawing any marble. But any marble drawn at random will be either black or white, and since the simple probability of drawing the former is 5/20, and the latter 15/20, therefore *certainty* must equal the *sum of all the separate probabilities,* in this case

$$5/20 + 15/20 = 1.$$

This corollary that certainty equals the sum of all separate probabilities may be further illustrated by the familiar example of the coin. It is certain that a coin tossed into the air will come to rest on one side and this fact is represented by the value "1." Now, since the coin has but two sides, the sum of the separate probabilities that it will alight heads up or tails up must equal 1. The probability of falling heads up, determined by the above rule for valuing simple probabilities, is ½, since there are two possible sides with equal chances and one is heads; likewise the probability of falling tails up is ½, and the *sum* of these two fractions or simple probabilities equals 1.

The *compound probability* that both of two mutually independent events will happen is equal to the *product* of the simple probabilities that the events taken separately will happen. Suppose that two coins are tossed up and it is desired to know the chance that they will both fall heads up. By the statement of the law above it will be ½ × ½, or ¼, since it is known that the chance is ½ that each separate coin will fall heads up. The correctness of this result may be demonstrated easily. Suppose the two coins are a nickel and a dime. Then the different ways in which they may fall are:

	NICKEL	DIME
1.	Heads up	Heads up
2.	Heads up	Tails up
3.	Tails up	Heads up
4.	Tails up	Tails up

These four combinations comprise the only possible ones that can be made with the two coins and the first combination is the only one of the four that satisfies the stipulated conditions, namely, both coins heads up. Hence, there is one chance in four for this combination to appear, or the probability of its occurrence is ¼.

According to the law of compound probabilities, only when the two events are mutually independent will the product of simple probabilities equal the probability that both events will happen. The happening of the one must have no effect upon the occurrence or non-occurrence of the other; that is, it must neither make it necessary for the second to occur nor make it impossible. If the law were valid irrespective of this qualification, such absurd results as the following might be obtained. The chance that the coin will fall heads up is ½ and the chance that it will fall tails up is likewise ½. Therefore, the chance that it will fall both heads up and tails up is ½ × ½, or ¼. The absurdity results from the fact that the occurrence of the first named event makes it impossible for the second to occur simultaneously.

THE USE OF PROBABILITY TO FORECAST FUTURE EVENTS

These three laws of probability are useful in estimating the likelihood of future events. Future events can be foretold in one of two ways: (1) by *a priori* or deductive reasoning, and (2) by inductive reasoning, i.e., from knowledge of what has happened in the past under similar conditions. The validity of *a priori* reasoning depends on the completeness with which all the causes at work in the determination of any phenomenon are known. The limitations of the human mind are such that *a priori* reasoning does not furnish a safe basis upon which to develop a superstructure guaranteeing that degree of certainty which is required in insurance. Reasoning inductively, or on the assumption that what has happened in the past will happen again in the future if the same conditions are present, does not require an analysis of the causes of phenomena in order to predict future events. Underlying this statement is the assumption that all things are governed by law. In the coin illustration the *law of pure chance* underlies the predictions. It is an even chance one with another that either side of the coin may be "up." Then if in a great number of trials it has been found that the coin falls "heads up" one half of the time the conclusion follows that this result will follow approximately if the same number of trials is taken again.

Inductive reasoning can also be applied to life insurance. From data showing the length of life and ages at death in the past it is possible to predict probabilities of death and of survival in the future. This prediction is based on the assumption that, like the law of chance, there is a *law of mortality* by which human beings die; that certain causes are in operation which determine that out of a large group of persons at birth a definite number of lives will fail each year until all have died; and that the force of mortality could be measured if only the causes at work were known. But it is not necessary to analyze this law of mortality completely and to know all the operating causes in order to predict fairly accurately the rate of mortality in a group of persons. By studying the rate of death among any group (if sufficiently large) and noting all the circumstances that might, according to our best knowledge, affect that rate, it is possible to surround any future group of persons with approximately the same set of circumstances and expect approximately the same rate of death. Thus, a working basis is available for predicting future rates of death. It is necessary then to have mortality statistics in order to develop a scientific plan of life insurance.

ACCURACY OF MORTALITY FORECASTS— THE LAW OF LARGE NUMBERS

The accuracy with which the theoretical estimates approximate actual experience has important bearings on the success of any method of insuring lives. This accuracy depends on two factors:

(1) the accuracy of the statistics underlying the estimates, and

(2) the number of units or trials taken.

With reference to the first factor, it should be obvious that accurate data is fundamental if an accurate measure of the law of mortality is to be obtained. Mortality statistics, from whatever source, should be scrutinized carefully in order to detect inaccuracies in the original data.

The second factor which determines the accuracy of the estimates based upon the laws of probability is the number of units or trials taken. This may be illustrated by the coin example presented previously. It was stated that the probability of falling heads up is ½. There is no inaccuracy in the data on which this fraction is based, for there are two sides only to the coin and one is heads.[2] To illustrate the accuracy dependent on the number of trials, the following experiment was undertaken. An ordinary copper cent was flipped three hundred times and the results, whether heads or tails up, were recorded for each ten throws. If the probable experience had agreed absolutely with the actual, the results would have shown five throws heads and five throws tails for each ten trials. The actual results are recorded in Table 19–1.

Table 19–1 shows that in thirty trials of ten throws each the actual experience coincided with the probable in eleven cases, that in two instances

TABLE 19-1.   Results of Each 100 Trials
in Groups of Ten

First 100	Heads	8–2–6–4–3–4–3–5–6–4	=	45
trials	Tails	2–8–4–6–7–6–7–5–4–6	=	55
Second 100	Heads	5–6–5–5–8–5–6–6–2–5	=	53
trials	Tails	5–4–5–5–2–5–4–4–8–5	=	47
Third 100	Heads	7–5–1–5–5–6–7–5–5–6	=	52
trials	Tails	3–5–9–5–5–4–3–5–5–4	=	48

---

[2] While it is possible for the coin to rest on its edge, this possibility is negligible and is ignored for purpose of this example.

TABLE 19-2. Results of 300 Throws by Specified Groupings

Number of Throws in Each Group		Number of Times Heads or Tails	Number of Groups
20	Heads	10–10– 7– 8–10–11–10–13–12– 7–12– 6–11–12–11	15
	Tails	10–10–13–12–10– 9–10– 7– 8–13– 8–14– 9– 8– 9	
30	Heads	16–11–14–15–18–17–14–11–18–16	10
	Tails	14–19–16–15–12–13–16–19–12–14	
50	Heads	23–22–29–24–23–29	6
	Tails	27–28–21–26–27–21	
100	Heads	45–53–52	3
	Tails	55–47–48	
300	Heads	150	1
	Tails	150	

heads appeared eight times out of ten, and in one case only once. These results in groups of ten may be combined into groups of twenty, thirty, fifty, one hundred, or in a single group of three hundred, and comparisons may then be made of the fluctuations in those respective groups. Organized in this fashion the original data assumes the form shown in Table 19–2.

In Table 19–2 the data are arranged in fifteen groups of twenty throws each, ten groups of thirty, six of fifty, three of one hundred, and a single group of the three hundred throws and the number of times the coin fell heads or tails is shown for each group. The important fact to be considered is the *relation between the expected and the actual experience in each grouping* of the data. For instance, in twenty throws the probability is that heads will appear ten times, but the figures show that in one case this result occurred thirteen times and once only six; in thirty throws heads appeared as many as eighteen times in two instances and as few as eleven the same number of times. Table 19–3 shows the maximum and the minimum number of times the coin turned heads up in any single trial of the specified number of throws.

TABLE 19-3.   Fluctuations in Number of Times Heads

In Groups of	Number of Times Tried	Maximum Number Times Heads Appeared	Minimum Number Times Heads Appeared
10 throws	30	8	1
20 throws	15	13	6
30 throws	10	18	11
50 throws	6	29	22
100 throws	3	53	45
300 throws	1	150	150

If these data are now reduced to the form of percentages, the results can be more readily compared, for the amount of the fluctuations will then have a common basis. It is understood that the probability that the coin will fall heads up is ½, and this will be represented by 50 per cent. The variation of the actual percentage from 50 per cent will therefore be the measure of the variation. Table 19–4 gives the results obtained.

Table 19–4 furnishes the basis for an important generalization with reference to the theory of probability. It shows that where the coin was thrown ten times the results varied from a minimum of 10 per cent to a maximum of 80 per cent; that where twenty throws were made, the variation was less, namely, from 30 to 65 per cent; and that as the number of throws increased the variation became smaller and smaller and the percentage of times heads appeared approached 50, the true probable percentage. That

TABLE 19-4.   Percentage of Times Heads Up

In Groups of	Maximum Per Cent	Minimum Per Cent
10	80	10.0
20	65	30.0
30	60	36.7
50	58	44.0
100	53	45.0
300	50	50.0

the three hundred throws resulted in exactly one hundred and fifty heads must be regarded as an accident; but it can be said with equal certainty that it would be extremely unlikely out of any three hundred purely chance throws that as many as 80 per cent or as few as 10 per cent would fall heads up. The generalization referred to above is as follows: Actual experience may show a variation from the true "probable" experience but as the number of trials is increased this variation decreases, and if a very great number of trials are taken, the actual and the probable experience will coincide. Specifically, if the coin were flipped ten million times and it were a pure chance which way it would fall, the actual results would be so near five million times heads that the difference would be negligible. This generalization is called the *law of large numbers*.[3] This law is fundamental to all insurance. Premium rates are based on estimates of future probabilities of loss. These estimates will not be valid representations of future experience unless insurance is provided a sufficiently large number of cases to guarantee that large fluctuations in results will be minimized. Prediction of future mortality rates in life insurance based on what has happened in the past can be made for a large group of persons; it cannot be made for a single individual or even a relatively small number (such as 1,000) of such persons. When a mortality table shows that persons of a certain age die at the rate of 7 per 1,000 per year that does not mean that out of a group of 1,000 exactly 7 will die within a year, but that out of a large group, containing perhaps many thousands, the deaths will occur approximately at the rate of 7 per 1,000.

With reference to the prediction of future mortality rates the law of large numbers has a *double application*. Future mortality will be estimated on the basis of past mortality data. But the statistics used for this purpose must include a sufficiently large group of representative individuals to ensure the operation of the law of large numbers. Assuming that the collected data are approximately correct and based on a large enough sample, they may

---

[3] This statistical principle is known as Bernoulli's Theorem in mathematical terminology.

be used to estimate future mortality. Then, in applying these mortality rates, a large enough number of individuals must be involved if the law of large numbers is to operate and the actual experience in the future is to be reasonably related to past experience.

MORTALITY STATISTICS

The establishment of any plan of insuring against uncertain death requires some means of giving mathematical values to the probabilities of death. The preceding discussion of the laws of probability demonstrated that this can be accomplished through the application of the laws of probability to mortality statistics or data which show the course of past mortality. Mortality tables are presentations of such data organized in a form to be usable in estimating the course of future deaths.

The two basic sources of mortality statistics are:

(1) population statistics derived from census enumerations and the returns of deaths from registration offices, and

(2) statistics derived from insured lives.

Both census enumerations and death registration records contain significant elements of error. Census data, collected by a large number of individuals through personal interviews, is particularly susceptible to error. For example, misclassification of information is frequent, inaccurate information is provided by the respondents, either willfully or inadvertently, tabulation errors creep in, and not infrequently ages are reported as unknown. Records of death provided to the National Office of Vital Statistics are frequently incomplete and inaccurate.[4]

At best, mortality tables based on population and death registration returns only approximately represent the actual mortality of the period. On the other hand, the mortality statistics of insured lives tend to be quite accurate. The nature of the insurance process leads to a careful recording of both the date of birth and date of death of insured individuals. This facilitates derivation of accurate death rates for the various ages.

The mortality experienced among insured lives is significantly different from that of the general population, because the insured lives have been subjected to the "selection of risk" process of the insurance company. Therefore, virtually all mortality tables used today by life insurance companies are based on the experience of insured lives.

It is important to remember that no matter how accurate the underlying mortality data is, a substantial volume of such data is essential to permit reliable predictions based thereon.

---

[4] Ample evidence of this is the fact that qualification for recognition as a "registration area" only requires 90 per cent of the probable deaths in an area.

CONSTRUCTION OF A MORTALITY TABLE

The theory of probability is applied in life insurance through the use of a mathematical model known as a mortality table. It represents a record of mortality observed in the past and is arranged in a form to show the probabilities of death and survival at each separate age. A mortality table has been described as "a generation of individuals passing through time." [5] It shows a group of individuals entering upon a certain age and traces the history of the entire group year by year until all have died. Since any description will best be understood by reference to an actual table, the *Commissioners 1958 Standard Ordinary Mortality Table* is presented in Table 19–5. This table is commonly referred to as the *1958 CSO Table* and is referred to by this abbreviation hereafter.

The heart of the table is the column of "yearly probabilities of dying," the yearly probability of surviving simply being the difference between the yearly probability of dying and certainty or one. The other essential features of a mortality table are the two columns of the "number living" and the "number dying" at designated ages. In the case of the *1958 CSO Table* it is assumed that a group of 10,000,000 males comes under observation at exactly the same moment as they enter upon the first year of life (age 0). Of this group 70,800 die during the year (10,000,000 × .00708), leaving 9,929,200 to begin the second year. The table proceeds in this manner to record the number dying during each year of life and the number living at the beginning of each succeeding year until only 6,415 persons of the original group are found to enter upon the one hundredth year of life (age 99), these 6,415 dying during that year.

The development of the appropriate series of death rates upon which any mortality table is based is the first and most basic step in its development. Since such a table is the basis upon which a life insurance company judges its financial commitments, it is important to understand the process by which it is constructed.

Derivation of Death Rates

It is manifestly impossible for any insurance company to insure a group of 10,000,000 persons of exactly the same age and at exactly the same time, and it is equally impossible to keep any such group under observation until all have died. Insurance policies are written at all times of the year and on lives at various ages. It is possible, however, for one company or a group of

[5] Arthur Newsholme, *Elements of Vital Statistics*, 3rd ed. (New York: The Macmillan Co., London; Sonnenschein & Co., 1899), p. 255.

TABLE 19-5. Commissioners 1958 Standard Ordinary (CSO) Mortality Table

(Male Lives)

Age at Beginning of Year	Number Living at Beginning of Designated Year (l_x)	Number Dying During Designated Year (d_x)	Yearly Probability of Dying (q_x)	Yearly Probability of Surviving (p_x)
0	10,000,000	70,800	.00708	.99292
1	9,929,200	17,475	.00176	.99824
2	9,911,725	15,066	.00152	.99848
3	9,896,659	14,449	.00146	.99854
4	9,882,210	13,835	.00140	.99860
5	9,868,375	13,322	.00135	.99865
6	9,855,053	12,812	.00130	.99870
7	9,842,241	12,401	.00126	.99874
8	9,829,840	12,091	.00123	.99877
9	9,817,749	11,879	.00121	.99879
10	9,805,870	11,865	.00121	.99879
11	9,794,005	12,047	.00123	.99877
12	9,781,958	12,325	.00126	.99874
13	9,769,633	12,896	.00132	.99868
14	9,756,737	13,562	.00139	.99861
15	9,743,175	14,225	.00146	.99854
16	9,728,950	14,983	.00154	.99846
17	9,713,967	15,737	.00162	.99838
18	9,698,230	16,390	.00169	.99831
19	9,681,840	16,846	.00174	.99826
20	9,664,994	17,300	.00179	.99821
21	9,647,694	17,655	.00183	.99817
22	9,630,039	17,912	.00186	.99814
23	9,612,127	18,167	.00189	.99811
24	9,593,960	18,324	.00191	.99809
25	9,575,636	18,481	.00193	.99807
26	9,557,155	18,732	.00196	.99804
27	9,538,423	18,981	.00199	.99801
28	9,519,442	19,324	.00203	.99797
29	9,500,118	19,760	.00208	.99792
30	9,480,358	20,193	.00213	.99787
31	9,460,165	20,718	.00219	.99781
32	9,439,447	21,239	.00225	.99775
33	9,418,208	21,850	.00232	.99768
34	9,396,358	22,551	.00240	.99760
35	9,373,807	23,528	.00251	.99749
36	9,350,279	24,685	.00264	.99736
37	9,325,594	26,112	.00280	.99720
38	9,299,482	27,991	.00301	.99699
39	9,271,491	30,132	.00325	.99675
40	9,241,359	32,622	.00353	.99647
41	9,208,737	35,362	.00384	.99616
42	9,173,375	38,253	.00417	.99583
43	9,135,122	41,382	.00453	.99547
44	9,093,740	44,741	.00492	.99508
45	9,048,999	48,412	.00535	.99465
46	9,000,587	52,473	.00583	.99417
47	8,948,114	56,910	.00636	.99364
48	8,891,204	61,794	.00695	.99305
49	8,829,410	67,104	.00760	.99240

TABLE 19-5. (cont'd.)

Age at Beginning of Year	Number Living at Beginning of Designated Year (l_x)	Number Dying During Designated Year (d_x)	Yearly Probability of Dying (q_x)	Yearly Probability of Surviving (p_x)
50	8,762,306	72,902	.00832	.99168
51	8,689,404	79,160	.00911	.99089
52	8,610,244	85,758	.00996	.99004
53	8,524,486	92,832	.01089	.98911
54	8,431,654	100,337	.01190	.98810
55	8,331,317	108,307	.01300	.98700
56	8,223,010	116,849	.01421	.98579
57	8,106,161	125,970	.01554	.98446
58	7,980,191	135,663	.01700	.98330
59	7,844,528	145,830	.01859	.98141
60	7,698,698	156,592	.02034	.97966
61	7,542,106	167,736	.02224	.97776
62	7,374,370	179,271	.02431	.97569
63	7,195,099	191,174	.02657	.97343
64	7,003,925	203,394	.02904	.97096
65	6,800,531	215,917	.03175	.96825
66	6,584,614	228,749	.03474	.96526
67	6,355,865	241,777	.03804	.96196
68	6,114,088	254,835	.04168	.95832
69	5,859,253	267,241	.04561	.95439
70	5,592,012	278,426	.04979	.95021
71	5,313,586	287,731	.05415	.94585
72	5,025,855	294,766	.05865	.94135
73	4,731,089	299,289	.06326	.93674
74	4,431,800	301,894	.06812	.93188
75	4,129,906	303,011	.07337	.92663
76	3,826,895	303,014	.07918	.92082
77	3,523,881	301,997	.08570	.91430
78	3,221,884	299,829	.09306	.90694
79	2,922,055	295,683	.10119	.89881
80	2,626,372	288,848	.10998	.89002
81	2,337,524	278,983	.11935	.88065
82	2,058,541	265,902	.12917	.87083
83	1,792,639	249,858	.13938	.86062
84	1,542,781	231,433	.15001	.84999
85	1,311,348	211,311	.16114	.83886
86	1,100,037	190,108	.17282	.82718
87	909,929	168,455	.18513	.81487
88	741,474	146,997	.19825	.80175
89	594,477	126,303	.21246	.78754
90	468,174	106,809	.22814	.77186
91	361,365	88,813	.24577	.75423
92	272,552	72,480	.26593	.73407
93	200,072	57,881	.28930	.71070
94	142,191	45,026	.31666	.68334
95	97,165	34,128	.35124	.64876
96	63,037	25,250	.40056	.59944
97	37,787	18,456	.48842	.51158
98	19,331	12,916	.66815	.33185
99	6,415	6,415	1.00000	.00000

companies to keep a record of all insured lives, showing at each age the number of persons under observation, the period of observation for each, and the number who have died. If a sufficient volume of data is collected, therefore, showing (1) the age at which persons come under observation, (2) the duration of the period of observation, and (3) the number dying at each age, a mortality table may be constructed.

Suppose, for illustration, that the following data have been collected:

Age	Number of Life-Years Observed	Number Dying Before End of Year
0	10,000	80
1	30,000	90
2	150,000	600
3	80,000	360
etc.	etc.	etc.

From these figures, death rates may be computed for the respective ages in the following manner:

Age	Rate of Death Expressed as a Fraction	Rate of Death Expressed as a Decimal
0	$\dfrac{80}{10,000}$	.0080
1	$\dfrac{90}{30,000}$	.0030
2	$\dfrac{600}{150,000}$	.0040
3	$\dfrac{360}{80,000}$	.0045
etc.	etc.	etc.

If the period of observation is more than one year, which it usually is, the "number under observation" is adjusted to reflect this fact. Thus, if the period of observation is five years, one individual under observation would be observed at five successive ages unless he died during the period. The deaths occurring at each age must, therefore, be compared with the total "exposure" at that age. For similar reasons an allowance would have to be made for the fact that policies which lapse are "exposed" for only part of the year.

It is assumed here that the above data reflect these and other necessary technical adjustments.

The rate of mortality at any given age is *the quotient of the number of deaths and the corresponding exposure for the period of study.*[6] The rate represents the probability that a person who has just attained a given age will die before he attains the next age. The rate of mortality is usually expressed in terms of the number of deaths "per thousand." The mortality table may be constructed by using an arbitrary number of persons (known as the radix) assumed to be alive at the youngest age for which death rates are available, and successively applying the mortality rates at each age.

Applying the death rates developed above will illustrate the process:

(1) Age	(2) Number Living at Given Age	(3) Probability of Dying	(4) Number of Deaths at Given Age (2) × (3)	(5) Number Living at Next Age (2) − (4)
0	10,000,000	.0080	80,000	9,920,000
1	9,920,000	.0030	29,760	9,890,240
2	9,890,240	.0040	39,561	9,850,679
3	9,850,679	.0045	44,328	9,806,351
4	9,806,351	etc.	etc.	etc.

Since the probability of dying at age 0 is .0080, there will occur 80,000 deaths during the year among the 10,000,000 starting at age 0. This leaves 9,920,000 of the group to begin age 1 and these die at the rate of three per thousand (.0030), making 29,760 deaths during the year. In this way the original 10,000,000 are reduced by deaths year after year until all have died. Thus, the basis of the statement that the mortality table represents "a generation of individuals passing through time."

Since the radix of the table is arbitrary,[7] the numbers in the columns headed "number living" and "number of deaths" are not significant in and of themselves. They simply reflect the series of death rates, the real heart of a mortality table.

Sometimes a mortality table has an additional column showing the "expectation of life" or "life expectancy" at each age. The figure in this column

---

[6] The distinction between "mortality rates," as the above rates are called by actuaries, and "probabilities of death," and the method of obtaining the latter from the former cannot be explained in the space available here. For purposes of simplification, death rates and probabilities of death are therefore assumed to be identical. For the construction of a mortality table, *probabilities of death* are necessary and they have reference to rates of dying among a group of persons *beginning* a certain age of life.

[7] The radix for the *American Experience Table,* for example, was 100,000 at age 10; for the *1941 CSO Table,* it was 1,000,000 at age 1; and the *1958 CSO Table,* 10,000,000 at age 0.

opposite any age is the *average* number of years of life lived after attaining that age by all who reach that age. "Expectation of life" is a misleading term since it has no significance whatever for any individual and does not show the probable future lifetime of an individual. The probable future lifetime of any individual depends on many factors, including his state of health, and may be greater or less than average. It is quite commonly supposed that life insurance companies make their calculations of premium rates, etc., on the assumption that everyone will live for the period of his "life expectancy." That is not the case, as will be explained in the following chapters. In fact, the only practical use of the "expectation of life" is for the purpose of comparing one mortality table with another.

Adjustments to Mortality Data

A mortality table used by a life insurance company in calculating premium rates or reserves does not reflect the precise mortality rates developed from the basic mortality data. Due to the fact that the volume of experience is not uniform and is insufficient to provide completely creditable or reliable statistics, two types of adjustments may be made to the derived rates:

(1) the rates are "smoothed" into a curve by a process known as *graduation* and

(2) a *margin* may be added to the derived curve.

Graduation is performed to eliminate the irregularities in the observed data which are not believed to be true characteristics of the universe from which the sample experience was extracted. One of several methods of graduation is used, depending upon the judgment of the actuary, the nature of the data involved, and the purpose of the computation. The objective in all cases, however, is to introduce smoothness and regularity, while at the same time preserving the basic characteristics of the observed values.

The addition of a margin to the derived rates is done where the rates will be used as a *valuation table* [8] and is in the interest of safety. In a life insurance mortality table used to value policy liabilities this means showing higher death rates than those actually expected; in an annuity valuation table, on the other hand, it means showing lower rates of mortality than those expected. Thus, the *1958 CSO Table* [9] is a life insurance valuation table and has margins built into the table. It should be noted that such a margin may also be provided by adjusting the underlying data prior to the derivation of the basic rates themselves. In any case the insertion of such margins enhances the security behind life insurance contracts and is considered a sound practice. It should be noted, however, that where a table will be used for gross premium and asset share studies,[10] a "basic experience" table,

[8] See pp. 398–401.
[9] See pp. 325–326.
[10] See pp. 410–419.

representing the most probable level of mortality, is needed and no margins for conservatism are added to the basic derived table of rates.

KINDS OF MORTALITY TABLES

Select, Ultimate, and Aggregate Tables

Mortality tables may be classified as *select, ultimate,* and *aggregate.* These terms have reference to the extent to which the data used have been affected by medical selection. It is a well-known fact that lives which have been newly examined by an insurance company and have passed the medical and other tests required before becoming policyholders show a lower rate of mortality than lives not so examined. The number of deaths occurring among 10,000 policyholders aged 40 who have just passed a medical examination can be expected to be fewer than among 10,000 aged 40 who were insured at age 30, and have been policyholders for ten years. So it is important for a company in estimating the probable mortality to know whether it has a large number of newly selected lives.

A *select* mortality table is based on data of freshly selected lives only; an *ultimate* table excludes this early data, usually the first five to fifteen years following entry, and is based on the *ultimate* mortality among insured lives. *Aggregate* tables include all the mortality data, the early years following entry as well as the later. Since newly selected lives, therefore, furnish a lower mortality, it is generally considered the safer plan for a company to compute reserve liabilities on the basis of the mortality among risks for whom the benefits of fresh medical selection have passed.

Technically, a select mortality table is one which shows the rate of mortality both *by age* and also *by duration of insurance.* Since the greatest effect of selection usually wears off in about five to fifteen years, the mortality rates are usually differentiated by duration only for such a period. An example of a select mortality table is presented in Table 19–6. The rates shown in Column "6 & over" constitute the ultimate mortality level and could be used in the development of an ultimate mortality table.

Select tables are used for purposes of analysis and comparison. The *basic tables* prepared and published by the Mortality Committee of the Society of Actuaries from data supplied by a group of established companies are constructed to show both select and ultimate mortality since their primary purpose is to reflect mortality trends.[11]

The mortality tables used in expressing participating life insurance premiums are usually ultimate tables based on the "ultimate" mortality data. Select mortality is used frequently, however, in asset share calculations test-

---

[11] The *ultimate* rates of mortality reflected in these tables, however, are used widely in the calculation of nonparticipating premiums.

TABLE 19-6. Select Mortality Table—Rates per 1,000

Age at Issue	Year of Insurance						Attained Age
	1	2	3	4	5	6 & over	
25	0.71	0.82	0.88	0.93	0.97	1.01	30
26	0.72	0.82	0.89	0.96	1.00	1.06	31
27	0.73	0.83	0.92	0.99	1.05	1.12	32
28	0.74	0.84	0.93	1.03	1.11	1.21	33
29	0.74	0.84	0.97	1.08	1.20	1.32	34
30	0.74	0.86	1.02	1.16	1.31	1.44	35

ing tentative participating gross premiums, in dividend calculations, and in the calculation of nonparticipating gross premiums.[12]

Mortality Tables for Annuities

A mortality table based on life insurance experience is not suitable for use in connection with annuities for several reasons. One reason is that annuities are generally purchased only by individuals in good health. At the higher ages (particularly in the case of annuity contracts purchased by single premiums for immediate income), the rates of mortality experienced among annuitants are generally lower than among life insurance policyholders. A life insurance mortality table would overstate the mortality rates to be expected and would not be an appropriate basis for annuity premiums and reserves.

Another important reason is that the constant improvement in mortality rates provides a gradually increasing margin of safety for life insurance but has the opposite result in the case of annuities. In fact, it has now been generally recognized that no annuity mortality table based on past experience (a "static" table) can safely be used as is and that what is now needed is a table that will show the (lower) rates of mortality anticipated in the future rather than the rates which have been experienced in the past. Such a table is known as a "table with projection."

Static Tables vs. Tables with Projection

All life insurance mortality tables in use today are "static" tables in that they are based on data taken from a "static" period of time. As the secular trend toward mortality improvement has continued, periodically these "static" tables have been replaced by other "static" tables based on more recent experience. The improvement in mortality has led to increasing mar-

[12] See pp. 410–419.

gins in life insurance premiums, since the "postponement" in death payment enables the companies to earn *additional* interest on their invested funds and to collect additional premiums. The situation has been just the reverse in connection with annuity contracts. Here the improving mortality has led to smaller margins, since postponement of death has led to the payment of additional annuity payments. Nevertheless, until 1949, "static" annuity tables were used exclusively by United States life insurance companies. To avoid the large expense of constructing new static tables *frequently,* allowance was made for the decrease in mortality rates by using age "setbacks," i.e., the static table was continued in use, but the rates shown in the table were *assumed* to apply to lower actual ages.[13] Setbacks of one to four years are used by many companies. In 1949 a table (*The Annuity Table for 1949*) was published, together with projection factors on different bases which could be applied to the basic (1949) table to make allowance for future reductions in mortality rates. The construction of such projected tables is too technical to be discussed here, but such tables are now in general use. The importance of providing for mortality improvement in annuity mortality tables can be seen when it is noted that annuity business [14] constitutes a significant and growing proportion of a life insurance company's total business.

Published Tables in Use Today

There are a number of well-known ordinary mortality tables in use in the United States today by life insurance companies. The *Commissioners 1941 Standard Ordinary Table* (*1941 CSO Table*), which was used very extensively for policies issued between 1948 and 1966, is based on a compilation of mortality experience of a group of United States and Canadian companies for the decade 1930–1940. For many years prior to the advent of the *1941 CSO Table,* the *American Experience Table of Mortality* was widely used. The *1941 CSO Table* is still of great importance because a large proportion of insurance now outstanding is based on this table. The *American Experience Table* was published in 1868 by Sheppard Homans and was calculated from the mortality experience of the Mutual Life Insurance Company of New York. Another table, the *American Men Mortality Table,* which was published in 1918, also found limited use.

The first special mortality table based upon industrial life insurance experience was the *Standard Industrial Mortality Table* in general use until 1948. In 1941 a new table, the *1941 Standard Industrial Mortality Table,* was developed and adopted as the mortality basis for the calculation of

---

[13] For example, a person who is actually 65 is assumed, for purposes of premium calculations, to be subject to the mortality rates of a man of 64 or 63, thus increasing the premium for a given amount of income.

[14] Including, in addition to individual annuities, group annuities and settlement option arrangements amounting, in some companies, to more than half their business when measured in terms of policy reserves.

minimum reserve and surrender values for industrial life insurance policies. Effective January 1, 1968, however, the *Commissioners 1961 Standard Industrial Mortality Table* became the legal basis for the calculation of minimum reserve and surrender values for all new business. Each of these tables is what was described earlier as an ultimate table.

There are three well-known individual annuity tables in use, the *1937 Standard Annuity Mortality Table,* the *Annuity Table for 1949,* and the *1955 American Annuity Table,* which will be discussed further in connection with annuities.

There are two group tables in use today, the *Group Annuity Table for 1951* and the *Commissioners 1960 Standard Group Mortality Table,* both of which are referred to later.[15]

While of little practical importance, it is historically important to note that the *Actuaries'* or *Seventeen Offices Table,* which in large measure preceded the *American Experience Table,* was of British origin and was introduced into the United States by Elizur Wright as the standard for the valuation of policies in Massachusetts.

The *1958 CSO Table,* developed jointly by the Society of Actuaries and the National Association of Insurance Commissioners, is mandatory as the basis for minimum reserves [16] and nonforfeiture values [17] of ordinary business currently being issued. It was developed, among other reasons, in an effort to eliminate deficiency reserves [18] which had become a serious problem for many stock life insurance companies.

The basic data were derived from the mortality experience of fifteen large companies for the period 1950–54 and were compiled by the Society of Actuaries Committee on Mortality under Lives Individually Insured. Additional data were examined and compared before the *1958 CSO Table* was finally approved and so designated.

OTHER CONSIDERATIONS

Application of the Laws of Probabilities to the Mortality Table

The statement was made earlier in this chapter that risk in life insurance is measured by the application of the laws of probability to the mortality table. Now that these laws are understood and the mortality table has been explained, a few simple illustrations may be used to show this application. Suppose it is desired to estimate the probability of a man's death within one, two, or five years from age 35. This probability, according to the laws

[15] See Chapters 34 and 35.
[16] See pp. 398–400.
[17] See pp. 431–433.
[18] See pp. 400–401.

explained earlier, will be determined according to a selected mortality table and will be a fraction, of which the denominator equals the number living at age 35 and the numerator will be the number who have died during the one, two, or five years, respectively, following that age. According to the *1958 CSO Table,* 9,373,807 men are living at age 35, and 23,528 die before the end of the year. Hence, the probability of death in one year is $\dfrac{23,528}{9,373,807}$. During the two years following the stated age, there are 23,528 + 24,685 deaths, or a total of 48,213. The probability of dying within two years is therefore $\dfrac{48,213}{9,373,807}$. Likewise, the total number of deaths within five years is 23,528 + 24,685 + 26,112 + 27,991 + 30,132, or 132,448, and the probability of a man entering age 35 dying within five years is thus $\dfrac{132,448}{9,373,807}$.

Probabilities of survival can also be expressed by the table. The chance of living one year following age 35 will be a fraction, of which the denominator is 9,373,807 and the numerator is the number who have lived one year following the specified age. This is the number who are living at the beginning of age 36, or 9,350,279. These illustrations furnish an opportunity for an illustration of the law of certainty. The chance of living one year following age 35 is $\dfrac{9,350,279}{9,373,807}$, and the chance of dying within the same period is $\dfrac{23,528}{9,373,807}$. The sum of these two fractions equals $\dfrac{9,373,807}{9,373,807}$, or 1, which is certainty, and certainty represents the sum of all separate possibilities, in this case two, the probability of death and the probability of survival. In like manner many more instructive examples of the application of these laws to the mortality table could be made, but they need not be carried further at this point, for the subject is fully covered in the chapters on net premiums.

Use of Mortality Tables in Rate-Making

The discussion in the following chapters utilizes the *1958 CSO Table* in illustrating the principles involved in rate-making. The *1958 CSO Table* is not, however, used by life insurance companies as the primary basis for establishing premium rates. They use tables reflecting up-to-date experience (often based upon the company's *own* most recent experience) in establishing premium rates, despite the fact that they may use the *1958 CSO Table* for reserve valuation and nonforfeiture value purposes. As is explained in a later chapter, gross premiums and estimated dividend scales (in the case of participating policies) are both tested through asset share studies under realistic assumptions before they are used.

Fundamental Principles | 20
Underlying Rate-Making |

As POINTED OUT earlier, the level premium plan of providing life insurance protection leads to the accumulation of large sums of money which are held by the companies many years before being paid in satisfaction of their liabilities. The funds are invested in income-producing assets and these earnings permit life insurance companies to "discount" premiums in advance in anticipation of such earnings.

Interest plays such a vital role in the actuarial calculations and the actual operations of a life insurance company that it is essential to consider some of the more important concepts associated with the interest function before proceeding with an analysis of life insurance rate-making.

INTEREST

Basic Terminology

Interest may be defined as the price paid for the use of money. The original investment, referred to as the *principal,* accumulates by the end of a specified term to a sum, referred to as the *amount.* The interest earned for this particular period is the difference of the amount less the principal.

The most common way of expressing interest is as a per cent of the principal on an annual basis. For example, if $2.50 were paid for the use of $100 for one year, interest amounting to $2.50/$100, or 2½ per cent, per year would be earned. This interest earnings rate could be expressed as being at a 2½ per cent *rate per annum.*

335

In order to abbreviate terms such as principal, amount, and rate per annum when working with investments, symbolic codes may be used for ease. Certain codes are used throughout the majority of interest texts and tables, and these codes will be presented with explanations such as follows:

$$I = \text{Interest}$$
$$S = \text{Amount}$$
$$P = \text{Principal}$$
$$i = \text{Rate per Annum}$$

By use of these symbolic codes, the statement that *amount* is equal to *principal* plus *interest* may be expressed as: $S = P + I$. The statement that interest is equal to principal times rate per annum may be expressed as: $I = Pi$. By rewriting our statement for amount using our new codes for I from our statement defining interest, we obtain: $S = P + Pi$ or $S = P(1 + i)$. The equation $S = P(1 + i)$ states that the amount to which principal will accumulate in one year at a given rate per annum is equal to the principal multiplied by one plus the rate per annum.

If interest is paid to the investor at the end of each interest period, assumed to be one year in this section, the interest is described as *simple interest*. In many cases, as is the case for life insurance calculations, interest earnings will be left with the original principal in order to earn interest on the interest already earned. When interest is not distributed but used to earn additional funds, it is described as *compound interest*.

Basic Compound Interest Functions

Four basic compound interest functions are often used in insurance rate-making. An understanding of these functions is important for all interested in the area of insurance as well as any other area of finance.

From time to time it is necessary to be able to project values to answer questions as follows:

(1) To what amount will $1 grow in N years at a given rate per annum?

(2) What principal must be invested now at a given rate per annum in order to accumulate $1 in N years?

(3) To what amount will $1 of principal deposited at the beginning of each year grow in N years at a given rate per annum?

(4) What principal must be invested now at a given rate per annum in order to obtain payments of $1 at the end of each year for N years?

Volumes of interest tables have been computed for answering these four major interest questions. By knowing interest values for $1, it is necessary only to multiply the appropriate interest value for $1 by the actual amount involved.

Accumulated Value of $1

The amount to which principal will accumulate in one year at a given rate per annum has been expressed earlier as: $S_1 = P (1 + i)$. Upon investing this amount for an additional year, the interest for the second year would be i times S_1. The amount at the end of the second year could then be expressed as: $S_2 = P (1 + i) + i S_1$, or, $S_2 = P (1 + i) + i P (1 + i)$, or, $S_2 = P (1 + i) (1 + i) = P (1 + i)^2$.

By continuing to use simple algebra, it may be shown that the accumulated value of P at the end of N years may be expressed as: $S = P (1 + i)^N$. Since interest tables are shown for $1 of principal in this case, the values $(1 + i)^N$ may be found in the appropriate interest table and multiplied by the principal in order to determine the amount.

Present Value of $1

In all financial areas it is often necessary to set a particular amount required at the end of a particular period and invest now to achieve this goal.

Since we have determined that $S = P (1 + i)^N$, it is only necessary to divide both sides of this equation by $(1 + i)^N$ to determine an expression for P as: $P = S / (1 + i)^N$. In order to determine the present value of the amount, the principal, it is only necessary to divide the amount, S, by $(1 + i)^N$.

Noting that $S / (1 + i)^N$ is equivalent to S times $1 / (1 + i)^N$, tables for the value $1 / (1 + i)^N$ were computed. These tables are referred to as the present value of $1 and are at times labeled as V^N rather than $1 / (1 + i)^N$ with V being a code given to the term $1 / (1 + i)$. The V tables must have been designated in order that a multiplication rather than division could be performed to obtain present value results.

Accumulated Value of $1 Per Year

In order to determine the accumulated amount when equal annual payments are made at the beginning of each year for N years, it is only necessary to add the amounts to which each of the payments will grow. For example, suppose an investment of $1 at the beginning of each year is made for 3 years. The first $1 will grow to an amount of $(1 + i)^3$. The second $1 will grow to an amount of $(1 + i)^2$, and the third $1 will grow to an amount of $(1 + i)$. The total amount at the end of three years may be expressed as: $\ddot{S}_{\overline{3}|} = (1 + i) + (1 + i)^2 + (1 + i)^3$ where $\ddot{S}_{\overline{N}|}$ is a code meaning the accumulated value of $1 invested at the beginning of each year for N years.

Present Value of $1 Per Year

The present value of equal annual payments obtained at the end of each year for N years may be computed by summing the present value of each payment. For example, suppose we wish to find the present value of $1 payable at the end of each year for three years. The present value of the first, second, and third payments are V^1, V^2, and V^3 respectively. The total present value may be expressed as: $a_{\overline{3}|} = V^1 + V^2 + V^3$ where $a_{\overline{N}|}$ is a code meaning the present value of $1 paid at the end of each year for N years.

Interest Tables

Table 20–1 is an example of how the four basic compound interest functions may be exhibited. Such tables are readily available in published form for various assumed rates of interest. Table 20–2 shows the present value of $1 function for three different rates of interest.

Interest Table Usage

After an explanation of the basic compound interest functions, certain examples utilizing interest tables may be helpful as a review:
1. To what amount will $100 grow in 20 years at 2½ per cent per annum?
    $$\$100 \ (1 + i)^{20} = \$100 \ (1.63862) = \$163.82$$
2. What principal must be invested now at 2½ per cent per annum in order to accumulate $100 in 20 years?
    $$\$100 \ (V^{20}) = \$100 \ (.61027) = \$61.03$$
3. To what amount will $100 deposited at the beginning of each of 20 years accumulate at 2½ per cent per annum?
    $$\$100 \ (\ddot{S}_{\overline{20}|}) = \$100 \ (26.18327) = \$2,618.33$$
4. What principal must be invested now at 2½ per cent per annum in order to obtain $100 at the end of each of 20 years?
    $$\$100 \ (a_{\overline{20}|}) = \$100 \ (15.58916) = \$1,558.92$$

TABLE 20-1. Interest Table for Four Basic Compound Interest Functions Rate, Per Annum 2.5 Per Cent

Year	Accumulated Value of $1	Present Value of $1	Accumulated Value of $1 Per Year	Present Value of $1 Per Year
1	1.02500	0.97561	1.02500	0.97561
2	1.05062	0.95181	2.07562	1.92742
3	1.07689	0.92860	3.15252	2.85602
4	1.10381	0.90595	4.25633	3.76197
5	1.13141	0.88385	5.38774	4.64583
6	1.15969	0.86230	6.54743	5.50813
7	1.18869	0.84127	7.73612	6.34939
8	1.21840	0.82075	8.95452	7.17014
9	1.24886	0.80073	10.20338	7.97087
10	1.28008	0.78120	11.48347	8.75206
11	1.31209	0.76214	12.79555	9.51421
12	1.34489	0.74356	14.14044	10.25776
13	1.37851	0.72542	15.51895	10.98319
14	1.41297	0.70773	16.93192	11.69091
15	1.44830	0.69047	18.38022	12.38138
16	1.48451	0.67363	19.86473	13.05500
17	1.52162	0.65720	21.38635	13.71220
18	1.55966	0.64117	22.94600	14.35336
19	1.59865	0.62553	24.54465	14.97889
20	1.63862	0.61027	26.18327	15.58916
21	1.67958	0.59539	27.86285	16.18455
22	1.72157	0.58086	29.58442	16.76541
23	1.76461	0.56670	31.34903	17.33211
24	1.80873	0.55288	33.15776	17.88499
25	1.85394	0.53939	35.01170	18.42438
26	1.90029	0.52623	36.91199	18.95061
27	1.94780	0.51340	38.85979	19.46401
28	1.99649	0.50088	40.85629	19.96489
29	2.04641	0.48866	42.90269	20.45355
30	2.09757	0.47674	45.00026	20.93029
31	2.15001	0.46511	47.15026	21.39541
32	2.20376	0.45377	49.35402	21.84918
33	2.25885	0.44270	51.61287	22.29188
34	2.31532	0.43191	53.92819	22.72379
35	2.37320	0.42137	56.30139	23.14516
36	2.43253	0.41109	58.73393	23.55625
37	2.49335	0.40107	61.22728	23.95732
38	2.55568	0.39129	63.78296	24.34860
39	2.61957	0.38174	66.40253	24.73035
40	2.68506	0.37243	69.08759	25.10278
41	2.75219	0.36335	71.83978	25.46612
42	2.82099	0.35449	74.66077	25.82061
43	2.89152	0.34584	77.55229	26.16645
44	2.96381	0.33740	80.51610	26.50385
45	3.03790	0.32917	83.55400	26.83303
46	3.11385	0.32115	86.66785	27.15417
47	3.19170	0.31331	89.85954	27.46748
48	3.27149	0.30567	93.13103	27.77316
49	3.35327	0.29822	96.48431	28.07137
50	3.43711	0.29094	99.92141	28.36231

TABLE 20-2. Present Value of $1 to Be Received at End of Various Periods
at Various Rates of Compound Interest

End of Year	2 Per Cent	2½ Per Cent	3 Per Cent
1	0.980392	0.975610	0.970874
2	0.961169	0.951814	0.942596
3	0.942322	0.928599	0.915142
4	0.923845	0.905951	0.888487
5	0.905731	0.883854	0.862609
6	0.887971	0.862297	0.837484
7	0.870560	0.841265	0.813092
8	0.853490	0.820747	0.789409
9	0.836755	0.800728	0.766417
10	0.820348	0.781198	0.744094
11	0.804263	0.762145	0.722421
12	0.788493	0.743556	0.701380
13	0.773033	0.725420	0.680951
14	0.757875	0.707727	0.661118
15	0.743015	0.690466	0.641862
16	0.728446	0.673625	0.623167
17	0.714163	0.657195	0.605016
18	0.700159	0.641166	0.587395
19	0.686431	0.625528	0.570286
20	0.672971	0.610271	0.553676
21	0.659776	0.595386	0.537549
22	0.646839	0.580865	0.521893
23	0.634156	0.566697	0.506692
24	0.621721	0.552875	0.491934
25	0.609531	0.539391	0.477606
26	0.597579	0.526235	0.463693
27	0.585862	0.513400	0.450189
28	0.574375	0.500878	0.437077
29	0.563112	0.488661	0.424346
30	0.552071	0.476743	0.411987
31	0.541246	0.465115	0.399987
32	0.530633	0.453771	0.388337
33	0.520229	0.442703	0.377026
34	0.510028	0.431905	0.366045
35	0.500028	0.421371	0.355383
36	0.490223	0.411094	0.345032
37	0.480611	0.401067	0.334983
38	0.471187	0.391285	0.325226
39	0.461948	0.381741	0.315754
40	0.452890	0.372431	0.306557
41	0.444010	0.363347	0.297628
42	0.435304	0.354485	0.288959
43	0.426769	0.345839	0.280543
44	0.418401	0.337404	0.272372
45	0.410197	0.329174	0.264439
46	0.402154	0.321146	0.256737
47	0.394268	0.313313	0.249259
48	0.386538	0.305671	0.241999
49	0.378958	0.298216	0.234950
50	0.371528	0.290942	0.228107

TABLE 20-2. (cont'd.)

End of Year	2 Per Cent	2½ Per Cent	3 Per Cent
51	0.364243	0.283846	0.221463
52	0.357101	0.276923	0.215013
53	0.350099	0.270169	0.208750
54	0.343234	0.263579	0.202670
55	0.336504	0.257151	0.196767
56	0.329906	0.250879	0.191036
57	0.323437	0.244760	0.185472
58	0.317095	0.238790	0.180070
59	0.310878	0.232966	0.174825
60	0.304782	0.227284	0.169733
61	0.298806	0.221740	0.164789
62	0.292947	0.216332	0.159990
63	0.287203	0.211055	0.155330
64	0.381572	0.205908	0.150806
65	0.276051	0.200886	0.146413
66	0.270638	0.195986	0.142149
67	0.265331	0.191206	0.138009
68	0.260129	0.186542	0.133989
69	0.255028	0.181992	0.130086
70	0.250028	0.177554	0.126297
71	0.245125	0.173223	0.122619
72	0.240319	0.168998	0.119047
73	0.235607	0.164876	0.115580
74	0.230987	0.160855	0.112214
75	0.226458	0.156931	0.108945
76	0.222017	0.153104	0.105772
77	0.217664	0.149370	0.102691
78	0.213396	0.145726	0.099700
79	0.209212	0.142172	0.096796
80	0.205110	0.138705	0.093977
81	0.201088	0.135322	0.091240
82	0.197145	0.132021	0.088582
83	0.193279	0.128801	0.086002
84	0.189490	0.125659	0.083497
85	0.185774	0.122595	0.081065
86	0.182132	0.119605	0.078704
87	0.178560	0.116687	0.076412
88	0.175059	0.113841	0.074186
89	0.171627	0.111065	0.072026
90	0.168261	0.108356	0.069928
91	0.164962	0.105713	0.067891
92	0.161728	0.103135	0.065914
93	0.158556	0.100619	0.063994
94	0.155448	0.098165	0.062130
95	0.152400	0.095771	0.060320
96	0.149411	0.093435	0.058563
97	0.146482	0.091156	0.056858
98	0.143610	0.088933	0.055202
99	0.140794	0.086764	0.053594
100	0.138033	0.084647	0.052033

ASSUMPTIONS UNDERLYING
RATE COMPUTATIONS

When the problem of rate computation is approached, it will be found that several questions present themselves at once; the answers to them will exercise much influence upon the results to be obtained. For instance, how is the premium to be paid? Is it to be paid in a single sum which will cover the risk for the entire period, as is the case with most other kinds of insurance contracts, or will periodic payments be made annually, semi-annually, or otherwise? Again, when is it to be paid? In case of annual premiums, will they be paid at the inception of the risk and annually thereafter, or will some other time be found? Further questions are: What will be done with the money between the time it is received and the time it is paid out? How will mortality rates be determined for periods of less than one year's duration in case, for instance, monthly premiums are decided upon, since the standard mortality tables give nothing less than yearly rates of mortality? And finally, when will death claims be paid? Clearly these questions must be answered before beginning the computation of rates, and their answers will furnish a method of procedure in rate-making.

Premiums may be paid in a single cash sum, called the single premium, which pays for the entire risk incurred during the life of the policy, or they may be paid in periods ranging from one week to one year. Many policies are purchased by an annual premium. When actuaries first set themselves to the task of computing premium rates, they laid down the following working rules: (1) premiums will be paid at the beginning of each policy year; and (2) matured claims will be paid at the end of the policy year in which the policy matures.[1] Accordingly, if a policy is purchased by a single premium, this sum is to be paid at the inception of the risk; in the case of level annual premiums the first payment is to be made on the date of issue of the policy and equal amounts annually thereafter on the anniversary of this date.

It is evident in the case of single premiums, and it is true only in lesser degree with annual premiums, that the company will have the money on hand for some time before being called upon to pay matured claims. The question of the use of the money in the meantime therefore arises. This money is invested and made to earn interest while in the company's possession, and it is proper that these interest earnings be regarded as one

---

[1] When the *1958 CSO Table* was adopted, many companies assumed that claims are paid at the moment of death. This is done through the use of "continuous functions." The technical details of this practice are beyond the scope of this volume.

source of the fund available to pay claims. But since the company does not know in advance what rate of interest will be earned it is necessary to assume a rate which is reasonably certain of being earned each year throughout the long life of the policy. And since much of the premium money received by the company is held for a number of years before being paid out in the form of matured claims it will be possible to earn *interest* on interest. The importance of compound interest accumulations to an insurance company is evident from the following figures showing, first, the amount of money obtained from investing $1,000 at different rates of interest for fifty years and, second, the amount of money which must be invested in the beginning to equal $1,000 in fifty years, at different rates of interest:

Amount of $1,000 in 50 years	at 2 %	=	$ 2,692
	at 2½	=	3,437
	at 3	=	4,384
	at 4	=	7,107
	at 5	=	11,467
	at 6	=	18,420
Present worth of $1,000 due 50 years hence	at 2 %	=	$371.50
	at 2½	=	290.90
	at 3	=	228.10
	at 4	=	140.70
	at 5	=	87.20
	at 6	=	54.30

In other words, if 6 per cent interest can be guaranteed on an investment, $1,000 may be put away now and at the end of fifty years it will have accumulated to $18,420; or in order to pay a debt of $1,000 fifty years hence it is necessary to put away only $54.30 and earn *compound interest* on it at the rate of 6 per cent.[2] These facts are highly important to the insurance company, which is often called upon to keep policies in force for fifty years. Table 20–2 shows discounted values for typical interest assumptions.

In determining the interest rate to be assumed in computing premiums it is necessary to select a rate which the company is *sure* of earning on the average over a long period of years. The assumption that 5 or 6 per cent could be earned would most surely be disastrous, for while the company might conceivably earn that rate in an unusually prosperous year, this period might be succeeded by a decrease in earnings and in the market value of securities or real estate. If the company should fail to earn the assumed 5 or 6 per cent rate, it would be called upon to replenish its in-

[2] It should be noted that only $4,000 would result from using simple interest, and thus $14,420 of the $18,420 is a result of the compounding concept.

adequate earnings from surplus or, in the absence of the latter, might be forced into bankruptcy. This makes it necessary for the company to assume a rate of interest which can be earned on the average regardless of the temporary fluctuations of the investment market, even in times of business depression. Companies issuing participating insurance will generally select a very conservative interest rate, with the intention and expectation of returning to the policyholder, through dividends, excess interest earnings over the rate selected. A typical rate used by participating companies for original rate computations is 2½ per cent. Where policies are made participating it makes little difference what rate is used so long as it is not too large, since all earnings are eventually returned to the policyholder in the form of dividends; and the lower the rate used the better will a company be able to weather a period of low interest rates. Companies issuing nonparticipating insurance will select an interest rate which they estimate can safely be earned over a lengthy period. A typical rate used by nonparticipating companies at this time is 3¾ per cent.

The second rule referred to above stated that matured claims would be assumed to be paid at the end of the policy year. Some time for the payment of claims must clearly be determined in order to know how long the money will draw interest before being paid. If it can be assumed that there will be a fairly even distribution of deaths throughout the year, the payment of claims, then based on this assumption, would occur six months after death. In the early experience of life insurance companies this was not far from the truth, for it took about three months to make proof of death, and old policies allowed the company three months after proof before the claim was payable. At the present time, however, claims are paid promptly, one prominent company, for instance, advertising that over 95 per cent of its claims are paid within one working day of receipt of proofs of death. The importance of this consideration lies in the fact that the assumption is overly generous, to the extent of six months' interest, in discounting claims. For, if deaths occur on the average at the middle of the year and proof of death requires one week, as is likely to be the case nowadays, claims are paid on the average at nearly the middle of the year. But by the assumption used in computing the premium, the claims are not paid until the end of the policy year. Computing premium rates at 2½ per cent, this would mean a loss of $12.50 on a $1,000 policy. The assumption that claims are paid at the end of the year, however, has been maintained by most companies in the calculation of net premiums.[3] This assumption is corrected by a small adjustment in the expense loading formula.

Another assumption made by the companies in their rate computations is that deaths are uniformly distributed throughout the year. Thus, if out of 100,000 persons of a certain age 600 die within one year, the assumption

[3] See previous footnote.

is that 50 die the first month, 50 the second month, and so on during the year. The fact is that the death rate decreases up to about age 10, when it begins gradually to increase, and this increase continues at a constantly accelerating rate to the end of life.[4] This assumption is of financial importance to the company primarily in the case of policies paid for by premiums at intervals more frequent than once a year. In the case of annual premiums a full year's premium is received in the year of death. In the case of monthly premiums, however, if only one twelfth of the annual premium is collected in advance, but one sixth of the total year's mortality should occur during the first month, the company will not have the funds on hand to pay losses.

This situation can occur only during the first ten years of life when the mortality rate decreases. But after age 10 the mortality rate is increasing, and the discrepancy between the assumption of uniform deaths and the actual situation is favorable to the company and therefore presents no dangers, for the company will collect one twelfth of the premium, but will experience less than one twelfth of the year's losses during the first month.

In addition to these assumptions, the following facts must be known in order to compute premium rates in life insurance:

(1) the age of the insured;
(2) the sex of the insured;
(3) the benefits to be provided;
(4) the mortality table to be used in measuring the risk;
(5) the rate of interest which the company proposes to guarantee on funds presumed to be in its possession; and
(6) the amount to be charged to cover the company's expenses of operation.

In addition to the above assumptions and facts, an assumption must be made as to the termination rates to be employed in testing tentative gross premiums through asset share studies. In practice, termination rates are usually differentiated only by plan of insurance. As will be pointed out later, termination rates are used in premium calculations only because of the disparity between surrender values and the funds available for distribution to withdrawing policyholders.

---

[4] Current experience shows that actual rates decrease again between ages 25 and 30. This is not shown in the valuation tables such as the *1958 CSO Table* but is reflected in the "basic experience" tables.

PREMIUMS CLASSIFIED

Single and Periodic

LIFE INSURANCE POLICIES may be purchased by a single premium, an annual premium, or a premium paid weekly, monthly, quarterly, or semi-annually. Premiums other than the single premium may continue until the death of the policyholder or the maturity of the policy, or may be limited to a definite number of years as in a twenty-payment life policy and a twenty-payment, thirty-year endowment. In the twenty-payment life policy, for instance, the premiums continue for twenty years provided death does not intervene before this period has elapsed, and after the twenty payments have been made, the policy requires no further payments and matures whenever death occurs. Few contracts with the exception of annuities are purchased by single premiums, although they may be so purchased and the companies will quote single premium rates for almost any kind of policy. Nevertheless, in taking up the subject of rate computation in life insurance it is necessary to begin with a thorough study of the single premium, inasmuch as it furnishes the method of approach in determining annual premiums.

Net and Gross

The premium charged for a life insurance contract depends on three factors, namely, mortality, interest, and expenses. Mortality cost has reference to that part of the premium which provides for the occurrence of the event or risk insured against, while the second element takes into account the interest which it is assumed will be earned on the funds of the company. The third element primarily covers the costs incident to the management of a company, such as salaries, rents, commissions, taxes, and so forth, which may be fairly charged against a particular policy. In computing premiums a *net* premium which takes into account the mortality and interest factors is always determined first and to this is added an amount, determined by a more or less scientific method, called loading, which provides for expenses and contingencies, and from these calculations is determined the premium charged the policyholder. Therefore, depending on whether the "premium" in question is "loaded" or not, it may be classed as *gross* or *net*. The net premium makes provision for interest and for mortality, while the gross premium contains these elements plus an addition, or a "loading," for expenses and contingencies. The gross premium is the only one known to the policyholder, but before it is obtained an actuary must have ascertained the *net* premium. If, therefore, the gross annual premium is the ultimate object of the study of rate computation, this study must begin by first determining the *net single premium*. From the latter, as is shown later, the *net annual premium* can be found. Following this it will be possible to study the various methods of loading in order to ascertain the gross annual premium.[1]

The computation of net premium rates on any kind of policy requires information as to (1) the age and sex of the insured, (2) the benefits to be provided, (3) the mortality table to be used in measuring the incurred risk, and (4) the rate of interest assumed on funds presumed to be in the hands of the insurance company. In the computations that follow, risks will always be measured according to the *1958 CSO Table,* the rate of interest assumed will be 2½ per cent, the face value of the policy will be $1,000, and the insured will be male unless otherwise stated. The age of the insured will be stated in each instance. It should be remembered that these rate calculations are also based upon the assumptions discussed earlier, namely, (1) premiums are paid annually at the beginning of each policy year; (2) matured claims are paid at the end of the year; and (3) the death rate is uniform throughout the year.

TERM INSURANCE

Term insurance is the simplest type of contract issued insuring against premature death. Term policies usually run for five, ten, fifteen, or twenty years, and promise to pay the sum insured if the policyholder should die within this period, nothing being paid if death does not occur during the designated term. Term policies are therefore a distinct type of *temporary insurance.* Attempts have been made to popularize a one-year term policy which is renewable from year to year at the option of the insured, thereby granting current cost insurance which is paid for at the beginning of each

[1] This sequence in procedure is not always followed but in any case the gross premium is always tested by asset share studies under realistic assumptions. See Chapter 25.

year, the premium furnishing protection for that year only, and a different rate being chargeable for the following year's insurance. This type of policy offers an excellent opportunity to explain the simple elements of rate-making. Suppose, therefore, that the net single premium is to be ascertained on a renewable one-year term insurance of $1,000 on a male life aged 45. Immediate use will now be found for two of the assumptions used in rate-making which were mentioned in the preceding chapter, namely, that premiums are paid at the beginning of each policy year and that matured claims are paid at the close of the policy year. Accordingly, it is required to find the amount of money which must be paid in at the beginning of the year by a policyholder in order to enable the company to return $1,000 at the close of the year in case the policy has matured. The question must now be asked: What is the risk insured against? It follows from the definition of term insurance that it is the chance of dying during the year. This will be determined by means of the mortality table. This shows that, of 9,048,999 males living at age 45, 48,412 die during the year. Suppose now that an insurance company should issue 9,048,999 one-year term policies to males aged 45. If the mortality experienced among this group coincides with the experience indicated in the mortality table, there will be 48,412 deaths during the year. Since each of these deaths represents a liability of $1,000 to the company, and since the claims are payable at the close of the year, the company must have on hand at that time $48,412,000 to pay claims. But this entire amount need not have been collected from the policyholders, since they were required to pay their premiums at the beginning of the year and the company was able to invest the money at interest for one year and earn 2½ per cent thereon. One dollar discounted for one year at 2½ per cent interest is equal to $0.9756. Therefore, the company needs to have on hand at the beginning of the year only $47,230,747.20 (0.9756 × 48,412,000) in order to have on hand at the end of the year sufficient funds to pay $1,000 for each of the 48,412 deaths. To obtain the premium which each individual should pay, it is only necessary to divide the total fund by the group of 9,048,999 to be insured, namely:

$$\$47,231,231.32 \div 9,048,999 = \$5.22$$

The net single premium for a one-year term insurance at age 45, or the amount of money that must be paid at the beginning of the year to supply each individual's contribution to the death losses of the group for the year is, therefore, $5.22.[2]

The same problem may be approached in a different way and a formula

---

[2] This method of determining individual net single premiums has been termed the *aggregate approach*, since it emphasizes the total fund necessary to meet death claims as they occur. The alternative approach which is discussed next is usually referred to as the *probability approach*. Either method may be used, but the probability approach is emphasized here. See also the algebraic approach in Appendix C.

stated for determining costs. The original assumption required the insurance of a group of 9,048,999 males of identical age. But this is impossible to obtain in practice. Suppose now that it is desired to insure a single individual aged 45 against death during the year and that the net single premium for this insurance is to be ascertained. Clearly, if the event occurs against which protection is desired, it will cost the insurance company $1,000. But what is the probability of death occurring during the year? It has been shown that 48,412 males aged 45 die out of a group of 9,048,999. Reference to the discussion of the theory of probabilities in Chapter 19 will show that this is equivalent to saying that the probability of death during the forty-sixth year is $\frac{48,412}{9,048,999}$. The cost to a single male, therefore, will be $\frac{48,412}{9,048,999}$ of $1,000. But since this value needs to be on hand at the end of the year and money earns 2½ per cent interest, the amount to be paid in by the insured will be the value of the above amount discounted for one year at 2½ per cent. This result is found as follows:

$$\frac{48,412}{9,048,999} \times \$1,000 \times .9756 = \$5.22$$

It must not be assumed from this that an insurance company can insure a single person; instead, it must always deal with a group sufficiently large to be sure, as was explained earlier, of the operation of the law of large numbers. But it does not need to insure this entire group with the same kind of policy or at the same age. Results will be satisfactory as long as the entire group of policyholders, including all ages and all kinds of policies is sufficiently large.

If the method used here in determining the cost of this insurance is carefully studied, it will be found to embody the following process: Multiply the probability insured against by the amount of the policy and then multiply by $1 discounted for one year at the assumed rate of interest. From this expression it is possible to construct a general expression to apply in computing the value of cost of benefits on a per year basis, namely, *the probability insured against multiplied by the amount of the policy multiplied by the value of $1 discounted for the period the money is held.* This expression is used hereafter in computing net single premiums. It would be possible now to compute the net single premium paid at the beginning of the second year for the second year's insurance under our renewable one-year term policy issued at male age 45. The probability of death during this year is the year probability of death at age 46, or $\frac{52,473}{9,000,587}$, and the cost of the year's insurance would be:

$$\frac{52,473}{9,000,587} \times \$1,000 \times .9756 = \$5.69$$

In like manner, the yearly cost of insurance can be computed for any age. Although much emphasis has here been placed upon the one-year term policy because of its appropriateness in developing the elementary principles of rate computations, the fact must be kept in mind that one-year term policies are rarely sold. The usual term policies extend for five years or longer, and this fact brings complications into the matter of rate-making. Suppose it is desired to compute the net single premium for a five-year term insurance issued at male age 45, that is, the amount of money which, paid in a single sum at age 45, will purchase insurance against death at any time within the next five years. Two facts are apparent upon a moment's reflection: (1) the premium is paid only once, in a single sum at the inception of the risk; (2) death claims will be paid at the end of the year in which death occurs and not at the end of the five-year period. This latter fact has an important bearing on the interest which will be earned and therefore, on the method of computing the five years' cost. Manifestly, the cost cannot be correctly determined by multiplying the total probability of dying during the five years by the face value of the policy and discounting this amount in one operation since some of the money collected will draw interest for only one year while another part will be earning interest for five years. It is necessary to compute the cost of each year's mortality separately. The probabilities insured against in this case are the chances that a male aged 45 will die during the first year following, during the second year, the third year, and so forth. These probabilities are, respectively,

$$\frac{48,412}{9,048,999}, \quad \frac{52,473}{9,048,999}, \quad \frac{56,910}{9,048,999}, \quad \frac{61,794}{9,048,999}, \text{ and } \frac{67,104}{9,048,999}.$$

Each of these figures must be multiplied by the amount insured and by the present value of $1 discounted in each instance by the length of time the money is held. The money available for the first year's claims will be held one year, for the second year's claims, two years, and so forth, the funds for the last year's claims being held five years. The discounted values of $1 for one, two, three, four, and five years at 2½ per cent interest are respectively $0.9756, $0.9518, $0.9286, $0.9060, and $0.8839. The cost of the five years' insurance, therefore, can be shown as follows:

$$\frac{48,412}{9,048,999} \times \$1,000 \times .9756 = \$5.2194 = \text{cost of 1st year's insurance}$$

$$\frac{52,473}{9,048,999} \times 1,000 \times .9518 = 5.5193 = \text{cost of 2nd year's insurance}$$

$$\frac{56,910}{9,048,999} \times 1,000 \times .9286 = 5.8401 = \text{cost of 3rd year's insurance}$$

$$\frac{61,794}{9,048,999} \times 1,000 \times .9060 = 6.1869 = \text{cost of 4th year's insurance}$$

$$\frac{67,104}{9,048,999} \times 1,000 \times .8839 = 6.5547 = \text{cost of 5th year's insurance}$$

Net Single Premium = $29.3204 = cost of five years' insurance

This computation shows that ignoring expenses and taxes, $29.32 paid to the company by each policyholder and placed at 2½ per cent interest will furnish enough money to pay all the death claims on this five-year term policy. By simply continuing the process of calculating the cost of insurance on a per year basis, the net single premium for a term insurance contract of longer durations may be determined.

WHOLE-LIFE INSURANCE

A whole-life policy continues for the whole of life and promises to pay its face value upon the death of the insured to his estate or his beneficiary. There is a possibility that the insured may live to an advanced age and this must be taken into consideration in computing the premium. This policy is like the term contracts just considered with the exception that, instead of being limited to a definite number of years, it continues for the longest possible length of life and will certainly be paid at some time. Since the *1958 CSO Table of Mortality* assumes that all males die by the end of the one hundredth year, the maximum possible age for which insurance against death needs to provide will be 99. The net single premium on a whole-life policy issued at male age 45 must, therefore, provide against the possibility that the insured will die during his forty-sixth year, his forty-seventh year, and so on during every year up to and including his one hundredth. The separate probabilities insured against will be fifty-five in number, that is, for ages 45 to 99 inclusive.

The chance of dying in each separate year will be multiplied by the face value of the policy ($1,000) and this amount discounted for the number of years between the issue of the policy (that is, the payment of the single premium) and the payment of death losses, thus:

$$\frac{48,412}{9,048,999} \times \$1,000 \times .9756 = \$5.2194 = \text{cost of term insurance during age 45}$$

$$\frac{52,473}{9,048,999} \times 1,000 \times .9518 = 5.5193 = \text{cost of term insurance during age 46}$$

$$\frac{56,910}{9,048,999} \times 1,000 \times .9286 = 5.8401 = \text{cost of term insurance during age 47}$$

$$\frac{61,794}{9,048,999} \times 1,000 \times .9060 = 6.1869 = \text{cost of term insurance during age 48}$$

$$\frac{67,104}{9,048,999} \times 1,000 \times .8839 = 6.5547 = \text{cost of term insurance during age 49}$$

. . . .

. . . .

. . . .

$$\frac{34,128}{9,048,999} \times 1,000 \times .2838 = 1.0703 = \text{cost of term insurance during age 95}$$

$$\frac{25,250}{9,048,999} \times 1,000 \times .2769 = 0.7727 = \text{cost of term insurance during age 96}$$

$$\frac{18,456}{9,048,999} \times 1,000 \times .2702 = 0.5511 = \text{cost of term insurance during age 97}$$

$$\frac{12,916}{9,048,999} \times 1,000 \times .2636 = 0.3762 = \text{cost of term insurance during age 98}$$

$$\frac{6,415}{9,048,999} \times 1,000 \times .2572 = 0.1823 = \text{cost of term insurance during age 99}$$

Net Single Premium = $517.4862

This amount, $517.49, is the discounted value of all the death claims payable from age 45 until the age at which the mortality table assumes that all males will have died and is, therefore, the net single premium which will purchase a whole-life policy issued at age 45. It is true that a few men outlive their one hundredth year, but since the computations assume that the insured will not have survived this age and since sufficient money will have been accumulated to pay the claim at the close of the one hundredth year of life, the policy may then be surrendered for its full face amount.

ENDOWMENTS

Pure Endowments

A pure endowment contract promises to pay the insured value in case the holder survives a specified period. Thus, a ten-year pure endowment will pay the holder the amount named in the contract if he be living ten years from the date of issue. The mortality table shows that 9,048,999 males are living at age 45, and that 8,331,317 are still living at age 55, leaving 717,-682 as the number dying during the ten years. A policy issued to a man aged 45, insuring against survival during this period must itself contribute $\frac{8,331,317}{9,048,999}$ of the amount of the contract discounted to allow for the interest to be earned during the period. Or it may be stated in this way: The probability insured against is $\frac{8,331,317}{9,048,999}$ and since the money paid as a single premium will be held ten years before the policy matures, the formula for determining the net single premium is:

$$\frac{8,331,317}{9,048,999} \times \$1,000 \times .7812 = \$719.24.$$

The decimal, .7812, is the present value of $1 discounted for ten years at 2½ per cent.

A clear distinction must be made between a pure endowment and a savings-bank account which is left to accumulate at an agreed rate of interest. The insured cannot get possession of the money invested in a pure endowment before the expiration of the endowment period. If he should die during this period all the money paid is lost to him, that is, it remains in the fund which will be needed to pay the survivors. A savings-bank account on the other hand is not lost through death of the investor. This fact makes it possible to divide the $1,000 which will be paid *in case of survival through the endowment period* into two funds, one of which might be called the tentative investment fund, and the other the speculative fund. The tentative investment fund in a ten-year pure endowment, issued at age 45, will equal $719.24 plus interest compounded for ten years at 2½ per cent.

$$\$719.24 \times 1.2801 = \$920.70$$

This $920.70 is the amount which would be obtained by investing the net single premium of this pure endowment policy at 2½ per cent interest for ten years. The remainder of the $1,000, or $79.30, comprises the survivor's share of the amounts left by those policyholders who died before their policies matured. The latter amount is technically the "benefit of survivorship," here called the speculative fund. The possibility of thus losing the entire amount of one's investment by death before the endowment period has expired makes the pure endowment a policy that finds little favor with the insuring public.[3] For this reason it is combined with, or con-

---

[3] In some jurisdictions pure endowment contracts are prohibited by law.

stitutes a feature of, some other kind of policy. It is interesting to note, however, that a life annuity is merely a series of pure endowments (see below).

Endowment Insurance

The combination in which pure endowments figure most frequently is technically known as endowment insurance. This policy is popularly referred to as an endowment. It promises to pay a certain sum to the insured in case he should die within the term of the policy or a like sum at the end of the term in case of survival. Analysis of this contract shows that it includes the pure endowment feature just discussed and, in addition, insurance against death during the term of the endowment. For illustration, a five-year endowment insurance policy issued at male age 45 will pay the sum insured if the policyholder dies during the first, the second, the third, the fourth, or the fifth years, and it will pay the same sum if he survives the fifth year. The cost of this insurance, therefore, will equal the following:

$$\frac{48,412}{9,048,999} \times \$1,000 \times .9756 = \$ \quad 5.2194 = \text{cost of 1st year's term insurance}$$

$$\frac{52,473}{9,048,999} \times 1,000 \times .9518 = \quad 5.5193 = \text{cost of 2nd year's term insurance}$$

$$\frac{56,910}{9,048,999} \times 1,000 \times .9286 = \quad 5.8401 = \text{cost of 3rd year's term insurance}$$

$$\frac{61,794}{9,048,999} \times 1,000 \times .9060 = \quad 6.1869 = \text{cost of 4th year's term insurance}$$

$$\frac{67,104}{9,048,999} \times 1,000 \times .8839 = \quad 6.5547 = \text{cost of 5th year's term insurance}$$

$$\frac{8,762,306}{9,048,999} \times 1,000 \times .8839 = 855.8960 = \text{cost of five-year pure endowment}$$

Net Single Premium = $885.2163 for five-year endowment insurance

Contracts known as semi-endowments or double endowments are sometimes issued. They differ from the policy just explained only in the fact that the amount due in case the insured should survive the term of the policy (that is, the pure endowment element) is one half, or is double, the amount paid in event of maturity by death. The cost of a five-year semi-endowment insurance of $1,000 at male age 45, therefore, would differ from the cost of the policy just computed only by the cost of the pure endowment, which in this case would be as follows:

$$\frac{8,762,306}{9,048,999} \times \$500 \times .8839 = \$427.9480$$

This amount, added to the cost of the five-years' term insurance, would give the net single premium for the semi-endowment.

Net Single Premiums: II | 22

THE PREMIUMS COMPUTED thus far relate to contracts which embody only two kinds of risks, the risk of death and the risk of survival. These two types are sometimes referred to as insurance and endowments, since insurance, as such, is generally needed against premature death whereas endowments resemble investments accumulated for the future. Every life insurance contract covers one or both of these features, namely, protection against death or accumulation in case of survival.

INSTALLMENT INSURANCE

In the policies studied thus far it has also been assumed that the face value of the policy (generally $1,000 or multiples of that amount) is payable at maturity in a single sum. But it has become a common practice to make provision for the payment of policies in periodic installments. Thus, there are policies paid in monthly installments extending over a period of years, or in ten, fifteen, or twenty yearly installments. These contracts differ in cost from those paid in a single cash sum and it is necessary to determine wherein this difference lies. Such installment contracts are of two kinds: one stating that the face value, $1,000, will be paid in a definite number of installments; and the other maturing regularly as a single-payment policy, but giving the insured or his beneficiary the option of choosing the installment-payment plan. A policy which promises payment of $100 on the death of the insured and $100 per year thereafter until ten payments have been made is an example of the first; the contract in the second case would mature for $1,000 payable at once, but would allow the beneficiary to receive in lieu thereof a certain sum annually for ten years, this sum not being $100 but that which can be purchased by $1,000 in hand at maturity.

In the case of the first contract it is evident that the company is going to pay out a total of only $1,000, but during the ten years given the company in which to pay this sum, it will be earning interest on the funds in its possession. It must have on hand, therefore, at the time of maturity only such funds as, *with interest added,* will yield $100 at each of the ten annual periods. The payments are made as follows: $100 immediately, $100 at the end of one year, $100 at the end of two years, and so forth, the tenth payment being made at the end of nine years. The first $100 will be paid at once upon the maturity of the contract and therefore earns no interest. A part of the funds will draw interest for one year, another part for two years, and so on, the last portion drawing interest for nine years. Consequently, the funds which must be available at the maturity of the contract will equal $100 plus such amounts as with interest for one year, two years, three years, and so forth, will respectively equal sums of $100. These amounts are the discounted values of $100 for one, two, three years, and so forth. The present value of these ten payments is found as follows:

		Present Value
$100 paid immediately		$100.00
100 one year hence = 100 X 0.9756 =		97.56
100 two years hence = 100 X 0.9518 =		95.18
100 three years hence = 100 X 0.9286 =		92.86
100 four years hence = 100 X 0.9060 =		90.60
100 five years hence = 100 X 0.8839 =		88.39
100 six years hence = 100 X 0.8623 =		86.23
100 seven years hence = 100 X 0.8413 =		84.13
100 eight years hence = 100 X 0.8207 =		82.07
100 nine years hence = 100 X 0.8007 =		80.07
Present value of $1,000 in ten installments =		$897.09

If the company, therefore, has $897.09 on hand at the time the policy matures and continues to earn 2½ per cent interest on all funds in its possession it will be able to pay the ten installments of $100 each as they come due. To determine the net single premium for a policy so paid, it is necessary to regard the policy as having a face value of $897.09, instead of $1,000. Thus, a term policy, a whole-life policy, a pure endowment, or an endowment insurance might be paid in ten installments, and the only change from the computations already made would consist in the substitution of $897.09 for $1,000 as the amount of insurance.

Where the policy matures for $1,000 but gives the further option of receiving payment in installments, it is clear that the premium must provide for $1,000 payable in a single cash sum at maturity, since the insured or beneficiary may choose this option. There will be no difference, therefore, in the computation of the net single premium for this policy from the usual $1,000 policy. But since $897.09 only is necessary at maturity to provide ten installments of $100 each, $1,000 in hand at maturity will enable the company to pay ten installments, each greater than $100. A simple proportion will show how the amount of these payments may be determined. Since $897.09 will provide installments of $100 each, $1,000 will provide installments greater than $100 in the same proportion that $1,000 is greater than $897.09. Thus, letting x equal the amount of the installment to be found, we have:

$$\$1{,}000 \; : \; 897.09 \; : : \; x \; : \; 100$$
$$\text{or} \quad \frac{1{,}000}{897.09} \; = \; \frac{x}{100}$$
$$x \; = \; \frac{100{,}000}{897.09}$$
$$x \; = \; \$111.47$$

A policy maturing for $1,000 and giving the option of receiving it in ten annual installments could therefore pay $111.47 in each installment. By the principles here laid down the cost can likewise be determined for contracts paid in any number of installments, such as five, fifteen, or twenty.

The contracts explained thus far have invariably involved but one life. Life insurance companies, however, will issue policies covering risks on two or more lives, or joint-life policies as they are called. But the computation of costs on joint-life risks will carry us more deeply into actuarial science than is appropriate here, since the purpose of our premium analyses is merely to give an adequate idea of the risk involved in the most usual types of policies and the impact of interest and survivorship on the cost of insurance. Premium computations, therefore, have not been made for ordinary joint-life, last-survivor, and contingent or survivorship insurances.[1]

WHOLE-LIFE ANNUITIES

The remaining class of contracts to be analyzed is known as whole–life annuities.[2] Life annuities promise to pay the possessor a stated income at intervals of one year or more frequently during the lifetime of said person. It will be seen, therefore, that they furnish a type of investment whereby the recipient whose sole dependence is upon invested capital can be assured of an income for life.

Annuities covering a single life are of two kinds, *immediate* and *deferred,* Immediate life annuities may be temporary, that is, limited to a term of

[1] The computation of costs for joint-life contracts is effected by the application to the mortality table of the law of compound probabilities in determining the probability that joint-lives will fail, that they will survive, etc.

[2] This discussion will relate only to single-life annuities. As pointed out earlier, however, annuities may be issued on any number of lives on a "joint" basis.

years during the lifetime of the annuitant, or may continue for the whole of life, or may promise a minimum number of payments irrespective of whether the recipient be living or not. The cost of each of these contracts will be considered in turn.

Immediate Whole-Life Annuities

An immediate temporary life annuity of $100 purchased, say, at age 70 and continuing for a period of ten years, will promise to pay the annuitant $100 one year from date of purchase, if then living, and $100 at each anniversary of that date if still living until ten payments have been made. The cost of this contract will be the sum of money paid at the time of purchase, namely, age 70, which will furnish these annual payments, and the net cost will be the amount necessary to provide merely for the payments of the sums promised to the annuitant without assessing against the contract anything for expenses. The formula used in computing the net single premiums on insurances can again be used here, namely, net cost will equal the probability insured against multiplied by the sum insured (the amount of the annuity) multiplied by the value of $1 discounted for the time the money is held. Since, therefore, a payment is made to the annuitant, if surviving, at the end of each year, the cost for each year must be determined separately and these sums added to obtain the total cost. The probability insured against is the probability that the annuitant will survive through the first year, through the second year, the third year, and so forth. It will be seen, therefore, that the annuity under consideration is equivalent to a series of ten pure endowments, one maturing in one year from date of purchase, one in two years, one in three years, and so on, until ten have been paid. However, although the formulas are equivalent to those for insurance, the mortality table is different, since insurance companies find that annuity mortality experience produces lower mortality rates than does insurance mortality experience. *The Annuity Table for 1949,* without projection (Table 22-1), is a table used currently for annuities. According to this table, the probability that the first annuity payment will be made, will equal the probability that a man aged 70 will survive one year, or expressed in the form of a fraction, $\frac{6,479,691}{6,715,346}$. The $100 paid in case of survival is paid one year from the date of purchase of the annuity and therefore the net cost of the first payment will be the value of this sum discounted for one year at 2½ per cent and multiplied by the probability of survival. Thus, the total operation of the first year is as follows:

$$\frac{6,479,691}{6,715,346} \times \$100 \times .9756 = \$94.14\text{—net cost of first annuity payment}$$

TABLE 22-1. Annuity Table for 1949 (without projection)

(Male Lives)

Age	Number Living at Beginning of Designated Year (l_x)	Number Dying During Designated Year (d_x)	Yearly Probability of Dying (q_x)	Yearly Probability of Surviving (p_x)
10	10,000,000	4,830	.000483	.999517
11	9,995,170	4,918	.000492	.999508
12	9,990,252	5,015	.000502	.999498
13	9,985,237	5,112	.000512	.999488
14	9,980,125	5,230	.000524	.999476
15	9,974,895	5,357	.000537	.999463
16	9,969,538	5,493	.000551	.999449
17	9,964,045	5,650	.000567	.999433
18	9,958,395	5,816	.000584	.999416
19	9,952,579	6,001	.000603	.999397
20	9,946,578	6,207	.000624	.999376
21	9,940,371	6,441	.000648	.999352
22	9,933,930	6,695	.000674	.999326
23	9,927,235	6,969	.000702	.999298
24	9,920,266	7,272	.000733	.999267
25	9,912,994	7,613	.000768	.999232
26	9,905,381	7,984	.000806	.999194
27	9,897,397	8,403	.000849	.999151
28	9,888,994	8,861	.000896	.999104
29	9,880,133	9,356	.000947	.999053
30	9,870,777	9,910	.001004	.998996
31	9,860,867	10,522	.001067	.998933
32	9,850,345	11,190	.001136	.998864
33	9,839,155	11,935	.001213	.998787
34	9,827,220	12,746	.001297	.998703
35	9,819,474	13,652	.001391	.998609
36	9,800,822	14,642	.001494	.998506
37	9,786,180	15,726	.001607	.998393
38	9,770,454	16,932	.001733	.998267
39	9,753,522	18,259	.001872	.998128
40	9,735,263	19,714	.002025	.997975
41	9,715,549	21,569	.002220	.997770
42	9,693,980	24,051	.002481	.997519
43	9,669,929	27,114	.003804	.997196
44	9,642,815	30,732	.003187	.996813
45	9,612,083	34,844	.003625	.996375
46	9,577,239	39,420	.004116	.995884
47	9,537,819	44,418	.004657	.995343
48	9,493,401	49,802	.005246	.994754
49	9,443,599	55,528	.005880	.994120
50	9,388,071	61,558	.006557	.993443
51	9,326,513	67,869	.007277	.992723
52	9,258,644	74,421	.008038	.991972
53	9,184,223	81,189	.008840	.991160
54	9,103,034	88,136	.009682	.990318
55	9,014,898	95,242	.010565	.989435
56	8,919,656	102,496	.011491	.988509
57	8,817,160	109,862	.012460	.987540
58	8,707,298	117,340	.013476	.986524
59	8,589,958	124,915	.014542	.985458

TABLE 22-1. (cont'd.)

Age	Number Living at Beginning of Designated Year (l_x)	Number Dying During Designated Year (d_x)	Yearly Probability of Dying (q_x)	Yearly Probability of Surviving (p_x)
60	8,465,043	132,580	.015662	.984338
61	8,332,463	140,560	.016869	.983131
62	8,191,903	149,084	.018199	.981801
63	8,042,819	158,170	.019666	.980334
64	7,884,649	167,809	.021283	.978727
65	7,716,840	177,997	.023066	.976954
66	7,538,843	188,697	.025030	.974770
67	7,350,146	199,873	.027193	.972807
68	7,150,273	211,484	.029577	.970423
69	6,938,789	223,443	.032202	.967798
70	6,715,346	235,655	.035092	.964908
71	6,479,691	247,991	.038272	.961728
72	6,231,700	260,304	.041771	.958229
73	5,971,396	272,415	.045620	.954380
74	5,698,981	284,106	.049852	.950148
75	5,414,875	295,116	.054501	.945999
76	5,119,759	305,184	.059609	.940391
77	4,814,575	313,987	.065216	.934784
78	4,500,588	321,198	.071368	.928632
79	4,179,390	326,465	.078113	.921887
80	3,852,925	329,437	.085503	.914497
81	3,523,488	329,774	.093593	.906407
82	3,193,714	327,174	.102443	.897557
83	2,866,540	321,376	.112113	.887887
84	2,545,164	312,213	.122669	.877331
85	2,232,951	299,613	.134178	.865822
86	1,933,338	283,638	.146709	.853291
87	1,649,700	264,501	.160333	.839667
88	1,385,199	242,582	.175124	.824876
89	1,142,617	218,412	.191151	.808849
90	924,205	192,682	.208485	.791515
91	731,522	166,196	.227192	.772808
92	565,326	139,823	.247332	.752668
93	425,502	114,443	.268960	.731040
94	311,059	90,866	.292118	.707882
95	220,193	69,764	.316834	.683166
96	150,428	51,615	.343122	.656878
97	98,813	36,657	.370973	.629027
98	62,156	24,884	.400352	.599648
99	37,271	16,071	.431199	.568801
100	21,200	9,824	.463415	.536585
101	11,375	5,652	.496870	.503130
102	5,723	3,041	.531389	.468611
103	2,682	1,520	.566757	.433243
104	1,161	700	.602714	.397286
105	462	294	.638956	.361044
106	167	112	.675143	.324857
107	54	38	.710898	.289102
108	16	11	.745822	.254178
109	4	3	1.000000	.000000

In like manner, the net cost for the remaining nine payments will be found by multiplying the probability of surviving through two, three, four years, and so forth, by the amount of the annuity of $100, discounted respectively, two, three, four years, and so forth. The entire computation for ten years, based on the *Annuity Table for 1949,* is as follows:

$$\frac{6,479,691}{6,715,346} \times \$100 \times .9756 = \$94.1364 = \text{net cost of 1st annuity payment}$$

$$\frac{6,231,700}{6,715,346} \times 100 \times .9518 = 88.3250 = \text{net cost of 2nd annuity payment}$$

$$\frac{5,971,396}{6,715,346} \times 100 \times .9286 = 82.5726 = \text{net cost of 3rd annuity payment}$$

$$\frac{5,698,981}{6,715,346} \times 100 \times .9060 = 76.8877 = \text{net cost of 4th annuity payment}$$

$$\frac{5,414,875}{6,715,346} \times 100 \times .8839 = 71.2727 = \text{net cost of 5th annuity payment}$$

$$\frac{5,119,759}{6,715,346} \times 100 \times .8623 = 65.7415 = \text{net cost of 6th annuity payment}$$

$$\frac{4,814,575}{6,715,346} \times 100 \times .8413 = 60.3171 = \text{net cost of 7th annuity payment}$$

$$\frac{4,500,588}{6,715,346} \times 100 \times .8207 = 55.0029 = \text{net cost of 8th annuity payment}$$

$$\frac{4,179,390}{6,715,346} \times 100 \times .8007 = 49.8327 = \text{net cost of 9th annuity payment}$$

$$\frac{3,852,925}{6,715,346} \times 100 \times .7812 = 44.8213 = \text{net cost of 10th annuity payment}$$

Net Cost = $688.9099 for a ten-year annuity

The temporary annuity for a man aged 70, therefore, will cost net $688.91, the sum composed of the net costs of each of the separate yearly payments.

If the contract issued at age 70 promises to pay an annuity for the whole of life, the computations must continue until the life surely fails, and this occurs, according to the *Annuity Table for 1949,* during the one hundred and tenth year of age. The net cost of a whole-life annuity, or an immediate life annuity, as it is usually called, will, therefore, equal the net cost of a series of pure endowments, the first maturing at age 71 and the last at age 109, since all lives are assumed by the table to have surely failed before the end of the one hundred and tenth year. The computation of the cost of this annuity is as follows, the first ten years being the same as for the term annuity just computed:

$$\frac{6,479,691}{6,715,346} \times \$100 \times .9756 = \$94.1364 = \text{net cost of 1st annuity payment}$$

$$\frac{6,231,700}{6,715,346} \times 100 \times .9518 = 88.3250 = \text{net cost of 2nd annuity payment}$$

$$\frac{5,971,396}{6,715,346} \times 100 \times .9286 = 82.5726 = \text{net cost of 3rd annuity payment}$$

$$\frac{5,698,981}{6,715,346} \times 100 \times .9060 = 76.8877 = \text{net cost of 4th annuity payment}$$

$$\frac{5,414,875}{6,715,346} \times 100 \times .8839 = 71.2727 = \text{net cost of 5th annuity payment}$$

$$\begin{array}{ccccc} \cdot & \cdot & \cdot & \cdot & \cdot \\ \cdot & \cdot & \cdot & \cdot & \cdot \\ \cdot & \cdot & \cdot & \cdot & \cdot \end{array}$$

$$\frac{462}{6,715,346} \times 100 \times .4214 = .0029 = \text{net cost of 35th annuity payment}$$

$$\frac{167}{6,715,346} \times 100 \times .4111 = .0010 = \text{net cost of 36th annuity payment}$$

$$\frac{54}{6,715,346} \times 100 \times .4011 = .0003 = \text{net cost of 37th annuity payment}$$

$$\frac{16}{6,715,346} \times 100 \times .3913 = .0001 = \text{net cost of 38th annuity payment}$$

$$\frac{4}{6,715,346} \times 100 \times .3817 = .0000 = \text{net cost of 39th annuity payment}$$

Net Cost = $935.0743 for a life annuity for a man, age 70

The sum of $935.07, therefore, represents the net amount which, paid at age 70, will enable the insurance company to pay $100 per year to the annuitant *during life*, according to these mortality and interest assumptions.

If this same annuity guaranteed that the first five payments were to be certain, that is, not affected by the death of the annuitant before their completion, this fact would have to be taken into consideration in computing the net cost. The distinction would lie in the fact that these five payments would not be affected by death, or to put it in actuarial terms, the risk would equal *certainty* or 1. The net cost of the first five payments would therefore be:

$$1 \times \$100 \times .9756 = \$97.56 = \text{net cost of 1st year's annuity}$$
$$1 \times 100 \times .9518 = 95.18 = \text{net cost of 2nd year's annuity}$$
$$1 \times 100 \times .9286 = 92.86 = \text{net cost of 3rd year's annuity}$$
$$1 \times 100 \times .9060 = 90.60 = \text{net cost of 4th year's annuity}$$
$$1 \times 100 \times .8839 = 88.39 = \text{net cost of 5th year's annuity}$$

$$\$464.5828 = \text{Total Cost of Annuity Certain}$$

The sixth and all subsequent payments would be dependent on the probability of survival, and their net cost would therefore be computed in the same manner as in the previous problem.

Deferred Whole-Life Annuities

Immediate life annuities are purchased by persons of advanced age, and contemplate the payment of benefits at periodic intervals following the date of issue. It is necessary, therefore, that the person considering investment in such a contract shall have accumulated the fund with which to make the purchase. This fund is presumably created from savings over the productive period of a man's lifetime. The experience of probate courts leads to the conclusion, however, that most men dying after age 60 leave little or no capital accumulated. Realizing this and knowing how easy it is to neglect the future, some men are interested in an annuity contract that will furnish an income during old age, as do the contracts just described, but which can be purchased by annual sums laid aside during their productive years; in other words a contract that will enable them to create this fund by annual payments, say, between ages 40 and 70, so the fund can then be returned to them as an annuity after age 70. The *deferred life annuity* offers this opportunity. It bears a close resemblance to private pension plans under which money is accumulated year by year in small amounts from the wages of the employees and contributions by the employer and is paid periodically during the lifetime of the employee after he has attained retirement age.

The deferred life annuity is the only type of single-life annuity sold by insurance companies which can be purchased by an annual premium. Of course, it is also possible to pay for such a contract by a single premium paid at the date of purchase of the contract. It is necessary, however, in this instance, as in the computations previously made, to compute the net single premium before determining the net annual premium.

If, therefore, it is desired to find the net single premium payable for a man at age 40 which will purchase the right to receive a whole life annuity of $100 beginning at age 70, there are two possible ways of approaching the problem. In the first place it may be asked, What is the amount of money that must have been accumulated by the company by the time the annuity begins? This is equivalent to asking how much money must be on hand at age 70 to furnish $100 annually during life, the first payment to be made when the annuitant reaches age 70. The problem at this point is, therefore, identical with that of the immediate whole-life annuity just discussed, with the single exception that here the first $100 payment is made at age 70 while in the former case the first payment was made at age 71. If, therefore, the insurance company has on hand at the time the annuitant becomes 70 years of age the amount of money necessary to purchase an immediate life annuity, the first payment being at age 71 plus an additional $100 for the payment made on arriving at age 70, or, taking the figures from our previous computations, $935.07 + $100.00, or $1,035.07, this amount may be considered as the net cost at *age 70* of a whole-life annuity the first payment of which is made to the annuitant at that age.

It is now necessary to determine how much must be paid to the insurance company by the purchaser who takes such a contract when 40 years of age. The cost of this contract may be computed on the assumption that the single premium paid at age 40 or the annual premium paid from ages 40 to 70 is a sum laid aside for use at age 70, the purchaser relinquishing any right to his contributions in case he fails to survive to that age. By this means he is able in case of survival to share proportionately in all funds relinquished by other annuitants who failed to live to age 70. Clearly the chance that a man aged 40 will collect any portion of his annuity is the chance that he will survive this period. In other words, the period of deferment is a pure endowment period.

It is now possible to state the problem in actuarial terms. In case of survival from age 40 to age 70 the annuitant must have standing to his credit the *then present value* of the whole-life annuity payments beginning at age 70. This amount was found to be $1,035.07. The amount payable by a man at age 40 which will furnish this sum if living at age 70 will be the present value of this sum discounted for thirty years at the assumed interest rate and multiplied by the probability of surviving the thirty-year period of deferment, namely:

$$\frac{6,715,346}{9,735,263} \times \$1,035.07 \times .4767 = \$340.36$$

The problem of computing the net single premium for the deferred annuity in question can be approached in a different way. It consists of dealing with each separate annual income payment by itself instead of obtaining the *combined* value at age 70 of all these payments and then discounting this value in one operation to its value at age 40. By considering each annuity payment separately it is possible to find the amount of money to be paid as a single premium at age 40 which will furnish a payment at age 70 *if living,* another at age 71 if living, and so on until according to the mortality table the annuitant will surely have died.

Thus, if $100 is to be paid at age 70, if surviving, its cost or present value at age 40 will be equal to the present value of $100 discounted for thirty years and multiplied by the probability of surviving to age 70. In like manner, the present value at age 40 of the second annuity of $100 will equal $100 discounted for thirty-one years and multiplied by the probability of surviving from age 40 to age 71. This process will be continued to the end of the mortality table and the net single premium for the deferred annuity will be equal to the total sum of these present values. The computations are shown herewith:

$$\frac{6,715,346}{9,735,263} \times \$100 \times .4767 = \$32.8826$$

$$\frac{6,479,691}{9,735,263} \times 100 \times .4651 = 30.9566$$

$$\frac{6,231,700}{9,735,263} \times 100 \times .4538 = 29.0485$$

$$\frac{5,971,396}{9,735,263} \times 100 \times .4427 = 27.1542$$

$$\frac{5,698,981}{9,735,263} \times 100 \times .4319 = 25.2833$$

$$\cdot \qquad \cdot \qquad \cdot \qquad \cdot$$

$$\cdot \qquad \cdot \qquad \cdot \qquad \cdot$$

$$\cdot \qquad \cdot \qquad \cdot \qquad \cdot$$

$$\frac{462}{9,735,263} \times 100 \times .2009 = 00.0009$$

$$\frac{167}{9,735,263} \times 100 \times .1960 = 00.0003$$

$$\frac{54}{9,735,263} \times 100 \times .1912 = 00.0001$$

$$\frac{16}{9,735,263} \times 100 \times .1865 = 00.0000$$

$$\frac{4}{9,735,263} \times 100 \times .1820 = 00.0000$$

Net Single Premium = $340.3577

The total obtained equals the net single premium for the annuity purchased at age 40 with benefits deferred until age 70. Comparison of this result with that found by the first method used will show that they are equivalent. For analytical purposes the former method has an advantage over the latter in bringing out in a more striking manner the pure endowment nature of the period of deferment from age 40 to age 70 wherein the insured leaves his contributions for the survivors in case of death before age 70.

Of course, a deferred annuity is usually purchased on a basis which eliminates the speculative element whereby all accumulations are left in event of death before age 70. Private pension programs normally include a provision that in case of death or withdrawal before the first annuity payment is made, the insured employee may receive a return of all his individual contributions with interest compounded at a nominal rate. Likewise, an individual deferred annuity usually has a provision that in case of prior death the insured shall have returned to him a sum at least equal to all the premiums paid in, without interest, and a comparable surrender benefit is also usually provided. Thus, if a particular annuity, such as that considered above, cost $15 a year between ages 40 and 70 and the insured died after having paid fifteen premiums, his estate would receive at least fifteen times $15, or $225. This return premium feature would, of course, cost an extra premium beyond that necessary to purchase the pure deferred annuity by itself.

THE LEVEL-PREMIUM SYSTEM

INSURANCE POLICIES MAY be purchased by a single cash sum or by periodic payments made weekly, monthly, quarterly, semiannually, or annually. The method of computing the net single premium has been described in Chapters 21 and 22. Therein it was explained that policies are ordinarily purchased by annual or periodic premiums but that the determination of the latter is possible only after the single premium has been ascertained.

It requires but a brief comparison to show why most insured persons choose the annual- rather than the single-premium method of paying for insurance. The net single premium on a $1,000 whole-life policy issued at male age 35 (*1958 CSO* 2½ per cent basis) is $420.13, while the net annual level premium is only $17.67. Two reasons favor the choice of the latter method of payment. In the first place most persons insure to protect their earning capacity from the risk of death or disability which enables them to assume certain definite family or business responsibilities. It is a man's earning power which enables him to marry or to engage in business with assurance of his ability to meet his responsibilities, for the majority of people do not obtain their capital by inheritance. It is from current income, therefore, that insurance premiums must ordinarily be paid. If the protection of a $4,000 income requires $10,000 of insurance, this amount on the single-premium plan for whole-life insurance at age 35 would run $4,201.30, while on the annual-premium plan it would mean an outlay of $176.70 per year. The former sum would normally be impossible to pay from a single year's income, while the latter would occasion no special hardship.[1]

A second reason for the choice of annual- rather than single-premium payments for life insurance lies in the reduced cost of a policy purchased by the former in case of early death of the insured. If the insured in the above illustration should die within one year after the issue of his policy, this insurance would cost him $4,201.30 under the one plan and but $176.70 under the other. This difference cannot be lightly overlooked. Disregard-

---

[1] It should be remembered that this discussion is in terms of *net* premiums.

ing interest, it will require the payment of twenty-four annual premiums before the amount paid in will equal the single premium, and therefore, the annual plan of premium payments is the cheaper to the policyholder whenever death occurs before the twenty-fourth year of insurance is begun. There is a corresponding disadvantage in the annual premium plan if the insured lives beyond the payment of his twenty-fourth premium for he will then pay more than would have been the case with the single premium. The two methods of payment, however, are actuarially equivalent.

A third reason has been brought out previously, namely, the basic concept of the level-premium plan is to avoid the formidable costs of insurance at the higher ages.[2]

Analogy Between Periodic Premiums and Annuities

If a policyholder is given the choice of payment for his insurance by a single or an annual premium, the amount of the latter must be determined on such a basis that with a large group of policyholders the company will receive the same amount of money under the one plan as under the other. Since the manner of computing the net single premium is known, the problem can be solved by finding a series of net annual level premiums mathematically *equivalent* to the net single premium. In order to do this it is necessary to inquire into the circumstances affecting the payment of annual level premiums. They are paid regularly during the life of some person, generally the insured, or for a limited number of years, but always *cease upon his or her death.* This is the same definition as that of an annuity, as stated in the previous chapter.

Annual premiums, therefore, are annuities, but they differ in four important respects from the annuities thus far considered: (1) They are annuities paid by the insured to the company, whereas regular annuities are paid by the company to the annuitant. (2) Annuities were found to be purchased, ordinarily, by a single premium, that is, a single cash sum. If annual premiums are analogous to annuities, how, then, are annual premiums purchased? Or, to state the proposition directly, in what way does the company return value received for the annual premiums it collects? Obviously, not as a cash sum to the insured upon the issue of the policy. Rather it pays for them *with the policy*, which promises cash upon the happening of some future event and this future promise of money has a *present value* which can be expressed in money. This present value is comparable to the cash payments for annuities. (3) Annuitant mortality is considerably lower than insurance mortality, and the mortality tables used for annuity calculations reflect that lower mortality; this consideration, however, does

[2] See pp. 9–11.

not apply to the annuities represented by the annual level premiums, and regular insurance mortality tables are used in the calculations regarding life insurance annual level premiums. (4) The time when annual level premiums and annuities begin represents a fundamental difference. It will be remembered that the cost of an immediate life annuity is computed on the assumption that the first payment of annual income is received one year from the date of issue of the contract. In practice the first annual premium is payable *when the policy is issued,* and not one year later, as is the case with annuities. The series of annual premiums is, therefore, equal to the usual annuity plus one payment made immediately. The distinction between the two is expressed by calling this series a *life annuity due.* Life annuities due are not sold as annuity contracts and the sole purpose of this term is to have a convenient expression to describe an annual premium in terms of an annuity.

It should be noted that the net level premium cannot be obtained simply by dividing by the number of installments agreed upon. The net single premium is a discounted value and the net annual level premium must reflect (1) the possibility that the insured may die prematurely and not pay future premiums; and (2) the smaller sum which will be invested at compound interest, with the resultant loss of interest earnings to the company.

The problem stated previously may now be restated in the following terms: The series of net annual level premiums will be a life annuity due equivalent to the net single premium.

Whole-Life and Limited Premiums

It was found in the previous discussion of life annuities that the cost of a whole-life annuity provides for the payment of annuities in some cases as late as the highest age in the mortality table. Are we to assume, therefore, since annual premiums are life annuities due, that they are invariably paid to the highest age in the table if the insured lives to that age? Of course this is not the case. Annual premiums are never paid after the termination of a contract, whether it terminates by expiry or by maturity; and a large majority of insurance contracts are certain to be closed before the holder reaches old age. The whole-life policy is the sole contract insuring against death which may continue to the end of the mortality table. Term and endowment contracts usually do not extend beyond age 65 or 70 of the insured. Therefore, the majority of annual premiums will be life annuities due, not for the whole of life but for a temporary period, the maximum length of which will be the maximum length of the insurance contract.

With respect to the period during which premiums are paid, insurance policies are of two kinds: policies with premiums payable throughout the life of the contract; and so-called *limited-payment policies,* where the premiums are limited to a term shorter than the maximum life of the contract. For instance, a whole-life policy with premiums payable for life, technically known as an ordinary life policy, will require payment of premiums until the contract matures by death. A thirty-year endowment-insurance policy usually requires payment of premiums for thirty years or for a shorter time in case the contract matures by death in less than thirty years. But a policy is often sold on a limited-payment basis. A twenty-payment life policy, for example, will mature and its face value be paid only upon death, but premiums will continue for a maximum of twenty years and fewer than twenty will be paid in case of death before the twentieth year. In the illustration cited, the series of annual premiums will be a life annuity due, not for the term of the insurance contract, but limited in this case to twenty years. It is possible, therefore, in view of these facts, to modify the definition given for the net annual premium again. The new statement may be defined in these terms: The series of net annual level premiums is a life annuity due *for the premium-payment period* which is equivalent to the net single premium on the particular policy.

COMPUTATION OF THE NET ANNUAL LEVEL PREMIUM

Term Insurance

In computing net annual level premiums it is first necessary to ascertain the net single premium. This has been done in Chapters 21 and 22 for the usual types of policies. The second step will be to define carefully the *premium-payment period* over which the annual premium is to be paid and for which the *life annuity due* is to be ascertained. Suppose it is desired, therefore, to compute the net annual level premium which will purchase a five-year term insurance policy of $1,000 at male age 45, *1958 CSO*, 2½ per cent basis. It was found on page 351 that the net single premium on this policy was $29.32. Beginning at date of issue the annual level premium will be paid over a five-year period, or until prior death, and is therefore a five-year temporary annuity due.

Since the amount of the annual level premium is the unknown quantity, it will be impossible to proceed directly to the computation of its present value, but it is feasible to take any assumed premium, such as $1, and compute the present value of an annuity due for this amount. An annuity due of $1 on the policy in question will be equal to a temporary immediate annuity for four years plus $1 paid initially, and its present value is computed in the following manner (note that the *1958 CSO Table*, not the *Annuity Table for 1949*, is used because the calculation is required for an *insurance* policy):

$$\$1 \text{ due immediately} = \$1.000000$$

$$\frac{9,000,587}{9,048,999} \times 1 \times .9756 = .9704$$

$$\frac{8,948,114}{9,048,999} \times 1 \times .9518 = .9412$$

$$\frac{8,891,204}{9,048,999} \times 1 \times .9286 = .9124$$

$$\frac{8,829,410}{9,048,999} \times 1 \times .9060 = .8840$$

$$\text{Present Value} = \$4.7080$$

The present value of a five-year annuity due of $1 at age 45 is, therefore, equal to $4.7080 and the annuity due, or annual level premium, of $1 for this period will purchase any policy the net single premium of which is equal to $4.7080. But the net single premium on the policy in question was found to be $29.32. If the present value of the $1 annuity due be divided into the net single premium on this policy, the resultant factor will show how many times the annual level premium of $1 must be taken to obtain an annual level premium the present value of which will equal the net single premium, or $29.32. Stated in other words, the annual level premium desired is as many times $1 as the net single premium on the policy is times the present value of a $1 annuity due for the premium-paying period. From this analysis it is possible to state a general rule for ascertaining the net annual level premium on any policy: *Divide the net single premium by the present value of a temporary life annuity due of $1 for the premium-paying period.* Thus, the net annual level premium on a five-year term insurance of $1,000 issued at age 45 is $6.23, computed as follows:

$$\frac{\text{NSP}}{\text{PVLAD of } \$1} = \frac{\$29.32}{4.708} = \$6.23$$

Ordinary Life Insurance

The net single premium for a whole-life policy of $1,000 issued at age 45 is $517.49 according to the figures on page 352. To find the net annual level premium this sum must be divided by the present value of a life annuity due for the whole of life, since premiums are paid continuously through the life of this policy. The method of ascertaining the present value of the life annuity due of $1 follows herewith:

$1 due initially = $1.00000000

$$\frac{9,000,587}{9,048,999} \times 1 \times .9756 = .9704$$

$$\frac{8,948,114}{9,048,999} \times 1 \times .9518 = .9412$$

$$\frac{8,891,204}{9,048,999} \times 1 \times .9286 = .9124$$

$$\frac{8,829,410}{9,048,999} \times 1 \times .9060 = .8840$$

. . . .

. . . .

. . . .

$$\frac{97,165}{9,048,999} \times 1 \times .2909 = .0312$$

$$\frac{63,037}{9,048,999} \times 1 \times .2838 = .0198$$

$$\frac{37,787}{9,048,999} \times 1 \times .2769 = .0116$$

$$\frac{19,331}{9,048,999} \times 1 \times .2702 = .0058$$

$$\frac{6,415}{9,048,999} \times 1 \times .2636 = .0019$$

Present Value = $19.7831

If, therefore, $19.7831 is the present value of a life annuity due of $1, it is possible for an annual premium of $1 paid throughout life to purchase any whole-life policy on which the net single premium is $19.-7831; and the net annual level premium necessary to purchase a life policy for $1,000 will be found, according to our formula, by dividing this sum into $517.49, the net single premium, as shown in the following example:

$$\frac{\$517.49}{19.783} = \$26.16 \text{ net annual level premium}$$

The net annual level premium for an ordinary life policy of $1,000 issued at male age 45, *1958 CSO* 2½ per cent basis, is therefore $26.16.

Limited-Payment Life Policy

If it is desired to pay for the above whole-life policy in twenty annual payments instead of allowing them to continue throughout life, it is required to compute the annual level premium, which, continued for twenty years or ceasing upon prior death, will purchase this policy. In accordance with our formula the annual level premium in this case will be found by dividing into the net single premium the present value of a temporary life annuity due for a term of twenty years following age 45.

The calculation of the present value of the life annuity due at male age 45 for twenty years would be:

$$\$1 \text{ due initially} = \$1.00000000$$

$$\frac{9,000,587}{9,048,999} \times 1 \times .9756 = .9704$$

$$\frac{8,948,114}{9,048,999} \times 1 \times .9518 = .9412$$

$$\frac{8,891,204}{9,048,999} \times 1 \times .9286 = .9124$$

$$\frac{8,829,410}{9,048,999} \times 1 \times .9060 = .8840$$

$$\cdot \qquad \cdot \qquad \cdot \qquad \cdot$$

$$\cdot \qquad \cdot \qquad \cdot \qquad \cdot$$

$$\cdot \qquad \cdot \qquad \cdot \qquad \cdot$$

$$\frac{7,698,698}{9,048,999} \times 1 \times .6905 = .5875$$

$$\frac{7,542,106}{9,048,999} \times 1 \times .6736 = .5614$$

$$\frac{7,374,370}{9,048,999} \times 1 \times .6572 = .5356$$

$$\frac{7,195,099}{9,048,999} \times 1 \times .6412 = .5098$$

$$\frac{7,003,925}{9,048,999} \times 1 \times .6255 = .4841$$

Present Value = $14.7219

The net annual level premium, therefore, for a twenty-payment whole-life policy issued at age 45 is $\dfrac{\$517.49}{14.722}$, or $35.15. It should be noticed that in all cases the net single premium for the whole-life policy (the numerator in the formula) is the same regardless of the premium paying period selected. In the case of a thirty-pay whole-life or a life paid-up at 65 policy, the same principle would be followed, dividing the net single premium ($517.49 at age 45) by the present value of a life annuity due for the appropriate premium-paying period.

Deferred Annuity

Deferred annuities are ordinarily paid for by means of annual rather than single premiums, and the premium may continue through the entire period of deferment or, as in the case of the whole-life policy above, may be limited to a stated number of years. As with premiums on insurances, the annual level premium on these contracts is paid only during survival. If, therefore, the deferred annuity issued at age 40 begins the payment of an annual income of $100 at age 70 if living, and if the net single premium for it is $340.36 as determined on page 366, the annual premium on this policy may be paid until one year prior to the beginning of the annuity, or until the holder of the contract is aged 69. In this case the series of annual premiums becomes a temporary annuity due for a term of thirty years, ages 40 to 69 inclusive. The amount of this net annual premium will be found, therefore, by dividing the net single premium by the present value of a life annuity due of $1 computed for the term stated. Since this is an annuity premium, it is necessary to use the same annuity mortality table used in calculating the net single premium for the policy. This life annuity due is computed using the *Annuity Table for 1949* and 2½ per cent interest as follows:

$1 due initially = $1.00000000

$\dfrac{9,715,549}{9,735,263}$ X 1 X .9756 = .973624

$\dfrac{9,693,980}{9,735,263}$ X 1 X .9518 = .947763

$\dfrac{9,669,929}{9,735,263}$ X 1 X .9286 = .922368

$\dfrac{9,642,815}{9,735,263}$ X 1 X .9060 = .897397

.   .   .   .

.   .   .   .

$$\frac{7,716,840}{9,735,263} \times 1 \times .5394 = .427566$$

$$\frac{7,538,843}{9,735,263} \times 1 \times .5262 = .407481$$

$$\frac{7,350,146}{9,735,263} \times 1 \times .5134 = .387618$$

$$\frac{7,150,273}{9,735,263} \times 1 \times .5009 = .367897$$

$$\frac{6,938,789}{9,735,263} \times 1 \times .4887 = .348320$$

Present Value = $19.7612

The result obtained represents the present value of an annual level premium of $1 paid over the same term as the premiums on the deferred annuity, and this figure divided into the net single premium for the deferred annuity will give a net annual level premium of $17.22, as follows:

$$\frac{\$340.36}{19.761} = \$17.22$$

The annual level premiums computed to this point should afford a sufficiently clear analysis of the subject of the level premium. The principles thus developed can be applied in ascertaining annual premiums on all policies involving risks on a single life. There remain still to be considered two special instances of the periodic premium, or two modifications of the annual premium, namely, premiums paid at intervals of less than one year, and premiums on policies which promise in the event of certain contingencies to return to the purchaser the premiums paid without interest.

OTHER ASPECTS

Premiums Paid at Intervals of Less Than One Year

By an extension of the principles laid down heretofore in computing single and annual premiums, it would now be possible to ascertain weekly, monthly, quarterly, and semiannual premiums. It would be necessary to make the time unit the proper fractional part of a year instead of one year. One difficulty with this method lies in the fact that none of the mortality tables in existence is graded for periods of less than one year. To illustrate, the probability that men arriving at age 25 will die within one week, one month, or six months has not been calculated from any of the tables in use.

We can only readily determine for example, that the chance that he will die *within one year* equals $\dfrac{18,481}{9,575,636}$ according to the *1958 CSO Table.* Thus, the true weekly, monthly, or quarterly premium cannot easily be ascertained, and some method of approximation to the correct result must be used. One method is to make a percentage addition to the annual premium, based on a careful study of past experience, and then divide this result into the requisite number of parts. By this plan the premium is looked upon as an annual premium paid in installments that do not cease upon death. That is, at the beginning of any policy year the entire premium for the policy is considered to be due and payable, but the insured is given the privilege of paying it in installments; then if the contract should mature by death before the total installments for the year are paid, those remaining still due will be deducted from the matured value of the policy and the balance only will be paid to the policyholder.[3] Thus, a policy for $1,000, being paid for by quarterly premiums of $10 might mature by death shortly after the payment of the first $10 installment of the year's premium. Deduction of the remaining three installments of $10 each from the face amount results in the payment to the beneficiary of $970. Most policies currently issued, however, provide that, even if death occurs before all installments of the year's premium have become due, no premiums are deducted from the amount due the beneficiary. This additional "nondeduction" benefit is usually provided by charging, for policies with premiums payable more frequently than annually, a slightly higher amount than would otherwise be required.

The percentage added to the annual premium to obtain the semiannual premium varies with different companies. Some add 2 per cent, some 2½ per cent, 3 per cent, or even 4 per cent. Thus, one company quotes a gross annual [4] premium on an ordinary life policy, age 45, of $32.35. Adding 2 per cent of this amount, or $0.65, gives $33.00, and this result divided by 2 equals $16.50, the semiannual premium quoted in this company's rate book. Another company (which is a participating company, so that the policyholder's cost will be reduced by dividends) quotes an annual premium of $39.55 for the same policy and a semiannual premium of $20.57. This latter figure is obtained by adding 4 per cent and dividing by 2. The same method is used likewise on twenty-payment life policies. At age 45, the annual premiums of the two companies referred to are, respectively, $43.20 and $51.06. If 2 per cent is added to the first and 4 per cent to the second and these results are divided by 2, the amounts obtained for the semiannual premium will be respectively $22.03 and $26.55. These are the quotations found in the rate books.

---

[3] This deduction of unpaid installments is done very seldom today. The waiving of these balances is sometimes referred to as the "nondeduction benefit."

[4] It will be noted that the premiums here quoted are *gross* premiums. The methods of loading for expenses to obtain the gross premium are taken up in Chapter 25, but these methods in no way affect the problem discussed here and therefore a knowledge of them is not necessary to an analysis of the principle involved.

The same method is used in computing quarterly or monthly rates, of course varying the percentage added in each case. From 4 to 6 per cent is usually added to the annual premium and this result divided by 4 to obtain the quarterly premium. Thus, to the annual rate of $32.35 quoted above for an ordinary life policy is added 4 per cent, or $1.29, making a total of $33.64, and this sum divided by 4 gives $8.41, the quoted rate for quarterly payments.

The increase in the rate on premiums paid more frequently than annually is justified on four grounds:

(1) the greater the expense of collection, where collection must be made two, four, or more times yearly instead of only once;

(2) the loss of interest, due to the assumption made in computing annual premiums that the premium is paid in at the beginning of the year and draws interest from that time;

(3) some of the companies justify this increased rate because of the greater tendency to lapse policies where premiums are paid twice or four times yearly instead of only once; and

(4) the cost of providing the nondeduction benefit described above.

Return-Premium Policies

Policies sometimes will include a provision whereby on the death of the insured the premiums paid in will be returned to the payer. This privilege is added to policies to balance some objectionable feature in the contract that militates against its ready sale. For instance, much objection is found to the pure endowment policy because of the possibility of losing one's entire investment in case of death before the maturity of the endowment. In other cases, it is simply added to make a regular contract more salable. These policies sometimes promised the return of the exact premium paid and sometimes a specified amount slightly less than the premium. For instance, if a certain pure endowment costs $50 per year, the company might promise a return of $40 for every premium paid to date of death. Suppose now a company issues a ten-year pure endowment for $1,000 to a male aged 45. It was found on page 353 that the net single premium for this policy is $719.24. The net annual level premium for the same policy will be found by dividing the above sum by the present value of a temporary life annuity due of $1 limited to a term of ten years, beginning at age 45, and this latter value can be found by adding the first ten terms of the appropriate whole-life annuity. This value is $8.712. If, therefore, the following computation is made,

$$\frac{\$719.24}{8.712} = \$82.56$$

it is found that the net annual level premium for the ten-year pure endowment is $82.56. Suppose furthermore that the company promises in event of the death of the policyholder before the ten-year period has elapsed to return to his estate $80 for every premium paid. It is desired to find the extra premium that must be paid to obtain this benefit. The benefit consists in the return of a single $80 if the insured should die during the first year after the contract is issued; if he should die during the second year he gets twice $80; in the third year three times $80; and so on, his death between the payment of his tenth premium and the time when the endowment would have matured entitling his estate to a return of ten times $80, or $800. The chances that any of these payments will be made, therefore, consist in the separate chances or probabilities that he will die within ten years. It is equivalent to the addition to the pure endowment of an increasing term insurance of $80, that is, an insurance of $80 the first year, $160 the second year, and so on. The method of computing the cost of this increasing insurance is, therefore, as follows: The net single premium for an increasing insurance of $80, *1958 CSO* 2½ per cent, male age 45:

$$\frac{48,412}{9,048,999} \times 1 \times \$80 \times .9756 = \$0.4176$$

$$\frac{52,473}{9,048,999} \times 2 \times 80 \times .9518 = 0.8831$$

$$\frac{56,910}{9,048,999} \times 3 \times 80 \times .9286 = 1.4016$$

$$\frac{61,794}{9,048,999} \times 4 \times 80 \times .9060 = 1.9798$$

$$\frac{67,104}{9,048,999} \times 5 \times 80 \times .8839 = 2.6219$$

$$\frac{72,902}{9,048,999} \times 6 \times 80 \times .8623 = 3.3345$$

$$\frac{79,160}{9,048,999} \times 7 \times 80 \times .8413 = 4.1212$$

$$\frac{85,758}{9,048,999} \times 8 \times 80 \times .8207 = 4.9778$$

$$\frac{92,832}{9,048,999} \times 9 \times 80 \times .8007 = 5.9142$$

$$\frac{100,337}{9,048,999} \times 10 \times 80 \times .7812 = 6.9297$$

Net Single Premium = $32.5816

The net single premium for the return-premium feature, namely, $32.58, will be divided by $8.712 to ascertain the net annual level premium as follows:

$$\frac{\$32.58}{8.712} = \$3.74$$

This result, $3.74, is therefore the amount to be added to the net annual level premium for the pure endowment, or $82.56, giving $86.30 as the net premium for the pure endowment with the return-premium feature included.

It would be possible to compute the net annual premium which would return the total or gross premium paid by the insured instead of some arbitrary sum, as was used above, but this would involve processes more complicated than it is appropriate to discuss here. The principles developed have been applied to all kinds of policies, but the return-premium feature is ordinarily added to policies in cases where it may be balanced against some seemingly objectionable characteristic whereby the insured apparently loses. Thus, any policy containing the pure endowment provision and not having a corresponding insurance element offers a good opportunity for the return-premium privilege. Policies involving survivorship likewise make use of it. Cases in point are the deferred annuity and the reversionary annuity.

Life Insurance Reserves | 24

NATURE OF THE RESERVE

ONE OF THE most difficult subjects for the layman to understand in connection with the administration of a life insurance company is the existence of the enormous assets possessed by the different companies and the reasons why these funds must be held. The fact is that virtually all of these assets stand behind liabilities of the company to its policyholders. Without these assets accumulated to assure payment of the companies' liabilities to policyholders, the security of life insurance protection as we know it would not be possible. The chief such liability is known as the *policy reserve*.

Financial Importance

The *Life Insurance Fact Book for 1971* shows that United States' life insurance companies held on December 31, 1970, total admitted assets amounting to $207,254,000,000 and of this sum $167,556,000,000, or 80.9 per cent, stand behind their policy reserve liabilities. A comparison of the total admitted assets and the policy reserves of five of the largest life insurance companies in the United States is also furnished in Table 24-1.

TABLE 24-1. Comparison of Total Admitted Assets and Policy Reserves of Five U.S. Life Insurance Companies

Company	Admitted Assets December 31, 1970 (000,000 omitted)	Policy Reserves December 31, 1970 (000,000 omitted)	Per Cent of Policy Reserves to Admitted Assets
A	$29,134	$22,877	78.9%
B	27,366	23,205	83.3
C	14,371	11,770	81.9
D	10,741	8,355	77.8
E	10,048	7,969	79.3

These figures likewise show that around 80 per cent of the total funds held by these companies represent funds held to support their reserve liabilities. Such vast resources justify a careful analysis of the nature and purposes of the reserve liabilities.

The Origin of the Reserve

The preceding chapters stated that life insurance policies may be purchased by a single payment or by annual premiums paid over a period of years during life. It was also pointed out that mortality rates generally increase with increasing age. Thus, in the early policy years, level premiums exceed the annual cost of insurance. These level premiums bring into the possession of the company funds which are not used immediately to pay policy claims but which must be accounted for by the company and set aside for all the policyholders until needed at some future date. In like manner, when a policy is purchased by a single premium, this premium becomes the total contribution of the insured toward claims paid under contracts of this class, and in the early years of the policy a large share of this single premium must be held by the company to meet future obligations.

Definition of the Reserve

The simplest way in which to define the reserve is to say that it is that amount, which together with future premiums, interest, and benefit of survivorship, will be sufficient, according to the valuation assumptions, to pay future claims. This is the so-called *prospective definition* of the reserve.

The calculation of a net single premium involves an equation, one side of which represents the present value of the benefits promised under the contract and the other the present value of the sum of money required to provide the benefits. At the inception of the contract, the two sides of the equation must be in balance. Once a premium (net single or net level) has been paid, however, the situation is changed. The present value of future benefits is no longer equal to the present value of future net premiums. The former has increased since the benefits are nearer to maturity while the latter has decreased since less premiums remain to be paid, the difference being the accumulating reserve. Consider, for example, a twenty-year annual premium endowment contract at the end of its eighteenth year. The fund on hand (as measured by the reserve) must be a large proportion of the face amount, because only two premiums, and two years' interest and benefit of survivorship remain, whereas the entire face amount must be paid out in two years, or possibly earlier, if death should occur. Thus, the reserve may be defined, prospectively, as *the difference, at any point in time, between the present value of future benefits and the present value of future net premiums.*

Another way of looking at the reserve is the so-called *retrospective view,* under which the reserve is considered as the difference between the accumulation at interest and survivorship of the net premiums received in the past and the accumulation at interest and survivorship of the claims paid. In the example above, this would be the accumulation at interest and survivorship of all eighteen net premiums that have been paid, less the accumulation at interest and survivorship of the death claims that have occurred during the eighteen-year period.

Before reserve calculations or valuation of policy liabilities can be made it is first necessary to select a mortality table (such as the *1958 CSO Table*) and an interest rate (such as 2½ per cent). It is then necessary to calculate the valuation net premium, on the basis of the table and rate selected,[1] and in the manner that has been described in preceding chapters. Then, if the policy duration for which the reserve is needed is selected (eighteen years in the example above), the calculation may proceed, using either the prospective or retrospective method. The retrospective and prospective reserves are always exactly equal to each other, assuming the same set of actuarial assumptions.

It is important to realize that the retrospective (and therefore the prospective) reserve has nothing to do with a company's *actual* past experience. It is always calculated on the assumption that experience has been in accordance with the mortality table selected and interest rate assumed. The term "reserve" has come to have a technical meaning in life insurance, due to the fact that most of the states have passed minimum reserve standards establishing definite methods of valuing policy liabilities.[2]

Reserve Is a Liability

The word "reserve" is somewhat misleading since it does not have the same use here as in the usual commercial dealings where "reserve" is often synonymous with "surplus." The policy reserve of a life insurance company is a *liability.* It represents an *obligation* to the policyholders. As will be brought out in the following discussion, if the company does not maintain the proper policy reserves, it may become insolvent and may eventually be unable to pay claims. The policy reserve is the most important of a life insurance company's liabilities and, as mentioned above, may constitute as much as 80 per cent or more of the total assets of a well-established company.

[1] It is also necessary to select a specific valuation of method. See pp. 398–400.
[2] See pp. 398–402.

TABLE 24-2. Progression of Reserves Under Retrospective Method of
Valuation, Level Annual Premium Basis; 1958 CSO Table and
2½ Per Cent Interest; $1,000 Ordinary Life Issued at
Male Age 35; Net Level Premium, $17.671

Duration	(1) Number Living at Beginning of Designated Year	(2) Number Dying During Designated Year	(3) Premium Paid at Beginning of Year [(1) X 17.671]
1	9,373,807	23,528	$165,644,543
2	9,350,279	24,685	165,228,780
3	9,325,594	26,112	164,792,572
4	9,299,482	27,991	163,331,146
5	9,271,491	30,132	163,836,517
6	9,241,359	32,622	163,304,055
7	9,208,737	35,362	162,727,592
8	9,173,375	38,253	162,102,710
9	9,135,122	41,741	161,426,741
10	9,093,740	44,741	160,695,480
11	9,048,999	48,412	159,904,861
12	9,000,587	52,473	159,049,373
13	8,948,114	56,910	158,122,122
14	8,891,204	61,794	157,116,466
15	8,829,410	67,104	156,024,504
16	8,762,306	72,902	154,838,709
17	8,689,404	79,160	153,550,458
18	8,610,244	85,758	152,151,622
19	8,524,486	92,832	150,636,192
20	8,431,654	100,337	148,995,758
21	8,331,317	108,307	147,222,703
22	8,223,010	116,849	145,308,810
23	8,106,161	125,970	143,243,971
24	7,980,191	135,663	141,017,955
25	7,844,528	145,830	138,620,654
26	7,698,698	156,592	136,043,692
27	7,542,106	167,736	133,276,555
28	7,374,370	179,271	130,312,492
29	7,195,099	191,174	127,144,594
30	7,003,925	203,394	123,766,359
31	6,800,531	215,917	120,172,183
32	6,584,614	228,749	116,356,714
33	6,355,865	241,777	112,314,490
34	6,114,088	254,835	108,042,049
35	5,859,253	267,241	103,538,860
36	5,592,012	278,426	98,816,444

(4) Interest for Year	(5) Death Claims	(6) Reserve at End of Year	(7) Reserve per Survivor at End of Year
$\begin{bmatrix} 0.025\,((6)\,\text{prior} \\ \text{year} + (3)) \end{bmatrix}$	[(2) × 1,000]	[(6) prior year + (3) + (4) − (5)]	$\begin{bmatrix} \dfrac{(6)}{(1)}\,\text{following} \\ \text{year} \end{bmatrix}$
$ 4,141,114	$ 23,528,000	$ 146,257,657	$ 15.64
7,787,161	24,685,000	294,588,598	31.59
11,484,529	26,112,000	444,753,699	47.83
15,227,121	27,991,000	596,320,966	64.32
19,003,937	30,132,000	749,029,420	81.05
22,808,337	32,362,000	902,519,812	98.01
26,631,185	35,362,000	1,056,516,589	115.17
30,465,482	38,253,000	1,210,831,781	132.55
34,306,463	41,382,000	1,365,182,985	150.12
38,146,962	44,741,000	1,519,284,427	167.90
41,979,732	48,412,000	1,672,757,020	185.85
45,795,159	52,473,000	1,825,128,552	203.97
49,581,267	56,910,000	1,975,921,941	222.24
53,325,960	61,794,000	2,124,570,367	240.63
57,014,872	67,104,000	2,270,505,743	259.12
60,633,611	72,902,000	2,413,076,063	277.71
64,165,663	79,160,000	2,551,632,184	296.35
67,594,595	85,758,000	2,685,620,401	315.05
70,906,415	92,832,000	2,814,331,008	333.79
74,083,169	100,337,000	2,937,072,935	352.54
77,132,744	108,307,000	3,053,121,383	371.29
79,983,720	116,849,000	3,161,564,913	390.02
82,585,376	125,970,000	3,261,424,260	408.69
85,109,154	135,663,000	3,351,888,369	427.29
87,246,571	145,830,000	3,431,925,594	445.78
89,215,793	156,592,000	3,500,593,079	464.14
90,819,992	167,736,000	3,556,953,626	482.34
92,216,569	179,271,000	3,600,211,687	500.37
93,181,615	191,174,000	3,629,373,896	512.19
93,784,239	203,394,000	3,643,520,494	535.77
94,108,480	215,917,000	3,641,884,157	553.09
93,986,765	228,749,000	3,623,478,636	570.10
93,363,867	241,777,000	3,587,379,993	586.74
92,366,739	254,835,000	3,532,953,781	602.97
90,917,624	267,241,000	3,460,169,265	618.77
88,997,717	278,426,000	3,369,557,426	634.14

TABLE 24-2.   (cont'd.)

Duration	(1) Number Living at Beginning of Designated Year	(2) Number Dying During Designated Year	(3) Premium Paid at Beginning of Year [(1) X 17.671]
37	5,313,586	287,731	$ 93,896,378
38	5,025,855	294,766	88,811,884
39	4,731,089	299,289	83,603,074
40	4,431,800	301,894	78,314,338
41	4,129,906	303,011	72,979,569
42	3,826,895	303,014	67,625,062
43	3,523,881	301,997	62,270,501
44	3,221,884	299,829	56,933,912
45	2,922,055	295,683	51,635,634
46	2,626,372	288,848	46,410,620
47	2,337,524	278,983	41,306,387
48	2,058,541	265,902	36,376,478
49	1,792,639	249,858	31,677,724
50	1,542,781	231,433	27,262,483
51	1,311,348	211,311	23,172,831
52	1,100,037	190,108	19,438,754
53	909,929	168,455	16,079,355
54	741,474	146,997	13,102,587
55	594,477	126,303	10,505,003
56	468,174	106,809	8,273,103
57	361,365	88,813	6,385,681
58	272,552	72,480	4,816,266
59	200,072	57,881	3,535,472
60	142,191	45,026	2,512,657
61	97,165	34,128	1,717,003
62	63,037	25,250	1,113,927
63	37,787	18,456	667,734
64	19,331	12,916	341,598
65	6,415	6,415	113,359

METHOD OF CALCULATION

Retrospective Reserve

The retrospective method of valuation may be explained in terms of either an individual policy or a group approach.

(4) Interest for Year $\begin{bmatrix} 0.025\ ((6)\ prior \\ year + (3)) \end{bmatrix}$	(5) Death Claims [(2) × 1,000]	(6) Reserve at End of Year [(6) prior year + (3) + (4) − (5)]	(7) Reserve per Survivor at End of Year $\begin{bmatrix} (6) \\ (1)\ following \\ year \end{bmatrix}$
$86,559,676	$287,731,000	$3,262,282,480	$649.10
83,790,027	294,766,000	3,140,118,391	663.72
80,593,843	299,289,000	3,005,026,308	678.06
77,109,091	301,894,000	2,858,555,737	692.16
73,263,564	303,011,000	2,701,787,870	706.00
69,244,880	303,014,000	2,535,643,812	719.56
64,950,407	301,997,000	2,360,867,720	732.76
60,448,591	299,829,000	2,178,421,223	745.51
55,759,526	295,683,000	1,990,133,383	757.75
50,911,839	288,848,000	1,798,607,842	769.45
45,986,461	278,983,000	1,606,917,690	780.61
41,087,220	265,902,000	1,418,479,388	791.28
36,255,287	249,858,000	1,236,554,399	801.51
31,591,431	231,433,000	1,063,975,313	811.36
27,183,229	211,311,000	903,020,373	820.90
23,062,830	190,108,000	755,413,957	830.19
19,288,231	168,455,000	622,326,543	839.31
15,886,489	146,997,000	504,318,618	848.34
12,868,358	126,303,000	401,388,979	857.35
10,240,781	106,809,000	313,093,863	866.42
7,988,164	88,813,000	238,654,708	875.63
6,086,751	72,480,000	177,077,725	885.07
4,515,951	57,881,000	127,248,148	894.91
3,244,216	45,026,000	87,979,021	905.46
2,241,948	34,128,000	57,809,972	917.08
1,473,679	25,250,000	35,147,578	930.15
894,951	18,456,000	18,254,263	944.30
465,196	12,916,000	6,145,057	957.92
156,584	6,415,000	—	—

Group Approach.   The reserve arises out of the use of the level-premium plan of payment.[3] Under this plan, premiums in the early policy years are almost always more than sufficient to take care of the death claims that are assumed, creating a fund that can be used in later policy years, when death rates rise sharply and the level premiums are insufficient

[3] The single-premium policy, while not technically a "level premium," involves the same principle of advance funding of the pure insurance costs leading to the need for a reserve.

to meet the claims submitted. The retrospective reserve can be thought of as an *unearned premium reserve* representing the provision in early premiums for advance funding of the benefits of surviving policyholders and is shown on the company's financial statement as a liability item. The manner in which reserves arise is shown in Table 24–2.

Table 24–2 shows the progression of reserves on a group of ordinary life contracts issued at age 35 and written in the amount of $1,000. According to the *1958 CSO Table,* 9,373,807 persons would be alive at age 35 out of an original group of 10,000,000 individuals alive at age 0. In order to simplify the illustration, it is assumed that the group of persons taking out an ordinary life contract at age 35 is composed of the survivors of the original group of 10,000,000. The net level annual premium for an ordinary life contract issued at male age 35, assuming the *1958 CSO Table* and 2½ per cent interest, is $17.671 per $1,000 of face amount.

Individual Approach.   The retrospective method of reserve valuation may also be illustrated with reference to an individual policy. Consideration of the process by which the net level reserve is built up involves an understanding of the *"cost of insurance"* concept. Reference was made in previous chapters to the net amount at risk, which is the amount of death benefit minus the terminal reserve at the end of the policy year.[4] When a policyholder dies, the reserve held on account of his policy is no longer required, and the amount of assets corresponding to that reserve is freed to help pay the claim. The balance of the claim, or the amount at risk, is paid for through charges to all policyholders, including those who die.

The contribution which each policyholder must make as his pro rata share of death claims in any particular year is called the cost of insurance based upon the net amount at risk. It is the amount each must pay for insurance *protection.* For any particular policy year it is determined by multiplying the *net amount at risk* at the end of such year (face of the policy less the terminal reserve)[5] by the tabular probability of death during such year. Thus, assuming the reserve under an ordinary life policy issued at male age 35 of $167.90 at the end of the tenth year, the cost of insurance

based upon the net amount at risk, for the tenth year is $\dfrac{\$832.10 \times 4.92}{1,000}$

or $4.09. The net amount at risk is $832.10 (1,000 — 167.90) and the year's probability of death at male age 44, according to the *1958 CSO*

---

[4] See p. 11.

[5] In order to determine the net amount at risk and hence the cost of insurance based on the net amount at risk, it is necessary to know the terminal reserve for the year, the very value being sought in a retrospective reserve determination. This is no problem utilizing algebraic or other methods, but creates an apparent impasse arithmetically. The purpose here is to demonstrate the cost of insurance concept and its role in a retrospective reserve determination. In order to avoid complicating the presentation, this arithmetic contadiction is ignored here.

Table is 4.92 per 1,000. Therefore, the policy's share of death claims during the tenth year of insurance is $4.09 per $1,000 of face amount.

The process of accumulation illustrating the determination of the retrospective reserve for an individual policy during the tenth year will be as follows:

Terminal reserve for ninth year	$150.12
Add net level annual premium	17.67
Initial reserve for tenth year	$167.79
Tabular interest at 2½ per cent	4.20
Fund end of tenth year	$171.99
Deduct cost of insurance based on the net amount at risk	4.09
Terminal reserve for tenth year	$167.90

Thus, the retrospective terminal reserve for any particular policy year can be obtained by adding the net level annual premium for the year in question to the terminal reserve of the preceding year, increasing the combined sum (called the initial reserve for the current year) by one year's interest at the *assumed* rate, and deducting the cost of insurance for the current year utilizing the *assumed* mortality table. It should be noted that if the policy is paid up, there are no annual premiums to consider and the cost of insurance is provided from the tabular interest on the reserve.

Table 24–3 shows the cost of insurance for a $1,000 ordinary life policy issued at age 35 for each policy year to the end of the mortality table. The cost of insurance increases steadily until the fifty-seventh year, after which it declines due to the fact that the net amount at risk is decreasing at a more rapid rate than the death rate is increasing.

Reserves on Individual Policies.   It is important to understand that neither the assets nor the total or aggregate reserve of a life insurance company, in theory, can be allocated to individual policyholders. It is only through the cooperation of large numbers of persons that life insurance is possible; insurance is a group concept and the reserve is also. If an equitable apportionment of the aggregate assets of a company were required to be made (for example, in the event of liquidation), such an allocation should, strictly speaking, consider the relative state of health of the various policyholders and their respective chances of survival. A policyholder in poor health should be entitled to a relatively greater share than one who is in good health, since his policy actuarially has a greater value, that is, his relative chance of death would be greater. Since it would be impractical to determine the relative value of the policies, the reserve under a particular policy is considered to be its pro rata share of the aggregate

TABLE 24-3. Cost of Insurance for $1,000 Ordinary Life Policy, Age 35, 1958 CSO Table and 2½ Per Cent Interest, Net Level Premium Reserves

(1) Policy Year $[t]$	(2) Attained Age at Beginning of Policy Year $[= 35 + (t-1)]$	(3) 1958 CSO Mortality Rate $[= q_{35} + (t-1)]$	(4) Amount at Risk During Year $[= 1,000\,(1 - {}_tV_{35})]$	(5) Cost of Insurance $[=(3) \times (4)]$
1	35	.00251	$984.36	$ 2.47
2	36	.00264	968.41	2.56
3	37	.00280	952.17	2.67
4	38	.00301	935.68	2.82
5	39	.00325	918.95	2.99
6	40	.00353	901.99	3.18
7	41	.00384	884.83	3.40
8	42	.00417	867.45	3.62
9	43	.00453	849.88	3.85
10	44	.00492	832.10	4.09
11	45	.00535	814.15	4.36
12	46	.00583	796.03	4.64
13	47	.00636	777.76	4.95
14	48	.00695	759.37	5.28
15	49	.00760	740.88	5.63
16	50	.00832	722.29	6.01
17	51	.00911	703.65	6.41
18	52	.00996	684.95	6.82
19	53	.01089	666.21	7.26
20	54	.01190	647.46	7.70
21	55	.01300	628.71	8.17
22	56	.01421	609.98	8.67
23	57	.01554	591.31	9.19
24	58	.01700	572.71	9.74
25	59	.01859	554.22	10.30
26	60	.02034	535.86	10.90
27	61	.02224	517.66	11.51
28	62	.02431	499.63	12.15
29	63	.02657	481.81	12.80
30	64	.02904	464.23	13.48
31	65	.03175	446.91	14.19
32	66	.03474	429.90	14.93
33	67	.03804	413.26	15.72
34	68	.04168	397.03	16.55
35	69	.04561	381.23	17.39
36	70	.04979	365.86	18.21
37	71	.05415	350.90	19.00

TABLE 24-3.   (cont'd.)

(1)	(2)	(3)	(4)	(5)
Policy Year $[t]$	Attained Age at Beginning of Policy Year $[= 35 + (t - 1)]$	1958 CSO Mortality Rate $[= q_{35} + (t - 1)]$	Amount at Risk During Year $[= 1,000 (1 - {}_tV_{35})]$	Cost of Insurance $[= (3) \times (4)]$
38	72	.05865	$336.28	$19.72
39	73	.06326	321.94	20.37
40	74	.06812	307.84	20.97
41	75	.07337	294.00	21.57
42	76	.07918	280.44	22.21
43	77	.08570	267.24	22.90
44	78	.09306	254.49	23.68
45	79	.10119	242.25	24.51
46	80	.10998	230.55	25.36
47	81	.11935	219.39	26.18
48	82	.12917	208.72	26.96
49	83	.13938	198.49	27.67
50	84	.15001	188.64	28.30
51	85	.16114	179.10	28.86
52	86	.17282	169.81	29.35
53	87	.18513	160.69	29.75
54	88	.19825	151.66	30.07
55	89	.21246	142.65	30.31
56	90	.22814	133.58	30.47
57	91	.24577	124.37	30.57
58	92	.26593	114.93	30.56
59	93	.28930	105.09	30.40
60	94	.31666	94.54	29.94
61	95	.35124	82.92	29.12
62	96	.40056	69.85	27.98
63	97	.48842	55.70	27.20
64	98	.66815	42.08	28.12
65	99	1.00000	0.00	0.00

reserve for all identical policies of the same age of issue and duration. In terms of a continuing company, this is reasonable in any case since all lives in a given class have essentially the same characteristics *at issue*.

Prospective Reserve

Although the retrospective method of computation provides a clear exposition of the origin and purpose of the reserve, it is seldom used in practice. State valuation laws express minimum reserve requirements in terms of the prospective method mentioned earlier, and there is a preference for the prospective method because of its simplicity.

Basic Prospective Relationship.   As mentioned earlier, the reserve is the balancing factor in the basic insurance equation, that is, in prospective terms, the reserve is the difference between the present value of future benefits and the present value of future premiums.

The prospective net level terminal reserve under a policy issued at age (x) at the end of any given number of years (t) is equal to the net single premium for the policy in question at the age of valuation (x + t) minus the net level annual premium at age of issue (x) multiplied by the present value of a life annuity due of $1 for the remainder of the premium-paying period calculated at the age of valuation (x + t), that is (for an ordinary life policy),

$$_t V_x = 1,000\, A_{x+t} - P_x\, \ddot{a}_{x+t}$$

Thus, an ordinary life insurance policy for $1,000 issued at age 35 would have a *tenth*-year reserve formularized using accepted notations as follows:

$$_{10} V_{35} = 1,000\, A_{35+10} - P_{35}\, \ddot{a}_{35+10}$$
or
$$_{10} V_{35} = 1,000\, A_{45} - P_{35}\, \ddot{a}_{45}$$

Substituting known values in the formula, the computation of the reserve is a simple arithmetic process:

$$_{10} V_{35} = \$517.49 - (\$17.671 \times \$19.783) = \$167.90$$

The same concept and calculation can be presented in less formal symbolism as follows:

Net Level Terminal Reserve Age of valuation		NSP Age of valuation		(NLP Age of issue	×	PVLAD of $1 for remaining premium-paying period)
Net Level Terminal Reserve = Age of valuation	=	NSP Age of valuation	−	(NLP Age of issue	×	PVLAD of $1 for remaining premium-paying period)

or

Net Level Terminal Reserve Age 45	=	NSP Age 45	−	(NLP Age 35	×	PVLAD of $1 for remaining premium-paying period age 45)

and

Net Level Terminal Reserve Age 45	=	$517.49	−	($17.671	×	$19.783) = $167.90

At the inception of a contract the present value of future benefits (PVFB) is exactly equal to the present value of the future premiums (PVFP). Thus,

$$\text{PVFB} = \text{PVFP at } \textit{date of issue.}$$

But as soon as the contract goes in force and one premium (single or annual) has been paid, the present value of future benefits (PVFB) almost always[6] exceeds the present value of future premiums (PVFP). This should be apparent since fewer premiums (or no premiums) remain to be paid and the present value of future benefits is greater since the policy is nearer to maturity. The difference between these two is a reserve obligation of the company. Thus,

Net Level Terminal Reserve Age of valuation	=	PVFB Age of valuation	−	PVFP Age of valuation

It has already been shown that the net single premiums (NSP) for a given policy is equal to the present value of future benefits, and the equation may be written,

Net Level Terminal Reserve Age of valuation	=	NSP Age of valuation	−	PVFP Age of valuation

Also, the present value of future premiums must necessarily be equal to the net level annual premium (NLP) for the contract under consideration multiplied by the present value of a life annuity due (PVLAD) of $1 for the *remaining* premium-paying period. Finally, then, the equation may be written,

Net Level Terminal Reserve Age of valuation	=	NSP Age of valuation	−	(NLP Age of issue	×	PVLAD of $1 Remaining Premium-paying period)

Considering the equation, the computation of the twentieth year net level reserve on a fifteen-payment whole life policy issued at age 35 is

Net Level Terminal Reserve 55	=	NSP 55	−	(NLP 35	×	0)	=	NSP 55

The result illustrates the principle that on a paid-up policy there are no future premiums and, consequently, the reserve *must* be equal to the present value of future benefits which can be measured by the net single premium of the given policy at the attained age of valuation. The principle is even more graphically illustrated by the single-premium policy which is paid-up after the payment of the first premium. Thus, a single-premium whole-life issued at age 35 would produce an identical twentieth-year reserve and be equal to the net single premium for a whole-life policy at age 55. The reserve at a given attained age on all paid-up policies of the same type and amount are, at the age of valuation, equal to each other and all equal the net single premium for that type of policy.

Considering a policy which is not fully paid, the computation of the present value of future premiums involves the determination of the original

---

[6] This is true in general of ordinary life policies, but at issue age 0 on 1958 CSO Ordinary Life, the first year terminal reserve is negative. The statement is also often not true for decreasing term insurance.

net level annual premium charged for the contract which is multiplied by the present value of a temporary life annuity due of $1 for the remaining premium-paying period. Thus, the twentieth-year net level reserve on an *ordinary* life policy issued at age 25 would be,

$$\text{Net Level Terminal Reserve}_{45} = \text{NSP}_{45} - (\text{NLP}_{25} \times \text{PVLAD of \$1 for life})_{45}$$

The tenth-year net level reserve on a twenty-payment whole-life policy issued at age 25 would be,

$$\text{Net Level Terminal Reserve}_{35} = \text{NSP}_{35} - (\text{NLP}_{25} \times \text{PVLAD of \$1 for 10 years})_{35}$$

Finally, the tenth-year net level reserve on a twenty-year endowment policy issued at age 25 would be,

$$\text{Net Level Terminal Reserve}_{35} = \text{NSP}_{35} - (\text{NLP}_{25} \times \text{PVLAD of \$1 for 10 years})_{35}$$

Computation of Reserves. Table 24–4 shows the actual computation of these reserves utilizing the principles developed here and in the earlier chapters concerning rate calculations.

TABLE 24-4. Computation of Prospective Net Level Reserves

(1958 CSO Table and 2½ Per Cent Interest)

	Net Single Premium			Present Value of Life Annuity Due of $1		
Age	Whole-Life	20-Year Endowment	10-Year Endowment	Life	20 Years	10 Years
25	$339.65	$617.92	$783.10	$27.074	$15.665	$8.893
35	420.13	623.77	784.01	23.774	15.425	8.856
45	517.49	640.95	787.52	19.783	14.721	8.712
55	624.55	678.56	796.21	15.393	13.179	8.355

$$\text{Net Level Terminal Reserve Age of Valuation} = \text{NSP Age of Valuation} - (\text{NLP age of issue} \times \text{PVLAD of \$1 for remaining premium paying period})$$

Computation

1. *Twentieth-Year Net Level Terminal Reserve, Ordinary Life Issued at Age 25:*

$$\text{Net Level Reserve}_{45} = \text{NSP}_{45} - (\text{NLP}_{25} \times \text{PVLAD of \$1 for life})_{45}$$

$$\text{Net Level Reserve} \atop 45 = 517.49 - \left[\frac{339.65}{27.074} \times 19.783\right]$$

$$\text{Net Level Reserve} = \$269.31$$

2. *Tenth-Year Net Level Terminal Reserve, Twenty-Payment Life Issued at Age 25:*

$$\text{Net Level Reserve} \atop 35 = \frac{\text{NSP}}{35} - \frac{\text{(NLP}}{25} \times \frac{\text{PVLAD of \$1 for 10 years)}}{35}$$

$$\text{Net Level Reserve} \atop 35 = 420.13 - \left[\frac{339.65}{15.665} \times 8.856\right]$$

$$\text{Net Level Reserve} \atop 35 = \$228.12$$

3. *Tenth-Year Net Level Terminal Reserve, Twenty-Year Endowment Issued at Age 25:*

$$\text{Net Level Reserve} \atop 35 = \frac{\text{NSP}}{35} - \frac{\text{(NLP}}{25} \times \frac{\text{PVLAD of \$1 for 10 years)}}{35}$$

$$\text{Net Level Reserve} \atop 35 = 784.01 - \left[\frac{617.92}{15.665} \times 8.856\right]$$

$$\text{Net Level Reserve} = \$434.69$$

SIGNIFICANCE OF ACTUARIAL ASSUMPTIONS

In measuring or valuing its liabilities under outstanding contracts, a life insurance company must make assumptions as to the rate of mortality among its policyholders and the rate of earnings on the assets standing behind the reserves. These assumptions are reflected in the mortality table and rate of interest assumed in making the valuation. The preceding discussion assumed the *1958 CSO Table* and 2½ per cent interest. Other assumptions, however, can and are being used in reserve valuations. It is important, therefore, to consider the impact on reserves of the choice of the mortality table and interest rate used.

Mortality

During the premium-paying period, the chief factor which governs the size of the reserve is the *rate of change from age to age* or the *slope* of the mortality curve. The steeper the slope of the mortality curve, the greater will be the reserve. Thus, a given mortality table, at a given age, may show a much lower *level* of mortality than another mortality table and still result in a considerably larger reserve. It is further important to note that the reserves under a specified table may be higher at some ages and durations than those of another table, and lower at other ages and durations.

In practice, it is frequently impossible to determine by a review of the mortality rates which mortality table will result in the larger reserve at a given age. In fact, the determination of the effect on reserves of a change in mortality assumptions is a complex mathematical problem and is beyond the scope of this volume.[7]

Table 24–5 shows a comparison of reserves under the *1941 CSO Table* and the *1958 CSO Table,* assuming an interest rate of 2½ per cent in each case. In general, *1958 CSO* reserves are slightly lower than *1941 CSO*

TABLE 24-5.   Net Level Terminal Reserves per $1,000

*(1941 and 1958 CSO Mortality Tables at 2½ Per Cent Interest
Issued at Male Age 35)*

Ordinary Life			20-Year Endowment		
Duration	1941 CSO	1958 CSO	Duration	1941 CSO	1958 CSO
1	$ 16.49	$ 15.64	1	$ 38.42	$ 39.17
10	174.39	167.90	5	202.29	204.66
20	362.45	352.54	10	430.62	435.31
30	546.80	535.77	15	692.05	696.65
50	824.54	811.36	20	1,000.00	1,000.00
60	906.44	905.46			

reserves on life plans and slightly higher on endowment plans. In the aggregate, *1958 CSO* reserves will generally be slightly lower than *1941 CSO* reserves.

Interest

In contrast to a change in mortality assumptions, the impact on reserves of a change in interest assumption can be more easily visualized. Thus, if the rate of interest assumed is decreased, the result will be an increase in reserves. This may be explained simply by the fact that the smaller anticipated earnings must be offset by a larger reserve at any point in time if the face amount is still to be accumulated within the same period of time.

An explanation of the impact of the change in interest assumption in terms of the conventional prospective and retrospective methods of calculation is not as easily grasped. Such an explanation is complicated by the

[7] See C. Wallace Jordan, Jr., *Life Contingencies,* 2nd ed. (Chicago: Society of Actuaries, 1967), pp. 118–123.

fact that *both* the earnings on the reserve and the net premiums are affected by the change, and the net effect of these modifications leads to the final reserve level.

The impact of a change in interest assumptions on the reserves of an individual contract utilizing the *1958 CSO Table* is presented in Table 24-6.

In view of the decline in the general level of interest rates during the decades of the 1930's and 1940's, virtually all life insurance companies lowered the rate of interest assumed in premium and reserve computations for new life insurance and annuity contracts.

TABLE 24-6. Terminal Reserve per $1,000—1958 CSO Table
Varying Rates of Interest

(Ordinary Life, Male Age 35)

Duration	2½ Per Cent	3 Per Cent	3½ Per Cent
1	$ 15.64	$ 14.30	$ 13.08
10	167.90	156.29	145.49
20	352.54	334.23	316.81
30	535.77	516.21	497.20
50	811.36	799.12	786.82
60	905.46	898.40	891.21

Today, most new participating life insurance contracts are being written on a 2½, 2¾, or 3 per cent interest basis, with the 2½ per cent basis still predominating. The current higher general level of interest rates has led to a significant number of changes in interest assumptions on new business, many companies doing so at the time they adopted the *1958 CSO Table* for reserve and nonforfeiture purposes.[8]

During the forties, many companies reduced the interest assumption on *old* business for reserve valuation purposes (resulting in increased reserves) despite the fact that no change could be made in the guaranteed premium rates. This was ordinarily accomplished by charging accumulated earnings of prior years, at one time or over a period of years. Once adequate amounts had been transferred to the reserves, the policies were then treated as if they had been written on the lower interest basis from the beginning, except that in some cases surrender values were not increased.[9] With the larger reserves, the companies were then able to meet their reserve requirements with a lower rate of earnings on their invested funds, and their reserves represented a more conservative appraisal of their liabilities to such policyholders.

[8] See p. 399.
[9] If the change in interest assumption was in excess of ½ per cent, in most states, consideration had to be given to increased surrender values. See pp. 435–436.

Plan of Insurance

The relative reserves for various plans of whole-life insurance are illustrated in Table 24–7.

TABLE 24-7. Terminal Reserves, Whole-Life Policies of $1,000, Male Age 35

(1958 CSO Table and 2½ Per Cent Interest)

Duration	Ordinary Life	Life Paid-up at 65	20-Pay Life	10-Pay Life
1	$ 15.64	$ 19.12	$ 25.47	$ 46.23
2	31.59	38.63	51.52	93.62
3	47.83	58.54	78.14	142.19
4	64.32	78.81	105.32	191.94
5	81.05	99.43	133.05	242.90
10	167.90	207.59	280.22	517.49
20	352.54	448.66	624.55	624.55
30	535.77	730.81	730.81	730.81
40	692.16	821.49	821.49	821.49
50	811.36	890.61	890.61	890.61
60	905.46	945.17	945.17	945.17
65	1,000.00	1,000.00	1,000.00	1,000.00

Table 24–7 demonstrates the fact that all limited-payment policies, assuming the same age of issue and amount, have the same reserve as a single-premium policy after they have been fully paid. In terms of the formula discussed earlier, the temporary life annuity due becomes zero after all premiums have been paid and the reserve becomes the net single premium in question at the insured's attained age. Similar principles apply to endowment contracts.

OTHER ASPECTS

Statutory Regulation of Reserves

Life insurance premiums as such are not generally subject to regulation by the various state regulatory authorities. The adequacy of such premiums is regulated indirectly by regulation of reserve liabilities. Because of the regulation of policy reserves, they have come to be known as *legal reserves* and the term "legal reserve life insurance company" has come to be commonly applied to companies carrying such reserve liabilities in their financial statements. Actually, the states only prescribe the basis on which *minimum* reserves are to be calculated, the companies being permitted to use any other basis which results in reserves equal to or greater than those produced by the statutory method. The basis is stated in terms of the *mortality table to be used,* the *maximum rate of interest to be assumed,* and the *valuation method to be applied.* The requirements differ as between life insurance and annuities and as between ordinary, group, and industrial life insurance. Supplementary agreements relating to proceeds left with the insurance company are subject to special rules.

Prior to 1948, the legal minimum standard in most states for computing reserves for ordinary insurance was the *American Experience Table* and 3½ per cent interest. In most jurisdictions some modification[10] of the net level premium reserve was permitted. The minimum basis for valuing reserves for newly issued ordinary policies was changed (adopted by individual companies no later than January 1, 1948) to the *1941 CSO Table* and 3½ per cent interest.[11] Although this Standard Valuation Law is still the minimum basis for reserves in all states, the *1958 CSO Table* and 3½ per cent interest was made mandatory in all states for ordinary policies issued on or after January 1, 1966.[12] As described in a later chapter, in both the original Standard Valuation Law and the new Standard, a *modified reserve,* not the net level premium method, is prescribed as the minimum basis.

Annual valuation of policy liabilities is required in every state. In practice, life insurance companies often use a reserve basis more conservative than that required by law. Even though state laws permit the use of a 3½ per cent interest assumption many companies use the same interest assumption as that on which their final gross premiums are expressed, currently 2½ per cent in the majority of participating companies. It will be explained later[13] that gross premiums are actually calculated on up-to-date, realistic mortality, interest, and expense experience, rather than on the assumptions used in calculating the net premium underlying the final gross premiums or the valuation net premium. In any case, computing reserves on the *1941* or *1958 CSO Table* and 2½ per cent interest is conservative, and actually provides a greater margin of safety than the minimum required by valuation laws.

Another factor which provides an additional margin of safety through reserve regulation is the requirement of a *net* premium method of valuation. Under this method of valuation, it is assumed that only the net premium on

---

[10] See pp. 422–426.

[11] In New York, the interest assumption was limited to 3 per cent.

[12] The minimum valuation standard is the *1961 Commissioners Standard Industrial Table of Mortality* and 3½ per cent interest for industrial life insurance issued after January 1, 1968.

[13] See Chapter 25.

the reserve basis is available year by year, including the first year, for the payment of claims. *Loading,* the addition to the net premium for expenses, contingencies, profits, and in some cases dividends, whether in connection with past or future premiums, is not taken into account.

At one time *gross* premium valuation was widespread. Furthermore, it was customary, in this regard, to ignore future expenses and to assume that the entire gross premium would be available for the payment of claims. The present *net* premium method of valuation assumes that none of the loading[14] will be available to pay claims. Actually, the truth usually lies somewhere between these two extremes, depending upon the mortality and interest assumptions underlying the gross premium. The loading in excess of that required for expenses could be considered in evaluating a company's financial position, but the present practice leans in the direction of conservatism, a practice looked on with favor when valuing liabilities.

Deficiency Reserves

The requirement of so-called deficiency reserves has long been a feature of state insurance laws, but has become much more significant in recent years. It was a prime cause in the move to develop the *1958 CSO Table* and the new valuation legislation.

If the *gross premium* charged by a life insurance company for a particular class of policies should be *less* than the *valuation net premium,* the company is required to maintain for such policies a supplemental reserve, a so-called *deficiency reserve.* The valuation net premium is the net premium used in the calculation of the company's policy reserves, and historically this has been considerably less than the gross premium for the various classes of policies issued. In recent years, however, continued improvement in mortality and increasing price competition brought gross premium levels down to levels approaching or even below valuation net premiums. This was particularly a problem for those smaller companies issuing nonparticipating business, with limited surplus available to establish such supplemental reserves.

Deficiency reserve laws are founded on the fact that the use, in the prospective reserve formula, of a valuation net level premium larger than the gross premium which will actually be received overstates the present value of future premiums and, consequently, understates the amount of the reserve. The deficiency is represented by the present value of the excess of the valuation net premium over the gross annual premium. In contrast to the regular policy reserves which increase with duration, deficiency reserves for a given class of policies decrease over time, disappearing altogether at the end of the premium-paying period.

---

[14] Under the Commissioners Reserve Valuation Method, the whole loading is released only on policies with a net premium equal to or smaller than a 20-pay whole-life. See pp. 425–426.

Consideration has been given to amending the deficiency reserve laws to authorize the use of the valuation net premium for *minimum* reserves regardless of the actual valuation assumptions adopted by a particular company.

Terminal, Initial, and Mean Reserves

Depending upon the point of *time* within the policy year that valuation occurs, reserves may be classified as *terminal, initial,* and *mean.* The calculations illustrated earlier have been concerned primarily with the terminal reserve, that is, the reserve at the end of any given policy year. The initial reserve for any particular year is the reserve at the beginning of the policy year and is equal to the terminal reserve for the preceding year increased by the net level annual premium (if any) for the current year. The mean reserve is the arithmetic average of the initial reserve and the terminal reserve for any year of valuation, but never less than half the net annual premium.

The *initial reserve* is used principally in connection with the determination of dividends under participating policies. The initial reserve is generally selected as the basis for allocation of interest earnings in excess of that assumed in the reserve.

The *terminal reserve* is also used in connection with dividend distributions, since the mortality savings are allocated on the basis of the "net amount at risk," and the terminal reserve is used to determine the net amount at risk. The terminal reserve concept is also used to determine nonforfeiture values, although since 1948, a so-called adjusted premium is used rather than the net level premium in such determinations.[15] The terminal reserve is also used in connection with that form of reinsurance which is based on yearly renewable term insurance for the "net amount at risk."

The *mean reserve* is used in connection with the annual statements of life insurance companies. Since policies are written at different points throughout the year, and company annual statements are prepared as of December 31, it would be extremely complicated and expensive to attempt a precise calculation for each individual policy. Consequently, for purposes of the annual statement, it is assumed that policy anniversaries are uniformly distributed throughout the calender year of issue, and the mean reserve is used for such valuation purposes.

Other Reserves

Special Benefits. The law requires that a minimum reserve liability be maintained for accidental death and waiver-of-premium

[15] See pp. 432–435.

benefits and an appropriate liability for supplementary contracts without life contingencies, dividend accumulations and similar benefits.

Accidental death benefit minimum reserves are determined in the same manner as ordinary policy reserves, using a mortality table (currently, the *1959 Accidental Death Benefits Table*) based on specific cause of death.

Reserves for waiver of premium are, of course, based upon appropriate morbidity and mortality tables. These form the basis for predicting the joint probability of dying or becoming disabled and, assuming the waiver-of-premium annuity has been entered upon, the joint probability of death or recovery.

Supplementary contracts without life contingencies, dividend accumulations, and similar benefits are easily valued, involving only compound interest calculations.

Voluntary Reserves. In addition to the legal reserves, which are held to meet specific policy obligations, life insurance companies set aside various *voluntary* reserves which really represent earmarking of surplus for particular purposes, and may or may not be liabilities. These surplus reserves are discussed in Chapter 42.

Gross Premiums | 25

THE NET PREMIUM, or that portion of the premium which cares for policy claims, was analyzed at length in preceding chapters. The gross premium includes the above plus an amount called loading, the purpose of which is to provide for expenses incurred and a margin for possible contingencies. Chief among the latter are unfavorable mortality experience, failure to earn interest at the rate assumed, and losses arising from surrenders. Also the practice of paying dividends has become so firmly established that the loadings on participating policies are almost invariably made with the further idea of reasonably rapid recoupment of sales and acquisition expenses and creating a surplus for future dividends.

Loading and the distribution of surplus share the distinction of furnishing insurance actuaries some of their most difficult problems. This is due to the complexity of the expense item and the difficulty of charging it proportionately against any policyholder in such a way as to obtain substantial equity. With the enormous size attained by many of our largest life insurance companies, with the various activities carried on by them, and with agency organizations covering the entire United States, the aggregate of expenses incurred within a single year totals a vast sum. This money, of course, must come from policyholders through their yearly contributions of premiums or from interest which the companies earn by investing part of the premiums collected. The problems arise in large part through the difficulty of determining what portion of particular items of expense shall be charged against one policy as compared with another.

GENERAL CONSIDERATIONS

Nature of Insurance Company Expenses

Many classifications of life insurance expenses have been developed, often in a more or less formal way or with no other purpose than to abbrevi-

403

ate a long and complex list of items. But classifications of any sort can be justified only on the ground that they serve to clear up points at issue, and one purpose of a classification of life insurance expenses should be a clear statement of the problems of gross premium derivation. In the following division of expenses the first step is to divide expenses into "investment" expenses and "insurance" expenses. The former class includes the cost of making, handling, and protecting investments and, since they are directly related to the production of investment income by the company, they are deducted from the gross income on investments. They are, therefore, taken into account in determining the net rate of interest to be used in calculating premiums and are not considered in connection with the loading.

Insurance expenses are expenses of a non-investment nature and may be classified as follows:

1. Selling, underwriting and issuance of new policies (for example, commissions, advertising, medical examinations, cost of approving applications, and cost of preparing policies for issue)

2. Premium collection and accounting

3. Service (for example, cost of approving claims, cost of paying surrender and maturity values, cost of policyholder correspondence)

4. General (for example, research, accounting, general actuarial and legal expenses)

For purposes of determining a proper amount for "loading," these various insurance expenses may be analyzed further and assigned to three major groups:

1. Expenses which vary with the amount of premiums, for example, agents' commissions and taxes. These are primarily a percentage of premiums.

2. Expenses which vary with the amount of insurance, for example, the cost of medical examinations and of approving applications. These tend to vary somewhat with the size of the policy.

3. Expenses which vary with the number of policies, for example, the cost of preparing policies for issue, establishing the necessary accounting records, sending of premium notices, and so forth.

In summarizing these different factors of expense it is found that some tend to vary with the size of the premium charged, some with the amount of insurance carried, and some with the number of policies. One group of expenses is incurred wholly within the first year of insurance, other groups annually during the policy term, and still others only at the time when the policy terminates. This statement sets in relief the factors that determine expenses attributable to any policy and makes possible a statement of the two major problems of loading, aside from the mere matter of collecting sufficient money to pay all expenses. These problems are respectively (1) the equitable distribution of expenses between *different classes* of policies and between policyholders at *different ages*—the problem of making each policy pay its own cost; and (2) the incidence of expense, or the problem of meeting the expense when it is incurred. The solution of these problems is complicated by the necessity of maintaining a level premium, of living up to statutory requirements as to reserves, of maintaining a consistent policy regarding surrender values and dividends, and finally of meeting the competition of other companies.

Because the objectives of adequacy and equity sometimes are in conflict with the objective of maintaining or improving the competitive position of the company, final gross premiums normally represent a compromise. Nevertheless, in the aggregate, adequacy must be maintained.

Nature of the Loading Formula

An equitable system of loading should require every policyholder to pay the expenses which his policy costs the company, as nearly as this amount can be determined. The foregoing analysis of insurance company expenses suggests that the loading to a net premium should consist partly of a percentage of the premium, partly of an amount for each $1,000 of insurance, and partly of an amount for each policy. If the loading formula were to be so constructed, the fixed "per policy" expenses would constitute a smaller and smaller percentage of the total premium as the face of the policy increased. The result would be a system of premium rates which varies with the size of the policy.

United States life insurance companies have not until recently graded premiums by size of policy. The use of graded premiums is now widespread. Many companies introduced special rates for certain types of policies issued in specified minimum amounts. A substantial number adopted premium schedules which grade premium rates for all plans of insurance in accordance with multiple size classifications or by means of a flat additional periodic premium per policy (a policy fee).[1] Among the former group, four or five classifications are usually established, with the rates per $1,000 being uniform *within* each classification.

Whether or not premiums are graded by size, "per policy" expenses are converted to an amount per $1,000 by relating them to the *average-size policy* issued. For example, if the cost studies of a company indicate that the share of each policy in the annual overhead of a company is $5.00, an

[1] See pp. 419–421.

average-size policy of $5,000 would result in a $1 per $1,000 constant addition to the loading formula whereas an average-size policy of $10,000 would result in a $0.50 per $1,000 constant. In order to provide greater equity between classes of policies where the *average-size policy* issued varies considerably, most companies utilize a separate average-size policy for each of the principal plans of insurance and age groups in their premium calculations.

With the "per policy" expenses converted to an "amount per $1,000" basis, the hypothetical loading formula may be reduced to two factors: (1) a percentage of the premium and (2) a constant per $1,000.

Gross Premium Levels

While the gross premium may be viewed as a net premium augmented by an amount called loading, in determining the *level* of gross premiums it is more frequently regarded as an amount derived independently of the valuation net premium, based on all the factors that enter into the gross premium. The six elements basic to the calculation of gross premiums are[2] (1) a suitable mortality rate, (2) an appropriate rate of interest, (3) a rate of withdrawal or a persistency rate, (4) factors of unit expenses out of which appropriate expense margins will be defined, (5) a factor for contingencies and fluctuations in experience, and (6) a factor to provide a margin for profit. Assumptions as to each of these elements can be selected, a formula embodying all of them derived, and a premium rate calculated. These tentative gross premiums are tested by asset share studies (see below) to be certain they are consistent with company objectives. The final gross premium is expressed in terms of the valuation net premium (or other net premium) and a mathematically derived loading formula which will reproduce the levels of gross premiums established through the asset share studies.

Probably the most complicated part of the premium calculation process is the determination of appropriate factors of expense. It is important to note that whether premiums are graded by size of policy or whether a single rate per $1,000 is used regardless of policy size, the principles of gross premium calculation remain the same. This also holds true with respect to differentiation by sex. The differences in premium levels for the various classes will arise by reason of the *differing experience rates* in the various subdivisions of the basic materials and the use of specific factors made applicable to each element by influence of differing average size policies.

[2] Alfred H. Guertin, "Life Insurance Premiums," *The Journal of Risk and Insurance,* Vol. XXXII, No. 1 (March, 1965), p. 24.

The following sections of this chapter will discuss the development of tentative gross premiums for pivotal ages, the use of asset share calculations to test the gross premium levels derived, and the recasting of tentative gross premiums by developing a loading formula which when added to the net premium (usually the valuation net premium) will reproduce the gross premium *levels* established for the principal plans and target ages.

DEVELOPING TENTATIVE GROSS PREMIUMS

Tentative gross premiums may be established by carefully developing a loading formula reflecting all categories of expense and allowances for contingencies and dividends, to be added to the net premium. They also may be based on any set of actuarial assumptions or none at all. Since the tentative gross premiums are tested by an asset share calculation (see below) regardless of how they were derived, their method of development is not critical and companies follow varying procedures. If the calculations are a phase of a general rate revision, the tentative premium for any particular policy and age of issue is usually the premium currently being charged, modified, where appropriate, to reflect changes known to have taken place in various factors since the last rate revision.

Where a loading formula, based on up-to-date experience, is developed to establish tentative gross premiums, the chief difference between the derivation of gross participating premiums and gross nonparticipating premiums is that the point of departure for the former is frequently a net premium based on the same mortality and interest assumptions underlying the valuation net premium, while the starting point for the latter is a net premium based on realistic assumptions as to mortality and interest earnings. Both procedures involve the development of reliable expense rates, the addition of these expense rates to the net premium to produce a tentative gross premium, and the testing of the tentative gross premium by an asset share calculation.

Basic Principle

The basic principle underlying the derivation of the loading formula is the same as that utilized in the computation of the net single and net level premiums. It will be remembered, in the case of net level premiums, the present value of the benefits under the contract is computed, and the sum, the net single premium, is converted into equivalent annual installments by dividing it by the present value of a life annuity due of $1 for the premium-paying period.

Similarly, the present value of the individual items of expense to be incurred under a particular policy is spread over the premium-paying period by dividing by the appropriate life annuity due. Conceptually, it is helpful to view the problem as the combination of the *present value* of benefits *and* expenses spread over the premium-paying period. The major problem involves a careful analysis of operating costs and probable future trend of such costs. The basic process involves allocating direct and indirect expenses to a predetermined set of functional classifications and the conversion of the allocations to unit expense rates, such as a percentage of premium, a dollar amount per $1,000 of insurance, or a dollar amount per policy. As with any cost analysis, the allocation of joint costs (e.g., general overhead) involves considerable judgment.

Expense Factors

Unit expense rates expressed as a percentage of the premium, such as commissions and state premium taxes, are by nature expressed directly or indirectly as a percentage of the premium and are easily obtained. The real task lies in the development of rates for all other types of expenses. Since the objective is to determine the *present value* of these expenses, they must be further classified as to their incidence or time of occurrence. A typical classification of such expenses might be as follows:

(1) Expenses expressed as a percentage of the premium
    (a) Incurred at time of issue
    (b) Incurred only during a limited number of renewal years
    (c) Incurred every year, including the first
(2) Expenses expressed as an amount per $1,000 of face amount
    (a) Incurred prior to time of issue
    (b) Incurred each year
    (c) Incurred only in year of maturity.

The determination of unit expense rates involves, then, both the amount of expense incurred, as shown by the cost study, and the time of its occurrence. Although the derivation of the individual unit expense rates is beyond the scope of this volume, some additional comments might be appropriate.[3] Claim expenses and costs of paying surrender values are usually accounted for separately and treated as *additional benefits*. The cost of writing the policy and establishing records would be assessed on a per policy basis; valuation fees paid the state insurance department would

[3] See *ibid.*, pp. 38–40.

be on a per $1,000 basis; and underwriting expenses would be split two ways with one part on a per $1,000 basis and one part on a per policy basis. As mentioned above, commissions and taxes would be treated as percentages of premiums. Salaries would be allocated on the basis of the nature of the work done, using time studies or other appropriate measures. Rent, light, heat, etc., would usually follow the salary distributions.

Once all unit expense factors are developed, they are then combined so as to give a pattern of (1) per policy, (2) per $1,000, and (3) percentage expenses for the first year and renewal years, the latter reflecting the acquisition expense patterns.

The unit expense rates developed on the basis of careful cost studies can be tested for accuracy by applying them to the appropriate elements of operation of the company. If such application results in *total expenses* approximating those reported in the company's annual statement, it may be presumed that they do in fact represent the operating costs of the company. Judgment modifications can of course be made, depending upon management's optimism or pessimism regarding the future.

Having determined the present value of all expenses and spread them over the premium-paying period, it is only necessary to include a margin for profit and contingencies and, in the case of participating companies, dividends, to produce the tentative gross premium by adding the total to the appropriate net premium.

Margins

As mentioned above, an allowance for profit and contingencies must be included in the loading formula. Even though the basic assumptions as to interest, mortality, and expenses are conservative for a participating company, a specific increment to the loading is usually made to meet unusual contingencies. Since any margins not needed can be returned through the dividend formula, the additional margin of safety is considered justified. Such an allowance might run from 1 to 3 per cent of the premium.

Participating companies customarily insert an additional allowance in the loading for the specific purpose of creating a surplus from which dividends can be paid. In most cases provision is made for a minimum dividend to be augmented by favorable deviations from the conservative assumptions underlying the premium rate. Such decisions involve broad managerial policy and vary from company to company. A moderate provision might be 5 per cent of the gross premium, or alternatively the equivalent amount expressed per premium and per $1,000.

The loading formula, for participating business, is usually expressed in terms of the tabular, i.e., the reserve basis, net premium.

TESTING THE TENTATIVE GROSS PREMIUMS

The set of gross premiums derived by applying the loading formula to the net premiums developed previously are only tentative and must be tested at various pivotal issue ages, such as 0, 15, 25, 35, 45, and 55, to see whether under *realistic* assumptions as to mortality, interest earnings, expenses, and terminations, they would develop sufficiently high asset accumulations to provide the surrender values promised under the contract, to meet the reserve requirements of the company, and to assure that the resulting net costs are reasonable and consistent. The gross premiums would also be compared with the gross premiums at key ages and plans of competing companies to see whether they are at a competitive level.

Asset Share Calculations

The adequacy tests are based on so-called "asset share calculations," the purpose of which is to determine, for any block of policies (same plan and age at issue), the expected fund per $1,000 of insurance held by the company at the end of each policy year (usually the test is for a maximum of twenty or thirty years) after payment of death claims, expenses, dividends, and surrender values and allowance for actual interest earnings. The accumulated *fund* at the end of any policy year is divided by the number of exposure units represented by the surviving and persisting policyowners. The process is similar to a retrospective reserve calculation but is based on a realistic forecast of experience, rather than tabular experience, and with allowance for terminations. For the same reasons that the surrender value ought to be less than this average asset share, the comparisons described below between average asset shares and surrender values produce nominal rather than actual gains and losses.

If the surrender values promised at each duration were precisely equal to the asset share at each duration, termination rates could be ignored in the calculation. Since in the usual case, surrender values are in excess of the asset share accumulation in the early policy years, it is necessary to take such terminations into account.[4] The final premium must reflect the losses created when a terminating policyholder receives a surrender value greater than the asset share allocable to his policy. After the early policy dura-

---

[4] It should be noted that the *ideal* surrender value should not be greater than the asset share at any time. Indeed, it should be something less than the asset share. See pp. 429–430.

tions, the asset share will normally exceed the surrender allowance and terminations result in a gain or profit.

Although the company may experience a gain on surrenders after the first few policy years, the amount taken from surplus to cover excess first-year expenses is not fully recovered until the asset share equals or exceeds the reserve. Up to that point, funds must be "borrowed" from surplus. The extent of the strain on surplus may be mitigated through a modified reserve system.[5] The duration at which the full policy reserve is to be accumulated (when the asset share equals or exceeds the net level reserve) is a management decision influenced by the competitive situation. The shorter the period over which the excess expenses are to be amortized, the larger must be the gross premium.

It is not unusual for a well-established company to take twenty or twenty-five years to amortize the acquisition expenses of a particular class of policies. Companies with a large volume of new business relative to their total volume in force usually amortize their acquisition expense within a much shorter period, such as five to ten years.

At the point the asset share exceeds the full reserve, the policy has not only returned the surplus "borrowed" to place it on the books, but begins to make a net, positive contribution to surplus.[6] All policies are expected to make some contribution to surplus, the extent of contribution being a management decision limited by considerations of safety, equity, and competition.[7]

Adjusting Tentative Gross Premiums

In the event the asset shares produced by the tentative gross premiums are deficient in light of company objectives, the premiums must be increased in some fashion or some specific item of expense decreased. If the fund accumulation appears to be excessive—if the asset share exceeds the surrender value by too great a margin or equals the reserve in too brief a period—the premiums must be reduced. Naturally, a participating company may also adjust the available asset share by modifying the tentative dividend scale.

The important purpose of the asset share calculation is to evaluate the level of the gross premium in relation to company objectives, incidence of expense and profit, etc. Asset share calculations taken on all blocks of policies also serve as a check on the basic equity as between classes.

---

[5] See pp. 422–426.

[6] Actually, as soon as assets increase in a policy year by more than the increase in liabilities, a policy can start contributing to surplus by making its negative surplus less negative.

[7] The State of New York regulates the contribution which participating policies can make to surplus in the aggregate.

Recasting Gross Premiums

Participating.   Having established the level of gross premiums at pivotal ages for each of the principal plans, the final step in the process for a participating company is to take the valuation net premium (at date of issue, the mortality and interest assumptions are often the same for the rate book and valuation net premiums) and by trial determine a particular loading formula (percentage and constant factors) which will reproduce the gross premiums levels established for the principal plans and target ages. Thus, a participating company might have its final gross premiums expressed in terms of the *1958 CSO Table*, 2½ per cent, and a loading formula which provides for a specified percentage of the net premium for the plan in question and a specified percentage of the net premium for an ordinary life plan issued at the same age and a constant amount per $1,000 insurance. The use of two elements in the percentage phase of the formula reflects the fact that expenses do not vary directly with the net premiums of the plans in question; that is, the expenses on a twenty-year endowment would not be in the same ratio to the expenses on an ordinary life as are the respective net premiums. Thus, the use of two elements in the percentage phase of the formula tends to reflect the varying commission scales paid on various plans of insurance.

Nonparticipating.   In the case of nonparticipating companies, the final step in the process of developing final gross premiums can be somewhat different. Having established the proper level of gross premiums at pivotal ages for each of the principal plans, these can be interpolated to establish the intermediate premiums with no effort made to express the premiums in terms of a valuation net premium and a loading formula. Today, however, with the availability of modern computer equipment, few companies use interpolation and most follow the same process as outlined above for participating companies.

ILLUSTRATIVE ASSET SHARE CALCULATION

Selection of Most Probable Assumptions

If the asset share calculations are to be a reasonable test of premium adequacy and equity between blocks of policies, the factors entering into the calculation must be chosen with great care. The assumptions underlying any mathematical model are critical to its effectiveness as a predictive device.

Mortality: Selection of the most probable assumption as to mortality is complicated by the secular trend toward mortality improvement. It might be argued that nonparticipating premiums should reflect anticipated improvement in future mortality. The vast majority of companies do not reflect such mortality improvement in their life insurance premiums although a growing number of companies are beginning to adjust *annuity* rates in anticipation of future longevity gains. Regardless of this feature, all companies utilize the latest available *past* experience.

The best source of information on the current trends, incidence, and level of mortality among ordinary policyholders has been the *Reports* of the Committee on Mortality Under Ordinary Insurances and Annuities, published annually by the Society of Actuaries. These data are compiled by the Committee on Mortality from statistics supplied by sixteen of the largest life insurance companies. The experience is published on a select basis for the first fifteen policy years and also on an ultimate basis for all policies with a duration of sixteen years or more. The death rates are shown for all ages on juvenile lives, but at only quinquennial age groups with respect to adult lives. Periodically, the Committee publishes a graduated mortality table based on these data (the latest based on the period 1955–60) and such tables are widely used by smaller companies in the calculation of nonparticipating premiums and the calculation of dividends under participating policies.

Most larger companies construct mortality tables from their own experience and use them in the determination of premiums and, in participating companies, dividends.

Interest. The rate of interest used in asset share calculations must be selected with great care. It involves an estimate as to rates at which investments will be made over the next twenty to fifty years. This estimate must be made with knowledge of the fact that the long-range impact of interest on life and endowment insurance is great. From the standpoint of the stockholder in a nonparticipating company, the leverage based on the margin between actual and assumed interest rates is enormous.

The rate selected will normally fall within a range of possible rates, the upper limit of which (during a period when interest rates are increasing) is the rate being earned on *new* investments and the lower limit the valuation rate of interest for policies currently being issued. Participating companies normally use the same rate for expressing final gross premiums and in reserve calculations since they are both subject to the same considerations. Many nonparticipating companies adopt a higher rate for expressing final gross premiums than for reserve calculations. A typical assumption for expressing final gross premiums and in reserve calculations for participating companies today is 2½ per cent; a frequent combination for nonparticipating companies is 3¾ or 4 per cent for premiums and 3 per cent for reserve calculations. Participating companies, however, still use 3¾ or 4 per cent interest after Federal income taxes in testing the level of tentative gross premiums. For both participating and nonparticipating companies, allowance is made in selecting these rates for the impact of United States Federal income taxes. Furthermore, recognition can be given to the possibility of changes in earned interest rates in future years. For example, 4 per cent can be assumed for years 1 to 10, with 3 per cent thereafter.

Operating Expenses.　　Both participating and nonparticipating companies compute their expense rates in the same manner. The average size of new policies is computed by plan and age at issue, and applied to the constant expense per policy to permit the expression of expense rates in terms of a percentage of the premium plus a number of dollars per $1,000 of insurance. Since the expense factors are based upon the *average* collection frequency of the company's business, the final premiums must be adjusted to reflect the particular frequency with which it will be paid. If the tentative gross premiums were based on a detailed analysis of current expenses, these same expense rates could be used as a basis for estimating future expense for purposes of the asset share calculation. Otherwise, a detailed cost study must precede the asset share calculation. Allowance may also be made for the impact on operating expenses of pending computer developments.

Termination Rates.　　Predicting future termination or lapse rates is usually found to be the most difficult task involved in an asset share calculation. The difficulty is caused by the extreme fluctuations over the years, largely as a result of economic conditions. While lapse rates are not as important to the adequacy test as the other three factors, for small companies with extremely high lapse rates during the early policy years the financial implications can be quite significant.

As in the case of the other factors, it is customary to use termination rates based on the company's individual experience, although published studies naturally provide a guide.[8] Termination rates are influenced by many factors, including the quality of the agency force, age of issue, plan of insurance, amount of premium, frequency of premium payment, and others. In practice, termination rates are usually differentiated only by

---

[8] See M. A. Linton, *The Record of the American Institute of Actuaries,* Vol. XIII (1924), pp. 283–316; see also C. F. B. Richardson and John M. Hartwell, *Transactions of the Society of Actuaries,* Vol. III (1951), pp. 338–372; for a recent study see Ernest J. Morehead, "The Construction of Persistency Tables," *Transactions of the Society of Actuaries,* Vol. XII (1960), pp. 545–563.

plan of insurance and *age of issue* and *frequency of premium payment.* Under all plans, the termination rate is high the first two years and decreases with duration, leveling out at the longer durations.

It should be noted again that termination rates are used in premium calculations only because of the disparity between surrender values and the asset shares available for distribution to withdrawing policyholders.

Asset Share Calculation

The process by which a set of gross premiums is tested can be explained most effectively by means of an illustrative asset share calculation. For this purpose, a tentative gross premium of $23.59 for an ordinary life insurance policy issued at age 35 has been selected. As pointed out earlier, the tentative gross premium could be based on any set of actuarial assumptions, or none at all. If the calculations are a phase of a general rate revision, the tentative premium for any particular policy and age of issue could well be the premium currently being charged. It could be the premium charged by a competing company. It could also be a net premium developed and loaded on the basis of a careful review of the company's own experience. In any case, the assumptions underlying the asset share formula are chosen with great care and are based on realistic "most probable assumptions" for the particular company involved.

For purposes of this illustration, the assumptions about mortality rates, termination rates, expense rates, and interest rate are somewhat arbitrary to simplify the example. The surrender values and dividend scales assumed are, of course, separate management decisions. They are also being "tested" by this asset share calculation.

With a set of assumptions as to the number and volume of premiums that will be received each year, the number of death claims of $1,000 each that will be incurred each year (based on the same death rates as those used to determine the number of premiums to be received), the number and amount of surrender payments that will be disbursed each year, and the rate of interest that will be earned on accumulated funds the raw materials are available (columns [1] through [8], Table 25-1) for the construction of the main body of the asset share calculation. The various assumptions are combined in Table 25-1 (columns [9] through [17]) to arrive at the asset share per $1,000 at each duration.

The asset share fund is analogous to an income-outgo account. Each year premiums and interest earnings are credited to the account as income, and death claims, surrender and dividend payments, and expense disbursements are charged against the account. The account balance at the end of each year (column [16], Fund at End of Year) is divided by the

TABLE 25-1. Asset Share Calculation $1,000 Ordinary Life Issued at Age 35 Gross Premium per $1,000

Policy Year	Number Paying Premiums at Beginning of Year	Number Dying *	Number Withdrawing †	Number Alive at End of Year After Withdrawals = (2) − (3) − (4)	Expense Rate per $1,000 ‡	Cash Value per $1,000 on Withdrawal	Dividend per $1,000
(1)	(2)	(3)	(4)	(5)	(6)	(7)	(8)
1	100,000	99	9,990	89,911	$27.01	—	—
2	89,911	98	5,389	84,424	2.83	$ 15.18	$2.59
3	84,424	106	4,216	80,102	2.83	33.28	2.88
4	80,102	113	3,520	76,469	2.83	51.68	3.15
5	76,469	122	3,054	73,293	2.83	70.38	3.46
6	73,293	131	2,634	70,528	2.83	89.36	3.75
7	70,528	142	2,252	68,134	2.83	108.59	4.05
8	68,134	155	1,971	66,008	2.83	128.10	4.34
9	66,008	170	1,778	64,060	2.83	147.86	4.62
10	64,060	186	1,597	62,277	2.83	167.90	4.87
11	62,277	205	1,490	60,582	2.83	185.85	5.24
12	60,582	224	1,388	58,970	2.83	203.97	5.58
13	58,970	246	1,292	57,432	2.83	222.24	5.95
14	57,432	270	1,200	55,962	2.83	240.63	6.29
15	55,962	296	1,113	54,553	2.83	259.12	6.67
16	54,553	325	1,085	53,143	2.83	277.71	7.03
17	53,143	353	1,056	51,734	2.83	296.35	7.40
18	51,734	383	1,027	50,324	2.83	315.05	7.79
19	50,324	414	998	48,912	2.83	333.79	8.18
20	48,912	447	969	47,496	2.83	352.54	8.58
21	47,496	—	—	—	—	—	—

* Deaths based on select and ultimate experience mortality table. Deaths assumed to occur in middle of policy year on the average.
† Withdrawals based on Linton A lapse rates. Assumed to occur on anniversary at end of policy year.

TABLE 25-1. (cont'd.)

Policy Year	Fund at Beginning of Year = (16) pr Year	Premium Income = ($23.59) X (2)	Expense Disbursements = (2) X (6)	Death Claims $1,000 X (3)	Amount Paid on Surrender (4) X (7)	Total Dividends Paid = (5) X (8)
	(9)	(10)	(11)	(12)	(13)	(14)
1	—	$2,359,000	$2,701,000	$ 99,000	—	—
2	$ -456,660	2,121,000	254,448	98,000	$ 81,805	$218,658
3	1,065,865	1,991,562	238,920	106,000	140,308	230,694
4	2,452,125	1,889,606	226,689	113,000	181,914	240,877
5	3,741,593	1,803,904	216,407	122,000	214,941	253,594
6	4,949,279	1,728,982	207,419	131,000	235,374	264,480
7	6,096,202	1,663,756	199,594	142,000	244,545	275,943
8	7,197,451	1,607,281	192,819	155,000	252,485	286,475
9	8,259,330	1,557,129	186,803	170,000	262,895	295,957
10	9,282,590	1,511,175	181,290	186,000	268,136	303,289
11	10,275,829	1,469,114	176,244	205,000	276,917	317,450
12	11,227,980	1,429,129	171,447	224,000	283,110	329,053
13	12,144,445	1,391,102	166,885	246,000	287,134	341,720
14	13,023,634	1,354,821	162,533	270,000	288,756	352,001
15	13,868,402	1,320,144	158,372	296,000	288,401	363,869
16	14,677,191	1,286,905	154,385	325,000	301,315	373,595
17	15,435,689	1,253,643	150,395	353,000	312,946	382,832
18	16,144,656	1,220,405	146,407	383,000	323,556	392,024
19	16,801,160	1,187,143	142,417	414,000	333,122	400,100
20	17,404,219	1,153,834	138,421	447,000	341,611	407,516
21	—	—		—	—	—

TABLE 25-1. (cont'd.)

Policy Year	Interest Earned During Year = .04 [(9)+(10)−(11)−½(12)] (15)	Fund at End of Year = (9) +(10)−(11)−(12) −(13)−(14)+(15) (16)	Asset Share at End of Year (16)÷(5) (17)	Reserve ** at End of Year (18)	Surplus per $1,000 at End of Year = (17)−(18) (19)
1	$−15,660	$ −456,660	$ −5.08	$ 15.64	$−20.72
2	54,436	1,065,865	12.63	31.59	−18.96
3	110,620	2,452,125	30.61	47.83	−17.22
4	162,342	3,741,593	48.93	64.32	−15.39
5	210,724	4,949,279	67.53	81.05	−13.52
6	256,214	6,096,202	86.44	98.01	−11.57
7	299,575	7,197,451	105.64	115.17	−9.53
8	341,377	8,259,330	125.13	132.55	−7.42
9	381,786	9,282,590	144.90	150.12	−5.22
10	420,779	10,275,829	165.00	167.90	−2.90
11	458,648	11,227,980	185.34	185.85	−0.51
12	494,946	12,144,445	205.94	203.97	1.97
13	529,826	13,023,634	226.77	222.24	4.53
14	563,237	13,868,402	247.82	240.63	7.19
15	595,287	14,677,191	269.04	259.12	9.92
16	625,888	15,435,689	290.46	277.71	12.75
17	654,497	16,144,656	312.07	296.35	15.72
18	681,086	16,801,160	333.86	315.05	18.81
19	705,555	17,404,219	355.83	333.79	22.04
20	727,845	17,951,350	377.95	352.54	25.41
21	—	—	—	—	—

** Net Level Premium Reserves, 1958 CSO 2½ per cent.

number of surviving *and* persisting policyholders to obtain the pro-rata share of the account for each surviving and persisting policyholder—his asset share. Table 25–1 shows that at the end of the tenth year, the 62,277 surviving and persisting policyholders each have an asset share in the amount of $165.00.

A number of significant facts are shown by the asset share study. First, the asset share is negative at the end of the first year, reflecting the relatively high first-year expenses involved in selling, underwriting, and issuing new business.

Comparison of columns (7) and (17) will show that the surrender value granted on withdrawal is greater than the asset share until the twelfth policy year. This means that the company would suffer a loss on any policy in this class terminating prior to the twelfth policy year. From the twelfth year on, the company would experience a net gain on policies which are surrendered.[9]

Column (18) shows the net level reserve (*1958 CSO,* 2½ per cent) which is assumed to be set up for this block of policies. Column (19), shows, year by year, the net effect on surplus. Under these assumptions a strain on surplus occurs until the twelfth policy year. From the twelfth policy year on, this block of policies will have positive accumulated surplus, having repaid fully the amounts "borrowed" from surplus in the early policy years.

As mentioned earlier, the asset share calculation also is testing the effect of the proposed surrender value and dividend scales. It could be used to test a proposed terminal dividend scale as well. The advent of the computer has facilitated asset share research, permitting prompt and economical analysis of the impact of proposed changes in any factor affecting the financial experience of a block of life insurance business.

PREMIUM RATES GRADED BY SIZE OF POLICY

It was pointed out earlier that there are certain expenses that vary with the *number of policies*, such as the cost of issuing policies, establishing the necessary accounting records, the sending of premium notices, and others. If the premium formula were to incorporate a constant for this element which did not vary by amount of insurance, the premium rate per $1,000 would vary inversely with the face of the policy.

---

[9] Viewed another way, the company still loses the present value of future profits and the ability to spread its overhead over a larger volume. It is difficult to demonstrate that surrendered policies result in a real "gain" to the company.

British life insurance companies have graded their premiums by size of policy for many years. In the United States, however, with elaborate governmental regulation of life insurance, recognition of policy size as an independent variable in premium rates has been slow in developing. Although in the past there has been no specific legal prohibition against grading premiums by size of risk, doubts were raised in view of the provisions against discrimination. For many years, however, companies have issued special or preferred risk policies in specified minimum amounts, such as $10,000 or $25,000. The companies avoided the discrimination provisions by making particular plans of insurance available only in amounts above the minimum size established. For example, a company might have a $25,000 minimum preferred risk ordinary life with a preferential rate. If this policy was made available, then, the company could not issue an ordinary life policy for less than the minimum amount. In practice, the company would issue smaller amounts on a "different" plan, such as endowment at 85 or life paid up at 85. Technically, no discrimination was involved, since all ordinary life and all life paid up at 85 policyholders were charged the same rate by *class*. Practically, however, there is very little difference in a life paid up at 85 and an ordinary life policy, but there is a difference.

In most jurisdictions where doubts as to the question of discrimination and gradation of premiums by size had been raised, these doubts have been resolved by insurance department rulings. Furthermore, the National Association of Insurance Commissioners has passed a resolution which, in effect, states that there is no inherent discrimination in the principle of gradation of premiums by size of policy. As long as the gradation of premiums is applied across the board to all plans and all ages, a company may now freely grade premiums by size of policy, and the principle has been widely adopted in the United States and Canada.

In the case where multiple size classifications are being used, two systems have developed in practice:[10]

1. *The Quantity Discount System.* Under the Quantity Discount System a number of "size bands," usually four, are established, with different premium rates applying within each class. The following would be a typical arrangement under this system:

SIZE BAND	PREMIUM PER $1,000 FOR A PARTICULAR PLAN AND AGE
2,000– 4,999	$20.00
5,000– 9,999	18.00
10,000–24,999	17.25
25,000 and over	17.00

[10] Elgin G. Fassell, "Premium Rates Varying by Policy Size," *Transactions of the Society of Actuaries*, Vol. VIII, No 22 (November, 1956).

2. *The Policy Fee System.* Under the Policy Fee System, the *premium* for a policy is expressed as the product of the amount of the policy and a "basic" rate per $1,000, plus a flat amount (known as the "Policy Fee"). For a particular plan and age, the premium might be $7.00 plus $16.50 per $1,000. This would work out to $40.00 for a $2,000 policy, for example: $89.50 for a $5,000 policy; $172.00 for a $10,000 policy, and so forth.

In both cases the loading formula has been modified so that the amount of expense which is *deemed* to be independent of size is charged only once each year regardless of the size of the policy. It should be remembered, however, that the total amount necessary to cover expenses is not changed by such gradations and the lower amount policies must of necessity pay a higher rate to offset the "discount" granted to the larger amount policies.

LOADING AND THE INCIDENCE OF EXPENSE

The problem of making each policy pay its own cost, as just discussed, is a matter of doing justice to each insured person. From the standpoint of the company, however, this factor is not of the same immediate importance as that of the incidence of expense, or the problem of meeting the expense when it occurs. The primary difficulty is that the expenses of the first policy year greatly exceed those of any subsequent year and, in fact, will usually exceed the entire premium. That first-year expenses will be high can be seen by considering that selling expenses, such as agents' commissions, expenses of medical examination, expenses of approving applications and preparing policies for issue, as well as the expenses of setting up records for new policies, are all incurred in the first policy year. Thus, the major problem of the incidence of expense is that policies cannot pay their first-year expenses from the loading available from the first premium. These expenses must be met when incurred and yet the company faces the necessity of maintaining the regular level premium, of paying death claims at the close of the first year, and of holding in reserve the remainder of the net premium. The net premium of $17.67 on an ordinary life policy at age 35 increased at 2½ per cent interest accumulates to $18.11 at the close of the policy year. Of this amount $2.47 is necessary to pay the estimated cost of insurance for the year and $15.64 constitutes the reserve that should be held in anticipation of future claims against the policy. The loading is the only portion of the first premium that is available, therefore, to pay the first year's expenses. For this reason a company cannot maintain its level premium and hold the full net level premium reserve from the start, and at the same time make every policy pay its own way at every duration. The first year's requirements are greater than the funds on hand. These first-year costs must be provided from some outside source, or some modification of the system of level reserve valuation must be made. For an old and well-established company, with a large surplus accrued, the solution of the problem is comparatively simple, for it can pay expenses of new business from surplus and depend on replacing the amount from margins in the loadings of the later premiums. This, however, is not possible for new companies, for they have relatively little surplus from which to borrow; and it results in slow growth of small companies whose surplus is insufficient to supply the demands of a rapidly increasing business.

MODIFIED RESERVE SYSTEMS

There exists the further possibility of dealing with this problem through some modification of the system of valuing reserves, whereby the policy reserve of the first year or of the first few years can be reduced. Two important methods of modifying the full net level premium reserves used in the United States today are known respectively as the full preliminary term method and the Commissioners' Reserve Valuation Method (modified preliminary term).

Full Preliminary Term Method

The full preliminary term method of valuation involves the assumption that the entire first-year valuation annual premium (except for the first-year cost of insurance) can properly be used to help meet the excess of first-year expenses over first-year loading, regardless of the type of contract involved or the age at issue. (Thus, under this method of valuation there is no first-year terminal reserve and the amount of reserve reduction can be amortized over the entire premium-paying period.)

The germ of the preliminary term concept was introduced into the United States from Europe. The technique is to treat the first year of insurance as term insurance, irrespective of the type of contract actually involved, and to assume that the original permanent contract goes into effect at the beginning of the second policy year. Hence, the title "preliminary term" is a logical one.

This method of valuation provides that the first year's premium under any form of policy shall pay for term insurance for one year, and that the regular policy, for reserve purposes, is to come into operation one year later than the age of issue, and will be for a premium-payment period one year shorter. By this means the company is relieved of the necessity of establishing a terminal reserve against the policy for the first year, and the entire premium becomes available for payment of current claims and expenses. Since the amount required for first-year claims is the net premium for one-year term insurance (which, for example, is $2.45 at age 35), the total amount available for expenses is the loading plus the excess of the net premium for the particular plan over the net term rate. In other words, by using this method an additional amount for expenses equal to the excess of the net premium for the particular plan over the net premium for one year's term insurance is made available. On the ordinary life policy at age 35 the additional amount for expenses is the excess of the net premium for ordinary life of $17.67 over $2.45, or $15.22; on the twenty-payment life plan at the same age the corresponding excess is $24.79, whereas on the twenty-year endowment plan it is $37.99. The *net* premium for the later years of the policy is then increased and, correspondingly, the loading is reduced, since the gross premium paid by the policyholder does not change. The net premium becomes the net premium for an insurance issued at an age one year higher, at a date one year later, and for a term one year shorter; and the reserves held on the policy for the second and later years are the reserves based on this new net premium. Thus, an ordinary life at age 35 becomes one-year term insurance plus ordinary life at age 36; a twenty-payment life policy becomes one-year term plus nineteen-payment life at age 36; and a twenty-year endowment becomes one-year term and a nineteen-year endowment at age 36. The effect of this method is that the additional amount "borrowed" in the first year is repaid in later years by reducing the loading and increasing the net premium in the second and later years.

These relationships are depicted graphically in Figures 1, 2, and 3 of Graph 25–1.

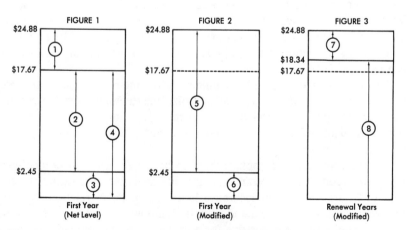

GRAPH 25-1. Preliminary term method of valuation, ordinary life, male age 35, $7.21 loading, 1958 CSO Table, 2½ per cent.

1. Normal net level loading for expenses and contingencies ($7.21)

2. Normal first-year net level reserve ($15.64)

3. Tabular cost of first year's insurance ($2.45)

4. Net level premium (remains constant throughout the life of the policy) ($17.67)

5. Modified loading available for expenses and contingencies, first year ($22.43)

6. Modified first-year net premium (i.e., premium for one-year term insurance) ($2.45)

7. Modified loading available for expenses and contingencies, renewal years ($6.54)

8. Modified net premium necessary to accumulate required reserve over remaining premium-paying period (i.e., net level O.L. premium for age 36) ($18.34)

Note that in Figure 1 the amount applied to the net level reserve (area [2]) plus the amount given to the cost of insurance for the year (area [3]) always equals the net level premium for the policy (area [4]). Therefore the amount available for expenses and contingencies is $7.21 (area [1]) for each year.

In Figure 2 the premium for one-year term insurance at age 35 (area [6]) plus the amount applied to first-year expenses (area [5]) equals the total gross premium, $24.88. This is permitted since no reserve is required at the end of the first year under this valuation method.

Under the full preliminary term method of valuation an ordinary life policy issued at age 35 is treated as the combination of a one-year term policy plus an ordinary life policy with level net premium issued one year later. Therefore, the renewal net premium (area [8]) is equal to the net level premium for age 36, and it is sufficient to provide benefits for an ordinary life policy with level net premium issued at age 36. The remainder of the gross premium (area [7]) is available each renewal year for expenses.

The net effect of the full preliminary term method, then, is to defer funding the first-year reserve and amortize this amount over the remaining premium-paying period of the contract. It is important to note that this method of valuation makes no distinction between various types of permanent contracts.

For most low-premium policies written by a typical life insurance company, the additional first-year loading made available by treating the first year of insurance as term insurance is not adequate in relation to heavy first-year expense. The remainder of the amount needed must be drawn from surplus. Thus, it is possible for a rapidly growing company to have a "capacity" problem, despite the fact that it is using the preliminary term plan.

On higher premium plans, on the other hand, the first-year reserve "borrowed" is correspondingly greater since the cost of one-year term insurance remains the same. Thus, on a ten-year endowment at age 35, $86.01 is the additional amount made available for expenses. If $15.15 in addition to the first year's loading is considered sufficient to pay new business expenses on an ordinary life policy, it should not require more than five times this amount on a ten-year endowment policy. The logic of this position has led regulatory authorities to prescribe the use of some modification of the full preliminary term method of valuation, the most important of which is known as the Commissioners' Reserve Valuation Method.

Commissioners' Reserve Valuation Method

The Commissioners' Reserve Valuation Method in effect makes the twenty-payment life policy the maximum basis on which deferred reserve funding is permitted, and, in doing so, divides policies into two groups:
(1) The preliminary-term method described above is used if the net premium for the second and subsequent years for the plan in question does not exceed the corresponding modified net premium for a twenty-payment life plan.

TABLE 25-2. Terminal Reserves per $1,000
Various Methods of Valuation

(1958 CSO Table and 2½ Per Cent Interest, Male Age 45)

Plan	Policy Year	Full Preliminary Term Method	Commissioners' Reserve Valuation Method	Net Level Premium Method
Ordinary Life	1	—	—	$ 21.58
	5	$ 90.00	$ 90.00	109.64
	10	204.74	204.74	221.90
	15	319.26	319.26	333.95
	20	429.80	429.80	442.10
20-Payment	1	—	—	30.85
Life	5	133.59	133.59	159.11
	10	312.61	312.61	330.84
	15	508.40	508.40	518.34
	20	730.81	730.81	730.81
20-Year	1	—	8.64	39.49
Endowment	5	172.57	179.72	205.25
	10	409.09	414.19	432.42
	15	677.54	680.33	690.27
	20	1,000.00	1,000.00	1,000.00

(2) For plans with higher premiums, the additional amount for expenses is limited to approximately the same amount as is permitted under the preliminary-term method for a twenty-payment life policy. It is not exactly the same as the twenty-payment life amount in the case of policies which require more or less than twenty years' premiums, because the amount "borrowed" is "repaid" by a level premium payable for each year of the premium-paying period including the first.

For example, for ordinary life at age 35 the Commissioners' Reserve Valuation Method calls for the full preliminary-term method, because the net premium at age 36 is less than the corresponding twenty-payment life preliminary-term basis premium for the second and subsequent years of $28.95 (that is, the nineteen-payment life rate at age 36).

However, in the case of the twenty-year endowment issued at age 35 the modified method applies, since the nineteen-year endowment rate at age 36 of $43.07 exceeds the nineteen-payment life rate at age 36 of $28.95. Following the method of paragraph (2) above, the additional amount available for expenses is found to be $24.79, which is equal to the amount given earlier for the twenty-payment life plan under the preliminary-term plan.

However, where the premium-paying period differs from twenty years the result will be slightly different, as in the case of the ten-year endowment at age 35 where the application of the method of paragraph (2) gives an additional amount available for expenses of $23.51.

Table 25–2 presents terminal reserve values under the several methods of valuation discussed above.

Surrender Values | 26

NATURE OF SURRENDER VALUES

IT HAS BEEN explained previously that the level-premium plan involves charging, during the early years of the policy, a net premium which is larger than necessary to pay for the insurance in those years, with a view to accumulating a fund sufficiently large to enable the company to meet the cost of insurance in the later years of the life of the insured when the net premium is insufficient to pay for the current cost of protection. Paralleling the growth of this fund, the reserve accumulates, as illustrated (page 384) in connection with a $1,000 ordinary life policy age 35, issued on the basis of the *1958 CSO Table* and 2½ per cent interest. It was seen that the net annual premium of $17.67 on this policy results in a reserve of $15.64 at the end of the first year, and that thereafter the accumulation to the credit of the policy continues to increase until, at the end of the sixty-fifth year of the contract, or the extreme limit of the insured's life according to the mortality table, it equals the face value of the policy.

Now what shall be done with these accumulations in case the insured wishes to surrender his policy or fails to pay his premium when due? It is clear that under such circumstances the company, since its future liability under the policy ceases, no longer requires the assets standing behind the reserve liability for the purpose originally intended. Experience has shown that it is not necessary for the protection of the company or the other policyholders to insist that the insured upon failing to continue his premium payments shall forfeit the entire reserve value of his policy. It has therefore become a universal practice to permit the insured, in case he surrenders or discontinues his policy, to receive a surrender value. During the early years of the policy, the surrender value is usually less than the full reserve. The difference between the surrender value and reserve has, in the past, been referred to as a *surrender charge*. This term is inappropriate because it suggests that the terminating policyholder is penalized, whereas, as will be explained later, payment of less than the full reserve as a surrender value is largely to protect continuing policyholders from loss rather than to exact a penalty from those who terminate.

427

Although the practice of allowing a surrender value in some form is an old one, for many years the matter was entirely optional with the companies, with some companies voluntarily granting cash surrender values and others not granting them. All states today have so-called "nonforfeiture laws" which define the minimum amount that must be returned upon surrender of a policy.[1] Today, most companies provide surrender values in excess of the minimums required by law.

COMPANY PRACTICE

In determining the proper value to be granted discontinuing policyholders, company practice is based on certain principles. Before examining the Standard Nonforfeiture Law these principles are considered briefly.

Concepts of Equity

The actual treatment of withdrawing policyholders can generally be based on any one of three possible concepts of equity. One possible view is that in the absence of legislation to the contrary the policyholder should receive *nothing* on the grounds that the sole function of a life insurance contract is to provide certain designated benefits in the event of the death of the policyholder or survival to the maturity date of an endowment policy. Premiums could be discounted for anticipated surrenders (dividends could also be increased in a participating contract) and thus, the forfeiture reflected in a reduction in the cost of insurance. In the early days of the business this extreme view was generally accepted and applied in many cases without an adjustment in the premium for the contract. Such practices led to the introduction of nonforfeiture legislation, and this approach would not be feasible today. Moreover, forecasts of future withdrawal rates are subject to wide fluctuations and would be of questionable reliability.

At the other extreme, the withdrawing policyholder might be considered as being entitled to the return of all premiums (less dividends) paid plus interest at the contractual rate less his pro rata share of assumed death claims and average expenses of the company; i.e., the *full reserve* under the contract, irrespective of the policy year in which the surrender occurs. This view, of course, ignores the question of the incidence of expense and assumes that unamortized acquisition expenses under policies surrendered during the early years after issue would be borne by existing policyholders or charged to the general surplus of the company.

Proponents of this latter philosophy argue that the healthy growth of a

[1] Under the leadership of Mr. Elizur Wright, the State of Massachusetts enacted the first such law on May 10, 1861.

company is essential for the welfare of all policyholders and consequently, the loss resulting from terminations at the early durations should be a charge on all policies and not specifically assessed against new policies. The strict application of this view, then, would provide a surrender value equal to the full reserve, even at the end of the first policy year. A modified form of this approach would have the acquisition expenses due to early terminations borne partially by the continuing policyholders and partially by the new policies, resulting in a surrender value something less than the full reserve and more than the asset share value (see below), until the acquisition expenses have been fully amortized, after which it would equal the full reserve.

The third concept of equity, and the one generally applied, is that the withdrawing policyholder should receive a surrender value as nearly as possible equivalent to his contribution to the funds of the company, less the cost of protection which he received, and less any expenses incurred by the company in establishing and handling his policy. This view has as its objective that the withdrawal of a policyholder should neither benefit nor harm the continuing policyholders. Under this concept the amount received by the withdrawing policyholder would be based on the pro rata share of the assets accumulated by the company on behalf of the classification of policies to which his policy belongs, that is, the so-called *asset share.*

Reasons Justifying Paying Less Than the Asset Share

It will be remembered that the asset share value is equal to the pro rata share of the assets accumulated by the company on behalf of the block of policies to which a particular policy belongs. This value reflects the incidence of expense and its relationship to policy duration. The actual surrender benefit may be somewhat less for several reasons, including: (1) adverse financial selection, (2) adverse mortality selection, (3) contribution to a contingency reserve or profits, and (4) cost of surrendering the policy.

Adverse Financial Selection.   A reason advanced for not allowing the insured to obtain the full asset share on the policy at any time is the possibility that during periods of financial stringency or business depression policyholders may avail themselves of the privilege of surrendering their policies to such an extent that the financial standing of the company may be greatly weakened to the detriment of remaining policyholders. In normal times life insurance companies have an excess of income over expenditures which is more than sufficient to meet demands for loans and cash values. In periods of economic crises and depressions, however, demands by policyholders may be so great that it becomes necessary to liquidate valuable assets at depressed prices. The right of the policyholder to demand the cash value of his policy at any time also necessitates a more liquid investment policy than would otherwise be required.[2] Many companies feel that those policyholders who surrender their policies should be charged with the loss of investment earnings, including capital losses, arising from their action and take this into account in fixing the amount of the termination value.

Adverse Mortality Selection.   A further argument advanced in favor of granting a surrender value less than the full asset share, although some writers question its correctness or importance, refers to the "adverse mortality selection" which it is assumed will be brought about by the allowance of very liberal surrender values. The position taken by the supporters of this view is as follows: A life insurance policy is a unilateral contract to which the company must always adhere but which the insured may terminate at any time by simply discontinuing his premium payments. Whenever, therefore, the payment of premiums seems a hardship, the healthy policyholder, not feeling the immediate need for insurance, will have no hesitancy in discontinuing premium payment. Policyholders in poor health, on the contrary, will appreciate fully the value of their insurance and will exert themselves to the utmost to pay the premium. Hence, according to this view policies on the good risks are likely to lapse on a large scale if surrender values are liberal, while impaired risks will stay with the company. The result is a reduction in the average vitality of the policyholders remaining with the company. It is therefore argued that retiring policyholders should receive less than the pro rata share of their policies in order to provide a fund to meet the higher death rate among the poorer risks that remain. It should be noted, however, that although seemingly logical, this tendency has been quite difficult to substantiate statistically.

Other Reasons.   Other reasons advanced for paying a smaller surrender value than would otherwise be indicated are based on the principle followed by some companies that each contract should make a contribution to the general contingency reserve or surplus of a company which is needed to absorb adverse fluctuations produced by occasional catastrophes, such as wars and epidemics, that may occur only once in several decades. To the extent of such a permanent contribution, the surrender allowance would have to be reduced.

Again, in a stock company an adjustment may be made in the surrender allowance to account for that policy's contribution to profits, which is in recognition of the risk borne by stockholders' investments.

Finally, there is a certain amount of expense incurred in processing the surrender of a policy. Some companies adjust the surrender allowance for

---

[2] Today, the company has the *legal right* to postpone payment of the cash surrender value for a period of six months. From a practical standpoint, however, this right could be invoked only under the most severe financial circumstances.

this factor rather than taking it into account in their premium loading formula.

Company Liberality

A major factor affecting a company's practices with regard to surrender allowances is competition. In recent years a significant number of companies have allowed surrender values far in excess of the minimum nonforfeiture values required by law. In some cases companies have allowed surrender values equal to the *full reserve* at the end of the second or third year. In fact, a few have allowed the *full reserve* at the end of the *first* policy year. In the event of the termination of such contracts prior to the point where the asset share equals the full reserve (ten to thirty years), the unamortized acquisition expenses of necessity must be borne by persisting policyholders. This would appear to be straining the argument that "new business is vital to the sound management of a life insurance company." As long as the values are equal to or greater than the minimum values required by law, the only question involved is the equity between terminating and persisting policyholders. The question of what constitutes "equity" in this case is a matter of company judgment.

STANDARD NONFORFEITURE LAW

As mentioned above, the early nonforfeiture laws were enacted to prevent the forfeiture of equities built up in level-premium policies. Traditionally, the values required to be returned have been called nonforfeiture values and the form in which these values may be taken are referred to as nonforfeiture options. The term "surrender value," except in reference to legislation, has increasingly been substituted because of its simplicity and better connotation.[3]

Purpose

The Standard Nonforfeiture Law, enacted to become effective on each company's "operative date" but no later than January 1, 1948, and generally referred to as the Guertin Legislation, was designed to effect four main changes as compared with previous nonforfeiture legislation.

1. It required the use of more up-to-date mortality table, the *Commissioners 1941 Standard Ordinary Mortality Table.* (Effective January 1,

---

[3] The terms "surrender" and "lapse" should be distinguished. Lapse refers to the termination of a policy through nonpayment of premiums at a time when the policy has no net surrender value.

1966, a new table, the *1958 CSO Table,* was made mandatory in calculating minimum nonforfeiture values.) [4]

2. It allowed substantial separation of reserves and nonforfeiture benefits. Previously, nonforfeiture benefits were linked directly to reserves, whereas under the new plan this close tie-up was obviated, with the result that greater equity could be maintained, as between policyholders at different ages and also with respect to different plans of insurance.

3. It established a new method of calculating nonforfeiture values. Under earlier methods nonforfeiture values were based directly on the reserve, although expenses were much higher in the first year than in later years because of such expenses as agents' first-year commissions, cost of underwriting, issuing of the policy form, and preparation of policy records. Therefore, the earlier legislation did not require the granting of nonforfeiture values during the first three years of the policy, and also authorized a surrender charge—a stipulated deduction from the reserve—for a considerable period thereafter. To meet the heavy initial expense, and at the same time to maintain reserves, insurance companies had to borrow from surplus, or, as was often done, employ preliminary-term or modified preliminary-term reserves. These were considerably smaller during the early years than the annual net level premium reserves. Yet, under the previous legislation, the same surrender charge deducted from the net level premium reserve could also be deducted from the smaller preliminary-term reserves. *The object of the Standard Nonforfeiture Value plan is to reflect with reasonable fidelity the asset shares accumulated under the policies.*

4. It gave recognition to the need for a margin of safety in reserves, by providing that a lower rate of interest could be used for reserve purposes (thus producing a higher reserve) than the interest rate used for nonforfeiture values, subject to the approval of the insurance commissioner. This differential in interest assumptions was based on the premise that exceptionally low interest rates in the investment market might make the accumulation of higher reserves a prudent step for the meeting of future claims. To avoid abuse, the new legislation provides that should the difference in the interest rate, assumed for reserve and nonforfeiture purposes, exceed ½ of 1 per cent, companies must either increase their nonforfeiture values under participating policies or prove the inadvisability of such an increase to the various state insurance departments.

Definition of Nonforfeiture Value

The minimum nonforfeiture value at any policy duration is the present value, at that time, of the future benefits under the policy less the present

---

[4] For industrial life insurance, *The Commissioners 1961 Standard Industrial Mortality Table* is used, effective January 1, 1968.

value of future "adjusted premiums." This is essentially the prospective reserve formula utilizing an "adjusted premium" in lieu of the regular net level premium. The "adjusted premium" is the level premium necessary to pay the benefits guaranteed by the policy (the net level premium) plus the level equivalent of a certain defined special first-year expense allowance. This is equivalent to the net level premium adjusted for the special first-year expense allowance, hence the name "adjusted premium."

In order to finalize the nonforfeiture values three additional factors used in the formula were defined; namely, (1) a specific mortality table (originally the *1941 CSO Table;* the *1958 CSO Table* became the mandatory standard on January 1, 1966); (2) a maximum rate of interest (3½ per cent); and (3) a maximum allowance for special first-year expense. For most plans of insurance the last factor is defined as a constant of $20 per $1,000 of insurance, plus a percentage (40 per cent) of the adjusted premium used, and a percentage (25 per cent) of the adjusted premium for a whole-life policy. According to the legislation, the special first-year expense may not exceed a maximum of $46 per $1,000 of insurance.

The percentage factors in the expense-limitation formula are designed to reflect those expenses which are dependent upon the premium and plan of insurance. The constant factor of $20 per $1,000 of insurance was intended to reflect those expenses which are dependent upon the number of policies or the amount of insurance. All the factors in the nonforfeiture value formula have margins and are set at a level which will provide ample margins for any well-managed company.

Illustration of Adjusted Premium Method

The first step in deriving surrender values under the Standard Nonforfeiture Law is to determine the special first-year expense allowance. This may be based on the company's expense situation, competitive pressures, or other considerations, but is limited by the maximum amount permitted under the law.

The second step in the process is to calculate the *adjusted premium.* This may be approached from two standpoints. It may be regarded as the net annual level premium required to amortize a principal sum equal to the present value of the benefits under the policy and the special first-year expense allowance. Thus, the present value of future benefits (PVFB) for an ordinary life policy issued at age 35 is equal to the net single premium for such a policy, $420.13. The maximum special first-year expense allowance for such a policy is $32.37.[5] The total of these two is a principal sum of

---

[5] For a clear exposition of how the expense limitation and the adjusted premium are derived algebraically, see Frederic P. Chapman, *The Standard Nonforfeiture and Valuation Legislation* (Philadelphia: American College of Life Underwriters, 1949), p. 8.

$452.50. The net annual level premium which will amortize this sum may be obtained by dividing $452.50 by $23.775, the present value of a life annuity due of $1 as of age 35. The result, $19.033, is the adjusted premium.

The second way of looking at the adjusted premium is that it is the sum obtained by adding to the regular net annual level premium the annual amount needed to amortize the special acquisition expenses over the premium-paying period. Thus, by dividing $32.37 (maximum special first-year expense allowance) by the present value of a life annuity due of $1 for the premium-paying period $23.775, the annual amount of $1.362 is obtained, which when added to the net level premium for an ordinary life policy issued at age 35, $17.671, gives $19.033, the same adjusted premium determined above.

The final step in determining the *minimum* surrender value is to substitute the adjusted premium for the regular net level premium in the formula employed in the computation of prospective reserves. Thus, the minimum nonforfeiture value is equal to the present value of future benefits at the attained age less the present value of future *adjusted* premiums.

The following summary of the calculation of the tenth-year minimum nonforfeiture value for an ordinary life policy issued at age 35 *(1958 CSO and 2½ per cent)* will illustrate the application of the principles developed here:

1. Find the net single premium for ordinary life policy age 35 $420.13
2. Find allowance for special first-year expenses   32.37
3. Add (1) and (2)   452.50
4. Find present value of life annuity due of $1 at age 35   23.775
5. Divide (3) by (4) to find adjusted premium   19.033
6. Find net single premium for ordinary life policy at age 45   517.49
7. Find present value of life annuity due of $1 at age 45   19.783
8. Multiply (5) by (7) to find present value of future adjusted
    premiums at age 45   376.53
9. Subtract (8) from (6) to find tenth-year minimum nonfor-
    feiture value $140.96

$$\begin{array}{ccc} \text{NFV} \\ \text{age of} \\ \text{valuation} \end{array} = \begin{array}{c} \text{Present Value of Future} \\ \text{Benefits} \end{array} - \begin{array}{c} \text{Present Value of Future} \\ \text{Adjusted Premiums} \end{array}$$

$$\begin{array}{c} \text{NFV} \\ \text{age of} \\ \text{valuation} \end{array} = \begin{array}{c} \text{NSP} \\ \text{age of} \\ \text{valuation} \end{array} - \left(\frac{\begin{array}{c}\text{NSP} \\ \text{original} + \begin{array}{c}\text{Special} \\ \text{Expense} \\ \text{Allowance}\end{array} \\ \text{age} \end{array}}{\text{PVLAD of \$1 PPP}} \times \begin{array}{c}\text{PVLAD of \$1 for} \\ \text{remaining premium-} \\ \text{paying period}\end{array} \right)$$

$$\begin{array}{c} \text{NFV} \\ 45 \end{array} = \begin{array}{c} \text{NSP} \\ 45 \end{array} - \left(\frac{\begin{array}{c}\text{NSP} \\ 35 \end{array} + \begin{array}{c}\text{Special} \\ \text{Expense} \\ \text{Allowance}\end{array}}{\text{PVLAD of \$1 PPP}} \times \begin{array}{c}\text{PVLAD of} \\ \$1 \text{ for life} \\ \text{at age 45}\end{array} \right)$$

$$\text{NFV}_{45} = 517.49 - \left(\frac{420.13 + 32.37}{23.775} \times 19.783 \right)$$

$$\text{NFV}_{45} = \$140.96$$

It should be noted that the only difference between this formula and the minimum reserve formula utilized earlier is the addition of the expense factor to the original net single premium resulting in a net level *adjusted* premium. Thus, in prospective terms, the nonforfeiture value is the present value of future benefits less the present value of future *adjusted premiums*.

The minimum nonforfeiture value may also be found by a retrospective process, but this is not considered here.

Modifications of the Adjusted Premium Method

The above illustration demonstrates the calculation of minimum surrender values under a 2½ per cent interest assumption. As mentioned earlier, many companies provide surrender values in excess of those required by law. This may be accomplished either by (1) assuming lower first-year expenses than the maximum permitted or by (2) assuming the maximum expenses and amortizing them at an uneven rate over the premium-paying period or by (3) a combination of (1) and (2).

If lower first-year expenses are assumed, the "adjusted premium" will be smaller making the "present value of future adjusted premiums" smaller and hence, resulting in larger surrender values. Similarly, in the case of amortizing the maximum permitted excess first-year expense over a shorter period or at an uneven rate, the "adjusted premium" is adjusted, resulting in appropriately modified surrender values. In those cases where the "adjusted premium" is adjusted to produce higher surrender values, the modified "adjusted premium" is known as a *"nonforfeiture factor."* Similarly, the term "adjusted premium method" refers to the derivation of *minimum* values only. Where larger values are derived through the use of nonforfeiture factor(s), the term, "standard nonforfeiture value method," is applied. It is important to remember that the law only requires that values no less than those derived by the adjusted premium method be provided.

Surrender Dividends

In any well-managed company the asset share allocable to any particular policy will normally exceed the surrender value provided within a reasonable period. Eventually, it will even exceed the reserve, the length of time necessary depending, among other reasons, upon the philosophy adopted in establishing the level of the gross premium for the particular block of policies. The justifications for paying a surrender value which is less than the asset share were discussed earlier. At that time, it was pointed out that each policy could be expected to make a permanent contribution to the surplus or contingency reserve of the company. Since the surrender value is usually equal to the reserve after a number of years, the asset share in the normal case must exceed the reserve to permit such a contribution to be made. To the extent the asset share exceeds the reserve by more than is necessary as its equitable contribution to the permanent surplus of the company, a withdrawing policyholder would seem to be entitled to take any "excess" surplus with him. Such a final settlement with a withdrawing policyholder is called a *surrender dividend*.

Although the Standard Nonforfeiture Law does not require surrender dividends, the Standard Valuation Law specifies that if the rate of interest used in the calculation of reserves under participating policies is more than ½ per cent lower than the rate underlying surrender values, a plan *must* be adopted for providing such "equitable increases" in surrender values as the Commissioner of Insurance shall approve. It should be noted that in the State of New York, if there is *any* differential in the interest rates underlying the reserve and surrender value calculations, the company *must* make provision for a surrender dividend or satisfy the Commissioner of Insurance that no increase in surrender values is justified.

RELATION BETWEEN SURRENDER VALUES, RESERVES, AND ASSET SHARES

The previous discussion has attempted to delineate between surrender values, reserves, and asset shares.

The *surrender value* represents the amount made available, contractually, to a withdrawing policyholder. This value is intended to represent an equitable distribution, as compared with persisting policyholders, of the net amount accumulated on behalf of the particular policy.

The *reserve* is a more conservative value, representing the liability of the company to its policyholders. As in the case of the surrender value it reflects the plan of insurance, age at issue, and policy duration. Except where some form of modified reserves is involved, it does not reflect the expense element. The surrender value, on the other hand, does reflect the incidence of expense, in keeping with the company's philosophy regarding the period over which excess first-year expenses are to be recovered, competition, etc.

The *asset share* is simply the pro rata share of the assets accumulated on the basis of the company's actual experience on behalf of a block of policies to which the particular policy belongs.

It has been pointed out that the asset share is less than the reserve in the early years due to the uneven incidence of *expense outlay* as compared with *expense provision* in the level premium. The length of time it takes the asset share to equal the reserve is a function of the management decision as to how soon they wish to recover their acquisition costs as reflected in the level of gross premiums adopted and/or the scale of dividends adopted. After the asset share equals the reserve, both continue to increase, but with the asset share frequently growing at a slightly faster rate.

As has been pointed out in the present chapter, the surrender value is a somewhat more arbitrary value, reflecting the elements of expense incidence, competition and the company's philosophy with regard to equity as between persisting and withdrawing policyholders. In the early years it usually lies somewhere between the asset share and the net level premium reserve. After the portion of acquisition expense allocated to withdrawing as well as continuing policyholders has been substantially amortized, the surrender value is usually equal to the net level premium reserve for that and later policy durations, for companies valuing reserves by that method.

Table 26–1 and Graph 26–1 show the relationship between these three values assuming acquisition costs are to be fully amortized within ten years.

TABLE 26-1. Relationship Between Surrender Values,
Net Level Terminal Reserves, and Asset Shares; Ordinary Life,
Male Age 35, $1,000 Basis

Policy Year	Surrender Value	Reserves	Asset Shares
1	–	$ 15.64	$ −5.08
2	$ 15.18	31.59	12.63
3	33.28	47.83	30.61
4	51.68	64.32	48.93
5	70.38	81.05	67.53
6	89.36	98.01	86.44
7	108.59	115.17	105.64
8	128.10	132.55	125.13
9	147.86	150.12	144.90
10	167.90	167.90	165.00
11	185.85	185.85	185.34
12	203.97	203.97	205.94
13	222.24	222.24	226.77
14	240.63	240.63	247.82
15	259.12	259.12	269.04
16	277.71	277.71	290.46
17	296.35	296.35	312.07
18	315.05	315.05	333.86
19	333.79	333.79	355.83
20	352.54	352.54	377.95

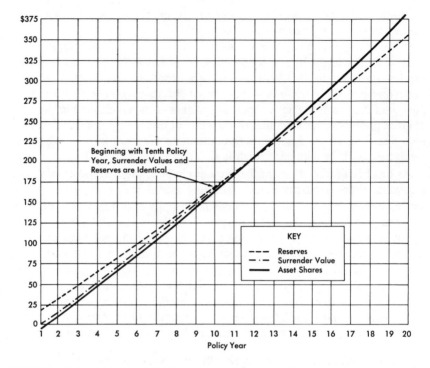

GRAPH 26-1. Relationship between surrender values, reserves, and asset shares per $1,000, ordinary life, male age 35.

Examination of Graph 26–1 will show (1) gain (no loss) to statement surplus; (2) gain (or loss) to company and (3) position of policyholder relative to the company in the event of withdrawals at various durations.

SURRENDER OPTIONS

The surrender options relate to the surrender value discussed above. Most policies stipulate that the nonforfeiture value may be taken in one of three forms: cash; reduced amount of paid-up insurance of the same kind as the original policy; paid-up extended term insurance for the full amount.

Cash

The policy may be surrendered for the cash value shown in the policy as of the date of surrender. When the option is elected, however, the protection ceases and the company has no further obligation under the policy. Consequently, though this provides a ready source for emergencies or other need for cash, it should be elected only after careful consideration. Essentially, the same amount of cash may be obtained through a policy loan, and consideration should be given to this alternative before a policy is surrendered. In general, a policy that has been surrendered for cash cannot be reinstated.

Under the nonforfeiture legislation, the surrender value of a policy is *required to be available in cash only* at the end of three years in the case of ordinary insurance and five years in the case of industrial insurance. This provision was intended to relieve the companies of the disproportionate expense of drawing checks for the relatively small values in the early years It does not, however, relieve them of the obligation of granting the surrender value in the form of some paid-up benefit.

The law *permits* a company to postpone payment of the *cash* surrender value for a period of six months after the policyholder requests it. The provision, known as the *delay clause,* is mandatory and is intended to protect the companies against any losses that might otherwise develop from excessive demands for cash in an economic crisis. The clause would be invoked only under the most unusual circumstances.

The available surrender value is the tabular value shown in the policy, decreased by the amount of any policy loan outstanding.

Reduced Paid-up Insurance

A second option permits the insured to elect to exchange the net amount of the cash value[6] for the equivalent in paid-up insurance of the same type as the original policy for a reduced face amount. The paid-up insurance is of the same type as the original basic policy exclusive of any term rider, except that the face amount is reduced, all riders and supplementary benefits such as for disability and accidental death are eliminated, and no further premiums are payable. It should be noted that the exchange is made at *net rates*.

Table 26–2, for example, shows that after ten years, the then cash value of $140.96 may be exchanged for $272.40 of paid-up whole-life insurance. This option would be appropriate where a smaller amount of permanent insurance would be satisfactory and it is desirable to discontinue premium payments. This elimination of premium payments may be particularly attractive as an insured approaches retirement where, normally, his income would be reduced.

---

[6] Cash value less any outstanding policy loans plus any dividend credits.

TABLE 26-2. Minimum Nonforfeiture Values

(1958 CSO Table, 2½ Per Cent Ordinary Life, Male Age 35)

| End of Year | Cash Value | Paid Up | Extended Term* | |
			Years	Days
3	$ 17.00	$ 37.97	4	38
4	34.03	74.40	6	363
5	51.31	109.84	9	47
6	68.81	144.27	10	268
7	86.53	177.72	11	354
8	104.47	210.21	12	338
9	122.61	241.76	13	245
10	140.96	272.40	14	91

*Extended Term is based on 1958 CET Table.

Extended Term Insurance

The third option permits the insured to exchange the cash value for paid-up term insurance for the full amount.[7] The length of the term insurance is that which can be purchased with the net cash value applied as a net single premium at the insured's attained age. Referring again to Table 26–2, the tenth-year cash value of $140.96 may be exchanged for term insurance for the full face amount running for 14 years and 91 days. If the insured does not make a specific election after default of premiums, this option is usually set up to go into effect automatically. This option would be appropriate where the need for insurance protection continues, but where the financial capacity to meet payment of premiums becomes impaired.

The period for which term insurance would be provided for various durations under an ordinary life and a twenty-year endowment policy, issued at male age 35, is shown in Table 26–3.

In the case of endowment policies, term insurance is not provided beyond the maturity date of the policy. Since the surrender value under all endowment policies eventually exceeds the sum needed to purchase term insurance to the end of the endowment period, provision is made to apply the excess to purchase a paid-up *pure* endowment with a maturity date the same as that of the original policy. Thus, the net single premium for the paid-up

---

[7] If a policy loan or paid-up dividend additions are outstanding, the face amount is decreased or increased accordingly.

TABLE 26-3. Minimum Paid-up Surrender Benefits at Various Durations Under Ordinary Life and Twenty-Year Endowment Policies

(1958 CSO Table and 2½ Per Cent Interest, Male Age 35)

Dura-tion	Cash Values	Extended Term Years	Extended Term Days	Re-duced Paid-up	Cash Values	Extended Term Years	Extended Term Days	Pure Endow-ment*	Re-duced Paid-up
3	$ 17.00	4	38	$ 37.97	$ 84.12	14	313	–	$125.76
5	51.31	9	47	109.84	172.42	15	–	$119.14	246.02
10	140.96	14	91	272.40	412.23	10	–	462.39	523.45
15	235.14	15	183	412.25	684.38	5	–	755.79	772.52
20	331.58	15	72	530.91	1,000.00			at maturity	
25	427.84	14	60	630.46	–	–	–	–	–
30	520.74	12	310	712.57	–	–	–	–	–

*Based on 1958 CET Table.

term insurance and the net single premium for the corresponding pure endowment would equal the full surrender value.

Other Aspects

Surrender Value and Settlement Options.   In addition to these nonforfeiture options, most companies permit the insured to apply the surrender value under the settlement options in the form of an annuity or retirement income. In the past this has been a matter of company practice, but recent contracts of many companies provide the insured with the *right* to take the cash value in the form of a life income purchased at net rates, usually at age 55 or later. Increasingly, individuals are purchasing low premium permanent life insurance to protect their family during the child raising period, but with the specific objective of using the cash values for their own retirement. For policies issued between the ages of 25 and 40, the cash value at age 65 will be from 50 to 60 per cent of the face amount. Thus, at age 65, the cash value of a good life insurance program, when supplemented by Federal OASDI benefits, will provide a reasonable amount of retirement income for the insured.

Automatic Premium Loan.   The automatic premium loan is sometimes considered as an additional option available in lieu of surrendering a policy for cash. Under this plan each premium is paid automatically as it comes due by the creation of a loan which, with interest, becomes a lien upon the insurance until paid. Premiums may be paid in this manner until the surrender value has been entirely utilized, at which time the insurance ceases to exist. A majority of the companies either provide or will permit the insertion of this provision in their contracts.

The automatic premium loan arrangement provides for a continuation of the insurance in cases where the insured, through either carelessness or inability, fails to pay his premiums, and it allows the insured at any time the right to attain his original status by repaying the amount which he owes the company. No evidence of insurability is necessary in reverting to the original status, whereas if either the extended term insurance or paid-up option is elected, the insured, in order to attain his former position, must furnish the company with satisfactory evidence regarding his insurability. In addition, use of the automatic premium loan continues supplementary life insurance and other benefits such as waiver of premium and accidental death benefits. These are not continued under the typical extended term option.

This method of using surrender values has some serious drawbacks, however. Policyholders may take advantage of this method of paying premiums when they are able to meet their payments, because of the fact that it works automatically. Also, when payments of premiums are made in this way, the insurance protection decreases each time the amount of the loan increases, since the money borrowed is a lien against the policy. Again, the period of coverage is shorter than if extended term insurance option is elected, and finally, the plan is troublesome and more costly for the company to operate than are the others.

NATURE OF SURPLUS

IT IS FUNDAMENTAL that due to the long-term nature of the life insurance company's obligations and the use of fixed premiums, such premiums should be calculated on a conservative basis. Consequently, it is expected that all companies will normally show a gain from operations. The immediate result of a gain, of course, is to increase the surplus position of the company. The size and disposition of this gain will depend upon whether the business written by the company is "participating" or "nonparticipating." Nonparticipating policies are those written at a fixed premium which guarantee the sum insured and do not entitle the insured to receive any other benefits than those expressly set forth in the contract. Although participating policies also are written at a fixed premium, they usually require the payment of a premium large enough to enable the company to meet its obligations on each class of policies at actual cost *for each class* under any plausible future experience. As a consequence the insured is allowed contractually from time to time to "participate," that is, to receive periodic distributions to the extent that management feels that experience warrants such adjustments. Since most participating insurance is written by mutual companies and most nonparticipating insurance by stock companies,[1] the following discussion will assume that reference to a mutual company and participating insurance will be synonymous unless expressly stated otherwise.

The gain in the case of a stock company (nonparticipating) may arise from either a specific provision in the gross premium for profit or as a result of favorable deviations of actual experience from assumed experience, or both. Such surplus is available to be paid to the stockholders as a dividend as compensation for the use of their capital funds, or used to finance the acquisition of new business to produce further gains, or kept as surplus to provide greater security to policyholders against future adverse contingencies.

[1] See Chapter 39.

The increase in surplus, prior to dividend distribution, in a participating company will normally be greater than in the case of the stock company, since their premiums are deliberately made more conservative. The mutual company can properly make its premiums conservative, since it can adjust the final charge to the policyholders by means of a dividend. The use of the term "dividend" here is unfortunate since the distribution, to a considerable extent, does not arise primarily from the deviations of actual from expected experience but from margins provided in the premium rates.

In any given year it is possible, of course, for a company to experience a loss or net decrease in surplus due to unfavorable experience relative to one or more of the basic assumptions entering into the gross premium. The great majority of companies, for example, suffered such losses during the influenza epidemic of 1917–18, when the actual deaths far exceeded the anticipated death rates. Nevertheless, the normal operations of a company should produce a net gain in surplus from year to year.

The remaining discussion in this chapter will be devoted exclusively to the surplus of mutual life insurance companies and its distribution under participating contracts.

SOURCES OF SURPLUS

In the aggregate, surplus will develop only if a company accumulates funds in excess of those that are needed to establish policy reserves and other liabilities. The sources of surplus, arising out of favorable deviations from the assumed experience as to mortality, interest, and loading entering into the gross premium, constitute the primary source of additions to surplus and are usually designated as *mortality savings, excess interest, and loading savings.* The word "savings" is used here to connote both the residue arising from more efficient and economical operations than were anticipated, and the margins *intentionally* provided for in fixing the premiums. It is important to remember that even though the premium is made conservative, capable management can make a significant difference in the amount added to surplus at the end of each year.

Earlier,[2] an analysis was given of the individual approach to the retrospective method of reserve accumulation. An examination of this approach will be instructive in demonstrating the three main sources of surplus. In the discussion, it was made clear that the terminal reserve at the end of any policy year could be projected to the terminal reserve at the end of the next policy year by the following formula:

[2] See pp. 388–389.

Initial Reserve

$$\left[\left(\begin{array}{c}\text{Terminal Reserve}\\\text{at End of Year }t\end{array} + \begin{array}{c}\text{Net Premium}\\\text{Calculated on}\\\text{the Reserve}\\\text{Basis}\end{array}\right)\left(\begin{array}{c}\text{Accumulated by}\\\text{One Year's Interest}\\\text{at the Reserve}\\\text{Interest Basis}\end{array}\right)\right] -$$

Cost of Insurance

$$\left[\left(\begin{array}{c}\text{The Rate of}\\\text{Mortality for}\\\text{this Policy}\\\text{Duration According}\\\text{to the Reserve}\\\text{Mortality Table}\end{array}\right)\left(\begin{array}{c}\text{The Face of the Policy}\\\text{Minus the Terminal}\\\text{Reserve at the End}\\\text{of Year}\\t+1\end{array}\right)\right] = \begin{array}{c}\text{Terminal Reserve at}\\\text{End of Year }t+1\end{array}$$

1. The function in the first parenthesis is known as the Initial Reserve. It is clear that if the company maintains funds on hand at least level to the Initial Reserve, and if the company earns a higher rate of interest on such funds than "one year's interest at the reserve interest basis" it will have developed surplus on policies in this group at this duration. Therefore, *excess interest*, over the reserve interest basis, is one of the main sources of surplus.

2. Similarly, it is clear that if the actual rate of mortality is lower than "the rate of mortality for this policy duration according to the reserve mortality table," the company will have developed a gain or *mortality savings*. This is a second main source of surplus.

3. Thirdly, note that the premium required in the formula is the "net premium calculated on the reserve basis." The actual gross premium charged by the company will be in excess of this, and the excess is available to the company for its expenses. If the actual expenses are less than this excess, the company will have developed surplus for this reason. This third main source of surplus is known as *loading savings*.

The surplus of the company arising from a given block of policies (a given plan, at a given age of issue, and at a particular duration), therefore, consists of the sum of the excess interest, mortality savings, and savings from loading plus gains from minor sources.

It should be mentioned again that for some policies, ages at issue, and durations some or all of the three gains could be *negative*. In particular, it is almost always the case for the savings from loading to be negative in the first policy year, when the company's expenses are higher relatively than in renewal years.

There are several minor sources of surplus additions which may be quite significant under certain circumstances.

1. Surplus may arise from capital gains. These arise from the *sale* of assets for more than the value at which they are carried on the company's

books, or the *writing up* of asset values. Capital losses can also occur, of course, and asset values may be *written down*.

2. Voluntary termination of policies during early durations when surrender values are less than reserves established on the company's books. To the extent that the reserves released as a result of surrenders exceed the amounts disbursed as surrender allowances, statement surplus, but not necessarily divisible surplus, will be increased.[3]

3. Supplementary benefits, such as disability or accidental death, may be an additional source of surplus gain or loss, and are sometimes taken into account as additional factors in dividend formulae.

Gain from Investment Earnings

Since life insurance policies are written for a long term of years, it is essential that the companies assume a rate of interest for their net premium and reserve computations so conservative as to assure its being earned throughout the life of the contract. If a company has based its reserves on the assumption that it will earn 3 per cent but actually earns 4 per cent (after the expenses connected with the making and maintenance of investments), that difference of 1 per cent represents the excess of investment earnings over and above the return necessary to the solvency of the company and may, if considered advisable, be returned to the policyholders who contributed the same. Frequently, a company may have profits from appreciation or losses from depreciation in the value of its investments. Such capital gains or losses may be taken into account in selecting the excess interest factor of the dividend formula; or, more commonly, they may be earmarked in a special surplus account to be used in offsetting future capital gains or losses.[4] It is frequently the case that the investments which produced the capital gains (losses) will be replaced with lower (higher) yielding assets.

Gain from Mortality

This gain arises from the fact that participating life insurance companies in the United States do not experience, normally, as heavy a mortality as is indicated by the mortality table employed by them in reserve calculations. The reserve, it will be recalled, was defined as the difference between the present value of future benefits and the present value of future premiums. In view of the fact that the reserve mortality table is deliberately made con-

---

[3] It should be noted that this does not necessarily constitute a true gain or profit. The relationship between the asset share and the surrender value allowed will determine this. See pp. 436–438.

[4] See pp. 718–719.

servative, it is natural that a gain results from normal operations. It is important not to place too much reliance on one year's mortality experience, since it tends to fluctuate from year to year. In the interest of stability and safety, therefore, most companies average mortality experience over a period of years.

Gain from Loading

Sound management in life insurance dictates that the gross premium should be more than sufficient to meet normal requirements so that the company and its policyholders may be protected against exceptional conditions. In fact, as pointed out above, the loading frequently includes an amount for dividends to the policyholder together with the gains from other sources. Competitive conditions, especially in the matter of agents' commissions, as well as inflationary pressures on expenses, have at times caused expenses to exceed loadings in the aggregate. In recent years, utilizing increasingly sophisticated computer systems, there has been a marked effort toward economical management in life insurance, and at present most companies manage, by exercising rigid economy, to make their annual expenses less than their allowance (the difference between the gross premium and the valuation net premium) for expenses and contingencies. Hence, they are able to credit a saving to surplus, and this saving serves the twofold purpose of protecting the company against financial disturbances and of furnishing an additional fund out of which to pay dividends to its policyholders.

Gain from Surrenders

Surrender values, as previously explained, are less than the reserves held by the company on those policies which are surrendered or lapsed within a designated number of years. The difference between the reserves released as a result of surrender and the surrender values allowed constitutes another source of statement surplus, although owing to the high expense of securing new business, this factor can scarcely be regarded as yielding a true gain. Such a gain frequently represents, in whole or in part, amounts returned to surplus which were originally taken from it in order to establish the reserves.[5] Furthermore, if any gain should be derived from this source, it is usually treated as an offset to expenses when calculations are made to apportion the divisible surplus to policyholders.[6]

[5] See Chapter 24.
[6] In the apportionment of surplus, as will be explained in a later section, it has been found that it is more practical to treat all surplus as coming from the three

Two other reasons have been advanced to show that the so-called gain from surrenders is only an apparent and not a real gain. In the first place it is believed that where *conservative* surrender values are allowed, the apparent gain to the company is offset in part by an unfavorable mortality experience, attributed to the adverse selection resulting from the fact that healthy policyholders tend to show a greater disposition to discontinue restrictive contracts while those who are ailing will remain in the company irrespective of the limited policy provisions. *But of much greater importance,* it is argued, is the expense of replacing the old policy with a new one. Not only did the company incur the heavy initial expenses in securing the discontinued policy, but in replacing it with a new policy it incurs this initial expense a second time.

DISTRIBUTION OF SURPLUS

Divisible Surplus

Following each year's operations, the question of how much of the *total* surplus (previously existing plus additions for the year) should be retained as a contingency fund or other special surplus appropriation [7] and how much should be distributed to policyholders must be determined. It is important to note that there may be no fixed relationship between the surplus gain in a particular calendar year and the dividends distributed to policyholders on the next policy anniversaries. The directors or trustees of the company, as a matter of business judgment, make the decision. The amount earmarked for distribution is designated *divisible surplus,* and once set aside by action of the directors or trustees loses its identity as surplus and becomes a *liability* of the company.

In deciding what portion of the total surplus should be retained as contingency funds, a balance must be maintained between the need for a general contingency fund and the competitive advantages of a liberal dividend *scale.* When the surplus earned for any given year is not sufficient to permit the company to maintain its current dividend scale, the management may decide to use a portion of the general contingency fund [8] for this purpose. On the other hand, if during a temporary period additions to surplus are

---

main sources previously mentioned, that is, loading, interest earnings, and mortality. Surplus from other sources, such as forfeitures and appreciation in the value of assets, therefore, are not treated separately, but are considered in connection with expenses and interest earnings.

[7] The term "reserve" sometimes is used here as an earmarking of surplus rather than as a liability in the sense of policy reserves.

[8] A given company may earmark a special fund for "dividend fluctuations" but the principle is the same.

more than adequate to support the existing dividend scale, the excess will usually be added to the general contingency fund in order to avoid the expense and complications involved in changing the *scale*. If the excess is substantial and is expected to continue over a reasonable period, consideration will usually be given to changing the *scale*. It should be remembered, however, that the decision is a matter of business judgment and is made by the directors or trustees of the company.

Security of benefit and good management require that the life insurance company maintain a surplus and general contingency fund which bears a reasonable relationship to its liabilities. As the policy reserves of the company increase through new business and the natural accretion under old policies, the surplus and general contingency funds of the company must necessarily also increase. It is important to note, again, that, under the surplus distribution systems of some mutual companies, each policy is expected to make a *permanent* contribution to the surplus of the company which will not be returned to the insured except in the event of the remote possibility that the company is liquidated while his policy is still in force in the company. Consequently, the aggregate dividend distributions[9] made to the class of policies to which his belongs over their entire duration will normally be somewhat less than their contributions to surplus. This is another way of saying that, for a block of policies, the asset share should eventually exceed the reserve and that each policy is expected to make a permanent contribution to the surplus of the company. These contributions to surplus are regarded as premiums which will ultimately enable the company to fulfill its contractual obligations even in the face of a severe catastrophe of the type that may occur only once in several decades. Just because a severe catastrophe does not occur during the lifetime of a particular policy should not exempt that policy from making its contribution to the surplus which is needed to withstand such a catastrophe. On the other hand, some companies take a somewhat different view and have a dividend practice which results in substantially complete liquidation of each generation's contributions to surplus by the time that generation of policyholders is extinguished from the books.

While the companies may, in the absence of legislation, use their discretion in determining the amount of surplus to be distributed, some states regulate this matter by statute. Thus, as a result of the New York insurance investigation of 1906, that state limited the amount of surplus which a company may withhold from policyholders, the limit varying from 20 per cent of the reserve liability or $10,000—whichever was greater in the case of smaller companies—to 5 per cent of the reserve liabilities where it exceeded $75,000,000. These limits have been changed since, and the present law

---

[9] This includes, in addition to the usual dividends distributed annually, extra dividends and settlement or terminal dividends. See p. 458.

provides that a life insurance company doing a participating business may accumulate and maintain a surplus, over and above all of its policy reserves and policy liabilities, in an amount not exceeding $850,000, or 10 per cent of its policy reserves and other policy liabilities, whichever is greater. The purpose of this legislation is to prevent the company from retaining more surplus than is necessary to offset factors, such as fluctuations in the mortality rate and in interest earnings, which are apt to interfere with the payment of stable dividends. It was felt not only that life insurance is not subject to catastrophic losses such as are experienced in fire insurance, and that the aforementioned limits are therefore conservative, but that a large surplus furnishes a constant temptation for extravagance in the conduct of business.

Frequency of Distribution

Dividends on participating policies may be paid either annually or on the deferred-dividend plan. The annual-dividend plan is used in connection with the sale of practically all participating policies at the present time, and in many states it is required by statute. Statutes of this nature were passed after the New York insurance investigation in 1906 disclosed certain abuses in connection with the payment of dividends on the deferred plan. Some policies are still in existence on which deferred dividends are paid.

Deferred dividends, as distinguished from annual dividends, refer to those which, according to the terms of the policy, are not payable until the close of a stipulated number of years, such as five, ten, fifteen, or twenty years. Policies providing for payment of dividends in this manner are commonly called deferred-dividend, accumulation, distribution, or semitontine policies. The underlying principle of the plan is that those policyholders who fail to continue premium payments to the end of the designated period because of death, surrender, or lapse, lose the dividends which they would have received under the annual-dividend plan, and that the dividends thus lost revert to those policyholders who continue their premium payments throughout the deferred-dividend period. The system, as used in recent years, must not be confused with the so-called tontine plan, which was, at one time, used in the United States and which provided for a forfeiture of both dividends and surrender value upon failure to pay a premium with the entire forfeiture accumulations being divided among the persisting policyholders at the close of the designated dividend period. As distinguished from this plan, the deferred-dividend system applies the forfeiture idea to dividends only, and thus reduces the chance of large gains being derived from the surrender of policies.

Even in this latter form the deferred-dividend plan lost favor with the public, and, as stated before, it has been almost wholly superseded by the annual-distribution system. The latter plan, it is argued, is not only well adapted to the policyholder who wishes to keep his annual net outlay to the lowest possible figures, but also serves the purpose of making the company economical in the management of its business, since extravagance will likely be revealed by a reduction in the annual-dividend distribution.

The deferred system in a modified form is still used to some extent in Canada. Under Canadian law, dividend distributions must be made every five years, but the amount of surplus set aside for deferred dividends during a five-year period must be carried as a *liability* until it is paid. Most Canadian companies pay an interim dividend in event of death during the period but not in the event of lapse or surrender.[10]

Principles of Allotment

The allocation of divisible surplus among the various policyholders is a complex matter. Obviously, equity is the basic objective, but consideration must be given to flexibility and simplicity. Flexibility is in reality a facet of equity, since adaptability to changing circumstances is essential if equity is to be attained. Simplicity is desirable both from an expense viewpoint and from the viewpoint of understanding by the agency force and policyholders. The earlier discussion of the sources of surplus would suggest that one way of obtaining reasonable equity would be to return to each class of policyholders a share of the divisible surplus approximately proportionate to the contribution of the class to the distributable surplus. It should be noted that such a plan does not require the return of *all* contributions to surplus. It merely requires that the *divisible surplus* be allotted to the policyholders in the approximate *proportion* in which they contributed to the total divisible

[10] Briefly outlined, the arguments advanced against and in favor of the plan are the following:

Against the plan it is argued:

a. That it is the reverse of insurance, the fortunate survivors benefiting at the expense of those who die.

b. That the plan is frequently not understood by the insured at the time the contract is issued, or, if understood, its significance is not properly appreciated.

c. That the plan furnishes a temptation toward extravagance in that it gives the company possession of large unassigned surplus funds. This is especially true where an accounting to policyholders is deferred until the end of the dividend period, whereas under an annual-distribution plan such extravagance would not be likely to occur, since it would come to the immediate notice of policyholders. It is for this reason that many of the companies which used the plan gave an annual accounting to their policyholders of the amount of surplus standing to their credit, thus enabling them to judge whether the company was being managed properly.

d. That the plan has been responsible in the past for extravagant estimates on the part of agents as to the amount of dividends that would be realized by policyholders who would continue premium payments to the end of the dividend period. In fact, much of the opposition to the system was occasioned by the fact that the estimates surplus. This plan under one or another of its modifications is used by practically all companies in this country.[11]

The Contribution Plan

The contribution plan is based upon an analysis of the sources of surplus and develops dividends which vary with the plan of insurance, age of issue, and duration of the policy. In the interest of simplicity, consideration is usually limited to the three major sources of surplus: excess interest, mortality savings, and loading savings. A system which recognizes these three sources of surplus is called the three-factor contribution plan. Where special benefits are involved, such as disability and accidental death, an additional factor is sometimes included for these features. The following sections will consider briefly the operation of a three-factor contribution system.

Interest Factor.   The interest factor is the simplest element of the dividend, consisting of the excess interest on, usually, the initial reserve [12] for the policy period at the end of which the dividend is payable. Assume that reserves have been calculated on the *1958 CSO Table* with interest at 2½ per cent and that the rate used in dividend calculations is 3½ per cent.[13] Under such circumstances, the rate of excess interest would

---

far exceeded the results obtained, thus causing many policyholders to labor under the impression that they had been deceived by the companies.

In favor of the plan it is argued:

a. That it represents an understanding between the insured and the company which is clearly set forth in the contract and which should be known to the insured at the time the contract is issued. It follows that the plan is not morally wrong and works no injustice to the policyholder since he has the right to have his dividend payments deferred and conditioned upon the payment of premiums during the whole of the stipulated dividend period.

b. That with reference to a company's solvency the plan is more advantageous than the annual-distribution system in that it enables the company to retain control of a large fund which is free from any definite liability and which will serve as a protection against the depreciation of the company's assets in time of financial panic or business depression. The shortcoming of the annual-distribution system, it is argued, lies in the fact that the company, owing to the strenuous competition prevailing in the business, may possibly endanger its solvency by too liberal a distribution of its surplus funds. Furthermore, an annual distribution is costly to the company and thus to the policyholders.

[11] Another method of computing dividends is the so-called experience-premium method which is used by a number of companies in this country. Its purpose is to avoid decreases in dividends on any plan even with a very low excess interest factor. See Joseph B. Maclean, *Life Insurance,* 9th ed. (New York: McGraw-Hill Book Co., Inc., 1962), pp. 159–160.

[12] Many companies utilize the mean reserve on premium paying policies and the initial reserve on policies where premiums have been fully paid up.

[13] This is not always the actual net rate earned.

be 1 per cent, and the interest factor for a given dividend would vary depending upon the size of the initial reserve for the contract under consideration. Thus, on a $1,000 ordinary life policy issued at age 25 which had been in force twenty years, the *interest factor* of the dividend would be 1 per cent multiplied by the initial reserve of $266.25, or $2.66. Policies with different initial reserves, because of plan of insurance, age of issue, or duration, would, of course, produce different initial reserves and hence, different interest contributions. Since the initial reserve will increase yearly under almost all permanent forms of insurance, the contribution of the interest factor will usually increase with duration assuming no change in the excess interest factor. It should be noted that the interest factor has a strong influence on the dividend. An increase in the above company's interest earnings from 3½ per cent to 4½ per cent would *double* the excess interest factor in every case. This would make a substantial difference in the dividends, particularly at long durations where the initial reserve is relatively high.

Although the interest factor is simple in concept, several complications arise in application. Aggregate investment earnings are readily available from the company's financial and accounting records, but there are several bases [14] which could be and are used to compute the *rate* of investment yield. For purposes of asset share studies underlying the dividend formula it is common to use a base consisting of the *interest-bearing liabilities* and surplus. Interest-bearing liabilities include policy reserves, funds held under settlement agreements, dividend accumulations [15] and advance premiums.[16] Where certain items such as dividend accumulations have a minimum guarantee, some companies credit such items with only the guaranteed rate and increase the net effective rate for regular policy dividend purposes. The final rate utilized in the dividend formula may well be less than the rate used in the asset share studies. This results in a contribution to the general contingency reserve, part of which may ultimately be distributed as a settlement or termination dividend. It is important to remember that the excess interest factor should reflect the *general trend* of the company's investment earnings and be set at a level which, according to the best judgment of the company, should be appropriate for a number of years. For short periods of time the factor could be based on a higher rate than is actually being earned.

There is also a difference in practice in the treatment of capital gains and losses on assets other than stocks and bonds. Some companies take these into account in fixing the excess interest factor when they reflect actual market transactions as opposed to unrealized gains or losses arising out

[14] For example, the base logically could be ledger assets, admitted assets, or invested funds.

[15] See p. 460.

[16] Most companies will permit policyholders to prepay premiums by discounting them at a given rate of interest. The discounted premiums so paid are applied as of the appropriate premium due dates. In the event of the death of the insured all unapplied premiums (less unearned discount) are returned to the beneficiary.

of adjustments in book value. The more common practice, however, is to transfer such gains and losses to an investment fluctuation fund or to a general contingency reserve where over a period of time the gains and losses tend to offset each other. This stabilizes net interest earnings and is consistent with the long-term nature of the life insurance contract.

There are also differences among companies as to the treatment of investment expenses. Companies particularly differ in their treatment of general overhead and Federal income taxes. This can make a significant difference in the "net rate earned" and although this should not affect the aggregate amount of surplus distributed, it does affect the pattern of distribution as between blocks of policies.

Even after the excess interest factor has been fixed, there remains the question to which actuarial value (initial reserve, mean reserve, or other) it is to be applied. The theoretically correct base is the initial reserve less one-half year's cost of insurance. The difference between this theoretically correct base and the mean reserve is quite small [17] and the mean reserve is considered a satisfactory approximation. While the mean reserve would be a more accurate measure of the policy funds available for investment, the difference in results is so insignificant that many companies continue to use the initial reserve without the adjustment for one-half year's cost of insurance.

Table 27–1 shows the interest contribution to annual dividends per $1,000 provided by an excess interest factor of 1 per cent under ordinary life, twenty-payment life, and twenty-year endowment policies issued to men aged 35 and 55, and in force for various durations. The factor is applied to the appropriate initial reserves [18] and demonstrates the impact of applying a fixed interest factor to a steadily growing reserve.

TABLE 27-1.   Contribution to Annual Dividend per $1,000 from
Excess Interest Factor of 1 Per Cent

Number of Years in Force	Ordinary Life, Age at Issue:		20-Payment Life, Age at Issue:		20-Year Endowment, Age at Issue:	
	35	55	35	55	35	55
5	$0.82	$1.56	$1.33	$1.93	$2.02	$2.15
10	1.68	2.96	2.77	3.81	4.27	4.32
15	2.58	4.27	4.37	5.81	6.82	6.83
20	3.51	5.43	6.14	8.13	9.76	9.76

[17] One-half year's interest at the valuation rate on the initial reserve.
[18] Based on full net level premium reserves computed in accordance with the *1958 CSO Table* and 2½ per cent interest.

The excess interest contribution increases with duration if reserves increase, and at all ages of issue and durations is larger for the higher premium forms than for the lower premium policies. It can be seen in the table that, assuming the same duration and age of issue, excess interest makes a greater contribution to the total dividend of a twenty-year endowment policy than it does for an ordinary life, particularly at longer durations.

Mortality Factor.   The *mortality factor* of the dividend in the three-factor formula is normally a percentage of the assumed "cost of insurance." [19] The percentage for any block of policies generally depends only on the attained age of the policyholder and the company's experience among *all policyholders* at that age and duration. The mortality factor of the formula normally takes the form of a scale of percentages of the assumed cost of insurance, decreasing with attained age, and reflecting the company's actual mortality experience age by age as compared with the rates shown in the mortality table assumed in calculating premiums and reserves.[20] The percentage may range from a high of 40–50 per cent at the younger ages to a low of 5–10 per cent at the older ages. Since mortality experience under term policies is considerably higher, age by age, than under permanent plans, a separate, lower scale of mortality savings would be applied to such classes of policies.

Some companies express the factor in slightly different form, but the effect in each case is to provide a mortality savings which, as a percentage of the assumed or tabular cost of insurance, declines with increases in attained age. Applied to the entire volume of business, the scale of mortality factors will reproduce approximately the aggregate amount of mortality savings for the period under consideration.

The percentage utilized in the final dividend calculation is normally based on the *ultimate* mortality experience although the select experience is utilized in the asset share underlying the development of the dividend distributions. Otherwise, a decreasing dividend scale by duration could result due to large mortality savings at early durations. The savings from the effect of selection are assumed to be applied toward the payment of excess first-year expenses and hence, are distributed indirectly in accordance with the method used to assess expenses to the various blocks of policies.

The mortality contribution per $1,000 of insurance provided by an illustrative scale of mortality factors under ordinary life, twenty-payment life, and twenty-year endowment policies, issued at ages 35 and 55 and in force for various durations, are shown in Table 27–2.

The mortality savings are assumed to range from 40 per cent at age 35 down to 10 per cent at attained ages 65 and over, diminishing at the rate

[19] See pp. 388–389.
[20] If the reserve basis mortality assumption is different from that used in expressing final gross premiums for this particular block of policies, the reserve basis mortality table is used.

TABLE 27-2. Mortality Contribution per $1,000 of Insurance Provided by an Illustrative Scale of Mortality Factors

Number of Years In Force	Ordinary Life, Age at Issue:		20-Payment Life, Age at Issue:		20-Year Endowment, Age at Issue:	
	35	55	35	55	35	55
5	$1.05	$2.39	$0.99	$2.28	$0.90	$2.21
10	1.23	2.08	1.06	1.82	0.83	1.67
15	1.41	2.69	1.06	1.93	0.58	1.48
20	1.54	3.24	0.89	1.22	—	—

of 1 per cent per year at attained age. It can be seen from the table that the mortality contribution normally decreases with duration and is smallest on the higher premium plans and ages of issue. This is so because of the fact that the declining *percentage factor* is applied to a steadily smaller net amount at risk and hence, in the usual case, a smaller cost of insurance. The higher the premium (due to plan or age at issue) the more pronounced is the decline in mortality savings. This is not invariably so, however. The cost of insurance actually *increases* at the higher ages under certain types of policies such as ordinary life. In these cases, the increase in the rate of mortality, at these ages, more than offsets the decrease in the net amount at risk resulting in an increased mortality cost for the year. In general, however, the mortality factor results in a decreasing contribution with greater durations.

In contrast to the interest factor the mortality contribution is very significant for term insurance policies. The percentage factor (normally a different scale applies) is applied here to a larger net amount at risk and hence, cost of insurance, resulting relatively in a greater proportionate contribution to the dividends distributable to term policies.

Loading Factor.   The loading factor of the dividend consists of the difference between the gross premium and the *valuation net premium,* less an expense charge. The assessment of expenses probably presents the greatest difficulty connected with the distribution of surplus. By far the greatest part of the expenses of a life insurance company is the initial expenditure incurred for the procurement of new business. With respect to this large initial expense some hold that it should be assessed against the new business while others maintain that the new business is for the benefit of the company as a whole and that the initial expense should therefore be assessed against the company's entire business. Furthermore, many expenses, such as rent, office supplies, salaries, office expense, advertising, postage, and so forth, are of a joint nature and it is difficult to identify these for the purpose of assessing them upon the numerous blocks of policies carried by an insurance company.

In general, the expense charge is frequently in the form of "a percentage and a constant," that is, a percentage of the premium and a constant of so many dollars and cents per $1,000 of face amount. The constant may vary to allow for differences in the average amount of policy by plan of insurance. The percentage element of the expense charge is usually on a decreasing basis, at least for the first few years, to reflect the lower expenses after the first few years. There are wide differences among companies both in gross premiums charged and in the manner of computing the expense charge. Consequently, the importance of the loading factor will vary considerably, the *amount* being much higher in a company with "high" gross premiums than in a company utilizing "low" gross premiums. The pattern in most cases, however, is for the loading factor to increase for the first few years and thereafter to increase slightly or remain relatively constant.

The trend of the contribution from loading during the early policy years will depend upon the period over which excess first-year expenses are to be amortized and whether they are amortized at a uniform rate or at a decreasing rate.

In the case of level amortization the contribution will be fairly level during the period of amortization, after which it will increase sharply and then level off. In the case of a decreasing rate of amortization the contribution will increase each year during the amortization period, after which it will level off. In the unusual case where a company treats acquisition expenses as a charge against all policies, the loading contribution should be relatively constant at all durations.

Dividend Pattern. For most plans of insurance the dividend scale under the contribution plan will usually show an increase with duration. This is entirely aside from an increase in the *scale* itself. The normal increase of dividends with duration is due to the fact that the interest factor normally increases with duration and the loading factor either increases or remains approximately constant. In the usual case these more than offset the tendency for the mortality factor to decrease with duration, but it is important to remember that this is not always so. An unfavorable investment market may well cause just the opposite to occur as happened in the 1940's when the average return dropped below 3 per cent.

It has been pointed out earlier that due to the high initial expense and the necessity of establishing the first-year reserve, a policy, normally, does not of itself produce any surplus in the first year. In view of this many companies make payment of a dividend at the end of the first year contingent upon continuation of the policy in force. In fact, some companies simply do not pay a dividend at all until the end of the second policy year. Many companies, however, pay a dividend at the end of the first year regardless of whether the policy is continued in force.

Special Forms of Surplus Distribution

Some companies pay *extra* dividends or settlement dividends in addition to the regular annual dividends.

Extra Dividends.   Extra dividends may be either a single payment made after a policy has been in force a specified number of years or a payment made periodically at stated intervals. The single-payment extra dividend is usually used where no first-year dividend is paid, the extra dividend serving as a substitute. This policy has the practical advantage of reducing the strain of initial expenses and also may have a tendency to reduce the first-year lapse rate. This procedure has the effect of assessing a larger share of first-year expense against those policies which terminate prior to the time when the extra dividend is paid.

Extra dividends paid periodically (say, at every fifth year) have little justification in theory unless it is that regular dividends have been calculated on a *very* conservative basis and equity insists that extra dividends be paid periodically to the surviving and persisting policyholders as the experience develops. A practical advantage, however, lies in the fact that illustrative net costs over a period of years are reduced by these extra amounts; only those policies remaining in force get the additional payments. This is particularly true of an extra dividend payable only at the end of the twentieth year.

Settlement Dividends.   Some companies pay a settlement or terminal dividend in the event a policy terminates by maturity, death, or surrender. In most cases such dividends are payable only if the policy has been in force a minimum length of time. Settlement dividends usually have the purpose of returning to terminating policyholders part of the general surplus to which they have contributed or to adjust for a guaranteed cash value which is something less than the asset share. Some companies, however, feel that the policyholder should make a *permanent* contribution to the surplus of the company as one of the normal expenses of operation.

It is important to note the distinction between a *post-mortem* or mortuary dividend and a settlement dividend payable at death. A post-mortem dividend is payable at death but is either paid in proportion to the part of the policy year of death for which premiums have been paid, or represents a method of distribution of surplus, mainly on term insurance, in lieu of dividends on each policy anniversary while the insured was living.

DIVIDEND OPTIONS

It is customary for companies to allow the insured, at his option, to use his dividends in one of a number of ways. The four basic dividend options are (1) cash; (2) reduction of premiums; (3) paid-up additions; and (4) accumulation at interest.

The policyholder may elect an option at the time the policy is applied for and the plan so elected remains effective until changed by the insured. Unless the owner of the policy elects some other plan, the application usually provides for the purchase of paid-up additions.

Cash and Part Payment of Premium

Most states require that the dividend be made available in cash; policyholders, however, usually find one of the other options more attractive.

Although applying the dividend toward the payment of the next premium under the policy is really the equivalent of cash, a substantial number of policyholders elect this option to reduce their current outlay of funds. They could, of course, take the dividend in cash and remit the full premium, obtaining the same net effect.

Purchase of Paid-up Additions

The insured may have the dividend applied to the purchase of nonforfeitable paid-up additions to the policy. Under this option the dividend is applied as a single premium at the insured's attained age to purchase as much paid-up insurance of the same type as the basic policy as the dividend will provide. It is customary to make the paid-up insurance available at net rates.[21]

The right to purchase a series of paid-up additions at net rates should be attractive to any policyholder. In the first place the policyholder has already incurred the acquisition costs on the amount of the dividend, since commission rates and certain other expenses vary with the premium and are levied against the *gross* premium. The attractiveness of this option is further enhanced for a policyholder whose health has become impaired. Usually, evidence of insurability is not required as a condition precedent to the exercising of the option and, if required, need be furnished only at the time

---

[21] It should be noted that, practically, this option resembles the reduced paid-up insurance available in connection with surrender values.

of election. Where paid-up additions are purchased, both the amount of insurance payable in case of death and cash values will increase at a greater rate each year if the paid-up additions are participating.

It should be noted that few individuals can afford to buy single premium life insurance and many consider it a wiser move to use dividends to reduce current premiums in order to permit the purchase of additional annual premium insurance and hence, a more adequate program.

Accumulate at Interest

Dividends may be allowed to accumulate to the credit of the policy at a definite rate of interest or at such a rate as may be determined by the company, and are withdrawable at the will of the policyholder or sometimes only on any anniversary of the policy. If death occurs, the face of the policy is paid plus dividend accumulations, and in the event of surrender, the cash value plus dividend accumulations will be returned. It should be noted, however, that if the basic policy ultimately terminates other than by death, and if Federal income taxes on the interest are not a factor, the purchase of paid-up additions was not as advantageous as accumulation at interest.

Term Additions

In recent years many companies have made available an option to apply the dividend to purchase one-year term insurance. This has taken two forms. One simply applies the dividend as a net single premium to purchase as much one-year term protection as it will buy. The other form purchases one-year term insurance equal to the surrender value of the policy with the excess portion of the dividend accumulated at interest until needed in later policy years. The latter form was introduced in connection with certain sales presentations involving the sale of permanent life insurance where the policy was paid for through loans against the policy. The object was to assure the beneficiary of the full face amount of the policy in the event of the insured's death even though the surrender value was fully pledged against the loans.

Other Options

Paid-up Contract.   Dividends may be used to make the policy a paid-up contract. This means that whenever the surrender value on the policy and existing dividend accumulations at the end of any policy year shall equal or exceed the net single premium for the attained age of the insured, according to a given mortality table and a stipulated rate of interest, for an amount of insurance equal to the face amount of the policy, the company, at the request of the insured, will endorse the policy as paid-up.

Endowment Option.   Dividends may be applied to convert the policy into an endowment, or in the case of endowment insurance to shorten the endowment term. The insured may arrange for this plan in one of two ways. Under the usual arrangement he may allow his dividends to accumulate at interest, and whenever the surrender value of the policy and the existing dividend additions at the end of any year equal the face amount of the policy, the company, upon its surrender, will pay the same as a matured endowment. If the insured should die while this plan is in force and before the policy matures, the company will pay the face amount of insurance plus the accumulated dividends. Under this plan, therefore, the insured does not exercise the endowment option until his surrender value and dividends equal the face of the policy. In this respect the option is similar to that explained in connection with making the policy paid-up. However, the insured must continue premium payments and dividend accumulations past the point where the policy could be made paid-up if he wishes to have it mature as an endowment.

The other plan by which dividends may be used to make the policy mature as an endowment or to shorten the endowment period is sometimes called the accelerative endowment plan. Under this plan each dividend, as it is paid by the company, is applied at once to reduce the endowment period with the understanding that said dividend will not be paid in the event of death. Because of this lessened liability of the company, this plan of using dividends will cause the policy to mature as an endowment more quickly than will the first plan.

BIBLIOGRAPHY

The Mathematics of Life Insurance

Attwood, James A. "Premiums Net and Gross," *Life and Health Insurance Handbook,* 2nd ed. (Homewood, Ill.: Richard D. Irwin, Inc., 1964), Chapter 11.

Belth, Joseph M. "Price Competition in Life Insurance," *Journal of Risk and Insurance,* Vol. XXXIII, No. 3 (September, 1966), pp. 365–379.

Fassel, Elgin G. "Premium Rates Varying by Policy Size," *Transactions of the Society of Actuaries,* Vol. VIII, No. 22 (November, 1956), pp. 390–419.

Guertin, Alfred N. "Life Insurance Premiums," *Journal of Risk and Insurance,* Vol. XXXII, No. 7 (March, 1965), pp. 23–49.

Larson, Robert E., and Gaumnitz, Erwin A. *Life Insurance Mathematics* (New York: John Wiley & Sons, Inc., 1951).

Maclean, Joseph B. *Life Insurance,* 9th ed. (New York: McGraw-Hill Book Company, Inc., 1962), Chapters 5–8.

McGill, Dan M. *Life Insurance,* rev. ed. (Homewood, Ill.: Richard D. Irwin, Inc., 1964), Part 3.

Menge, Walter O., and Fischer, Carl H. *The Mathematics of Life Insurance,* 2nd ed. (New York: The Macmillan Company, 1965).

Richardson, C. F. B. "Cost Analysis," *Record of the American Institute of Actuaries,* Vol. XXXV, pp. 49–73.

Sellers, Richard M. "The Calculation of Gross Premium Rates for Nonparticipating Life Insurance," *Journal of the American Society of Chartered Life Underwriters,* Vol. VII, No. 4 (September, 1953).

Sternhell, Charles N. "The New Standard Ordinary Mortality Table," *Transactions of the Society of Actuaries,* Vol. IX, No. 23 (March, 1957), pp. 1–24.

VI The Mathematics of Health Insurance

PREMIUM RATES FOR health insurance, like life insurance, should be adequate, reasonable, and equitable. Many more factors affect health insurance premium rates than affect the rates for life insurance and it is difficult to measure all such factors reliably and consistently.

At least three recognized methods of rating individual health insurance policies are in general use today.

1. *The flat-rate basis.*[1] Under this method of rating, the average benefit cost is determined for a particular type of benefit in a broad age class, such as ages 20 through 59, and appropriate premium rates are developed from these cost data. Under this method, the premium increases when a person attains age 60.

2. *The step-rate plan.* Under this method of rating, a flat premium is used until all persons insured under a certain age reach the age at which premiums increase. Such a rating plan may require only one or two changes in the rate level, such as at age 50, or the rates may be based on more frequent changes, such as decennial or 10 year age groups. If the latter method is used, the basis of rating is similar to that used under a Ten-Year Renewable Term Life policy, under which the insured pays an increased rate for the coverage based on his then attained age at the beginning of each new ten-year period of coverage.

3. *The level-premium basis.* Under this method of rating, premiums are generally based on the initial age at issue and are designed to be adequate to cover the increasing incidence of cost to be experienced as the age of the insured increases during the period the coverage will be in effect. This method is similar to the method used in level-premium life insurance and requires the establishment of reserves out of the excess premiums paid in the early years to offset the increasing average net annual claim cost to be expected in later years.[2]

---

[1] This basis is normally used only for optionally renewable policies where claim cost does not vary much by age.

[2] The expression "average net annual claim cost" is the product of the annual claim frequency and the average claim size.

Each of these methods has certain advantages and certain disadvantages over the others. They all have the common problems of (1) risk measurement and assignment of the appropriate risk charge; (2) loading for commissions, taxes, administrative expenses, and profit (or contribution to surplus); and (3) providing margins, allowances, or controls to allow for unfavorable fluctuations from the experience expected at the time the rates are initially determined. Each of these factors is analyzed in greater detail in this chapter.[3]

THE MEASUREMENT OF RISK

Health insurance premiums on individual policies are affected by many factors such as the assumed rates of mortality, interest, expense, and lapse. However, there are other factors, such as the method of selling used, the underwriting philosophy, and the claims administration policy as well as the overall philosophy and objectives of the insuring company which may result in a different experience by several companies issuing similar types of coverage. Likewise, changes and variations in hospital administration and medical practice, both geographically and from time to time in the same locality, and the impact of varying economic and business conditions make it difficult to predict reliably the future net annual claim costs.

Sources of Morbidity Statistics

As indicated earlier, determining and expressing rates of disability by frequency and severity is a complex problem in health insurance. Most population studies do not develop separate frequency and severity rates. Thus, the derivation of a net annual claim cost for a benefit with a particular elimination period from data about a benefit with a different elimination period, which would be simple if the frequency of disability were known, is difficult. Moreover, much data do not give sufficient consideration to age differentials[4] or exposure, making the data of little value for health insurance purposes. Even statistics derived from records of insured lives are of limited use because of the heterogeneity of individual company products and operating practices. The subjectivity of the health risk itself complicates even further the utilization of what data are available.

[3]See Edwin L. Bartleson *et al., Health Insurance,* 2nd ed. (Chicago: Society of Actuaries, 1968); see also Jesse F. Pickrell, *Group Health Insurance* (Homewood, Ill.: Richard D. Irwin, Inc., 1961).

[4] Even where it is appropriate and possible to get net annual claim costs by age groups, the results are often statistically unreliable so that even with a large volume of experience, great care must be exercised in utilizing the data.

The principal sources from which morbidity data are available can be classified in relation to (1) individual health policies, (2) life insurance disability riders, and (3) group health policies.

Individual Health Policies.   In many cases, companies entering the individual health insurance field initially base their premium rates on assumptions as to what claim frequencies and severities might be. Because of inadequate claim data, the contingency allowance or margin in the gross premium is much larger than it would otherwise be. Since the volume of claim data under this type of coverage develops rapidly, it is possible to determine whether the premium rates are producing expected results. Through a careful analysis of the loss experience, adjustments can be made where needed to make the premium adequate or equitable. As the volume of business develops, the *company's own experience* is the most important source of data for itself.[5]

In the area of *intercompany experience,* the best and most reliable source of statistics is that compiled by the Society of Actuaries' Committee on Experience Under Individual Health Insurance.[6] It publishes biennial reports of individual policy experience under disability income, hospital and surgical expense, and major medical expense insurance.

For *disability income* insurance, reports began with the 1959 Reports which covered experience over the years 1955–57. The biennial reports give experience for a one-year maximum benefit period; by sex, age group, occupational class, and elimination period. Accident and sickness are studied separately. A limited amount of experience is also shown for the second year of the benefit period.

The *hospital and surgical* reports analyze experience by age and sex, and for hospital room and board, miscellaneous hospital expenses, maternity, and surgery.

The *major medical* reports show recent claim experience of contributing companies.

The Health Insurance Association of America has established an Actuarial Statistical Committee with two subcommittees primarily interested in obtaining statistical information on which new forms of coverage can be based. These subcommittees are also interested in developing statistics which will permit the extension of coverage to risks not considered insurable because of either age or health. In addition, there has been considerable research, innovation, and implementation in these areas by individual companies.

[5] See, for example, Lowell Dorn, "New York Life Morbidity Experience Under Individual and Family Major Medical Policies," *Transactions of the Society of Actuaries,* December, 1963, pp. 275–286.
[6] See 1970 Reports published in June, 1971.

The Health Insurance Association of America[1] developed and published the *1964 Commissioners Disability Table* which many companies have adapted, with appropriate modifications, for rate-making purposes. The *1964 Table* was prepared separately for accident experience and sickness experience, faciliating the calculation of net premiums for accident policies, and for policies providing for different elimination periods and maximum benefit durations for disabilities caused by accidents as opposed to sicknesses.

The entry of the large life insurance companies into the health insurance field and the development of sophisticated electronic computing equipment have opened the way for major progress in the development of statistical information in this field. With such progress should come greater stability in pricing, greater equity, and sound product innovation.

Life Insurance Disability Riders.   As in the case of individual health insurance policies, many larger companies have developed a substantial volume of experience in this line and use their own experience as the basis for the rates being charged for these benefits.

In the area of intercompany data, the most significant studies include those prepared by committees of the Society of Actuaries and published in 1926 and 1953. The experience studied, for the most part, involved a waiting period of three to six months and terminated coverage at age 55 or 60. For coverage with other patterns it was necessary to extrapolate from the data for shorter waiting periods and for longer periods of coverage. The 1926 study, with modifications, has served as the primary base for determining premium rates for relatively long term disability benefits for more than two decades.[8] The 1953 study[9] has served as the basis for most waiver of premium and income disability morbidity rates.

In addition to being used for rate-making for individual disability income policies, the *1964 Commissioners Disability Table* can be used for rate-making for life insurance disability riders. The Society of Actuaries also conducts studies of double indemnity experience which have a bearing on the accidental death benefit.[10]

---

[7] The Table was based on the studies of the Committee on Experience Under Individual Health Insurance.

[8] The most commonly used of these modifications has been the modification of the Class (3) (the class which showed the highest claim rates) figures developed and published by the Health and Accident Underwriters Conference known as the "Conference Modification."

[9] See "Report of the Committee on Disability and Double Indemnity," Society of Actuaries, Chicago, April, 1953, pp. 70–182.

[10] See "Report of the Committee on Disability and Double Indemnity," Society of Actuaries, 1958 Reports, p. 45.

Group Health Policies.   Since 1947, group insurance statistics have been published regularly as part of the reports of the Committee on Group Mortality and Morbidity of the Society of Actuaries. In addition, the experience of a number of individual companies has been published in the *Transactions of the Society of Actuaries.* These have included studies of disability income, hospital, surgical, and medical expense data. Most group writing companies maintain their own statistics and tend to rely on these rather than on intercompany data. Intercompany experience, however, is studied carefully to detect broad trends in benefit costs which may not be evident in the company's own data. Naturally, intercompany data are extremely valuable to a company entering a line for the first time.[11]

Deficiencies of Available Morbidity Experience

Prior to considering the several approaches used in *measuring* morbidity experience it may be well to remind ourselves of the deficiencies of the available data and the fact that no single source of expected morbidity costs is sufficiently reliable for rate-making purposes.

Heterogeneity of Data.   In order for intercompany data to be meaningful, the data must be homogeneous. This would involve data based on risks of the same year of issue, the same sex, the same age or age groups, the same occupational hazard, the same elimination period, and ideally the same indemnity time limit and amount of monthly indemnity. In hospital and surgical coverage and many similar benefits, such refinement is not feasible, because the fragmentary data available would give little credibility within any one grouping. Most companies change their benefit patterns from time to time, so that the volume of compatible data that can be analyzed is not sufficient to produce meaningful results. Again, each waiting period produces a unique level of disability and there is little tendency toward convergence at later durations

---

[11] Five valuable papers containing extensive data on group experience are:
(1)   *Group Weekly Indemnity Continuation Table Study,* M. D. Miller, TSA III, p. 31.
(2)   *1957 Study of Group Surgical Expense Insurance Claims,* M. D. Miller, TSA X, p. 359.
(3)   *A Reinvestigation of Group Hospital Expense Insurance Experience,* S. W. Gingery, TSA XII, p. 564.
(4)   *An Investigation of Group Major Medical Expense Insurance Experience,* S. W. Gingery and R. J. Mellman, TSA XIII, p. 513.
(5)   *Development of Expected Claim Costs for Comprehensive Medical Expense Benefits and Ratios of 1959 and 1960 Actual Experience Thereto,* B. E. Burton and D. W. Pettingill, TSA XV, p. 10.

of disability such as at the end of the eighth, fifteenth, or thirty-first day of disablement. Consequently, a judgment factor must be applied in most cases where the waiting period under consideration differs from that upon which the available data are based.

Time Lag.   There is a time lag between the period selected for developing the statistics and the time this information will be used as a measure of morbidity costs in the future. For coverages such as hospital expense, surgical expense, medical expense, and major medical expense benefits, the combined secular trend in costs has been between two and three times the increase in the cost of living index.[12] Accordingly, a judgment factor must be introduced in using available statistics.

Measures of Morbidity Experience

In establishing premium rates for any type of health insurance coverage, it is necessary to begin by providing a measure of the expected net annual claim cost per policy.

Unit Benefit Costs.   The net annual claim cost of any benefit is the product of the frequency of occurrence and the amount of the average claim (severity). The unit benefit cost method entails the calculation of the cost of providing a standard or unit benefit so that the net annual claim cost of benefits actually provided can be determined by multiplying the unit benefit cost by the appropriate benefit amount.

The unit of exposure may be $1 of hospital daily benefit, $1 of monthly income disability benefit, a standard maximum surgical schedule, or other suitable units selected. Unit costs can be broken down by age, sex, occupation, geographic location, etc. If the unit benefit in question is $1 of daily hospital benefit, if the frequency of occurrence is .2 per famly per year. and if the average claim costs (severity) is $11, then the cost of this unit benefit is $2.20. Therefore, the net annual claim cost of $30 per day hospital benefit would be $30 x $2.20, or $66.00.

It is possible to obtain the net annual claim cost without separately determining the frequency and average amount of claim for the benefit under consideration.[13] For example, all hospital miscellaneous benefits paid during the year under policies providing the same maximum benefit can be divided by the appropriate exposure to determine the net annual claim cost

---

[12] The introduction of Medicare could have a significant impact on this trend in coming years.

[13] It can be done the other way, however, using one body of data for *frequency* and another for *claim size.*

per life. In like manner, if interest is ignored, the net annual claim cost per dollar of monthly income, under disability income insurance with a uniform elimination period and maximum benefit limit, may be determined by dividing the value of total incurred claims at each age of disablement by the total monthly indemnity exposed. The result will be the same as the rate of disability (frequency) multiplied by the value of the disabled life annuity, computed without interest (average amount of claim).

Continuance Tables.   The determination of (1) the expected claim rate among insured lives and (2) the incidence of claims cost are two important problems which confront the actuary. The mathematical measurement of the effect on claims cost of various elimination periods is usually handled by developing a continuance table which shows the probabilities of claim continuance for various durations or amounts.[14]

Hospital confinement, for example, may be expressed as the number of patients remaining in the hospital at the end of *t* days out of an assumed initial number of patients confined to a hospital, such as 10,000. Graph 28-1 reflects a study of the probability of *continuance of hospital confinement* among 10,000 lives confined (adult males).[15]

In disability income insurance, the elimination period has a dramatic effect on the rate level required. Graph 28-2 reflects a study of the probability of continuance of disability among 10,000 lives disabled at age 40.[16]

In like manner, a major medical continuance table could express the probability that the claim experience will equal or exceed *t* dollars, from which the effect of varying deductibles and varying maximum amounts can be determined.

Continuance tables are very helpful in computing the average size claim. Such average claim values, in combination with the expected claim frequency (rate of claims), produce the expected net annual claim cost for the pattern of benefits under consideration. The method is quite straightforward and easy to apply in practice where a single benefit, such as a monthly disability income benefit, is being considered. When benefits are combined in various ways with different elimination periods, different deductibles, and different maximum benefit limitations, the problem of measuring the expected net annual claim cost becomes exceedingly complex.[17]

[14] For an explanation of the development and utilization of continuance tables see Bartleson *et. al., op. cit.,* pp. 192–196.

[15] See Gingery, "Group Hospital Expense Insurance Experience," *TSA,* Volume IV, 87, Table VI-1, 10 X Miscellaneous Benefit 31-Day Plans.

[16] See Conference Modification of 1926 Class 3 Disability Table. See also the *1964 Commissioners Disability Table* and the *Reports of the Society of Actuaries* for a good discussion of the effects of elimination periods.

[17] For an excellent paper dealing with the mathematical concepts of developing continuance functions for complex benefits, see E. Paul Barnhart, *TSA,* Vol. XI, 1959, pp. 649–718.

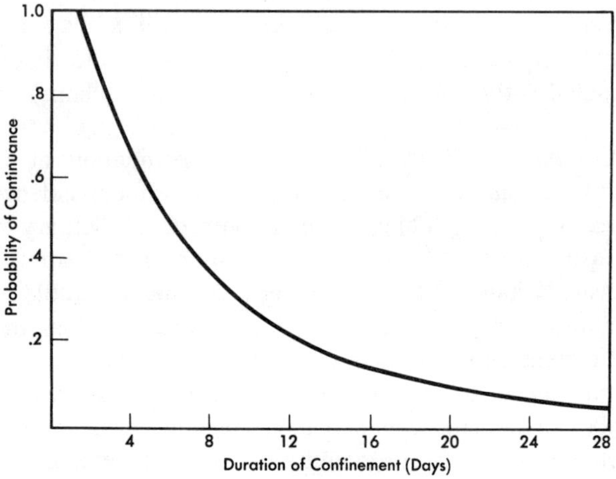

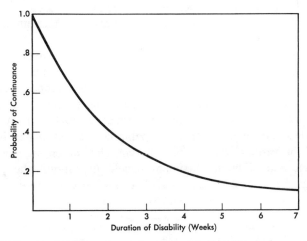

GRAPH 28-1.   **Probability of continuation of hospital confinement among 10,000 lives confined (adult males).**

GRAPH 28-2.   **Probability of continuation of disability among 10,000 lives disabled at age 40.**

Pension Fund Methods.   This method involves the development of commutation functions based on assumed claim frequencies at each age and assumed claim values for such ages. The method is usually used when an interest discount is introduced in determining the present value of a claim annuity, such as is required for waiver of premium or long-term disability income benefits.

The net-level premium for a disability income contract, as in the case of life insurance, is the level annual payment needed to pay benefits if (1) future claims exactly follow the average claim amounts assumed as well as the frequency rates shown in the morbidity table adopted, (2) deaths among persons insured occur at the rates given by the assumed mortality table, and (3) the rate of interest earned is that assumed in the rate basis.[19] Thus, at date of issue

$$\text{Net Level Premium} = \frac{\text{present value of future net annual claim costs}}{\text{present value of a life annuity due of \$1 per annum for the premium paying period}}$$

The present value of future net annual claim costs is the value at date of issue of all claims that are expected until the terminal date of the contract appropriately discounted with interest.

Table 28–1 illustrates the calculation of a net level premium for a five-year term guaranteed renewable hospital expense policy issued to a male, aged 60.

In connection with short-term benefits, where interest can be ignored without greatly distorting the results, the use of a Continuance Table in evaluating the expected claim liability is usually preferable.[20]

Loss Ratios.   This method of establishing the level of morbidity costs is based on the ratio of benefits incurred to premiums earned. It is an acceptable method for developing premium rates on business issued on a one year term basis but not for business issued on a level-premium basis. The loss ratio method should be used with great caution when comparing morbidity costs between different companies. Such comparisons are usually meaningless because of differences in (1) premium levels for the same type of benefits; or (2) types of policies with varying benefits; or (3) reserve requirements; or (4) lapse ratios; or (5) rates of company growth.[21]

[19] For a detailed explanation of the so-called "Pension Fund Method," see *Actuarial Studies No. 5* (Chicago: Society of Actuaries).

[20] Many companies also take into account voluntary terminations or lapses.

[21] See Bartleson *et al., op. cit.,* pp. 121–122.

TABLE 28-1. Illustrative Calculation of Net Level Premium Five-Year Guaranteed Renewable Hospital Expense Policy

(Male Age 60)

(1) Attained Age	(2) Annual Claim Cost During Year Following Attained Age	(3) Average Period from Date of Issue of Contract to Commencement of Claim *(in years)*	(4) Proportion of Those Insured Who Will Survive Average Period	(5) Amount of 1 Discounted at 2½ Per Cent per Annum for Average Period	(6) Present Value of Claim Cost (2) X (4) X (5)
60	$18.10	0.5	.9898	.9877	$17.695
61	18.70	1.5	.9688	.9636	17.457
62	19.32	2.5	.9462	.9401	17.186
63	19.96	3.5	.9222	.9171	16.881
64	20.62	4.5	.8965	.8948	16.541

Total of Column 6, present value of future annual claim costs $85.760

Present value of a five-year annuity due of $1 per annum at age 60 (1958 CSO 2½ per cent) $4.5595

Net Level Premium = $\dfrac{\$85.760}{4.5595}$ = $18.81

THE USE OF MORBIDITY EXPERIENCE IN RATE-MAKING

Compared with Life Insurance Rate-Making

Premium rates for health insurance depend on benefit costs, lapse rates, interest return, and expense of doing business, in much the same manner as for life insurance. In addition, the economic cycle and variations in the cost of providing benefits in different geographical locations, together with the effect on cost brought about by various elimination periods and front-end or other types of deductibles, create problems not inherent in the calculation of life insurance premiums.

Application of Morbidity Experience in Rate-Making

As indicated earlier, the claim cost may be broken down in relatively small groups to reflect the cost for various age groups, various types of benefits, and to reflect the increasing incidence of cost under a level-premium concept or may be developed to reflect the average net annual claim cost of a particular type of benefit for all ages or broad age classifications. The relative advantages and disadvantages of the different methods of classifying morbidity statistics for rate-making purposes will be discussed later.

Select vs. Ultimate Experience. Most morbidity tables used to calculate net annual claim costs of disability income benefits exclude the experience of the first few policy years. Attempts to identify the influence of underwriting on experience of these first few policy years—select experience—have not been too successful in contrast to the success of this practice for life insurance. The pattern of select experience under disability insurance is quite different from that for mortality under individual life policies. At ages 40 and under, the benefits of selection in the early policy years are almost negligible. This is probably due to the fact that for ages below 40 the sickness costs tend to increase by policy durations but the accident costs tend to decrease by policy duration. Thus, the two tend to cancel each other. At ages 50 to 65, studies show that there is a substantial increase in morbidity by policy duration, which continues for at least twenty years after issue. Applicants who becc ne insured in their 50's and 60's do not develop the same high level of morbidity as those who become insured in their 20's or 30's do when they attain advanced ages. Furthermore, the experience varies considerably depending on the type of benefit under consideration.

Obviously, consideration should be given to the relationship of select to ultimate experience in establishing gross premiums, in order that the premiums for insurance issued at advanced ages may properly reflect the savings from selection.

Very little is known at this time about the characteristics of hospital, surgical, and medical expense insurance experience in relation to policy duration. As more studies are conducted through the individual and group mortality and morbidity committees of the Society of Actuaries, it is reasonable to assume that greater refinement can be introduced into the premium rate calculations for these coverages on both an individual and a group basis.

On the other hand, the great difficulties brought about by the rapid cost increases in hospital and medical expenses are a serious limitation on such gains in refinement.

Role of Interest.   Interest is of less significance in the calculation of health insurance premiums than in calculating life insurance premiums. The ratio of claims to premiums under health insurance during the early policy years is substantially greater than under level-premium life insurance. Accordingly, more of the premium is used for claim payments soon after it is received by the insurance company and is, therefore, not available for investment and the accumulation of substantial reserves, such as is true of level-premium life insurance. Interest does enter into the claim liability required under long-term disability income benefits. Whereas interest is frequently ignored in disability income benefits payable for a short duration only, it is customary to introduce a disability life annuity (reflecting interest) in measuring the average claim cost under long-term disability income coverage. The value of the disabled life annuity is less on account of the interest discount than would be the case if interest were ignored.

Effect of Lapses.   Lapses have an important effect on health insurance rates for two reasons. First, expenses are higher during the first year than in subsequent years due to the expenses of issuing the policy or certificate, a higher first-year commission rate (if commissions are payable on other than a level basis) and for other obvious administrative expense reasons. Also, claim rates under health insurance tend to increase as the age of the insured increases. In view of these factors, which vary by age at issue and policy duration, the premium rate level will depend on the rate of lapse—or its complement, the rate of persistency, which is one minus the lapse rate.

The rate of lapse on individual health policies is usually higher than for life insurance and there is considerable variation by type of coverage. Companies transacting both life insurance and health insurance business have found their overall health insurance lapse rates to be from one and one half to two times as great as for permanent forms of life insurance.

Significance of Judgment.   The morbidity statistics used by an actuary who is assigned the job of computing the health insurance rates for a new company about to enter the business may come from several sources and may involve several modifications of the basic data based on experience and judgment. In view of the lack of reliable data and the multiplicity of factors producing variable cost levels, informed judgment plays an important part in health insurance rate-making.

BASIC PRINCIPLES OF RATE-MAKING

Rating Process

THE PROCESS OF rate-making involves the analysis of available data and the development of premium rates for the various classifications of insureds which are adequate, reasonable, and equitable. It is essential to differentiate between insureds on the basis of all important factors affecting morbidity costs and expenses of operations. Thus, in assigning morbidity costs and pricing benefits, a company must, depending upon the type of benefit involved, classify by age, sex, geographic area, type of coverage, and occupation. Such classifications are necessary if reasonable equity is to be realized between policyholders.

If an average rate were charged all policyholders regardless of the risk presented by the individual, serious antiselection would set in and the insureds with a lower risk cost, in the absence of compulsory participation, would leave the insured group. The remaining policyholders would then *on-the-average* present a higher risk cost and the premium would have to be raised to be adequate. This would lead to still further antiselection. It should be noted, however, that there are practical limitations on the process of refining classifications in the interest of equity. The parameters are established by the increasing administrative expense of dealing with multiple classes and the need to have a sufficient volume of business within a class to provide reliable experience and stability in the rate structure.

Competition in general will keep premium rates reasonable in relation to the benefits provided, but this is not always the case. Some states require filing of health insurance rates, but there is no regulation of rates as in the case of the property and liability insurance field. A number of states have enacted laws providing for the disapproval or withdrawal of approval of policy forms "if the benefits provided therein are unreasonable in relation to the premium charged," but this legislation was not intended to establish rate regulation.[1]

[1] Edwin L. Bartleson *et al., Health Insurance,* 2nd ed. (Chicago: Society of Actuaries, 1968), p. 121. But Pennsylvania has rate approval authority and, as of 1967, so does the state of Connecticut.

In the insurance process, clearly, adequacy of premiums is the most important criterion against which a premium rate should be measured. In a new line based on relatively unreliable experience, the margin of safety built into the premium is larger than in an established line with its own body of experience upon which to project cost estimates. As discussed below, the company normally tests the level of its premiums with asset share studies utilizing various assumptions as to expense rates, lapses, and interest where appropriate. The availability of electronic calculating equipment has made feasible refinements in developing and testing premiums—gross or net—that would not have even been thought of several years ago.

It should also be noted that, in addition to developing premium rates for new policies, there is the problem of revising rates on *existing* individual policies where they are issued on a variable-premium guaranteed renewable basis.[2]

Gross Premiums[3]

The gross premium must provide for benefits, expenses, and contingency margins in the event the claim experience and expenses are actually higher than anticipated. Gross premiums are usually calculated on the basis that the premiums are payable annually, but they may be paid on a semiannual, quarterly, or monthly basis. Gross premiums on individual health insurance policies are usually paid on a level basis, which means that the same premium is payable each year, from date of issue to the end of the term period of the policy, such as to age 65. Gross premiums may also be paid on a one-year term basis and a step-rate basis.

Factors Affecting the Premium.   The premium rates for a particular benefit depend upon such factors as (1) morbidity, (2) expenses, (3) persistency, (4) interest rate, and (5) contingency margins.

(1) Morbidity. The annual claim cost for a given age, sex, occupational class, etc., is the product of the *annual frequency* of a particular event times the *average claim* when such an event occurs. For example, the annual frequency of hospitalization for a given age and sex might be 10 per cent, the average stay in the hospital seven days and therefore the annual claim cost for a $40 daily hospital benefit would be $28 ($.1 \times 7 \times 40$). In health insurance, while mortality costs are involved at times, the primary consideration is the morbidity cost. As will be pointed out later,

---

[2] See also Paul Barnhart, "Adjustment of Premiums under Guaranteed Renewable Policies," *TSA* XII, pp. 472–498.

[3] See Health Insurance Association of America, *Principles of Individual Health Insurance I* (New York, 1968), pp. 138–150.

the annual claim costs may vary according to such factors as age, sex, occupational class, and geographical area. But these variations also depend upon the kind and amount of benefits, and inasmuch as most policies contain more than one benefit, it is necessary to obtain separate annual claim costs by type of benefit.

(2) Expenses. In order to obtain suitable expense rates for the determination of premium rates, it is necessary to make detailed cost studies in which all of the various expense items are expressed as (1) a percentage of the premium, which is called a *per premium* type of expense (e.g., premium taxes and agents' commissions); or (2) as an amount per policy, which is called a *per policy* type of expense (e.g., cost of underwriting and issuing a policy); or (3) as an amount *per claim* paid (e.g., cost of investigating and verifying a claim.)

(3) Persistency. The persistency rate for a group of policies is defined as the ratio of the number of policies that continue coverage on a premium due date to the number of policies that were in force as of the previous due date. Thus, if out of 100 policies which are in force, 75 policies are continued on the next due date, the annual persistency rate is 75 per cent. The persistency rate usually improves with policy duration and for some types of coverages the annual persistency rate will be 95 per cent or higher after the fifth policy year. Naturally, other factors affect persistency rates. In general, persistency rates are usually higher at the older issue ages and better for the less hazardous occupations. In connection with major medical expense and disability income coverages, persistency is usually better than on basic hospital expense coverages.

(4) Interest. When a level premium is used, the company will have, after the first few policy years, an accumulation of funds arising from the excess of premium income over the amounts paid for claims and expenses. As in level premium life insurance, the funds accumulated during the early policy years will be needed in the later policy years when the premium income is not sufficient to pay claims and expenses. In computing premium rates, therefore, it is necessary to assume a suitable interest rate to reflect the investment earnings on these accumulations.

(5) Contingency Margins. Again, as in the case of life insurance rates, it is necessary to introduce margin for contingencies into the premium rate calculation. One method is to calculate a premium on the basis of most probable assumptions and then to increase the premium by a percentage to provide some margins for contingencies. Another method is to introduce somewhat more conservative morbidity, expense, and interest rate assumptions and to determine a premium on that basis. Both approaches can produce approximately the same aggregate results.

Derivation of the Gross Premium.   Having determined all of the assumptions for a given issue age, type of benefit, and amount of benefit as to expenses, claims, persistency, and interest rate, the actuary makes a "ballpark" guess at what the gross premium will be. This tentative gross premium is tested against highly realistic expense, claim, persistency, and interest assumptions over an arbitrary period, commonly twenty years. If the tentative gross premium produces a fund accumulation that is too high or too low at the end of the projected period of coverage, an appropriate adjustment is made in the tentative premium to establish the appropriate gross premium level needed to support the particular policy under consideration.[4] In the case of participating policies, if it is determined that the accumulated fund at any time is in excess of the amount needed together with future premiums to pay for future claims and expenses, dividends may be paid. Similarly, if the policies are nonparticipating, the company will realize a profit which they are entitled to for insuring the risk. In general, the margins in the premium rates are more conservative on nonparticipating plans than in the case of participating policies.

Gross premium levels are not usually derived for every age by the method described above but possibly for every decennial age, such as ages 20, 30, 40, 50, and 60. Premiums for intervening ages can then be derived by fitting a smooth curve through the premiums for these ages. Another approach utilized by some companies is to determine net level premiums (based only on morbidity, mortality, and an interest rate) for each age and to find a loading formula which is usually in the form of a percentage times the net level premium plus a constant, which will approximately reproduce the gross premiums which are obtained for decennial ages.

ANNUAL CLAIM COSTS

The net annual claim cost can be considered as the claim frequency multiplied by the average claim value. Since many types of benefits with varying claim values are issued in the field of health insurance, it is necessary to consider each type of benefit separately in developing the necessary formulas and in applying the appropriate morbidity data for rate-making purposes.

---

[4] It is also possible to solve the asset share formula, with the appropriate assumptions and parameters, with the gross premium as the unknown and thus arrive at the appropriate gross premium directly.

Accidental Death and Dismemberment

Dismemberment claims usually represent about 10 per cent of total accidental death and dismemberment claims. Therefore, if r_x represents the accidental death rate at age x and the principal sum death benefit provided is $1,000, and if we let k equal the percentage of total claims that are dismemberment claims, then we can write an equation which expresses the pure premium for accidental death and dismemberment as

$$(1 - k) \ P_x^1 = \$1,000 \ r_x$$
$$P_x^1 = \frac{\$1,000 \ r_x}{1 - k}$$
$$\text{If } k = 10\%, \text{ then: } P_x^1 = \frac{\$1,000 \ r_x}{.90}$$

Since accidental death rates vary only slightly with age, at most ages at which this benefit is issued, it is usual to charge the same premium at all ages of entry, unless the coverage is issued on a limited-payment basis under which premiums cease before the coverage terminates.

Medical Expense Benefits

Hospital Benefits.   The average net annual claim cost varies considerably with the type of hospital benefit, the level of benefits provided, the duration of the maximum period of hospitalization, and the age and sex of the insured. Separate annual claim costs may be developed from available statistics for males, females, and children, on the basis of $1 of hospital benefits payable for varying durations, and these data will be used as the pure premium for the benefit before appropriate loading is added for expenses. Additional hazards such as those arising from occupation or geographic area may be taken care of by adjusting the net annual claim cost. This method might be used on individual health insurance; in the case of group insurance, adjustment factors might be applied to the gross premiums.

Hospital Fringe Benefits.   The cost for hospital extras may be related to the room and board rate, or an average benefit per insured family member per year may be computed and added to the room and board premium to determine the total pure premium required for hospital benefits. Maternity benefits are normally handled separately since they form a separate cost pattern and may or may not be included in the coverage being provided under the policy. Hospital room and board and miscellaneous expense benefits, until recently, were determined independent of geographic location. Since on regular hospital and surgical coverage an individual buys so many dollars' benefit per day, he tends to buy what he needs for *his area*, and geography is not too important. On the other hand, with the unallocated maximum benefit of major medical it is quite important. There is now a definite trend toward adjusting the charges for miscellaneous hospital extras by geographic location. This trend has developed since the introduction of major medical coverage, where experience studies have borne out the necessity for such refinement in order to establish equity between various policyholders, both for individual and for group coverages.

Surgical Benefits.   The surgical benefit schedules in common use have been similar, and costs of providing these standard benefits are fairly well established. In addition, the relative frequencies of certain procedures have been recorded on a basis unrelated to the benefit schedule. It is possible, therefore, to develop rates for varying surgical benefits quite reliably. The process includes examining enough claims to determine the expected average claim cost under the new schedule as compared with the standard schedule and adjusting the rate used for the standard schedule by multiplying it by the ratio of the average net annual claim cost under the new schedule to such average net annual claim cost under the original schedule. Such cost variations are usually determined for adult males, adult females and for children separately for nonmaternity surgical benefits. The additional cost for maternity and obstetrical claims is determined separately.

Major Medical Benefits.   The most difficult part of determining realistic rates for major medical coverage, whether on an individual or group basis, has been the problem of adjusting available morbidity statistics, much of which have been developed from base plan coverages, to the type of benefits provided under major medical coverage.

As experience developed under this relatively new line of coverage, most companies writing major medical insurance found their initial premiums inadequate. This was due to many factors which were not clearly apparent based on experience developed under base plan hospital, surgical, and medical care coverages. Such unique factors on which data were not available and are being developed include:[5]

[5] See, for example, S. W. Gingery and R. J. Mellman, "An Investigation of Group Major Medical Expense Insurance Experience," *TSA*, Vol. XIII (presents claim costs under comprehensive major medical coverage issued on a group basis in the calendar year 1957). See also, D. W. Pettengill and B. E. Burton, "1960 Tabular Costs for Comprehensive Medical Expense Plans," *TSA*, March, 1963.

1. The difference in the level of cost between "per illness" plans vs. "all cause" plans.

2. The effect on claim ratios of increased earnings of the insured.

3. The effect of geographic area on benefit costs for both employee and dependent coverages.

4. The effect on benefit costs of various recognized deductibles and percentage participation (coinsurance) factors.

5. The effect of inflation on medical care costs (by far the most important item).

6. The effect on benefit costs of inside limits, such as (a) a maximum hospital daily room and board benefit, or (b) a maximum surgical fee schedule. Such limits tend to affect the utility of private room facilities in the hospital as well as the amount payable for standard surgical procedures, where the charges of such items may vary greatly depending on the geographical location and the nature of the individual hospital confinement or surgical procedure required.

Cost Variations by Benefit Type.   The cost variations according to the type of benefit are illustrated in the tables which follow showing annual claim costs for hospital and surgical, maternity, major medical, and disability income benefits.

Table 29–1 shows that the annual claim costs for hospital and surgical benefits generally increase by age. The annual claim costs for females as compared to males are quite a bit higher at the younger ages. With increasing age, however, the costs converge and eventually after age 60 the costs become lower for females than for males. Usually, no distinction is made by sex or age in deriving the annual claim costs for children.

Table 29–2 shows the annual claim costs for a $100 maternity benefit. The cost of maternity benefits decreases by age. The experience is based on policies after they have been in force for three or more years. The cost of the benefits during the first policy year will be low because of the effect of the maternity waiting period. The maternity claim rates during the early policy years are much greater than at the later policy durations and, therefore, the cost of the maternity benefits is higher at the early policy durations.

Table 29–3 shows the annual claim costs for major medical benefits. The costs of the benefits increase with age, but the increase is much greater for major medical benefits than for the basic hospital and surgical benefits shown in Table 29–1. The costs for females are greater than for males up to age 55, but after age 55 the costs for females are less. As indicated in the heading for Table 29–3, the costs shown are for a particular plan and the costs will be different for other plans, depending upon the specifications of the other plans.

TABLE 29-1. Annual Claim Costs for Certain Hospital and Surgical Benefits

Attained Age	$10 Daily Hospital Benefit Max. Benefit Period 90 Days		Misc. Hospital Expense Benefit $200 Max. Benefit		$100 of Max. Surgical Benefit Standard Schedule	
	M	F	M	F	M	F
20-24	$ 4.84	$ 5.66	$ 8.52	$11.37	$1.18	$1.47
25-29	4.20	3.67	7.61	12.48	1.14	1.70
30-34	4.63	7.99	8.43	15.16	1.19	2.19
35-39	5.72	9.85	10.07	17.81	1.33	2.88
40-44	7.21	11.44	12.03	19.63	1.52	3.24
45-49	8.92	12.31	14.09	20.04	1.79	3.20
50-54	11.11	12.73	16.59	19.57	2.11	2.99
55-59	13.63	13.43	19.41	19.07	2.54	2.66
60-64	17.07	15.29	22.75	19.81	3.08	2.71
	Child		Child		Child	
All ages	$3.59		$7.03		$1.22	

Source: *Transactions of the Society of Actuaries–1969 Reports* from the following pages: 92, 95, 107.

TABLE 29-2. Annual Claim Costs for $100 Maternity Benefit
(Based on Calendar Duration 3 and Later)

Attained Age	Annual Claim Costs
20-24	$28.80
25-29	21.90
30-34	12.80
35-39	5.10
40-44	1.60
45-49	.20

Source: *Transactions of the Society of Actuaries–1969 Reports*, page 112.

As pointed out below, there is a variation in the cost of medical care by geographical area. Under hospital and surgical expense coverages, benefits are usually subject to a daily hospital benefit limit and to a surgical schedule and, therefore, there is usually no need to vary premium rates by area. In the case of major medical expense coverages, however, the cost of the benefits will be higher in high cost areas. To a certain extent this can be controlled by using so-called inside limits for room and board benefits and by the use of a surgical schedule. If inside limits are not used, consideration has to be given to varying premium rates by geographical area.

TABLE 29-3. Annual Claim Costs—Major Medical Expense Benefits
($500 Deductible Amount—$7,500 Maximum Amount
75 Per Cent Coinsurance—No Hospital Room and Board Limit
Calendar Duration 3 and Later)

Attained Age	Males	Females	Child (All Ages)
20–24	$ 10.61	$15.12	$7.57
25–39	11.36	20.92	
30–34	15.17	28.13	
35–39	19.16	37.80	
40–44	27.43	43.33	
45–49	38.62	49.98	
50–54	60.22	57.44	
55–59	82.40	77.14	
60–64	115.30	81.94	

Source: *Transactions of the Society of Actuaries—1969 Reports,* page 116.

TABLE 29-4. Annual Claim Cost Per $100 of Monthly Disability Income Benefit
Maximum Benefit Period—One Year
Elimination Period—None for Accident, 7 Days for Sickness

Attained Age	Accident	Sickness	Accident and Sickness
	Male—Occupation Group I		
20–29	$ 6.10	$ 4.70	$10.80
30–39	5.50	6.70	12.20
40–49	4.50	11.30	15.80
50–59	4.50	20.50	25.00
60–69	4.80	34.30	39.10
	Male—Occupation Group II		
20–29	12.00	6.90	18.90
30–39	12.30	9.10	21.40
40–49	10.40	15.10	25.50
50–59	10.00	26.40	36.40
60–69	9.90	43.70	53.60
	Female—Occupation Group I		
20–29	3.40	9.60	13.00
30–39	4.80	17.60	22.40
40–49	6.20	22.60	28.80
50–59	6.00	23.60	29.60
60–69	6.00	27.80	33.80

Source: *Transactions of the Society of Actuaries—1969 Reports;* Accident from page 68; Sickness from page 70.

Disability Income

The annual claim costs for a disability income benefit vary significantly by occupational classes. Table 29–4 shows the annual claim costs for one particular disability income benefit. For disability income plans the costs will vary according to age, sex, occupational class, elimination period, and maximum duration of benefits. If the elimination period and maximum duration of benefits are different for sickness benefits from those for accident benefits, it is necessary to develop separate costs for accident and for sickness.

PREMIUM RATE VARIABLES

Age Classifications

Age is of major importance in almost all forms of health coverage. The rate of increase in costs by age under accident coverage, however, is considerably less than for sickness coverages.[6]

Sex Classifications

The premium rates for females for hospital, surgical, and medical expense benefits are higher than for males. The difference varies with age and tends to disappear entirely at ages over 60. The average difference, exclusive of maternity benefits, is usually at least one and one-fourth times that for males. The relationship on group but not on individual also varies between employed females and dependent wives. Rates may be a percentage increase over the male rate or may be based on an analysis of actual experience on female lives.

Disability income benefits for women are usually issued to regularly employed females only. The rates for such coverage generally range from one and a half to two times the male rate; most companies are also hesitant to issue noncancellable coverage to females for benefit periods longer than one or two years although there has been a distinct trend recently toward increasing benefits to females.

[6] Bartleson, et al., op. cit., p. 139.

Occupational Classifications

Most hospital and surgical plans exclude benefits payable under Workmen's Compensation. Since this exclusion eliminates much of the adverse effect of hazardous occupations, it is customary to charge the same premium for hospital and surgical benefits regardless of occupation.

Accidental death and dismemberment benefits and disability income benefits may be insured on other than a non-occupational basis. In such cases it is customary to subdivide the various occupations into at least three classes and sometimes more with appropriate extra charges depending on the degree of extra morbidity expected. Some occupations may be eliminated entirely because of the undue occupational hazard.

Geographical Area Classifications

Within the United States, location of the insured individual is rarely a classification factor for disability income or accidental death insurance.[7] It is of greater significance in medical insurance costs, however, mainly because of wide variation in hospital rates and other medical care expenditures. Variations in claim rates also occur in some areas.

Elimination Periods

The elimination of income benefits for varying periods (such as 7, 14, 30, 60, 90, 120, 180, or even 365 days) is a method used to produce varying rate levels for disability income benefits and at the same time provide benefits which suit the various income replacement needs of the insureds in event of disability.

In like manner, under some group plans, a portion of the hospital expenses incurred on the first day of hospital confinement or possibly on the next one or two days of such confinement may be eliminated from plan benefits if the experience has been unsatisfactory and a rate increase would otherwise be required. Major medical benefits generally provide for the elimination of the first dollars of hospital or medical expense incurred, the amount of the deduction depending on the type of plan being offered.

If a continuance table is used in either case, it is quite easy to make the necessary adjustments in rates for various elimination periods. Since the effect on rates of a relatively short elimination period or small dollar amount does not vary much by age, a uniform adjustment at all ages is

[7] *Ibid.*, p. 141.

sometimes made, even though the basic premiums for the coverage are graded by age. Ideally, however, there should be a continuance table for each elimination period since the experience for policies with elimination or waiting periods as deductibles may not always be simply related to experience on policies without one.

Dependent Classifications

For individual insurance it is customary to charge a rate for each child rather than a rate for all children as is done in group.[8] The premium varies by type of plan but not by age. The hospital stay is usually short for most surgical procedures performed on children; therefore, the level of miscellaneous benefits provided by the plan affects the claim costs most dramatically and may vary the relationship between the cost of coverage for adults and children.

The premium rate for dependent coverage under group insurance may or may not be independent of industry and age, depending upon the company. Such coverage may include insurance on the spouse only, on the spouse and one child, or on the spouse and two or more children. Unlike individual insurance, there is no additional charge for children after the first under group coverages, whether the plan is basic hospital and surgery or major medical. Although such refinement would produce greater equity, it complicates administrative procedures. Since a portion of the premium is normally paid by the employer, the insured employees still receive equitable treatment under a properly designed group plan covering their dependents.

Other

Increasingly companies are permitting the issuance of individual noncancellable and guaranteed renewable policies to impaired risks, subject to the payment of an extra premium.

Numerical morbidity ratings have been established for each insurable impairment, varying from approximately 125 per cent to 300 per cent. Two ratings are required for each impairment—one for accident only policies and another for accident and sickness including hospital and surgery and major medical. Some impairments are standard for accident only but are rated for accident and sickness coverage.

It also should be noted that some relatively undesirable hospital and surgical risks can be accepted for disability income coverage if there is, say, a thirty-day waiting period. On the other hand, there are some poor disability income risks which are acceptable hospital risks.

---

[8] On major medical it is feasible to use an all-children rate on individual insurance because of the cost reduction effect of a large deductible. This effect is lacking on basic individual coverages and, hence, a per child rate is usually considered necessary.

Health Insurance Reserves | 30
and Surplus Distribution

HEALTH INSURANCE RESERVES[1]

Introduction

IN HEALTH INSURANCE, as in life insurance, it is important that proper provision be made in the company liabilities for all the obligations assumed by the company under its contracts, whether or not required by law. Reserves are usually established as liability accounts for present or future claims against the company's assets that must come from the premiums already received. Health insurance reserves may be broadly classified as:

1. *Policy reserves* include those amounts necessary for the fulfillment of contract obligations as to future claims, which includes pro rata unearned premium reserve and additional reserve for noncancellable policies.

2. *Claim reserves* include those amounts necessary to cover future payments on claims already incurred.

3. *Expense reserves* include those amounts necessary to pay expenses and taxes under obligations developed by the company from operations prior to the date of the reserve determination.

Table 30–1 shows a hypothetical company statement illustrating the various health insurance reserves which are discussed below.[2]

Policy Reserves

Pro Rata Unearned Premium Reserve. In determining the amount of the unearned premium reserve to be inserted in the annual state-

[1] For an excellent treatment of this subject see Edwin L. Bartleson *et al., Health Insurance,* 2nd ed. (Chicago: Society of Actuaries, 1968), pp. 121–160; see also John M. Bragg, "Health Insurance Claim Reserves and Probabilities," *Transactions of the Society of Actuaries,* Vol. XVI, p. 17.

[2] In the Life Insurance Company Annual Statement Form provision is made for a breakdown of health insurance in Exhibit 9, p. 11. See Chapter 42.

TABLE 30-1. XYZ Insurance Company
Annual Statement of Financial Condition
December 31, 1970

Assets:		
Cash	$170,000	
Bonds	675,000	
Stocks, preferred	75,000	
common	25,000	
Real estate owned	40,000	
First mortgage loans	316,000	
Premiums due and unpaid	43,000	
Total assets		$1,344,000
Liabilities, Capital, and Surplus:		
Unearned premium reserve	$320,000	
Additional reserve for noncancellable policies	35,000	
Reserve for premiums paid in advance	40,000	
Reserve for claims in course of settlement	140,000	
Reserve for claims incurred but unreported	50,000	
Present value of future amounts due on claims	110,000	
Reserve for future contingent benefits	20,000	
Reserve for dividends declared	20,000	
Reserve for expenses and taxes due and accrued	85,000	
Mandatory security valuation reserve	36,000	
Capital	250,000	
Unassigned surplus	238,000	
Total liabilities, capital, and surplus		$1,344,000

ment, the pro rata portion of the full gross premium from the statement date to the end of the period for which premiums have been paid on the policy is required to be set up as a reserve regardless of the renewal provisions of the policy. In establishing the appropriate amount to be set up for a large block of business, approximation methods are often used. This is normally the largest item among the policy reserves unless the company has large amounts of noncancellable or guaranteed renewable business.

The unearned gross premium reserve automatically provides a reserve allowance for the payment of expenses that will be incurred after the statement date, as well as for the benefit payments which will be incurred and must be paid out of the premiums already received by the company. Premiums paid beyond the next premium due date are separately classified as premiums paid-in-advance.[3]

[3] Advance premiums are not a part of the unearned premium reserve but appear as a separate liability because the premium paid is not yet due. The insured may change his mind and request the return of the premium and sound accounting practice indicates separate treatment.

Additional Reserve for Noncancellable Policies.   Noncancellable health insurance policies usually provide coverage to a specified age, such as 60 or 65, and are issued on the basis of level premiums payable each year after the date of issue.

Due to increasing morbidity costs at the older ages and the use of a level premium, it is necessary to accumulate excess funds in the early years, as measured by the reserve, which will eventually be consumed through increased claim costs by the expiration date of the benefits in much the same manner as reserves on Term to Age 65 life insurance policies are built up in the early years and later decreased to zero at age 65. As in life insurance, the so-called active life reserve calculated prospectively, is equal to the difference between the present value of future benefits and the present value of future premiums.

The *1964 Commissioners Disability Table* was adopted by the National Association of Insurance Commissioners in 1964 as a minimum standard for the valuation of disability income benefits due to accident and sickness.[4] The Conference Modification of the Class 3 Disability Table had been adopted by the National Association of Insurance Commissioners in 1941 as the minimum standard. As in the case of life insurance reserves, to establish a minimum standard for active-life reserves, state regulatory authorities must specify particular morbidity and mortality tables, and a maximum rate of interest.

In 1956, the National Association of Insurance Commissioners adopted a minimum morbidity standard for hospital and surgical benefit reserves based on the 1956 Intercompany Hospital and Surgical Tables.[5] Companies are permitted to use as an interest assumption the maximum rate currently permitted by law for the valuation of new life contracts and for mortality any table permitted by law in the valuation of currently issued life insurance. Companies may also use a preliminary term method of valuation [6] for active-life reserves.[7] For accidental death benefits, the minimum standard is the *1959 Accidental Death Benefits Table*.

Although the additional reserve is required only on noncancellable or

[4] This table was part of a report of an Industry Advisory Committee on Reserves for Individual Health Insurance Policies which made recommendations covering all reserve requirements for all classes of individual health insurance policies. By the end of 1967, six states had adopted the report by law or regulation as the minimum standard. Others were already using the so-called Task Force 4 recommendations.

[5] See *Transactions of the Society of Actuaries*, Vol. IX, pp. 334–410.

[6] A two-year preliminary term period may be used.

[7] Includes the following types of contracts: (1) contracts which are guaranteed renewable for life or to a specified age, such as 60 or 65, at guaranteed premium rates; (2) contracts which are guaranteed renewable for life or to a specified age, such as 60 or 65, but under which the insurer reserves the right to change the scale of the premium rates; (3) contracts other than franchise contracts in which the insurer has reserved the right to cancel or refuse renewal for any reason but has agreed implicitly or explicitly that prior to a specified time or age it will not cancel or decline renewal solely because of deterioration of health after issue.

guaranteed renewal policies,[8] the need for such a reserve exists on any level-premium type of coverage where the incidence of cost increases with advancing age.

Reserve for Future Contingent Benefits. If a hospital policy, whether individual or group, creates a contingent liability for pregnancies which exist at the time of termination of the policy, it is necessary to set up the value of such contingent liability. There are a number of acceptable methods of estimating such liability.[9] Some companies carry this reserve as a claim reserve instead of carrying it as a part of the policy reserve. In either case, however, it is segregated and designated as the *reserve for future contingent benefits.*

Claim Reserves and Liabilities

There are many acceptable methods of estimating the liability of the company for outstanding claims which have not been paid in full on the date the annual statement is being prepared. Any method selected to determine the amount of outstanding claim liability should be one that will produce an adequate liability and fairly reflect the actual liability which will later be developed after sufficient time has passed to permit the company to tabulate the actual results which occur subsequent to the statement date.

Present Value of Amounts Not Yet Due on Claims. Disability income benefits, with the problem of determining the reserve liability for disabled lives, provide the best example of the complicated nature of this claim liability item. The rate of recovery decreases with increasing duration of disability, so that the value of the claim annuity normally increases as the duration of any particular disability becomes greater until on a long benefit limit claim the death rate takes over. In estimating this liability item, it is, therefore, desirable to show for each claim the attained age on the valuation date, the age at date of disability, the number of months or years the claimant has been disabled, and the number of years of benefit remaining in order to be able to apply the appropriate claim annuity factor to the amount of the monthly benefit being provided. If the monthly income is not payable for more than one year, the claim annuity valuation factors may be based on an average age and on average durations which vary with the type of benefit being considered.

Hospital, surgical, and medical expense benefits are usually settled in a

---

[8] See footnote 7.

[9] See *Examination of Insurance Companies,* Volume 3, New York State Insurance Department; and the N.A.I.C. Instructions which accompany the Annual Statement Blank. See also Bartleson *et al., op. cit.,* pp. 157–158.

single sum, so that it is possible to determine the amount of the average claim and to apply this average to the number of claims outstanding. In some cases, where only a small volume of business is involved, the claims manager may establish a value, based on his judgment, of the expected claim liability.

Claims Due and Unpaid.   This item is normally small or nonexistent for health insurance claims. Most companies will pay any amount due on a claim as soon as the amount can be determined and the claim approved.

Claims in the Course of Settlement.   The liability shown for this item will be based on claims on which notice of claim has been received but on which all of the proofs of loss or other papers have not been received so that the claim cannot be approved on the statement date. Some companies examine each claim individually and prepare a list showing each item involved. Others use approximate methods in various ways. One method is to add the total amount of insurance and apply to it a factor obtained from the experience on previous valuation dates. Another method is to analyze a sample of claims and determine a percentage factor which is applied to the total liability for claims, including both accrued and unaccrued amounts.[10]

Claims Incurred but Unreported.   Experience will show that many claims are paid after the statement date each year which were actually incurred prior to the statement date, but the company had no knowledge of the claim until after such statement date. It is usual to tabulate such claims each year and relate the amount to some base, such as volume of business in force or earned premiums on the type of coverage involved. The total liability for incurred but unreported claims is divided into two parts: *accrued* and *future*. The accrued liability is reported as "incurred but unreported" as part of the policy claim liability. The future liability accruing *after* the valuation date is included under "Present Value of Amounts Not Yet Due on Claims."

Expense Reserves

It is necessary to provide in the company liabilities on the statement date a reasonable estimate of the claim expenses which will be incurred on unpaid losses occurring prior to the statement date. Such liability may be computed as a cost per claim or as a percentage of the liabilities for claims incurred or as a combination of both. In major medical coverage where the

[10] See Bragg, *loc. cit.*

cost of settling claims may be much higher per claim than under base plan coverage, it will usually be necessary to develop separate factors for each type of coverage, based on actual studies of handling the various types of claims.

The reserve for expenses other than claim expenses may either be accounted for in the Unearned Gross Premium Reserve, or if such reserve is not adequate, an additional amount may be set up in the expense reserve. This might be true during the first year if unpaid commissions or other expenses will be greater than the loading provided in that year's premium calculation.

Group Reserves

A company's liabilities under group health contracts create the need for the same types of policy and claim reserves as do individual health insurance contracts. The amounts of the reserves, however, are usually smaller. In general, premiums are paid monthly under group health contracts and the company reserves the right to adjust premium rates on any policy anniversary. Nevertheless, it is important to keep the level of premiums and, therefore, the insured's costs, on a stable basis.

Other Reserves

Reserve for Dividends Payable.   On the statement date participating health insurance policies will have dividends declared which will not be payable until after the statement date. The liability for such payments should be set up as a liability on the statement date.

Reserves Under Compulsory Disability Laws.   California, Rhode Island, New Jersey, and New York have compulsory non-occupational disability income insurance laws in effect which require the accumulation of reserves as prescribed in the various laws.

Surplus and Contingency Reserves.   Contingency reserves, which are *not* liabilities, are sometimes established on a voluntary basis to allow for the possibility of an upward trend in claim costs or an unusual occurrence. In state disability plans they may be established as an offset to decreasing premiums without a corresponding decrease in liability where premiums are paid on current wages while benefits depend on wages during a base period. Some states require the accumulation of a contingency reserve for group health business.[11]

[11] For example, see Missouri Department Order #30, December 15, 1961.

SURPLUS DISTRIBUTION

The great majority of individual health insurance policies have been issued on a nonparticipating basis. In recent years, however, an increasing number of large mutual life insurance companies have entered the health insurance field and have marketed a large volume of participating policies. Group health insurance policies are virtually always "participating" through a variety of "experience rating devices." The concepts underlying both dividends and experience rating are similar, but may differ somewhat in basic philosophy. In any case, the process should take into consideration the surplus position of the policyholder or class, the extent to which losses are pooled (averaged) between cases, the expenses incurred as between policyholders or classes, and the total surplus available for distribution.

For the larger group health cases it is practicable to develop the appropriate dividend or premium refund on an asset share basis. As in the case of life insurance, this involves the accumulation from date of issue of the premiums paid, increased in some cases by interest earnings. From this amount losses incurred, accumulated expenses incurred directly or allocated to the case, and allowances for contingencies and profit are deducted. From this net accumulation total dividends paid previously are deducted and the result is the surplus amount *available* for distribution.

Individual Policies

In the case of individual policies, funds are accumulated separately for each *class* of policy (sometimes referred to as policy form). In this way the amount of surplus accumulated for any dividend class is ascertainable. The dividend formula used is usually very simple, taking into account only broad equities. For example, for policies which have been in force for, say, three years, a specified percentage of the premiums, varied in some companies by duration, may be returned as a dividend. In connection with dividends, the asset share calculation is used principally as a test of the adequacy of the accumulation for any dividend class. As pointed out earlier, the adequacy of the company's contingency reserve for this type of business will affect the proportion of current earnings which are added to the contingency reserve for a particular class of policies.

Group Policies

An approach, similar to that used for individual classes, is used in dealing with small group cases. Here groups are classified and surplus distribution is based on asset share calculations applied to the classes of groups. Again, only a limited number of variables are considered. In small cases morbidity experience must be averaged due to the very low credibility or reliability of the individual case's experience. Expenses, particularly acquisition expenses, are relatively high but because of the smaller size discounts granted such cases they may develop reasonable dividend distributions over a period of time.

In the case of large groups the asset share approach is applied to the individual case. The chief problems involve the development of unit expense charges for indirect expense items, the determination of the period of amortization of acquisition expenses, and the individual case contribution to contingencies and/or profits. In all but the largest cases it is necessary to establish a limit on the maximum level of losses which will be considered in the experience rating formula. This is usually achieved by imposing a limit on an aggregate basis or, in some cases, an aggregate limit and a maximum for a single claim during a given experience period.

In all cases, the experience rating formula will give consideration to (1) premiums paid, (2) incurred losses (modified by loss limits and credibility), (3) direct and allocated expenses, and (4) allowances for contingencies and/or profits.

BIBLIOGRAPHY

The Mathematics of Health Insurance

Bartleson, Edwin L., *et al. Health Insurance,* 2nd ed. (Chicago: Society of Actuaries, 1968).

Dickerson, O. D. *Health Insurance,* 3rd ed. (Homewood, Ill.: Richard D. Irwin, Inc., 1968), Chapters 16 and 17.

Faulkner, E. J. *Health Insurance* (New York: McGraw-Hill Book Company, Inc., 1960), Chapters 11 and 12.

Health Insurance Association of America, *Principles of Individual Health Insurance I* (New York: 1968).

————, *Principles of Individual Health Insurance II* (New York, 1970).

————, *Principles of Group Health Insurance I* (New York, 1968).

————, *Principles of Group Health Insurance II* (New York, 1966).

MacIntyre, Duncan M. *Voluntary Health Insurance and Rate Making* (Ithaca, New York: Cornell University Press, 1962).

VII

Selection, Classification, and Treatment of Life and Health Insurance Risks

Selection and Classification of Life Insurance Risks: I

PURPOSE OF SELECTION

IN ANY INSURANCE plan, each insured person contributes to a common fund from which the unfortunate ones, who suffer losses caused by the peril insured against, are paid a certain amount. In order to maintain equity between different classes of policyholders, each insured should contribute according to the risk which he transfers to the common fund. If one person is allowed to pay less than his share, it will necessitate an overcharge against other persons in order to keep the common fund solvent and enable it to meet all claims. In each instance, therefore, it becomes the task of the insurance company to determine the risk which it assumes and to make a fair premium charge therefor. This cannot be accomplished without careful selection and classification of risks.

In any group of individuals *of the same age,* some are near death, some are disabled, some are exposed to unusual risks of death because of occupation or other activity, the great majority are "normal," and some few are free of even the slightest impairment. It is knowledge and understanding of the way the various factors influence mortality that enables the company to classify applicants into groups that will give relative mortality rates very close to those that are anticipated.[1] Those groups subject to a higher than normal mortality are said to be "substandard" or "special class."

Graph 31–1 depicts the degrees of anticipated future mortality represented in a randomly selected group of persons of the same age with 100 per cent representing average mortality for the group.

The chart portrays the wide range of future mortality for a group of persons falling within risk classifications measured by age alone. It should be clear that all applicants should not be offered insurance on the same terms. The life insurance company must establish a range of mortality expectations within which applicants will be regarded as normal and hence, insur-

---

[1] Pearce Shepherd and Andrew C. Webster, *Selection of Risks* (Chicago: The Society of Actuaries, 1957), p. 2.

able at standard premium rates, or conversely, the limits beyond which applicants will be considered substandard and subject to higher rates.[2] In addition to establishing the limits for the various classes of risk, the company must adopt selection and classification procedures that will permit the placing of applicants for life insurance into the proper categories. The process is complicated by the fact that applicants for life insurance do not constitute a randomly selected group as depicted in Graph 31–1. An

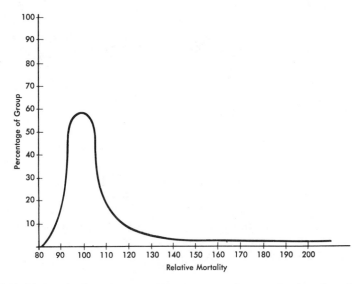

GRAPH 31-1.   Anticipated mortality represented in randomly selected group of the same age with 100 per cent representing average mortality for group.

applicant's or policyholder's decisions with regard to insurance are often based on his knowing or suspecting more about his condition of health than the company. It is only natural that he will "decide" on the most favorable basis to himself. This tendency is known as *adverse selection* or *antiselection* and will appear whenever an individual has freedom to buy or not to buy, to choose the amount or plan of insurance, and to persist or to discontinue as a policyholder. A company's underwriting procedures must attempt to screen out such applicants or classify them in appropriate substandard groups. In addition to separating and classifying substandard risks,

---

[2] Some companies offer special policies subject to "preferred" underwriting; i.e., cases free of virtually all the most minor unfavorable features, but this is relatively rare.

a significant purpose of selection in life insurance is to protect the company against such adverse selection.

More broadly, the purpose of selection can be expressed as the determination of a premium rate for the risk which is satisfactory to both the company and the buyer.[3] The principles and factors underlying a given company's selection philosophy are outlined in the following section.

SELECTION PHILOSOPHY

In formulating a selection philosophy, there are certain fundamental principles and factors which govern sound selection procedures, some of which are mutually inconsistent. The life insurance company's philosophy is the resultant balance between these opposing principles and considerations.

The Standard Group

It is an accepted principle that the standard group, i.e., those regarded as "normal" and insurable at standard rates, should be broad enough to encompass the great percentage of applicants. Evidence of this in practice in life insurance is the fact that currently 91 per cent of the applicants for ordinary insurance are being accepted at standard rates.[4]

Overly exacting selection standards and procedures would result in an excessive number of rejections or "rated" cases. This would undermine the morale of the agency force, tend to increase the cost of operation, and involve public relations considerations. The insurance business is based on the "averaging process," and apart from the practical considerations mentioned, the broader the base of standard risks the more stable the mortality or morbidity experience of the standard group will be. The extension of this principle is limited by considerations of equity and competition.

The Substandard Groups

The substandard classes or gradations of risk to be recognized in a company's premium rate structure are a function of the balance between the need to minimize the number of classifications for the purposes of stability

[3] Shepherd and Webster, *op. cit.*, p. 3.
[4] Of the remaining 9 per cent only 3 per cent are declined, with the remaining 6 per cent being insured at substandard rates. See *Life Insurance Fact Book 1971*, p. 94.

in mortality and morbidity experience and administrative considerations, and the need to maximize the number of classifications to avoid competitive disadvantages and to achieve reasonable equity. Naturally, the size of the company, marketing objectives, and other company policies are involved in the decision to provide substandard insurance and the classifications to be established.

Balance Within Each Risk or Rate Classification

Having defined its risk classifications, a company must also obtain and maintain a reasonable balance among the risks accepted in each rate classification. If the overall mortality experience of the risks within each classification is to approximate the predicted average for the group, every risk which is worse than the average for that class must be offset by one which is better than average. If each risk classification is over-balanced with risks whose mortality expectations are less favorable than the assumed average for the classification, the company will end up with excessive mortality costs, and consequently, a less favorable competitive position.[5]

In attempting to maintain the proper balance within the standard classification, it would appear that a company which does not offer substandard insurance would have a more difficult task than a company which does offer such insurance. In considering a borderline application a home office underwriter, who must either reject an application or accept it at standard rates, is tempted, by reasons of agency pressures, desire for business, and human nature, to approve the application rather than reject it. If he could place the risk in a substandard classification with a slightly higher premium, he would appear to be under less pressure to relax his standards. This tendency, however, is even present in classifying borderline cases where substandard insurance is available. This is evidenced by the fact that mortality studies consistently show that the distribution of risks within each substandard classification is skewed toward the top limit of the class. This fact is considered, of course, in establishing the premium rate for the class but it demonstrates the human element in the selection process.

Emphasis on the Unique Impairment

The selection process is primarily concerned with the hazards or impairments which are not common to all persons seeking insurance. Impairments

---

[5] In practice, companies accept business on the presumption that there will be a reasonable spread of risks within the class. Presumably, the extra premiums charged by class will be based on average mortality rating for each class which in turn would be based on a study of past experience.

which are common to the applying group operate to increase the mortality among all lives and are reflected in the general mortality levels assumed. The use of airplanes for passenger travel is so widespread that the accidental deaths or disabilities which result are regarded as a part of the general hazards of life and provided for in the general mortality levels underlying the rate structures. Not everyone, however, is an airplane pilot and it is the additional hazard of engaging in piloting a plane that would be of concern from an underwriting standpoint. The process of selection, then, constantly strives to ascertain *significant* factors which set a given applicant apart from the normal members of a group.

Equity Among Policyholders

The manner in which applicants are grouped for rating purposes must recognize the principle of equity. Some grouping of risks is inevitable due to the need to have a reasonable volume of experience within a given classification and due to expense considerations. On the other hand, to be satisfactory to the applicant, the spread between the worst and best risks within a classification should not be so broad as to produce significant inequity or hurt in competition. In practice, the width of rating classes tends to vary directly with the degree of rating with which, in turn, the accuracy of predicted extra mortality also varies. Hence, the width of class is to some extent a function of the dependability of the available mortality data on impaired lives. Differences between companies, in practice, are the result of different judgments as to what is best overall policy.

Recognition of Underlying Mortality Assumptions

An overall factor, which operates as a fundamental control in setting selection standards, is found in the mortality assumptions entering into the company's objectives as to insurance costs. The classification of the risk must reflect the mortality levels assumed in determining the premium rate to be applied. If the risk is to be considered at "standard rates," the mortality risk must be comparable to that of the lives in the experience used in determining the standard premium rates.

In practice some of the companies, especially the large ones, continually study their mortality experience and evaluate their classification rules. They combine their experience on lives accepted standard and compare their experience on impaired lives with the standard experience. Based on such study and analysis each company adjusts its classification rules where indicated. The basic objective is to assure reasonable homogeneity of risks.

Since insured experience is made up of selected lives, at least as effective selection must be exercised in the future as in the past, if mortality is to be kept within the mortality provided for in the premium. But a situation of *generally improving mortality* might permit acceptance of some impaired lives without exceeding the mortality assumed in the premium calculations. Such action, however, would adversely affect the company's competitive position if other companies continued to accept only "standard" risks at their standard rates. Furthermore, such a course of action would violate the principle of equity discussed previously.[6]

FACTORS AFFECTING THE LIFE RISK

In order to treat all policyholders equitably and to maintain the solvency of the insurance plan as a whole, the companies give careful consideration to a number of significant factors when each application for insurance is presented. The information which the companies obtain relating to these factors aids them in determining the extent of the risk involved.

Age

The age of the applicant is important, since the probability of death increases as a person grows older. For practical reasons the applicant is not required to furnish proof of age at the time he takes out insurance. Such a requirement would cause delay in the issuance of the policy, and such proof is usually easy to obtain if it is needed.

It should be noted, however, that in the case of an immediate annuity the relationship between the annuitant's age and the amount and nature of the benefit payments is so direct and immediate that proof of age is required at the time of purchase of the annuity.

If a question of age arises when a claim is made under a policy, proof of age will be required before payment is made. If a misstatement of age is discovered after a claim is made under the policy, the amount of the claim is adjusted in accordance with the misstatement-of-age clause.

Today, most companies will insure children at birth. Since a minor generally cannot make a binding contract, policies on the lives of minors up to age 15 or 16 are usually applied for and owned by a parent or other adult.

After age 15 or 16, depending on the various state laws, a minor may make a binding life insurance contract on his behalf, but these applications, as with all applications, are underwritten carefully as to the purpose of the

[6] Shepherd and Webster, *loc. cit.*

insurance. The mortality experience for this class of business has been excellent.

It is a common practice to place maximum limits on the amount of insurance obtainable in a given company. Individual company limits vary as to the maximum they will risk on one life. The amount will depend on age, company size, philosophy, reinsurance arrangements, and other factors.

Build

The *build* of an applicant is most significant in underwriting a life insurance risk. Build includes the applicant's height, weight, and distribution of the weight; it is one of the basic determinants of his mortality expectation.[7] Experience has shown that overweight increases the risk at all ages. The highest mortality rate because of overweight is experienced at the middle and older ages but the experience is worse than normal at all ages. Moreover, overweight can magnify the significance of other physical ailments such as cardiac conditions. Most companies use a table showing average weights according to height, age, and sex. The table is then extended to show the extra mortality as a per cent of standard for each age and height. At the "best" weights—less than the "average"—the tables indicate a better than standard mortality rate.

Physical Condition

The physical condition of the applicant, other than build, is an extremely important factor. Therefore, the company is careful to satisfy itself that the applicant is in good physical condition. The company knows from experience that the predicted future mortality of an applicant will depend, in varying degrees, upon abnormalities present in one or more of the important systems of the body—nervous, digestive, cardiovascular, respiratory, genitourinary and glands of internal secretion. The defects and disabilities which may be found in the organs of the body and the methods of ascertaining them are necessarily medical in character and cannot be explained here. However, some of the more common of these which usually increase

[7] The first comprehensive statistical study of the relationship between build and mortality covered the experience on policies issued by the principal companies from 1885 through 1908 and was published in 1913 as the *Medico-Actuarial Mortality Investigation*. The most recent investigation was made by the Society of Actuaries encompassing the ordinary issues of twenty-six companies for the years 1935 through 1953 and published in 1959 in a study entitled, *Build and Blood Pressure Study, 1959*. Build tables in use today are based on the 1959 study. For a summary of the study and its findings, see Edward A. Lew, "Build, Blood Pressure and Mortality," *Journal of the American Society of Chartered Life Underwriters*, Vol. XV, No. 1 (Winter, 1961), p. 19.

the risk may be mentioned. Thus, an examination of the circulatory system may reveal elevated blood pressure, a heart murmur, either organic or functional, or a high or intermittent pulse rate. An analysis of the urine may disclose the presence of albumin, sugar, or red blood cells. When there are indications of any of these or similar conditions, further examination may be necessary before the application can be definitely rejected or the risk insured upon terms satisfactory to both parties.

Personal History

The insurance company will investigate facets of the applicant's background which will have a bearing on his expected mortality. This may include the health record, habits, driving violations, insurance history, etc.

The health record is usually the most important of the personal history factors. If the applicant has at some time in the past suffered from a serious illness or accident, a careful appraisal of its probable effects on future life will be made. Such appraisal will frequently require that in addition to the medical history given by the applicant, reports will be obtained from the personal physician or from hospitals.

Insurance history is important. The applicant may have been refused life insurance by some company or offered insurance under special terms. If so, this implies an extra hazard which formerly existed and which may still be present. Also, the applicant may have such a large amount of insurance already in force on his life that a request for more must be regarded as speculative.

Family History

Family history is considered important by some companies because of the transmission of certain characteristics by heredity. If the history shows that most members of the family live to old age, and have been free from heart disease, insanity, diabetes, and other similar diseases, it may be inferred that the applicant will not be susceptible to such diseases and may be entitled to "credits" to offset some "debits." In most companies, however, family history is not used directly to rate an applicant unless it reveals a family characteristic that appears *also* in the applicant. For example, two or more deaths below age 65 because of cardiovascular disease in the family may be considered cause for an additional rating in the case of an applicant with elevated blood pressure, but would not be so considered in the absence of elevated blood pressure or other impairments of the cardiovascular system.

Occupation

The occupation of the applicant may affect the risk. Occupational hazards may increase the risk in at least three different ways. First, the occupation may present an environmental hazard such as exposure to violence, irregular living, a temptation to experiment with drugs or to overindulge in alcohol. This would be evident in portions of the entertainment and liquor industries. Second, the conditions surrounding an occupation have a decided bearing upon the health and longevity of the risk, e.g., persons who work in close, dusty, or poorly ventilated quarters or are exposed to poisons. Finally, and most important, there is the risk from accident such as is faced by electrical high-tension linemen working with high voltages, auto racers, pilots, and so forth. The various classes under this heading are too numerous to mention, but persons engaged in mining, logging, and similar industries are subject to serious accidents which must be considered in determining fair and equitable rates.

An applicant who has changed within recent years from a hazardous occupation to a safer form of employment is underwritten carefully since he may still retain ill effects therefrom. Also, he is more likely to return to the former occupation than another person without such a history. The usual practice is to ignore prior occupation if the applicant has been removed from it for a period of one or more years.

It should be noted, however, that occupational risks have declined in importance as a factor in life insurance underwriting. Ratings have been reduced or eliminated for many occupations since the end of World War II. Although people in some occupations must still be charged higher premiums, a study conducted during 1967 among seventeen life insurance companies representing 54 per cent of all individual life insurance in force in North America reflected substantial improvement in occupational mortality.[8] Occupational risks are no longer considered a *major* factor in life insurance underwriting.

Habits

Information is usually sought regarding the applicant's use of habit-forming drugs and intoxicating liquors. If it is found that the applicant uses alcoholic liquors in large amounts, he may be declined or offered sub-

[8] See Joseph C. Sibigtroth, "Occupational Risks as a Factor in Life Underwriting," Annual Meeting, Home Office Life Underwriters Association, Hot Springs, Virginia, April 4–6, 1968.

standard insurance, depending upon the degree of his apparent use. Use of drugs not prescribed by a physician, or drug abuse, may call for a decline depending upon the type of drug. A history of abuse or nonsupervised use may require a rating depending upon the length of time since the drug or drugs were used.

Moral Hazard

Since it is possible for an applicant to take advantage of the company when applying for insurance, the company finds it advantageous to investigate his character and financial standing. Information sought about character includes business as well as personal activities. The applicant's reputation for meeting his obligations and fairness in dealings may indicate the type of moral risk involved. Probably the financial status, as represented by the amount of assets, size and sources of income, and permanency of the income, is as important as any factor. The amount of insurance applied for may not be large, but if the applicant appears to have sufficient protection already, the case will bear more investigation. If, in addition to the suspicion of overinsurance, there is anything else unsatisfactory about the risk, such as an important physical defect, or dangerous occupation, the company may decline the risk entirely.

Speculation must be avoided, not only when the insured takes out the insurance on his own life, but when one person wishes to insure the life of another. The law gives an individual an unlimited insurable interest in his own life, and hence the need for insurance, as determined from such factors as financial status and dependents, largely governs the maximum amount the company will sell to him. Where, however, the insurance is applied for by one person on the life of another, the company will want to know about the insurable interest—the extent of the economic loss which the death of the insured will cause the applicant. Applications for life insurance for speculative purposes are rare when compared with total insurance sold, but the cases are frequent enough to be of importance.

Today, most companies will insure children at birth, but these applications, as with all applications, are underwritten carefully as to the purpose of the insurance. The mortality experience for this class of business has been excellent. Some companies will issue whatever amounts are justified on a child's life provided that the parents (if insurable) have a suitable insurance program and provided that all children in the family are insured for comparable amounts. The underwriting problem is to guard against one child's being selected for insurance.

Comparatively few persons at advanced ages can qualify as good risks. Many are already adequately insured. The earning power of the individual has usually decreased or ceased, thus reducing the insurable value and the need for protection. Companies insure older persons only after the most careful selection tests have been applied and then usually to provide liquidity to meet the estate taxes and other cash needs following the death of a person with substantial property holdings. Insurance of older persons by those on whom they are dependent is often speculative, whether intentional or not.

Sex

Years ago it was the rather general practice to refuse to insure women on the same terms as those offered to men. This action, based largely on the risks related to childbirth and weak insurable interest, has been changed by improved mortality and the fact that many women are gainfully employed. Still, many companies question the need for anything except small amounts of insurance on women unless they are employed or are in possession of wealth which would require insurance for estate tax purposes.

Aviation

It is usual to ask the applicant directly if he engages in aviation activities. Flights as a fare-paying passenger on regularly scheduled airlines are not sufficiently hazardous to affect the risk, particularly since such travel has become so widespread. But where there may be a definite aviation hazard involving commercial, private, or military flying the applicant may be requested to fill out a supplementary questionnaire devoted entirely to this subject. The company may then charge an extra premium to compensate for the aviation hazard, or the aviation risk may be excluded from the policy entirely. If the risk is excluded and if death occurs from aviation activities, the company is liable only for a return of premiums paid or the reserve accumulated on the policy, and sometimes whichever of the two produces the larger figure, depending on the company.

Military Service

In the absence of hostilities, contracts are issued with no exclusion or limitation on the military service risk. The adverse selection involved with applicants engaged in or facing military service during a period of armed conflict constitutes the underwriting problem. Underwriting action taken in the past has been either outright declination, a limitation on the amount of insurance issued, or the attachment of a so-called war clause, which limits the insurer's obligation to return of premiums with interest.

To date, the most common method of dealing with the extra hazard of military or naval service has been the war clause. Some companies have used a so-called status war clause, which limits the insurer's obligation to return of premium if the insured should die while in military service outside the territorial boundaries of the United States, whether or not the *cause* of death could be attributed to military service. Others have used a rider, referred to as a "results" clause, which limits the insurer's obligation only if the insured's death was a *result* of war. Generally regarded as more liberal to the insured than the "status" clause, this clause invokes the limitation of liability even though the insured was no longer in a war zone at the time of his death. Most companies have been willing to waive these clauses for an appropriate extra premium.

American involvement in "local wars," such as those in Korea and Viet Nam, has once again presented the companies with the problem of underwriting the war risk. A variety of approaches have been followed by the companies in dealing with the marked antiselection and the inherent persistency problems presented by the noncareer service man in the lower pay grades.

Other Factors

Residence.   In many countries the mortality rate is higher than in the United States and Canada, mostly due to climate and general living conditions. Individuals moving to the United States and Canada from a country with a higher mortality rate may bring with them a portion of the extra mortality. When a United States or Canadian applicant intends to reside in a foreign country, the possible increased hazards of climate, general living conditions, and political unrest must be considered.

Hobbies or Avocations.   With a high and steadily rising standard of living and increasing leisure time, hobbies and avocations are becoming inportant underwriting factors in some cases. Such activities as skin-diving, mountain climbing, competitive racing, and sky-diving clearly involve a significant hazard to be considered in the underwriting process. If there is a hazard which will cause increased expected mortality and the applicant is insurable on some basis, he is usually charged a flat extra premium commensurate with the risk. Occasionally, a rider excluding death from participation in the hazardous activity may be employed.

SOURCES OF INFORMATION CONCERNING
LIFE RISKS

The sources which a company may utilize in obtaining information concerning the factors affecting a life risk include: (1) the application, (2) the medical examination, (3) the agent's report, (4) attending physicians, (5) the inspection report, and (6) intercompany data. It should be noted that the data from these sources overlap on some factors; the "double check" is amply justified by experience.

The Application

Application blanks used by the various life insurance companies are by no means uniform in their content or arrangement. Generally, however, the blank consists of two parts. Part I contains questions requesting information of a nonmedical nature. Thus, the applicant must usually give information regarding the following: his name, address, former and contemplated future places of residence, occupation, date of birth, marital status, name and relationship of his beneficiary, amount and kind of insurance for which application is made, amount of life insurance already carried on his life, companies which have issued such insurance, any company which has ever modified or refused to issue insurance on his life, past and contemplated aviation activities, avocations, and plans for foreign residence.

Part II consists of medical history furnished by the applicant to the medical examiner in response to questions which the latter is instructed to ask. Thus, questions are asked regarding the illnesses, diseases, injuries, and surgical operations experienced since childhood; and regarding every physician or practitioner whom the applicant has consulted in the past five (or some other number) years. Other questions relate to the present physical condition. For example, questions are asked about the state of health, and bodily deformities (loss of arms or legs, impairment of hearing, and hernia). Some companies ask questions relating to the applicant's use of alcohol and drugs. Finally, questions are asked about the applicant's parents and siblings, including the number now living, their present condition of health, and the date and cause of any deaths which have occurred.

Some companies now write nonmedical insurance on applicants for amounts as high as $40,000 on younger ages and lesser amounts on ages to 40 or 45. In such cases a nonmedical declaration of insurability is used in lieu of the medical examination. Questions similar to those asked by the examiner in medically examined cases are asked and recorded by the agent and signed by the applicant.

The Medical Examination

In addition to recording the applicant's answers about his medical history, the medical examiner reports the findings of his examination. The examination includes height and weight, pulse and blood pressure readings, chest and abdomen measurements, condition of heart, lungs, nervous system, and urinalysis. In the case of large life policies more detailed examinations involving chest x-ray and electrocardiograms are used, and a second medical examination may be required. The medical examination is not, however, a foolproof safeguard against adverse selection. The applicant may go to considerable effort to appear at his best through rest and diet and may deliberately or unintentionally not disclose important items of health history. It is only through the use of all of the available information from all sources that an underwriter creates the picture of the applicant and arrives at his decision.

There is increasing use today by insurance companies of paraprofessionals in lieu of physicians. *Paramedical-type centers* are emerging in many areas of the country. The trained technicians will take the applicant's medical history and test him for height, weight, blood pressure, pulse and give a urinalysis for albumin, sugar, and occult blood. For an additional charge a test for vital capacity, a phonocardiogram, an electrocardiogram and an SMA 12 blood test may also be given. In addition, some centers have medical doctors available. The principal reason for the increasing popularity of paramedical care is a combination of cost, and lack of trained physicians who will give insurance exams. Most insurance companies availing themselves of this service will use it with policies not exceeding a certain size or will use it in lieu of a second medical exam where one is required.

The Agent's Report

Most companies include on the back of the application Part I blank certain questions which the agent must answer. The company will probably ask the agent how long he has known the applicant and whether or not he unqualifiedly recommends him as a sound risk.

The company may want to know if the life insurance applied for is intended to replace insurance in another company and whether or not there will be or has already been any cancellation of insurance in any company which the insurance applied for is designed to replace.[9] The agent may also be asked to express his opinion about the applicant's financial standing, character, and environment.

When a company does not require an àgent's report, it relies on its general instructions to its agents to prevent them from receiving applications on persons who are not acceptable risks. If the agent believes the risk is doubtful, he may be instructed to submit a preliminary inquiry. If the applicant has ever been refused insurance by any company, the agent may be instructed to report this fact to his company.

Attending Physicians

The attending physician's report is used only where the individual application and/or the medical examiner's report reveals conditions or situations, past or present, about which more information is desired. Because professional ethics prevent a physician from divulging such information without the consent of the patient, the consent of the patient is always obtained; he usually signs an authorization at the time of the application.

The Inspection Report

Life insurance companies obtain inspection reports for all persons who apply for significant amounts of insurance. In the case of modest amounts (e.g., $5,000 and less) and at the younger ages many companies do. not routinely get inspection reports. This report contains information bearing on the insurability of the applicant. Most companies use the service of an independent agency which maintains a staff of inspectors to make these and similar reports for other purposes.

When the company receives an application, if the rules call for an inspection report, one is promptly ordered giving the applicant's name, age, occupation, and place of residence. In some companies the request for the report is made by the agency. The report is sent directly to the home office. Because of the Fair Credit Reporting Act, it is now necessary to notify the applicant that such an inspection may or will be made. This notification may be part of the application form or it may be a separate notice. When the amount of insurance is not large, the investigator will make a rather general inquiry into the habits, character, financial condition, occupation, avocations, health, home and business life of the applicant. If the amount of insurance is large, a more careful and detailed report is obtained. In order to get the necessary information, the investigator may interview the

[9] This is now required by a number of states over the applicant's signature.

applicant's employer, neighbors, banker, business associates, and others who may be able to contribute the information desired and sometimes the applicant himself. A second report may be required in order to gather additional information or to recheck the first in unusual cases.

Intercompany Data

A final source of underwriting information is the Medical Information Bureau (MIB). This organization, an unincorporated nonprofit trade association, is a clearing house for confidential data of a medical nature on applicants for life insurance. The information is reported and maintained[10] in code symbols, and every effort is made to preserve its confidentiality.

Member companies are required to report most impairments designated on the official list. The impairments designated cover a broad spectrum of health conditions and other factors that could be of some significance to the home office underwriters. The members do not, however, indicate whether an application has been declined or rated or postponed or accepted. They do not state the amount of insurance applied for, nor do the Bureau's records show that an application has been received. *In sum, the underwriting evaluation is not reported to the Bureau.*

A company normally screens all of its applicants against the checking files of the Recording and Statistical Company, MIB's servicing organization. If the company finds an impairment and wants further details, it must submit its request through the Recording and Statistical Company.

The rules of the MIB stipulate that a company shall not take unfavorable underwriting action *solely* on the basis of information in the MIB files. The member company must, through other sources, have additional facts and information which substantiate an unfavorable underwriting decision. In many cases the information available through MIB permits favorable underwriting action by increasing the available data regarding a particular condition. MIB is a positive underwriting aid increasing the medical information available to permit each member company to make its own underwriting evaluation of a particular application.

---

[10] For a discussion of the operational procedures and controls utilized, see J. C. Wilberding, "The Medical Information Bureau," *The Journal of the American Society of Chartered Life Underwriters,* Vol. XX, No. 2 (Spring, 1966), pp. 176–181.

METHODS OF CLASSIFICATION

Once all available underwriting information about an applicant for life insurance has been assembled, the data must be evaluated and a decision reached as to whether the applicant is to be accepted at standard rates, treated as a substandard but acceptable risk, or rejected entirely. Occasionally, a risk is postponed for a period of time until the effect of a condition or impairment is resolved, e.g., if the applicant is expecting imminent major surgery he would be postponed until after the surgery. Ideally, the evaluation and classification system used by a company should (1) measure accurately the effect of each factor affecting the risk; (2) assess the combined impact of interrelated factors, including those in conflict; (3) produce equitable results; and (4) be relatively simple and inexpensive to operate.

The Judgment Method of Rating

Originally, and for many years, the companies used the judgment method of rating. Under this method the company depended upon the combined judgment of those in the medical, actuarial, and other departments who were qualified for this work. The judgment method of rating functions effectively when there is only one unfavorable factor to consider or where the decision was simply one of accepting the applicant at standard rates or rejecting him entirely. Where multiple factors (some possibly in conflict) were involved or a proper substandard classification was needed, it left something to be desired. Moreover, it required the use of highly skilled personnel to achieve proper risk appraisal. To overcome the weakness of the judgment method of rating, the life insurance business evolved the so-called numerical rating system.[11]

The Numerical Rating System

The numerical rating system is based upon the principle that a large number of factors enter into the composition of a risk and that the impact of each of these factors on the longevity of the risk can be determined by a statistical study of lives possessing that factor. Under this plan it is assumed

[11] See Arthur H. Hunter and Oscar H. Rogers, "The Numerical Method of Determining the Value of Risks for Insurance," *Transactions of the Actuarial Society of America,* Vol. XX, Part II (1919).

that 100 per cent represents a normal or standard risk—one which is physically, morally, and financially sound, and has a need for the insurance.

Each of the factors that might influence a risk in an unusual way is considered a debit or credit. In practice, values are usually assigned. The factors include: (1) build, (2) physical condition, (3) personal history, (4) family history, (5) occupation, (6) habits, (7) morals, (8) plan of insurance, and (9) other factors.[12] The values assigned to the factors considered are based on judgment supported by mortality studies among groups possessing such characteristics and other information. For example, if the mortality of a group of insured lives, reflecting a certain degree of overweight or a certain degree of elevated blood pressure, has been found to be 150 per cent of that among all standard risks, a debit or addition of fifty percentage points will be assigned to such degree of overweight or blood pressure.

A hypothetical illustration will help make clear the operation of the numerical rating system. Suppose a clerk, age 35, applies for thirty-year endowment insurance. Information obtained by the company reveals the following facts: height, 5 feet, 9 inches; weight, 205; family history, slightly better than average; habits, good; personal history shows recent medical attention for ulcer of the stomach, which has apparently been cured. From tables developed for this purpose the company will first ascertain the basic rating for this individual. This depends upon the build (height, weight, and girth). In this case the basic rating may be assumed to be 125, because the individual is overweight. In other words, the overweight in such cases is expected to result in mortality which equals 125 per cent of normal. To this basic figure 35 per cent is added for unfavorable personal history. The total is 160. On the other hand, the following credits are allowed for the favorable factors: family history, 5; and plan of insurance, 10. The net result, 145, represents an expected mortality 45 per cent greater than that which is expected for standard or normal risks.

The analysis is summarized below:

Base = 100		
Factor	Debit	Credit
Build: Overweight	25	
Personal History: Ulcer	35	
Family History		5
Plan of Insurance, 30-Year Endowment	—	10
Total	60	15
Rating = 145		

12 See pp. 506-512.

The ratings obtained by this method range in most companies from a low of 75 to a high of 500 or more. In most companies the ratings that fall between 75 and 125 are classified as standard. Some companies, particularly those that do not write substandard insurance, may broaden the standard category to include ratings up to 130. Risks which produce a rate in excess of the standard limit are either assigned to appropriate substandard classes or declined.

The scale of ratings produced by the numerical rating system might be classified in a particular company as follows:

	Standard				Substandard			...		Uninsurable
75	85	100	115	125	135	145	155		485	500

SCALE OF RATINGS

As is explained in the following chapter, the broad category of substandard risks is divided into a number of classifications, each with its own scale of premiums. The spread of fifty percentage points in the standard classification points up the need to balance the risks within the class if the average result is to be 100. This same concept is applicable to each substandard class established.

Judgment enters into the operation of the numerical system, primarily in the assignment of numerical values to each factor, and, when it occurs, in determining the effect of two or more factors which are related to each other in some way. Regarding the first point, the company generally derives the numerical weight of each factor from statistical data, interpreted in the light of experienced judgment. Regarding the second point, when two factors are so related that one affects the other, judgment and past experience may dictate an addition which is greater or smaller than the mere addition of the numerical factors. For example, if family history shows several deaths from heart disease, this adverse factor may be nullified somewhat by a good physical condition, good build, good environment, and similar favorable factors. On the other hand, such a family history plus findings of overweight or elevated blood pressure will probably warrant a larger addition than the sum of the two adverse factors.

In North America generally, the numerical method is universal practice and has been for many years. Even in experimental underwriting, where numerical debits are determined purely from the same sort of medico-actuarial judgment formerly used for case underwriting, actual cases handled are placed in a numerical rating system context, both for consistency and for setting a foundation for future statistical study.

The system in practice is applied with common sense and has the advantages of greater consistency of treatment and of permitting lay underwriters to process all applications other than those requiring detailed medical analysis. Also important is the fact that it helps minimize the expense of the selection process.

Selection and Classification of | 32
Life Insurance Risks: II

TREATMENT OF SUBSTANDARD LIFE INSURANCE RISKS

IN THE INSURANCE of substandard life insurance risks, provision must be made for the higher death rate expected. In general this is done by charging an extra premium in addition to the premium developed by the standard rate. This and other methods of providing for the extra mortality expected are discussed hereafter.

Developments in recent years have made life insurance companies better equipped to provide insurance on substandard lives. In treating substandard risks, statistical information on past experience is essential in order to develop an equitable basis for providing insurance on lives subject to different types of impairments. Companies have now accumulated a considerable volume of statistics on impairments, which have aided in determining their influence on mortality with increased precision. In addition, advances in medical science have developed new diagnostic procedures and improved treatment of numerous medical impairments. Similarly, the wide experience of reinsurers,[1] especially with substandard risk appraisal, has assisted direct writing companies in making proper classification of applicants.

Incidence of Extra Risk

While there are a number of factors which may cause a risk to be substandard, more than 65 or 70 per cent are rated because of various physical defects such as heart murmurs, overweight, albumin in the urine, and elevated blood pressure.[2] It is impractical, however, for the companies to at-

[1] See pp. 531–536.
[2] Based on a recent study of ordinary insurance the reasons for extra ratings showed the following distribution: heart disease, 33 per cent; weight problems, 16 per cent; other physical impairments, 29 per cent; hazardous occupations, 12 per cent; other reasons, 10 per cent. See *Life Insurance Fact Book, 1971*, p. 94.

tempt a classification and treatment of substandard risks which attempts to follow precisely the manner in which the extra mortality of each impairment occurs. Although equity is an objective to be sought, such an approach would result in prohibitive expense and is impracticable because knowledge of substandard mortality is not sufficiently detailed. The majority of companies, therefore, categorize substandard risks into three broad groups: (1) a group in which the extra risk remains approximately the same in all years following the issue of the policy; (2) a group in which the extra risk increases as the policyholders grow older; and (3) a group in which the extra risk decreases with time. Examples of the constant type of extra risk would be partial blindness, deafness, or occupation. An example of an increasing risk would be a person with untreated high blood pressure, whereas a person who had just undergone a supposedly successful operation would represent a decreasing risk. Such a classification permits the company to assess premiums according to the incidence of the extra deaths; that is, if the company expects the same number of extra deaths to occur in two groups over a particular period of time, different types of extra premiums will be needed for the extra risk in a group where the extra deaths occur early (decreasing risk) than where the deaths occur later (increasing risk).

Methods of Rating

A number of methods have been devised for rating impaired lives. In general, an effort is made to adapt the method to the type of risk represented by the impaired individual, but departures from theoretically correct treatment of the risk are frequently made for practical reasons. The objectives in establishing an extra premium structure are that it be (1) equitable between impairments and between classes; (2) easy to administer; and (3) easily understood by the agency force and the public.

Flat Extra Premium. This plan is used where the extra risk, measured in extra deaths per thousand, is considered to be constant, temporary or permanent, and largely independent of age. Under this plan a regular policy is issued but an extra premium is charged to provide for the additional expected mortality. Especially if the required extra premium is not large, the policy is treated as standard for the purpose of dividends, nonforfeiture values, and so forth.

The plan is most appropriate for most occupational risks, since much of the extra risk is independent of age. The plan is also appropriate to cover temporary extras (running for a specified period) used where most of the extra risk falls in the early years after an operation, such as for cancer or stomach ulcers.

The use of a flat extra premium for constant risks is theoretically correct for level term plans since the *net amount at risk* and the *face amount* are practically the same. On the other hand, for permanent plans and *decreasing* term insurance, the net amount at risk decreases as the reserve increases. Here the flat extra premium really provides for an increasing extra risk. It would entail disproportionate expense to attempt to decrease the extra charge from year to year and, in practice, a suitable flat extra premium is charged which takes into account the *average* extra amount of risk involved. For example, a company might charge a smaller extra premium for a twenty-year endowment policy than for a whole-life policy.

Usually, participating policies do not pay additional dividends on account of the additional premiums collected. Also the flat extra premiums paid do not increase the cash or other nonforfeiture values and may be easily removed where the decrease in risk so warrants.

Extra-Percentage Tables. By far the most common method used for the insurance of substandard risks is the so-called extra-percentage table plan. All substandard risks are divided into broad groups according to their numerical rating, and premium rates are based on the average numerical ratings in each class. A few of the larger companies also use special tables of nonforfeiture values and dividends, although most companies use standard values and usually do not issue the extended term insurance option with the higher rated cases. It will be remembered that standard risks with numerical ratings ranging up to about 125 are grouped together as one class and pay the same rates of premium. The procedure in setting up a substandard class is identical except the average rating of each additional substandard class established will be progressively higher than that for the standard class. Companies usually provide for at least four and sometimes as many as six or seven such substandard classes when special nonforfeiture values are used, and as many as sixteen classifications or more when standard values are used. Applicants are then placed in the appropriate class (standard or substandard) in accordance with their numerical ratings. The average numerical rating within these classes may range from about 135 to as high as 500 or even higher. An example of a scale of substandard classifications is shown in Table 32–1.

Under this method a special mortality table, reflecting the experience of each substandard classification, is developed for each substandard classi-

TABLE 32-1. Illustrative Scale of Substandard Mortality Classifications

Class	Mortality (per cent)	Class	Mortality (per cent)
A	130–150	E	310– 400
B	155–185	F	405– 500
C	190–235	G	505–1,000
D	240–305		

TABLE 32-2.   **Illustrative Substandard Gross Participating Premium Rates**
Ordinary Life

Age	Rate for Standard Risks	A 130%–150%	B 155%–185%	C 190%–235%	D 240%–305%
15	$16.78	$18.76	$ 19.95	$ 21.40	$ 23.22
20	18.38	20.62	21.98	23.65	25.74
25	20.54	23.09	24.66	26.58	29.00
30	23.20	26.16	28.00	30.27	33.14
35	26.55	30.07	32.26	35.01	38.52
40	30.84	35.11	37.80	41.21	45.65
45	36.31	41.58	44.92	49.25	54.97
50	43.42	50.01	54.22	59.78	67.31
55	52.76	61.02	66.37	73.57	83.56
60	65.26	75.47	82.17	91.38	104.48
65	82.92	94.69	102.47	113.30	128.99

fication and a set of gross premium rates is computed for the classification.

Table 32–2 shows illustrative gross premium rates for an ordinary life contract under substandard Tables A, B, C, and D. The standard rates are also shown for purposes of comparison.

It should be noted that these substandard premiums do not increase in proportion to the degree of extra mortality involved. This is due to the fact that the loading does not increase in proportion to the degree of extra mortality involved, the extra mortality is computed on the basis of *actual* mortality, not the *tabular* mortality as reflected by, say, the *1958 CSO Table*, and the premium calculation takes into account the decreasing net amount at risk by policy duration under the ordinary life plan.

The extra-percentage tables do not differentiate between the various types of substandard risks with different incidence of extra mortality (that is, increasing, decreasing, or constant). The assumption of a *constant percentage* of the standard mortality rates implies a number of extra deaths per thousand which increase with age for all types of cases rated on this basis. Although theoretically this plan may not exactly reflect, then, the incidence of extra risk, this procedure is justified on an expense basis and, on the average, is reasonably accurate. Also, the treatment here is no less refined than that utilized in classifying and rating standard risks.

Notwithstanding the fact that many companies will write insurance on persons subject to 500 per cent of standard mortality, there is a point beyond which the degree of extra mortality is so high that the insurance principle of averaging will not apply. As the ratings increase, there will normally be fewer applicants willing to pay the necessarily higher premiums, and it will become increasingly difficult to produce a sufficiently large group to secure average results. In addition, as the premium is increased, if the policy is for personal insurance, then the likelihood of adverse selection increases markedly.

Rated-up Age Plan.   Under this plan the insured is assumed to be a number of years older than his real age and the policy is written accordingly. The extra number of years to be added is determined by adding to the net premium for the real age an amount to provide for the extra risk and then comparing the result with the premium (and age) on the standard table which approximates the premium result in question. For example, if the net premium for ordinary life insurance age 25 is $14.60 and $4.17 is added to cover the additional mortality, the result will be $18.77. The net premium on the standard table which is the nearest to this amount is $18.44, which is the net premium at age 32. Therefore, the risk is rated up seven years on the ordinary life plan. Policies written on this plan are usually similar to other policies written on standard risks at the same ages. Cash, loan, paid-up, and extended insurance values as well as dividends are allowed at the increased age. Where the rating is high, the extended term option is frequently deleted.

The rated-up age plan is best adapted to the increasing type of extra risk, although it does not deal equitably with all risks of this type unless the plan is varied somewhat. Thus, suppose a group of substandard risks, each at age 25, is insured at the rated-up age of 30. The *1958 CSO Table* shows that the number of deaths is 1.93 per 1,000 persons at age 25 and 2.13 per 1,000 at age 30. During the first year of such insurance, provision is thus made for but .20 of one extra death per 1,000 insured. Ten years later, however, the extra mortality increases but the amount at risk is decreasing and the combined result may be a fairly level extra mortality.

In general, this plan has certain advantages. It is easy for the insured to understand and it appeals to him because of the increased surrender values and increased dividends which may be paid. It is simple for office purposes, since it does not involve any complicated record system. On the other hand, there are certain defects and disadvantages. The insured may take advantage of the higher values and surrender his policy in the early years, thus getting back a substantial part of the extra payments he has made to cover this additional risk. Competition may also offer him a less expensive policy on the extra-percentage plan without explaining the fact that his cash values and dividends will not be as high. To overcome adverse selection in the exercising of this option, the company may add a slightly higher loading to the original extra premiums. In order to use the plan in connection with endowment policies, particularly those of short term or those which mature at the younger ages, the company must rate up the insured a considerable number of years in order to provide for any substantial amount of extra risk. In other words, if a person is rated up five years under an ordinary life policy at age 30, the extra premium will be much greater in dollars and cents than for the same number of years rating-up on an endowment policy at this age. This is true in a reverse order when ordinary life insurance is compared with term insurance. In most cases the extra premium desired by the company will not be too great to permit the use of this plan in connection with endowment policies. In some cases it would cause the age to be rated up to ridiculous extremes so that flat extra premiums might be used for endowment plans while the age advance system is applied to other plans. This plan is used less frequently today since most physical impairments can be satisfactorily rated under the extra-percentage tables.

Lien Plan.   One of the first problems encountered in the sale of substandard insurance was the difficulty of convincing the applicant that provision must be made for the extra risk. To meet this problem the company in some cases offered to issue a regular policy at standard rates with a lien against it, to be deducted in the event of the death of the insured. If adequate statistics are available, it is possible to calculate the term and amount of the lien which would be the actuarial equivalent of the extra risk involved. The amount of the lien can be kept constant or the method refined to provide for a yearly reduction in the amount of the lien. The plan was best adapted to a decreasing risk, however, and it was used chiefly for this class of risks.

The plan had some advantages. It appealed to many insureds because it was easily understood; many were willing to accept the lien against their insurance because of their optimism regarding the future; and often the agent would sell additional insurance to cover the lien. On the other hand, the plan had such serious defects that it has never been used extensively in this country and is, in fact, illegal in some states. In most instances the amount of the lien, of necessity, was large compared with the face of the policy, and the insured often did not understand or realize that his protection was smaller than the face of the policy. Furthermore, in the case of decreasing risks to which it was usually applied, the lien reduced the protection at the time the insured needed it most, that is, during the early years following the issuance of the policy when the need was the greatest. In fact, its overall use in the United States is negligible today except in some individual policy pension trust plans.[3]

Special Dividend Plans.   In addition to the plans already explained, substandard risks are sometimes insured in a special class containing similar risks. The purpose of this classification is to adjust premiums (which are higher than for the standard class) and dividends according to the mortality experience. This plan has never been used extensively since the company must have a sufficient number insured in each class to permit the law of averages to work.

[3] The lien system, however, is used extensively in Great Britain and Canada.

In some cases the company may be willing to treat the applicant as standard if he will purchase a high premium policy, usually of the endowment type. Such a policy will have a higher reserve than the lower premium forms, thus lessening the risk assumed by the insurer. The object of the company is usually to get off the risk before the extra hazard becomes serious. Most companies refuse to issue term plans at very high ratings, e.g., above 200 to 300 per cent, primarily because of adverse selection.

Improvement in the Risk

After a policy has been issued to an impaired risk under the permanent flat extra premium, extra-percentage, or rated-up age plan, the policyholder may become eligible to purchase insurance at standard rates, or under better terms than those which govern the rated policy. Under such circumstances, the policyholder expects reconsideration. Most reconsiderations are noncompetitive. Many are "automatic," in the sense that the rating is reduced in conjunction with a repeat sale which has a lower or no rating. In some cases, the offer of standard insurance is made by another company. The insured usually appeals to the company issuing the existing insurance to meet the terms offered by the second company. Even without competition being involved, companies will entertain a request from the policyholder to improve the rating under his policy. In order to prevent insured persons from withdrawing, the first company generally makes some provision for handling improvement in the risk. In order that the company may remove the extra charge without loss to itself, the extra charge in the first instance must have been computed with data from which the improved lives were eliminated. If the extra premium for the impairment was calculated from data which included lives that improved, the company could not theoretically remove the extra charge. In this latter case, some of the risks will no doubt improve but others will grow worse, and since the company cannot increase the charges against those which deteriorate, it would be unable to reduce charges to those which improve. As a practical matter, however, most companies anticipate such withdrawals and will reduce the premium if they are convinced the risk is lower or remove the rating if standard.

When there is an apparent reduction in risk due to a change in residence or occupation, the usual practice is to require a probationary period of one or two years. At the end of this period, the company makes a retroactive refund of the extra premium dating from the time when the change in occupation or residence occurred. This protects the company against the possibility that the insured will return to the occupation or residence which he gave up.

SPECIAL PROCEDURES AND PROBLEMS

Nonmedical Life Insurance

A substantial proportion of all new life insurance is written today without the benefit of a medical examination. For example, neither group nor industrial life insurance normally requires a medical examination. In addition, an increasing proportion of ordinary life insurance is being sold without a medical examination.[4] The expression "nonmedical life insurance" normally refers to ordinary insurance sold in this manner.

Development.   For many years after its establishment as an underwriting device, the medical examination was considered a necessity. Toward the end of the nineteenth century, life insurance companies in England began to experiment with nonmedical underwriting on a limited basis. It was not until 1921, however, that several Canadian companies began to experiment with nonmedical as it is practiced today. The motivation for the development was the shortage of medical examiners, particularly in the rural areas, and the desire to reduce the expense rate on the predominantly small policies issued at that time. The practice spread to the United States' companies about four years later and is firmly entrenched today in both Canada and the United States.

Theory of Nonmedical Underwriting.   While nonmedical underwriting has the advantages of lessening the demands on the time and talent of the medical profession and facilitating the sale and processing of an application, the primary justification lies in the savings in expense. As long as the cost of the extra mortality brought about by the elimination of the medical examination is less than the expenses saved, it is economically sound. Detailed actuarial studies underlie the nonmedical rules utilized by the life insurance companies, and appropriate modifications are needed in the rules from time to time as indicated by the emerging experience, including the increasing costs of medical examinations in recent years.

Underwriting Safeguards.   Perhaps the most important safeguard built into the nonmedical underwriting rules is a *limit on the amount* which will be available to any one applicant. In the early days this limit was $1,000. When the experience turned out to be more favorable than anticipated, the limits were gradually raised. Today, most companies will

---

[4] About two out of every three policies of ordinary insurance are currently being written on a nonmedical basis. These policies account for approximately one third of the amount of new ordinary insurance written.

provide up to $30,000 on a nonmedical basis, some even higher, subject to appropriate age limitations, while virtually all will issue to $10,000 or even $15,000 on that basis. The limit varies by age groups, the largest amounts being permitted at the younger ages.

The above limits are applicable to any one application. Subject to an aggregate limit, some companies will issue additional amounts after a specified period of time has elapsed. In applying their rules most companies are willing to ignore all nonmedical insurance issued to a person *prior* to the time of a medical examination satisfactory to the company. After such an examination, additional amounts would be made available up to the applicable limits.

A second safeguard built into the rules is a *limit on the ages* at which the insurance will be issued. Normally, nonmedical insurance is not available beyond age 40 or 45, except in special situations, such as salary savings groups, where the age limits may be higher. Most companies impose no lower age limit, offering it down to age 0.

Other safeguards built into the nonmedical underwriting rules include the general limitation of nonmedical insurance to *medically standard risks* and the *refusal of many companies to write short-duration term insurance* on such a basis. Companies will usually consider occupations where the extra hazard is largely accidental and all aviation and avocation risks on a nonmedical basis.

The application form used contains the questions which would normally be asked by the medical examiner as well as the usual questions completed by the agent under a medical application. In those cases where adverse medical information is developed from other sources, the company may require a complete medical examination. It has been estimated that this occurs in about 10 per cent of the nonmedical applications.

It is understandable that the privilege of submitting nonmedical business is not bestowed indiscriminately on the members of the agency force. It is normally restricted to established agents, who have demonstrated good judgment and integrity in their submitted business.

Guaranteed Insurability Option

Most companies are now offering a so-called *guaranteed insurability* option, which permits the holder of a standard policy, at stated intervals, to purchase specified amounts of additional insurance *without evidence of insurability*. The additional insurance may be any standard life or endowment insurance plan issued by the company. If the original policy contains a waiver-of-premium provision and accidental death benefits, the new policies will, at the insured's option, contain the same features. In the event premiums are being waived in the original policy at the time an option for additional insurance is exercised, under some contracts premiums on the new policy are also waived from the beginning. The new insurance is issued at standard rates on the basis of the insured's attained age when the option is exercised.

As in the case of nonmedical rules, the options available vary as to details but follow the same general pattern. A typical plan permits the insured to purchase additional insurance at three-year intervals beginning with the policy anniversary nearest his age 25 and terminating with the anniversary nearest his age 40. The amount of additional insurance which can be obtained on each specified anniversary is limited to the face of the original policy or $10,000, *whichever is smaller.*[5] The option is usually restricted to policies of a specified minimum size (typically $5,000) and can be attached to only one policy issued by the company. Similar options may, of course, be added to policies issued by other companies. It should also be noted that some companies provide additional option dates at marriage and at birth of the insured's children.

The option is available for an extra premium which varies only *with the age at issue.* One company charges $0.50 per $1,000 at age 0 increasing to $2.00 per $1,000 at age 37. These premiums reflect the company's estimate of the average amount of extra mortality which will be experienced on policies issued without evidence of insurability. They represent to the insured the cost of "insuring his insurability."

Insurance at Extremes of Age

Applications for life insurance at both extremes of ages are underwritten very carefully. In both cases, the primary problem is that of limited insurable interest.

As was pointed out earlier, most companies will write life insurance on the lives of very young children, even down to 1 day old. They attempt to deal with the lack of insurable interest by (1) limiting the amounts of coverage, particularly at the early ages, (2) seeing that the life insurance on the child bears a reasonable relationship to the amounts in force on the breadwinner, (3) requiring that similar amounts of insurance be in force on all children in the family, and (4) aggressively seeking a large volume of such business to minimize the effect of adverse selection. The mortality experience on juvenile business has been very favorable. In general, the insurance is sold without medical examination since the amounts requested are usually within the nonmedical limits.

At the older ages, additional complicating factors, other than the lack of insurable interest, are involved. Here the volume of insurance written (above ages 60 or 65) is not large enough to develop an average experience. The restricted writings at these older ages reflect the high cost of

[5] In the last year or two considerable differences in company practices have developed with regard to this limitation.

the insurance, the difficulty of qualifying for standard insurance, and the limited need for new insurance. An additional problem is the relative ineffectiveness of the medical examinations because of many degenerative conditions which are not revealed in a routine medical examination. The limited amounts of insurance written are suggestive of adverse selection and when combined with high premium payments, the problem is considerably enlarged.

As a consequence of these circumstances, some companies establish an age limit, typically 65 or 70, beyond which they will not accept applications. The amounts which will be issued at the older ages may also be limited. It should be noted that many companies do not set an arbitrary limit beyond which they *categorically* refuse to consider an application. All, however, have ages beyond which rates are not published, 65 or 70 being common. Also, all have increasingly severe underwriting standards and medical tests.

REINSURANCE

Reinsurance may be defined as a device by which a life insurance company transfers all or a portion of its risk exposure under a life insurance policy to another company. The company which issued the policy originally is known as the *direct-writing* or *ceding* company, while the company to which the risk is transferred is called the *reinsuring* or *assuming* company. The process of transferring the risk from the ceding company to the reinsurer is known as a *cession*.

Concept of Retention

A life insurance company deals with a type of risk which, in the aggregate, may be measured and predicted with a remarkable degree of accuracy, the closeness of the approximation depending on the number and homogeneity of the individuals in the group. On the other hand, the exposure of one individual may be $100,000 and the exposure of another $5,000, depending on the amount of insurance taken. In general, the probability of death for either may be the same, but the impact on the surplus of a company could be much greater in the case of the $100,000 policy.

In the case of a recently organized or small company the need for a maximum limit on the amount of insurance which it will carry at its own risk on any individual should be obvious. In companies with a relatively small total number of policyholders the mortality experience may fluctuate rather widely from year to year. In such companies the surplus funds available to absorb an unusual loss are usually relatively small, and a single large death claim or several significant claims might have a marked effect on the operations of the year.

As a company increases in size, with an increasing total volume of insurance in force, and increasingly large surplus funds, the chance of significant fluctuations in its overall mortality experience will decrease and the company's ability to absorb unusual losses will increase. Thus, it can gradually and safely increase its maximum *retention* on any one life.

There is no simple formula for fixing a retention limit since that limit will depend in each case on a number of factors peculiar to a company's economic position and manner of operation. Such factors include (1) the size of the company's unallocated surplus; (2) the quality and distribution of its agency force; (3) the quality of the home office underwriting staff; (4) the distribution of insurance in force (by amount, number of policies, grouping by age, proportion substandard, etc.); and (5) the probable distribution of new business and average amount per policy. In general, the smaller the group of exposed risks and the less homogeneous the insured risks, the sharper and more sudden will be the fluctuations and, therefore, the lower should be the company's limit of retention. The limits may range from $5,000 in small, recently established companies to $1,000,000 or more in the largest companies. There may be various limits within a given company depending upon plan, age at issue, sex, and substandard classification.

Despite the need to have retention limits, a company must also provide competitive facilities to its agency force and accept virtually all of the cases written by its agents. Thus, it can be seen that some system of "insurance for life insurance companies" is necessary. This "insurance" is known as *reinsurance.*

While the primary purpose of reinsurance is to avoid too large a concentration of risk on one life, it may also be used to take advantage of the underwriting judgment of the reinsurer; to transfer all or certain classes of substandard business; [6] to reduce the drain on surplus caused by writing new business; to stabilize the overall mortality experience of the ceding company; and in the case of newly organized companies to obtain advice and counsel on underwriting matters, rates, and forms.

The traditional plans of reinsurance developed to deal with individual risks may be broadly described as *proportional reinsurance.* Recently, *nonproportional reinsurance* plans have been developed with the objective of stabilizing the overall mortality experience of the ceding company. Nonproportional reinsurance usually takes one of three forms, *stop-loss* rein-

---

[6] Life reinsurance may also be undertaken to transfer all or a specific portion of a company's existing liabilities. This is known as "assumption reinsurance" and might be utilized where a company wishes to withdraw from business entirely or from a particular territory. See Pearce Shepherd and Andrew C. Webster, *Selection of Risks* (Chicago: The Society of Actuaries, 1957).

surance, *catastrophe* reinsurance, and *spread-loss* reinsurance. The basic characteristic which differentiates them from traditional proportional reinsurance plans is that this approach relates the reinsurer's liability to the mortality experience on all or specified "blocks" of the ceding companies' business, rather than to individual or specific policies of insurance. In addition, the proportion in which the ceding company and the reinsurer will share losses is not determinable in advance. These forms are adaptations of property and liability reinsurance, none of which have been widely utilized as yet in the life field.[7] In view of the predominance of proportional reinsurance, the remainder of this discussion relates to that form.

Reinsurance Arrangements

Agreements.   Reinsurance may be arranged on a *facultative* or an *automatic* basis. Under the *facultative plan,* each excess risk is handled separately at the time it is incurred. When the original company receives an application for a policy for more than the amount it wishes to assume, it negotiates with another company for a transfer of that part of the risk which is over and above its own limit. This facultative method has certain advantages. It is flexible, in that there are no prearranged rules or agreements. Hence, new circumstances or conditions regarding the original insurance may be covered in the reinsurance negotiations without difficulty or restraint. The original insurer also gets the advice of the reinsurer with whom it negotiates. The major disadvantage is the additional time required for completing the transaction, which may result in loss of business to competitors.

The *automatic plan* provides that the original company *must* transfer any excess risk to the reinsuring company immediately upon payment of premium and the issuance of the policy. Also, the reinsurer *must* accept transfer of risk, which falls within the scope of the automatic treaty. The agreement always provides that not more than a certain amount of risk may be transferred to the reinsuring company, and the automatic agreement may provide for a distribution of the excess to more than one reinsuring company. Most, if not all, "split accounts" are split on systems under which any one case goes only to one reinsurer. The usual split is based on the first letter of applicant's surname—reinsurer #1 gets letters A-M, and #2 gets N-Z. It should also be noted that when application exceeds the limits of the automatic treaty, facultative reinsurance can be used for the excess.

It should be noted that the original insured, the person taking out the life insurance, is in no way a legal party to any reinsurance contracts which

[7] See Walter W. Steffen, "Recent Developments in Life Reinsurance," *Journal of Risk and Insurance,* Vol. XXXI, No. 2 (1964), pp. 265–271.

may result therefrom. He must look solely to the direct-writing company for any payments to which he is entitled under his policy, and the direct-writing company is liable for such payments regardless of the existence and terms of any reinsurance contracts to which it may be a party.

Plans.   In connection with use of either the facultative or the automatic type of agreement there are two usual methods of determining the extent of the reinsurer's liability in case of a loss. One of these is the *coinsurance plan* used principally by the larger ceding companies. Under this plan the reinsurer assumes a share of the risk according to the terms which govern the original policy. If a loss occurs, the reinsurer is liable for a part thereof, determined according to the size of the insurance assumed in relation to the amount of original insurance. Thus, if the reinsurer has accepted one half the original insurance, he becomes liable for one half of any loss. In return for this guarantee the reinsurer receives a pro rata share of the original premium less a ceding commission the purpose of which is to reimburse the direct writing company for an appropriate share of the agent's commissions, premium taxes paid to the state of domicile of the insured, and a portion of the other expenses attributable to the reinsured policy. Likewise, the reinsurer pays his share of dividends paid. In general, the contract which is the subject of the reinsurance agreement is a duplicate of that entered into by the original company with the insured.

The other plan of determining the liability of the reinsurer is the *yearly renewable term plan*, particularly appropriate for the smaller ceding companies because it results in larger assets for the direct writing companies and is simpler to handle than the coinsurance plan. Under this plan, the original company each year transfers to the reinsurer all or a portion of the net amount at risk and pays premiums on a yearly renewable term basis. Thus, a flat amount of retention such as $5,000 results in a decreasing amount reinsured each year due to the decreasing net amount at risk (except on level term plans). If a loss occurs, the reinsurer is liable for the amount that it has assumed that year, and the original insurer is liable for its retention plus the full reserve on the reinsured portion of the policy. In the interest of retaining control over the funds arising out of its own policies, a *modified coinsurance plan* has been developed. Under this arrangement, the ceding company pays the reinsurer a proportionate part of the gross premium, as under the conventional coinsurance plan, less whatever allowances have been arranged for commissions, premium taxes, and overhead. At the end of each policy year, the reinsurer pays over to the ceding company an amount equal to the net increase in the reserve during the year, less one year's interest on the reserve at the beginning of the year. The net effect of the plan is to return to the ceding company the bulk of the funds developed by its policies. Aside from the reserve adjustment, the modified coinsurance arrangement follows that of the regular coinsurance plan.

Source of Funds

Table 32–3 includes an example of the distribution of liability between the direct-writing company and the reinsurer where an age 35, ordinary life policy in the amount of $25,000 is reinsured under either the coinsurance, yearly renewable term or modified coinsurance plan. In each case a retention of $5,000 is assumed.

TABLE 32-3. Source of Funds for Paying a Death Claim Under the
Coinsurance, Yearly Renewable Term, and Modified
Coinsurance Plans, Ordinary Life Age 35,
Policy Amount $25,000

Year	Direct-Writer Reserve	Direct-Writer Surplus	Reinsurer Reserve	Reinsurer Surplus	Total
			Coinsurance		
1	$ 78.20	$4,921.80	$ 312.80	$19,687.20	$25,000
2	157.95	4,842.05	631.80	19,368.20	25,000
3	239.15	4,760.85	956.60	19,043.40	25,000
4	321.60	4,678.40	1,286.40	18,713.60	25,000
5	402.25	4,594.75	1,621.00	18,379.00	25,000
10	839.50	4,160.50	3,358.00	16,642.00	25,000
20	1,762.70	3,237.30	7,050.80	12,949.20	25,000
			Yearly Renewable Term		
1	$ 391.00	$4,921.80	$ .00	$19,687.20	$25,000
2	789.75	4,842.05	.00	19,368.20	25,000
3	1,195.75	4,760.85	.00	19,043.40	25,000
4	1,608.00	4,678.40	.00	18,713.60	25,000
5	2,026.25	4,594.75	.00	18,379.00	25,000
10	4,197.50	4,160.50	.00	16,642.00	25,000
20	8,813.50	3,237.30	.00	12,949.20	25,000
			Modified Coinsurance		
1	$ 78.20	$4,921.80	$ 312.80	$19,687.20	$25,000
2	478.57	4,842.05	311.18	19,368.20	25,000
3	886.75	4,760.85	309.00	19,043.40	25,000
4	1,302.12	4,678.40	305.88	18,713.60	25,000
5	1,723.81	4,594.75	302.44	18,379.00	25,000
10	3,916.96	4,160.50	280.54	16,642.00	25,000
20	8,605.39	3,237.30	208.11	12,949.20	25,000

*Assumes 1958 CSO 2½% NLP Reserve Method and claim paid on last day of policy
year prior to any reserve payment from the reinsurer to the direct-writer.

Selection and Classification of | 33
Health Insurance Risks[1]

MANY OF THE basic principles of selection discussed in the preceding chapters are applicable to health insurance underwriting. In order to avoid duplication, the following discussion of the selection and classification of health insurance risks attempts to concentrate on the unique aspects of health insurance underwriting.

FACTORS AFFECTING THE HEALTH RISK

In underwriting health insurance risks the hazards which affect the probability of loss must be evaluated. In contrast to life insurance the multiplicity of benefit types has an important bearing on the evaluation of the hazards. The probability of disablement and the average severity are affected by many of the same factors as those discussed for the life risk, but their significance varies.

Age

Age affects disability rates differently, depending on the type of benefit involved, although both frequency and severity increase with advancing age for all types of benefits. In the case of long-term disability, the increase in risk is as rapid as that found in death rates. For medical care expense coverages and short-term disability income contracts, the increase is not marked until about age 55. Thus, guaranteed renewable and noncancellable policies and life insurance disability riders are usually issued with net level premiums graded according to age of issue. Other types of policies, such as those which are optionally renewable by the applicant or the insurance company, often utilize a flat premium from, say, age 18 to 55, with

[1] See O. D. Dickerson, *Health Insurance*, 3rd ed. (Homewood, Ill.: Richard D. Irwin, Inc., 1968), Chapter 17; see also E. J. Faulkner, *Health Insurance* (New York: McGraw-Hill Book Company, Inc., 1963), pp. 292–363. These were the basic sources used in preparing this chapter.

sharply higher rates for renewals or new issues at higher ages. In general, policies have in the past not been available at ages materially higher than age 65, although there has been considerable extension in recent years of medical care expense coverage to these older ages. There is normally little need for income replacement coverage at advanced ages, since some form of retirement income is available to most insureds. Currently, some modern policies provide for continuance to age 70, subject only to full-time employment.

There is a severe problem of adverse selection at older ages, but considerable medical expense protection is provided for retiring persons under group policies and under Federal Medicare coverage. Most individual policies currently available are usually limited as to amount and type of coverage after a certain age, such as 65 or 70, although some companies have made lifetime coverage available.

Sex

Sex, as in the case of life insurance policies, is of considerable significance. Females show definitely higher disability rates in most studies. This is true even for policies which exclude coverage of pregnancy, miscarriage, abortion, and similar problems. Underwriters feel that there is greater moral hazard in connection with women since they are not normally the breadwinner. Women who are not employed outside the home are usually ineligible for disability income insurance. Companies are reluctant to issue such coverage to working women because their employment is frequently temporary and intermittent. Where issued, such coverage provides shorter and lower income benefits than would be issued to men. Life insurance disability income riders and long-term noncancellable disability income policies are seldom issued to women. For all types of policies, women usually are charged a higher rate than men, even if the maternity risk is excluded. Where such coverage is included, rates for the child-bearing ages are even higher. Many policies provide for reduced benefits if the female insured is not actively employed away from her residence immediately prior to the claim.

Occupation

The probability of disablement is materially affected by occupation, particularly as regards the peril of accidental injury. Certain occupations such as test pilot, steeplejack, sandhog, and the like are normally uninsurable on an individual basis. The duties of an occupation will also affect a claimant's ability to return to work and this, as well as the accident peril, is a basis for classifying and rating occupations.[2] A few companies have special-risk departments and will write such cases but only at very high premium rates. Lloyd's of London also will consider such hazardous risks.

Insurable occupations are classified into broad groups of about the same average claim cost with appropriate scales of premium rates applying to each class. The number of classes may vary from two (insurable and uninsurable) to thirty, depending on the type of company and the types of coverage provided. There is considerable diversity among the companies in this regard.

The complexity of occupational classifications is greatest in the noncancellable policies. Limited and industrial contracts are usually sold at a uniform rate for all occupations except those excluded by policy provisions. It is not uncommon for companies to restrict sales of noncancellable policies to the more favorable occupations. Some companies having no such restriction will have limitations as to benefit periods and amounts available to the less favorable occupations.

Physical Condition

Obviously, the present and potential physical condition of the applicant is important. The present physical condition and past health record must be evaluated to predict the probability of future disability. Naturally, an applicant who is currently disabled or undergoing medical treatment for a significant ailment at the time of application is not eligible for insurance against losses resulting from the current existing disability. In the case of minor impairments, the policy may be issued in view of the provisions in the policy relating to pre-existing conditions and the probationary period. If the impairment is serious, the application will be rejected, perhaps to be considered at a later date.

Build is of considerable significance. Extremes of weight will be rejected or given special treatment. Generally, a variation of 15–20 per cent in either direction from the average for the age is acceptable for standard coverage. Extreme height is also considered to involve a significant increase in risk. Underweight, especially if marked, is also an underwriting consideration which should be viewed in the light of the applicant's history, e.g., ulcer, bronchitis, tuberculosis, frequently recurring colds or pneumonia, colitis, etc. It could also be an indication of an undiagnosed condition which would call for a medical examination by the company. However, underweight of and by itself is usually not considered significant.

---

[2] For example, after a coronary, it would be easier for a desk clerk to return to work than, say, a construction worker.

Personal History

The importance the underwriter attaches to a history of past illness or accident will vary, depending upon the severity of the original ailment, the frequency of attacks, the degree of permanent impairment, and the length of time which has elapsed since recovery. All of these factors are considered in conjunction with the applied for benefits. This is important for both accidental injury and sickness coverages. For example, a history of epilepsy and vertigo would increase the probability of accident, and diabetes, hemophilia, overweight, or cardiovascular conditions would increase the duration of disability from injury or sickness.

Particular attention is paid to chronic conditions where the probability of recurrence is high. Less attention is necessary for acute conditions, even if quite serious, if recovery has been good, permanent impairment is not evident, and a reasonable time has elapsed without recurrence. Thus, a chronic condition such as asthma will be regarded more seriously than a history of pneumonia or appendicitis. Naturally, conditions which are both chronic and serious, such as heart disease, hypertension, tuberculosis, and cancer, will be underwritten very carefully and frequently declined altogether.

Family History

The health history of the family is sometimes taken into account in underwriting health risks. The application normally requests information on the age and health status of living parents, brothers and sisters, and on age at death and cause of death for those deceased. Such data, while not conclusive in and of themselves, may shed light on the case and, in combination with other factors, contribute toward a decision.

Moral Hazard

The moral hazard is a particularly serious problem in health insurance. The subjective nature of the disability risk and the difficulties in defining the insured events complicate the problem considerably. The character of the insured is one of the most important determinants of claim rates. Insurers must contend with such conditions as psychosomatic illness, accident proneness, and hypochondria, as well as deliberate malingering. In addition to the primary safeguard of limiting the amount of benefit to something less than the amount of loss, companies scrutinize all aspects of the selection process for evidence of moral hazard.

When an applicant voluntarily approaches the company for insurance, this is considered a warning signal. Experience has indicated that there is a better-than-average chance that he has knowledge of some condition which will make the insurance particularly valuable to him. In most cases where the occupation is characterized by unstable earnings, work performed at home, irregular and seasonable work, or any connection with illegal or dubious activities, underwriters will be hesitant to approve the risk. In the event the personal history of the applicant shows evidence of fraud or bad debts, a poor risk is indicated. Such activities as extramarital entanglements, dishonest or questionable business practices or ethics, questionable associates, criminal activity, and poor personal habits all present danger signals. Poor personal habits include gambling, excessive drinking, drug addiction, and the like. Any evidence of fraud or misrepresentation in the application will also be considered most significant.

Other Factors

Other factors which affect physical hazard to some degree include residence, habits, and avocations. In addition, the health insurance plan involved and the relation of insurance benefits to loss are important underwriting considerations.

Residence, Habits, and Avocations.   As in life insurance, only foreign residence is considered in underwriting health risks. Location in the United States is sometimes considered in group cases. Habits of drug addiction or excessive use of alcohol are, of course, quite significant. These affect both the physical and moral hazard and normally lead to rejection. Special treatment is usually given an individual who participates in particularly hazardous sports. Private aviation activities are excluded by policy wording from many disability contracts. For companies granting unrestricted aviation coverage such activities, including the type and frequency of flying, become an underwriting consideration.

Plan of Insurance.   As was pointed out earlier, one of the most important factors affecting actual observed claim rates is the type of policy and the type and amount of benefit. In this regard the definition of disability itself is important (e.g., "own occupation," "any occupation," or "any reasonable occupation"). In medical care expense coverages it may be in terms of admission to a hospital or treatment by a physician and/or the incurring of an expense. For other benefits it will be presumptive disability for certain specific disablements. The length of the elimination period, or the amount of the deductible, or the extent of percentage participation will be a major factor in determining claim rates for disabilities of short duration.

Over and above the differences in rates due to different definitions of covered events, differences in type and amount of benefit will produce different claim rates. This is a reflection of moral hazard. Under exactly the same definition of disability and waiting period, for example, higher claim rates result for a disability income benefit than for a waiver-of-premium benefit. In general, the greater the prospective benefit in terms of both amount and duration, the greater will be the claim rate, other things being equal. Naturally, where the potential benefit exceeds the loss, particular difficulties arise. In such a case the insured can make a profit from disability, and the motivation for malingering and a slow recovery is greatest.

The underwriter's primary concern with differences in disability definition is to be careful to apply appropriate criteria to specific types of insurance. When a policy or life insurance disability rider is noncancellable, higher standards are usually applied in initial underwriting. There can be no renewal underwriting as can be done with optionally renewable individual health insurance. More conservative selection standards must also be applied to contracts providing high benefits in regard to amount or duration or both. Similarly, stricter standards must be applied for policies covering sickness than for those covering accidental injury only.

In practice, the strictest underwriting standards are applied to the long-term noncancellable disability income policies and to life insurance disability riders. In the case of medical expense coverages, similar high standards are applied to major medical expense contracts. Disability income contracts and medical expense contracts other than major medical, renewable at the option of the company, are underwritten more liberally. The most lenient underwriting standards are applied to industrial and limited policies where benefit amounts are small and durations are short.

Relation of Insurance to Loss. The most significant underwriting safeguard against moral hazard is a reasonable relationship between the insurance benefit and the amount of potential loss. Underwriters feel that the situation is sound only if the *insured shares in the loss.* This may be accomplished by limited benefit amounts, limitations on the amount of insurance issued, by eliminating certain types of loss, and by policy provisions limiting the amount which may be collected in relation to the loss.

In medical expense coverages, for example, the amount of benefit for each type of expense is conservative and stated in the contract. Also, the policy will sometimes exclude such expenses as nurses' fees, drugs, appliances, prosthetics, and blood plasma.

In major medical expense policies such items as dental services, services in government hospitals, and services primarily for rest or diagnosis are usually not covered. Such contracts also commonly include deductible and percentage participation (coinsurance) provisions. The deductible serves mainly to avoid duplication with underlying basic policies, but the percentage participation (coinsurance) provision causes the insured to participate directly (20–25 per cent) in all loss payments above the deductible.

In disability income contracts the main reliance is on limiting the amount of benefit in relation to earned income. Most companies will not issue coverage for more than a portion of the applicant's income. This portion may be a straight percentage of the income or a percentage plus or minus a stated amount. It was not uncommon in the past to insure as much as 75 or 80 per cent of the insured's earned income but with disability benefits offered by the Federal and some state governments and the effect of taxes on take home pay, this percentage has rapidly decreased.

Some companies will also test the need and incentive to return to work by scrutinizing the applicant's unearned income and gross worth. This can be very important when application is made for sizeable amounts of disability insurance.

For applicants with higher incomes and coverages involving long-benefit durations, noncancellable or guaranteed renewable features, and life insurance disability income riders, even stricter standards are applied. In noncancellable policies the "average earnings clause" is sometimes used, particularly where the benefit duration is long. Since many companies do not use the clause, and since it takes no account of take home pay, it is of limited value. Prorating provisions are rarely found in medical expense policies, and there is no protection against duplication of benefits in the usual policy. Rising health insurance claims and the advent of disability coverage under Social Security have directed attention to the underwriting problems in these areas, and safeguards against such situations may well be developed in the future.

SOURCES OF INFORMATION CONCERNING HEALTH RISKS

The sources which a company may utilize in obtaining information concerning the factors affecting health risks, as in the case of life insurance risks, include: (1) the application, (2) the agent, (3) the medical examiner, (4) attending physicians, (5) the inspection report, and (6) intercompany data.

The Application

The health insurance application consists of the applicant's statement of certain information about himself and members of his family if a family policy is applied for and a description of the policy for which application is being made. It is usually quite detailed and complete for noncancellable or guaranteed renewable insurance, and progressively less so for optionally renewable individual, industrial, and limited policies. In its most complete form it will include the applicant's name, address, date of birth, height, weight, occupation, business, and employer. Normally, the application will also call for information as to present earnings and health insurance carried in all companies, including the one to which application is being made. At times life insurance in force must be listed, particularly if there are any disability income riders involved. Such coverages are often described completely, including any applicable waiting periods and deductibles. The applicant is required to state whether any life or health company has ever rejected or modified his application, cancelled, or refused to renew a policy, or refused payment of a claim.

A second portion of the application, at times designated Part II, as in the case of the life application, has to do with the applicant's personal health history and often that of his family. Where the application is "nonmedical," the agent fills out this part of the application also. Where there is a medical examination, these questions are asked and are filled in by the medical examiner. In either event, and as with the life application, the entire application is normally made a part of the contract. This is made clear to the applicant by requiring him to sign a statement that the answers recorded are complete and true to the best of his knowledge and belief and that he understands that they are material to the issuance of the contract.

The health information is similar to that requested in the life application. The questions relate to a series of various specific diseases and medical and surgical procedures. In addition, there are the usual general questions such as whether he has had, within the past five or perhaps ten years, any medical or surgical advice or treatment or any departure from good health. Specific details of such advice or treatment are requested. Where questions as to family health history are included, the information requested is similar to that provided in the life application.

Other Sources

As in the case of life insurance, most companies include on the back of the application blank certain questions which the agent must answer. In the case of some health applications, the names and addresses of two or three intimate friends may be called for in addition to the usual information. This can be useful as underwriting information, but also can be a source of prospects for the agent.

The *medical examination* is the best source of information about the current health of the health insurance applicant but also is quite expensive.

In health insurance it is used regularly in applications for long-term non-cancellable income policies and life insurance disability income riders and sometimes for major medical coverage at the older ages. In most other types of health insurance it is used in doubtful cases. In the case of limited policies it is virtually never used. The examination itself is quite similar for both life and health cases and includes pulse and blood pressure readings, chest and abdomen measurements, height and weight, condition of heart, lungs, nervous system, and frequently, urinalysis. In the case of large health policies more detailed examinations involving x-ray and electrocardiograms may be used. In general, the frequency of use of the medical examination and the detail involved is not as great for health insurance applications as for life cases.

The *attending physician's report* is used, as in life applications, where the individual application and/or the medical examiner's report reveals conditions or situations, past or present, about which more information is desired. However, requests for such reports are more common in health insurance than in life insurance, since relatively minor conditions can have a decided effect upon morbidity.

Health insurance companies obtain *inspection reports* for most persons who apply for individual health insurance. The inspection report is an important tool in underwriting many types of health coverages, especially disability income. It is most useful in verifying the occupation, earnings, and general financial record of the applicant. It is also helpful in determining the applicant's character, habits, and past and present physical impairments.

Intercompany data are utilized in all cases where the application reveals that the health applicant has been declined or rated, ridered or nonrenewed or if a history of impaired health is discovered from other sources. In general, the information obtained will relate to physical defects discovered but will not indicate the action of the other company. This may be obtained from the other company directly or from intercompany agencies, such as the Medical Information Bureau (MIB) or the inspection companies.

TREATMENT OF SUBSTANDARD HEALTH INSURANCE RISKS

As in the case of life insurance, the health insurance company can either reject an application, accept it at standard rates on a regular policy form, on a restricted policy form, or accept it on a regular policy form with an extra premium. In recent years there have been significant advances in underwriting substandard health insurance, and only a very small proportion of such risks are ineligible for insurance on some basis. Techniques for handling substandard risks include (1) waivers, (2) extra premiums, and (3) limitations on the type of policy which will be issued.

Waivers

In contrast to life insurance, *waivers* are a common method of handling physical impairments in health insurance. A waiver or impairment rider is an endorsement or rider attached to a policy which excludes from coverage any loss arising from a named disease or physical impairment. With such losses excluded and other aspects of the case normal, full coverage can be issued for other types of losses at standard rates. The waiver is normally broader than the condition which leads to its use. For example, an applicant with a history of kidney stones might be offered a policy excluding all diseases of the kidneys or genito–urinary tract. Such an approach is considered essential because a kidney stone condition might aggravate another related disease, and it also avoids possible problems in the event a claim based on a slightly different manifestation of the same condition is filed. On the other hand, a broad exclusion rider seriously impairs the value of the coverage. Despite the elimination of such possible sources of loss, no reduction in premium is granted for a ridered policy. The existence of the impairment can often produce disability even from unrelated ailments. Conditions which commonly require waivers include back injuries, appendicitis, hernias, and optionally elective surgical procedures.

Extra Premiums

A number of companies including some of the largest writers are now offering coverage to impaired risks at an extra premium. There are several variations in approach. Some companies will offer coverage only on selected impairments or selected plans. Others will offer on all bases. Some will reduce benefits and/or increase the elimination period for certain impairments and/or charge an extra premium in addition.

As might be expected, there are a multitude of problems in obtaining morbidity statistics which accurately reflect the increased risk. Yet the prospect of giving the widest coverage possible for pre-existing conditions which could cause disability or hospitalization to the greatest number of people has encouraged many companies to change their underwriting practices and grant more complete coverage for an extra premium. Many impairments which could not be satisfactorily waivered in the past because they were either too broad in scope, e.g., psychoneurosis, or had too many systemic complications, e.g., many heart conditions, diabetes, etc., can now be covered for a price. The increasing use of the extra premium approach does not mean that the use of waivers will soon fade away. Rather it means that in future years waivers will likely be resorted to less frequently. As of now there are still problems in granting unrestricted coverage in all instances, but it is a fast changing area of underwriting and perhaps before long the obstacles will be surmounted.

Modification of Type of Coverage

The third major method of handling substandard health insurance risks is to modify the type of policy. In the case of borderline applications, health insurance underwriters frequently will settle the problem by offering a different and more limited form of coverage. This limitation may be a lower amount, a shorter benefit period, or a longer waiting period. The latter device is particularly useful for cases where there is a history of minor chronic ailments.

Renewal Underwriting

Renewal underwriting is concerned with the health history of the insured, and also changes in occupation, income, residence, or habits, all of which may have made him an undesirable risk. With optionally renewable policies the company has an opportunity to re-evaluate its insureds periodically. Some companies do not avail themselves of their right to re-underwrite optionally renewable policies unless or until the loss ratio reaches a point where action must be taken. Cancellation and re-underwriting may seem unfair because the insured often does not understand all the terms of the contract or, if he understands them, he might not appreciate their full importance. This is one reason so many companies, especially life insurance companies, are now charging more and guaranteeing renewal of their policies to a specified age rather than emphasizing one-year term plans.

Reinsurance

Some of the health insurance coverages involve very substantial liability. As in the case of life insurance, reinsurance is utilized to avoid disruptive fluctuations in experience and company operating results. Reinsurance is also used for experimental coverages or for the writing of unusual lines where the spread of risk is not expected to be adequate.

There are many different bases of retention and oftentimes a combination of bases is used, depending upon the needs of the company. The reinsurance may be applied to all policies or to special policies or may apply to a particular benefit in a policy. With *quota share* reinsurance, the ceding company and the reinsurer share in a predetermined percentage of each individual risk. *Excess of risk or surplus share* means that the ceding company is retaining a fixed predetermined amount on each individual, ceding the excess over that amount to the reinsurer. With *extended elimination* or *extended wait*, the reinsurer assumes a large predetermined percentage of future disability claim payments on an individual after his claim has persisted for a predetermined period of time, e.g., two years or five years. A similar approach can be used on major medical which is referred to as *extended deductible*. With this basis the reinsurer assumes a large percentage of future claim payments on an individual, when a given claim exceeds a predetermined amount.

Catastrophe reinsurance reimburses a company up to a fixed dollar amount, in excess of a predetermined dollar amount, for multiple losses incurred as a result of an accident or occurrence. Usually this applies to accidents where two or more people are killed. With *loss ratio reinsurance* sometimes referred to as *excess of loss,* the reinsurer pays aggregate claims which exceed a predetermined percentage of the premium income over a given period of time. While this is an attractive basis of reinsurance to the ceding company, the disadvantage and problems from the reinsurance company standpoint make this a basis rarely offered by reinsurers.

As in the case of life reinsurance, health reinsurance may be on an automatic or facultative basis.

BIBLIOGRAPHY

Selection, Classification, and Treatment of Life and Health Insurance Risks

Bartleson, Edwin L., *et al. Health Insurance,* 2nd ed. (Chicago: The Society of Actuaries, 1968), Chapter 4.

Dickerson, O. D. *Health Insurance,* 3rd ed. (Homewood, Ill.: Richard D. Irwin, Inc., 1968), Chapter 17.

Dingman, Harry W. *Risk Appraisal* (Cincinnati: The National Underwriter Company, 1954).

Faulkner, E. J. *Health Insurance* (New York: McGraw-Hill Book Company, Inc., 1960), Chapter 10.

McGill, Dan M. *Life Insurance,* rev. ed. (Homewood, Ill.: Richard D. Irwin, Inc., 1967), Chapters XVIII–XXI.

Shepherd, Pearce, and Webster, Andrew C. *Selection of Risks* (Chicago: The Society of Actuaries, 1957).

Wickman, J. M. *Evaluating the Health Insurance Risk* (Cincinnati: The National Underwriter Company, 1965).

VIII Special Forms of Life and Health Insurance

Group Insurance | 34

GROUP INSURANCE IS a plan of insurance which provides coverage to a number of persons under one contract. Originating in the early years of this century to provide life insurance benefits on a yearly renewable term basis, the group approach has been applied to an increasing variety and number of groups and is now utilized to underwrite permanent life insurance, health insurance, and annuity benefits, as well as term life insurance. It is the youngest but fastest growing branch of the life insurance business. As of the end of 1970, there were approximately 316,000 plans of group life insurance in operation covering over 97 million persons and providing over $545.1 billion of protection.[1] These figures do not reflect the $87.9 billion of credit life insurance in force, of which $70.3 billion on 74.2 million individuals is group insurance. These figures also do not reflect the tremendous developments of the other group areas, group health insurance and group annuities. Taken in the aggregate, the group business has become a major and growing segment of life insurance company operations.

DISTINGUISHING CHARACTERISTICS [2]

In contrasting group insurance with other forms of insurance underwritten by a life insurance company, a number of unique features are evi-

[1] For an excellent and comprehensive study of group life insurance see Davis W. Gregg, *Group Life Insurance*, 3rd ed. (Homewood: Richard D. Irwin, Inc., 1962). This study was the basic source of material in the preparation of this chapter.

[2] Unless noted to the contrary, all statistical aggregates used in this chapter are taken from the *Life Insurance Fact Book 1971*.

dent: (1) the substitution of group selection for individual selection; (2) the use of a master contract; (3) low administrative cost; (4) flexibility in contract design; and (5) the use of experience rating.

Group Selection

Probably the most significant distinguishing characteristic of group insurance is the substitution of group selection for individual selection. Group insurance is usually issued without medical examination or other evidence of insurability. Of course, ordinary life and industrial life insurance may be written without medical examination, but in the case of nonmedical life and industrial life insurance, evidence of individual insurability usually must be furnished. In both cases, lives which are below standard are insured on a "substandard" basis or rejected entirely. In group insurance no individual evidence of insurability is usually required, and all lives are covered if the group risk is underwritten.[3]

Selection methods, medical and otherwise, used in connection with individual policies, are necessary to assure that the group of individuals insured will afford an "average rate of mortality" (or disability), that is, an actual rate of mortality near that expected from a group if individuals were taken at random from the same statistical universe. But for these safeguards, individuals in poor health would have the opportunity to select against the insurer and "profit" by the insurance.

Group selection, on the other hand, is normally not concerned with the health, morals, or habits of any particular individual; instead group selection is aimed at obtaining a group of individual lives or, what is even more important, an aggregation of such groups of lives, which will yield a certain predictable rate of mortality or morbidity. If a sufficient number of groups of lives is obtained, and if these groups are reasonably homogeneous in nature, then the mortality or morbidity rate is predictable. The point is that the group becomes the unit of selection, and insurance principles may be applied to it just as in the case of the individual. To assure that the groups obtained will be reasonably homogeneous, the selection process in group insurance is aimed at avoiding adverse selection by entire groups or a large proportion of the individuals within a given group.

---

[3] In recent years there has been a trend toward large amounts of group life coverage on individual lives—a violation of the basic concept of group selection—with a consequent reintroduction of evidence of insurability as in the case of ordinary insurance. This is a significant development. See pp. 566–567.

In underwriting group insurance, then, certain essential features must be present which are either inherent in the nature of the group itself or may be applied in a positive way to avoid serious adverse selection.

Insurance Incidental to Group.   *The insurance must be incidental to the group,* that is, the members of the group must have come together for some other purpose than to obtain insurance. For example, group insurance furnished the employees of a given employer would be only a secondary or unessential feature motivating the formation and existence of the group.

Flow of Persons Through Group.   There should be a *steady flow of persons through the group;* that is, there must be an influx of new young lives into the group and a flow out of the group of the aged and impaired lives. In the case of groups of actively working employees, it may be assumed that they are in average health. In fact, many employers impose pre-employment physical examinations which provide another screening device. In the case of nonworking groups, these latter inherent features would not be present.

Automatic Determination of Benefits.   In addition to the factors inherent in the nature of the group, insurance companies apply further positive safeguards to reduce adverse selection. Thus, group insurance underwriting requirements insist on an *automatic basis for determining the amount of benefits* on individual lives beyond the control of the employer or employees. If the amount of benefits taken were optional, obviously it would be possible to select against the insurer, since those in poor health would tend to insure heavily and the healthy ones would tend to elect minimum coverage.

Minimum Participation by the Group.   Another underwriting control is bound up in the requirement that *substantially all eligible persons in a given group be covered by insurance.* In contributory plans, at least 75 per cent of the eligible employees must join the plan if coverage is to be effective. In the case of noncontributory plans 100 per cent participation is required.[4] By covering a large proportion of all of a given

---

[4] In those cases where employees refuse the insurance for religious or other such legitimate reasons, which do not involve any element of "selection," this rule is relaxed.

group, the insurance company gains a positive safeguard against an undue proportion of substandard lives.

Third-Party Sharing of Cost.   A portion of the cost of a group plan should be borne by the employer or some third party other than the members of the plan. This *third-party sharing of the cost* tends to improve participation by eligible employees by making the plan more attractive to the individual. It also permits a stable rate of contribution from the employees, with fluctuations in cost being absorbed in the contribution of the employer, who in turn has an incentive to make the plan operate along sound lines. Where the employees pay part of the cost, the plan is said to be contributory.

Efficient Administrative Organization.   There must be a *single administrative organization* able and willing to act on behalf of the insured group. In the usual case this is the employer. In the case of a contributory plan there must be a reasonably simple method, such as payroll deduction, by which the master policyholder can collect premiums. An automatic method is essential from both an administrative and an underwriting standpoint.

There are, of course, a number of miscellaneous controls typically used in group insurance plans which are of underwriting significance, but the above discussion will permit an appreciation of the theory of group selection.

Master Contract

A second unique characteristic of group insurance is the use of a master contract with certificates in lieu of individual policies. This is, of course, one of the sources of economy under the group approach. The master contract is a detailed document carefully setting forth the contractual relationship between the group policyholder and the insurance company. The insured persons under the contract, usually employees and their beneficiaries, are not actually parties to the contract, although they may enforce their rights as third-party beneficiaries. The four-party relationship (employer, insurer, employee, and beneficiaries) found in a group insurance plan is unique, and it serves to create a number of interesting and unusual problems common only to group insurance.

Low Cost

A third feature of group insurance is that it is essentially low-cost whole-sale protection. The very nature of the group approach *permits* the use of mass distribution and mass administration methods which afford group insurance important economies of wholesale operation not available in individual insurance. It should be noted, however, that such economies are significant only in larger cases. In the case of some smaller group cases administrative unit expenses could conceivably be higher than in individual insurance.

Probably the most significant savings in the cost of marketing group life insurance lies in the fact that group commissions absorb a much smaller proportion of net income than for individual contracts. Because the marketing system relieves the agent (or broker) of many of the duties, responsibilities, and expenses normally connected with selling and servicing individual insurance and also because of the large premiums involved in many group insurance cases, a scale of commissions is paid which is considerably lower than for individual contracts. In addition to being lower, the commission rates are usually graded by the size of the premium developed by the case.

The nature of the administrative procedures permits simplified accounting techniques. The mechanics of premium collection are less involved, and dividend procedures are much simplified, since there is only one party to deal with—the master policyholder. Of course, the issuance of a large number of individual contracts is avoided, and due to the nature of group selection, the cost of medical examinations and inspection reports is minimized. Finally, administrative procedures are also simplified because a large proportion of group coverage is on a term basis as opposed to a permanent level-premium form, which requires special records for reserve and non-forfeiture value purposes.

Flexibility

In contrast to the individual contract which must be taken essentially as written, the larger policyholder may have a voice in the design and preparation of the group insurance contract. True, the contracts follow a pattern and include certain standard provisions, but there is considerably more flexibility here than in individual contracts. The group insurance program usually is an integral part of an employee welfare program, and in most cases the contract can be molded to meet the objectives of the policyholder as long as the requests do not entail complicated administrative procedures, open the way to possible serious adverse selection, or violate legal requirements.

Experience Rating

Another special feature of group insurance lies in the fact that premiums are subject to experience rating. The experience of the individual group may have an important bearing on dividends or premium rate adjustments. The larger the group, and hence the more reliable the experience of the individual group, the greater the weight attached to its own experience in any single year. The possibility that premiums may be increased or reduced by dividends or premium rate adjustments because of an employer's own experience gives him a vested interest in maintaining a favorable loss and expense record. It is most important to keep this factor in mind in understanding group insurance practices.

Advantages and Limitations of Group Mechanism

Advantages. The group insurance mechanism has proved to be a remarkably effective solution to the need for employee welfare benefits for a number of reasons. The utilization of mass distribution techniques has extended protection to large numbers of persons with little or no life or health insurance. The increasing complexity of our industrial economy has brought increasingly large numbers of persons together, and the group mechanism has enabled the life insurance industry to reach vast numbers of individuals within a relatively short period and at a very low cost. Group insurance has also extended protection to a large number of uninsurable people who cannot qualify for individual insurance because of health or hazardous occupation.

Another factor of significance and one of the more cogent motivations for the rapid development of group insurance in recent years has been the threat of Federal encroachment in this area. The Federal Old-Age, Survivors' and Disability Insurance program has expanded rapidly in this country, but many competent observers believe that had not group insurance provided substantial sums of life insurance, health insurance, and old age protection, the social insurance plan would have developed much more rapidly. Title XVIII of the Social Security Amendments of 1965 established Medicare. Although Medicare benefits became effective on July 1, 1966 (except for extended care services after hospitalization, which began on January 1, 1967), there are pressures to liberalize and extend the benefits further. These efforts undoubtedly will be successful, and the Medicare program will be broadened over the years.

Limitations. From the viewpoint of the employee, group insurance has one great limitation—the temporary nature of the coverage. An employee loses his insurance protection in the event the group plan is terminated, in the event of termination of employment, and also, at retirement, group life protection ceases in some cases. Most employees shift jobs at one time or another, and many fail to take advantage of their privilege to convert their group coverage. Naturally, this is no problem if they attain similar coverage in a new group.

Group life protection is continued after retirement in an increasingly large proportion of cases today. Where such protection is not available, however, the temporary nature of the coverage is a serious limitation. It should be noted that group health insurance, e.g., major medical expense, often may be continued after age 65 as a supplement to Medicare.

Another problem of significance involves individuals, especially supervisory and top management employees, who may be lulled into complacency concerning their life insurance programs by having large amounts of group life insurance during their working years. Many of these persons fail to recognize the need for or are unwilling to face the cost of permanent life insurance. Perhaps of even greater significance is the fact that the flexibility of the group approach is limited to the design of the master policy and does not extend to the individual covered employees. Further, it fails to provide any analysis of the financial problems of the individual, a service normally furnished by the individual underwriter. It should be noted, however, that many life underwriters discuss group insurance coverage with individuals as a foundation for discussing the need for additional amounts of individual life insurance.

Revenue Act of 1964

Under the Revenue Act of 1964 the employer's contribution for group term life insurance is normally not considered income to the employee for Federal income tax purposes, except where an employee is covered for more than $50,000. If an applicable state limit law provides a lower statutory maximum, that limit applies for Federal tax purposes.

An employee must include in his gross income the cost (determined from tables prescribed by the Internal Revenue Service) of employee group life in excess of $50,000, or an applicable state limit law, under all policies carried by his employer(s). However, the employee may deduct from this cost his own contribution, if any, towards his entire amount of group life.

If insurance on the lives of dependents exceeds $2,000, the employer's contribution is also considered taxable income to the employee.

FORMS OF GROUP INSURANCE

Today the group mechanism is applied in three broad areas to provide: (1) death benefits, (2) disability benefits, and (3) old age benefits. The remainder of this chapter gives considerable attention to the application of the group mechanism to provide life insurance benefits. Health insurance and retirement benefits are considered in separate chapters, and consequently less attention is directed here to group health insurance and group annuities.

GROUP LIFE INSURANCE

Legal Definition of Group Life Insurance

In 1917, the National Association of Insurance Commissioners (NAIC) promulgated a standard definition of group life insurance which was adopted, with varying modifications, by most states. Individual states, of course, are free to accept, reject, or modify recommendations of the NAIC. This original standard definition was revised in 1946, and from time to time since then under a "model law" proposed by the Association. The great majority of the states now have group legislation conforming substantially with the current model law, but a few of the state laws still are modeled after the 1917 definition. It is interesting to note, however, that a few states do not have any group insurance laws.

The original standard definition was concise and simple. It presents a condensed summary which includes the basic features of group life insurance and will serve as background for the following discussion of group life insurance. It reads as follows:

Group life insurance is hereby declared to be that form of life insurance covering not less than fifty employees with or without medical examination, written under a policy issued to the employer, the premium on which is to be paid by the employer or by the employer and employees jointly and insuring only all of his employees, or all of any class or classes thereof determined by conditions pertaining to the employment, for amounts of insurance based upon some plan which will preclude individual selection, for the benefit of persons other than the employer; provided, however, that when the premium is to be paid by the employer and employee jointly and the benefits of the policy are offered to all eligible employees, not less than seventy-five per centum of such employees may be so insured.

Coverage

Eligible Groups.   The definition, previously quoted, restricted group coverage to employees of a common employer. As the business developed, it became desirable to liberalize the standard definition to permit application to certain groups of persons who were not employees of a common employer. For example, the revised definition permits, in addition to individual employer groups, multi-employer groups, labor union groups, and creditor–debtor groups. Individual states provide for a great variety of groups not provided for under the NAIC model definition. A sizeable number of states also will permit limited group life coverage for the spouse and children of the employees insured under the group contract.[5]

[5] See Gregg, *op. cit.,* pp. 137–139. A significant but unique group is covered by a Federal Employees' Group Life Plan. See Gregg, pp. 139–143. Servicemen's Group Life Insurance (SEGLI), the largest single group life case ever written, went into effect September 29, 1965. At the end of 1970, it covered members of the uniformed services on active duty, or within 120 days of separation, for a total of $17.1 billion.

From the standpoint of number of group contracts, number of persons insured, and amount of life insurance in force, the individual employer group is by far the most important type of eligible group. The remainder of this chapter is directed toward this type of group.

Minimum Size and Proportion.   As was pointed out earlier, it is highly important that the group under consideration meet certain fundamental conditions regarding size and composition. The original requirement that at least fifty lives be insured has been reduced in later standard definitions to ten or fewer. In addition, a minimum proportion of the eligible employees must be insured under the group contract. Requirements of this nature are necessary in order to assure the maintenance of an average age with a view to preventing a rise in total premiums from year to year and also to protect the insurance company against the contingency of the group's becoming substandard through adverse selection. Also, the larger the group the less the expense per person insured. It is for these reasons that the various state statutes prescribe a minimum number of employees; and that all employees or all of any class thereof, determined by the conditions of employment, must consent to be insured; or where the employees contribute a portion of the premium, at least 75 per cent of the employees must be included under the plan. If the entire group of eligible employees is insured by the employer under a master policy without regard to the individual wishes of the employees with respect to insurance, or if at least 75 per cent of the eligible group comes under the plan, the danger of adverse selection will be minimized. A comparatively low and uniform average age will also be reasonably assured, with the result that the premium will also remain fairly low and uniform. On the other hand, if employees are permitted to accept or reject the insurance at will, this may lead to an undue inclusion of impaired risks and an undue refusal of acceptance on the part of the healthy ones. For this reason the composition of the group must not overly depend upon the voluntary action of the employees.[6]

Individual Eligibility Requirements.   In general, only regular active full-time employees are eligible for group life insurance. All such employees or all such employees in certain classes determined by conditions

---

[6] As the types and size of group covered have expanded, the minimum participation requirements have become a function of size, legal requirement, and rate basis. So-called Association cases commonly insure less than 75 per cent of the eligible groups, reflecting a rate basis somewhat higher than normally used on employer groups. Similarly, in the 10–25 life range many companies require a participation of 85 per cent.

pertaining to their employment (for example, "all salaried employees" or "all hourly-paid employees") must be included in the group as eligibles.

Another individual eligibility requirement for coverage is that an employee must be actively at work and must work a normal number of hours per week at his job, usually thirty, on the date he becomes eligible for his coverage. The requirement, of course, assures a reasonable minimum of health and physical well-being and protects the insurer against serious adverse selection.

A waiting or probationary period is usually applied to new employees (usually one to six months) before they become eligible for insurance. The probationary period minimizes the record keeping and administrative expenses involved in setting up records for employees who remain with the employer for a very short period.

After the completion of the probationary period, the employee is given a period of time, known as the eligibility period, during which he is entitled to apply for insurance without submitting evidence of insurability. This period is limited, usually to thirty-one days, in order to minimize selection against the company by the employee. For the same reason, it is customary to require evidence of insurability from employees who have dropped their coverage and desire to rejoin the plan or who did not enroll during the eligibility period. In the event the plan is written on a noncontributory basis these rules do not apply, since all employees (or all employees within the designated classes) are automatically covered.

Duration of Coverage. Once the insurance becomes effective for a particular employee, the protection continues as long as he remains in the service of the employer. The master contract usually gives the employer the right to continue premium payments for employees temporarily off the job, provided he does so on a basis which precludes individual selection. Upon permanent termination of service, the employee's coverage continues for thirty-one days beyond the date of termination. During this extension of coverage, the employee has an opportunity to replace the expiring protection with individual insurance, to obtain employment with another firm with group insurance, or to convert the expiring term insurance to a permanent form of insurance.

The conversion privilege and the continuance of coverage under those plans providing disability benefits is discussed in the following section on benefits. At this point, however, it might be well to discuss the problem of *continuing coverage on retired lives.*

An increasing proportion of plans continue after retirement at least enough insurance to take care of the employee's last illness and funeral expenses. In the past, many plans continued full benefits on retired lives with no special provision for pre-funding the rapidly rising costs as the number of retired employees covered increased. Once the employee has reached age 65, every $1,000 of insurance ultimately costs $1,000 (plus the cost of administration), and it matures generally within a period of fifteen years, whereas $1,000 of insurance on an active employee is in force over a period of thirty to forty years, and the accumulative gross premium is $200 to $300 and after experience credits may be no more than $100 to $150. When these facts are combined with rapidly rising pay levels which cause more employees to reach retirement age with larger and larger amounts of insurance, the effect on cost can be and has been catastrophic for some employers who didn't anticipate the increased cost in some appropriate manner.

There are three general approaches within the framework of group insurance which can be used appropriately to provide life insurance protection to retired employees. The simplest is to *continue a portion* of the group term insurance for the retired employee, with the employer paying the entire premium on behalf of the employee. Unless the original amount of coverage was very modest, the percentage to be continued generally varies from a minimum of 25 per cent to a maximum of 50 per cent.

A second approach that can be used to provide protection to retired employees is for the employer to *purchase a paid-up individual policy* in the appropriate amount for each employee. The advantages of this approach are the assurance to the employee and the ease of administration since there is no need for the employer to maintain contact with retired employees. On the other hand, the taxability of employer contributions (premium payments) to the employee in the year in which they are made and possible fluctuations in annual cost make this approach less desirable.

The third approach involves some form of permanent insurance financed throughout the active working period of the covered employee. The two basic arrangements for *group permanent insurance* were developed specifically to meet the problem of retired life coverage and are generally considered to represent the ideal approach to the problem. They are discussed further in a later section.

Benefits

In order to preclude individual selection, the employees to be covered under a group life insurance plan are broken down into various categories, and all employees placed in a particular category receive the same amount of insurance. The four bases for classification used are: (1) flat amount, (2) amount of compensation, (3) type of position, and (4) length of service.

Flat Amount.   The use of a flat amount benefit plan places all employees in one category. It has the advantage of simplicity, but it also has the important disadvantage of placing all employees on an equal level. If group insurance is to serve as a means of rewarding workers in the interest of stabilized labor, and this is one of the strong arguments, it seems neither wise nor fair that low-paid or new employees should obtain the same benefits as those that are skilled or have served the employer for years. This type of benefit has been principally used for union welfare funds. It should be noted, however, that where there is a flat amount of insurance per person, the possibility of adverse selection is greatly minimized and thus costs are stabilized.

Amount of Compensation.   The most widely used plan or schedule is that which bases the amount of insurance on an employee's earnings. A simplified scale utilizing earnings classes might be as follows:

ANNUAL EARNINGS	INSURANCE
Less than $5,000	$ 5,000
$5,000 or more, but less than $10,000	10,000
$10,000 and over	15,000

The plan could be based on any common earnings unit. This plan has the advantage, in a contributory plan, of relating cost to ability to pay and also recognizes, to some extent, the increase in human life value represented by increases in compensation. The schedule established quite frequently attempts to replace lost earnings for one or one-half years. More recently there has been a tendency to adopt a benefit formula of two times earnings or higher. It should be pointed out that the survivorship values payable under the Social Security Act adopted in 1967 are worth $25,000 to $40,000, depending on the age and number of the survivors. This is so significant as to justify coordination with private benefits. This is, of course, possible where benefits are based on compensation.

Position.   When the salary or wage is difficult to determine, as in the case of piece workers or salesmen, the insurance may be set according to the position held by the employee. Thus, officers, superintendents, and managers may receive $10,000 each; foremen and salesmen $7,500 each; and all other employees $5,000 each. This plan of determining the amount of insurance is used quite frequently, and also tends to reflect ability to pay and need.

Service.   Under the so-called service plan the amount of protection is increased in accordance with the length of time that the employee has been in the employer's service. Credit usually is given for the period of service prior to the time that the group policy is effected. If the plan is contributory, the service plan is not recommended because of the increasing amounts which the employee has to contribute for his insurance. Also, the plan is defective in that it makes no distinction between employees with high wages and those with low wages. This defect may be removed, however, by insuring different classes of employees for different amounts. For example, the lowest paid class may be given $500 insurance for the first year of service following the probationary period of six months and $100 additional insurance for each year of service thereafter, until a total of $2,500 is reached. Higher paid classes may be given larger amounts, and if it is desired, the highest paid class, such as officers and superintendents, may be given insurance under a combination of the salary and service plans.

Service plans have declined in popularity in recent years because of cost implications and the fact that the amounts of insurance grow inversely in relation to the employee's needs. As the plan provides increasing amounts of insurance based upon length of service, it tends to result in progressively higher premium costs.

Survivor Benefits.   Survivor benefits are a form of monthly income which become payable upon the death of an employee who may be covered under either a pension plan or a group life insurance plan. Several major carriers are marketing survivor-benefits group life insurance products in an effort to meet better the income needs of the surviving dependents of a deceased employee. There are three characteristics which distinguish true survivor benefits from other types of group life insurance: (1) the proceeds are payable only in the form of monthly income; (2) the covered employee does not name his beneficiary, as benefits are payable only to specified beneficiaries; and (3) benefits are usually payable only so long as there is a living survivor beneficiary.

The survivor benefit concept is not new. The first life insurance sold in the United States was actually a form of survivor benefits because proceeds were payable as periodic income. Modern pension plans frequently include a form of survivor benefits commonly referred to as "widow's benefits." Social Security includes survivor benefits which are payable to widows and to dependent children of qualified wage earners. Outside of a small lump-sum death benefit, this is the only form in which death benefits are payable.

In 1964 the survivor benefits concept received renewed interest when the United Auto Workers bargained with their employers for survivor benefits. Since 1964, the survivor benefit trend has evolved rapidly. Other unions have adopted UAW-type benefits. However, because UAW benefits are designed as a Social Security supplement to meet the needs of lower paid hourly workers within a relatively narrow earnings range, they are limited both in the amount of monthly benefit payable and the duration for which it is paid. Survivor benefits of the UAW type are not adequate for most salaried groups and, therefore, employers are turning to other kinds of survivor benefits for their nonhourly employees.

This interest has been stimulated by the following considerations. Most group life insurance plans today provide amounts which are a uniform multiple of annual earnings of employees without regard to age or family status. This means that generally, the older the employee, the more group life insurance he has, since earnings tend to steadily rise over his working career. However, it is also true that older employees normally have a smaller life insurance need when their children are grown, mortgages paid, and other forms of savings have been accumulated. On the other hand, the young employee with small children and a large mortgage has a substantial need, but his group life insurance benefit is at the bottom of the scale because his earnings are lowest in the early years of his employment. This paradoxical relationship of amounts of coverage and employee needs is the underlying factor in the growing survivor benefit trend.

As marketed by one major carrier, the survivor benefits product was designed around the aforesaid three characteristics but other features were added which are specifically aimed at meeting the needs of employees with the greatest family responsibilities:

(1) Although single employees are covered by the underlying regular group life insurance, they are not eligible for survivor benefits.

(2) The only permissible beneficiaries are an employee's spouse and/or children.

(3) Benefits are normally expressed as a percentage of the employee's pre-death earnings and are payable in two forms: a spouse benefit and a children benefit. The most common spouse benefit percentage is between 20 and 40 per cent of an employee's pre-death earnings, and the children benefit ranges between 5 and 15 per cent. The children benefit percentage can be significantly lower in most cases because of the presence of Social Security Survivor Benefits which are payable when there are children in the surviving family unit.

(4) The spouse benefit is normally payable until the spouse reaches age 62 or 65. The children benefit is payable until the youngest unmarried child reaches age 19 or alternatively age 23, if in school.

(5) A key feature is that benefits are payable only so long as there is a demonstrated need. If the spouse remarries or dies before the end of her benefit period, her benefit ceases. When the youngest unmarried child reaches the limiting age for children, the children benefit ceases. Thus, the situation of large amounts of insurance being payable either to an estate or to persons with whom the insured had a non-dependency relationship is avoided.

Life insurance protection for the American family provides less than two years of income continuance following a wage earner's death. Its proponents think survivor benefits will play an important role in filling this gap in the amount of insurance protection, and that the product will be the accepted way of providing death benefits in group plans of the future.

Minimum and Maximum Amounts.   Regardless of the plan used, some provision is always made to keep the amounts of insurance extended to executives and others with high salaries in line with the total amount of protection extended to the whole group. Thus, insurance companies will not usually write less than $500 or $1,000 on any one insured, nor more than a certain maximum amount, determined by both the number of persons insured and the average amount of insurance per employee. Of course, the maximum amount of insurance which may be written on any group is subject to the limits prescribed by the applicable state law.[7]

Underwriting limitations on amounts are necessary in smaller groups to minimize adverse selection, and in larger groups, where the group's individual experience has a strong effect on the level of dividends, a maximum is highly desirable in order to avoid undue fluctuations in cost from year to year.[8]

Virtually any company will write as much as $40,000 on an individual life under proper underwriting circumstances, and, in some cases, as high as $100,000 and over is being provided on individual lives. Many insurance companies will permit individual amounts in excess of their normal maximums, providing evidence of insurability is submitted for the excess amounts, or other safeguards are established to protect against severe adverse selection.[9]

The willingness of some insurance companies to superimpose a schedule of life insurance benefits on an already existing plan provided by another company has led to the writing of amounts of group life insurance on a single life far beyond what one company's underwriting rules will permit. The question of how much group life insurance should be provided on a single life has been a point of controversy in the life insurance field.[10]

---

[7] As of the end of 1971, twenty-seven states did not have any specific regulation limiting the amount of group life insurance which could be written on an individual life. The other twenty-one states and the District of Columbia have limitations varying up to a maxium of $100,000.

[8] In many cases companies will place a maximum on the amount of coverage on a single life which will be charged to the experience of the individual case with any excess coverage being pooled among cases.

[9] Other safeguards include obtaining inspection reports on one or more individual; extra premium charged on the case; excess amounts reinsured; special reserves built up for case; and excess amount risks pooled for experience purposes.

[10] See Gregg, *op. cit.*, pp. 57–62.

Conversion Privilege. An insured employee has the privilege of converting the face amount of his group term protection to an individual policy of permanent insurance under certain conditions. Normally, the employee may convert within thirty-one days after termination of employment or cessation of membership in an eligible classification, to one of the company's regular permanent forms at standard rates for his attained age. The most significant advantage to the employee lies in the fact that no evidence of insurability is required.[11]

Coverage During Conversion Period. The death benefit provided under a group life insurance contract is continued for a short period (usually thirty-one days) after an employee withdraws from the eligible group. In the event of the employee's death during this period, a death benefit is paid under the policy.

Disability Benefits. Until about 1932, group life insurance contracts contained a so-called maturity value benefit. This benefit usually provided that an employee becoming totally and permanently disabled prior to age 60 was to be paid the face amount of his certificate, sometimes in a lump sum but more often in installments over a short period such as sixty months. Following the very poor underwriting experience under this coverage in the years just preceding 1932, group companies began to limit disability benefits severely. For a number of years following 1932, group companies normally provided a so-called extended-death or a one-year waiver-of-premium benefit for all new groups. The extended-death benefit provides for the payment of the full face amount upon death occurring within one year after termination of employment and prior to age 65, if the employee was totally disabled at the time of termination and continued disabled until death.

In 1935, many insurance companies liberalized their disability provisions and began to provide coverage under the so-called lifetime waiver-of-premium benefit. This clause, which is the most common today in new contracts, in effect, eliminates the one-year restriction and lowers the disability insurance age limit to 60. As long as the insured proves his disability periodically, this clause provides coverage indefinitely.

It should be noted that the latter clauses leave the death benefit intact

[11] A conversion privilege is also available on the termination of the master contract under slightly different conditions. See *ibid.*, pp. 69–70. In view of the importance of group insurance as a factor in the security of most employees, some liberalization of the conversion privilege would be desirable. Although adverse selection is a problem, the improved service to insured employees would appear to justify a continuing effort to liberalize the conversion privilege.

for the benefit of the originally intended beneficiary rather than being utilized as disability income. Although the favorable underwriting experience of recent years had led to some increase in the use of the maturity value clause, the waiver-of-premium benefit is clearly the most common form in new contracts. In fact, the introduction of group long-term disability has led to the dropping of maturity value coverage from some older contracts.

Financing

A group insurance plan may be either contributory or noncontributory.[12]

The noncontributory plan is simple, and it gives the employer full control over the plan. It provides for the insurance of all eligible employees and it thus eliminates any difficulties involved in connection with obtaining the consent of a sufficient number of employees in order to meet the 75 per cent requirement. Also, there is no problem of distributing the cost among the various employees, as in the contributory plan.

The contributory plan is less costly to the employer. Hence, with employee contributions he is likely to arrange for more adequate protection for the employees, and also to keep the insurance in force longer. It can also be argued that if the employee contributes toward his insurance, he will be more impressed with its value and will appreciate it more. On the other hand, the contributory plan has a number of disadvantages. It is more complicated in operation. Each employee must consent to contribute towards his insurance, and as stated before, at least 75 per cent of the eligible group must consent to enter the arrangement. New employees entering the business must be informed of their insurance privilege. Usually, if the plan is contributory, the employee is not entitled to the insurance until he has been with the company, say, three months, and then, if he does not give consent to the plan within a period of thirty-one days, he must provide satisfactory evidence of insurability in order to become eligible.

Plans of Insurance

Yearly Renewable Term Insurance.   The basic plan of insurance under which group life insurance is provided is yearly renewable term insurance. This insurance protection has the same characteristics as

---

12 Only in the most exceptional cases will an insurance company underwrite a plan in which the employees are to bear the entire cost—a so-called employee pay-all plan. Such a plan is illegal in most states and is avoided for underwriting reasons in those states where it is legal.

that provided through individual policies. With respect to any covered employees, the protection expires at the end of each year but is automatically renewed without evidence of insurability. The premium rate for a unit of protection increases at an increasing rate from year to year as in the case of individual coverage. Despite this, however, the employee's contribution (if the plan is contributory) remains at the same level regardless of his attained age. The level contribution by the employee is practicable because the employer absorbs the portion of the cost in excess of the employee's annual contribution. Thus, the employer's contribution for any individual employee increases year by year. On the other hand, the employer's total contribution to the plan may well remain stable or even decline, depending upon the benefit formula, the age and sex composition of the group, and the experience of the plan.

The simplest way to comprehend the relative roles of the employer and employees in financing a term plan is through the calculation of the average annual premium for the plan.

The calculation of the average annual premium for $1,000 for the first year of group term insurance on a hypothetical employee group is presented in Table 34–1. Each employee is assumed to have insurance equal to two years' salary, subject to a maximum of $20,000.

The first step in calculating the average annual premium is to determine

TABLE 34-1. Calculation of Average Annual Premium per $1,000 of Group Term Life Insurance

Attained Age	Number of Employees	Insurance per Employee	Total Amount of Insurance	Annual Premium per $1,000*	Total Premium
20	5	$ 5,000	$ 25,000	$ 2.75	$ 68.75
25	5	7,000	35,000	2.97	103.95
30	10	11,000	110,000	3.15	346.50
35	10	13,000	130,000	3.74	486.20
40	20	15,000	300,000	5.28	1,584.00
45	20	17,000	340,000	8.08	2,747.20
50	10	19,000	380,000	12.51	4,753.80
55	10	20,000	200,000	19.55	3,910.00
60	5	20,000	100,000	29.72	2,972.00
65	5	20,000	100,000	44.67	4,467.00
Total	100		$1,720,000		$21,439.40

*The 1961 Standard Group Life Insurance Premium Rates (1960 Commissioners Standard Group Mortality Table at 3 per cent loaded by Basic Loading Percentage)

Total Annual Premium	$21,439.40
Addition for "Policy Constant" (40 × $2.40)	$ 96.00
Aggregate Annual Premium	21,535.40
Advance Expense Adjustment (12 per cent)	18,951.15
Average Annual Premium per $1,000	($18,951.15 ÷ 1,720), or $11.02

the total premium payable at each age represented by the group of covered employees. The sum of these values, as shown in Table 34–1, is $21,-439.40. To this sum must be added a so-called policy constant, which is $2.40 per year per $1,000 but is applied only to the first $40,000 of insurance. This recognizes the minimum expenses associated with any group. The total aggregate annual premium, then, is $21,535.40 and it is only necessary to apply an advance expense adjustment factor to derive the *initial annual premium*. In this instance, the group qualifies for a 12 per cent discount and the initial annual premium is $18,951.15. The final step in deriving the average annual premium per $1,000 simply involves dividing $18,951.15 by the number of $1,000 units of insurance—namely, 1,720 —which gives $11.02. Assuming the employees' contributions are $7.20 per $1,000 the employer must bear the difference of $3.82 per $1,000 or $6,570.40. In practice these premiums and contributions would normally be converted to a monthly basis.

However, if the experience under the plan is favorable, the dividend or retroactive rate adjustment will reduce the employer's cost. Under some plans, the dividend might equal and occasionally exceed the employer's contribution. In the latter instance, the excess of the dividend is at times applied in some manner for the benefit of the employees.[13]

Group insurance premiums may be paid by the employer annually, semi-annually, quarterly, or monthly; but all adjustments in the amount of insurance during the year, arising out of new employees, terminations, and reclassifications, are made on the basis of the average-annual-premium rate (or average-monthly-premium rate), regardless of the actual ages of the employees involved. At the end of each policy year, a new average-annual premium is computed. If premiums are to be paid on a less-than-annual basis, the annual premium rates are increased to provide for the loss of interest and the additional expenses of collection.

In harmony with the experience rating philosophy followed in group insurance, yearly renewable term insurance rates are guaranteed for only one year. From a practical standpoint, companies try to avoid rate increases since they are disturbing to the policyholder and, where possible, prefer to make adjustments in cost through the experience rating process.

Where group term life plans are on a contributory basis, employee contributions normally are at a uniform rate per $1,000 regardless of age. In setting the level of contributions the important principle is to see that the cost to the employee is such that the insurance is an attractive buy in comparison with insurance available to him under individual policies.

New York and Michigan have set a maximum limit on the amount of employee contributions, such as 60 cents per month per $1,000. Limitations also arise in other states, depending upon company underwriting philosophy.

[13] This is required by law in some states.

It should be noted that much group life insurance is not written on a yearly renewable term insurance basis. Many contracts continue in force from month to month. Dividends or experience rating credits are determined on anniversary dates and there are provisions for the dates on which the company can redetermine premium rates. While technically this would not be "yearly renewable term insurance," the basic principles remain the same.

Permanent Life Insurance.   Several different types of group life plans providing permanent insurance have been devised. Group insurance plans involving permanent life insurance fall into two major classes: (1) group term and group paid-up and (2) level-premium group permanent life insurance.

The most popular form of group life plan providing permanent insurance is written on the *group term and paid-up plan*.[14] This plan is a combination of accumulating units of single-premium whole life insurance and decreasing units of group term life insurance. Group term and paid-up insurance provides the same death and disability benefits as regular employer group term plans. Each premium paid by the employer consists of the individual employee's contributions and the employer's contribution. Employee contributions are usually applied to purchase increments of paid-up single-premium whole-life insurance, the amount of which is determined by the individual employee's attained age. The employer's contribution is applied to provide an amount of decreasing term insurance, which when added to the accumulated amount of paid-up permanent life insurance purchased by the employee under the plan, equals the total amount for which he is eligible. There is no statutory limitation on the amount of employee contribution for group paid-up insurance; but it should compare favorably with the cost to the employees of an individual whole-life policy. The most common rate of contribution is $1.30 per month per $1,000 of total insurance. Table 34–2 illustrates the paid-up insurance and surrender value accumulations created by such contributions.

In general, the group term and paid-up plan follows the pattern of the regular group term plan except for adjustments necessary to account for the accumulated surrender values in the permanent insurance. Ordinarily, at retirement the portion of the insurance that is still on a term basis will be discontinued, the paid-up permanent insurance remaining in force for the balance of the employee's lifetime. The employee may then have the right to convert the difference between the amount of paid-up insurance and the face of his certificate, on the same basis as under a regular group term contract. When an employee terminates employment and withdraws from the group, prior to retirement, similar provisions apply. He may withdraw the surrender value in cash if he wishes to terminate his insurance entirely.

[14] This plan is also known by the designations, "group life with paid-up values," "group paid-up and decreasing term," and "group paid-up."

TABLE 34-2. Illustrative Paid-up Life Insurance and Surrender Value Under Group Term and Group Paid-up Plan Based on Employee Monthly Contribution of $1.30

Paid-up Life Insurance

Years in Plan	Age When Entering Plan								
	20	25	30	35	40	45	50	55	60
1	$ 50.08	$ 44.93	$ 40.25	$ 36.19	$ 32.60	$ 29.48	$ 26.83	$ 24.49	$ 22.46
2	99.06	88.92	79.56	71.60	64.58	58.34	53.20	48.52	44.62
3	147.11	131.98	118.09	106.24	95.94	86.58	79.09	72.07	66.46
4	194.06	174.10	155.84	140.09	126.67	114.35	104.52	95.16	87.98
5	239.93	215.28	192.82	173.32	156.78	141.65	129.48	117.94	109.20
10	455.21	408.10	366.13	330.10	298.43	271.13	247.42	227.14	
15	648.02	581.41	522.91	471.74	427.91	389.06	356.62		
20	821.34	738.19	664.56	601.22	545.84	498.26			
25	978.12	789.84	794.04	719.16	655.04				
30	1,119.77	1,009.32	911.98	828.36					
35	1,249.25	1,127.26	1,021.18						
40	1,367.18	1,236.46							
45	1,476.38								

Paid-up accumulations purchased by employee monthly contribution of $1.30.

TABLE 34-2. (cont'd.)

Cash Surrender Values

Years in Plan	Age When Entering Plan								
	20	25	30	35	40	45	50	55	60
1	$ 15.60	$ 15.60	$ 15.60	$ 15.60	$ 15.60	$ 15.60	$ 15.60	$ 15.60	$15.60
2	31.20	31.20	31.20	31.20	31.20	31.20	31.20	31.20	31.20
3	46.80	46.80	46.80	46.80	46.80	46.80	46.80	46.80	46.80
4	62.40	62.40	62.40	62.40	62.40	62.40	62.40	62.40	62.40
5	78.00	78.00	78.00	78.00	78.00	78.00	78.00	78.00	78.00
10	162.97	163.65	164.03	164.39	164.14	163.76	162.80	161.27	
15	259.86	260.47	260.41	259.46	258.46	256.00	253.20		
20	367.96	367.62	365.51	363.14	359.16	353.76			
25	487.10	483.91	479.60	473.21	465.08				
30	615.87	609.63	600.08	588.14					
35	754.55	741.74	725.04						
40	899.60	877.89							
45	1,048.23								

Cash value accumulations created by employee monthly contribution of $1.30.

Under *level-premium group permanent* utilizing either the whole-life, endowment, or retirement income form, level premiums are most frequently payable for life or to age 65. On termination of employment the employee will have certain cash or paid-up privileges and also may have the option of continuing the full amount of insurance in force by paying the appropriate level premium directly to the insurance company. Level-premium group permanent plans represent the complete blending of group underwriting and administration and the mechanics and techniques of individual level-premium contracts. Level-premium group permanent has had its greatest use in the funding of pension benefits, where special tax treatment is applicable, rather than for the sole purpose of providing life insurance protection. This had been due to the fact that, in general, employer contributions made for permanent life insurance are considered taxable income to the employee in the year of contribution. In contrast, employer contributions toward group term life insurance benefits had not been so taxed, prior to the enactment of the Revenue Code of 1964. Even so, present Federal Income Tax Regulations exclude contributions for generous amounts of employer provided group term life insurance from being considered as income to the employee. This tax disadvantage to level-premium group permanent has led to emphasis on group term life and group term and paid-up plans where the term insurance benefits provided are in a more favorable tax position from the viewpoint of the employee.

Terms of Policy and Certificates

Various important features of group life insurance policies have already been discussed, such as the term of the contract, renewal, the promise of the insurance company to insure new employees as they become eligible, and so forth. In connection with the term of the contract and renewal, where the policy is issued on the yearly renewable term plan, the insurance company cannot refuse to renew each year if the employer wishes to continue the contract and pays the premium. It should be remembered, however, the premium rates may be increased to such an extent that for all practical purposes the right to renew may not be of any value. In contrast, the group paid-up coverage is usually written with a five-year rate guarantee subject to annual renewal thereafter. Level-premium group permanent contracts may have an initial rate guarantee of three or five years subject to annual adjustment at the end of the guaranteed period. It is important to note that the level premiums for the latter type of plan are guaranteed permanently for the benefits purchased prior to a rate change. This is similar to the rate guarantee applicable to individual permanent life insurance contracts.

The master policy also provides that if at any time the number of employees does not equal the required number of ten, or if the plan is contributory and the required 75 per cent of employees are not under the plan, the policy may be cancelled.

Other provisions of the policy should be referred to here. The laws in most states require certain standard provisions. Thus, the employer must deliver to the employee a certificate showing the amount of insurance in the given company, the name of the beneficiary, and containing a clause permitting the employee, in the event of termination of employment for any reason, to file application within thirty-one days, without evidence of insurability, for as much insurance (under any regular permanent type of policy, and at rates for the then attained age) as he is carrying at the time of such termination. Although few employees, relatively, take advantage of this privilege to convert their insurance, it is nonetheless a valuable option to the employee in bad health.

Another required clause provides for an adjustment in premiums and insurance in case the age of an employee has been misstated. The usual provision of this kind specifies that the correct amount of insurance will be paid by the insurance company and that the employer must make an adjustment in premium payments for the period on the basis of the true age. If the age has been overstated, the employer will receive a refund; if the age has been understated, the employer will be required to pay the necessary extra amount by which past premiums have been deficient. It should be noted that this method of adjusting policies for misstated ages differs somewhat from the adjustment made when an individual life policy has been issued at an incorrect age.

Group life insurance policies also contain an incontestable clause although it is of less significance than in individual insurance. In addition, the policy usually provides for: (1) a grace period of thirty-one days in connection with premium payments; (2) a right to have the proceeds paid in installments; (3) the necessity for making claims within one year following the last premium payment for the employee in question; (4) the continued insurance, for the period provided by the contract, of employees laid off because of illness, poor business, and so forth, provided that the employer continues to pay the necessary premium; and (5) extension of the insurance to employees who are eligible but have been reported ineligible because of clerical error.

Group Credit Life Insurance

Group credit life insurance is a special form of group term insurance issued to a creditor covering the lives of his debtors in the amount of their outstanding loans. The insurance is payable to the creditor should they die before loans are repaid. Group credit life insurance has shown a prodigious growth during recent years. At the close of 1970, there was over $74.2

billion of group credit life insurance in force in the United States.[15] Except for the modifications[16] necessary to account for the fact that credit life insurance is designed for one specific objective, the contract and pattern of operation are essentially the same as other group coverages.

Relationship of Wholesale Insurance

The original limitation of group insurance to groups of at least fifty lives gave rise to a modification of the plan known as wholesale insurance, under which groups as small as ten lives were insured. The reduction in the minimum number of lives for group insurance has led to a trend reducing the minimum for wholesale insurance to five or fewer.

The general method of issuing and administering wholesale insurance is similar to that for group life insurance. Under the wholesale plan, each employee applies for and receives an individual policy from the insurance company, there being no master policy issued to the employer, as in the case of group life insurance. All insured persons, however, must be employees of a common employer and the employer must file an application and agree to pay all or a part of the premiums. The amount of insurance which each employee is to receive is not optional with the employee, but is determined according to one of the various plans used in group life insurance for this purpose. Also, the maximum amount which may be carried by any one employee is limited by underwriting rules.

In view of the reduction in the minimum number of lives which may be insured under a regular group policy, wholesale insurance is now of very much less significance than formerly. Interestingly enough it has been used by some insurance companies to provide high limits of coverage where the maximum is regulated by state law.

Relationship to Salary Savings Insurance

While the majority of wage earners in the United States are protected under some form of individual life insurance, most of those insured have on the average small amounts of coverage. One reason for this situation is that many lower income individuals usually cannot afford to buy life insurance in large amounts and hence agents have had no great incentive to solicit this type of prospect. Another reason is that ordinary forms of insurance are sold in units of $1,000 each on an annual level-premium basis.

[15] There was also over $13.7 billion in force under individual credit life policies. *Life Insurance Fact Book 1971*, p. 34.

[16] These modifications are important, however. For example, no conversion privilege is provided, minimum rates may be quoted independent of age, maximum rates are regulated, the policyholder may legally be beneficiary, and in some states there are substantially lower legal amount maximums.

Salary savings insurance, developed chiefly since 1925, is a means of selling ordinary insurance to workers under a convenient and economical arrangement. Under this plan the regular forms of individual life insurance are sold to groups of employees, either to supplement existing group or wholesale insurance, or to provide benefits where group forms of insurance cannot be placed. The distinguishing characteristics of this form of insurance are the collection of premiums on a monthly basis from the employer, who deducts the necessary amounts from the wages of the insured employees, and the necessity for individual evidence of insurability to be furnished. The most common underwriting requirements are a minimum of from ten to twenty-five employees, stability of employment, and centralized accounting. Additionally, most insurance companies would require at least six to ten applications, with two months' prepayment of premiums, on four to eight lives. Finally, many companies will require that a minimum number of these applications, for example five to seven, must be acceptable on a standard underwriting basis within a specified period of time, for example thirty-one days.[17] More than one kind of policy may be sold to the members of a group and premiums may be paid quarterly, semiannually, or annually if desired.

GROUP HEALTH INSURANCE

The basic theory of group underwriting and group administration applies to group health insurance just as it applies to group life insurance. Much of the earlier discussion of individual health insurance [18] likewise applies to group health insurance. Consequently, here, attention is directed toward the distinguishing characteristics of group health insurance and deals with the various types of coverage available only in the most general terms.

Distinguishing Characteristics

In contrast to individual health insurance policies, group coverage usually provides benefits only for nonoccupational accidents and illnesses. This is so since occupational disabilities are normally covered under the state Workmen's Compensation laws. The standard provisions for individual health insurance contracts are not applicable to group health insurance. In general, insurance company practices under group contracts are considerably more liberal than under individual contracts. There are, however, certain standard provisions required for group contracts in the laws of some states.

[17] Nonmedical insurance is not peculiar to salary savings insurance. Both salary savings and nonmedical insurance, however, have been developed largely since 1925.

[18] See Chapters 16, 17, and 18.

The insuring clause for short-term disability income benefits (up to 104 weeks) is more liberal than that found in most individual health insurance policies in that disability is defined in terms of the employee's own occupation rather than in terms of any occupation. For long-term coverage "his occupation" is used for the first one or two years and "any occupation" thereafter. Group provisions and practices, in general, can be more liberal in view of the facts that (1) the benefits usually are payable for a shorter period and are relatively smaller than those under individual policies, and (2) experience rating is utilized. The ability to adjust the rate up or down periodically gives the employer an interest in preventing claim abuse and maintaining a reasonable loss experience.

It was pointed out earlier that a significant amount of individual health insurance is written on an optionally renewable basis. The insurance company may have a right to refuse to renew the master group health insurance contract, but no individual participant may be cancelled or denied renewal except by termination of the entire group. There are, of course, other minor differences, but basically group health insurance benefits, except as indicated above, follow the pattern of individual health insurance benefits with some modification to recognize the principles of group underwriting and group administration.

Types of Coverages

Group insurance can be written to provide virtually any combination of health insurance benefits. As with individual policies, group health insurance benefits may be broadly classified as: (1) disability income, (2) medical expense, and (3) accidental death, dismemberment, and loss of sight. The ever growing list of group health insurance types (benefit arrangements) includes coverages such as the following:

> Accidental Death and Dismemberment Insurance
> Voluntary Accident Insurance
> Travel Accident Insurance
> Weekly Indemnity Insurance
> Long-Term Disability Insurance
> Hospital Indemnity Insurance
> Hospital Expense Insurance
> Surgical Expense Insurance
> Physicians' Expense Insurance
> Diagnostic Expense Insurance
> Dental Insurance
> Vision Care Insurance
> Prescription Drug Insurance
> Polio Expense Insurance
> Major Medical Expense Insurance
> Comprehensive Major Medical Expense Insurance

Range of Benefits and Arrangements of Coverage

Accidental Death and Dismemberment. Benefits payable are normally in a lump sum for the accidental loss of life or any two body members such as two arms, two legs, two hands, two feet, two eyes, a hand and a foot, etc. Installment payments may be provided as may payments equal to one-half the face amount in the event of the loss of one body member. This coverage may be underwritten in essentially three forms:

1. *Basic.* It is fairly common for the group life insurance schedule to be accompanied by an identical or a reduced schedule of AD & D benefits. For want of more descriptive terminology, this might be said to be a basic schedule.

2. *Voluntary Accident.* This coverage, which varies widely from company to company, provides accident coverage in amounts up to about $100,000 in increments of $10,000 on a purely voluntary basis. In some cases coverage equal to five times the annual salary may be offered with a maximum of $250,000. This coverage is presently offered on a 24-hour basis. Additionally, some insurance companies offer coverage for the spouse and children, as a percentage of the employee's coverage and/or as a fixed amount.

3. *Travel Accident.* Many life insurance companies have borrowed from the portfolio of the casualty insurance companies and now offer excess amounts for accidental death or dismemberment while employees are on employer business. This may be written on various bases ranging from coverage while on business travel only to 24-hour coverage while out of town on employer business.

Disability Income. There are essentially two approaches to the provision of disability income benefits which can be described as Short-Term Disability and Long-Term Disability benefits.

1. *Short-Term Disability.* This coverage is intended as income replacement for a relatively short period of time, more often payable from the first day of disability resulting from an accident and from the eighth day when resulting from sickness. (It is important to note that many combinations of waiting periods are utilized.) Income benefits for both accident and sickness usually are payable for up to thirteen, twenty-six, or fifty-two weeks, except for disabilities from pregnancy, which are more limited or excluded.

2. *Long-Term Disability.* Benefits are here provided in recognition of the continuing need of income for the duration of a long-term disability arising from either accident or sickness without regard to whether or not it is job-connected in nature. (It is important to note that the disability definition is not so severe as to require total and permanent disability.) Benefits normally are not provided until the expiration of a probationary period which

may run from seven days to six months. The duration of benefits, assuming the continuation of disability, would usually be until age 65, but again alternate approaches, such as lifetime accident, are not uncommon. (It should be noted that again the size of the group in question is a most important underwriting consideration, and when the group is significant in size, considerable latitude in underwriting is prevalent.)

Hospitalization.   As in the case of individual insurance, group hospital expense insurance normally treats separately the expense of room and board charges and the expenses for other hospital services.

With regard to the daily room and board charge, most plans are underwritten on the basis of paying the actual charges up to a specified maximum. Some plans provide a benefit which is indefinite as to amount, being equal to the hospital's actual charge but not to exceed the charge for a room in a specified classification, e.g., semiprivate. The daily room and board benefit is payable up to a maximum number of days, such as 31, 70, or 120, and occasionally 365.

The miscellaneous hospital expense benefit may be written on an unscheduled basis up to a maximum of fifteen, twenty, or more times the daily room and board rate, or it may be written on a scheduled basis with dollar limits. Occasionally, plans affording an "unlimited" miscellaneous hospital expense benefit are written. In connection with the unscheduled miscellaneous expense benefit, it is common to increase the limit (above a basic area of 100 per cent reimbursement) substantially beyond the usual fixed multiple of room and board allowance, but with a percentage participation (coinsurance) factor under which the company pays 75 per cent and the insured employee pays 25 per cent.

Maternity benefits are usually limited in one way or another. For example, many plans limit benefits for room and board and miscellaneous expense to ten times the daily room and board benefit.

By definition, group hospital expense insurance is intended to deal only with the expenses in cases requiring actual hospital confinement. In order to implement this objective some companies have a requirement that a person be confined at least 18 hours in order to qualify for benefits while others require that a room and board charge be made. This is not usually required if treatment is for emergency care due to an accident or if a surgical operation is performed.

Surgical Expense.   Surgical insurance provides reimbursement for the charges made by physicians for surgical procedures. The schedules of benefits are similar to those used in individual health insurance. The maximum benefit payable under the schedule may vary from $500 to $1,500.

It is important to remember that the schedule of amounts of reimbursement is not usually intended to indicate what the physician's charge will or should be in a particular case. In a few areas, however, special arrangements have been worked out in cooperation with medical groups under which a prepared schedule of benefits is accepted by participating physicians as the full fee for insured persons whose incomes do not exceed specified amounts.

A relatively new approach involves full payment of charges for physicians' services, without using a limiting schedule. Payments are limited to the physician's normal charge, but not more than the prevailing fee for the surgical procedure in the geographical locality. This type of plan recognizes that there will be differences in physicians' charges because of such features as the prevailing fee levels of charges in a geographical locality, the skill of the physician, and the complexity of the service performed. This type of benefit has recently been bargained by several large unions.

Other Medical Expenses. A variety of different plans are available to cover other types of medical expenses. Some are intended to provide benefits for specific kinds of expense, e.g., the cost of diagnostic x-ray examinations and laboratory tests when these services are rendered in a physician's office or as an out-patient at a hospital. Such plans may take several forms. One fairly typical arrangement is to establish an annual maximum such as $50 with benefits limited by type of service according to a prescribed schedule (e.g., x-ray $25).

Other plans undertake to provide reimbursement of physicians' fees, other than surgeons' fees. Such coverage is usually written on an "in-hospital" basis. However, it can be written "while totally disabled" or on a comprehensive basis regardless of the nature of the disability, covering the physician's visits at home or in his office, subject to a maximum per call and a maximum total either in dollars or in duration of time. Usually, the first two or three calls are excluded—a deductible provision.

Finally, note should be taken of some special plans which provide a substantial level of benefits in cases of severe illness. In this category are various kinds of polio expense coverage (rarely written now with the advent of Salk vaccine) and so-called "dread disease" insurance. In such cases, the frequency of illness is quite low but may well involve substantial costs. Because of the low frequency, premiums appear to be low and, where major medical expense insurance is not available, this coverage serves a need. It should be noted, however, that such "dread disease" coverage may be misleading and lull employees into thinking they have broader coverage than they really have—when major medical is what they really need.

Major Medical Expense.   Major medical expense insurance may be of a "supplemental" variety being superimposed on a basic plan of hospital and surgical benefits or such coverage may be a "comprehensive" type providing benefits for the less severe cases as well as the more severe ones and dealing with expenses as a whole.

Where the plan is of the "supplemental" type, there can be a "corridor deductible" between it and the basic plan. The "corridor" is usually defined as a fixed dollar amount, such as $100. In such cases, the objective is to make the insured responsible for the "corridor deductible" regardless of the benefits provided by the base plan. Expenses above this corridor are covered by the plan but are subject to the percentage participation (coinsurance) provision under which the insurance company and insured share the expenses in a certain proportion. Usually, as in individual health insurance, this proportion is 75–25, 80–20, or rarely 85–15. The 80–20 basis is by far the most prevalent.

Under a comprehensive plan, a small deductible, such as $25, $50, or $100, would be applicable after which the plan would pay 80 per cent of all covered expenses above this amount. In some cases certain expenses may be payable in full with the percentage participation provision applying with respect to expenses in excess of the paid-in-full area.

It has become common to limit the number of deductibles in a calendar year to two or three per family, or to apply a dollar maximum to the deductibles within a calendar year for the family.

In ascertaining benefit payments under a major medical expense plan, the period of time used as a basis for determining eligible expenses arising out of a given illness or injury satisfying any deductible provisions, etc., may be either a calendar year or, alternatively, a period of not more than twelve months measured from the time expenses were incurred for a particular injury or illness. In some cases benefits are related to each separate period of disability or cause of disability. Most major medical expense plans have an overall maximum running up to as high as $25,000, $50,000, or even $100,000 on either a lifetime basis (with reinstatement possible subject to evidence of insurability) or a per cause basis.[19] In recent years, many plans automatically reinstate each calendar year $1,000 of used covered expenses without requiring evidence of insurability.

Dental Expense.[20]   Recently insurance companies have commenced issuing group dental expense insurance. The contracts of some

---

[19] A number of large employers have changed their plans to provide a $50,000 maximum for each separate illness, and a $100,000 lifetime maximum. Others have increased their plans to provide a maximum of $100,000 per illness.

[20] For a survey of available dental care coverage, see J. F. Follmann, Jr., "Dental Care Coverage," *Best's Insurance News,* Life Edition, December, 1962, p. 24.

insurance companies have been written on a comprehensive medical basis with all types of dental expenses, above a deductible, covered on a percentage participation (coinsurance) basis up to a maximum dollar amount. In the plan of one insurance company, the deductible *does not apply* to routine oral examinations. This particular company feels that such examinations are a sound investment to keep overall costs down. Many companies make available a "basic dental expense program," as contrasted with the comprehensive or major medical approach. These programs represent first dollar coverage with scheduled limits. Most union welfare funds have purchased dental expense coverage on this basis.

In most plans the percentage participation feature follows the pattern of major medical with the percentage being set at 75 per cent or 80 per cent. There is a maximum amount of benefits which are payable under the program to any one covered person. As might be expected, this maximum amount and how it is applied varies from company to company. For example, one insurer provides benefits for covered expenses up to $1,000 or $2,500 in any calendar year, or $50,000 in any lifetime. On the other hand, another provides a maximum of $1,000, but not more than $500 in any one calendar year applied separately to each covered member of the family. It should be noted that orthodontia is typically handled separately, with a separate maximum and increased participation in cost by member (frequently, 50–50 percentage participation).

The basic exclusions are dental services for purely cosmetic purposes, losses caused by war, occupational injuries, or sicknesses, or losses for which other insurance plans or agencies are responsible.

This dental expense coverage may or may not be packaged with other health insurance benefits because of the newness of the coverage and lack of experience. In underwriting these cases, the insurance companies have been very selective, with a minimum participation of 100 and a minimum contribution of 50 per cent on the part of the policyholder. However, there is a trend towards reducing these requirements.

This new coverage represents an important development in the group health field. It should be noted that these initial plans were developed in close cooperation with the American Dental Association.

GROUP ANNUITIES

The other major area in which the group mechanism has been applied is in providing annuity benefits in connection with private pension programs. It will be appropriate to discuss group annuities in the following chapter, which is devoted to the subject of insured pension contracts.

THE ECONOMIC STATUS of the aged has been a problem throughout every period of human history. Certainly, the problem has been a continuing one during the lifetime of this country.

A number of factors have contributed to the tremendous growth in pension plans in this country. The move from a rural to an urban society has contributed very heavily to the need for pension plans as a means of solving a problem which in a rural civilization was handled by providing a place for aging parents in the homes of their children. The produce of the farm provided most of the necessities of life on a relatively inexpensive basis. Within the urban community there has been a movement toward smaller homes and apartments which do not always provide sufficient living space for large family units. The increased mobility of the population, influenced heavily by the development of the automobile, has scattered family units over wide areas. This has also contributed to a desire for independence on the part of retired individuals.

There are also several forces which have contributed to a change in the size of the problem and hence have indicated a need for an orderly solution. The great medical advances which have increased the longevity of the general population have increased both the proportion of families with an aged member and the period of time during which the aged member must be provided for. In addition, while persons at older ages are in better health than ever before, the pace of change and increasing technical knowledge and changing knowledge necessitate either retiring or retraining older employees. Some of the improvements in industrial procedures (i.e., automation) have made it possible to reduce the required work force by retiring some of the older members, and some of the improvements have placed greater emphasis on the use of younger persons in the work force. The trend towards a shorter work week has educated the population to the pleasures of leisure time and has helped to create an atmosphere in which people look forward to retirement because of the increased leisure time which accompanies it.

The Federal income tax laws have made it very difficult for an individual to accumulate adequate funds to provide for his own retirement and, on the other hand, have encouraged employers to finance pension plans for their employees. The high tax rates of the early 1940's gave a strong push to this move. The restrictions on wage payments in these war years combined with the famous Inland Steel decision influenced the unions to emphasize so-called fringe benefits at a time when employers could well afford to meet the demands.

Today, the individual, private industry, and government are all playing a vital role in seeking a solution to this problem encountered by our elder citizens, although considerable debate is now occurring regarding the size of the role government should play.

Each individual has the primary responsibility for his own welfare—our society so decrees. Personal thrift has played and always should play a major role in providing for old-age security. Government efforts for the most part have been directed toward providing a basic minimum benefit, as a matter of right, through the various forms of Social Security legislation. With assurance of a minimum benefit, the employee, through his own individual effort and supplemented by any benefits his employer may provide, can seek to raise his old-age income to an "adequate" level.

One of private industry's most significant contributions toward old-age security lies in the development of private pension plans. Although employer objectives in establishing pension programs for their employees have lacked uniformity, the rapidly increasing number of plans are of growing economic significance. Many of the early plans began either as a move to meet the needs of individual retiring employees or as a reward for long and faithful service. While philanthropy was a motivation for some of these early plans, employers providing such benefits soon found that they led to increased production through improved morale, lower turnover, and systematic retirement. Gradually, increased production came to be an important motive in framing new plans. The original theory underlying this motive was that an organization is so stimulated by retiring older employees and promoting younger people to positions of responsibility that younger employees can increase production sufficiently to easily offset any increased pension cost that is borne to retire older people. It has proven sound.

Every established firm must eventually face the problem of superannuated workers and at that point must choose between three alternative procedures: (1) to discharge them; (2) to leave them on the payroll; or (3) to grant them a retirement income. For business as well as humanitarian reasons, the first choice is not practicable; and the second procedure is expensive, because retirement costs are hidden in the payroll. Because its flexibility permits the private pension system to meet the particular needs of various industries, a well-planned program of an employer for his employees is the most efficient way to take care of superannuated workers.

Probably one of the most important arguments advanced for a planned pension program is that it keeps the organization virile and able to meet active competition. The retirement of top management at a fixed retirement age keeps the promotional lanes open and encourages talented and ambitious employees to seek their opportunities within the company. Thus, an adequate pension program facilitates the retirement of older workers, including those in supervisory capacities who might retard the work of others, and systematically replaces them with more vigorous, more efficient workers. Indeed, the trend to replacing older employees with younger more efficient workers has become so significant that there is a trend to substantially lower the ages at which older people are being retired.

In making the decision to install a pension plan, an employer naturally considers the value of the increased efficiency and production arising from its installation against the cost of such a program. Due to favorable tax treatment for "qualified" plans, the cost of a pension program to an employer has been relatively lower. This has been a significant factor in the rapid development of private pensions plans.

Although the basic motivation for the installation of a pension plan by an employer may be that it will help attract and hold employees and generally improve the operation of his business, *social philosophy* and *union pressure* have been appreciable forces in the development and growth of private pension plans. While expecting to improve the operation of his business, an employer may also be fulfilling a genuine desire to contribute to the security and welfare of his employees. Similarly, the presence of a union does not necessarily mean that the employer would not have established the plan without union pressure. Since 1949 when the Supreme Court of the United States refused to review the Inland Steel decision, it has been necessary to distinguish between those plans arising out of collective bargaining and those where a union is not involved. This decision provided that pensions were a proper subject for collective bargaining, and that an employer could not install a pension plan unilaterally, without the union's approval.

Under today's conditions the employer is probably motivated primarily by competitive forces of the labor market and the pressures of conformance to industry patterns.

The rapid growth of private pension plans serves as evidence not only of the employee's interest in, but also of industry's acceptance of, the desirability of a planned pension program. As of December 31, 1970, it was estimated that over 34,520,000 persons in this country were covered by privately financed pension plans, either insured or noninsured. As of December 31, 1970, there were 289,510 insured pension plans in effect covering 10,980,000 participants.[1]

Even though private pension programs have played an increasingly important role in providing retirement security to the working population,

---

[1] *Life Insurance Fact Book 1971*, pp. 35–38.

and would continue to do so, if permitted, the existence of the private pension system is now being challenged. These challenges come from those who believe the job of providing "adequate" retirement income should be performed by the Social Security System, and from those who would legislate severe restrictions that could curtail the private pension system. As a result, the future role of the private pension system could be limited to providing supplemental benefits to relatively few employees. A detailed discussion of these challenges is beyond the scope of this text.[2]

FUNDAMENTAL CONCEPTS

In order to visualize the nature of the contracts issued by insurance companies under which pension plans are funded, there are certain fundamental concepts which should be understood. Before discussing the various insured pension contracts, these basic concepts are considered briefly.

Impact of Federal Income Tax Law

In establishing the pattern of a pension program, the Federal income tax law relating to "qualified" pension plans is most significant for the following reasons: (1) employer contributions are considered a reasonable and necessary business expense which is deductible from corporate income in determining the income tax; (2) employer contributions are not taxable to the employees as income in the years in which contributed but rather at such time as they are received in the form of benefits (which is usually after retirement at what would normally be a lower tax rate and usually with double exemptions); (3) the earnings of a qualified pension plan are exempt from income taxation. As a practical matter, very few funded plans have been installed which have not qualified within the meaning of the tax law.

The general requirements of a qualified plan may be summarized as follows: (1) there must be a *legally binding arrangement,* in writing and communicated to the employees; (2) the plan must be for the *exclusive benefit* of the employees or their beneficiaries; (3) it must be impossible for the principal or income of the trust to be *diverted* from these benefits to any other purpose; (4) the plan must benefit a broad class of employees and *not discriminate* in favor of officers, stockholders, supervisory personnel, or highly paid employees.

The law and regulations regarding the qualification and taxation of pen-

[2] See W. Lee Shield and Arthur S. Fefferman, "The Challenge to the Private Pension System," *The Journal of the American Society of Chartered Life Underwriters,* Vol. XX (Summer, 1966), p. 269; Joseph W. Satterthwaite, "The Private Pension System—Why It Should Be Preserved," *The Journal of the American Society of Chartered Life Underwriters,* Vol. XXV, No. 4 (October, 1971).

sion plans are very complex, and beyond the scope of this text.[3] It should be remembered, however, that they are nonetheless important and play a major role in every aspect of the creation, design, and operation of a pension plan.

Pension Plan Design

Eligibility.   A pension plan, of course, must set forth rules to determine who will be covered by the plan. Relatively few plans cover all employees. For example, part-time or seasonal employees are almost always excluded from coverage. Coverage may also be restricted to employees of a given plant or division or to unionized employees. In addition to determining the class or classes of employees to be covered, pension plans make coverage for the individual employee contingent upon a minimum length of service (waiting period) and/or attainment of a certain minimum or maximum age. Numerous variations of service and age requirements for coverage may be designed, but one way or another, all are intended to reduce cost by eliminating certain groups of employees which show a record of high turnover, excluding employees hired close to retirement[4] and simplifying administration of the plan. In any case, the eligibility provisions must be carefully drawn to meet the objectives intended, taking into account the non-discrimination requirements of the Internal Revenue Code, and The Civil Rights Act of 1964, which has been interpreted to require identical provisions for male and female employees.

Normal Retirement Age.   Every pension plan must establish a *normal retirement age.* This is necessary, since a fixed age or schedule of ages for retirement[5] is fundamental in estimating costs, determining the appropriate rate of accumulating funds for retirement benefits, and as important, to permit organization and planning for the retirement of employees. Virtually all pension plans make provisions for "early" or "deferred" retirement subject to certain conditions. The most common retirement age is 65, selected to conform to the Social Security retirement age.

[3] See Dan M. McGill, *Fundamentals of Private Pensions,* 2nd ed. (Homewood, Ill.: Richard D. Irwin, Inc., 1964).

[4] The purpose of eliminating employees who are hired close to retirement is to hold down the cost of the pension program. The cost of providing a pension increases with the age of the employee. In addition, an employer normally feels little responsibility for the retirement needs of a person who was in his service for only five or ten years before retirement.

[5] It is possible, of course, to establish a range of ages at which employees may retire, such as 65 to 68. In such cases an assumption is made, in estimating costs, as to the distribution of employees retiring at each age. Many negotiated pension plans do not have a "normal" retirement age in the usual sense.

Benefit Formula.   Since an employee's standard of living is normally related to his earnings, it is important that retirement benefits bear a reasonable relationship to those earnings.[6] In order to have an adequate income at the time an employee retires, it has been generally considered necessary to have a scale of benefits which will provide the average employee with a benefit, including Social Security, which is approximately 40 to 60 per cent of his average compensation in the five to ten years immediately preceding retirement. Because of inflation and the fixed nature of most pension arrangements, a problem that is now receiving attention is maintaining the adequacy of income after retirement. Some possible approaches to this problem are: (1) "variable" or "equity" annuities, (2) "cost of living" or "wage indexed" benefits, and (3) periodic increases in benefits for retired employees on a judgment basis.[7]

Traditionally, benefit formulae have been classified into two broad categories: (1) defined benefit, and (2) defined contribution. Under a defined benefit type of formula, the benefit developed by the formula is fixed, and the cost, based on a given *normal* retirement age, will depend upon the age and sex distribution of eligible employees. A defined contribution plan establishes a rate of contribution by the employer (noncontributory) or employee and employer (contributory), and the amount of benefit provided for each employee will vary depending on the age, sex, and length of covered service prior to *normal* retirement age.

The main differentiating characteristic between the defined benefit and the defined contribution types of plans is the fact that in the defined benefit formula the benefit is fixed and the contribution varies, while in the defined contribution approach the employer's contribution is fixed and the benefit varies.

Because of the increasing popularity of benefit formulae based on "final salary," this traditional distinction has lost some of its significance. Although the so-called defined benefit formula may produce a fixed amount of benefit for a given year of service, the final retirement benefit is a function of the employee's compensation in his final years of service prior to retirement. Thus, the "defined" benefit isn't really definite as to dollar amount until it has been recomputed based on the employee's "final salary," which frequently is based on the average of his last five years of credited service prior to retirement. It is true, of course, that the employer must increase his contributions on behalf of the employee because of the recomputation of benefits.

[6] It is important to note that while the great majority of union-negotiated plans provide benefits which are tied to length of service rather than earnings, it is assumed that the duration of employment within the collective bargaining unit is such that the average employee will have a retirement benefit which is comparable, as a percentage of earnings, to that of salaried employees.

[7] See John K. Dyer, Jr., "Better Than Money?" *The Journal of the American Society of Chartered Life Underwriters,* Vol. XXI, No. 1 (January, 1967), pp. 39–43.

The defined contribution type of formula has not been widely adopted by private industrial organizations.[8] Many collective bargaining agreements call for a "cents per hour" contribution by the employer. These so-called "Taft–Hartley" plans are not really defined contribution plans; the benefit formula is one in which benefits are related to years of service. The interesting feature of these plans is the tenuous relationship that sometimes exists between the employer's payment into the fund which is governed by the bargaining agreement and the pension benefit formula which is subsequently announced to the members of the union. Since the employer has not agreed to provide the funds necessary to support the benefit formula, the employee's expectations are dependent upon the restraint exercised by the plan trustees in approving actuarial assumptions and the ability of the union to bargain for increased payments by the employer if the benefit formula has been established on an overly optimistic basis. Many of these formulas, of course, depend upon an estimate of the probable average number of hours of employment over a long period of future years and a little over-optimism can substantially overstate the probable payments into the trust from which the benefits must be supported.

Defined benefit formulae may be a flat dollar amount, related to earnings, to service, or to a combination of earnings and service. Thus, a given formula may provide a retirement benefit of $125 a month regardless of earnings or service, 30 per cent of "final average salary," 1½ per cent of annual salary for each year of credited service, or others. In any case, where appropriate, earnings and service are carefully defined. Defined benefit formulae based upon earnings are frequently "integrated" with Social Security benefits. An integrated benefit may provide a larger benefit on earnings in excess of the Social Security wage base per annum to offset the fact that Social Security benefits are weighted in favor of the lower income groups. The extent of the differential in benefits permitted on earnings in excess of the Social Security wage base is closely regulated by the Internal Revenue Service.

Benefit formulae based on service normally give credit for both *past service,* that is, service prior to the installation of the plan, and *future service.* The sum total cost of the credits granted for past service represents the so-called *initial past service liability* at the date of the installaton of the plan. Credit for past service is sometimes limited by using a smaller percentage credit than for future service, by only counting service after a given age, such as 35 or 40, or by limiting the number of years' credit for past service to, say, fifteen or twenty. In any case, an employee's retirement benefit is the total of past and future service credits accumulated at retirement. For example, an employee with fifteen years' credited past service and five years' future service credits under the pension plan at retirement under a 2 per cent future and 1 per cent past service formula, would receive

[8] McGill, *op. cit.,* p. 61.

a retirement benefit equal to 15 per cent for past service (15 × 1 per cent) plus 10 per cent for future service (5 × 2 per cent), or a total of 25 per cent of average salary as a retirement income under the plan.

Supplemental Benefits. In addition to a retirement income, many pension programs include death, withdrawal, disability, or other supplemental benefits during the preretirement period. While it is important that such supplemental benefits not be included at the expense of an adequate retirement income, they form an important part of a well-designed employee benefit program. Naturally, what supplemental benefits are provided will depend on the personnel policy, finances, and other individual circumstances of the employer. The more commonly provided supplemental benefits are based on death or disability.

The portion of the supplemental benefits to be provided under the retirement plan and that to be provided under a separate group insurance program is another decision for the individual employer, with the help of expert guidance from his independent consultant, the insurance company, or both. Management has come to recognize that to the maximum extent possible there must be a coordination of all sources of income available to the employee from both employer and governmental plans. Such coordination is challenging since supplemental benefits may be provided in a number of ways. It should be noted, however, that, historically, coordination of all forms of employee benefits with governmental programs has been rather poor. Chapter 34 describes supplemental death and disability benefits provided under group insurance contracts separate from a contract providing retirement benefits. This chapter (35) concentrates on the provision of such benefits under the retirement plan.

The disability benefits that plan managers are now including in their benefit programs have become more generous and available to more members. Such benefits have taken a wide variety of forms and further development is likely in the future. At the lower range of benefit amounts, a totally and permanently disabled employee who qualifies for early retirement under the retirement plan would receive the same disability benefit as he would have received had he elected to retire early and receive an immediate retirement benefit. Under some of the more generous plans a disabled employee who meets the age, service, and degree of impairment conditions of eligibility may receive a benefit for life from all sources equal to the pension he would have received had he continued in employment until his normal retirement date at the same salary as when he became disabled.

The other main type of supplemental benefit, the death benefit, is also experiencing widespread use, more generous benefits, and a variety in the methods of providing the benefit. The traditional form of preretirement death benefit under pension plans was the refund of employee contributions, if any, with interest. If the employee died in active service, the beneficiary would also receive the proceeds of a separate group life insurance plan. After retirement the plan had an option which, if the employee survived to elect it, enabled him to guarantee his spouse a life income by taking a reduced pension on a joint and survivorship basis. This pattern is still prevalent in many plans today.

As time passed, however, a weakness gradually became apparent in most pension plans. The thoughtful employer found himself with the situation of husbands dying shortly before retirement as well as afterwards. Because the pension plan usually did not provide any substantial pre-retirement death benefit and the group life insurance benefits were not sufficient to provide survivors with an adequate income, the widow found herself in a desperate economic plight. Many employers, spurred on in some cases by union pressures, acted to alleviate this situation by amending the pension plan to provide a benefit to the survivor of an employee who died in active service within ten years of his normal retirement date. The beneficiary was usually the widow plus, in some cases, her dependent children. Although pensions may also be provided to widows of employees who die after retirement, the more pressing need is for the period prior to retirement, since an option may be used to take care of the period after retirement. To assure compliance with The Civil Rights Act of 1964 it is most desirable to provide the benefit to all dependent spouses rather than only to widows.

The survivor benefit has been provided by such methods as the purchase of an annuity from the fund under a deposit administration contract,[9] or by the purchase of an insured contract separate from the contract under which the retirement benefits for the participants are provided. Substantial supplemental death benefits can be subject to wide cost variations unless a special insurance arrangement is used. Insurance companies are developing a variety of solutions to the question of how best to fund these benefits. Regardless of the funding used, how large a pension the widow should receive is a matter calling for serious consideration on the part of the employer. As in any employee benefit plan, it should be simple and easy for the employee to understand.

The amount of widow's pension can be related to the formula used to determine the employee's retirement benefit. Some suggest that the formula be so selected that the widow of an employee who dies as late as one day before retirement receives about the same pension as if her husband had retired under the plan and then died with a joint and survivorship pension in operation. This way widows of employees for whom the survivor benefit is effective can receive equitable treatment regardless of when their husbands died.

Two basic approaches to selecting the formula are to relate the amount of widow's pension: (1) to the ultimate (or expected) pension which her husband would receive if he were to remain in the plan until normal retirement, and (2) to the pension credits earned to date of death. Many variations of these basic approaches have been adopted. Ideally, a formula should provide adequate widow's pensions at younger ages and equate with the annuity value of the employee's benefit at normal retirement.

Employee Contributions. From the standpoint of source of financing, pension plans may be contributory or noncontributory. Under a contributory plan the employee provides part of the funds necessary to purchase his benefits, with the employer assuming the remaining cost. Under a noncontributory plan the employer bears the total cost of the program. Although the proportion of contributory plans has not been constant, traditionally, the majority of plans, other than those which are a result of collective bargaining, have been written on a contributory basis. In many cases, such contributions permit the installation of a plan where the employer's financial position is such that unless they are utilized no plan would be installed at all. In other cases, employee contributions are used to enlarge the benefits provided or are used on the theory that employee appreciation will be greater if they bear part of the cost of their benefits.

Most employees are covered under noncontributory plans, and the current trend in industrial pension plans continues toward noncontributory plans.

The theoretical case for noncontributory plans rests largely on the deferred wage concept.[10] If retirement benefits can be regarded as deferred wages, the argument that the employer should assume the total cost of such benefits is logical. On the other hand, if they are not considered deferred wages, the rationale for unilateral financing tends to fail. But apart from the philosophical aspects of the question, there are strong practical arguments in favor of a noncontributory approach to financing. For example, it is argued that noncontributory plans permit greater efficiency in administration and flexibility in funding. A more significant reason, however, lies in the fact that employer contributions to a qualified pension plan are deductible for income tax purposes. On the other hand, an employee's contributions toward his own retirement benefits must be made from his income after taxes.

Vesting. It is a well-established principle of pension planning that an employee must be permitted to recover his contributions, with or without interest, if he withdraws from employment. The term "vesting" refers to the interest which an employee acquires in employer contributions. The rights of a withdrawing employee in employer contributions depend upon the vesting provisions, if any, in the pension agreement. Recently, the

---

[10] McGill, *op. cit.,* pp. 18–20.

term "portable pensions" has found some acceptance in pension literature to describe vested pension benefits that would follow the employee and be put into any new plan under which he is covered, or vested benefits that would be transferred to some central pension clearing house.

The vesting provisions of pension plans can be classified according to at least four different bases:[11] the *time,* the *amount,* the *form,* and the *type* of vesting. From the standpoint of *time,* employer contributions may become vested in the employee immediately or, as is usually the case, the vesting may be deferred until certain age and service requirements have been met. As regards *amount,* the employer's contribution may vest in full or only in part. A graded vesting provision, which provides an increasing percentage of vesting based on service up to 100 per cent, is in reality partly a time and partly an amount classification. With reference to *form,* the employee may be permitted to take the employer's contributions in a number of ways, including a lump sum, or he may be restricted to a deferred paid-up annuity without residual value in event of death prior to reaching retirement age. A final basis for distinction may be as to whether the vesting is *absolute* or *conditional.* Certain conditions may be established under the plan whereby the individual employee may lose his rights in the vested contributions of the employer. For example, the employee's right to employer contributions may be subject to the condition that he does not withdraw his own contributions in cash. In virtually all cases, vesting is based on service or a combination of service and age. The requirements from a service standpoint may be five, ten, fifteen, or twenty years. Where an age requirement is utilized, either age 45, 50, or 55 is normally used. In recent years there has been a trend towards liberalization of vesting provisions, and there have been proposals by government officials and others to establish minimum standards of vesting as a condition for qualification of the plan under Section 401 (a) of the Internal Revenue Code.

METHODS OF FINANCING

Funding Procedure

Once the basic features of a pension plan have been determined, consideration must be given to the various techniques used to measure the accrual of costs and liabilities under a pension plan. These techniques are usually referred to as *actuarial cost methods.* An actuarial cost method is "a particular technique for establishing the amount and incidence of the annual actuarial cost accrued for pension plan benefits, or benefits and expenses,

---

[11] *Ibid.,* pp. 92–96.

and the related actuaiial liability." [12] The legal instruments, such as pension contracts issued by insurance companies, under which the actuarial cost arrangements operate, are referred to as *funding media or financing vehicles.* Many pension contracts issued by insurance companies incorporate *both* the *actuarial cost method* and the pension *plan,* although there is a technical distinction. A given pension plan might have one document relating to the pension *plan* and a separate legal instrument under which the funding method operates, the plan being incorporated only by reference. With separate documents it is possible to amend the plan and not alter in any way the funding method or vehicle being employed. The essence of the funding process is the accumulation of assets to offset the liabilities arising under the pension plan as measured by the actuarial cost method utilized. The term "advance funding" may be applied to any arrangement to accumulate assets, in advance of the date of retirement, for the payment of retirement benefits. *Terminal funding arrangements* provide that no funds will be accumulated (formally) until an employee retires, at which time the single sum necessary to provide that employee's earned pension benefit will be deposited.[13] In other words no formal arrangements are made to build up the funds needed at retirement to purchase the accrued benefits for a retiring employee.

Only a few plans operate on a pay-as-you-go basis.[14] Under this arrangement, known also as the disbursement method, retirement benefits are paid as a "supplementary payroll." Payments are taken out of current operating revenue and are charged to operating costs. No funds are set aside in advance for the payment of pension obligations even at retirement. This type of arrangement furnishes the smallest degree of security to the employee, since neither the active nor the retired employees can look to a segregated fund or a third-party guarantee for satisfaction of their pension claims.[15] The former, advance funding, is the conventional financing technique used in pension plans today. The several patterns of advance funding may be broadly classified as (1) accrued benefit and (2) projected benefit cost methods.[16] Although given pension benefits can be funded by several methods usually one or the other will be more appropriate, depending upon the benefit formula and other characteristics of the plan.

[12] Definition adopted by the Committee on Pension and Profit-Sharing Terminology of the Commission on Insurance Terminology.

[13] This single sum may be applied to purchase an immediate annuity under an insured pension contract or by the transfer to a trust company of the principal sum, actuarially estimated to be sufficient to provide the benefits promised.

[14] Under Opinion 8 issued in 1966 by the Accounting Principles Board of the American Institute of Certified Public Accountants, neither pay-as-you-go nor terminal funding is an accepted principle of accounting for the cost of pension plans in financial statements.

[15] Dan M. McGill, "Public and Private Pension Plans," *Pensions: Problems and Trends* (Homewood, Ill.: Richard D. Irwin, Inc., 1955), p. 39.

[16] McGill, *Fundamentals of Private Pensions, op. cit.,* pp. 256–276

Accrued Benefit Actuarial Cost Method.   This method of funding, also known as the "single premium" method, involves the setting aside, in one sum, of the amount of money needed to fund in full one unit of benefit. In practice this unit of benefit is almost always related to a year of service, i.e., it is the benefit earned during one year of service. Thus, if an employee age 30 should earn currently an annual benefit at age 65 of $35, a paid-up annuity in that amount would be funded for that employee. Thereafter, this particular employee would have a paid-up annuity in the appropriate amount funded each year at an increasing cost per dollar of benefit based on his attained age at the time of each purchase. At retirement, this employee's income would be the total of each of these annual increments of benefits provided by a series of paid-up deferred annuities funded over his thirty-five years' participation in the plan.

The accrued benefit method assumes that the normal cost[17] of a pension plan for any particular year is precisely equal to the present value of the benefits credited to the employee participants for service during that year. Thus, a funding policy geared to this cost method funds future service benefits fully as they accrue. Past service benefits are funded according to a schedule adopted by the employer, usually over a period of years.[18]

The accrued benefit method of funding is virtually always used in connection with group deferred annuity contracts and may be used with other types of plans.

Projected Benefit Actuarial Cost Methods.   The other category of funding patterns is known as Projected Benefit Methods, which can be used with any type of benefit formula but which are especially adaptable to the type of formula which provides a composite benefit as opposed to a series of unit benefits.

(1) *Individual Level Cost Methods.* In contrast with the accrued benefit method of funding, the individual level cost method, without supplemental liability (see below), is one under which the total benefits to be paid to an employee are estimated and the sum required to provide the benefits is accumulated through level amounts contributed over the remaining years of service.

The most familiar form of the individual level cost method is the "individual level premium" method which is employed in connection with individual and group permanent insurance contracts. This funding method provides for an amount exactly adequate to provide the benefits that would be payable to the employee if his rate of compensation remained un-

---

[17] The normal cost under any actuarial cost method is the cost that would be attributable to the current year of a plan's operations if, from the earliest date of credited service, the plan had been in effect and costs had been accrued in accordance with the particular actuarial cost method. See *ibid.*, pp. 222–223.

[18] See *ibid.*, p. 257.

changed to normal retirement age. The premium here is, of course, a function of the entering age of the employee. In the event the rate of compensation and benefits increases, an adjustment in the amount of insurance is made and the funding of the increase in benefits is accomplished by a separate and additional level premium, payable from the date of increase and based on the age at that time. Contracts funded by this method are written in amounts designed to provide benefits for the entire period of credited service and, consequently, no distinction is made between past and current service costs, i.e., the supplemental liability for past service is not separately determined and handled.

The individual level cost method with supplemental liability (past service liability determined separately) serves as the funding guide for most trust fund plans and deposit administration contracts. The rationale here is that benefits are funded at a level amount basis over the employee participant's entire working lifetime. The supplemental liability for past service benefits is separately ascertained. It may be viewed as the accumulated value, with the benefit of both interest and survivorship in service, of the normal cost contributions assumed to have been made in respect of all participants with credited past service. Widely known as the "entry age normal" method, this funding method permits a flexible policy with regard to funding the past service or so-called supplemental liability.

(2) *Aggregate Level Cost Methods.* The aggregate cost methods are analogous to the individual level cost methods, except for the calculation of costs and contributions on a collective rather than individual basis. As in the case of the individual level cost methods, the annual cost accruals may be determined with or without supplemental liability.

Under this method, without supplemental liability, the total employer cost of all future benefits for present employees, less employer funds on hand, is expressed as a level percentage of future payroll of present employees. Each year as new employees enter, the "level" percentage must be recalculated. The actual calculation is made by dividing the present value of the future compensation of the employees entering into the funding calculations, or the present value of the appropriate portion thereof, into the present value of the estimated amount of benefits, less any employer funds on hand. This determines what is generally called the accrual rate or aggregate cost ratio. The annual premium is determined by multiplying the compensation, or appropriate portion thereof, paid during the year to employees entering into the funding calculations, by the accrual rate. In contrast to the above, the actuary can create a supplemental liability to provide greater funding flexibility.

Aggregate cost methods are most widely used in trusteed (noninsured) plans although they are equally adaptable to group deposit administration and immediate participation guarantee contracts.

Pension Costs

Advance funding involves the setting aside of funds for the payment of pension benefits in advance of their due date. Because of this, the cost of providing the benefits must be estimated years in advance. In *estimating* pension costs, some of the factors that may be taken into account include: (1) mortality, (2) interest, (3) expense of operations, (4) turnover, (5) age of retirement, and (6) changes in compensation. It should be clear that these factors will vary considerably over time and that the use of the word "estimate" is appropriate. The ultimate cost of a pension plan is equal to the benefits paid out, plus the costs of administration, less the earnings (including capital gains and losses) on any funds set aside for the payment of benefits.[19] This is not, however, the true cost to the employer. In order to obtain the true cost of a plan, this cost or net financial outlay must be adjusted for such factors as reduced labor turnover, retirement of inefficient employees, improved morale, and others. Because these factors are difficult to evaluate, the net financial outlay is generally assumed to represent the cost of the plan. It is important to remember that a pension plan is a long range venture and ultimate costs cannot be determined accurately in advance. This is true even in an insured pension plan, since contracts are experience rated[20] and the employer's own experience will have a marked effect on the level of dividends or experience rate credits.

Financing Vehicles

Broadly speaking there are two financing vehicles for funding pension plans: (1) the insured plan and (2) the noninsured plan. Noninsured plans are often referred to loosely as "self-administered" or "trusteed." A trust is virtually always used in noninsured plans with a trustee being responsible for the investment and management of the funds accumulated under the plan. On the other hand, where separate insurance policies on the lives of the covered individuals are used as a funding medium, the plans are often called "pension trusts." To avoid confusion in terminology the original distinction of "insured" and "noninsured" is used in this discussion.

---

[19] Some authors would include an item for "pooling gains and losses" arising out of the fact that investment and mortality results under all insured plans and some noninsured plans involve some averaging of results.

[20] Plans employing individual life insurance contracts under a pension trust are not experience rated but are treated as other individual life insurance policies. See pp. 601–602.

The noninsured plan usually involves the establishment of a trust for the benefit of the employees. Under such plans a consulting actuary is employed to make estimates of the sums which should be put into the trust. A bank, acting as a trustee, invests the funds so deposited, and when employees retire, the bank pays out a monthly check to the retired employee on the direction of the employer. The employer and employees assume all of the risks—investment, mortality, and expense—under the trusteed plan. The consulting actuary takes no responsibility for investment and mortality results but uses commonly accepted assumptions in estimating pension costs. Similarly, the trustee takes no responsibility except to invest the money in accordance with the law and his best judgment or at the direction of the employer (depending on the trust indenture). The employer is in a sense a self-insurer. But it should be noted that under a noninsured plan, the employer or, in the event of insolvency of the employer, the employee assumes risks which are assumed by the insurance company under an insured plan. The plan provisions usually limit the employer's liability (whatever his intentions) to whatever monies happen to be in the trust. Thus, in the final sense the employee assumes much of the risk in a noninsured plan. It should be noted, however, that the risks are usually on the younger group of employees and such risks are relatively less significant on the retired employees or those in the latter parts of their working careers since the assets are usually pledged on an oldest-age-first basis. Since the noninsured plan is a self-insured plan, it follows from the basic principles underlying all self-insurance schemes, that this approach has the least risk for large companies (or groups of companies) with sufficient spread to obtain predictable results, and to keep administrative costs reasonable.

The trusteed approach may have advantages for those corporations large enough to self-insure the pension risk. The advantages advanced include (1) economy of operation, (2) greater flexibility in both funding and plan provisions, and (3) the possibility of better investment results because of great investment freedom. While trusteed plans are noninsured in the sense that no guarantees are provided to covered individuals, the use of insurance company services is not precluded. Several insurance companies have developed contracts, for issuance to trusts, which permit the use of the insurance company's investment services, and, if desired, its administrative and actuarial services, but do not involve irrevocable guarantees to individuals. While such contracts do not fall within the traditional definition of insured pension plans, these arrangements have proved to be an increasingly important source of business for insurance companies. Noninsured pension arrangements are worthy of more comprehensive treatment, but in view of the nature of this text the remaining discussion is concerned primarily with insured pension plans.

INSURED PENSION CONTRACTS

The life insurance company offers considerable flexibility in tailoring a funding vehicle appropriate to meet individual employer needs. This flexibility makes it difficult to describe the available arrangements in simple terms. In this discussion names are attached to various types of insured pension arrangements but it should be understood that the contracts are modified to fit particular requirements.

The life insurance company is in the business of accepting risks and is willing to underwrite several different risks associated with pension plans and to underwrite them to varying degrees depending upon the employer's wishes. Some of these risks are as follows:

1. More people may live to retire than the assumed mortality tables anticipated.
2. Those who retire may live longer than the assumed mortality tables anticipated.
3. The rate of interest earned on investments may fall below the anticipated level.
4. There may be defaults in the investment portfolio or it may be necessary to sell particular investments at a loss.
5. Expenses of handling the plan may be higher than anticipated.[21]

The life insurance company is also in the position of providing a variety of services, many of which may be varied to suit the employer's wishes. An incomplete list of these services is as follows:

1. Advice as to plan design.
2. Advice as to obtaining maximum employee relations value.
3. Drafting necessary legal documents.
4. Providing literature for employees.
5. Determining annual payment to fund the plan.
6. Evaluating adequacy of accumulated funds to provide future benefits.

[21] It should be noted that in a well-designed employee benefit program, which provides death, disability, and retirement benefits with reasonably comparable values, the actuarial experience will not be significantly different whether more employees become disabled, more die, or more live and retire. However, if just one function like death is isolated, obviously, a higher or lower rate than expected can significantly change the experience with respect to that one plan. As companies develop more sophisticated benefit programs, the effect of risk will become less significant.

7. Holding and investing the accumulated funds.
8. Maintaining permanent records of pension credits.
9. Computing employee benefits.
10. Interpreting plan provisions.
11. Providing nationwide claim services.
12. Searching for terminated employees.
13. Keeping employers aware of current trends affecting pensions.
14. Providing income tax information to employees.
15. Providing miscellaneous actuarial services.

To the extent that the life insurance company does not underwrite all of the risks or provide all of the services, there is a possibility that the employee will not receive the full value of the pension which he anticipates will be available, or alternatively, there is a possibility that the employer will be faced with providing funds to cover a benefit which has presumably been funded by earlier payments.

Single-Premium Annuity Contract

Probably the insurance company rises to its maximum usefulness in the rather unusual situation where the employer determines the benefit which will ultimately be payable to each of his employees and makes a *single payment* to an insurance company to guarantee that all of these benefits will be paid as they become due. Such an arrangement is frequently used for a body of employees who have already retired. It is unusual with respect to employees who are still working except in the situation where an uninsured trusteed arrangement is terminated for one reason or another and the monies in the trust are used, insofar as they are sufficient, to purchase deferred annuities for the employees covered by the trust. The trust may be discontinued because the business has failed or because it has been purchased by another corporation or because the trust has run into financial difficulties. The insurance contracts written under these circumstances are commonly referred to as "Nonparticipating Single-Premium Group Annuity" contracts.

Level-Premium Annuity Contracts

Sometimes an employer makes an estimate of the amount of pension that will be payable when the employee reaches his normal retirement age, and the insurance company is asked to quote a *level annual payment* for each employee which can be guaranteed to provide the estimated amount of pension. The insurance company guarantees that if the indicated premium is paid each year until the employee retires, the insurance company will pay the indicated amount of benefit. Customarily, the estimate of the amount of pension is revised from time to time, most frequently because of changes in level of compensation, and additional units of annuity are established to take care of any increase in the estimate; or portions of the coverage (units of annuity) are cancelled if the estimate proves to be excessive. In the event that the employee terminates employment before the indicated retirement date, the insurance company may guarantee a paid-up deferred annuity based upon the amount of premiums which have been paid, depending on the vesting provisions of the plan. An arrangement of this type can be provided either through separate policies issued on the lives of the individual employees or through a master group annuity contract issued to the employer with certificates of coverage being given to the employees. In either event, it is quite common to provide a life insurance feature during the period prior to retirement. Where separate policies are issued on the lives of the employees, the policies are generally issued to and held by a trustee and the arrangement is called an *Individual Policy Pension Trust.* Where a group vehicle is used, it may be called a *Group Permanent contract,* or a *Level-Premium Group Annuity contract,* or a *Level-Premium contract with lifetime guarantees.* Under this type of arrangement, the insurance company assumes all of the risks and provides all of the services which were listed previously and, in particular, it guarantees a price structure which relates to premiums which may not be received for twenty or thirty years in the future at a time when investment conditions, mortality levels, and expense considerations may be quite different from those at the time a contract was entered into.

Single-Premium Deferred Annuities

A very substantial portion of pension reserves have been built up under *Group Deferred Annuity contracts.* Under this form of contract, the employee's pension is broken down into pieces which are associated with years of employment. Thus, for each year of service the employee might be entitled to an annual pension at retirement of 2 per cent of his year's salary or he might be entitled to a flat amount, such as $4 of monthly income for each year's service. Each year the employer then purchases a single premium unit of deferred annuity which will become payable when the employee reaches his normal retirement date. The employee's pension is the sum of the units which' had been purchased for him. Once the annuity has been purchased, the insurance company assumes all of the risks and provides all of the services which were listed earlier. While the company's risk with respect to any individual may extend for forty, fifty, or sixty years with respect to the premium it *has received,* the life insurance company has not guaranteed the price it will charge for additional units *to be pur-*

chased several years in the future. It is customary, however, for the insurance company to guarantee its rate structure with respect to the first five years of the contract.

A basic characteristic of all the previously described insurance arrangements is that each employee can be told with certainty that a benefit has been purchased or is being purchased for him and the life insurance company guarantees that it will be paid. The employer is in the secure position of knowing that he is not placing on future management any risk that the promised benefits will turn out to have been inadequately funded, with future management having the responsibility of making up a deficiency or incurring employee dissatisfaction by reducing the promised benefits.

It is characteristic of this type of arrangement that monies are set aside to provide pensions for some employees who will not stay with the employer until they have satisfied the vesting provisions, and furthermore, the employer must meet each year's pension obligation (based on current service) in full. Many employers indicated a desire for some method by which the employer could have greater latitude in the determination of his annual payments into the pension fund and could also discount his payments to allow for the probability that some of his employees would not persist in his employment and augment his payments to anticipate future pay increases. Out of these needs have grown the Deposit Administration contract, which is the most popular arrangement being issued by the insurance companies for new pension plans at the present time.

Deposit Administration Contracts

Under the *Deposit Administration contract,* the life insurance company takes all of the risks and provides all of the services enumerated earlier in this chapter but *only with respect to employees who have retired.* With respect to those employees who have not yet reached their retirement dates, the life insurance company provides no direct guarantees from employer contributions to the employees except that pensions will be provided to the extent that monies are available at the time the employees retire. The life insurance company or a consulting actuary supplies the employer with estimates of the amount of money which should be set aside each year in order to be reasonably certain that sufficient funds will be on hand to purchase annuities for employees as they retire. These monies are turned over to the life insurance company for safekeeping and investment. The life insurance company guarantees that there will be no capital impairment and that at least a specified minimum rate of interest will be earned on the funds. It also guarantees that a particular price structure will be used to establish annuities for the employees as they retire. Customarily, this package of guarantees applies to all monies set aside during the first five years of the contract and is applicable to this block of funds as long as the funds remain with the life insurance company. The life insurance company reserves the right to establish a new set of guarantees with respect to monies received in the sixth and subsequent years. The life insurance company has not assumed the risk of the number of persons who will stay with the employer until retirement but has assumed all of the other risks listed above. The insurance company may not provide all of the services which were listed since the employer or his consultant may maintain employee records, determine the amounts to be paid into the plan, and evaluate the adequacy of funds to provide for future retirements.

Immediate Participation Guarantee Contract

Another form of contract is referred to as an *Immediate Participation Guarantee contract* (IPG). This form of contract is also sometimes called a Pension Administration contract. These contracts are similar to Deposit Administration contracts in that the employer's contributions are placed in an unallocated fund and the life insurance company guarantees that the annuities for retired employees will be paid in full. They differ from these contracts in the extent to which, and the time at which, the insurance company assumes mortality, investment, and expense risks with respect to retired lives. The IPG contract may be said to have two stages of existence. The first or active stage continues for as long as the employer makes contributions sufficient to keep the amount in the fund above the amount required to meet the life insurance company's price to provide guaranteed annuities for employees who have retired. The contract enters its second stage if the amount in the fund falls to the so-called critical level.

In the active stage, the contract fund is charged directly with the contract's share of the life insurance company's expense and credited directly with its share of investment income (minus a small risk charge). The fund is also credited or charged directly with the contract's share of the company's capital gains and losses and with the difference between actual and assumed mortality and the investment and expense experience with respect to retired employees. If the employer allows the fund to fall to the critical level and the contract enters the second stage, the amount in the fund is used to establish fully guaranteed annuities and the fund itself ceases to exist.

Under an IPG contract, as long as the employer's contributions are sufficient to maintain the contract in active status, the life insurance company is relieved of investment, mortality, and expense risks with respect to all employees, both active and retired. If and when the contract enters the second stage, all these risks will be assumed by the insurance company.

Of course, the company is under a substantial risk during the active status of the contract since it has provided a guaranteed price structure which the employer can unilaterally decide to take advantage of at any time that he feels the probable future course of investment, mortality, and expense risks will be such that it will be to his advantage to shift the risk to the life insurance company.

Separate Accounts

Under recent law changes, insurance companies have secured authority to set up separate accounts. Such accounts are held separately from the other assets of the company and are not subject to the usual investment restrictions on insurance companies. The insurance company issues contracts under which the investment results credited directly reflect the investment results of the separate account.

The most common form of separate account is one in which the funds of many contract holders are pooled for investment in common stocks. However, some insurance companies have set up pooled accounts invested in bonds and mortgages and a large contract holder who does not wish to participate in a pooled separate account may request the insurance company to establish a special separate account for his exclusive use.

The most common use of separate accounts is for the accumulation of employer money held to provide the benefits of employees who have not yet retired. Use of separate accounts for employee money is not practical under current Security and Exchange Commission regulations. Provisions for the use of a separate account may be included in both Deposit Administration and Immediate Participation Guarantee contracts.

Separate accounts may also be used to provide variable annuity benefits. Amounts placed in the account are usually converted into units, and the amount of each employee's benefit is measured in terms of units. The money of each monthly annuity payment is equal to the product of the number of units to which he is entitled and the unit value for the month.

Split Funding

There are pension programs where two or more types of contracts are combined or an employer makes use of an insurance contract in conjunction with a noninsured trusteed arrangement. All such variations are called *Split Funding contracts*. Frequently, a bank will be used to hold and invest a part of the monies in the active life fund and monies are moved from the bank to the life insurance company to provide guaranteed annuities as the employees retire. If the life insurance company does not hold any of the monies prior to retirement and only receives money as employees retire to purchase the guaranteed annuities, the arrangement is called a *Terminal Funding* contract.

Profit Sharing Contracts

Profit sharing arrangements present different problems since the amount of annuity to be provided at retirement is not usually known but instead what is known is the amount of profits allocated to each employee each year. Such amounts are usually handled in a manner very similar to employee contributions, although the return in the event of termination of employment may be dependent upon a vesting provision. The amounts of money made available each year are used as single premiums to purchase whatever amounts of annuity can be provided on the basis of a price structure guaranteed by the insurance company.

Where the profits allocated to each employee are placed in an individual account for him under a noninsured trust, his accumulation at retirement may be used to purchase a guaranteed annuity under an arrangement similar to the Terminal Funding contract described in the preceding section.

Self-Employed Persons and Their Employees

Public Law 87–792, the Self-Employed Individuals Tax Retirement Act of 1962 (commonly referred to as "H.R. 10" or "Keogh") is effective for taxable years beginning after December 31, 1962. The primary purpose of this Act is to allow self-employed individuals to be covered by qualified plans and to extend to them some of the favorable tax benefits which have been available to employees of corporations under plans meeting the requirements of section 401(a) of the Internal Revenue Code. The plan must cover all full-time employees of the self-employed individual who have three or more years of service. Effective for taxable years beginning after December 31, 1967, the Act was liberalized in several respects so as to make the establishment of plans conforming to the Act quite advantageous to self-employed individuals. Due to provisions of the Act relating to maximum contributions and deductions on behalf of self-employed persons, most such plans are of the defined contribution type. Various types of insurance contracts, individual and group, are used as the funding vehicle for benefits under such plans.[22] These plans should prove to be a very important market for insurance contracts in the future.

[22] Other types of funding media, such as an exempt noninsured trust, face amount certificates, custodial accounts with a bank, and bond purchase plans, may also be used.

Employees of Charitable Organizations and of Public Educational Institutions

Employees of a charitable organization described in section 501(c) (3) of the Internal Revenue Code which is exempt from tax under section 501(a), and employees of a public educational institution, are entitled to special tax treatment on monies used by their employer to purchase an annuity for them. Federal tax law and regulations provide that such an employee may agree with his employer to have a portion of the money that would otherwise be part of his pay set aside by his employer in an annuity contract for him. These funds will eventually be subject to tax, but not until the money, with accumulated interest, is actually received, either as a cash withdrawal or as annuity payments. This arrangement is commonly called "403(b) annuities" (from the applicable section of the Internal Revenue Code) or "tax-sheltered annuities."

The regulations governing the maximum amount of money that may be set aside each year on behalf of an employee are quite complex; however, in general the maximum contribution payable on behalf of an employee is equal to 20 per cent of his current year's total compensation times the total period of employment with his employer (expressed in years and fractions thereof), less the sum of prior contributions and certain other tax-deferred employer contributions on his behalf. Various types of insurance contracts, individual and group, are used as the funding vehicle for such contributions, which have proven to be a substantial source of business for many insurance companies.

Employee Contributions

In the foregoing discussion, little has been said about *employee contributions* toward pension plans. Where employees pay a part of the cost of the pension plan, it is customary to maintain a very detailed record and frequently these monies are kept separate from the employer monies. In any event, the life insurance company guarantees that if an employee terminates employment or dies before retirement, he will be entitled to a return of at least his own contributions with some minimal rate of interest. Plans frequently guarantee that if the employee dies after annuity payments have begun, there will be a death benefit payable equal to the excess, if any, of the death benefit which would have been paid if the employee had died immediately before retirement, over the sum of the annuity payments that have already been made.

NATURE

INDUSTRIAL LIFE AND health insurance was originally designed for low-income families who could not afford the amounts of protection and premium payments associated with ordinary life insurance and individual health insurance. This branch of the life insurance business represents a significant proportion of the life insurance in force in the United States despite the fact that the average amount of insurance per policy is small, averaging around $500.[1] As of the end of 1970, there were 79 million industrial life insurance policies in force aggregating over $39.2 billion in coverage.[2] This represented about 2.8 per cent of the total amount in force, the remainder being 52.1 per cent for ordinary, 38.8 per cent for group, and 6.3 per cent for credit life insurance.[3] It should be noted, however, that due to the much greater rate of growth of ordinary, group, and credit life insurance, as well as a leveling off of industrial life purchases, the relative position of industrial life insurance has been declining steadily. Industrial health insurance has always represented a very small percentage of total health insurance in force in the United States. The relative decline in industrial insurance has been due partly to the economic gains of American workers, who need and can afford more protection than is normally available under industrial policies. Another important factor has been the rapid expansion of group insurance.

Definition and Purpose

Industrial life insurance has been defined by the model law on industrial life insurance as "that form of life insurance the policies for which include

[1] *Life Insurance Fact Book, 1971,* p. 32.
[2] *Ibid.*
[3] *Ibid.,* pp. 27–34.

the words *Industrial Policy* as part of the descriptive matter; and (a) under which the premiums are payable weekly, or (b) under which the premiums are payable monthly or oftener, but less often than weekly, if the face amount of the insurance provided by such policy is $1,000 or less."

Many states have not so limited industrial life insurance and will, for example, permit companies to issue larger amounts up to $5,000. Expense limitations and other regulatory influences have limited the issuance of new industrial contracts in New York. It is clear that industrial life and health insurance is adjusting to changing market conditions and therefore the following discussion should be read with this in mind.

In the past the primary purpose of industrial life insurance has been to provide for a large portion of our population a certain method of acquiring the funds necessary to assure a decent burial and the payment of the expenses for medical attendance during last illness. Today, to a limited degree, industrial life insurance is also serving to replace income, to provide funds for college education, and for many other uses. This is a natural result of the fact that the earnings level of the lower-income groups has steadily increased and hence, their ability to provide for a more adequate insurance program. In addition, industrial life insurance, as in the case of ordinary life insurance, constitutes a powerful factor for inculcating thrift, so the weekly premium or monthly premium plans used in industrial life insurance have been one of the important means of involving in systematic saving a large segment of our society which ordinarily finds it difficult to provide for contingencies. The payment of weekly or monthly premiums to meet the cost of insurance soon develops a habit of saving which has a wholesome effect in other directions. Industrial life insurance also renders the further service of familiarizing the masses with the benefits of insurance, and has thus been responsible for greatly increasing the uses of other kinds of insurance. The wage-earner, as his income level increases and he becomes acquainted with the beneficial results of industrial life insurance, is in a much better position to appreciate the value of other forms of insurance, and the value of developing a sound insurance program.

Industrial health insurance involves minimum benefits, frequently tied to an industrial life insurance policy. This health insurance coverage may take the form of weekly income or hospital and surgical benefits.

Development

Industrial life insurance had its beginning in 1875, when the Prudential Insurance Company of America issued its first policy of this type. By 1879, the John Hancock Mutual Life Insurance Company and the Metropolitan Life Insurance Company had also started the sale of this type of life insurance. A large number of other companies have entered the field since these early beginnings, but these three original companies, until recent years, wrote a vast majority of the total amount of industrial life insurance written. Their position is changing drastically, however. In 1940, these three companies had in force approximately 79 per cent of all industrial life insurance in force in the United States. Progressively, their relative position has declined until today they have less than 40 per cent of the total.[4] The shift in emphasis in these three companies from industrial to ordinary is even more evident from the fact that they have all ceased to write new industrial business. As these companies have reduced emphasis on industrial, a large number of stock life insurance companies have become very active in this field and today are writing close to 90 per cent of the new industrial life insurance being written. Virtually all of these stock companies issue nonparticipating policies, and their policy provisions and practices differ in many respects from the original three large industrial life companies.[5] This changing pattern will be given consideration in the following analysis of industrial life insurance.

Other factors have also affected the amount of new industrial life insurance being written. Thus, the rapid growth of group insurance, the survivorship benefits under Social Security, and the economic gains of American workers have shrunk the market for industrial life insurance significantly.

Industrial health insurance developed from two sources. One was the English "Friendly Society" and the mutual benefit associations of our early immigrant groups. The other was the expansion of some of the large industrial life companies into the health field in the early part of this century. A few of the smaller industrial insurance companies first started in the health insurance field and later expanded to include industrial life insurance.

Comparison with Other Forms of Life and Health Insurance

Although industrial life and health insurance is a modified form of ordinary level-premium life insurance and individual health insurance, and is, in most instances, written by companies which also write ordinary life and individual health insurance, there are certain fundamental characteristics which distinguish it from all other forms of insurance. Perhaps the most important distinctive characteristics are: (1) the frequency of premium payment, (2) the collection of premiums by the agent in the field, and (3) the relatively small units of insurance involved.

Frequency of Premium Payment.   Industrial insurance premiums are payable weekly or monthly whereas, in ordinary life and in-

[4] 1945, 71 per cent; 1950, 63 per cent; 1955, 53.6 per cent; 1960, 44.7 per cent, 1965, 30.8 per cent.

[5] Virtually all companies writing a significant volume of industrial life insurance also write ordinary insurance. Industrial agents write both forms of insurance and are usually referred to as combination agents. It is also quite common to refer to such companies as "combination companies."

dividual health insurance, they are usually payable annually, semiannually, quarterly, or monthly. This is one of the most important differences, since the feasibility of industrial insurance depends upon, and the organization of the company's agency system must be adapted to, this particular method of paying premiums. Experience has demonstrated the necessity of very frequent premium collections if life and health insurance is to be widely disseminated among a substantial portion of the lower-income groups. It should be noted, however, that there is a trend away from the weekly basis and toward the payment of premiums on a monthly basis, reflecting improved economic conditions among lower-income groups.

Premium Collection.   The premiums for industrial insurance, instead of being collected at the office of the company, as is usually the case in ordinary life and individual health insurance, are in the great majority of instances collected weekly or monthly *by the companies' agents at the homes of the insureds.* This characteristic is most significant, since it accounts for much of the increased cost of industrial insurance. It should be recognized that but for the regular and frequent contact between the industrial agent and his policyholders, many of them would have little or no insurance protection.

Relatively Small Units of Insurance.   Until recent years, industrial life insurance was written not on the basis of a "face amount" but rather in terms of a unit of premium, that is, the amount of insurance was adjusted to the unit of premium. Thus, an individual bought five-, ten-, or fifteen-cent policies, and the amount of insurance obtainable for that weekly premium varied according to the age of entry and represented odd amounts. This was essential when manual accounting methods were employed. In recent years, however, with the advent of machine accounting, it has become feasible to handle industrial life insurance on the same basis as ordinary despite the relatively small amounts and premiums involved. Although some business is still written with the premium as the unit, increasingly companies are utilizing face amounts as the unit of purchase for industrial life insurance.

Industrial health policies are written on the basis of benefits per week for disability due to sickness or accident, for a designated sum per day for hospital confinement and scheduled amounts for surgical operations, usually not in excess of $150.

Industrial insurance is also more and more being written on a monthly premium basis. This monthly premium business (in amounts from $250 to $5,000 for life coverage) has some of the characteristics of both industrial and ordinary forms of insurance.[6] As is brought out hereafter, as the

---

[6] Where state law limits industrial life insurance to $1,000, the business is written as "intermediate" or "monthly debit ordinary."

size of the policy and premium increases, the provisions of the industrial policy can more nearly conform to those in the ordinary contract and the individual health policy.

The relatively small size of the policy has other effects. For example, virtually all industrial insurance is sold without a medical examination. It simply would not be good economics to incur the cost of a medical examination[7] where the total premium is very small. As the size of the larger industrial policies increases, however, underwriting scrutiny will become more detailed and significant. Similarly, since adverse selection is less likely, policy restrictions as to suicide, aviation risks, and war hazards are not as necessary. In fact, the entire industrial operation is designed in keeping with the small, average size policy. This is essential in order to keep the expense factor reasonable in relation to the protection provided.

Other Characteristics

Another unusual characteristic of industrial life and health insurance as compared to ordinary and individual health insurance is the fact that the insuring age usually is determined on the basis of the *next* birthday, rather than *nearest* birthday.[8]

Industrial insurance is sometimes called "family insurance"[9] since it is written on all members of the family from birth to age 70 or 80. For many years insurance on small children was obtainable only under industrial policies. Formerly, insurance could not be effected in some states on the lives of children below the age of 1 year, but all such limitations have been removed. Today insurance may be issued in all states on the lives of children from birth.

Plans of Insurance

In keeping with the need to hold expenses to a minimum, the number of different plans of insurance available is limited and much less than in the case of ordinary and individual health insurance. A whole-life policy with premiums payable to an advanced age, such as 65, 70, or 75, and a twenty-payment life are issued by most companies. Endowment policies are usually available with premiums payable for fifteen or twenty years or until a stated age, such as 60 or 65. Term insurance is not issued by the industrial department because it would be impracticable in such small amounts.

[7] Companies in general, however, reserve the right to require a medical examination under certain conditions.

[8] There is a recent trend toward the use of *last* birthday as the basis for determining the insurance age for ordinary and industrial insurance.

[9] This term should not be confused with the "family policy."

Some companies offer so-called intermediate policies. Originally, these were ordinary policies in amounts of $500 or more and with provision for quarterly or *less* frequent premiums. Today many companies write industrial policies in amounts as large as $2,000, and many write ordinary policies in amounts as low as $500. The increasing use of monthly premiums both for ordinary, regular individual health and industrial policies has led to considerable overlapping, and the term "intermediate" has no generally applicable definition today.

Limits on weekly health policies are generally lower than monthly policies and in both they are much lower than the maximum available on commercial individual health policies. Some companies include the surgical benefits only on monthly policies.

Some industrial life companies operating mainly in the southern states issue health insurance policies that include a small amount of life insurance. The health insurance is usually written on a cancellable basis.[10] There are several million such policies in force, a large proportion of which are on Negro lives.

Premium Rates

In recent years there has been a tendency to limit weekly premium policies to the lower premium plans and to limit the amount of insurance sold to one individual in a specified period. Weekly premium industrial life insurance is, of necessity, more expensive to the policyholder than where premiums are payable less frequently. Those who purchase policies on endowment plans or other higher premium plans or who can buy policies of, say, $500 or more, or who purchase higher limits of health and hospitalization coverage, do not usually require a weekly payment basis. In recognition of the unnecessarily higher cost of paying on that basis, some companies now limit the issue of weekly premium policies to plans with premium rates not greater than for a twenty-payment whole-life policy and for amounts less than $500 and with weekly premiums of not more than twenty-five cents. The effect of such limitations is that a good deal of insurance which would formerly have been issued as industrial weekly premium business is now being issued on a monthly premium basis.

Specimen weekly premium rates currently used by one of the large writers of industrial life insurance are shown in Table 36–1.

These premium rates are nonparticipating and somewhat lower than would be charged for a comparable participating policy. Also, the premiums for these same contracts written on a monthly basis would be somewhat lower per week, than indicated here. Table 36–2 shows comparable

[10] See pp. 292–293.

TABLE 36-1. Weekly Premium Rates for Adult Industrial Life,
Insurance per $500*

Age Next Birthday	Whole-Life Paid-up at 85	20-Year Payment Whole-Life	Endowment at 65
20	$0.20	$0.31	$0.24
30	0.26	0.39	0.33
40	0.36	0.48	0.51
50	0.53	0.63	

*Includes special disability and accidental death benefits.

TABLE 36-2. Monthly Premium Rates for Adult Industrial
Life Insurance per $500*

Age Next Birthday	Whole-Life Paid-up at 85	20–Year Payment Whole-Life	Endowment at 65
20	$0.82	$1.30	$0.99
30	1.08	1.60	1.39
40	1.51	2.00	2.10
50	2.20	2.59	

*Includes special disability and accidental death benefits.

monthly premium rates. These rates include the cost of the double indemnity and disability benefits provided by the policies.

Table 36–3 shows specimen monthly premium rates for industrial hospital and surgical coverage offered by a large industrial company. These same benefits, subject to a $15 deductible, are available at lower premium rates.

The premiums for weekly or monthly industrial life and health insurance policies are, of course, higher than for ordinary insurance. This higher cost of industrial insurance results from both the higher rate of expense and the higher rate of mortality and morbidity.

TERMS OF THE POLICY

In its basic features the industrial policy is similar to that issued to ordinary life and individual health policyholders, and the contracts of the various leading industrial companies do not differ much in their essential terms. Because of the small amounts of insurance involved, the industrial policy cannot offer some of the options and the flexibility of the ordinary contract. On the other hand, these small amounts make it possible to offer a greater degree of liberality in some provisions than can be offered in ordinary contracts.

Industrial health contracts, however, are more restrictive than regular individual health insurance contracts. The insuring clause for the collection of income benefits for disability requires that the insured be unable to perform any function whatsoever pertaining ". . . to any occupation or employment, *whether gainful* or otherwise." This discussion is directed to those provisions of the industrial policy which are distinctive in nature.

Option to Return Policy

Until recently many industrial policies contained a provision which gives the policyholder the opportunity to examine the policy and return it if not satisfied. The policy usually provides that the insured has the right to return the policy within a specified time (two or three weeks) from the date of issue and have the premiums paid refunded. In the event the policy is returned, insurance *without cost* has been extended from the date of application to the date of cancellation. Today, only a few companies include such a provision in their life policies. It should be noted, however, that it is a *required* provision of industrial health insurance contracts.

TABLE 36-3. Monthly Premium Rates for Industrial Hospital and Surgical Coverage

Age Next Birthday	$6 Room and Board $150 Surgical	$10 Room and Board $250 Surgical	$14 Room and Board $250 Surgical
Males			
20	$3.08	$5.13	$ 6.40
30	3.47	5.78	7.26
40	4.25	7.08	8.97
50	5.18	8.63	11.04
60	5.76	9.60	12.37
Females			
20	$5.08	$8.47	$10.61
30	5.08	8.47	10.61
40	5.08	8.47	10.61
50	5.52	9.20	11.73
60	5.89	9.82	12.64
Each Child			
under 17	$1.64	$2.73	$ 3.26

Conversion Privilege

Some companies also give the insured the option of converting, on an attained age basis, his industrial policy into some other kind of contract. This may simply involve a shift from the more expensive weekly premium plan to the less expensive monthly premium plan or it may involve the conversion of a number of his industrial policies to an ordinary plan.

Disability and Accidental Death Benefits

Disability benefits of the usual type found in ordinary policies would not be practicable in view of the small amounts insured under industrial policies.

The disability benefits usually included in the industrial policy continue throughout the life of the insured, instead of ceasing at some age (such as 60) as they do in the ordinary forms of insurance.[11] The policy usually provides that if the insured loses, by severance, two hands or two feet, or one hand and one foot, or loses permanently the sight of both eyes, the company will pay at once, in cash, the full amount of insurance in force at the time such loss occurs. Furthermore, in such a case the insurance for the full amount still remains in force with premiums waived,[12] and is payable at death or at maturity, if an endowment. Some companies promise one half of the amount of insurance if the insured loses one hand or one foot by severance; or the whole amount if he loses two hands or two feet, or one hand and one foot, or loses permanently the sight of both eyes; and, in either event, a waiver of premium and payment of the full amount of insurance at death or maturity.

An accidental death benefit, similar to the double indemnity benefit contained in ordinary life insurance policies, has been included in industrial policies on adults since 1929. The clause of a well-known company provides that if the insured dies by accidental means prior to age 70, an additional payment will be made equal to the face of the policy, less the amount of any disability payments for the same injury which have already been made under the policy. This additional payment is not made if death occurs more than ninety days after the accident, and the benefit is subject to certain exclusions as in the case of the double indemnity benefit available to ordinary policyholders.

These "special benefits"[13] are included in the industrial contract with-

[11] Some industrial life companies do limit this coverage to age 65 or 70.

[12] Some companies do not provide for waiver of premiums in the event of payment for specific losses.

[13] Some weekly premium policies also provide for a travel accident benefit.

out specific extra charge. The cost of these benefits is included in the regular premium payable.

Emergency Draft. A few companies include a provision in each of their industrial policies that provides for the immediate payment of a given sum upon the death of the insured, provided the policy has been in force for one year. Payment will be made immediately by a bank or the home office or a district office upon presentation of the Emergency Draft form which is a part of each policy. Maximum payment under the draft is $500. The immediate availability of cash can be quite helpful to families of modest means which are faced with unusual financial problems following the death of the breadwinner.

Premium Payments

The first premium is always payable with the application, and the insurance takes effect immediately, provided the application is found to be acceptable. A grace period of four weeks is allowed policyholders in the payment of premiums on weekly premium policies, whereas the normal thirty-one day grace period is allowed on monthly premium business.

There is also a provision in the policy which allows the direct payment of premiums in contrast to the usual arrangement of collection by the agent at the home of the policyholder. A typical provision allows a 10 per cent discount if premiums are paid directly to the company continuously for a year. The amount of the discount is refunded at the end of the year, provided all premiums have been paid within the grace period. At least one company will also allow a 5 per cent discount when the premiums have been so paid for twenty-six weeks. Again, some companies will grant similar discounts for annual or semiannual payment of premiums under such contracts even where made directly to the agent.

Reinstatement

Lapses are naturally more frequent under weekly (or monthly) premium policies than where premiums are payable less frequently. The reinstatement clause in industrial policies recognizes this and also is more liberal than that in ordinary. Reinstatement may generally be effected within two or three years of lapse, subject to evidence of insurability and, on life insurance, payment of overdue premiums *without interest*. Interest is not charged because it would generally be smaller in amount than the expense involved in collecting it. In practice, reinstatements are sometimes permitted when premiums are in arrears for longer periods, although in such cases the company may charge interest on the premium in default. If the policy has been in force for more than five years and the lapse is less than six months, some companies require no evidence of insurability for reinstatement.

Health insurance policies can be reinstated upon evidence of insurability and the payment of two weeks' premiums.

Incontestability and Voidance.   Normally, industrial policies are contestable for only one year as contrasted to the usual two-year period in the ordinary contract. In addition, the application is not normally attached to and made a part of the industrial contract.[14] In order to provide a safeguard against improper or fraudulent claims, the industrial policy contains a provision for "voidance" to supplement the incontestable clause. This clause provides, in effect, that the policy can be voided, during the contestable period, if the insured fails to report on the application form any treatment received for a serious physical condition within the two years preceding the date of the application.[15] After the policy has been in force for one (or two) years during the lifetime of the insured, it is incontestable except for nonpayment of premiums.

It should be noted that most policies contain no limitation on liability in the event of suicide except with regard to accidental death benefits.

Assignment and Loans

Industrial policies either prohibit or provide for only a restricted form of assignment. This restriction is in keeping with the desirability of eliminating complications and reducing expense. Where assignment is allowed, the policy may usually *only* be assigned to a national bank, state bank, or trust company. This enables the policyholder to borrow on his policy from such institutions.

In view of the very small amounts obtainable and the high rate of expense which would be involved, it would not be practicable for most industrial life insurance policies to include a loan privilege. Banks on the other hand can make very small loans, since they can vary the interest charges with the size of the loan, and impose other conditions on the loan which are not permitted under the state insurance laws. It should be noted, however, that with the increasing size of the larger industrial policies there is a tendency to provide such a privilege in monthly premium policies.

[14] The application is attached to all industrial contracts by one of the largest companies.

[15] Sixteen states have specific statutes regarding such a provision. The significant thing about the statutes is that the burden of proof is shifted to the insured. He must show that the treatment was not material to the risk. South Carolina now refuses to approve a policy form with such a provision on the theory that the burden of proof is shifted from the company to the insured.

Nonforfeiture Provisions

The requirements of the Standard Nonforfeiture Law[16] are the same for industrial as for ordinary life policies except (1) that a different mortality table[17] is used in determining minimum values, and (2) that, in the case of industrial policies, a *cash* value need not be provided until premiums have been paid for *five* (instead of three) years. A *paid-up insurance value* (extended-term or reduced paid-up insurance) must be provided, as for ordinary policies, whenever the formula of the "adjusted premium method" produces one.

The industrial companies usually provide cash values after only three years and also allow a paid-up extended-term insurance value after six months. As in the case of ordinary, extended-term insurance is the usual *automatic* nonforfeiture benefit.

Dividends

There are three important differences in the dividend provisions of a participating industrial life insurance policy as compared with that in an ordinary policy. First, for reasons of economy, it is not possible to apply to the calculation of dividends on industrial policies the same degree of refinement as to individual policies or classes of policies which is possible for ordinary contracts. Second, the policy provides for only one method of allotment, there being no "divided options" as found in the participating ordinary contract. There are in use two general bases for applying dividends on industrial policies, namely, premium credits and paid-up additions. Under the premium credit system the annual dividend consists of a specified number of weeks' premiums, the number usually depending only on the year of issue and, occasionally, also on the plan of insurance. Under the paid-up addition system dividends are declared each year in the form of a *percentage* addition to the face of the policy rather than an actual *amount* of additional insurance. Finally, dividends are not usually paid until after three or more years, whereas participating ordinary policies, normally, receive dividends at the end of the first year.

Settlement Options

Again, because of the small amounts of insurance involved, weekly premium policies usually do not provide for settlement options. They may in-

---

[16] See Chapter 26.
[17] *The Commissioners 1961 Standard Industrial Mortality Table.*

clude a limited option available only if the face amount is more than a specified minimum, usually $250. In the case of monthly premium policies some companies make available the interest and installment time options.

Beneficiary and Facility of Payment

Industrial policies now commonly provide for naming a beneficiary just as in the case of ordinary policies. Provision is made, however, that if the beneficiary named in the policy does not submit a claim within a fixed period (thirty or sixty days) after the death of the insured, or if the beneficiary (1) is the estate of the insured, (2) is not legally competent (a minor, for example), or (3) predeceases the insured, the death benefit may be paid under the *facility-of-payment* clause. This clause permits the *company* to make payment to the executor or administrator of the insured, or to a named beneficiary, or to any relative, by blood or connection by marriage, of the insured appearing to the company to be equitably entitled to the benefit. The purpose of the clause is to simplify the contract and permit an equitable settlement without undue expense or delay. This provision is in keeping with the small amounts of insurance usually involved in industrial life insurance contracts.

It should also be noted that the company reserves the right to withhold approval of any original designation or change of beneficiary when the proposed beneficiary does not appear to have an insurable interest in the life of the insured. This clause is invoked only where there is evidence of abuse of the insurance and is consistent with the general objectives of industrial life insurance.

OTHER ASPECTS OF INDUSTRIAL LIFE AND HEALTH INSURANCE

Cost of Industrial Life and Health Insurance

Industrial insurance is naturally more expensive to the policyholder than ordinary insurance. The relatively greater cost of industrial insurance has been reduced substantially in recent years, however, by economies, improvements in administrative methods, and increased liberality in the terms of the contract. In addition, any appraisal of the relative costs of industrial insurance and other forms of insurance should consider *all the benefits* and *services* provided the industrial policyholder.

In general, the cost of any type of life insurance depends upon the rate of interest earned, the mortality or morbidity experience of the group insured, the benefits provided by the contract, and the expense of selling and servicing the business. Since the funds of the industrial department of a company are commingled with all other funds for investment purposes, no significant difference in cost should arise on account of differences in interest earnings. There are, however, considerable differences between industrial insurance and ordinary insurance with regard to both the rate of mortality and the rate of expense.

Mortality and Morbidity.   For several reasons mortality and disability rates among industrial policyholders are higher than among ordinary life or individual health insurance policyholders. First, industrial insurance is written almost exclusively on the lives of persons in the lower income groups who are usually subject to higher mortality and morbidity rates than those with a higher standard of living. It should be noted, however, that this differential has been steadily decreasing over the years due to the public health activities in this country and the steady rise in the standard of living at all income levels. Second, the selection of risks[18] is on a different and much more liberal basis than for ordinary insurance. Because of the small amounts of insurance involved, the cost of medical examinations and/or inspection reports, if generally required, would far exceed any mortality savings that would result. Consequently, the company generally relies upon the application and the agent to furnish it with underwriting information to replace that usually derived from a medical examination and/ or inspection report. It is only natural that this procedure, though economically sound, should result in a somewhat higher rate of mortality.

Finally, the "standard" group for rating purposes is much broader than that found in ordinary insurance because of the need for simplicity and economy. Many groups, which would be charged an extra premium[19] for ordinary or individual health insurance, are rated standard under industrial underwriting standards. Formerly, in many southern states, only two classifications were used for industrial health insurance—one for Negro and the other for white. Today, underwriting is based on so-called "socio-economic underwriting" with emphasis on the environmental conditions which are believed to materially influence mortality and morbidity. These basic classifications are further subdivided into male and female.

As in the case of ordinary and individual health insurance there has been a steady improvement in the mortality and morbidity experience among industrial policyholders over the years. With regard to percentage, the improvement has been greater for industrial, however, due to the fact that there was a greater margin for improvement.

Expense.   The rate of expense is also naturally higher in industrial than in ordinary insurance due to: (1) the smaller average size

[18] See Chapters 31 and 32.
[19] See Chapter 32.

policy and premium involved; (2) the cost of *additional* service to the policyholders; and (3) the disability and double indemnity benefits which are automatically included in life policies *without specific extra charge*.

The average size industrial life policy in force with United States companies is about $500, as compared with an average ordinary policy of $6,100.[20] Since many of the expenses in life insurance are independent of the amount of the policy, the cost per $1,000 of insurance of issuing and handling smaller units is increased. As was pointed out before, the methods of operation utilized are designed with full recognition of this smaller average size policy.

The weekly (or monthly) collection of premiums at the home of the policyholder is probably the most significant "additional service," causing industrial insurance to have a greater rate of expense than ordinary insurance or individual health insurance. This is evidenced by the policy provision which allows a 10 per cent discount in premium if the weekly (or monthly) premiums are mailed or carried directly to the company's office for a full year. At one time it was quite common for some industrial companies to provide free nursing service as part of a general health program for their industrial policyholders, but this has largely been discontinued due to the improvement in the standard of living and consequent improvement in the mortality and morbidity experience of industrial policyholders. There are other additional services provided, but they do not have a significant impact on cost.

Lapse.   Critics of industrial insurance sometimes allege that it is subject to an excessive lapse rate, resulting in a higher cost to policyholders. This criticism overlooks or ignores some important facts. It is only logical that weekly premium industrial insurance should have a somewhat higher rate of lapsation than ordinary insurance or individual health insurance. There are fifty-two opportunities every year for the industrial policyholder to lapse a weekly premium policy as compared with the lesser number of such opportunities of the ordinary life or health insurance policyholder. Furthermore, persons who carry weekly premium industrial insurance are more vulnerable to financial reverses than are ordinary policyholders and, therefore, should be more prone to lapse their policies.

The disability and double indemnity benefits which are included in industrial life policies without specific extra charge naturally result in a higher cost.

When all proper factors are considered, the difference in cost between industrial and ordinary insurance is reasonable. It should be remembered that industrial insurance was designed for those who either could not or would not purchase and retain ordinary life or individual health insurance.

[20] *Life Insurance Fact Book, 1971*, p. 23.

Organization and Management of the Field Force

Due to the weekly collection of premiums at the homes of the insured, it is necessary to organize the agency system in industrial insurance with special reference to the needs of the business. To facilitate the efficient handling of the enormous volume of details necessarily connected with weekly collections, the company's territory is divided into districts which are usually made to coincide with the leading cities, although in large cities like New York, Philadelphia, Atlanta, and so forth, several districts exist. Each district is supervised by a manager who has a number of assistant managers and numerous agents under him. The agents are expected to collect all outstanding premiums, and, according to the system, each has assigned to him a "weekly debit" which equals the total premiums on all policies assigned to him for collection. This debit includes both life and health business if the company issues both types of insurance.

On the average an agent is expected to collect each week $350 or more in premiums on 500 to 1,000 policies. In addition to this collection service, the agent is also required to solicit new business on the industrial, intermediate, and ordinary plans.

Compensation of Agents and Managers

The industrial agent's compensation is made up of three factors: (1) a commission on new business, (2) a conservation commission, and (3) a collection or servicing commission. Thus, the agent's basic compensation is based upon the size of the "debit" collected each week, the lapse ratio experience, and the amount of new business sold. On the amount of new industrial business sold during the week, the agent is paid a commission. In addition to this, the agent of the larger companies receives a collection commission of usually 10 to 12 per cent. Furthermore, in a typical plan a conservation commission, ranging usually from $2 to $12 a week, will also be paid, depending upon the agent's lapse ratio as measured by a base rate applicable to the company as a whole. It should be noted that commissions vary with companies, and sometimes with length of service. The agent is also paid under a similar plan for collections on monthly policies. In the case of some companies, the so-called "times" method of compensation is still used. Under this method the agent is paid a certain number (twenty or thirty) times the *increase* in his debit and a collection commission ranging from 15 to 20 per cent. This "times" method of compensation was once widely used but was discarded in the 1930's due to the reduction in agents' earnings during the depression brought about by the abnormally high lapse rate of that period.

The remuneration for ordinary and regular individual health insurance sold is computed in a manner similar to that used for agents who write only ordinary and individual health insurance business—a commission basis.

Managers and assistant managers are generally compensated by salary with a bonus based upon such evidences of performance as the amount of net new business developed and the relative persistency of the business under their supervision. Some compensation agreements also take into account relative costs of producing a given volume of business.

Future Growth

Industrial insurance has not shown the growth rate of other forms of insurance over the past 20 years. At the end of 1970, there was nine times the amount of group life insurance in force and four times the number of group certificates as in 1950. Ordinary life insurance in force had increased four times since 1950, and the number of outstanding contracts had doubled. During the same time period, however, the amount of industrial life insurance in force increased by only approximately 15 per cent, and the number of outstanding industrial contracts decreased by almost one third.[21] In fact, the amount of industrial life insurance in force and the number of contracts reached a peak in 1957 and have declined gradually since. This decline indicates that, since 1957, lapses, death claims, and surrenders have exceeded new sales.

For a number of reasons, including the steady expansion of governmental economic security programs, the steady improvement in family incomes, and, more recently, the marked interest in consumerism, it is likely that industrial insurance, *per se,* will continue to decline in importance and well may eventually be eliminated in most, if not all, sections of the country. Many insurers which formerly marketed industrial insurance exclusively have recognized this development and have become combination companies and made other adjustments in attempting to meet the needs of the current day consumer.

It is important to remember that the volume of monthly debit ordinary and regular ordinary written through the *debit system of marketing* has grown enormously. In contrast to industrial life and health insurance *per se,* the future of the debit system as a viable system of marketing is both

---

[21] These figures are for the entire industry and are heavily weighted by the withdrawal of the Metropolitan, Prudential, and John Hancock life insurance companies. Many individual companies have made significant gains during this same period.

excellent and positive. As product lines are remolded and broadened (e.g. development of one contract for both ordinary and "industrial," addition of mutual funds and homeowners insurance) and income levels continue to improve, premium growth, agency compensation and all elements of the system should improve. The closer supervision of the agent, the support role of the manager in the sales process, and the assignment of policyholders to a specific agent for servicing are all strengths of the debit system of marketing life and health insurance.[22]

[22] See *Study of the Debit System of Marketing* by the Center for Insurance Research, School of Business Administration, Georgia State University. The study, conducted by Eli A. Zubay and Robert A. Marshall, will be published in 1972.

GOVERNMENT LIFE INSURANCE[1]

GOVERNMENT LIFE INSURANCE in this country had its development during World Wars I and II and the Korean Conflict, and has been commonly discussed under two programs, United States Government Life Insurance and National Service Life Insurance. Two Acts of Congress, (1) the Servicemen's Indemnity Act of 1951[2] and (2) the Servicemen's and Veterans' Survivor Benefits Act of 1956,[3] have had an important effect on these government life insurance programs and are also considered here. The oldest of the government life insurance programs, United States Government Life Insurance (USGLI), was established by Act of Congress in 1919, and granted renewable term insurance to a maximum of $10,000 to those in the military and naval services for the benefit of a limited number of types of beneficiaries only; namely, wife, child, grandchild, parent, and brother or sister, although the insured was also entitled to the protection in the event of total and permanent disability. Later, the right of conversion to permanent policy plans was accorded to the holders of term insurance until July 2, 1927. By the War Veterans' Act of 1924, the USGLI was extended to all members of the armed forces, and in 1928, previous beneficiary restrictions were eliminated and a special disability income rider was made available.

The second of these programs, called National Service Life Insurance (NSLI), was established by the National Service Life Insurance Act of 1940, which terminated the privilege of those in active military service of applying for USGLI except with respect to World War I veterans. Its

[1] For an excellent summary of government life insurance, see Life Insurance Agency Management Association, *Veterans' Benefits,* 14th ed. (Hartford: May, 1968). See further a comprehensive study of government life insurance: Dan M. McGill, *An Analysis of Government Life Insurance* (Philadelphia: University of Pennsylvania Press, 1949).

[2] Public Law 23, 82nd Congress, April 25, 1951.

[3] Public Law 881, 84th Congress, August 1, 1956.

purpose was to serve veterans of World War II.[4] During World War II, the NSLI became the largest single life insurance operation in history with a peak of over $121,000,000,000 life insurance in force. Unfortunately, following World War II, only a relatively small percentage of those insured renewed their term insurance or exercised their privilege of converting to certain permanent forms of life insurance made available to them.

The Servicemen's Indemnity Act of 1951 was passed following a long series of investigations into the operation, cost, and justification of the entire government life insurance program. The law essentially ended the sale of new National Service Life Insurance and United States Government Life Insurance to those in service. It substituted a system of gratuitous indemnity ($10,000) for all members of the armed forces serving on and after the commencement of the Korean Conflict.[5]

The gratuitous indemnity benefit was payable only in monthly installments for ten years, and only to a restricted group of beneficiaries.[6] No provision was made for disability benefits, and the life insurance coverage which could be continued after return to civilian life was limited. Owners of regular NSLI and USGLI in the active service were permitted either to cancel their old policies in order to come under the gratuitous indemnity plan (re-acquiring them after discharge), or to continue NSLI or USGLI in force, with the pure insurance risk part of the premium waived by the Government. The law also provided two new types of insurance for veterans: Veterans Special Term Insurance available through December 31, 1956, and Service Disabled Veterans Insurance (SDVI), the only Government life insurance program still open to new business.

The Servicemen's and Veterans' Survivor Benefit Act of 1956 made sweeping changes in the entire benefit program for servicemen and veterans. The Act among other things terminated the gratuitous indemnity program (January 1, 1957) except as to provisions protecting those who had obtained pure insurance risk waivers or cancelled regular NSLI or USGLI and provisions for post-service insurance for *disabled* veterans.[7] In another major innovation, Social Security old–age, survivors, and disability benefits were extended to cover service members and dependents on a full contributory basis. With the incorporation of service personnel under the OASDI

---

[4] In 1930, the administration of all veterans' benefits was combined under an independent government agency called the Veterans Administration, under the headship of the Administrator of Veterans Affairs, who is directly responsible to the President. The duties of this agency were greatly expanded because of legislation for World War II and Korean Conflict veterans and the consequent increasing number of persons eligible for government benefits.

[5] June 27, 1950.

[6] The beneficiaries were limited to closely related persons including the insured's spouse, children, parents, and brothers and sisters. Payment could *not* be made to an *estate.*

[7] See p. 632.

program, the extension of government life insurance benefits to *new* persons terminated (except SDVI mentioned above). There is still, however, a considerable amount of government life insurance in force, particularly under the NSLI program. Consequently, the following sections review, briefly, the provisions of NSLI with some reference to USGLI and the insurance in force on certain veterans disabled while covered under the Gratuitous Indemnity Program.

National Service Life Insurance (NSLI)

Under NSLI the face of the insurance issued ranges from a minimum of $1,000 to a maximum of $10,000, in multiples of $500. It should be noted that some individuals may have insurance in force under both NSLI and USGLI, but the maximum government life insurance permitted at any one time under all plans combined or considered separately is $10,000.

Types of Contracts Available.   In addition to a five-year term policy, NSLI makes available seven permanent forms: Modified life, Ordinary life, Thirty-payment life, Twenty-payment life, Endowment at 65, Endowment at 60, and Twenty-year Endowment.

The term insurance is renewable indefinitely and may be converted at any time to one of the permanent forms without evidence of insurability. The term insurance may be converted to the permanent (except endowments) plans without evidence of insurability, even while the insured is totally disabled. This is particularly advantageous, since waiver of premiums for *total* disability is included without extra premium charge. Any permanent plan of insurance may be exchanged for another *permanent* form with a lower reserve element (for example, endowment to whole-life); however, evidence of good health must be furnished. The financial basis of such exchanges and those to permanent plans with a higher reserve is the difference in reserves under the two plans. The modified life plan was created[8] to make it financially easier for insureds to step up to permanent plan insurance. It is available only through insurance age 60. Dividends are small. At age 65, the insurance is automatically reduced to 50 per cent of the face, without a reduction in premium. The amount of insurance lost at age 65 may be replaced by the same or lesser amount of special ordinary life insurance for an extra premium. No medical examination is required.

Nonforfeiture Provisions.   Permanent NSLI policies provide for nonforfeiture options similar to those in commercial contracts.

[8] Public Law 88–664, 88th Congress, October 13, 1964.

Provision is made for extended term insurance (which is automatic in the absence of other election), reduced paid-up insurance, and the right to surrender the policy for its cash value.[9] A loan provision is available differing from the commercial contract clause in that a maximum of 94 per cent of the cash value may be borrowed. Such loans carry a rate of 4 per cent for loans obtained up to January 11, 1971, and 5 per cent on and after that date. It should be noted that an NSLI policy may not be assigned by the insured, except in connection with a loan on the policy itself.

Beneficiary Provisions. Under NSLI, by the Insurance Act of 1946, beneficiary provisions and settlement obligations were changed and made applicable to policies maturing on or after August 1 of that year. All beneficiary restrictions were removed and any person, firm, corporation, or the estate may be designated, by either name or class, and in any order desired. Should no designated beneficiary survive the insured, the insurance benefits are paid to the insured's estate in a lump sum. Where a lump-sum settlement was not authorized, the present value of any remaining unpaid guaranteed installments, following the death of all named beneficiaries, is paid to the insured's estate, unless the policy provides otherwise.

Settlement Options. NSLI policies permit four settlement options, namely: (1) lump-sum payment, elected by the insured only; (2) equal monthly installments ranging from 36 to 240 months, and in multiples of 12; (3) equal monthly installments for life for the first beneficiary, with 120 months certain; and (4) equal monthly installments in the form of a refund life income, with a face value certain, except where the settlement involves fewer than 120 monthly payments. With certain limitations the insured is free to select any one or a combination of the modes of settlement, as well as to change them at will. It should be noted that under the life income options (3) and (4) no distinction is made between male and female lives. In commercial contracts a given face amount will usually provide a smaller life income for females in view of their greater longevity. Options (3) and (4) are not available if the beneficiary is a firm, corporation, trustee, or legal entity (including the estate of the insured). If option (2), (3), or (4) is selected by the insured, any guaranteed amounts payable after the death of all beneficiaries will go to the insured's estate unless otherwise specified. In the event no option is selected by the insured, settlement is automatically made in 36 equal monthly installments, unless the designated beneficiary elects to receive settlement over a longer period of time.

---

[9] It should be noticed that insurance surrendered for cash *or* paid-up value can *never* be reinstated or repurchased except under the special provisions applicable to cancellations under the gratuitous indemnity program.

An insured may take the cash value of his NSLI or USGLI policy or the proceeds of an endowment in cash, monthly installments from 36 to 240 months, or as a refund life annuity.[10]

Disability Benefits.   The Insurance Act of 1946 authorized a total disability income provision, prior to a delimiting age, for any NSLI policy upon evidence of good health and the payment of an extra premium. Total disability is defined as "any impairment of mind or body which continuously renders it impossible for the insured to follow any substantially gainful occupation." Such disability for insurance purposes is also occasioned by the permanent loss of the use of both feet, both hands, both eyes, or by any combination of two of the aforementioned members, or by total loss of hearing, or the organic loss of speech. Originally, the total disability benefit amounted to $5 monthly for each $1,000 of insurance for life provided the disability occurred before the insured reached age 60. Effective November 1, 1958, a $10-a-month benefit per $1,000 of insurance was made available and on January 1, 1965, holders of the $10 rider became eligible to apply for extension of coverage to age 65 for a small additional premium. Holders of the $5 rider are now eligible to apply for the $10 rider with coverage to age 65, subject to evidence of good health. Application for either the exchange or a new $10 rider must be made before age 55.

As mentioned earlier, waiver-of-premium total disability is granted without extra premium. Premiums are waived after a period of six months' continuous total disability commencing before the age 65.[11]

Actuarial Basis.   NSLI premium rates, reserves, and life-income settlement options are all based upon the *American Experience Table of Mortality,* with 3 per cent interest. Surrender values under NSLI policies are based on the full net level reserve (AET and 3 per cent) and are available at any time after one year without regard to the "incidence of expense" problem, since all expense of operation is borne by the U.S. Government.

NSLI is participating, and dividends declared by the Administrator of Veterans Affairs may be (a) taken in cash, (b) used to *prepay* premiums, (c) accumulated at no less than 3 per cent interest (currently 4¼ per cent), or (d) accumulated at 3 per cent interest (currently 4¼ per cent) subject to automatic use to prevent lapsation of the policy. NSLI dividends have been very liberal, and the net cost of such policies has been very favorable because the U.S. Government absorbs *all* administrative ex-

---

[10] Public Law 91–291, 91st Congress, June 25, 1970.
[11] Extended from age 60, effective January 1, 1965.

penses and reimburses the NSLI Trust Fund for certain service-connected deaths.[12]

Financing the Plan.   NSLI is operated financially through the National Service Life Insurance Trust Fund. Premiums are paid into this fund, and claims are met out of the fund, the balance of income over outgo being retained for reserves, surplus, and dividends. But it should be noted that claims attributable to extra military service hazards are reimbursed to the fund by the government through a so-called NSLI appropriations account. The fund is maintained as a separate trust fund, the government acting as the trustee. The Secretary of the Treasury is authorized to invest all of the funds in United States interest-bearing securities, and no operating profit is derived by the government.

Relationship to Commercial Life Insurance.   In view of the far reaching extent of this particular governmental operation, many feared that NSLI would interfere seriously with commercial insurance. Such fears proved largely unfounded, partly because the government's system made the younger generation more life insurance minded, partly because a maximum of $10,000 insurance is relatively small when viewed in the light of normal family needs, and partly because a relatively small proportion of the servicemen retained their government insurance after discharge. It is estimated that war veterans and their dependents will soon represent a third to a half of the nation's population. Possessing at the most only $10,000 of government life insurance, many were educated to their need for a larger amount of life insurance.

United States Government Life Insurance (USGLI)

In view of the relatively small amount of USGLI in force, space does not warrant any substantive discussion in this volume.[13] USGLI and NSLI have a similar pattern except that the USGLI disability provision is somewhat more liberal. As in the case of NSLI, the Servicemen's Indemnity Act terminated the sale of new USGLI as of April 25, 1951.

---

[12] See D. M. McGill, "The Source of National Service Life Insurance Dividends," *The Journal of the American Society of Chartered Life Underwriters* (December, 1949).

[13] For details of current USGLI provisions, see V.A. Pamphlets 29–1 available at local V.A. offices.

Gratuitous Indemnity Program

As was pointed out earlier, the gratuitous indemnity program automatically insured persons on active duty between June 27, 1950, and January 1, 1957, for $10,000 (less the amount of any NSLI and/or USGLI *maintained in force* on any basis).[14] Beneficiaries were limited, and there was only *one* settlement plan for death benefits—monthly installments for ten years.[15]

Gratuitous protection was continued for 120 days after separation from service,[16] except for persons ordered to active duty for less than 30 days. The post-service insurance permitted was limited. Within 120 days following separation, *without evidence of insurability,* any veteran who was entitled to Servicemen's Indemnity could apply only for five-year renewable, *nonconvertible, nonparticipating* insurance called Veterans Special Term Insurance. In 1958, Congress liberalized certain aspects of this program. Commencing January 1, 1959, the former nonconvertible term insurance could be exchanged for another form of term insurance at a lower premium rate, not renewable after the insured's 50th birthday, or converted to any of the seven "modernized" permanent plans. This marked a reversal of a trend toward restriction of government life insurance for the veteran. The rate basis was on a "modernized" basis.[17]

In the case of eligible disabled veterans, all NSLI standard plans are available on a modernized rate and nonparticipating basis. No disability income rider is available. A veteran with a service-connected or service-aggravated disability has one year from the date he is rated by VA to apply for this type of insurance called Service Disabled Veterans Insurance (SDVI). This latter coverage for disabled veterans was the only type of post-service insurance available until January 1, 1959.

New NSLI Law

In October, 1964, a new law relating to NSLI was enacted, allowing certain disabled veterans a period of one year beginning May 1, 1965,[18] to buy a new form of National Service Life Insurance.

---

[14] Coverage was also extended to persons enroute to active duty, and to Reservists and National Guardsmen on training flights.

[15] $9.29 per month per $1,000 of proceeds (2¼ per cent interest basis).

[16] Prior to January 1, 1957.

[17] *Commissioners 1941 Standard Ordinary Mortality Table (1941 CSO)* and 2¼ per cent interest. Settlement options based on 2¼ per cent interest and on the *Annuity Table for 1949* where life contingencies are involved.

[18] Public Law 88–664, 88th Congress, October 13, 1964.

A veteran who was eligible to buy National Service Life Insurance after October 7, 1940, and before January 1, 1957, and who did not have Government life insurance or had less than $10,000 was eligible for the new insurance if: (1) He had a service-connected disability, whether or not he was receiving compensation, or (2) He had a nonservice-connected disability which, alone or in combination with a service-connected disability, made him uninsurable by commercial companies.

The cost of this plan was lowest for those veterans having a service-connected disability who met the V. A.'s good health standards, higher for those who did not meet these standards solely because of their service-connected disabilities, and very high for veterans unable to get commercial insurance at the highest rates because of nonservice-connected disabilities.

This insurance was made available on any of the regular permanent plans. Term insurance was not issued.

Servicemen's Group Life Insurance (SGLI)

Servicemen's Group Life Insurance was established by Public Law 89–214, approved September 29, 1965,[19] to provide members of the Uniformed Services on active duty with insurance written on a group basis through private life insurance companies. Similar in concept to the Federal Employees Group Life Insurance (FEGLI) plan, the program is administered through a "primary insurer" licensed in all 50 states and the District of Columbia. Other companies may participate as reinsurers even though not so widely licensed, subject to Veterans Administration approval of the criteria for selecting such companies. Approved companies may elect to participate in converting SGLI to individual policies, whether or not they act as reinsurers of the group plan.

Premiums paid by servicemen are designed to cover normal peacetime mortality costs and administration expenses. All costs attributable to the extra hazards of military service will be paid by the Federal Government through appropriations from the various Uniformed Service departments to a revolving fund, according to a formula determined by the Veterans Administration.

The insurance granted under this program is entirely separate from and in addition to any U. S. Government, National Service, or Federal Employees Group Life Insurance the individual may have or acquire. The amount of group insurance payable will not be reduced as a result of any other insurance on the individual's life.

    Eligibility.   Insurance is provided automatically for all persons on full-time active duty in the Uniformed Services in a commissioned,

[19] Amended by Public Law 91–291, June 25, 1970.

warrant, or enlisted rank, under orders that do not specify a duty period of 30 days or less. The Uniformed Services comprise the Army, Navy, Air Force, Marine Corps, Coast Guard, Public Health Service, and the National Oceanic and Atmospheric Administration, formerly the Environmental Science Services Administration (the merged Weather Bureau and Coast and Geodetic Survey), cadets or midshipmen of the ROTC, performing full-time active duty or activity duty for training under calls or orders not limited to 20 days or less.

Under the amended law, coverage was extended to all reservists, members of the National Guard, and ROTC members while engaged in authorized training duty.

Plan of Insurance.   Each eligible person will be covered *automatically* for $15,000 (increased from $10,000 effective June 25, 1970) of group term insurance without evidence of insurability, unless he or she takes affirmative action *in writing* to elect either: (1) to have no insurance at all under the program; or (2) to be covered for $10,000 or $15,000. There are no other choices.

The insurance will remain in effect during active duty and for 120 days after separation from service, unless terminated earlier at the insured's request. Coverage will also cease if the insured is absent without leave for a period of more than 31 days.

Evidence of good health is required to obtain insurance if the individual previously declined insurance or to increase coverage from $5,000 to $10,000 or to $15,000. Insurance lost as a result of the member being AWOL for more than 31 days is automatically revived as of the date the member is restored to duty with pay. Prior to the June 25, 1970, amendment, reinstatement required an application and evidence of good health.

Monthly premiums are deducted from the insured's service pay, without a formal allotment request being filed, at rates determined by experience with the program. Tentative rates were set for the first year of operation at $2 per month for $10,000 and $1 per month for $5,000, regardless of age. These are still in effect, plus the new $3 rate for $15,000. Basic coverage premiums are payable only during active duty. Unless previously terminated or converted, the group coverage will be continued during the 120-day period after separation without further premium payment. The amount of contribution required of the members for Reservist Coverage during the limited periods the coverage is provided has been established at $1.80 per year for $15,000 insurance, $1.20 for $10,000, and $.60 for $5,000. This amount is payable once each fiscal year and is not reduced if coverage is provided for less than a full year.

Beneficiary and Settlement Provisions.   The insured may designate any person or legal entity as beneficiary of the group insurance by request in writing to the office designated by his branch of service. If no beneficiary is designated or if no designated beneficiary survives the insured, proceeds will be paid to the following, in the order of preference indicated:

1. Widow or widower
2. Child or children and descendants of deceased children by representation
3. Parents
4. Executor or administrator of the estate
5. Next of kin under laws of the insured's state of domicile.

If any beneficiary entitled to proceeds fails to make claim within one year after the insured's death, payment will be made to the next beneficiary in the above line of preference.

Group insurance proceeds may be payable in one of two ways, either in a lump sum or in 36 equal monthly installments. If the insured has not elected either method of payment, the beneficiary may choose the method; if the insured elected the lump-sum option, the beneficiary may choose the 36-month installment plan instead (but not vice versa).

Conversion Privilege.   At any time while the group insurance is in force—within 120 days after separation—the insured may convert to an individual policy by applying to any approved company, on any approved plan then being written by the company. Such converted policy will be issued without medical examination in an amount not in excess of the amount of group insurance converted, and without war clause restrictions. The June 25, 1970, law modified this privilege to provide that the effective date of the converted policy is limited to the 121st day following separation or release from active duty. An exception to the 120-day limitation is the member who is totally disabled at separation. In that event, the member has up to one year, while totally disabled, to exercise the conversion privilege.

Under Reservist coverage, generally there is no conversion privilege except in the case of certain disabilities. Conversion in these cases will be effective the day after the end of the 90-day period after such duty.

Approximately three weeks after separation the member receives from VA a pamphlet (SGL–133) listing the companies approved to participate in the program.

GOVERNMENT HEALTH INSURANCE

Government programs dealing with income loss and medical care costs during periods of disability are of various types. They include Federal programs aimed at providing medical care through publicly financed health programs and facilities designed to provide essential medical care for certain groups of the population. In addition, Federal grant-in-aid programs exist to assist in financing joint Federal-state programs of the same type. At the state level, departments of public health as well as specialized agencies, including rehabilitation facilities related to the workmen's compensation programs, have been organized to deal with other aspects of the problem. In addition, a number of local government agencies, particularly in the large cities, have begun increasingly to develop unified programs for dealing with the problems of ill health, including provision of financial aid in some cases.

At the same time that programs providing for medical care were developing, others designed to replace some part of the lost personal income were being established. One of the oldest and broadest of these programs is workmen's compensation, which provides coverage against medical care costs and lost income due to industrial injury, and in many cases occupational disease in one form or another, in each of the several states. Coverage against wage losses resulting from nonindustrial accidents or disease is provided in five states through temporary disability insurance programs.

Several special programs have been developed by the Federal government. For example, disability income and in some cases medical care costs have been provided for some years for Federal civilian employees under terms of the Civil Service Retirement Act and the Federal Employees Compensation Act, and for railroad employees under the Railroad Retirement Act. More recently, beginning in 1954, under the terms of the Old-Age, Survivors, and Disability Insurance Program, a broad attempt to minimize the effects of lost time due to disability has been provided for all covered under that Act. This began with the "disability freeze," a provision allowing for elimination of lost time due to disability in computing the average wage for OASI benefit purposes. Subsequently, beginning in 1956, a benefit was made available to workers who are unable "to perform substantial gainful employment" for more than six months, if otherwise qualified. The benefit is computed in the same manner as the primary benefit under OASI, as discussed in the following section.

FEDERAL OLD-AGE, SURVIVORS, AND DISABILITY INSURANCE AND THE MEDICARE PROGRAM[20]

Purposes of the Legislation

The Social Security Act of 1935 (effective January 1, 1937), motivated largely by the severe business depression of 1930–36,[21] gave to this nation, for the first time, an old-age benefit system. At first, however, the benefits were available only to the worker, but in 1939 the system was enlarged to provide insurance protection also to the worker's family. The new enlarged system then assumed the name of Old-Age and Survivors Insurance (OASI).

Subsequent amendments included a provision (1946) for dependents of deceased World War II veterans, a major liberalizing amendment in 1950, and further liberalizing amendments in 1952 and 1954. An amendment in 1956 made disability income part of the bundle of benefits provided in the Act (so that the system was then Old-Age, Survivors, and Disability Insurance, OASDI); extended coverage to the armed forces and to certain other minor groups on a regular contributory basis; reduced the minimum retirement eligibility age for women to age 62; and extended children's benefits beyond age 18 if the child was disabled before age 18. In 1958 the Act was amended again, providing for increases in benefits.

Further amendments to the Act were made in 1960 and 1961. In 1960 the changes liberalized the provisions relating to disability benefits, earnings test, requirements for insured status, covered occupations, the benefits for surviving children, and the determination of the average monthly wage. In 1961 the age of eligibility for men for retirement benefits was lowered to age 62, and, in addition, minimum benefits, fully insured status, certain sur-

[20] See Robert J. Myers, *Summary of the Provisions of the Old Age, Survivors, and Disability Insurance System, the Hospital Insurance System, and the Supplementary Medical Insurance System* (Washington: Social Security Administration, 1970); see also David A. Ivry, Laurence J. Ackerman, and Walter C. McKain, *Fundamentals of the Federal Old-Age, Survivors, and Disability Insurance System and the Medicare Program*, rev. ed. (American College of Life Underwriters, 1968).

[21] The 1935 Social Security Act was a broad attack on the problems of insecurity. In addition to old-age insurance benefits, the Act covered other areas including aid to the blind, orphans, and aged and unemployment insurance. The discussion here will be concerned only with the present old-age, survivors, and disability insurance system initially established by the Social Security Act of 1935 and modified by subsequent legislation.

vivorship benefits, and the earnings test were liberalized.

In 1965, benefit levels and the definition of total disability and the earnings allowed while drawing benefits were liberalized. The 1965 Act also provided for an increase in the earnings or tax base to $6,600 effective in 1966 and introduced a new Title XVIII to the Social Security Act. This title initiated a health insurance program for the aged, popularly referred to as Medicare. Thus, the present program can be called Old-Age, Survivors, Disability, and Health Insurance (OASDHI). In the 1967 Act benefits were again liberalized and the earnings base was increased to $7,800 effective in 1968. In 1969 a 15 per cent benefit increase was enacted without raising tax rates or the earnings base as the existing actuarial surplus was assumed to be sufficient. In 1971, an additional 10 per cent benefit increase, effective retroactively on January 1, 1971, was enacted, and this increase was accompanied by an increase in the earnings base to $9,000 to become effective January 1, 1972.

The reasons for this governmental plan of protection were essentially four in number; namely: (1) the transformation of the national economy from a family self-sufficiency basis, where the aged still continued to contribute to the family support, to a complex urban system under which the self-sufficiency of the family largely ceased; (2) the increasing tendency, under the new urban system, to require the old to have money for room and board without having the opportunity to contribute substantially in return; (3) the increasing specialization and efficiency of industrial establishments, which made it difficult for the old to retain their jobs and next to impossible to secure new jobs if the old ones were lost; and (4) the very rapid increase, both absolutely and relatively, in the number of old people in the population. From 1900 to 1940, the percentage of the population aged 65 or over increased from 4.1 to 6.9 per cent, and authoritative estimates predicted a further increase to 9.7 by 1970, almost doubling from the 5.4 per cent prevailing in 1930.

Coverage

Coverage under Federal Old-Age, Survivors, and Disability Insurance (hereafter cited as OASDI) is conditioned on attachment to the labor market. The program is not based on the principle of universal coverage of all residents in the country, but rather aims to cover all gainfully employed persons.

Virtually all occupations are covered today, although certain occupations are subject to special eligibility rules because of administrative or constitutional reasons. The excluded occupations are made up of (1) certain types of family employment (e.g., child under 21 in the employ of his father); (2) border-line "occupations," such as newsboys under age 18 and full-time college students working in college fraternities; (3) certain employees of nonprofit organizations (e.g., student nurses and students); (4) the majority of Federal government employees, who are covered under a separate system; (5) policemen and firemen who are already protected under a state or municipal retirement system;[22] and (6) railroad workers, who are covered under the Railroad Retirement Act.[23] At the present time about 90 per cent of the gainfully employed are covered under OASDI. Coverage under present legislation is virtually as broad as is possible of attainment, short of a universal pension scheme.

Benefits

  Eligibility for Benefits.   The benefits derived from OASDI depend upon the insured status of the individual worker. Eligibility for the benefits under OASDI requires that the worker be *fully insured, currently insured,* or both *fully and currently insured.* Whether an individual is currently insured or fully insured depends upon his number of "quarters of coverage" and when they were earned.

  A "quarter of coverage" is a period of three calendar months ending on March 31, June 30, September 30, or December 31, generally one in which a worker has at least $50 in wages or is credited with self-employment income.[24]

  1. *Fully insured status.* An individual can attain fully insured status by (a) being credited with forty quarters of coverage earned at any time after 1936 (a worker who fulfills this requirement remains fully insured even if he spends no further time in covered employment), or by (b) being credited with at least *one* quarter of coverage (whenever earned) for every calendar year elapsing after 1950 (or after the year in which he attains age 21, if later) up to the year in which he reaches age 65 (age 62 for women), dies, or becomes disabled.

  It is important to note that even when a man retires at 62, the period up to age 65 is used in determining fully insured status. A minimum of six quarters of coverage is required in any case. Subject to certain requirements set forth in the law, a year during which a worker is disabled does not adversely affect his eligibility for fully insured status.

[22] In some states, such policemen and firemen can also be covered.

[23] Coverage for railroad workers under the Railroad Retirement Act is closely related to the coverage under Old-Age, Survivors, and Disability Insurance because of the provisions for the transfer of wage credits for those with less than ten years of service, as well as the social security minimum provisions applicable to all railroad employees and the financial interchange provisions between the two systems.

[24] Fundamentally, a wage earner must be paid at least $50 in covered employment during each quarter for which credit is granted; a self-employed person receives credit for four quarters in each year in which he earns net at least $400. There are other refinements of these rules, however. See Ackerman and Ivry, *op. cit.,* pp. 5–6.

2. *Currently insured status.* An individual can attain currently insured status by being *credited* with a minimum of six quarters of coverage during the thirteen-quarter period ending with (a) the quarter in which he died, (b) the quarter in which he first became eligible for old-age or disability insurance benefits, or (c) the quarter in which he actually retired.

It is important to note that fully insured status is related to the *length* of attachment and currently insured status to the *recency* of attachment to the labor market.

Nature of Benefits.   The OASDI program provides retirement, survivorship, and disability benefits. All benefits, however, are based on the insured worker's "primary insurance amount."

1. *Retirement benefits.* The insured worker's retirement benefit, a life income, is referred to as the "old-age insurance benefit" and is identical with the Primary Insurance Amount (P.I.A.) for retirement at or after age 65.[25] The wife of a retired worker (wife's benefit) is entitled to a benefit equal to 50 per cent of the Primary Insurance Amount if she is 65[26] or over, or, regardless of her age, if she has under her care a dependent and unmarried child of the worker under age 18 or regardless of age if the child is disabled and has been so since age 18 (mother's benefit). In addition, each dependent and unmarried child under 18 (or under the age of 22 if attending an educational institution on a full-time basis) is entitled to a benefit equal to 50 per cent of the Primary Insurance Amount (child's benefit). The maximum benefit which can be paid to an individual and his dependents—or to his survivors—is dependent upon the insured worker's average monthly wage with an absolute maximum of $517 per month, and these benefits are exhibited in Table 37–1. These retirement benefits are available only to *fully insured* persons and their dependents.

2. *Survivorship benefits.* The unmarried widow of a fully insured worker is entitled to a benefit equal to 82½ per cent of the Primary Insurance Amount if she is 62[27] or over or if she is disabled and is aged 50-59[28] (widow's benefit), or, regardless of her age, if she has under her care a dependent and unmarried child of the worker under age 18 or regardless of

[25] A man or woman who retires as a worker can elect to retire at age 62 with a permanently reduced benefit equal to 80 per cent of his or her full benefit (P.I.A.). Benefits are prorated for retirement between ages 62 and 65.

[26] The wife of a retired worker may qualify for benefits as early as age 62, but with a reduced benefit—75 per cent of the full benefit is payable at age 62 and proportionately more if benefits are first claimed between ages 62 and 65.

[27] If the widow is at least age 60 and less than age 62, she can elect to receive actuarially reduced benefits (71½ per cent at age 60).

[28] If the widow is age 50 at disability, her benefit is 50 per cent of the P.I.A., with proportionately higher benefits for older ages at disability (up to 71½ per cent at age 60).

age if disabled since before age 18, she is entitled to a benefit equal to 75 per cent of the Primary Insurance Amount (mother's benefit). In addition, a dependent and unmarried child under 18 (under the age of 22 if attending an educational institution on a full-time basis) or regardless of age if disabled before age 18 is entitled to a benefit equal to 75 per cent of the Primary Insurance Amount (child's benefit). Dependent parents 62 and over may be entitled to a benefit equal to 75 per cent of the Primary Insurance Amount (parent's benefit).[29] In addition to the income benefits, a lump-sum benefit is paid on death of the worker equal to three times the Primary Insurance Amount or $255, whichever is smaller (death benefit).

All of these survivorship benefits are available to the dependents of a *fully insured* worker. The dependents of a *currently insured* worker are eligible only for (1) the mother's benefit; (2) the child's benefit; and (3) the lump-sum death benefit. As was mentioned before, workers who are only currently insured and their dependents are not eligible for retirement benefits.

Dependent widowers and the dependent husband of a retired worker, if age 62 and over, and disabled dependent widowers age 50–61 are entitled to benefits only if the insured woman worker was fully insured.

3. *Disability benefits.* The 1956 Amendments to the Social Security Act included disability income benefits in the OASDI program for the first time, and they have been liberalized since then. An individual worker is eligible for cash disability benefits if he (1) is fully insured, (2) has at least twenty quarters of coverage out of the last forty quarters prior to disability; and (3) has been disabled for at least six months and has a disability that is so serious that it keeps him from engaging in "any substantial gainful activity" and such disability has lasted or may be expected to last at least twelve months or is expected to result in death. For persons under age 31, the coverage requirements are reduced. The disabled individual must also be willing to accept state vocational rehabilitation services.

The disability income benefit is the same as the Primary Insurance Amount, but continues only as long as disability exists. The determination of disability is made by state agencies with the right of review by the Social Security Administration. The determination of *continuance* of disability is made by the Social Security Administration.

Monthly benefits are payable to the dependents of persons receiving disability insurance benefits. The dependents eligible for these benefits are the same as the ones who would qualify as dependents of persons receiving retirement benefits.

It should be noted that the 1960 Amendments accented the importance of rehabilitation in the disability program. Thus, a disabled beneficiary who

---

[29] If only one parent is entitled to this benefit, the benefit is 82½ per cent of the deceased's Primary Insurance Amount.

performs services despite severe handicaps can continue to receive benefits for twelve months. In addition, the law also provides a period of adjustment for beneficiaries who medically recover from their disabilities.

An unmarried child of a deceased, disabled, or retired worker, disabled prior to age 18, is eligible for a cash disability benefit at age 18 or after. The child's disability benefits are payable as long as the disability continues and are the same as the benefit received by a dependent child of a deceased or retired worker. There is also a mother's benefit, payable to the mother who has in her care a disabled child receiving benefits. This applies if she is the wife of a disabled, retired, or deceased worker. The rehabilitation features of the disability program also apply to a disabled child.

Level of Benefits.   As noted earlier, all benefits are based on the Primary Insurance Amount which, in turn, is derived from the average monthly wage. The average monthly wage, a technical concept, is essentially obtained by dividing the insured's total covered earnings[30] for a number of years equal to 5 less than the number that have elapsed since January 1, 1951, or the first day of the year in which the insured reached age 22, whichever is later, and before the year in which the insured becomes 65 if a man (62 if a woman), dies or becomes disabled, by the number of months in those years. The years that are used are those with the highest earnings (but if the individual does not have as many years with earnings as must be used, then he must use zeros for the remaining years). Those periods during which an insured individual is totally disabled are to be omitted in the calculation of the number of years used in determining the average monthly wage. The effect of the "drop out" and "disability freeze" provisions is to increase the average monthly wage and, consequently, the benefits to be provided. In retirement cases, the number of years used cannot be less than five. Earnings in any years after 1950 can be used including years before age 22 and years after age 65 for men and age 62 for women.

The benefit formula applied to the average monthly wage to determine the Primary Insurance Amount is heavily weighted in favor of the low income worker. During the evolution of the Social Security Act a number of formulas for computing the Primary Insurance Amount have been in use.

A Consolidated Benefit Table (Table 37–1) now is used to determine the Primary Insurance Amounts. This table also includes other important information relating to family benefits.

The Primary Insurance Amounts included in the table, except those based on very low average monthly wages, are based approximately on the

---

[30] Since January 1, 1972, covered earnings include all earnings in covered employment up to a maximum of $9,000 a year. Maximums of $3,000, $3,600, $4,200, $4,800, $6,600, and $7,800 apply for earlier periods.

following formula:

(1) 90% of the first $110 of average monthly wage
plus
(2) 33% of the next $290 of average monthly wage
plus
(3) 31% of the next $150 of average monthly wage
plus
(4) 36% of the next $100 of average monthly wage
plus
(5) 20% of the next $100 of average monthly wage.

TABLE 37-1. Consolidated Benefit Table

Insured Worker's Average Monthly Wage	1971 Primary Insurance Amount*	Maximum Monthly Family Benefits	Insured Worker's Average Monthly Wage	1971 Primary Insurance Amount*	Maximum Monthly Family Benefits
$100	$ 91	$136	$520	$230	$421
150	112	168	530	235	427
200	129	193	540	237	431
250	146	223	550	240	435
300	161	264	560	243	438
320	168	284	570	247	443
340	175	301	580	251	448
350	178	309	590	254	452
360	181	318	600	258	457
370	184	326	610	262	461
380	189	338	620	265	465
390	191	346	630	268	469
400	194	355	640	272	476
410	197	363	650	276	483
420	200	371	660	277	486
430	203	379	670	279	489
440	206	386	680	281	493
450	209	390	690	283	496
460	213	396	700	285	500
470	216	400	710	287	503
480	219	404	720	289	507
490	222	408	730	291	510
500	225	412	740	293	514
510	227	416	750	295	517

*Monthly benefit for retired worker at age 65 or disabled worker at any age.

The sum of 1, 2, 3, 4, and 5 equals the Primary Insurance Amount. Examination of the table will show that the maximum Primary Insurance Amount is equal to $295. The minimum Primary Insurance Amount is $70 even though average monthly wages may be less than $75.

Loss of Benefits.   1. *Earnings Test.* If an eligible person is under age 72 and receives earnings of more than $1,680 a year from covered or noncovered *employment* or self-employment, some or all benefits will be lost for that year. There is no loss of benefits for $1,680 of earnings. Subject to the monthly test described hereafter, there is a loss of $1 in benefits for every $2 of earnings on the portion of earnings between $1,680 and $2,880; one dollar of benefits is lost for every $1 of earnings on the portion of earnings above $2,880. It should be noted that no benefits are lost for any month in which the individual neither earns more than $140 in wages nor renders substantial services in self-employment. Thus, if a fully insured worker, 66 years of age, earned $10,000 in continuous employment in 1968, no Social Security benefits would be payable. But if he earned $140 of wages (or less) in each of four months and did not engage in substantial self-employment then, benefits would be paid in those four months.

The earnings test applies to all payees under age 72 except disabled beneficiaries. The earnings of a person who is receiving benefits as a dependent or as a survivor affect only his own benefits and will not affect payments to other members of his family. Thus, if the wife of a deceased worker loses her benefit because of the earnings test, her children (under age 18, disabled since age 18, or to age 22 if they meet the school attendance requirement) normally will continue to receive their benefits.

2. *Dual Eligibility.* A person eligible for more than one benefit will receive in effect the highest benefit for which application has been made. Thus, a wife, eligible in her own right as an insured worker, can draw benefits under her husband's insured status only to the extent they exceed the amount of her old-age benefit.

3. *Changes in Family Status.* Social Security benefits are terminated when changes in family status, such as marriage or divorce, alter the conditions under which payments are made. For example, payments to a nondisabled child stop when he reaches age 18, or 22 if attending school, and payments to a widow generally stop if she remarries.

4. *Failure to File.* Failure to file for benefits after eligibility may deprive a person of benefits for a period of time. The Act grants monthly benefits retroactively for a period of twelve months.

5. *Incorrect Records.* The responsibility is placed on the individual to check into the accuracy of the Social Security Administration's records relating to his account. After three years, three months, and three days, no

corrections are permitted. Unfortunately, relatively few people are aware of this potential loss to themselves and their families.

6. *Other.* Benefits may be lost due to certain work outside the United States and also if the individual is convicted of certain subversive crimes.

Medicare Program [31]

As mentioned earlier, the 1965 Amendments to the Social Security Act added Title XVIII, initiating a health insurance program for the aged. Medicare represents one of the most sweeping changes ever made in the history of the Social Security Act.

Medicare is, in general, a two-part program of Federal health insurance. Under "Part A," the *Hospital Insurance Plan,* essentially all persons age 65 or over are covered for extensive hospitalization benefits. "Part B," which is *optional,* provides a supplementary program of surgical, doctors' care, and certain other benefits for persons over age 65 who enroll at a monthly premium of $5.80 for the period beginning July 1, 1972. The increasing trend in monthly premium is as follows:

Period	Monthly Premium
July, 1966 — March, 1968	$3.00
April, 1968 — June, 1970	$4.00
July, 1970 — June, 1971	$5.30
July, 1971 — June, 1972	$5.60

Basic Plan-Hospital Insurance. The basic hospital plan benefits include:

(1) *Inpatient hospital services* for up to 90 days in each "spell of illness." There is also a provision for a lifetime reserve of 60 days that can be used after the 90 days in a spell of illness. The patient pays a deductible amount of $60 for the first 60 days plus a deductible of $15 a day for the next 30 days for each spell of illness plus a deductible of $30 a day for the lifetime-reserve days; hospital services include all those ordinarily furnished by a hospital to its inpatients; however, payment is not made for private duty nursing or for the hospital services of physicians except services provided by medical or dental interns or residents in training under approved teaching programs. Inpatient psychiatric hospital service is included, but a lifetime limitation of 190 days is imposed.

(2) *Posthospital extended care* (in a facility having an arrangement with a hospital for the timely transfer of patients and for furnishing medi-

[31] See draft of Study Note, Part 8, Society of Actuaries prepared by Paul Barnhardt.

cal information about patients) after the patient is transferred from a hospital (after at least a 3-day stay) for up to 100 days in each "spell of illness." But after the first 20 days, patients pay a deductible of $7.50 a day for the remaining days of extended care in a spell of illness.

(3) *Posthospital home health services* for up to 100 visits for each spell of illness, within one year after discharge from a hospital (after at least a 3-day stay) or extended care facility. Such a person must be in the care of a physician and under a plan established by a physician within 14 days of discharge calling for such services. These services include intermittent nursing care, therapy, and the part-time services of a home health aide. The patient must be homebound, except that when certain equipment is used, the individual can be taken to a hospital or extended care facility or rehabilitation center to receive some of these covered home health services in order to get advantage of the necessary equipment.

No service is covered as posthospital extended care or posthospital home health services if it is of a kind that could not be covered if it were furnished to a patient in a hospital.

A *"Spell of Illness"* is considered to begin when the individual enters a hospital and ends when he has not been an inpatient of a hospital or extended care facility for 60 consecutive days.

The deductible amounts for inpatient hospital and extended care facility services will be increased to keep pace with increases in hospital costs. The coinsurance amounts for long-stay hospital and extended care facility benefits may be correspondingly adjusted. Increases in the hospital initial deductible will be made only when a $4 change is called for.

Payment of bills under the basic plan is made to the providers of service on the basis of "reasonable cost" incurred in providing care for beneficiaries.

Supplementary Medical Insurance Plan.   The supplementary plan provides, subject to a $50 annual deductible and a 20 percentage participation (coinsurance) above the deductible, the following benefits:

(1) *Physicians' and surgeons' services,* whether furnished in a hospital clinic, office, in the home, or elsewhere. Inpatient radiology and pathology services are not subject to the cost-sharing provisions.

(2) *Home health service* (with no requirement of prior hospitalization) for up to 100 visits during each calendar year.

(3) *Medical and health services* including: diagnostic x-ray, diagnostic laboratory tests, and other diagnostic tests; x-ray, radium, and radioactive isotope therapy; ambulance services, and surgical dressings and splints, casts, and other devices for reduction of fractures and dislocations; rental of durable medical equipment such as iron lungs, oxygen tents, hospital

beds, and wheelchairs used in the patient's home, prosthetic devices (other than dental) which replace all or part of an internal body organ; braces and artificial legs, arms, and eyes, physical therapy treatments, and so forth.

(4) *Psychiatric care* subject to a special limitation on outside-the-hospital treatment of mental, psychoneurotic, and personality disorders. Payment for such treatment during any calendar year is limited, in effect, to $250 or 50 per cent of the expenses, whichever is smaller.

If any of the services outlined above are covered under the basic plan, they are excluded from coverage under the supplementary plan.

The law provides for special rules regarding enrollment periods and the time when coverage commences.

Financing

The Old-Age, Survivors, and Disability Insurance System and the Hospital Insurance System are financed on a contributory basis shared equally by employee and employer.[32] The employee pays a tax on the wages he receives, and the employer pays a tax on his payroll. The 1971–72 rate of contribution was 5.2 per cent of covered wages and payroll or a total contribution of 10.4 per cent of covered payroll. As mentioned earlier, the tax is calculated on the first $9,000 of wages paid to an employee during the calendar year 1972. The employer withholds the employee's tax from his pay and remits the employee's tax and his own to the United States District Director of Internal Revenue for that district.

The tax pattern is somewhat different for the self-employed covered under the Act. To finance this phase of the program, the self-employed pay a tax equal to about one and one-half times the rate imposed on employees for OASDI, but the same rate for Hospital Insurance. This tax, currently 7.5 per cent, is imposed on self-employment income up to $9,000. If an individual has both covered wages and self-employment income, all covered wages are deducted from the $9,000 maximum to determine the taxable self-employment income. The self-employed person pays his tax on the basis of a special schedule attached to his Federal income tax return.

In considering the financing of the Social Security System, it is important to note the *increasing* schedule of contribution rates contained in the law.

---

[32] The Federal Insurance Contributions Act, Ch. 21, Internal Revenue Code.

The rates of tax payable by the employer *and* by the employee are:

Calendar Year	Earnings Base	HI Rate*	Combined OASDI and HI Rate Employer– Employee	Combined OASDI and HI Rate Self- Employed
1971	$7,800	$0.60	10.4%	7.5%
1972	9,000	0.60	10.4	7.5
1973–75	9,000	0.65	11.3	7.65
1976–79	9,000	0.70	11.7	7.7
1980–86	9,000	0.80	11.9	7.8
1987 and after	9,000	0.90	12.1	7.9

*Rate for employee; same for both employer and self-employed.

The premium for the Supplementary Medical Insurance is paid equally by the participant and by the Federal Government. It is payable by those 65 and over who choose this coverage. The initial premium rate was $3 monthly for the participant (the total monthly premium was $6). Premiums are at a rate determined by the Secretary of Health, Education and Welfare. A higher rate is to be paid by those enrolling late, i.e., after their initial point of eligibility—10 per cent additional for each full year of delay.

When paid, the funds collected for the several programs are allocated to the Old-Age and Survivors Insurance Trust Fund, the Disability Insurance Trust Fund, the Hospital Insurance Trust Fund, and the Supplementary Medical Insurance Trust Fund. They are managed by Boards of Trustees consisting of the Secretary of the Treasury, the Secretary of Labor, and the Secretary of Health, Education and Welfare. The Secretary of the Treasury is known as the Managing Trustee and as such has wide powers of management over the trust funds. The funds must be invested in securities which are the direct obligation of or guaranteed by the United States Government. Funds are disbursed from these accounts to cover benefit payments and administrative expenses.

The complete Social Security law now comprises several hundred pages. In a condensed digest of this nature, it is obviously impossible to cover the many hundreds of potential circumstances and situations which might arise. Individuals should always contact their local Social Security Office for information on any point that concerns them.

Current Developments.   Owing to the rapid increase in earnings levels and the cost of living some dissatisfaction seems to exist with reference to the present Social Security Act. There are those who favor an increase in the earnings base from $9,000 to a higher figure, and an increase in the benefits.

There are also those who favor replacing the present system with a plan of universal coverage, shifting to a flat benefit approach; others favor having part of the financing for OASDI and Hospital Insurance (Medicare) come from general revenues.

Currently, much attention is being directed toward the development of a comprehensive National Health Insurance Plan. Among the most crucial problems faced by a family seeking medical care today are high and rapidly rising costs, a chronic shortage of doctors and nurses, and unevenly distributed health facilities which result in some communities and even entire counties having neither doctor nor hospital. A number of comprehensive solutions to the nation's health care crisis have emerged over the past year. While a detailed discussion of these plans is beyond the scope of this text, Exhibit 37–1 summarizes the five major proposals under discussion currently.

Whatever direction is taken in connection with the health care proposals and other recommended expansions of the over-all Social Security program, the Social Security Act marks a definite milestone in the evolution of American life. Its influence on the economic security of the American people is significant, and the program deserves the attention of all.

EXHIBIT 37-1. Five Comprehensive National Health Insurance Proposals

	The Benefit	Patient Pays
HEALTHCARE (BURLESON-McINTYRE PROPOSAL) *(Developed by Health Insurance Association of America)*	Progressively expanding comprehensive coverage including hospital stays; extended care; nursing home treatment; surgery; diagnostic services; general and special physician services; preventive checkups; maternity care; well-baby care; prescription drugs; rehabilitation services; dental and visual care; and psychiatric care in and out of hospital.	Patient pays nominal co-payments for hospital, nursing home, home care, physician and surgeon services, drugs, inhospital psychiatric services. Co-payments for other services range from none for preventive checkups, to 50 per cent for out-of-hospital psychiatric care. For poor and near poor, total co-payments are eliminated or limited by income.
NATIONAL HEALTH INSURANCE STANDARDS PROGRAM FAMILY HEALTH INSURANCE PLAN *(Developed by the Nixon Administration)*	Comprehensive coverage including hospital; surgical; extended care; diagnostic workups, general and special physician services; maternity and well-child care; health maintenance services, low income family counselling; vision care for children; acute hospital psychiatric services.	Patient pays first $100 of expenses and cost of first two days of hospital care, plus 25 per cent co-payment on first $5,000 of expense. The $100 deductible is eliminated for well-baby care and child vision care. Deductible as well as co-payments are eliminated for the poor and scaled down for near-poor. Part B Medicare monthly premium costs are eliminated.
NATIONAL HEALTH SECURITY PLAN (KENNEDY-GRIFFITHS PROPOSAL) *(Developed by Committee for National Health Insurance and AFL-CIO)*	Immediate comprehensive coverage, including hospital stays; extended care; surgical; general and special physician services; diagnostic workups; preventive care; maternity and well-baby care; prescription drugs; rehabilitation services; vision care; dental care for young; psychological and psychiatric services; health and nutrition counselling; prosthetic devices.	Patient pays nothing.
NATIONAL HEALTH INSURANCE AND HEALTH SERVICES IMPROVEMENT PROGRAM *(Developed by Sen. Jacob K. Javits)*	Comprehensive medical coverage, including hospital stays; extended care; surgical; diagnostic workups; general and special physician services; annual physical exams; maternity; long term prescription drugs for chronic conditions; dental care for young children; psychiatric care in and out of hospital; medical appliances.	Patient pays first $52 of hospital stay and some co-payments for long term hospitalization and convalescent care. For other services patient pays first $50 plus 20 per cent of the bill. Drug co-payments are limited to $1 per prescription.
MEDICREDIT (FULTON-HANSEN PROPOSAL) *(Developed by American Medical Association)*	Limited comprehensive coverage, including hospital stays, extended care; surgery, radiation therapy, physician services; diagnostic services; preventive checkups; maternity; well-child care; psychiatric services in and out of hospital; hospital rehabilitation; catastrophic illness coverage.	Patient pays first $50 per hospital stay, plus nominal co-payments for other services. Patient also pays up to 20 per cent of adjusted gross income before catastrophic illness coverage takes over.

Several other plans have also been proposed. They include: Minimum Health Benefits and Health Services Distribution and Education Program, sponsored by Sen. Pell and Sen. Mondale; Ameriplan, developed by the American Hospital Association; National Health Insurance Plan, sponsored by Rep. Dingle: A catastrophic illness insurance measure developed by Sen. Long;

Financed by	Underwritten by	The Approach
For most, employers and employees will share premium costs. For the poor and near poor, states and Federal Government will subsidize premium costs up to 100 per cent.	Private carriers regulated by state insurance commissions, except for Medicare benefits	Establish upgraded benefit standards and provide access to health care financing for all. Phase in benefits to prevent overloading the health care delivery care system. Phase poor and near poor into the benefit program faster. Use co-payment system to hold down premium costs and prevent over-utilization. Use grants, loans and other incentives to expand health manpower, to distribute manpower and facilities properly and to create system of comprehensive ambulatory care centers. Absorb Medicaid and supplement Medicare benefits for over 65 population.
Employers and employees will share premium costs with employers eventually paying 75 per cent. Group-rate pools will be set up for state and local government employees, self-employed, small employers and people outside of labor force. For the poor the plan would pay all costs. A sliding scale of subsidies would apply to costs for families with incomes of $3,000 to $5,000. Social Security and Railroad Retirement recipients will be financed through Social Security taxes and Railroad Retirement contributions.	For employed persons, private carriers working under Federal regulations. For poor with dependent children—a Federal program. For all other poor—the present Federal State Medicaid Programs.	Mandate health insurance coverage through the employer-employee mechanism and establish civil court procedures for non-compliance. Establish risk pools for groups not covered by other means. Encourage with grants and loans the development of health maintenance organizations and permit families to elect this type of service. Increase output of health manpower with per-capita grant program to medical-dental training centers. Encourage proper distribution of health personnel under existing incentive legislation. Continue Medicare for aged.
One half with general federal revenues; one half with employer-employee wage taxes, self-employed tax, and tax on unearned income.	Department of Health, Education and Welfare through a Federal health security board and state health agencies.	Scrap private health insurance plans and finance costs publicly through new and existing federal taxes. Scrap co-payment system. Absorb Medicare and Medicaid into the new system, to complete federal administration of all health care financing. Encourage group practice and preventive medicine through an incentive system. Establish funds to increase health manpower. Empower HEW secretary to promote proper distribution of health manpower and facilities. No phasing.
General revenues and new Social Security taxes, shared in three equal parts by employers, employees and the Federal Government. Individuals and employer-employee groups can establish alternative private plans, with benefits equal or superior to the government plan and the financing by employers and employees on a 75 per cent-25 per cent basis.	The Department of Health, Education and Welfare with private carriers as intermediaries. Alternative private plans would be underwritten by private carriers working under HEW guidelines.	Liberalize and extend to the general population provisions of the Medicare Program, retaining the use of private carriers to administer claims. Provide for alternative, or superior plans in the private sector. Encourage organization or comprehensive health care centers through incentives. Phase poor, disabled and unemployed into system first, then extend plan to rest of population. Control costs by establishing interplay between private and public systems.
Sliding scale of tax credits based upon income. Poor and near poor would receive assistance through premium payment vouchers.	Private carriers under a national health insurance advisory board, chaired by secretary of Health, Education, and Welfare, and including commissioner of Internal Revenue Services, working through state insurance departments.	Support voluntarily purchased private health insurance premiums for the poor and near-poor with payment vouchers. Subsidize these costs for others with a sliding scale of tax credits based upon income. Set minimum federal standards for health insurance plans. Retain present Medicare program for people over 65.

A catastrophic illness insurance measure introduced by Rep. Hall; National Catastrophic Illness Insurance Program, introduced by Rep. Hogan.

Source: Health Insurance Institute.

Other Forms of Life Insurance | 38

FRATERNAL LIFE INSURANCE

LIFE INSURANCE BENEFITS are furnished to their members by many fraternal benefit societies on a basis similar to that utilized by the commercial life insurance companies. This was not always so. During their early history, these organizations, which exist for other purposes besides providing insurance for their members, conducted their insurance operations almost entirely according to the assessment premium plan [1] and issued contracts with many restrictions contained therein.[2] Today, however, the leading fraternal life insurance societies, writing the greater proportion of new fraternal life insurance, offer a contract with essentially the same terms as the commercial companies, develop new business through an agency system, and are subject to regulation by the states. With a possible few exceptions among the smaller ones, all of these societies maintain legal reserves on their life insurance obligations.[3]

In order to understand the unique characteristics of the fraternal benefit societies, and their current practices, it will be helpful to consider the nature of a fraternal order and to examine briefly their development as life insurance carriers.

Nature of Fraternal Benefit Societies

Fraternal benefit societies have existed in this country for over 100 years. The early fraternal societies were formed on a localized basis purely for

---

[1] See p. 656.

[2] It might be noted that the early contracts issued by the commercial companies also were much less liberal than they are today. See Joseph B. Maclean, *Introduction to Life Insurance* (New York: Life Office Management Association, 1948), pp. 198–201.

[3] Any society having as much as $5 million insurance in force usually operates on a legal reserve basis.

social and benevolent purposes. Members and their families were provided various forms of relief during sickness and unemployment or at death on an informal basis. In many societies, eligibility for membership depended on such factors as nationality, language, membership in some religious denomination or sect, or occupation. Many modern societies now accept members without regard to such factors but the greater number of them retain membership prerequisites such as those enumerated. Today some of the societies have both "social" and "beneficial" members with only the latter participating in the insurance benefits. This makes clear the fact that fraternals have basic functions which are not in the nature of insurance. It is the existence of the "fraternal" side of their operations which provides the basis for their favorable tax treatment.[4]

Fraternal benefit societies are defined and their supervision provided for in all of the states and the District of Columbia by special sections or chapters of their respective insurance codes, and except for the minimum reserve requirements, the provisions and requirements are somewhat less comprehensive than those sections or chapters pertaining to commercial companies. In this connection it is important to note that the commissioners of insurance of the several states have broad, general statutory powers which *enable* them to regulate and supervise all insurers to an extent greater than is evident from the specific enactments of the insurance codes. New York law defines a fraternal benefit society as follows: [5]

Fraternal benefit society, defined. Every incorporated society, order, or supreme lodge, without capital stock, formed, organized, and carried on solely for the benefit of its members and of their beneficiaries and not for profit, operating on a lodge system and having a representative form of government, which obligates itself for the payment of insurance or annuity benefits or both in accordance with this article, is hereby declared to be a fraternal benefit society within the meaning of this chapter.

The definition is self-explanatory except with regard to (1) "operating on a lodge system" and (2) what is meant by a "representative form of government." The New York Law in another section outlines the essentials of "operating on a lodge system" as follows: [6]

Lodge system, defined. Every such society having a supreme governing or legislative body and subordinate lodges, by whatever names known, into which members shall be elected, initiated, or admitted in accordance with its constitution, bylaws, rules, and regulations, which subordinate lodges shall be required by the constitution and bylaws of such society to hold regular or stated

[4] See p. 661.
[5] Article XIV, Section 450, New York Insurance Law.
[6] Article XIV, Section 451, New York Insurance Law.

meetings at least once in each month, and either to conduct prescribed ritualistic ceremonies for the initiation of new members or to carry on other altruistic, educational, fraternal, or recreational activities, shall be deemed to be operating on the lodge system.

A "representative form of government" connotes a supreme controlling body composed of representatives, elected either directly by the members or by delegates from the local lodges or intermediate bodies chosen in accordance with the society's constitution or bylaws. It is important to note that proxy voting is generally prohibited thus minimizing the use of this device as a means of perpetuating a management group. In addition to the interweaving of insurance and fraternal functions and their being managed through a representative form of government, another distinctive characteristic of fraternal benefit societies is characterized by their use of the so-called open contract. Under this contract the society's constitution and bylaws, and any future change therein, are or become a part of the contract with the member. In the "closed" contract of the commercial companies, the terms of the life insurance contract and the application therefore constitute the entire agreement between the company and the policyholder. This distinction and its advisability will be considered in more detail below.

Development of Fraternal Life Insurance. Fraternal life insurance made its appearance about the same time as industrial life insurance and in answer to the same needs—those of the low income groups of the population. The volume of life insurance written by the fraternals grew rapidly, particularly during the 1880's and 1890's, and in fact, during a part of this period, the amount of fraternal life insurance in force actually exceeded the ordinary insurance in force in all the commercial companies.

There were two main reasons for the prodigious growth of fraternal life insurance in the period from 1875 to 1895. The first of these was the number of failures of commercial life insurance companies about this time. The well-established commercial companies had always operated on sound business lines, but after the Civil War a large number of companies were organized, many of which were operated on unsound lines. In addition, state regulation at that time was, in general, inadequate. The panic of 1873, and the subsequent period of depression saw a large number of failures, leaving the public disappointed and distrustful of level-premium life insurance as furnished by the commercial companies.

The second reason leading to the growth of fraternal life insurance was the widely publicized view that insurance on the level-premium plan was unnecessarily expensive and, in view of the series of failures, hazardous to the purchaser. The fraternals claimed that reserves were unnecessary and that life insurance could be provided far more cheaply by operating under an "assessment system." The level-premium system is technical and complicated, and, in view of the many failures among those using it, it is not surprising that the public came to consider the insurance offered by the fraternals safer and more reasonable, particularly since it appeared to be much cheaper. In its early stages of development, fraternal life insurance was provided on a pure assessment basis with uniform assessments, irrespective of age, each time a death occurred. The inherent defects in this system did not become evident until later.[7]

Since 1919, fraternal life insurance has, until recent years, shown a steady decline in volume of insurance in force and now accounts for a far smaller share of the total life insurance in force than formerly. The prime reason for the spectacular decrease in the amount of fraternal life insurance in force was the relentless compounding of difficulties by a fundamentally defective idea—the assessment plan of insurance.

Another reason for the decline was the introduction of group life insurance by the commercial companies in the 1920's. One authoritative writer has expressed the impact as follows: [8]

Group insurance is probably the greatest blow ever received by fraternal societies. It has supplied the need for cheap term protection. In search of business the fraternals are being forced more and more to adopt the benefits granted by life insurance companies. They are criticized for so doing and are warned of the penalties they may expect in the shape of taxation. They are told to keep to their original simple forms of insurance, but on adequate rates, and find their prospects taken from them under these simple plans, by the coverage given by the group policies of the life insurance companies.

Since 1940, the volume of fraternal life insurance in force has shown a gradual increase, although at a much lower rate than that shown by the ordinary, industrial, and group insurance of commercial companies. In part, this increase is accounted for by the larger average certificate amount written because of inflation. But the greater part is due to the facts that today the fraternals operate on a legal reserve basis and that those societies writing the majority of the new business are operating on much the same basis as the commercial insurers as to the system and plans of insurance offered, the terms of their contracts, and the utilization of promotional and training methods for their agents.

At this writing, over $25 billion of life insurance is in force in fraternals, and this represents about 1.6 per cent of the total life insurance in force in the United States and Canada.[9]

---

[7] In passing, it is well to note that had the early fraternalists given the least attention to the available literature describing the disasters of the English friendly societies, the unsoundness of the assessment systems would have been clearly evident.

[8] S. H. Pipe, "History of Fraternal Insurance," *Record of the American Institute of Actuaries*, 1927, Vol. 16, p. 29.

[9] *Statistics of Fraternal Benefit Societies*, 1971.

Period of Transition

The Assessment System.   Fundamental in the assessment system is the assumption that there will be an annual influx of new members at the younger ages, thus tending to maintain the same average age for the whole group, which would prevent the cost of insurance from increasing.[10] The inequity of equal assessments, irrespective of age, is eventually bound to become apparent and to have some effect on the ability to secure and retain new members at the younger ages. But even if the average age were maintained, the assessment would increase as the original members began to reach older ages, because of the higher mortality cost at these older ages. Despite its inherent defects, some of the societies were able to continue operating under the assessment system for remarkably long periods, the result, probably, of the small insurance benefit provided by these societies resulting in increased assessments which were small and of the feeling that life insurance was not the only or even the most important reason for membership. Under such circumstances the inequities were not as obvious and did not have as great an impact at first as might otherwise have been the case.

The defects of the uniform-assessment system led to the adoption of the "graded-assessment system" under which assessments were graded upward by *age at entry*. This modification still failed to recognize the basic fact that the cost of insurance on a year-to-year basis depends on the *current age*. A few of the societies, realizing that the cost of insurance is related to current age, adopted the "natural premium" or "step-rate" plan for assessments. This was a financially sound plan, but as the commercial companies had discovered, prohibitive costs develop at the older ages and even yearly renewable term insurance on an adequate rate basis ultimately breaks down because of adverse selection at the higher ages.

Legislative Efforts.   Gradually, many of the societies came to realize that life insurance benefits must be based either on an adequate "natural premium" plan or, if *permanent* insurance was to be provided, on the level-premium plan with its attendant reserves. The ultimate transition to a sound actuarial basis, which has been accomplished by all the fraternal societies of consequence, was aided by legislation initiated by the fraternals themselves through action by their organizations, the National Fraternal Congress and the Associated Fraternities of America.

In 1892, after much virulent internal opposition was overcome, a uniform bill was drafted by the National Fraternal Congress (NFC) and recom-

---

[10] It might be noted that the system could be utilized successfully if all people of a given large political entity were required through taxation to contribute.

mended for enactment by the states. This first model bill did not deal with rates or actuarial solvency. Basically, it defined a fraternal benefit society, and provided for the licensing by and annual reports to the state and granted exemption of fraternals from most of the provisions of the state insurance law applicable to commercial companies.

In 1898, the *National Fraternal Congress Table of Mortality* was constructed on the basis of the experience of both fraternal benefit societies and commercial companies. In spite of its hasty construction and then imperfections, the *NFC Table* served for a considerable period as the basis for rates and the valuation of life insurance liabilities of fraternal societies. Its adoption evidenced recognition by the societies of the need for an actuarial basis for life insurance benefits. It probably had a greater educational result than any other mortality table has had. As one writer expressed it: [11]

It probably had a greater educational result than any other mortality table. . . . The maneuvers used in the construction of their own table had the appearance of a pseudo-actuarial setting to produce a desired result. But in its accomplishments the result was worth while. The fraternal societies had a great faith and a still greater courage to reform their system.

Following the construction of the *NFC Table,* an amendment to the uniform bill was prepared in 1900 which would have required *new* societies to charge rates based on that table but would have made no such requirement for societies already in existence. Wide disagreement over the amendment (known as the Force Bill) prevented any action from being taken, but the issue evoked considerable discussion concerning the actuarial aspects of fraternal life insurance.

In 1910, committees of the National Convention of Insurance Commissioners and of the fraternal organizations agreed on a new model bill. This bill, the Mobile Bill,[12] prescribed the *NFC Table* as the minimum basis for rates and provided for standards of actuarial solvency. The bill, which was enacted in thirteen states, required societies to attain adequate actuarial reserves gradually, or face dissolution or loss of license. Opposition to this bill soon appeared, and in 1912 another model bill, the New York Conference Bill, was agreed on. It modified the provisions of the Mobile Bill and added a provision permitting the separation of adequate and inadequate rate groups. Under the bill, members in an "inadequate-rate" class could transfer to an "adequate-rate" class by agreeing to pay the rates required. The New York Conference Bill was enacted by a substantial majority of the states.

The above review shows that even after the fraternals recognized the in-

[11] Pipe, *op. cit.*

[12] The meeting of the National Convention of Insurance Commissioners out of which this bill arose was held in Mobile, Alabama.

herent weaknesses in the assessment system, it required a considerable period of transition to bring about reform. This is understandable if it will be remembered that fraternals operate through a representative form of government and members had to vote to raise their own premiums, or *to reduce their own benefits*. Human nature being what it is and in face of a technical subject and a complete about face (albeit, a courageous one) on the part of management, it is not surprising that the early efforts to reform were not very successful, nor that final accomplishment took a considerable period. More recently, the National Fraternal Congress developed a model bill, The Uniform Fraternal Code, which has been approved by the National Association of Insurance Commissioners. Since its approval in 1955, with amendments, this Uniform Fraternal Code has been enacted in twenty-three states and Puerto Rico.

Modern Fraternal Life Insurance

Operate on Legal Reserve System.   With a few minor exceptions fraternal benefit societies now operate on a level-premium basis, charging adequate rates and maintaining reserves on a legal reserve basis. Virtually every state has a minimum valuation basis for fraternals and in some respects the requirements are more restrictive than for commercial companies.

The Fraternal Contract.   In contrast to the brief certificate, which was used earlier, that attested to the fact of membership and recited the contract of insurance, the modern fraternal life insurance certificate or contract is similar in most respects to the commercial company form and contains most of the provisions found in such policies. Although some state laws regulating fraternal certificates are not as restrictive as those applying to the commercial companies, the forces of competition and the desire on the part of the fraternals to provide "the best life insurance protection" to their members has led to the adoption, by either contract provision or company practice, of privileges essentially the same as those granted to commercial policyholders. For example, although the fraternal contract may not necessarily include a provision for assignment or as wide a range of settlement options, the right of assignment is generally recognized and settlement requests nòt specifically provided for are usually granted as a matter of society practice. It should be noted, however, that many societies do provide for assignment and a full range of settlement options in their certificates.

One of the unique features of the fraternal contract is the fact that it is an "open" contract. This means that unlike the commercial policy, which with the application constitutes the entire agreement, the fraternal contract includes the constitution and bylaws of the society and is subject to their provisions and to any amendments or additions thereto. In this connection one researcher stated:[13]

With fraternal societies collecting assessments in accordance with actuarial principles, as is largely the case today, the difference between the closed and open contracts lies in the procedure to be followed by the insurance organizations in time of financial stress. Under the *closed* contract the corporation must reinsure, merge or be forced into receivership. In any event, if there is a significant deficiency, the closed contract must be "opened" by either joint agreement of the parties or by a court of law so that appropriate liens may be levied. This is in contrast to the *open* contract where, under the same conditions, the supreme lodge of the society may act. The fraternal procedure is claimed to be quick, simple, and inexpensive.

The merits of the open contract have been much debated. As pointed out in the above quotation, the open contract permits assessments, but these would only be permitted in the event of insolvency, a condition which would necessitate a receivership for or the reinsuring of a commercial carrier.

It is pretty well established by case law that a fraternal benefit society cannot, under any circumstances, reduce the benefits promised without the consent of the individual members, each one as to his own case. This is not to say that a member cannot be required to pay, in the event of a reserve impairment, an equitable assessment in order to prevent a de facto reduction in the benefit to him.

Should the reserves of a society become impaired, the Board of Directors or the supreme governing body may levy an assessment on each member in an amount equal to his equitable proportion of the deficiency. The member may pay the assessment, in which case all is well. He may not pay it. Two alternatives then appear: the member, at his own option, may allow the unpaid assessment to become an interest-bearing lien against his certificate or he may accept a certificate with a reduced benefit, free of any lien, the present value of the reduction being equal to the assessment levied.

In all fairness to the fraternal system, it should be remembered that a commercial insurer is just as apt to find itself in a situation of reserve impairment as is a fraternal society operating on a legal reserve basis. When that situation obtains in a commercial company, the receiver, with the consent of the court, will establish liens and alternatives thereto no different in effect from those established by the Board of Directors or governing body, with the approval of the insurance commissioner, of an impaired fraternal

---

[13] Richard de R. Kip, *Fraternal Life Insurance in America* (Philadelphia: College Offset Press, 1953), pp. 112–113.

benefit society. Thus, in New York, only in the case of insolvency could a society exercise the open contract feature to reduce in any way the benefits guaranteed by the contract. In other states the approval of the insurance commissioner would undoubtedly be necessary before such a move could be taken.

Contrary to what is usually believed, use of an open contract is not restricted to fraternals. Commercial companies utilize this principle both in the noncancellable health insurance field and in group insurance coverages. In view of the purposes of fraternal life insurance, and governed as they are by a representative form of government, the fraternal benefit societies feel that the open contract is an attractive feature.[14]

The leading fraternals offer all of the ordinary life and endowment insurances including family income and the retirement income. For the most part they have not issued annuities except in connection with settlement arrangements. It should be noted, however, that many of the larger societies now issue annuities, some are issuing health insurance contracts, and at least one has set up a mutual fund outlet.

Field Organization.   Today, fraternal benefit societies are utilizing promotional methods similar to those of the commercial carriers. The more aggressive fraternals operate on an agency system built around so-called state managers and district agents. Training programs for new agents have been adopted by the leading fraternals, and in general, the sales organization of these societies resembles that of the commercial companies. In this regard, the fraternals concentrate their attention on their entire membership, as contrasted with ordinary companies who usually organize their marketing efforts toward those with higher than average incomes. It should be noted, however, that there are many fraternals who still depend essentially upon lodge members for new entrants. Naturally, their progress has been considerably less than those operating on an agency system.

Fraternal agents must be licensed in forty-one states, and are required, in at least eighteen states, to pass an examination as a prerequisite to obtaining a license.

Tax Exempt Status.   The fraternal benefit societies have continued to be exempt from premium taxation. Exemption for fraternals under the tax laws of most states stems from the fact that fraternals engage in community endeavors and charitable enterprise for their members, in

---

[14] One member of the fraternal field has suggested that the fraternals might create better understanding of their contract by referring to it as a "complete" contract rather than as an "open" contract. "Complete" indicates what happens in case of a reserve impairment, as opposed to the incomplete nature of the "closed" contract which does not indicate what happens in case of a reserve impairment.

addition to the insurance benefits provided. These activities take many forms, from extending financial aid to needy members, to hospitals, sanitoriums, old peoples' homes, youth development programs, and many other types of noncontractual fraternal benefits.

Thus, the "fraternal" in fraternal benefit societies is the primary justification for their favorable tax position. As the insurance operations of the fraternals have developed to a sound actuarial basis, the relative emphasis on the "fraternal" and "insurance" aspects has tended to differ from society to society, with the "insurance" aspect heavily predominating in some of the leading fraternals. There are those who feel that care should be taken to keep the "fraternal" in fraternal benefit societies. As one society official expressed it: [15]

For sixty-seven years we have found pride in a combined allegiance to business and fraternal principles. We believe our success as a leader in the insurance industry and as the outstanding institution among fraternals has come because we have not sought to emphasize one over the other. Rumblings are rightfully heard from the offices of regulatory bodies in the insurance field concerning those who stray from a proper adherence to the fraternal laws. Let us be careful that we are not the cause of such noises and let us look with scorn upon any who by such action would bring us into disrepute. Providing unselfishly for those we love and for release from the fear of deprivation finds its highest development in our activity as a true Fraternal Society.

Assessment Associations

There are a number of assessment and other similar associations operating on many different plans.[16] Although most of them utilize the level-premium plan and do not operate solely on an assessment basis, many of them do not set up any actuarial reserve as such. The larger associations maintain a large surplus which is some protection but may not be adequate to meet future liabilities. The right of the association to charge additional assessments is often not known to the insured. Under the laws of some states, adequate premiums and reserves are required in respect to new members of existing assessment associations, and a separation of assets is also required. In some states organization of new assessment associations is prohibited. It is doubtful that these associations supply any life insurance need which is not better supplied by the commercial life insurance companies or the fraternals.

[15] Howard M. Lundgren, Report of President, 31st Biennial Convention Sovereign Camp, Woodmen of the World Life Insurance Society, New York, July 22–25, 1957.
[16] For example, some operate by collecting one dollar from each member every time a member dies and the total collected is paid to the beneficiaries.

SAVINGS BANK LIFE INSURANCE [17]

Origin and Purpose

In 1907, Massachusetts passed a law empowering mutual savings banks in that state to establish life insurance departments for the purpose of providing life insurance and annuity benefits over-the-counter to residents or those working in the state. Since then, similar laws have been enacted in the State of New York in 1938, and in the State of Connecticut in 1941. The Massachusetts law was the result of proposals made by Louis D. Brandeis following the Armstrong Investigation [18] in New York. The testimony taken in the investigation had emphasized the excessive amounts spent by some of the companies at that time for commissions on new business and had also brought out the comparatively high cost of weekly premium industrial insurance which was due to the facts that premiums were collected weekly at the home of the policyholder and that industrial insurance was subject to a high rate of lapsation. Another fact contributing to the higher cost of industrial insurance was that it covered mainly low-income groups subject to relatively high mortality rates and was issued generally without medical examination.

The purpose of the Massachusetts law was to provide a system of low cost over-the-counter insurance to all residents of the commonwealth who were willing to avail themselves of life insurance and who exercised habits of thrift. *The reduction in cost under the savings-bank system depended primarily* on the elimination of the sales costs incurred by commercial companies, chiefly through eliminating commissions to soliciting agents and the benefit of a lower rate of lapsation. In addition, the "home collection" feature of industrial insurance was eliminated. On the other hand, in most cases the savings-bank system required a medical examination.[19] Consequently, although the savings-bank system originally provided insurance of small amounts at much lower cost than under industrial insurance, it *did not provide the same services* nor did it cover the same classes of people. Today, however, amounts up to $41,000 are available and surveys show that about the same classes of people purchase savings bank life insurance as do commercial life insurance. It should also be noted that the

[17] For a detailed treatment, see Donald R. Johnson, *Savings Bank Life Insurance* (Homewood, Illinois: Richard D. Irwin, Inc., 1963).

[18] An investigation by the State of New York, 1905, into many phases of life insurance company operations. Louis D. Brandeis acted as counsel for the Policyholders Protective Committee which had been formed as a result of the insurance investigation then under way in New York.

[19] Savings bank life insurance is available today on a nonmedical basis subject to age and amount restrictions.

mortality experience of savings bank life insurance plans has been very favorable.

The Massachusetts law provided that savings banks could participate either as "issuing" or as "agency" banks. Only a minority of the mutual savings banks, however, have taken advantage of the power to establish "issuing" insurance departments. In Massachusetts there are forty-one banks issuing policies and maintaining insurance departments. *One hundred thirty-four* others, however, act as agencies for the issuing banks. In New York there are fifty-eight issuing banks and fifty-four agencies; in Connecticut there are thirteen issuing and thirty-nine agency banks.

Bills for the establishment of savings bank life insurance have been introduced in a number of other states where the savings banks are not quite as strong and numerous, but since the Connecticut bill in 1941, none has passed. Quite naturally the most active opposition to savings bank life insurance has come from the life insurance agents' organizations, which consider savings bank life insurance an unfair threat to their means of livelihood. In the past, the commercial life insurance companies opposed such bills mainly on the ground that these earlier bills were discriminatory in that, under their provisions, the insurance departments of the banks were not made subject to the same conditions and requirements as the companies. More recent legislation has generally provided for the same requirements and conditions as apply to the commercial companies.

Nature

The distinctive feature of savings bank life insurance is that it is transacted on an over-the-counter basis, or by mail and without the use of soliciting agents. This normally results in considerable savings in expense, fewer lapses, and a low cost to policyholders.

Since a savings bank is not equipped to handle many of the technical details of the administration of a life insurance business, there is, in each state, a central organization which furnishes the actuarial, medical, and certain other services for the banks. The central organization computes the premium rates, which are the same for all issuing banks in a given state, and also prepares policy forms, application blanks, and so forth. Thus, in some ways the savings bank life insurance system is similar to a single life insurance company with the central organization serving as the "home office" and the individual banks the "branches." Each issuing bank, however, is an independent unit which issues its own contracts, maintains records, and retains and invests the assets of its own "insurance department." The surplus funds belonging to the insurance department of a bank are available only to the policyholders of that bank. In addition, the assets of the banking and insurance departments of a given issuing bank are kept separate from each other and the assets of one are *not* available for the liabilities of the other. Further, an equitable allocation of expenses between the savings department and the life insurance department is required. The central organization, however, maintains a contingency or "guaranty" fund, established by the contributions of the insurance banks, which is available, if needed, to protect policyholders of all participating banks.

An important feature of savings bank life insurance which lends stability to the system is the so-called unification of mortality. In view of the relatively small amounts of insurance issued or in force in many of the banks, the mortality experience of individual banks is subject to relatively large fluctuations from year to year. To lend stability to the individual banks, mortality costs for all participating banks in a given state are pooled or averaged and, in effect, each bank experiences proportionately the same mortality cost. Thus, by this process death losses are unified.

The banks have authority to sell the usual types of ordinary policies, annuities, and group insurance. Where the legal limits have been restrictive (see below), much of the insurance has been sold on women and children, but where they have been raised, more of the insurance is sold to men. Sales of term insurance, especially decreasing term insurance to cover the unpaid balance of a mortgage, have been proportionately higher than in the commercial companies. Waiver-of-premium benefits, in event of total disability, are available in all three states, but disability income and double indemnity benefits are not available under the ordinary forms of policies issued.

The terms of the contracts are similar to those of the commercial companies and all contracts are participating. Cash and loan values and non-forfeiture options are available after one year [20] and, in the early years, are on a more liberal basis than in the usual commercial company contract. These favorable values, of course, reflect the much lower first-year expense due to the absence of agents' commissions and other agency expenses and low overhead costs.

The amount of insurance obtainable by any one applicant is limited by law. Originally, the Massachusetts law limited policies to $500 in any one bank upon the life of an individual. The limit was later raised to $1,000 in each bank and in 1951, to $5,000 subject to an aggregate limit of insurance issued or in force at any time on any one life in all savings banks of $1,000 times the number of such banks. Under the law it is possible to obtain a total of $41,000 (the former limit of $1,000 per bank times the number of issuing banks). This is a larger amount of insurance than can be obtained under either the New York or the Connecticut system by an individual applicant. In the event more than $5,000 of insurance is desired, it is not necessary to go to more than one bank, since any participating bank can handle the whole application, acting as agent for the other banks.

Under the New York law the limit of insurance, whether in one bank or

[20] In Connecticut the cash value is available after six months' premiums have been paid.

in a number of banks, was originally $3,000 but was increased to $5,000 in 1948. In 1958 the basic limit for New York was increased to $10,000 with an exception in the case of decreasing term insurance permitting an additional $20,000. In 1967 the limit was increased to $30,000. In Connecticut the limit of insurance obtainable by one applicant, in one bank or more than one bank, was originally $3,000 but was increased to $5,000 in 1957. The minimum policy in Connecticut and Massachusetts is $500. The minimum in New York is $1,000 for adults and $500 for children.

Premium rates vary considerably among the three states but are all relatively low. Premiums may be paid monthly or less frequently and may be paid to any bank operating an insurance department or acting as a collecting agency for the system, or to other organizations serving as collection agencies for the system. In many cases, arrangements can be made to withdraw premiums automatically from a savings account.

Savings bank life insurance is available only to residents of or workers in the state but, of course, remains in force if the policyholder should leave the state.

Administration and Supervision

In Massachusetts there are, in effect, three "central organizations," namely, (1) the Division of Savings Bank Life Insurance; (2) the Savings Bank Life Insurance Council; and (3) the General Insurance Guaranty Fund.

The general supervision and regulatory control of the savings bank life insurance system in Massachusetts is in the hands of the Division of Savings Bank Life Insurance, one of the three divisions of the Department of Insurance and Banking. The Division employs a state actuary and a state medical director who serve all issuing banks. Under present law, expenses of the State Division are assessed upon the issuing banks and paid from policyholders' funds. The law forbids the use of soliciting agents, but since 1915, the division has employed two "instructors" whose duties are to "educate workers" throughout the state as to the advantages of savings bank life insurance.

In 1938, the issuing banks formed an association, the Savings Bank Life Insurance Council, and since then advertising and promotional activities and many operational functions have been gradually assumed by the Council. Formerly, many of these activities were conducted by the Division of Savings Bank Life Insurance. Today, the activities of the Division, in addition to supervision and administration, consist of furnishing actuarial, underwriting, and policy-making functions.

The General Insurance Guaranty Fund is an incorporated body of trustees appointed by the governor and forms part of the Division of Savings Bank Life Insurance. The primary function of the trustees is to serve as the governing body of the system. In addition, the *trustees* maintain and administer the joint contingency fund formed by the contributions which the law requires each individual insuring bank to make. Originally, the rate of contribution was 4 per cent of premiums. Currently, no contributions to this fund are being collected since growth by addition of income to the principal of the fund is deemed adequate. At the end of 1970, the amount in the Guaranty Fund was about $2,620,000. This fund is available in the event any participating bank experiences financial difficulties in its insurance operation, but no bank to date has ever had to call on the Guaranty Fund for assistance. Thus, the security of savings bank life insurance policyholders is represented by the assets of the insurance department of the bank in which they are insured, together with the guarantee of the General Insurance Guaranty Fund.

In New York all the administrative functions performed in Massachusetts by the three organizations described above are combined in the Savings Banks Life Insurance Fund. Supervision of the Fund and of the insurance departments of the issuing banks is the responsibility of the Superintendent of Banks in the same way as for commercial companies. In addition, they are subject to the supervision of the Superintendent of Insurance.

The Connecticut Law, which was enacted in 1941, was, in effect, identical in all important respects with the New York law until the Spring of 1963. Legislation enacted in Connecticut then changed the picture considerably.

The 1963 legislation provided for the merger of the Savings Banks Life Insurance Fund into The Savings Bank Life Insurance Company, a company chartered by the General Assembly of Connecticut.

The charter of the Savings Bank Life Insurance Company gives it the same corporate form and powers as other legal reserve life insurance companies authorized in Connecticut. The Company may issue policies on applications taken by savings banks acting as agencies of the Company, and it may reinsure the mortality and morbidity risks of policies issued by savings banks. In addition, the Company is empowered to serve savings banks in life insurance by providing them with the actuarial and medical underwriting services, formerly provided by the central fund.

The Company's charter authorizes it to serve mutual savings banks organized pursuant to the laws of the United States or any state, territory, or possession thereof. Therefore, any savings bank in any state having the authority to sell or write savings bank life insurance may utilize the Savings Bank Life Insurance Company as a central facility. It was not contemplated, however, that either New York or Massachusetts would utilize this facility,[21] the systems in these states being structured in accordance with existing state laws.

[21] For a discussion of the new facility for Savings Bank Life Insurance and its implications, see Walter E. Rapp, "New Horizons for Savings Bank Life Insurance," *Savings Bank Journal*, August, 1963.

Extent and Growth

As of December 31, 1970, the total volume of savings bank life insurance in force was about $4,114 million.[22] A great part of this total was in Massachusetts and New York. The amount in force in Massachusetts ($1,512 million) and in New York ($2,477 million) is growing at a steady rate while the growth in Connecticut (presently, $125 million in force) has been relatively slow due in part, at least, to the relatively small amount of life insurance permitted on one life under state law.

Admitted assets as of December 31, 1970, totaled $481 million of which $258 million were in Massachusetts, $203 million in New York and $20 million in Connecticut.

These figures indicate that, while the business and assets of savings bank life insurance are substantial, they are relatively insignificant when compared with the aggregate figures for the commercial life insurance companies. On the other hand, there will undoubtedly be a continued healthy growth in savings bank life insurance in force even if the program continues to be restricted to these three states.

[22] *Life Insurance Fact Book, 1971,* p. 99. Unless otherwise indicated, all statistics in this section were taken from this source.

BIBLIOGRAPHY

Special Forms of Life and Health Insurance

Bernstein, Merton C. *The Future of Private Pensions* (New York: The Free Press of Glencoe, 1964).

Biegel, Herman C., *et al. Pensions and Profit Sharing,* 3rd ed. (Washington, D. C.: BNA Incorporated, 1964).

Black, Kenneth, Jr. *Group Annuities,* S. S. Huebner Foundation Studies (Philadelphia: University of Pennsylvania Press, 1955).

Blicksilver, Jack. *Industrial Life Insurance in the United States* (Richmond: Life Insurers Conference, 1968).

Brinker, Paul A. *Economic Insecurity and Social Security* (New York: Appleton-Century-Crofts, 1968).

Davis, Malvin. *Industrial Life Insurance* (New York: McGraw-Hill Book Company, Inc., 1944).

Graham, W. J. "Group Insurance," *Transactions of the Actuarial Society of America,* Vol. XVII, Part II (October, 1916).

Gregg, Davis W. *Group Life Insurance,* 3rd ed. S. S. Huebner Foundation Studies (Homewood, Ill.: Richard D. Irwin, Inc., 1962).

Johnson, Donald R. *Savings Bank Life Insurance,* S. S. Huebner Foundation Studies (Homewood, Ill.: Richard D. Irwin, Inc., 1963).

Kip, Richard deR. *Fraternal Life Insurance in America* (Philadelphia: University of Pennsylvania Press, 1953).

Melone, Joseph J., and Allen, Everett T., Jr. *Pension Planning* (Homewood, Ill.: Richard D. Irwin, Inc., 1966).

McGill, Dan M. *An Analysis of Government Life Insurance,* S. S. Huebner Foundation Studies (Philadelphia: University of Pennsylvania Press, 1949).

_____. *Fulfilling Pension Expectations,* Pension Research Council, University of Pennsylvania (Homewood, Ill.: Richard D. Irwin, Inc., 1962).

_____. *Fundamentals of Private Pensions,* 2nd ed., Pension Research Council, University of Pennsylvania (Homewood, Ill.: Richard D. Irwin, Inc., 1964).

Pickerell, Jesse F. *Group Health Insurance,* rev. ed. S. S. Huebner Foundation Studies (Homewood, Ill.: Richard D. Irwin, Inc., 1961).

Pipe, S. H. "History of Fraternal Insurance," *Record of the American Institute of Actuaries,* Vol. XVI, 1927.

Satterthwaite, Joseph W., "The Private Pension System—Why It Should Be Preserved," *The Journal of the American Society of Chartered Life Underwriters,* Vol. XXV, No. 4 (October, 1971).

Taylor, Maurice. *The Social Cost of Industrial Insurance* (New York: Alfred A. Knopf, Inc., 1933).

Turnbull, John G., Williams, Arthur C., Jr., and Cheit, Earl F. *Economics and Social Security,* 3rd ed. (New York: The Ronald Press Company, 1968).

Whittaker, E. B. *The Social Responsibility of the Group Insurance Industry* (New York: Prudential Insurance Company of America, 1948).

IX Organization, Management, and Regulation of Life Insurance Companies

ORGANIZATIONS PROVIDING LIFE insurance may be broadly classified as (1) commercial, (2) governmental, and (3) other.

The role of government carriers, both Federal and state, has already been considered in connection with earlier discussions of Social Security benefits, government life insurance, and certain forms of accident and sickness benefits. Similarly, savings bank life insurance, fraternal life insurance, assessment associations, and certain nonprofit organizations providing death and accident and sickness benefits have each been treated as an institutional unit considering, in addition to the insurance protection provided, the characteristics of the organizations providing such benefits. The great portion of this book has been concerned with the contracts, coverages, and practices of commercial life insurance companies and this chapter, likewise, is devoted primarily to a discussion of the organizational, financial, and operational characteristics of this class of companies.

COMMERCIAL LIFE INSURANCE COMPANIES

The commercial life insurance companies may be classified as *stock* or *mutual*.

At times attempts have been made to classify companies on the basis of whether they issue insurance on the participating or nonparticipating plan. This seems inappropriate since stock companies may write participating insurance, nonparticipating insurance, or both plans of insurance. A number of states, including New York and New Jersey, still prohibit the sale of nonparticipating insurance by a mutual company but even here exceptions are permitted on such items as reinsurance, annuities, nonforfeiture options, dividend options, and the like. The distinguishing characteristic of a stock company is its stockholders. If a company has stockholders, it is a stock company; if it has not, it is a mutual company irrespective of the kinds of policies it issues.[1] The following discussion considers these from the point of view of (1) organization, (2) control, (3) financial stability, and (4) cost of insurance.

Organization

Although it is theoretically possible for a life insurance business to be undertaken by an individual or by a partnership, the form of organization required for a life insurance business should be one which will provide both permanence and a high degree of security of payment. Only a corporation has the inherent characteristics to meet these requirements and under the various state insurance laws that is the only form of business organization which is permitted to undertake a life insurance business.

Thus, from a practical and legal viewpoint the operation of the life insurance business requires the formation of a corporation. There are two different types of life insurance corporations, the stock company and the mutual company.

Stock Company. A stock life insurance company is one which is organized for the purpose of making profits for its stockholders. If the policyholders or "customers" of the company pay, each year, a fixed premium stated in their policies for their insurance protection, their policies are referred to as *nonparticipating,* since the policyholders share neither in any savings or profits nor in any losses which may arise in the operation of the business. Their fixed premiums represent both the initial and final cost to them for their insurance coverage. Stock companies, as pointed out below, sometimes issue *participating* as well as nonparticipating policies. In fact, some stock companies issue *only* participating insurance. When stock companies issue participating policies, either exclusively or in conjunction with the sale of nonparticipating policies, some states impose certain limitations on the extent to which the stockholders of the company may benefit from the participating business. The majority of states, however, impose no special regulation upon the participating insurance sold by stock companies.

The life insurance business is highly specialized and is subject in every state to special *insurance laws.* As in other respects, the formation of a life insurance corporation is regulated by these insurance laws. Under the state insurance laws a company must have a minimum amount of capital and surplus before it can secure a license to operate as a life insurance company.

---

[1] One author believes the criterion ought to be voting rights and recommends "mixed company" for companies in which both stockholders and participating policyholders have voting rights. See Joseph M. Belth, "Types of Life Insurance Companies," Chapter in Dan M. McGill, *Life Insurance,* rev. ed. (Homewood, Ill.: Richard D. Irwin, Inc., 1967), p. 790.

For instance, under New York law, a stock life insurance company must have a minimum of $1,000,000 capital and an initial surplus of 200 per cent of the initial capital. Where the initial capital is the minimum of $1,000,000, the initial surplus must be at least $2,000,000. These minimum capital requirements are intended to assure that the new company can make the required deposits,[2] has sufficient funds for normal operations, and has a "contingency fund" to meet any adverse fluctuations in experience which occur during the initial development period. Once the stock has been subscribed and the various state requirements met, the company can be organized by the stockholders and begin business.

Mutual Company.   A mutual life insurance company is a *corporation,* but has no capital stock and there are no stockholders. The company is organized and owned by its *policyholders* from whom all its resources are derived. The policyholder in a mutual company is both a "customer" *and* an "owner" of the company in contrast to the policyholder in a stock company who is a "customer" only. The policyholder in a mutual company is a member of the company and has the right to vote in the election of the board of directors or trustees.

Technically, the assets and income of a mutual company "belong" to the company. The policyholders are contractual creditors, with the right to vote for directors as provided by law. The company is administered, and its assets are held, for the benefit and protection of the policyholders and beneficiaries. In a broader sense, all of the assets and income belong to the policyholders and beneficiaries and either are held for their benefit and protection as reserves, surplus, or contingency funds or are distributed to them as dividends to the extent that management deems warranted as a result of the company's experience. Thus, in a mutual company, the policyholder pays, each year, a fixed premium stated in his policy (usually higher than the premium for a similar nonparticipating contract in a stock company), but the actual or net cost to the policyholder will depend on the amount of earnings of the company and on the amounts of any dividends allocated to his policy each year by the board of directors of the mutual company. The policies usually issued by a mutual company are, therefore, referred to as "participating," that is, policies eligible for dividends. The fixed premium stated in their contract is the initial cost and while it represents the maximum, the final actual cost would be less by the amount of dividends paid on the contract.

Normally, mutual companies issue only *participating* policies. Sometimes, however, mutual companies also issue nonparticipating policies, but these policyholders, as with policyholders of stock companies, are simply customers of the mutual company owned by the participating policyholders.

[2] See pp. 781–782.

The organization of a new *mutual* company presents some serious practical problems. As in the case of the stock company, funds are needed to cover the expenses of operation, make the required deposits with the state insurance department, and provide a surplus or contingency fund to meet any unusual fluctuations in experience before the company has had time to accumulate such funds from its operations.

In the case of a stock company, funds for all of these purposes are obtained from the sale of stock; but in a mutual company the only source of money income at the beginning will be the first premiums paid in by the original member-policyholders or funds borrowed to get the company going. The lack of profit incentive is undoubtedly a significant factor in the decision to form a mutual company, but, in addition, the statutory requirements for the formation of a new mutual life insurance company are so difficult as to make it almost impossible. For instance, the State of New York requires that a mutual company cannot *begin* operation as a going concern unless it has applications for not less than $1,000 each from 1,000 people with the full amount of one annual premium for an aggregate amount of $25,000, *plus* an initial surplus of $150,000 in cash. It should be apparent that there would be great practical difficulty in finding a large number of persons who are "insurable" and who are willing to apply for insurance in and to pay the first premium to a company which is not yet in existence, and not yet able to issue policies. These difficulties of organizing a new mutual company are so great that none has been organized for many years and no new mutual company is likely to be formed. The only practical way of organizing a new life insurance company is on a stock basis. A stock company, after it has been fully established and attained adequate financial stability, can be converted into a mutual company.[3]

Procedure.　　In general the procedure in organizing a new life insurance company is the same for both stock and mutual companies. Both types of carriers are corporations and must be organized in accordance with the provisions of the state laws applying to corporations generally, or, as is usually the case, in accordance with special insurance laws regulating the organization of insurance corporations.[4]

The various state laws as regards the organization of insurance companies are very similar, and the pattern prescribed by the law of New York

[3] Many of the large mutual companies in existence today (e.g., Metropolitan, Prudential, and Equitable of New York) were, in fact, originally stock companies that were "mutualized." At one time some states provided for a guaranty capital put up temporarily by those persons interested in forming a mutual company. This guaranty capital was to be retired as soon as the mutual company's operations stabilized financially. Sometimes the stock remained outstanding for some period while the company operated on the mutual idea. But this would hardly justify a separate classification as a type of carrier.

[4] At one time insurance companies were organized by a special act of the legislature which became the "charter" of the company.

is representative of the general procedure. In that state the incorporators (at least thirteen persons) first apply to the state for a charter setting forth the name of the company, its location, the type of business to be transacted, its powers and how they will be exercised, the method of internal control, the amount of capital (if a stock company), and any other essential particulars. In addition to advertising, in a prescribed manner, their plan to incorporate themselves as an insurance company, the organizers must file a "certificate of intention" and a copy of the charter with the superintendent of insurance for approval before they become a corporation. They then receive subscriptions to the capital if the company is to be a stock company or receive applications for insurance and the premiums therefor if the company is to be mutual. It is important to note that they may still not issue policies. When the legal minimum capital has been subscribed, or when the premiums on the necessary minimum amount of insurance in the case of a mutual company have been paid in, and when the statutory deposit has been made with the superintendent, the organization may be completed. At this point the subscribing stockholders or initial applicants for insurance elect the directors who in turn authorize the issuance of the stock or the policies as the case may be. At this organizational meeting the owners adopt bylaws covering such matters as the duties of officers and committees, regulations on investments, maximum amount of insurance to be written on a single life, the territory in which business is to be transacted, and others. The newly elected directors then meet to elect officers and set up committees of the board to take charge of particular departments of the general administration of the company, delegating powers appropriately. At this point, assuming the company's application for a license to do business in the state has been approved by the state insurance department, staff, supplies, and equipment may be secured and business begun formally.

Control

In comparing stock and mutual carriers, a second point to be considered is the question of control and the responsibility of management to the policyholders.

Stock Company. Since a stock company is owned by the stockholders, the directors and officers are responsible to them and not to the policyholders. As in all stock corporations, the actual control lies with the holders of the majority of the stock.

Technically, unwise or even unscrupulous handling of the affairs of the company are beyond the control of the policyholders. It should be noted that, as in the case of other large national corporations, a stock company with a large number of widely scattered stockholders is controlled by its management group through proxy arrangements. In such cases the effective control, in fact, is not in the hands of the stockholders or the policyholders but in the hands of the management group operating the company. The likelihood of management ignoring the interest of the policyholders, however, is largely hypothetical in the case of substantial and well-established stock life companies because of the comprehensive state supervision to which all life insurance companies are subject. In some cases limited participation by the policyholders in the management of a company is permitted. For example, policyholders may be given the right to elect a number of directors, although naturally a minority of the whole. It is also possible for a company to pass completely from stock control to mutual control.

(1) Mutualization of Stock Companies.   Some stock companies have been converted from their stock form into mutual form through a procedure that is called "mutualization." In essence, mutualization involves the retirement of the outstanding capital stock of the company coupled with the transfer of control of the company from the stockholders to the policyholders. The motivations for such a move vary widely, including, for example, a desire to prevent control of the company from falling into undesirable hands through a change in stock ownership.

The officers of the company usually initiate mutualization proceedings by submitting a proposal to the board of directors. The key factor is, of course, the price to be paid for each share of stock and the manner of payment. The price must be attractive enough from the viewpoint of the stockholders to induce them to relinquish their rights of ownership and control. On the other hand, from the company's viewpoint, the price must be limited practically by the fact that the remaining surplus, after mutualization, must be adequate to permit sound operation of the company. Sometimes it is quite important that the payment for the shares be spread over a period of time so as not to impose an undue burden on current surplus.

If the plan, including the price to be offered to the stockholders, is approved by the board of directors, the plan must be submitted to the state insurance department for the approval of the commissioner of insurance. Assuming the proposed plan is approved by him, it will then be submitted to the policyholders and stockholders in accordance with the requirements of the applicable state insurance law.

In executing a mutualization plan approved by the necessary majorities, the company takes up the stock to the extent feasible. Some of the stockholders may object to the plan for one reason or another, and the process of taking up the stock will usually require some time. As the stock is bought up, it is not cancelled but transferred to trustees for the policyholders, who vote the stock in their behalf. Normally, a substantial majority of the total stock can be purchased immediately, so that effective ownership and control are obtained by the policyholders. Ultimately, when all the shares of stock have been purchased, the stock may be cancelled and the company becomes fully mutualized.[5]

(2) *The Holding Company.* In recent years, the use of holding companies has been the central theme of the intercorporate reorganizations that have occurred in managements' attempts to help their organizations improve their earnings and long-term growth possibilities through diversification. For the most part, the holding companies are financial corporations owning or controlling one or more insurers, mutual fund broker-dealer organizations, mutual fund management investment research companies, consumer finance companies, and other financially related corporations. Some stock life insurance companies are owned or controlled by nonfinancial holding companies and conglomerates that group together companies in unrelated fields.

This latter development has been viewed with alarm by some. A Special Committee on Insurance Holding Companies appointed by the Superintendent of Insurance of the State of New York concluded[6]

that the holding company device, when it involves affiliation with non-insurance enterprises, jeopardizes the interest of both the public and the policyholder, and especially will do so if its development is indiscriminate and without benefit of close regulatory supervision.

The Committee went on to recommend the relaxation of some restraints, traditional in insurance practice and insurance law, which they felt had unnecessarily added to the pressures to organize noninsurance holding companies. These recommended changes related to the formation and acquisition of subsidiaries, disclosure of intercorporate relationships among parents and subsidiaries and their affiliates to the Superintendent of Insurance, the liberalization of investment regulations, and greater freedom in raising capital through the sale of senior securities and securities convertible into equities.[7]

---

[5] For a recent study of mutualizations, see Linda Pickthorne Fletcher, "Mutualization of Stock Life Insurance Companies" (Ph.D dissertation, University of Pennsylvania, 1964). Although rare, a few mutual companies have converted to stock form. See, for example, "Memo Explains How Mutual Life Company Switched to Stock," *The National Underwriter* (Life ed.), March 27, 1965, p. 21.

[6] *Report of the Special Committee on Insurance Holding Companies,* State of New York Insurance Department, 1968, p. 7.

[7] For a summary of developments in the holding company area, see Kenneth Black, Jr., and John F. Adams, "Insurance Company Organization and Finance," Working Papers, International Insurance Seminar, Tokyo, Japan, July 26–30, 1970, pp. 53–70.

Mutual Company.   In a mutual company the policyholders theoretically own the company and control the management; in practice, this is true only to a limited extent. The limited effectiveness of the policyholders' control of a mutual company is due to the facts that (1) policyholders are numerous; (2) they are widely scattered geographically; (3) they have little capacity for intercommunication; (4) the stake of each policyholder in the company is proportionately small; and (5) many policyholders do not understand the nature of a mutual company or know that they have a right to vote at elections of directors. The fact of the matter is that the *directors and officers,* in effect, control the mutual company. As in the case of the well-established stock company, a well-established mutual is controlled by its management group through proxy arrangements. Again, lack of control by the policyholders is not serious, particularly in view of the character and extent of the supervision exercised by state authorities. In view of the highly technical nature of the business, it is probably best that it is not too easy for policyholders or stockholders to interfere in the management of the company.

The relationship of mutual insurance companies to the holding company device is somewhat different from that of the stock insurance company. The holding company formed by one or more stock companies has been called an "upstream" holding company. It sits at the top of the intercorporate structure; it is owned by stockholders, and, in turn, it owns subsidiaries. A so-called downstream holding company is usually formed by a mutual insurance company;[8] it sits in the middle of the intercorporate structure; it is owned wholly or in part by the mutual which sits at the top; and it owns subsidiaries. The significance of the distinction is that the downstream holding company presents few regulatory problems to state insurance departments, because the parent mutual is directly subject to insurance regulations. As a consequence, a downstream holding company is a viable device only if the parent mutual has a very strong surplus position, and, under present laws,[9] can never have the flexibility available to an upstream holding company.

The large mutual life insurance company with a significant surplus position is capable of diversification through acquisition or otherwise by simple management decision, provided the activity is permitted by the state insurance department. It would not appear that the holding company

---

[8] Downstream holding companies may be formed by a stock company also.

[9] This may well be legislated at the state level both by the demand for equality of opportunity by mutuals and some of the excesses in the withdrawal of insurance company assets by some conglomerates. See James S. Kemper, Jr., "Rush to Diversify: New Ideas for Old Money," *Conglomerates and Congenerics—Their Impact on the Insurance Industry,* Society of CPCU, New York Chapter Clinic, *CPCU News* (March, 1969), p. 39.

device is significant to such organizations if greater flexibility, such as was recommended by the "Report of the Special Committee on Insurance Holding Companies" in New York,[10] is granted. It should be noted that there has been some interest on the part of mutual life insurance companies to attempt conversion to stock insurers.

Security

In comparing stock and mutual companies the question of security of benefit is a point to be considered. In the initial period of development of a stock company, the capital and surplus paid in by the stockholders is a significant factor in the company's guarantee of payment. In later years this element of security becomes much less important. In most stock life insurance companies, the capital stock and paid-in surplus are eventually very small compared with the total liabilities of the company. A contingency or guarantee fund is still necessary to absorb unfavorable fluctuations and losses, but it will be primarily composed of surplus earnings and profits accumulated over the years. In a mutual company, of course, no capital stock exists and its guarantee fund will be entirely made up of surplus earnings. In a mutual company all the assets and all earnings arising from these assets and from the operations of the business are held by the company for the benefit and protection of the policyholders. These earnings will be available to reduce the cost of insurance or may be added to the company's surplus as additional safety funds.

The relative security of stock and mutual companies is largely an academic question. As between stock and mutual companies, the more conservative assumptions underlying the premium rate structures of mutual companies afford a safety margin and, therefore, an additional element of security to policyholders in mutual companies. The value of this additional margin will often be much larger than the capital of stock companies. The basic issues underlying security, however, are sound and efficient management and adequate supervision and control by governmental authorities. Incompetent management can be disastrous to policyholders, but this has seldom occurred. But this is true of any new business enterprise and is not solely a function of the method of organization and control of the corporation. In general, the policyholder in any well-established company, whether stock or mutual, need not concern himself with the question of security as such.

---

[10] *Ibid.*, pp. 39–41. See also John T. Fey, "Markets and Marketing in the Age of Conglomerates and Congenerics," *Best's Review,* Life/Health Insurance edition (January, 1970), p. 26.

Cost

From the policyholder's viewpoint, a significant point of comparison between stock and mutual companies is the relative cost of life insurance. Stock companies usually issue nonparticipating policies, that is, policies which do not provide for dividends so that the annual cost to the policyholder is fixed by the premium rate. For the most part, mutual companies issue policies at premium rates higher than those of the stock companies but carrying the right to participate in earnings through dividends which may or may not result in a lower "net cost" than in the stock company.

In general, stock company nonparticipating rates are fixed on a basis which is expected to cover the cost of the insurance and a margin for profit to compensate stockholders for the risk they incur. In mutual companies, participating rates are set at more conservative levels, but policyholders, through dividends, receive their insurance at "cost" with no element needed to compensate stockholders. As between participating and nonparticipating policies (including those issued by the same company), it seems clear that the cost of nonparticipating policies is lower in the early years, but the net cost of participating policies is normally distinctly lower thereafter and over the long run.

Since a stock company may, and many do, issue participating policies, a stock customer holding a participating policy may be in essentially the same position as a mutual company customer as far as *cost* is concerned except for any profits flowing to the general company account. Similarly, some mutual companies issue nonparticipating contracts. Consequently, the comparison of relative costs depends on the systems of providing insurance —participating and nonparticipating—as well as on a comparison of types of companies as such. It is true, however, that most of the participating insurance is issued by the mutual companies and most of the nonparticipating insurance by the stock companies.

Participating and Nonparticipating Systems.   The gross premiums charged by mutual companies for participating insurance include a margin which not only covers all expenses, but also usually includes an additional amount to safeguard the company against any possible contingencies. Then, as earnings emerge, they are, to the extent that the board of directors may authorize, returned to policyholders in the form of dividends, thus giving them protection at substantially actual cost. The stock company normally follows the plan of discounting the future—that is, of paying its dividends in advance—by charging a guaranteed low premium, whereas the mutual company asks a higher premium to start with and subsequently reduces the cost through the payment of dividends.[11] In practice, therefore, a comparison of the showing which stock companies make from the standpoint of ultimate cost of insurance to the policyholder and the showing made by a mutual company requires a comparison of the net annual cost of the policy in the two companies over a long period of time.

(1) Cost Comparisons.   There are a number of ways of presenting cost comparisons.[12] The most widely used method has been labeled the "traditional method." Its process is to add together the premiums for a period of years, usually twenty, and to subtract the cash value at the end of the period and the sum of all policy dividends shown in the life insurance company's illustration for the period. The result is averaged over ten or twenty years and the result described as "Average Surrendered Net Cost." An industry committee, in its report on life insurance costs, summarized the Traditional Method when it is used as an index of comparative net cost as follows:[13]

(1) It assumes that the current dividend scale will continue unchanged, a clearly artificial assumption and certainly not an expectation. Nobody knows what dividends will be paid on participating policies in years ahead. Illustrative dividends do not represent estimates of what a company will pay. They are nothing more than just the company's current dividend scale as it would apply to a currently issued policy.

(2) It assumes that future changes in dividend scales will affect all companies in roughly the same manner or degree. Again, this is most unlikely to be the case since it disregards changing patterns within companies as to investment yields, underwriting results, and expenses of operation.

(3) By ignoring interest it fails to give any recognition to the *time* when a dollar is paid either by or to the policyholder. The effect of this generally is to attribute a lower cost to a participating policy than to a like nonparticipating policy, to a policy with high premiums and high cash values than to a like policy with low premiums and low cash values, and to a policy with low early and high later dividends than to a policy with a "flatter" dividend pattern.

(4) It is based on the artificial assumption that the purchaser will keep his policy in force for exactly 20 years (or other period used) and then surrender it.

[11] The modified life policy was introduced by a mutual company to meet the competition of nonparticipating policies. See pp. 95–96.

[12] See Price Gaines, Jr., editor, *Cost Facts on Life Insurance* (Cincinnati, Ohio: The National Underwriter Company, 1969).

[13] *Report of the Joint Special Committee on Life Insurance Costs,* Report to American Life Convention, Institute of Life Insurance and Life Insurance Association of America (New York: Institute of Life Insurance, May 4, 1970), p. 6.

(5) In many cases it carries an implication that may strike a buyer as puzzling, that is, if he keeps his policy in force for the indicated period his insurance will have cost very little, or less than nothing.

After a careful review of the various cost comparison methods that have been suggested, the Committee recommended that the so-called *Interest-Adjusted Method* be utilized in making cost comparisons. The Committee felt that this method was most suitable because:[14]

(1) It takes time of payment into account.

(2) Of all the methods that take time of payment into account it is the easiest to understand.

(3) It is possible to use this method without having recourse to advanced mathematics.

(4) It does not suggest a degree of accuracy that is beyond that justified by the circumstances.

(5) It is sufficiently similar to the Traditional Method so that transition could be accomplished with minumum confusion.

The steps required to apply the Interest-Adjusted Method to a policy with level annual premiums are as follows:

1. Select the period over which the analysis is to be made (10 or 20 years).

2. Select the interest rate to be used (currently 4 per cent).

3. Accumulate the annual dividends, if any, at interest to the end of the selected period, and add to them the cash value (and terminal dividend, if any) available at the end of the period.

4. Divide the result of Step 3 by an interest factor that converts it into a level annual amount accruing over the selected period. If the period is 20 years and the interest rate is 4 per cent, this factor is 30.969, or, with sufficient accuracy, 31.

5. Subtract the result of Step 4 from the annual premium. This is the Interest-Adjusted Cost. Divide by the number of thousands of the amount of insurance to arrive at the Interest-Adjusted Cost per thousand.

The Committee report gave a series of comparisons[15] of results obtained by the Traditional Method and by the Interest-Adjusted Method. Many company rankings remained about the same under either method, but there were enough substantial changes to justify making allowance for interest by using the Interest-Adjusted Method instead of the Traditional

[14] *Ibid.*, p. 21.
[15] *Ibid.*, Appendix C.

average surrendered net cost method. The relatively high rates of interest prevailing make the development of the Interest-Adjusted Method particularly appropriate at this point in time.

All methods of presenting the "cost of life insurance" have advantages and disadvantages. There is, however, a specific problem inherent in participating insurance brought on by the use of projected net cost figures. Net cost proposals, of necessity, illustrate an ultimate net cost or cost index which is usually based on the *current* dividend scale of the company. The companies issuing participating policies caution their agents to tell prospects that projections of dividend scales are illustrative only, and, in fact, include a statement accompanying dividend illustrations, which clearly states that such illustrations neither imply nor guarantee future experience. Dividend projections commonly reflect experience current at the time, and if dividends actually paid by a company over a subsequent period of years are more or less favorable, this reflects improved or worse actual experience with respect to such things as interest earnings, mortality, expenses, and so forth, in relation to what was assumed in the projection. A comparison of earlier projected dividends with the actual dividend histories on a particular plan with a particular company may show a consistently conservative projection. It would appear reasonable to place more credence in a company's projected net payments or net cost presentations where they have consistently paid more in dividends than they have projected. Naturally, these comments on net cost are appropriate whether the cost comparisons are between a participating policy and a nonparticipating policy or between two participating policies.

Much has been written concerning the question as to which system, participating or nonparticipating, will give the cheaper protection to the insured. The showing made under the two plans will depend upon the companies under consideration, and the future experience under the two types of contracts. The controversy concerning the subject consists primarily of a discussion of companies and their management. It should be recognized that a true comparison of the two plans as regards the cost of insurance—a comparison of systems and not of companies—requires that the companies used for illustrative purposes should operate under precisely the same conditions, that their managements should have equal ability and integrity, that they should do approximately the same amount of business yearly, and that their policies should be alike in their provisions. There are no two such companies!

(2) *Advantages and Limitations of Systems.* The advantages of nonparticipating policies are (1) a guaranteed and fixed annual cost and (2) a lower immediate premium payable for a nonparticipating policy. Since nonparticipating premiums are not subject to adjustment, they must be as low as safely possible in order to meet the "net cost" competition of participating policies. In view of the long-term nature of the contract, the non-

participating premium must contain some margin over anticipated costs and also some provision for profit to the stockholders or a provision for contribution to the general surplus of the company if the nonparticipating policy is issued by a mutual company. This contribution to the general surplus of the mutual company is essential to maintaining an adequate surplus to provide unquestioned security for the company's policyholders in general and, normally, will not be returned to the policyholder. The premiums charged for participating policies, on the other hand, are large enough to generate earnings. Refunds in the form of policy dividends are made, usually annually, based on the company's actual experience in rates of interest, mortality, and expense. The actual outlay for insurance by a participating policyholder is thus measured by the premium less the dividend, that is, the *net payment* mentioned earlier.

Assuming the companies were equally efficient and well managed, there is no automatic cost advantage to either system. In the nature of things interest, mortality, and expense experience may produce entirely different results over different periods of time. The higher gross premium on the participating plan may result in a higher commission amount payable and unless dividends are applied to purchase paid-up additions, will result in a slightly higher rate of expense per unit of coverage. Some companies may also have a lower commission rate, plan for plan, and a nonparticipating policy does not have to bear the cost of the complex system of calculation and general accounting for dividends themselves. Finally, the greater margin in the participating premium earns interest until refunded as a dividend, thus increasing the amount available for distribution as a dividend. The nonparticipating policyholder has the use of this overcharge and the value of the right to use this money is an additional factor to be considered in comparing participating and nonparticipating policies. As pointed out earlier, however, the nonparticipating policyholder's premium includes a charge for profits to stockholders and this kind of a charge is not made to participating policyholders.

The participating plan has the general advantages of (1) giving an added margin for safety and (2) making greater equity among all policyholders possible. In the event adverse experience develops, dividends can be reduced, thus providing a stabilizing factor not available in nonparticipating premium rates on old policies where premium rates, to some extent, would have to be increased on new business to make up losses suffered on business already in force. Theoretically, at least, participating policies should permit the attainment of greater equity among policyholders.

Competition within the industry is such that the leading companies have to hold their rates reasonably in line, whether they are participating or nonparticipating, if they want to maintain their position in the industry. It should be pointed out, however, that price competition, to the extent it is effective, applies only at the point of sale. Once a nonparticipating contract is issued, it is fixed for better or worse, depending upon the experience as it develops. The first premium on a nonparticipating policy fixes the price for all time whereas, on a participating policy, old policyholders share in the experience of the company as reflected in annual dividends. Assuming other things equal and improving conditions as to interest, mortality, and expenses, the policyholder who wants to participate in such improved conditions should buy a participating policy. On the other hand, assuming a worsening of the experience, the policyholder who wants to fix his outlay should buy a nonparticipating policy. It should be remembered, however, that other factors (the agent, the importance of fixed cost compared with experience cost, policy benefits, service, and so forth) are equally if not more important in choosing a participating or nonparticipating policy.

From the viewpoint of the participating policyholder, he has the cost advantage of applying his dividends to purchase paid-up additions at net rates without evidence of insurability.[16] The other dividend options also lend flexibility to his contract. Whether these privileges have a cost value to the policyholder depends upon how he uses his dividends.

In summary then, there is no automatic cost advantage either to a particular type of company or to the participating or nonparticipating system of providing insurance. The buyer's appraisal of future economic conditions and the quality of service to be provided by a company and his objectives and planned utilization of the policy benefits are all important factors in making a decision to purchase a particular policy under a particular system from a particular company. The ultimate experience with regard to interest, mortality, and expense, the actual quality of management of a particular company, and the actual utilization of the policy benefits by a policyholder all will have a bearing on each individual case.

INDIVIDUAL COMPANY CHARACTERISTICS

From the buyers' viewpoint, a company's individual management, philosophy, and practices are much more significant than whether the company is a stock, mutual, or other type of carrier. Probably the only way to measure the management of a company is in terms of performance. Consequently, such factors as the nature of the product, cost, service, and security are the fundamental yardsticks for measuring the quality and appropriateness of a given company. The problem is complicated, however, by the fact that these factors are interrelated. For example, it should be clear that a company providing life insurance at a low cost may reflect excellent management or it may reflect little service or a restrictive contract.

---

[16] This is also true of substandard insurance; dividends are applied at *standard* net rates.

Nature of the Product

Individual life insurance companies do not always attempt to serve the same markets. For example, many companies do not write industrial life insurance or group insurance. Others may operate solely or for the most part in these or other specialized areas. Again, individual company managements may differ strongly on the advisability of providing health insurance coverage. The point is that the organizational structure, service facilities, and cost of operation for these areas of coverage differ widely, and one area of operation may have an impact on the cost of another. In addition, the mass distribution philosophy of group insurance at some points comes into apparent if not real conflict with the basic philosophy underlying the sale of ordinary insurance. The advantage of greater premium income and spread of risk brought about by multifield operations might be offset by the extreme competition in areas such as group insurance and the greater risk to the company inherent in the subjective nature of the sickness risk. Further, once a company has attained a sufficient size to realize fully the economies of scale, further expansion into multifield activity might lead to increasing costs because of management problems.

In addition to varying philosophies about fields of operation, individual companies vary considerably in the range and type of contracts made available. The need for product differentiation may well make it virtually impossible for the average buyer to make any comparison between the contracts of two individual companies. For example, the premium redistributions involved in modified life contracts, return of premium provisions, variations in early cash values, dividend scales, and other modifications all complicate any such comparisons. Package or combination policies likewise further complicate the problem of which contract is the most appropriate for a particular set of circumstances. The contracts of individual companies also differ with regard to liberality. Thus, many companies do not include a change of plan provision as a matter of *contract right,* although most will permit it as a matter of practice. Again, the settlement options included in an individual contract may be more liberal than in that of another company. The guaranteed cash values may differ considerably from company to company and even within a given company on different contracts. It should be remembered that there is no standard life insurance contract and except for the standard provisions required by state law, only competition causes a tendency toward uniformity. Thus, when a new benefit or contract feature is introduced successfully by one company, others tend to adopt it also. It should be noted, however, that competition also works against uniformity. It serves as an incentive for companies to develop distinctive and improved contract features to differentiate their product and be able to make the best possible competitive showing. The point here is not that a standard contract is necessarily desirable, but that inadequate comparisons of cost and coverage may be grossly misleading because of product differences.

A final factor of significance in regard to the product, as regards individual companies, is the underwriting practices of the individual company. Many companies issue substandard business and all differ as to what constitutes a "standard" risk. Some companies are much more liberal than others in regard to the flexibility permitted in utilizing settlement options. It is axiomatic that, other things being equal, greater liberality in company practices implies more service and higher costs.

Service

Service is, of course, a nebulous term. In terms of individual companies, variations are primarily a matter of management philosophy rather than the type of carrier. In some companies a request for information, a policy loan, processing a death claim, or other aspects of the "performance" of a life insurance contract will be handled much more quickly than in other companies. This greater service implies greater cost, and may result from broader authority in local field offices or from other specific emphasis in terms of planning and personnel. In terms of service by the life underwriter, there is even greater variation in service. Some companies place great emphasis on the training of the agents and spend large sums keeping them fully informed in regard to legal, tax, and other changes which vitally impinge on the service which a given underwriter is *capable* of rendering. A separate question, in regard to the amount and adequacy of service from any underwriter, is his *desire* to serve.

Cost

The factor of cost in measuring the performance of individual companies is the one which receives considerable attention by buyers. Actually, as the preceding discussion has indicated, it is virtually impossible for the layman to compare the cost of two individual companies because of the many variables which are involved. Too often it is assumed that a simple comparison of premium rates is all that is needed. Actually, the premium rate reflects the management philosophy in terms of safety, service, liberality of contract provisions, and other factors.[17] Obviously, it would be misleading

[17] Companies not using agents can offer insurance at lower rates. The question of the value of an agent's service may be debated, but it does have a definite money cost and value.

to compare the initial premium rates of a participating and a nonparticipating plan of insurance, since the participating premium includes a margin for payment of dividends.

But there is no way in advance to know what level of dividends will actually be paid on participating insurance, since this will depend on the experience of the company in future years in terms of investment yields, mortality experience, and expense of operation. Consequently, it is impossible to know in advance with certainty which company or contract will have the lowest net cost.[18]

Over and above the possibility that net cost illustrations may be misleading, they place emphasis on "cost" buying to the exclusion of the real needs of the buyer and the appropriateness of the particular contract under consideration. Due to the emphasis on cost in sales presentations, very inefficient companies have been able to market contracts with very limited benefits and contract provisions at what appear to be startlingly low rates. It is fundamental that a $20,000 house and a $40,000 house may be equally good "buys."

Security

The final yardstick in measuring the performance of a given company is the question of security of benefit. Again, it is difficult to lay down any general rules as to what makes a company safe. The amount of insurance in force has little to do with safety. Insurance in force represents the amount of money the company has contracted to pay at the maturity of all outstanding policies. The policy reserves underlying the insurance in force are liabilities and certainly do not measure the safety of the company. Again, the size of the company in terms of assets has little to do with safety even though the relative conservatism of the valuation basis has a direct relationship to security. Assets are largely a result of building up policy reserves which represent the company's present estimate of the amount necessary with future premiums to meet its contract obligations as they fall due. Minimum reserves are established by state law, but most well-established companies hold reserves much in excess of the minimum reserves established by state law. The extent to which a company holds reserves in excess of the minimum is a function of management philosophy and judgment.

Other factors affecting security are underwriting standards and underwriting practices, quality of investments, and the amount of surplus. The

[18] In fact, a limited sample of prices for straight life policies issued in 1962 to standard males age 35 showed that both the absolute and relative variation in participating straight life prices were substantially greater than the corresponding measures in the nonparticipating straight life prices studied. See Belth, *op. cit.,* p. 73.

ratio of policyholders' surplus to total assets is one measure of safety, usually quoted, but the reserve policy of the company will have a direct effect on this ratio, since the surplus position of a company will appear stronger in face of a minimum reserve policy. State law sets the minimum safety standard for investments. The investment skill of a given company lends an extra margin of safety. It must be remembered that the objective of investment policy is the maximum rate of return consistent with absolute safety. Judgment is, of course, an element in setting such policy.

The factor of safety is not subject to absolute objective measurement. If it were, state insurance departments would be able to guarantee absolute safety, which they in fact have not been able to guarantee through present modes of regulation. If a rating institution or a state insurance department gives a bad rating to a company, this is worthy of consideration. On the other hand, a good rating by such organizations is not conclusive in terms of safety as evidenced by past experience.[19]

The preceding discussion indicates two important points. In the first place it is very difficult for a well-informed person to compare individual companies, their contracts and their costs of operation; secondly, it is virtually impossible for the average layman to do so.

Then what course is open to the layman in utilizing the services of the life insurance industry? The complex nature of the business, its social implications, and the inability of the average layman to cope with the problem have led to comprehensive state regulation and a demand for professionalization of the vocation of life underwriting. The buyer of insurance has the problem of determining his need for life insurance, selecting appropriate contracts, and setting them up in a way to maximize the effectiveness of his premium dollars. By carefully selecting an underwriter who will consider him a client and render a truly professional service, a buyer will have the best chance that he will solve his life insurance problems in a satisfactory manner. If insurance is purchased from a well-established company, state regulation will provide assurance that security of benefit will be obtained.

---

[19] See Chapters 42 and 43 for a more thorough discussion of interpreting annual reports and other sources of information regarding a particular company's operations.

Organization of Companies | 40

HOME OFFICE ORGANIZATION

FUNDAMENTALLY, THE ORGANIZATION of a life insurance company home office follows the pattern of other corporations which are concerned with the collection, investment, and disbursement of funds. Organization possesses three main elements: (1) levels of authority, (2) departmentalization, and (3) functionalization. Each of these elements plays an important role in establishing an efficient organization structure and also in insuring efficient co-ordination of effort within that structure. The organization of a life insurance company is no different in that it possesses these elements. In terms of total organizational structure, life insurance companies are most frequently *line-staff-functional* organizations. Individual segments of a life insurance company, however, may well be organized on a *line* or a *line and staff* basis. For example, branch offices are usually organized on a line basis with all operations directly under the control of the manager. The agency department, on the other hand, is normally organized on a *line* and *staff* basis where the agency vice-president is supported by line assistants (directors of agencies) and also by staff assistants (for example, directors of research and training).

Companies differ widely by size, fields of operation, objectives, and other factors. Their actual organizational patterns likewise differ, since a company rarely selects a pattern consciously, but rather develops an organizational pattern as a matter of evolution. Subject to this limitation, it is the purpose of this chapter to outline the more important official positions, committees, and departments of the average well-established life insurance company, and to describe briefly their respective functions and duties.

Levels of Authority

There are usually four levels of authority in a life insurance organization. The board of directors and its various committees are, of course, the top or *directorial* level of authority. The president and senior officers of the company are found at the *executive* level. In addition to serving as part of the executive management team, the senior executive officers are given authority and responsibility for particular functions. Each of the vice-presidents has subordinate officers at the *managerial* level who are responsible for the day to day functions of their departments. These subordinate officers, who may serve in line, staff, or functional relationships, make decisions on all matters within the limits of authority delegated to them. Finally, the supervisors in charge of subdivisions of the departments are found at the *supervisory* level of authority.

The Board of Directors

The board of directors and the several committees of the board constitute the top level of authority in a life insurance company. In a mutual company the directors are elected by the policyholders from among their own number, whereas in a stock company they are elected by the stockholders and in order to qualify must be the owners of a designated number of shares. But whatever the method of election, the board possesses complete supervisory powers over those who manage the company. It is not only empowered to select the president and other principal officers, but may delegate to them such powers as it sees fit. It also meets at stated intervals to approve or disapprove the recommendations of officials, the findings of committees, and to consider and pass judgment upon all important matters concerning the general business conduct of the company. Since the transactions of a life insurance company assume a great variety of forms, it is usually considered desirable that the directorate should be composed of men who represent various callings and possess wide experience.

To expedite the proper fulfillment of its functions, and to bring its members into close touch with the business affairs of the company, the board divides itself into a number of standing committees. In many companies the president and other officers are members of the board of directors and hence are entitled to membership on important committees. Where the executive officers are not directors, they are invited to various meetings in an advisory capacity. These committees vary in the different companies but usually include an *executive* or *insurance committee,* a *finance committee,* a *claims committee,* and an *auditing committee.* The executive committee, consisting of the president and certain members of the board, has for its purpose the consideration and ratification of such matters as bear a vital relation to the general business policy of the company. For example, the committee determines the kinds of insurance contracts which the company will sell, the provisions of the contracts, the premium rates, the territory in which the company will operate, and so forth. The finance committee, consisting of the president and treasurer of the company and a certain number of the directors, exercises supervisory control over the company's investment policy and practices. In larger companies it is quite common to have a separate committee to deal with real estate and mortgage loans. The claims committee has general control over the payment of claims and, in particular, determines policy in regard to doubtful or contestable claims. The auditing committee maintains general supervision over the company's accounting system and records.

In general, the officers of the company who carry on its active management initiate action, the function of the directors being to approve or disapprove the recommendations made. For the most part, directors' committees will be guided by the recommendations of the officers of the company directly concerned. This is particularly true in the case of committees dealing with technical details of the business.

Executive Officers

The executive officers are responsible for the carrying out of the policies determined by the board of directors and for the general management of the business. These officers usually comprise the president, one or more vice-presidents, each of whom has charge of a department, and the treasurer. The president is usually entrusted by the board of directors with large executive powers, and should not only be well versed in financial matters but also have a wide experience in the life insurance business so as to interpret properly the results attained in the respective departments of the company, advise the board of directors in supervising the general business conduct of the company, determine the best policy for it to pursue, and direct the work of the subordinate officials. He is also entrusted with the duty of selecting subordinate officials and departmental heads. The several vice-presidents, each of whom usually has charge of a department of the company, must also keep up with the general business operations of the company so as to be in a position to assist the president in his duties, to assume his responsibilities (or those of a ranking vice-president) during his absence, and to be prepared to assume the office in the event of promotion.

Functional Areas

The operations of life insurance companies involve three basic functions: to sell, to service, and to invest. But to carry out these basic functions properly, there must be high-quality professional advice from an actuary, a lawyer, a doctor, and an accountant. Consequently, most companies operate with seven major functional areas: actuarial, agency, accounting and auditing, investments, law, underwriting, and administration.

Departmentalization

Departmentalization simply means the division of the work to be performed into logical sections or assignments. Business organizations are normally departmentalized on either a *functional, geographical,* or *product* basis. Examples of all three types of departmentalization are to be found in many life insurance companies. Thus, the actuarial department is established on the basis of function; a southern department follows from a geographical viewpoint, and the ordinary or group departments are established on the basis of product. In any case a given company will usually follow an individual pattern. The following discussion of functional departmentalization will illustrate the internal organization and activities of a life insurance company.

The *actuarial department* establishes the company's premium rates, establishes reserve liabilities, nonforfeiture values, and generally handles all of the mathematical operations of the company. This department also is responsible for analyzing earnings and, in a participating company, furnishes the statistical data from which the annual dividend scale is established. Again, the actuarial staff designs new policies and forms and is responsible for filing these with the various state insurance departments. The department also makes mortality studies and supervises the underwriting practices of the company. It works closely with the agency department in considering policy design and other factors which affect the competitive position of the company's field force. Finally, because of the importance of the technical actuarial element in group insurance and group annuities, this department frequently handles the administration of such business or exercises a considerable degree of functional responsibility over it. The role of the actuary is vital to the operation of a life insurance company. In many smaller companies the actuary will in effect serve as executive vice-president and exercise a considerable influence over all areas of operations.

The *agency department* is responsible for the sale of new business, conservation of existing business, and field service to policyholders. This department supervises the activities of the company's field force and is also responsible for advertising, sales promotion, market analysis, recruiting, selection and training of agents, and controlling agency costs.

The *accounting and auditing department* under the direction of the vice-president and comptroller is responsible for establishing and supervising the company's accounting and control procedures. Auditing, both in the field and home office, is done by an independent unit of this department. The actual preparation of the annual statement is handled here, although the actuarial department exercises considerable functional control in this regard. The accounting department is, of course, responsible for matters concerning Federal, state, and local tax laws and regulations. Also, it is responsible for expense analysis and other operational statistics not handled by the actuarial department.

In recent years the introduction of *electronic data processing equipment* (EDP) and the increasingly sophisticated applications of such equipment to company operations has caused organizational realignments. In many companies the original installation has been under the direction and control of the actuarial department or the accounting department. In either case, eventually an overall control of electronic research and planning has become necessary with the result that a number of companies have established *EDP* departments independent of the usual *functional* departments.

The *investment department,* usually under the direction of the treasurer, handles the company's investment program under policies laid down by the board of directors. The department, besides passing on the merits of the company's investments preparatory to presenting them to the finance committee for final approval, is usually the custodian of the bonds, stocks, and other investments held by the company, and is entrusted with the duty of collecting the interest and dividends thereon. To invest the company's money in securities that are safe and yet will yield a return somewhat higher than the rate assumed for premium and reserve computations requires skill and a wide knowledge of the various classes of investments in which life insurance companies are permitted to invest their funds. Great care must be exercised, especially with regard to investments in real-estate mortgages. Sound acceptance of these involves a knowledge of values, the character of the mortgagor, and an examination of the mortgages and abstracts of title. Since real-estate mortgages constitute so large a proportion of the total investments in life insurance, it is common for large companies to have a special department—a real-estate department—to manage and supervise them.

The *legal department* is charged with the responsibility of handling all of the company's legal matters. These include, among other things, the conduct of court cases growing out of the contested claims, foreclosure proceedings, imperfect titles, and so forth; the sufficiency and correctness of policy forms, agency contracts, bonds, notes, and so forth; the inspection of titles to property purchased by the company or upon which it has granted loans; and the analysis and interpretation for the benefit of the company of the statutory and court law governing life insurance in those states where the company operates.

The *underwriting department* is responsible for establishing standards of selection and for passing judgment on applicants for insurance. In some companies the medical department is given separate status. The medical director supervises the company's force of medical examiners and may be the final authority to pass upon the insurability of applicants. In some instances, however, general underwriting control may rest in the hands of a vice-president who is not a physician. The department makes use of many specialists known as "lay underwriters" who are not physicians. Many underwriting decisions do not depend upon a physician's opinion, since "insurability" connotes much more than "good health."

The *administration department,* often headed by the secretary, is responsible for providing home office service to the company's field force and policyholders. This usually includes the issuance of new policies, premium and commission accounting, claims, loans, surrenders, policy changes, and other similar transactions. This department is also responsible for the personnel administration and home office planning. The secretary has charge of the company's correspondence, the minutes of the board of directors and its various committees, and the company's records.

It should be noted that many companies also departmentalize on the basis of product, having separate departments for *ordinary, industrial, health* and *group* insurance, depending upon which lines they write.

In addition to committees of the board of directors, a number of *interdepartmental committees* may be appointed by the executive officers to coordinate the efforts of the various departments. These committees normally report their findings to the officer responsible for their appointment. Some of the inter-departmental committees which might be appointed are: an insurance committee, a budget committee, a public relations or advertising committee, a man-power and employee-benefit committee, a research committee, and a personnel and management training committee.

While the above description of home office organization is representative, it should be noted that the above description may not fit any particular company; it is presented merely to illustrate one possible type of home office organization.

MARKETING LIFE AND HEALTH INSURANCE

The degree to which a life insurance company succeeds reflects the consolidated effort of all the activities of the organization. Of the three major operational areas—marketing, investment, and administration—marketing is the largest in terms of both manpower requirements and costs. Both in servicing current policyholders and in producing new policyholders and premium income, the marketing department's role in contributing to a company's well-being is vital.

Top Management's Responsibility for the Marketing Function

The top management of a life insurance company bears the ultimate responsibility for the effectiveness of the organization's marketing operations. Top management has the responsibility for determining a number of basic policies in the sales area. Important among them are the kinds of markets to be reached, the type of organization to conduct the business, the amount of resources to be allocated for new business, and expansion and personnel policies.

The implementation of the policies established by top management is the job of the principal marketing executive, as head of the marketing department and the agency force. He also has the obligation to top management of sensing the ever-changing requirements of the company's markets, both present and future, and making suitable recommendations based upon these requirements.

The Marketing Organization

The marketing management organization of a life insurance company includes a number of middle management positions that lie between the senior marketing executive and the agency supervisors of the field representatives. In a company operating over a wide geographical area, the number of middle management executives may be fairly large even when a reasonable span of control is maintained. Adequate staff assistance must be available to handle the details of operating the business and to provide the research and development activities that must be maintained in a progressive, forward-looking organization. Even in a small company the principal marketing executive must have the support of both competent line and staff people.

Although the duties of sales management are numerous, as shown above, they may be classified into six major areas of responsibility:

1. Developing and maintaining a sales program
2. Recruiting and selecting personnel
3. Training personnel
4. Motivating personnel
5. Directing administrative work
6. Developing and maintaining good public relations.

These major areas of responsibility apply throughout the marketing management hierarchy of a life insurance company. Although some positions may involve all six areas, other positions may be concerned with less. The duties are pervasive. They apply equally well, however, to the supervisors of the sales personnel in the field as well as to the executive in charge of the entire marketing operation.

Developing and Maintaining a Marketing Program

The development and maintenance of a company marketing program is the primary responsibility of the senior marketing executive. His decisions and recommendations in this area provide the basis for all actions in his remaining areas of responsibility.

The first and most basic decision underlying the development of a company marketing program is the *type of market* to be sought. A company can, for example, restrict its marketing to selected geographical areas, or it can be nationwide or even international in scope. It can decide on an urban operation or a rural one; it can concentrate on high-, middle-, or low-income groups. Similarly, decisions must be made with respect to the *product line* as they relate to special policy features, such as term insurance riders, special purpose policies, or the sale of group or health insurance.

Once a decision has been made regarding market orientation, the type of marketing organization to be formed must be determined. Some life insurance companies choose to work through general agents, while others conduct their business through company-operated branches. The question of the *magnitude* of a company's sales organization is also basic. Assuming the relative share-of-the-market position is to be maintained or increased, it may be necessary to develop and maintain programs for the horizontal expansion of the field force. On the other hand, if the company's decision is to increase total sales by upgrading the capabilities of the present agency organization, a different plan of action must be formulated. The environment for life insurance marketing, both internally and externally, is constantly changing. Consider, for instance, the changes affecting the life insurance industry that have evolved as the result of social security legislation, and, more recently, Medicare. Population shifts, from rural to urban areas, from the cities to the suburbs, and from eastern to western states, all have materially affected the marketing programs of life insurance companies. Similarly, rising standards of living, changing life styles, and other changes have had major impacts on the way of doing business. These changes are felt slowly, but they must be anticipated as early as possible to cope with the challenges of ever-changing marketing conditions.

To a considerable degree the sales operation is dependent on local economic conditions and the extent to which prospects have funds for the purchase of insurance. As population shifts occur and new marketing opportunities emerge, agencies or branch offices as well as sales personnel must be repositioned. This process involves the creation of new agencies or the expansion of existing ones in growth areas and the elimination or consolidation of agencies where the sales potential is diminishing. The senior marketing executive has the job of determining the basic framework and program within which the changes in field structure will occur.

An integral part of the development and maintenance of a marketing program is the quantification of expected sales performance, based on a common understanding of the company's direction and a knowledge of long-range commitments to the chief executive. The senior marketing executive's job in this area is to establish the company and territorial sales objectives. Finally, the marketing plan must provide a series of control reports to serve as signals and reminders to management at all levels to instigate corrective action when necessary.

FIELD ORGANIZATION

Need for a Field Organization

Notwithstanding the almost universal need for life insurance, relatively few persons voluntarily apply for it; most people have to be solicited by an agent. The reasons are not difficult to explain. Life insurance provides for the future, and the individual, if he desires to be insured, must turn over to the insurance company money which could be used for the satisfaction of present wants. This sacrifice naturally causes many to procrastinate in obtaining life insurance, and salesmen are necessary in order to get action before it is too late. Life insurance does not have the same appeal to the average individual as does an automobile, a television set, or some other tangible product. Objects of this kind may be used in the present and shown to friends, thus giving to the possessor immediate pleasure and satisfaction. One of the main functions of insurance is to provide against premature death, and people instinctively do not like to think of dying, or becoming disabled. Retirement, for younger people, is a long way off. The services of a salesman aid in motivating the prospect, thus bringing about the purchase of insurance which would not be obtained otherwise. Finally, due to our complex manner of living, many perplexing questions arise at the time life insurance is to be purchased. Agents are necessary to render service in ascertaining the prospect's needs and properly fitting the insurance to those needs. Due to rapidly changing conditions, agents are also necessary for the servicing of policies after they are sold. Life insurance needs are not static but require frequent review and adjustment to meet changing conditions. The policyholder also depends largely on the agent for other types of services including such things as policy loans, assignments, changes in plans of insurance, reinstatements, and others. Finally, at death or maturity of an endowment policy, the agent assists claimants and beneficiaries. The agency system undoubtedly adds to the cost of insurance, but it is a mistake to assume that the elimination of that cost and the related services would be beneficial to the public.

Attempts have been made to sell life insurance directly to the public through advertising and through the medium of savings banks and certain governmental agencies such as the post office, but such methods have met with little success. At the present time only one company of importance in the United States is operating without agents. Even though it uses the mails and advertises through other means, the volume of business has been relatively small. The oldest regular life insurance company in the world and one of the strongest financially operates without agents, but the policies sold annually do not exceed a few hundred. The policies, however, are usually for large amounts. Massachusetts has had a system of selling life insurance to its citizens through savings banks since 1907, but the amount of insurance obtained is relatively small as compared with the insurance written by commercial companies. A law was passed in Wisconsin in 1911 authorizing the sale of life insurance by the state, but the amount of insurance sold has been negligible. On several occasions, England has offered to sell life insurance and annuities to her citizens through the post office savings banks, with poor results. No agents were provided and the insurance plans were voluntary and permissive in character. After many years of operation under the Act of 1882, the total number of annuity contracts and the total insurance contracts were relatively negligible as compared with the business written by the regular companies.[1]

---

[1] The War Risk Insurance plans pursued by the United States Government during World Wars I and II have been more successful than any other state plan, but the large amount of insurance in force was sold on favorable terms and by aggressive methods.

While the amount of individual life insurance sold without agents has increased with the development of mass marketing schemes (viz., marketing through credit cards, associations, mutual funds, and lending organizations), the amount of new insurance individually marketed through agents continues to dominate the field by a wide margin.

The need for agents is not merely a matter of securing the largest possible amount of new insurance. The need also arises from the social responsibility of the companies to provide adequate life insurance protection for all who need it and thus to perform to the maximum extent possible the function for which they are organized.

In addition to housing the agents representing the company and those supervising them, a field organization of offices, distributed throughout the country, is essential to handle efficiently important functions such as the collection of premiums, the settlement of claims and others.

The Structure of the Field Organization

The agent is the foundation of the field organization. He generally operates under the training and supervision of an assistant manager or agency supervisor. The next echelon of management is the branch manager or general agent. This, then, is the management structure in the field. The man who supervises and controls field branch managers or general agents may bear a title such as regional vice president, regional director of agencies, or superintendent of agencies. The regional supervisor may be located either in the home office or in the appropriate regional office. At the top of the agency hierarchy is the agency vice-president, who has direct contact with the president. In some of the large companies, in order to relieve the agency vice-president of some of his many duties, the position of senior vice-president for marketing has been created as the top position of the field structure. In many companies the president devotes a large part of his time and interest to marketing.

The effectiveness of the field organization is determined in large part by the recruiting of new agents and by the management and direction which the new and old (i.e., experienced) agents receive.

The manager or general agent has the important job of instilling in his organization the desire and will to learn, to serve, to sell, and to succeed. In addition to this important duty of leadership, he must recruit new agents if the agency is to grow; he must train them in prospecting and selling and give counsel and advice where needed. He is responsible not only for the work performed by the clerical staff but also for the correctness of applications and forms turned in by the agency force for transmission to the home office. Frequently, he is expected to do some life insurance selling himself. A few companies discourage this feature because it may interfere with the recruitment and development of agents. Of course, most companies desire that he, as a leading businessman in the community, participate in civic affairs. In doing so, he not only helps fulfill the company's social responsibilities but builds prestige for his agency.

Types of Agency Organization

The two main types of agency systems used in the life and health insurance business are the general agency system and the branch office system. In addition, there is the direct agency system, under which agents are appointed and supervised from the home office with or without the assignment of exclusive territory. This system is probably the oldest, since it works best with small companies in limited territories. A few mutuals use it exclusively at the present time, but the great mass of companies have an agency system either of the general agency or the branch office type or one with some of the characteristics of both.

Much life insurance is also sold by brokers, although this method is of much less importance relatively than the two main agency plans. Insurance brokers are found in the large cities, and they serve their clients by procuring insurance of all kinds to fill their needs. In obtaining life and health insurance for his customer, a broker may be acting as an agent of the company or as an agent of the insured, depending upon the law in the state in which the operation is conducted. Thus, in some states, such as Pennsylvania and New York, the law requires the broker, before he can place life or health insurance with any company, to secure an agent's license from the state. In states with a requirement of this nature a broker may have an agent's license (which runs for one year) with a number of companies, as a result of his activities in filling his clients' needs. In all states the broker usually places his insurance through regularly licensed agents rather than directly with the home office.

The General Agency System.   The pure general agency system, which is only theoretical today, is the oldest of the systems and aims to accomplish through general agents what the managerial system is designed to do through branch offices. According to the plan, the company appoints a general agent to represent it within a designated territory over which he is given control, and by contract the company agrees to pay him a stipulated commission on the first year's premiums plus a renewal on subsequent premiums. In return, the general agent usually agrees to devote himself to the building of the company's business in his territory. He is empowered to engage agents on such terms as he may deem best. Thus, he may pay them all of his first year's commission plus a renewal somewhat smaller than that which he receives from the company, or he might pay all of the commission on the first year's premium and retain the renewals himself, or, again, he may retain a portion of both the first year's premium and the renewals. The difference between what the general agent receives from his company and the amount he pays his agents is known as his override or overriding commission. If the agency is already established when the general agent is appointed, the company will usually pay him collection fees on the premiums turned in on the business which his predecessors developed, expecting that this income will be utilized for the building of the agency. If the agency, however, is just being established, the company will often advance to the general agent the capital necessary for development and reimburse itself out of the commissions accruing under his contract. Frequently, the contract requires the general agent to produce a stipulated amount of business within a designated time. The general agent is also frequently responsible for the collection of premiums and interest on loans, the receipt of loan applications and proofs of loss, and other clerical work which naturally arises in connection with insurance sold in his territory. Routine matters of this nature, however, may be handled by a separate force of persons located in the general agent's office but directly responsible to the home office. An arrangement of this nature relieves the general agent of details not directly related to production and at the same time offers the advantages which accrue from close contacts with such matters.

It should be noted that agents' contracts are made with the general agent and not with the company. In the pure general agency contract, the company, theoretically, has no control over the appointment of his agents, although in practice the company usually specifies the form of contract to be used and reserves the right to reject agency appointments.

There are two classes of general agencies: (1) those where the general agent relies chiefly upon his own personal business for his main profit and considers the income derived from his subagents as of minor importance; and (2) those where the general agent subordinates his personal business and aims to develop a large force of subagents with a view to deriving his chief profit from the marginal difference between the commissions and renewals paid by him to such agents and those which he receives from the company. If belonging to the first class, the general agent will consider his personal business of greatest importance and will select those prospective applicants which he can handle best himself. Needless to say, such an agency is not as advantageous to subagents as the second class where, although it should always be the aim of the general agent to obtain some personal business, he will nevertheless promote the welfare of his agents in preference to the interests of himself or his office.

The Branch Office System.   As contrasted with the general agency system, the managerial system is gaining in relative importance, especially among the large companies. Its purpose is to establish branch offices in various districts in charge of a manager and cashier. The manager, usually selected because of his success as an agent, is charged with the responsibility of securing and directing agents within his territory and of instructing and otherwise helping and encouraging them in their work as solicitors. The function of the cashier, on the other hand, is to collect premiums and the interest on policy loans and to keep all office records. He is expected to look after all correspondence in connection with applications and policies, notify delinquent policyholders of their obligations, attend to filling in proofs of loss, applications for policy loans, and payment of maturing endowments, and answer all communications from policyholders which are not of sufficient importance to be referred to the home office. He is also charged with the supervision, efficiency, and conduct of the clerical staff. As in the case of the officials at the home office, the managers, cashiers, and clerks at the branch office are paid by salary, although the manager sometimes receives extra payments (bonuses) for increasing the volume of business through his office and for adding to the number of productive agents.

The Systems Compared. The separate treatment accorded the two main agency systems up to this point should not lead the reader to conclude that a company will use one or the other in the manner just described. The branch office or managerial system, as stated before, has been gaining in popularity over the general agency plan. There has been a trend, also, in recent years toward the formation of agency systems which have some characteristics of both. These trends are due, no doubt, in part to the fact that agency development work has been pretty well accomplished and pioneering profits are no longer as great as formerly. Thus, in the matter of agency expenses the companies, in many instances, are allowing the general agent certain amounts of money for named expense items. Also, some companies are now assuming responsibility for the training and development of agents, a matter formerly left entirely to the general agent. On the other hand, managers of branch offices are being encouraged to work harder by means of a reward system under which the amount of compensation varies with the volume of business produced.

Much has been written about the relative merits of the general agency and branch office systems, some supporting one plan and some the other, and it may be well to indicate the principal contentions. The general agency system, it is argued, has the two-fold advantage of definitely fixing the cost which the company incurs in securing its business; and of relieving the company of the trouble connected with the supervision of many agents and the risks incident to the financial relations into which the company would otherwise have to enter with numerous agents. The supporters of the branch office system, on the other hand, maintain that it is more economical because of the more prompt collection and remittance of premiums, agents under this system being required to make prompt payments, and all collections of premiums and interest being deposited at once to the credit of the company and thus made available for immediate investment. This contention has reference to the practice of allowing general agents frequently a considerable period of grace in making their collections and remittances, thus leading to significant bank balances in favor of the agency, or to slackness on the part of policyholders in paying their premiums. It is further argued that the general agency system causes a lack of uniformity, since the general agent can control and compensate agents as he pleases, while under the branch office system the company conducts all its agency affairs directly from the home office through its own branch offices, rented in the company's name, and placed in charge of managers under salary.

Other Aspects

Contracts with Agents.   Agents may be hired by the company or, in a pure general agency, by a general agent to whom the company has given exclusive right to the business in a certain territory. In either case, the agent is asked to sign a written contract and, in both cases, the legal relationship between the company and the agent is the same.

A good portion of the *ordinary* agent's contract is devoted to the compensation which he is to receive.[2] Ordinary agents' compensation is usually on a commission basis [3] calling for high commissions on the first year's premium with a much smaller commission on future premiums. The "New York scale," for example, provides first-year commissions of as high as 55 per cent on policies such as ordinary life,[4] grading down to as low as 15 per cent on some forms of term insurance and 3 per cent on single-premium contracts. Renewal commissions are 5 per cent for all policy forms, payable for nine years. Under a so-called New York Contract the total commission payable is a maximum of 100 per cent of one year's premium (55 per cent plus 9 × 5 per cent).[5]

[2] For a survey of research by the Life Insurance Agency Management Association relating to field compensation, see LIAMA, *Cost and Compensation in Life Insurance* (Hartford: LIAMA, 1967), pp. 103–144.

[3] A few companies of reasonable size use other than a commission plan of compensation. These contracts provide salary in lieu of or in addition to commission. The salary is weighted by and must be validated by production, however, and this is tantamount to a commission level of compensation.

[4] The "top commission" contracts vary with companies.

[5] There are variations from company to company, since New York insists only that the aggregate compensation be the actuarial equivalent of the normal plan or less. Any company licensed to do business in New York State must comply substantially to this limitation in every state in which it operates. Companies not licensed in New York may pay more. Smaller companies and others which feel that their competitive situation is such that they must pay more to attract and hold agents often offer contracts which range as high as 90 per cent of first-year commission with some such renewal arrangement as nine at 7½ per cent and five at 5 per cent.

The contract provides for the "vesting" [6] of renewal commissions if the agent achieves certain levels of production or completes a minimum period of service such as five, ten, fifteen, or perhaps twenty years.

In recognition of the service which an agent is called on to give long after the renewal commissions have expired, many companies pay a "service fee" which commences after renewals stop and continues as long as the agent remains with the company and the policy stays in force. The service fee is a small percentage, usually 2 or 3 per cent, and never vests in the agent.

Many companies also pay additional commissions or bonuses per $1,000 of new business, basing the bonus on a satisfactory average-size policy or rate of persistency or a combination of both. The presence and nature of such additional compensation varies widely and is a function of the philosophy of the company involved.

In addition to direct compensation, fringe benefits such as retirement, life, and disability benefits are provided by many companies.

Under a straight commission contract the agent earns nothing until he starts making sales. As a result, a new agent will have to draw on another source of income until his commissions build up to a reasonable level. It has become common today for the companies or general agents [7] to finance a new agent's first months or years in the business.

Financing plans differ widely but may be illustrated in general terms. For example, the drawing account approach simply means that the new agent is extended credit by the company or general agent either on a stipulated weekly or monthly basis or as he needs it. The agent must pay the money back as he is able and usually even if he terminates his contract. Many companies agree to provide a stipulated salary against which any commissions earned are credited. Subject, usually, to certain minimum production or validation requirements, the agent may continue under this plan for a period up to, say, three years, but may go off the plan at any time he chooses. In case the agent leaves the company he may or may not be responsible for any debit balance outstanding. Other financing plans attempt to provide a level base salary and also guarantee part of the commissions from the beginning. The variations are almost infinite. But in any case it should be remembered that, regardless of the financing plan, an agent must sell life insurance to make his living selling life insurance.

The agents' contract also contains provisions regulating the territory in which the agent must operate; the duties of the agent in the collection of premiums; the right of the agent to hire subagents; the right of the agent to alter or change the insurance contract; the maintenance and ownership of books of records; and numerous other provisions relating to the various

---

[6] *Vesting* refers to the ownership of the renewals. Practically, vested renewals means the agent's renewals will continue to be paid to him even if he terminates his connection with the company.

[7] Losses are usually shared by the company and the general agent.

things which might arise while the agent is devoting his time and energy to the sale of life and health insurance.

Training of Agents.   Much progress has been made in raising the standards of and in increasing the efficiency of life insurance agents. In most states the agent must procure a license and in some he must pass a written examination before he is allowed to operate. The companies have become increasingly careful in their selection of new agents. They also devote much attention to the training of their agents in the nature and uses of life insurance and in the methods of salesmanship. Many companies conduct special training programs on the principles of life and health insurance and salesmanship. Many others issue training materials explanatory of the various types of contracts and their uses, various aspects of the sales process (e.g., prospecting, approach, handling objections, the close, etc.), and much other information of value to the agent in his daily work. It should be pointed out that the agent, if he is to render the greatest service to his client and function as a professional, should be well informed concerning the technical phases of life insurance, such as the principles of rating, the operation of the policy reserve, the nature and sources of the surplus, and so forth, all of which are important to the agent in serving his client properly. To render expert service he should possess a thorough knowledge of the types of policies available, their usefulness under various family and business circumstances, and the settlement options and their advantages, so that he may intelligently fit the policy to the determined needs of his prospective client. He should be thoroughly informed with regard to his company's investments and its treatment of policyholders, and should be in a position to present the benefits of insurance clearly and forcibly. There are also many legal phases of life insurance such as the naming or changing of the beneficiary and the assignment of policies, an understanding of which will greatly enhance the agent's ability to serve his client. Furthermore, the agent should not consider his service to his client completed when the sale of a policy has been effected. Instead, his advisory relationship to the insured and the beneficiary should extend, if at all possible, throughout the life of the policy and, as regards the conservation of the proceeds, even after it matures.

One of the most important educational developments in agent training was the formation of the American College of Life Underwriters, chartered on March 22, 1927. The purpose of this organization is to raise the educational and ethical standards of those engaged in life underwriting to a level where the business will be regarded in the same light by the public as are the other well-known professions of law, medicine, and accounting.[8]

---

[8] See Ernest J. Clark, "The American College: Its Founding," *Journal of the American Society of Chartered Life Underwriters* (March, 1947); see also Raymond C. Johnson, "Higher Education in Insurance—Our Growing Strength," *Journal of the American Society of Chartered Life Underwriters* (March, 1951).

To achieve its purpose, the American College each year gives a series of ten examinations of two hours each, covering a wide range of subjects, such as life insurance fundamentals, economics, government, psychology, sociology, taxation, commercial and insurance law, the law pertaining to wills, trusts, and estates, corporation finance, banking, credit, and investments. If the candidate successfully passes these examinations and meets certain other requirements, he is awarded the designation, Chartered Life Underwriter (CLU) which he may use in a proper manner to indicate that he is qualified according to high standards to render valuable service in the sale of life insurance. The College encourages and fosters the training of students in educational institutions for the career of professional life underwriter, and cooperates with universities and colleges in general life insurance education for laymen.

Relations Between the Home Office and the Field Force. The agency department is often characterized as the most important branch of the home office. Successful agency work requires not only the most effective organization but a close co-operative relationship between the home office and those in the field. To this end united action is emphasized as much as possible. Not only are all important agency questions considered by special committees at the home office, but agents' meetings and conventions are organized with a view to enabling a free discussion of important questions vitally related to the agents' work and equipment.

The Investments of | 41
Life Insurance Companies |

NATURE OF INVESTMENT ACTIVITY

Need for Investment

IT HAS BEEN SHOWN earlier that, under the level-premium plan of providing life insurance protection, the insurer will accumulate policyholders' funds at a contractual rate of interest until the policy matures. It should be apparent that as the rate of return on invested assets increases, other things being equal, the company can increase the contractual rate of interest and therefore charge a lower premium rate for a given insurance contract or increase dividends if the contract is participating. Since premium rates and net costs are important competitive considerations, the investment function is a significant factor in maintaining and improving a company's competitive position in the business. In the aggregate, the magnitude and direction of insurance company investment activity establish the life insurance business as a significant factor in the capital markets.

Scope of Investment Activity

Sources of Investable Funds. In a life insurance company, investable funds arise from both insurance and investment operations. The cash flow from insurance operations arises out of the difference between cash receipts (premiums, annuity considerations, and other deposits) and cash disbursements (benefits and expenses). The cash flow from existing investments develops from current income (earnings from net interest, dividends, and *realized* capital gains), maturities, prepayments, redemptions, calls, and sales. The relative magnitude of these cash flows presents a significant investment task.

Magnitude of Investment Activity. The magnitude of life insurance company investment activity can best be illustrated by considering the figures in Table 41–1. On December 31, 1970, the assets of all U. S. life insurance companies approximated $207,254 billion (nearly four times those at the close of World War II), an increase during that year of $10,046 billion. The 1970 asset growth exceeded the total assets of all U. S. life insurance companies at the close of World War I, ample testimony to the regard in which this unique protection and savings mechanism is held by the insuring public.

As staggering as the 1970 asset increase of $10,046 billion may seem, it does not tell the whole story, for during that year the companies were obliged to make investments far in excess of that figure. The industry acquired $62,292 billion of new investments during 1970.[1] The substantial differential between the gross investment and the net asset increase is accounted for by a number of factors which necessitate reinvestment of company assets. Among these are the "roll-over" (reinvestment at maturity) of Treasury bills and other short-term paper, the sale, redemption, or exchange of securities already owned, and mortgage loan principal amortization and prepayments.

Through life insurance company investment operations another pooling arrangement is brought to bear on the welfare of the nation. Millions of policyholders contributing relatively small amounts of premiums annually create a fund to be invested by professional investors. So invested, the funds provide the financial basis for more and better homes, utility systems and schools, and a more rapidly advancing industrial technology. All of this accrues at least indirectly to the benefit of the policyholder, just as the proceeds of his policy enhance the economic security of himself and his beneficiary.

TABLE 41-1. Total Admitted Assets of United States Companies
(000,000 Omitted)

Year	Amount	Year	Amount
1900	$ 1,742	1940	$ 30,802
1905	2,706	1945	44,797
1910	3,876	1950	64,020
1915	5,190	1955	90,432
1920	7,320	1960	119,576
1925	11,538	1965	158,884
1930	18,880	1969	197,208
1935	23,216	1970	207,254

Source: Institute of Life Insurance; used by permission.

[1] *Life Insurance Fact Book, 1971*, p. 71.

Functions of the Investment Department

The life insurance company investment department is charged with making recommendations which underlie the formulation of investment policy by top company management. The liabilities of a life insurance company are largely composed of the policy reserves established to stand behind its outstanding insurance and annuity contracts. The bulk of liabilities (80 to 90 per cent) represent long-term fixed dollar obligations that must be increased periodically by an assumed rate of interest. The nature of these liabilities dictates that the corresponding assets should be invested in long-term fixed dollar investments with a yield at least equal to the interest rate guaranteed in the outstanding contracts. The remainder of the assets would appropriately be short-term investments and cash to provide the liquidity necessary to meet current demands. Some attention is given to the distribution of maturities, but the basic objective seems to be the acquisition of the longest maturities compatible with the risk, yield, and liquidity considerations associated with a company's current investment strategy.

Basic Investment Objectives.   The primary quality sought in life insurance company investment policy is *safety of principal.* Within the constraints necessary to maintain a safe investment portfolio, life insurance companies seek to maximize the yield obtained on their investments. *Socio-economic* considerations also influence life insurance investment decisions. *Liquidity,* the ability of an asset to be converted into cash immediately and without loss of value, is relatively of less importance to a life insurance company than many other financial institutions.[2] Nevertheless, it is a factor in investment planning, particularly for smaller organizations.

Viewed from a risk standpoint, the fundamental concern of life insurance companies is the risk of legal insolvency, that is, a condition in which admitted assets[3] are less than the liabilities required by law. The primary concern is with the aggregative or portfolio risk in contrast to the risk on individual investment proposals. In recent years, some companies have demonstrated a willingness to sacrifice some safety of principal through the acquisition of investments with slightly higher risk but higher expected returns. This reflects the increasing sophistication of investment planning, the effect of competition, and the greater emphasis on portfolio rather than individual risk. The significance of a competitive yield will

[2] James E. Walters, *The Investment Process* (Boston, Mass.: Division of Research, Harvard University, 1962), p. 40.
[3] See p. 735.

undoubtedly grow in relative importance with the recent development of investment-oriented contracts like variable annuities and life insurance and pension funding instruments in direct competition with other financial institutions for the saving or investment dollar. Balancing the traditional concern for the safety of principal with the need to maximize the portfolio yield is a basic policy decision which will reflect individual life insurance company investment philosophy.

Since liabilities are relatively stable and predictable, the primary insolvency risk centers on the potential loss of value of assets. The National Association of Insurance Commissioners annually promulgates guidelines for the valuation of assets for annual statement purposes.[4] These rules and procedures will be reviewed below in connection with the discussion of the various categories of life insurance company investments. Further, all states have laws and regulations which limit the scope of life insurance company investment activity. These constraints will also be discussed below.

For the average established life insurance company, legal insolvency is not the major problem for the company; it is rather a level of surplus low enough to place the company in possible jeopardy or to damage its image with either the public or its marketing organization. In a company writing participating business, a reduction in the dividend scale because of a low level of surplus would be perceived by the agency force as a serious problem. The actuarial department would tend to perceive the investment risk in terms of the level of surplus. While both situations may reflect the same basic conditions, it points out that, in essence, it is not investment risk but attitudes toward it that shape investment objectives into investment strategy.

Operational Responsibilities.   The life insurance company investment staff is charged, beyond its broad general function of implementing the company's investment policy, with the dual responsibility of acquiring, supervising, and maintaining its currently invested assets and keeping up a constant search for new outlets for its investable funds. The former implies a continuing study of the financial and general economic status of companies and individuals to whom loans have already been made or whose securities are already owned as well as the "money markets" in general. The latter involves the determination of that moment when a given industry or a given company within an industry has achieved sufficient stature to be worthy of investment consideration. Further, it implies an awareness of constant socio-economic change which results in altered investment patterns and media. How these have altered since 1900 is discussed later.

[4] See pp. 715–720.

REGULATION OF INVESTMENTS

The investment activities of life insurance companies must be conducted within the limitations prescribed by state insurance regulations. There is a significant degree of uniformity among the several states primarily due to the role of the National Association of Insurance Commissioners in the formulation of investment regulation. The concentration of domiciled insurers in a number of leading "insurance states" makes it possible to emphasize the provisions of a few states and still have the discussion representative of the regulatory environment within which the great majority of investment decisions are made.[5] Nevertheless, individual state statutes and regulations should be examined when specific situations are under consideration.

In general, state laws provide limitations aimed at (1) preserving the safety of the assets standing behind policyholder reserves and (2) preventing undue control by the life insurer through proportionately large investment in one firm. Thus, investment regulations specify eligible types of investments and the minimum quality criteria for individual investments within the eligible categories. In addition, there are quantitative limitations imposed on the amounts that can be placed in eligible investments.

Types of Investments

The major categories of life insurance company investments include (1) bonds, (2) mortgages, (3) preferred and common stock, and (4) real estate. The following discussion of the types of investment outlets will illustrate the limitations mentioned above. Consideration will also be given to the valuation of assets for annual statement purposes, an additional constraint which must be considered in investment decisions.

    Bonds.   Bonds of various types currently constitute the largest single investment of life insurance companies. All of the states permit ownership of U.S. Government bonds and the bonds of states and their political subdivisions. In this latter case some states restrict municipal bond ownership to general obligation bonds while others permit ownership of

---

[5] The New York State Insurance Law is particularly significant because of the extraterritorial provisions which require companies *licensed* to do business in the state to "comply substantially" with New York regulations. See *New York Insurance Law,* sec. 42 (5), 90 (1).

limited liability tax bonds and revenue anticipation bonds as well. Generally speaking, the states permit ownership of the mortgage bonds, debentures, and notes of solvent U.S. and Canadian corporations. A typical limitation (Nebraska) requires that an issuing public utility company must have earned the fixed charges on all of its debt at least 1¾ times during the past year. Another (Illinois) limits public utility bond investment to 33⅓ per cent of admitted assets. Another (Connecticut) prohibits purchase of bonds on which there has been a default in payment of interest on the bond during the five years preceding the purchase of the bond. Another (Ohio) restricts public utility bond purchases to first mortgage bonds of those companies which have earned their fixed charges an average of 1½ times during each of the preceding five years. There are many more restrictions of a similar statistical nature, but the above demonstrate the lack of uniformity in detail in achieving a common goal. All of these limitations plus those to be cited below were conceived with a single purpose in mind, the protection of the policyholder's deposits with the insurance company. Suffice it to say that their existence has not impaired the ability of the typical investment department to earn a satisfactory return on its invested assets.

Mortgages.   First mortgages on residential, commercial, and industrial real estate comprise the next largest single area of investment for life insurance companies. The need for funds to finance the building of homes has led the several states to permit virtually unrestricted investment in these loans. The advent of the Federal Housing Administration insured loan and the Veterans Administration guaranteed loan drew the life insurance industry back into the residential mortgage field to a considerably greater degree than was the case after the depression of the early 1930's and prior to World War II. Recently, the higher yields available in multiple family apartments and commercial and industrial real estate have slowed the flow of life insurance funds into individual family dwellings. The most general legal restriction on "conventional" (uninsured, nonguaranteed) first mortgage loans is that the loan not exceed a percentage of the value of the improved real estate. Some states permit loans in amounts up to 80 per cent of value; others limit the amount to 75 per cent.

At the close of 1970, investments in the above two categories (bonds and mortgages) represented slightly more than 76.5 per cent of the assets of U.S. life insurance companies. The changing social and economic structure of the country plus the greatly increasing flow of investment funds has obliged the companies to seek additional outlets for investment. While the use of remaining categories is small relative to the companies' bond and mortgage activities, the dollar amounts involved are significant enough to the nation's economy to justify mention of some of the more frequently encountered legal restrictions on their use.

Preferred and Common Stock.   An increasing number of states are enacting laws permitting investment in preferred and/or common stock. This type of investment had, in many instances, been barred as a result of the New York insurance investigation of the early 1900's which uncovered speculative excesses, interlocking directorates, and other undesirable features which are potential outgrowths of large equity investments. Typical restrictions in use by the states in this area are the following: limiting total stock investment to a small percentage of assets of the insurance company or to a percentage of its capital and/or surplus; limiting ownership of the stock of a given company to a very small percentage of that company's outstanding shares; and prohibiting ownership of the stock of a given company to a very small percentage of the insurer's admitted assets; and prohibiting ownership of shares which cannot meet a variety of statistical requirements which relate primarily to the companies' earnings and dividend records.

It is possible to build a case against equity investment by a life insurance company. It should be apparent, however, that permission to use this medium enables insurers to invest in those corporations whose operations do not require the use of the credit type of security which is the more typical life insurer investment. It also increases the ability of the industry to meet the varying capital demands of the nation and provides an additional source of diversification.

Real Estate.   For many years investment in real estate for other than operational purposes was forbidden to most life insurance companies. The dynamic nature of the post-World War II economy, however, has resulted in an increasing demand for capital from commerce and industry. A company which can maintain its competitive position in a static economy with a large percentage of its capital tied up in fixed assets often finds itself in need of capital to finance increased plant and inventory requirements in order to keep pace with its competition. Such circumstances have led to the increased use of the so-called Sale–Leaseback or Purchase–Leaseback transaction. Here a company builds a plant or warehouse or office and, on completion, sells it to a long-term investor, at the same time leasing the property back from the purchaser. Life insurance companies, as a large source of capital, naturally have been approached to make this type of investment and many of the states have enacted permissive legislation in this area. Typically, companies are allowed to have only a small portion of assets invested in "investment" real estate; 5 per cent is a common figure. Most states require that rentals received be adequate to amortize the cost of the property over a given period of time, typically the term of the lease or a specified number of years. Most states also require that the lease be "net," i.e., the tenant is responsible for normal maintenance, insurance, and taxes in addition to his rental payments.

A number of states include a "leeway law" or "basket clause" in their insurance codes which alleviates in part any strain that restrictive statutes may impose on company investment operations. The code of Connecticut includes the following provision: "Any domestic life insurance company may loan or invest its funds to an amount not exceeding the aggregate of eight per cent of its total admitted assets in loans or investments not qualifying or not permitted under its charter or under any section of the general statutes."

Valuation of Assets

Although not strictly speaking direct legal limitations, the Mandatory Security Valuation Reserve and corollary regulations of the National Association of Insurance Commissioners and the codes of the various states as they relate to the valuation of assets serve to discourage companies from investing too extensively in securities of less than generally recognized investment quality.

To understand the basis of the values that are placed on assets for financial statement purposes, it will be helpful to classify them broadly as (1) marketable securities and (2) other property.

Marketable Securities. In view of the fact that a substantial proportion of life insurance company assets are invested in readily marketable securities, problems involved in valuing such investments are significant. In this case, a daily market quotation is available, but if used as the basis for valuing such securities, a company's financial position could fluctuate frequently due to the volatile nature of such market values. Such a financial statement would have little real meaning or usefulness. This fact has been recognized by the state regulatory authorities and most of the states have provided by law (or by ruling) for a method of valuation of a substantial part of the securities independent of current prices in the securities markets.

The law of the State of New York is representative and provides in connection with the valuation of marketable securities, that (1) no stock or bond that is in default in either principal or interest or that is not amply secured and no "perpetual bond" (i.e., without maturity date) shall be valued above the market value; and (2) all other bonds, i.e., those which are amply secured and not in default, shall be valued on the basis of the purchase price adjusted so as to bring the value to par at maturity and so as to yield meantime the effective rate of interest at which the purchase was made. The values produced by the method in the second category are known as *amortized values*. The process of deriving such values is discussed below, but, for present purposes, it will be sufficient to classify marketable securities into amortizable and nonamortizable securities.

1. *Amortizable Securities.* For some years the Committee on Valuation of Securities, appointed by the National Association of Insurance Commissioners, has supplied specific bases for determining the eligibility of various classes of bonds for amortization. This committee submits an annual report which sets these requirements forth in great detail. Since these requirements are quite complex and are subject to change from year to year, only a very general description of them will be given here.

(A) *Eligibility.* Bonds[6] *other than corporate bonds* are amortizable if they are issued or guaranteed by the United States or Canada or political subdivisions thereof and are "legal" investments by insurance companies. Foreign government bonds are amortizable provided they are deemed by the Committee to be amply secured. *Corporate bonds*[7] not in default are subject to two statistical tests to determine their eligibility for amortization.

The first test, applying for the most part to all corporate bonds, relates to (1) the rating given to the bond by recognized bond-rating agencies, (2) the proportion of net earnings available over a five-year period to meet fixed charges, and (3) the ratio of "long-term debt" to total capitalization.

The second test, applicable only to railroad bonds, requires that current assets must be not less than 125 per cent of current liabilities.

For bonds in still other categories, there are additional requirements as to earnings and the relation between "working capital" and "long-term debt."

(B) *The Amortization Process.* The use of the amortized value for a bond is based on the assumptions (1) that the amounts of interest and principal will be paid when due and (2) that it will not be necessary to sell before maturity.

The expression "amortized value" applies, strictly speaking, only to those bonds bought at a premium (above par), but it is also generally used in connection with bonds bought at a discount (below par). It refers to the adjustments of the original cost (original book value) by which that value is reduced or increased by successive stages until it equals the *par value* on the *maturity date*.

Table 41–2 illustrates the amortization process for a $1,000 bond having two years to run and upon which the nominal interest rate payable is 6 per cent (semiannual coupon rate of 3 per cent). It is assumed that bond was purchased for $1,018.81 to yield 5 per cent.

---

[6] Except perpetual bonds.
[7] Except perpetual income bonds.

The principles illustrated are equally applicable to the accumulation of discount for a bond purchased below par.

The amortized value of a bond bears no necessary relation to the amount which could be obtained by the sale of the bond in the open market. Under this system it is assumed that the principal of the bond will be paid at maturity and that all coupons will be paid. The only elements entering into the valuation of a bond on the amortization plan are, therefore, the rate of interest involved in the transaction (the yield corresponding to the purchase rate—5 per cent above), the amounts receivable (whether as principal or interest), and the length of time until these amounts are due. Where the bond is fully secured and no doubt exists about payment of principal and interest, no other factors need be considered.

It should be apparent that the use of amortized values for bonds involves applying the same principle to the valuation of assets as is used in the valuation of liabilities. In both cases, given an amount payable at a future date, the operation of interest or discount is applied on the basis of a fixed yield as determined by the price paid.

2. *Nonamortizable Securities.* As mentioned earlier, all stocks and all bonds which are not deemed to be "amply secured" or are currently in default *must* be valued at the *market* price. From time to time, during a period of abnormal economic conditions, the requirement of market values has been questioned due to their abnormally low levels and the fact that life insurance companies had no intention or need of selling at the temporarily depressed prices. In the years 1917, 1921, and again from 1931 to 1933 resolutions were adopted by the NAIC recommending the adoption of higher values for nonamortizable securities than the actual market prices on December 31. Such arbitrary "market values" were known as *convention values* or *commissioners' values*. While most states approved the higher values and most companies put them into use, some states did not permit the use of these convention values.

TABLE 41-2. Illustration of Premium

Period (in half-years)	Book Value at Beginning of Half-Year	Coupon Payable at End of Half-Year	Six Months Interest at 5 Per Cent on Book Value at Beginning of Half-Year	Excess of Coupon over Interest Required (amortization)	Book Value at End of Half-Year (amortized values)
1	$1,018.81	$30	$25.46	$4.53	$1,014.28
2	1,014.28	30	25.36	4.64	1,009.64
3	1,009.64	30	25.24	4.76	1,004.88
4	1,004.88	30	25.12	4.88	1,000.00

The principle adopted in determining the convention values was to substitute for the actual market prices an *average* price based on the normal "range of the market." Although the use of such arbitrary values may be questionable, in the years when these special values were permitted, the use of market values would have represented a material understatement of the true values, especially since most companies had no need to dispose of their holdings.

A satisfactory method of valuation of "nonamortizable securities" poses a difficult problem. The only available "nonarbitrary" value, the current price in the market, may be affected temporarily by many factors which have little relation to the true value. Use of such market values may lead to an apparent loss or gain in surplus which might be completely reversed a few weeks later. The answer may be the use of some relatively stable though artificial values in conjunction with special investment reserves. This remains a key area of investigation for life insurance research. A satisfactory solution to the problem will have significant ramifications, not only for investment policy, but in terms of product design, the company's ability to supply capital to the economy, the industry's relative competitive position, and in other ways.

3. *Mandatory Securities Valuation Reserve.*[8] In trying to deal with the problems of valuing marketable securities, regulatory authorities introduced in 1951 the Mandatory Security Valuation Reserve (MSVR). This reserve was introduced primarily as a means of preventing undue surplus changes arising from fluctuation in the market value of securities owned. The MSVR also absorbs, within certain specified limits, fluctuations in surplus caused by increases and decreases arising out of *realized* capital gains and *realized* capital losses.

The amount of the MSVR each year consists of (1) the previous year's balance, (2) capital gains less capital losses for the current year, and (3) an additional amount added each year in accordance with a formula.

A maximum amount is established for the MSVR. Until this maximum is reached, capital gains and losses are absorbed by the reserve so that they have no effect on surplus. After the maximum is reached, capital *gains* directly increase surplus and capital *losses* cause the reserve to decrease. If the MSVR balance becomes zero, subsequent capital *losses* would directly decrease surplus.

The maximum MSVR and annual additions to it are calculated by multiplying the admitted values of each of several different types of bonds or stocks by specified percentages. The exact method of calculation is complex and will not be presented here.

Although the MSVR absorbs surplus fluctuations arising from both

[8] Charles L. Van House, Sr., and W. Rogers Hammond, *Accounting for Life Insurance Companies* (Homewood, Ill.: Richard D. Irwin, Inc., 1969), pp. 180–183.

bonds and stocks, it is more useful in connection with changes in the market value of common stocks, even though the proportion of insurance company funds invested in stocks is relatively small when compared to that invested in bonds. There are three reasons why this is so: (1) most bonds are eligible for amortization, and their values as presented in the Annual Statement are not, therefore, subject to market fluctuations; (2) the degree of rise and fall in market price is much greater for common stocks than for bonds or preferred stocks; and (3) while common stock holdings of most life insurance companies are a small percentage of total assets, they constitute a large percentage of surplus so that changes in market price could be the cause of substantial surplus changes.

Since U.S. life insurance companies must value common stocks at market for Annual Statement purposes, they must be concerned with unrealized gains or losses on stocks which they own. If no investment reserve were maintained, surplus would fluctuate widely, and persons not familiar with this aspect of insurance company statements would assume incorrectly that these swings indicated instability. The protection afforded by the MSVR, therefore, is very important to companies that find it expedient to invest in common stocks.

Since there is no direct change in surplus because of change in market value of amortizable bonds and since most bondholdings are in this category, a lower percentage annual addition to the MSVR is required for bonds owned than for stocks owned. However, some reserve is required to absorb gains or losses when bonds are sold and to absorb changes in market value of nonamortizable bonds.

Since the assets standing behind these reserves would presumably be available for other purposes if any need or emergency arose, it would seem that they should actually be considered surplus funds. However, in view of the fact that their amount is determined by regulation and their maintenance is mandatory, they appear in financial statements as a liability.

It is important to remember that the MSVR relates only to stocks and bonds. It is not intended to protect against depreciation in the values of other types of investments, such as mortgages and real estate whose valuation problems are discussed below.

Other Property. Property other than securities comprises real estate, transportation equipment, mortgage loans, policy loans, and cash. The value placed on such assets is normally the *book value*, i.e., in the case of real estate and transportation equipment the *cost* (subject to any adjustments which have taken place) and in the case of loans the *unpaid principal balance*.

Real estate may or may not actually be worth the original cost or the present book value. An *appraisal* could be made periodically as a basis for formally adjusting the book value, but such appraisals are themselves only an estimate. Thus, some companies establish an offsetting liability in the form of a special contingency reserve for revaluation of real estate to cover expected losses on sale. On the other hand, if the book values are definitely excessive, they should be written down. The same procedure may be applied to mortgage loans if the security is deemed questionable.

In connection with mortgage loans, an important question is the extent to which credit should be taken as an asset for *interest due and unpaid*. Under present New York law, interest due and accrued on mortgage loans may be included as an asset to an amount not exceeding the value of the property *less* the unpaid loan and *less* any delinquent taxes. No credit is permitted, however, for interest overdue more than eighteen months or for *any* overdue interest if any taxes are in default more than eighteen months.

Unpaid interest may be capitalized, i.e., added to the loan, but this is justified only where the security is sufficient to protect the additional loan.

INVESTMENT PERFORMANCE

The rate of return on invested assets is considered the basic criterion in measuring the investment performance of a life insurance company. The portfolio rate of return is the weighted average of investments made over time at different rates of return. This composite rate is a summary measure of past *and* current investment decisions. Table 41–3 illustrates the average net rate of interest that has been earned by United States life insurance companies over the years. Individual company performance, naturally, varies both above and below the average for the industry.

Current investment performance is primarily determined by allocation strategy based on risk, return and other considerations, and the availability of desirable investments. The relative amount of funds available for investment (cash flow) depends on factors such as past investment decisions (e.g., average length of maturities), company growth (premium and annuity considerations), and so forth. Since the rate of return is a weighted average of returns on investments made in different time periods, the rate is clearly influenced by the timing of cash flows with respect to market interest rates. It should be remembered that the portfolio rate of return is determined by factors which in the short run are largely out of the control of the investment officers; for this reason, the rate of return on *new* investments is an additional and important criterion for measuring investment performance.

TABLE 41-3. Net Rate of Interest Earned on Invested Funds
U.S. Life Insurance Companies

Year	Rate	Year	Rate	Year	Rate	Year	Rate
1915	4.77%	1938	3.59%	1949	3.06%	1960	4.11%
1920	4.83	1939	3.54	1950	3.13	1961	4.22
1925	5.11	1940	3.45	1951	3.18	1962	4.34
1930	5.05	1941	3.42	1952	3.28	1963	4.45
1931	4.93	1942	3.44	1953	3.36	1964	4.53
1932	4.65	1943	3.33	1954	3.46	1965	4.61
1933	4.25	1944	3.23	1955	3.51	1966	4.73
1934	3.92	1945	3.11	1956	3.63	1967	4.82
1935	3.70	1946	2.93	1957	3.75	1968	4.95
1936	3.71	1947	2.88	1958	3.85	1969	5.12
1937	3.69	1948	2.96	1959	3.96	1970	5.30

Source: Institute of Life Insurance. The net interest rate is calculated using industry aggregates, and represents the ratio of (1) net investment income to (2) mean invested assets (including cash) less half the net investment income. Before 1940, some Federal income taxes were deducted from net investment income; beginning with 1940, the rates are calculated before deducting any Federal income taxes. The data include the assets and earnings (less capital gains and losses) of the Separate Accounts.

PATTERNS OF INVESTMENT 1900-70

Having explained the purposes of the life insurance investment operation and delineated the legal and self-made framework within which the typical investment department performs its function, we may next consider the portfolio as constituted throughout the past seventy years and examine for cause the periodic rise to and fall from prominence of the various investment media.

Government Securities

Government Bonds.   There is probably no better example of the life insurance industry's willingness to adjust itself to the changing capital demand patterns of the nation than that to be found in an examination of the government bond account. In 1900, life insurance company holdings of government securities represented only 0.4 per cent of total assets. This figure rose abruptly from 1.2 per cent in 1917 to 8.6 per cent in 1918 and 11.5 per cent in 1919 as the industry helped meet the capital needs of World War I. From 1919 until 1931 the relative significance of government bonds dwindled to 1.8 per cent of assets. The antidepression activities of the Federal government placed a demand on the industry again which was to result in continually increasing investment in government bonds, both absolutely and relatively, throughout the economic recovery of the 1930's and the World War II years, 1941–45. At the close of 1945, the industry had 45.9 per cent of its assets invested in U.S. government bonds. Subsequent to that year, the demand pattern shifted again and Treasury bonds declined in absolute and relative significance. The 1970 figure was 3.8 per cent of assets. The decline has been brought about by the ever-increasing capital needs of business and industry in the postwar era, the need for greater investment diversification, and the industry's recognition of a need for a greater yield than that obtainable from Treasury securities. The bulk of current new investment in government bonds is either for purposes of liquidity or to earmark funds to be used in meeting advance commitments too large to be handled in the normal cash flow pattern.

State, Provincial, and Local Bonds. Life insurance company ownership of securities of this category has never been of great relative significance. The highest percentage of assets that the industry has ever had invested in this area was 7.8 per cent in 1940. The following year witnessed our entry into World War II and, as municipal financing came to a standstill, life insurance company investment in municipal bonds dwindled, ultimately to 1.8 per cent of assets in 1947. For the next five years, purchases of these securities were in an uptrend and at the close of 1962 represented 4.0 per cent of the assets of the industry.

The effect of the Life Insurance Company Income Tax Act of 1959 has been to reduce the desirability of this type of security from an income standpoint and holdings declined to 1.6 per cent of total industry assets at the close of 1970. These funds have been used to provide schools, utility systems, and roads to meet the needs of our ever-increasing population.

Foreign bonds are also included in this category and are represented largely by the bonds of the Dominion of Canada. These bonds never have represented a significant proportion of life insurance company assets (1.5 per cent at the close of 1970).

Corporate Securities

Bonds and stocks of business and industry have, since 1935, constituted the largest single area of investment of life insurance companies, representing 42.7 per cent of assets at the close of 1970.

Bonds. Corporate bond holdings amounted to $73.1 billion at the end of 1970, and were 35.5 per cent of all assets. These investments have increased steadily for many years and doubled between 1955 and 1970. They have, however, remained between 35 per cent and 40 per cent as a proportion of all life insurance company assets for the past 20 years.

The bulk of corporate bond holdings at the end of 1970 was invested in United States organizations with $4.4 billion invested in corporations in foreign countries, chiefly in Canada.

Corporate bonds include the bonds of railroads, public utilities, and industrial and miscellaneous corporations. Public utility bonds have traditionally been an important medium for life insurance company funds. Such investments have helped to provide the nation with the power for industrial expansion and the means to distribute it. They have also backed expanded communications facilities and underwritten water, sewerage, fuel, and local transportation facilities for a growing and increasingly mobile population.

Preferred and Common Stocks.   Investments in stocks account for the other part of corporate securities owned by U.S. life insurance companies and amounted to $15.4 billion at the end of 1970. Common stocks account for approximately two-thirds and preferred stocks one-third of the total. Common and preferred stocks together represent 7.4 per cent of total company assets at year-end 1970.

Historically, stocks have been a small percentage of total assets for reasons rooted both in the investment philosophy of the business and in the laws regulating life insurance. They have not been heavily used as a major investment medium for funds backing life insurance policies, in view of contractual guarantees for specified dollar amounts. Legal restrictions on stock investments have also been quite specific.

The recent entry of the industry into the mutual fund and variable annuity fields, plus the increasing current use of stocks in companies' segregated pension fund accounts presages a relatively higher rate of common stock investment than has heretofore been the case. State laws now generally permit certain assets of these pension and other plans to be maintained in an account separate from a life company's other assets, with up to 100 per cent invested in stocks or other equities. Some of the recent increase in common stock holdings is the result of these developments. At year-end 1970, common stocks in separate accounts amounted to nearly $4.0 billion.

Mortgage Loans

During the early 1900's, residential and commercial mortgage loans constituted the largest single area of investment of U.S. life insurance companies. This medium of investment grew in relative significance until, in 1927, it represented 43.1 per cent of total industry assets. Subsequent to this date and until the close of World War II, these loans declined in relative significance in life insurance company investment operations. The exigencies of the Great Depression of 1929–32 were the largest single causative factor in the decline, followed by postdepression and wartime governmental capital demands. The historical low point of 14.8 per cent of assets was reached in 1945 and 1946. Since that time, the average American family's desire to own its own home, combined with the needs of business and industry in terms of increased office and production space, has given rise to a record-shattering construction boom. The life insurance companies, through their mortgage loan activities, have provided much of the financing necessary to this expansion. More than half of the mortgage holdings at year-end 1970 were in apartment developments and commercial properties; residential loans represented about 35 per cent of the mortgage debt held by life insurance companies, with farm properties the security on the balance. Slightly over 20 per cent of these loans are either guaranteed by the Veterans Administration or insured by the Federal Housing Administration.

A new emphasis in life insurance mortgage loans and other investments was introduced in the fall of 1967 with a commitment by the life insurance business to invest $1 billion to help alleviate the problems of the cities' conditions. A second $1 billion pledge was added to this program in 1969. By the end of 1970 a total of nearly $1.6 billion had been placed or committed in mortgages under this program.

Real Estate

As was noted earlier, life insurance companies for many years and in most states were prohibited from owning real estate for other than operational purposes. In the early years of the period under consideration, home and branch office investment could and did represent a substantial portion of assets (9.1 per cent in 1900); however, normal depreciation charge-offs plus the growth in other assets resulted in a long-term relative downtrend through 1926 (2.3 per cent). The early 1930's witnessed a substantial increase in the companies' holdings as a result of foreclosures on mortgaged homes and business properties, and holdings reached a post-depression peak of 8.6 per cent of assets in 1935 and 1936. The disposal of foreclosed properties resulted in an absolute and relative downtrend in this area through the end of World War II (1.5 per cent of assets at the close of 1946). The postwar advent of the purchase–leaseback type of transaction discussed above, coupled with an ever-increasing operational investment, has reversed this trend again. The industry had 3.0 per cent of its assets invested in various types of real estate at the close of 1970. Between 1952 and 1970, the industry increased its investment in home and branch office properties over 300 per cent.

Policy Loans and Other Assets

Although the policy loan, since it is an income-generating asset, is an "investment," its status in the life insurance company statement is not the normal province of the investment department. As would be expected, the relative significance of these loans as an industry asset fluctuates inversely with the availability of credit from other sources. At year-end 1970 policy loans constituted 7.8 per cent of life company assets, the highest proportion since the 1940's.

Cash, due and deferred premiums, and collateral loans comprise the remaining assets of the industry. The first two are obviously not investments except as they relate to the companies' liquidity position, and the latter, infrequently made today, have never occupied a position of any prominence in life insurance company investment operations.

LIFE INSURANCE COMPANIES IN
THE CAPITAL MARKETS

The leading financial institutions in the United States are commercial banks, life insurance companies, savings and loan associations, mutual savings banks, corporate pension funds, nonlife insurance companies, finance companies and mutual funds. Table 41-4 shows that the commercial banks

TABLE 41-4. United States Financial Institutions

Institution	Assets in 1970
Commercial Banks	$570,560,000,000
Life Insurance Companies	207,254,000,000
Savings and Loan Associations	179,383,000,000
Mutual Savings Banks	78,946,000,000
Corporate Pension Funds	94,000,000,000
Nonlife Insurance Companies	55,000,000,000
Finance Companies	31,123,000,000
Mutual Funds	47,618,000,000

Sources: Various annual institutional fact books.

are the most significant of these with over $570 billion in assets in 1970. The life insurance industry ranked second in assets and is obviously a major factor in the capital markets. Its role is particularly significant in that, despite relatively close regulation, life insurance companies are able to utilize a wider range of loan instruments than many of the other financial institutions. Despite an extremely favorable rate of growth in life insurance in force since World War II, the relative rate of savings through life insurance has decreased. This is reflected in a shift to term insurance, both individual and group, which have little or no savings element. The life insurance and banking industries both have failed to keep pace in competition for the savings dollar, particularly in relation to savings and loan associations and corporate pension funds. Current life insurer interest in equity-based products and other marketing developments are indicative of the life insurance industry's concern and intention to improve its relative share of the savings dollar. The industry should continue to be a major factor in the capital markets.

Interpreting Life Insurance | 42
Company Financial Statements: I

INTRODUCTION

THERE ARE TWO fundamental financial statements: (1) the *balance sheet* which presents the financial condition of an enterprise as of a particular day and (2) the *statement of income and disbursements* which summarizes the financial operations of the enterprise during a stated period of time.

Financial statements become useful instruments of management, investment, and even of regulation only when they are intelligently interpreted. Meaningful statement interpretation is accomplished by a systematic analysis of the statements themselves and through the use of supplemental sources of information.

Financial statements are included in the *annual report* published by the enterprise for its owners and for others. The purpose of this chapter is to provide a background for interpreting annual statements and reports of insurance companies.[1] The annual reports of insurance companies differ from those of most other organizations. These differences are a natural result of (1) the nature of the life and health insurance business and (2) governmental regulation. Before proceeding, however, it might be useful to examine these differences briefly.[2]

The long-term and generally increasing nature of the risks assumed by a life and health insurance company requires that, out of the level annual premiums, amounts be set aside each year on each policy to assure the company's ability to pay claims in later years when claim costs may exceed premiums received. These set-aside amounts are discounted values of future benefit payments and are *liabilities* measured by the *policy reserves.* These reserves change continuously with the passing of time, so that it is neither practical nor useful to carry them on the formal ledger itself. It is

[1] See B. Franklin Blair, *Interpreting Life Insurance Company Annual Reports,* American College of Life Underwriters, 1965. Much of the material in this chapter is based on Mr. Blair's paper.

[2] See Robert G. Espie, "Financial Statements," chapter in Dan M. McGill, *Life Insurance,* rev. ed. (Homewood, Ill.: Richard D. Irwin, Inc., 1967).

far simpler to value these policy reserves only at the time a financial statement is being prepared and to record the amounts of these reserves directly on the statement without ever recording them in the books of account.

Life insurance accounting, reflecting government regulation generally and the NAIC Annual Statement specifically, is conditioned by an *emphasis upon solvency*. This emphasis is aimed at assuring that companies will always be able to meet their obligations at any and all times. This emphasis upon solvency is essential also because a failure of management to maintain real solvency may not be readily discernible before losses have been suffered by policyholders or others. This emphasis on solvency, and the difficulty of ascertaining whether such a state exists, have led to the adoption of very conservative valuation standards, both for liabilities and for assets.

The usefulness of the NAIC Annual Statement as a measure of year-to-year earnings is also affected by these conservative valuation standards since they affect both earnings and the change in surplus from one year-end to another. Measurement of the true earnings of a life insurance company from one year to another is also made more difficult by that facts that

(1) a relatively long time must pass before it can be determined whether the sale of a block of insurance policies has been profitable;

(2) the pattern of mortality rates found in *valuation mortality tables* normally is quite different from those found in the individual company *experience tables* used in establishing premium rates; and

(3) the usual net level premium and modified net level premium valuation formulas *release expense margins* in premiums in a pattern quite different from the *actual incidence of expenses*.

It should be clear that each of these situations leads to an actual or potential distortion of the *current earnings* of a life insurance company.

It should be apparent from the above that there are significant differences between life insurance accounting practices and so-called "generally accepted accounting principles." In a more specific sense the major differences in accounting practices include the following:

(1) Commissions and other costs of acquiring premium income are charged to operations as they are incurred, rather than being deferred and charged to operations as the related income is produced. As a result, there is usually a substantial drain on surplus for each new policy sold (particularly if reserves are set up on the net level premium basis). Consequently, an increase in the amount of new insurance sold may produce the anomalous result of a decrease in the net gain from operations, and a decrease in the new insurance sold may result in an increase in the net gain from operations.

(2) The asset values used for most bonds are amortized values rather than either current market values or cost.

(3) The "nonadmitted assets" are arbitrarily excluded from the admitted assets.

(4) The asset values used for stock owned of an insurance company affiliate is the latter's book value without recognition of market value or of any excess of cost over book value.

(5) The Mandatory Securities Valuation Reserve is set up as a liability, rather than being subtracted from the assets although the latter method is a more generally accepted way of handling reserves set up to reflect decreases in the values of assets. Moreover, the amount of the Mandatory Securities Valuation Reserve may not be directly related to the quality and current value of the securities.

(6) No liability is set up for future income taxes on any accrued but unrealized net capital gains.

These distinctions and complications should be kept in mind in considering this and the following chapter relating to the interpretation of life insurance company financial statements.

SOURCES OF INFORMATION ON OPERATIONS

Annual Statements and Triennial Examinations

NAIC Statement Blank.   The principal financial statements of a life insurance company are presented annually in a report called the *NAIC Statement Blank.* This report, known colloquially as the "Convention Blank" or "NAIC Blank," must be filed with the insurance department of the home state of the company and with that department of each of the other states in which the company is licensed to conduct business. The NAIC Statement is a standard form prescribed by The National Association of Insurance Commissioners. Some states require a few minor variations from the standard form.

The NAIC Statement is intended to provide the technical information required for proper supervision by the state department of all of the operations and activities of the company.[3] The nature and quantity of data required for regulatory purposes makes the NAIC Statement a very complex and lengthy report covering in considerable detail the condition and operations of the company.

The NAIC Annual Statement is not intended to be, and is not, a suitable direct source of information for policyholders, owners, or the general public. Condensed and simplified financial statements are included in the

[3] See pp. 755–757.

published *Annual Report* issued by each company to its policyholders and/or its stockholders. These statements and the excerpts from the Annual Report are also used by many companies in their advertising and other publicity activities.

> *Triennial Examinations.*   A regular financial *audit* or *examination* is made of each company, usually every third year, by the insurance commissioner of the company's home state. Representatives of other states also may participate in this examination. To simplify the participation of other states, these examinations are conducted on a *zone* basis. Under arrangements made by the National Association of Insurance Commissioners, the United States is divided, at present, into six zones. If a company is licensed in one or more states in a zone, the zone may send a representative to participate in the examination. The supervision of the examination is the responsibility of the home state commissioner.

The triennial examinations are very comprehensive. The state examiners not only verify the accuracy of the NAIC Annual Statement, they investigate such matters as claims practices and other relations with policyholders as well. The insurance departments of many states make the report of their examinations available to the public upon request.

The NAIC Annual Statement and the triennial examination are two devices used by the state in its supervision of the insurance industry. There are other regulatory *tools,* among which are the requirements that certain types of transactions be reported by the companies. The fact that information reported to the state is, presumably, available to the public brings to bear, potentially, the potent force of public opinion. An example will demonstrate this point. There are no statutes directly limiting the salaries of company officials but companies are required to report the compensation of all persons receiving more than $20,000 a year as well as the ten highest salaries, regardless of amount. The publicity which might be given this information may be a significant factor in preventing improperly excessive salaries.

Trade Publications

Another source of financial information about insurance companies is found in what are often called the *trade publications*. A number of publishers issue annual volumes which contain summaries of the data reported in the Annual Statements of most of the life insurance companies doing business in the United States.[4]

These books include all the important companies. They make available, at a relatively slight cost, summaries covering most, if not all, of the com-

---

[4] See pp. 755–757.

panies in which one might be interested. Some of these volumes include other information about the company, such as analyses and comments not found in the Annual Statement.

The material is somewhat different in the several publications, but these comprehensive volumes usually contain the following about each of the companies covered:

1. Assets listed by categories such as bonds, stocks, mortgages, and real estate.

2. Liabilities listed by categories such as reserves, dividend accumulations, and accrued taxes.

3. Income for the year and disposition of the income.

4. Analysis of the surplus account.

5. Interest rates on several different bases.

6. Historical schedule of insurance paid-for, insurance in force, assets and surplus funds.

7. List of executive officers and directors.

Annual Reports to the Policyholders

The *Annual Reports* published by life insurance companies for their policyholders and/or their stockholders were mentioned earlier. These reports are prepared, in part, from information in the NAIC Annual Statement. The financial statements in the Annual Report are, in a sense, relatively condensed versions of those in the Statement and of those which might be prepared for managerial use within the company.

The scope of Annual Reports and the kind and detail of the information included in them, in addition to the fundamental financial statements, varies greatly from company to company and from year to year, even for the same company. Most of these reports contain supplementary information on the company's operations, plans, and other matters usually found also in the trade press. Among other things there is frequently a narrative presentation of a promotional nature.

The Annual Report can serve its purpose only when it is read and understood. Most companies apply significant attention and resources to the preparation of a report which is readable and which is useful in maintaining good public relations.

The remainder of this chapter is concerned with: (1) an analysis of the type of information found in the typical Annual Report, (2) a brief, general outline of the NAIC Annual Statement, and (3) some of the elements in the evaluation of the performance of an individual company.

The material which follows is generally applicable to both *stock* and *mutual* companies. The material is based, however, on the assumption that, in general, the company under discussion is a *mutual* company which issues participating insurance. This assumption simplifies the presentation. The choice of a mutual with participating insurance reflects the fact that over 61 per cent of the total insurance in force in U.S. companies at the close of 1970 was participating and that 52 per cent of the total was in mutual companies.[5]

A second assumption is that the company's premium income from health insurance is small relative to its total premiums. This assumption also reflects the more common situation in the industry. Proper consideration is given, however, to both *life* and *health* insurance throughout the discussion.

ANNUAL REPORTS

Nature of the Balance Sheet

The most significant feature of an Annual Report is probably the statement of financial condition or balance sheet (Table 42–1). This consists of a list of the assets and liabilities of the company and its capital and surplus.

An idea of the capital and surplus margins available for contingencies can be obtained from the balance sheet, assuming that the *assets have been properly valued* and that the *liabilities have been correctly stated*. If the liabilities plus capital were to exceed the assets, the company would be technically insolvent. The assets virtually always exceed the liabilities by substantial amounts, and, as a matter of record, life insurance companies rarely become insolvent.

The excess of the assets over the liabilities consists of capital (in a stock company) and surplus, both earmarked and unassigned.

As is explained hereafter, a rough measure of the financial stability of the company is indicated by the relation of the capital and surplus to the liabilities.

In order to understand the sample balance sheet presented in Table 42–1, it will be helpful to consider briefly certain technical terms which appear in the NAIC Annual Statement, even though some of the terms appear infrequently in Annual Reports.

Ledger Assets.   Ledger assets are those which have been entered on the books (ledgers) of the company. Cash and investments are the main ledger assets.

[5] *Life Insurance Fact Book, 1971*, p. 26. On the other hand, it should be noted that there are many more stock than mutual life insurance companies operating in the United States today.

TABLE 42-1. Sample Statement of Financial Condition, December 31, 1970

(Balance Sheet)

Assets		
Bonds: *		
United States Government	$ 4,400,000	
Canadian Government (includes political		
subdivisions)	500,000	
State, County, and Municipal	3,900,000	
Public Utility	13,000,000	
Railroad	2,600,000	
Industrial and Miscellaneous	23,100,000	
Total Bonds		$ 47,500,000
Stocks: *		
Preferred and Guaranteed	$ 1,500,000	
Common	3,200,000	
Total Stocks		4,700,000
Mortgages:		
Insured under Federal Housing Act	$ 8,000,000	
Guaranteed in Part by Veterans Administration	5,000,000	
Others *(conventional)*	22,200,000	
Total Mortgages		35,200,000
Real Estate and Other Property:		
Home Office	$ 950,000	
Real Estate Held as an Investment	2,045,000	
Real Estate Acquired in Satisfaction of Debt	55,000	
Transportation Equipment	160,000	
Data Processing Equipment	50,000	
Total Real Estate and Other Property		3,260,000
Other Assets:		
Loans on Policies of the Company	$ 4,700,000	
Collateral Loans	60,000	
Cash and Bank Deposits	1,300,000	
Investment Income Due and Accrued	850,000	
Net Premiums Due and Deferred	2,000,000	
(fully covered by policy reserves)		
Miscellaneous Assets	430,000	
Total Other Assets		9,340,000
TOTAL ASSETS		$100,000,000

*Bonds subject to amortization according to state laws are carried at their amortized values. Other bonds and all stocks are carried at values prescribed by the National Association of Insurance Commissioners.

TABLE 42-1. (cont'd.)

Liabilities

Reserves for Policies and Supplementary Contracts:		
Life Insurance	$58,500,000	
Annuities and Supplementary Contracts with		
Life Contingencies	17,500,000	
Supplementary Contracts Without Life		
Contingencies	3,750,000	
Disability Benefits	500,000	
Accidental Death Benefit	300,000	
Health Insurance	750,000	
Total Reserves for Policies and Supplementary		
Contracts		$ 81,300,000
(This fund, together with future premiums and interest earnings, is to provide for payment of future benefits.)		
Dividends Left to Accumulate at Interest		2,900,000
Policyholder Dividends Declared for Following Year		1,600,000
Premiums Received in Advance		1,550,000
Claims in Course of Settlement		800,000
(includes amount set aside for claims incurred but unreported)		
Taxes Accrued, Payable in Following Year		800,000
Miscellaneous Liabilities		1,100,000
Mandatory Securities Valuation Reserve		1,350,000
Total Liabilities		$ 91,400,000
Capital		750,000
Special Surplus Funds		1,750,000
Unassigned Surplus		6,100,000
TOTAL LIABILITIES, CAPITAL, AND SURPLUS		$100,000,000

Note: In an actual annual report, the reserves for policies and supplementary contracts would probably be shown simply as one lump sum and not broken down as above.

Nonledger Assets.   For practical reasons, some assets are usually never entered into the ledgers of the company. The most significant of these include: (1) *overdue investment income* (usually small), (2) *accrued investment income* (earned but not received), and (3) *net premiums due* (or uncollected) on all types of insurance, and deferred premiums on ordinary insurance and annuities. The latter class of nonledger assets arises from the fact that policy reserve liabilities are normally stated on the assumption that premiums are payable annually in advance. This is an overstatement of the reserve where policies are payable monthly, quarterly, or semiannually,[6] or where premiums are due before the statement date but have not been paid. This asset offsets the excess reserve liability so that the net effect on the balance sheet is proper.

Admitted Assets.   Assets approved by state regulatory authorities as sound assets and accepted as such in the NAIC Annual Statement are known as *Admitted Assets*. Admitted assets are made up of both ledger and nonledger assets. All of the assets shown in an Annual Report are admitted assets.

Nonadmitted Assets.   This category, of course, includes all assets which are not considered as sound assets for purposes of the NAIC Annual Statement. While some of these assets are considered sound in other businesses, they are not admitted here in the interest of conservative reporting of a company's financial position. Nonadmitted assets include: (1) *furniture and equipment,*[7] (2) *agents' balances* (advances to agents), and (3) *overdue and accrued interest on mortgages* on which the interest is *overdue* more than a specified period. Companies have a certain amount of choice in determining the length of the period after which such interest will be treated as a nonadmitted asset. Some nonadmitted assets are ledger assets (e.g., agents' balances) and some are nonledger assets (e.g., overdue interest).

Accrual Basis vs. Cash Basis.   The *cash basis* of accounting (which most individuals use for their personal income tax returns) assumes that reported income and disbursements include *only* items which have been actually received or disbursed and entered on the books. On the other hand, if items are included which have not been actually received or disbursed but which are attributable to the current accounting period, the income and disbursements are said to be on an *accrual basis*. Examples of *income items* which have not actually been received are "accrued interest" and "due or uncollected premiums"; examples of *disbursement items* which have not been actually disbursed are "claims in the course of settlement" and "taxes payable in the following year on current year's operations." The "summary of operations" [8] contained in the NAIC Annual Statement (and

---

[6] Assume a policy dated September 15 with quarterly premiums paid to December 15. On December 31, the December 15 premium is due and its net amount is counted as an asset. The premiums due next March 15 and June 15, required to complete the policy year, are "deferred" premiums and their net amounts are also counted as assets.

[7] A number of states make an exception for large-scale data processing equipment, allowing its value after depreciation to be counted as an admitted asset.

[8] See pp. 745–752.

in many Annual Reports) shows income and disbursements on an *accrued basis*.

Interpreting the Balance Sheet

The sample balance sheet shown in Table 42–1 is a hypothetical stock company writing participating insurance. If this were a mutual company, there would be no item of "Capital." Again, there would be no items concerned with dividends to policyholders in a stock company writing *only* nonparticipating business. On the other hand, there could be an item for dividends to stockholders in stock company statements.

The assets and the liabilities in this company roughly reflect the average assets and liabilities of all U.S. life insurance companies at the end of 1970. To present some concepts for discussion purposes, reasonable assumptions were made as to the breakdown of certain items where the information was not readily available for all companies.

Assets. The values to be placed on various types of assets are very important in the financial picture presented by the balance sheet. The subject of valuation of assets was discussed in the preceding chapter. For purposes of the present discussion, assets as shown in a financial statement may be broadly classified as follows:

1. Cash
2. Investments
3. Net premiums deferred and overdue
4. Interest and rents due and accrued
5. Miscellaneous assets

1. *Cash.* The cash consists of (a) actual cash held at the date of the statement in the company's home office and branch offices and (b) amounts on deposit in banks. These amounts are shown as a single sum in the Annual Report by most companies and separately by others. It is essential for companies to maintain bank accounts in cities throughout the country where they transact business. Part of these deposits may be "at interest" (generally at a very low rate) but this is not the usual practice. Although "actual cash" is of relatively small amount, cash in banks may amount to as much as ½ to 2 per cent of the total assets. Since this asset is nonproductive, an unusually large amount of cash would warrant investigation as to its cause. As was pointed out in the previous chapter, a very significant problem for life insurance company management is the projection of cash flows to facilitate investment and maximizing the income arising from invested assets.

2. *Investments.* The investment portfolio of a life insurance company usually includes (a) bonds, (b) stocks, (c) mortgage loans, (d) real estate, and (e) policy loans.[9]

The values placed on each of these classes of investments are determined as explained in the preceding chapter; i.e., bonds, if fully secured and not in default, are included at their amortized values; other bonds and all stocks [10] are listed at current market values (as determined by the NAIC Committee on Valuation of Securities); mortgage and policy loans are entered at the amounts of the loans unpaid; [11] and real estate is shown at book or market value, whichever is lower. It is quite common to write down the book value regularly each year. In many cases, the write-downs may exceed normal depreciation. Normally, the book value will be lower than the fair market value.

Since the asset page of an Annual Report does not reveal the quality of the assets, the most useful information which can be derived from the asset page is some idea of how the distribution of the assets of a particular company compares with the distribution for the life insurance industry as a whole. If the percentage of the assets in each category for a given company approximates that for the industry, the company's investment program is probably somewhere near the middle of the road compared with the programs of other life companies. If, however, there are significant differences between the percentages for a particular company and those for the industry, it would be well to consider a more thorough investigation of the investment program of the company. In any such investigation, the comparison of the interest rate earned by the company with the average rate for the industry is one very important factor to consider.

In evaluating a company's investment program, it is necessary to consider general business and economic conditions and the effects they might be having on a "prudent" investment program. It should also be remembered that "hindsight is better than foresight"; only time can give an accurate appraisal of the soundness of a particular investment program.

U.S. Government securities should not loom large relative to the industry in a company's statement today (at the end of 1970, 3.8 per cent). Such a condition might imply that the company is putting undue emphasis on safety and liquidity at the expense of yield.

Corporate bonds, constituting about 35.3 per cent of the aggregate assets of all companies, represent, in general, a middle-of-the-road position with respect to security, yield, and liquidity.

Tax-exempt bonds (state, county, municipal, and authority issues) repre-

---

[9] In some companies there are other special types of investments including various types of loans (e.g., "collateral loans") other than mortgage and policy loans.

[10] Preferred stocks "in good standing" are shown at their "adjusted values" as determined by the Committee on Valuation of Securities. See pp. 717–718.

[11] Mortgages bought at a premium or discount are shown, in many circumstances, at values which take the premiums or discounts into consideration.

sent only a small percentage of assets (about 1.6 per cent in 1970), but may increase in view of the treatment of earnings from such bonds under current Federal income taxation of life insurance companies.

Most companies either include in the Annual Report or make available on request a list of the securities owned. The increasing proportion of securities which are obtained by direct placement has made it increasingly difficult for an outsider to form any valid judgment of their quality.[12] It is possible, however, to determine whether a life insurance company has invested excessively in the securities of any one corporation and to obtain a rough idea of the *diversification* within the portfolio.

Stocks usually constitute a small percentage of total assets. Preferred and guaranteed stocks make up about 1.7 per cent of the total assets of life insurance companies and common stocks about 5.7 per cent. The amount of common stocks, although still relatively small, has increased considerably in the past decade. A significant proportion of assets invested in common stocks might indicate an investment program with too little attention to safety. Most state laws limit common stock investment to a small percentage of the assets, and it would be rare that a national company could or would attain the maximum usually permitted. A company operating in a limited geographical area with a high percentage of capital and surplus in relation to assets could conceivably approach the legal maximum but a limiting factor is that the legal maximum is based, not on cost, but on current market and a company would undoubtedly try to leave a safety margin between the amount invested and the amount permitted.

One of the main objections to larger holdings of common stocks (and one of the reasons for the state limitations) is the fact that a satisfactory method of valuing them which is independent of short-term changes in market values has never been developed. Life insurance obligations have been measured, traditionally, in fixed amounts, and stocks are not satisfactory for extensive investment because they tend to fluctuate with the market and economic conditions, leaving the company with the possibility of "becoming insolvent" during a time of depression, even though it might recover with a substantial surplus when the market price of equities again started rising. Legislation permitting segregated funding, however, may see an increasing proportion of life company assets invested in common stocks with still new problems for the individual analyzing life insurance company financial reports.[13]

Mortgages usually constitute the second largest category of investments, representing 35.9 per cent of the assets of the life insurance industry in

---

[12] Primarily due to the problems involved in determining proper values for many privately placed bonds and for common stocks, life companies are required to set up a Mandatory Securities Valuation Reserve. See pp. 718–719.

[13] See pp. 718–719. See also Harold G. Fraine, *Valuation of Securities Holdings of Life Insurance Companies* (Homewood, Ill.: Richard D. Irwin, Inc., 1962).

1970. Mortgages are often regarded as less liquid than bonds because mortgages are usually not traded as freely. Here again a balance between liquidity and the higher yield available from mortgage investments must be considered in evaluating a company's portfolio. A major consideration, of course, is the percentage of the mortgages which are FHA or VA mortgages. These "insured" mortgages are typically more marketable than are conventional mortgages. Also, most mortgages now being issued provide for complete amortization over a period of years. This practice has greatly improved the investment standing of mortgages in respect to safety and liquidity. If investments are made in mortgage loans, it is desirable that they be in significant volume. The higher fixed costs usually involved in servicing mortgages make the returns unattractive on a small volume.

Investment real estate is a comparatively minor item on the balance sheets of most companies. It is an unsuitable investment medium for any large proportion of the assets because of its special characteristics, including lack of liquidity and possible tax disadvantages under the current Federal income tax law.

The amount of real estate owned which was acquired because of *mortgage foreclosure* is negligible today. In most companies, the *home office* (land and buildings) also represents only a small proportion of the assets. Occasionally, a small company will have a home office which does constitute a significant proportion of assets. This may be an indication of overexpansion or lack of prudent management. There is also a danger that the book value at which such a property is carried may be higher than the amount which could be realized upon sale, especially in times of business depression. It is probably much more common, however, for the book value of a home office property to be lower than its fair market value. Many companies write down the book value of their home office property regularly each year to take care of depreciation and obsolescence; "write-downs" in most cases exceed the actual depreciation.

Transportation equipment in moderate amounts makes a suitable investment medium. The advantages and disadvantages of this type of investment are somewhat similar to those for investment real estate.

Policy loans represented, at year-end 1970, 7.8 per cent of life insurance company assets as compared with a peak of 18 per cent in 1932 and 1933. This represents, however, the highest level of policy loans since the 1940's. As policy loans are usually made only on ordinary insurance, the percentage of policy loans for a particular company might be higher or lower than the industry average, depending on the proportion of its policy reserves which are for ordinary insurance.

In general, economic conditions are the major factors affecting the amount of policy loans outstanding. The percentage for a certain company might be considerably higher than the industry average, as the result of factors not of any special significance. On the other hand, a high percentage might be an indication that the company operates in a depressed area and that its business is likely to be more vulnerable to lapse or surrender than the business of an average company. The recent development of the market interest rate for loans to levels exceeding the policy loan rate guaranteed in most outstanding contracts has led to a higher percentage of policy loans outstanding.

3. *Net Premiums Deferred and Uncollected.* As we pointed out earlier, this item is taken as an asset to offset the overstatement of the policy reserve liability brought about by the difference between the assumptions as to premium payments in reserve calculations and the actual modes of paying premiums. In essence there is an overstatement of both assets and liabilities, leaving the resultant position of the company's surplus unchanged. This item also accounts for premiums which are overdue since the reserve is overstated in this case also.

4. *Interest and Rents Due and Accrued.* A complete statement of assets must include not only assets actually in the possession of the company but also assets represented by amounts due to the company, whether these have actually become receivable or are merely the accrued part of payments to be received later.

In the case of overdue receivables, a sound asset exists only if the payment is secured (the usual case in connection with mortgage or other loans).

Accrued interest (where there has been no default) is a sound asset. In the case of bonds, for example, if the bond were sold, the sale price would be subject to addition of accrued interest. During normal times, overdue interest is likely to be very small; it is often reported in combination with the much larger item of accrued interest. In periods of economic depression, overdue interest on mortgages may become sizable.[14] In such periods, its size may be helpful in giving some indication of the quality of the mortgage portfolio. Its usefulness as such an indicator, however, is impaired by the fact that company practices, relative to charging off overdue interest as a nonadmitted asset, vary considerably. It is possible for a company with a portfolio of excellent quality to have proportionately more overdue interest shown in its Annual Report than a company with a portfolio of a lesser quality. This could occur if the first company included most of its overdue interest as an admitted asset and the second company treated most of its overdue interest as a nonadmitted asset, perhaps because its ultimate collection was more doubtful than in the case of the first company.

5. *Miscellaneous Assets.* The other assets usually found in a statement are chiefly (a) other amounts due to the company but not yet received (e.g., reinsurance claim settlements) and (b) collateral loans, neither of which constitute a significant amount in the usual statement. Some companies also include large scale electronic data processing equipment in this category.

---

[14] No item of overdue interest is carried as an asset on bonds in default, as the market value of such bonds reflects any interest in default.

Liabilities.   The liabilities as they appear in the usual statement may be broadly classified as follows:

1. Policy reserves
2. Amounts held on deposit for policyholders and beneficiaries
3. Dividends (to policyholders or stockholders) which have been allocated but are not payable until after the date of the balance sheet
4. Claims incurred but not yet paid
5. Other amounts payable
6. Amounts held for account of others
7. Special reserves treated as liabilities

1. *Policy Reserves.* Policy reserves are amounts which, on the basis of the assumed mortality tables (or other tables) and rates of interest, are needed, less future net premiums receivable, to provide the benefits included in the company's life, annuity and health insurance contracts. This includes the reserves for the "special benefits," i.e., benefits in event of total and permanent disability or accidental death.

As indicated by the balance sheet in Table 42–1, by far the greatest proportion of the liabilities of a life insurance company is represented by the single category "Policy Reserves." *Minimum standards* for the calculation of most policy reserves are prescribed by the state insurance laws. For the types of coverages for which minimum standards are not prescribed, a company must satisfy the commissioner that the reserve basis used is adequate. The details of the basis of the policy reserves are reported in the NAIC Statement. In addition, a number of insurance departments make a duplicate calculation of most of the policy reserves of domestic companies. Therefore, the policy reserves can usually be assumed to be adequate.

Unfortunately, an Annual Report seldom gives any indication of the mortality, morbidity, and interest bases or the method (net level premium method or a modified preliminary term method) used in the calculation of policy reserves.[15] Consequently, it is virtually impossible to tell from an Annual Report whether the reserve basis is at or near the prescribed minimum or whether the basis used gives larger, and thus more conservative, reserves than minimum. Some of the trade publications mentioned earlier provide information on the interest rates used in reserve calculations and also on the extent to which the net level premium method or other methods are used to determine the life insurance reserves. They contain virtually nothing about the basis of health insurance reserves.

Other things being equal, the lower the interest rate used for valuation, the larger is the reserve. A low valuation interest rate, therefore, is usually

---

[15] The question of the valuation method applies primarily only to life and health insurance reserves because the other large category of reserves—annuities and supplementary contracts—are mostly not subject to further premium payments so that this question does not arise with respect to these categories.

regarded as conservative and indicative of a strong basis of valuation. Also, the reserves are larger on a net level premium basis than on a preliminary term or modified preliminary term basis so that, other things being equal, the net level premium basis is the more conservative. It should be remembered, however, that there are a number of other factors—such as the margins in the gross premiums and the size of the surrender benefits guaranteed—which should be taken into consideration in appraising the relative conservatism of a valuation basis for policy reserve liabilities.

2. *Amounts Held on Deposit for Policyholders and Beneficiaries.* This category includes (a) amounts held by the company under supplementary contracts, (b) dividends held under the accumulation option, and (c) premiums paid in advance.

Supplementary contracts include settlements both with and without life contingencies. Those which provide incomes based on life contingencies are, an effect, life annuities and are included as a part of the policy reserves mentioned above. The remainder—funds held at interest or under the fixed period and fixed amount options—are included here.

Policyholder dividends may be accumulated at interest under participating contracts, and in most mutual companies a large amount is held under this option. The liability shown on the balance sheet will include interest accrued (but not yet payable) to the date of the balance sheet.

Premiums paid in advance do not loom large relative to the policy reserve liability but can be a significant amount in a particular company. The right to pre-pay premiums is permitted as a matter of company practice, but most companies will permit limited advance payments, allowing a moderate discount. The amount of the total liability as shown on the balance sheet is the discounted value of all the premiums so held and which have not yet become payable.

3. *Dividends Allocated but Not Yet Payable.* In respect to policyholders' dividends, the generally accepted practice, except on group business, is to set up as a liability the estimated amount of dividends to policyholders for the entire following calendar year. This is done on the theory that dividends in a given calendar year should be paid out of surplus actually earned in the preceding calendar year. Some companies, however, do not actually take formal action before December 31 on their dividends for the entire following year. They set up as a liability the estimated amount of dividends to policyholders for only part of the following year, such as three months. In any case when the directors or trustees take action to allocate a specific sum for dividends, that sum becomes a liability and should be shown on the balance sheet as such.

In the case of stock companies, dividends to stockholders become a liability at the time they are declared by the Board of Directors of the company.

4. *Claims Incurred but Not Yet Paid.* This class of liabilities includes (a) claims due but unpaid, (b) resisted claims, (c) claims in process of

being settled, and (d) *estimated liability* for claims *incurred* on or before the date of the statement (normally December 31) but *not reported* by that date.

The first two categories are very small since claims usually are paid as soon as the completed papers are received and a very small proportion of life and health insurance claims are litigated. The third category likewise is small and represents those claims which are still under investigation or for which complete papers have not been received. The final category, claims *incurred but not reported,* is estimated on the basis of the experience of prior years.

5. *Other Amounts Unpaid.* In addition to unpaid claims, liability will exist for other incurred but unpaid items, such as expenses, taxes, surrender values, and others. An important item in this category is the amount estimated to be payable for Federal income tax in the following year on the income of the current year.

6. *Amounts Held for Account of Others.* As mentioned earlier, deposits by mortgagors to pay taxes, insurance premiums, and the like not yet due, amounts due to reinsurance companies, amounts withheld on payroll deductions, and other funds held temporarily must be shown as liabilities.

7. *Special Reserves.* The distinction between some special reserves which are labeled *liabilities* by some companies and those which are merely *earmarked surplus* by other companies is a rather fine one. For example, a special reserve for a particular purpose may be shown by one company as a liability and by another as part of the surplus account.

The Mandatory Securities Valuation Reserve is now required by law in most states and must be shown as a liability although its nature is basically that of a contingency fund or earmarked surplus. The purpose of the requirement is to accumulate a reserve over a period of years to protect against adverse fluctuations in the values of securities (bonds and stocks) and against losses on their sale. The reserve is built up by annual increments until it reaches a maximum determined by the rules. The amount of the increment for any one year depends on the values of the bonds and stocks held and on the net capital gains on bonds and stocks during the year. Companies are permitted, within limits, to add to the reserve more than the required increment. The reserve relates only to stocks and bonds and is not intended to protect against declines in the values of other types of investments.

As a result of the liberal terms of the optional settlements in policies formerly issued, many companies have established a *special reserve for unmatured settlement options.* This reserve is much more clearly a liability and, in fact, might well be included as a part of the policy reserve. Similarly the special reserve generally established by companies with group insurance in force to cover the catastrophic risk borders on the nature of a liability. Many companies, however, treat the group insurance reserve as earmarked surplus (see below). The matter of the treatment of special reserves either as liabilities or as surplus is one about which more uniformity would be desirable. The present lack of uniformity makes it difficult to evaluate the balance sheet of particular companies.

Companies occasionally set up other special liability items to cover a variety of special situations where there is greater uncertainty than usual as to whether there actually will be any additional liability. Special items of this type, if small, would probably be included in the term "Miscellaneous Liabilities"; if large, they might be shown separately in the Annual Report. In either case, they would be shown separately in the NAIC Statement.

It is difficult to tell how to appraise such special liabilities for a particular company. If no such liabilities appear on the balance sheet, it could be because the reserve basis is so conservative that no special liabilities need to be set up. It might, on the other hand, be because the company's surplus position is not strong enough to permit setting up such special liabilities even though they are badly needed. It would take a very thorough actuarial appraisal of the company's structure to enable one to tell which (if either) of these situations was the more likely. Even then much would depend on the individual judgment of the person making the appraisal. Moreover, where such liability items do appear on a statement, it is virtually impossible to tell whether the amount set up is on a conservative basis or not.

Capital and Surplus.   As indicated above, the excess of assets over liabilities consists of capital and surplus.[16] Capital, naturally, appears only on the balance sheets of stock companies. Although the capital item represents the interest of the stockholders in the company, it nevertheless is available for the protection of the policyholders. In the event of financial difficulties, the policyholders' interest comes *before* that of the stockholders.

Surplus appears in the Annual Report (and also in the NAIC Statement) in one of two forms:

1. *Special Surplus Funds.* In some companies, part or all of the surplus is earmarked to cover special contingencies. The following examples taken from actual Annual Reports are illustrative of the types of contingencies covered:

"Voluntary reserve for further strengthening of policy reserves"

"Group life insurance reserve for epidemics"

"Special reserve for possible loss or fluctuation in the value of investments"

"Voluntary reserve for contingencies"

---

[16] There is some tendency in the annual reports of companies (in other types of business as well as in insurance) to replace the word "surplus" by some term such as "contingency reserve" on "margin for contingencies." This tendency stems from the possibly unfavorable connotation of "surplus," which implies an excess or more than is needed. This term might imply to policyholders that a company was retaining larger funds than necessary and paying smaller dividends than it should.

Some companies even carry their entire surplus as one special surplus fund to cover all unforeseen contingencies.

2. *Unassigned Surplus.* This represents either the entire surplus or the part of surplus which has not been assigned to cover specific or general contingencies.

The earmarking of surplus to cover special contingencies can, naturally, be changed from year to year. Thus, a special reserve for investment fluctuation set up at the end of one year could, if necessary, be used during the following year to absorb mortality fluctuations arising from an epidemic or a war.

Summary of Operations (Income and Disbursements)

An important feature in the Annual Reports of many life companies is the "summary of operations" or "statement of the operations" for the year. The general pattern of the "summary of operations" in the NAIC Annual Statement [17] is usually followed. As explained hereafter, however, the "summary of operations" in typical Annual Reports frequently differs from that in the NAIC Statement with respect to the treatment of certain details, such as investment expenses. As might be expected, there is considerable diversity in practice in presenting the "summary of operations" in Annual Reports.

A sample "Summary of Operations" is shown in Table 42–2. As in the case of the sample balance sheet, the items shown for this hypothetical company are in roughly the same proportions as the corresponding aggregates for all U.S. life companies in 1970. The first part of the summary is an analysis of income.

Income.   The income of a life insurance company consists primarily of:

1. Premiums
2. Considerations for supplementary contracts and deposits
3. Investment income
4. Capital gains
5. Miscellaneous income

1. *Premiums.* Premium income includes, in addition to regular premiums from policyholders, (a) dividends taken by policyholders in the form of paid-up additional insurance and (b) policy proceeds (as from death claims, matured endowments, and surrenders) *left* with the com-

---

[17] The NAIC Annual Statement also contains an "Analysis of Operation by Line of Business" exhibit, which is an analysis of the year's operations broken down by "line of business," that is, by the various categories of business, such as industrial, ordinary, annuities, group, health, and so on.

TABLE 42-2. Sample Summary of Operations for 1970

(Accrued Basis)

Income

Premiums from Policyowners:		
Life Insurance	$10,200,000	
Annuities	1,520,000	
Health Insurance	3,080,000	
Total Premiums		$14,800,000
Net Earnings from Investments:		
Interest, dividends, and rents less investment expenses and taxes		3,300,000
Funds Left with the Company:		
Policy proceeds placed under supplementary contracts and dividends left to accumulate		1,860,000
Other Income		40,000
TOTAL INCOME		$20,000,000

Disposition of Income

Benefits to Policyowners and Beneficiaries:		
Death Benefits	$ 3,000,000	
Matured Endowments	600,000	
Annuity Benefits	600,000	
Health Insurance and Disability Benefits	2,400,000	
Surrender Benefits (insurance)	1,200,000	
Dividend Accumulations Withdrawn	400,000	
Supplementary Contract Benefits	800,000	
Dividends to Policyowners	1,500,000	
Total Benefits		$10,500,000
Operating Expenses and Taxes (excludes investment expenses and taxes):		
Agency Expenses, Including Commissions	$ 2,000,000	
Home Office Insurance Operations	1,500,000	
Premium, Payroll, and Other Insurance Taxes	150,000	
Federal Income Taxes	350,000	
Total Expenses and Taxes		4,000,000
Increase in Required Reserves Held for the Benefit of Policyowners and Beneficiaries		4,500,000
Transfer to Surplus Account		1,000,000
TOTAL DISPOSITION OF INCOME		$20,000,000

TABLE 42-2.   (cont'd.)

Changes in Surplus Account

Unassigned Surplus, December 31, 1969		$5,800,000
Additions:		
Transferred from Insurance Operations	$1,000,000	
Net Increase in Values of Assets	480,000	
Increase in Surplus of Separate Account Business	20,000	
Total Additions		$1,500,000
Deductions:		
Dividends to Stockholders	$ 100,000	
Net Losses on Sale of Assets	300,000	
Increase in Reserves on Account of Change in Valuation Basis	200,000	
Increase in Mandatory Securities Valuation Reserve	500,000	
Increase in Special Surplus Funds	100,000	
Total Deductions	1,200,000	
Net Additions		300,000
Unassigned Surplus, December 31, 1970		$6,100,000

Note: Life insurance premiums shown include premiums for disability and accidental death benefits.

pany as consideration for supplementary contracts *with* life contingencies. Premiums, naturally, constitute by far the largest source of income.

2. *Considerations for Supplementary Contracts and Deposits.* A substantial proportion of all policy proceeds from death claims, matured endowments, and surrenders is left with the company under optional settlements *without* life contingencies. Although no cash payment by the company (other than the first installment) takes place at the time the claim is settled, the amounts shown in the disbursements for death and other claims would be understated if amounts left with the company were omitted. These amounts are properly treated *as if* they were first paid to the policyholder in cash and then immediately repaid to the company. They are therefore *entered both as disbursements and as income.* Since no cash payment is involved (payment of the first installment being treated as a separate transaction), the total amount of the company's assets is not affected.

The same situation exists with regard to dividends left with the company under the accumulation option. In order to show the true total amount of dividends "paid," a dividend deposited must be included with other dividends among the disbursements and also entered as income.

3. *Investment Income.* Investment income is comprised of: (a) interest on bonds and loans as well as miscellaneous interest such as interest on agents' balances; (b) dividends on stocks; and (c) rents from real estate or transportation equipment owned, including the rent which the company charges itself for occupancy of property owned, such as its home office. The latter item is necessary in order to show a proper yield on the investment.

The amount of "interest" in the case of amortizable bonds is normally not the amount of the coupon but is the effective interest returned by the bond.

In the Annual Report investment income may be shown on a "gross" basis *before* deducting investment expenses and taxes. In this case, investment expenses and taxes are included with other expenses and taxes in the "disposition of income." However, the NAIC Annual Statement calls for reporting investment income on a "net" basis, that is, *after* deducting investment expenses and taxes. Many companies in their Annual Reports follow the precedent of the NAIC Annual Statement and show net investment income. Due to the diversity in the practice of companies, it is often difficult to make consistent comparisons of companies by using figures from their Annual Reports. This is only one of a number of areas where a similar difficulty arises.

4. *Capital Gains. Realized capital gains* arise through the sale of an asset for an amount greater than the value at which it is carried on the books.

Unrealized capital gains may arise from revaluation of assets and changes in the market values of nonamortizable securities. It will be remembered that nonamortizable securities, except for preferred stocks "in good standing," are valued in the balance sheet at current market prices. While these gains or losses are unrealized, they result in a change in the amount of assets and must necessarily be treated as income (or disbursements) for the purposes of the financial statements.

Some companies in their Annual Reports include in regular income some or all of their net capital gains (capital gains minus capital losses). The NAIC Annual Statement, however, now includes all capital gains and losses in the "surplus account," discussed below. Consideration of the surplus account will be simplified if it is assumed that Annual Reports also include all capital items in the surplus account.

5. *Miscellaneous Income.* This is usually quite small in relation to total income; it includes minor items which do not fit clearly into one of the first three categories described above.

Disbursements.   Disbursements by a life insurance company consist of:

1. Contractual payments
2. Payments from funds on deposit
3. Policyholder dividends
4. Expenses of operation
5. Capital losses

1. *Contractual Payments.* Contractual payments are all benefit payments including, in addition to regular death, endowment, and annuity payments, cash surrender values, payments under supplementary contracts, and waiver-of-premium, disability income, and health insurance benefits.

The full amount of claim payments will be included where the amount is left under a settlement option. This will also be the case where a policy loan is deducted, since the disbursement is offset or balanced by the asset (policy loan) cancelled and the net cash payment. In the case of disability income benefits (paid in cash) and premiums waived (not paid in cash), both are included in full as disbursements. The waiver of premium is treated as if the premium were first paid to the company and then refunded. This procedure is necessary in order to show the proper amount of premium income and benefit payments.

2. *Payments from Funds on Deposit.* This class of disbursements includes primarily the regular payments under supplementary contracts *without* life contingencies and the amounts of dividend accumulations withdrawn or paid with death claims, matured endowments, or surrenders. These payments could logically also be classified as "Contractual."

3. *Policyholder Dividends.* If the dividend year is assumed to be the same as the calendar year, the total amount of *dividends payable* in any calendar year is derived from surplus existing at the end of the *previous calendar year.* At the end of a given calendar year, a new allotment will be made (from surplus) for dividends to be distributed in the following year. On the incurred or accrued basis the new allotment, less any excess of the allotment at the end of the previous year over the actual dividend payments during the past year, is applicable "disbursement" for the coming year.

4. *Expenses of Operation.* The principal categories of expenses have been discussed previously in connection with gross premium derivation. It should be pointed out here, however, that taxes (other than real estate taxes) consist primarily of the Federal income tax and state taxes on premiums, both of which are substantial in amount. Other taxes include miscellaneous license fees, Social Security taxes, and the like.

5. *Capital Losses.* Capital losses, whether realized or unrealized, must be treated as disbursements for the reasons already explained in connection with capital gains. As mentioned there also, the NAIC Annual Statement now includes all capital gains and losses in the "surplus account." We have assumed for this discussion that this same treatment is applied in Annual Reports.

Sample Summary of Operations.   The previous review of the income and disbursement items for a life insurance company should simplify the interpretation of the Summary of Operations Statement.

As mentioned earlier, in the operation of a life insurance company, much of the income does not actually "go out" in the same year it is received. Instead, much of the income is retained for the benefit of policyholders and beneficiaries in the form of increased reserves and increased surplus (if the company is growing satisfactorily). Therefore, a more descriptive term such as "Disposition of Income" or "How the income was applied" is often used in Annual Reports instead of "outgo" or "disbursements."

Most of the items shown under "Disposition of Income" in the sample "Summary of Operations" are self-explanatory. As mentioned above, the figures for death benefits, matured endowments and surrender benefits each include policy proceeds left with the company under settlement options as well as proceeds paid out in cash; similarly, the figure for dividends to policyholders includes dividends left to accumulate.

In the sample, the expenses and taxes shown exclude investment expenses and taxes, which have been deducted from investment income in the "Income" section. It should be noted again that a company which owns a home office building is required to charge itself rent on a reasonable basis (so that home office rent is counted both as an expense and as an offsetting income item). This requirement arises from the desirability of having expenses on a reasonably comparable basis regardless of whether the home office is owned or rented. In general, life insurance companies own their home offices.

The item "Transfer to Surplus Account" in the sample "Summary of Operations" in Table 42–3 is essentially a balancing item.[18] In some Annual Reports, it is called "Net gain from operations after dividends." Table 42–3, which is a rearrangement of some of the principal items in the sample "Summary of Operations," may clarify the nature of this last item and show why it may be called by either name.

Dividends to policyholders are not included with the other benefits paid to policyholders and beneficiaries in some Annual Reports. In such cases, the net gain from operations may be shown both *before* and *after* dividends. Table 42–4, which is based on the operating results used in Table 42–2, illustrates this. (Table 42–4 parallels the treatment of these items in the NAIC Annual Statement.)

The term "net gain" implies that the company, as distinguished from the policyholders, is profiting from the gain. Due to this incorrect connotation, there is some feeling that using the term "net gain" is inadvisable. This is particularly applicable to "net gain before dividends," which is almost al-

---

[18] In a stock life insurance company, gain from operations is regarded as an important measure of operations and is more than a "balancing item."

TABLE 42-3.   Alternative Presentation of Disposition of Income on Summary of Operations

Total Income		$20,000,000

Disposition of Income

Total Benefits to Policyowners and Beneficiaries (including Dividends)	$10,500,000	
Total Expenses and Taxes	4,000,000	
Increase in Required Reserves	4,500,000	
		19,000,000
Net Gain from Operations after Dividends or Transfer to Surplus Account		$ 1,000,000

TABLE 42-4.   Alternative Presentation of Disposition of Income

Total Income		$20,000,000

Disposition of Income

Total Benefits to Policyowners and Beneficiaries (excluding Dividends)	$9,000,000	
Total Expenses and Taxes	4,000,000	
Increase in Required Reserves	4,500,000	
		17,500,000
Net Gain from Operations before Dividends		$ 2,500,000
Dividends to Policyowners		1,500,000
Net Gain from Operations after Dividends		$ 1,000,000

ways a comparatively large figure in companies issuing participating insurance. A number of companies, therefore, prefer the method of presentation used in Table 42–2.

It is quite common to provide in Annual Reports a graphical analysis of the "income dollar" for the current year. These charts or graphs differ greatly as to format, but their fundamental features are fairly well standardized. A typical chart is shown here in Graph 42–1.

In connection with these charts, it is often pointed out that the money paid to or retained for policyholders and beneficiaries exceeds the funds received from them because the earnings from investments exceed the operating expenses and taxes.

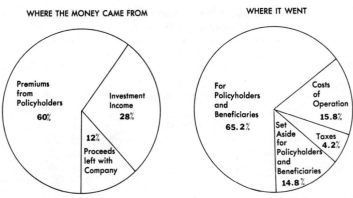

WHERE THE MONEY CAME FROM

Premiums from Policyholders 60%

Investment Income 28%

12% Proceeds left with Company

WHERE IT WENT

For Policyholders and Beneficiaries 65.2%

Costs of Operation 15.8%

Set Aside for Policyholders and Beneficiaries 14.8%

Taxes 4.2%

GRAPH 42-1. The 1970 income dollar.

Surplus Account

In many Annual Reports, the "Summary of Operations" is accompanied by an analysis of the surplus account, which reconciles the surplus at the beginning and end of the year. A sample surplus account is shown in Table 42–2 below the sample "Summary of Operations." The basic mechanics of the reconciliation can be explained as follows:

To the unassigned surplus at the beginning of the year, add any additions during the year, such as:

1. Net gain from operations after dividends to policyowners
2. Net capital gains (if not included in Income)
3. Decrease in Mandatory Securities Valuation Reserve
4. Decreases in other special reserves included in liabilities
5. Decreases in special surplus fund
6. Decreases in separate account business

From the sum, subtract any deductions from unassigned surplus during the year, such as:

1. Dividends to stockholders
2. Net capital losses (if not included in Disposition of Income)
3. Increase in reserves on account of change in valuation basis (reserve strengthening)
4. Increase in Mandatory Securities Valuation Reserve
5. Increases in other special reserves included in liabilities
6. Increases in special surplus funds
7. Increases in separate account business

The balance is equal to the unassigned surplus at the end of the year.

The surplus account is very helpful in giving insight into the success of the current year's operations. The question of the size of the surplus in relation to the size of the company is discussed below.

Other Statistical Information

In addition to the basic materials described above (balance sheet, summary of operations, surplus account), additional statistics are found in many Annual Reports. The types of information usually presented include:

1. New business figures, showing amount of insurance and number of policies paid for. Figures may be shown separately for the different lines of insurance, i.e., ordinary, group, industrial, and health insurance.[19] For ordinary insurance, the figures are sometimes broken down into life, endowment, term, and paid-up additions; the average amount of insurance per policy is also often shown.

2. Insurance in force, often according to the subdivisions mentioned above.

3. Benefits paid to policyholders and beneficiaries during the year and total benefits paid since organization.

4. Analysis of death claims during the year according to cause of death.

For each of these items, figures are usually shown for the current year and the previous year. Frequently, some of them (as well as analyses of the assets by type) also are shown for each of the last five, ten, or twenty years or at five-year intervals over a period of years. From the new business and insurance in force figures for prior years some idea of the rate of growth of the company can be obtained. Changes in the distribution of deaths by causes are frequently of interest to the policyholders.

The new business and insurance in force figures are usually presented on the same basis as the corresponding information in the NAIC Annual Statement. This leads to duplication in some cases because the insurance in force figures in the NAIC Annual Statement include reinsurance assumed from another company in addition to all directly written business, whether or not any part of it has been "ceded" to another company as reinsurance. Thus, these figures, if added up for all the companies, include duplication to the extent that business has been reinsured.[20]

In appraising a company, it is helpful to know the nature of the business being written. One of the more important aspects traditionally was the proportion of term insurance. Due to its temporary nature and its low pre-

---

[19] Premium income is the usual measuring rod for amounts of health insurance.

[20] The Balance Sheet and Summary of Operations do not involve any duplication, since they include data for reinsurance assumed but exclude data for business ceded to another company.

miums and low commissions per $1,000 of insurance, term insurance ordinarily does not mean as much in the way of permanent growth of a company as an equal face amount of whole-life or endowment business.[21]

The proportion of new term business may affect materially the average amount of insurance per new ordinary policy. The average face amount of term policies is almost always substantially higher than the average for whole-life and endowment policies. This is the result of a number of factors, which include the lower premiums per $1,000 on term, the different age distribution of term buyers, and the smaller proportion of women among the term buyers.

The average amount of insurance per policy is important. Some expenses depend on the number of policies rather than the amount of insurance, so that the expense rate per $1,000 ordinarily will be somewhat lower on a large policy than on a small one. Thus, if all other factors are the same, a company with a high average amount of insurance per policy will have a lower expense rate per $1,000 than a company with a low average amount of insurance per policy. Since all other factors are never the same in two companies, great caution must be exercised in using comparisons of the average amounts of insurance per policy in different companies as an indication of their relative expense rates.

The significance which can be attached to the proportion of term insurance or to the average amount of insurance per policy has been greatly reduced by two developments:

1. The popularity of the family policy, which usually consists of a combination of whole-life insurance on the father and a lesser amount of term insurance on the mother and on each child. In some companies, this term insurance is included with other term insurance; in other companies the entire family policy is treated as a permanent life insurance policy.

2. The increasing use of premiums graded by size of policy and of "special" policies with high minimum amounts. Thus, the buyer of a large policy receives the benefit of the low expense rate per $1,000 on his policy even though the average amount of insurance per policy may be quite low in the company in which he is purchasing insurance.

[21] Bases for measuring the growth of a company are discussed on p. 720.

Interpreting Life Insurance Company Financial Statements: II | 43

THE NAIC ANNUAL STATEMENT

As INDICATED EARLIER, the financial condition and management of an insurance company are concerns of state law and are subject to constant review by state regulatory authorities. In order for state insurance departments to obtain information which will enable them to evaluate a company's financial condition, each company is required to submit a highly detailed annual statement. These statements are filed with the insurance department in each state and territory in which the company is licensed to do business. In Canada, they are filed with the Dominion Department, which assumes the primary responsibility for the solvency of companies licensed by it.

In 1871, by securing the agreement of the states to adopt the *uniform* annual financial statement, the National Association of Insurance Commissioners (then known as the National Insurance Convention of the United States) rendered one of its most valuable contributions to the insurance business. This so-called *NAIC Blank* is subject to revision by a committee of the Association annually, but usually only minor changes are made. Special blanks are prepared for different classes of insurance (e.g., life, casualty, etc.). The life blank was significantly revised last in 1951.

Although a thorough analysis of the NAIC Annual Statement Blank is beyond the scope of this volume, it is worthwhile to review, *generally,* the major elements of the prescribed form and, broadly, the types of information included. For purposes of this analysis the discussion is divided into two parts:

1. The financial statements, and
2. Supplementary exhibits and schedules.

The Financial Statements

The *financial statements* consist of a *balance sheet* and a *summary of operations*. With regard to the major items, the statements of assets and liabilities are in summary form. Thus, in the statement of assets, the amount of each main category (such as bonds or stocks) is shown only in total, while in the statement of liabilities the policy reserves are similarly shown in total. Detailed breakdowns of these items are furnished in subsidiary exhibits and schedules which are discussed below.

The form of the *summary of operations* in the NAIC Annual Statement is somewhat different from the one illustrated earlier in connection with Annual Reports. It shows the net increase in surplus from all sources except (1) capital gains, (2) increases or decreases in special reserves, (3) increases or decreases arising from separate account business, (4) dividends to stockholders, and (5) increases or decreases in reserves on account of change in valuation basis (reserve strengthening). These items, excluded from the summary of operations, are shown in the *surplus account*.

The Summary of Operations statement is accompanied by two supplementary reports:

1. An analysis of *operations by lines of business,* and
2. An analysis of *changes in policy reserves* during the year.

The analysis of operations by lines of business is merely an allocation by line of business of the figures shown for all lines combined in the first part of the summary of operations mentioned above. It shows how the total net gain for the company, after allocation of dividends to policyholders, is distributed among the different lines of business, namely, life insurance (ordinary, industrial, and group), annuities (individual and group), the "special benefits" (disability and accidental-death benefits), and health insurance (individual and group).

The report, relating to changes in policy reserves, is a purely technical statement for the use of the actuaries of the State Insurance Department in verifying certain gains and losses and for other purposes.

Supplementary Exhibits and Schedules

In general, the subsidiary exhibits and schedules provide analyses, breakdowns, or further details in regard to some of the items which appear only in total in the financial statements.

Among the *exhibits,* the more important are those furnishing detail or classified information about (1) premium income, (2) investment income, (3) capital gains and losses, (4) expenses, (5) taxes, (6) policy reserves, (7) policy claims, (8) life insurance issued, terminated, and in force (the "policy exhibit"), and (9) annuities issued, terminated, and in force (the "annuity exhibit").

Following the exhibits, there is a series of general interrogatories. A statement of the company's business in the state in which the report is being filed is now shown at the end of the statement following "schedules." The statement shows the numbers and amounts of policies issued, terminated, and in force together with a statement of premiums collected and claims incurred in the state. Naturally, the necessity of furnishing such information by state requires the insurance company to maintain its records in such a way as to allocate its business by state.

The most important *schedules* found in the NAIC Statement are those relating to real estate, mortgage loans, and securities (bonds and stocks). The schedules for real estate and securities show, in detail, the amounts owned at the end of the year and the purchases and sales during the year. Somewhat similar information is given for mortgage loans but without much detail. Other important *schedules* show detailed information regarding (1) December 31 bank balances; (2) resisted claims; (3) expenses incurred in connection with legal matters or appearances before legislative bodies, etc.; and (4) proceedings at the last annual election of directors.[1]

EVALUATING THE INDIVIDUAL COMPANY

In an earlier chapter,[2] some of the variables affecting individual company performance were reviewed. The criteria considered were (1) nature of the product, (2) service, (3) cost, and (4) security. In reviewing the information available in the usual Annual Report, it will be helpful to consider the principal factors affecting the cost of life and health insurance as well as some of the other statistical measures presented as indicators of company performance and strength.

In making any comparison involving two or more companies it is important to be careful to compare *like things* and to use suitable *measuring*

---

[1] As was pointed out earlier, the primary purpose of the NAIC Statement is to supply the supervisory officials with information which they need or desire in regulating the insurance business. It should be noted, however, that the annual filing of the Statement Blank also provides a permanent year to year record of the company's operations for the use of management, stockholders, employees, potential buyers of the company and the public at large. The Statement Blank has been described only in outline in this discussion. On the other hand, the reader who wishes to study it in greater detail may be able to obtain a copy of the current blank either from the State Insurance Department or from the home office of a life insurance company domiciled within his state.

[2] See pp. 688–689.

rods. An Annual Report does not provide the information needed to make a reliable comparison between companies.

It was pointed out earlier that companies differ widely in the composition of their business, in accounting practices and in method of reporting operational results. Unless allowance is made for such differences, comparisons between companies have little, if any, validity. Unfortunately, sufficient information is usually not available to permit such adjustments. As a practical matter, however, such comparisons are made and it is important for the student of life and health insurance to be acquainted with the limitations of such comparisons.

Principal Factors Affecting the Cost of Life Insurance

As was brought out in the discussion of premiums and dividends, the three basic factors influencing the cost of life insurance are interest, mortality, and expense.

Interest.   1. *Rate on Total Portfolio.* The rates for the total portfolio are usually based on the formula specified for calculating interest rates in the Annual Statement filed with the state insurance departments.[3] This formula produces a compound interest rate by reflecting the effect of interest earned during the latter part of a year on interest received earlier in the year and reinvested.

Interest rates based on the portfolio for the past year are often referred to as "earned" rates. They are likely to be reported on one or more of the following bases:

(a) *Gross.* In computing this rate, "investment income" or "I" is the gross investment income before deducting any investment expenses and taxes.

(b) *Net before Federal income tax.* In computing this rate, "I" is the *net* investment income *before* Federal income tax, i.e., the gross investment income minus all investment expenses and minus investment taxes other than Federal income tax.

(c) *Net after Federal income tax.* In computing this rate, "I" is the gross investment income minus all investment expenses and all investment taxes *including* the portion of the Federal income tax charged to investment expenses. Since the Federal income tax of a life insurance company is based

---

[3] This formula is: $i = \dfrac{2I}{A + B - I}$ where i is the interest rate, I is the investment income for the year and A is the sum at the beginning of the year of (a) invested assets, (b) cash, and (c) overdue and accrued investment income, while B is the corresponding sum at the end of the year.

partly on its net investment income and partly on its net "underwriting income," some companies treat part or all of the Federal income tax as a tax on insurance operations and not as a tax on investment income.

Because of the diversity of practice with regard to treating Federal income tax as an investment or insurance expense, the net interest rates of various companies *after* Federal income tax simply are not comparable without additional information not available in the Annual Report.

The net rates *before* Federal income tax, as given in Annual Reports, are a sounder basis for comparison and represent one of the more satisfactory measures of the success of a life insurance company's investment policy. The rate of interest on this basis for 1970 for United States life insurance companies was 5.30 per cent. Even this measure of investment results does not reflect the tax advantages of tax-exempt securities and of stocks, since this net interest rate is *before* tax.

In view of the fact that expense rates vary greatly on different types of investments, the gross rate is not satisfactory. For example, the expense rate on mortgages, caused by the greater cost of servicing such investments, may well be at least 0.2 per cent higher than the expense rate on bonds and stocks, since the latter are usually purchased in relatively large blocks. With the significant variations in expense rates for various types of investments, comparisons of the *gross* rates for companies with different asset distributions are not reliable indicators of how the more significant *net* rates would compare.

The ratio, "investment expenses to mean assets," is sometimes quoted as a measure of investment expense.[4] This ratio is not a good basis for comparing the investment expenses of two or more companies. Variations in the ratio from company to company may well be caused solely by differences in the composition of the investment portfolio and not by actual differences in the rates of investment expense on each asset classification.

2. *Rate on New Investments.* As a measure of the effectiveness of the current investment activity, the average rate on the new investments made during the year is usually reported in the Annual Report to policyholders. This rate is often reported on a *gross* basis rather than a net basis despite the disadvantages of gross rates as a basis for comparisons. To compute the rate of yield on new investments on a net basis would necessitate an estimate of future average investment expenses and taxes. It is usually considered preferable to avoid such projections.

3. *"Interest-Bearing Liabilities."* As pointed out in the discussion of dividends,[5] the total invested income may be related only to those assets which stand back of or offset those liabilities which are assumed to be credited

---

[4] "Mean assets" is the average of the admitted assets at the beginning of the year and at the end of the year.

[5] See pp. 452–455.

yearly with interest at a specified rate, the so-called interest-bearing liabilities. An interest rate computed on the basis of this restricted group of assets would naturally be higher than one based on total assets.

4. *"Required Interest."* Although of doubtful value because of the differences in reserve bases, the results of the investment operations of life insurance companies are sometimes measured by comparing the actual net investment income with the interest "required" to be earned on the "interest-bearing liabilities." Thus, the actual rate earned on the total assets may be compared with the average rate required to maintain the "interest-bearing liabilities."

5. *Capital Gains or Losses.* Normally, capital gains or losses do not enter directly into the determination of any of the interest rates discussed above, although they can have a considerable effect on the success of a company's investment program. As pointed out earlier, the net capital gains for the *current year* usually are reported in the Annual Report (in the analysis of the surplus account or in the summary of operations). Some trade publications also show such net capital gains, but neither source reports them over a period of years. The results for an individual year give a misleading picture because these gains, particularly in a company owning common stock, can fluctuate widely.

Capital losses also may be misleading because sound securities are sometimes sold at losses in order to reinvest at higher interest rates, with the result that a particular year's capital losses will be more than offset by higher earnings in the future. Conversely, capital gains may be misleading if they arise from the calling of bonds at a time when reinvestments can only be made at lower interest rates.

Mortality.   No really satisfactory basis for comparing the mortality experience of different companies is available. Theoretically, the mortality experience on life insurance can be measured by comparing the ratio of the "actual" mortality experienced to the "expected" (or "tabular") mortality according to a given table of mortality. Misleading ratios may result, however, unless the table of mortality being used as the basis for the expected mortality shows about the same pattern of variation, according to age and according to the number of years the policy has been in force, as does the actual mortality experience. Moreover, the same table must be used by the companies being compared.

Many years ago, the ratio of the actual mortality to the expected mortality was widely used to compare mortality experience of companies. At that time, practically all companies used the *American Experience Table of Mortality* (1868) as the basis for the expected mortality for most of their business. The introduction of the *1941 CSO Table* in 1948 and more recently, the *1958 CSO Table* as the basis for expected mortality for future business has made any such comparisons completely invalid today. The proportion of different companies' business valued on these different bases, would produce rates of actual expected mortality on a hybrid basis totally unsuitable for comparing companies.

Further, the rate of growth and stage of development of individual companies mitigate against valid comparisons. A relatively new company with most of its business still in the "select period" (ten to fifteen years) would show a much lower actual rate of mortality and hence a lower rate of actual to expected mortality than many other companies. In some cases, such a situation might actually hide very poor underwriting performance.

Still another reason why the aggregate ratio of actual to expected mortality for one company should not be compared with the aggregate ratio for another company is that both the actual mortality rates experienced and the expected mortality rates assumed are likely to be considerably different for each of the three main classes of business—ordinary, group, and industrial. The aggregate ratio would clearly be affected by the different proportions of ordinary, group, and industrial business.

Mortality ratios are also affected by the proportions of medically examined and non-medical business, and the proportions of men and women insured. Mortality on business written on a non-medical basis is usually somewhat higher (particularly during the "select period") than on otherwise comparable business underwritten with a medical examination. Also, male mortality is distinctly higher than that of females. Thus, a company which writes a significant proportion of its business on a non-medical basis would expect to experience higher mortality rates than another company which writes a relatively insignificant proportion of non-medical business. The additional mortality costs on non-medical business usually are offset roughly by the savings in expense through eliminating the medical examination and additional underwriting costs and this fact would have to be taken into account to make a valid comparison.

A similar situation exists in connection with the relative proportions of male and female business. Male mortality is distinctly higher than female mortality, but this is usually compensated for in many companies either by using regular premiums and "setting back" the ages of women or by developing separate lower premiums for women.

As pointed out earlier, mortality rates on term insurance and on conversions from term insurance are usually higher than average. Therefore, the relative amount of a company's total business which is term insurance or conversions from term will affect the ratio.

In view of all these complicating factors, the ratio of actual to expected mortality for a company is rarely reported either in Annual Reports or in trade publications.

TABLE 43-1. Evaluation of Various Expense Ratios

$\dfrac{\text{Expenses}}{\substack{\text{Amount of Insurance}\\\text{in force}}}$	1. It gives no weight to annuities, supplementary contracts, health insurance, and disability and accidental death benefits. 2. It gives no weight to miscellaneous operations which are conducted on a basis which is usually self-supporting. Examples of such operations are handling dividend accumulations or prepaid premiums. 3. It makes no allowance for the difference between first year and renewal year expenses unless some arbitrary adjustment is introduced such as multiplying the amount of new business by a factor of, say, 5 or 10. 4. It makes no allowance for the difference between expenses on ordinary, group, and industrial business unless some arbitrary weighting of the three categories is introduced. 5. It makes no allowance for variations in expenses with age and plan of insurance. 6. It makes no allowance for differences in methods of operation. For example, a company doing little or no non-medical business might have a high expense rate but this presumably would be offset by more favorable mortality experience.
$\dfrac{\text{Expenses}}{\text{Premiums received}}$	1. 2, 3, 4, and 5 above. 2. Gives some weight (but not necessarily the proper weight) to annuities, health insurance, and disability and accidental death benefits. 3. *No* weight to supplementary contracts.
$\dfrac{\text{Expenses}}{\text{Total income}}$	1. 3, 4, and 6 above. 2. Gives weight to supplementary contracts. 3. Raises questions about handling of investment expenses.

Expenses.   The dollars spent for expenses by a life company may be obtained from its Annual Report or from trade publications, but it is practically impossible to find a suitable measuring rod to tell whether the rate of expenses is high or low. The measuring rods used for purposes of comparisons are: (1) amount of insurance in force, (2) premiums received, or (3) total income. None of these is entirely satisfactory. Expenses vary with many different things, and the ideal measuring rod would have to take all of them into consideration. For example, the varia-

TABLE 43-2. Calculation of Various Expense Ratios

Ratio of Expenses to Insurance in Force (Total expenses excluding taxes, licenses, etc., $3,500,000 ÷ insurance in force $750,000,000) Expenses per $1,000 of insurance in force		$4.67
Ratio of Expenses to Premium Income (Expenses $3,500,000 ÷ Premium Income $14,800,000)	Ratio	23.6%
Ratio of Expenses to Total Income (Expenses $3,500,000 ÷ Total Income $20,000,000)	Ratio	17.0%

Note: Total insurance in force calculated at the rate of $1,000 of insurance per $20 of premium income of $15,600,000 in Ta' le 42-2. All data taken from Table 42-2.

tion between first year expense and renewal year expense is so significant that it must be considered. First year expenses are usually many times those incurred in a renewal year. Expense rates also vary significantly among various lines of business.

Table 43–1 shows expense ratios based on the three measuring rods mentioned above and indicates the weaknesses of each ratio. Table 43–2 shows these ratios calculated on the basis of the data shown in Table 42-2. The aggregate rate of expense of a company is a poor indicator as to the expense rate which will be charged against various classes of policies in calculating dividends. The increasing use of special policies with high minimum amounts and of premium and/or dividend scales which vary with the size of the policy has reduced the value of the overall expense rate as a guide to the expense rate likely to be charged per $1,000 on a particular plan.

Expense rates published in trade publications are of relatively little value for purposes of comparison. Annual Reports of life insurance companies usually convey little or no real information about the level of expenses. References to expense rates deal with the expense question in only the most general terms.

Other Measures of Operating Results

Lapse Rates.   In view of the incidence of expense problem [6] a low lapse rate is desirable. Some measure of the lapse rate is frequently shown in Annual Reports and trade publications.

The pattern of lapse rates and the factors affecting them were discussed earlier. They are generally comparatively high in the first year, somewhat lower in the second year and then decrease gradually until they level off

[6] See pp. 421–426.

around the fifth or tenth year.[7] Lapse rates also tend to vary with issue age, plan of insurance, and mode of premium payment. In general, the lapse rate is low at the juvenile ages and high at the younger adult ages, decreasing gradually at the middle and higher ages as the age at issue increases. It is usually considerably higher on term plans than on whole-life or endowment plans and higher on monthly premium policies than on annual premium policies.

Because of the several variable factors, any comparison of the lapse rates of various companies can be misleading unless the composition of the business of each company is similar. Such a similarity is rarely found, and comparisons of lapse rates should be used cautiously, if at all.

The problem of comparing lapse rates is much the same for ordinary and industrial business, although the actual pattern of the rates may be quite different. Obviously, the lapse rate of a company writing no industrial business should not be compared with the lapse rate of a combination company writing ordinary and industrial with a considerable part of its business on the industrial basis.

Rate of Growth. Most companies take pride in their growth and Annual Reports usually present a record of the company's growth in the last five or ten years. If the growth rate of a company is less than the average for the industry, it may be an indication of poor management or high costs. On the other hand, it may also be an indication that management is satisfied that the company is growing at an efficient rate and feels that money spent to increase the rate of expansion might not be justified. A very rapid rate of growth may indicate undue expansion without regard to costs or it may indicate a vigorous and capable management. Although it would be helpful to have information on the size and caliber of the sales force, it is practically impossible to obtain such information for different companies on a consistent basis. Finally, small, recently established companies would be expected to grow at faster *percentage rates* than older, larger companies.

The items used most frequently in measuring growth are (1) amount of new insurance paid-for, (2) amount of insurance in force, (3) premium income, and (4) assets.

Considerable analysis is desirable before drawing any conclusions from the comparative growth rates of companies. Except in a depression, however, a decrease in items (2), (3), or (4) should be interpreted as a warning signal.

Annuities and Supplementary Contracts. The gains or losses on annuities and supplementary contracts usually are not shown separately in Annual Reports, although such gains or losses are reported in some trade publications. As a result of the decline in the average net in-

[7] See pp. 414–415.

terest rate earned by life insurance companies during the 1930's and 1940's and the secular trend toward mortality improvement, many companies have had large losses on annuities and supplementary contracts. The interest rate, however, has improved considerably in recent years and some companies are now reporting gains on annuities and supplementary contracts, particularly those which strengthened their reserves to a reasonably conservative basis.[8]

The single-premium annuity business is usually nonparticipating and deferred annuities and supplementary contracts involving life contingencies are often nonparticipating after the end of any refund or certain period. Therefore, policyholders in a participating company can benefit from the gains on annuities and supplementary contracts, and would be interested in the experience of this class of business. Similarly, they would be interested in any health insurance business written on a nonparticipating basis.

Health Insurance.   Using premium income as the criterion, the health insurance business of life insurance companies is growing more rapidly than their life business. In some medium-sized and small life insurance companies, health insurance premium income is considerably larger than life insurance premium income.

The operating results of the health insurance business are usually expressed in terms of (1) the loss ratio and (2) the expense ratio.

1. *Loss ratio.* The ratio of claims "incurred" during the year to premiums "earned" during the year constitutes the *loss ratio.* As in the case of fire insurance, a premium paid during the year for a period which runs beyond the end of the calendar year is regarded as split into two portions, an "earned" portion from the premium due date to December 31 and an "unearned" portion from December 31 to the next premium due date. The term "incurred" reflects both losses *paid* during the period plus an adjustment for the change in claim reserve over the period. The ratio then shows the proportion of every premium dollar earned during the period which was needed to meet all losses allocated to the period.

2. *Expense ratio.* The ratio of expenses "incurred" during the year to "earned" premiums[9] is known as the expense ratio. This ratio is affected by the composition of the business. The types of health insurance issued

---

[8] It should be remembered that the strengthening of reserves does not, *in the long run,* have a material effect on the gains or losses of a company; the main effect is to *change the incidence* of the gains and losses. A large bookkeeping loss is shown in the year when reserves are strengthened, but on the other hand the losses shown in future years will be somewhat smaller (or the gains will be somewhat larger) than would have been the case if reserves had not been strengthened. By the time all of the block of business has gone off the books, the accumulated net effect is small.

[9] This formula is used in the NAIC Annual Statement as the basis for computing the expense ratio. Many trade publications, however, use the ratio of expenses incurred during the year to "written" premiums ("written" being used in a specialized sense to denote premiums paid adjusted for premiums due but unpaid at the beginning and end of the year). The difference between the expense ratio based on "earned" premiums and the ratio based on "written" premiums is usually small.

have a particularly important effect on expense ratios. For example, travel accident and other limited policies tend to have high expense ratios because of the low average premium per policy; broader coverage policies with larger average premiums per policy would tend to have lower expense ratios.

The sum of the loss and expense ratios is an approximate indication of whether the company had an underwriting profit or an underwriting loss in its health insurance business, depending on whether the sum is under or over 100 per cent. In the case of participating health insurance, the ratio of policyholders' dividends to earned premiums should also be considered in evaluating overall results. For example, assuming a loss ratio of 55 per cent and an expense ratio of 35 per cent, a 10 per cent ratio of dividends to earned premiums would indicate that the health insurance operations of a particular company were almost exactly at the break-even point, since the sum of the three ratios is 100 per cent.

These health insurance ratios are given in several trade publications, but they are not usually reported in the Annual Reports of life insurance companies. Morbidity rates and, hence, loss ratios fluctuate considerably and ratios for more than one year should be examined to form any conclusions about a company's health insurance operations.

The Annual Reports usually give considerable information on the types and volume of health insurance business, but references to the operating results are brief and so indefinite as to be of relatively little value.

Dividends to Policyholders. The Annual Reports of companies issuing participating insurance virtually always report the amount set aside for dividends in the coming year and how it compares with dividends in the past year. This is particularly so if the dividend scale has been increased for the coming year.

The percentage increases often presented with such comparisons can be misleading. Assuming a company paid out $1,000,000 in dividends during a given year and its insurance in force increased 10 per cent during the same year, it might expect to pay out $1,100,000 in dividends during the coming year *if it did not increase its dividend scale.* If it increases its dividend *scale* by 20 per cent, the dividend liability for the coming year will be $1,320,000 (120% $\times$ $1,100,000), a further increase of $220,000. The total liability, $1,320,000, is greater than the $1,000,000 paid the previous year. In press releases and trade magazines, this is frequently reported as a 32 per cent increase in dividends when actually it is only a 20 per cent increase in the dividend scale. If no change had occurred in the dividend *scale,* dividends would still have gone up $100,000 due to the increase in insurance in force. Frequently, careful reading is necessary to tell whether the reference is to the average percentage increase in the dividend scale itself or to the increase in total amount to be paid including the effect of any increase in the insurance in force.

Percentage increases can be misleading in another way. Assume two companies of the same size and exactly alike in every respect except that the loading in one company's premiums was $500,000 greater for the past year than the loading in the other company's premiums.[10] Since the net cost of insurance is assumed to be the same in the two companies, the dividends for the past year in, say, company A would have been $500,000 greater ($1,500,000) than in company B. For the coming year, they would go up 10 per cent to $1,650,000 [11] because of the increase in insurance in force. The increase in the scale in company A (to keep the net premium payments the same as in company B) will result in an increase of $220,000, the same amount as in company B. This will make company A's liability for the coming year $1,870,000 on the new scale. But the ratio of $1,870,-000 to $1,650,000 is only 113 per cent, indicating an increase in the scale of only 13 per cent as compared with 20 per cent for company B. Thus, comparisons of the percentage increases in different companies can be very misleading unless the level of the gross premiums (and also the distribution of business according to plan, age, and duration) is approximately the same in the two companies.

Comparisons based on the average increase per *$1,000 insurance* in the dividend *scale* take care of any discrepancies between the level of the gross premiums, but even here no allowance is made for any distortion due to differences in the distribution of business. Comparisons of the average *dividend* per $1,000 insurance in different companies are pratically worthless because of differences in premium levels and in distributions of business.

Dividends to Stockholders.   In many stock companies, the dividends to stockholders are relatively small in relation to the company's operations. For example, one medium-sized, successful stock company paid out thirty-four times as much in 1970 in dividends to policyholders as in dividends to stockholders. Where such a relation exists, the cost to the policyholder is certainly little greater, if any, than in a mutual company.

The Strength of a Company

Balance Sheets Are Conservative.   The great majority of life insurance companies, which have been established long enough to have the margins required, have a basic policy of valuing assets low and liabili-

[10] In connection with this reference to difference in the loading, it might be appropriate to point out here the weaknesses of a ratio which is quoted by at least one trade publication—"loading to gross premiums (life insurance)." As between participating and nonparticipating business, and as between companies with a high premium philosophy and companies with a low premium philosophy, this ratio can vary so widely as to be almost meaningless.

[11] $1,500,000 + 10% of $1,500,000.

ties high. This does not mean that management arbitrarily place a low value on assets and a high value on liabilities but simply that management tends, given a choice, to choose the low value for an asset item and the high value for a liability item. This is considered sound accounting practice and state regulatory authorities often have encouraged this attitude to provide an additional measure of protection for the policyholders. Therefore, it can be assumed in the case of established companies that there is probably some understatement of surplus.

Measures of Strength.   Although the entire financial picture, as measured by assets, liabilities, insurance in force, level of premiums, mortality experience, and so forth, is helpful in appraising the strength of a life insurance company, total surplus is the item which is most indicative of the strength of a company.[12] Total surplus (including special surplus funds as well as unassigned surplus) is compared in most Annual Reports with the corresponding figure for the previous year, and the significant factors resulting in the change from one year to the next are reviewed.[13] A suitable analysis is particularly important if there has been a decrease in surplus.

The adequacy of a given amount of surplus can only be determined in relation to some measuring rod. As an absolute figure, the amount of the surplus has relatively little meaning. The two ratios most commonly used are:

1. Surplus as a percentage of liabilities, and
2. Surplus per $1,000 insurance in force

1. *Surplus as a Percentage of Liabilities.* The ratio of surplus to liabilities has received the quasi-approval of regulatory authorities as a basis for evaluating a particular surplus position. This is evidenced by the fact that the State of New York limits surplus in life insurance companies writing participating policies to $850,000 or 10 per cent of *"policy reserves and policy liabilities,"* if greater.[14] Nevertheless, this ratio is not completely satisfactory, because the surplus needed in relation to particular liabilities varies by type of business. In the case of group and health insurance, for example, reserves are usually quite small in relation to the amounts at risk. Therefore, a surplus of 10 per cent of the reserves might be inadequate on group or on health insurance. On the other hand, on other types of business,

---

[12] The term "surplus," as used here, includes capital in a stock company. Due to a special tax situation in New Jersey, a company domiciled in that state may have surplus which is proportionately smaller than that of other companies, but this is offset by additional reserves.

[13] This is done automatically if the changes in the surplus account are presented in tabular form as in Table 42–2; see p. 747.

[14] The general purpose of this New York law is to prevent an undue accumulation of surplus at the expense of policyholders and to assure *annual* dividend distributions.

which do not involve mortality or morbidity contingencies, such as funds held under interest options or dividends left to ‘accumulate, surplus is needed only to protect against investment contingencies. In such cases a comparatively small surplus in relation to the liability would be entirely satisfactory.

The ratio of surplus to liabilities, expressed as a percentage, makes no allowance for the proportions of the various types of liabilities and is less than satisfactory for comparing companies which differ significantly in the composition of their business. Despite this limitation, this ratio is probably the most nearly satisfactory simple measure of the financial strength of a company. Since the Mandatory Securities Valuation Reserve is not a true liability, it can be argued that it should be subtracted from liabilities and added to surplus before calculating the ratio of surplus to liabilities. This refinement, while theoretically justifiable, is not usually made.

2. *Surplus per $1,000 Insurance.* The second measure of a company's surplus position, surplus per $1,000 insurance in force, has the advantage of giving greater weight to group insurance than does the ratio of surplus to liabilities. But surplus per $1,000 insurance in force also has disadvantages. In fact this ratio probably gives too much weight to group insurance. Also, it does not give any weight to annuities, supplementary contracts, health insurance, and the minor types of liabilities, all of which need surplus held for them. In calculating this ratio a decision must be made as to how to handle reinsurance. As mentioned earlier, business ceded to another company as reinsurance *is usually included* in the amount of insurance in force, but clearly there is need for relatively little surplus on business ceded to another company.

To a certain extent, these ratios complement each other. Probably a more accurate picture can be obtained by comparing companies on the basis of both figures than by comparing them on the basis of either ratio alone.

3. *Effect of Mandatory Securities Valuation Reserve.* The Mandatory Securities Valuation Reserve, when it reaches its permitted maximum, may represent as much as 2 per cent or even 3 per cent of the assets. Reserves of this size may be expected to have some long-term influence on the amounts retained as surplus. Other things being equal, a company with a large Mandatory Securities Valuation Reserve would be likely to hold a smaller surplus than an equally conservative company with a small valuation reserve. Therefore, it seems reasonable to assume that the existence of the Mandatory Securities Valuation Reserve may tend, over a period of years, to decrease gradually both the ratio of surplus to liabilities and the amount of surplus per $1,000 insurance in force.

4. *Other Measures of Strength.* Two other ratios which are used at times as measures of company strength involve the substitution of "assets" instead of surplus in the ratios discussed above. These ratios are (a) assets as a percentage of the liabilities, and (b) assets per $1,000 insurance in force.

Since the assets are equal to the liabilities plus the surplus, the ratio for assets as a percentage of liabilities is simply 100 per cent more than the figure for the surplus as a percentage of liabilities. Therefore, a comparison of companies upon the ratio of surplus to liabilities or the ratio of assets to liabilities will produce similar results.

In contrast, the amount of assets per $1,000 insurance in force is almost completely meaningless as a measure of the strength of a company. This figure, rather than measuring the strength of a company, reflects the age and composition of the company's business.

A company with large reserves for annuities and supplementary contracts could conceivably have assets of over $1,000 per $1,000 insurance in force and yet be in serious financial difficulty.

Adjusted Figures for Stock Companies. Placing a proper price for a share of stock in a life insurance company is of concern to all those interested in buying and selling such shares. The book value of the stock may not necessarily be a good indicator of its fair market value, partly because there is usually a drain on surplus when new business is sold, and partly because in many companies (particularly the older ones) there is probably some understatement of surplus as a result of valuing assets low and liabilities high.

To attempt to arrive at a better indicator of reasonable prices for insurance company stocks, many stock analysts and some insurance trade publications calculate "adjusted book values" and "adjusted earnings" for each company, taking into consideration by rough rules of thumb the value of (1) the insurance in force and (2) the increase during the year in the insurance in force.

The values assigned vary by the type of insurance. Typical schedules used for nonparticipating insurance might be somewhat as follows:

Individual life and endowment	$15 to $25 per $1,000 insurance
Individual term	$5 to $7.50 per $1,000 insurance
Group life	$2 to $5 per $1,000 insurance
Individual health	25 to 35 per cent of premiums
Group health	0 to 10 per cent of premiums

The value assigned to participating business would depend in part on any statute or charter limitations on the earnings that stockholders may derive from participating business.

So-called "conditional reserves" and their increase during the year may also be treated as equivalent to surplus in calculating "adjusted book values" and "adjusted earnings." These conditional reserves include the Mandatory Securities Valuation Reserve and amounts voluntarily set aside by management as reserves for possible future contingencies.

These rules of thumb for determining "adjusted book values" and "ad-

justed earnings" overlook many factors which have a marked effect on the proper value of the insurance in force. Among the more important of these factors are: (1) the level of the gross premiums, (2) the interest rates assumed and earned, (3) the recent mortality experience, (4) the recent lapse rates, (5) the level of expenses, (6) the bases for valuing the insurance and annuity reserves, and (7) the quality of the assets.

The use of empirical schedules of the value of insurance as described above is by no means the only method used by analysts. Unfortunately, few of these methods take into consideration the characteristics of a particular company. Moreover, these methods generally involve the implicit assumption of the continuance of past trends for the life of the company. Hence, the analyst is merely substituting different assumptions for those used by the company itself either by choice or by requirement of regulatory authorities.

While a security analyst may calculate "adjusted" figures, a company itself may not calculate them. In a number of states a company cannot publish the amount of its surplus on any basis other than that in the NAIC Statement filed with the insurance department. Therefore, such adjustments necessarily have the weakness that they are made by persons outside rather than inside the company.

Currently, there is considerable discussion about using generally accepted accounting principles for preparing financial statements for publication and for reporting to stockholders. A joint committee of the American Life Convention (ALC) and the Life Insurance Association of America (LIAA) is now working with a committee of the American Institute of Certified Public Accountants (AICPA) to prepare an audit guide that will specify certain approaches that must be used in auditing financial statements that may be certified as having been prepared in accordance with generally accepted accounting principles. Their most significant achievement to date is the development of a "natural reserve" concept for valuing life insurance policy liabilities. These developments will undoubtedly have a significant impact on interpreting life insurance company financial statements.[15]

---

[15] For a review of the overall situation, see Charles L. Van House, Sr., "Can Life Insurance Accounting Be Modernized?" Parts I, II and III, *Best's Review*, Morristown, N. J.: A. M. Best Company, Vol. 71, Nos. 11 and 12 (March and April, 1971); Vol. 72, No. 1 (May, 1971).

Government Regulation 44
and Taxation of
Life and Health Insurance

INTRODUCTION

FEW, IF ANY, business institutions have been subjected to such strict and detailed government supervision as life and health insurance. The reasons for this become clear when we consider the vital relationship which personal insurance bears to the family and the community. Its mission is security; millions of people rely upon it as the principal means of protecting the home against the deprivations occasioned by premature death, disability, and the expenses of medical care.

The great majority of life insurance contracts, and an increasing number of health insurance contracts, run for many years before maturing or expiring and frequently involve an obligation on the part of an insurer extending over forty to seventy-five years. Huge reserve funds are created by the company to meet these obligations. These funds must be safeguarded adequately. Further, the size of the industry as a financial institution means that it plays a vital role in our national economy.

The nature of the insurance transaction involves the utilization of a technical-legal document which makes a present promise of future performance upon the occurrence of stipulated events. Few policyholders read their contracts, and among those who do, perhaps even fewer understand what they are reading. In a nontechnical sense, the insurance product is purchased in good faith by the great majority of policyholders. These insureds, in a very practical way, rely upon the integrity of the insurance company and those who act as its representatives.

Despite the almost universal belief in the need for life and health insurance, and its vital importance to all who purchase this insurance, few persons take a direct interest in acquainting themselves with the management, business policy, and practices of the insurers behind their contracts. Even assuming that a considerable portion of the vast number of policyholders could be induced to take an interest in the condition of their insurers, very few would be sufficiently knowledgeable about insurance matters to ascertain intelligently the true state of affairs. Life and health insurance is necessarily a technical and complicated subject and, as pointed out in the preceding chapters, the true financial condition of an insurance company can be determined only by expert and laborious examination.

Without question, the greatest volume of life and health insurance is sold by reputable companies striving to meet their legal and moral obligations. However, for all of the reasons enumerated above, the activities and operations of life and health insurance companies are a fit subject for government regulation designed to protect the public adequately against unjust practices and mismanagement as they may arise.

The *protection* of the insuring public is, by far, the most important objective of regulation. Other objectives, peculiar to state as opposed to Federal regulation, might include *revenue* and *retaliation*.

Retaliation as an objective of regulatory activities is defensive in nature, i.e., retaliatory statutes have been enacted against foreign insurance companies in an effort to protect domestic companies from undue burdens and limitations which might be imposed by other states in which the domestic company desires to do business.[1]

Such statutes usually provide that when the laws (usually tax laws) of another state or foreign country create a greater burden upon domestic insurance companies (their representatives, etc.) than domestic laws impose upon similar foreign insurers (representatives, etc.), then the commissioner of the state of domicile shall impose similar obligations upon foreign companies (representatives, etc.) seeking to do business in his state. Retaliation as an objective of insurance regulatory legislation, though still present, is far less important today because of the efforts of the insurance companies, the individual insurance commissioners, and the National Association of Insurance Commissioners (see below) in developing uniform state laws.

It is difficult to understand why revenue is listed commonly as an *objective of regulation*. Life and health insurance companies and their representatives are subject to a great variety of license fees, charter fees, and statement fees at the state level, and in some states, municipal license fees. Generally, these fees are not of sufficient size to prevent undesirables from being licensed. Fines are rarely levied. It would appear that the principal justification for the taxation of the insurance business must be to raise revenue, a small part of which supports regulation in the public interest. Revenue is not a regulatory device. It is not a reason for regulation.

Personal insurance *is* subject to heavy taxation. Some states levy a tax on all or part of the insurer's assets. Others tax their net receipts; but by far the greater number tax the gross premiums, with the rate varying from 1¾

---

[1] A *domestic* company is generally considered to be one domiciled in the state involved. A *foreign* company is an American company whose state of domicile is other than the state involved. An *alien* company is one which is domiciled in a foreign country.

to 4 per cent. In addition, the Federal Government imposes an income tax which currently accounts for about 60 per cent of the taxes paid by insurance companies.

The present heavy taxation of personal insurance is due chiefly to general ignorance on the part of the public and the lawmakers of the true nature of legal reserve insurance, and to the fact that taxes on this business, especially those levied on gross premiums and assets, are so easily collected. Probably not more than one out of every twenty policyholders understands the true function of the reserves in life and health insurance. The general public and the lawmakers see only the billions in assets that are being accumulated, and naturally conclude that such huge funds should be taxed like any other property. They overlook the fact that premium reserves merely represent the funds of millions of policyholders which are held in trust for them and are necessary for the fulfillment of the company's obligations to them and their beneficiaries. They overlook the fact that claim reserves in the field of health insurance represent obligations which must be discharged to the insured and his family. To a large extent, the heavy tax burden is also traceable to the fact that, as regards most states, the companies operating therein are foreign in nature and for that reason, especially when it is believed that they take millions out of the state, are not regarded as entitled to leniency.

LEGAL STATUS OF
STATE INSURANCE REGULATION

In the governmental structure of the United States, both the Federal and the state governments exist within the same territory. Prior to 1944, governmental regulation of insurance was almost exclusively the responsibility of the states. Since the historic South-Eastern Underwriters Association decision, when Congress was given nearly complete control over insurance, the legal right of individual states to regulate the business has been based upon (1) the determination by Congress that the states rather than, and in some instances together with, the Federal Government shall regulate insurance, and (2) the state police power.

In the United States of America all sovereign powers are vested in the people. The people have created governmental bodies to serve them and have vested powers in these bodies. The people granted broad *general powers* to their state governments. All powers not reserved by the people in the respective state constitutions are vested in the state. In creating a Federal government, the people delegated to it certain *specific limited authority* to act on matters affecting the welfare of the entire nation. Since no provision of the United States Constitution specifically limits the authority of the states to legislate on matters over which the Federal Government was given specific authority, both governments may exercise power in these areas. However, *any conflict in legislation or regulation* must be resolved by consideration of the fact that the delegation of a *specific power* to the Federal Government impliedly limits a *general state power. The power of the Federal Government to act on matters over which it has specific authority is supreme.*

The framers of the United States Constitution, recognizing that the economic welfare and the safety of the nation would be jeopardized by trade barriers restricting the free flow of trade between the states, incorporated Article 1, Section 8, which gives Congress the exclusive power to regulate commerce with foreign powers and among the several states and Indian tribes. In general, the right to regulate intrastate commerce was reserved for the states. However, Congress, through the commerce clause, also has the implied power to regulate matters which affect interstate commerce, i.e., Congress may regulate intrastate commerce insofar as that intrastate commerce affects interstate commerce. Since the power of Congress is supreme, no state may restrict or impede interstate commerce, or matters affecting interstate commerce, where Congress has taken action. No state laws are valid which contradict or contravene Federal law regarding interstate commerce or matters affecting interstate commerce. Yet traditionally, insurance has been regulated exclusively by the states. Traditionally, insurance was not deemed by the United States Supreme Court to be commerce within the intent of the United States Constitution.

In 1868, in the famous case of *Paul vs. Virginia,* the United States Supreme Court refused to declare an insurance contract an instrumentality of commerce, and asserted the doctrine that there was no doubt of the power of the state to prohibit foreign insurance companies from doing business within its limits. To quote the Court:

> Issuing a policy of insurance is not a transaction of commerce. . . . These contracts are not articles of commerce in any proper meaning of the word. They are not subject to the trade and barter. . . . They are like other personal contracts between parties which are completed by their signature and the transfer of the consideration. Such contracts are not interstate transactions, though the parties may be domiciled in different states. . . . They are, then, local transactions, and governed by the local law. They do not constitute a part of the commerce between the states.[2]

For three quarters of a century, following the *Paul vs. Virginia* case, it was the accepted practice to regard the general supervision of all forms of insurance as falling solely within the jurisdiction of the several state governments. Repeatedly, the Supreme Court reasserted its view of 1868. In the

---

[2] (1868) Wall (U.S.) 168. See also, *New York Life Insurance Co. vs. Deer Lodge County* (1913), 231 U.S. 495.

absence of national supervision, the entire regulation of the insurance business was relegated to the several state governments. On June 4, 1944, the United States Supreme Court in the case of the *United States vs. the South-Eastern Underwriters Association*,[3] *et al.*, abandoned the view that insurance was not commerce and therefore was not properly the subject of Federal regulation under the terms of the commerce clause of the United States Constitution. In holding that insurance was commerce—interstate commerce for the most part—the Court swept away the foundations on which the structure of state regulation of insurance had been built. It appeared that insurance was subject to any regulations which Congress desired to impose.

Congress, on the theory that it had the power to redefine the distribution of authority over interstate commerce and consistent with the granting to other industries of complete or partial protection from antitrust laws, passed Public Law 15, 79th Congress, known as the *McCarran–Ferguson Act*. The purpose of this act may be found in its title:

An Act to Express the Intent of the Congress with
Reference to the Regulation of the Business of Insurance.

In this act, Congress took control over the regulation of insurance, redefined the authority of the states, and established a plan for cooperative regulation. It seems clear, in retrospect, that Congress desired that there be collaboration between Federal and state governments in a complete system of regulation. Today, there is *joint jurisdiction* over the business of insurance, with the states charged with the greater responsibility.

According to the terms of the McCarran–Ferguson Act, the Federal Government retains exclusive control over certain matters which it deems are *national in character,* that is, matters where regulation is (or should be) uniform throughout the states. Employer–employee relations (National Labor Relations Act) and fair labor standards (Fair Labor Standards Act), as well as agreements for or acts of boycott, coercion, and intimidation (Sherman Act) are deemed by the McCarran–Ferguson Act to be matters of national character and thus subject to the exclusive control of Congress. In effect, certain portions of these laws were related by the Congress specifically to insurance.

Further, it is important to note that Congress may expand this area of exclusive control by an act of Congress relating *specifically* to insurance. Such a Federal law would be applicable to the business of insurance to the exclusion of all other state statutes in conflict therewith. Prior to 1964, the principal acts relating specifically to insurance were limited in application to the District of Columbia. In 1964, the Securities and Exchange Act of 1934 was amended to relate specifically to the business of insurance.

[3] 332 U.S. 533 at 553 (1944).

Although the McCarran–Ferguson Act declares that the continued regulation of insurance by the states is in the public interest, *the law states that certain existing Federal statutes (the Sherman Act, the Clayton Act, and the Federal Trade Commission Act) which are general in nature and do not deal with insurance specifically are made specific to the business of insurance to the extent that "such business is not regulated by state law."* Hence, an implied purpose of Public Law 15 was to encourage improved and more uniform state regulation of insurance in the public interest.

In the years following the enactment of Public Law 15, the National Association of Insurance Commissioners (see below) together with representatives of the insurance industry undertook to draft model legislation intended to place the regulation of insurance among the several states on a more uniform and adequate basis, i.e., to meet the challenge of the *proviso* clause of Public Law 15.

Today, the great burden of regulation over the insurance industry rests with the states. The following discussion of governmental regulation will emphasize the regulation as practiced by the states. Federal regulatory activities will be discussed in relation to state regulation.

Given the jurisdictional authority to regulate the business of insurance, the basis for state insurance regulation is the state police power as applied to private property and private business affected with the public interest.

THE MECHANISM OF STATE REGULATION

State regulation of the insurance business is conducted by three agencies of government—the courts, the legislature, and the insurance commissioner or other administrative official. In addition, the National Association of Insurance Commissioners performs a vital role in the development of needed regulatory law and in the coordination of the activities of the legislatures and commissioners among the various states.

The role of the judiciary in state insurance regulation is three-fold. Most obvious to the average insured is the function of deciding cases of conflict between companies and policyholders. In a limited sense, a judicial decision interpreting a contract provision regulates the duties of the insurer under that class of policies. The courts further protect the insured by enforcing criminal penalties against those who violate the insurance law. Finally, insurance companies and their agents may occasionally resort to the courts in an effort to overturn arbitrary or unconstitutional statutes or administrative regulations or orders promulgated by the insurance department.

The role of the court in the regulatory process (although very important to individual and corporate rights) is becoming relatively minor when compared with the role played by the legislature and the insurance commissioner. Within Constitutional limitations, and with the permission of Congress, the state legislatures have the ultimate power to make and amend insurance law. They establish the broad legal framework and prescribe the general standards which govern the activities of the administrative agencies.

The legislatures have not taken this power lightly, for one out of every ten bills introduced pertains to insurance. During the last quarter century, a substantial number of jurisdictions have enacted comprehensive revisions of their insurance laws. These new insurance "codes" have swept away the accumulated layers of legislation of previous decades and reduced the insurance law to a uniform style and fairly systematic order.

Even though the insurance law may not have been revised and codified, the law of a particular jurisdiction usually relates to the requirements, procedures, and/or standards for (1) the organization and operation of the state insurance department; (2) the formation and licensing of the various types of companies for the various kinds of insurance and reinsurance; (3) the licensing of agents and brokers; (4) the filing and approval of property insurance rates; (5) unauthorized insurers and unfair trade practices; (6) company financial solvency; and (7) the liquidation and rehabilitation of insurers. Most jurisdictions also incorporate in the insurance law certain standards for the insurance contract with specific standards for certain lines of insurance, i.e., individual life and health insurance, group life and health insurance, industrial insurance (life, health, and property) and fire insurance. In addition, the code usually prescribes penalties for the violation of the insurance law.

Administrative Officials

The state legislatures, recognizing the need for specialized attention, discretion, and flexibility, established agencies or departments whose duties are limited to insurance supervision. In industrial economies, even highly developed general courts are not equipped to give protection in matters in which only experts can be informed; and legislatures, in addition to their lack of experience, find it impossible and impractical to pass laws involving every phase of a highly technical and rapidly changing industry which might need regulation. Thus, state departments or agencies were created with broad administrative, quasi-legislative, and quasi-judicial powers over the insurance business.

These insurance departments (the first was formed in Massachusetts in 1852) are usually under the direction of a chief official who may have the title of commissioner, superintendent, or director. In Texas, the responsibility of direction is placed in a three-man board. In many states the state official who has this responsibility also has other duties, such as state auditor, comptroller, or treasurer; or the department of insurance is associated with some other department, such as the department of banking.

Since the right to do an insurance business, or represent a company in doing an insurance business, or to represent the public in placing insurance, is considered to be a privilege, it is limited to those who qualify by obtaining a license. Thus, insurance is brought under the control and supervision of the insurance commissioner by means of the licensing function.

In granting a license, the state has the power to prescribe numerous conditions and limitations which must be observed by companies as a condition precedent to exercising the privilege of doing business within the state. In implementing these various standards the insurance commissioner is given numerous powers and duties. The principal powers of the commissioner are: (1) the power to make administrative regulations; (2) the power to grant or revoke any license; (3) the power to examine; (4) the power to require an annual statement of condition; (5) the power to approve; (6) the power to investigate complaints; (7) the power to order liquidation or rehabilitation; and (8) the power to initiate original investigations. His duties involve the enforcement of all of the insurance laws of the state and the administration of the department.

National Association of Insurance Commissioners

The National Association of Insurance Commissioners (formerly National Convention of Insurance Commissioners) was organized in 1870. The objectives of the Association are (1) to promote uniformity in legislation and administrative rulings affecting insurance; (2) to increase the efficiency of officials charged with the administration of insurance laws; and (3) to protect the interest of policyholders.

The Association has been successful and has served as a unifying and harmonizing force. Some of its more significant accomplishments include (1) the adoption by all states of a uniform blank for companies' annual financial reports; (2) the acceptance by most states of a certificate of solvency by a company's home state, thus eliminating much duplication and expense; (3) acceptance of the principle that a deposit of securities should be required only in a company's home state; (4) adoption of uniform rules for valuation of securities; (5) development of the zone system for the triennial examination of insurance companies; (6) the preparation of new standard mortality tables; (7) the preparation of a standard valuation law and a standard nonforfeiture law; and (8) the drafting of many other model laws in the fields of life and health insurance. There can be no question of the important role which the NAIC has played in the regulation of the insurance industry by the states. Although no state is bound to follow the recommendations of the NAIC, a reasonable degree of uniformity has resulted in the pattern of state regulation.

AREAS OF STATE REGULATION

Having outlined in a general way the duties and powers of the officials entrusted with the supervision of insurance companies, this section will outline the particular functions which it is the purpose of governmental regulation to perform. Because of the peculiar nature of the insurance business and the position of public trust which it holds, the authority of the state over the activities of the insurance company is exerted from the moment of birth to the moment of death. The insurance enterprise, whether it be corporation or association, must meet certain requirements in order to be organized and to obtain a license in the various jurisdictions in which it wishes to do business. Its agents and brokers must be licensed, its contract forms approved, and in some instances in the case of health insurance, rates may be scrutinized. Advertising and sales practices are considered and standards of fair competition are established. Company expenses may be regulated. Deposits may be required in various jurisdictions as a guarantee of the willingness of a company to comply with state statutes and to discharge the obligations under its contracts.

The solvency of an insurance company is carefully regulated. There may be limitations upon the size of risk which may be accepted by a single company. Specific requirements are established for reserve liabilities, the minimum size of capital and/or surplus, and investments and the proper valuation thereof. Finally, the state presides over the conservation or liquidation of those companies whose solvency is in danger.

It is impossible to discuss all of the subject matter of regulation in the few pages allotted in this volume. Only those areas particularly important to the field of life and/or health insurance will be considered.

This volume has attempted to provide a parallel treatment of life and health insurance in all of its aspects. This parallel description and explanation will be continued in the field of regulation. However, it must be understood that the regulatory problems associated with health insurance often differ from those in the field of life insurance and sometimes each must be treated as a separate and distinct line of insurance.

Space forbids a detailed discussion of the legislation which has been adopted in the various states. Practically all of the important laws may be grouped conveniently within the following areas: (1) organization and licensing of companies; (2) supervision of the product; (3) supervision of company practices; (4) supervision of financial solvency; and (5) conservation and liquidation.

Organization and Licensing of Companies

Although the organization of insurance companies is governed largely by the law applying to the organization of corporations in general, most states have seen fit to supplement their general corporation law with special acts pertaining only to insurance companies. State insurance laws describe specifically the requirements for the organization of a life company. Health insurance may be written by either a life, a casualty, or a mono-line company specializing in the field. Generally, where health insurance is written by a life company, the requirements for organization and licensing of a life company apply. Where health insurance is written by a casualty company, the requirements for a casualty company apply. Generally, a mono-line or specialty health company may organize under either the life or casualty sections of the law.

State insurance codes require the drafting of a charter which specifically describes the name and location of the company, the lines of insurance which it plans to write, the powers of the organization and its officers. Frequently, the method of internal organization must be specified. Minimum amounts of paid-in capital and surplus for stock companies are stated varying from $100,000 to $1,000,000 of capital plus an initial surplus varying from 50 to 200 per cent of the minimum paid-in capital for each line of insurance (life or health) to be written. Minimum surplus and participation requirements for mutual insurers are also specified and, increasingly, the minimum surplus requirement is similar to the minimum capital and surplus requirement for stock companies. Before issuing the certificate of incorporation, a responsible state official will investigate the character of the incorporators of the new firm. Companies are required frequently to deposit with the state approved securities to the value of $100,000 or some other designated sum or percentage of the minimum capital or surplus required.

Even when these requirements have been met and the directors and officers have been chosen and approved and a certification of incorporation issued by the state in which the company is domiciled, the company may not commence to do business. Generally, all companies doing business within the state must be licensed. The requirements for licensing domestic companies may be identical with those for its organization. Sometimes a single license for organization is all that is required. Often the license must be renewed periodically.

The requirements for licensing foreign and alien companies may be similar to those for domestic companies—sometimes they are more stringent. All companies (domestic, foreign, or alien) are required to maintain a substantial deposit of securities of a specified quality in trust with the state. To meet this requirement, foreign or alien companies may substitute a certificate from the insurance commissioner of another state in which they are licensed to the effect that a deposit is being maintained in trust in that state for the purpose of protecting policyholders and/or creditors. The deposit in trust for alien companies is usually quite substantial, and must be equal in value to its liabilities in the United States, plus a surplus which is at least equal to the minimum capital required for a domestic company licensed to transact the same kinds of business. In addition, several states require a small security deposit with the treasurer of the state for the purpose of protecting the policyholders of that particular state.

A foreign or alien company must generally appoint a resident of the state, in which it wants to do business, as its attorney for purposes of serving a legal process.

Unauthorized Insurance

One of the most vexatious problems (in the light of the McCarran–Ferguson Act) confronting state insurance regulation involves the question of control over the activities of unauthorized insurance companies. By refusing to apply for a license, the unauthorized insurer escapes regulation in all states except the state of domicile. To be more specific, since these out-of-state companies have no representatives within the state, they are not legally "doing business" within the state, and thus are not subject to state regulation. They make no reports to the state insurance department; they are not subject to examination; policy forms are not subject to state approval; interstate mail advertising is not subject to state control; and the state commissioner is powerless to render any service to the policyholder in the adjustment of claims.

At present, five principal types of regulation are utilized by the states to control the operations of unauthorized insurers:

1. The state may prohibit these insurers from "transacting business" within the state without first procuring a license to do so. Similarly, with certain obvious exceptions, no person shall (a) represent an unauthorized insurer in the solicitation, negotiation or effectuation of insurance, inspection of risks, fixing of rates, investigation or adjustment of losses, collection of premiums or in any other manner in the transaction of insurance with respect to the subjects of insurance, resident, located or to be performed in the state involved; or (b) represent any person in the procuring of insurance in such an unauthorized insurer upon or with relation to any subject of insurance.
2. Several states make such contracts legally voidable by the insured unless

during the life of the contract the insurer becomes licensed to transact the class of insurance involved (i.e., life or health insurance).

3. Advertising originating within this state, and which is designed to solicit insurance from persons located within this state may be prohibited. Usually, this prohibition is aimed at the publisher, or radio station, etc., as well as the insurer.

4. Under the NAIC Uniform Unauthorized Insurers Service of Process Act, as adopted by almost all jurisdictions, the insured may bring a legal action involving a claim against an unauthorized out-of-state insurer by serving process upon the insurance commissioner of his home state.

5. The NAIC Non-Admitted Insurers Information Office—a central clearing house for the collection of information about insurers not licensed in the jurisdiction.

Despite the existence of laws of this type, numerous difficult problems of regulation exist. They arise largely because the state of domicile does not control adequately the practices and financial solvency of these companies. The principal problem seems to be the regulation of misleading advertising and solicitation conducted through the mails. The Post Office Department has broad powers to control the use of the mails, but these are usually exercised only where there is evidence of fraud. The Federal Trade Commission in 1950 promulgated a set of "Trade Practice Rules Relating to the Advertising of Mail Order Insurance." (See "Unfair Trade Practices," p. 791, for a further discussion of this problem.)

Insurance Company Operations

Once the company is organized and/or licensed to transact business in the state, almost every phase of its operation is subject to state supervision. Policy forms must be approved, business-getting methods must exclude certain practices, and it must meet the prescribed standard of financial solvency.

Policy Forms.   In most lines of insurance, the various policy forms are subjected to some regulation in an effort to protect insureds, policyholders, and beneficiaries against unfair and deceptive provisions and practices.[4] Life, and especially health, insurance are no exceptions for, perhaps, the greatest amount of regulation and supervision pertaining to these lines involves the contract.

State supervision over life and health insurance contracts follows the

---

[4] The definition of "approval" varies by jurisdiction. Many jurisdictions require approval of a form prior to its utilization with the added provision that the form is approved by default at the end of thirty (forty-five) days if the commissioner has not taken action. Other states utilize the "file and use" technique with the commissioner having the power of subsequent disapproval after hearing.

same pattern, i.e., there is no statutory standard policy, and no statutory standard benefit or coverage provisions. Briefly stated, the system of state contract regulation involves (1) the requirement that a policy form may not be used until it is filed with and approved by the state insurance department, and (2) the various requirements or standards for its approval.[5]

The insurance commissioner utilizes both *general* and *specific* legal standards designed to serve as a guide in his effort to determine the appropriateness of forms in the public interest. Much of this statutory and administrative law is based upon recommendations of the National Association of Insurance Commissioners.

Briefly stated, the principal type of *general* standard which a form must meet in order to obtain the commissioner's approval establishes *general standards* for *policy format and language* and may be applicable to both life and health insurance contracts. For example, in the field of health insurance, the recommended NAIC Accident and Health Regulation Law of 1946 provided that the contract must not be unjust, ambiguous, unfair, misleading, or encourage misrepresentation. Since the application of this general standard creates problems for both the commissioners and the industry, the NAIC and the various commissioners have developed *specific standards* which are designed to implement the general standard.

1. *Specific Standards—Life Insurance.* Every jurisdiction requires (or will accept) life insurance contract forms which contain, *in substance,* certain provisions which are set forth in the laws of most of the states. The commissioner may approve forms containing these provisions in a language more favorable than that of the statute. These minimum standard statutory provisions, as recommended by the NAIC, include: grace period, premium, incontestable clause, "entire contract," misstatement of age, annual apportionment of dividends, surrender values and options, policy loan, settlement options, and reinstatement. The standard provisions for group life insurance contracts and certificates, as well as those for industrial life insurance contracts are treated separately.

2. *Specific Standards—Health Insurance.* In 1946, following the SEUA decision and the passage of the McCarran–Ferguson Act, the NAIC and the All-Industry Committee recommended to the states the Accident and Health Regulatory Law mentioned previously. In addition to establishing the requirement that contract forms, classifications, rates, and endorsements must be filed and that forms and endorsements must be approved (see above), this law establishes the *general* standards that contracts must not be unjust, ambiguous, unfair, misleading, or encourage misrepresentation. Futher, the model law states (though this provision was omitted by some jurisdictions as they passed the legislation) that forms may be disapproved

---

[5] Much contract regulation actually arises because of undesirable claims, advertising, and other practices surrounding the use of the contract by a few insurers.

if "benefits are unreasonable in relation to the premium charged" (see below).

Nearly all jurisdictions [6] have adopted the Uniform Individual Accident and Sickness Policy Provisions Law as recommended by the NAIC in 1950. This law includes *specific* standards for both required and optional provisions. The twelve required provisions, which are designed primarily to protect the interest of the insured after a loss, include provisions for notice and proof of loss, time of proofs, payment of claims, time limit on certain defenses, and change of beneficiary. The eleven optional provisions, which need not be included unless the company so desires, cover such subjects as change of occupation, misstatement of age, reduction in benefits where other insurance exists, relation of insurance to earnings, and cancellation. As regards both the required and optional standard provisions, the insurer may use wording of its own choosing so long as it is no less favorable to the insured or beneficiary than the provisions as stated in the law. Additional flexibility in contract design is permitted since these provisions may be included either with other provisions to which they may be logically related, or they may be incorporated in the policy as a unit in the order provided by the law. Further, the law provides that, subject to the approval of the commissioners, the insurer may omit from the policy any inapplicable provision or part of a provision, and modify any inconsistent provision or part of a provision, in order to make the provision contained in the policy consistent with the coverage provided by the policy.

In addition to the specific statutory standards contained in the 1950 Law, the insurance commissioners of each jurisdiction have developed numerous specific standards by administrative regulation. These regulations include the 1944–47 *Official Guide* and the *Statement of Principles—1948*. Requirements are established for the clear labeling of limited policies, certain types of provisions are prohibited or restricted, and certain practices with respect to the policy contract are controlled. These standards are too numerous and varied to be considered here.

In 1952, the NAIC recommended an administrative regulation regarding the renewal and cancellation provisions of the contract. This recommended regulation required, in the absence of a brief description on the face of the policy or a separate statement printed on the first page, that the provisions of the contract relating to renewability shall be placed on the face of the policy and captioned clearly. The regulation specifies the proper place and caption for the cancellation provision, and where the provision is not printed on the face, reference must be made on the face to the cancellation provision contained within.

---

[6] Forty-seven states and the District of Columbia have adopted the Uniform Individual Accident and Sickness Policy Provisions Law; in addition, Georgia, Louisiana, and Alaska have adopted similar statutes. See Berkeley Cox *et al., Law Notes, Life and Health* (Hartford: International Claim Association, 1964), pp. 306–307.

In 1956, the NAIC Cancellation Sub-Committee of the Accident and Health Committee recommended a uniform model amendment to the 1950 Uniform Accident and Sickness Policy Provisions Law which provides that individual health (as opposed to accident) insurance contracts which are renewable at the option of the company shall restrict the right of the company to refuse renewal to each anniversary date of the contract. Where the contract lapses and is reinstated, this renewal date begins with the anniversary of the last reinstatement. A thirty-day written notice must be given to the insured of the company's intention not to renew. This recommended modification has been adopted in the code of several jurisdictions.

In 1958 the New York State Legislature passed a statute restricting the right of the insurance company to refuse to renew or cancel hospital and medical expense contracts as follows:

6. After two years from its date of issue or the date of its last reinstatement and before the attainment of the age limit, or date or the expiration of the period, if any, stated in the policy in accordance with the provisions of paragraph (B) (9) of subsection two of this section, no insurer shall refuse to renew a policy of hospitalization or surgical or medical expense insurance or refuse to renew any other policy in which one-third or more of the total premium is allocable to hospital, surgical or medical expense benefits, or any combination thereof, except for one or more of the following reasons: fraud in applying for the policy or in applying for any benefits under the policy, moral hazard, over-insurance or duplication of benefits according to standards on file with the superintendent of insurance, discontinuance of a class of policies, and such other reasons, including but not limited to, the filing of false or improper claims, as the superintendent of insurance may approve; however after such two year period in no event shall any insurer refuse to renew any such policy because of a change in the physical or mental condition or the health of any person covered thereunder. Furthermore, after such period no insurer shall require as a condition for the renewal of any such policy any rider, endorsement or other attachment which shall limit the nature or extent of the benefits provided thereunder. In the case of an individual converted policy such two year period shall commence from the date the insurance as to such person became effective under the policy from which conversion was made. The superintendent may require every insurer to file with him such documents, statistics or other information regarding the refusal to renew permitted by this subsection as he may deem necessary for the proper administration of this subsection.

7. This section shall not apply to or affect (1) any contract of noncancellable disability insurance which is governed by or excepted from section one hundred fifty-eight; or (2) any policy or contract of reinsurance; or (3) any policy of group or blanket insurance which is governed by section one hundred sixty-two; or (4) any policy providing disability benefits pursuant to article nine of the workmen's compensation law; or (5) any policy of a cooperative life and accident insurance company except as provided in section two hundred thirty-seven; or (6) life insurance, endowment or annuity contracts, or contracts supplemental thereto which contain only such provisions relating to accident

and sickness insurance as (a) provide additional benefits in case of death or dismemberment or loss of sight by accident, or as (b) operate to safeguard such contracts against lapse, or to give a special surrender value or special benefit or an annuity in the event that the insured or annuitant shall become totally and permanently disabled, as defined by the contract or supplemental contract.[7]

The insurance company must give thirty days' written notice of its intention not to renew where such renewal meets the requirements of the law. It is possible that a company may be permitted to cancel within ninety days after the policy is issued, if it so desires.

The New York Law specifies certain minimum benefits for medical care expense contracts and, in addition, permits the conversion of family medical care expense policies to individual contracts without evidence of insurability.

The law of the State of North Carolina provides that, with regard to commercial health insurance contracts, no contract may be cancelled nor may renewal be refused unless the insurer notifies the insured sufficiently well in advance to meet the requirements of the law. This period of notice varies from one month to two years, depending upon the period during which the policy has been in force.

Separate provisions regarding the terms of the contract apply to group insurance contracts.

Rates. The supervision of the product involves, in many lines of insurance, the regulation of rates—the product price. The various states regulate rates in most of the property-liability insurance lines. Usually, rates for these contracts and the applicable policy forms must be filed with the commissioner. Although a few jurisdictions follow the "file and use" concept, generally, rates must be approved (in a technical sense) prior to use. In nearly all jurisdictions after a hearing, the commissioner may set aside or disapprove a filing where the rates are excessive, inadequate, or unfairly discriminatory.

Life (occasionally) and health insurance rates must be filed with the contract forms to which they apply. Generally, they are not subject to approval (see below). They are filed principally to make them a matter of public record for the benefit of those persons who come under the misstatement of age and other provisions involving a proration of premium.

1. *Life Insurance.* Life insurance rates for individual insurance are regulated only in a most indirect sense. It is felt that competition is an adequate regulator over any tendencies toward rate excessiveness. As a practical matter, rate *adequacy* may be a problem and it is felt that minimum reserve requirements (see below) and expense limitations are an adequate safe-

---

[7] Insurance Law of the State of New York, Laws of 1939 as amended, Chapter 882, Section 164, 5 (6) (7).

guard. The states of New York and Wisconsin have complex laws limiting the amount of expenses that can be incurred in the production of new business and the maintenance of old business in force.

The laws of most jurisdictions assume that, for stock companies issuing nonparticipating contracts, competition is an adequate guarantor of rate equity among the different classes and generations of insureds. However, a mutual company is owned by and operated for the benefit of all of its insureds. Often mutual insurance companies are prohibited from issuing nonparticipating policies. Where premiums prove to be redundant, equity demands that the excess be returned in the form of a dividend to each class or generation of insureds in proportion to their contributions to the surplus. Most states require that dividends be apportioned and paid (when earned) annually. A few states limit the amount of aggregate surplus which may be accumulated to an amount not to exceed (usually) 10 per cent of the legal reserve. Although announced specific standards do not exist, the commissioners do review dividend apportionment formulas from time to time—generally at the time of the examination of the company.

These limitations upon the dividend policy of the insurance company further serve as a restriction upon the too rapid expansion of new business at the expense of current insureds.

Stock insurance companies issuing participating contracts may be required to limit the amount of dividends payable to stockholders in the interest of fairness to insureds under such contracts.

2. *Health Insurance.* One of the *general* standards for the approval of health insurance contract forms is basically an attempt to regulate the benefit provisions. It attempts the task by relating benefits to premium, i.e., forms must not be approved (or approval must be withdrawn) if "benefits are unreasonable in relation to the premium charged." This standard, found in the laws of only a few jurisdictions, is very general in nature and is difficult to implement in specific instances. This general standard arose as a part of the flood of state law which was developed following the passage of the McCarran–Ferguson Act. Although health insurance may be written by casualty insurers, it was excluded from the provisions of the All-Industry —NAIC Model Casualty Rate Regulatory Bill. However, certain commissioners felt that the abuses of certain health insurers surrounding the coverage or benefit provisions could best be handled through some form of rate regulation. Strong industry opposition made it apparent that a health insurance rate regulatory bill would not receive legislative support, and thus a compromise was devised—the 1946 Accident and Health Regulatory Law was developed and recommended to the various state legislatures.

Although the distinction is somewhat tenuous, this law appears more nearly to establish standards (the general standard that *policies* shall be disapproved if benefits are not reasonable in relation to premium) for the approval of policy forms than for rates. It is the *policy form* that is subject to being disapproved—not the rates—in the event that there is a question about the reasonableness of benefits. However, the specific standard which the NAIC recommended to implement this general standard could provide some degree of surveillance over rates. The recommended administrative procedures include:

1. The filing of actual loss experience by policy form as a part of the annual statement.
2. The filing of estimated loss experience by policy form. Although this procedure is not specifically recommended by the NAIC, it is followed in a few jurisdictions.
3. In 1953, the National Association of Insurance Commissioners adopted a report which suggested as "bench marks" certain minimum loss ratios for the various types of policy forms. The report stated that where the benefits of a policy (including dividends to policyholders) produced an ultimate credible loss ratio lower than the reasonably average percentages indicated, there is created a *possible* presumption that the "benefits are unreasonable in relation to the premium charged."

So far as the author can determine, few jurisdictions have formally established this or other similar standards in disapproving new forms, or withdrawing approval of old forms.

Business-Getting Methods

Broadly interpreted, state regulation of business-getting methods includes control over the licensing of agents and brokers, and unfair trade practices.

Licensing of Agents and Brokers.   The statutes of nearly all jurisdictions contain provisions for the licensing of agents and brokers. A few jurisdictions license counselors. No person may act as agent, broker or counselor within the jurisdiction without first obtaining a license; no company may issue a contract through or remunerate any person who acts as agent, etc. (other than on renewal business, or other deferred compensation where the agent has ceased to participate in the development of new business), unless such a person shall have a currently valid license.

The procedure which must be followed in obtaining a license is similar for all lines. In addition to the filing of the application by the licensee (in which the licensee must give detailed information regarding his character, experience, and general competence), each insurer for which he is to be licensed must submit a notice of appointment (or intention of appointment) together with a certificate of trustworthiness and competence signed by a responsible officer of the insurance company. In many states, the new applicant (usually defined as a person who has not held a license in the recent past—two years) meeting these requirements is given a temporary license, with a permanent license being issued following the successful completion of an examination, or such other test of competency in the line for which he is seeking a license as may be required by the insurance commissioner. In addition to establishing a minimum standard of competency, these examinations serve to reduce turnover and thus contribute further to the general upgrading of insurance representatives.

The agent's license may be perpetual until revoked, or subject to renewal at stipulated intervals. Because of the large number of licenses, administrative expediency has dictated that the perpetual license gain in popularity. Where the license must be renewed, the insurer usually handles the details (no examination is required) although the licensee may be required to pay the license fee in those states which make a charge for the license. The license may be refused, revoked, or suspended by the commissioner, after notice and hearing, on the grounds that the agent willfully violated the law in his capacity as an agent, conducted fraudulent or dishonest practices, was proved untrustworthy or incompetent, or made a material misrepresentation in the application for his license. In addition, the license is terminated by death or termination of the agent's appointment by the insurance company. In states making provision for brokers, the requirements and procedures for obtaining a broker's license are, in general, very similar to those already discussed. In the State of New York, completion of a series of courses in insurance is required as a condition precedent to obtaining a broker's license. Usually, the broker's license must be renewed periodically, subject to a renewal fee which may be higher than that charged the agent. The grounds for refusal, revocation, or suspension of the license are similar to those applicable for the agent.

Although life insurance and reinsurance contracts are not included, some jurisdictions include health insurance with the property and liability lines as regards the counter-signature law. Although the provisions of these laws vary, the central feature of nearly every counter-signature law is that foreign or alien companies are prohibited from issuing policies covering risks (personal or property) within the regulating states that have not been issued through, or countersigned by, a licensed resident agent. A counter-signing fee or commission, which ranges from 5 to 100 per cent of the producing agent's commission, must be paid to the resident agent. Somewhat retaliatory in nature, the counter-signature requirements serve to (1) fix the situs of the insurance contract and thus the jurisdiction of contract interpretation; (2) facilitate the detection and control of rebating; (3) assist the state in collecting the premium tax on foreign companies; (4) minimize unfair competition through the erroneous quotation of rates; and (5) protect local agents from "unfair competition" from out-of-state producers on large multi-state risks.

It is interesting to note that among those jurisdictions exempting health insurance from the counter-signature requirements, a few have adopted a reciprocal law providing that a person not resident in the regulating state may be licensed as an agent in that state provided that the state in which such person resides will accord the same privileges to the citizens of the regulating state. The commissioner of the regulating state may be authorized to enter into reciprocal agreements to waive the written examination requirements of such state where the nonresident already holds a valid license in his home state.

Unfair Trade Practices. While the states have long exercised control over certain unfair practices, especially misrepresentation, twisting, rebating, and unfair discrimination, the impact of the SEUA decision and the McCarran–Ferguson Act led many jurisdictions to adopt the NAIC model Unfair Trade Practices Act which, although differing in philosophy, was designed to be sufficiently comprehensive to oust the Federal Trade Commission from jurisdiction over these matters. All unfair trade practice acts identify and define certain unfair trade practices. Usually, they give the commissioner the power to investigate and examine, and after notice and hearing, to issue cease and desist orders with penalties for violations. In addition, the NAIC model act gives the commissioner the authority to seek a court injunction, through the attorney general (and thus the validity of the commissioner's charges is examined by a court), to restrain insurers from using any other methods which he believes to be unfair or deceptive.

The recommended NAIC Unfair Trade Practices Act specifically includes the following as being unfair trade practices in the business of insurance:

Misrepresentation and False Advertising of Policy Contracts and Twisting
False Information and Advertising Generally
Defamation
Boycott, Coercion, Intimidation
False Financial Statements
Stock Options and Advisory Board Contracts
Unfair Discrimination
Rebates

The various state unfair trade practices acts are made applicable generally to all lines of insurance (they were designed with the problems of health insurance specifically in mind).

Unfair Advertising Practices. As indicated in the discussion of unauthorized insurance, the Federal Trade Commission's *"Trade Practices Rules Relating to the Advertising of Mail Order Insurance"* represented the first attempt of the Commission to regulate the practices of insurance companies (other than actions regarding boycott, coercion, and intimidation) under the "proviso clause" of the McCarran–Ferguson Act. Although many states had already done so, this attempt by a federal agency spurred the adoption by the NAIC of the model Unfair Trade Practices Act.

In 1954, the FTC began another investigation of health insurance advertising. The investigation, which was precipitated by a "flood of complaints," resulted in the issuance of complaints against forty-one companies alleging the use of false and deceptive advertising regarding such matters as the extent of coverage, period of protection and probationary period, required health status of the applicant, benefit amounts, cost, and cancellation and renewal provisions. The insurance companies, the trade associations, and the NAIC defenses to these complaints included the following:

1. The FTC did not have jurisdiction since health insurance advertising was adequately regulated by state law in the various jurisdictions involved (see Unfair Trade Practices Act above). In some cases the advertising was actually approved by state authorities.

2. The complaints were based upon advertising which was voluntarily submitted, two years old, and long since withdrawn from use.

3. The statements were misleading only when quoted out of context.

4. There had been no intention to mislead.

5. There was no evidence that the applicants had actually been misled by the statements.

In order to strengthen their contention that advertising was adequately regulated by the state law, the NAIC recommended the *NAIC Advertising Code* in December, 1955. This Code is composed of specific standards designed to serve as a guide to the commissioners in the implementation of the general advertising standards contained in the model Uniform Trade Practices Act. It is interesting that the Federal Trade Commission held a trade practices conference to consult with the industry and the NAIC representatives, and then promulgated its own code early in 1956. The two codes are very similar in content.

The *NAIC Advertising Code* specifies (1) certain words and phrases considered deceptive, (2) the necessity for disclosing provisions relating to renewability, cancellation, and termination, and (3) rules regarding the use of testimonials, identification of the policy, use of statistics, contract inspection offers, comparisons with other contracts, identification of the insurer, introductory or special offers, and service facilities. Every insurance company must maintain for examination by the state insurance department a complete file of all advertising material utilized. Further, each company must file with its annual statement a certification that it has complied with the rules.

In 1956 a joint industry NAIC committee developed an *Interpretative Guide* to be used by the industry and the commissioners in following and administering these rules.

The jurisdictional matter has not been fully settled. The complaints against several insurance companies were dismissed. In some cases, the courts held that the Federal Trade Commission did not have jurisdiction. However, where the company sends direct-mail advertising into states where it is not licensed and therefore cannot be reached by state authorities, the courts have held that the FTC does have jurisdiction. The Federal Trade Commission has moved slowly because of jurisdictional questions. It is known that investigations have been made into the direct-mail advertising practices of several major health insurance companies and a few life companies specializing in mail-order solicitation campaigns geared to the military market. Further, the FTC is compiling a set of "trade practice guides" or "administrative interpretations of law administered by the commission for the use of the commissioner's staff and the guidance of businessmen in evaluating certain types of practices." At this writing, the FTC has submitted a draft of these "guides" to the NAIC for comment.

Financial Condition

As previously indicated, one of the important objects of regulation is the financial soundness of insurance companies. This concern is most obvious in the various statutory and administrative standards and regulations surrounding the financial management of an operating company. Briefly, insurance supervisory authorities desire that an insurance company maintain at all times assets at least equal to its presently due and prospectively estimated liabilities (including minimum, capital, and/or surplus requirements). Further, in order that the relationship between assets and liabilities will have some meaning, there is a large body of law specifically relating to these items.

Assets.   Although there is a decided lack of uniformity in the insurance codes of the various states as they pertain to company assets, all jurisdictions are concerned with the types of investments which are permitted and the techniques of asset valuation.

In general, the funds of life insurance companies (including the income derived from health insurance operations) may be invested in obligations of the Federal, state, or local governments, corporate bonds, real estate mortgages, and policy loans. Although policy loans are not now payable to insureds under health insurance contracts, the commingling of insurance company assets means that such loans must be included among the types of investments available to the life insurance company for health insurance funds.

In general, the types of investments permitted casualty insurers (which may write health insurance) include those permitted life insurers without many of the numerous restrictions regarding stock holdings.

The law in a number of jurisdictions includes a "leeway provision" which provides that any domestic insurance company (primarily life insurers) may loan or invest its funds to an amount not exceeding a stipulated percentage of its total admitted assets in loans or investments not qualified under any section of the law. This percentage may vary from 2 to 10 per cent. The law is designed to alleviate any strain that the restrictive statutes may impose on company investment operations.

Nearly all jurisdictions distinguish between capital and reserve investments. New York follows the traditional pattern and requires that funds equivalent to the minimum capital or surplus required by law for the line or lines of insurance being transacted be invested in certain very secure types of investments (cash, government bonds, and mortgages). Life insurance companies may invest all remaining funds in "reserve investments," i.e., "capital investments" plus other permitted investments of second quality. In addition to the "capital investments," casualty insurers must invest at least 50 per cent of assets equal to the amount of their reserve liabilities (loss and unearned premium reserves) in "reserve investments," with the remaining funds invested in any of the securities recognized by the law. Investments must be income producing and not in default at the time of purchase.

The law in most jurisdictions requires that no insurance company shall make any investment or loan unless the same is authorized or approved by the company's board of directors, or by a committee authorized by such a board and charged with the supervision or making of such investments. The law further requires that the minutes of any such committee shall be recorded and regular reports of such committee shall be submitted to the board of directors. The directors and officers must not have a personal interest in the investments or in their sale to the insurance company.

The law in some jurisdictions is vague as regards standards to be imposed upon a mono-line health company where such company may be organized and licensed under either the life or casualty requirements. However, it would appear that the competitive situation would dictate that the new mono-line company attempt to acquire a casualty status.

Generally, foreign companies must meet substantially similar investment standards as domestic companies in order to qualify for a license to do business within the state.

The valuation of the assets held by an insurer for annual statement purposes is a complicated and detailed procedure. Most insurance statutes state that the commissioner may specify the rules for determining the value of securities, subject (in some cases) to the limitation that such rules shall not be inconsistent with those established by the National Association of Insurance Commissioners.[8]

Liabilities.   The principal true liabilities in the insurer's balance sheet are the insurance policy reserves. An insurance policy reserve is a balance sheet account established to reflect actual and potential liabilities under expired and outstanding contracts.

1. *Life Insurance.* Life insurers are required by law to charge themselves the minimum reserve as a liability. In this regard the Standard Valuation Law and the Standard Nonforfeiture Law have been enacted or otherwise made effective in all jurisdictions. Their provisions are applicable, in general, to all policies issued since their enactment or amendment. The valuation of life insurance reserves was discussed earlier.[9]

2. *Health Insurance.* Those reserves provided specifically in the annual statement for the health insurance business include the unearned premium reserve; the additional reserve (active life reserve) for policies where the insurer's right of termination is restricted by the terms of the contract or company practice; the reserve for future contingent benefits; the reserve for the present value of amounts not yet due on approved claims; the reserve for claims in the course of settlement; the reserve for incurred or unreported claims; and the claim expense reserve.

While the continued financial soundness of an insurer depends upon proper investments, together with the correct valuation of all assets, the establishment and proper valuation of reserves is just as important and, in the health insurance line, a much more difficult task. And, while the laws of the various jurisdictions establish rigid controls over the assets of health insurers, and while the National Association of Insurance Commissioners' forms for the annual statement (Life and Accident and Health, and Fire and Casualty) specifically provide for most of the reserves mentioned above, the specific standards for the valuation of these health insurance reserves are notable by their general absence. The insurance laws of most jurisdictions specifically establish standards for the unearned premium reserve. Further, the laws of most jurisdictions grant the commissioner the power to require or to establish standards for such additional reserves as may be consistent with the practice formulated by the National Association of Insurance Commissioners. A few states specifically require, and establish standards for, the active life reserve and the disabled life reserve under disability income policies. In most jurisdictions, the standards utilized in measuring the adequacy of the various health insurance reserves are left to individual company determination, with many companies making this de-

---

[8] See pp. 715–720 for a discussion of the valuation of assets.
[9] See pp. 398–400 for a discussion of the valuation of policy reserve liabilities.

termination in consultation with the actuary of the respective state insurance departments.[10]

Rehabilitation and Liquidation

When, regardless of other regulatory efforts, an insurer is in serious financial or other difficulties, the state insurance department in most jurisdictions has the further responsibility of assuming control over the assets and management of domestic and alien insurers (where the largest amount of the United States assets of the alien insurer are located within the state) or over those assets of foreign insurers located within the state. The usual procedure requires that when he deems it necessary, the insurance commissioner must petition the proper court for a court order appointing him (in his official capacity) receiver for the purpose of rehabilitation, conservation, or liquidation.

Under a rehabilitation order, the commissioner is granted title to the domestic insurance company's assets and is given the authority to carry on its business until he is able to return it to private management after the grounds for issuing the order have been removed. In those jurisdictions adopting the NAIC Uniform Insurer's Liquidation Act, rehabilitation refers to reorganization—a more drastic procedure whereby the commissioner disposes of the company to a successor corporation. In all cases, the commissioner, acting under a rehabilitation order, attempts to preserve the intangible assets of the company, such as the agency plant and good will by maintaining the company as a going concern. This procedure, where successful, also results in maintaining policyholder confidence in the insurance institution. The numerous statutory grounds under which the commissioner must apply for a rehabilitation order include (1) the impairment of capital or financial insolvency, (2) a finding that further operations would be hazardous to policyholders, creditors, or the public, and (3) a determination that its officers and/or directors are guilty of certain acts or omissions. In most jurisdictions, the insurance company is insolvent when its admitted assets are less than the sum of its required true liabilities and the minimum (as opposed to the initial) capital or surplus required for a licensee to write the various lines for which it is licensed.[11]

When it is not found advisable to attempt rehabilitation, or if rehabilitation becomes impracticable, the commissioner must petition the proper court for a liquidation order. The grounds which demand such an order are similar to those for rehabilitation. As a receiver under a liquidation order,

---

[10] See pp. 490–495 for a discussion of health insurance reserves.

[11] Some jurisdictions make the distinction between an impairment of capital and insolvency. The latter exists only when admitted assets are less than the sum of the required true liabilities and the minimum capital or surplus requirements by a stipulated percentage, such as 25 per cent.

the commissioner must collect and conserve the assets, and where possible reinsure the outstanding contracts, pay all admitted claims due, and pay other admitted obligations. The law may state a priority for the payment of claims. The Georgia Insurance Code, for example, lists the following priority of claims for the distribution of assets:

(1) Claims for the cost of administration and conservation of the insurer's assets.

(2) Claims under policies for losses incurred, including claims of third parties under liability policies.

(3) Claims for unearned premiums.

(4) Compensation actually owing to employees, other than officers of the insurer, for services rendered within three months prior to the commencement of a proceeding against the insurer, but not exceeding $500 for each employee.

(5) Claims of general creditors.

In a technical sense, the statutes of several jurisdictions use the term "conservation order" to refer to the court order directing the commissioner to act as receiver for the conservation of the assets of a foreign or alien insurance company which is located within the jurisdiction. The grounds forming the basis for the insurance commissioner's request are similar to those for liquidation and rehabilitation. Usually, prior to, or concurrent with, being named receiver under an order of conservation, the commissioner will revoke or suspend the insurer's license to do business within the state.

The procedure of naming the insurance commissioner (rather than another person) as receiver was developed to reduce the delay and expense associated with the ordinary receivership procedure and thereby speeding the return of a larger dividend to the creditors and policyholders of the company. In some cases, it makes possible the rehabilitation of a company so that there will be little or no loss to those involved. Some jurisdictions still apply the usual procedures utilized in the liquidation of a business firm, i.e., the commissioner must petition the proper court for the appointment of a receiver (other than the commissioner), who will then liquidate the company under the direction of the court. Under such circumstances (delay, lack of technical ability, etc.), the possibility of rehabilitation may not exist.

TAXATION OF LIFE AND HEALTH INSURANCE COMPANIES

Life and health insurance companies are taxed by the Federal and state and local governments. The basis for this taxation differs from the basis of taxes levied on other corporations. This difference stems primarily from two factors. First, a large part of the life insurance premium is in the nature of a deposit of funds by the policyholder and, therefore, is not earned income to the life insurance company. Second, the life insurance contract is long-term in nature and the usual approach of annual income taxation is not as appropriate for life insurance companies as for other companies whose contracts are usually completed in a relatively short time.

State Taxation

The most important form of state tax levied on life insurers is the tax on life and health insurance premiums and annuity considerations discussed earlier in connection with the revenue objective of state regulation.[12] Today, all states impose a premium tax of some sort and the imposition of this tax has developed into a revenue measure rather than a method for financing the regulation of the business. Only about 5 per cent of the total premium tax collected is utilized to defray the cost of supervising insurance companies. The tax rates on life and health premiums vary among states from about 1¾ per cent to 4 per cent, with the most common rate being 2 per cent.

In determining the tax base to which the premium tax rate will apply, it is necessary to include only those premiums received from policies insuring risks domiciled in the state, excluding, however, premiums paid to reinsurers which are not included in the tax base in any state. In over half the states annuity considerations are not included in the tax base and in those states taxing annuity considerations the rate is usually lower than that applied to life and health premiums. Some states exempt both life insurance premiums and annuity considerations received in connection with qualified retirement plans.

About three-fourths of the states allow dividends paid to policyholders to be deducted from the tax base except those dividends applied to purchase additional insurance or to shorten the premium paying or endowment periods of the policies. The remaining states do not allow a deduction for policyholder dividends but most of these states do not require dividends applied to purchase additional insurance or to shorten the premium paying or endowment periods to be included in the base.

Several states allow other taxes, such as ad valorem taxes paid on real estate within the state and state income taxes paid, to be offset against the premium tax. A few states allow a reduction in the premium tax if a designated portion of the company's assets are invested within the state. Such measures are designed to benefit the insurers domiciled in the state. This together with the fact that some states either do not levy premium

[12] See pp. 773–774.

taxes on domestic companies or else tax them at a lower rate than that on foreign insurers means that a majority of states have tax regulations favoring domestic companies.

The premium tax laws of most states have a retaliatory feature as pointed out earlier. These provisions have had the effect of promoting uniformity in the rate of premium taxation among the states by discouraging increases in the tax rate charged by a state on foreign insurers since such an increase by a state would result in its domestic companies having to pay the same rate in other states.

In the majority of states the premium tax is in lieu of other specified taxes. In many states the premium tax is in lieu of all other state and local taxes except those on real estate and tangible personal property, and license fees.

In most jurisdictions, the states have preempted the taxation of life and health insurance companies as a source of revenue and have not permitted their subdivisions to impose taxes on the companies. Wherever local taxes are permitted and imposed, the maintenance of special records and the filing of reports constitutes a serious administrative burden that is disproportionate to the revenue produced.

Federal Income Taxation

Since the advent of Federal corporate income taxation, life insurance company tax formulas have undergone frequent revisions designed to make them acceptable to all segments of the industry and at the same time to produce the revenues expected by the Treasury Department. In order to be equitable, a tax formula to be applied to life insurance companies must (1) recognize the long-term nature of the life insurance contract and the difficulty in determining the operating gain in any one year; (2) tax both mutual and stock companies fairly without disrupting the existing competitive balance; and (3) provide an acceptable method for determining the interest required to maintain policyholder reserves. Prior to the enactment of the present law, tax formulas failed to meet one or more of these criteria and also in many years produced revenues far below the level acceptable to the Treasury.

Evolution of Present Tax Legislation.   Prior to 1921, life insurance companies were taxed on the same basis as other corporations, i.e., net income, and at the corporate tax rate. All premiums received, all investment income except interest on tax-exempt securities, and all capital gains were considered as gross income. In determining taxable income, life insurance companies were permitted to deduct from gross income all investment and underwriting expenses, payments other than dividends made to policyholders within the tax year under insurance and annuity contracts, the net increase in policyholder reserves and other contractual obligations, and dividends to policyholders paid in cash or applied to pay premiums currently due. Clearly this approach did not consider the long-term nature of the life insurance contract and the possibility that an underwriting gain in any given year could not be considered entirely as profit since it could be offset by a loss in a future year. By 1921 the problems associated with this approach to life company taxation were of such magnitude that the tax formula applicable to life insurance companies was changed.

Between 1921 and 1942 life insurance companies were taxed on their investment income only. Underwriting gains arising from favorable mortality experience were ignored, as were losses from adverse experience. Net investment income was determined by deducting investment expenses and the interest required to maintain policyholder reserves from gross investment income. Capital gains and interest on tax exempt securities were not included in gross investment income during this period.

The interest required for policyholder reserves was determined by having each company apply the same rate to its reserves. From 1921 through 1931 this rate was set at 4 per cent and from 1932 through 1941 it was reduced to 3.75 per cent.

This approach to life insurance company taxation was more applicable to mutual companies than to stock companies since theoretically any underwriting gains in a mutual company are eventually distributed to the policyholders as dividends. The exclusion of underwriting gains of stock companies from the tax base was justified on the grounds that both stock and mutual companies must be taxed on the same basis in order to preserve the competitive balance existing between them.

As interest earnings declined in the 1930's many insurance companies lowered their reserve interest rates on new business (thus producing higher reserves). The combined effect of these two events was drastic reduction in life insurance company tax revenues; so, in 1942 a new formula for the taxation of life insurance companies was adopted.

During the period from 1942 through 1948 the taxable investment income concept in existence since 1921 was retained but the method of determining the tax base was changed. During this period, the Secretary of the Treasury determined from data for the entire industry the ratio of the reserve interest required to the net investment income. The resulting percentage, known as the "Secretary's Ratio," was applied to each individual company's investment income net of expenses to determine the amount required to maintain its reserves. The remainder of the investment income was subject to Federal income taxation at regular corporate rates. The continued downward trend in the investment earnings of life insurance companies and an attendant reduction in reverse interest rate assumptions produced Secretary's Ratios in excess of 100 per cent in 1947 and 1948, and thus no Federal income taxes on life insurance operations in those years. To overcome this disadvantage in taxable year 1949 and 1950 the Ratio was calculated using more realistic reserve interest assumptions for the companies involved and companies whose investment earnings and reserve interest requirements were such that they would produce a negative amount of taxable income were eliminated from the calculation.

For the years 1951 through 1954 the deduction for interest required to meet reserve obligations was disallowed altogether, but the net investment income of the companies was taxed at a rate lower than the regular corporate tax rate. The effect of the reduced tax rate was the same as that which would have been produced by a Secretary's Ratio of 87½ per cent.

In 1955 Federal taxation was based on a method similar to that used from 1942 through 1948 except that the proportion of net investment income assumed to be required to maintain reserves corresponding to the Secretary's Ratio was fixed. This method was continued until 1958.

1959 Federal Income Tax Law.   When the Life Insurance Company Income Tax Act of 1959 was enacted its provisions were applied retroactively to 1958. The income of life insurance companies is presently taxed under this statute. This act, as amended, represents a so-called *total income approach* which involves not only the investment income but also the gain from operations and the capital gains income. The 1959 Tax Act made life insurance companies taxable on all their income at full corporate rates. The only deviation is that a portion of that income is not taxed currently in recognition of the fact that it is quite difficult to determine the income of a life insurance company on an annual basis because of the long-term nature of its contracts.

Under current law, operating gains and losses other than those resulting from investments are recognized for tax purposes. If the net gain from operations is equal to or less than the taxable investment income, then the net gain from operations is the tax base. There is no tax liability if there is a loss from operations, other than that which might arise from payment of dividends to shareholders described later as Phase III income. Policy dividends are deductible in computing the net gains from operations but not to the extent that this would reduce the net operating gain below the taxable investment income by more than $250,000.

The taxable income computation is divided into three phases and the total taxable income is the sum of the taxable income under each phase.[13]

[13] Initially, the law provided that net long-term capital gains in excess of short-term capital losses were to be taxed separately at a 25 per cent rate. This was usually labeled Phase IV. After the taxable year 1962, however, long-term capital gains are included in taxable investment income. They are not taxed separately when tax at the 25 per cent rate would be less than the tax at the regular corporate rate. This is identical to treament accorded other corporate taxpayers.

(1) *Taxable Investment Income.* Phase I determines the taxable investment income. First the adjusted reserves rate is determined by taking the lesser of the current year's investment earnings rate or the average of such rates over the last five years of operation ending with the current year. Next, the reserves are reduced 10 per cent for each 1 per cent that the adjusted reserves rate exceeds the company's average reserve interest rate assumed. The reserves so adjusted are then multiplied by the adjusted reserves rate, and the result is the reserve interest deduction for the year. Taxable investment income is determined by reducing the net investment income by the reserve interest deduction, and other reduction items allowed by the law.

The amount of interest needed to meet reserve and other policy contract obligations, and deducted from investment income to arrive at taxable investment income, is determined separately for each company; this is in contrast to the previous tax laws which required the deduction of a fixed percentage of investment income based on an industry average.

In computing taxable investment income there is a special deduction for investment income on qualified pension plan reserves. This special deduction is in recognition of the fact that the income of qualified pension plans held by trust companies is exempt from taxation.

(2) *Taxable Underwriting Gain.* Phase II determines the taxable underwriting gain. This is one-half of the excess of the gain from operations over the taxable investment income determined in Phase I. The current taxation of only half of the excess of the operating gain over the taxable investment income (this might be considered as a sort of adjusted underwriting gain) is based on the long-term nature of the insurance business and the resulting difficulty of making a final determination of profits from mortality in any one year. The tax on the other half of such income is postponed for as long as the income is kept in the company. This other half is taxed in Phase III when it is paid out to shareholders or when it exceeds certain limits.

(3) *Taxable Stock Company Distributions to Shareholders.* Phase III applies to stock companies only since it taxes certain distributions to shareholders. The law provides for the establishment of two accounts: a shareholders' surplus account into which all monies on which taxes have been paid or which are tax exempt are placed, and a policyholders' surplus account into which is placed that portion of Phase II income which was not taxed. Any shareholders' dividends paid from the policyholders' surplus account are considered Phase III taxable income.

(4) *Sample Calculation of Taxable Income.* The sections of the law describing these procedures do not refer to them as phases, but most writers divide the discussion into phases or "steps" to facilitate understanding. The following simplified example of the calculation of life in-

surance company taxable income should further assist the reader in understanding these complex procedures.[14]

In order to calculate the Phase I taxable investment income, all allowable deductions for investment expenses, real estate, depreciation, and a few other expenses related to the earning of investment income are deducted from the gross investment income. The resulting figure is called the net investment income.

This net investment income is divided into the policyholders' share and the company's share. The company's share, after some deductions, is the taxable investment income (Phase I income). The following calculation to arrive at the taxable investment income should clarify the above statement.

1. The first step is to compute the net investment income:

Gross Investment Income:		
Taxable interest		$1,000,000
Tax-exempt interest and 85 per cent of dividends received		100,000
Rental income		200,000
Short-term capital gain		50,000
Total Gross Investment Income		$1,350,000
Deductions:		
Salaries of investment department	$ 50,000	
Service fees paid for collecting mortgage interest	50,000	
Investment services, etc.	10,000	
Tax on rental property	20,000	
Other investment expenses	20,000	
Total Deductions		150,000
Net Investment Income		$1,200,000

2. The next step is to determine the rate of return earned on the invested assets of the company.[15] If the assets were $29,000,000 at the beginning of the year and $31,000,000 at the end of the year, then there has been an average investment of $30,000,000 of assets, and the net in-

[14] This example is based essentially on an excellent summary of the law by Dr. Stuart Schwarzschild. See Schwarzschild and Zubay, *Life Insurance*, Vol. II (Homewood, Illinois: Richard D. Irwin, Inc., 1967), Chapters XLIV and XLV.

[15] Assets counted are all assets except the real estate and personal property (excluding money) used in conducting the life insurance operations.

vestment income represents a current earnings rate of 4 per cent.

$$\frac{\$\ 1,200,000}{\$30,000,000} = .04$$

3. The third step is to determine an average of the current earnings rates of the past 5 years.

Year	Current Earnings Rate %	Average Earnings Rate %
1970	4.0	
1969	4.1	$\dfrac{20.5}{5} = 4.1$
1968	4.1	
1967	4.1	
1966	4.2	
	Total 20.5	

4. The fourth step is to select the lower of the current earnings rate or the average earnings rate. Since the current (1970) earnings rate of 4 per cent is lower than the average earnings rate of 4.1 per cent, the adjusted reserves rate is 4 per cent. The adjusted reserves rate is used to compute the deduction for interest needed to maintain reserves.

5. It is now necessary to compute the average interest rate assumed which the company owes on its reserves. This computation is illustrated below for the various blocks of reserves which might be held by a life insurance company:

(a) Assumed Rate (%)	(b) Reserve Dec. 31, 1969	(c) Reserve Dec. 31, 1970	(d) Mean Reserves $\dfrac{b + c}{2}$	(e) Product of Rate x Mean Reserve (a x d)
3.5	$ 9,000, 000	$11,000,000	$10,000,000	$350,000
3.0	4,000,000	6,000,000	5,000,000	150,000
2.5	8,000,000	12,000,000	10,000,000	250,000
	$21,000,000	$29,000,000	$25,000,000	$750,000

$$\text{Average interest rate assumed} = \frac{\$\ 750,000}{\$25,000,000} = .03$$

6. Next, it is necessary to compute what the law calls the adjusted life insurance reserves. The mean of the life insurance company's reserves for the current and previous years is reduced by 10 per cent for each 1 per

cent that the adjusted reserves rate exceeds the average interest rate assumed.[16]

Mean of life insurance reserves =
$$\frac{\$21,000,000 + \$29,000,000}{2} = \$25,000,000$$

Therefore:

Adjusted life insurance reserves =
$$\$25,000,000 \times .90 = \$22,500,000.$$

In order to see what has been done up to this point, below are listed items that have been calculated and which are now needed in order to finish computing the taxable investment income.

Net Investment Income	$ 1,200,000
Adjusted Reserves Rate	4%
Average Interest Rate Assumed	3%
Adjusted Life Insurance Reserves	$22,500,000

7. The next step necessary is to compute the reserve interest deduction for 1970 by multiplying the adjusted life insurance reserves by the adjusted reserves rate.

Adjusted Life Insurance Reserves	$22,500,000
Adjusted Reserves Rate	× .04
Reserve Interest Deduction	$ 900,000

---

[16] The use of this formula was suggested by Walter O. Menge and as a result is known as the "Menge Formula." The policy reserves are adjusted to the extent that the adjusted reserves rate differs from the average reserve interest rate assumed. This adjustment is designed to make the reserves consistent with the deduction rate (adjusted reserves rate). If the deduction rate is higher than the assumed rate, as in the example above and in almost all actual cases, the reserves are adjusted downward. If, however, the converse were true, the reserves would be increased. Since the deduction is a combination of the earned and assumed rates of interest, the effect of varying reserve interest assumptions on the deduction would appear to be minor. Consequently, this provision of the law serves to minimize the possibility of reserve manipulation for tax reasons.

8. The next step is to deduct the reserve interest deduction from the net investment income giving the company's share of the net investment income.

Net Investment Income	$1,200,000
Subtract Reserve Interest Deduction	900,000
Company Share of Net Investment Income	$ 300,000

9. The company gets a further deduction for a portion of tax-exempt interest received and 85 per cent of dividends received which is proportionate to the company's share of the net investment income. The ratio of the company's share of the net investment income to the total net investment income is:

$$\frac{\$300,000}{\$1,200,000} = .25$$

The tax-exempt interest received and 85 per cent of dividends received was $100,000. Therefore:

$100,000 Tax-exempt interest received and 85 per cent of dividends received

$\times$ .25 Company's share of net investment income

$ 25,000 Company's share of tax-exempt interest and of 85 per cent of dividends received

10. From the company's share of net investment income (step 8 above) the company's share of tax-exempt interest and 85 per cent of dividends received is subtracted. One further reduction item, the small business deduction, is available to all companies. This deduction is equal to 10 per cent of the net investment income of the company up to the maximum allowable deduction of $25,000. The remainder of the net investment income after these deductions is taxable investment income.

Company's share of net investment income (step 8)	$300,000
Less company's share of tax-exempt interest and 85 per cent of dividends (step 9)	25,000
Less small business deduction	25,000
Taxable investment income (Phase I income)	$250,000

The second type of income which is recognized for Federal income tax purposes is that income which results when the aggregate premiums received and the net investment income exceed the amounts needed for claims, expenses, special deductions,[17] dividends to policyholders, and increases in the policy reserves. This is known as the gain from operations. If the gain from operations exceeds the Phase I taxable investment income, one half of the excess amount is known as Phase II taxable income and is added to the taxable investment income (Phase I) to produce the taxable income (tentative). The following example should clarify the above explanation:

Gain from operations	$500,000
Less taxable investment income (Phase I)	250,000
Difference	$250,000
Phase II income ½ of the $250,000 difference	125,000
Add taxable investment income (Phase I)	250,000
Taxable income (tentative)	$375,000

Of the company's $500,000 gain from operations shown above, $125,000 is not carried to taxable income; the remaining $375,000 is taxable income (tentative). Let us assume that the tax (tentative) on the $375,000 of taxable income is $182,000. The $375,000 taxable income (tentative) minus the $182,000 tax thereon leaves $193,000, which sum is added to the shareholders' surplus account and is available for corporate dividends. The $125,000 of the $500,000 gain from operations which was not carried to taxable income goes to the policyholders' surplus account.

If the company exhausts its shareholders' surplus and wants to use the policyholders' surplus account for shareholders' dividends, the sum so used from policyholders' surplus is called Phase III income and is added to the taxable income (tentative) to give the final taxable income for the year. If a company paid dividends to shareholders from the policyholders' surplus account, it would develop taxable income to the extent of the payment even if there were no other taxable income.

(5) *Summary.* The procedures described are designed to tax the investment income and one-half of the excess of gain from operations over investment income and not to tax the other half of this excess as long as it is left in the company. This technique of taxing only 50 per cent of the gain from operations other than investment income is used because most life insurance policies are long-term contracts, and whether a gain in one

[17] The special deductions allowed are: (1) The larger at 10 per cent of the increase in the nonparticipating reserves or 3 per cent of nonparticipating premiums. (2) Two per cent of group insurance premiums and individual accident and health premiums. (3) Dividends paid to policyholders up to an amount which would reduce the total taxable income base to a level equal to the taxable investment income less $250,000. The sum of these special deductions cannot exceed an amount equal to $250,000 plus the excess of the gain from operations over the taxable investment income.

year will be offset by a loss in a later year will not be known for a long time. However, when the company feels that the untaxed earnings can be paid out to shareholders, the government feels that it is entitled to collect income taxes on the amount paid out.

The given explanation covers only the main outlines of the life insurance company tax law. Further treatment of this tax law is beyond the province of this text, but is, nevertheless, a major factor influencing the management of life insurance companies.

BIBLIOGRAPHY

Organization, Management, and Regulation of Life and Health Insurance Companies

Bartleson, Edwin L., *et. al. Health Insurance,* 2nd ed. (Chicago: The Society of Actuaries, 1968), Chapters 6 and 8.

Black, Kenneth, Jr., and Adams, John F. "Insurance Company Organization and Finance," *Working Papers,* Sixth Annual International Insurance Seminar, International Insurance Seminars, Inc., Tokyo, Japan, July 26–30, 1970.

1968).

Eilers, Robert D. *Regulation of Blue Cross and Blue Shield Plans.* S. S. Huebner Foundation Studies (Homewood, Ill.: Richard D. Irwin, Inc., 1963).

Fey, John T. "Markets and Marketing in the Age of Conglomerates and Congenerics," *Best's Review,* Life/Health Insurance ed. (January, 1970).

Fletcher, Linda Pickthorne. "Mutualization of Stock Life Insurance Companies" (Ph.D. Dissertation, University of Pennsylvania, 1964).

Fraine, Harold G. *Valuation of Securities Holdings of Life Insurance Companies* (Homewood, Ill.: Richard D. Irwin, Inc., 1962).

Huebner, S. S., and McCahan, David. *Life Insurance as Investment* (New York: D. Appleton-Century Company, Inc., 1944).

Kemper, James S., Jr. "Rush to Diversify: New Ideas for Old Money," *Conglomerates and Congenerics—Their Impact on the Insurance Industry,* Society of CPCU, New York Chapter Clinic, CPCU News (March, 1969).

Life Insurance Agency Management Association. *Cost and Compensation in Life Insurance* (Hartford: LIAMA, 1967).

————. *Markets in Life Insurance* (Hartford: LIAMA, 1966).

————. *Recruiting, Selection, Training and Supervision* (Hartford: LIAMA, 1966).

Life Insurance Association of America. *Life Insurance Companies as Financial Institutions* (Englewood Cliffs: Prentice-Hall, Inc., 1962).

McGill, Dan M. *Life Insurance* (Homewood, Ill.: Richard D. Irwin, Inc., 1967).

————, ed. *Life Insurance Sales Management.* S. S. Huebner Foundation Lectures (Homewood, Ill.: Richard D. Irwin, Inc., 1958).

Mehr, Robert I. *Life Insurance: Theory and Practice* (Austin, Texas: Business Publications, Inc., 1970).

"Memo Explains How Mutual Life Company Switched to Stock," *The National Underwriter* (Life ed.), March 17, 1965.

New York Insurance Law, sec. 42 (5), 90 (1).

Patterson, E. W. *The Insurance Commissioner in the United States* (Cambridge: Harvard University Press, 1927).

Report of the Special Committee on Insurance Holding Companies, State of New York Insurance Department, 1968.

Russell, G., Hugh, and Black, Kenneth, Jr. *Human Behavior and Life Insurance* (Englewood Cliffs, Prentice-Hall, Inc., 1963).

Schultz, Robert E. *Life Insurance Housing Projects.* S. S. Huebner Foundation Studies (Homewood, Ill.: Richard D. Irwin, Inc., 1957).

Snider, H. Wayne. *Life Insurance Investment in Commercial Real Estate.* S. S. Huebner Foundation Studies (Homewood, Ill.: Richard D. Irwin, Inc., 1957).

Van House, Charles L., Sr. "Can Life Insurance Accounting Be Modernized?" Parts I, II, III, *Best's Review* (Morristown, N. J.: A. M. Best Company), Vol. 71, Nos. 11 and 12 (March and April, 1971); Vol. 72, No. 1 (May, 1971).

Walters, James E. *The Investment Process* (Boston: Division of Research, Harvard University, 1962).

Appendices

A Specimen Copies of Life and Health Insurance Policies

Application for Life Insurance Policy I

PART ONE OF APPLICATION FOR INSURANCE

№ 768727

| Your Full Name as Proposed Insured *(Print)* | ☐ Male ☐ Female | 4a. AMOUNT and PLAN? *(Check provisions desired)* |

b. ☐ Waiver of Premium

c. ☐ Additional Indemnity of $................

d. ☐ Insurability Agreement for $................

1a. Date of Birth? *(month, day and year)*   b. Birthplace? *(City and State)*

c. ☐ Single   ☐ Married   ☐ Widowed   ☐ Divorced   ☐ Separated

5a. Beneficiary? *(If an individual, print first name, initial, surname, and state relationship. If a corporation, print full corporate name.)*

d. RESIDENCE

No. & St.............................. Yrs.

City........................ State.......... Zip............

Former: No. & St.................................

City........................ State..........

BUSINESS

No. & St..................................

City........................ State.......... Zip............

Former: No. & St..................................

City........................ State..........

Unless otherwise stated above, if no individual designated as a beneficiary survives the Insured, payment shall be made to the executors or administrators of the Insured. If a corporate beneficiary is designated, payment shall be made to the corporation or its successors or assigns.

b. Owner?   ☐ Insured   ☐ Applicant

☐

or his executors or administrators (or its successors or assigns, if a corporation).

2a. Occupation? *(Give job title and duties)*

Owner's Social Security or Identification number   Owner's name and address—if other than insured

Employer's Name

6a. Use of Dividends   ☐ Buy additional insurance   ☐ Buy One Year Term Insurance with   ☐ Accumulate   ☐ Balance—Additional Insurance   ☐ Apply on premiums   ☐ Balance—Accumulate   ☐ Cash   ☐ Balance—Apply on premiums

b. Any change of occupation contemplated?   ☐ Yes ☐ No

c. Is travel or residence outside United States contemplated?   ☐ Yes ☐ No

d. In the past two years have you flown other than on a scheduled airline?   ☐ Yes ☐ No

e. In the past five years have you flown as a pilot, student pilot or crew member, or is such flying contemplated? If so, submit Aviation Supplement.   ☐ Yes ☐ No

f. In the past three years have you participated in any hazardous avocation such as motor vehicle racing, parachute jumping, or skin or scuba diving, or is such activity contemplated? If so, submit Avocation Supplement.   ☐ Yes ☐ No

g. In the past three years have you been in a motor vehicle accident, or charged with a "moving" violation of any motor vehicle law, or had your license suspended?   ☐ Yes ☐ No

h. Are you a member of or do you contemplate joining any branch of the armed forces? If so, submit Military Supplement.   ☐ Yes ☐ No

i. Have you negotiated for other life insurance within ninety days?   ☐ Yes ☐ No

j. Have you ever been declined, postponed, or charged an extra premium for Life or Health Insurance?   ☐ Yes ☐ No

b. Premiums Payable   ☐ Annually   ☐ Quarterly   ☐ Semi-annually   ☐ Monthly   ☐ M.C.S.   ☐ Allotment

c. Premium Notices to: ☐ Insured at residence   ☐ Insured at business   ☐ Other *(Give Name and Address under Number 8 below)*

d. Premium Loan Provision to be effective, if available.   ☐ Yes ☐ No

e. Payment of Premium (and Interest) by Accumulated Dividends Provision to be effective, if available.   ☐ Yes ☐ No

7. Has any insurance on your life terminated within six months or is termination of any now contemplated? If so, submit Form 108.   ☐ Yes ☐ No

8. Use this space to explain any "Yes" answer to Questions 2b, c, d, g, i, and j, and to give any special instructions. *(If space inadequate, use Form 16)*

3. Existing life insurance? If group, identify by (G)

Company	Amt. of Ins.	Year of Issue	Additional Indemnity

9. Premium paid?   ☐ Yes ☐ No   If "Yes", state amount paid $................

Unless otherwise provided in a Conditional Advance Premium Receipt duly issued and delivered and bearing the same printed number as this Application, it is understood and agreed that any policy issued on this Application, consisting of Parts 1 and 2, shall take effect only if the first full premium is paid and such policy is issued and delivered while the health, habits and occupation of the proposed insured and other conditions affecting insurability remain as described in this Application. Upon issuance of the policy applied for, this paragraph shall be subject to the provision therein entitled 'Incontestability.'

Dated at.................... this.......... day of.................... 19.......

Witness to Signature.................   Signature of Proposed Insured.......................

The applicant agrees to be fully bound by all statements, answers and agreements contained in Parts 1 and 2 of this Application.

Dated at.................... this.......... day of.................... 19.......

Witness to Signature.................   Signature of Applicant.......................

(For use only if Applicant is other than proposed insured)

(State relationship, if any, to proposed Insured)

DO NOT WRITE BELOW THIS DOUBLE LINE

F 10—66

CONDITIONAL   ADVANCE PREMIUM   RECEIPT

IF PREMIUM IS PAID AT THE TIME OF APPLICATION, THIS RECEIPT SHOULD BE COMPLETED AND GIVEN TO THE PAYOR. NO OTHER RECEIPT WILL BE RECOGNIZED BY THE COMPANY. IF PREMIUM IS NOT PAID, THE RECEIPT SHOULD NOT BE DETACHED.

Received the sum of.................... Dollars, on an application bearing the same number and date as this receipt for insurance with.................... in the amount of....................

Dollars, on the life of..................... If all evidence of insurability requested by the Company is furnished within sixty days from the date of this Receipt, and if the proposed Insured is insurable in the Company as a standard risk in accordance with the Company's established practice in the selection of risks for the amount (subject to Limits Provision below) and on the plan applied for without modification, and such insurability exists on the latest date of (1) Part 1 of the application, (2) Part 2 of the application, (3) the effective date of the Policy, if any, which may be requested in the application, the Company will issue the policy applied for and such policy shall relate back and be effective from the latest of said dates. If the proposed Insured is not insurable as a standard risk as above provided, or if any evidence of insurability requested by the Company shall not be furnished within sixty days from the date hereof, then the Company shall be under no obligation to provide any insurance coverage under this Receipt and the amount paid hereon shall be repaid upon return of this Receipt.

Limits Provision — The maximum amount of Life Insurance cannot be in excess of $500,000, inclusive of all life insurance already in force or applied for in the Company. The maximum amount of Additional Indemnity payable as a result of death by accidental means cannot be in excess of $25,000 at ages under 10, or $50,000 at rated ages 10-24, or $150,000 at rated ages 25-65, inclusive of all such Additional Indemnity already in force or applied for in the Company.

If any check or draft given in exchange for this Receipt is dishonored when presented for payment, this Receipt shall be null and void.

Dated at.................... this.......... day of.................... 19.......

Agent, at....................

№ 768727

BUSINESS INSURANCE DATA — to be completed in all cases where insurance is being purchased for a business purpose.

1a. Amount of insurance on Proposed Insured already payable to this business beneficiary?	3. Purpose(s) of Insurance: ☐ Keyman ☐ Deferred Compensation ☐ Salary Continuance ☐ Split Dollar ☐ Stock Retirement
b. His annual compensation from this business?	☐ Stock Purchase ☐ Partnership Entity Buy-Sell ☐ Partnership Criss-Cross Buy-Sell ☐ Secure Credit
2a. Other executives already insured in favor of this beneficiary? (Give names and amounts)	☐ Proprietorship Buy-Sell ☐ Other (explain)
b. Names of other executives currently being insured in C. M. L.	4. Describe value of Proposed Insured's services, duties, skills, financial resources, etc., which warrant the amount of insurance desired. (If space inadequate, give full details in a letter)
c. If other key executives are not insured, explain why.	

AGENT'S REPORT — to be completed by agent in all cases.

1a. To what company do you give your first line of life insurance? ☐ ☐ .... (Name of Company)	5. If proposed Insured is a married woman, dependent child or dependent parent a. Who will pay for this insurance?
b. If not .... has insurance been applied for in your first line company? ☐ Yes If "yes," give amount and date. ☐ No If "no," explain why.	
2a. How long have you known proposed insured? ....Yrs. ....Mos.	b. Amount of insurance in force on life of payor of premiums?
b. Is he a: ☐ Relative ☐ Friend ☐ Acquaintance ☐ Stranger	
3a. Estimated financial worth $................... Annual income $...................	6. Do you know anything about the proposed insured's character, habits, reputation or health, which might make this risk undesirable? ☐ Yes ☐ No If "Yes", explain by letter.
b. Is financing of first or subsequent premium by loan contemplated? ☐ Yes ☐ No If "yes", submit Form 104	7. If residence is rural, give directions regarding location.
4. To your knowledge, has any insurance on the life of the Proposed Insured terminated within six months, or is termination of any now contemplated? ☐ Yes ☐ No If "yes," submit Form 108.	Located..................miles in a.................direction from........................on R. F. D. No...................

MARKET RESEARCH DATA — to be completed by agent in all cases:

1. Proposed Insured's County of residence?	4. Estimate of his education? ☐ High School or less ☐ Some College ☐ College Graduate ☐ Graduate School ☐ Professional School
2. Number of his dependent children?	5. Basis of sale: Identify sales plan (e.g., Axiom, HM & WK, Funnel, Designed for Young Men & Women, Capitalization & Discount, etc.) or otherwise describe (e.g. savings, education, program, mortgage, estate liquidity, keyman, audit, etc.)
3. Estimate of his total annual premiums for life insurance?	

THIS SECTION TO BE COMPLETED BY AGENCY NEW BUSINESS CLERK

1. Have you checked this application for errors or omissions? ☐ Yes	4. Is the agent properly licensed in the state in which this application was written? ☐ Yes ☐ No
2. If non-medical, does agent have non-medical privilege? ☐ Yes ☐ No	5. Residence code:
3. If examined, was appointed examiner used? ☐ Yes ☐ No If not, submit explanation on Form 1281.	☐ State ☐ County ☐ City

AGENT'S COMMISSION CERTIFICATE   For Agent's Plate(s)

The undersigned are the sole parties entitled to commissions on any insurance issued pursuant to said application. Commissions, and service fees if any, shall be paid subject to agency agreements which may be in effect when commissions become payable.
No other agreement for remuneration in connection with such insurance shall be made unless authorized in writing by the Company.

SIGNATURE OF SOLICITING AGENT	FORM OF CONTRACT ☐ FULL-TIME ☐ BROKER-1st Line ☐ SINGLE CASE AGREEMENT ☐ PART-TIME ☐ BROKER	
TYPE OR PRINT ABOVE NAME HERE	FIRST COM. RATE %	RENL. COMS.-% OF TOTAL RATE %
ASSISTING AGENT'S SIGNATURE (IF ANY)	FORM OF CONTRACT ☐ FULL-TIME ☐ BROKER-1st Line ☐ SINGLE CASE AGREEMENT ☐ PART-TIME ☐ BROKER	
TYPE OR PRINT ABOVE NAME HERE	FIRST COM. RATE %	RENL. COMS.-% OF TOTAL RATE %

....   BY..
GENERAL AGENT'S SIGNATURE   ATTORNEY

USE BLACK
INK ONLY

NON-MEDICAL
PART 2

DECLARATIONS IN LIEU OF MEDICAL EXAMINATION
Every Question in Part 2 must be fully answered by the Proposed Insured in the presence of the Agent.

Part 2 of Application for insurance on life of ....

10. a. FAMILY RECORD	Age if living	HEALTH—If not good state why	Age at death	CAUSE OF DEATH
Father				
Mother				
Husband or Wife				
Brothers & Sisters				
No. living............				
No. dead............				

b. Have there been any cases of diabetes, cancer, tuberculosis, or mental disease among your parents, brothers, or sisters?

c. Have you within the past 2 years lived with or been regularly associated with a person having active tuberculosis?

ESTIMATED		Actual, BY AGENT	
11. a. Height ....ft...............in.		Height ....ft...............in.	
b. Weight ....lbs.		Weight ....lbs.	

When build nears borderline on table in Medical Guide, secure actual height and weight.

c. Change of weight in past 6 months?
Gain.............lbs. or Loss.............lbs.

If loss, explain and state how long weight has remained stationary.

13. a. To what extent do you use alcoholic beverages?

b. Have you ever used any of them to excess?

c. Have you ever been treated for alcoholism or drug habit?

14. a. Have you had any surgical operations?

b. Are any contemplated?

c. Have you ever been in a hospital or institution for observation or treatment?

d. Have you ever had any special studies completed, such as X-rays, electrocardiograms, blood sugar studies, Wassermann or Kahn tests, or other blood chemistry?

15. a. Have you, within the last year, applied to any other company for life insurance without medical examination?

b. Have you any impairment of vision not fully corrected by glasses, or any impairment of hearing?

c. Have you any deformity or amputation or any physical or mental disability?

d. Have you ever made claim for or received any disability benefits or government pension? (*If government pension, state for what condition, amount received, and what changes in rating.*)

If proposed insured is a female:
16. a. Have you now or have you ever had any disorder of the generative organs or breasts?

17. Have you ever had, or consulted a physician about:

a. Heart murmur, high blood pressure, chest pain, angina pectoris, coronary artery disease, cardiac irregularity or any other heart condition?

b. Nervous breakdown, insanity, epilepsy, convulsions, severe headaches, paralysis, or any disease of the brain or nervous system?

c. Tuberculosis, spitting of blood, asthma, chronic bronchitis or cough, pleurisy, pneumonia, or any disease of the lungs or throat?

d. Indigestion, gastric or duodenal ulcer, gallstones, gallbladder trouble, jaundice, appendicitis, dysentery, rectal trouble, hernia?

e. Kidney stones or colic, Bright's disease, syphilis, albumin, sugar, blood, or pus in the urine?

f. Chronic disease of the eyes, ears, nasal sinuses, skin, or bones?

g. Cancer, tumor, goitre, diabetes, rheumatism or arthritis?

18. a. Have you consulted, or been under treatment by, any physician in the past 5 years for any symptoms or diseases not mentioned above?

b. Do you to the best of your knowledge, now have any disease, disorder or infirmity not mentioned above?

IF ANY QUESTION 13b to 18b HAS BEEN ANSWERED "yes," GIVE FULL DETAILS BELOW, SUCH AS NAME OF AILMENT, NUMBER OF ATTACKS, DATES, DURATION, SEVERITY, RESULTS, AND NAMES OF ALL ATTENDING PHYSICIANS. (Specify number of question.)

I HAVE READ ALL THE STATEMENTS AND ANSWERS IN THIS APPLICATION (consisting of Parts 1 and 2 and any amendments thereto) AND I HEREBY DECLARE THAT ALL SUCH STATEMENTS AND ANSWERS ARE TRUE AND FULL and agree that they shall be the basis of and a part of the consideration for the Insurance applied for.

I EXPRESSLY WAIVE, on behalf of myself and of any person having any interest in any policy issued hereunder, all provisions of law preventing any physician or other person from disclosing any information as to my health known to him and I authorize any physician or person to disclose any such information to the Company. This waiver and authorization is subject to any limitation of law.

Dated at.., this..day of....................................19.......

Witness:... Signature of Proposed Insured : X...
Form 2077   (Signature of Proposed Insured to be witnessed by Agent.)   AGENTS' FORM NO. 147   (Ed. 2-57) +   (Write the name in full.)

This authorization should be
signed by Proposed Insured.

AUTHORIZATION TO CONSULT PERSONAL PHYSICIAN, HOSPITAL OR CLINIC

I hereby authorize any physician or practitioner who has observed me for diagnosis or treatment, or any disease or ailment; or any hospital or clinic where I have been a patient for such diagnosis, treatment, disease or ailment, to give full particulars thereof, including any prior medical history, to
A photostat of this authorization shall be as valid as the original.
to whom I am making application for insurance.

.... X...
          Witness   Proposed Insured's Signature

....
          Date

AGENT'S CERTIFICATION AND RECOMMENDATION

A. How long have you known the proposed insured?	............years ....months	**B.** How well do you know him and how frequently do you see him?	
C. Did he seek this insurance without previous approach on your part?		**D.** Was the soliciting of this application suggested to you by a broker or agent of this or any other life insurance company? (If so, give details.)	
E. Do you know anything about the proposed insured's character, habits, reputation, personal history, family history, or physical condition which might make the risk undesirable?			**F.** If proposed insured is a married woman not regularly employed outside her home, state amount of insurance on husband's life.
G. Has any life insurance on this proposed insured terminated within one year, or have you discussed with him termination of any insurance at some future date? (If so, give full particulars.)		**H.** Did you ask of and carefully explain to the proposed insured each question, and record his answer in his presence?	
a. In the			
b. In any other Company? (Name Company — date of termination.)			
I. If proposed insured lives in a country district, answer the following question:	Located...................miles in a...direction from..on R.F.D. No...............		

I hereby certify that I personally solicited and secured this application, that I know of nothing against the risk which is not fully set forth in these papers, and I UNQUALIFIEDLY RECOMMEND THE PROPOSED INSURED as a desirable subject for insurance.

....
(Date)   (Signature of Agent)

Note. If the above agent is not qualified under the Company's rules to submit non-medical business, a qualified agent must be present and subscribe to the following declaration.

I was present at the solicitation and witnessed the entire filling in and completion of this application.

....
(Date)   (Signature of Qualified Agent)

Rules Governing Insurance without Medical Examination

1. Only those agents who are authorized under the Company's rules may submit applications on the non-medical basis.

2. AGENT'S RESPONSIBILITY. The application must be fully completed by him in the presence of the proposed insured — never by mail. Questions should be carefully explained and answers accurately recorded, with names and addresses of physicians and dates. All answers must be written in ink — never by typewriter. Ditto marks or similar symbols should not be used. Erasures and alterations should be initialed by the proposed insured (not by the agent).

3. AGE LIMITS. Applicants must not be older than 40 years of age, taken at the age nearest birthday — except that higher age limits apply on (1) Pension Trust "Additions" (see back of Pension Trust Addition, Form 10D) and (2) Payor Clauses applied for in connection with insurance on children (see back of Juvenile Part 1, Form 10B).

4. NON-MEDICAL LIMITS.

	Without G. I. A.			With G. I. A.
Ages	Within Any 12 Months' Period	Over-All Limit	Ages	
0-5	$10,000	$25,000	0-5	$10,000 (With G. I. A. on $10,000)
6-30	25,000	25,000	6-20	25,000 (With G. I. A. on 10,000)
31-35	15,000	15,000	21-30	15,000 (With G. I. A. on 10,000)
36-40	5,000	10,000	31-37	5,000 (With G. I. A. on 5,000)

5. PLAN LIMITS. The above table applies to all plans of insurance except the Insurance Builder, the basic Term plans (Initial Term, 5 Year Term, etc.) and Level Term Agreements. Where Family Income or Decreasing Term is involved the initial amount of such risk must not be more than twice the amount of the base policy.
The limit on the Insurance Builder is ten units (i.e. $10,000 basic face amount increasing to $50,000 ultimate face amount).
On the basic Term plans (Initial Term, 5 Year Term, etc.) and Level Term Agreements the non-medical limit is $10,000 and the top age limit is 30.

6. All cases coming within the age, amount and plan limitations, as outlined above, submitted by agents privileged to handle non-medical business must be presented first on a non-medical basis, and the Company may then require an examination wherever deemed advisable. If a medical examination is made without authorization from the Home Office on a case coming within the non-medical classification, the examiner's fee may be charged to the General Agency, unless a satisfactory explanation is submitted.

7. This form is for use where proposed insured is age 16 or over. For children under that age, Agents' Form No. 397 should generally be used.

(Ed. 12-62)+

Whole-Life Policy   II

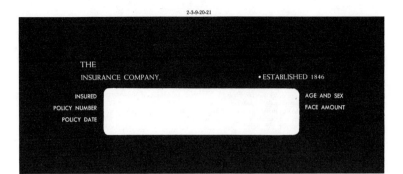

2-3-9-20-21

THE

INSURANCE COMPANY,   • ESTABLISHED 1846

INSURED   AGE AND SEX

POLICY NUMBER   FACE AMOUNT

POLICY DATE

The   Life Insurance Company will pay the Face
Amount to the Beneficiary, subject to all provisions of this Policy,
upon receipt at its Home Office of due proof of the Insured's death.

This Policy is issued by the Company at its Home Office,
on the Date of Issue.

REGISTRAR

GUIDE TO POLICY PROVISIONS   PAGE

Extra Benefit Agreements, if any, and a copy of the application
appear after Page 8.

WHOLE LIFE POLICY
Payable at Death
Premiums Payable for Life unless previously Paid-up by Dividends
Annual Dividends

DEFINITIONS

Definitions. Every reference in this Policy to: "dividend credits" means any dividends due and unpaid and any outstanding dividend accumulations; "indebtedness" means any policy or premium loan indebtedness to the Company on or secured by this Policy plus any interest due or accrued on such loan; "written request" means a request in writing satisfactory to the Company and filed at its Home Office.

OWNER AND BENEFICIARY

Rights of Owner. During the Insured's lifetime and unless otherwise provided in this Policy, the right to receive all cash values, loans, dividends and other benefits, to change the Beneficiary, to assign this Policy, to exercise all privileges and options, and to agree with the Company to any release, modification or amendment of this Policy, shall belong exclusively to the Owner.

Beneficiary. If no Beneficiary designated under this Policy shall survive the Insured and if the Policy does not provide otherwise, the Beneficiary shall be the executors or administrators of the Insured.

Any beneficiary may be changed by written notice in form satisfactory to the Company. Such notice, when received at the Home Office, shall make the change effective as of the date on which the notice was signed. The Company's liability under the Policy shall be discharged, however, to the extent of any payment which it makes in accordance with the last recorded beneficiary designation or income settlement option election made prior to the receipt at the Home Office of notice of change of beneficiary. The interest of any beneficiary shall be subject to any assignment of this Policy which is binding upon the Company and to any Optional Settlement Agreement which may be in effect at the Insured's death.

CASH VALUE, EXTENDED AND PAID-UP INSURANCE

Cash Value. This Policy may be surrendered to the Company for its Cash Value less indebtedness at any time after premiums have been duly paid on it to or beyond the end of the period for which it first has a Cash Value, in full settlement of the Company's liability under it. The Company may defer such surrender payment for a period not exceeding 6 months after application for surrender, but if payment is deferred for 30 days or more, interest at the rate of 2¾% a year will be paid for the period of deferment.

The Cash Value at any time while this Policy is in force as a premium-paying policy, and all premiums due have been paid, shall be the reserve on this Policy, plus the reserve on any paid-up additions. Such deduction at the end of the first policy year shall be the Cash Value Factor shown at the bottom of the Table of Values. Thereafter, the deduction shall decrease uniformly so as to be eliminated at the end of the policy year shown at the bottom of the Table of Values. The Cash Value at any time during a policy year will be computed with allowance for the time elapsed in such year and the date to which premiums have been paid. In no event shall this Policy have a Cash Value if premiums shall have been paid for less than one full policy year.

If this Policy becomes fully paid-up under the Paid-up or Matured by Dividends provision, the Cash Value shall be the then reserve plus the reserve on any paid-up additions.

If, after premiums have been duly paid for one full policy year or more, this Policy is in force under the Automatic Extended Insurance or Paid-up Insurance provision, the Cash Value shall be the then reserve plus the reserve on any paid-up additions. However, such Cash Value within 3 months after the due date of the premium in default shall be computed as of such due date, and such Cash Value within 30 days after any subsequent policy anniversary shall be not less than the Cash Value on such subsequent anniversary.

Automatic Extended Insurance. If any premium due is not paid by the end of the grace period from dividend credits, by premium loan, or otherwise, this Policy will be automatically continued in force as Nonparticipating Extended Insurance unless the Paid-up Insurance benefit has been elected.

The amount of Extended Insurance shall be the Face Amount, plus any paid-up additions and dividend credits, less indebtedness. Such insurance will start as of the due date of the unpaid premium and will continue for such term as the Cash Value (or, if premiums have been paid for less than a full policy year, the reserve on this Policy less $25 for each $1000 Face Amount), plus dividend credits, less indebtedness, will purchase as a net single premium. If no value is available under this provision as a net single premium, no Extended Insurance shall be available. If such value available as a net single premium would purchase a smaller amount of Extended Insurance than of Paid-up Insurance, then Paid-up Insurance will be provided instead.

Paid-up Insurance. This benefit will be effective instead of Extended Insurance if (1) written request is made within 3 months after the due date of the unpaid premium, (2) premiums have been paid on this Policy for one full policy year or more, and (3) a value is available as a net single premium under the Automatic Extended Insurance provision. If these conditions are met, this Policy will be continued in force as Participating Paid-up Life Insurance for the remainder of the term of this Policy in the amount which such value available as a net single premium will purchase as of the due date of the unpaid premium.

Table of Values. The Values in the Table of Values on Page 3 apply if all premiums have been paid to the end of the policy year shown and if there is no indebtedness. Values will be increased by dividend credits and any paid-up additions only as specifically provided in this Policy. The Loan Values are the Maximum Loan Values available at the end of the policy years specified. Loans may also be obtained at any time during such policy years as set forth in the Policy Loan provision. Values for any policy years not shown will be furnished by the Company upon request. All Values are greater than or equal to those required by any statute of the state in which this Policy is delivered. No Value is provided under the terms of this Policy until premiums are paid to the time such Value is first shown in the Table of Values.

SPECIFICATIONS

BENEFICIARY MARY DOE, WIFE OF THE INSURED.

INSURED	JOHN DOE	35 MALE	AGE AND SEX
POLICY NUMBER	0,000,000	$10,000	FACE AMOUNT
POLICY DATE	APR 15, 1967		

DATE OF ISSUE   APR 3, 1967
OWNER THE INSURED

BENEFITS AND PREMIUMS

BENEFIT	ANNUAL PREMIUM	YEARS PAYABLE
WHOLE LIFE POLICY	$234.20	FOR LIFE
TOTAL FIRST YEAR ANNUAL PREMIUM	$234.20	

POLICY YEARS, MONTHS AND ANNIVERSARIES ARE COMPUTED FROM THE POLICY DATE

TABLE OF VALUES (SEE PAGE 2)

POLICY YEARS ELAPSED	CASH OR LOAN VALUE	PAID-UP LIFE INSURANCE	EXTENDED INSURANCE YEARS	DAYS
1/4	$ .00	$ 0	0	0
1/2	.00	0	0	0
3/4	.00	0	0	0
1	5.60	10	0	60
2	180.50	410	4	215
3	364.20	800	7	301
4	550.40	1,190	10	66
5	739.20	1,560	11	344
6	930.20	1,930	13	101
7	1,123.40	2,280	14	116
8	1,318.60	2,620	15	47
9	1,516.00	2,950	15	276
10	1,715.30	3,270	16	87
11	1,898.80	3,550	16	180
12	2,083.90	3,820	16	243
13	2,270.50	4,080	16	281
14	2,458.40	4,340	16	296
15	2,647.40	4,580	16	291
16	2,837.20	4,820	16	269
17	3,027.70	5,050	16	231
18	3,218.80	5,270	16	181
19	3,410.20	5,490	16	119
20	3,601.70	5,700	16	47
AGE 60	4,554.40	6,630	14	329
AGE 65	5,473.80	7,400	13	167

CASH VALUE FACTOR $160.00 – DECREASING TO ZERO AT END 10TH YEAR

$34.10 MONTHLY LIFE INCOME TO INSURED AT ATTAINED AGE 65 WITH 120 MONTHS
CERTAIN PROVIDED BY CASH VALUE AND SUBJECT TO INCOME SETTLEMENT OPTION PROVISIONS

Plate 147

PREMIUMS

Premium Payments. This contract is made in consideration of the application and the payment of all premiums as provided in this Policy. All premiums are payable in advance either at the Company's Home Office or to an agent of the Company on delivery of a receipt signed by its President or Secretary and countersigned by the agent. Possession of such receipt shall be sole evidence of the authority of any agent to receive any premium due on this Policy. If any premium is not paid as provided in this Policy, all liability under this Policy shall terminate except as otherwise provided in this Policy.

Annual premiums shown in the Schedule of Benefits and Premiums on Page 3 are payable on the Policy Date and annually thereafter during the Insured's lifetime for the period stated in the Schedule. Upon written request, the method of premium payment may be changed on any policy anniversary to the annual, semiannual or quarterly basis using the applicable published rates for this Policy. Premiums payable annually are due on the first day of each policy year. Premiums payable semiannually are due on the first day of each policy year and 6 months thereafter. Premiums payable quarterly are due on the first day of each policy year and every 3 months thereafter.

Payment of any premium for any extra benefit agreement shall not increase any cash, loan, paid-up or extended insurance value or dividend under this Policy.

Grace Period. A grace period of 31 days after its due date will be granted for the payment of each premium after the first, during which period the Policy will continue in force.

Premium Adjustment. If the Insured dies while this Policy is in force on a premium-paying basis, premiums for the policy year of death will be refunded or charged as may be required to effect premium payments to the end of the policy month in which the Insured died. Such refund or charge will be made by adjustment in the death proceeds.

Payment of Premium and Interest by Accumulated Dividends.
If requested in the application, or by written request while this Policy is premium-paying, any premium including any extra benefit agreement premium, or policy loan interest, or both, remaining unpaid at the end of the grace period shall be paid automatically from the then dividend credits, if such credits are sufficient. If such credits are insufficient to meet the required payment and the Premium Loan provision is operative, said credits shall be applied toward the payment if the premium loan value is sufficient to cover the balance of such payment. If such credits are insufficient to meet the premium required and the Premium Loan provision is not operative, the method of premium payment shall be changed automatically to quarterly, unless such credits are insufficient to meet the quarterly premium, in which event this paragraph shall not apply. Any request that this provision be operative may be revoked by written request as to premiums thereafter becoming due.

Premium Loan. If requested in the application, or by written request while this Policy is premium-paying, the amount of any premium on this Policy (including the premium for any extra benefit agreement) falling due after the first policy year, and not paid in cash or by application of dividends, will be paid by being charged as a loan, provided that the loan, together with existing indebtedness, shall not exceed the Maximum Loan Value.

If the available loan value is insufficient to pay the premium or balance of premium due, the method of premium payment shall be changed automatically to quarterly, unless the available loan value is insufficient to pay a quarterly premium (or balance of quarterly premium), in which event this provision shall not apply. If a premium is paid under this provision and dividends are on the accumulative basis, future dividends shall be applied automatically against premiums unless otherwise requested. If premiums are payable more frequently than annually, and if two or more successive premiums have been paid in whole or in part by Premium Loan, the Company may change the method of premium payment to annual if the available loan value is sufficient to pay the annual premium (or balance of annual premium).

Any premium loan shall bear interest from the due date of the premium to which the loan value was applied and shall be subject to the policy loan terms of this Policy, but without other loan agreement or delivery of this Policy. Any request that this provision be operative may be revoked by written request as to premiums thereafter becoming due.

DIVIDENDS

The Dividend. Upon payment of the premium for the full second policy year, and thereafter at the end of the second and each later policy year, this Policy, while in force other than as Extended Insurance, will be credited with such share of the divisible surplus, if any, as may be apportioned to it by the Company as a dividend. At the option of the payee, each dividend shall be applied under one of the following:

(1) CASH — Paid in cash.

(2) ACCUMULATION — Left with the Company, subject to withdrawal, to accumulate at interest, credited annually, at the rate declared by the Company but not less than $2\frac{3}{4}\%$, but with no interest allowed for any fraction of a policy year.

(3) PREMIUM PAYMENT — Applied on a premium due on this Policy.

(4) PAID-UP ADDITION — Converted into a participating paid-up addition to the sum insured under this Policy. Any such additions outstanding may at any time be surrendered to the Company for cash in an amount equal to their reserve.

Unless the Company is otherwise directed in writing within 31 days after a dividend becomes payable, that dividend will purchase a paid-up addition under option (4).

Any dividend credits and paid-up additions outstanding at the maturity of this Policy, and any post-mortem dividend apportioned by the Company, shall be payable as part of the proceeds of this Policy. Any dividend credits outstanding at the surrender of this Policy shall be paid at the time of such surrender.

Paid-up or Matured by Dividends. Whenever the reserve on this Policy and on any paid-up additions, with any dividend credits, (1) shall equal the net single premium for a fully paid-up policy of this same kind and face amount for the then age of the Insured, upon release of such dividends and paid-up additions, the Company will endorse this Policy as fully paid-up, or (2) shall equal the Face Amount, then upon payment and release of such dividends and paid-up additions the Company will pay the Face Amount as a matured endowment, less any indebtedness.

POLICY LOAN

The Company will loan any sum up to the Maximum Loan Value less existing indebtedness upon submission to the Home Office of a loan agreement satisfactory to the Company, at any time after this Policy first has a Cash Value, and while it is in force other than as Extended Insurance. This Policy shall be the sole security for the loan but need not be presented at the Home Office for endorsement or inspection unless required by the Company. Lack of endorsement shall not indicate that the Policy is free from loans. Any premium due at the time the loan is made shall be paid in cash or deducted from the proceeds of the loan.

The Maximum Loan Value is the amount which, with interest at 5% a year, shall equal the Cash Value on the next policy anniversary or on the next premium due date if that is earlier.

The Company may defer making the loan for a period not exceeding 6 months after application unless the loan is to be used to pay premiums to the Company.

The loan shall bear interest at the rate of 5% a year, payable annually, not in advance, on the policy anniversary. Principal and interest are payable at the Home Office. Indebtedness may be repaid in whole or in part at any time prior to maturity if it has not been deducted under the Automatic Extended Insurance or Paid-up Insurance provision.

Any interest not paid when due shall be added to the loan and shall bear interest at the same rate. Whenever indebtedness equals or exceeds the Cash Value, this Policy shall terminate and have no further value 31 days after notice has been mailed to the last known address of the Insured, or of such person as may have been designated to receive such notice, and of any assignee of record at the Home Office.

CHANGE OF PLAN

This Policy, while premium-paying, may be exchanged on any policy anniversary, or within 31 days thereafter, without evidence of insurability, for a premium-paying policy for the same Face Amount, on any other whole life or endowment form (except Graded Premium Whole Life) and at the published premium rate in use by the Company at the issue of this Policy, upon written request and payment of 103% of the difference in reserves. If any premium or premiums falling due after a proposed change of plan date have been paid in advance, the amount of such prepayment may, upon proper authorization, be applied to the cost of the plan change on such date.

The Policy issued in exchange shall not involve any other life, and any extra benefit agreement shall be available only with the Company's consent, unless otherwise provided in an agreement issued with this Policy. The Policy issued in exchange shall be written with the same Policy Date and Age as this Policy and be subject to any limitations of risk and to any indebtedness and assignments outstanding against this Policy.

GENERAL PROVISIONS

Incontestability. This Policy will be incontestable after it shall have been in force during the lifetime of the Insured for a period of 2 years from the Date of Issue, except for non-payment of premium. This provision shall not apply to any agreement providing benefits in event of disability or in event of death from accidental means.

Age and Sex. The Insured's Attained Age on any policy anniversary is the age listed on Page 3 following the Insured's name increased by the number of policy years elapsed. If the Insured's age or sex has been misstated, the amount payable under this Policy shall be such as the premium paid would have purchased using the correct age and sex according to the Company's rate basis effective on the Date of Issue. Any age reference in the Table of Values on Page 3 means the policy anniversary on which the Insured's Attained Age is that stated.

Assignments or Transfers. The Company shall not be required to take notice of or be responsible for any transfer of any interest in this Policy by assignment, agreement or otherwise unless and until a written notice of the terms of the transfer, or copy of any assignment, is filed at its Home Office. The Company will not be responsible for the validity of any assignment. Any assignment made after the Insured's death will be valid only with the Company's consent.

Reserves and Net Single Premiums. The Commissioners 1958 Standard Ordinary Mortality Table is used to compute all reserves and net single premiums referred to in this Policy except those for extended insurance for which the Commissioners 1958 Extended Insurance Table is used. Calculations are based on the net level premium method, continuous functions, and compound interest at 2½% a year.

Suicide. In event of the death of the Insured within 2 years from the Date of Issue by suicide, whether sane or insane, the amount payable under this Policy shall be limited to a sum equal to the premiums paid under this Policy.

The Contract. The Policy and the application, a copy of which is attached to and made a part of this Policy, constitute the entire contract. All statements in the application shall be deemed representations and not warranties. No statement shall be used to avoid this Policy nor to defend against a claim under it, unless contained in the application and unless a copy of the application is attached to the Policy when issued.

Agents of the Company have no authority to alter or modify any of the terms, conditions or agreements of this Policy, or to waive any of its provisions.

Proceeds. Death proceeds payable under this Policy will be the Face Amount (or the amount of any Extended or Paid-up Insurance if effective as provided in this Policy) plus any outstanding paid-up additions and dividend credits and any post-mortem dividend apportioned by the Company, less indebtedness, and adjusted by any refund or charge under the Premium Adjustment provision.

Policy Settlement. All sums payable by the Company under this Policy are payable only at its Home Office. In any settlement of this Policy, indebtedness will be deducted from the amount payable, and the Company may require return of the Policy.

Interest will be paid on proceeds paid in one sum in event of the Insured's death, at the rate declared by the Company but not less than 2¾% a year from the date of death to the date of payment, except that such interest will not be paid for a period in excess of one year.

Reinstatement. This Policy may be reinstated at any time within 5 years after default in premium payment if it has not been surrendered for its cash value, upon evidence of insurability satisfactory to the Company and payment of overdue premiums with compound interest at the yearly rate of 5% and also upon payment or reinstatement of indebtedness which existed at the date of default, increased by interest in accordance with the loan provisions to the date of reinstatement.

Plate 149

INCOME SETTLEMENT OPTIONS

Death proceeds payable under this Policy, or endowment or surrender proceeds, if any, may be paid under one of the following options instead of being paid as otherwise provided in this Policy. To elect an option, an Optional Settlement Agreement on the Company form must be completed and effective in accordance with its terms. If no such Agreement is in effect when the proceeds become payable, any one of the following options will be available to the payee of the proceeds, provided the proceeds are not less than $1000.

Option 1. Instalments for a Specified Period. Equal instalments for a specified number of years, not exceeding 30, as stated in the Option 1 table.

Option 2. Life Income. Equal monthly instalments during the payee's lifetime, as stated in the Option 2 table, with or without instalments certain as may be elected.

Option 3. Interest. Interest earnings during the payee's lifetime or for a shorter fixed period, as may be specified. Interest is payable at an effective rate of 2¾% a year ($27.50 annually, $13.66 semiannually, $6.81 quarterly, $2.26 monthly, for each $1000), plus whatever additional interest earnings the Company may apportion.

Option 4. Instalments of Specified Amount. Equal annual, semiannual, quarterly or monthly instalments in the amount specified until the proceeds and interest are exhausted. The total yearly amount payable may not be less than 5½% of the original proceeds. Unpaid balances remaining with the Company will be increased by interest at 2¾% a year, plus whatever additional interest earnings the Company may apportion.

Option 5. Life Income with Instalment Refund. Equal monthly instalments, as stated in the Option 5 table, payable until the total amount paid equals the proceeds, and as long thereafter as the payee lives.

Alternate Life Income. If Option 2, 5 or 6 is elected, in place of income payable according to the following tables, the payee may, at the time of commencement of such income, elect to receive a monthly life income which is equal to 104% of a monthly annuity based on the published rates of the Company then in use for new single premium annuities, first payment immediate.

Payment Provisions. If any instalment is less than $10, the Company may change the payment basis to equivalent quarterly, semiannual or annual payments. If the proceeds are less than $1000, the Company may discharge its obligation by paying the proceeds in one sum to the then payee of income named in the Optional Settlement Agreement.

Payments under Options 2, 5 and 6 shall be subject to satisfactory proof of age of the payees.

The first instalment under Options 1, 2, 4, 5 and 6 is due as of the date the proceeds become payable.

Instalments certain under Options 1, 2, 5 and 6 are computed on the basis of 2¾% interest compounded annually, except when the Alternate Life Income is elected. Instalments certain, after the first, will be increased by whatever additional interest earnings the Company may apportion, but if the Alternate Life Income is elected under Option 2, 5 or 6, the instalments certain will not be increased by additional interest earnings.

No endorsement of the Policy is required when an Optional Settlement Agreement is completed. When proceeds become payable under the terms of any Optional Settlement Agreement, the Policy and the Agreement shall be exchanged for an instrument evidencing the rights and benefits provided under that Agreement.

Option 1 — Instalments Certain for each $1000 of Proceeds

Number of Years	Annual Instalment	Monthly Instalment
1	$1000.00	$84.37
2	506.78	42.76
3	342.42	28.89
4	260.26	21.96
5	211.00	17.80
6	178.17	15.03
7	154.74	13.06
8	137.19	11.57
9	123.54	10.42
10	112.64	9.50
11	103.73	8.75
12	96.32	8.13
13	90.06	7.60
14	84.70	7.15
15	80.06	6.75
16	76.01	6.41
17	72.44	6.11
18	69.28	5.85
19	66.45	5.61
20	63.91	5.39
21	61.62	5.20
22	59.55	5.02
23	57.66	4.86
24	55.93	4.72
25	54.35	4.59
26	52.89	4.46
27	51.54	4.35
28	50.29	4.24
29	49.14	4.15
30	48.06	4.06

Semiannual instalments are 50.34% of the annual instalments. Quarterly instalments are 25.25% of the annual instalments.

Monthly Life Income for each $1000 of Proceeds

Male Payee Age Nearest Birthday	Option 2 — Without Instalments Certain	Option 2 — 60	Option 2 — 100	Option 2 — 120	Option 2 — 240	Option 5 — With Instalment Refund	Female Payee Age Nearest Birthday	Option 2 — Without Instalments Certain	Option 2 — 60	Option 2 — 100	Option 2 — 120	Option 2 — 240	Option 5 — With Instalment Refund
15 and under	$2.85	$2.84	$2.83	$2.82	$2.77	$2.70	15 and under	$2.77	$2.76	$2.75	$2.74	$2.69	$2.62
16	2.87	2.86	2.85	2.84	2.79	2.72	16	2.79	2.78	2.77	2.76	2.71	2.63
17	2.89	2.88	2.87	2.86	2.81	2.74	17	2.81	2.80	2.79	2.78	2.73	2.65
18	2.91	2.90	2.89	2.88	2.83	2.75	18	2.83	2.82	2.81	2.80	2.75	2.67
19	2.94	2.93	2.92	2.91	2.85	2.77	19	2.85	2.84	2.83	2.82	2.77	2.69
20	2.96	2.95	2.94	2.93	2.87	2.80	20	2.87	2.86	2.85	2.84	2.79	2.71
21	2.99	2.98	2.97	2.96	2.90	2.82	21	2.89	2.88	2.87	2.86	2.81	2.73
22	3.01	3.00	2.99	2.98	2.92	2.84	22	2.91	2.90	2.89	2.88	2.83	2.75
23	3.04	3.03	3.02	3.01	2.95	2.87	23	2.93	2.92	2.91	2.90	2.85	2.77
24	3.07	3.06	3.05	3.04	2.98	2.90	24	2.95	2.94	2.93	2.92	2.87	2.79
25	3.10	3.09	3.08	3.07	3.00	2.93	25	2.98	2.97	2.96	2.95	2.89	2.82
26	3.13	3.12	3.11	3.10	3.03	2.95	26	3.00	2.99	2.98	2.97	2.92	2.84
27	3.16	3.15	3.14	3.13	3.06	2.98	27	3.03	3.02	3.01	3.00	2.94	2.86
28	3.19	3.18	3.17	3.16	3.09	3.01	28	3.05	3.04	3.03	3.02	2.97	2.89
29	3.23	3.22	3.21	3.20	3.12	3.05	29	3.08	3.07	3.06	3.05	2.99	2.92
30	3.27	3.26	3.24	3.23	3.16	3.08	30	3.11	3.10	3.09	3.08	3.02	2.94
31	3.30	3.29	3.28	3.27	3.19	3.12	31	3.14	3.13	3.12	3.11	3.05	2.97
32	3.34	3.33	3.32	3.31	3.23	3.15	32	3.17	3.16	3.15	3.14	3.08	3.00
33	3.39	3.38	3.36	3.35	3.27	3.19	33	3.20	3.19	3.18	3.17	3.11	3.03
34	3.43	3.42	3.40	3.39	3.30	3.23	34	3.24	3.23	3.22	3.21	3.14	3.06
35	3.48	3.47	3.45	3.44	3.34	3.27	35	3.27	3.26	3.25	3.24	3.17	3.10
36	3.53	3.51	3.50	3.49	3.39	3.31	36	3.31	3.30	3.29	3.28	3.20	3.13
37	3.58	3.57	3.55	3.54	3.43	3.36	37	3.35	3.34	3.33	3.32	3.24	3.17
38	3.63	3.62	3.60	3.59	3.47	3.40	38	3.39	3.38	3.37	3.36	3.28	3.21
39	3.69	3.67	3.65	3.64	3.52	3.45	39	3.43	3.42	3.41	3.40	3.32	3.25
40	3.75	3.73	3.71	3.70	3.57	3.50	40	3.48	3.47	3.45	3.44	3.35	3.29
41	3.81	3.80	3.77	3.76	3.62	3.55	41	3.52	3.51	3.50	3.48	3.39	3.33
42	3.88	3.86	3.84	3.82	3.67	3.61	42	3.57	3.56	3.54	3.53	3.44	3.37
43	3.95	3.93	3.90	3.88	3.72	3.66	43	3.62	3.61	3.59	3.58	3.48	3.42
44	4.02	4.00	3.97	3.95	3.78	3.72	44	3.68	3.66	3.65	3.63	3.53	3.47
45	4.10	4.08	4.04	4.02	3.83	3.78	45	3.73	3.72	3.70	3.68	3.58	3.52
46	4.18	4.16	4.12	4.10	3.89	3.85	46	3.79	3.78	3.76	3.75	3.63	3.57
47	4.26	4.24	4.20	4.17	3.95	3.92	47	3.86	3.84	3.82	3.81	3.68	3.63
48	4.35	4.33	4.28	4.26	4.01	3.99	48	3.92	3.91	3.88	3.87	3.74	3.69
49	4.44	4.42	4.37	4.34	4.08	4.06	49	3.99	3.98	3.95	3.93	3.79	3.75
50	4.54	4.51	4.46	4.43	4.15	4.14	50	4.06	4.05	4.02	4.00	3.85	3.81
51	4.64	4.61	4.56	4.52	4.21	4.22	51	4.14	4.12	4.10	4.08	3.91	3.88
52	4.75	4.72	4.66	4.62	4.27	4.30	52	4.22	4.21	4.17	4.16	3.98	3.95
53	4.87	4.83	4.76	4.72	4.34	4.39	53	4.31	4.29	4.26	4.24	4.04	4.02
54	4.99	4.94	4.87	4.82	4.41	4.49	54	4.40	4.38	4.35	4.32	4.11	4.10
55	5.12	5.07	4.98	4.93	4.48	4.58	55	4.50	4.48	4.44	4.41	4.18	4.19
56	5.24	5.19	5.09	5.04	4.55	4.68	56	4.60	4.57	4.53	4.50	4.24	4.27
57	5.37	5.31	5.21	5.15	4.61	4.78	57	4.70	4.67	4.62	4.59	4.31	4.35
58	5.51	5.45	5.33	5.26	4.67	4.88	58	4.81	4.78	4.72	4.69	4.38	4.44
59	5.66	5.59	5.46	5.38	4.73	4.98	59	4.92	4.89	4.83	4.79	4.44	4.52
60	5.82	5.74	5.60	5.51	4.79	5.09	60	5.04	5.01	4.95	4.91	4.51	4.61
61	5.99	5.90	5.74	5.64	4.85	5.20	61	5.18	5.14	5.07	5.02	4.58	4.71
62	6.17	6.07	5.89	5.78	4.90	5.33	62	5.32	5.27	5.19	5.14	4.65	4.82
63	6.36	6.25	6.05	5.93	4.96	5.46	63	5.47	5.42	5.33	5.27	4.71	4.93
64	6.57	6.44	6.21	6.08	5.01	5.59	64	5.63	5.58	5.47	5.41	4.78	5.05
65	6.79	6.64	6.39	6.23	5.06	5.74	65	5.81	5.74	5.63	5.55	4.84	5.17
66	7.03	6.86	6.57	6.39	5.10	5.89	66	6.00	5.92	5.79	5.70	4.91	5.30
67	7.29	7.09	6.76	6.56	5.14	6.05	67	6.20	6.11	5.96	5.86	4.96	5.44
68	7.56	7.33	6.96	6.73	5.18	6.22	68	6.42	6.32	6.14	6.02	5.02	5.59
69	7.86	7.59	7.16	6.90	5.22	6.39	69	6.66	6.54	6.33	6.19	5.07	5.74
70	8.18	7.86	7.37	7.07	5.25	6.58	70	6.91	6.77	6.53	6.37	5.12	5.91
71	8.52	8.15	7.58	7.25	5.27	6.78	71	7.19	7.02	6.73	6.55	5.16	6.08
72	8.88	8.46	7.80	7.42	5.30	6.98	72	7.48	7.29	6.95	6.73	5.20	6.26
73	9.28	8.77	8.02	7.60	5.32	7.20	73	7.80	7.57	7.17	6.92	5.24	6.45
74	9.70	9.11	8.24	7.77	5.33	7.43	74	8.15	7.87	7.40	7.11	5.27	6.66
75	10.16	9.45	8.46	7.93	5.35	7.67	75	8.52	8.19	7.63	7.30	5.30	6.88
76	10.64	9.81	8.68	8.09	5.36	7.93	76	8.93	8.52	7.87	7.49	5.32	7.11
77	11.16	10.18	8.89	8.24	5.37	8.19	77	9.36	8.87	8.11	7.68	5.34	7.35
78	11.72	10.56	9.10	8.39	5.37	8.47	78	9.83	9.23	8.35	7.86	5.35	7.60
79	12.31	10.97	9.30	8.53	5.38	8.77	79	10.33	9.61	8.59	8.04	5.36	7.88
80	12.99	11.40	9.50	8.65	5.38	9.08	80	10.86	10.00	8.82	8.21	5.37	8.17
81	13.68	11.80	9.68	8.76	5.39	9.41	81	11.42	10.40	9.03	8.37	5.38	8.47
82	14.40	12.19	9.86	8.88	5.39	9.76	82	12.03	10.81	9.28	8.52	5.38	8.80
83	15.15	12.57	10.02	8.98	5.39	10.13	83	12.69	11.24	9.52	8.67	5.39	9.14
84	15.94	12.93	10.18	9.07	5.39	10.52	84	13.40	11.68	9.70	8.80	5.39	9.51
85 and over	16.75	13.32	10.32	9.15	5.39	10.93	85 and over	14.18	12.13	9.90	8.92	5.39	9.91

(P2-Ed. 66)

Page 8

ADDITIONAL INCOME SETTLEMENT OPTION

The following additional option will be available only for surrender proceeds, or endowment proceeds if any, and may be elected by the payee of such proceeds if the proceeds are not less than $1000.

Option 6. Joint Life Income for Insured and One Other Person with Two-Thirds to Survivor. (One Hundred and Twenty Months Certain). Based on the following table, a joint monthly income is paid to the Insured and the beneficiary designated at exercise of this option for 120 Months Certain, and as long afterwards as both of such payees are living. After the death of either payee, and following payment of any remaining income certain, monthly payments equal to two-thirds of such monthly income will be continued to the surviving payee for life. The "Alternate Life Income" and "Payment Provisions" paragraphs apply to this option.

MONTHLY INCOME FOR EACH $1000 OF PROCEEDS — OPTION 6

FEMALE PAYEE Age Nearest Birthday	MALE PAYEE — Age Nearest Birthday																				
	50	51	52	53	54	55	56	57	58	59	60	61	62	63	64	65	66	67	68	69	70
45	$3.84	$3.87	$3.90	$3.92	$3.95	$3.98	$4.00	$4.03	$4.05	$4.08	$4.11	$4.13	$4.16	$4.19	$4.21	$4.24	$4.27	$4.29	$4.32	$4.34	$4.37
46	3.88	3.91	3.93	3.96	3.99	4.02	4.04	4.07	4.10	4.12	4.15	4.18	4.21	4.23	4.26	4.29	4.32	4.34	4.37	4.39	4.42
47	3.92	3.94	3.97	4.00	4.03	4.06	4.09	4.11	4.14	4.17	4.20	4.23	4.26	4.28	4.31	4.34	4.37	4.40	4.42	4.45	4.47
48	3.95	3.98	4.01	4.04	4.07	4.10	4.13	4.16	4.19	4.22	4.25	4.28	4.31	4.34	4.37	4.39	4.42	4.45	4.48	4.51	4.53
49	3.99	4.02	4.05	4.09	4.12	4.15	4.18	4.21	4.24	4.27	4.30	4.33	4.36	4.39	4.42	4.45	4.48	4.51	4.54	4.57	4.59
50	4.03	4.07	4.10	4.13	4.16	4.19	4.22	4.26	4.29	4.32	4.35	4.38	4.41	4.45	4.48	4.51	4.54	4.57	4.60	4.63	4.66
51	4.07	4.11	4.14	4.17	4.21	4.24	4.27	4.31	4.34	4.37	4.40	4.44	4.47	4.50	4.54	4.57	4.60	4.63	4.66	4.69	4.72
52	4.11	4.15	4.19	4.22	4.25	4.29	4.32	4.36	4.39	4.43	4.46	4.49	4.53	4.56	4.60	4.63	4.66	4.70	4.73	4.76	4.79
53	4.15	4.19	4.23	4.27	4.30	4.34	4.37	4.41	4.45	4.48	4.52	4.55	4.59	4.62	4.66	4.70	4.73	4.76	4.80	4.83	4.86
54	4.18	4.23	4.27	4.31	4.35	4.39	4.43	4.46	4.50	4.54	4.58	4.61	4.65	4.69	4.73	4.76	4.80	4.83	4.87	4.90	4.94
55	4.22	4.27	4.31	4.35	4.40	4.44	4.48	4.52	4.56	4.60	4.64	4.68	4.72	4.75	4.79	4.83	4.87	4.91	4.94	4.98	5.01
56	4.26	4.31	4.35	4.40	4.44	4.49	4.53	4.57	4.61	4.65	4.69	4.73	4.77	4.81	4.85	4.89	4.93	4.97	5.01	5.05	5.08
57	4.30	4.35	4.39	4.44	4.49	4.54	4.58	4.62	4.66	4.71	4.75	4.79	4.83	4.88	4.92	4.96	5.00	5.04	5.08	5.12	5.16
58	4.34	4.39	4.44	4.49	4.54	4.59	4.63	4.67	4.72	4.76	4.81	4.85	4.90	4.94	4.98	5.03	5.07	5.11	5.16	5.20	5.23
59	4.38	4.43	4.48	4.53	4.58	4.64	4.68	4.73	4.77	4.82	4.87	4.91	4.96	5.01	5.05	5.10	5.14	5.19	5.23	5.27	5.31
60	4.42	4.48	4.53	4.58	4.63	4.69	4.73	4.78	4.83	4.88	4.93	4.98	5.02	5.07	5.12	5.17	5.22	5.26	5.31	5.35	5.40
61	4.47	4.52	4.57	4.63	4.68	4.74	4.79	4.84	4.89	4.94	4.99	5.04	5.09	5.14	5.19	5.24	5.29	5.34	5.39	5.44	5.48
62	4.51	4.56	4.62	4.68	4.73	4.79	4.84	4.89	4.95	5.00	5.05	5.11	5.16	5.21	5.27	5.32	5.37	5.42	5.47	5.52	5.57
63	4.55	4.61	4.67	4.72	4.78	4.84	4.90	4.95	5.01	5.06	5.12	5.17	5.23	5.29	5.34	5.40	5.45	5.51	5.56	5.61	5.66
64	4.59	4.65	4.71	4.77	4.83	4.90	4.95	5.01	5.07	5.12	5.18	5.24	5.30	5.36	5.42	5.48	5.54	5.59	5.65	5.70	5.76
65	4.64	4.70	4.76	4.82	4.89	4.95	5.01	5.07	5.13	5.19	5.25	5.31	5.37	5.43	5.50	5.56	5.62	5.68	5.74	5.80	5.85
66	4.68	4.74	4.81	4.87	4.94	5.01	5.07	5.13	5.19	5.25	5.32	5.38	5.44	5.51	5.58	5.64	5.70	5.77	5.83	5.89	5.95
67	4.73	4.79	4.86	4.92	4.99	5.06	5.12	5.19	5.25	5.32	5.38	5.45	5.52	5.59	5.66	5.72	5.79	5.86	5.92	5.99	6.05
68	4.77	4.83	4.90	4.97	5.04	5.11	5.18	5.24	5.31	5.38	5.45	5.52	5.59	5.66	5.73	5.81	5.88	5.95	6.02	6.09	6.15
69	4.81	4.88	4.95	5.02	5.09	5.17	5.23	5.30	5.37	5.44	5.52	5.59	5.66	5.74	5.81	5.89	5.96	6.04	6.11	6.18	6.25
70	4.85	4.92	5.00	5.07	5.14	5.22	5.29	5.36	5.43	5.51	5.58	5.66	5.74	5.82	5.89	5.97	6.05	6.13	6.21	6.28	6.36

The rate for any combination of ages not stated in the table or for two payees of the same sex will be furnished on request.

Inspection Report Form III

LIFE REPORT

Acct. No. _____

Dist., Agcy., or Br. _____

OFFICE

Date: _____

Pol. No. _____

INSURANCE HISTORY

NAME: _____

| Date | Acct. No. | Amt. or Type Coverage | Fam. or Indiv. |

Address:
Occupation on
Inq. & Employer:

Date of Birth: _____ A _____ Health App'd for $ _____ Per _____ ☐ Hospitalization ☐ Major Medical Exp.

	NO	YES	
1. ANY REASON FOR NOT RECOMMENDING APPLICANT?	☐	☐	Feature(s)

2. On what date was this inspection made? _____

IDENTITY 3—A. How many years has each of your sources known applicant?   A.
      B. How many days since you or your sources have seen applicant?   B.
           (If not within two weeks, explain fully.)

AGE 4. Is there any reason to doubt accuracy of birth date given?

FINANCES 5—A. What would you estimate net worth?   A. $
      B. What is annual earned income from work or business?   B. $
      C. Has applicant any income from investments, rentals, pension, etc.?   C.
           (If so, state source, amount.)

	NO	YES	
OCCUPATION 6—A. Does the occupation or job differ in name from that given in heading of this report?	A.		
B. Does applicant change jobs frequently?	B.		
C. Any part-time or off-season occupation? Does applicant plan work or travel in foreign countries?	C.		
D. Does applicant or employer sell or manufacture beer, wine or liquor?	D.		
DRIVING RECORD 7. Is applicant a fast, reckless, or careless driver?			IF YES, See Questions on Back.
AVIATION—8—A. Has applicant taken flying lessons, either as member of armed forces or as civilian, owned or piloted a plane, or flown in planes not operated by scheduled airlines?	A.		
SPORTS—AVOCATIONS B. Does applicant engage in hazardous sports or avocations (racing, skin or scuba diving, sky diving, mountain climbing, cave exploring, etc.)	B.		IF YES, See Questions on Back.
HEALTH 9—A. Is there anything unhealthy about appearance, such as being very thin or having excess weight?	A.		
B. Any deformity, amputation, blindness, deafness, or other defects?	B.		IF YES, See Questions on Back.
10. Do you learn of any illness, operation, or injury, past or present?			
11. Do you learn applicant was ever rejected for military service or discharged for medical reasons?			
12. Do you learn of any member of family (blood relation) having had heart trouble, cancer, diabetes, tuberculosis or mental trouble? *(If so, who and which disease.)*			
HABITS 13—A. Is applicant a steady, frequent drinker (daily, almost daily, several times a week)?	A.		
IF SO, { B. How often?	B.		
C. How many drinks does applicant take on these occasions?	C.		
D. What does applicant usually drink (beer, wine or whiskey)?	D.		
14. Does applicant now or has applicant in the past used beer, wine or whiskey to noticeable excess or intoxication?			IF YES, See Questions on Back.
ENVIRONMENT 15. Anything adverse about living conditions or neighborhood?			IF YES, See Questions on Back.
REPUTATION 16. Do any of following apply to this applicant: Heavy debts? Domestic trouble? Drug habit? Connection with illegal liquor? Irregular beneficiary?			
17. Is there any criticism of character or morals?			
IF FAMILY POLICY:	Answer only if Family Policy	{ ☐ NO ☐ YES	
18. Anything adverse on health or physical condition of other family members? (If so, cover in Remarks.)			

REMARKS: 19. COMMENT BELOW ON TOPICS LISTED AT LEFT; GIVE DETAILS OF "YES" OR INCOMPLETE ANSWERS.

A. BUSINESS:
Employer's name, line
and size of business?
Name of applicant's
job? How long so
employed? Cover any
indication of frequent
job changes or insta-
bility of employment.

B. ANSWER HANDY
GUIDE QUESTIONS,
IF APPLICABLE.

C. PERSONAL: Mar-
ried, single, or di-
vorced? Any children?
Type of associates. IF
WOMAN, name of
father or husband;
his occupation, worth
and income.

Signature of person making report_____

Form 1—5-68 U.S.A. ★★★★   **OVER—SEE ADDITIONAL QUESTIONS ON BACK**   LIFE REPORT

#19 Continued

DETAILS OF APPEARANCE:

20—A. How does applicant appear unhealthy (complexion, weight, or what)?_____B. Describe. (If overweight or underweight, give details.)

DETAILS OF HEALTH HISTORY ON APPLICANT:

21. Nature of illness, operation or injury?_____

22. Approximate date it occurred?_____

23—A. How long confined or "laid up"?_____

  B. Completely recovered? _____

24—A. Attended by Dr. (Name)_____

  Address _____

  B. Confined to hospital?_____If so, name and address:

  Name _____

  Address _____

25. Any effect on present health?_____Details:

DETAILS OF DRIVING RECORD:

26. When, where, and under what circumstances does applicant drive in a fast or reckless manner? (Open highway, congested areas, etc.—if known to drive considerably in excess of speed limit, cover.)

27. Any evidence of unsupervised racing?_____ Give details:

ANSWER THESE IF LEARNED IN INVESTIGATION

28. Any arrests?_____(Approximate dates)_____

29. Charges? _____

  If convicted, approximate dates?_____

30. Any accidents?_____If so, approximate dates and details:

31. License ever suspended or revoked?_____If so, cause, date and whether applicant drove without a license?

DETAILS OF ENVIRONMENT:

32. LIVING CONDITIONS:
A. Over-crowded, dirty, unsanitary, etc.?_____
        (If so, give details.)

  B. If apartment, dark or dirty halls, broken or littered stairs, etc.? (If so, give details.)_____

33. NEIGHBORHOOD: Deteriorating physically, poor sanitation, vice and crime, vandalism, etc.? (If so, give details.)_____

DETAILS OF DRINKING HABITS: Give these additional details to show drinking habits as definitely as possible:

34. Classify excessive drinking: ☐ Present ☐ Past

		How often? (Once a week, once a month, etc.)
A. Getting "drunk," stupefied, entirely out of control of usual faculties?	A._____	A._____
B. Loud, boisterous, or obviously under influence, although still in possession of most of faculties?	B._____	B._____
C. Mild excess, just getting "feeling good"; exhilaration or stimulation?	C._____	C._____

35. Do (did) these occasions last for an evening, a day, two days, a week, or for how long?

36. How long has (had) applicant been drinking to this extent?

37. WHEN WAS THE LAST OCCASION OF THIS SORT?

38. If applicant is an excessive drinker at present, does applicant drive a car during periods of excess?

39. Has applicant ever taken any "cure" for liquor habit? (If so, when? Any subsequent lapse?)

40. Tell how applicant drinks, if social or solitary, or if because of domestic or other trouble, how it affects applicant, whether ever arrested, and details to give clear picture of drinking habits; if habits have changed, tell how and how long since change; if reformed, what led to reformation (ill health, domestic trouble or what)?

INSPECTOR: Do not write in this space.
(Use Continuation of Report, Form 5166, for additional remarks.)

1-R—5-68

15-517 Rev. 1-50—LIFE INSURANCE ASSIGNMENT

FORM APPROVED BY
BANK MANAGEMENT COMMISSION
AMERICAN BANKERS ASSOCIATION

ASSIGNMENT OF LIFE INSURANCE POLICY AS COLLATERAL

A. *For Value Received* the undersigned hereby assign, transfer and set over to _____

_____ of _____

its successors and assigns (herein called the "Assignee"), Policy No. _____ issued by the

_____

(herein called the "Insurer") and any supplementary contracts issued in connection therewith (said policy and contracts being herein called the "Policy"), upon the life of _____

of _____, and all claims, options, privileges, rights, title and interest therein and thereunder (except as provided in Paragraph C hereof), subject to all the terms and conditions of the Policy and to all superior liens, if any, which the Insurer may have against the Policy. The undersigned by this instrument jointly and severally agree and the Assignee by the acceptance of this assignment agrees to the conditions and provisions herein set forth.

B.   It is expressly agreed that, without detracting from the generality of the foregoing, the following specific rights are included in this assignment and pass by virtue hereof:
1. The sole right to collect from the Insurer the net proceeds of the Policy when it becomes a claim by death or maturity;
2. The sole right to surrender the Policy and receive the surrender value thereof at any time provided by the terms of the Policy and at such other times as the Insurer may allow;
3. The sole right to obtain one or more loans or advances on the Policy, either from the Insurer or, at any time, from other persons, and to pledge or assign the Policy as security for such loans or advances;
4. The sole right to collect and receive all distributions or shares of surplus, dividend deposits or additions to the Policy now or hereafter made or apportioned thereto, and to exercise any and all options contained in the Policy with respect thereto; provided, that unless and until the Assignee shall notify the Insurer in writing to the contrary, the distributions or shares of surplus, dividend deposits and additions shall continue on the plan in force at the time of this assignment; and
5. The sole right to exercise all nonforfeiture rights permitted by the terms of the Policy or allowed by the Insurer and to receive all benefits and advantages derived therefrom.

C.   It is expressly agreed that the following specific rights, so long as the Policy has not been surrendered, are reserved and excluded from this assignment and do not pass by virtue hereof:
1. The right to collect from the Insurer any disability benefit payable in cash that does not reduce the amount of insurance;
2. The right to designate and change the beneficiary;
3. The right to elect any optional mode of settlement permitted by the Policy or allowed by the Insurer;
but the reservation of these rights shall in no way impair the right of the Assignee to surrender the Policy completely with all its incidents or impair any other right of the Assignee hereunder, and any designation or change of beneficiary or election of a mode of settlement shall be made subject to this assignment and to the rights of the Assignee hereunder.

D.   This assignment is made and the Policy is to be held as collateral security for any and all liabilities of the undersigned, or any of them, to the Assignee, either now existing or that may hereafter arise in the ordinary course of business between any of the undersigned and the Assignee (all of which liabilities secured or to become secured are herein called "Liabilities").

E.   The Assignee covenants and agrees with the undersigned as follows:
1. That any balance of sums received hereunder from the Insurer remaining after payment of the then existing Liabilities, matured or unmatured, shall be paid by the Assignee to the persons entitled thereto under the terms of the Policy had this assignment not been executed;
2. That the Assignee will not exercise either the right to surrender the Policy or (except for the purpose of paying premiums) the right to obtain policy loans from the Insurer, until there has been default in any of the Liabilities or a failure to pay any premium when due, nor until twenty days after the Assignee shall have mailed, by first-class mail, to the undersigned at the addresses last supplied in writing to the Assignee specifically referring to this assignment, notice of intention to exercise such right; and
3. That the Assignee will request forward without unreasonable delay to the Insurer the Policy for endorsement of any designation or change of beneficiary or any election of an optional mode of settlement.

F.   The Insurer is hereby authorized to recognize the Assignee's claims to rights hereunder without investigating the reason for any action taken by the Assignee, or the validity or the amount of the Liabilities or the existence of any default therein, or the giving of any notice under Paragraph E (2) above or otherwise, or the application to be made by the Assignee of any amounts to be paid to the Assignee. The sole signature of the Assignee shall be sufficient for the exercise of any rights under the Policy assigned hereby and the sole receipt of the Assignee for any sums received shall be a full discharge and release therefor to the Insurer. Checks for all or any part of the sums payable under the Policy and assigned herein, shall be drawn to the exclusive order of the Assignee if, when, and in such amounts as may be requested by the Assignee.

G.   The Assignee shall be under no obligation to pay any premium, or the principal of or interest on any loans or advances on the Policy whether or not obtained by the Assignee, or any other charges on the Policy, but any such amounts so paid by the Assignee from its own funds shall become a part of the Liabilities hereby secured, shall be due immediately, and shall draw interest at a rate fixed by the Assignee from time to time not exceeding 6% per annum.

H.   The exercise of any right, option, privilege or power given herein to the Assignee shall be at the option of the Assignee, but (except as restricted by Paragraph E (2) above) the Assignee may exercise any such right, option, privilege or power without notice to, or assent by, or affecting the liability of, or releasing any interest hereby assigned by the undersigned, or any of them.

I.   The Assignee may take or release other security, may release any party primarily or secondarily liable for any of the Liabilities, may grant extensions, renewals or indulgences with respect to the Liabilities, or may apply to the Liabilities in such order as the Assignee shall determine, the proceeds of the Policy hereby assigned or any amount received on account of the Policy by the exercise of any right permitted under this assignment, without resorting or regard to other security.

J.   In the event of any conflict between the provisions of this assignment and provisions of the note or other evidence of any Liability, with respect to the Policy or rights of collateral security therein, the provisions of this assignment shall prevail.

K.   Each of the undersigned declares that no proceedings in bankruptcy are pending against him and that his property is not subject to any assignment for the benefit of creditors.

Signed and sealed this _____ day of _____, 19_____

_____   _____ (L. S.)
            Witness   *Insured or Owner*

                                                  _____
                                                                Address

_____   _____ (L. S.)
            Witness   *Beneficiary*

                                                  _____
                                                                Address

INDIVIDUAL ACKNOWLEDGMENT

STATE OF_____
COUNTY OF_____ } ss:

On the_____day of_____, 19_____, before me personally came
_____, to me known to be the individual___ described in and who
executed the assignment on the reverse side hereof and acknowledged to me that ___he___ executed the same.

My commission expires_____

_____
Notary Public

CORPORATE ACKNOWLEDGMENT

STATE OF_____
COUNTY OF_____ } ss:

On the_____day of_____, 19_____, before me personally came_____
_____, who being by me duly sworn, did depose and say that he resides in_____
that he is the_____of_____, the corporation described in and which executed the assignment on the
reverse side hereof; that he knows the seal of said corporation; that the seal affixed to said assignment is such corporate seal; that it was so
affixed by order of the Board of Directors of said corporation, and that he signed his name thereto by like order.

My commission expires_____

_____
Notary Public

· · · ·

Duplicate received and filed at the home office of the Insurer in_____, this_____day of_____, 19_____

By_____
Authorized Officer

NOTE: When executed by a corporation, the corporate seal should be affixed and there should be attached to the assignment a certified copy of the resolution of the Board of Directors authorizing the signing officer to execute and deliver the assignment in the name and on behalf of the corporation.

RELEASE OF ASSIGNMENT

The debt which this assignment was given to secure having been paid in full, we hereby release all our right, title and interest in and to the policy thereby assigned to us.

This_____day of_____, 19 _____

By_____
By_____

STATE OF_____
COUNTY OF_____ } ss:

I, _____, Notary Public in and for said county and state, do hereby certify that
_____and_____
the persons whose names have been signed to the foregoing instrument, appeared before me this day in person and acknowledged that having
read the said instrument, they signed, sealed and delivered the same as their free and voluntary act and as the deed and pursuant to authority
conferred upon them by_____

Given under my hand and notarial seal this_____day of_____, 19_____

_____(SEAL)
Notary Public

My commission expires_____

Application for Hospital Expense Plan   V

Application to		Dist. Code	Staff Letter	Debit Number
THE **INSURANCE** **COMPANY**				

1 a. Kind of Policy?
"HOSPITAL EXPENSE" PLAN II

1 b. Deductible?
$ .... ☒ None

1 c. Maximum Daily Hospital Benefit?
$ 30,-

(PRINT First name, Middle initial and Last name)

2. Proposed Insured? JOHN J. DOE

3. Sex? ☒ Male ☐ Female

4. ☐ Single? ☒ Married? ☐ Widowed? ☐ Divorced? ☐ Separated?

5. Address for Communications? No. 15 .... Street BLANK .... City (NAME OF CITY) .... Zone 1 .... State STATE)   (NAME OF (NAME OF

6. Birth date? Mo. 6 Day 1 Year 1930 | **7. Age last birthday?** 35 | **8. Birthplace?** (NAME OF STATE)

9. Height? 5 ft. 10 in. | **10. Weight?** 175 lbs. | **11. Change in weight during past year?** ☒ None; Gain ......lbs.; Loss ......lbs. Explain change. | **12. All present occupations?** OFFICE CLERK

13. Is the spouse of the proposed Insured to be included for coverage? Yes ☒ No ☐ | If "Yes", questions 14-21 apply to such spouse and are to be completed. | **14. Name of Spouse?** (PRINT First name, Middle initial and Last name) MARY J. DOE

15. Birth date? Mo. 7 Day 10 Year 1930 | **16. Age last birthday?** 35 | **17. Birthplace?** (NAME OF STATE)

18. Height? 5 ft. 3 in. | **19. Weight?** 120 lbs. | **20. Change in weight during past year?** ☒ None; Gain ......lbs.; Loss ......lbs. Explain change. | **21. All present occupations?** HOUSE WIFE

22. Dependent children proposed for coverage? (PRINT First name, Middle initial and Last name)

		23. Relationship to applicant?	24. Birth date? Mo. Day Year	25. Age last birthday?	26. Am't paid in advance?
a.	NONE				$ NIL
b.					
c.					
d.					**27. Premium mode?** ☒ Ann. ☐ Semi-Ann.
e.					☐ Quar. ☐ Mo.

28. Has any person to be covered ever:
a. been in any hospital, clinic, dispensary, sanitarium, or other institution for observation, rest, diagnosis, treatment or advice? ☐ Yes ☒ No
b. had any surgical operations? ☐ Yes ☒ No
c. had any known mental or nervous disorder or abnormality? ☐ Yes ☒ No
d. had any known impairment of sight or hearing? ☐ Yes ☒ No
e. had any known deformity? ☐ Yes ☒ No

29. Has any person to be covered, within the past 5 years, ever:
a. been advised by any physician or other practitioner to enter any hospital, clinic, dispensary, sanitarium, or other institution for observation, rest, diagnosis, treatment or advice but has not done so? ☐ Yes ☒ No
b. been advised by any physician or other practitioner to have an operation which has not been performed? ☐ Yes ☒ No
c. had any known close association with anyone having tuberculosis? ☐ Yes ☒ No
d. made claim for or received benefits or a pension on account of sickness or injury? ☐ Yes ☒ No

30. Other than as disclosed in the answers to Questions 28 and 29, has any person to be covered, within the past 5 years, ever consulted or been attended by or been examined or had a check-up by any physician or other practitioner? ☐ Yes ☒ No

31. Does any person to be covered have any known indication of any physical disorder, disease, defect, or abnormality not disclosed in the answers to Questions 28, 29 and 30? ☐ Yes ☒ No

32. Does any person to be covered have:
a. any individual or group plan of Hospital, Surgical or Medical Expense insurance in this or any other company, or in any hospital plan or service organization? ☐ Yes ☒ No
b. any other individual or group Hospital, Surgical, Medical Expense, Income Protection or Life insurance application(s) or reinstatement(s) pending or being negotiated for in this or any other company, or in any hospital plan or service organization? ☐ Yes ☒ No

33. Has any person to be covered ever:
a. made application for a Life or Health insurance policy and been declined, postponed, rated up or had a policy issued for a smaller amount than applied for? ☐ Yes ☒ No
b. withdrawn an application for a Life or Health insurance policy, or had a policy modified, canceled, or its renewal or reinstatement refused? ☐ Yes ☒ No

34. Will any coverage be discontinued if this policy is issued? (If "Yes", give name of insurer, kind and amount of coverage and date on which this coverage will be terminated.) ☐ Yes ☒ No

35. With respect to each person to be covered, what are the full particulars of each and every part of Questions 28 through 33 to which the answer is "Yes"?

Name of Person and Question No.	Condition and Complications, or Other Reason (If operated, so state)	Onset Mo. Yr.	How long disabled?	Full Recovery Mo. Yr.	Names and Addresses of Physicians and Hospitals

I hereby declare that the above statements and answers to the above questions are complete and true and include full particulars of each and every part of Questions 28 through 34 to which the answer is "Yes". I agree that: (1) that this application and any medical examination, designated as Part 2 of this application, required by the Company on myself, my spouse or any dependent child now proposed for coverage, and any amendment of this application and any supplementary declaration thereto shall constitute the application for insurance and become a part of the policy hereby applied for; (2) that no agent has the authority to waive the answer to any question in the application, to waive a condition of any policy issued as a result of the application, or to waive any of the Company's rights or requirements with respect to the application, to modify the application, or to bind the Company by making any promise or representation or by giving or receiving any information; (3) that if the full initial premium according to the premium mode selected is paid at the time of signing this application and if this application and any medical examination(s) and any other information required by the Company are received at one of its Home Offices, and the applica-

tion is approved by the Company, then insurance under the policy, when issued, shall take effect in accordance with its terms as of the date of this application, except that if on request and permitted by the Company's rules the policy is to bear a date later than the date of this application, no insurance shall take effect until such later date and then only if all of the answers to the questions in the application are living and all of the answers to the questions in the application and in said medical examination(s) continue to be true and complete answers as of such later date. I further agree that unless insurance takes effect in accordance with the immediately preceding agreement "(3)" no insurance shall take effect unless: (a) a policy is issued by the Company and delivered to and accepted by me during the lifetime of the persons now proposed for coverage, and (b) the full initial premium thereon is paid, and (c) all of the answers to the questions in the application and in any medical examination(s) continue to be true and complete answers as of the date of delivery of the policy, in which case the insurance shall be deemed to have taken effect on the effective date stated in the policy.

Application made at (NAME OF CITY) State STATE)   (NAME OF

Date AUGUST 10 ...., 1965

Signature of Applicant X *John J. Doe*

I certify that I have truly and accurately recorded hereon the information supplied by the Applicant, and that I witnessed the above signature.

Signature of Writing Representative *Richard R. Roe*

SA 1—ED 9-62

Hospital Expense Policy VI

INSURED		POLICY NUMBER
PREMIUM PERIOD		POLICY DATE
INITIAL PREMIUM		EFFECTIVE DATE
AGENCY		

The _____ Insurance Company of America will pay the benefits stated in this Policy, in the event of sickness or injury as hereinafter defined, subject to all the provisions and exceptions contained herein, endorsed hereon, or attached hereto.

Notice of Ten Day Right to Examine Policy: Within ten days after its delivery to the Insured, this Policy may be surrendered by delivering or mailing it to an office of the Company or to the Agent through whom the Policy was purchased. Upon such surrender, the Company will return any premium paid.

Initial Period of Coverage: This Policy is issued in consideration of the Application, a copy of which is attached to and made a part of this Policy, and of the payment in advance of the Initial Premium, receipt of which is hereby acknowledged. Coverage shall begin as of the Effective Date which date shall be no later than the Policy Date. The Policy shall continue in force for the duration of the Premium Period, such period to commence with the Policy Date.

Policy Guaranteed Continuable to Age 65, Subject to Company's Right to Change Table of Premium Rates; Coverage on Children Ceases at Age 23 or Prior Marriage or Cessation of Dependency: The Insured, while less than 65 years of age, shall have the right to continue this Policy in force in accordance with and subject to its terms for successive premium periods, each of the same number of months as the Premium Period, by the payment of premiums as specified in the provision entitled "Premiums". The Company reserves the right to change at any time and from time to time the table of rates applicable to premiums thereafter becoming due under this Policy. In the event of a change in the table of rates, such change shall be made only on a class basis.

The Company promises and agrees that while this Policy continues in force, the Company shall not have the right to cancel this Policy or place any restrictive riders or endorsements hereon with respect to coverage already in force or to change the classification of any Covered Person on account of any physical impairment or on account of any claims incurred under this Policy.

The Insured, and the spouse of the Insured if a Covered Person, in each case shall cease to be a Covered Person at the end of the premium period in which such person attains his or her 65th birthday, and a child shall cease to be a Covered Person at the end of the premium period in which such child attains his or her 23rd birthday or, in the event of prior marriage or cessation of dependency, at the end of the premium period in which the earlier of such marriage or cessation of dependency occurs; provided, however, that subject to the provision entitled "Misstatement of Age", the acceptance by the Company of a premium with respect to any Covered Person after the date upon which such person would have ceased to be a Covered Person as provided herein, shall serve to continue such person as a Covered Person until the end of the period for which such premium is paid. If the Insured dies or ceases to be a Covered Person as provided herein, the spouse, if then a Covered Person, shall automatically become the Insured under this Policy, and all references in this Policy to the Insured shall thereafter mean such spouse, otherwise this Policy shall cease to be in force at the end of the period for which the premium has been paid. All persons shall cease to be Covered Persons under this Policy when it ceases to be in force.

The provisions, exceptions and schedules set forth by the Company on this and the following pages are a part of this Policy.

In witness whereof, THE _____ INSURANCE COMPANY _____ has caused this Policy to be executed on the Policy Date, which is the date of issue of this Policy.

832   Appendix A

GENERAL PROVISIONS

Premiums: Premiums subsequent to the Initial Premium are due periodically, each on the first day of the premium period to which the premium applies during the continuance of this Policy. Each premium shall be in accordance with the Company's applicable table of rates in effect on its due date using the original insuring age of each person who is then a Covered Person under this Policy. The original classification of each Covered Person shall also be used except that, on any due date, the classification of a woman with respect to whether she has a husband who is covered under this Policy, shall be determined as of such date.

Premiums shall be payable at the Home Office or to an authorized Agent of the Company but only in exchange for an official receipt signed by the President or Secretary of the Company and countersigned by the Agent receiving the premium. Upon written request and subject to the Company's approval, the premium period may be changed to one, three, six, or twelve months. Except as provided in the provision entitled "Grace Period", the payment of any premium shall not maintain this Policy in force with respect to any Covered Person beyond the end of the last day of the premium period to which such premium applies.

Premium Refund: If a Covered Person dies before the end of a period for which a premium has been paid with respect to such person, the Company, upon written proof of death, will refund that part of the premium paid with respect to such person for the period beyond the end of the policy month preceding that in which death occurs.

Covered Persons: Only the Insured, the spouse of the Insured, and dependent children more than 14 days but less than 18 years of age are eligible to become Covered Persons under this Policy.

Those eligible persons named for coverage in the application shall become Covered Persons hereunder from the Effective Date of the Policy. Any eligible person who is not a Covered Person on the Effective Date of this Policy shall become a Covered Person upon written acceptance by the Company of the Insured's written request and appropriate increase in the premium then and thereafter becoming due. Evidence of insurability satisfactory to the Company in accordance with its then current underwriting rules shall be required except in the case of a child of the Insured born after the Effective Date of this Policy for whom coverage is requested in writing and the required premium paid within the 45-day period following the date of birth.

Definitions: Wherever used in this Policy:

"Sickness" means only sickness or disease of a Covered Person contracted and commencing after such person becomes covered under this Policy except that with respect to a child of the Insured born after the Effective Date of this Policy, who becomes a Covered Person within the 45-day period following the date of birth, "sickness" means sickness or disease requiring care and treatment by a licensed physician after such child becomes covered under this Policy.

"Injury" means only accidental bodily injury of a Covered Person sustained after such person becomes covered under this Policy except that with respect to a child of the Insured born after the Effective Date of this Policy, who becomes a Covered Person within the 45-day period following the date of birth, "injury" means accidental bodily injury requiring care and treatment by a licensed physician after such child becomes covered under this Policy.

"Hospital" means only (1) an institution which is operated pursuant to law and is primarily engaged in providing on an inpatient basis for the medical care and treatment of sick and injured persons through medical, diagnostic and major surgical facilities, all of which facilities must be provided on its premises under the supervision of a staff of licensed physicians and with twenty-four hour a day nursing service, or (2) an institution not meeting all the requirements of (1) but which is accredited as a hospital by the Joint Commission on Accreditation of Hospitals. In no event shall the term "hospital" include a convalescent nursing home or any institution or part thereof which is used principally as a convalescent facility, rest facility, nursing facility or facility for the aged or for the care of drug addicts or alcoholics.

"Convalescent nursing home" means only an institution operated pursuant to law for the care and treatment of persons convalescing from sickness or injury, with organized facilities for medical supervision and twenty-four hour a day nursing service. In no event shall the term "convalescent nursing home" include a hospital or any institution or part thereof which is used principally as a rest facility, or facility for the aged or for the care of drug addicts or alcoholics.

"Surgical procedure" means only procedures which are listed in the Schedule of Surgical Procedures, and the following procedures: cutting, suturing, electrocauterization, removal of stone or foreign body by endoscopic means, or injection of sclerosing solution.

POLICY SCHEDULE

INSURED	JOHN J. DOE	HO 000 000	POLICY NUMBER
PREMIUM PERIOD	12 MONTHS	AUG 17, 1965	POLICY DATE
INITIAL PREMIUM	$313.15	AUG 17, 1965	EFFECTIVE DATE
AGENCY	R-NK 1		

HOSPITAL CONFINEMENT BENEFITS (PART 1)
   MAXIMUM DAILY BENEFIT   - $30.
   MAXIMUM DURATION   - 120 DAYS

ADDITIONAL HOSPITAL EXPENSE BENEFITS (PART 2)
   MAXIMUM BENEFIT   - $600.

PHYSICIANS' IN-HOSPITAL CALLS BENEFITS (PART 3)
   MAXIMUM DAILY BENEFIT   - $6.
   MAXIMUM BENEFIT   - $300.

CONVALESCENT NURSING HOME EXPENSE BENEFITS (PART 4)
   MAXIMUM DAILY BENEFIT   - $15.00
   MAXIMUM DURATION   - 60 DAYS

SURGICAL EXPENSE BENEFITS (PART 5)
   MAXIMUM SURGICAL BENEFIT   - $900.

RADIOTHERAPY EXPENSE BENEFITS (PART 6)
   MAXIMUM RADIOTHERAPY BENEFIT - $600.

ENDORSEMENT

THE   INSURANCE COMPANY   is a mutual life insurance company incorporated under
the laws of the State of   with principal office in the City of

SA 31673   ED 1-66

Printed in U. S. A.

CONVERSION PRIVILEGE

When a child ceases to be a Covered Person hereunder while this Policy continues in force, such person shall, subject to the conditions hereinafter stated, be entitled to have issued without evidence of insurability a policy of insurance (hereinafter referred to as the converted policy) by making written application therefor and paying the first quarterly premium, or at the option of such person a semi-annual or annual premium, to the Company not later than 31 days after such person ceases to be a Covered Person hereunder. Such premium shall be in accordance with the Company's table of premium rates in effect on the date of application for the converted policy, and applicable to the class of risk to which such person belongs and to such person's age and to the form and amount of insurance provided. The effective date of the converted policy shall be the date such person ceases to be a Covered Person hereunder. The converted policy shall be such as is provided for by the rules of the Company pertaining to insurance obtainable under this privilege and in effect when the application for such policy is made to the Company.

The Company shall not be required to issue a converted policy covering any person if such person is covered by another policy of hospital or surgical or medical expense insurance or hospital service or medical expense indemnity corporation subscriber contract providing similar benefits or is covered by or eligible to be covered by a group policy or contract providing similar benefits or is provided with similar benefits required by any statute or provided by any other plan or program (whether insured or not), which together with the converted policy, would result in overinsurance according to the Company's standards relating to converted policies.

ENDORSEMENT

Option to Continue Coverage of Dependent Child Incapacitated When Specified Age Limit for Children Is Attained:
If a dependent child is mentally or physically incapable of earning a living on the date the child's coverage under this Policy would terminate due to attainment of the specified age limit for children, and if within thirty-one days of such date the Company receives due proof of such incapacity, then, at the option of the Insured, the coverage of such child under this Policy may be continued while the Policy remains in force and such incapacity continues, by payment of premiums in accordance with the provision of this Policy entitled "Premiums".

THE   INSURANCE COMPANY

ESP 31476—ED 10-65

BENEFIT PROVISIONS

Services Furnished and Surgical Procedures Performed by Other Than a Licensed Physician: When a service or surgical procedure, for which this Policy provides a benefit if furnished or performed by a licensed physician, is furnished or performed by any other practitioner who is duly licensed and acting within the scope of his license, such benefit shall be payable to the same extent that it would have been payable had the service or surgical procedure been furnished or performed by a licensed physician.

Part 1. Hospital Confinement Benefits: If sickness or injury requires the confinement of a Covered Person as a resident inpatient in a hospital and the confinement commences while this Policy is in force with respect to such person, the Company will pay the amount of the charge made by the hospital for room, board and routine hospital services, including general nursing care, up to the Maximum Daily Benefit specified for this Part 1 in the Policy Schedule, for each day of such confinement but not to exceed, for all hospital confinements of such person due to any one accident or occurring during any one period of sickness, the Maximum Duration specified for this Part 1 in the Policy Schedule.

Part 2. Additional Hospital Expense Benefits: If benefits are payable under Part 1 of this Policy with respect to hospital confinement of a Covered Person as a resident inpatient, or if a Covered Person, while this Policy is in force with respect to such person, is confined in a hospital, but not as a resident inpatient, for a surgical procedure required by sickness or injury or for emergency treatment of an injury within 48 hours after such injury is sustained, the Company will pay the amount of the charges incurred:

(a) during such confinement as a resident inpatient;

(b) at the time such surgical procedure is performed;

(c) within 48 hours after the injury is sustained for which such emergency treatment is provided;

for local transportation by professional ambulance service to and from a local hospital, anesthetics and the administration thereof, use of operating room, and all other medical services received during such confinement except charges for room, board and routine hospital services including general nursing care and except charges for radiotherapy or services of physicians, nurses and physiotherapists, but the total amount payable under this Part 2 with respect to all confinements of a Covered Person due to any one accident or occurring during any one period of sickness shall not exceed the Maximum Benefit specified for this Part 2 in the Policy Schedule.

Part 3. Physicians' In-Hospital Calls Benefits: If charges are incurred for licensed physicians' calls made on a Covered Person during a hospital confinement of such person with respect to which benefits are payable under Part 1 of this Policy, the Company will pay the amount of such charges up to an amount equal to the number of days of such hospital confinement times the Maximum Daily Benefit specified for this Part 3 in the Policy Schedule, provided, however, that if during such hospital confinement a surgical procedure is performed for which benefits are payable under Part 5 of this Policy, the number of days of hospital confinement within the four week period immediately following the performance of such surgical procedure and charges for physicians' calls made during hospital confinement within such four week period shall not be included in the determination of the amount of benefits payable under this Part 3 unless the Insured elects to

have such days and charges included in lieu of receiving benefits under Part 5 with respect to such surgical procedure. The total amount payable for all physicians' calls made on a Covered Person during all hospital confinements due to any one accident or occurring during any one period of sickness shall not exceed the Maximum Benefit specified for this Part 3 in the Policy Schedule.

Benefits under this Part 3 shall not be payable for any charge for performance of a surgical procedure or for any charge for which benefits are payable under Part 6 of this Policy.

Part 4. Convalescent Nursing Home Expense Benefits: If sickness or injury requires the confinement of a Covered Person in a convalescent nursing home commencing while this Policy is in force with respect to such person and within 7 days following confinement of such person as a resident inpatient in a hospital for a continuous period of at least 5 days, the Company will pay the amount of the charge made by the convalescent nursing home for room, board and routine convalescent nursing home services, including general nursing care, up to the Maximum Daily Benefit specified for this Part 4 in the Policy Schedule, for each day of such confinement but not to exceed, for all convalescent nursing home confinements of such person due to any one accident or occurring during any one period of sickness, the Maximum Duration specified for this Part 4 in the Policy Schedule.

Part 5. Surgical Expense Benefits: If sickness or injury requires a Covered Person to undergo one or more surgical procedures performed by a licensed physician while this Policy is in force with respect to such person or while benefits are payable under Part 1 with respect to such person, the Company will pay the amount of the charges incurred for such procedure or procedures, other than any procedure performed for the administration of radiotherapy, not to exceed a maximum amount determined in accordance with whichever one of the following paragraphs (a) through (d) is applicable, provided, however, that the total amount payable under this Part 5 with respect to all surgical procedures performed on a Covered Person due to any one accident or during any one period of sickness shall not, in any event, exceed twice the amount of the Maximum Surgical Benefit specified in the Policy Schedule.

(a) The maximum amount payable when one surgical procedure is performed will be the Maximum Payment applicable to such procedure according to the Schedule of Surgical Procedures.

(b) The maximum amount payable when a combination of surgical procedures is performed for which combination the Schedule of Surgical Procedures provides a Maximum Payment, will be the maximum so provided.

(c) The maximum amount payable when, at one operative session, two or more surgical procedures are performed in the same operative field or through the same incision, will be the Maximum Payment applicable, according to the Schedule of Surgical Procedures, to the procedure performed for which such Schedule provides the largest Maximum Payment. For the purposes of this paragraph (c), a combination of procedures for which combination the Schedule of Surgical Procedures provides a Maximum Payment will be considered as one procedure and two or more procedures performed through the same natural body orifice will be considered to have been performed in the same operative field.

(Continued on following page)

BENEFIT PROVISIONS (Continued)

(d) The maximum amount payable when, at one operative session, two or more surgical procedures are performed, not all in the same operative field and not all through the same incision, will be determined as follows: The Company will determine, with respect to each operative field, the maximum amount that would have been applicable in accordance with paragraph (a), (b) or (c) above for the surgical procedure or procedures performed in such operative field had there been no surgical procedure performed in any other operative field, and, for the purposes of this paragraph (d), the maximum amount payable will be the largest of the maximums so determined plus 50% of each other maximum so determined. For the purposes of this paragraph (d), two or more procedures performed through the same natural body orifice will be considered to have been performed in the same operative field.

Part 6. Radiotherapy Expense Benefits: If sickness or injury requires a Covered Person to undergo, other than for diagnostic purposes, radiotherapy which is administered while this Policy is in force with respect to such person or while benefits are payable under Part 1 of this Policy with respect to such person, the Company will pay, in accordance with the Schedule of Radiotherapy, the amount of the charges incurred for such radiotherapy not to exceed the applicable Maximum Payment specified in such Schedule, provided, however, that the total amount payable under this Part 6 for all radiotherapy administered to a Covered Person due to any one accident or during any one period of sickness shall not exceed the Maximum Radiotherapy Benefit specified in the Policy Schedule.

Part 7. Hospital Confinements, Convalescent Nursing Home Confinements, Surgical Procedures or Radiotherapy During One Period of Sickness: For the purposes of Parts 1 through 6 of this Policy, two or more hospital confinements of a Covered Person due to sickness, two or more convalescent nursing home confinements of a Covered Person due to sickness, two or more surgical procedures performed on a Covered Person due to sickness and all radiotherapy administered to a Covered Person due to sickness shall be considered as occurring, being performed, or being administered during one period of sickness unless (a) due to the same or related sickness and separated by a resumption of full normal activities for a continuous period of at least 6 full months, or unless (b) due to entirely unrelated sicknesses and separated by a resumption of full normal activities.

EXCEPTIONS

This Policy does not provide benefits with respect to:

1. Sickness or injury covered by any workmen's compensation act or occupational disease law;

2. Sickness or injury resulting from war or any act of war. As used herein, "war" means declared or undeclared war and includes resistance to armed aggression;

3. Hospital confinement or convalescent nursing home confinement in, or services or supplies provided in, any facility contracted for or operated by the United States Government for the treatment of members or ex-members of the armed forces;

4. Hospital confinement or convalescent nursing home confinement of or services or supplies provided for a Covered Person within 6 months after such person becomes covered under this Policy if such confinements, services or supplies are (a) for repair of inguinal, femoral or umbilical hernia, (b) for removal or treatment of hemorrhoids, (c) for removal of tonsils or adenoids, or both, (d) caused or contributed to by any condition of the female generative organs, or (e) for removal of appendix concurrent with an operation on the female generative organs performed through the same incision;

5. Hospital confinements, convalescent nursing home confinements, services or supplies to the extent to which they are provided for under any national or state government program or law that is not restricted to the employees of such government or to such employees and their dependents;

6. Physicians' services in connection with:

   (a) Mouth conditions due to periodontal or periapical disease, or involving any of the teeth, their surrounding tissue or structure, the alveolar process or the gingival tissue; unless for the treatment or removal of malignant tumors with respect to which benefits would, except for this subparagraph (a) of Exception 6, be payable under this Policy;

   (b) Weak, strained or flat feet, any instability or imbalance of the foot, or any metatarsalgia or bunion; unless for a surgical procedure with respect to which benefits would, except for this subparagraph (b) of Exception 6, be payable under this Policy;

   (c) Corns, calluses or toenails; unless for the following services with respect to which benefits would, except for this subparagraph (c) of Exception 6, be payable under this Policy: (i) the partial or complete removal of nail roots, or (ii) services prescribed by a licensed physician who is treating the patient for a metabolic or peripheral-vascular disease;

7. Hospital confinement or convalescent nursing home confinement of or services or supplies provided for a Covered Person during pregnancy or within 6 months after termination of pregnancy, if such confinements, services or supplies are caused or contributed to by pregnancy, resulting childbirth, abortion or miscarriage, but if such pregnancy commences more than 30 days after such person becomes covered under this Policy, this Exception 7 shall not apply to such confinements, services or supplies which are directly related to (i) a surgical procedure which is performed for extrauterine pregnancy, (ii) an intra-abdominal surgical procedure which is performed subsequent to the birth of a child provided such procedure is required because of complications of pregnancy occurring at the time of such birth, or (iii) pernicious vomiting of pregnancy (hyperemesis gravidarum) or toxemia with convulsions (eclampsia of pregnancy);

8. Hospital confinement or convalescent nursing home confinement of or services or supplies provided for a Covered Person (a) while such person is on full-time active duty (other than active duty for training purposes only, for two months or less) as a member of any military, naval, or air force of any country, combination of countries, or international organization, or (b) as a result of sickness contracted or injury sustained by such person while on such full-time active duty. The Company will refund upon written notice all premiums paid with respect to such person for any such period of full-time active duty.

Page 6 (BH—65)

SCHEDULE OF SURGICAL PROCEDURES

This Schedule shows the Maximum Payments applicable to the respective surgical procedures specified below when the Maximum Surgical Benefit specified in the Policy Schedule is $600 or $900. For any surgical procedure neither specified nor expressly excluded, the Company will objectively determine a consistent Maximum Payment not to exceed the Maximum Surgical Benefit specified in the Policy Schedule.

	Maximum Payment when Maximum Surgical Benefit is: $600	$900
CARDIOVASCULAR SYSTEM		
Pericardiectomy	$400	$600
Thromboendarterectomy of abdominal aorta	600	900
Valvulotomy or commissurotomy		
Aortic, pulmonic or tricuspid	600	900
Mitral	480	720
Varicose veins		
*Injection of sclerosing solution into vein(s) of leg	6	9
Cutting operation with or without injection		
Ligation and division and complete stripping		
long or short saphenous veins,		
unilateral	120	180
bilateral	200	300
long and short saphenous veins		
unilateral	160	240
bilateral	240	360
Ligation and division of short saphenous vein at sapheno-popliteal junction	50	75
DIGESTIVE SYSTEM		
Adenoidectomy	40	60
*Anal papillectomy, one or more	20	30
Appendectomy	160	240
Appendicial abscess, transabdominal incision and drainage	120	180
*Aspiration biopsy of liver	20	30
Cholecystectomy	240	360
With open exploration of common duct	280	420
Cholecystotomy	200	300
Colectomy		
Partial resection of large intestine in two stages including first stage colostomy or cecostomy	400	600
Enterectomy		
Resection of small intestine with anastomosis or enterostomy	280	420
Excision of submaxillary gland, tumor, or both	160	240
Fissurectomy with or without sphincterotomy	80	120
Fistulectomy or fistulotomy		
subcutaneous	40	60
submuscular	160	240
Gastrectomy with or without vagotomy		
Subtotal or hemi-gastrectomy	320	480
Total gastrectomy	400	600

	Maximum Payment when Maximum Surgical Benefit is: $600	$900
Gastroduodenostomy or gastrojejunostomy	$240	$360
Gastroscopy or esophagoscopy		
Diagnostic, with or without biopsy	60	90
Gastrotomy or gastrorrhaphy	200	300
Hemorrhoids		
*Excision of external hemorrhoidal tabs	20	30
*Incision of external thrombotic hemorrhoid	12	18
*Injection of sclerosing solution	8	12
Hemorrhoidectomy		
External, complete	80	120
External and internal, or internal	120	180
With submuscular fistulotomy or fistulectomy	160	240
With fissurectomy	120	180
Hernioplasty, herniorrhaphy, or herniotomy		
Epigastric, femoral, inguinal	140	210
Inguinal with orchiectomy or excision of hydrocele	160	240
Umbilical, under age 5 years	120	180
Umbilical, age 5 years or over	140	210
Incision and drainage of ischiorectal abscess	40	60
Laparotomy, exploratory	160	240
Marsupialization of cyst or abscess of liver	280	420
Pancreatectomy, total	560	840
Proctectomy complete, combined abdominoperineal, one or two stages	400	600
Proctosigmoidoscopy		
Initial	12	18
Subsequent	8	12
With biopsy	20	30
With removal of polyp	28	42
With removal of polyps	36	54
Tonsillectomy, with or without adenoidectomy		
Under age 18 years	60	90
Age 18 years or over	80	120
EAR AND EYE		
Cataract		
Discission: needling of lens		
Initial	80	120
Subsequent	40	60
Extraction of lens, intracapsular, extracapsular, or linear	320	480
Enucleation of eyeball	160	240

*When this procedure is performed during resident inpatient hospital confinement, the applicable Maximum Payment is increased by $8 when the Maximum Surgical Benefit is $600 and by $12 when the Maximum Surgical Benefit is $900.

(Continued on following page)

SCHEDULE OF SURGICAL PROCEDURES (Continued)

	Maximum Payment when Maximum Surgical Benefit is:			Maximum Payment when Maximum Surgical Benefit is:	
	$600	$900		$600	$900
Excision of pterygium	$100	$150	Excision of benign lesion of skin, subcutaneous tissue or mucous membrane, lesion diameter:		
Mastoidectomy, simple	200	300	¼ inch or less	$16	$24
*Myringotomy, tympanotomy, plicotomy	12	18	over ¼ but not over ½ inch	20	30
Reattachment of retina			Excision of malignant lesion of skin or mucous membrane of:		
Electrocoagulation, scleral resection, buckling or partial tubing	400	600	Trunk, arms or legs, lesion diameter:		
Light coagulation of retinal breaks	160	240	¼ inch or less	24	36
*Removal of foreign body embedded in conjunctiva	8	12	over ¼ but not over ½ inch	32	48
Stapes mobilization	280	420	Face, scalp, ears, neck, hands, feet, genitalia, lesion diameter:		
			¼ inch or less	40	60
ENDOCRINE, HEMIC, LYMPHATIC SYSTEMS			over ¼ but not over ½ inch	60	90
Biopsy or excision of lymph node			Eyelids, lips, mucous membrane, lesion diameter:		
Anterior scalene	60	90	¼ inch or less	60	90
Other	20	30	over ¼ but not over ½ inch	80	120
Excision of cyst or adenoma of thyroid	160	240	*Incision and drainage of sebaceous cysts, furuncle, carbuncle or any		
Thyroidectomy			other subcutaneous abscess	8	12
For malignancy with radical neck dissection	400	600	Suturing of wounds (all wounds combined)		
Total or complete	280	420	2½ inches or less	16	24
Total thyroid lobectomy	200	300	over 2½ but not over 5 inches	26	39
FEMALE GENITAL SYSTEM			**MALE GENITAL SYSTEM**		
Amputation of cervix	80	120	Circumcision, other than clamp, or dorsal slit	40	60
Biopsy of cervix or endometrium	12	18	Epididymectomy or excision of hydrocele or varicocele	120	180
Dilation and curettage of uterus			Orchiectomy, unilateral	80	120
under general anesthesia	60	90	Orchiectomy, bilateral	100	150
with conization	80	120	Prostatectomy (one or two stages, complete procedure)	320	480
Excision or cautery destruction of Bartholin's gland or cyst	60	90			
Hysterectomy			**MUSCULOSKELETAL SYSTEM**		
Radical for cancer, including regional lymph nodes	400	600	AMPUTATIONS, complete procedure		
Subtotal or supracervical	220	330	Ankle, with skin-plasty and resection of nerves	200	300
Total (corpus and cervix)	240	360	Arm through humerus or through radius and ulna	160	240
Repair of cystocele with or without urethrocele	140	210	Digit, with or without split or Wolff graft, skin-plasty, tenodesis, or defini-		
Repair of cystocele, rectocele and perineoplasty, with or without repair of urethrocele	200	300	tive resection volar digital nerves		
Repair of rectocele	120	180	Finger or thumb	60	90
Salpingectomy, oophorectomy or salpingo-oophorectomy, complete or partial, unilateral or bilateral	180	270	Toe	40	60
			Disarticulation of hip	320	480
INTEGUMENTARY SYSTEM			Disarticulation of knee	160	240
Breast			Disarticulation of shoulder	300	450
Mastotomy with exploration or drainage of abscess, deep	40	60	Foot, midtarsal or transmetatarsal	140	210
Partial mastectomy, or excision of cyst or tumor			Hand, midcarpal or transmetacarpal	160	240
Unilateral	60	90	Leg through tibia and fibula	200	300
Bilateral	100	150	Thigh through femur, including supracondylar	240	360
Radical mastectomy, including breast, pectoral muscles and axillary lymph nodes	280	420	BONES		
Simple mastectomy, complete	120	180	Excision of bone cyst or chondroma:		
			Humerus, radius, ulna, pelvis, femur, tibia, or fibula	200	300
			Carpal or tarsal bones	100	150

*When this procedure is performed during resident inpatient hospital confinement, the applicable Maximum Payment is increased by $8 when the Maximum Surgical Benefit is $600 and by $12 when the Maximum Surgical Benefit is $900.

(Continued on following page)

SCHEDULE OF SURGICAL PROCEDURES (Continued)

	Maximum Payment when Maximum Surgical Benefit is: $600	$900
Fractures, closed reduction of		
Ankle		
bimalleolar (including Pott's), simple	$100	$150
trimalleolar, simple	120	180
Astragalus or os calcis, simple	80	120
Carpal, one or more, simple	40	60
Clavicle, simple	60	90
Femur		
distal end, condyle(s), or both, simple	140	210
intertrochanteric, simple, with fixation or traction	180	270
neck, simple, with fixation or traction	200	300
shaft, including supracondylar, simple	160	240
Fibula		
distal end, malleolus, or both	60	90
shaft, simple	60	90
with tibia, shafts, simple	120	180
Humerus		
medial or lateral condyle	80	120
shaft, simple	100	150
surgical neck, simple	120	180
*Malar, simple or compound	20	30
Maxilla or mandible, simple or compound, with wiring of teeth	120	180
Metacarpal, simple or compound		
one	40	60
more than one	50	75
Metatarsal, simple	40	60
*Nasal, simple or compound	20	30
Patella, simple	48	72
Pelvis, simple	40	60
Phalanx or phalanges, simple, one finger, thumb, or toe	20	30
Radius		
head or distal end, simple	60	90
shaft, with or without ulna, simple	80	120
Ribs, one or more, simple	26	39
Scapula or sternum, simple	48	72
Tarsal (other than astragalus or os calcis) one or more, simple	40	60
Tibia		
distal end, malleolus, simple	60	90
shaft, or proximal end, with or without condyle(s), or intercondylar spines, simple	100	150
with fibula, shafts, simple	120	180
Ulna, shaft, with or without radius, simple	80	120
Vertebral body (other than sacrum), one or more	120	180
Vertebral processes, one or more	32	48
Spinal fusion, two or more segments	400	600
JOINTS		
Arthrectomy		
Excision of intervertebral disc, with spinal fusion	480	720

	Maximum Payment when Maximum Surgical Benefit is: $600	$900
Excision of semilunar cartilage, knee joint	$200	$300
Temporomandibular joint	300	450
Arthrotomy or capsulotomy with exploration, drainage, or removal of loose body		
Finger, thumb, or great toe	60	90
Hip	280	420
Shoulder, elbow, knee or ankle	200	300
Toe, other than great toe	40	60
Dislocations, closed reduction of		
Ankle or tarsal, simple	40	60
Clavicle, simple, with general anesthesia	40	60
*Wrist, elbow or shoulder (humerus), simple	20	30
*Finger, one or more joints, simple	12	18
Hip (femur) or knee (femoral-tibial joint), simple	80	120
*Metacarpal, one bone, simple	12	18
Metatarsal, one bone, simple	28	42
*Patella, simple	12	18
*Temporomandibular, simple	20	30
*Thumb, simple	16	24
*Toe, one or more joints, simple	8	12
Vertebra, simple, using traction and general anesthesia	220	330
Suture or repair of joint capsule for recurrent shoulder dislocation	280	420
TENDONS, TENDON SHEATHS AND FASCIA		
Excision		
Baker's cyst (synovial cyst of popliteal space)	120	180
Lesion of tendon or fibrous sheath, or ganglion		
finger, thumb, or toe	40	60
in other locations	60	90
Repair or suture		
Extensor tendon, single		
forearm or leg	72	108
hand or foot, distal to wrist or ankle	48	72
Flexor tendon, single, finger, hand, or forearm	120	180
Transfer, transplant, or free graft of tendon, single		
Elbow to shoulder, knee to hip	200	300
Distal to elbow, distal to knee	160	240
NERVOUS SYSTEM		
Craniectomy, suboccipital, for brain tumor	600	900
Craniectomy, suboccipital, for section of cranial nerves	500	750
Craniotomy for drainage of brain abscess	300	450

*When this procedure is performed during resident inpatient hospital confinement, the applicable Maximum Payment is increased by $8 when the Maximum Surgical Benefit is $600 and by $12 when the Maximum Surgical Benefit is $900.

(Continued on following page)

SCHEDULE OF SURGICAL PROCEDURES (Continued)

	Maximum Payment when Maximum Surgical Benefit is: $600	$900		Maximum Payment when Maximum Surgical Benefit is: $600	$900
Laminectomy for removal of intervertebral discs..................	$360	$540	Bronchoscopy with removal of foreign body or tumor....................	$100	$150
Skull, burr holes, one or more, for ventriculography..............	80	120	Nasal polypectomy *Single polyp......................	12	18
Splanchnicectomy, unilateral..........	260	390	Multiple polyps, unilateral or bilateral, one or more stages.....	28	42
Splanchnicectomy, bilateral..........	320	480	Pneumonectomy or lobectomy........	400	600
Sympathectomy, cervical, unilateral....	240	360	Tracheotomy......................	80	120
Sympathectomy, lumbar, unilateral.....	220	330			
Sympathectomy, lumbar, bilateral......	300	450	**URINARY SYSTEM**		
			Cystolithotomy....................	200	300
RESPIRATORY SYSTEM			Cystoscopy, while resident hospital inpatient:		
Antrotomy			Diagnostic.....................	32	48
Intranasal, unilateral..............	60	90	With ureteral catheterization......	60	90
Intranasal, bilateral................	100	150	Cystoscopy with biopsy..............	40	60
Radical (Caldwell-Luc), unilateral....	200	300	Excision or fulguration of		
Radical (Caldwell-Luc), bilateral.....	260	390	urethral caruncle..................	28	42
Bronchoscopy			Pyelotomy, pyelolithotomy,		
Initial...........................	60	90	pelviolithotomy..................	280	420
Subsequent.......................	40	60	Removal of kidney.................	320	480
With biopsy.......................	80	120			

*When this procedure is performed during resident inpatient hospital confinement, the applicable Maximum Payment is increased by $8 when the Maximum Surgical Benefit is $600 and by $12 when the Maximum Surgical Benefit is $900.

SCHEDULE OF RADIOTHERAPY

This Schedule shows the Maximum Payments applicable to the respective radiotherapies, including consultation, dosage calculation, materials and the preparation thereof, and the use of facilities. For any radiotherapy neither specified nor expressly excluded, the Company will objectively determine a consistent Maximum Payment not to exceed the Maximum Radiotherapy Benefit specified in the Policy Schedule.

	Maximum Payment			Maximum Payment
TELERADIOTHERAPY		RADIOISOTOPE THERAPY		
X-ray—1000 KVP and higher, radium, cobalt, betatron —per treatment..........................	$18	(NON-SEALED SOURCES)—administered internally, interstitially or intracavitarily. The maximum		
X-ray—less than 1000 KVP, telecesium —per treatment.........................	12	stated is for all charges incurred during any one series of treatments for the condition shown.		
RADIUM AND RADIOISOTOPE THERAPY (SEALED SOURCES)		Thyroid cancer............................		$300
Intracavitary or interstitial application of radium or radioisotope		Prostatic cancer...........................		360
—per treatment........................	150	Thyroid ablation for cardiac disease..........		270
Application of radium or radioisotope		Polycythemia vera.........................		120
plaque or mold		Chronic leukemia.........................		120
—per treatment........................	18	Metastatic cancer to bone..................		210
		Ascites or pleural effusion, or both..........		300
		Hyperthyroidism..........................		180

Printed in U. S. A. by

A COPY OF THE APPLICATION UPON WHICH THIS POLICY IS ISSUED
HAS BEEN ATTACHED TO AND MADE A PART OF THIS POLICY.

ADDITIONAL PROVISIONS

Entire Contract; Changes: This Policy, including the endorsements and the attached papers, if any, constitutes the entire contract of insurance. No change in this Policy shall be valid until approved by an executive officer of the Company and unless such approval be endorsed hereon or attached hereto. No Agent has authority to change this Policy or to waive any of its provisions.

Incontestable: (a) After this Policy has been in force with respect to a Covered Person for a period of two years during the lifetime of such person (excluding any period during which such person is disabled) it shall be incontestable as to the statements concerning such person, contained in the application for coverage of such person.

(b) No claim for loss incurred with respect to any person after two years from the date such person becomes covered under this Policy shall be reduced or denied on the ground that a disease or physical condition not excluded from coverage by name or specific description effective on the date of loss had existed prior to the effective date of coverage of such person.

Grace Period: A grace period of thirty-one days will be granted for the payment of each premium falling due after the initial premium, during which grace period the Policy shall continue in force.

Reinstatement: If any premium after the initial premium be not paid within the time granted the Insured for payment, a subsequent acceptance of premium by the Company or by any Agent duly authorized by the Company to accept such premium, without requiring in connection therewith an application for reinstatement, shall reinstate the Policy; provided, however, that if the Company or such Agent requires an application for reinstatement and issues a conditional receipt for the premium tendered, the Policy will be reinstated upon approval of such application by the Company or, lacking such approval, upon the forty-fifth day following the date of such conditional receipt unless the Company has previously notified the Insured in writing of its disapproval of such application. The reinstated Policy shall cover only loss resulting from such injury as may be sustained after the date of reinstatement and loss due to such sickness as may begin more than ten days after such date. In all other respects the Insured and the Company shall have the same rights thereunder as they had under the Policy immediately before the due date of the defaulted premium, subject to any provisions endorsed hereon or attached hereto in connection with the reinstatement.

Notice of Claim: Written notice of claim must be given to the Company within twenty days after the occurrence or commencement of any loss covered by the Policy, or as soon thereafter as is reasonably possible. Notice given by or on behalf of the Insured to the Company at the Home Office, or to any authorized Agent of the Company, with information sufficient to identify the Insured, shall be deemed notice to the Company.

Claim Forms: The Company, upon receipt of a notice of claim, will furnish to the claimant such forms as are usually furnished by it for filing proofs of loss. If such forms are not furnished within fifteen days after the giving of such notice, the claimant shall be deemed to have complied with the requirement of this Policy as to proof of loss upon submitting, within the time fixed in the Policy for filing proofs of loss, written proof covering the occurrence, the character and the extent of the loss for which claim is made.

Proofs of Loss: Written proof of loss must be furnished to the Company at its said office within ninety days after the termination of the period for which the Company is liable. Failure to furnish such proof within the time required shall not invalidate nor reduce any claim if it was not reasonably possible to give proof within such time, provided such proof is furnished as soon as reasonably possible and in no event, except in the absence of legal capacity, later than one year from the time proof is otherwise required.

Time of Payment of Claims: Benefits payable under this Policy will be paid immediately upon receipt of due written proof of such loss.

Payment of Claims: All benefits of this Policy are payable to the Insured. Any accrued benefit unpaid at the Insured's death will be paid to the estate of the Insured.

If any benefit of this Policy shall be payable to the estate of the Insured, or to an Insured who is not competent to give a valid release, the Company may pay such benefit, up to an amount not exceeding $1000, to any relative by blood or connection by marriage of the Insured who is deemed by the Company to be equitably entitled thereto. Any payment made by the Company in good faith pursuant to this provision shall fully discharge the Company to the extent of such payment.

Subject to any written direction of the Insured in the Application or otherwise all or a portion of any benefits provided by this Policy on account of hospital, nursing, medical, or surgical services may, at the Company's option and unless the Insured requests otherwise in writing not later than the time of filing proofs of such loss, be paid directly to the hospital or person rendering such services; but it is not required that the service be rendered by a particular hospital or person.

(Continued on following page)

Page 11   (BH—65)

ADDITIONAL PROVISIONS (Continued)

Physical Examinations: The Company at its own expense shall have the right and opportunity to examine the person of any Covered Person as to whose sickness or injury a claim is made hereunder when and as often as it may reasonably require during the pendency of such claim.

Legal Actions: No action at law or in equity shall be brought to recover on this Policy prior to the expiration of sixty days after written proof of loss has been furnished in accordance with the requirements of this Policy. No such action shall be brought after the expiration of three years after the time written proof of loss is required to be furnished.

Misstatement of Age: If the age of any Covered Person has been misstated, all amounts payable under this Policy shall be such as the premium paid would have purchased at the correct age.

If, as a result of misstatement of the age of a Covered Person, the Company accepts any premium or premiums for a period or periods beyond the date the coverage of any or all such persons would have ceased according to the correct ages, or if, according to the correct ages, the coverage provided by this Policy for any or all such persons would not have become effective, then the liability of the Company with respect to such person or persons for the period during which their coverage would not have been effective shall be limited to the refund, upon written notice, of all premiums paid for the coverage of such person or persons for such period.

Control: The person herein designated the Insured shall be entitled while covered under this Policy, without the consent and to the exclusion of any other person, to receive any amount payable under this Policy and to exercise any rights and privileges conferred by this Policy or allowed by the Company.

Assignment: Any assignment of interest under this Policy must be in writing. The Company shall not be considered to have knowledge of an assignment unless the original or a duplicate thereof is filed at the Home Office. The Company assumes no responsibility for the validity or sufficiency of any assignment.

Statements: All statements made in the Application for this Policy shall be deemed representations and not warranties, and no statement therein shall avoid this Policy or be used as a defense to a claim hereunder unless it is contained in such Application and a copy thereof is attached to this Policy when issued.

Participation: This Policy shall be entitled to participate in the divisible surplus of the Company in such manner, under such conditions, and to such extent as may from time to time be determined by the Board of Directors of the Company.

ENDORSEMENTS

(Endorsements may be made only by the Company at the Home Office.)

MAJOR MEDICAL EXPENSE POLICY— PREMIUM RATE SUBJECT TO CHANGE
See Policy Summary within for deductible, limits, and covered persons

Life Insurance Company

A MUTUAL COMPANY—INCORPORATED
BY THE STATE OF NEW YORK

hereby furnishes insurance to the extent provided in this Policy, subject to all the provisions printed or written by the Company on this and the following pages.

Secretary   President

CONSIDERATIONS, TERM PERIOD, DATE OF ISSUE

In consideration of the representations in the application, a copy of which is attached to this Policy and forms a part of it, and the payment of the Initial Premium specified in the Policy Summary, this Policy is issued for the Initial Term Period shown in the Policy Summary, beginning and ending at 12:01 A.M., Standard Time of the place where the Named Insured resides. The Date of Issue shown in the Policy Summary is the effective date of this Policy and is the date from which policy anniversaries are determined.

POLICY GUARANTEED RENEWABLE TO MEDICARE ELIGIBILITY AGE
PREMIUM RATES SUBJECT TO CHANGE

While this Policy continues in force, the Company shall not have the right to cancel it or to place any restrictive riders on it with respect to any coverage already in force. By timely payment of renewal premiums, the Policyowner is guaranteed the right to renew this Policy from term period to term period until 12:01 A.M. on the day after the youngest adult covered person reaches the age limit for an adult, at which time the Policy will terminate. The premium for the period from the last regular premium due date until the date when this Policy so terminates will be computed on the pro rata basis. The age limit for an adult is the day before he becomes entitled to coverage under Medicare, or would become so entitled unless ineligible by reason of factors other than age.

Renewal premiums shall fall due on the last day of each expiring term period. If the Company shall accept a premium applicable to an adult covered person after the date when premiums allocable to him should terminate as provided above, the coverage provided by this Policy will continue with respect to such person until the end of the period for which such premium shall have been accepted.

Renewal premiums shall be at the Company's applicable table of rates in effect on their respective due dates, but, except for premium changes arising from changes in the covered persons, no increase in premium rate may be made on this Policy until at least three years have elapsed from the Date of Issue or the date of the last preceding premium rate increase, whichever shall be the later. Premium changes arising from changes in the covered persons will be made in accordance with the provision on page two entitled Premium Adjustments. The ages and classes of risk used in determining any change in renewal premium rates shall be the ages and classes of risk of the appropriate covered persons at the time they become covered hereunder.

WAIVER OF PREMIUM DURING TOTAL DISABILITY
OF EMPLOYED HEAD OF FAMILY

If total disability of the head of family shall commence while this Policy is in force, and if such total disability shall continue without interruption for six months, the Company will waive the payment of each premium thereafter falling due during the period of continuous total disability and will refund any premium theretofore paid which shall have fallen due and have been paid during such period. Upon the waiver of each premium so falling due, this Policy shall be deemed to be renewed for an additional term period of the same length as the last term period for which premium shall have been paid. In the event of the termination of such total disability before termination of the Policy, the Policyowner shall have the right to resume the payment of premiums on the next regular premium due date.

If the head of family shall have been continuously totally disabled for at least six months during all of which this Policy shall have been in force, and shall die while so disabled, while a covered person, and while the Policy is in force, and shall leave a lawful wife who is then a covered person, the Company will waive the payment of any premiums falling due during the twelve months immediately following his death, but this paragraph shall not extend coverage to any person after she has attained the age limit for an adult.

For the purposes of this provision, a head of family is defined as one who at the time disability commences, (a) engaged in the regular pursuit of an occupation for gain, compensation or profit, (b) a covered person and (c) an adult male Named Insured, the husband of an adult female Named Insured, or an unmarried female Named Insured. A married female Named Insured may not be deemed the head of family, whether or not her husband is a covered person. This waiver of premium provision shall be inapplicable during any period in which no covered person meets this definition of head of family.

For the purposes of this provision, total disability means incapacity of the head of family, resulting from sickness or injury as defined in this Policy, which prevents him from performing substantially all the work pertaining to his occupation or any other occupation for which he is or may be suited by education, training or experience. The entire and irrecoverable loss of the sight of both eyes, or the loss of any two extremities by severance through or above the wrist or ankle joints, shall be accepted as constituting total disability.

No premiums shall be waived under this provision by reason of any disability which shall result from war or any act of war, whether or not declared or not, or which shall commence while the head of family is in the military (land, sea or air) service of any nation or international authority.

NOTICE OF TEN DAY RIGHT TO EXAMINE POLICY: We want you to be entirely satisfied with your Policy and to fully understand it. Read it carefully. If you have any questions, consult your agent. If you are not satisfied with the Policy for any reason, you may surrender it by delivering or mailing it, within ten days after it is received by you, to the Company's Home Office at New York, N. Y. 10003, or to the agent through whom it was purchased. Immediately upon such delivering or mailing, the Policy shall be deemed void from the beginning, and any premium paid for it will be refunded.

Form No. NC 46   THIS IS A PARTICIPATING POLICY

COVERED PERSONS

Covered Persons Identified: Covered persons are the individuals listed as such in the Policy Summary and any individuals who become covered persons under the provision below entitled Additional Covered Persons, but whose covered person status has not terminated. Covered person status of children reaching the age limit or marrying, or of a divorced or separated spouse of the Named Insured, terminates as provided in the provision below entitled Termination of Covered Person Status.

Premium Adjustments: There shall be a premium adjustment when an adult covered person is added or removed, when the first child in a household is added as a covered person, and when the last child in a household is removed. The Policyowner shall give the Company written notice at its Home Office,   New York, N. Y. 10003, if the last dependent child in a household containing covered persons shall marry before the policy anniversary next following his twenty-second birthday. If the Company, having received such notice, shall accept any premium allocable to such child after the date on which his coverage ceases as provided below, then the covered person status of that individual shall continue for the period for which such premium shall have been accepted.

ADDITIONAL COVERED PERSONS

A child born to the Named Insured and his spouse while this Policy is in force shall be a covered person from birth until the next regular premium due date. A child who, after the Date of Issue, is adopted by the Named Insured or becomes wholly dependent on the Named Insured for support and a permanent resident of the Named Insured's household, and who has not passed his 18th birthday, shall become a covered person when the Named Insured assumes custody of him and shall remain one until the next regular premium due date.

Subject to the limitations under the heading Divorce or Separation below, if the Named Insured shall marry after the Date of Issue of this Policy and while it is in force, his newly married spouse (if not at or over the age limit for an adult) and any unmarried, dependent children of such spouse not past their 18th birthdays becoming permanent residents of the Named Insured's household will then be covered persons until the next regular premium due date.

Covered person status from date of birth, custody or marriage until the next regular premium due date will be provided without additional premium charge. Thereafter, such individuals will remain covered persons only if they are within the eligible ages and if the Policyowner shall give the Company notice in writing of the additional covered person or persons together with sufficient information for identification and determination of eligibility, and shall pay any increased premium required, both before the end of the first grace period beginning after the date of birth, assumption of custody or marriage, whichever is applicable. In the absence of such timely notice and payment, such individuals may again be covered persons only upon application, acceptance thereof by the Company at its Home Office, and payment of the required premium.

The Company shall have the right to exclude a spouse newly married to the Named Insured from covered person status provided it shall notify the Policyowner in writing of its intention to do so within forty-five days after having received the above mentioned identification and eligibility information and shall refund any additional premium paid on behalf of said spouse. The exclusion of the spouse shall then take effect at the end of the first grace period beginning after the marriage, except with respect to a claim in connection with which the first covered charge is incurred during the period of automatic temporary coverage afforded above.

TERMINATION OF COVERED PERSON STATUS

Dependent Children: A dependent child shall cease to be a covered person on the policy anniversary date next following his twenty-second birthday or prior marriage, or, if earlier, upon the termination of this Policy.

Adults: An adult shall cease to be a covered person when he attains the age limit for an adult, and, if the Policy then continues in force on another covered person or persons, subsequent premiums will be appropriately reduced.

Death: Upon the death of an adult covered person, or of the only covered dependent child, an appropriate refund of unearned premium will be made on the pro rata basis, and subsequent premiums will be appropriately reduced. If all adult covered persons shall die, this Policy shall terminate, unless there are covered dependent children in which case it shall terminate on the next regular premium due date.

Divorce or Separation: Upon the divorce of the Named Insured and his spouse, the provision above entitled Additional Covered Persons shall cease to operate and shall be suspended until the covered person status of the former spouse of the Named Insured and of any dependent children not remaining members of the Named Insured's household shall have been terminated as provided below. During the period of suspension of such provision, any persons who otherwise would have become covered persons automatically may be added as covered persons only upon application in writing by the Policyowner, acceptance thereof by the Company, and payment of the required premium.

Upon written request by the Policyowner, the covered person status of a divorced or separated spouse of the Named Insured, or of such spouse and the dependent children eligible for covered person status who will live in the household of such spouse, may be terminated. Such termination will be effective on the premium due date next following the day the request is received by the Company at its Home Office.

CONVERSION PRIVILEGE

Upon the termination of the covered person status of any individual as provided in the foregoing provision for any reason except his death or attainment of the age limit for an adult, and subject to the following limitations, such person shall be entitled to have issued to him by the Company, without evidence of insurability, an individual policy of insurance called a converted policy.

In order to qualify for a converted policy, the person eligible must make written application to the Company and pay the first premium for such policy, both within thirty-one days after the termination of his covered person status under this Policy.

However, the Company shall not be required to issue a converted policy if the person eligible or the person applying:

(a) will have at that time in force on a group or individual basis another policy or hospital service or medical expense indemnity contract providing similar benefits, or

(b) shall at that time be eligible for such coverage under a group insurance policy or contract, or

(c) shall be provided with similar benefits by any statute or by any welfare plan or program, and

(d) if such other coverage as described in (a), (b) and (c), together with the converted policy, would result in overinsurance or duplication of benefits according to the Company's standards relating to individual policies then effective in the state where the Named Insured resided when this Policy was issued. If such state requires the filing of such standards, the applicable standards shall be those last filed with the official having supervision of insurance in such state.

The converted policy shall be on the policy form then being issued by the Company as a converted policy which most nearly approximates the coverage of this Policy and shall take effect upon termination of covered person status under this Policy.

BENEFIT PROVISION

The Company will pay benefits equal to all covered charges in excess of the Applicable Deductible Amount which are incurred for the medical care and treatment of a covered person by reason of a sickness or an injury, but not more than the Benefit Limit on behalf of any one covered person for any one sickness or injury, provided:

(1) covered charges at least equal to the Minimum Deductible are incurred within a period of four months (herein elsewhere referred to as a Claim Qualification Period), during all of which period he shall have been a covered person under this Policy; and

(2) only those charges will be paid which are so incurred within a Benefit Period. However, if the Benefit Limit for such sickness or injury has not been exhausted at the end of the Benefit Period, a new Benefit Period may be established, provided the Policy is in force and the patient is a covered person when the new Benefit Period begins, in the same manner as the original Benefit Period, including a new Applicable Deductible Amount, but in no event shall the maximum benefit for any one sickness or injury of any one covered person exceed the Benefit Limit, regardless of the number of Benefit Periods which may be established.

(3) covered charges with respect to a sickness or injury shall not be combined with covered charges incurred with respect to a different and unrelated sickness or injury for the purpose of satisfying the Applicable Deductible Amount.

Charges shall be deemed incurred when the services for which they are charged are performed or rendered or when the items for which they are charged are purchased.

ATTACH COPY OF APPLICATION AND RIDERS HERE

POLICY SUMMARY

POLICY NUMBER

ORIGINAL NAMED INSURED

POLICYOWNER (if other than the Named Insured)

COVERED PERSONS

INITIAL PREMIUM	$
INITIAL TERM PERIOD	MONTHS
DATE OF ISSUE	
APPLICABLE DEDUCTIBLE AMOUNT	The amount of benefits provided for covered charges by Other Medical Expense Coverage, or the Minimum Deductible set forth below, whichever is larger.
MINIMUM DEDUCTIBLE	$
BENEFIT LIMIT	$50,000 for any one covered person for any one sickness or injury.
HOSPITAL DAILY SERVICE CHARGE MAXIMUM	$40
SURGICAL FEES LIMIT	100% of the first $1,000 and 75% of the excess over $1,000.
CONVALESCENT HOME DAILY MAXIMUM	$20 for not more than 30 days.
CLAIM QUALIFICATION PERIOD	Four Months
PRIVATE DUTY NURSING LIMITS	Only 75% of charges qualify. Practical nurses' services following hospital confinement covered for not more than thirty days.

Examined by   Countersigned (where required) by

Registrar	Licensed Resident Agent

PRIVILEGE OF CHANGING THE MINIMUM DEDUCTIBLE

The Policyowner shall have the right to change the Minimum Deductible from the amount set forth in the Policy Summary, or from any amount to which the original Minimum Deductible shall have been changed, to any amount which was available to him when the Policy was issued, subject to the following conditions:

(1) If it is desired to reduce the Minimum Deductible, the reduction must be made effective on a policy anniversary; it will be granted subject to payment in advance of the required additional premium and to evidence of insurability satisfactory to the Company; and if all or part of the time limits in the Policy provision entitled Time Limit on Certain Defenses shall have expired, they will again become effective (as to to the amount of the reduction in the Minimum Deductible only) for a period of two years beginning on the date the reduction becomes effective.

(2) The Minimum Deductible may be increased upon the establishment of a Benefit Period, in which case the increased Minimum Deductible will be applicable to that Benefit Period, and the premiums for the Policy will be appropriately reduced retroactively for a period of one year, or for the period since the beginning of the last previously established Benefit Period if shorter.

Page three

GENERAL DEFINITIONS

COMPANY
Company means The _____ Life Insurance Company of America.

NAMED
INSURED
Named Insured means the person named as Original Named Insured in the Policy Summary while such person is living. Should the Named Insured die while this Policy is in force, the surviving spouse, if then a covered person, shall become the Named Insured. If an unmarried female named insured marries after the Date of Issue of this Policy, her husband may become the Named Insured under this Policy upon (1) written request by the Policyowner and (2) his acceptance by the Company as a covered person.

POLICYOWNER
Policyowner means the Named Insured in the absence of the designation in this Policy of any other party as Policyowner. Should more than one party be designated as Policyowner, they or the survivors or survivor shall act jointly unless otherwise provided.

APPLICABLE
DEDUCTIBLE
AMOUNT
The Applicable Deductible Amount is the amount of benefits provided for covered charges by Other Medical Expense Coverage as defined below or the Minimum Deductible set forth in the Policy Summary, whichever is larger. If two or more persons sustain injuries in a common accident or contract the same contagious disease within ten days of each other, the Applicable Deductible Amount for all such persons combined shall be either the amount of benefits provided with respect to all such persons together by Other Medical Expense Coverage or the Minimum Deductible set forth in the Policy Summary, whichever is larger. With respect to each Benefit Period, if the Applicable Deductible Amount exceeds the Minimum Deductible, then the Benefit Limit will be increased by an amount equal to three times the difference between the Applicable Deductible Amount and the Minimum Deductible, but not more than $5,000 as to any one covered person, whether such increases arise from one or more benefit periods, or one or more sicknesses or injuries. Any such increase in Benefit Limit will remain available to the covered person to whom it applies so long as he remains a covered person under this Policy and may be used in connection with any Benefit Period for any sickness or injury until the benefits actually paid on behalf of such person shall have exceeded the limits otherwise available for him by an amount equal to such increase or increases. If any such increase shall become applicable to two or more persons in common by reason of the common accident or contagious disease provisions above, the amount of such increase shall be apportioned according to the ratio of the Other Medical Expense Coverage available to each such person to the total Other Medical Expense Coverage.

MEDICARE
Medicare means the amendments to the Social Security Act enacted under Title I, Part 1, of Public Law 89-97, 89th Congress of the United States, known as the Health Insurance for the Aged Act, any substitutes therefor or amendments thereto.

OTHER MEDICAL
EXPENSE
COVERAGE
Other Medical Expense Coverage means all coverage provided during a Benefit Period for hospital, medical, surgical, dental, nursing, paramedical or other health care expenses by any other insurance or welfare plan or prepayment arrangement, or by Medicare or any other program (whether compulsory or voluntary) established under the public law of any state or of the United States, whether provided on an individual or family basis or on a group basis through an employer, union or membership in an association. If such coverage is on a provision of service basis rather than an indemnity basis, the amount of benefits provided thereby shall be deemed to be the amount which the services rendered would have cost in the absence of such coverage.

INJURY
Injury means accidental bodily injury sustained by a covered person while this Policy is in force as to such person. Such injury shall be deemed to include all injuries resulting from one accident and all complications arising from said injury or injuries.

SICKNESS
Sickness means a sickness or disease, suffered by a covered person, contracted and first treated by a physician while this Policy is in force as to such person, all complications thereof or therefrom, and all related conditions and recurrences thereof. If, while this Policy is in force and more than six months after he has become a covered person, a covered person shall donate an organ of his body for surgical transplantation during his lifetime to the body of another individual, otherwise covered charges incurred in connection therewith by such covered person shall be deemed to have arisen from such sickness.

BENEFIT LIMIT
The Benefit Limit is the amount set forth as Benefit Limit in the Policy Summary, plus any unused sums added thereto as provided in the definition of Applicable Deductible Amount.

BENEFIT PERIOD
A Benefit Period is a period not longer than three years which begins on the day on which is incurred the first covered charge applied against the Applicable Deductible Amount in connection with a given sickness or injury. However, each Benefit Period will terminate at the end of any period of three consecutive calendar months during which the total covered charges incurred with respect to the same sickness or injury do not exceed $50. If a Benefit Period shall so terminate less than three years after its inception, it may be reinstated for any unused portion of the period ending three years after its inception whenever additional covered charges equal to at least one-half the Minimum Deductible are incurred for the treatment of the same sickness or injury within a period of two months and before the end of said three year period. Nothing in this paragraph shall be held to (1) preclude the establishment of a new Benefit Period after the expiration of said three year period, as provided in the Benefit Provision, or (2) provide benefits exceeding the Benefit Limit for all covered charges incurred in connection with one sickness or injury.

CONVALESCENT
HOME
Convalescent Home means a lawfully operated institution maintained for the principal purpose of providing full time care, under the resident supervision of a physician or legally qualified nurse, for five or more patients requiring convalescent care, which has in effect a transfer agreement with one or more hospitals, and which is not primarily a place for the treatment of alcoholism, mental illness or drug addiction, or primarily a residence for the aged.

HOSPITAL
Hospital means a lawfully constituted and operated institution which has organized facilities for care and treatment of sick and injured people on an inpatient basis, twenty-four hour nursing service and medical supervision, and (except in the case of hospitals specializing in the care of tuberculosis) facilities on the premises for diagnosis and major surgery.

PHYSICIAN
Physician means a legally qualified physician or surgeon, other than a parent, spouse, brother, sister or child of the named insured or spouse.

NURSE
Nurse means a graduate, registered professional nurse, or a licensed practical nurse, other than a parent, spouse, brother, sister or child of the named insured or spouse.

COVERED CHARGES AND SPECIAL LIMITATIONS

Covered charges are charges of the kinds set forth and to the extent specified below, subject to the exclusions under the heading Charges Not Covered, for the payment of which the Named Insured or a covered person is legally obligated to the person or institution furnishing the services or supplies for which the charges are made.

(1) Charges by Physicians for medical treatment other than surgery.

(2) Charges by Physicians for surgery, or by dentists or oral surgeons for such dental care as is not hereinafter excluded, but not exceeding the Surgical Fees Limit specified in the Policy Summary for all surgery resulting from any one sickness or any one injury, including pre-operative and post-operative care.

(3) Charges for hospital room, board and general nursing care, but not exceeding the Hospital Daily Service Charge Maximum shown in the Policy Summary for each day of confinement for each covered person so confined.

(4) Charges for anesthesia, whether administered by a Physician or by a Hospital technician.

(5) Charges for room, board and routine care of a covered person in a Convalescent Home during a period of not more than thirty days which immediately follows necessary confinement of said person in a Hospital, but not more than the Convalescent Home Daily Maximum shown in the Policy Summary for each day of confinement for each covered person so confined.

(6) Three fourths of the charges made for private duty nursing recommended by a Physician and rendered by (a) registered professional nurses anywhere, or (b) licensed practical nurses in a hospital, or (c) licensed practical nurses for home care during the thirty days immediately following a period of hospital confinement.

(7) Charges of licensed physiotherapists for treatment administered on the advice of a Physician.

(8) Charges by a Hospital for miscellaneous medical services and supplies provided by the Hospital, and charges for local ambulance service.

(9) Charges for all drugs and medications purchased while the covered person for whom they are required is confined in a Hospital or in a Convalescent Home, and for such other drugs and medicines as may be purchased only upon a Physician's prescription.

(10) Charges for casts, splints, trusses, braces, crutches, surgical dressings, oxygen, or for rental of a wheelchair, hospital type bed, iron lung, or other mechanical equipment required for treatment of respiratory paralysis.

(11) Charges for original purchase of, and fitting with, necessary prosthetic appliances required for the replacement of natural parts of the body lost while this Policy is in force, but not dentures or dental prosthetics except those required as a result of injury to natural teeth.

CHARGES NOT COVERED

The Company will not pay benefits for any of the following charges, nor may they be applied to the satisfaction of the Applicable Deductible Amount.

(1) Any excess over the regular and customary charges for the services, supplies and treatment in the locality where rendered or provided.

(2) Charges for prenatal care, delivery and post partum care in connection with normal pregnancies and pregnancies terminating in abortion, miscarriage or surgical delivery. However, in the event of unusual complications of pregnancy other than those listed in the preceding sentence, charges otherwise within the definition of covered charges will be deemed covered charges. In the event that such complications occur in connection with a delivery, the Minimum Deductible shall be increased by $200, which shall be deemed the charge for normal delivery for the purposes of this provision.

(3) Charges incurred within ten months after the Date of Issue of this Policy for the care, treatment, or removal of any genital organ of any female covered person.

(4) Charges incurred for services, supplies or treatment not prescribed as necessary by a Physician.

(5) Charges incurred for care or treatment of sickness or injury caused or contributed to by war or act of war, whether war be declared or not.

(6) Charges for dentures, dentistry, dental surgery, or dental x-rays except as required for the treatment of injuries to natural teeth, and then not more than the Surgical Fees Limit.

(7) Charges for cosmetic surgery, unless performed to correct
(a) sequelae of an injury, or
(b) a congenital anomaly in a child born to the Named Insured and his spouse while this Policy is in force.

(8) Charges for drugs and medications purchased while the covered person for whom they are required is not confined in a Hospital or a Convalescent Home, unless they are obtainable only upon a Physician's prescription.

(9) Charges for communication or transportation expense or travel time of Physicians or Nurses, or of patients except local ambulance service.

(10) Charges for care or treatment for which benefits are payable under any workmen's compensation or occupational disease act or law.

(11) Charges made by persons or institutions for hospital or medical care or treatment which is customarily furnished without charge and without a means test.

(12) Charges incurred for care or treatment of sickness or injury suffered by a covered person while in the military (land, sea or air) service of any nation or international authority, and pro rata portion of any premium paid with respect to a specific covered person for the period while such person is in such service will be refunded.

(13) Charges for the care or treatment of mental or emotional illness, disorder or disturbance, except such charges incurred:
(a) during the first sixty days of a single period of confinement in a Hospital of a covered person specifically for the treatment of such mental or emotional illness, disorder or disturbance, which confinement lasts at least seven consecutive days; and
(b) within one month after the termination of such a single period of hospital confinement.
For the purpose of this provision, all periods of hospital confinement for the care or treatment of mental or emotional illness, disorder or disturbance shall be deemed a single period of confinement unless the periods of hospital confinement are each separated by twelve consecutive months or longer. All psychotherapy shall be deemed rendered for the treatment of mental or emotional illness, regardless of the nature of the symptoms. The benefits afforded under (a) and (b) above shall be available but once as to each such single period or periods of hospital confinement.

GENERAL POLICY PROVISIONS

CHANGES IN TERM PERIOD: On any premium due date of this Policy on which the head of family is not totally disabled, the Policyowner shall have the right to change the then current term period to twelve months, six months or three months, except that no change in term period will be allowed which would result in (a) a premium not being due on the policy anniversary date, or (b) a premium for the term period of less than ten dollars.

ASSIGNMENT: The Company shall not be charged with notice of assignment of any interest in this Policy until the original assignment or a duplicate has been filed with the Company at its Home Office. The Company assumes no responsibility as to the validity or effect of any assignment.

PARTICIPATION: This Policy shall be entitled to participate in the divisible surplus of the Company in such manner, under such conditions, and to such extent as may from time to time be determined by the Board of Directors of the Company.

RIGHTS OF POLICYOWNER: The Policyowner may exercise every right and enjoy every privilege conferred by this Policy or allowed by the Company, except that benefits payable hereunder shall be payable in accordance with the Payment of Claims provision.

SUSPENSION DURING MILITARY SERVICE: If the Named Insured shall enter active duty in the military (land, sea or air) service of any nation or international authority for a period exceeding ninety days, the Company upon written request of the Policyowner, will suspend this Policy for the period (if more than ninety days) subsequent to the receipt of such request at its Home Office during which the Named Insured shall remain on active duty in such service and will refund any premium paid for the period of such suspension on the pro rata basis. Upon termination of the Named Insured's tour of active duty in such service before the date when this Policy would terminate by reason of the attained ages of the covered persons, this Policy may be reinstated without evidence of insurability, effective upon written request therefor by the Policyowner and payment of the required premium, provided such request is made within sixty days after the termination of said period of active duty.

ENTIRE CONTRACT; CHANGES: This Policy, including the endorsements and the attached papers, if any, constitutes the entire contract of insurance. No change in this Policy shall be valid until approved by the President, a Vice President or Secretary of the Company and unless such approval be endorsed hereon or attached hereto. No agent has authority to change this Policy or to waive any of its provisions.

GENERAL POLICY PROVISIONS (Continued)

TIME LIMIT ON CERTAIN DEFENSES: (a) After two years from the Date of Issue of this Policy, no misstatements, except fraudulent misstatements, made by the Original Named Insured or Policyowner in the application for such Policy shall be used to void the Policy or to deny a claim with respect to an injury sustained or sickness first treated by a Physician after the expiration of such two year period.

(b) No claim in connection with which the first covered charge applied against the Applicable Deductible Amount is incurred after two years from the Date of Issue of this Policy, or for waiver of premium by reason of disability commencing after said two years, shall be reduced or denied on the ground that a disease or physical condition, not excluded from coverage by name or specific description effective on the date said first covered charge is incurred or such disability commences, had existed prior to the effective date of coverage of this Policy.

GRACE PERIOD: A grace period of thirty-one days will be granted for the payment of each premium falling due after the first premium, during which grace period the Policy shall continue in force.

REINSTATEMENT: If any renewal premium be not paid within the time granted for payment, a subsequent acceptance of premium by the Company or by any agent duly authorized by the Company to accept such premium, without requiring in connection therewith an application for reinstatement, shall reinstate the Policy; provided, however, that if the Company or such agent requires an application and issues a conditional receipt for the premium tendered, the Policy will be reinstated upon approval of such application by the Company or, lacking such approval, upon the forty-fifth day following the date of such conditional receipt unless the Company has previously notified the policyowner in writing of its disapproval of such application. The reinstated Policy shall provide benefits only with respect to covered charges or losses incurred in connection with such accidental injury as may be sustained after the date of reinstatement and in connection with such sickness as may begin more than ten days after such date. In all other respects, the Named Insured, Policyowner other than the Named Insured if any, and the Company shall have the same rights thereunder as they had under the Policy immediately before the due date of the defaulted premium, subject to any provisions endorsed hereon or attached hereto in connection with the reinstatement.

NOTICE OF CLAIM: Written notice of claim for benefits based on covered charges must be given to the Company within 30 days after the covered charges exceed the Minimum Deductible or as soon thereafter as is reasonably possible. Written notice of total disability on the basis of which premiums may be waived must be given to the Company within 30 days after the head of family has been totally disabled for six months, or as soon thereafter as is reasonably possible. Notice given by or on behalf of the Policyowner or a covered person to the Company at its Home Office, _____, New York, New York 10003, or to any authorized agent of the Company, with information sufficient to identify the Named Insured shall be deemed notice to the Company.

CLAIM FORMS: The Company, upon receipt of a notice of claim, will furnish to the claimant such forms as are usually furnished by it for filing proofs of claim. If such forms are not furnished within fifteen days after the giving of such notice the claimant shall be deemed to have complied with the requirements of this Policy as to proofs of loss upon submitting, within the time fixed in the Policy for filing proofs of claim, written proof covering the occurrence, the character and the extent of the loss for which claim is made.

PROOF OF CLAIM: Written proof of claim must be furnished to the Company at its said Home Office in case of claim for any covered charge within ninety days after such covered charge is

made, or for a waiver of any premium within ninety days after the due date of the first premium to fall due after the head of family has been totally disabled for six months, and within ninety days after each subsequent premium to be waived is due. Failure to furnish such proof within the time required shall not invalidate or reduce any claim if it was not reasonably possible to give proof within such time, provided such proof is furnished as soon as reasonably possible and in no event, except in the absence of legal capacity, later than one year from the time proof is otherwise required.

TIME OF PAYMENT OF CLAIMS: Benefits payable under this Policy will be paid immediately upon receipt of due written proof of claim.

PAYMENT OF CLAIMS: All benefits payable under this Policy will be payable to the Named Insured current at the time the benefits are payable. If no Named Insured is living to receive such benefits, payment may be made to the estate of the last Named Insured. If any benefits of this Policy shall be payable to the estate of a Named Insured, or to a Named Insured who is a minor or otherwise not competent to give a valid release, the Company may pay such benefits, up to an amount not exceeding $1,000, to any relative by blood or connection by marriage of such Named Insured who is deemed by the Company to be equitably entitled thereto. Any payment made by the Company in good faith pursuant to this provision shall fully discharge the Company to the extent of such payment.

Subject to any written direction of the Named Insured in the application or otherwise, all or a portion of any benefits provided by this Policy on account of hospital, medical or surgical services may, at the Company's option and unless the Named Insured requests otherwise in writing not later than the time of filing proofs of such claim, be paid directly to the hospital or person rendering such services; but it is not required that the service be rendered by a particular hospital or person.

PHYSICAL EXAMINATIONS: The Company at its own expense shall have the right and opportunity to examine the person of the covered person on whose behalf covered charges have been incurred or premiums are to be waived when and so often as it may reasonably require during the pendency of a claim hereunder.

LEGAL ACTIONS: No action at law or in equity shall be brought to recover on this Policy prior to the expiration of sixty days after written proof of claim has been furnished in accordance with requirements of this Policy. No such action shall be brought after the expiration of three years after the time written proof of claim is required to be furnished.

CANCELLATION BY THE POLICYOWNER: The Policyowner may cancel this Policy at any time by written notice delivered or mailed to the Company, effective upon receipt or on such later date as may be specified in such notice. In the event of such a cancellation which takes effect during the first policy year, the Company will return promptly one half of the pro rata unearned premium paid; if such a cancellation takes effect during a subsequent policy year, the Company will promptly return three fourths of the pro rata unearned premium paid. Cancellation shall be without prejudice to any claim originating prior to the effective date of cancellation. The Company may not cancel this Policy during any term period for which premium has been accepted, and it is renewable in accordance with the renewal provision on page one.

CONFORMITY WITH STATE STATUTES: Any provision of this Policy which, on its effective date, is in conflict with the statutes of the state in which the Named Insured resides on such date is hereby amended to conform to the minimum requirements of such statutes.

Page six

GUARDIAN NONCANCELLABLE DISABILITY INCOME POLICY — NONCANCELLABLE TO AGE 65
See Policy Summary within for coverage outline

Life Insurance Company

**A MUTUAL COMPANY—INCORPORATED
BY THE STATE OF NEW YORK**

hereby furnishes insurance to the extent provided in this Policy, subject to all the provisions printed or written by the Company on this and the following pages.

Secretary   President

INSURING CLAUSE

This Policy insures the person named in the Policy Summary as the Insured, subject to all the terms, conditions, definitions, exclusions and limitations printed or written by the Company on this and the following pages, all of which are a part of the Policy, (1) against loss resulting from sickness which first becomes manifest while this Policy is in force (hereinafter called such sickness), and (2) against loss resulting from accidental bodily injuries sustained while this Policy is in force (hereinafter called such injuries).

CONSIDERATIONS, TERM PERIOD, DATE OF ISSUE

In consideration of the representations in the application, a copy of which is attached to this Policy and forms a part of it, and of the total premium for the Policy Term Period shown in the Policy Summary, this Policy is issued for the Term Period shown in the Policy Summary, beginning and ending at 12:01 A.M., Standard Time of the place where the Insured resides. The Date of Issue shown in the Policy Summary is the effective date of this Policy and is the date from which Policy anniversaries are determined.

NONCANCELLABLE AND GUARANTEED RENEWABLE TO AGE 65
CONDITIONALLY RENEWABLE THEREAFTER TO AGE 70

The Company guarantees to the policyowner the right to renew this Policy from Term Period to Term Period by timely payment of renewal premiums at the Company's premium rate in force on its Date of Issue, but not beyond the Policy anniversary next following the Insured's 65th birthday. On the Policy anniversary next following the Insured's 65th birthday and on each Policy anniversary thereafter to which this Policy shall have been renewed, until the Policy anniversary next following the Insured's 70th birthday, the Company will permit the policyowner to renew this Policy for an additional year provided that on and until each such Policy anniversary the Insured shall have been actively and regularly employed full time. If the Company shall accept a premium applicable to any period after the Policy anniversary next following the Insured's 65th birthday, the Policy will continue in force until the end of any period or periods for which premium shall have been accepted. On and after the Policy anniversary next following the Insured's 65th birthday, premiums for renewal of this Policy shall be based on the Company's applicable table of rates for this Policy form then in effect for persons of the Insured's then attained age, occupation, and sex. While this Policy is in force, the Company cannot place any restrictive rider on it, except at the express written request of the policyowner. Renewal premiums shall fall due on the last day of each expiring Term Period.

GRACE PERIOD

A grace period of thirty-one days will be granted for the payment of each premium falling due after the first premium, during which grace period the Policy shall continue in force.

INCREASE IN AMOUNTS

If, on the date of (1) the commencement of a disability from sickness, or (2) an accident resulting in loss covered under this Policy, the then current Term Period is six months, the amounts of insurance provided in this Policy and in additional coverage riders attached to it, if any, shall be increased by five percent with respect to losses arising out of such sickness or such accident, as the case may be; if the then current Term Period is twelve months, said amounts shall be increased by ten percent.

WAIVER OF PREMIUM

If such sickness or such injuries shall totally and continuously disable the Insured for a period of at least ninety days during all of which period this Policy shall have been in force, the Company will refund any premiums paid during such ninety day period and will waive the payment of any premium thereafter falling due during the continuance of that period of total disability and before the Policy anniversary next following the Insured's sixty-fifth birthday. Upon the waiver of each such premium so falling due, this Policy shall then be deemed to be renewed for an additional Term Period of the same length as the last Term Period for which premium shall have been paid. In the event of the termination of such total disability, the policyowner shall have the right to resume the payment of premiums on the next regular premium due date. No premiums will be waived for any period after the Policy anniversary next following the Insured's sixty-fifth birthday.

EXCLUSIONS

This Policy shall not cover any loss caused or contributed to by intentionally self inflicted injuries, or by war or act of war, whether war be declared or not.

SUSPENSION DURING MILITARY SERVICE

If the Insured shall enter upon active duty (other than active duty for training lasting ninety days or less) in the military (land, sea or air) service of any country or international authority, the coverage of this Policy shall be suspended on the date of commencement of such military service, and the Company will refund any premium which shall have been paid for the period of such suspension on the pro rata basis. Upon termination of the Insured's tour of active duty in such service, this Policy may be reinstated without evidence of insurability at the original premium rate upon written application by the policyowner and payment of the required premium, both within sixty days after the termination of said period of active duty. If the policyowner prefers to pay premiums during the period of such military service, the coverage of this Policy will be automatically reinstated upon the termination of such military service and the Company will then refund the premiums allocable to the period of military service.

NOTICE OF TEN DAY RIGHT TO EXAMINE POLICY: We want you to be entirely satisfied with your Policy and to fully understand it. Read it carefully. If you have any questions, consult your agent. If you are not satisfied with the Policy for any reason, you may surrender it by delivering or mailing it, within ten days after it is received by you, to the Company's Home Office at   New York, N. Y. 10003, or to the agent through whom it was purchased. Immediately upon such delivering or mailing, the Policy shall be deemed void from the beginning, and any premium paid for it will be refunded.

Form No. NC 51   THIS IS A PARTICIPATING POLICY   Page one

DEFINITIONS

Total Disability

(a) For the first five years from the day benefits first become payable in any period of continuous disability (or until the end of the maximum benefit period if less than five years), the term total disability shall mean complete inability of the Insured to engage in his regular occupation or profession.

(b) After the first five years in any period of continuous disability, the term total disability shall mean complete inability of the Insured to engage in any reasonably gainful occupation for which he shall be fitted by education, training or experience, having due regard for the nature of his occupation at the time disability shall have begun and for his prior average earnings.

(c) However, the entire and irrecoverable loss of the sight of both eyes, or of the power of speech, or of the use of both arms or of both legs or of one arm and one leg shall always be accepted as constituting total disability as long as such loss continues; and upon the occurrence of any such loss as described in this subparagraph, any unexpired portion of the elimination period will be waived, and the benefits for total disability will begin from the date of such loss or from the end of the elimination period, whichever shall first occur. Speech means audible communication of words, with or without artificial assistance.

Maximum Benefit Period

The maximum benefit period is as provided in the Policy Summary.

Elimination Period

Elimination period means the number of days at the beginning of a period of total disability, commencing with the first day thereof, for which no indemnity is payable. The elimination period for total disability from sickness will be applied to any disability resulting from any kind of hernia.

Policyowner

The Insured is the policyowner in the absence of the designation in this Policy of any other party as policyowner. Should more than one party be designated as policyowner, they or the survivors or survivor shall act jointly unless otherwise provided.

Other Definitions

The word Company means The _____ Life Insurance Company of America. The word Insured means the person named as such in the Policy Summary, and as the proposed Insured in the copy of the application. The word physician means a legally qualified physician other than the Insured. The word sickness includes the meaning of the word disease.

BENEFIT PROVISION

A. **Total Disability**

If, commencing while this Policy is in force, such sickness or such injuries shall result in the continuous total disability of the Insured, the Company will pay periodically the monthly indemnity for total disability specified in the Policy Summary, beginning after the applicable elimination period specified in the Policy Summary, for the period of such continuous total disability, but for not longer than the maximum benefit period. The Insured will not be entitled to concurrent benefits for total disability contributed to or caused by both such injuries and such sickness or by more than one injury or more than one sickness.

B. **Fractional Months**

Disability for a fractional part of a month will be indemnified on the basis of one thirtieth of the applicable monthly benefit for each day of disability for which the Company is liable.

C. **Recovery and Recurrence**

This provision governs benefits payable under this Policy if the Insured, having received monthly indemnity under the Policy for total disability, subsequently recovers, and later suffers a recurrence of total disability while this Policy is in force, arising out of or contributed to by the same cause or causes as the original period of disability. For the purpose of this provision, the Insured will be deemed to have made a recovery when he has engaged in his regular occupation or profession or in any other gainful occupation or profession for which he is reasonably fitted and has performed all the important duties thereof on a full-time basis. When the Insured shall have engaged in any occupation or profession and shall have performed all the important duties thereof for a period of six months, that occupation shall thereafter be deemed to be his regular occupation or profession.

If the period of recovery shall be continuous for six months or more, the recurrent total disability shall be subject to a new maximum benefit period and a new elimination period. If the period of recovery shall be less than six months, this Policy will provide only the unexpended balance, if any, of the original maximum benefit period, but no new elimination period will be imposed.

If the cause of the subsequent disability shall be entirely unrelated to the cause of the prior disability, the subsequent disability will be subject to a new elimination period and will provide a new maximum benefit period.

D. **Rehabilitation**

Recognizing that economic rehabilitation is preferable to monetary compensation for disability from the standpoint of the Insured, the Company, and society, the Company declares that participation by a totally disabled Insured in a government sponsored or other professionally planned rehabilitation program approved by the Company in advance will not alone be deemed a recovery from total disability.

E. **Capital Sum Benefit**

If, while this Policy is in force (or, if the Policy shall have terminated, within ninety days after the date of an accidental cause occurring while this Policy shall have been in force), the Insured shall suffer the entire and irrecoverable loss of the sight of an eye or of the power of speech from a medically determinable physiological cause, or the loss of a hand or foot by severance through or above wrist or ankle joint by reason of sickness or injury, and if he shall survive such loss for thirty days, the Company will pay, in addition to any other indemnity payable under this Policy, indemnity in one sum equal to the monthly indemnity of this Policy (not including any attached rider) for one year of compensable total disability. The maximum indemnity payable under this provision for all such losses occurring during the lifetime of the Insured shall not exceed a sum equal to twice the indemnity for one such loss.

DISABILITY INCOME POLICY SUMMARY

POLICY NUMBER

INSURED

POLICYOWNER (if other than the Insured)

BASIC TERM PERIOD PREMIUM $

TERM PERIOD PREMIUM FOR
ADDITIONAL BENEFIT RIDERS, IF ANY $

TOTAL PREMIUM FOR POLICY TERM PERIOD $

TERM PERIOD   MONTHS

DATE OF ISSUE

MONTHLY INDEMNITY
FOR TOTAL DISABILITY $

MAXIMUM BENEFIT PERIOD   {   UNLIMITED IF IT BEGINS BEFORE AGE 50;
FOR TOTAL DISABILITY   TO AGE 65 BUT NOT LESS THAN TWO YEARS
(see details below)   IF IT BEGINS THEREAFTER

                FOR TOTAL DISABILITY FROM SICKNESS
ELIMINATION PERIODS   {
(see exception below)   FOR TOTAL DISABILITY FROM ACCIDENT

ADDITIONAL BENEFIT RIDERS

ADDITIONAL AND AMENDED POLICY PROVISIONS

Definition of Maximum Benefit Period

For a period of total disability which begins before the Policy anniversary nearest the Insured's fiftieth birthday, the maximum benefit period is unlimited during the continuous total disability and lifetime of the Insured. For a period of total disability beginning on or after the Policy anniversary nearest the Insured's fiftieth birthday, the maximum benefit period ends on the Policy anniversary next following the Insured's sixty-fifth birthday, except with respect to any period of disability for which monthly indemnity shall first be payable after the Policy anniversary next following the Insured's sixty-third birthday, in which case the maximum benefit period shall be two years.

Waiver of Elimination Period in Certain Cases

An elimination period will not be applied to any period of total disability which commences while this Policy is in force and within five years after the termination of a prior period of total disability (1) for which monthly indemnity shall have been payable under this Policy and (2) which shall have lasted more than six months.

This provision does not apply to any rider attached to this Policy, except a rider providing monthly indemnity for the duration of total disability to a specified age or for life, in which case it applies separately to each such rider under which monthly indemnity shall have been paid for total disability lasting more than six months.

Guaranteed Issue Option For Extended Benefit Rider (Accident)

This option is available on the Policy anniversary nearest the Insured's fiftieth birthday and on each subsequent anniversary until and including that nearest the Insured's fifty-fifth birthday. If, within the year prior to any such Policy anniversary and while the Insured is not disabled, the policyowner has made written application to the Company for an Extended Benefit Rider, such a rider, providing as follows, will be issued without evidence of insurability. Subject to payment of the required premium, it will take effect on such Policy anniversary and will provide that the Maximum Benefit Period with respect to total disability resulting directly and independently of all other causes from such injuries will be unlimited provided such injuries are sustained while this Policy and said Rider are in force and before the Policy anniversary next following the Insured's sixty-fifth birthday.

Examined   Countersigned (where required) by

_____   _____
         Registrar   Duly Licensed Resident Agent

AR 123-L

F. Medical Care Requirement

No monthly indemnity shall be payable under this Policy for any period of disability during which the Insured shall not be under the care of a physician, except that such care shall not be a requirement if total disability shall have resulted from loss of eyesight or of any two extremities by severance through or above wrist or ankle joints.

G. Transplant Surgery Benefit

If while this insurance is in force and commencing more than six months after the Date of Issue, the Insured shall become continuously and totally disabled as a result of the transplant of a part of his body to the body of another, such total disability will be indemnified, beginning after the elimination period, as a total disability due to such sickness.

GENERAL POLICY PROVISIONS

ENTIRE CONTRACT; CHANGES: This Policy, including the endorsements and the attached papers, if any, constitutes the entire contract of insurance. No change in this Policy shall be valid until approved by the President, a Vice President or Secretary of the Company and unless such approval be endorsed hereon or attached hereto. No agent has authority to change this Policy or to waive any of its provisions.

INCONTESTABLE: (a) After this Policy has been in force for a period of two years during the lifetime of the Insured, it shall become incontestable as to the statements contained in the application.

(b) No claim for loss incurred or disability (as defined in the Policy) commencing after two years from the Date of Issue of this Policy shall be reduced or denied on the ground that a disease or physical condition not excluded from coverage by name or specific description effective on the date of loss had existed prior to the effective date of coverage of this Policy.

REINSTATEMENT: If any renewal premium be not paid within the time granted for payment, a subsequent acceptance of premium by the Company or by any agent duly authorized by the Company to accept such premium, without requiring in connection therewith an application for reinstatement, shall reinstate the Policy, provided, however, that if the Company or such agent requires an application for reinstatement and issues a conditional receipt for the premium tendered, the Policy will be reinstated upon approval of such application by the Company or, lacking such approval, upon the forty-fifth day following the date of such conditional receipt unless the Company has previously notified the policyowner in writing of its disapproval of such application. The reinstated Policy shall cover only loss resulting from such accidental injury as may be sustained after the date of reinstatement and loss due to such sickness as may begin more than ten days after such date. In all other respects the Insured, policyowner other than the Insured if any, and the Company shall have the same rights thereunder as they had under the Policy immediately before the due date of the defaulted premium, subject to any provisions endorsed hereon or attached hereto in connection with the reinstatement.

NOTICE OF CLAIM: Written notice of claim must be given to the Company within thirty days after the occurrence or commencement of any loss covered by the Policy, or as soon thereafter as is reasonably possible. Notice given by or on behalf of the Insured to the Company at its Home Office, New York, N. Y. 10003, or to any authorized agent of the Company, with information sufficient to identify the Insured, shall be deemed notice to the Company.

CLAIM FORMS: The Company, upon receipt of a notice of claim, will furnish to the claimant such forms as are usually furnished by it for filing proofs of loss. If such forms are not furnished within fifteen days after the giving of such notice the claimant shall be deemed to have complied with the requirements of this Policy as to proofs of loss upon submitting, within the time fixed in the Policy for filing proofs of loss, written proof covering the occurrence, the character and the extent of the loss for which claim is made.

PROOFS OF LOSS: Written proof of loss must be furnished to the Company at its said office in case of claim for loss for which this Policy provides any periodic payment contingent upon continuing loss within ninety days after the termination of the period for which the Company is liable and in case of claim for any other loss within ninety days after the date of such loss. Failure to furnish such proof within the time required shall not invalidate or reduce any claim if it was not reasonably possible to give proof within such time, provided such proof is furnished as soon as reasonably possible and in no event, except in the absence of legal capacity, later than one year from the time proof is otherwise required.

TIME OF PAYMENT OF CLAIMS: Indemnities payable under this Policy for any loss other than loss for which this Policy provides any periodic payment will be paid immediately upon receipt of due written proof of such loss. Subject to due written proof of loss, all accrued indemnities for loss for which this Policy provides any periodic payment will be paid at the expiration of each thirty days, and any balance remaining unpaid upon the termination of liability will be paid immediately upon receipt of due written proof.

PAYMENT OF CLAIMS: All indemnities of this Policy will be payable to the Insured, and any accrued indemnities unpaid at the Insured's death will be payable to the estate of the Insured.

If any indemnity of this Policy shall be payable to the estate of the Insured, or to a person who is a minor or otherwise not competent to give a valid release, the Company may pay such indemnity, up to an amount not exceeding $1000, to any relative by blood or connection by marriage of the Insured who is deemed by the Company to be equitably entitled thereto. Any payment made by the Company in good faith pursuant to this provision shall fully discharge the Company to the extent of such payment.

PHYSICAL EXAMINATIONS: The Company at its own expense shall have the right and opportunity to examine the person of the Insured when and so often as it may reasonably require during the pendency of a claim hereunder.

LEGAL ACTIONS: No action at law or in equity shall be brought to recover on this Policy prior to the expiration of sixty days after due written proof of loss has been furnished in accordance with the requirements of this Policy. No such action shall be brought after the expiration of three years after the time written proof of loss is required to be furnished.

MISSTATEMENT OF AGE: If the age of the Insured has been misstated, all amounts payable under this Policy shall be such as the premium paid would have purchased at the correct age. If, according to the correct age of the Insured, the coverage provided by this Policy would not have become effective, or would have ceased prior to the acceptance of such premium or premiums, then the liability of the Company shall be limited to the refund of all premiums paid for the period not covered by the Policy.

Page three

GENERAL POLICY PROVISIONS (Continued)

CONFORMITY WITH STATE STATUTES: Any provision of this Policy which, on its effective date, is in conflict with the statutes of the state in which the Insured resides on such date is hereby amended to conform to the minimum requirements of such statutes.

PARTICIPATION: This Policy shall be entitled to participate in the divisible surplus of the Company in such manner, under such conditions, and to such extent as may from time to time be determined by the Board of Directors of the Company.

ASSIGNMENT: The Company shall not be charged with notice of assignment of any interest in this Policy until the original assignment or a duplicate has been filed with the Company at its Home Office. The Company assumes no responsibility as to the validity or effect of any assignment.

CHANGES IN TERM PERIOD: On any premium due date of this Policy, the policyowner shall have the right to reduce the then current Term Period from twelve months to six months or three months, or from six months to three months, as the case may be. On any Policy anniversary, if the Insured is not then disabled, the policyowner shall have the right to increase the Term Period from three months to six months or twelve months, or from six months to twelve months, as the case may be.

RIGHTS OF POLICYOWNER: The policyowner may exercise every right and enjoy every privilege conferred by this Policy or allowed by the Company, except that benefits payable hereunder shall be payable in accordance with the Payment of Claims provision.

CHANGE OF PLAN OR POLICY FORM: At any time prior to the Policy anniversary next following the Insured's sixtieth birthday while this Policy is in force with no premium in default, the policyowner shall have the right, upon written request to the Company and surrender of this contract, to change this Policy without evidence of insurability to a disability policy on any policy form which could have been issued by the Company in the state where the Insured resided on the Date of Issue of this Policy and which does not provide a longer maximum benefit period, larger monthly indemnity or shorter elimination period than this Policy, or any benefit not contained in this Policy, and which does not require a higher premium rate than this Policy. The changed policy shall bear the same number and Date of/Issue as this Policy and shall be issued at the premium rate for its coverage and class of risk applicable to the Insured on the Date of Issue of this Policy, but its coverage shall replace the coverage of this Policy on the premium due date next following surrender of this Policy and proper written request for the change, subject to the payment of the required premiums when due.

SPACE FOR ENDORSEMENTS

Page four

Life Insurance Company

is a mutual Company   There are no stockholders.

The annual election of Directors is held at the Home Office of the Company on the second Wednesday in December. Voting privileges may be exercised by policyholders of the Company in accordance with, and as defined by, the Insurance Law of the State of New York. For particulars, apply to the Secretary, New York, N. Y. 10003.

Notify the Company promptly of any change in address. In communicating with the Company, please give the Insured's name, your post office address and the number of the Policy.

IMPORTANT

Your Policy contains many valuable benefits and provisions. Be sure to consult the Company if anyone advises you to lapse it.

It is not necessary to employ anyone to present a claim under this Policy. If you are in doubt as to your rights and privileges, full information may be obtained from the nearest Agency Office or from the Home Office in the City of New York.

Life Assurance Society of the United States

NAME OF EMPLOYEE	GROUP NO.	CERTIFICATE NO.	EFFECTIVE DATE

BENEFICIARY: THE BENEFICIARY SHALL BE THE PERSON OR PERSONS SO DESIGNATED, IN ACCORDANCE WITH THE ELECTION OF THE EMPLOYEE ON THE INSURANCE RECORDS MAINTAINED IN CONNECTION WITH THE INSURANCE UNDER THE POLICY.

Certificate of Group Insurance

SPACE FOR ATTACHMENT OF
COVER PAGE
IDENTIFYING THE INSURED EMPLOYEE

If any prior Certificate describing the same kind of group insurance has been issued to the Employee named herein such Certificate is void.

The   Life Assurance Society of the United States

Subject to the terms and conditions of
Group policy(ies) No. 0700, 0700D and 0700M
the Employee named on the cover page, an Employee of

RICHARD ROE CORPORATION

(Herein called the Employer)
is insured for the benefits described in this certificate.
AMOUNTS OF INSURANCE

Non-Contributory Life Insurance.......................$1,000
Non-Contributory Accidental
Death and Dismemberment Insurance $1,000

For additional benefits, see subsequent pages hereof.

The Contributory insurance benefits for the Employee, which are described in this certificate, are not in effect unless the Employee elects to become insured and is making the required contributions for such insurance. In addition, if such election is made more than thirty-one days after the date he is first eligible he must submit evidence of insurability, at his own expense, satisfactory to the Society before such insurance shall become effective. If the Employee is not actively at work on the date his Contributory insurance would otherwise become effective it shall not become effective until he returns to active work.

INDIVIDUAL TERMINATIONS: The insurance of any Employee under a Group policy shall cease automatically upon the occurrence of any of the following events:

(a) the termination of the policy, (b) the cessation of premium payments on account of the Employee's insurance thereunder, (c) the termination of his employment in the classes of Employees insured thereunder.

Note: In case of cessation of active work the Employee should consult the Employer to see what arrangement, if any, can be made to continue the insurance.

This individual certificate is furnished in accordance with and subject to the terms of the Group policy(ies). Each policy, and the respective application of the Employer therefor, constitute each entire contract. This certificate is merely evidence of insurance provided under the policy(ies), which insurance is effective only if the Employee is eligible for insurance and becomes and remains insured in accordance with the provisions, terms and conditions of each respective policy.

(3.401C)

(For additional provisions see subsequent pages hereof)
LIFE ASSURANCE SOCIETY OF THE UNITED STATES

PF 4441A Amended by PF 18505   Printed in U. S. A.

NOTE: The insurance described in this certificate for Dependents is void and of no effect unless the insured Employee has eligible Dependents and such Dependents become insured in accordance with the terms set forth below.

INSURANCE FOR DEPENDENTS

This is to certify that the Group Hospital Expense policy includes benefits as therein limited for the Dependents of the Employee.

DEFINITION OF DEPENDENT. The word Dependent means any of the following not eligible for insurance as an Employee of the Employer:

(a) An insured Employee's wife or husband not legally separated from the Employee.

(b) An insured Employee's unmarried child who has attained the age of two weeks but has not attained the age of nineteen years.

ELIGIBILITY AND EFFECTIVE DATES OF INSURANCE FOR DEPENDENTS. Each Dependent shall be eligible for insurance under the policy on the latest of (a) the date set forth on the cover page (b) the date of the Employee's eligibility and (c) the date the Dependent first becomes a Dependent of the Employee. If on the date a Dependent would otherwise become eligible, he is confined to a hospital, he shall not become eligible until the termination of such confinement.

The insurance of the Dependents of any Employee shall become effective on the date of their eligibility.

TERMINATION OF INSURANCE FOR DEPENDENTS. The insurance of any Dependent shall cease automatically upon the occurrence of any one of the following events:

(a) The cessation of premium payments on account of the insurance of such Dependent.

(b) The termination of the Employee's insurance under said Group policy.

(c) When he ceases to be a Dependent as defined.

(5.900C)

PF 4441 (1.2)

LIFE INSURANCE

The Group Life Insurance policy provides that upon receipt of due proof of the death of the Employee occurring while insured thereunder, the Society will pay to the Employee's designated beneficiary the amount of life insurance then in force on the life of the Employee.

BENEFICIARY. The Employee may change the beneficiary from time to time by written request filed through the Employer, but any such change shall take effect only upon its entry on the insurance records maintained in connection with the insurance under the policy. Any part of the insurance for which there is no beneficiary designated by the Employee or surviving at the death of the Employee will be payable in a single sum to the first surviving class of the following classes of successive preference beneficiaries: The Employee's (a) widow or widower; (b) surviving children; (c) surviving parents; (d) surviving brothers and sisters; (e) executors or administrators.

In the absence of the appointment of a legal guardian, any minor's share may be paid at a rate not exceeding $50 a month to such adult or adults as have in the Society's opinion assumed the custody and principal support of such minor.

OPTIONAL MODES OF SETTLEMENT. By giving proper written notice, the Employee may elect (with the right to revoke or to change such election) to have the whole or any part of the amount of life insurance which would otherwise be payable to the beneficiary in a single sum paid in instalments or in any other manner that may be agreed to by the Society. The amount and terms of payment shall be in accordance with those customarily offered by the Society for group life insurance policies at the time of election. If the Employee does not make an election, the beneficiary may do so after the Employee's death.

After the death of the Employee the beneficiary may designate (with the right to change such designation) a person or persons to receive any amount which in the absence of such designation would become payable to the beneficiary's executors or administrators.

CONVERSION PRIVILEGE. A. Upon Termination of Employment. If the Employee's employment is terminated in the class or classes of Employees insured under the Group policy, the Employee shall be entitled to have issued to him by the Society, without evidence of insurability, upon application made to the Society within thirty-one days after such termination and upon the payment of the premium applicable to the class of risk to which he belongs and to the form and amount of the policy at his then attained age, an individual policy of life insurance in any one of the forms then customarily issued by the Society (except a policy of Term insurance, or a policy providing benefits in event of total and permanent disability or additional benefits in event of accidental death) in an amount equal to, or at the option of the Employee, less than the amount of his insurance under the Group policy ceasing because of such termination, except that in the case of an Employee who upon such termination continues in the employment of the Employer but in a class not insured thereunder, the amount for which such individual policy may be issued shall not exceed the amount of insurance on his life under the Group policy ceasing because of such termination less any amount of life insurance for which he is or becomes eligible under any group policy within thirty-one days after such termination. Such individual policy, if issued, shall become effective upon the expiration of the thirty-first day following the day on which occurred such termination of his employment, provided the premium therefor is paid to the Society not later than such effective date.

B. Upon Termination of Policy. If the Group policy is terminated or amended so as to terminate the insurance of any class of Employees in which he is included, the Employee, if he has been continuously insured under said policy and under any policy issued by the Society which it replaces for five years or more immediately prior to such a termination, shall be entitled upon such a termination to the same benefits and upon the same conditions and limitations as set forth in the foregoing paragraph upon termination of employment, except that the amount of such converted life insurance shall in no event exceed the lesser of:

(1) $2,000, and

(2) the amount of the insurance on the Employee's life under the Group policy at the date of such a termination less any amount of life insurance for which he may become eligible under any group policy issued or reinstated by the Society or another insurer within thirty-one days after the date of such a termination.

MISSTATEMENT OF AGE. If the amount of insurance depends upon the age of the Employee and if there has been a misstatement of the Employee's age, there shall be an adjustment of the amount of his insurance to that determined by his correct age.

(6.01C)

PF 4441 (1E) (Amended by PF 7103-9517)

EXTENDED DEATH BENEFIT

A. During Conversion Period Following Termination of Employment. Upon receipt of due proof that an Employee whose insurance under the Group policy terminated due to termination of employment in the class or classes of Employees insured thereunder, died within thirty-one days after such termination of employment, the Society will pay to the Employee's beneficiary an amount of insurance equal to that for which such Employee would have been entitled to have an individual policy issued to him in accordance with the first paragraph of the provision hereof entitled "Conversion Privilege."

B. During Conversion Period Following Termination or Amendment of Policy. If an Employee's insurance is terminated due to termination or amendment of the Group policy, and if he has been continuously insured under said policy and under any policy issued by the Society which it replaces for five years or more immediately prior to such termination of his insurance, then upon receipt of due proof that the Employee died within thirty-one days following such termination, the Society will pay to the Employee's beneficiary the lesser of:

(1) $2,000, and

(2) the amount of insurance for which the Employee was last insured under the Group policy reduced by any amount for which the Employee became insured under any group policy issued or reinstated by the Society or another insurer within thirty-one days after the date of such termination.

C. During Total Disability Commencing Prior to Age Sixty. If an Employee before attaining 60 years of age and after the effective date hereof but before cessation of his insurance in accordance with the provision hereof entitled "Individual Terminations" becomes totally disabled by bodily injury or disease so as to be prevented from engaging in any occupation for compensation or profit, and

(1) the Employee remains continuously so disabled until his death, and

(2) death occurs either:

(a) within one year after the date of discontinuance of premium payments for the Employee's insurance, or

(b) more than one year after said date of discontinuance but prior to termination of this benefit because of failure of the Employee to submit due proof of continued total disability as required in the following paragraph,

then, upon receipt within one year after the Employee's death of due proof of such continued total disability and death, the Society, provided the Employee has complied with the conditions of this provision hereinafter set forth, will pay to the Employee's beneficiary the amount of insurance for which the Employee's life was last insured under the Group policy, but the amount so payable shall be reduced by any amount payable under Paragraph A or Paragraph B of this provision.

Extension of the death benefit hereunder beyond any anniversary of the date of discontinuance of premium payments for the Employee's insurance shall be subject to the Employee's submitting due proof in writing at the Home Office of the Society within three months prior to each such anniversary that he has been totally and continuously disabled since said date of discontinuance. If the Employee fails to submit such proof within three months prior to any anniversary the benefit shall terminate on that anniversary unless previously terminated because the Employee has ceased to be totally disabled as defined herein.

Extension of the death benefit hereunder shall also be subject to the following conditions:

(1) If an individual policy shall have been issued in conversion of the Employee's insurance under the Group policy, such individual policy must be surrendered to the Society at the time due proof of total disability is first submitted during the Employee's lifetime. Upon such surrender, the Society will refund any premiums theretofore received by the Society under the individual policy.

(2) The Society shall have the right and opportunity to have a medical representative of the Society examine the person of the Employee when and so often as it may reasonably require, but after the benefit has been continued for two full years under this provision, not more than once a year. Upon failure of the Employee to submit to any such examination this benefit shall terminate unless previously terminated because the Employee has ceased to be totally disabled as defined herein.

Upon termination of this benefit, the Employee, unless he becomes insured again under the Group policy within thirty-one days after such termination, shall be entitled to the rights and benefits set forth in Paragraph A of this provision and in Paragraph A of the provision hereof entitled "Conversion Privilege," as if employment had terminated on the date of such termination of benefit.

D. If a benefit becomes payable hereunder after an individual policy shall have been issued in conversion of the Employee's insurance under the Group policy, the amount, if any, paid as a death benefit under such individual policy shall be deemed to be a payment toward the amount of benefit becoming due hereunder and any premiums paid under the individual policy will be paid to the beneficiary thereunder upon surrender of the policy. The designation of a beneficiary under such an individual policy or in the application therefor (if such policy has not been issued) different from the beneficiary under the Group policy shall, notwithstanding any other provision of said Group policy, effect a change of beneficiary hereunder to the beneficiary so designated. While a benefit is continued under Paragraph C of this provision, an Employee may from time to time change the beneficiary by filing a written request with the Society at its Home Office, but such change shall take effect only upon receipt of the request for change at the Home Office of the Society.

(6.11C)

PF 4441 (1E) (Amended by PF 9517)

ACCIDENTAL DEATH AND DISMEMBERMENT INSURANCE

The Group Accidental Death and Dismemberment policy provides that upon receipt of due proof that the Employee, while insured thereunder, shall have sustained bodily injuries caused directly and exclusively by external, violent and purely accidental means, and, within ninety days after such injuries, and as a result, directly and independently of all other causes, of such injuries, shall have sustained any of the losses enumerated in the Schedule of Losses, the Society will, subject to the limitations and provisions set forth in said policy, pay to the Employee, if living, otherwise to the Employee's designated beneficiary, an amount determined in accordance with said Schedule.

Any part of the Accidental Death and Dismemberment insurance for which there is no beneficiary designated by the Employee or surviving at the death of the Employee will be payable in a single sum to the first surviving class of the following classes of successive preference beneficiaries: The Employee's (a) widow or widower; (b) surviving children; (c) surviving parents; (d) surviving brothers and sisters; (e) executors or administrators.

In the absence of the appointment of a legal guardian, any minor's share may be paid at a rate not exceeding $50 a month to such adult or adults as have in the Society's opinion assumed the custody and principal support of such minor.

Schedule of Losses

Life	The principal sum.
Two hands	The principal sum.
Two feet	The principal sum.
Sight of two eyes	The principal sum.
One hand and one foot	The principal sum.
One hand and sight of one eye	The principal sum.
One foot and sight of one eye	The principal sum.
One hand or one foot	One-half principal sum.
Sight of one eye	One-half principal sum.

With regard to hands and feet, loss shall mean dismemberment by severance at or above wrist or ankle joints respectively; with regard to eyes, total and irrecoverable loss of sight.

If the Employee shall sustain more than one of the aforesaid losses as a result of any one accident, payment shall be made only for that one loss for which the largest amount is payable.

Payment shall be made in accordance with the above Schedule for the specific loss resulting from an accident without reference to any previous loss.

LIMITATIONS.   No payment shall be made under the paragraph entitled Accidental Death and Dismemberment Insurance for any loss resulting from or caused directly or indirectly, wholly or partly, by

  (a) bodily or mental infirmity, hernia, ptomaines, bacterial infections (except infections caused by pyogenic organisms which shall occur with and through an accidental cut or wound) or disease or illness of any kind, or

  (b) self-destruction or self-inflicted injury, while sane or insane, or

  (c) war or an act of war, or service in any military, naval or air force of any country while such country is engaged in war, or performing police duty as a member of any military or naval organization, or

  (d) participation in or in consequence of having participated in the committing of a felony.

(8.01C)

PF 4441 (2) (Amended by PF 18505)

MAJOR MEDICAL EXPENSE INSURANCE

DEFINITIONS. BASE PLAN. As used herein and in the Group policy the term "Base Plan" shall include all plans providing benefits for the types of medical expense included in the term "covered charges" (as defined in the provision entitled "Major Medical Expense Benefits") provided they are plans toward the cost of which contributions or payroll deductions are made by the Employer.

MAJOR MEDICAL EXPENSE BENEFITS. The Group policy provides that the benefits hereinafter set forth are payable for "covered charges" (defined below) incurred on account of a non-occupational accidental bodily injury or a non-occupational sickness, and are subject to the other provisions and limitations of the Group policy applicable to Major Medical Expense insurance.

A. BENEFITS.

    1. AMOUNT OF BENEFITS. When an Employee or Dependent has incurred covered charges while insured for Major Medical Expense insurance and such covered charges during a calendar year exceed the deductible amount (defined below) the Society shall pay an amount of benefits equal to 80% of such covered charges in excess of the deductible amount during such calendar year, subject to a Maximum Amount of Benefits with respect to each person insured for Major Medical Expense Insurance of $5,000.

    2. REINSTATEMENT OF MAXIMUM AMOUNT OF BENEFITS. At any time after the payment of total benefits of $1000 or more with respect to an insured person, he may reestablish his Maximum Amount of Benefits by furnishing, without expense to the Society, evidence of his insurability satisfactory to the Society. Effective on the date of the Society's acceptance of such evidence, the amount of benefits previously paid for the person shall not be considered in applying the Maximum Amount of Benefits. If the Maximum Amount of Benefits has been paid, the person shall become insured again as of the date of the Society's acceptance of such evidence.

B. COVERED CHARGES. "Covered charges" shall consist of the following charges for services, supplies, and treatment:

    1. Charges made by a legally constituted and operated hospital for room and board and other services but not including any room and board charges for a private room in excess of a daily rate equal to the average room and board charge for semi-private accommodations made by the hospital.

    2. Charges made for diagnosis, treatment and surgery by a physician legally licensed to practice medicine and surgery.

    3. Charges made by a Registered Nurse for private duty nursing service.

    4. Charges for the following: local ambulance service, equipment, medication, appliances, x-ray services, laboratory tests, the use of radium and radioactive isotopes, oxygen, iron lung, physiotherapy.

    5. Charges made by a Doctor of Dental Surgery for the performance of oral surgery consisting of cutting procedures for the treatment of diseases or injuries of the jaw or extraction of impacted teeth, provided that such oral surgery is performed during a period of confinement in a legally constituted and operated hospital for at least eighteen hours.

The charges referred to shall in no event include any amount of such charges in excess of the regular and customary charges for the services, supplies and treatment furnished.

C. DEDUCTIBLE AMOUNT. The deductible amount for any calendar year shall be an amount equal to the sum of

    (1) a cash deductible of $100 , and

    (2) the total amount of benefits provided (including the value of benefits provided on a service basis) with respect to covered charges incurred during such calendar year under the Base Plan and any other Group plan or plans toward the cost of which any employer makes contributions or payroll deductions or any labor union makes contributions.

The deductible amount shall be applied separately to the amount of covered charges incurred during each calendar year by each person while insured under the policy, subject to the following exceptions:

    (i) The cash deductible shall be reduced by any amount of covered charges incurred for the insured person involved during the last three months of the preceding calendar year which were applied towards the cash deductible for such preceding calendar year.

    (ii) If two or more persons, while insured under the policy as members of the same family, incur covered charges on account of the same accident occurring while insured thereunder, a single cash deductible shall apply to the combined covered charges incurred by all such insured persons on account of the common accident during the calendar year in which such accident occurs and again during the following calendar year. Furthermore, any benefit paid that would not have been payable were it not for this provision, shall not be charged against the Maximum Amount of Benefits of the person involved. If during any calendar year one of the insured persons incurs covered charges not related to the common accident such person may apply towards the cash deductible applicable to such charges any covered charges which he incurred during such calendar year and which were applied towards the common-accident cash deductible.

If greater benefits should be payable without application of exception (ii), the greater amount shall be paid.

(46.272C)PF 4441 (24) (Amended by PF 13747-14339-21951)

MAJOR MEDICAL EXPENSE INSURANCE - (Cont'd)

ADDITIONAL LIMITATIONS APPLICABLE TO MAJOR MEDICAL EXPENSE BENEFITS.

In addition to the GENERAL LIMITATIONS applicable to the policy, the following limitations shall apply to MAJOR MEDICAL EXPENSE INSURANCE:

A. "Covered charges" shall in no event be deemed to include expenses incurred for services, supplies, or treatment
1. unless such services, supplies or treatment (including the entire period of hospital confinement) were prescribed as necessary by (a) a physician legally licensed to practice medicine and surgery or (b) a Doctor of Dental Surgery in connection with hospital confinement and oral surgery as herein provided,
2. if they were incurred on account of
   a. dental work, treatment, extractions, or dental x-rays, except as provided in 5. of "Covered Charges", unless such charges were made by a hospital as provided for in 1. of "Covered Charges" or were incurred on account of accidental injury of sound, natural teeth occurring while insured for Major Medical Expense Insurance,
   b. eye refractions, eyeglasses, or the fitting thereof,
   c. hearing aids or the fitting thereof,
   d. transportation, except for local ambulance service,
   e. war, declared or undeclared, including armed aggression,
   f. disease of a Dependent with respect to which benefits are payable under any workmen's compensation, occupational disease act or similar law,
   g. health examinations not required in connection with treatment of sickness or injury,
3. in any Federal hospital.

B. "Covered charges" shall in no event be deemed to include expenses incurred for services, supplies, or treatment if they were incurred on account of injury or sickness which existed within three months prior to the effective date of a person's insurance or any condition related to such injury or sickness, except that this limitation shall not apply to any such expenses incurred after the earliest of the following dates:
1. the date following the effective date of such person's insurance on which occurs the expiration of a period of three consecutive months during which no charges listed in the provision entitled "Covered Charges" were incurred on account of such injury or sickness or any related condition,
2. the date of the expiration of a period of six consecutive months during which the Employee was continuously actively at work and insured in the case of such injury or sickness of an Employee, and
3. the date of the expiration of a period of twelve consecutive months during which such person was continuously insured.
   This limitation shall not apply to a newborn child.

C. No payment shall be made under the provisions of the Group policy for any expenses incurred on account of pregnancy or resulting childbirth, abortion, or miscarriage, except that in the case of any complication arising out of such pregnancy, including a complication with respect to the newborn child, benefits shall be payable in accordance with the foregoing provisions, but with the following modifications:
1. Benefits shall be payable only for covered charges which are in excess of those which would have been incurred in the absence of complications, as determined by the Society.
2. Such covered charges with respect to the newborn child shall be added to those of the mother in determining the Major Medical Expense benefits.
3. If a person is pregnant on termination of her insurance under the Group policy, the benefits set forth in this paragraph shall be applicable with respect to covered charges incurred within a period ending on December 31 of the calendar year following the calendar year in which such termination of insurance occurs.

D. Payment for professional fees for psychiatric treatment while not confined to a hospital shall be subject to the provisions and limitations of the Group policy including the following additional limitations:
1. "Covered charges" shall not include any amount of such fees in excess of $20 per visit and shall not in any event include the fees of any practitioner other than a physician legally licensed to practice medicine and surgery.
2. Benefits for such professional fees shall be payable in accordance with the provision hereof entitled "Amount of Benefits" except that (a) the fraction in such provision applicable in determining the amount of benefits payable with respect to covered charges for such fees shall be limited to 50% and (b) benefits for such covered charges incurred during any period of twelve consecutive months shall not exceed $500.

(46.466C) PF 4441(25) (Amended by PF 14339-14790)

MAJOR MEDICAL EXPENSE INSURANCE - (Cont'd)

EXTENDED INSURANCE BENEFITS.

If a person's Major Medical Expense insurance terminates for cause other than payment of Maximum Amount of Benefits, and if at the date of such termination the person is totally disabled by bodily injury or disease so as to be continuously prevented from engaging in any occupation and performing all regular and customary duties, then benefits shall be provided, as if insurance had not terminated, for covered charges incurred solely on account of such injury or disease during the uninterrupted continuance of such disability and within a period ending on December 31 of the calendar year following the calendar year in which such termination of insurance occurs.

STANDARD PROVISIONS

(NOT APPLICABLE TO LIFE INSURANCE)

NOTICE OF CLAIM. Written notice of the event upon which claim may be based must be given to the Society at its Home Office in the City of New York within 90 days after the date of the loss or the beginning of the period, as the case may be, with respect to which claim is made. Failure to give notice within the time required by the policy shall not invalidate or reduce any claim if it shall be shown not to have been reasonably possible to give such notice within the required time and that notice was given as soon as was reasonably possible.

The Society, upon receipt of such notice, will furnish forms for filing proof of claim. If such forms are not furnished within fifteen days after the receipt of notice the claimant shall be deemed to have complied with the requirements of the policy as to proof of claim upon submitting within ninety days after the date of the loss for which claim is made, written proof covering the occurrence, character and extent of the loss for which claim is made.

PROOF OF CLAIM. Written proof of claim therein referred to must be furnished to the Society at its Home Office in the City of New York on the Society's forms within ninety days after the date of the loss or the end of the period, as the case may be, with respect to which claim is made. Failure to furnish written proof of loss within the time required by the policy shall not invalidate or reduce any claim if it shall be shown not to have been reasonably possible to furnish such proof within the required time and that proof was furnished as soon as was reasonably possible.

EXAMINATIONS. The Society shall have the right and opportunity through its medical representative to examine any person when and so often as it may reasonably require during the pendency of claim under the policy and also the right and opportunity to make an autopsy in case of death where it is not forbidden by law.

PAYMENT OF CLAIMS. Benefits are payable immediately upon receipt of due proof of claim except that if the policy provides weekly or daily benefits, all accrued benefits shall be paid at the expiration of each two weeks during the period for which benefits are payable thereunder, and any balance remaining unpaid at the termination of such period will be paid immediately upon receipt of due proof.

LEGAL PROCEEDINGS. No action at law or in equity shall be brought to recover under the policy prior to the expiration of 60 days after proof of claim has been furnished in accordance with the requirements of the policy, nor shall any such action be brought at all unless commenced within 2 years from the expiration of the time within which proof of claim is required by the provisions thereof.

PF 4441(8) Standard Provisions. (Amended by PF 21759), (25)(Amended by PF 13749)

B Uniform Individual Accident and Sickness Policy Provisions Law

A. Text

The following is the model bill adopted at the June, 1950 meeting of the National Association of Insurance Commissioners which, with the changes necessary to adapt it to the insurance codes of the various states, became the Uniform Individual Accident and Sickness Policy Provisions Law. The portions appearing in italics were not intended as language of the law, but rather as editorial comments on the proposed law or informative notations with respect to existing law. The portions printed in type of a smaller face than the body of the law were intended as part of it and to be enacted but were shown in smaller type to indicate that such portions were not to be included in the policy provisions themselves.

SECTION 1. DEFINITION OF ACCIDENT AND SICKNESS INSURANCE POLICY.

The term "policy of accident and sickness insurance" as used herein includes any policy or contract covering the kind or kinds of insurance described in ....
(insert here the section of law authorizing accident and sickness insurance).
(Note: If the insurance law of the state in which this draft is proposed for enactment does not have a section specifically authorizing the various types of insurance which may be written, this section should be modified to define accident and sickness insurance as "insurance against loss resulting from sickness or from bodily injury or death by accident, or both".)

SECTION 2. FORM OF POLICY.

(A) No policy of accident and sickness insurance shall be delivered or issued for delivery to any person in this state unless:
 (1) the entire money and other considerations therefor are expressed therein; and
 (2) the time at which the insurance takes effect and terminates is expressed therein; and
 (3) it purports to insure only one person, except that a policy may insure, originally or by subsequent amendment, upon the application of an adult member of a family who shall be deemed the policyholder, any two or more eligible members of that family, including husband, wife, dependent children or any children under a specified age which shall not exceed nineteen years and any other person dependent upon the policyholder; and
Note: In states having community property systems derived from the civil law it is suggested that in the foregoing subparagraph the words "an adult member" be replaced with "the head".)
 (4) the style, arrangement and over-all appearance of the policy give no undue prominence to any portion of the text, and unless every

printed portion of the text of the policy and of any endorsements or attached papers is plainly printed in light-faced type of a style in general use, the size of which shall be uniform and not less than ten-point with a lower-case unspaced alphabet length not less than one hundred and twenty-point (the "text" shall include all printed matter except the name and address of the insurer, name or title of the policy, the brief description if any, and captions and subcaptions); and

(5) the exceptions and reductions of indemnity are set forth in the policy and, except those which are set forth in section 3 of this act, are printed, at the insurer's option, either included with the benefit provision to which they apply, or under an appropriate caption such as "EXCEPTIONS", or "EXCEPTIONS AND REDUCTIONS", provided that if an exception or reduction specifically applies only to a particular benefit of the policy, a statement of such exception or reduction shall be included with the benefit provision to which it applies; and

(6) each such form, including riders and endorsements, shall be identified by a form number in the lower left-hand corner of the first page thereof; and

(7) it contains no provision purporting to make any portion of the charter, rules, constitution, or by-laws of the insurer a part of the policy unless such portion is set forth in full in the policy except in the case of the incorporation of, or reference to, a statement of rates or classification of risks, or short-rate table filed with the (*commissioner*).

(B) If any policy is issued by an insurer domiciled in this state for delivery to a person residing in another state, and if the official having responsibility for the administration of the insurance laws of such other state shall have advised the (*commissioner*) that any such policy is not subject to approval or disapproval by such official, the (*commissioner*) may by ruling require that such policy meet the standards set forth in subsection (A) of this section and in section 3.

SECTION 3. ACCIDENT AND SICKNESS POLICY PROVISIONS.

(A) Required Provisions

Except as provided in paragraph (C) of this section each such policy delivered or issued for delivery to any person in this state shall contain the provisions specified in this subsection in the words in which the same appear in this section; provided, however, that the insurer may, at its option, substitute for one or more of such provisions corresponding provisions of different wording approved by the (*commissioner*) which are in each instance not less favorable in any respect to the insured or the beneficiary. Such provisions shall be preceded individually by the caption appearing in this subsection or, at the option of the insurer, by such appropriate individual or group captions or subcaptions as the (*commissioner*) may approve.

(1) A provision as follows:

ENTIRE CONTRACT; CHANGES: This policy, including the endorsements and the attached papers, if any, constitutes the entire contract of insurance. No change in this policy shall be valid until approved by an executive officer of the insurer and unless such approval be endorsed hereon or attached hereto. No agent has authority to change this policy or to waive any of its provisions.

> (*Note: When enacted in states which prohibit amendment of a policy form by means other than attached printed rider upon a separate piece of paper the new law should contain (but not as a required policy provision) an added section defining "endorsement" in such a manner as to make the new law consistent with current statutes.*)

(2) A provision as follows:

TIME LIMIT ON CERTAIN DEFENSES: (a) After three years from the date of issue of this policy no misstatements, except fraudulent misstatements, made by the applicant in the application for such policy shall be used to void the policy or to deny a claim for loss incurred or disability (as defined in the policy) commencing after the expiration of such three year period.

(The foregoing policy provision shall not be so construed as to affect any legal requirement for avoidance of a policy or denial of a claim during such initial three year period, nor to limit the application of section 3 (B), (1), (2), (3), (4) and (5) in the event of misstatement with respect to age or occupation or other insurance.)

(A policy which the insured has the right to continue in force subject to its terms by the timely payment of premium (1) until at least age 50 or, (2) in the case of a policy issued after age 44, for at least five years from its date of issue, may contain in lieu of the foregoing the following provision (from which the clause in parentheses may be omitted at the insurer's option) under the caption "INCONTESTABLE":

After this policy has been in force for a period of three years during the lifetime of the insured (excluding any period during which the insured is disabled), it shall become incontestable as to the statements contained in the application.)

(b) No claim for loss incurred or disability (as defined in the policy) commencing after three years from the date of issue of this policy shall be reduced or denied on the ground that a disease or physical condition not excluded from the coverage by name or specific description effective on the date of loss had existed prior to the effective date of coverage of this policy.

(3) A provision as follows:

GRACE PERIOD: A grace period of .... (insert a number not less than "7" for weekly premium policies, "10" for monthly premium policies and "31" for all other policies) days will be granted for the payment of each premium falling due after the first premium, during which grace period the policy shall continue in force.

(A policy which contains a cancellation provision may add, at the end of the above provision,

subject to the right of the insurer to cancel in accordance with the cancellation provision hereof.

A policy in which the insurer reserves the right to refuse any renewal shall have, at the beginning of the above provision,

Unless not less than five days prior to the premium due date the insurer has delivered to the insured or has mailed to his last address as shown by the records of the insurer written notice of its intention not to renew this policy beyond the period for which the premium has been accepted,).

(4) A provision as follows:

REINSTATEMENT: If any renewal premium be not paid within the time granted the insured for payment, a subsequent acceptance of premium by the insurer or by any agent duly authorized by the insurer to accept such premium, without requiring in connection therewith an application for reinstatement, shall reinstate the policy; provided, however, that if the insurer or such agent requires an application for reinstatement and issues a conditional receipt for the premium tendered, the policy will be reinstated upon approval of such application by the insurer or, lacking such approval, upon the forty-fifth day following the date of such conditional receipt unless the insurer has previously notified the insured in writing of its disapproval of such application. The reinstated policy shall cover only loss resulting from such accidental injury as may be sustained after the date of reinstatement and loss due to such sickness as may begin more than ten days after such date. In all other respects the insured and insurer shall have the same rights thereunder as they had under the policy immediately before the due date of the defaulted premium, subject to any provisions endorsed hereon or attached hereto in connection with the reinstatement. Any premium accepted in connection with a reinstatement shall be applied to a period for which premium has not been previously paid, but not to any period more than sixty days prior to the date of reinstatement.

(The last sentence of the above provision may be omitted from any policy which the insured has the right to continue in force subject to its terms by the timely payment of premiums (1) until at least age 50 or, (2) in the case of a policy issued after age 44, for at least five years from its date of issue.)

(5) A provision as follows:

NOTICE OF CLAIM: Written notice of claim must be given to the insurer within twenty days after the occurrence or commencement of any loss covered by the policy, or as soon thereafter as is reasonably possible. Notice given by or on behalf of the insured or the beneficiary to the insurer at . . . .(insert the location of such office as the insurer may designate for the purpose) , or to any authorized agent of the insurer with information sufficient to identify the insured, shall be deemed notice to the insurer.

(In a policy providing a loss-of-time benefit which may be payable for at least two years, an insurer may at its option insert the following between the first and second sentences of the above provision:

Subject to the qualifications set forth below, if the insured suffers loss of time on account of disability for which indemnity may be payable for at least two years, he shall, at least once in every six months after having given notice of claim, give to the insurer notice of continuance of said disability, except in the event of legal incapacity. The period of six months following any filing of proof by the insured or any payment by the insurer on account of such claim or any denial of liability in whole or in part by the insurer shall be excluded in applying this provision. Delay in the giving of such notice shall not impair the insured's right to any indemnity which would otherwise have accrued during the period of six months preceding the date on which such notice is actually given.)

(6) A provision as follows:

CLAIM FORMS: The insurer, upon receipt of a notice of claim, will furnish to the claimant such forms as are usually furnished by it for filing proofs of loss. If such forms are not furnished within fifteen days after the giving of such notice the claimant shall be deemed to have complied with the requirements of this policy as to proof of loss upon submitting, within the time fixed in the policy for filing proofs of loss, written proof covering the occurrence, the character and the extent of the loss for which claim is made.

(7) A provision as follows:

PROOFS OF LOSS: Written proof of loss must be furnished to the insurer at its said office in case of claim for loss for which this policy provides any periodic payment contingent upon continuing loss within ninety days after the termination of the period for which the insurer is liable and in case of claim for any other loss within ninety days after the date of such loss. Failure to furnish such proof within the time required shall not invalidate nor reduce any claim if it was not reasonably possible to give proof within such time, provided such proof is furnished as soon as reasonably possible and in no event, except in the absence of legal capacity, later than one year from the time proof is otherwise required.

(8) A provision as follows:

TIME OF PAYMENT OF CLAIMS: Indemnities payable under this policy for any loss other than loss for which this policy provides any periodic payment will be paid immediately upon receipt of due written proof of such loss. Subject to due written proof of loss, all accrued indemnities for loss for which this policy provides periodic payment will be paid . . . . (insert period for payment which must not be less frequently than monthly) and any balance remaining unpaid upon the termination of liability will be paid immediately upon receipt of due written proof.

(9) A provision as follows:

PAYMENT OF CLAIMS: Indemnity for loss of life will be payable in accordance with the beneficiary designation and the provisions respecting such payment which may be prescribed herein and effective at the time of payment. If no such designation or provision is then effective, such indemnity shall be payable to the estate of the insured. Any other accrued indemnities unpaid at the insured's death may, at the option of the insurer, be paid either to such beneficiary or to such estate. All other indemnities will be payable to the insured.

(The following provisions, or either of them, may be included with the foregoing provision at the option of the insurer:

If any indemnity of this policy shall be payable to the estate of the insured, or to an insured or beneficiary who is a minor or otherwise not competent to give a valid release, the insurer may pay such indemnity, up to an amount not exceeding $ . . . . (insert an amount which shall not exceed $1000) , to any relative by blood or connection by marriage of the insured or beneficiary who is deemed by the insurer to be equitably entitled thereto. Any payment made by the insurer in good faith pursuant to this provision shall fully discharge the insurer to the extent of such payment.

Subject to any written direction of the insured in the application or otherwise all or a portion of any indemnities provided by this policy on account of hospital, nursing, medical, or surgical services may, at the insurer's option and unless the insured requests otherwise in writing not later than the time of filing proofs of such loss, be paid directly to the hospital or person rendering such services; but it is not required that the service be rendered by a particular hospital or person.)

(10) A provision as follows:

PHYSICAL EXAMINATIONS AND AUTOPSY: The insurer at its own expense shall have the right and opportunity to examine the person of the insured when and as often as it may reasonably require during the pendency of a claim hereunder and to make an autopsy in case of death where it is not forbidden by law.

(11) A provision as follows:

LEGAL ACTIONS: No action at law or in equity shall be brought to recover on this policy prior to the expiration of sixty days after written proof of loss has been furnished in accordance with the requirements of this policy. No such action shall be brought after the expiration of three years after the time written proof of loss is required to be furnished.

(12) A provision as follows:

CHANGE OF BENEFICIARY: Unless the insured makes an irrevocable designation of beneficiary, the right to change the beneficiary is reserved to the insured and the consent of the beneficiary or beneficiaries shall not be requisite to surrender or assignment of this policy or to any change of beneficiary or beneficiaries, or to any other changes in this policy.

(The first clause of this provision, relating to the irrevocable designation of beneficiary, may be omitted at the insurer's option.)

(B) Other Provisions

Except as provided in paragraph (C) of this section, no such policy delivered or issued for delivery to any person in this state shall contain provisions respecting the matters set forth below unless such provisions are in the words in which the same appear in this section; provided, however, that the insurer may, at its option, use in lieu of any such provision a corresponding provision of different wording approved by the (commissioner) which is not less favorable in any respect to the insured or the beneficiary. Any such provision contained in the policy shall be preceded individually by the appropriate caption appearing in this subsection or, at the option of the insurer, by such appropriate individual or group captions or subcaptions as the (commissioner) may approve.

(1) A provision as follows:

CHANGE OF OCCUPATION: If the insured be injured or contract sickness after having changed his occupation to one classified by the insurer as more hazardous than that stated in this policy or while doing for compensation anything pertaining to an occupation so classified, the insurer will pay only such portion of the indemnities provided in this policy as the premium paid would have purchased at the rates and within the limits fixed by the insurer for such more hazardous occupation. If the insured changes his occupation to one classified by the insurer as less hazardous than that stated in this policy, the insurer, upon receipt of proof of such change of occupation, will reduce the premium rate accordingly, and will return the excess pro-rata unearned premium from the date of change of occupation or from the policy anniversary date immediately preceding receipt of such proof, whichever is the more recent. In applying this provision, the classification of occupational risk and the premium rates shall be such as have been last filed by the insurer prior to the occurrence of the loss for which the insurer is liable or prior to date of proof of change in occupation with the state official having supervision of insurance in the state where the insured resided at the time this policy was issued; but if such filing was not required, then the classification of occupational risk and the premium rates shall be those last made effective by the insurer in such state prior to the occurrence of the loss or prior to the date of proof of change in occupation.

(2) A provision as follows:

MISSTATEMENT OF AGE: If the age of the insured has been misstated, all amounts payable under this policy shall be such as the premium paid would have purchased at the correct age.

(3) A provision as follows:

OTHER INSURANCE IN THIS INSURER: If an accident or sickness or accident and sickness policy or policies previously issued by the insurer to the insured be in force concurrently herewith, making the aggregate indemnity for . . . . (insert type of coverage or coverages) in excess of $ . . . . (insert maximum limit of indemnity or indemnities) the excess insurance shall be void and all premiums paid for such excess shall be returned to the insured or to his estate.

or, in lieu thereof:

Insurance effective at any one time on the insured under a like policy or for policies in this insurer is limited to the one such policy elected by the insured, his beneficiary or his estate, as the case may be, and the insurer will return all premiums paid for all other such policies.

(4) A provision as follows:

INSURANCE WITH OTHER INSURERS: If there be other valid coverage, not with this insurer, providing benefits for the same loss on a provision of service basis or on an expense incurred basis and of which this insurer has not been given written notice prior to the occurrence or commencement of loss, the only liability under any expense incurred coverage of this policy shall be for such proportion of the loss as the amount which would otherwise have been payable hereunder plus the total of the like amounts under all such other valid coverages for the same loss of which this insurer had notice bears to the total like amounts under all valid coverages for such loss, and for the return of such portion of the premiums paid as shall exceed the pro-rata portion for the amount so determined. For the purpose of applying this provision when other coverage is on a provision of service basis, the "like amount" of such other coverage shall be taken as the amount which the services rendered would have cost in the absence of such coverage.

(If the foregoing policy provision is included in a policy which also contains the next following policy provision there shall be added to the caption of the foregoing provision the phrase "—EXPENSE INCURRED BENEFITS". The insurer may, at its option, include in this provision a definition of "other valid coverage", approved as to form by the (*commissioner*), which definition shall be limited in subject matter to coverage provided by organizations subject to regulation by insurance law or by insurance authorities of this or any other state of the United States or any province of Canada, and by hospital or medical service organizations, and to any other coverage the inclusion of which may be approved by the (*commissioner*). In the absence of such definition such term shall not include group insurance, automobile medical payments insurance, or coverage provided by hospital or medical service organizations or by union welfare plans or employer or employee benefit organizations. For the purpose of applying the foregoing policy provision with respect to any insured, any amount of benefit provided for such insured pursuant to any compulsory benefit statute (including any workmen's compensation or employer's liability statute) whether provided by a governmental agency or otherwise shall in all cases be deemed to be "other valid coverage" of which the insurer has had notice. In applying the foregoing policy provision no third party liability coverage shall be included as "other valid coverage".)

(5) A provision as follows:

INSURANCE WITH OTHER INSURERS: If there be other valid coverage, not with this insurer, providing benefits for the same loss on other than an expense incurred basis and of which this insurer has not been given written notice prior to the occurrence or commencement of loss, the only liability for such benefits under this policy shall be for such proportion of the indemnities otherwise provided hereunder for such loss as the like indemnities of which the insurer had notice (including the indemnities under this policy) bear to the total amount of all like indemnities for such loss, and for the return of such portion of the premium paid as shall exceed the pro-rata portion for the indemnities thus determined.

(If the foregoing policy provision is included in a policy which also contains the next preceding policy provision there shall be added to the caption of the foregoing provision the phrase "—OTHER BENEFITS". The insurer may, at its option, include in this provision a definition of "other valid coverage", approved as to form by the (*commissioner*), which definition shall be limited in subject matter to coverage provided by organizations subject to regulation by insurance law or by insurance authorities of this or any other state of the United States or any province of Canada, and to any other coverage the inclusion of which may be approved by the (*commissioner*). In the absence of such definition such term shall not include group insurance, or benefits provided by union welfare plans or by employer or employee benefit organizations. For the purpose of applying the foregoing policy provision with respect to any insured, any amount of benefit provided for such insured pursuant to any compulsory benefit statute (including any workmen's compensation or employer's liability statute) whether provided by a governmental agency or otherwise shall in all cases be deemed to be "other valid coverage" of which the insurer has had notice. In applying the foregoing policy provision no third party liability coverage shall be included as "other valid coverage".)

(6) A provision as follows:

RELATION OF EARNINGS TO INSURANCE: If the total monthly amount of loss of time benefits promised for the same loss under all valid loss of time coverage upon the insured, whether payable on a weekly or monthly basis, shall exceed the monthly earnings of the insured at the time disability commenced or his average monthly earnings for the period of two years immediately preceding a disability for which claim is made, whichever is the greater, the insurer will be liable only for such proportionate amount of such benefits under this policy as the amount of such monthly earnings or such average monthly earnings of the insured bears to the total amount of monthly benefits for the same loss under all such coverage upon the insured at the time such disability commences and for the return of such part of the premiums paid during such two years as shall exceed the pro-rata amount of the premiums for the benefits actually paid hereunder; but this shall not operate to reduce the total monthly amount of benefits payable under all such coverage upon the insured below the sum of two hundred dollars or the sum of the monthly benefits specified in such coverages, whichever is the lesser, nor shall it operate to reduce benefits other than those payable for loss of time.

(The foregoing policy provision may be inserted only in a policy which the insured has the right to continue in force subject to its terms by the timely payment of premiums (1) until at least age 50 or, (2) in the case of a policy issued after age 44, for at least five years from its date of issue. The insurer may, at its option, include in this provision a definition of "valid loss of time coverage", approved as to form by the (*commissioner*), which definition shall be limited in subject matter to coverage provided by governmental agencies or by organizations subject to regulation by insurance law or by insurance authorities of this or any other state of the United States or any province of Canada, or to any other coverage the inclusion of which may be approved by the (*commissioner*) or any combination of such coverages. In the absence of such definition such term shall not include any coverage provided for such insured pursuant to any compulsory benefit statute (including any workmen's compensation or employer's liability statute), or benefits provided by union welfare plans or by employer or employee benefit organizations.)

(7) A provision as follows:

UNPAID PREMIUM: Upon the payment of a claim under this policy, any premium then due and unpaid or covered by any note or written order may be deducted therefrom.

(8) A provision as follows:

CANCELLATION: The insurer may cancel this policy at any time by written notice delivered to the insured, or mailed to his last address as shown by the records of the insurer, stating when, not less than five days thereafter, such cancellation shall be effective; and after the policy has been continued beyond its original term the insured may cancel this policy at any time by written notice delivered or mailed to the insurer, effective upon receipt or on such later date as may be specified in such notice. In the event of cancellation, the insurer will return promptly the unearned portion of any premium paid. If the insured cancels, the earned premium shall be computed by the use of the short-rate table last filed with the state official having supervision of insurance in the state where the insured resided when the policy was issued. If the insurer cancels, the earned premium shall be computed pro-rata. Cancellation shall be without prejudice to any claim originating prior to the effective date of cancellation.

(Note: In some states by statute termination of the in force status of the policy alone may not prejudice any claim for loss arising during and out of a disability which commenced while the policy was in force. The language here is susceptible of an interpretation consistent with such statutes.)

(9) A provision as follows:

CONFORMITY WITH STATE STATUTES: Any provision of this policy which, on its effective date, is in conflict with the statutes of the state in which the insured resides on such date is hereby amended to conform to the minimum requirements of such statutes.

(10) A provision as follows:

ILLEGAL OCCUPATION: The insurer shall not be liable for any loss to which a contributing cause was the insured's commission of or attempt to commit a felony or to which a contributing cause was the insured's being engaged in an illegal occupation.

(11) A provision as follows:

INTOXICANTS AND NARCOTICS: The insurer shall not be liable for any loss sustained or contracted in consequence of the insured's being intoxicated or under the influence of any narcotic unless administered on the advice of a physician.

(Note: Paragraphs (10) and (11) are suggested for states which desire such provisions.)

(C) Inapplicable or Inconsistent Provisions

If any provision of this section is in whole or in part inapplicable to or inconsistent with the coverage provided by a particular form of policy the insurer, with the approval of the (commissioner), shall omit from such policy any inapplicable provision or part of a provision, and shall modify any inconsistent provision or part of the provision in such manner as to make the provision as contained in the policy consistent with the coverage provided by the policy.

(D) Order of Certain Policy Provisions

The provisions which are the subject of subsections (A) and (B) of this section, or any corresponding provisions which are used in lieu thereof in accordance with such subsections, shall be printed in the consecutive order of the provisions in such subsections or, at the option of the insurer, any such provision may appear as a unit in any part of the policy, with other provisions to which it may be logically related, provided the resulting policy shall not be in whole or in part unintelligible, uncertain, ambiguous, abstruse, or likely to mislead a person to whom the policy is offered, delivered or issued.

(E) Third Party Ownership

The word "insured", as used in this act, shall not be construed as preventing a person other than the insured with a proper insurable interest from making application for and owning a policy covering the insured or from being entitled under such a policy to any indemnities, benefits and rights provided therein.

(F) Requirements of Other Jurisdictions

(1) Any policy of a foreign or alien insurer, when delivered or issued for delivery to any person in this state, may contain any provision which is not less favorable to the insured or the beneficiary than the provisions of this act and which is prescribed or required by the law of the state under which the insurer is organized.

(2) Any policy of a domestic insurer may, when issued for delivery in any other state or country, contain any provision permitted or required by the laws of such other state or country.

(G) Filing Procedure

The (commissioner) may make such reasonable rules and regulations concerning the procedure for the filing or submission of policies subject to this act as are necessary, proper or advisable to the administration of this act. This provision shall not abridge any other authority granted the (*commissioner*) by law.

SECTION 4. CONFORMING TO STATUTE.

(A) Other Policy Provisions

No policy provision which is not subject to section 3 of this act shall make a policy, or any portion thereof, less favorable in any respect to the insured or the beneficiary than the provisions thereof which are subject to this act.

(B) Policy Conflicting with this Act

A policy delivered or issued for delivery to any person in this state in violation of this act shall be held valid but shall be construed as provided in this act. When any provision in a policy subject to this act is in conflict with any provision of this act, the rights, duties and obligations of the insurer, the insured and the beneficiary shall be governed by the provisions of this act.

SECTION 5. APPLICATION.

(A) The insured shall not be bound by any statement made in an application for a policy unless a copy of such application is attached to or endorsed on the policy when issued as a part thereof. If any such policy delivered or issued for delivery to any person in this state shall be reinstated or renewed, and the insured or the beneficiary or assignee of such policy shall make written request to the insurer for a copy of the application, if any, for such reinstatement or renewal, the insurer shall within fifteen days after the receipt of such request at its home office or any branch office of the insurer, deliver or mail to the person making such request, a copy of such application. If such copy shall not be so delivered or mailed, the insurer shall be precluded from introducing such application as evidence in any action or proceeding based upon or involving such policy or its reinstatement or renewal.

(B) No alteration of any written application for any such policy shall be made by any person other than the applicant without his written consent, except that insertions may be made by the insurer, for administrative purposes only, in such manner as to indicate clearly that such insertions are not to be ascribed to the applicant.

(C) The falsity of any statement in the application for any policy covered by this act may not bar the right to recovery thereunder unless such false statement materially affected either the acceptance of the risk or the hazard assumed by the insurer.

(*Note: Section 5, or any subsection thereof, is suggested for use in states which have no comparable statutes relating to the application.*)

SECTION 6. NOTICE, WAIVER.

The acknowledgement by any insurer of the receipt of notice given under any policy covered by this act, or the furnishing of forms for filing proofs of loss, or the acceptance of such proofs, or the investigation of any claim thereunder shall not operate as a waiver of any of the rights of the insurer in defense of any claim arising under such policy.

SECTION 7. AGE LIMIT.

If any such policy contains a provision establishing, as an age limit or otherwise, a date after which the coverage provided by the policy will not be effective, and if such date falls within a period for which premium is accepted by the insurer or if the insurer accepts a premium after such date, the coverage provided by the policy will continue in force subject to any right of cancellation until the end of the period for which premium has been accepted. In the event the age of the insured has been misstated and if, according to the correct age of the insured, the coverage provided by the policy would not have become effective, or would have ceased prior to the acceptance of such premium or premiums, then the liability of the insurer shall be limited to the refund, upon request, of all premiums paid for the period not covered by the policy.

SECTION 8. NON-APPLICATION TO CERTAIN POLICIES.

Nothing in this act shall apply to or affect (1) any policy of workmen's compensation insurance or any policy of liability insurance with or without supplementary expense coverage therein; or (2) any policy or contract of reinsurance; or (3) any blanket or group policy of insurance; or (4) life insurance, endowment or annuity contracts, or contracts supplemental thereto which contain only such provisions relating to accident and sickness insurance as (a) provide additional benefits in case of death or dismemberment or loss of sight by accident, or as (b) operate to safeguard such contracts against lapse, or to give a special surrender value or special benefit or an annuity in the event that the insured or annuitant shall become totally and permanently disabled, as defined by the contract or supplemental contract.

(*Note: This provision may, if desired, be modified in individual states so as to be consistent with current statutes of such states.*)

SECTION 9. VIOLATION.

Any person, partnership or corporation willfully violating any provision of this act or order of the (*commissioner*) made in accordance with this

act, shall forfeit to the people of the state a sum not to exceed $ . . . .
for each such violation, which may be recovered by a civil action. The
(*commissioner*) may also suspend or revoke the license of an insurer or
agent for any such willful violation.

(*Note: This provision is to be used only in those states which do not
have similar legislation now in effect.*)

SECTION 10. JUDICIAL REVIEW.

Any order or decision of the (*commissioner*) under this act shall be
subject to review by appeal (writ of certiorari) to the . . . .
Court at the instance of any party in interest. The filing of the appeal
(petition for such writ) shall operate as a stay of any such order or decision
until the Court directs otherwise. The Court may review all the facts and,
in disposing of the issue before it, may modify, affirm or reverse the order
or decision of the (*commissioner*) in whole or in part.

(*Note: This provision is to be used only in those states which do not
have similar legislation now in effect.*)

SECTION 11. REPEAL OF INCONSISTENT ACTS.

(*Note: This section should contain suitable language to repeal acts or
parts of acts presently enacted and inconsistent with this act.
The repealing section should contain an appropriate exception
with regard to section 12 of this act.*)

SECTION 12. EFFECTIVE DATE OF ACT.

This act shall take effect on the . . . . day of . . . . ,
19 . . . . A policy, rider or endorsement, which could have been
lawfully used or delivered or issued for delivery to any person in this state
immediately before the effective date of this act may be used or delivered
or issued for delivery to any such person during five years after the effective date of this act without being subject to the provisions of sections 2, 3
or 4 of this act.

B. Variations in the Uniform Individual Accident and Sickness Policy Provisions Law as Enacted in Different States*

In certain instances the legal requirements applicable to a health insurance policy differ from the minimum requirements of the Uniform Law be-

* Edwin L. Bartleson *et al.*, *Health Insurance Provided Through Industrial Policies*,
rev. ed. (Chicago: Society of Actuaries, 1968), pp. 232–233. Used by permission.

cause of additional legislation or insurance departments' regulations. In addition to these supplementary laws, and sometimes incidental to them, there have been departures from uniformity in the various versions in which the law has been enacted. Some of the most important of these are indicated below.

1. *Form of Policy.*
   (a) In several states application for family coverage must be made by the head of the family. These states include California, Louisiana, Nevada, New Mexico, Pennsylvania and Washington.
   (b) In several states family policies must extend the coverage of unmarried dependent children who are unemployable by reason of mental retardation or physical handicap when they attain the age limit for coverage of children. These states are Arkansas, Hawaii, Illinois, Massachusetts, Michigan, Missouri, New Jersey, and New York.

2. *Time Limit on Certain Defenses.*
   (a) The limit is two years in Alabama, Colorado, Georgia, Illinois, Kansas, Kentucky, Maryland, Massachusetts, Michigan, Minnesota, Mississippi, Missouri, New Mexico, New York, Ohio, Oklahoma, North Carolina, South Carolina, South Dakota and West Virginia. In Missouri, a limit of three years may be used in the optional *Incontestable* clause.
   (b) In New Mexico no time limit is specified in the second paragraph of the *Time Limit* provision, so there can be no exclusion of pre-existing conditions. In Georgia, the phrase "except fraudulent misstatements" is omitted and in North Carolina it may be used only in policies meeting prescribed tests as to the benefits provided.

3. *Grace Period.* The time within which notice of intention not to renew must be given, which is referred to in the *Grace Period* provision, is 30 days in Alabama, Arkansas, Illinois, Maryland, Massachusetts, Montana, New York, Oklahoma, South Carolina, South Dakota, Utah, West Virginia, and Wisconsin. In North Carolina, the time is from 30 days to two years, and in Rhode Island, it is 10 days. In Mississippi nonrenewal of a hospital, medical or surgical policy in force four years or more is prohibited except upon one year's notice to insured.

4. *Reinstatement.* New Mexico reduces to 30 days the period during which an application for reinstatement may be disapproved.

5. *Notice of Claim.* In Mississippi, the time allowed for notice must be 30 days, and in Wyoming 60 days.

6. *Physical Examination and Autopsy.* The reference to autopsy is omitted in Massachusetts, Mississippi, and South Carolina.

7. *Legal Actions.* The maximum time limit within which legal actions

must be brought is one year in Louisiana, five years in Kansas and six years in South Carolina.

8. Other Insurance. The optional provisions dealing with insurance in the same or other insurers may not be used in hospital, surgical, or medical expense policies in South Dakota or West Virginia. The Mississippi law omits all of the optional *"other insurance"* provisions except the one dealing with *Relation of Earnings to Insurance* which applies to loss of time coverage.

9. Cancellation. No provision for cancellation may be used in Alabama, Arkansas, Georgia, Idaho, Maryland, Massachusetts, Montana, New Mexico, North Carolina, Ohio, Oklahoma, Utah, West Virginia or Wisconsin. In Rhode Island, 10 days' notice of cancellation is required and in New York and South Carolina, the permissible provisions are effective only during the first 90 days and first six months, respectively. In Mississippi cancellation of a hospital, medical or surgical policy in force four years or more is prohibited except upon one year's notice.

10. Illegal Occupation; Intoxicants and Narcotics. These are not given as optional provisions in Colorado, Connecticut, New Hampshire, New Mexico and South Dakota. Minnesota and Oklahoma include the optional provision for *Illegal Occupation* but omit the intoxicants part of the optional provision for *Intoxicants and Narcotics*.

C Mathematics of Life Insurance

IN THE SECTION of the volume relating to the mathematical aspects of life insurance, all calculations were arithmetical. In practice, symbols are used to calculate premiums and reserves. By using symbols and notations the actual calculation of premiums and reserves is much simplified. In order to understand the formulas used by the actuary in his work, one must learn the language of symbols and notations.

Furthermore, in order to minimize the actual computation work, commutation symbols, each representing a series of calculations and available in table form, are used in computing premiums and reserves.

In the following pages a summary of the mathematical approach of the actuary is presented on a basis which correlates with the arithmetical approach presented earlier.

NET SINGLE PREMIUMS

1. Accumulating and Discounting Money

The fundamental concepts of accumulating money (finding its value at a later date) and discounting money (finding its value at an earlier date) were introduced in Chapter 20. Each of these processes can be expressed by the equations (1) and (2), respectively:

Accumulating: $$S = A(1 + i)^n \qquad (1)$$

which states that a sum of money A growing at the rate of interest i per year will amount to S after n years.

Example 1. Find the accumulated value of $1,000.00 at the end of 50 years at the rate of 2½%.

Solution. Using equation (1)

$$S = \$1,000.00(1.025)^{50}$$
$$= \$3,437.11 \qquad \qquad Ans.$$

Discounting: Solving equation (1) for A,

$$A = \frac{S}{(1 + i)^n} = S \cdot v^n \cdot \left(v = \frac{1}{1 + i} \right) \qquad (2)$$

where A is the amount of money which will grow to S in n years at the rate of interest i per year.

Example 2.   Find the present value of $1,000.00 due in 50 years if money grows at the rate of 2½% per year.

Solution. From Table 20–2, the present value of $1.00 due in 50 years is 0.290942; therefore, the present value of $1,000.00 is

$$\$1,000.00(0.290942) = \$290.94 \qquad Ans.$$

The quantities $(1 + i)$ and v are known as the accumulation factor and discount factor respectively using an interest rate i.

2. Accumulating and Discounting With Benefit of Survivorship (WBOS)

The following definitions will be found useful in the work which follows:

$l_x =$ the number of individuals alive at age x as recorded in the mortality table.

$d_x = l_x - l_{x+1}$ is the number of individuals who die between ages x and $x + 1$ in a one-year period of time.

$q_x = \dfrac{d_x}{l_x}$ the probability that a person aged x will die between ages x and $x + 1$.

Assume that l_x persons each contribute $1.00 to a fund which will be invested at rate i per year and at the end of n years the accumulated fund will be divided among the l_{x+n} survivors. Each survivor will share in the accumulated interest earned on the fund and also by his portion of the funds contributed by those who failed to survive. This method of accumulating money is known as *accumulating with benefit of survivorship*. An expression will now be derived representing the accumulation factor WBOS.

The total fund invested by l_x persons is $1.00 l_x, and its value n years later is by equation (1)

$$\$1.00 \, l_x(1 + i)^n$$

which is shared equally among the l_{x+n} survivors, the share of each being

$$\frac{\$1.00 \, l_x(1 + i)^n}{l_{x+n}}$$

which is one form of the accumulation factor WBOS.

A simpler form can be obtained by multiplying the numerator and denominator of the fraction by v^{x+n} with the result,

$$\frac{\$1.00 \, l_x(1 + i)^n \, v^{x+n}}{v^{x+n}l_{x+n}}$$

Since

$$(1 + i)^n \cdot v^{x+n} = (1 + i)^n \cdot v^n \cdot v^x = 1v^x$$

the fraction may be written,

$$\$1.00 \, \frac{v^x l_x}{v^{x+n} l_{x+n}} = \$1.00 \, \frac{D_x}{D_{x+n}} \tag{3}$$

where D_x is defined to be $v^x l_x$, and is the first of a series of symbols known as commutation symbols which serve to simplify the calculation of annuity and insurance benefits, when tables of commutation functions are available.

Example 3.   Find the accumulated value of $1,000.00 WBOS for 50 years on a male life aged (a) 25 years, (b) 35 years, (c) 45 years. Use *1958 CSO Table*, 2½%.

Solution.

(a) $\$1,000.00 \, \dfrac{D_{25}}{D_{75}} = \$1,000.00 \, \dfrac{5,165,008.0}{648,112.3} = \$7,969.31$ *Ans.*

(b) $\$1,000.00 \, \dfrac{D_{35}}{D_{85}} = \$1,000.00 \, \dfrac{3,949,851.1}{160,764.2} = \$24,569.22$ *Ans.*

(c) $\$1,000.00 \, \dfrac{D_{45}}{D_{95}} = \$1,000.00 \, \dfrac{2,978,698.8}{9,305.6} = \$320,097.45$ *Ans.*

The problem of discounting $1.00 WBOS is most easily considered by answering the question: What sum, X, will grow to $1.00 in n years WBOS? The answer is simply that $X \cdot \dfrac{D_x}{D_{x+n}} = \$1.00$ by equation (3); therefore,

$$X = \frac{\$1.00}{\dfrac{D_x}{D_{x+n}}} = \$1.00 \, \frac{D_{x+n}}{D_x} \tag{4}$$

which is the discount factor WBOS = $1.00 $A X{:}\overset{1}{\overline{n}}$. The numeral 1 over the $\overline{n}$ is to indicate that the benefit is paid *only* if the period of n years expires before the life fails. The quantity $\dfrac{D_{x+n}}{D_x}$ is sometimes referred to as the net single premium *pure endowment* of 1 because it is the value at age x of a unit which will be paid at age $x + n$ if x is alive at that time.

3. Cost of Insurance

The *cost of insurance* is defined to be the premium paid at the begining of a year which will provide an insurance benefit of $1.00 at the end of the year if death occurs during the year. It is represented by the symbol c_x (not to be confused with C_x defined below).

Using the principle stated in italics on page 349,

$$\$1.00\ c_x = \$1.00\ q_x \cdot v = \$1.00\ v\ \frac{d_x}{l_x} \tag{5}$$

If the numerator and denominator are multiplied by v^x, the value of c_x becomes:

$$c_x = \frac{v^x \cdot v \cdot d_x}{v^x l_x} = \frac{v^{x+1} d_x}{v^x l_x} = \frac{C_x}{D_x} \tag{6}$$

where
$$C_x = v^{x+1} d_x$$

Because q_x increases continually after the age of 10 in the *1958 CSO Table,* the cost of insurance will increase slowly at first, but with increasing rapidity as the end of the mortality table is approached. This fact is exhibited graphically on page 10.

　　　Example 4.　　Calculate the cost of insurance for an insurance of $1,000.00 on a male life aged (a) 25, (b) 35, (c) 45. Use *1958 CSO Table,* 2½ per cent.

　　Solution.

(a) $\$1,000.00\ c_{25} = \$1,000.00\ \dfrac{C_{25}}{D_{25}} = \dfrac{\$1,000.00 \times 9,725.344}{5,165,008.0} = \$1.88$　　*Ans.*

(b) $\$1,000.00\ c_{35} = \$1,000.00\ \dfrac{C_{35}}{D_{35}} = \dfrac{\$1,000.00 \times 9,672.213}{3,949,851.1} = \$2.45$　　*Ans.*

(c) $\$1,000.00\ c_{45} = \$1,000.00\ \dfrac{C_{45}}{D_{45}} = \dfrac{\$1,000.00 \times 15,547.309}{2,978,698.8} = \$5.22$　　*Ans.*

4. Whole-Life Insurance

　　The net single premium A_x for a $1.00 whole-life insurance policy on a life aged x will obviously be the discounted value to age x of all of the natural premiums for each of the years from age x to the end of the mortality table. Therefore, using equation (4)

$$A_x = c_x + c_{x+1} \cdot \frac{D_{x+1}}{D_x} + c_{x+2} \frac{D_{x+2}}{D_x} + \cdots$$

Using equation (5)

$$A_x = \frac{C_x}{D_x} \cdot \frac{D_x}{D_x} + \frac{C_{x+1}}{D_{x+1}} \cdot \frac{D_{x+1}}{D_x} + \frac{C_{x+2}}{D_{x+2}} \cdot \frac{D_{x+2}}{D_x} + \cdots$$

$$= \frac{C_x + C_{x+1} + C_{x+2} + \cdots}{D_x}$$

$$= \frac{M_x}{D_x} \tag{7}$$

Where M_x is defined to be $C_x + C_{x+1} + C_{x+2} + \cdots$

Example 5.   Calculate the net single premium on a $1,000.00 whole-life policy on a male life aged 45. Use *1958 CSO Table,* 2½ per cent.

Solution.

$$\$1,000.00 \frac{M_{45}}{D_{45}} = \frac{\$1,000.00 \times 1,541,435.368}{2,978,698.8} = \$517.49 \qquad Ans.$$

5. Term Insurance

The net single premium for a *n-year* term insurance policy for $1.00 on a life aged x is represented by the symbol $A^1_{x:\overline{n}|}$. This premium is evidently equal to the discounted value of the first n natural premiums, so that

$$A^1_{x:\overline{n}|} = \frac{C_x + C_{x+1} + C_{x+2} + \cdots + C_{x+n-1}}{D_x}$$

$$A^1_{x:\overline{n}|} = \frac{M_x - M_{x+n}}{D_x} \tag{8}$$

The effect of the negative term is to eliminate all insurance benefits at and after age $x + n$. The numeral 1 over the x is to indicate that the benefit is paid only if the life fails before the expiration of the *n*-year term period.

Example 6.   Calculate the net single premium for a $1,000.00, 5-year term policy on a male life aged 45. Use *1958 CSO Table,* 2½ per cent.

Solution.

$$\$1,000.00 \; A^{'}_{45:\overline{5}|} = \$1,000.00 \; \frac{M_{45} - M_{50}}{D_{45}}$$

$$= \$1,000.00 \; \frac{87,334.855}{2,978,698.8} = \$29.32 \qquad Ans.$$

A concept which will be useful later in the study of policy reserves is the value of term insurance for *n* years on a life aged *x* evaluated at the end of the term which is represented by the symbol $_{n}k_{x}$ so that $_{n}k_{x}$ is the accumulated value WBOS of $A^{1}_{x:\overline{n}|}$ giving

$$_{n}k_{x} = A^{1}_{x:\overline{n}|} \cdot \frac{D_{x}}{D_{x+n}} = \frac{M_{x} - M_{x+n}}{D_{x}} \cdot \frac{D_{x}}{D_{x+n}} = \frac{M_{x} - M_{x+n}}{D_{x+n}} \qquad (9)$$

6. Endowment Insurance

The *n-year* endowment insurance policy combines the features of the *n-year* term insurance policy and the *n-year* pure endowment and is represented by the symbol $A_{x:\overline{n}|}$ therefore

$$A_{x:\overline{n}|} = A^{1}_{x:\overline{n}|} + A_{x:\overline{n}|}^{\;\;1}$$

The omission of a numeral 1 on the symbol $A_{x:\overline{n}|}$ indicates that the benefit is paid upon the occurrence of the first of two events—the failure of the life *x,* and the expiration of *n years.*

$$A_{x:\overline{n}|} = A^{1}_{x:\overline{n}|} + \frac{D_{x+n}}{D_{x}} = \frac{M_{x} - M_{x+n}}{D_{x}} + \frac{D_{x+n}}{D_{x}}$$

and,

$$A_{x:\overline{n}|} = \frac{M_{x} - M_{x+n} + D_{x+n}}{D_{x}} \qquad (10)$$

Example 7.   Calculate the value of a 5-year endowment policy for $1,000.00 on a male life aged 45. Use *1958 CSO Table,* 2½ per cent.

Solution. The 5-year pure endowment for $1,000.00 on a male life aged 45 is by equation (4),

$$\$1,000.00 \; \frac{D_{50}}{D_{45}} = \frac{\$1,000.00 \times 2,549,324.7}{2,978,698.8} = \$855.85 \qquad Ans.$$

When this result is added to the premium for the corresponding 5-year term policy in Example 6, we have,

$$\$1{,}000.00 \; A_{45:\overline{5}|} = \$29.32 + \$855.85 = \$885.17 \qquad Ans.$$

7. The Discounted Value of a Life Annuity Immediate

The symbol, a_x, is used to represent the discounted value at age x of an annuity of 1 paid at the end of each year during the lifetime of x. Using equation (4):

$$a_x = \frac{D_{x+1}}{D_x} + \frac{D_{x+2}}{D_x} + \frac{D_{x+3}}{D_x} + \cdots$$

$$= \frac{D_{x+1} + D_{x+2} + D_{x+3} + \cdots}{D_x}$$

$$= \frac{N_{x+1}}{D_x} \tag{11}$$

where, $\qquad N_{x+1} = D_{x+1} + D_{x+2} + D_{x+3} + \cdots$

Example 8. Calculate the discounted value of a_{40} using 2½ per cent and (a) the *1958 CSO Table,* (b) the *Annuity Table for 1949* (Male).

Solution. (a) Using equation (11)

$$(a) \; a_{40} = \frac{N_{41}}{D_{40}} = \frac{71{,}753{,}134.1}{3{,}441{,}765.1} = 20.848 \qquad Ans.$$

$$(b) \; a_{40} = \frac{N_{41}}{D_{40}} = \frac{8{,}036.4109}{362.5710} = 22.165 \qquad Ans.$$

8. The Discounted Value of a Deferred Life Annuity Immediate

The symbol $_n|a_x$ represents the value at age x of a life annuity due with the first payment at age $x + n + 1$.

The value at age $x + n$ of an annuity immediate first payment at age $x + n + 1$ is a_{x+n} and its value n years earlier is $\dfrac{D_{x+n}}{D_x} a_{x+n}$; therefore using equation (10)

$$_n|a_x = \frac{D_{x+n}}{D_x} \cdot \frac{N_{x+n+1}}{D_{x+n}} = \frac{N_{x+n+1}}{D_x} \tag{12}$$

Example 9.   Calculate the value of $_{30}|a_{40}$ using 2½ per cent and (a) the *1958 CSO Table*, (b) the *Annuity Table for 1949* (Male).

Solution. Using equation (12)

$$\text{(a)} \quad _{30}|a_{40} = \frac{N_{71}}{D_{40}} = \frac{8,006,177.3}{3,441,765.1} = 2.326 \qquad \textit{Ans.}$$

$$\text{(b)} \quad _{30}|a_{40} = \frac{N_{71}}{D_{40}} = \frac{1114.9209}{362.5710} = 3.075 \qquad \textit{Ans.}$$

9. The Discounted Value of a Temporary Life Annuity Immediate

A life annuity immediate on a life aged x, (an n year life annuity immediate) $a_{x:\overline{n}|}$, may be considered as the value of a whole-life annuity immediate minus an annuity immediate on life aged x, deferred n years, that is,

$$a_{x:\overline{n}|} = a_x - {}_n|a_x$$

Using equations (10) and (11)

$$a_{x:\overline{n}|} = \frac{N_{x+1}}{D_x} - \frac{N_{x+n+1}}{D_x} = \frac{N_{x+1} - N_{x+n+1}}{D_x} \qquad (13)$$

Example 10.   Calculate the value of $a_{40:\overline{30}|}$ using 2½ per cent and (a) the *1958 CSO Table*, (b) the *Annuity Table for 1949* (Male).

Solution. (a) Using the results in Example 8(a) and Example 9(a)

$$a_{40:\overline{30}|} = 20.848 - 2.326 = 18.522 \qquad \textit{Ans.}$$

(b) Using the results in Examples 8(b) and 9(b)

$$a_{40:\overline{30}|} = 22.165 - 3.075 = 19.090 \qquad \textit{Ans.}$$

10. Annuities Due

The annuity due differs from the annuity immediate by having the payments made at the *beginning* of each year rather than at the *end;* the symbols for annuities due are distinguished from the symbols for annuities immediate by having two dots placed above the a as, $\ddot{a}$.

The equations for the discounted values of the whole-life annuity due, the deferred annuity due and the temporary annuity due corresponding to equations (11), (12), and (13) are, respectively, represented by

$$\ddot{a}_x = \frac{N_x}{D_x} \tag{14}$$

$$_n|\ddot{a}_x = \frac{N_{x+n}}{D_x} \tag{15}$$

$$\ddot{a}_{x:\overline{n}|} = \frac{N_x - N_{x+n}}{D_x} \tag{16}$$

Example 11.   Calculate the values of (a) $\ddot{a}_{40}$, (b) $_{30}|\ddot{a}_{40}$ and (c) $\ddot{a}_{40:\overline{30}|}$ using the *1958 CSO Table* and 2½ per cent.

Solution.

(a) $\quad \ddot{a}_{40} = \dfrac{N_{40}}{D_{40}} = \dfrac{75,194,899.2}{3,441,765.1} = 21.848 \qquad\qquad Ans.$

(b) $\quad _{30}|\ddot{a}_{40} = \dfrac{N_{70}}{D_{40}} = \dfrac{8,999,059.0}{3,441,765.1} = 2.615 \qquad\qquad Ans.$

(c) $\ddot{a}_{40:\overline{30}|} = \dfrac{N_{40} - N_{70}}{D_{40}} = \ddot{a}_{40} - {_{30}|\ddot{a}_{40}} = 21.848 - 2.615 = 19.233 \quad Ans.$

In the study of net level terminal reserves it is desirable to have an equation representing $\ddot{s}_{x:\overline{n}|}$, the accumulated value at age $x + n$ of an n-year annuity due of 1 on a life aged x.

Equation (16) gives the discounted value of a temporary annuity of n payments on a life aged x, therefore the desired value of $\ddot{s}_{x:\overline{n}|}$, being the value of the same annuity n years later is given by the equation,

$$\ddot{s}_{x:\overline{n}|} = \ddot{a}_{x:\overline{n}|} \cdot \frac{D_x}{D_{x+n}}$$

and by equation (16), $\ddot{s}_{x:\overline{n}|} = \dfrac{N_x - N_{x+n}}{\cancel{D_x}} \cdot \dfrac{\cancel{D_x}}{D_{x+n}}$

$$\ddot{s}_{x:\overline{n}|} = \frac{N_x - N_{x+n}}{D_{x+n}} \tag{17}$$

To summarize the general annuity formula

$$\frac{N_a - N_b}{D_c}$$

represents the value at age c of an annuity with first payment at age a and the last payment at age $b - 1$.

NET LEVEL PREMIUMS

1. A Fundamental Equation

Life insurance was first placed on a scientific basis when it was recognized that the value of all net premiums received by an insurance company had to be equal to the value of all benefits provided by the insurance contract at its inception.

The net single premiums for standard insurance benefits were developed in Chapters 21 and 22. In Chapter 23 the net level anual premiums were studied. Using P in general to represent one of the net level premiums, $\ddot{a}$ to represent the discounted value of an annuity due, and A to represent the discounted value of the benefits, then since the present value of the premiums must equal the present value of the benefits,

$$P \cdot \ddot{a} = A \tag{18}$$

Solving for P,
$$P = \frac{A}{\ddot{a}} \tag{19}$$

2. Annual Premium for an n-year Term Policy

Using equation (19) and $P^1_{x:\overline{n}|}$ to represent the net annual premium for an *n-year* term policy,

$$P^1_{x:\overline{n}|} = \frac{A^1_{x:\overline{n}|}}{\ddot{a}_{x:\overline{n}|}} = \frac{\dfrac{M_x - M_{x+n}}{D_x}}{\dfrac{N_x - N_{x+n}}{D_x}} = \frac{M_x - M_{x+n}}{N_x - N_{x+n}} \tag{20}$$

Example 1.   Calculate the net annual premium for a $1,000.00, 5-year term policy on a male life aged 45. Use *1958 CSO Table,* 2½ per cent.

Solution. Using equation (20), $1,000.00 $P^1_{45:\overline{50}|}$ = $1,000.00

$$\frac{M_{45} - M_{50}}{N_{45} - N_{50}}$$

$$\$1,000.00 \ P^1_{45:\overline{5}|} = \$1,000.00 \ \frac{87,334.855}{14,023,612.9} = \$6.23 \qquad \textit{Ans.}$$

3. Annual Premiums for a Whole-Life Policy

The *ordinary life* policy provides a death benefit of $1.00 throughout life and is paid for by premiums which also continue through the life of the insured. From equation (7),

$$A_x = \frac{M_x}{D_x}$$

and if P_x represents the net level premium for an ordinary life policy, then

$$P_x \cdot \ddot{a}_x = A_x$$

and
$$P_x = \frac{A_x}{\ddot{a}_x} = \frac{\dfrac{M_x}{D_x}}{\dfrac{N_x}{D_x}} = \frac{M_x}{\cancel{D_x}} \cdot \frac{\cancel{D_x}}{N_x} = \frac{M_x}{N_x} \tag{21}$$

Example 2.   Calculate the net annual premium for an ordinary life policy for $1,000.00 on a male life aged 45. Use *1958 CSO Table*, 2½ per cent.

Solution. Using equation (21),

$$\$1,000.00 \, P_{45} = \$1,000.00 \, \frac{M_{45}}{N_{45}} = \$1,000.00 \, \frac{1,541,435.364}{58,927,803.1} = \$26.16 \quad \textit{Ans.}$$

In the case of the *limited-payment whole-life policy* the benefit is the same as for the ordinary life policy, A_x; however, the number of premiums is limited to n. Using $_nP_x$ to represent the net annual premium for such a policy,

$$_nP_x \, \ddot{a}_{x:\overline{n}|} = A_x$$

Solving for $_nP_x$,

$$_nP_x = \frac{A_x}{\ddot{a}_{x:\overline{n}|}} = \frac{\dfrac{M_x}{D_x}}{\dfrac{N_x - N_{x+n}}{D_x}} = \frac{M_x}{N_x - N_{x+n}} \tag{22}$$

Example 3.   Calculate the net annual premium for a $1,000.00, 20-payment life policy on a male aged 45. Use *1958 CSO Table*, 2½ per cent.

Solution. Using equation (18)

$$_{20}P_{45} \cdot \ddot{a}_{45:\overline{20}|} = A_{45}$$

Solving for $_{20}P_{45}$,

$$\$1,000.00 \, _{20}P_{45} = \frac{\$1000.00 \, M_{45}}{N_{45} - N_{65}} = \frac{1,541,435.364}{43,849,970.5} = \$35.15 \quad \textit{Ans.}$$

4. Annual Premiums for Endowment Insurance

From equation (10) the value of the benefits for the endowment insurance is

$$A_{x:\overline{n}|} = \frac{M_x - M_{x+n} + D_{x+n}}{D_x}$$

If the net annual premium for an n-year endowment policy is represented by $P_{x:\overline{n}|}$ then by equation (18)

$$P_{x:\overline{n}|} \cdot \ddot{a}_{x:\overline{n}|} = A_{x:\overline{n}|}$$

and $$P_{x:\overline{n}|} = \frac{A_{x:\overline{n}|}}{\ddot{a}_{x:\overline{n}|}} = \frac{M_x - M_{x+n} + D_{x+n}}{N_x - N_{x+n}} \qquad (23)$$

Example 4.   Calculate the value of $1,000.00 $P_{45:20}$ on a male life. Use *1958 CSO Table*, 2½ per cent.

Solution. Using equation (23)

$$\$1,000.00 \ P_{45:\overline{20}|} = \$1,000.00 \ \frac{M_{45} - M_{65} + D_{65}}{N_{45} - N_{65}}$$

$$= \$1,000.00 \ \frac{1,909,187.3}{43,849,970.5} = \$43.54 \qquad Ans.$$

5. The Net Annual Premium to Provide a Deferred Life Annuity Due

The problem of finding the net annual premium payable from age x to age $x + n$ to provide an annuity of $1.00 for life, first payment at age $x + n$ is one of considerable interest. Let $\pi_{x:\overline{n}|}$ represent the net annual premium and $_n|\ddot{a}_x$ the value of the deferred annuity benefit, then since the value of the premiums at age x must equal the value of the benefits,

$$\pi_{x:\overline{n}|} \cdot \ddot{a}_{x:\overline{n}|} = {}_n|\ddot{a}_x$$

and, $$\pi_{x:\overline{n}|} = \frac{{}_n|\ddot{a}_x}{\ddot{a}_{x:\overline{n}|}} = \frac{\dfrac{N_{x+n}}{D_x}}{\dfrac{N_x - N_{x+n}}{D_x}} \qquad (24)$$

In the evaluation of such a benefit it would be desirable to calculate the numerator on the basis of the *Annuity Table for 1949* and the denominator by the *1958 CSO Table*, to be conservative.

Example 5.   Calculate the annual premium, $\pi_{40:30}$, payable from age 40 to 69 inclusive to provide an annuity of $100.00 per year, first payment at age 70. Assume the individual is a male.

Solution. According to the *Annuity Table for 1949* (Male), 2½ per cent,

$$_{30|}\ddot{a}_{40} = \frac{N_{70}}{D_{40}} = \frac{1234.1543}{362.5710}$$

therefore $_{30|}\ddot{a}_{40} = 3.4039$

and from Example 4, Chapter 13, $\ddot{a}_{40:\overline{30}|} = 19.233$ (using the *1958 CSO Table*), therefore by equation (24),

$$\pi_{40:\overline{30}|} = \$100.00 \, \frac{3.4039}{19.233} = \$17.70 \qquad\qquad Ans.$$

RESERVES

The basic equation of life insurance states that the discounted value of the premiums must equal the discounted value of the benefits. If this is true at the inception of the contract it must be true at any other time during the life of the contract because the same rate of growth is assumed throughout.

On the tth anniversary of an ordinary life policy, for example, the accumulated value of the premiums which have already been paid, plus the discounted value of the premiums still to be paid at age $x + t$, must be equal to the accumulated value of the insurance benefits paid out over the first t years plus the discounted value of the benefits still to be paid.

Expressing this statement of equivalence in the form of an equation we have, by equation (17), the accumulated value of the first t premiums is $P_x \cdot \ddot{s}_{x:\overline{t}|}$ and by equation (14) the discounted value of the premiums still to be received is $P_x \cdot \ddot{a}_{x+t}$. Similarly the accumulated value of the benefits already paid out is, by equation (9), $_tk_x$ and by equation (7) A_{x+t} is the discounted value of the benefits still to be received. Equating the value of all of the premiums to the value of all of the benefits at age $x + t$, we have

$$P_x \cdot \ddot{s}_{x:\overline{t}|} + P_x \cdot \ddot{a}_{x+t} = {_tk_x} + A_{x+t}$$

Transposing the second term on the left side of this equation to the right side and the first term on the right side to the left gives

$$P_x \cdot \ddot{s}_{x:\overline{t}|} - {_tk_x} = A_{x+t} - P_x \cdot \ddot{a}_{x+t} \tag{25}$$

The excess of the accumulated value of the premiums over the accumulated value of the benefits paid out is evidently the tth terminal reserve on an ordinary life policy, represented by the symbol $_tV_x$ so that

$$_tV_x = P_x \cdot \ddot{s}_{x:\overline{t}|} - {}_tk_x \qquad (26)$$

and because of the equality expressed in equation (25),

$$_tV_x = A_{x+t} - P_x \cdot \ddot{a}_{x+t} \qquad (27)$$

The viewpoints taken in equations (26) and (27) are known as the *retrospective* and *prospective,* respectively.

The corresponding equations for the tth reserve on an *n*-year term insurance policy are,

$$_tV^1_{x:\overline{n}|} = P^1_{x:\overline{n}|} \cdot \ddot{s}_{x:\overline{t}|} - {}_tk_x \qquad (28)$$

$$_tV^1_{x:\overline{n}|} = A^1_{x+t:\overline{n-t}|} - P^1_{x:\overline{n}|} \ddot{a}_{x+t:\overline{n-t}|} \qquad (29)$$

Similarly the retrospective and prospective reserve formulas for the *n*-pay life policy are,

$$^n_tV_x = {}_nP_x \cdot \ddot{s}_{x:\overline{t}|} - {}_tk_x, \qquad (t \le n) \qquad (30)$$

$$^n_tV_x = A_{x+t} - {}_nP_x \cdot \ddot{a}_{x+t:\overline{n-t}|}, \ (t \le n) \qquad (31)$$

$$^n_tV_x = A_{x+t} \qquad\qquad (t \ge n) \qquad (32)$$

The corresponding formulas for the *n*-year endowment are,

$$_tV_{x:\overline{n}|} = P_{x:\overline{n}|} \cdot \ddot{s}_{x:\overline{t}|} - {}_tk_x, \qquad (t \le n) \qquad (33)$$

$$_tV_{x:\overline{n}|} = A_{x+t:\overline{n-t}|} - P_{x:\overline{n}|} \cdot \ddot{a}_{x+t:\overline{n-t}|}, \ (t \le n) \qquad (34)$$

Example 1.   Calculate the 15th net level terminal reserve on (a) a \$1,000.00 ordinary life insurance policy on a male life aged 21.

Solution. Using equation (26)

$$\$1,000.00 \ {}_{15}V_{21} = \$1,000.00 \ (P_{21} \cdot \ddot{s}_{21:\overline{15}|} - {}_{15}k_{21})$$

$$= \$1,000.00 \ \frac{M_{21}}{N_{21}} \cdot \frac{N_{21} - N_{36}}{D_{36}} - \$1,000.00 \ \frac{M_{21} - M_{36}}{D_{36}}$$

$$= \frac{1,794,622,238}{161,928,780.9} \cdot \frac{71,971,793.3}{3,843,841.0} - \frac{144,854,095}{3,843,841.0}$$

$$= (\$11.0828) \ (18.7239) - \$37.6847$$

$$= \$207.5132 - \$37.6847 = \$169.83 \qquad\qquad Ans.$$

Using equation (27)

$$\$1,000.00 \ {}_{15}V_{21} = \$1,000.00 \ A_{36} - \$1,000.00 \ P_{21} \cdot \ddot{a}_{36}$$

$$= \$1,000.00 \ \frac{M_{36}}{D_{36}} - (\$11.0828) \ \frac{N_{36}}{D_{36}}$$

$$= \frac{\$1,649,768,143}{3,843,841} - (\$11.0828)\,\frac{89,956,987.6}{3,843,841.0}$$

$$= \$429.1978 - (\$11.0828)\,(23.4029)$$

$$= \$429.1978 - \$259.3697 = \$169.83 \qquad Ans.$$

Example 2. Calculate the 15th net level terminal reserve on a \$1,000.00 (a) a 20-year term policy, (b) a 20-pay life policy and (c) a 20-year endowment policy on a male life aged 21.

Solution. (a) Using equation (28)

$$\$1,000.00 \; {}_{15}V^1_{21:\overline{20}|} = \$1,000.00 \; P^1_{21:\overline{20}|} \cdot \ddot{s}_{21:\overline{15}|} - \$1,000.00 \; {}_{15}k_{21}$$

$$= \$1,000.00 \, \frac{M_{21} - M_{41}}{N_{21} - N_{41}} \cdot (18.7239) - \$37.6847$$

$$= \frac{\$198,732,173}{90,175,646.8} \, (18.7239) - \$37.6847$$

$$= (\$2.2038)\,(18.7239) - \$37.6847$$

$$= \$41.2637 - \$37.6847 = \$3.58 \qquad Ans.$$

(b) Using equation (30)

$$\$1,000.00 \; {}^{20}_{15}V_{21} = \$1,000.00 \; {}_{20}P_{21} \cdot \ddot{s}_{21:\overline{15}|} - \$1,000.00 \; {}_{15}k_{21}$$

$$= \$1,000.00 \, \frac{M_{21}}{N_{21} - N_{41}} \cdot (18.7239) - \$37.6847$$

$$= (\$19.9014)\,(18.7239) - \$37.6847$$

$$= \$372.6318 - \$37.6847 = \$334.95 \qquad Ans.$$

(c) Using equation (33)

$$\$1,000.00 \; {}_{15}V_{21:\overline{20}|} = \$1,000.00 \; P_{21:\overline{20}|} \cdot \ddot{s}_{21:\overline{15}|} - \$1,000.00 \; {}_{15}k_{21}$$

$$= \$1,000.00 \, \frac{M_{21} - M_{41} + D_{41}}{N_{21} - N_{41}} \, (18.7239) - \$37.6847$$

$$= \frac{\$3,544,698,676}{90,175,647} \, (18.7239) - \$37.6847$$

$$= (\$39.3088)\,(18.7239) - \$37.6847$$

$$= \$736.0140 - \$37.6847 = \$698.33 \qquad Ans.$$

It is interesting to observe that the negative terms in the solution of (a), (b), and (c) above are identical for obvious reasons.

NONFORFEITURE VALUES

A description of the rationale and principles of the Standard Nonforfeiture Law was included in Chapter 26, along with an arithmetical example of the law's application. The formulas used in the determination of minimum statutory nonforfeiture values can easily be expressed in terms of mathematical symbols.

The following equation defines the "adjusted premium," which must be calculated prior to the actual determination of minimum values:

$$P^A \ddot{a}_{x:\overline{n}|} = A + .02 + .4 \left\{ \frac{P^A}{.04} \right\} + .25 \left\{ \frac{{}^{wl}P^A}{\frac{P^A}{.04}} \right\}$$

where P^A = the annual adjusted premium for the policy under consideration

n = the number of years in the premium-paying period

A = the net single premium for the policy at issue

${}^{wl}P^A$ = the annual adjusted premium for a whole-life policy issued at the same age as the policy being considered.

The *smallest* of the quantities enclosed by the brackets is to be used when applying the formula.

It should be clear from the formula that the special first-year expense allowance cannot exceed $46 per thousand dollars of face amount.

Depending upon the plan of insurance being considered, as well as the issue age, the foregoing formula can take on several different forms. For example, if a relatively expensive plan of insurance is considered at an age at which the ordinary life adjusted premium would be less than $40 per thousand, the expression for P^A would be

$$\frac{A + .036 + .25{}^{wl}P^A}{\ddot{a}_{x:\overline{n}|}}$$

However if the ordinary life adjusted premium at the age in question were greater than $40 per thousand, the expression for the adjusted premium for the same plan of insurance would be

$$\frac{A + .046}{\ddot{a}_{x:\overline{n}|}}$$

Often trial and error methods are necessary to determine which form of the basic equation is appropriate.

Example 1.   Find the adjusted premium for a $1,000, 25-payment life contract issued at age 40.

Solution. The first problem is to ascertain the whole-life adjusted premium at issue age 40.

$$^{wl}P^A \, \ddot{a}_{40} = A_{40} + .02 + .65 \left\{\frac{^{wl}P^A}{.04}\right\}.$$

Suppose we guess that $^{wl}P^A$ *is more than* $40 per thousand. Then, based on *1958 CSO Table,* 2½ per cent,

$$^{wl}P^A = \frac{A_{40} + .046}{\ddot{a}_{40}} = .02349 < .04.$$

Clearly we made an improper guess and we should have supposed that $^{wl}P^A$ was less than $40 per thousand. Thus the applicable formula for $^{wl}P^A$ is

$$^{wl}P^A = \frac{A_{40} + .02}{\ddot{a}_{40} - .65} = .02298.$$

Now that $^{wl}P^A$ has been determined, the expression for the adjusted premium for the 25-payment life policy under consideration is

$$P^A\ddot{a}_{40:\overline{25}|} = A_{40} + .02 + .4 \left\{\frac{P^A}{.04}\right\} + .25 \left\{\frac{.02298}{P^A}\right\}.$$

Let us make the educated guess that

$$.02298 < P^A < .04.$$

Then

$$P^A\ddot{a}_{40:\overline{25}|} = A_{40} + .02 + .4 \, P^A + .25(.02298).$$

Solving,

$$P^A = .02888.$$

It appears that our guess was correct in this case. Had it not been, the correct range for P^A could have easily been found. For a $1,000 policy, of course, the adjusted premium would be $28.88.

Example 2.   For the policy discussed in Example 1, find the minimum cash value at the end of the tenth policy year.

Solution:

$$_{10}CV^{MIN} = A_{50} - P^A\ddot{a}_{50:\overline{15}|}$$
$$= .23251$$

Thus, the minimum cash value after ten years on a 25-payment life policy of $1,000 face amount issued to a life aged 40 is $232.51.

This solution follows the general rule that the minimum nonforfeiture value is found by diminishing the present value of future benefits by the present value of future adjusted premiums.

Once the series of minimum cash values is determined, the amounts of coverage which could be provided by the other nonforfeiture options can easily be calculated by applying the principles of the mathematics of life insurance. The minimum reduced paid-up values would be based on the *1958 CSO Table* and the minimum extended term insurance values would be based on the *1958 CET Table*.

D Selected Compound Interest and Discount Functions

2 Per Cent

Years	Amount of 1 How $1 Left at Compound Interest Will Grow	Amount of 1 Per Annum How $1 Deposited Periodically Will Grow	Present Value of 1 What $1 Due in the Future Is Worth Today	Present Value of 1 Per Annum What $1 Payable Periodically Is Worth Today
1	1.020 000	1.000 000	.980 392	.980 392
2	1.040 400	2.020 000	.961 169	1.941 561
3	1.061 208	3.060 400	.942 322	2.883 883
4	1.082 432	4.121 608	.923 845	3.807 729
5	1.104 081	5.204 040	.905 731	4.713 460
6	1.126 162	6.308 121	.887 971	5.601 431
7	1.148 686	7.434 283	.870 560	6.471 991
8	1.171 659	8.582 969	.853 490	7.325 481
9	1.195 093	9.754 628	.836 755	8.162 237
10	1.218 994	10.949 721	.820 348	8.982 585
11	1.243 374	12.168 715	.804 263	9.786 848
12	1.268 242	13.412 090	.788 493	10.575 341
13	1.293 607	14.680 332	.773 033	11.348 374
14	1.319 479	15.973 938	.757 875	12.106 249
15	1.345 868	17.293 417	.743 015	12.849 264
16	1.372 786	18.639 285	.728 446	13.577 709
17	1.400 241	20.012 071	.714 163	14.291 872
18	1.428 246	21.412 312	.700 159	14.992 031
19	1.456 811	22.840 559	.686 431	15.678 462
20	1.485 947	24.297 370	.672 971	16.351 433
21	1.515 666	25.783 317	.659 776	17.011 209
22	1.545 980	27.298 984	.646 839	17.658 048
23	1.576 899	28.844 963	.634 156	18.292 204
24	1.608 437	30.421 862	.621 721	18.913 926
25	1.640 606	32.030 300	.609 531	19.523 456
26	1.673 418	33.670 906	.597 579	20.121 036
27	1.706 886	35.344 324	.585 862	20.706 898
28	1.741 024	37.051 210	.574 375	21.281 272
29	1.775 845	38.792 235	.563 112	21.844 385
30	1.811 362	40.568 079	.552 071	22.396 456
31	1.847 589	42.379 441	.541 246	22.937 702
32	1.884 541	44.227 030	.530 633	23.468 335
33	1.922 231	46.111 570	.520 229	23.988 564
34	1.960 676	48.033 802	.510 028	24.498 592
35	1.999 890	49.994 478	.500 028	24.998 619

	2 Per Cent			
	Amount of 1 How $1 Left at Compound Interest	Amount of 1 Per Annum How $1 Deposited Periodically	Present Value of 1 What $1 Due in the Future Is Worth	Present Value of 1 Per Annum What $1 Payable Periodically
Years	Will Grow	Will Grow	Today	Is Worth Today
36	2.039 887	51.994 367	.490 223	25.488 842
37	2.080 685	54.034 255	.480 611	25.969 453
38	2.122 299	56.114 940	.471 187	26.440 641
39	2.164 745	58.237 238	.461 948	26.902 589
40	2.208 040	60.401 983	.452 890	27.355 479
41	2.252 200	62.610 023	.444 010	27.799 489
42	2.297 244	64.862 223	.435 304	28.234 794
43	2.343 189	67.159 468	.426 769	28.661 562
44	2.390 053	69.502 657	.418 401	29.079 963
45	2.437 854	71.892 710	.410 197	29.490 160
46	2.486 611	74.330 564	.402 154	29.892 314
47	2.536 344	76.817 176	.394 268	30.286 582
48	2.587 070	79.353 519	.386 538	30.673 120
49	2.638 812	81.940 590	.378 958	31.052 078
50	2.691 588	84.579 401	.371 528	31.423 606
51	2.745 420	87.270 989	.364 243	31.787 849
52	2.800 328	90.016 409	.357 101	32.144 950
53	2.856 335	92.816 737	.350 099	32.495 049
54	2.913 461	95.673 072	.343 234	32.838 283
55	2.971 731	98.586 534	.336 504	33.174 788
56	3.031 165	101.558 264	.329 906	33.504 694
57	3.091 789	104.589 430	.323 437	33.828 131
58	3.153 624	107.681 218	.317 095	34.145 226
59	3.216 697	110.834 843	.310 878	34.456 104
60	3.281 031	114.051 539	.304 782	34.760 887
61	3.346 651	117.332 570	.298 806	35.059 693
62	3.413 584	120.679 222	.292 947	35.352 640
63	3.481 856	124.092 806	.287 203	35.639 843
64	3.551 493	127.574 662	.281 572	35.921 415
65	3.622 523	131.126 155	.276 051	36.197 466
66	3.694 974	134.748 679	.270 638	36.468 103
67	3.768 873	138.443 652	.265 331	36.733 435
68	3.844 251	142.212 525	.260 129	36.993 564
69	3.921 136	146.056 776	.255 028	37.248 592
70	3.999 558	149.977 911	.250 028	37.498 619
71	4.079 549	153.977 469	.245 125	37.743 744
72	4.161 140	158.057 019	.240 319	37.984 063

		2 Per Cent		
Years	Amount of 1 How $1 Left at Compound Interest Will Grow	Amount of 1 Per Annum How $1 Deposited Periodically Will Grow	Present Value of 1 What $1 Due in the Future Is Worth Today	Present Value of 1 Per Annum What $1 Payable Periodically Is Worth Today
73	4.244 363	162.218 159	.235 607	38.219 670
74	4.329 250	166.462 522	.230 987	38.450 657
75	4.415 835	170.791 773	.226 458	38.677 114
76	4.504 152	175.207 608	.222 017	38.899 132
77	4.594 235	179.711 760	.217 664	39.116 796
78	4.686 120	184.305 996	.213 396	39.330 192
79	4.779 842	188.992 115	.209 212	39.539 404
80	4.875 439	193.771 958	.205 110	39.744 514
81	4.972 948	198.647 397	.201 088	39.945 602
82	5.072 407	203.620 345	.197 145	40.142 747
83	5.173 855	208.692 752	.193 279	40.336 026
84	5.277 332	213.866 607	.189 490	40.525 516
85	5.382 879	219.143 939	.185 774	40.711 290
86	5.490 536	224.526 818	.182 132	40.893 422
87	5.600 347	230.017 354	.178 560	41.071 982
88	5.712 354	235.617 701	.175 059	41.247 041
89	5.826 601	241.330 055	.171 627	41.418 668
90	5.943 133	247.156 656	.168 261	41.586 929
91	6.061 996	253.099 789	.164 962	41.751 891
92	6.183 236	259.161 785	.161 728	41.913 619
93	6.306 900	265.345 021	.158 556	42.072 175
94	6.433 038	271.651 921	.155 448	42.227 623
95	6.561 699	278.084 960	.152 400	42.380 023
96	6.692 933	284.646 659	.149 411	42.529 434
97	6.826 792	291.339 592	.146 482	42.675 916
98	6.963 328	298.166 384	.143 609	42.819 525
99	7.102 594	305.129 712	.140 794	42.960 319
100	7.244 646	312.232 306	.138 033	43.098 352
		2½ Per Cent		
1	1.025 000	1.000 000	.975 610	.975 610
2	1.050 625	2.025 000	.951 814	1.927 424
3	1.076 891	3.075 625	.928 599	2.856 024
4	1.103 813	4.152 516	.905 951	3.761 974
5	1.131 408	5.256 329	.883 854	4.645 828
6	1.159 693	6.387 737	.862 297	5.508 125
7	1.188 686	7.547 430	.841 265	6.349 391
8	1.218 403	8.736 116	.820 747	7.170 137

			2½ Per Cent	
Years	Amount of 1 How $1 Left at Compound Interest Will Grow	Amount of 1 Per Annum How $1 Deposited Periodically Will Grow	Present Value of 1 What $1 Due in the Future Is Worth Today	Present Value of 1 Per Annum What $1 Payable Periodically Is Worth Today
9	1.248 863	9.954 519	.800 728	7.970 866
10	1.280 085	11.203 382	.781 198	8.752 064
11	1.312 087	12.483 466	.762 145	9.514 209
12	1.344 889	13.795 553	.743 556	10.257 765
13	1.378 511	15.140 442	.725 420	10.983 185
14	1.412 974	16.518 953	.707 727	11.690 912
15	1.448 298	17.931 927	.690 466	12.381 378
16	1.484 506	19.380 225	.673 625	13.055 003
17	1.521 618	20.864 730	.657 195	13.712 198
18	1.559 659	22.386 349	.641 166	14.353 364
19	1.598 650	23.946 007	.625 528	14.978 891
20	1.638 616	25.544 658	.610 271	15.589 162
21	1.679 582	27.183 274	.595 386	16.184 549
22	1.721 571	28.862 856	.580 865	16.765 413
23	1.764 611	30.584 427	.566 697	17.332 110
24	1.808 726	32.349 038	.552 875	17.884 986
25	1.853 944	34.157 764	.539 391	18.424 376
26	1.900 293	36.011 708	.526 235	18.950 611
27	1.947 800	37.912 001	.513 400	19.464 011
28	1.996 495	39.859 801	.500 878	19.964 889
29	2.046 407	41.856 296	.488 661	20.453 550
30	2.097 568	43.902 703	.476 743	20.930 293
31	2.150 007	46.000 271	.465 115	21.395 407
32	2.203 757	48.150 278	.453 771	21.849 178
33	2.258 851	50.354 034	.442 703	22.291 881
34	2.315 322	52.612 885	.431 905	22.723 786
35	2.373 205	54.928 207	.421 371	23.145 157
36	2.432 535	57.301 413	.411 094	23.556 251
37	2.493 349	59.733 948	.401 067	23.957 318
38	2.555 682	62.227 297	.391 285	24.348 603
39	2.619 574	64.782 979	.381 741	24.730 344
40	2.685 064	67.402 554	.372 431	25.102 775
41	2.752 190	70.087 617	.363 347	25.466 122
42	2.820 995	72.839 808	.354 485	25.820 607
43	2.891 520	75.660 803	.345 839	26.166 446
44	2.963 808	78.552 323	.337 404	26.503 849
45	3.037 903	81.516 131	.329 174	26.833 024

		2½ Per Cent		
Years	Amount of 1 How $1 Left at Compound Interest Will Grow	Amount of 1 Per Annum How $1 Deposited Periodically Will Grow	Present Value of 1 What $1 Due in the Future Is Worth Today	Present Value of 1 Per Annum What $1 Payable Periodically Is Worth Today
46	3.113 851	84.554 034	.321 146	27.154 170
47	3.191 697	87.667 885	.313 313	27.467 483
48	3.271 490	90.859 582	.305 671	27.773 154
49	3.353 277	94.131 072	.298 216	28.071 369
50	3.437 109	97.484 349	.290 942	28.362 312
51	3.523 036	100.921 458	.283 846	28.646 158
52	3.611 112	104.444 494	.276 923	28.923 081
53	3.701 390	108.055 606	.270 169	29.193 249
54	3.793 925	111.756 996	.263 579	29.456 829
55	3.888 773	115.550 921	.257 151	29.713 979
56	3.985 992	119.439 694	.250 879	29.964 858
57	4.085 642	123.425 687	.244 760	30.209 617
58	4.187 783	127.511 329	.238 790	30.448 407
59	4.292 478	131.699 112	.232 966	30.681 373
60	4.399 790	135.991 590	.227 284	30.908 656
61	4.509 784	140.391 380	.221 740	31.130 397
62	4.622 529	144.901 164	.216 332	31.346 728
63	4.738 092	149.523 693	.211 055	31.557 784
64	4.856 545	154.261 786	.205 908	31.763 691
65	4.977 958	159.118 330	.200 886	31.964 577
66	5.102 407	164.096 289	.195 986	32.160 563
67	5.229 967	169.198 696	.191 206	32.351 769
68	5.360 717	174.428 663	.186 542	32.538 311
69	5.494 734	179.789 380	.181 992	32.720 303
70	5.632 103	185.284 114	.177 554	32.897 857
71	5.772 905	190.916 217	.173 223	33.071 080
72	5.917 228	196.689 122	.168 998	33.240 078
73	6.065 159	202.606 351	.164 876	33.404 954
74	6.216 788	208.671 509	.160 855	33.565 809
75	6.372 207	214.888 297	.156 931	33.722 740
76	6.531 513	221.260 504	.153 104	33.875 844
77	6.694 800	227.792 017	.149 370	34.025 214
78	6.862 170	234.486 818	.145 726	34.170 940
79	7.033 725	241.348 988	.142 172	34.313 113
80	7.209 568	248.382 713	.138 705	34.451 817
81	7.389 807	255.592 280	.135 322	34.587 139
82	7.574 552	262.982 087	.132 021	34.719 160

Years	2½ Per Cent			
	Amount of 1 How $1 Left at Compound Interest Will Grow	Amount of 1 Per Annum How $1 Deposited Periodically Will Grow	Present Value of 1 What $1 Due in the Future Is Worth Today	Present Value of 1 Per Annum What $1 Payable Periodically Is Worth Today
83	7.763 916	270.556 640	.128 801	34.847 961
84	7.958 014	278.320 556	.125 659	34.973 620
85	8.156 964	286.278 570	.122 595	35.096 215
86	8.360 888	294.435 534	.119 605	35.215 819
87	8.569 911	302.796 422	.116 687	35.332 507
88	8.784 158	311.366 333	.113 841	35.446 348
89	9.003 762	320.150 491	.111 065	35.557 413
90	9.228 856	329.154 253	.108 356	35.665 768
91	9.459 578	338.383 110	.105 713	35.771 481
92	9.696 067	347.842 687	.103 135	35.874 616
93	9.938 469	357.538 755	.100 619	35.975 235
94	10.186 931	367.477 223	.098 165	36.073 400
95	10.441 604	377.664 154	.095 771	36.169 171
96	10.702 644	388.105 758	.093 435	36.262 606
97	10.970 210	398.808 402	.091 156	36.353 762
98	11.244 465	409.778 612	.088 933	36.442 694
99	11.525 577	421.023 077	.086 764	36.529 458
100	11.813 716	432.548 654	.084 647	36.614 105
	3 Per Cent			
1	1.030 000	1.000 000	.970 874	.970 874
2	1.060 900	2.030 000	.942 596	1.913 470
3	1.092 727	3.090 900	.915 142	2.828 611
4	1.125 509	4.183 627	.888 487	3.717 098
5	1.159 274	5.309 136	.862 609	4.579 707
6	1.194 052	6.468 410	.837 484	5.417 191
7	1.229 874	7.662 462	.813 092	6.230 283
8	1.266 770	8.892 336	.789 409	7.019 692
9	1.304 773	10.159 106	.766 417	7.786 109
10	1.343 916	11.463 879	.744 094	8.530 203
11	1.384 234	12.807 796	.722 421	9.252 624
12	1.425 761	14.192 030	.701 380	9.954 004
13	1.468 534	15.617 790	.680 951	10.634 955
14	1.512 590	17.086 324	.661 118	11.296 073
15	1.557 967	18.598 914	.641 862	11.937 935
16	1.604 706	20.156 881	.623 167	12.561 102
17	1.652 848	21.761 588	.605 016	13.166 118
18	1.702 433	23.414 435	.587 395	13.753 513

		3 Per Cent		
Years	Amount of 1 How $1 Left at Compound Interest Will Grow	Amount of 1 Per Annum How $1 Deposited Periodically Will Grow	Present Value of 1 What $1 Due in the Future Is Worth Today	Present Value of 1 Per Annum What $1 Payable Periodically Is Worth Today
19	1.753 506	25.116 868	.570 286	14.323 799
20	1.806 111	26.870 374	.553 676	14.877 475
21	1.860 295	28.676 486	.537 549	15.415 024
22	1.916 103	30.536 780	.521 893	15.936 917
23	1.973 587	32.452 884	.506 692	16.443 608
24	2.032 794	34.426 470	.491 934	16.935 542
25	2.093 778	36.459 264	.477 606	17.413 148
26	2.156 591	38.553 042	.463 695	17.876 842
27	2.221 289	40.709 634	.450 189	18.327 031
28	2.287 928	42.930 923	.437 077	18.764 108
29	2.356 566	45.218 850	.424 346	19.188 455
30	2.427 262	47.575 416	.411 987	19.600 441
31	2.500 080	50.002 678	.399 987	20.000 428
32	2.575 083	52.502 759	.388 337	20.388 766
33	2.652 335	55.077 841	.377 026	20.765 792
34	2.731 905	57.730 177	.366 045	21.131 837
35	2.813 862	60.462 082	.355 383	21.487 220
36	2.898 278	63.275 944	.345 032	21.832 252
37	2.985 227	66.174 223	.334 983	22.167 235
38	3.074 783	69.159 449	.325 226	22.492 462
39	3.167 027	72.234 233	.315 754	22.808 215
40	3.262 038	75.401 260	.306 557	23.114 772
41	3.359 899	78.663 298	.297 628	23.412 400
42	3.460 696	82.023 196	.288 959	23.701 359
43	3.564 517	85.483 892	.280 543	23.981 902
44	3.671 452	89.048 409	.272 372	24.254 274
45	3.781 596	92.719 861	.264 439	24.518 713
46	3.895 044	96.501 457	.256 737	24.775 449
47	4.011 895	100.396 501	.249 259	25.024 708
48	4.132 252	104.408 396	.241 999	25.266 707
49	4.256 219	108.540 648	.234 950	25.501 657
50	4.383 906	112.796 867	.228 107	25.729 764
51	4.515 423	117.180 773	.221 463	25.941 227
52	4.650 886	121.696 197	.215 013	26.166 240
53	4.790 412	126.347 082	.208 750	26.374 990
54	4.934 125	131.137 495	.202 670	26.577 660
55	5.082 149	136.071 620	.196 767	26.774 428

		3 Per Cent		
Years	Amount of 1 How $1 Left at Compound Interest Will Grow	Amount of 1 Per Annum How $1 Deposited Periodically Will Grow	Present Value of 1 What $1 Due in the Future Is Worth Today	Present Value of 1 Per Annum What $1 Payable Periodically Is Worth Today
56	5.234 613	141.153 768	.191 036	26.965 464
57	5.391 651	146.388 381	.185 472	27.150 936
58	5.553 401	151.780 033	.180 070	27.331 005
59	5.720 003	157.333 434	.174 825	27.505 831
60	5.891 603	163.053 437	.169 733	27.675 564
61	6.068 351	168.945 040	.164 789	27.840 353
62	6.250 402	175.013 391	.159 990	28.000 343
63	6.437 914	181.263 793	.155 330	28.155 673
64	6.631 051	187.701 707	.150 806	28.306 478
65	6.829 983	194.332 758	.146 413	28.452 892
66	7.034 882	201.162 741	.142 149	28.595 040
67	7.245 929	208.197 623	.138 009	28.733 049
68	7.463 307	215.443 551	.133 989	28.867 038
69	7.687 206	222.906 858	.130 086	28.997 124
70	7.917 822	230.594 064	.126 297	29.123 421
71	8.155 537	238.511 886	.122 619	29.246 040
72	8.400 017	246.667 242	.119 047	29.365 088
73	8.652 018	255.067 259	.115 580	29.480 667
74	8.911 578	263.719 277	.112 214	29.592 881
75	9.178 926	272.630 856	.108 945	29.701 826
76	9.454 293	281.809 781	.105 772	29.807 598
77	9.737 922	291.264 075	.102 691	29.910 290
78	10.030 060	301.001 997	.099 700	30.009 990
79	10.330 962	311.032 057	.096 796	30.106 786
80	10.640 891	321.363 019	.093 977	30.200 763
81	10.960 117	332.003 909	.091 240	30.292 003
82	11.288 921	342.964 026	.088 582	30.380 586
83	11.627 588	354.252 947	.086 002	30.466 588
84	11.976 416	365.880 536	.083 497	30.550 086
85	12.335 709	377.856 952	.081 065	30.631 151
86	12.705 780	390.192 660	.078 704	30.709 855
87	13.086 953	402.898 440	.076 412	30.786 267
88	13.479 562	415.985 393	.074 186	30.860 454
89	13.883 949	429.464 955	.072 026	30.932 479
90	14.300 467	443.348 904	.069 928	31.002 407
91	14.729 481	457.649 371	.067 891	31.070 298
92	15.171 366	472.378 852	.065 914	31.136 212

		3 Per Cent		
Years	Amount of 1 How $1 Left at Compound Interest Will Grow	Amount of 1 Per Annum How $1 Deposited Periodically Will Grow	Present Value of 1 What $1 Due in the Future Is Worth Today	Present Value of 1 Per Annum What $1 Payable Periodically Is Worth Today
93	15.626 507	487.550 217	.063 994	31.200 206
94	16.095 302	503.176 724	.062 130	31.262 336
95	16.578 161	519.272 026	.060 320	31.322 656
96	17.075 506	535.850 186	.058 563	31.381 219
97	17.587 771	552.925 692	.056 858	31.438 077
98	18.115 404	570.513 463	.055 202	31.493 279
99	18.658 866	588.628 867	.053 594	31.546 872
100	19.218 632	607.287 733	.052 033	31.598 905

Index

915